FIELDING™
TRAVEL GUIDES

FIELDING'S
THE WORLD'S
MOST DANGEROUS
PLACES™

Fielding Titles

Fielding's Alaska Cruises and the Inside Passage
Fielding's Asia's Top Dive Sites
Fielding's Amazon
Fielding's Australia
Fielding's Bahamas
Fielding's Belgium
Fielding's Bermuda
Fielding's Borneo
Fielding's Budget Europe
Fielding's Caribbean
Fielding's Caribbean Cruises
Fielding's Disney World and Orlando
Fielding's Diving Indonesia
Fielding's Eastern Caribbean
Fielding's England
Fielding's Europe
Fielding's European Cruises
Fielding's Far East
Fielding's France
Fielding's Freewheelin' USA
Fielding's Kenya
Fielding's Hawaii
Fielding's Holland
Fielding's Italy
Fielding's Las Vegas Agenda
Fielding's London Agenda
Fielding's Los Angeles
Fielding's Malaysia and Singapore
Fielding's Mexico
Fielding's New Orleans Agenda
Fielding's New York Agenda
Fielding's New Zealand
Fielding's Paradors, Pousadas and Charming Villages of Spain and Portugal
Fielding's Paris Agenda
Fielding's Portugal
Fielding's Rome Agenda
Fielding's San Diego Agenda
Fielding's Scandinavia
Fielding's Southeast Asia
Fielding's Southern Vietnam on Two Wheels
Fielding's Spain
Fielding's Surfing Indonesia
Fielding's Sydney Agenda
Fielding's Thailand, Cambodia, Laos and Myanmar
Fielding's Vacation Places Rated
Fielding's Vietnam
Fielding's Western Caribbean
Fielding's The World's Most Dangerous Places
Fielding's Worldwide Cruises

FIELDING'S THE WORLD'S MOST DANGEROUS PLACES™

Second Edition

Robert Young Pelton

Coskun Aral

Wink Dulles

Fielding Worldwide, Inc.

308 South Catalina Avenue

Redondo Beach, California 90277 U.S.A.

FIELDING WORLDWIDE INC.

PUBLISHER AND CEO **Robert Young Pelton**
GENERAL MANAGER **John Guillebeaux**
MARKETING DIRECTOR **Paul T. Snapp**
OPERATIONS DIRECTOR **George Posanke**
ELECTRONIC PUBLISHING DIRECTOR **Larry E. Hart**
PUBLIC RELATIONS DIRECTOR **Beverly Riess**
ACCOUNT SERVICES MANAGER **Christy Harp**
PROJECT MANAGER **Chris Snyder**

EDITORS

Kathy Knoles   **Linda Charlton**

PRODUCTION

Martin Mancha   **Ramses Reynoso**
Alfredo Mercado   **Craig South**

COVER DESIGNED BY **Digital Artists, Inc.**
COVER PHOTOGRAPHERS **Klaus Schönwiese**
INSIDE PHOTOS **Werner Funk, Jim Hooper, Franck Jolot, Anthony Mor-
land, Roddy Scott,
Blackstar: Sebastian Bolesch, Francois Charton,
Charles Crowell, Caren Firouz, Cindy Karp, Erica
Lanser, Vera Lentz, Malcolm Linton, Paul Miller, Debbi
Morello, Christopher Morris, Rob Nelson, Rogerio Reis,
Klaus Reisinger, Joseph Rodriguez, Robert Semeniuk,
Joao Silva, Jay Ullal, Munesuke Yamamoto
National Geographic: Rebecca Abrams, James P. Blair,
Bruce Dale, James Staufield
Sipa Press: Coskun Aral, Philippe Fabry, Albert Facelly,
Patrick Frilet, Andy Hernandez, Armineh Johannes,
Barbier A Kachgar, Francois Lehr, Richard Manin, John
Mantel, Marc Simon, Bob Strong, Sergio Zalis
Westlight: Robert Young Pelton**

Inquiries should be addressed to: Fielding Worldwide, Inc., 308 South Catalina Ave., Redondo
Beach, California 90277 U.S.A., Telephone ☎ *(310) 372-4474*, Facsimile *(310) 376-8064*, 8:30
a.m.–5:30 p.m. Pacific Standard Time.
Web Site: http://www.fieldingtravel.com
e-mail: fielding@fieldingtravel.com

ISBN 1-56952-104-2

Printed in the United States of America

Letter from the Publisher

Despite early predictions of folly, *DP* has become Fielding's fastest-selling travel guide and the rallying point for a new type of traveler. A traveler who is a lot like the authors: curious, intelligent and skeptical of the sound-bite view of the world's least traveled places—people who trust other travel guides as much as we trust infomercials.

Many people ask how we do the things we do. The answer is simple. We just do it. We may not always be successful in our quest, but we always have a good time.

So to those embassy workers in Algeria, U.N. peacekeepers in Rwanda, reporters in Cambodia and producers in Hollywood, keep wearing those Mr. DP shirts proudly, push those limits and keep your letters coming. No walls, no barriers, no bull.

RYP

Robert Young Pelton
Publisher and CEO
Fielding Worldwide, Inc.

Preface

Welcome to the second edition of *The World's Most Dangerous Places*. This book has been a long time in coming—combining research, personal experiences, opinions and countless adventures.

For this edition, authors and contributors have been on the ground in Afghanistan, Bosnia, Burundi, Cambodia, Chechnya, India, Indonesia, Iraq, Laos, Lebanon, Liberia, Pakistan, Paraguay, the Philippines, Russia, Rwanda, Sierra Leone, Somalia, Thailand, Turkey, and many other nasty places. We also have been doing our homework in the United States, in Los Angeles, Miami, New York and Washington, D.C.

Along the way, we have chatted and broken bread with some interesting characters—from the leaders of Hezbollah to the warlords in Liberia, to the Moros in the Philippines to the *taliban* in Afghanistan. We also have hit the books and tried to keep track of and make sense out of this rapidly changing world.

We have been to a lot of countries besides the ones mentioned here and managed to have a good time in most of them. And once again we are a whole lot smarter and a whole lot wiser than we were last year.

As our loyal readers know, we hold no political affiliations or any political agenda sacred. We have no axe to grind. We happily make fun of the pedantic and the fanatic. We are fascinated equally by the relevant and irrelevant facts we stumble across.

If you like what you read, send us a letter. If you don't, give this book to your worst enemy—maybe he or she will use it as a travel guide.

The *DP* Thing

To say that *DP* has become popular would be an understatement. In less than a year we have gone from laid-back travelers visiting the world's cesspools and hot spots to minor celebrities, complete with offers of TV and movie deals. Throughout all this, we have the bizarre sense of being Peter Sellers in *Being There* or Tom Hanks in *Forrest Gump*. "Dangerous is as dangerous does" might even be our motto. We didn't set out to be the poster boys for thrill seekers and professional adventurers, but things have changed since the first edition was published. Coskun now has one of the top television shows in Turkey, Wink keeps getting mistaken for Mel Gibson in Saigon, and I endure the hundreds of questions reporters throw at me in an effort to find out just what is so appealing about this book. To help folks out, here are answers to the top 10 questions I'm most frequently asked:

1) Who is Mr. DP?

Many people ask why we use the laughing skull as a mascot. Well, Mr. DP (as he is affectionately called) came into being because we needed something simple, memorable and small to give out as gifts to soldiers, freedom fighters and anyone who helps in our work. So we designed a mascot and printed a pile of stickers to slap on everything from AK-47s to APCs. He is sort of Kilroy for the nineties. The World Tour, All-Access and Do the World Right T-shirts were created to provide memorable clothing that we could give out to our favorite people. It also gave us something to wear in the field that didn't show dirt.

2) Do you do personal appearances and talk about your adventures?

No, I write books and run Fielding Worldwide. Neither I nor my coauthors have any interest in becoming celebrities or motivational speakers. Although I agreed to interviews on CBS, CNN and other television shows, I must say I do not enjoy losing my spectrelike anonymity as a result. Coskun is very well known in the Middle East but is as shy as I am. I do book signings with great reluctance but I prefer hanging around bookstores without being pestered. But I do enjoy meeting our readers since I am continually surprised at the amazing breadth and depth of their backgrounds.

3) Do you visit every one of these places every year?

Between the three of us and our correspondents, we get to most of the interesting ones. We travel to places that pique our interest or are changing dramatically. We use the phone a lot and take a lot of trips to find out exactly what is going on.

4) Why did you write the book?

This book exists because it is desperately needed and no one else would write it. Once I started, I became enthused with the absolute coolness of wrapping up the big bad world within a thousand pages. I would compare the experience to doing a hard tour in the worst of the world's war zones and writing a doctoral thesis at the same time.

5) How can I write for DP?

Send in whatever you want. But we just don't have the budget to pay more than a T-shirt if we like what we read and we publish it. We always need good travel tips from the world's wild places. We don't write this book for money or for fame. We do it because we live it. Some readers have said they are "itching for action" and want to get in on what we do. We don't engage in any armed combat, we do not carry any firearms, and we do not harm, injure or kill people in our travels. We get shot at, abused, scammed, beaten, blown up, sick, bored and bashed, but we don't reciprocate. (Sounds like a bad "Kung Fu" episode.)

6) Who reads this book?

We have no way of knowing everyone who buys the book, except when we meet readers or get letters. So tell us what you like and don't like. We do know that members of most of the governments profiled in DP are avid readers. Those in Cambodia, Colombia, Libya, Panama and Turkey have been among the more vocal.Our readers tend to be educated, high-income professionals who live on the east and west coasts. A fairly typical slice of book reader—including a whole mess of embassy staff, spooks, soldiers, skateboarders, housewives and college kids.

7) Do you encourage people to travel to the places in this book?

We are in the business of providing information, not promoting tourism. If any book could be criticized for discouraging travel, it is this one. The uniqueness of *DP* is that we rarely cover any attractions or provide any reasons to visit any of these countries. We only cover what is potentially dangerous and along the way open our readers' eyes. The underlying message of this book is to encourage people to better understand their world and not accept the traditional clichés put forth by the media machine or other travel guides. If that encourages you to brave the world's dangerous places, so be it.

8) How do you keep the book up to date?

We continually travel, research, check facts and interview. We are truly information junkies, scanning thousands of documents every month. We are also completely unafraid to get on a plane (or a camel) and go directly into a hot spot to find out what is really going on. Happily, the first edition exceeded our sales expectations and sold out four times in the first 12 months, also allowing us to sneak updates into each new printing. On a more depressing note, certain chapters continue to be prophetically accurate or portray a never changing scenario.We have yet to drop any regions.

9) Is *DP* a macho thing?

Some adventure magazines have tried to portray us as tough guys cruising the world looking for trouble. I can tell you that, from experience, trouble hurts and that tough is for leather and overdone steaks. I can't think of anything that is further from the truth. I now consider myself a seeker of knowledge, a far more cerebral occupation than my previous title of professional adventurer. The fact that the *DP* crew endures some hardships to get a fresh perspective does not make us macho. I can admit that we may be adrenaline junkies, but none of us has ever been bungy jumping, rock climbing or even windsurfing. I collect art, write books, love nature and have two beautiful twin daughters. Coskun likes to cook, Wink likes to play blues guitar, and together we don't exactly fit the hairy-chested, cigar-stomping adventurer profile.

10) What is the most dangerous situation you have been in?

I truly can't answer this. It might be as mundane as surviving a plane crash in Borneo, Coskun hitting a land mine in Afghanistan or Wink riding his motorcycle through war-torn Cambodia. We really never set out to do anything overly dangerous. But we do pride ourselves on knowing how to handle ourselves in dangerous situations, and we have done a lot of fast talking at gunpoint. I have been described as "very lucky," Coskun as "charming" and Wink as "crazy," so that's as far as I can analyze it. So far, the gods have been smiling on us. We must be doing something right.

A Message to Fellow Adventurers and Seekers of Knowledge

The response to the first edition of this book has been overwhelming. Governments have expressed their outrage, and readers have sent in their heartfelt thanks for creating a book that "tells it like it is." If this book can save one life or change a misconception, we did our job. As for the many readers who gave us the benefit of their experiences in dangerous places, we are very grateful and they now own a free book and a cool T-shirt. If you have any pearls of wisdom that may save another traveler from misfortune, please send it in and if we use it we will gladly send you a *DP* book and one of our politically incorrect (but heavy-duty) T-shirts.

—RYP

The Authors

Robert Young Pelton

Pelton has led an adventurous life. It started with being the youngest student ever (age 10) to attend a Canadian survival school in Selkirk, Manitoba. Whether it was canoeing 1000 miles in the early spring or snowshoeing marathons in 50 degrees below zero temperatures, Pelton had an early exposure to adversity and adventure. He has also worked as a lumberjack, boundary cutter, tunneler, driller and blaster's assistant. His quest for knowledge and understanding has taken him through the remote and exotic areas of more than 50 countries. Stories about Pelton or his adventures have been featured in publications ranging from *Soldier of Fortune* to *Outside Magazine*.

Some of Pelton's adventures include living with the Dogon people in the Sahel, breaking American citizens out of jail in Colombia, running forbidden rivers in Indonesia in leaky native canoes, traveling across East Africa with the U.S. team in the Camel Trophy, hitchhiking through war-torn Central America, setting up the world's first video taped interview of the *taliban* leaders in Afghanistan and completing the first circumnavigation of the island of Borneo by land.

Along the way, he survived car accidents, muggings, illness, attacks by everything from the PKK to African killer bees, even a plane crash in the central highlands of Kalimantan. He still faces each dangerous encounter with a sense of humor and an irreverent wit.

Pelton's approach to adventure can be quite humorous. Whether it's challenging Iban headhunters to a chug-a-lug contest, filling expedition members' packs with rocks, indulging in a little target practice with Kurdish warlords in Turkey or filling up the hotel pool with stewardesses, waiters and furniture in Burundi during an all-night party, he brings a certain element of fun and excitement to dangerous places.

Pelton is a Fellow of the Royal Geographical Society in London, a trustee of the Orange County Museum of Art and is also author or coauthor of *Borneo*, and *L.A. Agenda* for Fielding Worldwide.

Coskun Aral

Coskun Aral was thrust into the spotlight as a young photojournalist when he was caught aboard a Turkish 727 hijacked by terrorists in 1980. He risked his life to cover the hijacking from the inside. His career was launched.

Since then, Aral has made a living covering dangerous and forbidden places. One of the few people on earth who has photographed Mecca and been on first-name terms with the major warlords in Beirut during the '80s, he has seen many things, and his special relationships with some of the world's most dangerous people make him uniquely suited to contribute to this book.

He has covered wars on the front lines in Afghanistan, Azerbaijan, Bosnia, Cambodia, Chad, Iran, Iraq, Kuwait, Liberia, Libya, the Philippines, Nicaragua, Northern Ireland, Panama, Romania, Sri Lanka, Bosnia and many other areas. He is also the only ten -time participant of the Camel Trophy.

Aral was the only reporter in the world to interview the hijacker of the TWA plane in Beirut airport in 1985 and he spent over 10 years in Lebanon. He covered the Gulf War from downtown Baghdad and has two *TIME* covers to his credit, as well as numerous photo stories. His adventures for *DP* as well as other topics are currently featured in his hour-long show, "The Reporters," on ATV in Turkey.

Wink Dulles

Wink covers the Far East for *DP* and for other Fielding books. He has spent considerable time in Cambodia, Thailand and Vietnam, traveling by motorcycle. Dulles covered the 1993 elections in Cambodia and the subsequent breakdown of order in that besieged country, being in-country at a time when few foreigners dared. After the first edition of *DP* was published in 1995, he was "invited" back to Cambodia by the government to attend a personal tongue-lashing for his contribution to *DP's* Cambodia chapter. Articles on Wink's adventures have been published in *Newsday*, *National Geographic Traveler* and *Escape* magazines. In February 1996, Dulles guided the first American motorcycle tour of Vietnam. He lives in Los Angeles, Ho Chi Minh City and Bangkok and plays a mean guitar. Dulles is the author of *Fielding's Vietnam*, *Fielding's Southern Vietnam on Two Wheels* and *Fielding's Thailand, Cambodia, Laos & Myanmar*.

DP Contributors

Sedat Aral

Aral (coauthor Coskun's younger brother) has been a "hot spot" photojournalist for more than 12 years. He has covered Afghanistan, Azerbaijan, Bosnia, Chechnya, Georgia, Iran, Iraq, Lebanon, Malaysia, the Philippines and Syria, as well as news stories in his native Turkey. He has worked internationally for news agencies including Reuters and Sipa Press and works on assignment for *Time.* Currently he is a special assignment reporter for the Sabah Media Group in Turkey. He can no longer enter Iran by official routes, having been deported twice for taking photographs. He has had his life threatened in Tunceli for photographing burnt Kurdish villages in the region closed to the press, and has been seriously beaten by police after photographing armed attacks on unarmed protesters.

Jim Hooper

Hooper is a freelance journalist based in the U.K. Wounded twice in Africa, he is the coauthor of *Flashpoint! At the Frontline of Today's Wars* (with Ken Guest) and *Beneath the Visiting Moon,* a documentary account of his six months with a counterinsurgency unit in Namibia. During the war in Angola, Hooper accompanied UNITA forces on guerrilla operations against Soviet and Cuban-backed government forces. He has also covered conflicts in Chad, Sudan, South Africa and Uganda. His articles and photos have appeared in a wide range of publications including *Jane's Intelligence Review, The Economist* and *The Sunday Telegraph* of London.

Jack Kramer

Kramer has been sent to the world's most dangerous places on assignment for *TIME, Business Week* and *PBS.* He began his career by covering the civil rights movement in the Deep South during the mid-60s. In the late '60s, he went from covering the battles at home to experiencing and reporting on some of the bloodiest fighting of the Vietnam War, from Cam Lo to Khe Sanh. Later, his beat was the turbulent Middle East, including the Six-Day War, Sudan and Eritria. He worked as a television producer for PBS on "Behind the Lines" and was *Business Week's* Cairo bureau chief, covering Saudi Arabia, the Gulf States and Iran. He covered Iran before, during and after the revolution and then restarted the defunct *Beirut Daily Star* in 1984. Kramer has covered Kenya, Rhodesia (Zimbabwe), Tanzania, Laos, Thailand, Tunisia, Turkey, Syria, South Africa and the Somalia crisis. He has traveled with the Innuit in northern Canada and with the Polisario guerrillas in Morocco. He is author of *Our French Connection in Africa,* a major investigative report published in *Foreign Policy* and *Travels with the Celestial Dog,* a historical analysis of the 1960s. He lives in Washington, D.C., with his wife and their two children.

Anthony Morland

Morland was born in York, England, and grew up in London and Rome. He began his journalism career in Geneva and now works as an AFP correspondent for Agence France Presse in Abidjan, Ivory Coast.

Roddy Scott

Scott graduated from Edinburgh University and began his career as a journalist for a magazine in the Middle East. He writes for a variety of newspapers and magazines including *Soldier of Fortune* and *New African.* He also conducts radio interviews for BBC World Service and Radio France International.

TABLE OF CONTENTS

CRIMINAL PLACES

ADVENTURE GUIDE

LIST OF MAPS

Foreword

The standard first question most interviewers ask me is "What is the most dangerous thing in the world?" My answer is always "Ignorance." Many people make the assumption that they know the difference between dangerous and safe. Unfortunately, as travelers are kidnapped and executed in Cambodia, a recognized dangerous place, they also are hunted down and murdered in Los Angeles. As I checked into a Royal Air Cambodge flight to Phnom Penh, I asked if Cambodia is dangerous. The clerk looked at me, and in reference to the killing of Hang Ngor by LA gang members, replied, "Obviously a lot safer than Los Angeles."

Danger is all around us. It's found in the black hearts of junkies looking for a quick hit, terrorists looking for publicity, in the poorly maintained tin buckets that pass as airplanes you fly in across the Himalayas, the water you drink in Kenya, or even in the air-conditioning ducts on a cruise ship. Danger is what happens when you are not prepared or knowledgeable or unlucky.

Danger is all around, and, for the traveler faced with a new environment and strange cultures, it is important to at least have a level playing field. This book will not tell all, or even attempt to provide a comprehensive list. It *will* provide fairly candid appraisals of the dangers that await the unsuspecting. Along the way, you will learn and understand things and places that are rarely talked about in polite circles: how drugs are smuggled, how much money mercenaries make, the cost to bribe your way out of jail and much more. For those who have the common sense to read this book but have no intention of setting foot in the world's most dangerous places, you now will have plenty of reasons never to leave your armchair.

Who This Book Is For

Intelligence junkies

Those who have an unabashed curiosity about the world may be looking for a central source of information on dangerous places. This book can never compete with the files of the world's intelligence agencies, but it makes for good reading on a 20 hour plane trip. If you want real up-to-the-minute "intel," join the CIA. If you want to have a general grounding on the political complexities of the world, go to school.

Journalists

The hard-boiled scribes and shooters who travel to cover danger require a basic grounding in the regions' danger zones and a rudimentary background on the perils that await them. Some journalists know more about their destination than the people who live there. Others could care less. If nothing else, this book will confirm your darkest suspicion about your next assignment. For those in need of the latest info, call the local newspaper editor or the embassy and tap into the State Department's on-line incident reports. If you disagree with anything in this book or have something to add, drop us a line.

Expats

Expats are people who choose to work and live in a country other than their own. This means they are willing to overlook certain problems in direct proportion to the amount of tax-free benefits they receive. Expats tend to live in manicured ghettos, genteel compounds or secure buildings. They pride themselves on the amount of research they ingest before packing their bags. Little do they know that most of the info is provided by their future employer and the Western press.

Later, safely ensconced in their air-conditioned villas, they realize they might as well be on the moon. They quickly distance themselves from the shaggy unkempt backpackers, quick to point out they are "locals." All this means is that their "local" neighborhood liberation group has been clocking every shopping trip, intimidating the housekeeper and timing how long their children spend on the bus to school. *DP* will not tell you how to spend your weekends, but it is a starting point for your education.

Adventure travelers

The legions of healthy, young, urban professionals looking for a two-week recharge may or may not be aware of the dangers that await them in those ecogroovy destinations. The rapid increase in travel to exotic regions will continue to attract travelers as they venture to more and more far-flung countries. Many of the new countries currently in favor are "adventurer destinations" such as Cambodia, Kenya, India, Pakistan and Turkey. They all possess both dangerous and safe regions.

Most will return robust and suntanned. Some will die, the result of bus crashes, robberies, kidnappings, land mines and diseases. Most adventure travelers rely on politically correct but militarily naive guidebooks published by such companies as Lonely Planet, Moon Publications and Rough Guides. They provide minimal coverage of war zones (although there has recently been an attempt by some to provide anecdotes and tips on nasty places) or simply tell you to stay away. Very few backpacker guide writers will risk their lives for the paltry sums earned creating these books. Their hesitation in covering the untouristy subjects of land mines, street executions, kidnapping of foreigners and drug smuggling is also understandable, in light of the fact that book sales are based on the number of travelers who go there. Understandably we don't meet many travel writers or tourists on our research trips.

Adrenaline junkies and war freaks

There are people who look for nerve-tingling destinations. Some of those folks ask how to get a "job" with *DP*. Predictably, we reply to the many ex-Marines, ex-SEALS and ex-Rangers that writing for *DP* is "not a job but an adventure." The world has many areas that attract ghouls, mercenaries, thrill seekers and the intellectually curious. They swarm into small countries in their Banana Republic safari jackets and Tony Lama boots, bearing Halliburton briefcases and smeared tattoos. Soon all the good hotels are full of arms dealers, pilots, advisors, embassy attachés and spooks. This book can provide a basic grounding for those heading in harm's way but does not endorse travel to dangerous places. (See you at the bar.)

The curious and easily amused

The intellectual, the curious and the bored will find that this book contains information not available in any other guidebook—for example, where you shouldn't take your Barbie dolls, how much the Chechen mafia charges for battlefront tours, and even where to find pirates. If you manage to wade through the entire book, you might even come up with a few good screenplays.

A Polite Discourse on Liability (Ours) and Gullibility (Yours)

If you decide to wax up your VISA card and actually go to some of the locations described in this book, our advice is more likely to kill you than save your life. (On the other hand, since more people are injured in their homes than outside them, you may be safer traveling to some of the places in this book.) Areas of conflict change daily, land mines are laid every night, and dictators move in and out of the presidential mansion faster than summer replacement sitcoms. We have been taken to task by institutions like *Outside* magazine for our overly verbose disclaimer, but the bottom line in this book is about how to stay *away* from danger. If you want to fly in the face of common sense, you can ignore our warnings and be killed, kidnapped, robbed, beaten or all of the above.

Some of the information is gathered from secondhand sources, especially where we feel it is more accurate than our firsthand reports. War zones, Third World countries and nasty places are very mercurial places with no one really knowing what's going on at any one time. Situations change by the hour. We ask a lot of questions, and we write down the answers that make sense. We avoid interviews with politicians and zealots, and sometimes people tell us the wrong answer or, God forbid, just lie. We check out as much as we can, but we use a lot of common sense and street smarts in translating what we see and hear. So use this book and other sources as pieces of the puzzle. If you choose to travel to dangerous places, get your situation reports updated by everyone all the time. Ask the embassy, the police, locals, bus drivers and farmers what's going on. But remember, even if you have all the pieces, you're still left with a puzzle.

Our official disclaimer for people who didn't get the point of the paragraph above: Please understand that due to the nature of this book and the unusual sources of information, we ask that you do not make any decisions based on the material presented here. In fact, this book is about places where you should not go (they *are* dangerous). This book is written by a group of people with help from correspondents, friends and contacts around the world. To protect many of our sources (we do have to, uh, break, or rather bend, some laws), we have not credited all of them. We cannot guarantee this information is accurate or reliable simply because by the time we get back and write it down, the situation could reverse. Do not use this book for the planning of any activity. We encourage you always to investigate thoroughly and use as many sources of information as you can find regarding areas where you wish to travel. Although we have an uncanny knack for predicting wars, massacres and kidnappings, Fielding and the authors cannot take responsibility for any misfortune, liability or inconvenience due to your interpretation, application or even understanding of the information in this book. Let's do it again in all caps now:

THE AUTHORS AND PUBLISHERS ASSUME NO LIABILITY NOR DO THEY ENCOURAGE YOU TO DO, SEE, VISIT OR TRY ANY OF THE ACTIVITIES OR ACTIONS DISCUSSED IN THIS BOOK. THIS BOOK IS INTENDED FOR BACKGROUND INFORMATION ONLY AND MAY NOT BE RELIABLE AFTER PRESS TIME.

The Modest Goal of the Authors: Unemployment

This book is not all doom and gloom. There are sections on how to "Make a Difference" and "Save the Planet." We show you how to actually connect with other people and organizations to effect change. It might be clearing land mines in Cambodia, sleeping in a hammock high up in an Indonesian forest to fight off loggers, protecting diamond mines in Sierra Leone as a paid mercenary, or even teaching people how to vote. In all cases, I hope that this book encourages you to dig a little deeper into lesser-known regions and peoples of the world. We do not support any cause, back any fight or endorse any activity that uses violence. But like spectators at a Brazilian soccer game, however, we're not supposed to play but we get awfully close to the action sometimes. We can't afford to be partisan, but we encourage you to root and support your favorite cause. Don't be shy about contacting the resources listed to find out more.

This is our primitive formula for success: Educate people as to what is going on and then show them how to fix it. Knowledge fights fear, builds hope, exposes cowards, supports the just and makes the world a better place. We do not aspire to greatness, but we do hope that we intrigue enough people to want to know how to gather information and then do something with it.

It is our goal that sometime in the future we will not be able to find enough dangerous places in the world to justify writing a book about the subject. But, we are in our second edition and we continue to add countries.

—**RYP**

What Is Dangerous?

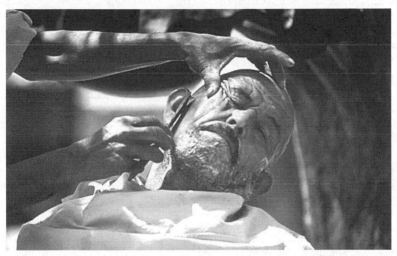

Everyone wonders how they will die or meet misfortune. Newspapers, magazines and television shows thrive on sensationalizing and personalizing a world full of tragedy and bringing it to your home every day. However, the reality is you will most likely die of natural causes, followed by disease and then because of an accident. Travel is way down on the list.

There are three danger zones in life. The first major hurtle is making it through the first year of life. The second is surviving until the ripe old age of 37, prior to which accidental death is the grim reaper's best friend. Unintentional injuries are the fifth-leading cause of death. The third stage is making it past the list of debilitating diseases that claim most people and surviving into old age. It's important to understand the relative dangers of normal living to appreciate the numbers that you will read about in later chapters. The dangers that face you when you travel are infinitesimal when compared to just surviving the dangers you face in the nine-to-five grind, running to the fridge to get your eighth beer, or just surviving the frenetic weekend activities that pass for relaxation.

So, what is dangerous and what isn't? Since this is a book about dangerous travel, let's look at the odds. There's a one in 10 million chance of dying in a plane crash. Not bad. The odds of getting killed on a train are 10 times higher, about one in a million. Still good but not great.

If you think that pilot error or cannibis-smoking railroad engineers are the cause of most accidents, try driving across the country. The chances of getting killed are one in 14,000—worse odds yet. That's dangerous, yet a full third of American drivers don't even bother to buckle up. The recent increase in American speed limits from 55 to 65 has jacked the accident fatality rate a whopping 44 percent. But we are speeding ahead of ourselves. So what will get you?

Time

The number-one killer is that kindly, grandfatherly looking fellow, Father Time. Although there is a slow lengthening of our lives as standards of living, safety, nutrition and health care spread to the lower incomes, we are all subject to deterioration of tissues. Most of us can expect to live to our mid-70s before getting nervous about getting our money's worth on a five-year carpet. In 1890, life expectancy was 31.1 years. In 1995, it was 75.4 years. Joining the century club is completely possible for the next generation.

How to cheat the grim reaper? First, don't let accidental causes get in the way. Second, exercise and eat right and maintain a positive mental attitude. How is that done? Travel, of course. People who live the longest seem to have an insatiable curiosity as well as a natural love for travel. There are a lot of those wiry little octogenarians that seem perfectly healthy, have inquiring minds, travel a lot and are always looking for a good time. Some of them started reading Fielding guides when they were 30! They stay out of the house as much as possible, fully understanding that the home is the world's most dangerous place (see "Accidents") for people over the age of 75.

Accidental Death

OK, you bought a stack of travel guides and stretched your finances to buy that round-the-world cruise ticket. But how do you live long enough to enjoy all your acquired common sense? You have to get through four stages:

Young and Tender

In 1994, there were 34,628 children who did not make it past the first year of life in the U.S. If you make it out of the womb (15,562 didn't) without a major congenital abnormality (7449 did), there's Sudden Infant Death Syndrome to deal with (4891). The next most dangerous incidents are choking (229), car crashes (160), ingesting a foreign object (103), burns or fires (98) and drowning (89).

Young and Reckless

Young male teenagers in cars seem to have a death wish. Eighteen may be a magic age for most people, but it is a very profitable target demographic for undertakers. Of every 100,000 eighteen-year-olds, 55.5 of them will die in car crashes.

Middle-aged and Reckless

What is the number-two accidental killer of people between the ages of 18 and 49 (after car accidents, of course)? Dying to know the answer? It's accidental poisoning—a curious manner of death, with a rate highest for men aged 37. Most of this poisoning is the result of the deadly side effects of ingesting normal medicines.

Old and Clumsy

The next time you send Gramps downstairs to find his glasses, don't be surprised if he doesn't come back. Falls collect a number of victims in the age group above 75. Although the number pales in comparison to heart disease, it is worth remembering: 8336 people died from falls last year vs. 438,873 from heart disease.

Disease

OK, the ballet and meditation lessons are paying off; you are a now a graceful, cautious, levelheaded person, you drive real slow, and tip your hat and smile at anyone who carries an automatic weapon. But there is an insidious killer that few of us have any control over. So add some items to your busy schedule like eating tofu burgers, exercising daily, staying out of the sun and following the advice of Bill Clinton: if you smoke anything, don't inhale, and if you have an affair, don't stick it in. AIDs is spreading at an alarming rate among young people, so if you are under 45, make sure you pack your leak-tested haz-mat suit with extra gaffers tape when you go to Club Med. HIV claimed 24,629 people between the ages of 25 and 44 and has become the number-one killer for those 25–34.

When the numbers were totalled up in 1995, the leading cause of death due to medical problems in America was heart disease (717,706 deaths). Cancer claimed 520,578 lives, strokes accounted for 143,769 fatalities, and chronic obstructive pulmonary disease claimed 91,938 victims. It's a long way down to the next killer. Are there any trends to give us hope? The rates of incidence of stomach, uterus and liver cancer have dropped since 1930. But lung cancer and leukemia cases have climbed dramatically. So don't smoke, don't work in coal mines, don't have unprotected sex, and stay away from nuclear waste sites.

OK, those numbers are great for the sedentary hordes who are content to watch "Wild Kingdom" reruns. What about us hairy-chested adventurers, slashing our way through the tropical jungle? Although adventure films have titles like *The Temples of Doom* or *Mars Attack*, they should more accurately be titled *Montezuma's Revenge* or *Kebab Attack*. The reality is that the only guaranteed discomfort adventurers will experience is that mad dash to sit and ponder the world's great and varied selection of evacuation devices. (How come Rambo and Indiana Jones never have the runs?).

Dr. Richard Dawood put together an interesting chart in *Condé Nast Traveler* using info from the World Health Organization and from a study by Professor Robert Steffen of the University of Zurich. The following table is the monthly incidence of health problems experienced by travelers to tropical destinations (based on a sample of 100,000 people):

Health Problems Experienced (per 100,000 Travelers)		
Experienced a health problem	55%	55,000
Felt ill	25%	25,000
Consulted doctor	.08%	8000
Stayed in bed	.06%	6000
Unable to work upon return	.02%	2000
Hospitalized while abroad	.004%	400

| Evacuated by air | .0006% | 60 |
| Died abroad | .00001% | 1 |

Source: Condé Nast Traveler

Dawood mentions the results of a study done by the British Consumers Association among 15,972 members which revealed that 15% of their members had been sick on vacation. The results are not that surprising when you look at countries where travelers became sick:

When it comes to Montezuma's revenge or Delhi Belly no surprises here. India (60 percent), Egypt (53 percent) and Mexico (40 percent) are the best places to get the runs. Most people will experience diarrhea or intestinal problems with about 25–40 percent of travelers to tropical places being afflicted. Sunburn affects about 10 percent of travelers with the Caribbean and Mexico being the most likely places to get fried.

Malaria affected a minuscule number of travelers (1036 in 1994 or about.0000345 percent of the 30 million U.S. residents who traveled abroad.) About 3 percent of those cases were fatal.

Top-Ten Cancer Killers

The number of cancer deaths has shot up over the last 15 years, with exceptions in very few areas.

	MEN	1971	1996*
1.	Lung	54,931	94,400
2.	Prostrate	17,772	41,400
3.	Colon/Rectum	22,410	27,400
4.	Pancreas	9967	13,600
5.	Lymphoma	7577	13,250
6.	Leukemia	8206	11,600
7.	Esophagus	4599	8500
8.	Liver	4711	8400
9.	Stomach	9421	8300
10.	Bladder	6075	7800
	WOMEN	**1971**	**1996***
1.	Lung	13,686	64,300
2.	Breast	29,969	44,300
3.	Colon/Rectum	23,924	27,500
4.	Ovary	9978	14,800
5.	Pancreas	7945	14,200
6.	Lymphoma	6016	11,560
7.	Uterus	12,216	10,900
8.	Leukemia	6263	9400
9.	Liver	7945	6800
10.	Brain	3518	6100

Source: American Cancer Society   ** projected*

Accidents

We weren't joking in saying that if you want to live longer, stay out of the house. But just don't leave too fast and don't take your car. People between the age of 70 and 90 are attracted to stairs like lemmings to cliffs. But even at younger ages, if you really want to live dangerously, stay at home. Yes Virginia, most accidents happen at home. Any student of statistics will tell you that home is where people spend the majority of their time. Each year slippery tile floors, cheap ginsu knives and trendy glass coffee tables will do more damage than all the world's terrorists.

When should you plan to spend a month in that Buddhist retreat? Well, the most dangerous month for accidents is August, with 9000 unintentional injuries versus a monthly incidence average of 7500. The safest month is February, with only 5700. Curious to know the other most dangerous months?

Cause of Death	Most Dangerous Month	#	Least Dangerous Month	#	Avg
Car Accidents	August	4243	January	2869	3628
Falls	December	1145	February	959	1055
Drownings	July	886	November	147	385
Firearms	November	164	September	83	120
Fire	January	539	June	194	343
Poisoning	August	572	January	412	475

Source: National Center for Health Statistics and National Safety Council

Domestic Accidents

A survey by the Department of Trade and Industry's Consumer Safety Unit brings us some bad news. When the Home Accident Surveillance Unit looked into what caused 17,726 accidents, they came up with a rogues' gallery of culprits and tools.

"All right drop that loofah, get up slowly out of that rocking chair, and hold that dustpan up where we can see it."

A partial list of objects that were the cause of a domestic accident:

Sofa	1422
Bathtub	1016
Toilet	398
Sink Taps	149
Washing Machine	201
Sponge/Loofah	25
Door Bell/Entry Phone	41
Dressing Gowns	33
Rocking Chair	25
Dustpan	7
Shoe Scraper	6
Chopsticks	3

Source: Department of Trade and Industry's Consumer Safety Unit

What Danger Awaits the Weary Traveler?

From the moment you grasp your airline seat with sweaty palms to the minute your cab rolls to a stop at your front door, most travelers have a nervous feeling that their life has become more dangerous. The reality is quite the opposite. Remember we told you that fewer accidents happen to people when they travel than when they are at home. Why?

Well, think of whom you trust your life to when you travel. If you survive the cab ride, you'll arrive in a well-designed, safe terminal, complete with sprinklers, emergency exits and, in many cases, on-site medical staff. (Does your house have this?) When you board the plane, you enter a multimillion dollar aircraft, the culmination of more than 100 years of aviation safety engineering. Every element and part of the computer-designed wonder is regulated, inspected, maintained and replaced. Up front, you have two pilots who are the best of their kind. Many American pilots are Vietnam-era pilots who have flown in combat. Many have racked up tens of thousands of hours in the air. Every pilot goes through intensive training and regular retraining to stay in top form. You are given flight safety procedures by individuals trained in emergency situations, first aid and other lifesaving procedures. After you are aloft, you are now under the control of a global traffic network that tracks all major aircraft and weather patterns using a system of computers and fail-safe devices. When you finally arrive at your destination, tired but safe, you meet your driver/guide.

From then on, you're on your own. The fact that your guide is drunk, blind in one eye and drives what used to be a 1957 Chevy still can't take your mind off his gold tooth and missing fingers. So it's off to the rebel camp to meet the guerillas. "Oh, by the way," he says in his aguardiente -laced breath, "the *gobermente* overran the camp yesterday, but I think *el jefe* is still alive."

Oops, we are getting ahead of ourselves again. Travel in the First World is pretty sedentary and predictable. Buses, trains and cars are subject to stringent safety laws in both construction and operation. Hotels have sophisticated sprinkler systems and emergency evacuation plans. Restaurants are inspected by health inspectors, and so on. You can even get your fare back if you are hijacked or killed. Now that's customer service!

The hordes of Tilley-hatted ecotourists have not always been with us. In the year I was born (1955), there were only 46 million people traveling from one country to another. Most of them were well-heeled folks "doing the continent" or "taking the sun." Ten years later there were 144 million and by the early nineties there were 455 million. That's a lot of Samsonite. In 1995 these travelers cleaned out their wallets to the tune of $315 billion. So what do half a billion people worry about when they travel? A recent survey of vacationers in Europe came up with the following:

What Me Worry?	%
Burglary of home while away	90%
Illness and accidents on holiday	40%
Family's safety	33%
Bad accommodation	26%
Bad weather	19%
Bad food	18%
Work	6%

By the very definition of travel, you will be forced to choose some form of transportation. Planes are the safest means; cars are the most dangerous. In America, the death rate per miles traveled is comforting for those who fly but unsettling for the majority of people who like to drive:

Type of Passenger Transport	Death Rate (per billion passenger miles)	Passenger Miles (in billions)
Passenger Cars	.89	2393.2
Intercity Buses	.03	23.7
Transit Buses	.01	20.6
Trains	.02	13.5
Airplanes	.01	354.3

Americans tend to be a little diffident about the goings-on in other countries. Very few Americans list any of their own tourist destinations as potentially dangerous places. You may be surprised to learn what Europeans think of as dangerous:

Europeans' Most Dangerous Places	%
Florida	42%
North Africa	9%
Turkey	7%
California	7%
Kenya	7%

Many fears people have are unfounded. But to help people better understand the dangers and by offering some safety measures (every travel guide must have tips!), we throw a little light on the world of travel.

Minibuses

Expect danger every time you decide to get into a taxi; but expect death in a small minivan. You may prefer to travel by bus, cab, rickshaw, trishaw, *becek* or even rollerblades after your first Third World minivan ride.

The most dangerous form of travel in the world is the fabled minibus. These Third World creations are small Japanese-made transports with a drive train that has a hard time pushing around a family of four but manage to carry up to 48 (yes, I have counted 48—24 inside and 24 on top). Most minivans are designed to seat 7–12 people.

Minivans are used primarily for rush-hour transportation of poor people to work. Unlike the large, regulated buses, minivans are run by entrepreneurs who make their money by carrying as many people as many times as they can. For example, in South Africa 60,000 accidents involving minibuses killed more than 900 people in 1993. In Peru, where they are called "killer combis," the death toll also includes nonpassengers trying to get out of the way of the weaving, speeding vans. The deadly driving style is a function of drivers who must make their money within the two hours of rush hour in order to make a profit on their rental owner's charge. Last year, 375 pedestrians were killed by the 30,000 or so minivans in Lima. The numbers are not available for most Third World countries. A rough estimate puts the chances of a fatality in a minibus, or *matatu* or combi, at about 30 times the normal U.S. accident rate. So, the next time you plunk down between a quarter to fifty cents for one of these rides, consider for how much you just sold your life.

Imagine what happens when your body decelerates from 60 to zero m.p.h. in two milliseconds. Not pretty. Having been at the site of many small bus crashes in my travels, I can best compare the scenes to putting a dozen mice in a coffee can along with glass and nails, slamming it against a wall and then shaking it for a few minutes more. Then spray the bloody contents across the path of oncoming traffic. That pretty much sums up the bloody and confused scene of a *matatu* accident.

HOW TO SURVIVE MINIBUSES

There is a reason for the multitude of religious symbols, slogans and prayers painted on Third World buses. Once they cram their doors shut and the wobbly wheels start forward, your life is in the hands of a supreme being. If you travel via small buses, remember the following:

- **Understand the potential danger before you get aboard. Is there a safer way?**

HOW TO SURVIVE MINIBUSES

- Avoid mountainous areas and/or winter conditions. Fly if necessary.

- Bring water and food with you, plan for the unexpected, delays and diversions.

- Ask whether the route goes through areas frequented by bandits or terrorist groups.

- Sit near an exit or on top. At least make sure you are near an open window.

- Don't antagonize anyone and follow the *DP* rule: Be friends to everyone—your seat mate might be a rebel commander.

- Remember your luggage is prey for rummagers, slashers and thieves. Put your luggage in a standard trash bag, a canvas duffle or under everyone else's.

- Watch for shirt slashers if you doze off; put your money in your shoes if necessary.

- Do not accept food or drink from male passengers but offer your own.

Taxis

Our esteemed founder, Temple Fielding, was reputed to have once lost a libel case wherein he described a particular cab company as the biggest crooks in Italy. The cab company easily won the case because they proved, not that they were innocent, but that there were bigger criminal operations in Italy at the time.

When you get into a taxi driven by a stranger in a strange land, watch out. The odds for damage to your body, your sense of well being and your wallet just jumped. Cabs in most countries have no seatbelts, no brakes, no license and no top end on what can be charged. In many countries, such as Colombia, you could get robbed in the bargain. Taxis can't always be controlled by telling the driver to drive slowly in his native language. I do remember a friend of mine, during one particularly terrifying cab ride, rummaging through his Greek phrase book, yelling what he thought meant "slower" at the top of his lungs. As the driver divided his time between staring at us incredulously and trying to maintain control of his over-revved cab, we thought we were in the hands of a lunatic. At the end of our ride, the wide-eyed cabdriver was visibly relieved to see the last of us. Upon closer examination, we realized in our haste to translate, we had been screaming, "Faster, faster!" To be fair, I also had a cabdriver in Malaysia carry around stacks of expensive luggage all day long for less than $20. Based on courtesy, cleanliness, knowledge and respect for human life, the world's best cabdrivers are in London and the world's worst cabbies are in New York City.

HOW TO SURVIVE TAXIS

- Never get into a taxi with another local already inside.

- Do not take gypsy cabs; ask the airline people how much it should cost to go to your destination and then agree upon a fare before you get in.

- Keep your luggage in the backseat and pay your fare after you've unloaded.

- Memorize the local phrases for "no," "yes," "stop here" and "how much?"

- Have the hotel doorman or guide negotiate cab fares in advance.

- Check your change before you get into the cab or get change. It seems to be a global law that cabbies never carry change.

- Many cabbies will rent themselves out for flat fees. Do not be afraid to engage the services of a trusted cabby as guide and protector of baggage.

- Do not tell cabbies where you are going during your stay, when you are leaving or any other particulars that could be of interest to bad people.

Automobiles

If you rent or drive a car, you can expect a few thrills and spills along the way. First, you should know the most dangerous places to drive in the United States:

U.S. Vehicular Deaths per 100,000 population	
South Carolina	25.2
Mississippi	31.3
New Mexico	27.9
Tennessee	23.4
Arkansas	27.0
Alabama	30.0
West Virginia	24.0
Wyoming	24.2
Idaho	24.3
Kentucky	22.1

The accident rate for international travel is clouded by lack of reporting and the skew in numbers caused by the large numbers of people who die in vehicle-related accidents and don't have the courtesy to fill out the paperwork after they are dead. Countries like Mexico, Pakistan, Australia, India, Egypt and China have horrendous accident rates but do not figure prominently in studies. Countries like Afghanistan, Zaire, Sierra Leone and Liberia wish they had enough cars or roads to have accidents. Obviously, in the U.S., travel "down South" behind the wheel of a car can be nasty business. Here's what it's like outside the country:

International Vehicular Deaths (per 100,000 population)	
India	34.6
South Korea	30.4
Portugal	28.1
Brazil	22.7
Hungary	22.7
Greece	22.0
Venezuela	20.7
Spain	20.5
Ecuador	20.0
New Zealand	19.5
Luxembourg	19.4
Poland	19.2
Belgium	18.4
United States	18.4

Trivia buffs might like to know that the first car accident was on May 30, 1896, in New York City (with a bicyclist); the first fatality was on September 13, 1889 (a pedestrian). The death toll caused by auto accidents in 1994 was 40,676 (from 6.5 million accidents)—not much numerical change from 1937 with a death toll of 39.643 people (out of 7 million accidents), but a significant statistical drop per person.

How to Get Killed Driving

If you have a death wish, you could find a 16-year-old to drive you around, go for drinks and take a back road on a Friday night. Sixteen-year-olds are the most dangerous drivers in America, being involved in 1200 deadly accidents during 1994. But more driving-related fatalities involve the use of alcohol. Many more. A recent study by Ford Motor Company revealed that secondary roads have an accident rate nearly twice as high and a fatality rate more than double that of interstate highways. On some rural roads on weekends after midnight, one out of three drivers are drunk. A nationwide organization of 25,000 sheriffs, deputy sheriffs and municipal, state and federal law enforcement officers were polled to find out what causes accidents:

Causes of Vehicular Accident	
Alcohol/Drugs influenced	90%
Speeding	83%

Causes of Vehicular Accident	
Running red traffic lights	78%
Not concentrating on driving	76%
Aggressive driving	68%
Tailgating	63%

Source: National Sheriff's Association

What are the chances you will be killed while driving overseas? Well, it depends. First off, most statistics for accidents are based on accidents that locals have. Second of all, the number of tourist fatalities is rather insignificant compared to domestic death rates. The average death toll outside the U.S. for Americans involved in traffic-related accidents during a typical year is 750 with 25,000 injured. If you compare that to the 40,000 or so who buy it Stateside, it really isn't a big deal.

Road deaths per 100,000 people	
France	15
Spain	14
Italy	12.5
Germany	12
Sweden	7.5
Britain	6

Source: WTO, Int. Road Federation

The general rules of common sense apply in every country in the world. The only major difference is the opportunity for bad roads, defective vehicles and bad drivers. Another big difference between First and Third World highways is the disparity in driver licensing standards. Many countries have licensing standards far below those of the United States, and in many Third World countries unlicensed drivers hit the roadways every day, posing a danger to everything in their path.

If there is one general rule that can help to save your life, it is to avoid driving or traveling by road at night and in bad weather. Nighttime reduces visibility and is also the witching hour for drunks. Bad weather doubles the danger. The other general rule is to reduce your speed, and the final is to be in control of your own vehicle.

HOW TO SURVIVE AUTOMOBILES

There is little to be said that hasn't been said in every driver's education class you have ever taken. Speed, booze, lousy roads and other drivers kill. Driving in the Third World is not safe, so if possible check out Hertz Rent-A-Yak.

HOW TO SURVIVE AUTOMOBILES

- Be familiar with road warning signs and laws. For example, in Borneo, there are signs telling you to stick to the left or right of the road to choreograph the intentions of oncoming logging trucks. In Europe, unless a road sign says otherwise, traffic to your right at any intersection has priority. In countries like Mexico, you are considered at fault in any accident and will be hauled off to jail while your cocrashee staggers back to the cantina to finish his drink.

- Avoid driving if possible. Nobody gets up in the morning and plans on having an accident. The fact that you are rubbernecking or checking maps while on the wrong side of the road dramatically increases your chances of an accident. Flying is safer than driving.

- Avoid driving in inclement weather conditions, nighttime or on weekends. Fog kills, rain kills, drunks kill, other tourists kill. It is estimated that after midnight on Friday and Saturday nights in rural America, three out of five drivers on the road have been drinking. That means if you are one of the sober ones, pray that the only other sober driver is coming the other way.

- Stay off the road in high-risk countries. You may think the Italians, Portuguese and Spaniards display amazing bravado as they skid around winding mountain roads. The accident rate says they are just lousy drivers.

- Secondary roads have an accident rate almost twice as high and a fatality rate that is double the interstates. You choose.

- Reduce your speed. To see the difference in impact at various speeds, try running as fast as you can into the nearest wall. Now walk slowly and do it again. See how much better that is?

- Wear a seat belt, rent bigger cars, use freeways, carry a map and a good road guide, etc. You're not listening, are you?

- If you can hire a driver with car, do so. Contact tour companies, embassy staff and hotel concierges. Many countries provide a driver when you rent a car, so make sure you feel comfortable with him. Try a one-day city tour first to see if the chemistry and his driving skills are to your tastes.

- Don't drive tired or while suffering from jet lag. Don't pull off to the side of the road to nap, don't leave possessions in plain sight, and try to park in lighted areas. I can see you're not listening, so just do whatever the hell you are going to do, but don't say I didn't warn you.

Boats

"Row, row, row your boat" may now be a little ditty you can use to strike terror into the heart of little children. "Ro-ro" is also short for "roll-on, roll-off" ferries that ply the frigid northern waters between Scandinavia, Russia, Europe and Great Britain. Ro-ros can also be found in Alaska, British Columbia, Washington and the Greek Isles as well as anywhere a lot of car traffic has to get to an island quickly and efficiently. There are about 2000 of these ferries, and the 1994 sinking of the *Estonia* brought some much needed attention to this dicey form of travel. Since cars must drive in the front and then out the back, the ships feature large doors that yawn open. No problem when you are tied to a dock, but when heavy seas start pounding and water enters the ship, these mammoth vessels will flip like a waterlogged rubber ducky. The chances of anyone finding a lifeboat or even getting outside to jump overboard are slim to none. For example, 900 people perished in the *Estonia* disaster, the *Herald of Free Enterprise* sank in the English Channel killing 193. Not a trend but a warning. Since then, maritime safety officials have demanded that bulkheads be installed to act as a second line of defense. Open-deck ferries are safer, since they allow water to run off.

Ferries in places like Bangladesh, Haiti, the Philippines and Hong Kong have had major disasters from capsizing due to overloading and collision. Between 1986 and 1994, there have been more than 360 ferry boat accidents killing 11,350 people.

In May of '96 as many as 549 people were killed on Lake Tangent in Tanzania in a ferry accident, in which 700 passengers were aboard a boat designed for 441. Crew members took bribes to let people aboard who did not have tickets. Within the same month, 77 people were drowned when two river ferries collided. In Bangladesh more than 50 ferry boats have sunk since 1981 killing more than 1000 people.

Cruise ships are much safer, with the occasional engine room fire and food poisoning problem. However, it doesn't provide much comfort to know that the *Achille Lauro* (site of the terrorist takeover that ended in the execution of a wheelchair-bound American, Leon Klinghoffer) sank off the coast of Africa but is now being dredged up and refurbished for use as a luxury cruise liner.

HOW TO SURVIVE BOATS

It is hard to provide general safety tips, considering the wide range of waterborne craft travelers can take. Large cruise ships have very different safety problems, when compared to pirogues. Here is a starting list.

- **Know how to swim, or at least how to float. Panic kills.**

- **Wear or have quick access to a life preserver. Don't assume that large chest labeled "Life Preservers" actually has usable life preservers in it.**

- **Do not take overcrowded boats. Charter your own, or ask when the boat will be less crowded. Overcrowding and rough seas are the number-one reason for sinking of small and medium-sized ships.**

- **Do not travel in rough weather, during monsoon or in hurricane season.**

- **Stay off the water in areas frequented by pirates. This is typically the Strait of Malacca and the coastal areas of the Philippines, Thailand and southern China.**

- **In cold weather, remember where the covered life rafts are. Understand the effects and prevention of hypothermia.**

- **On large ships, pay attention to safety and life boat briefings and practice going from your cabin to the life boat station with your eyes closed.**

HOW TO SURVIVE BOATS

- Keep a small carry-on or backpack with your money, papers and minor survival gear (water, energy bars, hat, compass and map). Make it waterproof by using one or two garbage bags as a liner.

- Prepare and bring items to prevent seasickness, sunburn, glare and chapped skin.

- Bring binoculars, books, coastal maps, pens and a journal to pass away the time.

Planes

North America is the safest place to fly. If you fly any First World airline, your chances of being killed in a crash are one in 4.4 million, according to Massachusetts Institute of Technology. If you are on a U.S. carrier, flying coast to coast, the odds are even better, one in 11 million. Other studies say that your odds of getting on a plane that is going to crash are one in every 20,000. About two-thirds of major airline crashes have been blamed on flight crew error. When you change from a big bird to a puddle-jumper you have just increased your chances of crashing by a factor of four. Commuter flights (flights with 30 or fewer seats) carry about 12 percent of all passengers. These small planes not only fly lower, take off and land more often, but are piloted by less experienced, more over-worked pilots and are not subject to the same safety standards as large airliners.

U.S. puddle-jumpers are as safe as houses compared to Third World airlines. If you are flying anywhere in Africa, the chances of crashing are multiplied by 20—about the same odds as getting killed in an automobile accident in the States. Get on a smaller plane or a charter, and the odds multiply again. About 700 people die in small plane crashes each year in America. Buddy Holly, Ricky Nelson, Stevie Ray Vaughan, Rocky Graziano, and a host of politicians, race drivers and other high flyers have died as victims of small plane crashes. There are so many crashes that the small airplane industry has evaporated, because of the litigation caused by each crash. There are 650,000 private pilots in the U.S., and only 700 out of the 13,000 U.S. airfields have control towers. The accident rate for a small plane is about 11 for every 100,000 aircraft hours compared to .8 for commercial jets. There are two fatalities for every 100,000 hours of operation for small planes.

Falling From the Friendly Skies

Some experts calculate that the odds of being killed in a plane crash are less than one in a million for North America, Canada and Western Europe versus one in 50,000 for the dark continent. Flying in Latin America, the Middle East, Asia and Eastern Europe are the next most dangerous areas of the world. Colombia's Avianca has one of the worst flight safety records in the world. Not surprising, considering that poorer countries fly old aircraft usually purchased from major carriers that have already wrung every useful mile from their airframes. The safety of these aircraft is aggravated by substandard maintenance programs and less-developed facilities.

Although we have shown that flying is safe on U.S. airlines, it might help to see how accidents have decreased over the years. At least in part this can be attributed to the newer, safer aircraft and more stringent maintenance for older planes. Other than a nasty blip in '95, the record looks good for U.S. carriers. Although age is cited by many doomsayers, it should be remembered that the Valujet crash in Florida was the first crash of the new low-budget, high-mileage (average age of Valujet's planes was over 26 years) airliners. At presstime, the 1996 TWA crash over Long Island that killed 230 was suspected to be caused by a bomb but still under investigation.

U.S. Airlines Accident Record		
	Accidents per year	Per 100,000 hours of flying
1985	22	.24
1986	24	.23
1987	36	.32
1988	29	.25
1989	28	.25
1990	24	.20
1991	26	.21
1992	18	.12
1993	23	.18
1994	23	.17
1995	35	.26

Source: FAA

To find out how to get the safety record for U.S. airlines, call the FAA's consumer's hot line at ☎ *1 (800) 322-7873.*

There are about 25 airlines banned from landing in the U.S., due to their poor safety and maintenance standards. What are the airlines? The list is kept under wraps to avoid diplomatic repercussions. Just look for flying goat logos or gaffer's tape around the windows.

The most dangerous places to fly are on local carriers in **China**, **North Korea**, **Colombia**, all countries in **Central Africa** and all countries in the **CIS**. It is wise to avoid all flights inside **India** and through the **Andes**. But faced with taking a clapped-out bus over rugged mountains, most people choose clapped-out airplanes. China has the world's worst air piracy record, and Russian flight crews are known to accept bribes to overload planes with extra passengers, baggage and cargo.

Russian Roulette

Aeroflot and the 500-odd new airlines created by the breakup of the Soviet Union have made Russia the most dangerous place to fly in the world. The U.S. State Department has instructed government employees to avoid using all Russian airlines unless absolutely necessary. Britain, Canada and other nations have issued similar warnings. The International Airline Passengers Association issued an unprecedented warning that flying anywhere in the former Soviet Union is unsafe. *DP* flew to Lake Baikal in Siberia, where the passenger exit of a Tupelov had to be sealed with gaffers tape before takeoff. It's said that if the flight doesn't nail you, the food will. To be fair, Russia is a big place and it takes a lot of flying in some of the world's worst conditions to get around. But even when the figures are evened out for miles flown, leaving the ground in Russia is a very scary feeling. There are about 15,000 airplanes operating in Russia at any one time, most of them ready to be turned into frying pans as soon as they get a buyer. Russian airports make inner-city bus stations seem like Taj Mahals. Traffic controllers would have a hard time refereeing a volleyball game, and the only time businessmen pick up stewardesses is when they fall over from drinking too much. Safety inspectors make about $100 a month, making it easier to bribe them to keep the planes flying than actually doing the necessary maintenance work. Safety demonstrations are a curious Western custom, and the only thing that will fall down from the overhead panel during decompression will be luggage. The only factor that may be keeping the carnage down might be the dramatic drop in passengers flying: 30 million in 1994 down from 90 million in 1990. The Russian airlines compete for these poor passengers by making more flights, pushing aircraft longer and cutting costs wherever they can.

FAA SAFETY CATEGORIES

The FAA assigns 180 countries to various categories based on the level of safety they enforce among their national carriers.

Category 1: Nations that maintain proper civil aviation standards.

Category 2: Countries that are on probation and whose carriers have operating restrictions. Aruba, Bolivia, Ecuador, Jamaica and Morocco.

Category 3: Airlines banned from the United States until standards are improved in their home countries. Belize, Haiti, Nicaragua, Suriname, Uruguay and Zaire.

Note: Russia and China have not been rated. And U.S. carriers can operate in Category 2 and Category 3 nations. Only two European countries have been assessed, Poland and Romania. For the latest check out http://www.faa.gov.

The only bright spot is that over 100 airline licenses were pulled in 1994 and radio equipment was upgraded, allowing a Europe-Asia fly-over ban to be lifted.

Worldwide, the fatality rate for commercial passengers is .8 in a million. In America we have a comforting 0.5 fatalities per million passenger miles flown. In Russia, the figure is 5.2 per million. You will not see Mutual of Omaha insurance machines in Russian airports. Other sources put the odds of dying in a Russian crash at seven times the global average. Based on miles flown, 10 times as many passengers died in Russian crashes than U.S. crashes. In one 18-month period, there were more than a dozen air crashes in the former Soviet Union, involving both commercial and military aircraft, killing more than 500 people.

Before the Soviet breakup in 1991, Aeroflot was the largest airline in the world with more than 4000 planes. Carrying more than 100 million passengers annually, it maintained a safety record in line with the international average. Now the CIS has more than 300 separate carriers. The Russian version of our national system of maintenance and safety inspections has been discontinued. The ITAR-Tass news agency reported: "The American flying public is entitled to know that we have concerns with the safety of the Russian air transportation system."

Russian pilots make as little as 20 dollars a day or 40,000 rubles. In May 1994, Alfred Malinovsky, president of the Russian Pilots' Association, commented during a one-day strike to protest lack of aircraft safety standards, "We are as scared as anyone to fly, perhaps even more, because we know more."

To give you a taste of just how bad it is, in March 1994, an Airbus A-310 crashed, killing all 75 people on board—apparently while the pilot was giving an impromptu flight lesson to his teenage son.

Colombian Roulette

In Colombia in May 1994 alone, there were seven accidents that resulted in 16 deaths. At Bogota's international airport, air traffic controllers sometimes work 12-hour shifts; many of the nation's aircraft navigation radio beacons have not been serviced since 1986.

Colombia has the worst air-safety record in the Americas, according to the International Airline Passengers Association, a consumer group based in Dallas. Citing aircraft accident rates, India and Colombia were declared the two most dangerous countries to fly in.

After deregulation in Colombia in 1990, the number of passenger and cargo airlines serving El Dorado Airport in Bogota surged from 24 three years ago, to 68 today. In the same four years, the volume of international passengers arriving in Colombia jumped by 55 percent. Last year El Dorado handled 170,000 take-offs and landings. By comparison, Gatwick Airport in London typically handled 180,000 takeoffs and landings.

Chinese Roulette

In June 1994, a Chinese Northwest airliner crashed after takeoff from the city of Xian, killing all 160 onboard. On the same day, a lone hijacker commandeered a China Southern Airlines plane to Taiwan, the 12th hijacking in the past year. In October of 1990, 128 people were killed when the pilot of a hijacked Xiamen Airlines plane struggled with the hijacker during landing. The plane crashed into two other fully loaded aircraft, even though the pilot had warned the airport 40 minutes earlier.

There are about 40 different airlines flying in China. China is a leading contender for the title of the most dangerous place in the world to fly. There are enough hijackings from the mainland to Taiwan to set up a hijack-only express service.

China's biggest problem is a shortage of pilots. Passenger air travel is expected to grow 20 percent annually until the year 2000. To keep up with demand, the country needs 600 new pilots a year. But China can only turn out less than half that number. Once a pilot is on the job, the workday is excruciating. Although Chinese regulations set the limit at 100 hours of flight time a month to avoid pilot fatigue, pilots average an astounding 280 hours. China's airspace is controlled by the military, and civilian airlines must request use of it; then they are allotted narrow air corridors. There is a severe shortage of radar and ground equipment. Some parts of the country have no IFR controls, meaning that flying can be done only in good weather. In 1994, 120 pilots and airport personnel were prosecuted for endangering passenger safety. Want more horror stories? In 1992 a China Northwestern flight from Guangdong to Beijing actually ingested a man through one of its engines while on the tarmac. The pilot said that he noticed some overheating on one of the engines but took off anyway. A crash of a Tupelov TU-154 was pinned on five ground crew who incorrectly installed an auto pilot unit. They could not understand the instructions which were written in Russian cryllic. It is estimated that there are 10 fatalities in China for every million passenger miles. For now, mountainsides and Chinese airlines will maintain their fatal attraction.

Domestic frequent flyers can breathe a little easier...or can they? If you attack the domestic odds of being on a flight that pancakes, it still is scary. There are seven million commercial flights a year in the States, giving you a year and a half after a major crash to fly with impunity–assuming that God starts the clock on your first flight.

HOW TO SURVIVE FLYING

If you have a choice of transportation when traveling long distances, jump on a plane. This applies even in Russia, China or South America. Yes, it is dangerous but not as dangerous as enduring the kaleidoscope of misery and misfortune that awaits you on the ground.

- Stick to U.S.-based carriers with good safety records.

- Fly between major airports on nonstop flights.

- Avoid bad weather or flying at night.

- You can sit in the back if you want to leave a good looking corpse (the rear 10 rows are usually intact in case of ground impact, but the passengers are usually dead), or above the wing (you may get thrown clear, seat and all) or near an exit (easier egress in case of fire or emergency landing) might be just as advisable.

- Avoid small charter aircraft, dirt strips and no instrument fields

- Avoid national carriers that are not allowed to fly into the United States.

- Avoid military cargo flights, tagging along on combat missions, or flying over active combat or insurgence areas. (You paid $19.95 to be told this!)

- Avoid older Soviet- or Chinese-made aircraft or helicopters.

- After all this, remember that travel by airliner is the safest method of transportation and that your odds of surviving plane crashes are about 50 percent.

Trains

Trains are supposed to be safe. After all, they run on rails, are usually pointed in one direction and are rumored to be immune to the inclement weather that plague airplanes, buses and cars. When trains do hit, they hit hard.

Heavy Sleepers on the Night Train

Beware of the 10-hour night train from Budapest to Vienna. The first two hours during the stretch between Gyoer on the Austro-Hungarian border and Budapest are the most dangerous. The train leaves from the west Vienna station. The railway line to Vienna via Hungary is one of the last links with Yugoslavia after United Nations sanctions were imposed. Several Serbians working in Germany, Switzerland and Austria take the route back home. The train is targeted because Serbs working in Germany and loaded with cash and gifts take the train. The bandits will inject sleeping gas into each compartment and then methodically rob each one. The criminals comprise a United Nations of crooks: Serbs, Croats, Russians, Hungarians, Slovaks and Albanians from Kosovo in Rump, Yugoslavia. Some suspect that the Hungarian conductors and engineers collaborate with the criminals. At some time after a robbery, the train will stop so that the robbers can escape.

Trains tend to run into substantial objects, like trucks stalled on crossings or trains coming the other way. The fact that trains have limited mobility makes them ideal targets for terrorists. Criminals enjoy the opportunities trains afford, as passengers leave their belongings in their seats or cabins when they leave for the dining car.

Using the death rate per billion miles as a guide, American trains are about twice as dangerous as flying, four times safer than driving and a lot safer than local buses. If they have a bar car, you can quickly douse your fears as you watch the war-ravaged countryside zip by.

HOW TO SURVIVE TRAINS

- **Ask locals whether the train is a target for bandits or (this is appropriate in Cambodia and Egypt), where terrorists, bandits and insurgents regularly target tourist routes).**

- **Beware of Eastern European train routes, where thieves are known to ride as passengers. When in doubt sleep, with the window cracked open to avoid being gassed.**

- **Stash your valuables in secret spots, making it more difficult for robbers to locate your belongings.**

- **The back of the train is traditionally the safest area in the event of a collision, unless your train is the one that gets rear-ended.**

- Keep your luggage with you at all times if possible. Be nice to the conductor, and he will look out for you.

- Trains are preferable to buses when traveling through mountainous areas, deserts and jungles.

- Select a piece of luggage or bag that you can leave on your seat but contains nothing valuable (a shopping bag or plastic sack full of newspapers will work).

- If you spot someone who looks suspicious, particularly if you detect the outline of a gun, let the conductor know immediately.

Making the Best of Nasty Situations: Dangerous Destinations

We have the rundown on the do's and don'ts of travel conveyances, but what if you take your favorite airline, your most trusted driver and safest vehicle straight into an emerging coup? This chapter will help you understand the dynamics of hot spots and ideally keep you out of the nastier ones. These days those who don't want to get killed shouldn't dodge the draft, they should sign up.

War Zones

Welcome to the War of the Innocents. According to the U.N., of the 82 armed conflicts that were fought in the past three years, only three were between nations. The rest were civil wars or insurgencies. Four million civilians have been killed in wars since 1990.

It is hard to define war today. No longer is war a series of well-planned battles between two opposing sides. There are few uniforms, few battlefields to become tourist attractions and even fewer marching songs and flying colors. In the past, 90 percent of casualties used to be soldiers; today, 90 percent of the casualties are civilians. This is the new face of war. Or is it war? In Rwanda, Somalia, Bosnia, Haiti and Azerbaijan, we see the mass graves, the frightened refugees, the crying babies, the atrocities, the horror—but where are the soldiers? The flags? The marching columns? Were these simply internal disturbances? In Algeria, Egypt, Turkey, Sri Lanka, Cambodia and Pakistan, there is no war, yet the body count in each country exceeds the total Americans killed in Vietnam. Worse yet, armed groups in these countries are specifically targeting unarmed Westerners. Is this a war or a turkey shoot?

In the words of General George S. Patton: "The idea is not to die for your country but to make the other poor bastard die for his." Patton never lived to see the sad irony of terrorism: where we die for our enemies' countries. Worse yet, in some cases we're dying so the poor bastards can have a country to die for.

Even though few U.S. travelers head for war zones, it is important to understand what is going on there. (See the chart on the following page.) Fewer Americans are victims of war but many groups target Americans (like Colombia and Cambodia). There are also runs on no-discount, full-fare business-class tickets by journalists whenever a war breaks out. Other travelers may find themselves in the middle of a revolution or firefight with little knowledge of who the players are. There is also the chance that war will find you. This is called terrorism. Various folks around the world are looking for a few good victims. The total number of deaths from international terrorism declined from 314 in 1994 to 165 in 1995, but the number of people wounded increased by a factor of 10 to 6291 people, according to the U.S. State Department. The gas attack on the Tokyo subway system injured 5500. Of the 440 terrorist attacks in 1995, Western Europe was the most popular venue with 272 attacks, the Middle East placed second, then Latin America. Ninety-nine terrorist attacks were directed at American interests. There are many more terrorist groups that operate in other countries. The list does not include narco/trafficking groups or criminal groups allied under a political banner.

Where are the hot spots? According to the U.N., the countries of Algeria, Afghanistan, Angola, Burma (Myanmar), Burundi, Egypt, Georgia, Haiti, Iraq, Liberia, Mexico, Mozambique, Nigeria, Sudan, Tajikistan, Rwanda and Zaire are in crisis and in danger of social disintegration. It is an interesting assumption that some of these countries have something to disintegrate from.

There are many other countries, such as Jamaica, Mexico and the United States, where there is just old-fashioned killing taking place on a daily basis. Ever wonder why you don't see some of these places on your 11 p.m. Eyewitness News shows? Apparently, being a reporter isn't the privileged, glamourous job it used to be. According to the Committee to Protect Journalists, in 1995, 150 journalists were killed on the job. A total of 125 journalists were detained by local governments who objected to their reports. Until war correspondents make as much as bleached-blonde anchors and gossip columnists, whose greatest risk is being punched out by Sean Penn, war reporting will only lure those who don't fear risking their lives to get a good story. Since our coverage of war isn't what it used to be, *DP* has compiled the mother of all charts to help you understand what is going on in our world:

COUNTRY	TYPE OF CONFLICT	CAUSE OF CONFLICT	SINCE	WITH	KILLED TO DATE
Algeria	War	Religious, Political	1991	Armed Islamic Group (GIA)	30,000
Afghanistan	War	Religious, Political, Drugs	1989	Taliban, Uzbeks, Tajiks, Iran	15,000
Angola	Unrest	Tribal	1975	UNITA	400,000
Armenia	Unrest	Religious, Ethnic	1988	Azerbaijan	N/A
Azerbaijan	Unrest	Ethnic	1988	Armenia	40,000
Bangladesh	Unrest	Tribal	1971	Shanti Bahini	8000
Bosnia-Herzegovina	Unrest	Ethnic, Religious	1991	Serbs vs. Bosnian-Croats & Muslims	210,000
Burundi	War	Ethnic	1988	Hutu vs. Tutsi	180,000

COUNTRY	TYPE OF CONFLICT	CAUSE OF CONFLICT	SINCE	WITH	KILLED TO DATE
Cambodia	Unrest	Ideology	1970	Khmer Rouge	1,500,000
Chad	War	Tribal, Religious	1965	Various ethnic & military groups	N/A
Congo	Unrest	Political	1993	Old Marxists vs. Govt.	2,500
Colombia	War	Ethnic, Political, Ideological, Drugs	1986	FARC, ELN, EZLN, DCM	20,000
Croatia	Unrest	Ethnic	1991	Croats vs. Serbs	N/A
Djibouti	War	Ethnic, Tribal	1991	Afar vs. Issa tribes	350
Egypt	Unrest	Religious	1992	The Islamic Group	700
Georgia	Unrest	Ethnic	1992	Abkhazia	30,000
	War	Ethnic	1991	South Ossetia	N/A
	Unrest	Political	1991	Mkhedrioni militia	N/A
Ghana	Unrest	Tribal	1994	Konkombas vs. Nunumba & Dagomba	6000
Guatemala	Unrest	Political	1968	URNG vs. Govt.	65,000
India	War, Unrest	Religious	1989	Kashmir: Muslim vs. Hindu	25,000
	War	Religious	1981	Punjab: Sikh vs. Hindu	14,000
	War	Ideological	1969	Andhra Pradesh: Maoist Naxalites Peoples War Group vs. Govt.	80
	War	Ethnic, Ideological	1954	Assam, Nagaland, Manipur: various groups	N/A
	Unrest	Ethnic	1975	Timor: Timorese FRETELIN vs. Govt.	210,000
Indonesia	Unrest	Political	1989	North Sumatra: Aceh Merdaka (Freedom Aceh) vs. Govt.	2,500
	Unrest	Ethnic	1963	Irian Jaya: Papua Independent Organization (OPM) vs. Govt.	1,200
Iraq	War	Religious	1991	Southern Iraq: Govt. Sunni vs. Marsh Arab Shi'a Muslim	250,000
	Unrest	Ethnic	1981	Northern Iraq: Kurds vs. Govt.	180,000
Israel	War	Religious	1948	Jews vs. Muslim	3000
Lebanon	War	Religious	1991	Jews vs. Hezbollah	700
Liberia	War	Tribal	1989	Tribal warfare	200,000

COUNTRY	TYPE OF CONFLICT	CAUSE OF CONFLICT	SINCE	WITH	KILLED TO DATE
Mali	Unrest	Ethnic	1990	North: Arab Turag vs. Black	220
Mexico	Unrest	Political	1994	South: Zapatistas	200
Myanmar	Unrest	Ethnic	1992	Royhinga Muslims	N/A
	Unrest	Ethnic	1948	Kachin Independence Army	N/A
	Unrest	Ethnic	1942	Karen National Union	N/A
	Unrest	Ethnic	1948	Karenni	N/A
	Unrest	Ethnic	1948	Mong Tai	N/A
Niger	Unrest	Ethnic	1991	North: Arab Turag vs. black Govt.	N/A
Papua New Guinea	Unrest	Political	1988	Bougainville Revolutionary Army (BRA) vs. Govt.	35
Peru	War	Border Dispute	1942	Peru vs. Ecuador	30,000
	War	Ideological, Drugs	1980	Maoists groups: Shining Path, Tupac Amaru	32,000
Philippines	War	Political	1969	Communist North: New Peoples Army	3,500
	War	Religious	1974	Muslim South: Abu Sayyaf, MILF	N/A
Rwanda	Unrest	Ethnic	1990	Hutu vs. Tutsi	500,000
Russia	Unrest	Ethnic	1994	Chechens	80,000
Senegal	Unrest	Tribal	1983	Casamance (Dioula) vs. Senegalese (Wolof)	1000
Sierra Leone	War	Religious	1991	United Revolutionary Front (RUF) vs. Govt.	20,000
Somalia	War	Tribal	1978	Clan warfare	500,000
	Unrest	Tribal	1991	Somalialand, Sanaay	120,000?
Sri Lanka	War	Ethnic	1983	Liberation Tigers of Tamil Eelam (LTTE) vs. Sinhalese	50,000
Sudan	War	Ethnic, Religious	1955	Muslim north vs. animist black south	1,300,000
Tajikistan	War	Ethnic	1991	Muslim Tajiks vs. Russians	50,000
Turkey	War	Ethnic	1984	Kurds in east vs. Govt. PKK, Dev Sol	14,000

COUNTRY	TYPE OF CONFLICT	CAUSE OF CONFLICT	SINCE	WITH	KILLED TO DATE
Uganda	War	Ethnic	1979	Lord's Resistance Army (LRA) West Nile Bank Front (WNBF)	1200

Source: Various, DP

So now that you know enough to stay out of war zones, you might want to know how to live a little longer should you end up in one. Remember that a civilian is more likely to get killed than a soldier, and that if you are not fighting for one side or the other, that includes you.

HOW TO SURVIVE WAR ZONES

If you are lucky (or unfortunate) enough to find yourself in a hot spot, remember that war is not a carefully planned or controlled activity. More importantly land mines, shells, stray bullets and booby traps have no political affiliation or mercy. To survive war zones, keep the following in mind:

- Avoid politics; do not challenge the beliefs of your host; be firm but not belligerent about getting what you need. Talking politics with soldiers is like reading *Playboy* with the Pope. It kills time but is probably not a rewarding pastime.

- Do not engage in intrigue or meetings that are not in public view. They still shoot spies. Be cautious about any invitations for dinner, tea or social activities. Getting to know your hosts is important. Do not gossip or lie.

- Travel only under the permission of the controlling party or governor. In many cases you will need multiple permissions from officers, politicians and the regional commander.

- Remember that a letter of safe passage from a freedom group presented to an army checkpoint could be your death warrant. Understand and learn the zones of control and protocol for changing sides during active hostilities.

- Carry plenty of identification, articles, letters of recommendation and character references. It may not keep you out of jail, but it may delay your captors long enough to effect an escape.

- Check in with the embassy, military intelligence, local businessmen and bartenders.

- Do not misrepresent yourself, and keep your story simple and consistent. Bring photographs of your family, friends, house, dog or car. Carry articles you have written or ones that mention you. Picture ID is important, but even a high school yearbook can provide backup to your story.

- Dress and act conservatively. Be engaging and affable, and listen a lot more than you talk. Your actions will indicate your intentions as the locals weigh their interest in helping you. It may take a few days for the locals to check you out before they offer any assistance.

HOW TO SURVIVE WAR ZONES

- Remember that it is very unusual for noncombatants to be wandering around areas of conflict. If you are traveling, make sure you have the name of a person whom you wish to see and a reason for passing through.

- Understand where the front lines are and, the general rules of engagement. Meet with journalists and photographers (usually found at the hotel bar) to understand the local threats.

- Carry a lot of money, and be ready to leave or evacuate at any time.

- Choose a place to sleep that would be survivable in case of a rocket or shell attack. Inside rooms on the second floor are good.

- Visit with the local Red Cross, U.N., embassy and other relief workers to understand the situation. They are an excellent source of health information and may be your only ticket out.

- If warranted, buy and wear an armored flak jacket. Carry your blood type and critical info (name, country, phone, local contact, allergies) on a laminated card or written on your vest. Wear a Medic-Alert bracelet if needed.

- Carry a first-aid kit with syringes, antibiotics, IV needles, anesthetics and pain killers as well as the usual medication. It might be wise to use auto-inject syringes. Discuss any prescriptions with your doctor in advance.

- Understand and learn the effects and consequences of land mines, mortars, snipers and other vagaries of war.

- Get insurance and don't lie. Tell them you are going to a war zone. Also check with the emergency evacuation services to see if they will go into a war zone to pull you out.

- Carry a military-style medical manual to aid in treating field wounds. Take a first-aid class and understand the effects and treatment of bullet wounds and other major trauma.

TIPS FOR JOURNALISTS

- Conduct yourself on the basis that people in war time are freaked out and often can have a blood lust. They may not respond rationally.You may look just like the guy that slaughtered their friends that morning. They may hate journalists. They may not need a reason. If things are dicey, leave quickly.

- Journalists are specifically targeted in many areas. Bosnia was a good example. If you need to show ID on your vehicle, use the local words for "press" or "journalist" instead of "TV" or "CNN" on your car or clothing.

- Carry and show your photos and articles. Do not show gory pictures or articles sympathetic to any side. Show work on nonpolitical topics. Point to your name and show them your passport. Do not double-cross anyone, and if you are not sympathetic, say so. Travel with an open heart and do not criticize or judge. Do not lie or suggest any affiliation you don't have. You will be checked out.

- Try to use auto-exposure, auto-wind cameras and zoom lenses. Many journalists will use remote video monitors or auto-release mechanisms to allow them to film out windows and around corners without becoming targets. Others just barge on out and hope they don't get hit.

- Keep a blank roll of film or video tape handy. When soldiers demand your film or tape, you can unload, make the switch and then reload the original.

HOW TO SURVIVE WAR ZONES

- Snipers hone in on lights, bright colors and even decals. Things like cigarettes, head flashlights, video eyepieces, strobe-ready lights and press decals can become targets.

- Arrive fully prepared for no electricity, food shortages, water shortages, no sheets, no laundry, no medicine and no banks.

- If possible, talk to other journalists who have returned to understand the special problems of the region. Placing a call to a paper that has carried a recent story on the zone you are heading for is a good start.

- Contact the various journalist protection groups like RSF and CPJ, listed in the back of the book, for very specific information on the region to which you will be traveling.

- Use a black SLR and blackout white type. Carry range finders or cameras with glass surfaces towards your body to avoid sunglints.

The Ugly American

Americans are such a polyglot culture that it is impossible to stereotype a nation of a quarter billion people who literally come from every country in the world (if you assume that the Indians came over the land bridge from Russia). Yet total strangers in many parts of the world have an itch to walk straight up to you and yell "Die American Pig!" or "Get out of Japan" or another slogan of the week. It is questionable whether it is America or the United Nations that relieves, aggravates or prolongs regional tensions. Do Russia and the United States have the right to militarily interfere in foreign countries? Do aid programs actually create starvation and suffering by artificially shifting populations to refugee camps and thereby increasing the birth rate? These may be questions your hosts expect answers to. Much of the world views American intervention as old-fashioned imperialism.

Anger toward Americans is a direct result of others' perception of our need to control foreign governments. If the government feels it lacks sufficient political clout in certain regions of the world, it brings out the checkbook. The U.S. bought peace in the Middle East by writing checks to both sides, thereby aggravating fanatics on both sides. We also support a wide variety of dictators, despots and other nondemocratically elected rulers because they are less antagonistic toward the U.S. than the opposition. We even tolerate folks like Saddam and Muammar because they are a buffer between a nasty enemy. This also creates animosity on your behalf. In addition, the U.S. wages moralistic, covert (and not so covert) operations against enemies of the state, such as the Islamic fundamentalists, drug dealers, unfriendly dictators and gangsters. We do this by supporting (or sometimes creating) opposition forces with money, weapons and military training. This creates a lot of ill will toward "Americans," regardless of their beliefs or background.

You may find it surprising to see how obvious the U.S. "covert" presence is in Third World countries. Terrorist groups keep very good tabs on CIA and other government agents in their countries.

The problem for the traveler is that in some areas, such as the Middle East, Southeast Asia, Central Africa and areas where Americans are rarely seen, you will be assumed to be working for or allied with American intelligence agencies. Although I'm Canadian, I have been accused on numerous occasions of being "CIA" in war zones, simply because I had no plausible explanation as to why I was there.

If you look and act like an American, you will be assumed to be gathering information. You'll run the risk of confrontation, kidnapping, detainment or harassment. Execution is rare, since Americans are worth more alive (financially and politically) than dead.

HOW TO SURVIVE BEING A YANKEE PIG

Whether you accept it or not, if you are of European extraction, or were raised on T-bones and Pepsis or even shop at Eddie Bauer, you will be taken for a "Yank" in most of Russia, Asia, Australasia or Central and South America. Africans will probably mistake you for being German or French, and the Chinese have a tendency to think all Westerners and Europeans look the same.

Even African-American travelers find themselves being simply regarded as rich Americans when they search for their roots in black Africa. In all cases, understand that, along with your American Tourister luggage and Nikes, you carry a different kind of baggage: about 200 years of enslavement, imperialism, covert action, warfare, occupation and political interference. Also a large part of the world just resents the fact that you are so damned affluent and healthy and they're not. You may not have bombed Laos, smart-bombed innocent Iraqi children, overthrown every Latin American dictator, shot Moros in the Philippines or cut down the rain forests to grow cows for your Big Macs, but the chances are good you will be blamed for it. So, to survive being a Yank, keep the following in mind:

- **Dress conservatively, stay away from obvious American brands and logos, and do not wear signs of wealth (gold watches, jewelry, expensive cameras, etc.).**

- **Learn or try to use the local language, even if only to say thank you and excuse me. Even learning the phrase "I love your wonderful country" can get you a lot farther than "Why the hell don't you wogs learn to speak American?"**

- **Call the local embassy to find out the do's and don'ts.**

- **Don't wear American flags, Uncle Sam decals or other U.S. symbols.**

- **Be compassionate, understanding and noncommittal about the current situation of the country. Do not belittle other nationalities.**

- **Simply wearing sunglasses, traveling in air-conditioned cars and lacking language skills can create barriers and misunderstanding.**

- **Say hello to everyone you meet on the street and in the course of your travels. Look people straight in the eye and smile. Be polite, patient and helpful.**

Revolutionary Places

Let's play out this scenario. A backward country emerges from decades under a totalitarian regime. Freedom is in the air. Tourist visas are as easy to get as Publisher's Clearinghouse entry forms. Hotels are hosed out and airlines change their names. You, being the adventurous type, are off in a heartbeat, eager to be the first to visit ancient temples, scenic wonders, etc. One week later, tanks fill the streets, surly men in cheap uniforms are thumping innocent bystanders, you hear shots every night. One morning someone kicks in your door, and it's not room service. You are officially an enemy of the people, and you will not be able to try out those bitchin' new Nikes in the mountains after all. You are eating cockroach soup and watching your bruises turn ten shades of purple and your teeth wiggle. What happened?

Students of history and readers of *DP* could tell you that you screwed up. You forgot that the countries most likely to be plunged into civil warfare are newly emerging democracies. Yes, you raving liberal, the most dangerous countries are the ones that still can't figure out how to operate a ballot box and lift repression.

Once the iron hand is lifted, every crackpot faction has a voice and begins organizing. Since there is no effective way to compromise, these well-meaning folks simply make their points more clearly to their opposition by using rifles and shovels. Every colonial entry in Africa has gone through this turmoil. Some, like Liberia and Angola, just don't know when to stop. Other countries, like Yugoslavia, Pakistan, Somalia, South Africa and India, have no clue as to how to deal with their ethnic masses. The most dangerous transition is from long-term dictatorship to democracy as was experienced in the Soviet Union. Technically, these are caused by special-interest groups putting restraints on leaders and not allowing them to deal with minor uprisings. Division is the natural outcome, splitting the military, religious, regional and business elements into their tiniest elements. Ideally, they form their own spheres of influence, creating the normal political structures found in First World countries. Unfortunately, they adopt the brutal tactics of their former leaders and usually have the tanks and population fired up within weeks. Other groups, like the Mafia, drug runners, terrorists and criminals, make good use of the division and confusion to quickly establish wide-ranging organizations and transportation corridors. The lesson is to remember that dictatorships are the safest countries, followed by well-established democracies. Save your "being part of the solution" urges for the PTA and antilitter campaigns.

HOW TO SURVIVE REVOLUTIONARY PLACES

Although no one can predict a sudden change in government, there are some things that could keep you from appearing on CNN wearing a blindfold:

- **Check in with the embassy to understand the current situation and to facilitate your evacuation if needed.**

- **Stay away from public demonstrations and avoid main boulevards, government buildings, embassies, radio stations, military installations, the airport, harbor, banks and shopping centers.**

- **If trouble starts, call the embassy immediately with your location. Stay off the streets, and, if necessary, move only in daylight in groups. Stay in a large hotel with an inside room on the second or third floor. Convert foreign currency into Western currency if possible. Book a flight out with multiple reservations and names (J. Smith, John Smith, Jacqueline Smith, etc.).**

HOW TO SURVIVE REVOLUTIONARY PLACES

- Understand the various methods of rapid departure. Collect flight schedules and train information, and ask about private hires of cars and planes. Do not travel by land if possible.

- Do not discuss opinions about the former regime or the current one.

- Keep your money in U.S. dollars. Do not depend on credit cards or traveler's checks.

- Do not store luggage or ship items out of the country.

- Hire a local driver/guide/interpreter to travel around town and/or to go out at night.

- Listen (or have your guide listen) to the local radio station or TV station. Have him update you on any developments or street buzz.

Radical Places

There are many countries, like Iran, Iraq, North Korea, Pakistan, Syria and Afghanistan, that would have Rush Limbaugh's head on a stick in less than 15 minutes for being too liberal. These countries might have a Bill of Far Rights, but if you are too outspoken, there's nothing to protect your butt from a lifetime of incarceration or summary execution. These countries fall into two general categories: fundamentalist regions and brutal dictatorships.

Fundamentalist Regions

What can be said about religious strife that hasn't been said before? Despite what most Americans assume, and the fact that there are more people listed as Christians or Buddhists, the most popular religious deity in the world has to be the prophet Mohammed. Over one billion of the world's inhabitants are Muslims. Only 18 percent are found in the Arab world. Most live east of Karachi; 30 percent of Muslims are found on the Indian subcontinent, 20 percent in sub-Saharan Africa, 17 percent in Southeast Asia and 10 percent in the CIS and China. There are an estimated 5 million Muslims in the United States. Now most Muslims will tell you that Jews, Christians and Muslims are all "people of the book" and that there is more to bind us than divide us. It just seems that message doesn't get to the top, where they sign the checks for all those weapons, explosives and training camp supplies.

This is not to say that there is a basic antagonism between Christianity and Islam. There tends to be much confusion and distrust generated by the media. Unable to understand the basic similarities between Islam and Christianity, the media focuses on the disparities and usually the most extreme examples. The presentation of Islamic fundamentalism as a religion rather than a political agenda is one example. Christian fundamentalism is just as dangerous and skewed as any other hard-core belief. Currently, there are dozens of conflicts between Hindus and Muslims (Kashmir), Muslims and Christians (Bosnia), Islamic factions and Christians and Marxists (Central America).

HOW TO SURVIVE FUNDAMENTALIST REGIONS

When traveling to a fundamentalist, religiously zealous country, remember to smile, mind your own business, respect their customs and leave your personal opinions at home. Certain religions tend to be somewhat tolerant of loudmouthed boorish outsiders, but areas like the Middle East and Far East can be very intolerant. Some tips on surviving fundamentalist regions:

- Do not proselytize, preach or conduct religious functions without permission of the local government. Do not wear religious symbols or use expressions that involve the name of Christ, Allah, God or other religious entities.

- Read about and respect the local religious beliefs, customs and places of worship. Read and understand the Koran and tenants of Islam or the religion of your chosen destination. Do not mishandle, drop or show disrespect to the actual Koran or other religious symbols.

- Feel free to admit your religious affiliation, but express your interest in knowing more about the Koran and Islamic way of life. But beware that students and older men are very pleased to proselytize the word of Allah to a potential convert.

- If you are Jewish and traveling in a fundamental Islamic area, your life may be at risk by identifying yourself as Jewish or discussing an opposing point of view.

- Do not squeeze hands when shaking; you may touch your chest after shaking hands in the traditional Muslim greeting.

- Dress cleanly and conservatively, and remove your shoes in mosques and temples. Do not point the soles of your feet at your host, and it's important to use your right hand to eat, greet and pass objects around. Expect to be kissed on both cheeks by men in some regions.

- Ask permission before taking pictures of men; do not insist or sneak photos. Do not take photographs of women. Do not take pictures of the infirm or elderly. Don't blow your nose in public. Don't eat walking around. Don't admire objects in a host's home (he will feel obligated to give them to you). Gifts are expected when visiting homes. Do not show open affection. Do not show undue attention to women. The list goes on.

- Read up on the cultures of each region, and ask permission when in doubt.

Brutal Dictatorships

There is a nice group whose backwater despots allow tourists into their countries so that their populace can see what they're missing under a democratic government (like good nutrition, high standards of living, and so forth). Iraq, Iran, North Korea, Cuba, Myanmar, Zaire, CAR (Central African Republic), and other little cranky, tin pot countries are furiously pushing their domains back into the Stone Age and dragging their neighbors along with them.

Why visit these countries? Where else can you take a time machine back to the '50s, the '20s or even the turn of the century (we mean the 12th century). Imagine meeting people who still herd sheep, break rocks, kill other people and even carve temples, all for no money, without an education and while they're on the brink of starvation. No Sirree, you won't see these places on "Lifestyles of the Rich and Famous." So why go?

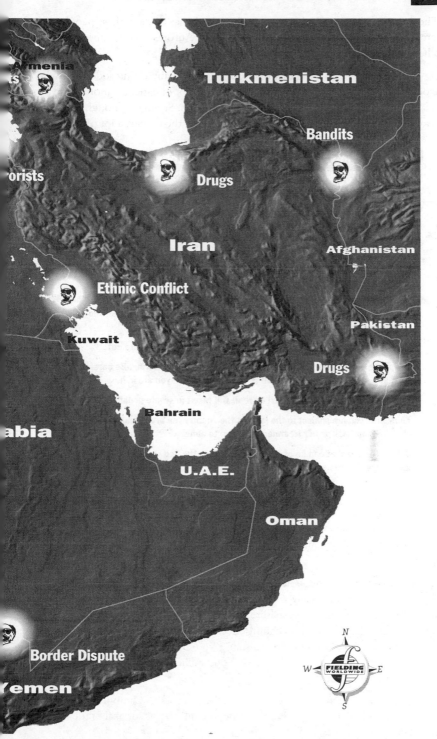

The answer is simple. You have to go. Somebody has to show these people that there is a world out there full of Pop Tarts, Buick Auroras, MTV, education, and fat happy people who actually die of natural causes.

If we don't go there, we will maintain our image of baby-eating sodomites who bayonet and barbecue old ladies for fun. It takes a lot of patience, money and *cojones* to travel through the last of the dark kingdoms. Strangely enough, many of these places are quite safe and, once the police turn the corner, a lot of fun.

HOW TO SURVIVE BRUTAL DICTATORSHIPS

Want to see George Orwell's *1984* in real life? Visit North Korea. What about watching live executions on "Saturday Night Live?" Go to Saudi Arabia or Nigeria. Here are a few tips to keep you safe:

- **Do not discuss politics with anyone. Better yet, do not continue conversations started by strangers. Yes, you can be paranoid in these places.**

- **If you stop to talk to locals, understand that they will be questioned later or come under suspicion.**

- **Most autocratic countries employ or encourage spying on foreigners. Do not be surprised if you are not only followed but your tails may even argue over who gets to follow you.**

- **Expect to have your room and your luggage searched while you are out.**

- **Telephone and mail are subject to interception and/or monitoring. Be careful of what you say. Make sure your room is very secure when you are in it.**

- **Any violation of the law (imagined or real) will result in severe penalties.**

- **Remember you are subject to the laws of the country you are in and the concept of rights, fair trial, or fair treatment are slim to none.**

- **Collect sources that can be of assistance such as the Red Cross, Amnesty International or Reporters Without Frontiers (see our reference section in the back).**

Nasty Places

Imagine a naked man walking down the street with $100 bills taped to his body. That's what the typical tourist looks like to the residents of most Third World countries.

The fact that you consider yourself the owner of your camera, wallet, luggage, watch and jewelry is not really a debating point with many of these folks. That you might need to be killed to expedite the transfer of those goods is also a minor detail to them. Even your well-thumbed copy of Somalia on a Shoestring or Birkenstocks won't fool them into thinking you are a culturally sensitive, eco-friendly, politically correct global traveler. You, my rich American friend, are meat and you just entered the butcher shop.

In many war-ravaged countries, such as Afghanistan, Cambodia, Somalia, Liberia, Zaire, Mozambique or Sierra Leone, the only law is survival of the fittest, fastest and meanest.

HOW TO SURVIVE NASTY PLACES

Many tourists are surprised to find themselves victims of attack in "recovering" regions where tour prices are low and the crowds at the temples are slim. Be aware that banditry is a very real danger in places like Kenya, Somalia, India, Cambodia, Pakistan, Myanmar and southern regions of Russia. Tips on surviving nasty places:

- **Meet with and discuss the situation with local embassy staff. Ask them specifically what to do if you are arrested, followed or hassled. Carry their card or at least number and address on you while in the country.**

- **Stay within well-defined tourist routes and lock all luggage and belongings in a secure place, like a major hotel.**

- **Never travel alone, and you should use a guide. Always hire a driver recommended by someone you trust.**

- **Stay inside major cities at major hotels, and eat at well-known, large restaurants. Never travel or go out late at night. Phone ahead to tell people you are coming over, and call anyone you may have left behind to let them know you arrived safely.**

- **Fly between cities, and prearrange transportation from the airport to the hotel.**

- **Beware of intimidation from police and military. Be firm about your innocence, and try to lead them to your embassy or safe place.**

- **Dress conservatively in plain clothing. Do not carry a camera or briefcase.**

- **Keep abreast of the political and military situation. Keep in mind that kidnapping, extortion and murder are very real possibilities.**

Poor Places

Not all countries are downright nasty. There are lots of places that are really nice—they just seem to have a lot of dead people on the side of the road in the morning. These places have a terminal funk to them. Hazy gray skies, the stench of rotting everything, snotty-nosed kids with hands outstretched. The kind of places that the Brits used to wear starched white linen suits in. These are the tough places, the hard countries that barely survive. Many of these places, like India, Egypt, Bangladesh, Kenya, Pakistan, Haiti, China and Indonesia, are like this because there are just too many people for the resources available. There is a lot of petty theft, minor muggings, infectious diseases, and scams and relatively few murders.

The trend in emerging dangerous places—normally, underdeveloped nations—is that exploding population rates are creating tensions.

On the African continent, 45 percent of the population is under the age of 15; in South America, it's 35 percent; in Asia, 32 percent. Only 21 percent of the population of the United States and 19 percent of Europe is under 15. Things are not going to get better in our lifetime.

Waterworld?

Nearly 50 countries on four continents have more than three-quarters of their land in international river basins; 214 river basins are multinational, while 13 are shared by five or more countries. And nearly 40 percent of the world's population lives in an international river basin. The Jordan, the Ganges, the Nile and the Rio Grande rivers have been at the center of international disputes. Since rivers in many areas serve as borderlines, water will continue to be a source of conflict. Europe needs more than 175 international treaties to regulate its four river basins shared by more than four countries. The Iraqis are busy draining their southern marches to displace people, while the Turks are busy building dams in east Turkey to flood out others.

In 1950, 33 percent of the world's population lived in the developed, industrialized nations. Today, that share is approximately 23 percent. By the year 2025, it will fall to 16 percent; Africa then will have 19 percent of the world's inhabitants. Today, western and Southeast Asia are home to more people than any other part of the world. The population of India will overtake that of China early in the next century. These underdeveloped nations are also home to the most diverse mix of languages, religions and peoples in the world; many of the people have been at war for centuries and will continue to fight over water, land, religion and tribal divisions.

The World Resources Institute reports that only 3 percent of the world's inhabitants lived in urban areas in the mid-18th century. By the 1950s, that proportion had risen to 29 percent. Today, it is more than 40 percent; by 2025, 60 percent of the world's people are expected to be living in or around cities. Almost all of that increase will be in what is now the Third World. The young people tend to migrate to major urban centers, seeking Western-style jobs instead of backbreaking menial labor. Once in the city, they find that the competition for jobs is fierce and petty crime against the wealthy is the only source of income. But despite this, the cities continue to grow. Mexico City, which had 17 million inhabitants in 1985, will have 24 million by the end of the century; Sao Paulo will jump from 15 million to 24 million.

As populations grow and standards of living drop, people will live at ever-greater densities, creating more tension. *The World Bank's World Development Report* noted that only Bangladesh, South Korea, the Netherlands and the island of Java had population densities of more than 400 people per square kilometer. By the middle of the next century, one-third of the world's people will probably live at these density levels. Given the current trends, the population density of Bangladesh will rise to a barely conceivable 1700 people per square kilometer. Population growth on such a large scale is intrinsically destabilizing. The wars in India show that even minor terrorist incidents can kill hundreds of people. The world's most dangerous places will also be the most crowded and impoverished places.

Poorest People	% of Population in Poverty
Bangladesh	80%
Ethiopia	60%
Vietnam	55%

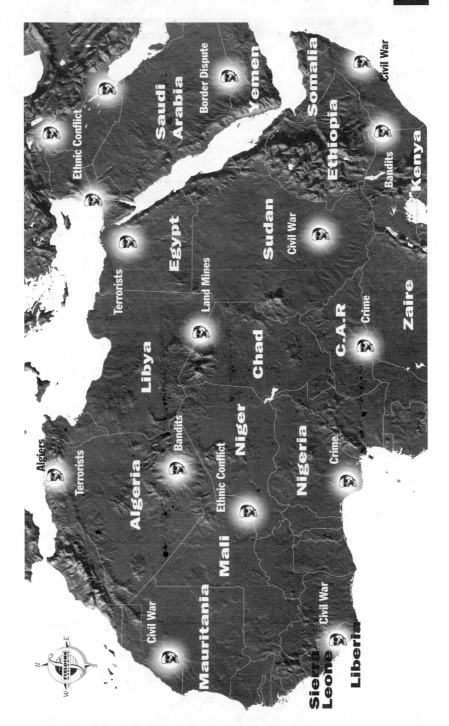

Poorest People	% of Population in Poverty
Philippines	55%
Brazil	50%
India	40%
Nigeria	40%
Indonesia	25%
China	10%

HOW TO SURVIVE POOR PLACES

- Treat all people, even the poorest beggar with respect.
- If you give money, put it in the person's hand and wish the person good health.
- Do not throw money or coins into crowds.
- Understand that people's need to survive may lead to attacks, theft or assaults.
- Do not wander through streets at night or without company.

Terrorist Places

There is no simple advice to give on how to avoid being the victim of a terrorist attack. Although terrorism is specifically designed to capture the world's attention, it poses a lesser threat than disease, car accidents, plane crashes and other afflictions that haunt the traveler. But having taken the lightly booked anniversary flight of Pan Am flight 103, I can attest to the effectiveness of terrorism in deterring tourists.

Statistics are meaningless in understanding terrorism. Like a protoplasmic liquid, terrorism flows around the world and reshapes itself according to pressures mounted against it. In fact, like water, the harder you hit it, the more it hurts. Just when experts figure they have it pegged, it assumes new, more frightening images—the World Trade Center, Oklahoma, Tokyo and Unabomber sagas.

The number of terrorist attacks in 1995 increased to 440, up from 322 in 1994—not an impressive figure in terms of the number of dangerous incidents compared to muggings. When you localize some of these activities though, it gets a little scarier.

The increase in terrorism was primarily due to activities of the Kurdistan Workers Party, or PKK, which launched hundreds of attacks, including indiscriminate bombings throughout Turkey, Western Europe and Germany. Fatalities from international terrorism worldwide resulted in 6291 people wounded in 1995; of those, 5500 were injured in a gas attack on the Tokyo subway system, which was masterminded by the Japanese cult, Aum Shinrikyo. The unleashing of nerve gas in a heavily occupied public place sent a chilling message worldwide on the potential deadly effects of terrorism directed at people simply going about their daily activities.

The number of anti-American attacks increased in 1995 to 99, up from 66 the previous year. In 1996 the bombing of a military compound in Riyadh, Saudi

Arabia, the fiery explosion over Long Island that killed all 230 passengers on a TWA jet, and the pipe bomb at the Centennial Olympics in Atlanta all sent strong messages that terrorism is an ever-present threat. Seven nations are currently designated as states that sponsor international terrorism: **Iran**, **Iraq**, **Libya**, **Syria**, **Sudan**, **Cuba** and **North Korea**. Most European adventure travelers consider these countries quasi-safe for travel, except for the southern region of Sudan and the rougher parts of Cuba. Most Americans have little or no interest in visiting these regions and, in most cases, couldn't visit if they wanted to.

There is an understandably high level of antagonism in Iraq, Iran and North Korea toward Americans, especially toward those who make it in—usually nuts or spooks. The fact that two Americans were slapped with eight-year jail sentences for illegally entering Iraq should keep most travelers out. Read the chapter "Terrorism" for more info.

Criminal Places

Travelers are ideal targets for crooks; they carry lots of cash and expensive equipment and keep it in handy luggage, cars or hotel rooms. They can't or won't hang around to pursue the case, and they are, in the majority of instances, unarmed and unsuspecting. The most likely bad experience you will face, war zone or not, is finding someone's fingers wandering through your pockets, or your luggage running down the street attached to a teenage kid.

Criminals are not all shifty-eyed opportunists. Criminals can also run countries, protecting drug smugglers, poachers, terrorists and even leaders of terrorist groups.

Americans like to think that they enjoy a certain level of safety because of their standard of living. They do. But if you don't have a certain standard of living, you live in one of the world's most violent and dangerous places. Crime is big business in some countries, and you are part of their expansion plan. Travel to these countries is laughably easy and getting whacked is even easier. Staying alive or solvent in these countries requires a lot of common sense (don't go out at night, travel in groups, don't stray off the beaten path, etc.).

Specifically what to look out for in high-crime places is detailed in the list that follows.

Angola

Bands of armed youths rule here. Many need the receipts of crime to survive. Although soldiers are supposed to be turning in their arms, they still can make a better living robbing folks than sitting around unemployed.

There is no functional police force in Angola. Carjacking and violent robbery are the norm here. There is a biweekly meeting at the embassy on security tips and the most recent developments.

Argentina

Hezbollah is busy here attacking political or religious targets. Street crime is normal for South America. Guns are brandished in robberies but rarely used. Daylight break-ins are common even in homes with bars and grilles. Auto theft and personal robbery against people with luxury cars or sport utilities are on the rise.

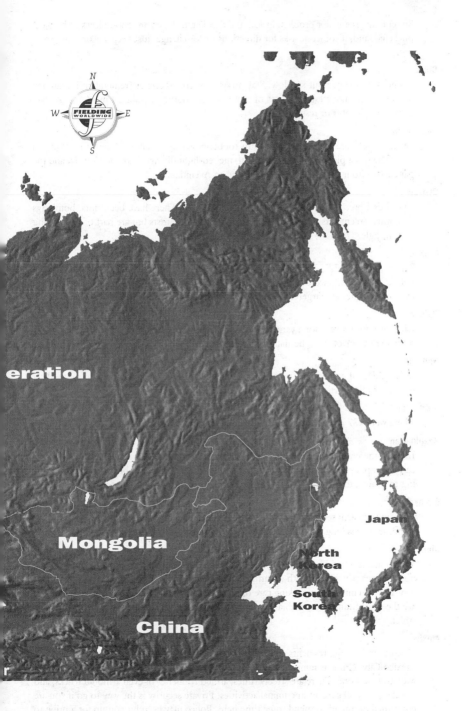

Brazil

Street crime is a major problem in Rio and São Paulo. Buses are good places to be pick-pocketed, and, if someone asks for directions or for change, just keep walking and smiling.

China

Crime is on the rise but still low. Stay away from crowd scenes (remember Tiananmen Square?), and don't take pictures of any criminal, traffic or political incidents. Always carry your passport or resident card.

Costa Rica

Sexual assaults are a problem here, with robberies averaging about three an hour in San Jose. The worst places are the bus station, the red-light district, Plaza de Cultura, and the park across from the Melico Salazar theater on Avenida 2.

Cyprus

Cyprus is a pretty laid-back place until the bars close. There have been riots, bombings and other violent acts. These are not targeted against tourists but are part of an ongoing turf struggle.

France

There were 3,492,712 crimes in France in 1990, a 7 percent increase from the year before. Most crimes were petty larceny and 250,000 were vehicular thefts. Cars with out-of-country plates are targeted by thieves. Theft of unattended baggage is common.

Guinea

Civil unrest can occur for a variety of reasons. One reason for riots was the rumor that a foreigner was involved in bestiality in 1992.

Holland

Minor thefts of car radios, briefcases and luggage from cars is common, and more likely to occur in the north and in Amsterdam.

Indonesia

There were 437 reported crimes against foreigners in Jakarta in 1990.

Kazakhstan

In 1995 there were 68 crimes against Americans reported to the embassy. Make sure you carry your passport, or you can be fined on the spot. This scam can be countered by offering to show it to the officer at the police station or manager at the hotel.

Malaysia

The only problem seems to be crimes against residents of wealthy neighborhoods. Police response time is long due to the snarled traffic in Kuala Lumpur.

Mali

Things are tense in Mali politically, and there is a definite danger when traveling in the north or near the border with Mauritania due to banditry. The safest way to get around is by air, with hired drivers taking care of ground transportation. Street crimes in Bamako are the usual thump, cut, grab and run type. Don't go out at night and stay to the main streets.

Mexico

Tourists and foreign residents account for 70 percent of all criminal reports in downtown Mexico City. Crime is rampant and there was a 32 percent increase in crime in 1995 in Mexico City alone. There are street crimes, armed robberies of even armored trucks, and violence is up 50 percent in criminal activities. Private security is the way to go if you are concerned or intend to spend some time here. Police may even hit you up for a bribe to help you out. Taxi robberies are the latest thing, where volkswagon cabdrivers stop and men swarm in to relieve you of your belongings. Many roving taxis in Mexico City are stolen, more are unlicensed. Use a hired driver, radio, or *sitio* cabs to get around.

Myanmar

Crime is low and of the petty type. It is illegal to change money on the black market and to purchase gems outside of government shops.

Namibia

There is an unusually high danger of rape in Namibia. Residential burglary is on the rise, and normal street crime is common. Car accidents are a danger here from wild-eyed drivers and the large amount of game that runs across the roads. There are plenty of land mines off the beaten paths.

Senegal

Casamance separatists are busy in the southern part of the country, especially in the Bignonia area. Roadblocks and violence are a danger.

Singapore

Despite the squeaky clean image Singapore wants to present, there are a number of gangs that operate throughout the city. Crimes tend to be snatch-and-run types.

A minor note for those who think caning is inhumane, there are 80 people on death row for a variety of offenses, mostly drug-related.

South Africa

Johannesburg is the murder capital of the world, with an average of 52 murders a day. In 1993 the Ministry of Law and Order indicated that an average day in South Africa results in 77 people being murdered, 68 raped and 775 assaulted. About 65 cars are stolen in the Joburg area every weekend. Carjackings are endemic with about 160 a month, 80 percent conducted at gunpoint. They usually take place when motorists leave or arrive at their home. A third of the carjackings took place at stoplights. Over half were during daylight. There were about 1600 thefts from cars every year. Driving is dangerous. The N2 highway between Cape Town and Somerset West is affectionately called "Hell Run" by the locals, because of the number of random attacks on vehicles.

Tourist crime is high along the beaches, in parks and in city centers. At night bars and nightclubs have high incidents of crime. Hiking in rural areas is not advised.

Six Americans were attacked in South Africa last year, and one, Amy Biehl, was killed.

Suriname

The eight-years old insurgency in the interior is over after a signed peace treaty, but street crime is on the rise.

Switzerland

Although Switzerland is safe, the tiny utopia does have a rash of burglaries in the summer tourist seasons.

In Geneva in 1993 there were 6524 car thefts, 3328 burglaries, 2372 pickpocketings, 214 armed robberies, 31 sexual assaults and three homicides.

Syria

Syria is safe for the simple reason that many of the world's terrorist groups are headquartered here. Assad keeps close tabs on every human, sheep and goat so there is little opportunity for crime. There are more soldiers than citizens sometimes. The only complaint by expats is the amount of sexual harassment shown Western women by the macho and bored Syrian men.

Tanzania

Crime is rampant. Expats are the favored target for muggers, theft, carjacking and currency scams. Policemen may pose as cops and ask for your money.

Trinidad and Tobago

Lots of tourist crime (about 75 percent takes place in Port of Spain), lots of nasty weapons ranging from machetes to handguns. Rape is also a danger here.

Tunisia

Women are hassled by Tunisian males. Street crimes are common, but violent crime is unusual.

Yemen

Some parts of Yemen are rough and ready. Tribes in the Saada, Marie, al-Jawf governates and Khowlon areas are a little xenophobic and should only be visited with a local guide set up by a travel agent who has good contacts in the specific area. Yemen is one of the most heavily armed countries on earth, according to the State Department. Depending on which political wing you sit on, this is good or bad news.

Zambia

Plenty of violent crime in addition to the usual street crime.

Zimbabwe

Lots of petty crime due to the deteriorating economy and influx of young kids into the strained job market. Tourists are targets for hit-and-run theft.

Macho, Macho, Blam!
Countries with murder rates of more than 20 per 100,000 people
Colombia
Mexico
Guatemala
Venezuela
Puerto Rico

Business Travelers: Professional Victims

We know that money makes the world go round. We also know that money makes businesspeople go round the world. And where there is money, there is crime. Many companies pay a premium for foreign expertise and will convince normally rational people to set out for the front lines in the new war against America. American workers in oil, mining, construction, technology and computer companies are in big demand abroad and are exposed to major risks on an increasing basis.

Business travel rather than adventure travel, is the most dangerous. Why? Namely, one becomes a target by most of the world's terrorists simply by representing an American company. You also lose the ability to be discerning about when and where to travel. Most tourists wouldn't consider flying into a Colombian war zone for a week. Yet folks from oil, computer, agricultural and food companies do it regularly. Most victims of terrorism tend to be working on a daily basis in a foreign country in areas where no sane traveler would go.

Finally, by doing business, you tend to frequent establishments and locations where thieves, terrorists and opportunists seek victims—luxury hotels, expensive restaurants, expat compounds, airports, embassies, etc. As a businessperson, you cannot adopt the cloak of anonymity, since you will more than likely be wearing an expensive suit, staying in expensive hotels and have scads of luggage, cash and gifts.

The Most Dangerous Places	
Algeria	Executions
Haiti	Street Crime
Cambodia	Kidnappings
Myanmar	Civil Disorder
Burundi	Violence
Pakistan	Ethnic rioting, street violence

Source: Control Risks Group

Business travel exposes you to frequent car and air travel and other means of transportation. Many trips are also undertaken in bad weather conditions and at congested travel periods (i.e., Monday out, Friday back). You are fed very carefully through a chain of businesses that cater to business travelers and become a high-profile target for criminals who prey on business travelers. I often shudder when I see oil field technicians, complete with cowboy hats, pointed ostrich leather boots and silver Halliburton briefcases, tossing beer-soaked profanities around the world's transit lounges. Can you think of a more inviting target?

Dangerous Places for Business Travel

Business travelers are by far the juiciest targets for terrorists and thugs alike. They make great kidnap victims as well as willing dispensers of cash. Any Third World country with oil should be considered dangerous.

Angola

Oil and diamonds shore up this shattered country. Angola is looking for investors to help dig it out. However, impotent cease-fires are signed as frequently as bad checks, and, although the heavy fighting has wound down, the countryside is lawless.

Algeria

Algeria is, by far, one of the countries most dependent on foreign expertise, and yet it is the most dangerous place in the world in which to provide this aid. In Algeria, about 12,000 people have died in political violence, and in a 10-month period 53 foreigners were killed, 14 of them during a four-day period in the beginning of July 1994. Foreign companies are paying top dollar for oil workers and technicians.

Cambodia

Cheap labor and an eager government attract plenty of Chinese garment manufacturers to Cambodia. The land of the Khmers is essentially lawless, except for a narrow strip around the temples of Phnom Penh and Siem Reap, thanks to the Khmer Rouge and banditry in rural areas. There is little business left to conduct in this postelection, war-torn country. Rising crime and armed carjackings in Phnom Penh are turning the capital into an anarchist's heaven.

Colombia

Colombia gets five stars for brutality and ingenuity. Strangely enough, we do plenty of business with this tough customer.

Nigeria

Nigeria is floating on oil, and its people are dirt-poor. I wonder where all that Shell money goes? For now, Nigerians could never be called lazy. They provide some of the best drug mules, scam artists, con men and extortion-based crime. In West Africa if you get a fax from Nigeria asking for a meeting, run (do not walk) to the nearest bunco squad.

Pakistan

Cheap, cheap, cheap is what draws Samsonite-packing deal-makers to this promised land of profits. The government is considered corrupt. Political stability is tenuous, and there is constant warfare and insurgencies.

Some tribes in Pakistan are insulted when you tell them that kidnapping for ransom is a crime. The climate for business is unhealthy, to say the least.

The Philippines

The southern Philippines is where a host of motley terrorists-turned-brigands compete for hostages. They prefer to kidnap the children of rich Chinese and priests but dabble

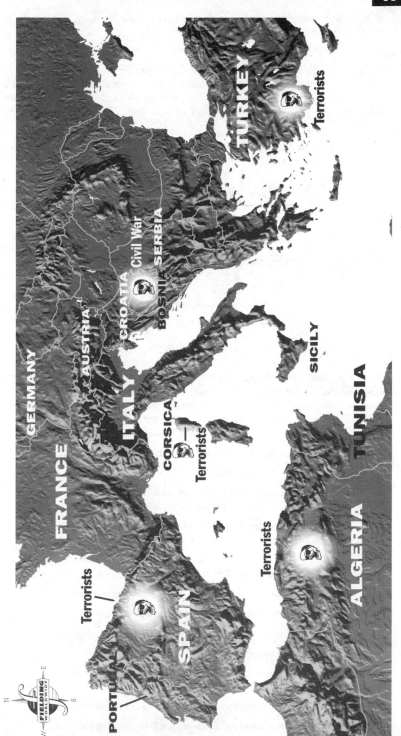

with Westerners when they get lucky. The Philippines should be doing a lot better with its cheap labor and democratic government.

Russia

Russia, specifically Moscow and St. Petersburg, is a quagmire for American businesspeople who are faced with extortion, lawlessness and political instability. There is growing disenchantment with the new Russian revolution. Many had a much better go at it with the communists. It's estimated that there will be more than 120 foreigners killed in Russia this year.

Business travelers in all Third World countries can expect to be hit up for tips, bribes, gifts and dinner checks.

Gangsters: The Businessman's Friend

Wherever there is money, there are gangsters. They have an amazing ability to ignore governments and streamline collection procedures. Do not be surprised if your business partner in Eastern Europe or Russia turns out to be a person of ill repute. Italian and Russian gangs are busy establishing links and are now working together in Germany to control a number of businesses: Of the 776 investigations into organized crime in Germany last year, 17 percent involved attempts to influence politics, big business or government administration. The main activities of organized crime were drug trafficking, weapons smuggling, money laundering and gambling. In 1992, police uncovered profits from organized crime in those areas alone totalling US$438 million, or 700 million Deutschemarks.

TIPS ON SURVIVING BUSINESS TRAVEL

- Spend very little time in dangerous places: airports, remote regions and inner cities. Stay inside after dark. Avoid American chain hotels, and stay on the lower, but not ground, floors.

- Avoid traveling in cars with foreign or rental identification plates and tags.

- Avoid restaurants frequented by expats and tourists.

- Be especially alert during dangerous times, such as public holidays, anniversary dates of terrorist attacks or political parties or during visits by foreign delegations.

- Retain copies of important papers, separate your credit cards in case you lose your wallet, and keep the numbers, expiration dates and the phone numbers to order replacements.

- Divide your money in half and keep it in separate places.

- Choose nonstop flights and stay in the transit lounge when stopping over.

- Do not show your name, country or hotel ID on luggage or clothing.

- Do not discuss plans, accommodations, finances or politics with strangers.

- Wear a cheap watch and no jewelry.

- Get used to sitting near emergency exits and fire escapes, locking your doors and being aware at all times.

- Avoid American symbols or logos. Wear drab colors with conservative accessories.

- Stay away from the front of the plane (terrorists use it to control the aircraft).

TIPS ON SURVIVING BUSINESS TRAVEL

- Do not carry unmarked prescription drugs.

- Leave questionable reading material at home (i.e., *Playboy*, political materials, financial magazines).

- Carry small gifts for customs, drivers and other people you meet.

- Do not take foreign women (or men) up on questionable offers.

- Watch your drink being poured.

- Do not hang the "Make Up Room" sign on your hotel room door. Rather, use the "Do Not Disturb" sign. Keep the TV or radio on, even when you leave.

If you're the kind of person who hums "I'd like to buy the world a Coke," and gets teary-eyed when you wear your hippie beads, you will be dismayed to know that a 43-year-old German multimillionaire was recently kidnapped and released after his family paid $20 million as a ransom. The man had sold his food and tobacco business, retired and was spending his time (and money) advancing social causes and writing books.

But cheer up, the chances of being kidnapped and returned home safe are the least of your worries. You could end up dead. According to International SOS Assistance in Geneva, Switzerland—a company that specializes in health, security and insurance for travelers—a deadly traffic accident is the most likely reason you'll be flown home dead. Cardiac arrest is the second most likely reason. Tropical diseases are the third. Have fun and save those receipts.

Tourists:
Fodder for Fiends

"The scenery is terrible but the people are interesting!"

Usually, when you are on vacation, you do a few things that make local police shudder. You carry a lot of money, you dress funny, you drive an easy-to-spot rental car, you stay in concentrated high-risk areas and you probably drink too much or stay out too late.

Criminals, given a choice between rolling a next-door neighbor or a Rotarian from Cleveland, don't have to think too hard. They know where, when and how to find tourists. And they know exactly what to say to them. They're nice. They'll ask you where you're from—and then jack you up for your wallet, camera and jewelry. You'll then have to leave town or spend all day in the police station filing a report. You'll have to rebook airline tickets and then hit the VISA or AMEX office to get new credit cards. You'll never be back to file a charge or testify. And this is the happy ending.

Think this is bad? In Kenya, bandits routinely rob tourist buses, perform violent carjackings and prey on tourists in the Masai Mara, the world's most popular safari park. In August 1993, a band of robbers shot a bus driver dead and robbed all 50 passengers between Malindi and Lamu. Tourists are robbed and beaten in most countries, but many never bother to report the incidents, knowing full well the futility.

Tourists congregate in the same places. They drive in a state of rubbernecking ecstasy. And they are terrified of local law enforcement. They're even more terrified of damaging that nice new rental car on which they were too cheap to take out insurance. In Florida, thugs looked for European tourists driving rental cars with "Y" and "Z" plates, until someone finally figured out that discretion is better than advertising. Route A46 south of Lyon, France, is the site of more than five robberies a month during the summer. Crooks race up behind cars with foreign license plates, rear-end them and then, when the unsuspecting tourists get out, rob them at gunpoint. In southwestern Turkey don't be surprised to see a carload full of swarthy men wave a pistol at you. They won't kill you, they just want your luggage. You'll get everything back from the police who expect a tip.

The chance of being injured or slain by a terrorist is much less than an attack by a common criminal. But as you will learn in this book, crooks in **Algeria**, **Egypt**, **Turkey**, **Cambodia**, **Myanmar**, **Colombia**, **the Philippines** and **Peru** are deliberately targeting tourists and foreigners as victims of kidnap and/or murder. Their need for negative publicity is designed to curtail tourism and the prosperity it brings in to convolute what they view as elemental societal disfavor with the present political structure. They also demand ransoms for the release of their hostages. In Cambodia, if you're abducted by the Khmer Rouge, you may as well kiss your life adios if their demands aren't met— and in some instances, even if they are.

Dangerous Places for Tourists

Despite the charming pictures of happy travelers having a good time in Third World countries, there is much to be said for the evils of tourism. As soon as you don that Hawaiian shirt or throw on that Eagle Creek backpack, you may as well paint a bull's-eye on your back. Nobody likes to be considered a tourist; we are travelers, cultural ambassadors yearning to soak up new experiences and sights. The first place to look for danger is in the eyes of the people who wait your table, drive your minibus or clean your toilet. Many countries simply refuse to let tourism interfere with their cultures. Brunei, Saudi Arabia, the Gulf States and North Korea all view tourism as an evil and do their best to restrict outside influences.

PLEASE COME TO SEE OUR LOVELY COUNTRY	
Afghanistan	Who you gonna call?
Belize	Petty crime
Benin	Street crime
Bolivia	Kidnapping
Brazil	Violent crime
Burundi	Violent crime in between massacres
Cambodia	Kidnapping, murder
Cameroon	Street crime
Central African Republic	Street crime
Chad	Banditry

UNITED ST

Crime

Crime

Crime MEXICO

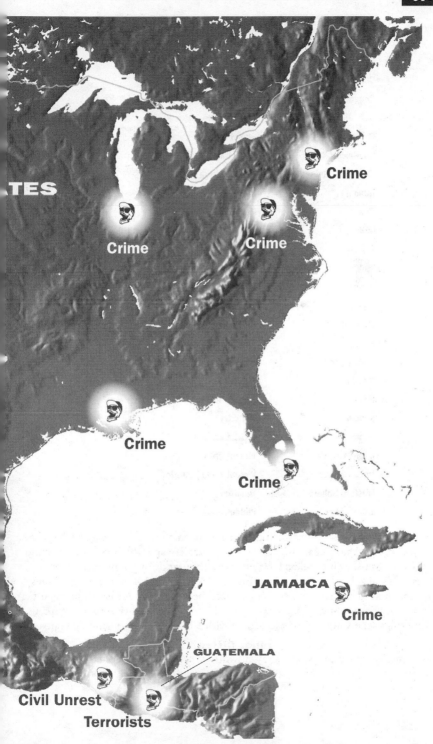

PLEASE COME TO SEE OUR LOVELY COUNTRY

Chile	Petty crime
China	Petty theft, robbery
Colombia	You name it
Congo	Street crime
Cote d'Ivoire	Street crime
Cuba	Street crime
Dominican Rep.	Petty theft
Equatorial Guinea	Violent crime
Ethiopia	Banditry
Ghana	Petty theft
India	Petty theft, kidnapping
Liberia	Lawlessness
Mali	Banditry
Morocco	Banditry
Nigeria	Con artists
Pakistan	Kidnapping, banditry
Peru	Murder, kidnapping
Philippines	Kidnapping
Russia	The works
Rwanda	Nobody left to steal anything
Somalia	Banditry
Spain	Tourist crime
Uganda	Violent crime
United States	Violent crime, murder
Western Sahara	Banditry
Zaire	Violent crime

Other countries are averse to tourism, but need the bucks. Tourism has destroyed places like Nepal, the Caribbean, Mexico and the Riviera. Invading armies of cash-spewing oglers have enslaved thousands of young girls as prostitutes in Thailand, Amsterdam, Hamburg, New York and Berlin. Entire villages, like Bagan in Myanmar, have been bulldozed because they cluttered the scenery. Hundreds of tiny rustic seaports have turned into T-shirt-spewing tourist traps, as cruise ships send waves of tourists armed with VISA cards off in landing crafts.

Inner Cities

In America, few local people stray downtown after dark. Unfortunately, many tourists stay in business hotels built downtown and go for early morning jogs or late night strolls. Are they crazy? No, they're just tourists.

Trains

In Russia, China, Central and Southeast Asia, Georgia and Eastern Europe, trains are a target of organized thefts and abductions. Bandits, terrorists and marauding militias use drugs injected into sleeping cars. Others place logs or vehicles across the tracks and then leisurely rob passengers one at a time. Others, such as the Khmer Rouge in Cambodia, simply rocket trains before they rob and kill the passengers.

Buses

Buses are prime targets of criminals and terrorists because they hold a lot of people in a confined area, have few exits and generally travel rural routes—the unarmed passengers are usually carrying most of their earthly belongings with them. Buses also follow regular routes along remote thoroughfares, which allows the civilized bandit to pull off an 11:30 a.m. ambush and make it home for lunch.

Resorts

If you are looking for tourists, what better place than where they sleep and store all their stuff? No need to kick in the door, since the criminals will already have a key; the manager splits the booty with them. Hotels are also convenient places to put bombs. The Kurdish separatist movement in Turkey (PKK) deliberately targets tourist resorts along the Aegean Sea, even though they're fighting a war in Eastern Turkey. The Basque separatists (ETA) wreak havoc along the Spanish Mediterranean coast, and Corsican terrorists (FLNC and MNA) have tried to scare away French tourists with random bombings in French resorts.

Here's a brief overview of where tourists are considered the daily sustenance for bad people.

More Dangerous Places for Tourists

North America/Mexico

The United States is plagued with inner-city crime. Guns are commonly used, and convenience store clerks should get combat pay. Tourists are under attack, often with more violent consequences than are found in many "uncivilized" countries.

After racking my brain for something dangerous in **Canada,** I finally stumbled onto an obscure study by the Italian Bankers Association (ABI) that says Canada has the highest number of bank raids per branch, with one branch in seven being robbed in 1994. After that, it's frostbite and roaming polar bears. So cash those traveler's checks at the Amex office next time you're in the frozen north.

European tourists love **Florida**. Never having seen an inner-city or rest-stop killing ground, they have little idea of what to avoid. Asian tourists love **California**. They usually stay in those fancy downtown hotels. The unsuspecting traveler can't figure out why no one else is on the streets when he staggers back to his hotel, drunk on American whisky and saki. Asian tourists carry lots of American money because it's so cheap. Crooks like rolling Asians, because they don't carry guns and they're so damn polite when they fork over all that cheap American green.

Mexico is still wild and woolly. Big, bad Mexican desperadoes still exist. Mexico's frontiers are rife with mean, dusty border towns, where anything can be had for a price. Corrupt *federales,* who will steal your money and piss on your shoes, abound. Cheap, dark bars still sell ammo, drugs and women. Convention hall–sized whorehouses feature nonstop knife fights. Petty crime flourishes in resort areas. Violent crime is always a threat in the boonies. And God help you if you get busted. The best advice is to stay out of the resorts and find the real Mexico. Thankfully, for every bad guy, there are a thousand Mexicans with hearts of gold.

South America

Mexico is Disneyland compared to **Colombia**. Terrorists in **Peru**, **Bolivia** and **Guyana** await you. Pickpockets and thugs in Brazil hope that tourism will pick up before the death squads kill them all. Coca is the crop of choice, and the resultant criminal infrastructure makes travel hairy in the valleys of the northwest part of the continent. **Brazil** is a zoo with street crime in Rio, and the number of land mines left over in the **Falkland Islands** discourages trekkers and bird-watchers.

Africa

North Africa is still a nasty place. The Tuaregs in **Mali** and **Niger** still feed off unsuspecting travelers. Tourism is an alien concept to these nomadic warriors. Tourist groups have been robbed at gunpoint, female members raped, and the victims left without transportation in the desert. Remember, in the Sahara, no one can hear you scream.

Islamic fundamentalists in **Egypt** have one of the most effective campaigns to scare away tourists. They have exploded bombs at the Great Pyramid and attacked tour buses, not to mention conducting sniper attacks on Nile riverboats. Luckily, the group el-Gama'a el-Islamyia wants to discourage tourism, not necessarily kill tourists. The machine-gunning of 19 Greek tourists in Cairo was considered to be "unusual."

In **Algeria,** Islamic fundamentalists are killing foreigners as fast as they can. The Polisario is still raising hell in **Morocco**. Nobody even thinks of going to **Mauritania**, unless they want to be kidnapped and sold off as a white slave. **Djibouti** still has rebel activity, and **Ethiopia and Somalia** have the meanest bandits in the world. The **Sudan** has a very vicious war being waged in the south.

Sub-Saharan Africa

Your best hope is that you stay in a place surrounded by wild animals and wilder mercenaries. At least it will keep the thieves away. The Hutu and Tutsis in **Rwanda** and **Burundi** are still whacking each other with *pangas*. The mean deeds of folks in **Zaire**, **Central African Republic**, **South Africa** and **Nigeria** would make a Russian gangster blush. Desperately poor urban thieves and roving bandits plaguing **Tanzania**, **Kenya** and **Uganda** are stepping up crimes against tourists, and **Madagascar** requires a cautious approach as it slides into anarchy. **Sierra Leone**, **Liberia** and **Angola** are strictly for soldiers of fortune, since even aid workers are fair game in these places.

Middle East/Mediterranean

The world still has a rotten core. **Bosnia** will be a mess for years to come. Ethnic and religious tensions make **Israel**, **Southern Lebanon**, **Cyprus** and the **Occupied Territories** hot spots for terrorism and violence. **Syria**, **Iraq** and **Iran** are relatively safe, in the sense that their brand of nastiness is for export only.

Eastern Turkey is a mess: The Kurdish Workers Party, or PKK, has the tourist-terrorism thing down pat. The PKK issued a warning that effectively broadens their battleground to hotels, beaches and other tourist attractions. They take

Crime

Crime

Crime

VENEZUELA

GUYANA

FRENCH GUIANA

SURINAME

Drugs

COLOMBIA

ECUADOR

Drugs

Border Dispute

PERU

BRAZIL

Drugs

BOLIVIA

CHILE

PARAGUAY

Crime

URUGUAY

ARGENTINA

Land Mines

FALKLAND ISLANDS

great pleasure in ensuring that the lives of all people visiting Turkey will be in danger. There are also nasty things being done by rival Kurdish factions, Armenian terrorists, the special ops groups, drug smugglers, Hezbollah, and more in Northern Iraq.

Europe

Europe is supposed to be a safe haven for tourists, but petty crimes in the tourist areas and central cities are common. Skinheads are busy in **Germany** bashing people with brown eyes and foreign accents. The Basque ETA in **Spain** likes to blow things up. **Paris** is crawling with Gypsies and petty thieves above ground and Algerian terrorist setting off bombs below ground when they get the chance. **Sicily** is still home to bandits who like to prey on tourists. They like to use *lupares* (sawed-off shotguns) and rob people—and kill them, of course. Petty thievery runs rampant along the beach resorts of **Spain**, **France** and **Italy** during tourist season.

South/Western Asia

The north is a seething mass of conflict, with separatist, ethnic and religious groups blasting each other into shreds. **Afghanistan** is a perpetual battlefield, and no tourists dare venture there (except *DP*, of course, who has a special affinity for that wasted place). **Pakistan** has roving bandits and hot-headed killers who will rob policemen and armed convoys just for their bullets. Northern **Sri Lanka** is a bona-fide war zone, even though the beaches are full in the south.

Southeast Asia

Cambodia has a continual game of push-me pull-you, as they play tug-of-war with the Khmer Rouge for control of the countryside. Meanwhile, there are still enough land mines to put Doctor Scholl out of business. Despite the government calling in *DP* to do a short arm inspection, we put it on our danger list. The Golden Triangle area of **Thailand** is still controlled by drug lords and hardwood timber smugglers, although not as much as in **Laos** and **Myanmar**. **Papua New Guinea** and **Irian Jaya** have local tribal wars and insurgents that break out around ecotrekkers. The sex tourism industry and prevalence of AIDS in Southeast Asia poses a whole other danger for the adventurous.

THE STING

When traveling through Asian countries, you could be the victim of over-zealous law enforcement agents. In India and Thailand, there have been reports of threats of arrest on drug charges, unless you give officers money. In Thailand, police officers make a monthly salary of about US$200. Thai police officers and their informants can receive a reward of 10,000 baht per kg of pure heroin recovered. It has been stated that after refusing these demands, some foreign travelers were booked and charged for using heroin.

Some travelers have paid US$150–200 to get these cops off their backs. If you are taken to court in Thailand, the odds are not good. No foreigner has been acquitted of an offense in more than 20 years. In India, there are 40 young Westerners serving lengthy jail sentences who claim they were sent to prison on bogus charges.

Due to the severity of sentences and the low salaries of officers, Thailand, Malaysia and India can be considered the most dangerous destinations for backpacking youngsters. Indonesia, the Philippines and Latin America are also danger spots. The only solution is to not look like a hippie, not travel alone and try to get witnesses if you feel you are being pushed into an unethical transaction.

China/Far East

China is pushing its people to desperation, and, despite more executions than there are daytime Emmys in Hollywood, the crime wave is increasing. All Dr. Kevorkian has to do is hand out free airline passes for Chinese airlines if he wants to legalize suicide. **South Korea** is the scene of anti-American demonstrations, as is **Japan** to a lesser extent.

Is It Safe?

Despite the concerted efforts of all these nations and groups to wreck your two weeks of vacation time, most of the world's travelers will have little more to complain about than cold French fries and lumpy mattresses. Are we being overly glum here? We put our heads together to come up with a list of the world's safest places and we couldn't come up with enough countries to put on a decent volleyball game.

THE WORLD'S MOST BORING PLACES

When I get old and feeble, I think I will write a book about safe places, but for now this is about it for my list of *not* dangerous places. *DP* has been accused of using creative license to prove its point, so do you think I can start a few civil wars with these descriptions?

Canada	Vicious, half-frozen hockey players whacked on fermented maple syrup can't find anybody to insult. Seems like everybody there already came from somewhere else. The French want to leave, but nobody cares. It just means cereal boxes will have fewer words on them.
The Caribbean	Toasted, ganja-bent natives spend their entire lives laughing, swimming and partying. Major fear is bad backs from too much limbo, and cirrhosis of the liver and cavities from too many piña coladas.
Costa Rica	Lush mountainous country, swarming with tree-hugging eco yuppies. Instant riots when locals throw gum wrappers on street or ask for nonrecycled coasters for their Perrier.
Mongolia	Flat dull place with no roads and less people. Would like to have more accidents, riots and civil unrest, but can't seem to get enough people in the same place at the same time.
New Zealand	Remote flyspeck island, where sheep have a terrified look in their eyes. In order to satisfy the Kiwi thirst for bloodshed and violence, they play a lot of rugby.
Pacific Islands	Can't steal anything, 'cause there's no one to sell it to. Can't overthrow anyone, because everyone is related to everyone else. Can't beat anyone up, since everyone is over 400 pounds and laid back. Can't complain about the government, because then you would have to wear a suit and go to work everyday.
The Vatican	The land of one house and one church pisses a lot of people off, but it seems like those funny-looking Swiss mercenaries in striped pantaloons and pig stickers keep everything under control.

PHILIPPINES

orism

Crime

Civil Unrest

**PAPUA
NEW GUINEA**

st

AUSTRALIA

Switzerland	Duck and cover is the word here. Too much money packed into this alpine paradise to start a fight.
Australia	Aussies like their beer and bash a few roos to work off their frustration. They'd like to start a ruckus, but they would have to get it all figured out in time for Sunday cricket.
Iceland	The land of fire and ice can't get up much steam when it comes to being mean. The fair-haired lads used to kick some booty in the Viking days, but now they are happy to make more fairhaired babies.
Antarctica	It's too damn cold to go outside and fight. This icebox is cut into neat little pie slices, until one of the slice owners finds oil. Then it's all settled with snowballs.

Also considered safe are Kuwait, Japan and Belgium. Let's keep it that way 'cause we're too damned tired of adding chapters to this book every year.

DANGEROUS PLACES

Dangerous Places
(Short and Sweet)

You know the world is a dangerous place (you watch "Frontline" reruns and "Cops" religiously, and down at Jerry's Elbow Inn they're always jabbering about Bosnia Whachamacallit or "Somellyia" or even all those dungholes owned by Stan: Afghanistan, Pakistan, etc.). But even if you know how to rattle off dangerous places, you still get shown up by some college punk who reads Cliffs Notes. So if you want to look like you read this book, here is a primer guaranteed to keep you in free beer and pretzels. The following is a short and opinionated list of the world's most dangerous places:

Afghanistan Civil war between northern Tajik fundamentalists and back-country Pahktun fundamentalists. The only country where religious students know how to drive tanks.

Algeria Muslim fundamentalists are mad because they were cheated out of a 1992 election victory. They take it out on Westerners and journalists.

Angola A civil war between pouting egos that is really about diamond mines protected by mercenaries. It's quiet for now, but that's only because they ran out of bullets.

Argentina Feuding with Chile over the Beagle Channel and with Paraguay over their northeastern border. They agree that the Pilcomayo river is the boundary, but the darn river keeps changing course.

Armenia The Armenians want it all, and they want it now (see Azerbaijan).

Azerbaijan Squabbling with Armenia about a little'ole chunk of land (about 20 percent of their country) that used to be theirs (see Armenia).

Bangladesh The home of Shanti Bahini, Chakma and 200,000 Royhinga refugees. Where's George Harrison when you need him? These folks are very nervous about tidal waves because they don't surf.

Bolivia Coca, Tupac (not the late Shakur) Katari and grinding poverty. Peasants still get more money for that white powder than those Alpaca blankets.

Bosnia-Herzegovina Mass graves in Europe (again). Nobody seems to care. The war to end all wars or start all wars? Hatred still simmers in a land where a lot of people will never be found.

Bougainville	Fuzzy-haired rebels with rusty shotguns fighting for a fly-speck-size island.
Burundi	Rwanda, the sequel. Same story, different location.
Cambodia	Land of the Khmer Rouge, folks who don't like progress or the West. Many mines and front lines awfully close to Angkor Wat. Kidnapped Americans are only worth 10 grand here and they don't take American Express.
Colombia	The nastiest place in the Western Hemisphere: drugs, kidnapping, murder, terrorism and great beaches.
China	Human rights, sweat shops, occupation of Tibet, the border with Bhutan and oppression of the Muslims in the northwest. Big place, big problems, still under a firm communist grip, which means you can still get free "Made in China" toys in your next Happy Meal.
Corsica	Swarthy men who want to have their own country of swarthy men. Unfortunately, the Legion likes Corsica (its base) and killing insurgents (their job). Tourists are guaranteed to have a blast.
Cyprus	Turks versus Greeks separated by a thin blue line. The oldest U.N. mission that keeps on going and going and going....
Djibouti	The hottest, lowest place in Africa doesn't seem like it would be worth fighting over, but the Afars and the French Foreign Legion do.
Ecuador	They lost a tiny sliver of land near Tiwinza to Peru in 1941, and they want it back. So it's time to rumble in the jungle with tear gas, flamethrowers and artillery.
El Salvador	You thought the movie *Salvador* was history. Same place, same problem, different time. Death squads and left-wing insurgents seem to be a permanent fixture here.
Egypt	Fundamentalists like to hide in the weeds along the Nile and take pot shots at tourists. When 18 Greek tourists died of lead poisoning, most folks figured the temples could gather a little more dust. Could this be an exciting new theme park ride?
Germany	Skinheads are blaming all the Middle East immigrants for their joblessness: Could it be the swastikas tattooed on their heads?
Georgia	Besieged by Armenians, Azeris, Abkazanians, South Ossetians and more people wanting freedom than prisoners at a San Quentin parole hearing.
Guatemala	With a name like URNG, you'd be mad too. Indians versus the rich folks. Political killings are cheaper than printing campaign posters.
Haiti	Decades of brutal dictatorship, crime and corruption briefly interrupted by some good old-fashioned gunboat diplomacy.
India	Seven revolts, hundreds of languages, countless religions and manufacturing more people daily than China in half the space. Great restaurants, lousy weather.
Indonesia	Half of East Timor used to be a Portuguese colony. Some folks in Aceh and Irian Jaya are not happy either. It is amazing Indonesia holds together at all.

Iran The big bad wolf of our times. Fundamentalism is the "in-thing," whether other countries like it or not. Baluchis and Kurds are not happy. Not getting along with Iraq either. Iran is heading backwards fast, and they don't even need H.G. Wells.

Iraq A punch-drunk dictator who doesn't know when to retire to Miami Beach (he must like sand) and write his memoirs. A starving impoverished country that picks fights with the wrong people (U.S., Iran, Kuwait, Kurds, Shiites and the dictator's own family).

Israel An occupying force that doesn't get along with the former landlords. Peace is at hand, but the war is not over. Plenty of sworn enemies to keep them busy (Hamas, Hezbollah, right wingers et. al.).

Kenya The northern border is a nasty place, thanks to Somali gangs. The nomadic Masaii and agrarian Kikuyu can't get along. Lots of crime, poverty, conflict, but it doesn't stop the tourists.

Laos Too poor to really have a good knockdown insurgency since the U.S. carpet-bombed it. Warlords still have Chao Fah rebels and a running feud with Thailand over the border.

Lebanon Northern Lebanon welcomes tourists, NASA wishes they had the rocket budget southern Lebanon has. Southern Lebanon is the nastiest place in the Middle East. Great beaches, great food. Hey, was that a rocket attack or is it a national holiday? Home of Hezbollah.

Liberia Dumb war, vicious leaders, no future. Teenagers killing teenagers with no idea why. You need a program to follow the bit players.

Malaysia Clean modern place surrounded by vicious seaborne pirates.

Mali The Tuaregs are not happy. The blacks shoot first, check nationality later. Don't go out on your camel after dark.

Mexico Nasty, party kind of place teetering between the Third and First World. The Zapatistas are now focused on cutting mean movie deals instead of throats. EPR might mean Extremely Pissed Radicals.

Morocco Polisario still conduct sand wars.

Mozambique More land mines than people. All sold out of "watch your step" signs.

Myanmar There are 30 different opposition groups, from drug rings to oppressed tribal minorities. More Generals than a GMC truck dealer.

Niger The Tuaregs are mad as hell, and they aren't going to take it anymore.

**Northern
Ireland** Keep your fingers crossed, and kiss your four leaf clover. Shopping in London just got more exciting.

Pakistan Fierce mountain tribes in the northwest. Fierce desert tribes in the south. Fierce Muslim tribes in the northeast. You get the picture. Karachi is most dangerous city in the world. Cheap guns and great climbing, nice people when they aren't killing each other.

Philippines In the South, Muslims vs. Christians. Didn't we figure this stuff out during the Crusades? In the North, it's communists vs. government. Didn't we figure this out in the eighties?

Peru The Shining Path and Tupac Amaru have lost some of their influence, but none of their nastiness. As long as folks keep tooting, the government will keep stomping.

Russia	Discos, limousines, drugs, gangsters, gunfights… where's Coppola and De Palma?
Rwanda	There is no one left to kill anybody. They'll need about 10 years to build up enough people to kill each other again. Will the Hutus ever get along with the Tutsis? Not likely.
Sardinia	Swarthy gangsters import drugs, kill people, make money. See Chechnya and Corsica and Russia and….
Senegal	*Casamance* is hiding in the swamps. Hey, that's my oil you're sitting on!
Sierra Leone	Whacked-out rebels who eat people and *then* kill them. White mercenaries backed by diamond mine owners. Steaming jungles, tough guys in beatup Russian attack helicopters. Is this a great "B" movie plot or what?
Somalia	Warlord central. Technicals equipped with 50 calibre guns rule. My Toyota can whip your Toyota. Each side has its favorite banana company. Brand loyalty is important here. Greed and hatred reign.
Spain	The Basques want to be free. Free to do what? Herd sheep?
Sri Lanka	Suicide frogmen and cyanide pendants are popular here.
Sudan	A two-decade war where starvation is a weapon. Black vs. Arab, Christian vs. Muslim. Nasty war, no end in sight.
Suriname	Rebels in the jungle, crime, corruption. Business as usual in the south Caribbean.
South Africa	Voted "most dangerous place" outside a war zone. Right wings, neo-Nazis, concentration camps, and more: 87 rapes and 50 murders a day, great surfing and game viewing too.
Tajikistan	What are those crazy Russians up to? They play both sides of the border and make money doing it. Great place for a "Wars'R. Us" franchise.
Turkey	The Kurds want their own country; Turkey says quit whining. The PKK like to kill people, blow things up and shoot schoolteachers. For now, come visit our sunny land (the west part at least).
Uganda	It is safe now, isn't it? Well, maybe after refugees from Rwanda, Burundi and Lord's Resistance group stop killing and go home. Oh yeah, Idi's still kicking back in the Saudi.
United States	Some days our inner cities can make Monrovia look like a Mormon suburb. Over 70 people killed a day and over 200 million guns ready to party. Do you feel lucky, punk?
Western Sahara/ Morocco	This sand ain't your sand, this sand is my sand. No, this isn't Coney Island on a long weekend. The Polisario Front, backed by Algeria, must own a beach umbrella concession.
Zaire	Dirty, nasty, corrupt, violent, but other than that, not bad. Just a typical central African hellhole.

Afghanistan
★★★★★

The Rockets' Red Glare

Watching the Katyushas make shallow arcs over Kabul used to be the only form of entertainment in this blown to hell town. Now that the *taliban* have their prize even that fireworks show is over. In September of 96 the *taliban* chased DP's buddy Massoud and Rabbiani out of Kabul, strung up Najibullah, former president and head of secret police under Karmal (got any bad puppet on a string jokes) and started chanting the Koran over megaphones; *taliban* Rap has come to Afghanistan and you definitely can't dance to it.

This is just one scene from one of the many conflicts that have shaped this country. If all the world's wars could be weighed on a scale of depression and misery,, the wars that have ravaged Afghanistan would tip the scales. Once united by a common enemy, the Afghans fought against the Russians in what was the hardest and fiercest war of the Soviet empire.

Modern Afghan misery began in 1978, when Noor Taraki attempted to import communism into Afghanistan with the aid of the Soviet Union. His successor,

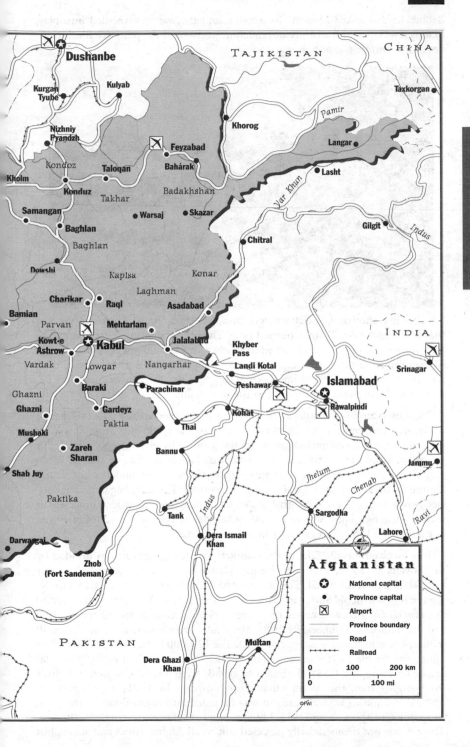

Afghanistan

- ✪ National capital
- • Province capital
- ☒ Airport
- Province boundary
- Road
- Railroad

| 0 | 100 | 200 km |

| 0 | 100 mi |

©FWI

Babrak Karmal, asked Moscow for troops, and the war was whistled into play. Marxism was met with mortars and machine guns—and the primitive flintlock rifles of the *mujahedin*, or holy warriors.

Eighty-five thousand Soviet soldiers invaded Afghanistan. Their pretext was that the puppet ruler, Karmal, needed help. The official demand for this intervention was sent from Kabul and signed by Karmal, who could not have been in the Afghan capital at the time because he was riding into Kabul with a Soviet army convoy. Meanwhile, Gulbuddin Hekmatyar spent the Russian war safely in Peshawar while Massoud was fighting in the mountains.

The conservative Muslim *mujahedin* put up an unexpected and bitter resistance to the new government. Soviet troops, armed to the teeth with Moscow's most modern materiel, were picked apart on the ground by elusive rebel *mujahedin* guerrillas, employing antiquated weapons that had been state of the art when Jane's first started publishing their guide to all the world's blunderbusses. Later, the rebels, backed by the CIA and supplied through Pakistan, began picking Soviet gunships out of the sky with U.S.-supplied Stingers and other surface-to-air rockets. The fighting was bloody, and both sides settled into a war of attrition, not unlike the U.S. effort in Vietnam a decade earlier.

How involved was the CIA in the conflict? When Afghanistan was invaded by the Soviets in 1979, President Jimmy Carter provided the *mujahedin* with US$30 million in covert aid. This manifested itself in the form of the CIA supplying the rebels with old Soviet arms procured from Egypt. As covert military aid to the *mujahedin* increased under the Reagan Administration, so did the carnage and the number of refugees. By 1985, the Afghan rebels were receiving US$250 million a year in covert assistance to battle the 120,000 Soviet troops. That 1985 figure was double 1984's amount. The annual amount received by the guerrillas reached a whopping US$700 million by 1988. Even after the Soviets withdrew from Afghanistan, the spook bucks kept flowing. In 1991, anywhere from US$180 million to US$300 million was funneled into Afghanistan by the CIA. In all, the CIA spent about US$3.3 billion in rebel aid over the course of the war. The aid was not democratically parceled out to all Afghan tribes and states, but deftly flowed only to the tribal and political leaders who were friendly with Pakistan. Under these conditions, the *taliban* emerged.

An initial agreement to end outside aid was signed in April 1988 by Afghanistan, the U.S.S.R., the U.S. and Pakistan. The accords were signed on the condition that the U.S.S.R. pull out its troops by the end of the year. The Soviets' withdrawal occurred in February 1989. Another agreement, signed between the Soviet Union and the U.S. in September 1991, also sought to arrange the end of meddling into Afghanistan's affairs by the two superpowers. By the middle of April 1992, *mujahedin* guerrillas and other Islamic rebels moved in on Kabul and ousted President Najibullah. A 50-member ruling council comprised of guerrilla, religious and intellectual leaders was quickly established to create an Islamic republic. Najibullah had lived under house arrest at a U.N. compound in Kabul until the *taliban* lynched him from a 20 foot tower. Few shed any tears since Najibullah was the head of the secret police before he became Moscow's stooge.

The *taliban* swept like a hot desert wind from the south (see "The Players") all the way to the outskirts of Kabul. They were checked in their advance and there they sat stalemated in their quest to conquer Afghanistan. Now it seems the ragtag army directed by the *taliban* (religious students) will likely remain confined to their power-base in the Durrani Pushtun provinces of southern Afghanistan. This area is the center of Pakhtun culture and coincidently the home of the monarchy. The Pakhtun or Pathans are a group of 15–17 million people of which 10 million live in Afghanistan and the rest in Pakistan.

The Pakhtuns have not forgotten that it was from Kandahar in 1747 that Ahmadshah Durrani created the Pushtun tribal confederacy that became what we call Afghanistan today. Since that time a Pakhtun has always ruled Afghanistan except for a brief period in 1929 when the Tajik, Habibullah called the shots. This was truly to be a grass roots uprising and a true jihad.

The *taliban's* main enemies were in Kabul. The government of Rabbani, Massoud and Hekmatyar were like three Western gunslingers forced together in fear of a massive Indian attack from the ridge outside of town. The Hizb-i-Islami (Islamic Party) of Islamist Gulbuddin Hekmatyar had been swept from the south by the *taliban* advance and its three-year siege of Kabul broken. Now Massoud is being forced north towards the country he helped defeat long ago. The Iranian-backed Shia Hizb-i-Wahdat-i-Islami (Islamic Unity Party) has similarly been driven from its stronghold in southwestern Kabul and reduced to a tiny organization based in northern Afghanistan. Uzbek warlord Abdul Rashid Dostam, weakened by a cutback in aid from Uzbekistan, has seen his own Kabul forces destroyed and his power-base confined to the northwest.

The *taliban* was started in the Maiwand district of Southern Afghanistan by a group of 30 former religious students who had studied together in the provincial madrassahs. Their leader was one-eyed 34-year-old Mullah Mohammad Omar. Most of the students were veterans of the war against the Russians and were unhappy with the power vested in a few warlords by their control of U.S.-supplied weapons. The leaders of the *taliban* remained enigmatic and the western press was terrified to enter into this new uncharted war. DP has been following the rise of the *taliban* from the *madrassahs* (religious colleges) of the south to their siege of Kabul. Their leaders are Pathans from the Kandahar and Helmand provinces. The uprising began when they attacked the highway checkpoints manned by their followers—extortion, robbery and rape were daily occurrences. These atrocities not only angered the common people but they cut into the business of influential traders based in Quetta in Pakistan and in Kandahar. These traders financed the initial campaigns of the *taliban* to clear Kandahar of the warlords.

They had support from the *madrassahs* (religious schools) in the refugee camps of Baluchistan and Peshawar where thousands of Afghan refugee youth were studying. The Pakistani *madrassahs* in the south were supported by businessmen and religious leaders who had connections with the Pakistani religious party Jamiat-i-Ulema Islami, led by a member of Bhutto's government, Fazlur Rahman. Their brand of Islam is the strict, old fashioned Sunni Deoband school—so strict that the leaders forbid their pictures from being taken. Their fervent brand of Islam and stern punishment methods have struck fear in the hearts of most western journalists.

The first area the *taliban* captured was the border town of Spin Baldak in October 1994. It didn't take long, about two to three hours. In two days the entire city of Kandahar fell to the *taliban* after weak resistance. In November and December, the provinces of Uruzgan to the north and Zabol were taken by troops riding in the back of pickup trucks waving the Koran.

In January, the *taliban* took over Afghanistan's major opium growing center; Helmand, without a single shot fired. The *taliban* are against drugs of any kind and things don't look good for the future of Afghanistan's largest cash crop. In late January and February, Ghazni and Maidanshahr came under *taliban* control. Maidanshahr fell on February 10 erasing Hekmatyar's supply line to his position at his base of Charasyab south of Kabul and in Logar province. On February 14, Hekmatyar fled Charasyab. All this was accomplished with an army of less than 3000 ill-equipped, ill-trained men using captured Russian arms.

The *taliban* fights in small groups called *lashkars*. This is the Afghan name for a tribal war party. The *taliban* is a movement of Tajiks, Uzbeks, Hazaras and other minorities and has no axe to grind with any minority or ethnic group.

Estimates put the *taliban* army at 10,000–15,000 men on both western and eastern fronts. Most of this rabble was used to fight in western Herat, not in Kabul in the east. Less than 3000 *taliban* fighters took Kabul.

The *taliban* didn't get much of an air force when they seized Kandahar airport;, they captured six MIG-21 'Fishbed' interceptors (only one of which can fly) and four Mi-17 helicopter transport (none are set up as gunships). Two additional Mi-17s were captured from the base of Hizb commander Sarkateb outside the city. The *taliban* is short of pilots but they have plenty of "tank drivers" to drive the captured battle tanks and armored fighting vehicles.

Massoud's forces included the muscular Central Corps with 15,000–20,000 men, the 6th Corps Kunduz covering the northeast; and the 5th Corps, formerly in Herat in the west. It's anybody's guess how they will be regrouped. He does get some help with the six Su-22 'Fitters' and a group of several Mi-24 Hind helicopter gunships flown by pilots trained in India.

For now the *taliban* have called upon their enemies to lay down their arms and follow them in a true Koranic jihad. This works fine on country folk but the people of Kabul are Farsi speaking Hazari's and Uzbeks and are rather sophisticated compared to the Pashto-speaking Southerners. The Pakistan Secret Service (ISI) is believed to be backing the *taliban*. Massoud did not accept ISI help during the Russian war, but Hekmatyar used their support not only during the Russian conflict but even while he was rocketing Kabul for three years. All DP saw wasPakhtunPakhtun phone lines and infrastructure being rebuilt within *taliban*-controlled areas and we noted a blind eye to cross border traffic. The *taliban* continue to gain and are feared in the west which is why DP made a point of getting to know these rather homespun revolutionaries.

The Scoop

War without end, amen. As if it wasn't bad enough that 2 million Afghans died during the Russian occupation between 1979 and 1989, now Muslim has set upon Muslim in a nihilistic struggle for control of this poor country. The civil war has claimed 70,000 lives since the Russians left, and countless others have been wounded by war and land mines. After 16 years of take-no-prisoners warfare, there is little to recommend about this rugged, shattered land. Few travelers other than aid workers and *DP* staffers go into Afghanistan. Nobody comes out without a few close calls. The *taliban*, a group of fundamentalists (surprised?) from the south, emerged as the new player in February of 1995, descending like locusts on the killing fields.

The *taliban* loom large in Kabul and it remains to be seen if they can switch over from being fighters to being politicians and administrators.

The Players

The *Taliban*

The black-turbaned *taliban* have been hard at work liberating Afghanistan from the bands of militia and warring factions that have choked the country and turned it into a lawless wasteland. They burst on the scene in the first week of October 1994 from their base in Kandahar. Their leaders are primarily selected from the Durrani tribes hailing from the backwater southern provinces of Helmand and Uruzgan, who have little allegiance to Pakistan and its Western supporters. They took over the capital of Kabul by simply entering the city in pickup trucks, concealing their weapons under their cloaks. They are considered a simple, pure people led by very religious but culturally isolated mullahs who've had enough of the oppression of the northern- and eastern-based warlords.

The *taliban* began in Kandahar where trucks driving towards Kabul were forced to pay a toll of 2 million Afghanis (about US$250–300) to cross the checkpoint. It is normal to charge tolls in Afghanistan but not to sodomize any young boys who have the misfortune to pass through. The gunmen would force young boys to undergo a mock public marriage and then sodomize them repeatedly. Outraged by the treatment the warlord dealt to his own people, the local *taliban* took action. Religious leader Maulavi Mohammed told his spiritual leader that he had a dream to create a new Afghanistan free of the cruel men created by outside interference. Omar then got together a group of 50 men and hung them from their tank barrels as a warning and a message that things were going to change.

Since then the *taliban* have swept through southern Afghanistan like a hot desert wind often meeting no resistance. The highest decision-making body in the *taliban* is the *Shura*, which reportedly numbers 30 but has grown to include leaders from areas that have come under the *taliban's* influence. The inner core of the Shura is limited to eight members, of which a group of four leaders, all from Kandahar (one eyed (left eye) Maulvis Umar, Mohammad Rabbani, Mohammad Abbas and Borjan) are considered the brains behind the *taliban*. In *taliban* areas, soccer, volleyball and even chess have been banned because they cause youths to miss some of their five daily prayers. Women must wear veils and men's hair must be kept short. The most grisly change is the practice of public executions where the victims' relatives get to execute the killer with a machine gun. In some cases the killer's father must do the killing and buy the bullets used to end his son's life. Public amputations of thieves are common and are performed by doctors who administer a painkiller first. Punishment for jaywalking and spitting will take some creativity but they'll think of something.

DP spent some time with these very focused folks. Their goal is to clean out the outside-supported factions and establish an Islamic government that would make Iran look like Fire Island on a holiday weekend. They have banned education for females. They are not wild about Shias, football, cocktail parties and women's lib. They are led by 41-year-old Maulana Mohammed Umar and a group of 22 imman who have created a *shura*, or parliament, to run the country. The two principal military leaders are Maulan Mohammed Rabbani (no relationship to President Burhanuddin Rabbani), based in Logar, and Maula Mashar, in Wardak. The fighters of the *taliban* are recruited from hundreds of religious schools in Afghanistan and Pakistan and look exactly as you would expect a grass roots militia to look; they possess neither uniforms nor training, and are completely devoted to their cause. The Iranians (predominately Shia) are hardly friendly with the hard-core Sunni *taliban*, and the border areas between Iran and Afghanistan will probably be major flash points in the coming years. The group currently operates a tiny radio station in Kandahar and, once in power, promises to permit the broadcasting of radio and television programs, as long as all media is devoted to spreading the word of Allah. At press time, the *taliban* were ringing Kabul with more than 100 new Saudi-supplied tanks, truck-mounted rocket launchers and thousands of armed militiamen. There are about 20,000 *taliban* fighters at the present time.

Direct telephone numbers to contact the taliban:

Lahore: ☎ *042-669087* (Dari spoken) Taliban office, Lahore

Quetta: ☎ *081-822422* (Pushtu spoken) Taliban HQ, Kandahar

Jamiat-i-Islami (Islamic Society)

Jamiat-i-Islami (Islamic Society) is influenced by the thinking of Pakistani theologian Abul Ala Maududi and Egyptian thinker Sayyid Qutb. Afghan Islamism began on the campus of Kabul University in the mid-1960s as a reaction to the Marxist trend among the students. Among the professors trained at Cairo's Al-Azhar University, among them Burhanuddin Rabbani, it attracted students of science, engineering and medicine. Hekmatyar (Kabul University) and Massoud (Kabul Polytechnic) are both engineering students who began their political careers on Kabul campuses. The party of Rabbani and Massoud pushes a revolutionary but modern form of Islamism.

Gulbuddin Hekmatyar

Hekmatyar is the leader of the Hezbi Islami and formerly was nurtured by the CIA in their efforts to give the Soviets a black eye. He was also once supported by the warlord Abdul Rashid Dostam (who once supported President Burhanuddin Rabbani but is now his enemy). Hekmatyar is the quintessential pissed-off rebel who wants Rabbani replaced by a *loya jirga*, a revolutionary council that would organize elections. Hekmatyar was once Rabbani's prime minister but broke away and began a yearlong siege of Kabul. His army was trashed in March 1995 by the *taliban*, but now he's back in Rabbiani's fold. He spent the Russian war safely in Peshawar while Massoud was fighting in the mountains. His forces were the major beneficiary of weapons from Pakistan and once bragged that he could fight a war for 25 years without ever needing supplies. His arms caches are now in the hands of the *taliban*. Hekmatyar still has a lot of fans in Pakistan but can't find a sugar daddy to replace the billions of dollars of arms he lost to the *taliban*.

President Burhanuddin Rabbani

Rabbani is a former professor and the former official political leader of Afghanistan (although his term has legally expired), although one wonders whom and what he has been leading. A highly educated man, Rabbani made an attempt to build a bridge between opposing forces when he named Hekmatyar prime minister in 1993 and again in 1996. But there is little room for compromise in this fundamentalist country. He is backed mainly by the Tajiks in the north (3.5 million people or about 25 percent of Afghanistan's population) and maintained his power only with the military might of Massoud. His Jemiaate Islami party is the only non-Pathan party in Afghanistan.

Ahmed Shah Massoud

The "Lion of Panjir" is credited with being the main reason the Russians high-tailed it out of Afghanistan. Rabbani's defense minister, Commander Ahmed Shah Massoud, is an old friend of *DP*'s Coskun Aral and controls a well-trained Tajik army. It remains to be seen if Massoud has political ambitions or like Shane will ride off into the sunset. He managed to repulse the *taliban* once in March 1995, but time and political support ran out in September 1996. Massoud was getting aircraft and pilots from India, ammunition from Russia and military training advisors from Iran. This one-time bitter enemy of Russia is now the recipient of massive shipments of weapons and ammunition from his former foe. On August 3, 1995, a Russian Illuyshin-76 cargo plane was forced down in Kandahar by the *taliban* air force. On board were 3.4 million rounds of ammunition bound for Kabul. The ammo came from Albania and was delivered through Dubai. Afghan politics is tricky stuff. It was a lot simpler when he got his ammo and supplies from dead Russians.

General Rashid Dostum

Everybody wants a chunk of Afghanistan, and the northern neighbor of Uzbekistan is slicing off a nice piece of the Afghan pie, thanks to its gun buddy, Rashid Dostum. The fact that their juicy piece contains the primo Afghan drug-growing region of Mazar-i-Sharif might just be a geographic coincidence; maybe also a coincidence is that nearby Mother Russia is home to more junkies than "Baywatch" viewers. Dostum is an Uzbek warlord who is kept brimmed with guns and ammo by Uzbekistan. He controlled the only major supply route, the Salang Highway from Kabul to Uzbekistan. Despite the geographic and ethnic proximity to Uzbekistan, Dostum is a still considered by the Uzbekistanis as a loose cannon. He has changed allegiances more times than his underwear in the last three years.

Mujahedin and the "Afghans"

The Pathans (called Pakhtuns in their own language) are a distinct group of tribes that make up 40 percent of Afghanistan's populace and 13 percent of Pakistan's. Years of war have created three new warrior castes in Afghanistan. The older generation of Afghani *mujahedin* spent their young adult lives in nomadic columns killing Russians; now they off other Afghanis. The second caste of "Afghans" (called "Afghans" because they are not Afghani) is a group of foreigners who came to Afghanistan (actually Pakistan first) armed to kill Russians. Well trained, impoverished and savvy in the arts of deception, marksmanship, explosives and terror, they have been in great demand in other parts of the world by Iran and Sudan for their absolute devotion to *jihad*. Today, both *mujahedin* and "Afghans" can be found around the world, from Bosnia to the Philippines, fighting as volunteers or mercenaries for Islamic forces. The older fighters, who remember what Afghanistan looked like, are giving way to the third generation of *mujahedin*, youngsters who grew up in the squalid, mud-walled refugee camps of Peshawar and Quetta in Pakistan. These are the young men who are heeding the call of the *taliban* and flocking to the front lines in Afghanistan and elsewhere.

Pakistan

If you look on most maps, you will see a distinct border between Afghanistan and Pakistan. It ain't so. Even though the Durand line was created as an official demarcation between the two countries, it is not recognized by Afghanistan and even less so by the

Pathan tribes whose homeland it divides. Pakistan has absorbed most of the refugees and keeps warm ties to whoever is in power. During the time Uncle Sam was supporting the *mujahedin*, Pakistan diverted arms to the mullahs rather than the various tribal chiefs, who were less religious but equally warlike. More specifically, the Pakistani government of General Zia—killed in a plane crash on July, 18, 1988—supported the Ghilzai tribe from eastern Afghanistan, where most *mujahedin* leaders herald from. The southern Durranis still support the Afghani royal family of former king Zahir Shah. Things may be changing; the Pakistani embassy was burned to the ground in Kabul in the fall of 1995, and Pakistan has not developed an official policy regarding the *taliban* other than one of tolerance. Pakistan is a country controlled by Punjabis, who permit the independence of the Pathans only because they know the region can never truly be occupied by any single entity. There is intense desire for statehood among the Pathans for "Pakhtunistan," with a bent toward Afghanistan that might remove most of the NWFP and the tribal areas from the map of Pakistan.

The 'Afghans'

After a recent tour of Afghanistan, we were amazed that everywhere we went—the coffee shops, the stalls, everywhere—we saw nothing but guys about 30 years old sitting around. They were all veterans of the war against the Soviet Union. Killers with hard faces, deeply lined. None of them have jobs. They're just sitting around, waiting. Imagine if you trained a bunch of steel workers in Pittsburgh to kill—and then took away their jobs.

Virtually every male in Afghanistan old enough to lift a rifle fought against the Russians. But Afghanis weren't the only ones. The other "Afghans" included more than 3000 Algerians who fought in Afghanistan, as well as 2000 Egyptians. Hundreds, if not thousands, of others arrived from Yemen, Sudan, Pakistan, Syria and other Muslim states.

In all, according to some estimates, 10,000 Arabs received training and combat experience in Afghanistan—of whom nearly half were Saudis. A big chunk of the financial backing for the Afghan warlords came—and continues to come—from the fundamentalist Wahhabi sect in Saudi Arabia.

The war in Afghanistan graduated a lot of students, and many are continuing their education in places as far apart as Bosnia, the Philippines and the U.S. In fact, fighters trained in Afghanistan have surfaced in at least a dozen different struggles, including conflicts in China, Kashmir, Chechnya and Algeria. More than 1000 veterans of the war in Afghanistan fought in Bosnia. Abu Sayyaf, a radical new Islamic group comprised of "Afghanis", has emerged as the principal Muslim guerrilla movement in the Philippines. Ramzi Ahmed Yousef, the mastermind behind the 1993 bombing of the World Trade Center in New York City, is an Pakistani who lived in Kuwait, who was trained in Afghanistan. In Algeria, the last two leaders of the radical Armed Islamic Group are Afghan veterans.

And where the 'Afghans' go, the conflicts become bloodier, the extremism more intense. Whereas nine journalists were killed in Algeria by Islamic extremists in 1993, more than 50 were assassinated in 1994–95. In the Philippines, Abu Sayyaf staged one of the most brutal attacks in the country's two decades of Muslim separatism when, in April 1995, 200 heavily armed Islamic guerrillas attacked the southern town of Ipil, killing 50 and razing the city. Yousef himself was involved in a plot to assassinate Pope John Paul II and was linked to the bombing of a Philippines Airlines plane in December 1994.

One can only wonder what will become of Afghanistan's taliban army. A new generation of fighters who only are fervently religious and eager to destroy infidels.

Travel Advisories

The Department of State warns all U.S. citizens against travel to Afghanistan. Fighting continues between opposing factions in the civil war, and indiscriminate rocket attacks, aerial bombardments, and other violence can occur without warning. Land mines are prevalent throughout the countryside. Westerners are vulnerable to politically and criminally motivated attacks, including robbery, kidnapping and the taking of hostages. All U.S. personnel at the U.S. embassy in Kabul were evacuated on January 31, 1989, relief workers were evacuated in September of 1996. No other diplomatic mission represents U.S. interests or provides consular services.

Getting In

If you hate crowds and want to impress your well traveled friends, this is the place. Under peaceful circumstances, you can get a tourist visa for three months for US$30 per visa application, but at press time only journalists and aid workers were officially allowed in-country. The borders with Iran, Tajikistan and most of Afghanistan's other neighbors are officially closed to Westerners. A passport and visa are required. For further information, the traveler can contact the following:

Embassy of the Islamic State of Afghanistan

2341 Wyoming Avenue, N.W.
Washington, D.C. 20008
☎ *(202) 234-3770/1*
FAX (202) 328-3516

The Embassy told us that "in Afghanistan there are safe places to travel and there are some places [that are] unsafe." Kabul is the least safe place for travel. All border crossings are technically open, but the embassy recommends that travelers use the crossings from Pakistan, Iran and Tajikistan only. *DP* didn't have the heart to tell the embassy spokesman that all those borders were closed to foreigners and that he'd better read his copy of DP next time. The pleasant embassy staff told us that entering illegally will "put you in jail for a while" before being deported. We were going to ask which police and which jails would be used for our detention, but with the ambassador's paymaster on the lam from Kabul, we thought we should be kind. Our latest vacations in-country reveal that even though there are military and police at official crossings, entry into Afghanistan is very easy. In fact, any body with a pair of hiking boots and a love of pack animals should have no problem. The hardest part is selecting your entry point from the many offers you will get from willing guides. The best way in is from Pakistan. Don't do it in the winter because of the bitter cold—and snow has a way of hiding the land mines. The intrepid can stroll into Afghanistan over the many mountain trails that connect the two countries in the north. It's a bit risky, however, due to tribal control of all lands. They could care less who is fighting who, they just want to trade you for some livestock or ammo. There are eight Pakistani checkpoints from the start of the Khyber area to the Afghan border. These are closed to all foreigners. To get in, just scoot north of the checkpoint in the Smugglers Bazaar and make a beeline past the drug sellers to the minibuses. Make sure you are traveling with someone who has pull with the players in the area. The area's biggest honcho is Yacoub Affridi, who—apparently through a comfortable arrangement with the Pakistani government—left his massive house in Landi Kotal for Jalalabad. This is a major smuggling route, and all travelers will be suspect. The local folks are quite hospitable and will offer food and whatever lodging they have. You are expected to reciprocate with some type of gift or remembrance. Photos of your family are great as well as flashlights, medicine or even clothes. Make sure you pick the right guide, one on good terms with the tribes who control the regions you will be passing through. You will probably be the only tourist in Afghanistan. Camels can be rented to carry heavy gear for US$10 dollars a day, and guides go for about US$20 a day, plus *baksheesh* (a tip). Travelers would be ill-advised to go gem hunting or arms collecting in the hills at this time due to the prevalence of land mines—still the number-one killer and maimer of humans and other living things—and the propensity of Afghans to kidnap foreigners for a few quick dollars.

Most of the country to the south and west of Kabul is in the hands of the *taliban,* who also control the entry and movement of all outsiders. The northwest is in the hands of the Dostums, and Rabbiani and his Tajiks (for now) and the Wahkan corridor is a mess because of drugs and fighting in Tajikistan (see Tajikistan chapter)

For more information on getting into Afghanistan, contact representatives of what will be the new government. Please keep in mind that it is busy fighting a war and does not have any official policy on tourism, time-share condos, bargain flights, youth hostels or package tours.

Taliban

> *Post Office 868*
> *Peshawar University*
> *North West Frontier Province, Pakistan*
> *Quetta* ☎ *(081) 447300 (fax and phone)*
> *Peshawar* ☎ *(0521)*

Peshawar

> ☎ *(0521) 42645; contact Abdul Ghafoor Afghani.*

Quetta (fax/phone)

> ☎ *(081) 447300. Contact: Mohammed Masoom Afghani*

Note: There is no street address supplied for the *taliban* for security reasons. They can also be contacted by asking anyone in the Afghan markets in Quetta and Peshawar. Currently, the *taliban* "extend an open hand to all peace-loving nations of the world," and hold no animosity toward Americans, even though the Yanks are responsible for much of the chasm that Afghanistan fell into after the war with the Russians.

Getting Around

There is little chance of safe travel in Afghanistan right now or in the distant future. Journalists can travel into Afghanistan under the protection of whomever can get you in at the time. The *taliban* is your best bet if you want to see the rest of the country, but they may get weary of dragging camera crews around in the future. When we went only the BBC and one other European crew had ever met with the students. Travel outside of any city is dangerous, and you will be stopped by numerous armed militias. The chances are high that these groups will be rather happy to see you and they will gladly lighten your load. Some may do you the favor of hastening your entry into the Eternal Kingdom. The Afghan embassy's *chargé d'affaires* in the States, Yar M. Mohabbat, either has a problem with English or total command of the language when he advises *DP* readers: "Tourists must have caution and be more careful where not to go [sic] and where not to go." The favored modes of travel are by minibus (cheap and available in all small towns), private car (not as available) and pack animals, which are slow and a great way to see what land mines can do. There is no law inside Afghanistan other than *sharia*, or local tribal law.

It is helpful if Westerners adapt Afghan dress and have a basic understanding of the Pakhtun (Pathan or Pashto) language; more importantly is knowledge of the customs of Islam. The *taliban* and most Afghans are absolutely fundamentalist in their beliefs in and love of Islam. Currently, there is little animosity toward Westerners, but you will be lectured continuously on Islam and considered an oddity for not embracing what is essentially the only accepted religion in Afghanistan. The *taliban* are against alcohol, drugs, photography and pornography, and they demand that all women be fully veiled. Any major affront to Islam could result in severe punishment or execution. Even taking photographs can create trouble, as devout Muslims abide by a law that forbids the re-creation of images of people. We were told to get decent jobs and stop insulting Allah when taking pictures of wounded Afghans. Understandably film, Fotomats and Blockbusters are alien concepts here.

Most people traveling in Afghanistan are soldiers, the wounded going to and from battle (via buses), and truck drivers who are either transporting food stuffs and basic goods (tires, cotton, fuel) or smuggling heroin, hashish, electronics or arms between the Gulf states, Iran, the CIS states, Pakistan and China. Many of the goods are sold in Pakistan or shipped out of Karachi. Needless to say, there is a paucity of tourists, and the *mujahedin* will assume you are smuggling hashish or heroin if you are stopped.

Embassy Location

Because there is no U.S. embassy in Afghanistan and no country represents U.S. interests here, the United States government is unable to provide normal consular protective services to U.S. citizens in Afghanistan. The nearest U.S. embassies and consulates are in Pakistan and Tajikistan. The telephone number for the U.S. embassy in Islamabad, Pakistan, is ☎ *(92) (51) 826-161/179.* There is little they can do for you once you are in Afghanistan.

U.S. Consulate in Peshawar, Pakistan
☎ *(92) (521) 279-801/2/3*

U.S. Embassy in Tashkent, Uzbekistan
☎ *(7) (3712) 771-407/771-081*

U.S. Embassy in Dushanbe, Tajikistan
☎ *(7) (3772) 21-0356/-0360/-0457*

U.S. Embassy in New Delhi, India
☎ *(91) (11) 600-651*

Getting Out

Leaving Afghanistan is a simple matter of hoping that the people who brought you in have enough resources to get you to the airport or back across the Pakistan border safely. Ariana, the Afghan airline, or more precisely, the afghan "airplane" is the single plane carrier that flies out of Afghanistan. The Red Cross flies in and out sporadically but is busy with wounded.

Dangerous Places

Kabul

With an average life expectancy of only 44 years, Afghans don't have much to look forward to in this bombed and gutted shell. More than a quarter-million of the 1.5 million residents have fled the battered city to Peshawar as refugees. Westerners are not welcome and even the ubiquitous Red Cross can do little with its skeleton staff. They've been intermittently open and closed as pro-President Rabbani forces use the closures to strengthen their positions.

Everywhere Else

The Russians took great pains to make Afghanistan a dangerous place for years to come. There are about 10 - 12 million land mines scattered by air and buried in the ground throughout Afghanistan. You will see many people with their leg (or legs) amputated just below the knee. Most of the maiming is caused by small, butterfly-like, plastic mines that were scattered from Soviet planes and helicopters. Designed to blow only the foot off the unfortunate guerrilla, the mines are hard to spot and continue to injure.

The Borders

Lawlessness and a lack of national infrastructure have made Afghanistan a major drug-trafficking route. Large armed convoys guard the transport of opium from Pakistan and areas within Afghanistan. When the Soviet Union stopped patrolling its Afghani border, the country became the second major conduit of opium and heroin (the Golden Triangle in Southeast Asia is the number-one source and conduit of poppy-based drugs) and the largest exporter of hashish in the world. Up to 14 metric tons of hashish have been seized by the border states of Uzbekistan, Turkmenistan, Kyrgystan, Tajikistan and Kazakastan. Badakhshan borders Russia's Tajikistan, where Russia has deployed at least 15,000 troops to help fight antigovernment Islamic guerrillas believed to have bases in Afghanistan. This will change with the taliban in charge. Drug rehabilitation now means a bullet to the head.

The Khyber Pass/Tribal Areas

The Khyber pass is still controlled by tribal chiefs (one of whom is keen on his son marrying both of my daughters) who make a living by shaving a few rupees from truck drivers and travelers that ply this historic route. Robbery, murder, extortion and/or kidnapping are an absolute guarantee for the unwary.

Dangerous Things

Tribes

Most people are unaware that Afghanistan is still a land of tribal chiefs and feudal kingdoms. This is the land of *badal*, where every Afghan man must avenge a wrong, no matter how slight and how long it takes. Every major tribal home in Afghanistan is a small stone-and-mud fortress, and each person must stand watch in the tower. Tribes have been keeping score over how many of each other they have whacked, with a rivalry that approaches USC-UCLA fervor. They also take their tribal codes and Islam seriously. When *DP* was cruising through one tribal area, we were told a tribe member had seen a young woman and a man from another tribe kissing on a hillside. The father of the girl captured a cousin of the object of her affection, tied them both to a tree and pumped 75 bullets into them.

The Taliban's Air Force

That's right, folks, this may be the only student union with its own airforce. On November 25, 1995, *taliban* jets bombed Kabul, killing at least 35 people and wounding more than 140. Nine bombs, including cluster and parachute bombs, were dropped on residential areas of the besieged capital by an unspecified number of jets. These jets were hot wired leftovers from other people's arsenals.

Guns

When it comes to gun love, the Afghanis make *Soldier of Fortune* readers seem like Brady Bill backers. And thanks to John Bull and Uncle Sam, Afghanistan has more guns per capita than anywhere else on earth. England allowed the Pathans to manufacture their own guns 200 years ago, and the CIA delivered enough weapons to keep Afghanistan not only armed, but legged. But this was all dwarfed by the stockpiles of weapons the Russians abandoned or lost in the 10 years of warfare. One Afghan gunman philosophically pointed out the unique relationship Afghanis have with their ballistic toys when he said, "You have your cameras, and we have our guns."

If the containers and warehouses full of pristine weapons aren't enough, the Affridi tribe of Afghanistan and Pakistan still pumps out about 900 to 1200 copies of modern weapons a day in its gun factories in Darra Adam Khel.

Happiness is a Worn Gun

For those who can't resist a bargain, the best place to buy guns is actually just outside Afghanistan in Pakistan. Take along an Afghan guide and go visit the Smugglers Bazaar (20 minutes east of Peshawar) in Darra (about 40 minutes south of Peshawar). DP did a little pre-Christmas shopping (peace on earth, goodwill to all men) to discover that you can buy a worn but serviceable AK-47 for 6,000 rupees (US$200). Pros know to buy the short Chinese-made assault versions, since their barrels don't heat up as much and they can be concealed under your shwalwar qamiz. These go for about 12,000-30,000 rupees (US$375-1000). Chinese- and Russian-made pistols are between 300 and 1200 rupees with the Afghan-made knockoffs at the low end of the price spectrum.

Happiness is a Worn Gun

Rambos can pick up Chinese and Russian rocket launchers for 30,000 rupees (just under a grand), and spare rockets by the case for 400 rupees (US$125) each. Grenades are a bargain at 100 rupees (US$3) each. Other items for sales at bargain basement prices include land mines, antiaircraft guns, bazookas, Stalin Organ-style rocket launchers (the self-propelled kind) and even new Russian tanks.

Wannabes who simply appreciate the smell of cordite and advanced hearing loss can arrange to fire automatic weapons. One banana clip of 30 bullets will set you back 200-300 rupees, about 10 bucks. Cheap even by Coney Island standards. The hottest-selling items are still the pen guns that fire a single bullet and can be used to write ransom notes. They are a measly 200 rupees, or six dollars. Naturally, you will need a complete Soviet era–uniform, bayonets, combat gear, watches, boxes of uncirculated rubles (wrapped and still in serial number order) and medals to complete your cold war GI Joe play kit.

Kidnapping

The Afghans are among the most hospitable people in the world. In fact, some may invite you to stay with them for a long, long time, unless you or your relatives or government can cough up the ransom. Kidnapping is actually a tribal tradition that goes back before recorded time. It is an easy way to get a wife, get your goats back or make some extra money in lean years. Recently, kidnapping has been a means to bring attention to tribal disputes or grievances. Locals, expats and tourists are routinely kidnapped in Afghanistan and the border areas with Pakistan. Ransoms run from US$2000 up to US$50,000 and more for foreign workers. The positive side to this is that if you're traveling under the protection of one tribe and are kidnapped by another, your host tribe has an obligation to free you. The people in the greatest danger are foreign workers who travel in a predetermined route or stay in a fixed place.

Drugs

Afghanistan is essentially a smuggling economy. Drugs represent the largest single hard-currency earner. Poppies and *sensimilla* products are easily grown and are in wide propagation. The best hashish in the world comes from Mazar-i-Sharif in the north, a major destination for Western drug smugglers before the Russians rolled in. The Russian army picked up the nasty habit of smoking opium and mainlining heroin while they were here (a practice that continues to this day in needle-strewn streets from Grozny to Moscow). Haji Ayub Afridi controls most of the traffic in heroin and hash from Afghanistan into Pakistan. His massive house in Landi Kotal is famous for its opulence. Instead of jockeys on the lawn, he has opted for antiaircraft guns. I was offered a job as one of his gunmen, but figured that 2000 Pakistani rupees a month (about $65) and a new Kalashnikov were not an upward career move. Ayub has about 100 gunmen and was forced to move to Jalalabad from Landi Kotal after the U.S. pressured Pakistan to "clean up the drug trade."

Most drugs are trucked directly through Peshawar and Quetta with the complicity of border guards and police. Other tribes like to pack the brown stuff the hard way (overland by mule through Iran and Turkey). Other middlemen use human mules. Freelance smugglers and stupid tourists still buy hashish and heroin in the smuggler's bazaar in Peshawar, Pakistan, and discover when it's too late that the government offers a 5000 rupee reward for turning in dope heads (your guide gets to keep your dope money). Other smugglers (usually Nigerians, Afghans and Pakistanis) end up losing their heads when caught flying through Saudi Arabia with dope poorly concealed in various luggage and orifices.

Flying Over Afghanistan

Because of safety concerns arising from the civil conflict in Afghanistan, all U.S. airlines and aircraft operators are prohibited by the Federal Aviation Administration from overflying Afghanistan. A faction in the civil conflict issued a warning on September 8, 1995, that they would shoot down any airliner that ventured into airspace over territory they control without acquiring clearance from them. At this time, many foreign air carriers continue to overfly Afghanistan on routes between Asia and Europe. There are no reliable communications with Kabul air traffic control who spends most of their time in bomb shelters. Should an air disaster occur in Afghanistan or an aircraft be forced to land there, ICAO advises that adjacent countries would most likely become aware only when an aircraft failed to exit Afghan airspace. In that event, because there is no U.S. embassy in Afghanistan and no third country represents U.S. interests there, you're up the creek. Moreover, any search-and-rescue efforts cannot be expected, as it is also not possible for neighboring states to obtain permission to enter Afghanistan in search of survivors.

Smuggling

There are no reliable figures for how much money and goods are smuggled through Afghanistan, but it would be safe to say that the crux of the country's GNP is earned through smuggling and through the various "tolls" smugglers have to pay along the way. Western travelers in Afghanistan will be assumed to be transporting something they would not claim on their customs forms. Accordingly, you will be searched and taxed by every gun-toting tribe, militia and group you come across.

Getting Sick

In Kabul, there are makeshift medical centers that provide limited care to the wounded and the sick. The Red Cross commutes by air from Peshawar about once a week. Outside Kabul, the more seriously wounded or very ill are evacuated by pickup truck or ambulance to Peshawar and Quetta. Medical facilities in Kabul are subject to random rocket attacks. Even the most basic medical care is limited or nonexistent, with extreme shortages of most basic medicines. The Red Cross has a presence in Kabul, but will be very unsympathetic to your problems. Items like syringes and bandages are reused, and there is a shortage of doctors and beds. Malaria is present below 2000 meters in the southern area. To get more info, U.S. citizens who register at the U.S. embassies in Pakistan, India, Tajikistan, or Uzbekistan can obtain updated information on security in Afghanistan.

Dangerous Days

9/27/1996	The *taliban* enter Kabul at 1 a.m. after two days of heavy fighting. Former President Najibullah and his brother are hanged. Eighty per cent of Kabul is in ruins and 30,000 of its civilians have died
10/17/1995	Thousands of the inhabitants of the capital fled the city in the wake of a *taliban* militia attack. The fierce fighting between *taliban* and Rabbani forces around Kabul compelled hundreds of families to leave the city. Families shifted from Kabul to Jalalabad, capital of Nangahar province, and stayed in camps. Many refugees headed towards Pakistan.
09/06/1995	The Pakistani embassy was set on fire in four places. At least 5000 Afghans marched on the embassy in protest of alleged Pakistani support for the Islamic *taliban* militia.
04/25/1992	Anniversary of the fall of the communist government. Islamic *mujahedin* guerrillas took power in Kabul in April 1992 from a collapsed former Soviet-backed communist government after 14 years of civil war that left 13,000 Soviet soldiers dead.

In a Dangerous Place

Afghanistan, March, 1983: In the Lion's Lair

An expedition into war-torn Afghanistan has developed in Paris. Three French doctors from Médecins sans Frontières decide to go to the Panshir Valley headquarters of the Afghan resistance. In addition to myself, two other journalists will join us: Philippe Flandrin, a Frenchman, and the Iranian-born photographer Reza Deghati. Deghati wants to go to east Kabul to meet the monarchists of leader Mahaze Melli. Flandrin will continue to Baktia outside Kabul to locate the Hezbe-Islami and their leaders, Yunus Khales and Abdul Haq.

We fly to Peshawar to meet the *mujahedin* organization. The Hezbe-Islami propose to bring us into Panshir, but we prefer to trust the people from Jemiaate-Islami, because this time they control the Panshir region. The leader of this organization is Muchai Barzali. The trek will cover about 450 kilometers and is expected to last one month.

The three doctors will bring in food and medicine, and the guerrillas will provide protection. We wait until March for the snow to start melting. We will climb the 4500-meter-high mountain of Hindi Kuch. On the other side, we are expecting jeeps to be waiting to provide us with transit to Peshawar. But after the long, grueling trek, we will find no jeeps.

The trip begins on March 10, 1983. We dress like Afghans because we are crossing tribal country. I bring along three cameras. Flat-footed and out of shape, I am always behind. Our convoy moves at night to avoid the Russian helicopters. Despite our stealth and our altitude, the group is often attacked by Soviet gunships. I have brought along some dry fruit to supplement the meager rice rations. As our food supply dwindles, I discover there is nothing in the countryside with which to replenish our supplies. Once in a while, we come across a small tea shop in the villages.

In my fatigue and hunger, I make the mistake of taking a leak while standing up. An Afghan spots me and the alarm goes out. Muslims always squat to urinate.

The group decides that I'm a Russian spy and that I am to be shot. Our body-guards come to my rescue and argue that Turkish Muslims always stand to piss, and that I am a true Muslim. The argument rages on; our explanation finally prevails. It is a close call. One of our convoy is not so lucky, and the cause for his execution is even more ridiculous. A young man is shot to death in the backyard of a village house, because the hairs on his arms are not pointing in the correct direction. If he had been cleaning himself five times a day in preparation for prayer, the hairs on his arms would have been pointing toward his hands. The sentence is passed by the leader of our column and he is shot to death out of sight of the others.

It is frigid in the mountains. Sometimes we have to cross ice-cold rivers fully clothed. I am amazed that I do not freeze to death. I am starving. I dream of greasy hamburgers and crisp french fries.

On the last leg of the journey to the Panshir Valley, we ride in a truck. The truck hits a land mine and rolls over, launching a piece of a metallic ladder into my jaw and knocking out three of my teeth. I lose a lot of blood and am saved only by the doctors.

We finally reach the Panshir Valley and set up a makeshift hospital. Wounded rebels are carried in, some from two to three days away. There is no anesthetic; bullet wounds are washed out with tea. During Ramadan, a Muslim fast lasting 40 days, the Afghans would not give blood, so I and the doctors give blood, depending on the blood type necessary.

The man named Massoud, "The Lion of Panshir," is the reason for our trip. The rebel leader has asked for medical help and the doctors come at great personal risk. Massoud and I became friends. Massoud was educated in the Lycée Istiqlal (a French high school) in Kabul. Now a resistance leader, he was considered to be very clever and was always on the move. He needed medical help because his men were dying slow, agonizing deaths from gunshot and shrapnel wounds. The doctor Gilles will accompany us. We take the injured back to Pakistan in a convoy. Since I am the least injured member of the group, I will be the leader. As a token of the rebels' appreciation, I am given a horse. I use it to help transport the wounded. When we arrive back in Pakistan, we are detained because we carry no identification papers. Finally, we are permitted entry.

I traveled back to Afghanistan two more times to cover the *mujahedin*. Gilles returned to Paris, and shortly afterwards committed suicide.

—**Coskun Aral**

Algiers

Algeria
★★★★★

You Can't Dance

Hey world, are you ready for Islam? Well, you'd better get ready, according to a crudely assembled and rambling four-page fax sent to *DP* from the Islamic Salvation Front (FIS). The FIS is calling out for the release of "martyrs" Abassi Madani, FIS council member, and Ali Belhadj, his deputy, both jailed in June 1991 for 12 years. The fax goes on to claim that all singers, artists, journalists, soldiers and policemen are nonbelievers and if you see them near the Kaaba in Mecca, it's okay to kill them. They ain't kiddin' around.

Algeria has become a dangerous place to hang out or do business in these days. Islamic fundamentalists opposed to the Western-backed military government of President Liamine Zeroual are wreaking havoc. In the wake of cancelled elections in 1991 and 1992, the fundamentalist FIS party has chosen terrorism because the ruling government has stolen their political voice. It seems that if FIS can't talk, then the people can't dance. Foreigners in Algeria are assassinated, often quite gruesomely, to frighten Western businesses and countries supporting Zeroual's

ALGERIA

authoritarian government. When the throat slitting, beheading and shooting of aid workers and local intellectuals stopped making foreign news, the FIS decided to employ the classic bad guys PR /political leverage and fund-raising tool—hijacking. On December 24, 1994, four Algerian terrorists of the Armed Islamic Group seized an Air France Airbus A300 jetliner in Algiers with 239 passengers and crew members aboard. Their demand, of course, was for the release of the two imprisoned FIS leaders. The gunmen killed three passengers, including a Vietnamese diplomat, before the plane was stormed by French commandos in Marseilles. The raid killed all four terrorists (the oldest was 20) and wounded 13 passengers. Since the cancelled 1992 Algerian elections, radical fundamentalists have assassinated more than 11,000 people, including over 100 foreigners, in an effort to topple the government. Among the victims are playwrights, artists, journalists, politicians, and even schoolgirls who refuse to don the *hejab*, or traditional Muslim head covering.

These guys brag that they have sent Cheb Hasni (a popular Algerian singer whom they recently shot to death) to hell. They kidnapped 38-year-old singer Lounes Matoub, but then, after having second thoughts, released him. Matoub is an ethnic Berber and had recorded a satirical song about the fundamentalists. The Berbers are the country's largest ethnic minority and not a group anyone wishes to mess with. The FIS communique went on to say, "Now we will start with the journalists, the poets and the soldiers. Belly dancing is a prayer to Satan. When Satan's messengers give a direction to people, they dance." They ask that if you dance, please stay out of Algeria. Not an entirely unfair request in post-disco Africa. (The FIS has said nothing about gangster rap.)

The fundamentalists' threats are not just the rhetoric of bored bullies. Journalists are under a direct threat of immediate execution if they enter the country; more than 70 have been killed and 700 have fled. Wearing glasses, Western clothes or even looking educated can make you a target of these nasties. Sounds a little like Cambodia of the 1970s. It is estimated that the entire wealth of this country of 28 million is in the hands of only about 5000 people. Reason enough for reform but not for mayhem.

Algeria is no stranger to hatred and death. Eight years of cruel warfare with the French started back in 1954 killed a quarter of a million people and forced out more than a million *pied noirs* (black foot), or white colonists. Despite its independent status, Algeria's 133-year marriage to France has made it more French than Arabic.

France has always had a love-hate relationship with Algeria, due more to its geographical proximity than to its cultural dissimilarities. In Algeria, Russia has found a major customer for its military hardware and expertise, and Italy makes sure Algeria continues to pump out the oil and gas it needs to keep those Fiats and Ferarris topped off.

In October 1993, two French technicians were kidnapped and murdered near Sidi-Bel-Abbes. In October, two Russian lieutenant colonels stationed at the air base in Laghuat (about 200 miles south of Algiers) were shot. Three days later, three Italian technicians were kidnapped and murdered. In Tiaret, merely a day after the Italians' murder, three employees of the French general consulate were kidnapped.

In 1992, at least 560 Algerian militants were training at military bases in Sudan, financially supported by Iran. Most of the trainees were veterans of the Afghan war and traveled to Sudan via Iran. These militants are trained to add to the core of the underground Islamic fundamentalist movement held responsible for the killing of more than 210 members of Algeria's security forces. The Algerian government suspended six Islamic groups: the Call and Conveyance of the Message, the Nahdha Association for Social and Cultural Reform, the Algerian Islamic Association for Civilization and Construction, the Women's League for Adherence to God's Way, the Algerian League for Islamic Literature, and the Islamic League for Fine Arts.

More than 50,000 people have been killed in this North African country since 1992. In addition, hundreds of people have been reported missing for months. The estimate of Muslim militants who have been killed is thought to be over 20,000. More than 100 foreigners have been killed and 23 others injured in Algeria by terrorist groups. In 1994 and 1995, Algerian security forces killed 5029 guerrillas; Muslim militants killed 1400 civilians, of which 500 were women. The victims include 52 journalists killed during the two-year period, 372 union activists, 184 magistrates and 84 Muslim religious workers.

The only bright spot? It seems the U.S. embassy staff are major fans of *DP* and wear their sense of humor well, along with *Mr. DP* "Tour of Duty" shirts and *DP* stickers.

The Scoop

The world's most dangerous place for foreigners. A country where wacked-out fundamentalists and burned-out Algerian veterans of Afghanistan's war with Russia like to cut throats and shoot expats. Why? Algeria's military, in a ridiculous move, stupidly decided to cancel the 1992 elections which the Islamic Salvation Front was going to win handily.

The goal of the FIS is to make Algeria an Islamic fundamentalist country by forcing out foreign interests and influence with Iran footing the bill. The FIS does this by deliberately murdering foreign workers and tourists. An ultimatum was handed out in November 30, 1993, demanding all foreigners to leave the country. Since then, it's estimated that about 15 assassinations occur each day, including those of politicians, intellectuals, journalists and non-Algerians. The mayhem continued in 1996. GIA guerrillas kidnapped and beheaded seven elderly French monks. The GIA and the FIS shot reporters, teachers, old ladies and government officials (as well as each other), partly in retaliation for the torture and "extrajudicial executions" of its members by the Algerian army. More than 100 were foreigners killed between 1992 and 1996. And the two rebel groups have taken to blowing each other away. In January 1996 alone, more than 50 radicals were killed when the FIS and GIA decided to take out each other. Of course, that helped the government, who snuffed an additional 259 rebels that month. In '94 and '95 an estimated 5029 guerillas were killed by the government.

Algerian fundamentalist rage is reaching other lands. A GIA armed robbery gang was blown away by French and Belgian police during a 24-hour-long firefight on March 28–29; and French police arrested another 10 Algerian radicals on the Riviera.

Since the termination of the heightened security operations for the elections in early 1996, there has been a return to the small unit killing tactics seen in October and early November 1995. The number of victims of terrorist attacks is increasing. The principal target of these attacks seems to be police, military and government officials. However, journalists and foreigners who present a security vulnerability have also been attacked. Since the beginning of the terrorists' assassination campaign in the fall of 1993, more than 70 journalists have been killed. Over 100 foreigners have been kidnapped and murdered since September 1993, sometimes in assaults involving dozens of attackers. None of these individuals were American citizens. Nonetheless, terrorists have threatened to kill all foreigners in Algeria. An Air France flight was hijacked at Algiers Airport on December 24, 1994, by heavily armed terrorists who threatened to blow up the aircraft.

There is not much reason for thrill seekers to travel here, since there is nothing visual or saleable for Western journos. Off-the-beaten-path travelers can get all the danger they need in Morocco or Egypt without being specifically targeted. Foreign workers take their chances, hoping they will get transferred to a nice quiet place like Somalia or Burundi.

The Players

FLN

The old guard revolutionaries who kicked the French out in 1962 are now the ones who have to go. They have held on to their power by simply cancelling an election that the newer and more vital Islamic Salvation Front won fair and square. The FLN tried everything, from adding seats in their strongholds and arresting FIS members to finally cancelling the elections altogether. The military is directly in control of the High Security Council, with General Khaled Nezar, the leader of the Algerian military, pulling the strings.

Islamic Salvation Front (FIS)

The FIS wants to make Algeria an Islamic state with the Koran as its constitution. Some FIS members are calling for a democratic society with Muslim values. In any case, the FIS was banned by the government after being the front runner in the aborted 1992 elections. The FIS has decided to make Algeria the most dangerous place in the world for foreigners. It's hard to say whether FIS terrorist activities or the management of the current regime have more severely damaged Algeria's economy. FIS leader Shaykh Abassi Madani and his hawkish deputy, Ali Belhadj, were released from jail and transferred to a cushy villa under house arrest in an effort to strike a compromise with the fundamentalists. About 400 members of the FIS were sent to the Bekáa Valley in Lebanon for training in 1990. FIS members have also been trained in the Sudan by Hezbollah. The FIS is not just a bunch of crazies. The party was a grass roots political and religious movement that originally attracted the dispossessed. The party has grown to involve the support of the majority of the country, including intellectuals and professionals. Keep in mind that the FIS is not one cohesive party but a mishmash of everything from tiny radical cells to large political machines, none of whom agrees on much. One thing they do have in common is their collective threat to foreigners in Algeria: Leave or die.

Armed Islamic Group (GIA)

The GIA is led by probably the most heartless and cruel group of men on earth: Algerian veterans of the Afghan war, or *mujahedin*. They're hard, brutal guys trained in Sudan, battle tested in Afghanistan and bankrolled by Iran. The GIA views the FIS as being soft. The GIA likes to cut throats and engage in cold-blooded murder. Their leader, Cherif Gousmi, 27, and his iron-fisted deputy were shot in September of 1994, so you missed out on the US$70,000 bounty the government was offering for their heads.

President Liamine Zeroual

He's doing his best to keep the lid on, but he isn't doing a very good job. His idea of building a coalition only works when both sides want to play, which isn't often. The GIA would rather kill people. In April 1993, he appointed 71-year-old statesman Abdesselem Habbachi as "mediator of the republic," to handle complaints about the government. We don't imagine he'll be spending much time out in the field.

The Army and the Death Squads

Groups of five to 10 men in plain clothes work the inner city, while 35,000 troops man an "infernal arc" in the Mitidja between Algeria, Blida, Laarba and Medea. Out in the countryside, small groups of soldiers travel in helicopters and armored personnel vehicles to track down fundamentalists. It's clobbering time in Algeria. The annual U.S. report on human rights said there was "convincing evidence" of systematic torture and executions of suspected GIA and FIS insurgents.

The Cops

Police and security forces in Algeria consist of three organizations: (1) the national police (DGSN), (2) an agency of the ministry of the interior, Gendarmerie (MOD), and (3) the communal guards, similar to village or small town police with limited training and equipment. There is an ongoing problem with the terrorists infiltrating the ranks of all three. In addition, the terrorists have obtained hundreds of police uniforms and badges and have masqueraded as police to carry out terrorist and criminal operations. Some of these operations have included assassinations of GOA officials by terrorists operating fake police checkpoints. Throughout the war, terrorists have targeted GOA officials, journalists, foreigners and randomly selected Algerian citizens. But the cops and security forces have borne a large proportion of the targeting and, as such, suffered numerous casualties. The large number of deaths within the police forces, coupled with the uncertainty about fellow officers' loyalties, have resulted in low morale in the police ranks.

Groupe Islamic Armee, Armed Islamic Group, El-Djama'a El-islamia El Mosalaha. (GIA)

An Algerian Muslim fundamentalist group determined to establish an Islamic state based on the Islamic jurisdiction, Hadith el Quran. The men of El-Djama'a, are veteran Afghani war fighters and supporters of Mostafa Bou'ali, the militant Islamic imam. The G.I.A. bases its whole ideological background on one aspect: a fatwa issued by Sheikh Abdel-Haq el-Ayadia, one of the founders and leaders of the ground. The fatwa says "The leaders of Algeria are all nowadays infidels, with no exceptions. Their minister, officers, aides, and everybody that followed their path, worked for them, accepted or did not react to their acts, fall with them under the same category. They are all infidels and getting rid of them is a glory to Islam and Muslims. This fatwas is interpreted as the unrestricted execution of intellectuals, journalists, government officials, military officials, diplomats, and foreigners working in Algeria.

The fighters are found in the Algiers region, the Atlas Mountains and along the border regions. The GIA have divided Algeria into three military zones, East, Middle, and West, each headed by a vice-emir, but they fall under the emir's leadership, whose rank is the highest. The emirs of the GIA are : El-Mansouri El-Miliani, Abudllah Qalek, Abdel-Haq Ayadia and Djafar El-Afghani. Djamel El-Zitouni, the most ruthless of the group, was killed by his own men on July 16, 1996. (A fitting end to the man who ordered the beheading of seven Trappist monks, the hijacking of an Air France plane and the subway bombings in Paris.) The GIA nowadays suffers from an internal conflict on the leadership of El-Djama'a.

Getting In

Passports and visas are required for U.S. citizens traveling to Algeria. However, Algeria does not give visas to persons whose passports indicate previous travel to Israel or South Africa. For more information concerning entry requirements, crazy travelers may contact the following:

Embassy of the Democratic and Popular Republic of Algeria

2137 Wyoming Avenue NW,
Washington, D.C. 20008
☎ *(202) 265-2800*

Getting Around

The two routes south across the Sahara are closed (there is an alternate route through Mauritania to Senegal). Algerian embassies are very reluctant to provide visas for Westerners.

More than 110 foreigners have been killed since 1993. Control Risks Group, a business consultant to companies doing business in foreign countries, rates Algeria as the most dangerous place in the world to do business. About 2000 French citizens, mostly businessmen and diplomatic staff, remain in the country. Every night an average of 50 people are killed in the city of Algiers.

DP's Tips on Surviving Algeria

1. The government of Algeria is not wild about tourists. Only accredited journalists will be allowed entry.

2. All accredited journalists are met on arrival by a protection team supplied without charge by the government.

3. Most journos stay at the Hotel St. George (also called the Hotel al-Jezzair) or the Hotel Sofitel. Both are guarded 24 hours a day.

4. During your stay, you will be escorted at all times. You will be driven to meetings and escorted back to your hotel. The teams only operate in Algiers. For trips outside the city, taxis can be hired for about $60 a day from your hotel.

5. Those who want to wander around town will be given walkie-talkies. Do not wear these conspicuously. Do not stay in one place any longer than 10 minutes (the time it takes locals to alert GIA gunmen)

6. You will be allowed to walk around town unescorted or to leave Algiers only if you sign a disclaimer.

7. The most dangerous place in Algiers is the Kasbah. A Western journalist went there unprotected and was shot within 5 minutes.

8. If you are in Algiers, say hello to the U.S embassy staff—major consumers of *DP* T-shirts and stickers as well as all around good sports.

If the GIA do grab you, the only known method of avoiding instant execution is to recite the Muslim prayers.

— *Roddy Scott, London, England,* DP *contributor*

Dangerous Places

With terrorists in the north and bandits in the south, most of Algeria is dangerous. The Zabarbar forest, Blida mountains and the Jijel region are frequently napalmed by the government in their quest to rid themselves of fundamentalist pockets. The favorite target of the FIS seems to be the airbase at Laghuat. MIG-23s regularly drop napalm on remote regions used by the terrorists for their bases of operations.

Algiers

In January 1995, a global study conducted by an international business group, Corporate Resources Group, rated Algiers the worst city in the world. The group based its findings on criteria such as quality of life, security, public services, mental and physical care and facilities, and political and social stability.

Schools

In addition to journalists, teachers are a favored target of Muslim militants. It's not unusual for two a week to be whacked in Algiers, and, as of mid-1996, some 700 schools have been razed by fire or sabotaged.

Dangerous Things

Bandits

As if the terrorists weren't enough, there are also numerous incidents of banditry and assault involving foreigners that have been reported in the far southern region of Algeria near the border with Niger. Bandits have robbed, assaulted, kidnapped and killed travelers in Algeria south of Tamanrasset.

Being a Journalist

At least 70 journalists have died in Algeria since 1993. Three were killed in January 1995.

Civil Disorder

Political, social and economic problems have created a climate of unrest and uncertainty in Algeria. Sporadic bombings and assassinations continue. The most prominent victim was President Mohammed Boudiaf, who was assassinated on June 29, 1994, in the eastern city of Annaba. An estimated 100 police and security officials have been slain. These disturbances have not taken an anti-American tone, with the exception of one small bomb that exploded harmlessly in the U.S. embassy compound on January 30, 1992. Anyone living in Algiers is exposed to the risk of being inadvertently caught in the wrong place at the wrong time when violence breaks out.

Criminals

As if getting your throat slit wasn't bad enough, the threat of theft is increasing in Algeria. The most frequent crimes involve the theft of auto parts from parked cars. Car windows and trunk locks are frequently broken in the hope that the thief will find something of value within. Home burglary is an increasingly serious problem, and most residences of foreigners are protected by alarm systems, watch dogs and/or guards. Experienced expatriate residents should venture out into the city with only a minimum amount of cash carried in a carefully concealed location. Vehicles are not generally parked in unguarded locations because of theft and vandalism.

Booby Traps

Booby traps proliferate in the country. One of the less ingenious but still surprisingly effective modes is the old "booby trap in the corpse trick." In January 1995, the booby-trapped corpse of a slain security force member exploded when it was picked up by two security force members, killing both of them.

Buses and Trains

Crime on Algeria's trains and buses is so serious that the government has prepared newspaper articles lamenting the dangers posed by pickpockets and thieves. Baggage must never be left unattended in a public place.

Hotel Rooms

Nothing of value should be left in a hotel room. There are reports of hotel staff helping themselves to the toiletries, appliances and food of the guests. Pedestrians are not likely to encounter armed robbers, but must be alert to the danger of pickpockets and purse snatchers near the major hotels.

Hassles with Police

Armed men posing as police have entered homes of foreigners, held the occupants at gunpoint and robbed them.

Police are highly visible. Roadblocks, especially at night, are located at many major intersections, and police vehicles are constantly patrolling the streets. The Algerian police are well trained and equipped. They are fully professional in their conduct and attentive to the needs of the foreign community. Police may be contacted in any city by dialing 17; rural areas are under the jurisdiction of the Gendarmerie Nationale.

ALGERIA

Getting Sick

Hospitals and clinics in Algeria are available, but limited in quality. If you are seriously wounded, you stand a better chance by being flown out to nearby France, Britain or Germany. Medicines can be hard to get or expensive. Don't expect much outside of the major cities.

Nuts and Bolts

The workweek in Algeria is Saturday through Wednesday, at least for those who work; 84 percent of Algerians between the ages of 15 and 30 are jobless, and inflation is at 55 percent. Factories are functioning at 50 percent of capacity. In addition, Algeria has the lowest farm yield of any Mediterranean country, forcing it to import two-thirds of its food.

Traveler's checks and credit cards are acceptable in only a few establishments in urban areas. Currently, the government of Algeria requires all foreigners entering the country to exchange US$200 into local currency. Documentary proof of legal exchange of currency is needed when departing Algeria.

Embassy Location

U.S. Embassy
> *In the capital city of Algiers.*
> *4 Chemin Cheikh Bachir El-Ibrahimi*
> *B.P. 549 (Alger-Gare) 16000*
> ☎ *69-11-86, 69-18-54, 69-38-75.*

Dangerous Days

05/05/1995   Islamic extremists killed five foreigners working at a pipe mill at an industrial zone in the Ghardaia region of northern Algeria. The victims were identified as two Frenchmen, a Canadian, a Brit and a Tunisian.

04/20/1980   Berber spring. Berber ethnic protests were held in Tizi Ouzou.

08/20/1955   Algerian independence fighters launched their first armed offensive against French forces in eastern Algeria.

11/08/1942   U.S. and British forces landed in North Africa.

ALGERIA

Luanda

Angola
★★★★

When Three Tribes Go to War...

Until Rwanda set a new standard for savagery, Angola held the title of having Africa's most bloody war. More than 400,000 people have been killed in the on-going battle since its independence from Portugal in 1975. The dead may be the lucky ones. The fighting has resulted in 50,000 orphaned children and 80,000 cripples. Today, Angola has the highest percentage of amputees in the world. Nearly 40 percent of the population is estimated to be missing limbs.

The United Nations estimates that, at the conflict's peak, 1000 people were dying a day in this war without end. The 20 million explosives left buried in the soil will continue to kill and maim for years to come. There are perhaps only 10 or 11 million people left in Angola and more than enough land mines, famine, drought and pestilence to kill every one of them. At least twice.

Angola was a valued source of slaves for 300 years after the area was colonized by the Portuguese in the late 15th century. But it wasn't until after the Second World War that Portugal attempted to bring Portuguese settlers into Angola.

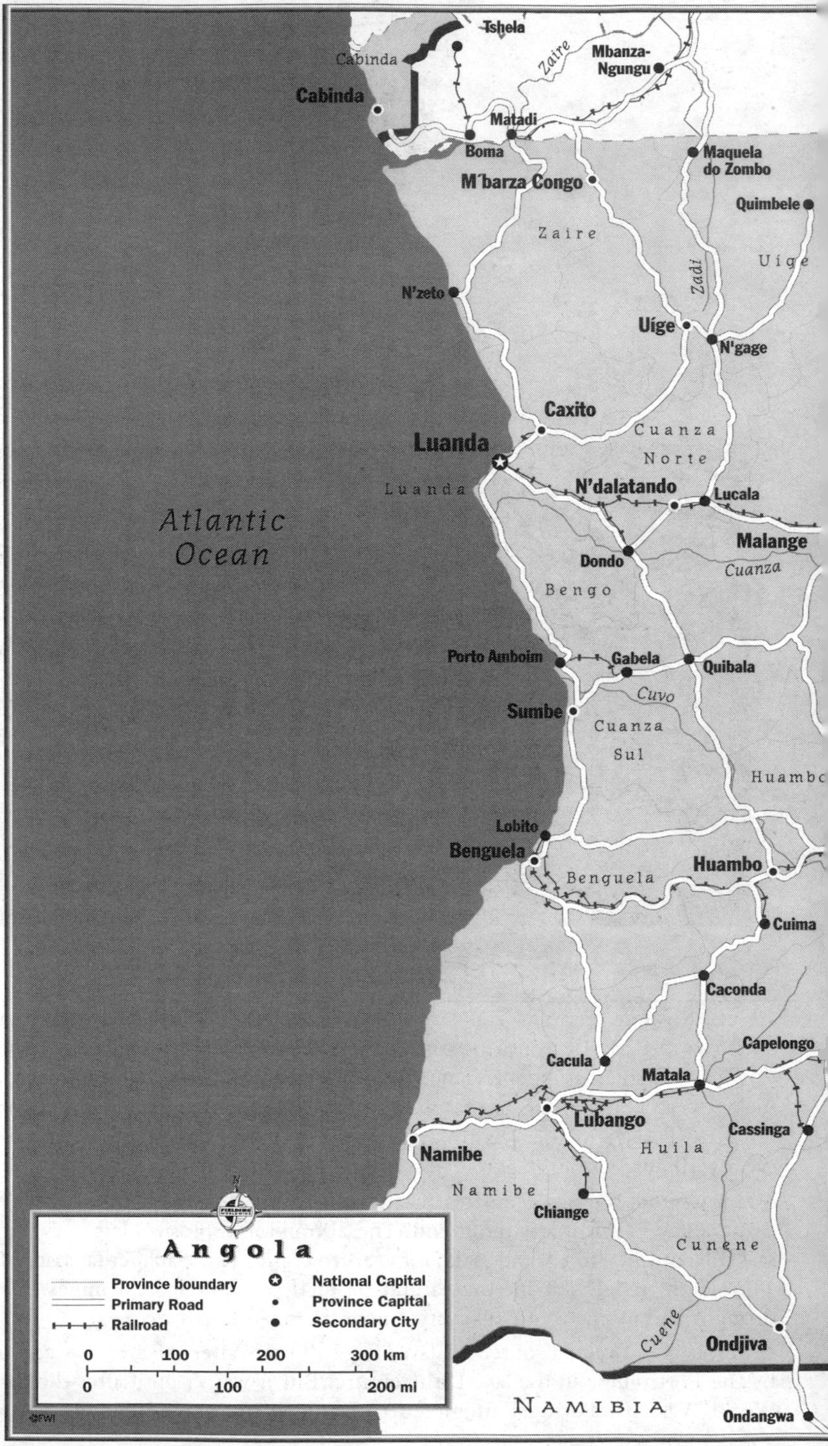
Tshela
Cabinda
Cabinda
Zaire
Mbanza-Ngungu
Matadi
Boma
Maquela do Zombo
M'barza Congo
Quimbele
Zaire
Uige
Zadi
N'zeto
Uíge
N'gage
Caxito
Luanda
Cuanza Norte
Luanda
N'dalatando
Lucala
Atlantic Ocean
Malange
Dondo
Cuanza
Bengo
Porto Amboim
Gabela
Quibala
Cuvo
Sumbe
Cuanza Sul
Huambo
Lobito
Benguela
Benguela
Huambo
Cuima
Caconda
Capelongo
Cacula
Matala
Lubango
Cassinga
Namibe
Huila
Namibe
Chiange
Cunene
Cuene
Ondjiva
Namibia
Ondangwa
Angola
Province boundary
Primary Road
Railroad
National Capital
Province Capital
Secondary City
0 100 200 300 km
0 100 200 mi
©FWI

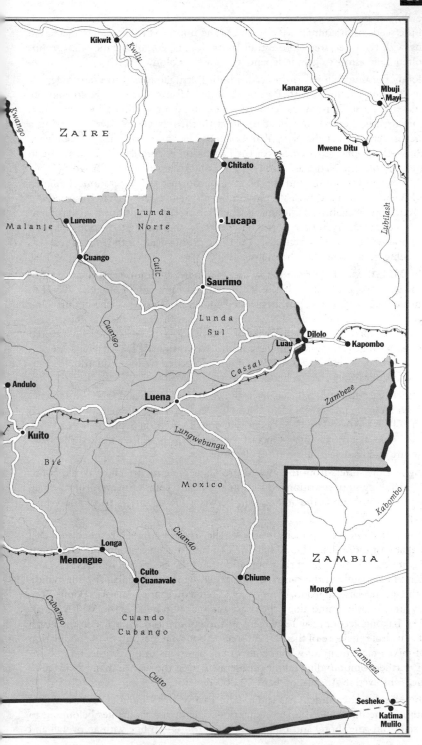

The Portuguese inhabitants of Angola established lucrative coffee plantations, and the seeds of discontent were sewn. As the number of Portuguese increased, along with their hectares of bountiful landholdings, Angolan nationalist groups revolted in an effort to gain independence for the colony.

Bloody fighting followed for decades until Portugal agreed to grant independence to Angola, along with Portugal's other African colonies. Following the course that most Third World countries trek along after gaining independence, the insurgents didn't know what to do with their freedom, save for taking a course in acronyms at the Navy War College. The three principal independence groups—the Popular Movement for the Liberation of Angola (MPLA), strong in central Angola; the National Union for the Total Independence of Angola (UNITA), based in the south; and the National Front for the Liberation of Angola (FNLA), which had the most strength in the north and had separately carried out the rebellion—began to clash among themselves. The transitional government that was established after the Portuguese forces withdrew in 1975 soon collapsed like a house of cards. The wrath that the three groups had for the Portuguese was now being directed among themselves.

The MPLA, with help from Cuba and the Soviet Union, seized the capital of Luanda and proclaimed itself the legitimate government of Angola. UNITA, with the help of South Africa, controlled the southern part of the country and waged, along with the weaker FNLA (and the help of the classified ad department at *Soldier of Fortune*), a 16-year civil war against the MPLA. The MPLA adapted a Soviet-style governing system. Agostinho Neto, the MPLA general secretary, became president. He died in 1979 and was succeeded by Jose Eduardo dos Santos, who successfully created better ties with the West.

A 1991 cease-fire ended the civil war between the MPLA and UNITA. However, UNITA instigated renewed hostilities in October 1992 after elections resulted in an MPLA victory. The U.N. Security Council voted on September 26, 1993, for sanctions against UNITA. On October 6, 1993, UNITA accepted the 1991 cease-fire and its defeat in the 1992 elections.

Angola now suffers from the myriad problems endemic to Third World countries, including poor nutrition, education and health care. However, the most serious social problem is the antagonism between the country's tribal and ethnic groups.

Ethnic hostilities, the principal cause of the strife in Angola, resulted in a civil war that cost more than US$30 billion. The largest ethnic group, the Ovimbundu, comprises 37 percent of the population (and the essence of the UNITA forces) and lives mainly in the central and southern parts of Angola. The Kimbundu are the second-largest group, comprising about a quarter of Angola's population. They are primarily found along the coast and make up most of the MPLA. Finally, the Bakong account for 13 percent of the population. They live in the north and constitute the core of the FNLA forces. About one percent of the population is of mixed race, many of whom control key positions in government and business, further compounding ethnic problems. Before the war, as many as 330,000 Caucasians lived in Angola; perhaps 30,000 remain.

The Angolan government has said it plans to privatize a number of state-owned groups in the hotel and tourism industry—some being companies belonging to the state-run Angohotel and Emprotel hotel groups—in line with an overall and urgent effort to liberalize its formerly Marxist economy. The Angotur tourism company would also be revitalized. Tourism has totally disappeared here in the 20 years of civil war. A significant number of residents in the capital city of Luanda live in hotels due to a severe shortage of decent housing.

Angola's ruling MPLA has promised sweeping reforms in its economy to bring it closer to a free market system. However, chaos due to the war with UNITA rebels has severely hampered these proposed moves.

In November 1994, UNITA's Jonas Savimbi capitulated to the government, thanks in no small part to the South African mercenary recruitment firm Executive Outcomes (see "The Players" section in the Sierra Leone chapter), whose training of the Angolan army after UNITA rearmed and restarted its battle against MPLA in 1992 turned the tide in the war. The group's contract with the Angolan government was reportedly worth US$23 million.

The Scoop

After three decades of war and a half-million dead Angolans, the guns are quiet. The only sound now is the sound of shovels and picks. In the north, diamonds are the new focus. Even during the last three years of war, diamonds were the fuel of UNITA forces, who extracted the shiny stones to pay for bullets and bombs. The Angolan Government tapped the petro bucks to fight the diamond dollars. Two of the country's northern provinces, Lunda Norte and Lunda Sul, produced more than half a billion dollars worth of diamonds in 1994.

The current bloodshed started when the Portuguese administration began to crumble in 1974. By March 1976, it had turned into a dirty, three-way war. As usual, the CIA is to blame for undermining the MPLA, whose platform was considered too radical.

Holden Roberto and the Kikongo-speaking people of the north (the FNLA) are backed by the CIA and Zaire. The Portuguese and South Africa back Jonas Savimbi's UNITA, which is comprised of Umbunda-speaking peoples and other tribes of the south and east. UNITA has also enjoyed the support of the CIA. The MPLA is backed by Cuba and is popular with urban Angolans. The MPLA technically runs the country but has been under attack from South Africa and the dissenting parties.

When the superpowers and other outside meddlers became tired of counting corpses, there were only two players left, both dazed and bloodied. The South African merc firm Executive Outcomes was called in by the government for US$23 million to clean up the mess. Supported by mining interests and tacitly by the British government, they mainly have.

The Players

Popular Movement for the Liberation of Angola (MPLA)

The Marxist regime held together by the soft-spoken and educated José Eduardo dos Santos. He was propelled to power via a slam-dunk election masterminded by a Brazilian public relations company. Dos Santos has promised to drop the unpopular dogma of Lenin and embrace free market principles. The MPLA won the September 1992 elections, supervised by 800 outside observers—his arch rival, Jonas Savimbi, went back to his base in Huambo and continued to kill his countrymen in the name of peace.

Dos Santos' government is propped up by petroleum and diamond exports extracted and managed by foreign firms and the Angolan Armed Forces (FAA). The FAA is busy packing over US$3.4 billion dollars in new weapons and deploying the 500 white mercenaries (mostly from South Africa). Also, 4500 U.N. peacekeepers have been baby-sitting the new peace agreement between UNITA and the ruling government.

National Union for the Total Independence of Angola (UNITA)

Headed by 61-year-old Jonas Savimbi. Considering the number of people his brand of socialist politics has killed, it may be surprising to learn that Savimbi was a graduate of the School of International Politics at Lausanne University in Switzerland. Educated in guerrilla tactics in China, he has vowed to topple the Cuban- and formerly Soviet-backed government. He is facing escalating pressure in terms of sanctions for his refusal to negotiate seriously with the government for peace.

Up until the middle of 1994, UNITA controlled about 70 percent of the country with its 40,000 troops and aid from South Africa and Zaire. However, Savimbi quickly lost ground after Executive Outcomes, the Gal Friday of private soldiering, sent in about 500 mercs to show MPLA how it's done. In August 1994, the government retook areas around Malanje and launched attacks in the northern diamond-producing area of Lunda Norte near Cafunfo. Savimbi's control of the diamond mines had funded his resistance movement. In 1993, UNITA pocketed about US$200 million from smuggling diamonds out of Angola. DeBeers calculates that, in 1992, about US$500 million worth of diamonds were smuggled out of Angola. Part of the 1995 peace deal allowed UNITA to legalize its diamond mining operations and turn many of the soldiers into construction workers.

Cabindan Democratic Front (FDC)

The northern region of Angola is oil-rich, and while the MPLA and UNITA were duking it out, no fewer than 10 different separatist movements started jockeying for siphoning rights on those petro dollars. Meanwhile, Chevron Corporation, which owns the production facility, will be the winner regardless of who's in control.

Executive Outcomes

EO is the hugely successful South African-based temp agency for international mercenaries. The Angolan government used about 500 EO "advisers" to fight against UNITA, and it paid off when the rebs made peace with the MPLA in November 1994. But it came with a price tag of about US$23 million. In Sierra Leone, EO is fighting for diamonds in payment. The company has diversified from simple soldiering in recent months. EO's sister and/or parent companies mine for gold in Uganda and drills boreholes in Ethiopia. In all, EO operates 32 companies, ranging from adult education facilities to computer software firms, in countries such as Angola, South Africa, Zambia, Botswana and Lesotho. If you want to enlist, the pay's not bad at US$2000 a month—plus all the bullets you'll need. Contact the following:

Executive Outcomes
Recruitment Officer
PVT. BAG X-105
Hennopsmeer 0046
South Africa
☎ *011-27-12-666-8429/7005*

Getting In

Passport and visa required. Persons arriving without visas are subject to possible arrest or deportation. Tourist/business visas take two days and require an application form, US$30, a letter stating purpose of travel, and two color photos. Applications by mail require prepaid return envelope. Yellow fever and cholera immunizations are required. The embassy was quite excited about the 7000 or so U.N. peacekeepers heading to their country. They estimate it will be one to two years before things settle down. For now, they still welcome tourists but advise strongly that you fly directly into Luanda and do not dillydally out of Luanda, Lobito, Benguela or Namibe. The Angolan Ministry of Hotels and Tourism is the best source for people looking to book Shriner Conventions there.

Land borders may or may not be under government control. Folks caught tiptoeing in will be incarcerated if they don't hit a land mine first.

For additional information, contact the following:

Embassy of Angola

1819 L Street, NW, Suite 400
Washington, D.C. 20036
☎ *(202) 785-1156*
FAX (202) 785-1258

The Permanent Mission of the Republic of Angola to the U.N.

125 East 73rd Street
New York, NY 10021
☎ *(212) 861-5656*

Getting Around

There is little infrastructure left in Angola. Most roads are closed or mined or both. Wandering bands of armed thugs will stop and rob any travelers found in the countryside.

Make sure you have extra passport-sized photos for special permits required to travel around the country outside Luanda. Permits are available at the Direcao de Emigracao e Fronteiras in Luanda. Most folks you run into here will be in the oil patch. There are plenty of roadblocks, and chances are one of them might be a group of thugs who want your car. There have been carjackings against foreigners coming from the airport. You can't blame these folks for being a little riled up at whitey. After all, the Portuguese yanked about 3 million mothers' sons from Angola during the slave days and the Western world has done a good job of killing whomever was left.

Dangerous Places

Travel throughout Angola is considered unsafe because of the presence of undisciplined, armed troops and land mines, as well as the possibility of sudden outbreaks of localized combat or a direct attack by armed soldiers or civilians. Travel in many parts of the capital city is relatively safe by day, but considered unsafe at night because of the increased incidence of armed robberies and carjackings. The presence of police checkpoints after dark, often manned by armed, poorly trained personnel, contributes to unsafe nighttime travel. Police at checkpoints actively solicit bribes and have used deadly force against vehicles for not stopping as requested.

The Northeast

Lunda Norte and Lunda Sul provinces in the northeast are extremely hazardous for foreigners. The diamond areas around Lucapa are major stages for violent crime. About 50 to 100 people used to be murdered in Lucapa each week. Despite the attempt to legalize and control diamond mining, most stones are smuggled out of the country, with only 20 percent of the hauls actually going through official channels.

Dangerous Things

Land Mines

It is estimated by Human Rights Watch that there are 20 million land mines in Angola. The U.N. figures there are 12 million. Halo Trust, a British mine clearing company, is one group that has the thankless job of clearing them out. They find a lot more unexploded ordnance than land mines. About 120 people a day are killed. There are no figures for maimings.

Thugs

Violent crime exists throughout the country. Armed robbery occurs in Luanda both day and night. Travel outside Luanda is not safe. In a country where police make the equivalent of $5 a month, there is little incentive to follow the straight and narrow. In Angola, crime does pay. At least a lot more than the cops make.

Shoplifting

Angola doesn't possess a formal prison or penal system. Most "law" offenders are simply executed or beaten.

Getting Sick

Don't. Travelers are advised to purchase medical evacuation insurance. Malaria in the severe falciparum (malignant) form occurs throughout the entire country and is chloroquine-resistant. Tungiasis is widespread. Many viral diseases, some causing severe hemorrhagic fevers, are transmitted by ticks, fleas, mosquitoes, sandflies, etc. Relapsing fever and tick-, louse- and flea-borne typhus occur. Sleeping sickness (human trypanosomiasis) is regularly reported. Food-borne and waterborne diseases are highly endemic. Bilharziasis is present and widespread throughout the country, as are alimentary helminthic infections, the dysenteries and diarrheal diseases, including cholera, giardiasis, typhoid fever, and hepatitis A and E. Hepatitis B is hyperendemic; poliomyelitis is endemic and trachoma widespread. Frequently fatal arenavirus hemorrhagic fevers have attained notoriety. Rats pose a special hazard; lassa fever has a virus reservoir in the commonly found multimammate rat. Use all precautions to avoid rat-contaminated food and food containers. Ebola and Marburg hemorrhagic fevers are present but reported infrequently. Epidemics of meningococcal meningitis can occur. Echinococcosis (hydatrid disease) is widespread in animal breeding areas. The health system has collapsed. Three million people are at risk of famine, and, at its peak, more than 10,000 people were wounded a day during the war. There is one doctor for every 13,489 people. Angola has the highest infant mortality rates in the world, as well as the greatest number of amputees—not from sickness, but from mines.

Money Hassles

There are a number of counterfeit Angolan $100 notes in Luanda. The notes are printed on the same paper that the real currency is. The counterfeit notes have 1990 and 1993 dates.

Nuts and Bolts

Angola is a developing African country that has been plunged into civil war since its independence from Portugal in 1975. On May 19, 1993, the U.S. recognized the government of the Republic of Angola, and a U.S. embassy was established in Luanda on June 22, 1993. Facilities for tourism are virtually nonexistent. There are severe shortages of lodging, transportation, food, water and utilities in Luanda and other cities in the country. Shortages result in a lack of sanitary conditions in many areas, including Luanda.

Per-capita income in Angola was only about US$770 back in 1993; 75 percent of the people are engaged in subsistence agriculture. Life expectancy is a low 44 years, and more than half of the population is illiterate.

Registration

U.S. citizens who register at the U.S. embassy's consular section, which can now extend full consular services, may obtain updated information on travel and security in Angola.

Embassy Location

U.S. Embassy
*On Rua Houari Boumedienne
in the Miramar area of Luanda.
P.O. Box 6468
☎ [244] (2) 34-54-81 and 34-64-18 (24-
hour number)
FAX [244] (2) 34-78-84*

Consular Section
*Casa Inglesa, First Floor
Rua Major Kanyangunla No. 132/135
Luanda
☎ [244] (2) 39-69-27
FAX [244] (2) 39-05-15*

ANGOLA

Yerevan

Armenia
★

Little Israel

Armenia has many similarities to Israel: They are both small, "ethnically pure" countries squeezed between Muslim giants. Much of Armenia's support comes from former natives who are now successful businessmen and influential people living outside their homeland. So it is not surprising that tiny (11,500 square miles) and oft-bullied Armenia has decided to defend itself by becoming the aggressor against much bigger enemies. Armenia has taken advantage of Moscow's preoccupation with its financial and political troubles and rolled through Azerbaijan into Nagorno-Karabakh, gobbling other areas along the way. During the occupation of these territories, Armenians made sure there would be a tidy political consensus for independence and pushed out most non-Armenians. Like the Jews, Armenians have endured a holocaust equal to or greater than that suffered by the Jews at the hands of the Nazis in WWII (April 24 is the commemoration of the WWI genocide of the Armenians by the Turks). Given this event, it is somewhat understandable that the Armenians, like the Jews, tend to be pugnacious

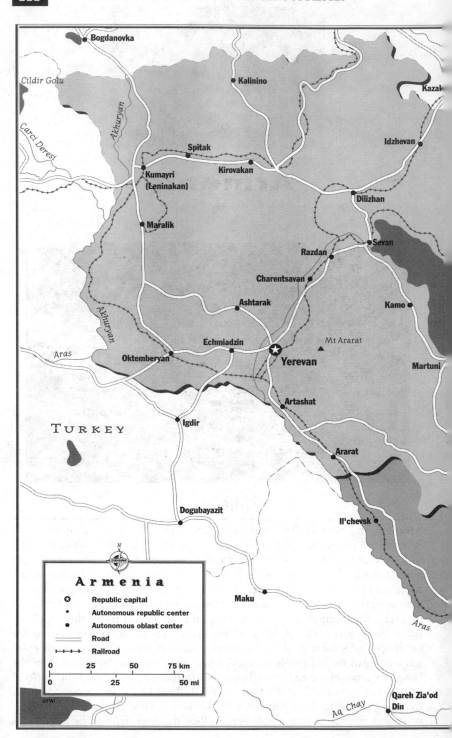

Armenia

⊕ Republic capital
• Autonomous republic center
● Autonomous oblast center
──── Road
╫┼┼┼ Railroad

0   25   50   75 km
0   25   50 mi

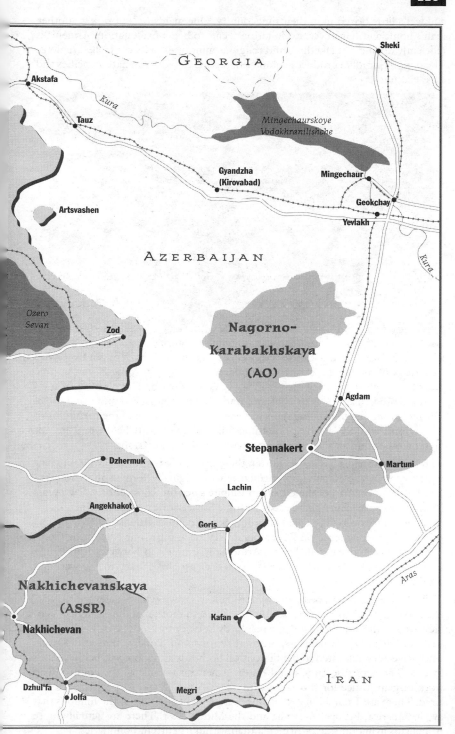

and feel a little boxed-in in their tiny country. One man's *Lebensraum* is another man's homeland. However, exploitation seems to beget exploitation. Armenia is efficiently driving out all ethnic and religious minorities in its controlled regions. The ongoing conflict produces volumes of reports of indiscriminate atrocities and mass executions.

So, if you are into visiting small, struggling countries that are creating new homelands, Armenia and its new territory of Nagorno-Karabakh might be for you (just think of the low hotel rates!). Be forewarned though, Armenia can best be described as gloomy in the classic Trans-Caucasian mold. There's a lot of mud and destroyed villages, bizarre cultures and strange languages—and not a lot of sun and swimming pools. Fog, rain and eternal chill are some of the highlights of the region's weather. Putting on ethnic folk dances or battlefield tours are not high on their tourism's development agenda in Nagorno-Karabakh.

To be fair, Armenia has always gotten the short end of the stick. Hayastani Hanrapetutyun, or the Republic of Armenia, was originally formed in November 1920. It had been part of the Ottoman Empire since the 16th century. Two years later, in 1922, Armenia disappeared into the Soviet vortex, until it gained its independence following the failed hard-line Soviet coup of August 1991. Armenia gained full independence on December 21, 1991, and became part of the Commonwealth of Independent States. Armenia is jammed in between Iran to the south, Georgia to the north, Azerbaijan to the east and Turkey to the west and southwest.

The Armenians have a bad habit of getting into brawls with equally proud, warlike and bigger neighbors, so it shouldn't come as a shock that the Armenian people have lost most of their land as a result. By hook or by crook, they would like it back. So there are Armenian-sponsored terrorists in Turkey, Iraq and Russia. They have been relegated to being political hotheads as opposed to being serious threats. There are also large numbers of Armenians outside of the country who work to gain justice for the various injustices Armenia and its people have suffered. There are 1.6 million Armenians in the CIS in addition to the millions that live in America, Europe, Australia and the Middle East. There are actually more Armenians living outside of Armenia than within its current boundaries.

Armenia is mad about a lot of things. One is the disputed ownership of the biblical ark. Armenia claims ownership of the ark (Armenia says that Noah founded the capital of Yerevan and that Mount Ararat was originally part of Armenia), but Iraq, Turkey and Russia also lay claim to the resting place of the ancient vessel. The Armenian claim has a lot more validity than the Armenians' recent real estate grab in Azerbaijan. The Christian Armenians view the Muslim Azeris as "Turks," thereby blaming them for the Turkish massacres of 200,000 Armenians in Turkey in 1895 and another million in 1915. The Azeris speak Turkish but definitely cannot be fingered for the death and destruction of the Armenian peoples in 1915.

The Scoop

Armenia is a grindingly poor but workable country that suffers from the emigration of its best and brightest. Not many people other than foreign Armenians bother visiting. Taking a lesson from Hitler and Serbia, they quickly chased out any ethnically or religiously impure folks in the occupied areas. Things seem better when there's no one left around to complain. However, Armenia—although beset with teething pain—is making the transition from communism to capitalism relatively smoothly. Economically, the country is self-disciplined; inflation is minimal—as is the foreign debt. And industrial output is on marked rise. Although these boys like battling with their neighbors, they don't blame their woes on the collapse of communism. Their troubles come mainly from the energy squeeze that neighboring Turkey and Azerbaijan put on the country over the dispute of the sovereignty of Nagorno-Karabakh. For now, things have cooled down in Nagorno Karabakh. The reason is that Armenia has run out of bullets and money.

Getting In

A passport and a visa are required. Without a visa, travelers cannot register at hotels and may be required to leave the country immediately via the route by which they entered. For current information on visa requirements, U.S. citizens can contact the Armenian embassy in Washington, D.C. (see the listing on the next page).

Getting Around

A natural gas and transportation blockade is causing severe food and medical supply shortages, frequent interruptions in electrical power and shortages of transportation fuel. Internal travel, especially by air, may be disrupted by fuel shortages and other problems. Tourist facilities are limited to some grody hookers and a smattering of public toilets, and Armenians, in general, are about as bilingual as members of the Northern Michigan Militia. Ask for directions in Armenia and you may get some pocket change in return. Many of the goods and services taken for granted in other countries are not yet available. Armenia's road system is surprisingly good; 6525 miles out of 7022 are paved.

Dangerous Places

Armed conflict is taking place in and around the Armenian-populated area of Nagorno-Karabakh, located in Azerbaijan, and along the Armenian-Azerbaijani border. Fighting continues on a daily basis, and the front lines change frequently, although things seem to be marginally cooling down in the region. The U.S. government has prohibited all U.S. officials from traveling overland between Georgia and Armenia due to the activity of bandits.

Getting Sick

Medical care in Armenia is limited. There are 43 doctors and 91 hospital beds per 10,000 people as of 1989. The U.S. Embassy maintains a list of English-speaking physicians in the area. There is a severe shortage of basic medical supplies, including disposable needles, anesthetics and antibiotics. Elderly travelers and those with existing health problems may be at risk due to inadequate medical facilities. Doctors and hospitals often expect immediate cash payment for health services. U.S. medical insurance is not always valid outside the United States. Travelers have found that, in some cases, supplemental medical insurance with specific overseas coverage has proved to be useful.

Nuts and Bolts

Armenia is a cash-only economy. Traveler's checks and credit cards are not accepted anywhere except as fuel and for lock-picks.

Currency in Armenia is the ruble, with 100 kopeks to 1 ruble. Yerevan is the country's commerce center. An ethnically and religiously pure country in contrast to its neighbors (it is 93.3 percent Armenian—1.7 percent Kurdish, 1.5 percent Russian and 3.5 percent other), Armenia is virtually entirely Christian, with 94 percent being practicing Armenian Orthodox. Armenian is the "official" tongue, but you can find people who speak Russian. The Kurds speak Kurdish. English is not common, except among business professionals. Armenia has cold winters and hot summers. The average temperature during the winter in Yerevan is 26° F, while summer enjoys a more comfortable average of 77° F. Annual rainfall in Yerevan averages 13 inches but is much higher in the mountainous regions, which also have cooler temperatures. Mud and drab characterizes the Nagorno and Karabak regions.

Americans who register at the consular section of the U.S. embassy may obtain updated information on travel and security within Armenia.

Embassy Locations

Armenian Embassy in the United States
  2225 R Street, N.W.
  Washington D.C. 20008
  ☎ (202) 319-1976

The U.S. Embassy
  18 General Bagramian Street
  Yerevan, Armenia
  ☎ [374] (2) 15-11-22

Dangerous Days

03/16/1921	Signing of the Soviet-Turkish border treaty that ended Armenian hopes of establishing an independent state.
04/01/1915	April is designated a "month of remembrance" to commemorate the anniversary of the claimed Turkish massacre of 1915.

Azerbaijan
★

The Russians' First "Wars R Us" Store

Oil-rich and sparsely populated Azerbaijan finds itself in the crosshairs of Russia, Georgia, Iran and Armenia. The region of Nagorno-Karabakh is now controlled by invading Armenians who want to grab back a predominantly Armenian region now inside Azerbaijan. The fact that Armenia is also the landlord of large tracts of Azeri and Kurdish regions doesn't seem to bother the Armenians.

At least 2500 people have been killed in seven years of fighting over the disputed 1700-square-mile mountain region of Nagorno-Karabakh, a part of Azerbaijan populated by Armenians but under Azeri control since 1923. The relative dominance of a single ethnicity in the country (Azerbaijani, 82.7 percent; Russian, 5.6 percent; Armenian, 5.6 percent; others, including Daghestani, 6.1 percent) normally wouldn't be a predicator of civil war, as the Muslim Azeris vastly outnumber the Armenians. The Azerbaijan Republic was a former province of Persia that was annexed by Russia in 1828. It gained its independence in 1917 but was invaded by the Soviet Army in 1920 and became a Soviet republic in 1936.

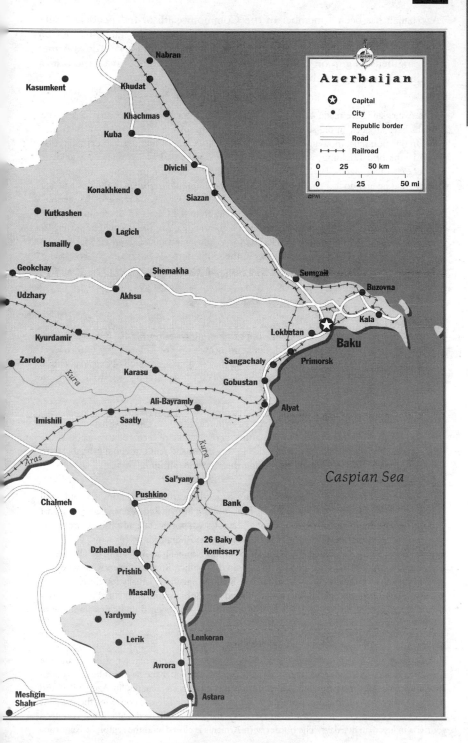

Azerbaijan

- ✪ Capital
- • City
- ····· Republic border
- —— Road
- ⊢+⊢+⊢ Railroad

0   25   50 km

0   25   50 mi

GFW

Kasumkent

Nabran

Khudat

Khachmas

Kuba

Divichi

Konakhkend

Siazan

Kutkashen

Lagich

Ismailly

Geokchay

Shemakha

Udzhary

Akhsu

Sumgait

Buzovna

Kala

Kyurdamir

Lokbatan

Baku

Zardob

Sangachaly

Primorsk

Karasu

Gobustan

Ali-Bayramly

Alyat

Imishili

Saatly

Kura

Aras

Kura

Sal'yany

Pushkino

Chalmeh

Bank

26 Baky
Komissary

Dzhalilabad

Prishib

Masally

Yardymly

Lerik

Lenkoran

Avrora

Meshgin
Shahr

Astara

Caspian Sea

Azerbaijan has been a member of the Commonwealth of Independent States (CIS) since December 21, 1991. Militarily weak, Azerbaijan stands to lose 25 percent of its land to the Armenians and will start marching backwards as Armenia strengthens its grip on occupied territories, and as refugees swell the rest of the country straining Azerbaijan's meager resources.

The Scoop

The Armenians have made an old-fashioned land grab for Nagorno—"Carry-back." The Russians have dropped an old-style Politburo member into Azerbaijan to kick out the Armenians. In the meantime, thousands of innocent people have been slaughtered and millions displaced in the brutal fighting, which featured an unusual scenario of Russian army soldiers battling each other. Azerbaijan President Heidar Aliev wants to turn the country into another Kuwait—and he may do it. Beneath the waters off the shores of Azerbaijan in the Caspian Sea lay some 68 billion gallons of oil. A deal was struck with the Kremlin in October 1995, permitting Azerbaijan to pump "early oil" through pipelines from the Caspian fields through southern Russia and Georgia. If the uneasy peace lasts with Armenia, Azerbaijan could be within 15 years of producing 700,000 barrels of oil a day for an annual income of about US$4.2 billion. That's if all goes well. Of the three republics in the southern region (Azerbaijan, Georgia and Armenia), Azerbaijan is the most vulnerable; it's the only republic that refuses to allow Russian soldiers on its soil.

The Players

The Armenians

The Armenians have about 50,000 troops occupying Nagorno-Karabakh. Unless someone big and ugly—and disciplined, unlike Moscow's troops—comes along to throw 'em out, they won't be leaving. In the meantime, they've done a good job of cleansing ethnic impurities by driving out all non-Armenians, not only from Nagorno-Karabakh but from other occupied areas.

The Azeris

They are little guys with an army the size of a church choir who can't do a helluva lot with two-thirds of the Armenian army squatting in the middle of their country. Luckily, the Russians know the value of the oil fields in the region and rent out enough hardware to the Azeris to keep the Armenians shelling their way into attrition.

The Russians

About 62,000 Russian troops are waiting patiently nearby, representing the only real threat to the Armenian army. Both sides accuse the former Red Army of acting against them. The 366th motorized infantry regiment, bored, poorly run and suffering from low morale and desertions, was ordered out of Nagorno-Karabakh by Moscow. Originally utilized to help expel Armenians out of Nagorno-Karabakh in the spring of 1991, they went freelance of sorts and aided both sides in the conflict. Russian officers went renegade in the war, with many choosing sides, and Russian units have actually fought each other with helicopters and tanks. The officers rented out tanks to both sides for about US$400 a day and even charged for soldiers, as the Russian Army opened up its first franchise of "Wars R Us."

Getting In

A passport and visa are required. Travelers without a visa cannot register at hotels and are subject to hassles and expensive (read that as bribes) treatment at the hands of local visa issuance authorities. Business travelers will need an invitation from someone in Azerbaijan, and travelers need telex confirmation from the hotel in Azerbaijan. There is no fee for the visa, but there is a $20 express handling (less than 10 days) charge. You will be dinged $75 if you need your visa in less than five days. The border with Armenia is closed, and the region of Nagorno-

Karabakh is considered unsafe due to the Armenian occupation and ongoing conflict. If you are caught entering the country illegally, you will be deported. U.S. citizens can contact the Azerbaijan embassy in Washington, D.C., for current information on visa requirements. There is a curfew in Baku from midnight to 5 a.m. Roadblocks and checkpoints are common. Travelers from Georgia to Azerbaijan can use the Georgian visas to enter Azerbaijan for five days. Travelers staying longer must get an Azeri visa after that.

Embassy Locations

Embassy of Azerbaijan
927 15th Street, NW, Suite 700
Washington, D.C. 20005
☎ *(202) 842-0001*
FAX (202) 842-0001

U.S. Embassy
Szadliq Prospect 83
☎ *[7] (8922) 96-00-19 or [7] (8922) 98-03-35*
FAX [7] (8922) 98-37-55

Getting Around

Of the total 22,805 miles of roadway in Azerbaijan, 19,760 of them are paved (as of 1990). If that was anywhere else, it might mean smooth sailing—but not here. Vehicles aren't available. There are 1299 railway track miles in Azerbaijan. Take a train and count on it being rocketed or bombed on. The major seaport is at Baku. There is virtually no civil aviation in Azerbaijan. Buses—those that are still running—have no spare parts. Nagorno-Karabakh is currently occupied by the Armenians.

Dangerous Places

Nagorno-Karabakh

The obscure and somewhat difficult to pronounce regions of Nagorno and Karabakh have been the locations of dirty and hate-filled fighting in Azerbaijan. Armenia has simply grabbed a quarter of Azerbaijan under the pretext that it wants to bring the predominantly Armenian region of Nagorno-Karabakh back into the fold. Formerly 94.4 percent of Nagorno-Karabakh's population was Armenian. Now the area is 100 percent Armenian. Armenia maintains that the Armenians of Nagorno-Karabakh voted for secession in a December 1991 referendum. They forget to mention that the Armenians cast 40,000 votes from a region of 160,000 people in a country of 7 million. Think of it as a small Cajun bayou town in Louisiana asking France to liberate them.

In the Armenians' enthusiasm to liberate their fellow Armenians, they managed to also occupy non-Armenian areas in Azerbaijan, such as the 4741-sq-km regions of Lachin, Shusha, Agdam and Kelbajar, which just happen to lie between the Armenians and Nagorno-Karabakh. The fact that there are 131,197-sq-kms of Azerbaijan under foreign occupation has not seemed to interest the world's press, other than to create little sidebars in annual roundups of small wars. Since the Armenians were on a roll, they also cleansed themselves of Kurds. In 1992, after forcing the 25,000 Kurdish residents out of Armenian-occupied areas, the historic Kurdish capital of Lachin was looted and burned. Kurdish monuments, libraries and cultural sites were razed. Armenia has also expelled Kurds in the occupied regions into Iran and what little of Azerbaijan still exists. All told, the war between the Armenians and Azeris has spawned more than 1 million Azeri refugees, 300,000 Armenians, tens of thousands of Kurds and countless other tribal and ethnic factions.

The local Russian Army has been backing both sides, depending upon the financial arrangement or ethnic alignment of the officers. The president of Azerbaijan, Abulfez Elchibey, fled the country on June 18, 1993, leaving the parliament leader—an old Brezhnev-era-former-head-of-the-Azeri-branch-of-the-KGB boss named Heydar Aliyev—to run the show. Technically, the CIS is an autonomous group of independent countries. But they usually go running to mother Russia when there is trouble. The Russian Army has bolstered the scrawny 5000-man Azeri army but has been losing in magnificent form to the Armenians.

Nakhichevan

Alikram Gumbatov and his supporters made a grab for power in seven southern areas of Talysh-Mugan. This area, also known as Nakhichevan, is a minuscule region in southeast Azerbaijan. Shoehorned between Armenia, Iran and Nagorno-Karabakh, it is not surprising that it declared its independence in August of 1993. The Nakhichevan People's Front has not announced when a new McDonalds will open or when postage stamps will go on sale. It remains to be seen whether the Azeris, Armenians or Iranians will remember to set up an embassy.

Dangerous Things

Money Hassles

Azerbaijan is a "cash only" economy. "Traveler's cheques" and credit cards are not accepted. While the local currency is the manat, the Russian ruble is in circulation and prices are often confusingly quoted in manats and rubles. U.S. dollars are required in most hotels and preferred in many restaurants.

Getting Sick

Medical care in Azerbaijan is dangerously limited. There were 40 doctors and 101 hospital beds per 10,000 people before the war. The U.S. embassy maintains a list of English-speaking physicians in the area. There is a severe shortage of basic medical supplies, including disposable needles, anesthetics and vaccines against communicable diseases. Doctors and hospitals often expect immediate cash payment for health services. Some recent health problems include cases of cholera in Baku and cases of anthrax in Nakhichevan. Malaria is found in some southern border areas near Iran.

Nuts and Bolts

The currency is the manat with a hundred gopik to the manat. The port city of Baku is the capital and major business center. It has a population of just over a million and not much else.

Many of Azerbaijan's people live in geographically isolated, ethnically pure pockets of topography, the result of years of wars, migrations and dubious, short-lived peace settlements. The 1828 Russo-Persian carved up a much larger Azerbaijan into two slices. Half went to Persia (about nine million Turkish-speaking Azerbaijanis comprise one-fifth of the Iranian population) and the rest went to Russia.

The country is 87 percent Muslim, 5.6 percent Russian Orthodox and 5.6 percent Armenian Orthodox. The language is Azeri (82 percent) with a smattering of Russian (7 percent) and Armenian (11 percent.) Azerbaijan has the same lousy weather that the rest of Caucasus enjoys: cold in the winter (average January temperature in the plains area is 34 degrees F) and baking in the summer (average 80 degrees F). There's a lot of rain and mud in the spring and fall. The Lenkoran plains area has an average rainfall of between 39 and 68.9 inches. The average annual rainfall in low-lying areas varies between 7.9 and 11.8 inches.

Embassy Location

Prospect Azadling 83
Baku, Azerbaijan
☎ *[7] (8922) 96-36-21, 96-00-19 or 91-79-57 (from outside Azerbaijan)*
☎ *96-36-21 or 96-00-19 (from within the country)*
FAX [7] (8922) 98-37-55.

In a Dangerous Place

Azerbaijan: Burning Down the House

The war had just begun in Azerbaijan. We catch an early morning flight into Baku on a beat-up old *TU-154*. I am with three other journalists and figure we can get past the Russian border guards with a minor bribe. The Aeroflot logo had been crudely painted over, and the plane now is called Azerbaijan Airways. On board are a motley crew: doctors and nurses on their way to the war zone, businessmen looking to set up import-export contracts and men on their way to the cheap sex vacations for which Baku is famous for.

When we arrive, $50 each is all it takes to get our passports stamped. We find a driver outside the airport who will make the 200km trip to Gendje southeast of Baku. This will take us close to the war zone on the Karabakh border. Along the way, we pass hundreds of Russian-made trucks carrying soldiers and tanks. Whatever the Russians had left behind after Azerbaijan declared its independence is now the official property of the Azeris. Despite Gendje's proximity to the war, the only complaint the people seem to have is how the prices had been driven up by the visiting soldiers and short supplies. That night we find another driver who will take us into the war area. We arrive in Agdam by midnight. The road is rough but, the ever increasing checkpoints make the journey tedious at best. The fact that we are Turkish means that we are among friends. Of all the Central Asian Turkic languages, the Azeri's is the closest to that of the Turks. Our arrival in Agdam looks like a Hollywood director's version of a war zone. It seems that every building is in flames or exploding. We are welcomed by a heavy barrage of Katusha rockets. Our driver is a volunteer member of "the Popular Front" and takes us to their local headquarters, a large house in the center of the besieged town. The place is teeming with soldiers and volunteers. They are talking anxiously on Russian-made walkie-talkies, counting, unpacking and distributing weapons for the front, and what makes it all unusual is that they are all speaking Russian. Even the older Azeris are using Russian, though they speak Azeri amongst themselves.

We are given beds on the upper floor of the headquarters. The fact that we are surrounded on all sides by burning buildings doesn't help us get to sleep. When we find out that the headquarters also doubles as the ammunition depot, sleep is soon forgotten. We listen to each explosion to hear if we will be next. We look at what is in the crates that hold up our mattresses and find that they are packed with grenades and rockets. Though we are worried, we fall asleep and wake a few hours later when a large explosion blows up a sawmill outside our window. We get up and walk the 200 meters to the sawmill to take photos. There is not much to photograph and the intense heat keeps us back. When we go back to our room to try to catch up on our sleep we find a clubfooted soldier in there setting up a radio and fiddling with the dial.

Wanting to get to the front to take some photographs, we arrange for two soldiers to take us there in a Russian jeep about 4.5 kms away. We join a tedious parade of trucks carrying ammunition, rations, men and other journalists. We arrive during an artillery barrage. The Azeris are positioned just below the summit of a hill that faces the Armenian position on another hilltop. The equipment they are

AZERBAIJAN

using to fight this war is cast off by the Russians, and it is obvious why they don't take it with them. The volunteers manning the artillery are surprisingly young, about 15 or 16; most of them have little idea of how to properly utilize the decrepit tanks and artillery. I watch the teenagers playing around with the colored rings of the mortar shells. Each ring sends the mortar 100-meters toward the target, but if the kids undo the knots that hold the explosive rings around the narrow tails of the mortar shells, they will go off like Chinese Crackers.

I notice what makes the tanks and artillery look so ridiculous. The Azeris had bent the barrels of the tanks into "S" shapes by improperly loading their tanks. The shortage of skilled soldiers and operational equipment had created a market for entrepreneurs. The Russians had kept their presence in Azerbaijan unofficial, but there is an ominous force that looks markedly different. These are the tanks manned by soldiers for hire. These are Russian soldiers who rent out their tanks for $100 a day; the crew cost $50 extra. The white Russian ID number is covered in mud. The comical part is that the same tank will show up on the opposite side a day or two later and shell their former employers.

We stay in our deadly accommodations, becoming indifferent to the explosions around us, even with the knowledge that we will be instantly atomized if a shell lands on our building. The deaf and clubfooted radio operator never returns, and his radio sits in the corner of our room untouched.

The next day we go to the cemetery to see the fighting that is raging where the Azeri cemetery butts up to the Armenian cemetery. We rent a minibus, and, when we arrive, the fighting is fierce and hand-to-hand. Both sides use the tombstones as cover as they shoot at each other and charge each other's position. We try to capture the fighting, while keeping our heads down behind a cemetery wall.

We are surprised by the arrival of the local Armenian commander. Middle-aged with snow white hair, Allahverdi (which translated means "God given") whips out a megaphone and begins shouting orders to his men in Russian. The fighting stops and one of the soldiers with him explains that he is negotiating for the release of 15 prisoners captured the day before. The Azeris are 250 meters away on the other side of the cemetery. The deal is a tanker full of gas in exchange for the prisoners. The answer comes back: "No. We want a tanker full of gas and 12 hours of electricity." A deal is cut and the prisoners are released the next day. We see the prisoners when they arrive at the headquarters building where we are staying. Most are old; they had their gold teeth yanked out and their toes had been broken when they were tortured. The women had been raped, while the young teenagers seem to be in shock and will not talk. The people who had done this had been their neighbors only 15 days before. Now they are sworn enemies.

We have seen enough. This is a dirty, stupid war. We hitchhike our way back to Gendje. We find a plane flying to Baku and ask the fare. It is the cheapest flight I have ever taken—$1. The plane is another ex-Aeroflot junk heap. We count over 80 passengers, not including goats, chickens and luggage. Just before takeoff, the pilot, mistaking us for Russians, turns to us and says, "For $20, I will fly us all to Moscow. Do you want to go now?" We passed.

—**Coskun Aral**

Bolivia
★

The Lure of Easy Money

Butch Cassidy and the Sundance Kid hung out here. So did other outlaws and bandits. It was a great place to hide, with rugged, inaccessible terrain. Police and the army were easy to pay off to ensure some protection and anonymity. Today, it's much the same.

Bolivia is undoubtedly the poorest country in South America with a per-capita annual income of a little over US$870. That's the official figure. If you include the amount thousands are making picking coca leaves, chewing coca leaves and turning them into white powder, then moving it to North America to be tooted, toked and mainlined by high school kids, gold-encased ghetto gangsters, sleazy Hollywood movie moguls and a few million decent people who've gotten caught up in a bad thing, then you'll see a huge number of wealthy Bolivians.

In the 1980s, Bolivia's economy took a nosedive. Surging unemployment (nearly 20 percent) forced a large segment of the population into the drug trade, and coca was an easy cash crop. Four yields can be harvested a year. It's easier to

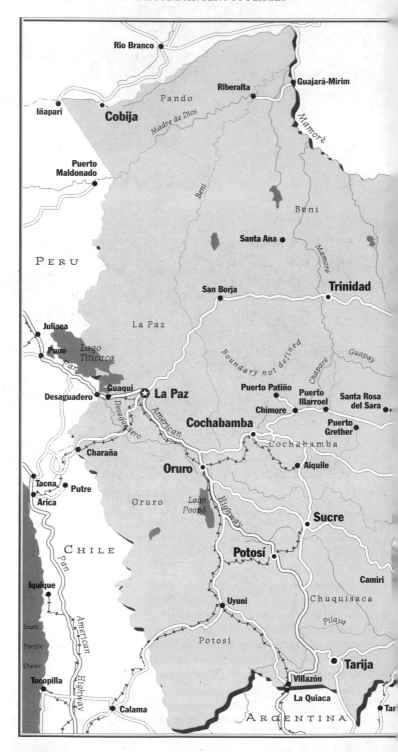

Bolivia

⊗ National capital
● Department capital
Department border
Road
Railroad

0   50   100 150 200 km
0   50   100   150 mi

©FWI

grow than grass. Bolivia's cocaine industry is a US$2 billion-a-year business. Who wants to go back to slashing sugar cane and picking cotton? Throw in a virtually lawless and uninhabitable topography along with a turbulent political history rooted in racial, ethnic and geographic strife, and you've got the fodder for rock'n' roll anthems. Not to mention a lot of death.

What else would you expect from the land of Ché?

Bolivia was sliced up and much of it divided among three neighboring countries. Bolivia lost several thousand square miles, and its outlet to the Pacific, to Chile, after the War of the Pacific in 1884. Brazil annexed Bolivia's rubber-rich province in 1903. In 1938, after a war between those two countries, nearly 100,000 square miles of the Gran Chaco was swallowed up by Paraguay.

Then in 1965, Ché (Ernesto) Guevara was dispatched from Cuba by Papa Fidel—not wanting to miss an opportunity to start an insurrection—to the revolutionary-fertile soil of Bolivia to off some fascists, wreak havoc and recruit anyone with a pop gun. The CIA—not one to miss an opportunity to quell an insurrection—smashed Ché's little red tag sale and executed the guerrilla on October 9, 1967.

Bolivia took a serpentine course toward democracy, but an attempt at a civilian government was quickly squelched in 1980 when despot General Luis Garcia Meza Tejada wrested power. In 1982, the military moved to restore civilian rule to Bolivia, after a succession of cigar-chomping generals followed Tejada. However, under President Hernán Siles Zuazo's rule, the country became paralyzed by strikes and work stoppages, including the processing of the nation's natural resources, such as gold, natural gas, lithium, tungsten and potassium. Inflation soared to 3000 percent. Enter the coca leaf.

The Scoop

Bolivia is a recovering country, its economy improving at a snail's pace. Although inflation has come down to 10–20 percent, unemployment continues at alarming rates, making tourists the frequent targets of petty crime, particularly in La Paz. Bolivia's acute poverty problem, along with widespread corruption, continues to create unrest. Although terrorist incidents are infrequent in comparison with Andean neighbors of Chile, Peru and Colombia, it should be noted that U.S citizens are the primary targets of Bolivian terrorist groups.

The Players

Nestor Paz Zamora Commission (CNPZ)

A radical leftist terrorist organization that first appeared in October 1990. It is named after the deceased brother of President Paz Zamora. It currently operates under the umbrella of the ELN (Bolivia) and is a violent, extremely anti-U.S., Marxist-Leninist organization. In June 1990, the Bolivian owner of the La Paz Coca-Cola Bottling Company was kidnapped by the CNPZ while he was being driven to work in downtown La Paz. The victim was murdered by his captors on December 5, 1990, during a rescue attempt by Bolivian police. In October 1990, the group attacked the residence of the U.S. embassy's marine security guard detachment in La Paz with automatic weapons and explosives. One Bolivian police officer standing guard at the marine house was killed and another officer was seriously wounded. None of the marines were injured. The same month, the CNPZ bombed a monument to U.S. President John F. Kennedy in La Paz. Today, the group is probably operating with fewer than 100 guerrillas. Peru's MTRA (Tupac Amaru) has provided training, limited funding and logistic support.

Getting In

A passport is required. U.S. citizens do not need a visa for a one-month stay. For current information concerning entry and customs requirements for Bolivia, travelers can contact the Bolivian Embassy (see below), or the nearest consulate in Los Angeles, Miami, New York or Houston.

Bolivian Embassy
3014 Massachusetts Avenue NW
Washington, D.C. 20008
☎ *(202) 483-4410*

Dangerous Places

Santa Cruz and Vicinity

A number of major narco-traffickers consider Santa Cruz their home. Crime in Santa Cruz is both more prevalent and more violent than in any other Bolivian city. Armed robbery has become commonplace in certain areas, and taxi drivers have even been murdered for their money. Vehicles traveling from Paraguay to Santa Cruz have been robbed by armed bandits. Large amounts of cocaine are smuggled out of both Santa Cruz and Cochabamba. Various sectors of Santa Cruz, Cochabamba and Beni regions are under the control of narco-traffickers.

Cochabamba and Vicinity

There are ongoing clashes between farmers and police, as the farmers try to prevent the government from destroying coca areas. The U.S. government demands that a certain percentage of coca acreage must be destroyed to avoid sanctions. The central region of Cochabamba possesses about 79,000 of Peru's 114,000 acres of coca plantations.

There has been a perceptible shift in public opinion and a rise in anti-American sentiment in Cochabamba over the last two years. These changes can be explained by drug-related interests having acquired access to mass media and leftist politicians having begun to organize the coca leaf growers. Furthermore, there is growing evidence of radical leftists linking up with the coca growers. As the COB (Bolivian Workers Central) membership has dwindled (due to layoffs in the miners' and factory workers' unions), radical organizers and union leaders increasingly organize and advise the coca growers. Leftist university students have consistently demonstrated in support of coca growers' demands. Between 1987 and 1988, Cochabamba businessmen were being kidnapped for varying periods of time and later released after paying substantial ransoms. The criminals responsible for these kidnappings have been imprisoned, and no other kidnappings have been reported since then. As far as drug-related violence is concerned, the press recently reported the forcible break-in to the house of a former Bolivian police colonel. Aside from that, all residents and foreign visitors are vulnerable to purse snatching and pilfering of objects. Burglaries are common, and there are continual reports of wallets and documentation being stolen at bus terminals, airports and hotels. Pickpockets are common in the open-air markets.

Dangerous Things

Street Crime

Street crime, such as pickpocketing and theft from parked vehicles, is common. Violent crimes or crimes involving weapons are rare, especially in La Paz, although there are indications of an increased incidence of such crimes in Santa Cruz. In downtown La Paz and the Calacoto region most frequented by Americans, crime consists of pickpocketing, vehicular break-ins and burglary. Robbery, assault and other violent crimes are almost unheard of in these areas. In the poorer areas of the city, especially the sprawling suburbs of El Alto, assault, rape and robbery are much more common. Americans are cautioned against staying in these areas at night.

Civil Disorder and Terrorism

All terrorist acts directed against U.S. citizens over the last five years have occurred in La Paz. Terrorist incidents are infrequent in comparison with the Andean neighbors of Chile, Peru and Colombia. U.S citizens are the primary targets of Bolivian terrorist groups. Of the Americans targeted, those at most risk are the ambassador, members of the military and DEA personnel. Some local employees have also been subject to harassment. U.S. corporations are also at risk, although not as often targeted as higher-profile U.S. government personnel. There have been isolated terrorist incidents against American officials, installations and resident missionaries.

There have been numerous bomb placements and bomb threats throughout La Paz. The La Paz bomb squad receives an average of three bomb threats a day. The great majority of these threats are false; however, a dozen or so bombs have been found throughout La Paz's commercial centers and three were found at the La Paz airport. To date, no one has been killed or wounded by a bomb blast. Demonstrations or strikes occur on an almost weekly basis in La Paz. The majority of these demonstrations are peaceful and not anti-U.S. in nature. All travelers are cautioned to stay away from these marches, due to the frequent detonation of small dynamite charges and rockets by protesters. For the most part, tourists and business travelers are not targeted in terrorist acts or civil disorders.

Bogus Cops

Bolivian law holds that police may only search your belongings at a police station. If you are asked to be searched, demand to be taken to a police station. If you're detained by an individual in plain clothes claiming to be a cop, insist on seeing an identity card or badge and note the date on it. There are numerous instances of tourists being robbed by bandits posing as police officers, particularly in La Paz and Sucre. If you are robbed, go to the nearest Departamento de Criminalistica.

Hassles with Police

There is police resentment in some Bolivian cities and towns toward Americans because of U.S. involvement in Bolivia's drug eradication efforts. Some police officers don't appreciate gringos messing with Bolivia's internal affairs. Their animosity may be taken out on you—not violently, but in the form of laxadaisical assistance.

Drugs

In the land of the coca plant, it takes a lot of persuasion to switch to something like bananas or pineapples. Farmers in the Chapare region are being paid $1000 an acre to dig up their coca bushes and eke out a legal living. The deterrent is that farmers can harvest up to four crops of coca a year and they have their crop sold before they plant it. Naturally, more coca is planted every year.

Extortion

There is an increase in extortions against visitors and foreign tourists by Bolivian government officials. Typically, Bolivian males who identify themselves as immigration or customs officers will extort US$10–20 from tourists who have not "registered" their video cameras or other equipment in their passports. Routinely, tourists are forced to pay bribes to expedite the issuance of visas or other permits by Bolivian government agencies.

Narcotics Activities

Because of antinarcotics activities in the Chapare region between Santa Cruz and Cochabamba, the potential for security risks exists here. Travelers to this area should consult with the consular section of the U.S. embassy prior to travel.

Demonstrations

La Paz and other cities have been the scene of frequent demonstrations by various local groups. Although there has been no violence specifically directed at foreigners during these demonstrations, there are occasional confrontations between police and demonstrators.

Getting Sick

Cholera is present in Bolivia. Visitors who follow proper precautions about food and drink are not usually at risk. For additional health information and information on high-altitude travel, travelers may contact the Centers for Disease Control's international travelers hotline at ☎ *(404) 332-4559.*

Nuts and Bolts

The country is about the size of California and Texas combined. It's bordered by Chile and Peru to the west, and by Paraguay and Argentina to the south. The western part of Bolivia is a great plateau—the *altiplano*, enclosed by two chains of the Andes—with an average altitude of 12,000 feet (3658 meters). The area is home to 80 percent of the population as well as the administrative capital of La Paz. Lake Titicaca, at 3812 meters, is one of the largest high lakes in the world. Ancient Inca ruins can be found on islands in the lake. The eastern portion of the country is a low alluvial plain drained by the Amazon and Plata river systems.

The principal language is Spanish; however, Quechua and Aymara are widely spoken. Roman Catholics comprise 95 percent of the country. The monetary unit is the boliviano (Bs). It's divided into 100 centavos. The local time is four hours behind GMT.

Business hours are normally between 9 a.m. and 12 p.m. (11:30 a.m. in La Paz) and between 2 p.m. and 6 p.m. Monday–Friday; 9 a.m.–noon on Saturdays. In the provinces, businesses generally open and close later. Banks are open from 9 a.m. to noon Monday–Friday and closed on Saturdays. Government offices are open during normal business hours but are closed Saturdays.

The best time of the year to visit Bolivia is during the dry season from May to November. Keep in mind, however, that May, June and July are the coldest months.

Embassy Location

Americans who register with the consular section of the U.S. embassy in La Paz, located one block from the Embassy on the second floor of the Tobia building on Calle Potosi near the corner with Calle Colon, ☎ *[591] (2) 356-685*, can obtain updated information on travel and security within Bolivia.

U.S. Embassy

Avenida Arce No. 2780
San Jorge
☎ *[591] (2) 430-251*
FAX [591] (2) 433-560

Consular Agents

In Santa Cruz:

Marilyn J. McKenney (acting)
in the Edificio Oriente
on Calle Bolivian, corner of Chuquisaca,
Room 313
☎ *[591] (2) 33-30725 (office)*
☎ *[591] (2) 33-23467 (home)*

In Cochabamba:

William Scarborough
1724 Libertador Bolivar Avenue
☎ *[591] (2) 42-43216 (office)*
☎ *[591] (2) 42-44775 (home)*

The consular agencies are open mornings Monday through Friday.

Important Phone Numbers:

Banco Popular Del Peru Building

Calle Colon No. 280
(Corner of Calle Mercado)
La Paz
☎ *[591] (2) 350-120 Or 350-251*

Comando General de La Policia Boliviana
☎ *[591] (2) 378-280*

Dangerous Days

07/04/1991   The Tupac Katari Guerrilla Army (EGTK) carried out its first terrorist act—blowing up two electric power pylons in the city of El Alto—on this date.

Sarajevo

Bosnia-Herzegovina
★ ★

See No Evil

Yugoslavia had been bound by the big bear hug of Tito for more than 45 years, but now it is a crazed blender of religious and ethnic groups forced to live together—all harboring long-standing grudges that go back to the Middle Ages.

The Western world, determined to believe they had made Europe safe, refused to admit the truth. During World War II and the Cold War, Europeans showed that not only could they make watches, cars and clothing, but could kill boys and old men with sickening cruelty. The U.N. sat by and watched Serbs methodically separate the men from the women and calmly noted in memos that there weren't as many refugees as they expected. Bosnia is about cruel death, missing people and deja vu.

Bosnia-Herzegovina is not one country, but two regions glued together. Without "Big Brother" around to settle disputes, the country erupted into a land grab for independence. The Serb minority called up the Serbian-run Yugoslav Peoples Army to wage an old-fashioned blood feud. The Muslims, located primarily in

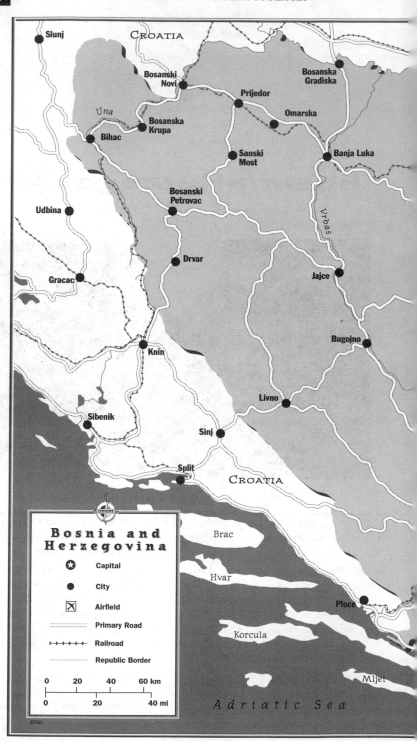

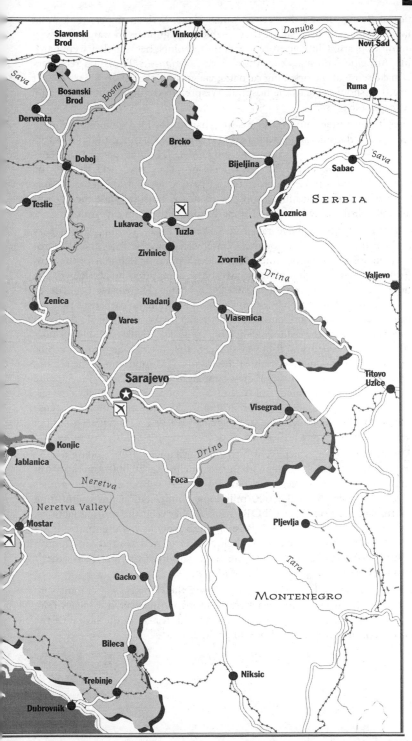

the cities of Bosnia, found themselves under siege. Serbian snipers took great pride in gut shots over head shots; they enabled the gunners to watch their victims squirm to death. Children were worth more points, because they were harder to hit. Atrocities and mass executions were *de rigueur*. Television reporters tried to make sense of the sickening carnage; viewers watched shoppers try to sort which leg they should take to the hospital. We preferred "Beavis and Butthead." At least that made sense.

The foes in this bitter conflict aren't sure what to do. Like siblings arguing at the table, they hurl insults and do disgusting things to each other until NATO arrives and holds them apart, still swearing and kicking. Hardly repentant, the enemies don't quite know how to kiss and make up. They never will, despite the U.S.-brokered Dayton peace accords. In the past, when outside peace brokers force the foes to suspend hostilities and discuss peace, both sides use the "downtime" to grab a little more land, and the Serbs did a little ethnic cleansing.

High in the mountains above tattered Sarajevo, once—seemingly in a fairy tale—the pristine, majestic site of the Winter Olympics, is Pale, the self proclaimed capital of the self-proclaimed Republika Srpska, or Republic of the Bosnian Serbians. Even though atrocities have been committed by all sides in the war, the Serbs have been getting most of the blame. There have been death camps run by the Serbs, examples of savagery and systematic barbarism that haven't been seen on the continent since the Nazis of World War II. Radovan Karadzic's Serbs, under the military leadership of Ratko Mladic, strangled Sarajevo's 300,000 or so residents for four years. The Serbs, in 1992, began their ethnic cleansing campaign, forcing hundreds of thousands of Muslims out of the region. Thousands died in the Drina River Valley campaigns of 1992 and 1993. Satellite photos of large bulldozed patches of earth where young Bosnian men were last seen provide haunting evidence that something was very wrong. Survivors accuse Mladic of personally attending some of the genocide sessions, and it's a good bet he'll face war crimes charges if the current peace in Bosnia holds.

The Dayton peace plan, which went into effect in January 1996 (calling for the stationing of 60,000 NATO troops in Bosnia, including 20,000 American soldiers), has been a relative success. On January 19, 1996, Bosnia's various armies pulled back 2.5 miles from the 600-mile-long confrontation line, permitting NATO's Implementation Force (IFOR) to move between the warring factions. The Dayton accord requires that the Bosnian Serb army leave the suburbs of Sarajevo; the Bosnian Croats have to cede their NATO air-raid-assisted conquests in the country's northwest. The armies were then permitted to enter each other's evacuated territories during the middle of March.

Muslims are forbidden by Serbs from reentering their homes, war criminals go on with their daily business, and bleached skeletons are uncovered by heavy rain. Land mines lurk in the dark woods, and hatred still festers in the hearts of the combatants. Nothing has changed or will change.

Sniper Alley: Rapid Transit in Sarajevo

The streetcars in Sarajevo may be old, but they were never dull. They were shut down by shelling when war broke out in April 1992. The tram system reopened in March 1994, after a local cease-fire ended the daily bombardment of Sarajevo. The trams became a daily target for Serbian snipers. They travel only 300 meters from Grbavica, a Serb-held district where snipers fire from high-rise apartment buildings. But they're a healthier alternative to running or walking the same distance. U.N.anti-sniper teams were deployed along the tram line and fire back to deter the shooters. The line's most dangerous stretch passed between the Bosnian parliament building and the Holiday Inn, a base for foreign diplomats and journalists.

The Scoop

Balkanization is the term used to describe "insurmountable factionalism." Starting in 1991, war in Yugoslavia spread like a cancer from the northwest to the southeast when Croatia and Slovenia declared independence. The Croats and the Serbian residents wanted to whack each other before they got whacked first. The rest is history and bad ratings. We have eaten our TV dinners to the images of children murdered, concentration camps, atrocities and sniper-stricken Sunday shoppers sliding around in their own blood. Most politicians don't remember much Balkan history, but some recall that this region has been the cornerstone of many a European conflict as well as World War I. Bill, John, Helmut and Boris didn't want to be remembered as the next Neville Chamberlain. So, they left the dirty work to the world's lowest-paid referees: the U.N. The U.N. acted like a chaperon at a high school dance, scolding, but turning its back when the kids started goosing each other. There were some get-tough NATO air strikes on Serb positions in 1995, and they gave the Croats a chance to grab some quick acreage while the Serbs ducked down in their bunkers. Thus, the way was opened for the Dayton peace accords.

This conflict has been a less glamorous version of the last great noble war: the Spanish Civil War. Mercs and volunteers from Great Britain, Russia, Iran, Iraq, Afghanistan, Egypt, Turkey, Canada, Greece and the U.S. have all put some time in fighting the good fight until they realized there was little goodness and even less money. War photographers, who initially covered Bosnia like flies on dog dung, jumped for joy when editors shipped them off to cover Somalia and Haiti—where there was more sun and they didn't have to get so damn muddy. A stupid war of greed, egos and hatred is in its umpteenth peace agreement with U.S. troops acting as cops again. For the next half year, the precarious peace will be kept by 60,000 international soldiers, including 20,000 Americans.

Just how shattered is Bosnia? By late-1996, about 210,000 people had been killed in this dirty little war, more than 200,000 wounded and some 2.2 million made refugees. Nearly 20 percent of Bosnia's homes have been destroyed and half of its schools. Forty percent of the country's bridges have been demolished. Big deal; you can't get to them anyway—a third of Bosnia's roads have been wiped out.

The Players

From a straight military perspective, the Bosnian army wouldn't have had a prayer against the Serbs had Uncle Sam, NATO and Croats not fired a few well-aimed rockets and taken a few key hectares of real estate. If the foreigners had stayed out, the Serbs would have run through the country. For those who want just the short version, it's the Serbs (Yugoslavs, Krajina Serbs, Bosnian Serbs and various renegade factions) against the Croatian-Muslims (Croatians, Bosnian-Croats and the Bosnian Government).

The Bosnians

Bosnia is really a a group of enclaves and pockets that have yet to be put under one administrative body. President Alija Izetbegovic runs the remaining pieces, about one-sixth of the actual country. Bosnia is a Muslim-dominated country with a very diverse group of residents: Bosnia-Herzegovinians, Bosnian Muslims, Bosnian Serbs and Bosnian Croats. At the rate they flee from the Serbs and Croats, it is hard to tell who is where anymore. The northwest part of Bosnia was scrubbed clean of Bosnian Muslims by the Serbs, who now make up most of the Seventh Corps. The Bosnian army has about 150,000 troops and vastly outnumbers the 64,000-man Bosnian Serb army. The Croats only have only 175 tanks to the Serbs 400, and 400 artillery pieces to the Serbs 500. Before IFOR came in, the Serbs could have tipped the scales totally if they had brought in the Yugoslav army with its 150,000 soldiers, 300 tanks and 800 artillery pieces. The Bosnian army is ill-trained, poorly paid (the average combat pay for a soldier is about $50 a month) and inadequately supplied. The Bosnians began this war with beat-up tennis shoes and hunting rifles against what was essentially the old Yugoslavian army. The Bosnian army, primarily Muslim, is outgunned and poorly trained. Their alliance with the Croatian army, as well as NATO airstrikes, finally brought the Serbs to Dayton.

The Croats

Croatia is the country to the north and west of Bosnia, comprised of 78.1 percent Croats. The Croatians confuse most Sunday paper readers, as the Serbs in the country (12.2 percent) are also called Krajina Serbs and are allied with the Bosnian Serbs. Many Krajina Serbs fled to Serb-held parts of Bosnia when the Croat army took back the Krajina area. The leader of the Croatian Serbs is Milan Martic.

The Croats also possess about a sixth of the territory inside Bosnia itself (about as much as the Bosnians themselves). The Croats hate the Serbs, and their relatively large and well-trained army has been fighting alongside the Bosnian army. They would be more than happy to kick the Serbs all the way to Russia if they could get away with it. Although the Croats are allied with the Bosnians, old-timers can't forget the Bosnians cleansing Muslims from Herzegovina in 1993.

The Croats possess an impressive military prowess: There are 115,000 regular soldiers, 175 tanks, 605 armored vehicles and 605 artillery pieces. It's thought that the Croats have brought into the war more than US$1 billion worth of weapons. The country's once dismally small airforce of three planes has been expanded to more than 40 since 1991. The Croats have been purchasing weapons from Russia and Eastern European countries through brokers and then shipping them from Hungary to get past the arms embargo.

Arms destined for the Muslims in Bosnia have also been shipped via Croatia, which pockets a healthy 40 percent "shipping and handling" charge. The Adriatic island of Kirk in Croatia has been utilized as the primary base for flights arriving with arms. In August 1993, the government had a hard time explaining why an Air Iran Boeing 747 showed up one day, considering there hadn't been a tourist charter to the Adriatic coast since 1991.

Croat-Muslims

Croatians and the mostly Muslim Bosnians, who comprise about 78 percent of Bosnia's population, formed an alliance with the Bosnian government to counter the Serb juggernaut. The group has tended to elicit sympathy from both the West and the Islamic world, but still generally get its ass kicked on the battlefield. Muslims have been supported by Iranian-backed *mujahedin* and Hezbollah fighters, as well as mercenaries and volunteers from a number of countries.

The Serbs

The bad guys. But, then again, 400 years of cruel occupation by the Turks would make anybody slightly ornery. The Serbs were supposed to mind their own business in Serbia to the east, but couldn't resist slamming an axe on a slow snake.

Under the guise of helping the Bosnian Serbs, Serbia created a brutal war of siege, torture, mass execution and deceit. The Serbs have made fools of the international community and the U.N. They had their hands slapped through token NATO air strikes. They continued to expand their control of Bosnia's Muslim regions and to lay siege on Sarajevo up until the Dayton accords. The Serbs controlled about a third of Croatia and two-thirds of Bosnia until the peace agreement. They have been rousted by Croats, showing that a bully always runs when you punch him in the nose. Their eternally pissed-off military leader, General Ratko Mladic, was in the hospital with kidney problems during their recent retreat. Their self-proclaimed Bosnian Serb republic is a transparent land grab, and the ethnic cleansing is good old medieval warfare at its finest. The Radovan and Ratko Show is fighting to create a country called Greater Serbia that would establish a Serbian state in Bosnia connected to Yugoslavia.

General Ratko Mladik

The Serb rebel commander and indicted war criminal. Ruthless, but loved by his soldiers. Has said that only an army that is defeated retreats. "Smash, don't sprinkle!" he proclaims. Although President Radovan Karadzic is theoretically in charge, Mladik calls the shots on the ground, where most of the "peace process" has traditionally taken place. He eats and sleeps with his soldiers, and leads them into combat in an armored personnel carrier. He has a lot of deadly toys that formerly belonged to the Yugoslav army. When things got slow among the regulars, his army practiced gunnery on the innocents in Sarajevo, a hobby that finally got him bombed by NATO planes. Despite Mladik's threat to send terrorist bombers to London and New York if his troops were to be bombed by NATO, he seems to be content killing old men, women and children. He may take his job too seriously, as he's been fingered as being present during mass executions of Muslims.

President Radovan Karadzic

Radovan Karadzic is a former psychiatrist turned indicted war criminal who is the self-proclaimed Bosnia Serb president of the self-proclaimed Bosnian Serb government, of the self-proclaimed country of Republika Srpska. He works out of a truck factory in the self-proclaimed capital of the self-proclaimed country. He even has a television show called: "Ask the President." Shouldn't it be called "Ask the self-proclaimed president"?

Although technically we (or the United Nations) are supposed to run right up to the truck factory and slap handcuffs on him, nobody wants to make the first move. To make matters worse, not only can you watch Karadzic on TV, but the IFOR folks are just down the road and know where he goes on a daily basis.

The U.N.

Bosnia has been the worst PR disaster in the U.N.'s history. Ineffective, insulted and frustrated, U.N. troops watched as the Serbs mercilessly pounded safe havens, as well as their own soldiers. U.N. forces have been the frequent targets of Serb snipers and other attacks.

NATO

Thank God the Soviets never rolled into Germany. NATO is military bureaucracy at its most intricate. In order to launch an air strike, it takes a green light from local U.N. commanders, NATO commanders and their boss in New York. When the jet fighters finally got busy in late August 1995, they discovered the Serbs like to keep artillery in hospitals, schools and village squares. Nonetheless, more than 100 warplanes and U.N. artillery took out fuel dumps, missile sites, communications centers and command sites. It worked. The old adage that bullies only understand force played out. The strikes sent the Serbs to the peace table in an effort to buy time and plot their next move.

The "Afghans"

About 1000 veterans of the war in Afghanistan against the Russians found their way into the Bosnian conflict—and nearly all have found their way back out again as NATO forces have shooed them away, as well as other mercenary forces. As things heat up, they'll be back. About 100 still remain.

Mercenaries/Volunteers

Some countries such as Iran view the Bosnian conflict as a Muslim-Christian thing and have sent in *mujahedin* guerrillas and members of Hezbollah. Others see it as a Serb-Croat fight, and volunteers from the U.S., Canada and Europe came in to take some pot-shots. Still others simply see Bosnia-Herzegovina as a great place to kill someone. For now, most of the mercs have gone home.

Tito

Tito went to the Great Socialist Republic in the Sky in 1980, and that was the last the world saw of Yugoslav unity. His hard-line policies kept the six republics together for 35 years. Tito was half-Slav, half-Croat and forced the Serbs into submission by splitting them and scattering them over five of the six republics.

Getting In

A passport is required. Permission to enter Bosnia has been granted at the border on a case-by-case basis. Journalists have a decent chance, but it's not as easy as it was when the U.N. had some say in the matter. It's best to make prior arrangements, illicitly or otherwise.

Getting Around

Journalists were the only ones trying during the war and are the only ones trying these days—and they need APC's to do it. Sygma, one of the world's top photo news agencies, acquired an armored personnel carrier in 1993 to protect its under-fire shooters in Bosnia, and to get them around. However, there isn't yet regularly scheduled armored personnel carrier service in Bosnia. Women journalists seem to be better able to get around in Bosnia than their male counterparts. Alain Mingmam, editorial manager of Sygma's Paris office, said that women were preferable to men in many instances because they'll go "where no man will ever go."

Their checkpoints throughout the country which were manned generally by militia personnel, but occasionally by undisciplined, untrained reserve militia groups are now in NATO hands. The militia groups frequently confiscated relief goods and trucks, and otherwise behaved unprofessionally. Although these guys have largely scattered back into the woods, they return from time to time to detain and rob Muslims and other unluckies. Travelers are expected to provide identification and cooperate fully at all checkpoints, whether they're manned by IFOR or others. Travelers should refrain from photographing police, buildings under police or military guard, border crossings, demonstrations, riots, and military personnel, convoys, maneuvers and bases.

Dangerous Places

The Entire Country

The civil war has completely ruined the tourist industry in Bosnia-Herzegovina. The cultural heritage of Bosnia's Muslim cities is no longer accessible. The fighting between the Serbs and the Croats has created massive social and economic problems, including mass homelessness and chronic unemployment. All plans for modernization and industrial growth have been shelved for at least the next decade.

Eastern Bosnia and Sarajevo

Travel to eastern Bosnia and the capital city of Sarajevo is particularly dangerous. The popular religious shrine at Medjugorje is located within Bosnia-Herzegovina's borders, but not a lot of tourists get a chance to see it these days.

Eastern Slovenia

A soon-to-be dangerous place that's not even in Bosnia-Herzegovina. Eastern Slovenia is not the place in the Lil' Abner cartoon strip, but instead the eastern sliver of acreage the Serbs stole from Croatia and then displaced all but ethnic Serbs to. Croatia's President Franjo Tudjman wants it back, and if he doesn't get it diplomatically, he'll fire up his battle wagons and try to kick some ass.

Kirk Island

Watch your step in this region. It is a major smuggling point for weapons and personnel from Muslim countries to the Muslim fighters in Bosnia. Iranian transport aircraft used the airport during the war to fly in shipments of small arms and equipment. Kirk Island is about 75 miles west of Zagreb, the Croatian capital.

Dangerous Things

Peace

The current plan is to slice Bosnia into a 51 percent Muslim Croat federation and a Bosnian Serb entity that will control the remaining 49 percent. IFOR has had to play cop. Minesweeping has been a terror for IFOR deminers. The country is littered with land mines.

Crime

General lawlessness and deteriorating economic conditions have brought an increase in crime. Adequate police response in the event of an emergency is doubtful. Murder has increased dramatically with many incidents in broad daylight and some at popular public places. Crime has increased markedly in the cities, particularly near railroad and bus stations and on trains. The possession of firearms has proliferated greatly. Effective police protection is almost nonexistent.

Being an American

Anti-American sentiments run high in many parts of the country, particularly in Serb-dominated areas.

Getting Sick

Health facilities are minimal or nonexistent. Many medicines and basic medical supplies as well as X-ray film often are unavailable. Hospitals usually require payment in hard currency for all services.

Nuts and Bolts

Bosnia-Herzegovina declared its independence from the former Yugoslavia in October 1991 and was subsequently invaded by the Federal Army, comprised primarily of Serbs. Bosnia is bordered by Serbia to the east, Croatia to the north and west, and Montenegro to the south.

The official language is Serbo-Croat, or Bosnian, written in Latin and Cyrillic. Ethnically, Bosnian Muslims comprise 44 percent of the population; Serbs, 31 percent; and Croats, 17 percent. Religiously, Slavic Muslims make up 40 percent of the population; Orthodox, 31 percent; Catholics, 15 percent; and Protestants, 4 percent.

The monetary unit is the dinar, with 100 paras to the dinar. It is impossible to use credit cards or to cash traveler's checks. German deutsche marks are the currency of favor at present.

The small coastal area of Bosnia enjoys a mild, Mediterranean climate with a mean temperature of 80° F in summer. The interior has a moderate, continental climate with warm summers and frigid winters.

Embassy Location

The U.S. embassy in Sarajevo opened in July 1994, but due to extremely limited staffing, the embassy is unable to provide consular services, except in extreme emergencies. U.S. citizens seeking assistance while in Bosnia can contact the U.S. embassies in Belgrade or Zagreb. The U.S. embassy in Belgrade has a limited ability to assist, however, because of conflict in the area, lack of communications and reduced embassy staffing. Both embassies are expected to beef up their staffs with the implementation of the Dayton accords.

The U.S. Embassy

Djure Djakovica 43
Sarajevo, Republic of Bosnia and Herzegovina
☎ *[387] (71) 659-992*

When no personnel are in Sarajevo, U.S. officials accredited to the Government of Bosnia and Herzegovina will be available in Vienna, where they have resided since the establishment of relations between the Government of Bosnia and Herzegovina and the United States. They cannot provide consular services in Vienna.

U.S. Embassy Vienna

Boltzmanngasse 16
Vienna, Austria
☎ *[43] (1) 31-339, extension 2173*
FAX [43] (1) 310-0682.

U.S. Embassy

Kneza Milosa 50
Belgrade, Serbia
☎ *[381] (11) 645-655*

U.S. Embassy

Andrije Hebranga 2
Zagreb, Croatia
☎ *[385] (41) 456-000*

Dangerous Days

01/1996	Dayton peace accords went into effect.
05/01–02	May Day
07/04	Fighter's Day
09/06/1994	Pope cancelled visit.
11/29–30/ 1991	Day of the Republic (Nov. 29–30)

In a Dangerous Place

Bosnia: Tea Before Mortars

It is odd for me to have to cover a war in Europe. I leave Paris with my ears full of the noise made by the French about the need to preserve Dubrovnik's architectural marvels. Nobody seems to care for the Serbs and the Croats, but talk about the ancient city of Dubrovnik and everybody yells about how it belongs to mankind's culture and should be preserved at all costs.

I spend only a week in Yugoslavia, enough to see a horrible war. In Belgrade everything seems normal. Then things start to change as we approach the frontier with Hungary in Zagreb and even more in Ossiek.

I travel to the war with a friend, American journalist Chris Morris. He takes me in his car to Vukovar. We spend three days there amidst the battles. We meet a Canadian mercenary known only as John, the commander of the place. That's one of the features of this war: There are lots of mercenaries. John is a Croatian by origin and commands the Croats.

Our biggest fear is the number of snipers here. John brings us to a mortar position. It is teatime first; after tea the bombing of the Serbs' position resumes, followed by an offensive with mortars made in Germany. The night comes. The situation becomes hellish. It is like the end of the world. We spend three nights in cellars with a Croatian family. The son keeps entertaining his girlfriend who lives nearby, through a walkie-talkie. The girl asks him to give her some cassettes to play on her walkman. The boy turns toward me and I agree to lend him two cassettes. He then proceeds to walk out in the middle of the night under the bombs, but does not come back. Everybody starts worrying. Some people go out to look for him, but they do not come back either.

The next morning we are awakened by shouting and loud sobs. We leave the cellar and there they are—dead bodies. I recognize the boy to whom I had loaned the tapes, and not far from him lies the headless body of his girlfriend. Her head had rolled away after it had been chopped off, either by shrapnel or by some other means.

We leave Vukovar to go to Ossiek. We see prisoners. Lots of them are to be executed.

We receive the news a few hours after our departure that Vukovar has just fallen. There is no story here, just killing and atrocities. The news magazines aren't interested in running more dull grey shots of people being killed.

—Coskun Aral

BOSNIA-HERZEGOVINA

BOSNIA-HERZEGOVINA

Bujumbura

Burundi

★★★★★

The "Problem"

Each day at nightfall in Burundi's capital of Bujumbura the streets are empty. Grenade blasts (grenades can be had for a mere US$7) and machine-gun fire from both the city and the surrounding hills, shatter the night silence. Occasionally, there is screaming and crying. The impression is suddenly being caught in the middle of an invasion. Then, in the morning, it is calm. You're surprised to discover that corpses do not litter the streets. There is little, if any, evidence of fighting. When inquiring among locals the cause of the evening's disturbance, you will be answered with two words: "Burundi's problem."

Burundi—which suffers the geographic misfortune of being Rwanda's closest neighbor—has never quite been the same since enduring one of Africa's worst tribal wars in 1972. War is not the right word. Genocide fits better. It all happened after King Ntaré V returned in April of that year. Usually, when the president of the country promises safe conduct to a returning monarch, the chances are pretty good the red carpet will be rolled out. Well, that wasn't exactly what

145

Burundi President Michel Micombero had in mind for the return of the man he overthrew. Not even a party. No sooner had Ntaré V stepped off the plane than he was judged and executed by Micombero. Hell of a homecoming. What happened afterward defies explanation.

Thousands of invading exiled Hutus attending Ntare V's return to Burundi were slaughtered by the rival Tutsis. But the Tutsis didn't stop there. Over the next eight weeks, nearly a quarter of a million native Burundi Hutus were massacred by the Tutsis. The genocide was followed by coup after coup after coup, until Burundi's first democratically elected leader, Melchior Ndadaye, assumed the presidency in June 1993. All's well that ends well? Hardly.

Tutsi paratroops overthrew Hutu President Ndadaye on October 21, 1993, abruptly ending the three-month experiment with democracy in the central African state. The predawn coup was led by Army Chief of Staff Colonel Jean Bikomagu and former President Jean Baptiste Bagaza, who was himself overthrown in 1987. The paratroops arrested Ndadaye and detained him at the Muha barracks on the outskirts of the capital city of Bujumbura before executing him. The coup was the fifth since the country's independence in 1962, and led to unprecedented violence and death in that year of Burundi's history. More than 200,000 deaths were caused by the unrest, equaling if not exceeding the casualties that occurred in the 1972 genocide that swept the country. Tribal massacres drove nearly a million Burundians into neighboring countries to escape the slaughter.

The coup collapsed, but it hardly made any difference. Burundi had already collapsed. Ethnic fighting between the Hutu tribe, which Ndadye came from, and the minority Tutsis, who controlled the military and have dominated politics for generations, continued to ravage the country. Pictures revealed hundreds of bodies, devastated towns, destroyed farms and a countryside that had been set on fire. Corpses littered the countryside, after the army stood by and watched as Tutsis and Hutu slaughtered each other. Thousands of Burundians marched through the streets of Bujumbura, urging the remnants of Ndadaye's government to emerge from hiding and lead the country from the chaos caused by the military revolt. As many as 500,000 refugees had fled to Rwanda alone.

The Trash War

The morning was foggy, and we had driven up the slippery slopes from Tanzania. When we camped for the night, we saw no one. Now we were surrounded by a circular wall of people. They pressed in slowly, curious to see what these visitors might have. They began to touch at first, and then grab. Fighting back, we chased them off. As they ran and tripped, they grabbed anything they could pry loose—empty water bottles, scraps of paper. As the bolder ones tried to grab and run back into the crowd, they were immediately pounced upon by other Hutus, who ripped and tore whatever meager trophy they had retrieved until they possessed minuscule scraps in their hands. The Hutus were stealing trash, fighting for trash. As we quickly jumped in our vehicles and drove off, we watched them continue to beat and fight each other for trash until, finally, the battle was lost in the fog.

But even the foiled coup failed to bring stability to Burundi. The presidents of both Burundi and Rwanda were aboard a plane that was blasted out of the sky by rocket and gun fire as it was landing at Kigali airport in Rwanda on April 6, 1994. Intense fighting broke out in neighboring Rwanda. During the ensuing 14-week

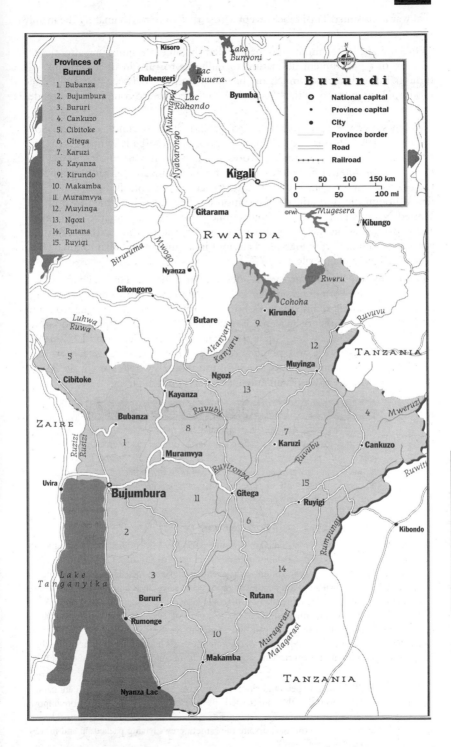

Provinces of Burundi

1. Bubanza
2. Bujumbura
3. Bururi
4. Cankuzo
5. Cibitoke
6. Gitega
7. Karuzi
8. Kayanza
9. Kirundo
10. Makamba
11. Muramvya
12. Muyinga
13. Ngozi
14. Rutana
15. Ruyigi

Burundi

⊕ National capital
• Province capital
• City
Province border
Road
Railroad

0   50   100   150 km
0   50   100 mi

©FWI

civil war in Rwanda, Tutsi rebels swept across the country, decimating the mainly Hutu government.

On April 29, 1994, hundreds of people fled shelling in Bujumbura, after the expiration of a government ultimatum to militants to turn in their weapons. Although Burundi escaped much of the 1995 fighting between the two ethnic groups, Hutu militants of the "People's Army" declined to comply and surrender their weapons.

Violence, perhaps a precursor to a total breakdown in Burundi, again broke out in January 1996, as Burundi government troops attacked a Rwandan Hutu refugee camp and killed 20, wounding scores of others. This sparked a mass exodus of more than 14,000 terrified Hutus who beat tail for Tanzania, already crammed to the brim with more than 700,000 Hutu refugees from both Burundi and Rwanda. Although the Burundi ruling coalition has been sternly warned by both the United Nations and the U.S. about ethnic violence, and the army particularly about overthrowing the precarious government, the raid in northeast Burundi was seen as a highly choreographed attempt in a multiphased plan to force Hutu rebels into permanent exile.

Pierre Buyoya, 46, became the president of Burundi in a Tutsi military-backed coup in July '96. Former president and Hutu Sylvestre Ntibantunganya hot footed it to the American ambassador's home, a place we remember well from our pleasant lunch. Another coincidence is that we also met the new prez (and former major in the army) at a whoop-up in'91 when he was president from 1987–1993. The only changes were an embargo from neighboring countries. His army of 16,500 men will be busy fighting the 3500 Hutu rebels who represent the 85% of Burundians who are Hutu. Gentlemen, sharpen your machetes.

The 1:30 to Paris

Our arrival was not an important event, but reason enough for lunch at the embassy. After a brief tour, including meeting the grizzled marine security officer, we had lunch high up in the hills overlooking Bujumbura. In between polite conversation, a silence would fall as an airliner took off from the airport. Without looking, our hosts would rattle off the flight and carrier, as if repeating a religious chant.

The Scoop

More than 180,000 people have died in Burundi since 1993 in conflicts between minority Tutsis and majority Hutus, and a million more made refugees as a result of ethnic violence between the Tutsis, who control the 18,000-man-strong military, and the Hutus. (According to some estimates, some half a million people are reported to have been killed—mostly Tutsis—in 1994 alone.) The war killed more than 2400 people between October 1995 and April 1996. A Hutu rebel offensive and army operations in the spring of 1996 forced between 55,000 to 100,000 people from their homes. To give you an idea how savage this carnival of death is, at least 458 people were killed in fighting in 48 separate incidents in April 1996 alone. More than 300 people—90 percent of them civilians, and most of those children—were killed over a two-week period that month.

The airport in Bujumbura opens and closes like an L.A. rave club. A per-capita annual income of around US$150 makes the country perhaps the poorest in Africa, even more impoverished than neighboring Rwanda. The nation suffered one of Africa's worst genocides—a duck shoot that continues to this day, despite the camera crews having packed up and moved to genocides closer to a Holiday Inn. Burundi is arguably one of the most dangerous places in Africa. Looting, raping, pillaging, maiming and murder are the norm. Gangs of youths from the minority Tutsi tribe occasionally paralyze the capital and, together with soldiers, hunt down and slaughter Hutu militiamen and civilians. The latest fighting stretches along a diagonal line from Kirundi province in the northeast to Nyanza-lac on Lake Tanganyika in the southwest. The Tutsi-dominated government army and Hutu rebels routinely kill civilians in revenge for attacks.

Latest figures put the 1994 Rwandan Massacre at 800,000 people. There is no reason why that scenario will not repeat itself here. In Burundi there is a 85 percent majority of Hutus dominated by a Tutsi elite. There are about 1.7 million refugees from Rwanda in camps in Burundi, Zaire and Tanzania who are afraid to go back to Rwanda for fear of being killed. The camps are being used as delivery points for weapons, training camps and security buffer zones that allow Hutu groups to make raids into Burundi and then return to vanish into the masses unmolested. There are three Hutu insurgencies and with all the people who have died in Burundi, the chemistry is just right for explosion.

The Players

The Hutus

Hutus comprise about 85 percent of Burundi's population and were the victims of a Tutsi-led mass genocide campaign in 1972. After President Ndadaye was overthrown and executed in an abandoned coup effort in October 1993, the Hutu went on a stampede. When it was over, nearly a quarter million corpses were left in the wake. The leader of the Hutu rebels, the National Council for the Defense of Democracy (CNDD), is Leonard Nyangoma, a former interior minister.

The Tutsis

The Tutsi-led military junta purged the military and bureaucracy of Hutus from 1964-1972. In 1972, a large-scale revolt by the Hutus killed several thousand Tutsis. The Tutsi machine followed with the mass extermination of selected and unselected Hutus. Any Hutu with an education, a decent job or any degree of wealth was arrested and murdered, most in a horrifying fashion. More than 200,000 Hutus were slaughtered in the ensuing three months. Tutsi army's makeshift trucks could be seen in the streets packed with mutilated corpses of Hutu victims.

Party for the Reconciliation of the People (PRP)

Led by Mathias Hitimana, now under house arrest, the Hutu dissident group opposes the oppression of the Hutu people by the government. The group, a champion of Hutu dissidents, is a frequent instigator of street clashes with government security forces.

National Liberation Front (NLF)

The armed wing of the Hutu Party of Liberation of the Hutu people is based and prevalent in the northwestern province of Cibitoke. They are hostile to foreigners, especially white expats, and killed three Swiss Red Cross workers when they ambushed and machined gunned a clearly marked Red Cross vehicle in June of '96.

Getting In

You can get into Burundi by air, road or lake ferry. By land from Rwanda, you can get in from Butare as well as Bujumbura. Expect to have your belongings searched on both sides of the border. From Zaire, you can get into Burundi from Bakavu via Uvira. You can also get to Bujumbura from Bakavu via Cyangugu in Rwanda. On Lake Tanganyika, you can get in from Tanzania. (Few travelers stay long in Burundi. Most are in transit between Tanzania and Rwanda.)

A passport and a visa are required. Only those travelers who reside in countries where there is no Burundian embassy are eligible for entry stamps, without a visa, at the airport upon arrival. These entry stamps are not a substitute for a visa, which must subsequently be obtained from the immigration service within 24 hours of arrival. Visas cost from US$30 to US$60, depending on anticipated length of stay. Travelers who have failed to obtain a visa will not be permitted to leave the country. Multiple entry visas valid for three months are available in Burundian embassies abroad for US$11. Evidence of yellow fever immunization must be presented. Also, visitors are required to show proof of vaccination against meningococcal meningitis. Additional information may be obtained from the following:

Embassy of the Republic of Burundi
2233 Wisconsin Avenue, N.W.
Suite 212
Washington, D.C. 20007
☎ *(202) 342-2574*

Permanent Mission of Burundi to the United Nations in New York
☎ *(212) 687-1180*

Getting Around

Burundi has a good network of roads between the major towns and border posts. Travel on other roads is hazardous, particularly in the rainy season. Public transportation to border points is often difficult and frequently unavailable, but it is improving. There has been a proliferation of modern Japanese-made minibuses in recent years. They're usually not terribly crowded and are far less expensive than taxis. These buses leave terminals (*gare routière*) in every town in the early morning through the early afternoon, and depart when they are full. They display their destinations on the windshield. The government-owned OTRACO buses are mainly found in and around the capital of Bujumbura. Total road miles are 3666; 249 of them are paved. There are six airfields in the country, only one with a permanent surface.

The border with Zaire is closed temporarily to prevent Hutu rebels from crossing into Burundi. Route One, the main highway linking Bujumbura with the rest of the country, is frequently closed because of land mines placed by Hutu rebels usually northeast of the capital. The road is also the site of frequent ambushes. More than 125 people, mostly civilians, were killed in over 20 ambushes in the first part of 1996.

There is an eight mile *cordon sanitaire*, or clean line, around the city of Bujumbura as well as a 9 p.m. curfew. Life may go on as normal during the day, but the killing begins at night. As many as 100 people die every week in Burundi, mostly because of attacks by Hutu insurgents who have their bases in the refugee camps in Zaire and because of Army reprisals against local Hutus.

Dangerous Places

Bujumbura

Sporadic violence remains a problem in the capital, Bujumbura—better known to locals as "Tutsiville", as the Tutsis have slaughtered most of the city's Hutus or sent them fleeing into the hills—as well as in the interior, where large numbers of displaced persons are encamped or in hiding. Renewed warfare in neighboring Rwanda has caused thousands of Rwandans to flee to Burundi and other countries in the region. The U.S. embassy has reiterated the importance of using extreme caution, with no travel to the troubled neighborhoods of the capital and none but essential travel in the city after dark. Armed Tutsi thugs and army soldiers comb the streets after dark, preying on the remaining Hutu militiamen. The Hutus, for the most part, have fled into the surrounding hills and each morning stream down into the capital to go to the market or do other chores before heading back to the hills before dark—to keep from being shot. As one journalist notes: "At 8 p.m., a Burundian must already be where he plans to spend the night." Burundi periodically has closed its land borders without notice and suspended air travel and telephone service in response to political disturbances.

Route 7

Strategic Route 7, which snakes southeast from Bujumbura, is closed, due to continued rebel attacks, effectively cutting off the entire south of the country.

Dangerous Things

Crime

Street crime in Burundi poses a high risk for visitors. Crime involves muggings, purse snatching, pickpocketing, burglary and auto break-ins. Criminals operate individually or in small groups. There have been reports of muggings of persons jogging or walking alone in all sections of Bujumbura, especially on public roads bordering Lake Tanganyika.

Bujumbura U.S. embassy sources report that dangerous areas for criminal activity in Bujumbura are the downtown section, the vicinity of the Novotel and the Source du Nil hotels, and along the shore of Lake Tanganyika. The majority of the criminal incidents in the Burundian capital consist of muggings, purse snatchings, and auto break-ins (to steal the contents).

Street Demonstrations and Clashes

Minority Tutsi youths regularly engage with the military and police in street protests in Bujumbura. Although the protests are not anti-U.S. in nature and Americans and other foreigners are rarely targeted, stay off the streets during any public rally. Relatively peaceful demonstrations can turn violent.

Hippos and Crocs

You may be surprised to find out that Burundians can't swim. The reason is crocs. You may also be surprised to see traffic held up at sunset as hippos leave the lake and waddle up to eat the grass on the soccer field in Bujumbura.

Getting Sick

There are 14 hospital beds and 0.5 doctors for every 10,000 people. Yellow fever and cholera immunizations are required. Inoculations for tetanus, typhoid and polio are also recommended, as are gamma globulin shots and malaria suppressants. Doctors and hospitals often expect immediate cash payment for health care services. U.S. medical insurance is not always valid outside the United States. Supplemental medical insurance with specific overseas coverage, including medical evacuation coverage, has proved to be useful. The Center for Disease Control recommends that travelers to Burundi receive the meningococcal polysaccharide vaccine before traveling to the area.

Nuts and Bolts

Burundi is a small, inland African nation (about the size of Maryland), passing through a period of instability. Facilities for tourism, particularly in the interior, are limited. The country is divided into 15 provinces, each administered by a civilian governor. The provinces are subdivided into 114 communes, with elected councils in charge of local affairs.

Burundi's climate varies from hot and humid in the area of Lake Tanganyika, with temperatures around 86° F, to cool in the mountainous north, about 68° F. The long rainy season runs from October through May.

Hutus comprise about 85 percent of the population. About 14 percent are Tutsi. Kirundi and French are the official languages; Swahili is also spoken; English is rare. Indigenous religions are held by 34 percent of the population; Roman Catholics make up 61 percent of the population; Protestants account for 5 percent. The literacy rate is about 50 percent.

The currency in Burundi is the Burundi franc (BFr): 250 BFr = $US1.00

Embassy Locations

U.S. Embassy in Burundi

Ave des Etats-Unis

B.P. 34, 1720, Bujumbura
☎ *[257] (2) 22-34-54*
FAX [257] (2) 22-29-26

Burundian Embassy in Canada

151 Slater Street, Suite 800
Ottawa, Ontario, Canada K1P 5H3
☎ *(613) 741-7458*
Telex: (369) 053-3393
FAX (613) 741-2424

Burundian Embassy in United States

2233 Wisconsin Avenue, N.W., Suite 212
Washington, D.C. 20007
☎ *(202) 342-2574*

Dangerous Days

04/25/1994 Failed coup. A military coup in Burundi failed when soldiers, fearing the triggering of a tribal bloodbath similar to the one in neighboring Rwanda, refused to participate in the military mutiny.

04/06/1994 A plane carrying the presidents of both Rwanda and Burundi was shot out of the sky as it attempted to land in Rwanda.

10/28/1993 Evacuations to Bujumbura. Foreigners in Burundi were evacuated to the country's capital, Bujumbura, as concern over tribal violence associated with a failed military coup grew.

10/28/1993 Six government ministers were confirmed murdered during a failed coup in Burundi.

10/21/1993 Paratroops overthrew President Melchior Ndadaye and executed him.

06/02/1993 Melchior Ndadaye became Burundi's first democratically elected president.

11/06/1976 Lieutenant Colonel Jean Baptiste Bagaye led a coup and assumed the presidency, suspending Burundi's constitution.

04/19/1972 Natré V returned to Burundi and was executed by President Micombero, sparking one of the bloodiest wars in African history.

BURUNDI

In a Dangerous Place

Burundi: Across East Africa by Land Rover

I have come to see Africa as well as to conquer it. The white man's idea of Africa has always been to test his mettle against this daunting land. We will be following the path of fellow Royal Geographical Society explorers, Burton and Speke, roughly tracing an old Arab slave trading route in four-wheel-drive expedition vehicles. Starting in the rough and tumble port of Dar es Salaam, we will travel a thousand kilometers to the source of the Nile, a tiny stream in equally minuscule Burundi. There is a rough track in the dry season, but we will attempt it in the height of the rainy season. If we succeed, we will gain nothing but a sense of accomplishment. If we fail, we will simply join the millions of people who understand that Africa, with all its death, pestilence, disease, hunger and poverty, will always be the dark continent.

As we cruise along country roads, singing stupid songs and dodging potholes the size of small lakes, it feels more like a vacation than an expedition. When we are delayed by overturned trucks or washouts, we amuse ourselves by handing out balloons, baseball cards and candy to delighted children.

BURUNDI

As the day progresses, the villages give way to farmland and farmland to grass-lands. As evening falls, we wait for the rest of the convoy at the turnoff that will take us onto our first remote trail. A heavy rain begins to fall with a foreboding vengeance; the easy part is over. As the scout in the lead car searches for the path in the tall grass, we watch the villagers stare at us from under the shelter of a giant mango tree.

There is some confusion. Where the road once was, there is now a wall of grass 20 feet high. You can feel the packed ground where a trail has once been. To the right are the remains of a drainage ditch, and along the road a clear area still ex-ists. Step one foot off on either side of the narrow path, and you sink into the bot-tomless, black mud.

We can imagine the thoughts of the villagers as they watch the long yellow column of vehicles idling at the entrance to what looks like a sea of tall grass. Who are these strange white men? Why are they going down that road?

Our scout keeps searching the wet, sucking mud for an entrance to, or even a trace of, a road, muttering that just three months ago on the pre-scout mission he drove this road at 60 miles an hour. The scout tries to convince himself that the tall grass is an illusion or just a temporary barrier. He has obviously not consulted with the locals, or has a hard time comprehending the growth rate of grass in Africa. Three months ago, in the dry season, the locals would have told him that, yes, there is a definite reason the grass grows so tall here and, yes, there was a road here once but probably only for a few days. We are standing knee-deep at the entrance to a swamp that stretches not for yards, but for miles.

Yes, there is a reason grass can grow 20 feet in three months. We are about to enter the great swamps of East Africa.

Into the Tall Grass

We decide to press forward, despite being faced with an endless sea of swamp and tall grass. We drive forward, testing the route. The rest of the convoy waits patiently behind, wondering what is going on. This is to be a common pattern over the next few days. At first, we try using machetes to clear the path. As we push deeper and deeper into the swamp, we realize that at this rate using machetes will get pretty old after a couple of days. We wonder what surprises await us in the long grass. There are to be quite a few.

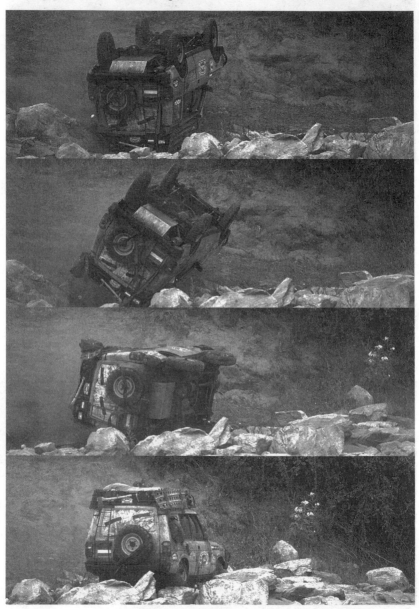

BURUNDI

The scout runs ahead to feel the path, while the drivers follow the lead car. We are 20 yards behind the red taillights, leaving enough room in case they need to be towed out of a gully or river. Suddenly, the scout comes screaming toward us, tearing his clothes off while swearing, "Bloody bastards. Get some water, get some water!" His thick accent and apoplectic state make it difficult for us to understand exactly what he wants. Since it is pouring rain, it seems a strange request. It is only after he is nearly naked that we realize he has been attacked by red ants. So we dump half of our precious water supply on him in order to ease the pain.

After our first run-in with African wildlife, we offer to cut trail. We take a more scientific, more team-oriented approach. I assign responsibilities. One person will ride on top with the spotlight, looking for the thin ridge of high grass that identifies the center of the road. We drive blind, sensing the camber of the road through the steering wheel and angle of the hood. I watch out the passenger side for the slight ridge caused by shorter grass that identifies where trucks that have passed in the dry season have slowed grass growth by soil compression. We decide to abandon the machete method and use our Discovery like a bulldozer to smash our way through the green wall of grass.

The Yellow Weed Whacker

The rain increases in intensity. It is nighttime and we are surrounded by a solid wall of grass 20 feet high like an ant walking through a lawn. The powerful driving lights bounce back off the wet grass and illuminate the car like a movie set. What I think is sweat running down my neck is really dozens of inquisitive insects. To say that there are a lot of insects would be an understatement. Not the big fluttery, elegant kind found in Asia but the weird, crawly bugs of Africa. As we slam through the thick, wet grass, bugs of every size and description are flicked through the window and inside the truck.

Soon, car and passengers are a furry carpet of prickly grass and crawling insects. It is a truly special and indescribable feeling to be soaking wet and covered from head to toe with insects of every variety. Hundreds of cockroaches, beetles, flies, mantises, spiders, ticks, moths, crickets, ants, earwigs, grasshoppers and walking sticks are crawling over and through our hair, up our noses and inside our clothing.

Giant praying mantises and walking sticks calmly crawl up our necks to stand next to our head-mounted flashlights and gorge themselves on the gnats, flies and moths that are attracted to the light. Despite our inquisitive friends, we still have to be alert to the other surprises that await us in the endless ocean of grass.

An incredible amount of stress comes from driving at high speed through a 12- to 18-foot wall of grass. It rains every night, swelling rivers, washing out make-shift bridges and deepening ravines. Fallen tree branches suddenly appear like lances straight out of the green wall. Stream beds present themselves quickly and dramatically, forcing us to slam on the brakes to avoid going head over heels into the water. We get our reconfirmation that this has been a road, or at least a bridge when we almost plunge into a 10-foot gap created by two naked bridge supports. We have to drive fast because driving slow means getting stuck, and each river we cross is running higher and faster, swollen by the heavy rains. As night turns to day and to night again, all we see is grass. Fording ravines and rivers offers our only break from the monotony.

We are in a hurry to reach Mikumi to make up lost time. Instead of building bridges and laying passable tracks for the teams behind, we decide to smash through swamps and washouts, leaving a gooey quagmire for those who follow. The rear of the column is getting farther and farther behind—a distance originally measured in hours and now in days. The heavy support vehicles require constant winching through the swamp, until the convoy is no longer driving but dragging itself every inch of the way.

The last time we see the rear of the convoy is at a point on the map where a shallow river crossing is marked. Tonight, or rather this morning, it is a raging river with a 20-foot-high waterfall where the road used to be. We decide to stop and sleep for three hours. As the sun comes up, I walk back to visit with the other teams just pulling in to the rear of the column. They are beginning to show the effects of constant driving and winching, of no sleep and the endless strain of fighting the swamp. In the weak light of morning, large blue crabs scuttle around the two water-filled ruts the vehicles have left behind us, as they hauled them-selves through the endless bog.

The Elephant Walk

The tedium of the seamless days and nights is punctuated by rain-swollen river crossings. During one wet and exhausting river crossing, we find an unusually large hole through the trees to winch the trucks up from the river. Once the ve-hicles are across, we collapse until the dawn comes an hour and a half later. While sleeping on the roof rack in the rain, I hear slow swishing in the grass and wake up to find elephants, obviously quite disturbed to find these metal intruders blocking their path to the river. Eye to eye with these giants, I keep desperately quiet as they slowly thread their way alongside our vehicles and down to the river.

That morning, the car windows are steamed up, the sleeping occupants appearing as if they have been shot dead in their seats, mouths gaping, heads sagging. We realize that we weren't dreaming when we see the huge elephant tracks around the trucks heading down to the riverbank.

We have lost radio contact with the rest of the convoy. At last check, we were four days ahead of the last vehicle. Our fuel indicators have been on empty for the last day and a half. In the last six days, we have slept exactly six and a half hours. Our eyes have given up focusing—they stare straight ahead. We look out through the rain-soaked windshield, hallucinating from lack of sleep. We are traveling up through a pass at night. Huge 50- to 150-foot trees bearing monstrous scars loom overhead. Elephants have ripped branches from the trees, leaving white flesh and jagged skeletons. Illuminated by our eight high-powered driving lights, they seem to dance and move. This is elephant, big elephant, country.

Finally, we emerge from the bizarre forest and re-enter the swamps. We run over what we first think is a giant toad, which turns out to be the head of a very long python. We know it is at least 15 feet long, since we can see only 15 feet at one time. Unharmed in the marshy ground, it slithers back into the grass. Later, we come across the skeleton of an elephant killed by poachers. We take turns taking pictures of each other standing inside the elephant's pelvis. We tie the massive bones to the fronts of our vehicles in a "skull and crossbones" and then decide to take off.

At last, we come to the long-awaited river crossing—the end of the wilderness and the beginning of the road that leads to Mikumi. The water rages under the heavy downpour. Too tired to walk the swollen river, we charge our vehicle across and immediately plunge over the edge of a steep rock ledge and submerge our car for the third time that week. We jump out of the truck and struggle through the heavy current to the opposite bank with the winch line. We hook it up and wait for the driver to pull us across. We wait...and wait. The vehicle is leaning at a grotesque angle. The water is rising and pouring through the open windows. We realize that the driver is fast asleep at the wheel, quite comfortably submerged up to his chest in the raging water. We bang on the hood, and he finally snaps out of it. We winch it out, our fuel running out 20 feet on the other side.

We don't have time to celebrate the fact that we have made it out of the swamps and are only a few miles from civilization. By now, we are zombies as we try to make it to a mission, 20 miles up the dirt track. Instead of a navigable dirt road, we experience a wet and furious roller-coaster ride through lake-sized potholes and muddy cane fields. We don't even notice. We drive straight through, not even caring how deep the holes are. We dive underwater again. By now, we are so wet, tired and cold we are oblivious to everything. We try to stay awake by talking to each other, but we miss chunks of sentences as we doze off and awake mid-sentence. Somehow we get to Mikumi in one piece.

We collapse on the cement floor, only to find ourselves wide awake an hour later and unable to sleep.

Boredom and Death in Mikumi

We have pushed hard for 144 hours (137 hours without sleep), and all we can do now is sit and wait for the others to make it through the swamps. The unforeseen delay and hardship have also depleted their fuel, water and vital spare parts.

A military cargo helicopter on loan from the Tanzanian government is pressed into service to fly the needed supplies to the depleted convoy.

We load up fuel, water and a replacement gearbox and wait in a school yard to load it onto the helicopter. We wait until the sun goes down. Still no helicopter. We find out the details later: Ten minutes after takeoff, it crashed into a mountainside, killing the copilot and seriously injuring the other two crew members. The battered old Huey was exactly 50 percent of the Tanzanian Air Force. Since some of the stuck convoy is a few kilometers from a rail line, we resort to commandeering a rail speeder car for a five-hour trip. The heavy gearbox and diesel fuel are carried in safari style on two poles to the stranded convoy. Later, we regroup and resume our journey.

Out of the Swamps and into the Scrub

We leave the mud and grass of the swamps far behind us and are now traveling through classic East African savannah. The horizon stretches in a virtually unobstructed 360° view, hindered only by gentle acacias and tortured, swollen baobab trees.

Puffy, white clouds form an endless pattern, accompanied by the lazy sound of tsetse flies, as giraffes watch shyly in the distance. Time seems to slow down, and your senses are sharpened. We begin to notice the thousands of purple and yellow flowers that carpet the land. Time passes even slower, as vultures aimlessly circle the convoy. We discover more bleached, tuskless skeletons of elephants killed by poachers. The heat paints swirls on the landscape, creating an Impressionist painting. The cruel African sun draws the moisture out of our bodies. Tiny sweat bees hungrily suck the beads of perspiration from our arms. We figure they are entitled to it.

Our once-soaked clothes are now dry. Our hands become hard, cracked and calloused, the nails and creases packed with black dirt. The hot sun begins to tan our skin and clear up our rashes, grass cuts and insect bites. We are adapting to the hot, dry savannah days and cool, crisp nights. We come to recognize the unique flora and fauna of the spear grass. Thousands of these sharp, barbed weapons are snicked off by the brush guard and embedded in our skin and clothing. However, spear grass pales in comparison to the various types of acacia thorns that grow up to five inches long. Just like porcupine thorns, these light, hollow daggers are everywhere and can pierce right through heavy boots. They become projectiles when they smack through an open window at 40 m.p.h., looking for soft flesh to penetrate.

We also become good friends with the scourge of Africa—the tsetse fly. Built like deer flies with mandibles designed to bite through water buffalo skin, they are vicious. Under constant attack, we smack'em, roll 'em, crush'em—and they just get up, shake their heads and attack again. Well-fed tsetse flies are easier to kill. We catch them on the windows. One smack and—blammo!—they explode in a shower of blood.

We are attacked by African killer bees that swarm out of their nests to rush at us again and again. They will attack even if we pass 20 to 30 meters from their nests. They charge at us in a horde, climbing up our noses, into our shirts. The next day, I feel like I have been beaten with a baseball bat.

We pass through many primitive and scenic areas populated by elephants, warthogs, baboons, giraffes, zebras, gazelles and other savannah animals. In the Selous, we stop to admire a family of elephants playing in the shade of a spreading acacia tree. The bull elephant suddenly takes exception to our intrusion, turning on us, ears flapping, shaking its head and loudly trumpeting its displeasure. After its false charge, it lowers its head like a locomotive and heads straight for us again. As we speed off, the ranger cocks his weathered rifle and only takes it down when the elephant gives up.

Finally, we find a faint trail, which soon becomes a dirt road. We have crossed the savannah and now see the hills and mountains of Central Africa dead ahead of us. Late that night, we pull into the ranger station in Rungwa to refuel, replace tires and sleep. The next morning, we are awakened by a glorious, 20-minute-long sunrise framed by an unusual double rainbow; it's almost as if the heavens are rewarding us for surviving the long journey.

Into the Heart of Africa

Although no signpost marks the spot, there is a distinct transition between Eastern and Central Africa. The soil turns from black loam to red clay, the air turns softer, more tropical—and even the people seem gentler and shyer. It is also darker and more foreboding. The wild, empty panoramas of Tanzania are replaced by the heavily populated, agricultural quiltwork of Burundi. Slipping and sliding through muddy banana plantations, the convoy labors over a mountain pass in dense fog. As we reach the crest, we are dazzled by the brilliant light and spectacular view.

Before us is a wide expanse of shimmering silver, fronting a mountainous wall of rich green. Stretching as far as the eye can see is a massive wall of dark mountains. Soaring above these magnificent mountains are huge, white thunderheads; below is the fabled Sea of Ujiji, now known as Lake Tanganyika, sparkling like a pool of diamonds.

This unforgettable sight has inspired awe in every explorer since Burton and Speke first set eyes on the lake:

"Nothing could be more picturesque than this first view of the lake," wrote Burton. "A narrow strip of emerald green, marvelously fertile, shelves towards a ribbon of yellow sand and bordered by sedgy rushes."

Like Burton, we had endured the swamps, the long, hot savannah, the wild animals, pests, and pestilence. But what had taken him seven and a half months, we have compressed into three weeks.

That night, we celebrate with the locals, among them the president of Burundi and whatever socialites and party animals Bujumbura can muster. Once the politicians and upper crust go home, 20 days of being in the bush with little sleep is erased by adrenaline and alcohol. One by one, the team members start throwing each other in the pool. Soon there are more people in the pool than outside. After we run out of khaki-clad people to toss in, everything else is fair game: Sabena stewardesses, lawn furniture, waiters, pots and pans. Laughing riotously, we pour what beer is left on top of each other's heads and jump into the seething pile of debris and people in the once sedate hotel pool. After the hotel runs out of beer, we migrate to an all-night disco on the shores of Lake Tanganyika.

Still dripping wet, we spend the rest of the night dancing and drinking with the local girls. Most try to stay out of fights with jealous boyfriends, who are determined to see just how tough we are. We didn't come to Africa to prove we were tough; we came here to have a good time.

As the dawn breaks over Lake Tanganyika, the few that can still walk stagger outside to get one last look at this magical lake in the heart of Africa. As the sun rises over the mist-covered mountains across the golden lake, we know we have seen the soul of Africa.

Five-Door, Turbo Diesel Discovery

For the East Africa journey, the vehicles used were Land Rover Discoveries. The equipment list (not including rations) was as follows: 2495 cc intercooled, turbocharged, direct-injection diesel with four cylinders in line; full-time, four-wheel drive with high/low and central diff lock; fuel capacity, 88.6 liters.

Factory Modifications

- Custom roll bar with integrated roof rack and light bar designed by Safety Specialists

- Dog guard for luggage area

- Two Hella fog lamps on bull bar

- Four Hella driving lights with rear work light

- Blacked-out hood for night glare from roof driving lights

- One hand spot

- Brush guard with lamp protectors

- Four sand ladders

- Two pintle hooks on front, one on rear

- Waterproof seat covers

- Inside and outside winch remote plug

- Waterproof box for winch solenoids under hood

- Alternator, 80-amp

- Heavy-duty shocks

- Wading plugs

- Michelin XCL radial tires

- Air-intake snorkel for deep wading

- Terratrip odometer

- Heavy duty 5.5" x 16" steel wheels

- Superwinch, 8000-lbs., with extra cable and winch kit (gloves, remote, shackles, snatch block and tree protector)

- Rear light protectors

- Ladder-to-roof rack on back door

- Skid plate, front and rear, with Neoprene padding

- Eight black Pelican cases with Camel Trophy logo

- Axe

- Pick and shovel

- Two water containers

- Two spare tires on rims

- Yellow (Sable) paint

- Hood locks

- Wire brush protectors with hood release

- Underhood, electrical cutoff switch

- Dual batteries (single system)

- Extensive spares kit

- Six inner tubes

- Two Zargas aluminum boxes (for food)

- Rear shelf with retainers

- Air jack

—RYP

BURUNDI

Phnom Penh

Cambodia
★★

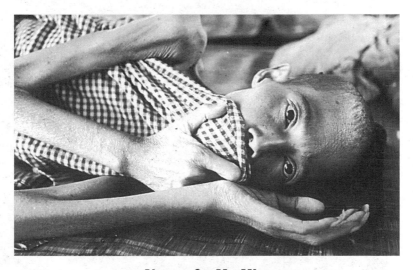

Always On My Mine

Perhaps no country on earth has so brutally suffered from as many forms of conflict over the past 30 years as has Cambodia. Civil wars, border wars, massive bombardment via a superpower's B-52s, a deforestation rate considered unparalleled anywhere in the world and an autogenicide unprecedented in its savagery—effectively eliminating a full seventh of the country's population—have ravaged this once proud and culturally influential empire.

With the help of the United Nations, Cambodia began crawling back into the world on its knees in 1993, literally, as so many of the country's citizens are missing limbs after accidental encounters with one of the perhaps 6-10 million land mines still buried beneath the surface of the countryside's topsoil. And those not missing arms or legs are most assuredly missing relatives, victims of Pol Pot's murderous Khmer Rouge regime of the mid- and late 1970s. The Khmer Rouge was responsible for more than a million deaths between 1975 and 1979 alone. Recent reviews of documents left by the Khmer Rouge put that total at twice that

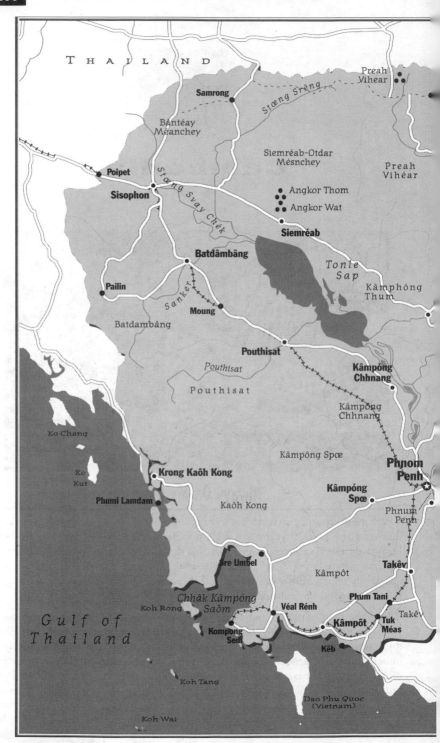

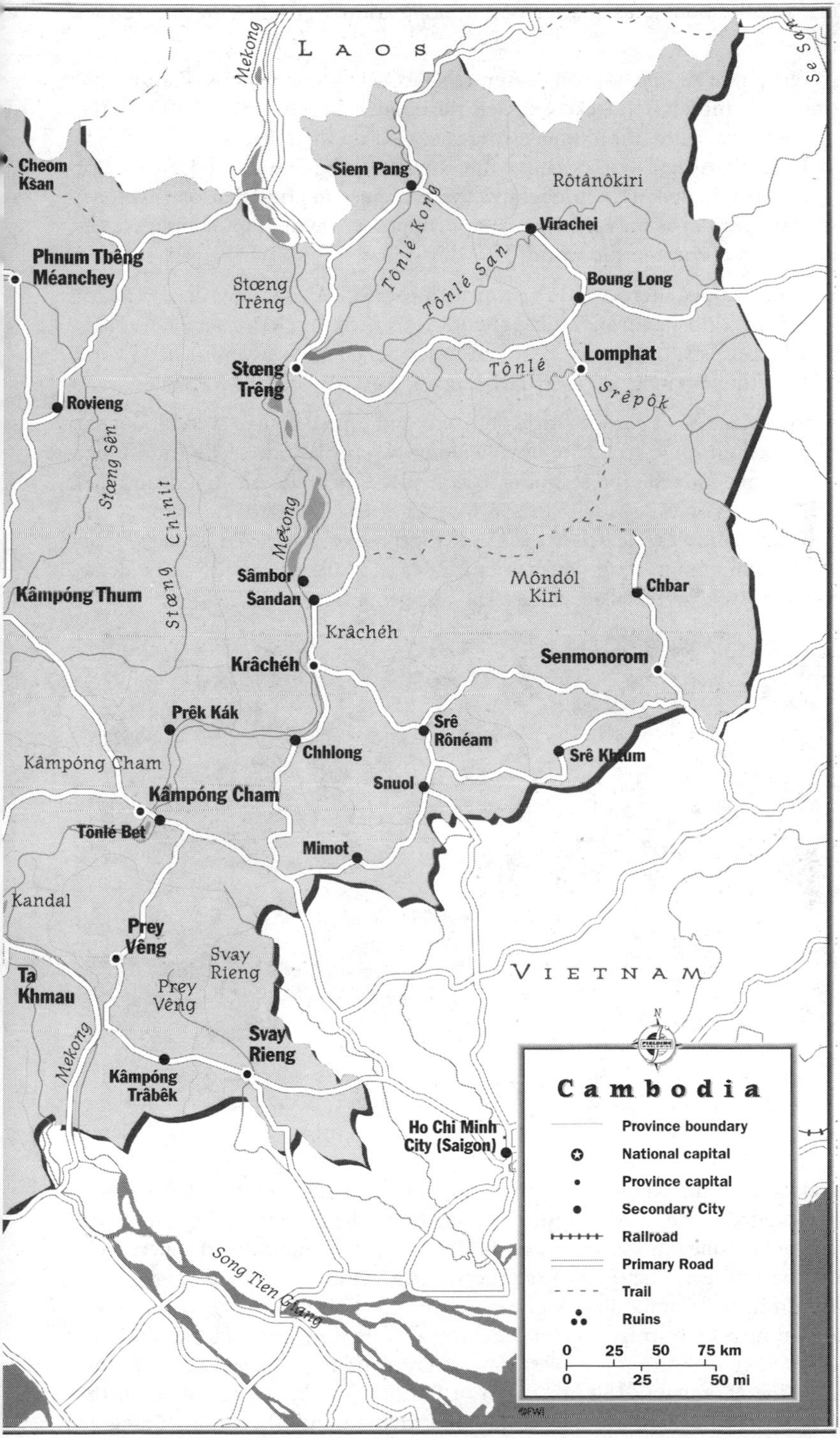

LAOS

Cheom Ksan

Siem Pang

Rôtânôkiri

Virachei

Phnum Tbêng Méanchey

Stœng Trêng

Boung Long

Tônlé Kong

Tônlé San

Stœng Trêng

Lomphat

Tônlé

Srêpôk

Rovieng

Stœng Sên

Stœng Chinit

Mekong

Kâmpóng Thum

Sâmbor

Sandan

Môndól Kiri

Chbar

Krâchéh

Krâchéh

Senmonorom

Prêk Kák

Srê Rônéam

Chhlong

Srê Khtum

Snuol

Kâmpóng Cham

Kâmpóng Cham

Mimot

Tônlé Bet

Kandal

Prey Vêng

Svay Rieng

VIETNAM

Ta Khmau

Prey Vêng

Mekong

Svay Rieng

Kâmpóng Trâbêk

Ho Chi Minh City (Saigon)

Song Tien Giang

Cambodia

	Province boundary
⊛	National capital
•	Province capital
•	Secondary City
┼┼┼┼┼	Railroad
═══	Primary Road
---	Trail
••	Ruins

0   25   50   75 km
0   25   50 mi

amount. In all, about one quarter of the population was killed by the Khmer Rouge.

However, peace didn't last long after UNTAC (United Nations Transitional Authority in Cambodia) peacekeepers left the country in November 1993. In the wake of their departure, the Khmer Rouge stepped up their attacks on the Cambodian People's Armed Forces (now the Royal Cambodian Armed Forces, or RCAF) and gained decisive battlefield victories against an army that one Western analyst characterized as the "most ill-equipped, poorly trained, undisciplined, officer-heavy and corrupt in the world."

And Khmer Rouge attacks didn't stop with the RCAF. In 1994, six Western hostages were kidnapped and subsequently executed by KR guerrillas. Their crime: being tourists. In January 1995, an American couple was ambushed by the KR while visiting a temple site north of Angkor Wat; the woman was killed.

On April 11, 1994, a pair of British citizens and an Australian were abducted from their taxi en route to Sihanoukville along National Route 4 by the Khmer Rouge, brought into the forest, and subsequently executed. An American relief worker, Melissa Himes, was released on May 11 after 41 days of captivity by the Khmer Rouge. She was released in exchange for three tons of rice, 100 bags of cement, 100 aluminum roofing sheets, medicines and 1500 cans of fish to be delivered to the KR-occupied village where she was being held.

Another incident that year received more world attention. Briton Mark Slater, 28, Frenchman Jean-Michel Braquet, 27, and Australian David Wilson were taken hostage by the Khmer Rouge on July 26, 1994, as they traveled by train from the capital to the seaside "resort" of Sihanoukville. The train was ambushed by the Khmer Rouge in southern Cambodia. At least 13 innocent travelers were killed in the ambush. The three Westerners, three ethnic Vietnamese, and an unknown number of Cambodians were marched into the forest. The ethnic Vietnamese are suspected to have been executed a short time later. Hopes lingered into November that the three Westerners were still alive at the Khmer Rouge camp at Vine Mountain (150 km south of Phnom Penh), as KR leaders in the area continued to demand first a ransom and then a political role (including an end to a ban on the guerrilla group) in Cambodia's government as a condition for their release. However, it was subsequently learned that the three Westerners had been summarily bound and shot or bludgeoned to death execution-style by KR soldiers at the command of KR General Nuon Paet near the end of September.

In many parts of Cambodia, Khmer Rouge 82mm mortars are still felt daily. In one attack, in October 1994, 46 Cambodians were slaughtered by KR marauders in Battambang. Ethnic Vietnamese villages, especially those along the banks of the Tonlé Sap River and the Great Lake of Tonlé Sap, are routinely ransacked, their inhabitants usually marched off into the woods and bludgeoned to death, as the guerrillas choose to save their bullets for the Cambodian army.

Even the spectacular and highly touristed ruins at Angkor are in occasional danger of attacks by Khmer Rouge guerrillas who, despite U.N.-supervised elections in May of 1993, still control fully 20 percent of Cambodia's landscape. Shortly before the polls that spring, armed guerrillas attacked a U.N. garrison at Siem Reap and injured a Portuguese tourist. A Japanese tourist fled the area on a motorcycle and streaked all the way to the Thai border, nearly 100 miles away.

In Siem Reap province itself, not more than about 20 km from the temple complex, Khmer Rouge guerrillas are busy "recruiting" soldiers and murdering ethnic Vietnamese. (There are about 5500 members of the Khmer Rouge, although 1200 fighters recently defected.) *DP* hooked up with an army colonel in March 1996. The colonel offered to bring us to the front lines near Phnom Bok, about 20 km northeast of Angkor Wat. We made the journey on a Sunday, the least dangerous day of the week to travel near Christian and Buddhist war zones. Activity was relatively light in the area, Colonel Heng told me. But I wouldn't get a chance to discover that for myself, as a general at the army's base camp at Phnom Bok turned me around and sent me packing back to Phnom Penh for formal government approval to travel with the army—permission we wouldn't get.

War is not far beneath the surface here. (Oh, by the way, we took a taxi from Siem Reap to the front.) In many areas across the lush Khmer countryside, bones spring from the earth like desert cacti, still shrouded with the tattered garments their owners were clothed in on the day they were slaughtered—a testament to Pol Pot's demonic wrath of the mid- and late 1970s. At mass grave sites, human teeth can be found among the rocks and grass like pebbles in an old parking lot. Many of these locations are not named, not enshrined by glass and concrete and tour guides and ticket booths. They're just there, baking in the same sun as the resin harvesters along the rutted, muddy roads nearby, toting Chinese-made AK-47 rifles and preparing to enter the fog-encased dark green jungle for another day's toil.

Rebel Etiquette

In 1992, UNTAC issued a pamphlet to its soldiers and workers listing helpful Khmer phrases for use in the event of being detained or robbed by the KR. Translated, a couple read:

- *That's a very nice gun, sir. I'd be honored to give you the gift of my truck.*

- *My watch is very expensive; that's why it makes me very happy to present it to you as a gift.*

Red signs depicting skulls and crossbones are tacked to trees, sharing the bark with bullet holes, warning of land mines. Tracers raining back and forth between government forces and the Khmer Rouge in the night sky can sometimes be witnessed by visitors to this exotic land. To the uninitiated, the orange tracers streaking in a large arc across the Asian twilight appear to be a display of grand fireworks that simply aren't functioning properly, some sort of defused celebration—which is in fact what Cambodia is.

Cambodia's most significant offering to the world today may not be its art, its dancing, its magnificent ancient temples; instead, it might be the testament to the country's horrific past. Cambodia's most popular attractions, apart from its ancient *wats*, are the museums and fields that depict the mass genocide of its people, although many simply don't have the stomach to visit the still bloodstained walls of schoolrooms turned torture chambers, or of longan fields turned open graves.

Many of Pol Pot's victims who survived the genocide today roam Phnom Penh's trash-laden boulevards like zombies out of a George Romero film. Some are hideously disfigured; nearly all are penniless and they follow Western tourists like gulls behind a shrimper, begging for handouts.

Cambodia belies itself; it's perhaps the greatest paradox on the planet in its contrast of human warmth and vile indignity. Its people are arguably the gentlest on the globe, sentenced by circumstance to an environment that's utterly raw and entirely untamed. They are struggling to enter the modern world by investing salaries that average as little as US$4 a month on English lessons along Phnom Penh's English Street. (It's English now—not French. The majority of people who were versed in French either fled the country or were executed by the Khmer Rouge.)

Passenger Justice

Halfway into town after arriving at Phnom Penh's Pochentong Airport, my taxi driver stopped. A police motorcycle carrying two of Phnom Penh's finest had pulled out onto Pochentong Boulevard from a side street directly in front of a small Toyota, which slammed into the rear of the bike. The bike was eaten by the sedan's grille and lay crumpled beneath the undercarriage. One of the cops staggered away in shock. The small Toyota was packed with perhaps eight Khmer passengers. The other cop bolted to his feet and raced to the right front door of the car. He opened it, dragged out a young, shock-stricken Cambodian man and began kicking the crap out of the poor soul, pummeling his rib cage with his military boots. It seemed to make no difference that the steering wheel of the Toyota was on the left-hand side, the actual driver of the car grimacing in either the realization of imminent pain and arrest or in the delight that his car had been smuggled into Cambodia from Vietnam (where they drive on the right side of the road) and not Thailand (where they drive on the left).

To the adventure tourists who don't heed King Norodom Sihanouk's 1994 call for Western tourists to stay out of his country, Cambodia is one of the last frontiers, the Wild West of East Asia, where one can hitchhike from Phnom Penh to Angkor Wat with a relatively good chance of being stopped and detained at rifle point by Maoist guerrillas or highway thugs. Where one can share a ferry ride in a raging storm across the Great Lake of Tonlé Sap on a dilapidated, rusted barge with a dozen sows, cockroaches the size of plums and a few soldiers and joke about the ferry that sank over the same reef the night before during a monsoon, killing 50. Where one can sneak across the border from Thailand aboard a speedboat manned by smugglers bound for Kompong Som (Sihanoukville), harboring a cache of Singaporean VCRs. Where one can ride a train from Phnom Penh to Sihanoukville with a high likelihood of being abducted and executed. Yippie-yai-yo-kai-yae!

Although the country is hardly stable politically (in November 1995, King Norodom Sihanouk's half-brother Prince Norodom Sirivudh was arrested for plotting to kill CoPremier Hun Sen), tourism seems to be on the rebound after falling off dramatically in the wake of the deaths of the foreigners in 1994 and early 1995. According to government statistics, tourist arrivals for the first six months of 1995 were up 35 percent over the same period the previous year. Although tourism officials have generally been successful in channeling and containing tourists to the Phnom Penh–Angkor route, hardier souls are journeying down to the coast along National Highway 4, which is in much improved condition after a U.S.-backed highway reconstruction program. The effort is being supported by Canadian-led units of the Cambodian Mine Action Committee (CMAC), which has been clearing the estimated 4000 land mines from the side of the road.

Is Cambodia safe?

Back in 1994, *DP* stated no. This year, we'll say it's as safe as you make it. Fly or take the speedboat to Siem Reap to visit Angkor, and you'll find the experience perfectly safe. Take the train to Kompot, on the other hand, and you may not come back. And stay off of Phnom Penh's streets after 10 p.m.—Every resident will warn you of the danger.

Cambodia's Interior Ministry has been completing plans to introduce tourist police units in Phnom Penh, Siem Reap and the seaside resort, Sihanoukville. Tourism Minister Veng Sereyvuth said the units would be on call 24 hours a day and trained to help tourists in situations ranging from emergencies and crime to simple requests for information. The problem is the bandits dress like cops or soldiers.

The Khmer Rouge Threat and The Thai Connection

The Khmer Rouge survive, despite a dwindling of their numbers due to defections. Estimates of their troop strength range from between 3500 to 5500 regular and militia soldiers, depending on who you believe. But they continue to be financed primarily through trade in hardwood and gems with Thai businessmen and corrupt elements of the Thai military, despite a United Nations ban on the commerce and the Thai government's well-intentioned but unsubstantiated claim that trade between Thais and the Khmer Rouge has ended. Most diplomats and Royal Cambodian Armed Forces officers agree that the RCAF could easily defeat the Khmer Rouge if Thai merchants and black marketeers ceased their support of and cooperation with the rebels.

The Khmer Rouge have made, by conservative estimates, hundreds of millions of dollars in dealings with the Thais—perhaps billions. The 700 km-plus border with Thailand is essentially lawless and is riddled with corrupt Thai army officials who freely permit the crossing of Cambodian (i.e., KR) hardwood and gems into Thailand—for a price, of course. As well, Cambodian military offensives against the KR have failed near the Thai border because, according to Cambodian military officials, the Thai border hasn't been sealed, allowing the rebels to regroup and attack the flanks of RCAF positions with artillery and small arms.

The late 1993 discovery by Royal Cambodian troops of a well-maintained dirt road leading from Ta Phraya, on the border of Thailand, a mile into the Khmer Rouge-controlled Cambodian town of Phnom Prak, revealed a massive, elaborate compound of spacious wooden homes and warehouses built by Thai contractors for none other then Pol Pot himself. Khmer Rouge defectors reported that one of the largest houses, hidden on a densely-foliaged hillside with a small garden, was Pol Pot's own home during his sojourns into Cambodia from his base in Thailand. He brought along both his wife and daughter during his frequent visits there. Even more shocking was the nearby discovery, within Cambodian territory, of offices belonging to the Royal Thai Army's Task Force 838, a military unit that worked secretly with the Khmer Rouge and acted as intermediaries between the KR and the Thai Army.

Although the compound was overrun by Cambodian troops, it only serves as further evidence of the Khmer Rouge-Thai connection, a thriving relationship that continues to this day.

Essentially the Thais and the Khmer Rouge forged their relationship after the Vietnamese overthrow of Pol Pot's Phnom Penh regime in January 1979, in mutual antagonism toward the Vietnamese, a traditional enemy of both countries. Failed assaults on both nearby Anlong Veng and the Khmer Rouge capital at Pailin in May 1994 have done nothing but intensify the guerillas' resolve—and strength.

And there have been recent accusations in Phnom Penh that the Khmer Rouge are acquiring outside military aid. *The Cambodia Daily* reported that the KR has started receiving tanks and other armored equipment from China, a country that once vigorously supported the Khmer Rouge with arms and financing until the Paris Peace Accords and subsequent attacks on Chinese UNTAC soldiers by KR units. But the Khmer Rouge contend they obtained their new tanks after the government's May 1995 assaults on both Pailin and Anlong Veng (another strategic KR stronghold in the west) failed.

A Khmer Rouge radio message monitored in Bangkok said that when the government troops withdrew from Pailin and Anlong Veng, the Royal Army "abandoned dozens of their tanks on the battlefield. Khmer Rouge forces captured them like crabs and then used them to attack government positions."

No one seems to know for sure why the strength of the Khmer Rouge continues and where this muscle is coming from. Perhaps most confused are government officials themselves. "The Khmer Rouge are using Chinese tanks," said Cambodian Copremier Prince Norodom Ranariddh, "the tanks that UNTAC, with all its helicopters and photographs, did not manage to discover. I want to know, where do all of these tanks come from?"

Although many sources say that the Khmer Rouge control only the Thai border regions (and indeed most of the fiercest fighting is occurring in Pailin, Battambang and the northwest) this information cannot be considered to be entirely reliable. Tourists have been abducted south of Phnom Penh by KR units, such as the July 1994 abductions at Vine Mountain. The Vietnamese border guards at the crossing at Ha Tien in the extreme southwest of Vietnam told me that the Khmer Rouge controls areas just across the border, which, if true, contradicts accounts given to me by the American embassy in Phnom Penh as well as Phnom Penh Tourism sources.

Cambodia's Chief Office of Military Intelligence said at the end of 1995 that the gradual strangle of supply routes and the government's Defector Program (which grants amnesty to Khmer Rouge deserters and the opportunity to join the RCAF), which will reduce the KR's strength by some 3000 guerrillas in 1995 alone, had whittled the rebels' strength to a mere 3500 soldiers and militia. The Cambodian military believes it is winning this war of attrition as evidenced by its claim that the 2664 guerrillas who defected in the first eight months of 1995 possessed an average three rounds of small ammunition each.

From January 1–August 15, 1995, the government had recovered 1061 AK-47s, 215 CKC assault rifles, 40 land mines and 6698 rounds of small ammunition from 2664 defecting Khmer Rouge.

In its own arsenal, the Cambodian military possesses six Czech L-39 Albatross ground attack aircraft, about two dozen MiG-21bis/UMs, most of which can't fly due to a lack of spare parts and maintenance. At last check, four of the MiGs had recently returned from Israel where they were undergoing repairs.

According to Battambang provincial police, the Khmer Rouge continue to receive intelligence on government troop positions and intentions from "Thai spies" along the border. One Thai army unit, Task Force 838 (mentioned above), has traded with the Khmer Rouge, while Thai army Task Force 315 supplied the KR with information on RCAF troop movements. These are allegations the Thai Army refutes as unfounded or outdated.

It is quite possible that the planned, three-prong February 1996 dry season offensive in Cambodia's northwest will be more effective than the RCAF's failed debacle of May 1995. And as far as a time frame for the complete defeat of the Khmer Rouge?

"Only a fool would say," said one Cambodian intelligence officer.

Cambodia's Train to Hell

One activity that remains decidedly unsafe in Cambodia is taking the train. Any train, anywhere.

After one leaves Pochentong by train heading south for Sihanoukville, the track cuts a swath through scenic rice fields accented by towering sugar palms before winding its way through the mountainous areas of the south. The route offers some of the most magnificent scenery in Cambodia. Rice farmers toil in the fields, coaxing their oxen to pull wooden ploughs. Bright Buddhist pagodas can be seen in the fields and on the hillsides, set far away from the track.

But this same route, formerly popular with adventure tourists and the curious alike, today is less than affectionately known as "The Death Railway."

Or "The Train to Hell."

"Safety features" on the Cambodian railway system include 1960s French-built locomotives sporting steel plates in front of the cab and two up-front "mine clearing" cars, where passengers with enough courage can ride for about 1500 riel (about US$.60).

Brackets welded into the plates are made from railway iron and resemble the "cowcatchers" on 19th-century U.S. locomotives. All this to protect passengers and crew from mines laid on the tracks by the Khmer Rouge and corrupt army soldiers and police. Not to mention rocket attacks spawned by one or more of the above.

Sixty cents seems like a small life insurance policy, and it is. But Cambodian trains are the only means rural Khmer farmers and other poor Cambodians have to get their produce, animals and other goods to markets from Sihanoukville to Phnom Penh.

On July 26, 1994, a Khmer Rouge attack on one such train left 13 people dead, with three Westerners taken hostage and ultimately executed two months later.

This certainly wasn't an isolated occurrence. More than one Cambodian railroad engineer has survived at least 10 train ambushes since the early 1980s, when the KR began their efforts in earnest to create anarchy in Cambodia after Pol Pot's fall to the Vietnamese in January 1979. But their numbers are diminishing rapidly.

On the day prior to the May 1993 elections, KR marauders formed a gauntlet on both sides of the track and rocketed a train, resulting in the deaths of at least 30 people.

On paper, at least, the trains aren't as defenseless as you might think. Usually, a "railway militia" team consisting of about two dozen government soldiers is on board each train. Their job? To repel bandits and raiders, typically KR guerrillas. For the initial leg of the journey from Phnom Penh southward, the guardian force can usually be found asleep or playing cards. But by the time the train reaches Kompong Trach (an area under marginal KR control), it's lock'n load. But, typically, when a firefight breaks out, the "militia" are the first to abandon their positions aboard the train and flee into the forest. Crew members tend to follow suit. Some crew members on board are heavily armed with assault rifles and grenades. But it's a lot to ask of a man who makes about US$20 a month to defend a Cambodian train against a disciplined and ruthless KR unit. Under attack, the forest is mighty appealing to even the toughest-skinned Cambodian railroader.

Many Cambodian engineers who were trained in the 1960s on steam trains aren't around anymore to recount their adventures, having either been slain in the mid-1970s during Pol Pot's regime, or by subsequent KR ambushes on their trains during the '80s and '90s.

So skip Sihanoukville, you say. The train to Battambang has got be a lot safer.

Is it safe? Maybe. Maybe not.

Probably not.

It takes a lot of nerve and bravery to crew a Cambodian train, and, these days, even more stupidity to buy a ticket to ride it.

The Scoop

In September 1993, a democratically elected government took office in Cambodia, following a two-year United Nations peacekeeping program. The country has enormous economic needs and faces a diminishing Khmer Rouge insurgency in several provinces. Defections have had an impact on the guerrilla group, who have resorted to attacks on defectors' families to deter further changes in allegiance. High levels of crime and banditry remain a persistent problem in Cambodia. Phnom Penh seems to be gripped with coup phobia, and nervous soldiers protecting Second Prime Minister Hun Sen gunned down four young Westerners in August 1995 in the mistaken belief that they were assassins. In November 1995, King Norodom Sihanouk's half-brother, Norodom Sirivudh, was arrested and ultimately exiled to France for plotting to kill Hun Sen, whose personal paranoia, political resiliency and thirst for absolute power threaten any semblance of democracy in the country. Hun Sen has been responsible for an increasing suppression of the press. On December 29, 1994, the U.S. government said it was satisfied that the Cambodian government had distanced itself from the Khmer Rouge and would provide increased military aid. There were some reports in 1995, none confirmed by *DP*, of sightings of U.S. Special Forces personnel on the front lines with Cambodian troops battling the Khmer Rouge. Limited military conflict, which frequently intensifies during the dry season (November through May) is possible in a number of areas, including along the border with Thailand, and especially in Battambang province.

On April 16, 1996, a gang of armed bandits attacked a group of several hundred Khmer tourists celebrating the New Year holiday at a waterfall about eight miles from Kampot city. Most people fled when shots were fired, but a number of persons were robbed. The only known injury was to a young child hit by a ricocheting bullet. Contrary to some wire service reports, no one was taken hostage and the attackers were not believed to be Khmer Rouge. No Americans (and possibly only two foreigners) were in the group of tourists at the waterfall.

The Players

The Khmer Rouge, or NADK (National Army of Democratic Kampuchea)

Outlawed in 1994 by the FUNCINPEC-led coalition Cambodian government, the Khmer Rouge are Maoists. The communist Khmer Rouge refuses to allow the disarmament of its fighters until certain conditions are met, including a prominent role in the coalition government. But most of these demands are rhetoric, as its real aims are apparently creating its own provisional government in as much of Cambodia as it can seize. The Khmer Rouge leader was Pol Pot, who, although based across the border in Thailand, makes frequent forays to a new home he has had built inside the Cambodian border. Khieu Samphan is the nominal leader of the Khmer Rouge. They are headquartered in Pailin, a power center that remains despite a spring 1994 government siege of the city. The Khmer Rouge is supported by oil, timber and gem trade with Thai businessmen and corrupt elements of the Thai Army and is backed by Thai generals, using Chinese weapons. They are striving to create a self-sustaining economy in the Cambodge Profound. Their attempts to create a completely agrarian community in the '70s resulted in the genocide of more than 1 million Cambodians. Today, with a somewhat weakening but still firm power base in northern and western Cambodia, the Khmer Rouge number between 3500 and 10,000 soldiers (according to which source you talk to) and control approximately 10 percent of the country, primarily in the north, the northwest, the west along the Thai border and pockets in the south (particularly in Kompot province) between Phnom Penh and the coastal port city of Sihanoukville. To counter the threat, there is an Australian-built jungle warfare school at the Pich Nil pass in southern Cambodia. The three-month course teaches Cambodian soldiers how to engage and attack KR troops in the nearby Elephant Mountains and along the Thai border.

Ieng Sary

Ieng Sary, known as Brother Number Two, is the Khmer Rouge's foreign minister. He is Pol Pot's successor and, some say, evil twin. Ieng Sary and Pol Pot studied Marx together in Phnom Penh and Paris, and later fought together in the 60s. He is now working with the government of Cambodia to create a political presence for the KR. He will create a party to run in the 1998 elections. (The Khmer Rouge blew their chance back in 1991 when they boycotted the election and there is little chance any sane person would ever vote for the killers of some 2 million Cambodians.) Some Khmer Rouge leaders, such as the one-legged Ta Mok (he stepped on a mine), are determined to fight to the end. Others want to live to spend the millions they've earned from smuggling gems and timber. When *DP* was lost in Cambodia, all it took was the promise of a Range Rover to tip the scales and convince a Khmer Rouge general to defect.

The Thai Army

Despite a ban on cross-border timber trade, the Khmer Rouge continues to finance themselves with the sale of hardwood and gems to Thai business firms, with the complicity of the Thai military. At least two different Thai army task forces have been implicated in both the cross-border illegal trade of logs and supplying the Khmer Rouge with intelligence information on RCAF troop movements.

King Norodom Sihanouk

In 1941, the French made Prince Sihanouk king of Cambodia, believing they had installed another loyal puppet on the throne who'd do anything the French asked of him for the price of a lavish existence. Instead, King Sihanouk moved in the direction of Cambodian independence. In 1953, he declared martial law and dissolved the parliament. On November 9, he proclaimed Cambodia an independent state. But internal divisions continued to hamper the solidarity among the nation's leaders. In 1955, Sihanouk abdicated the throne in favor of politics. Politically, Sihanouk has vacillated between the right and the left throughout his career (intermittently supporting the Khmer Rouge and its foes alike). Known for bending with the wind, he is nonetheless still worshipped by the core of the Cambodian people. Ill with cancer, he resides primarily in Peking and Pyongyang, North Korea. His relationship with the late North Korean leader Kim Il Sung was deep and lasted for decades.

Hun Sen

Hun Sen is a turncoat Khmer Rouge who was installed as Cambodia's puppet president by the Vietnamese after their defeat of the Khmer Rouge in 1979. He ruled alone until the 1993 elections but was named copremier despite losing the elections to Prince Norodom Ranariddh's FUNCINPEC party. Hun Sen has shown increasing antagonism toward the West in recent years and signs of dismissing "Western-style" democracy in Cambodia altogether. He is shrewd, power hungry and paranoid and disdains the press.

Prince Norodom Ranariddh

Cambodia's first prime minister and leader of the increasingly right-leaning FUNCINPEC party. Ranariddh has clashed frequently with Hun Sen since the two have shared office and was considered the more powerful of the two. But Cambodia's two leaders seem to be sharing an uneasy alliance these days in their battle against the press to keep their flunkyism a secret.

Sam Rainsy

In October 1994, the government performed a major housecleaning of its cabinet, including the firing of popular finance minister Sam Rainsy, a brilliant, French-educated free market reformer, outspoken government critic and ardent anti-corruptionist who became a darling of Western diplomats. Rainsy was subsequently stripped of his MP position in parliament and expelled from FUNCINPEC in May 1995. On November 9, 1995, Rainsy launched a new political party in Cambodia called the Khmer Nation Party (KNP). The party was immediately declared illegal by the government, although no direct action was taken immediately to dismantle it or throw its leaders in jail.

Getting In

A passport is required. An airport visa valid for a 30-day stay is available upon arrival at Phnom Penh's Pochentong Airport from the Ministry of National Security for US$20. You can also apply to:

General Direction of Tourism
> *Chief of Tour Service Office*
> *3 Monivong Street*
> *Phnom Penh*
> ☎ *855-23-24607 or 23607*
> *FAX: 855-23-26164 or 23-26140.*

You will need to send the following: full name, passport number, photocopy of the front section of your passport, date and place of birth, arrival and departure dates and itinerary. They will confirm receipt of application. Visas will then be issued on arrival at Pochentong Airport. You will need two passport-sized photos. Visas are good for stays up to 30 days.

That's the official line. But try and get to Bangkok first for the latest dope on getting over the border. Most travel agents there will say you've got to cough up anything from US$80 to US$120 and wait three days for your visa. But you can also try simply getting on a plane, as I have done, and pay US$20 U.S. cash at Pochentong for a 30-day visa.

Visa extensions can be applied for, but not necessarily granted, in Phnom Penh at the following:

Foreign Ministry
> *240 St. and Samdech Sothearos Boulevard*
> ☎ *24641 or 24441*

General Direction of Tourism
> *3 Monivong Street*
> *Phnom Penh*
> ☎ *855-23-4607 or 23607*
> *FAX: 855-23-26164 or 23-26140*

Phnom Penh Tourism
> *313 Samdech Sothearos Boulevard*
> ☎ *23949, 25349, or 24059*
> *FAX: 885-23-26043*

You can also arrange for visas in Vietnam. Allow three to five days for issue. Various Saigon tour operators run boats up the Mekong River from Vietnam to Phnom Penh. However, most of these excursions have been curtailed due to lawlessness and Khmer Rouge attacks on river-going vessels. Entry by land from Thailand is illegal, however an increasing number of travelers are reporting success entering Cambodia by sea from Trat, Thailand. Although this is illegal, it is expected by both Thai and Cambodian border authorities that this method of departing Thailand and entering Cambodia will soon be permitted for foreigners. In this anticipation, or for a bribe, they may stamp your passport.

Cambodia can be entered by land from several points, but legally only from one.

Through Vietnam

Crossing into Cambodia from Vietnam is very popular with budget travelers. There are several border checkpoints, but at the time of this writing only one is usable by foreigners, the Moc Bai-Bavet checkpoint on Route 1. A bus leaves at dawn daily except Sundays from both Phnom Penh and Saigon; it's a hellishly crowded affair, and very slow with frequent stops. Once the bus reaches the border there is a wait of several hours while the authorities on each side pore over travel papers, visas, and every box and basket on the bus in search of contraband. Total travel time is about 12 to 13 hours, if the bus doesn't break down. Verdict: not recommended

A better way is to catch a share taxi to the border from either side; from Phnom Penh the fare can be as low as US$5 per person if the car is full. Upon arrival at the border, simply walk to the other side and stick your thumb out for the next taxi or private car willing to ferry you the rest of the way. This cuts a good four hours off the bus trip, and is usually much more comfortable. Be sure the price is agreed upon before getting into the car.

Through Thailand

There was a time several years ago, when the UN was in town, when travelers could cross into Cambodia at the Klong Leuk checkpoint in Aranyaprathet. Then it was simply a matter of finding a taxi in Poipet and gritting your teeth for the 12 hours of "lambada road" to Phnom Penh ahead.

Not anymore. Foreigners are currently prohibited from crossing the Thai checkpoints due to security reasons, i.e. the almost daily skirmishes between the Cambodian government forces and the Khmer Rouge guerrillas. Don't even think of getting off the road and sneaking across unless you want to be called "Stubby;" the Thai-Khmer border is one of the heaviest mined areas in the world, and claims new victims nearly every day.

In mid-1994 people were still crossing into Koh Kong province from south of Trat town in Thailand. A few hundred baht was paid to the soldiers at the border, a speed boat taken to Kompong Som, and the traveller was home free. This is illegal, but was feasible at the time as the Cambodian authorities rarely checked visas. Of course, the same route must be taken when leaving the country. Ask around in the Trat guesthouses before attempting this.

From Cambodia into Thailand is not as easy. The Thai police are wise to this trick, and if they catch you in the country (most likely to happen in Trat town or the vicinity) without a properly stamped visa, you could win a free vacation in the Bangkok immigration jail. Best not to try this.

From Laos

To date, no one knows of any "tourist" who has made the crossing into Cambodia from Laos. This is probably because the northeast of Cambodia is mostly thick jungle with little population. Theoretically it should be possible, but again you would be entering illegally if your visa (assuming you had one in advance) was not stamped. If you must do it legally, the best route would be along the Mekong River, as there is sure to be a checkpoint for the locals, or along a well-travelled logging road.

Getting Around

Intercity buses and trains are out of the question for foreigners, due to the high probability of banditry and guerrilla attacks in the countryside. Intercity buses are officially off limits to foreigners and trains are often restricted to Cambodian citizens. Officially, travel in Khmer Rouge-controlled areas is restricted. By road, Siem Reap can be reached from Phnom Penh by road via share taxis, which take National Route 5 to Battambang and then swing east around the Tonlé Sap Lake. The trip is long and arduous, however, and security on the Battambang-Siem Reap leg is chancy. National Route 6, the most direct road from Phnom Penh, is still highly insecure between Kompong Thom and Siem Reap.

By air, Royal Air Cambodge (owned by Malaysian Air Service) flies new Boeing jets and ATR turboprops to Siem Reap from Phnom Penh several times daily and several times weekly to Sihanoukville, Battambang and Rattanakiri.

There are now several companies running a speedboat service to Siem Reap via the Tonlé Sap River. The trip takes about five hours from Phnom Penh; foreigners pay US$25, Khmers 50,000 riel one-way. Two types of boats make the run: long, enclosed boats bought second-hand from Malaysia, and comparatively new, smaller speedboats with twin outboard engines run by a Chinese company. The long boats are the more comfortable, with aircraft-like interiors, air conditioning, and real (if tiny) toilets. Be sure to bring toilet paper, as none is provided. Earplugs are also a good idea, as the drone of the engine competes with Chinese video dubbed in Khmer and played at top volume. The smaller speedboats are supposedly a bit faster, but the double-row bench seats get uncomfortable after an hour, and the "toilet" is a roofless box at the stern. Both boats depart every day at 7 a.m. from the Psar Toit area north of the Japanese Bridge. A free shuttle to the pier leaves at about 6:30 a.m. from the Capitol Hotel.

Travel to Siem Reap is also possible on the slow cargo boats, which depart Phnom Penh regularly and take a full 24 hours. The boat anchors in the middle of the river for the night; travelers must bring their own sleeping gear. Price is about 35,000 riel one way.

Dangerous Places

Southeast Cambodia has seen an upsurge in banditry and military activity. Several other areas, such as parts of Battambang Province, are also insecure. The temples at Angkor are safe to visit. But travel in other areas of Siem Reap province is highly dangerous, as the Khmer Rouge control or terrorize large parcels of the province. Americans traveling outside urban areas are urged by the U.S. embassy to exercise caution and restrict travel to daylight hours and to travel only in vehicle convoys to enhance security. Crime, including armed vehicle theft, is a serious problem in areas including the capital city, Phnom Penh. Travelers can register and obtain updated security information from the U.S. embassy upon their arrival in Phnom Penh.

Banteay Srei

One American—Susan Hadden, 50—was killed and another was wounded by bandits on January 15, 1995, in the vicinity of Banteay Srei Temple, a little visited site approximately 30 kilometers northeast of Siem Reap and Angkor Wat. The area surrounding Banteay Srei Temple continues to be unsettled and dangerous. Since January 16, 1995, the Cambodian government has prohibited travel to that temple.

Dangerous Things

Kidnapping

The Khmer Rouge have kidnapped 7 Westerners and have killed 6 of them. Do you feel lucky punk?

Land Mines

U.N. officials and demining experts estimate that between 6 and 10 million mines are scattered around the country. The Russian PMN2 antipersonnel mine is the most common mine in Cambodia. Three hundred people are killed or maimed every month. It is estimated that one person in 236 in Cambodia is an amputee because of an injury from land mines. The most heavily mined areas are Kampong Thom, Siem Reap, Kampong Chang, Kampong Speu, Koh Kong, Oddar Meanchey, Batneay Meanchey, Battambang and Pursat. Although mines are cleared out every day, more are planted by the Khmer Rouge in their efforts to create terror amongst the rural population.

Clearing Mines

While *DP* was in Cambodia, a group of 29 mine disposal workers were attacked by the Khmer Rouge in Siem Reap province. The employees of Mines Advisory Group were accused of laying mines. The 10 gunmen made off with an English mine clearer and his interpreter. A man who was arrested later said he was paid $20 to show the KR where the mine clearers would be working that day. A group of three women who went to negotiate the Brit's release were themselves taken hostage, and all five were taken to Anlong Veng, a KR camp run by General Ta Mok. For now the KR is not reading or following the rule book.

Crime

There are frequent armed thefts of vehicles, armed extortion attempts and numerous incidents of petty crimes, such as hotel theft and purse snatching. In October 1994, armed bandits, dressed as police officers, robbed an armored courier truck of about US$100,000 that was en route to Pochentong Airport for transfer of the funds to a

Bangkok bank. In May 1994, a police colonel was slain by armed bandits for his motor-bike. Foreigners are frequently targeted. Automatic weapons abound in Cambodia, and are possessed and used by numerous citizens, even within Phnom Penh. The Khmer Rouge does not have a retirement plan, so many former KRs are roaming the country with their weapons looking for spare change.

Hooligan Haven

The Interpol representative office in Cambodia believes that at least 100 of Interpol's most-wanted criminals are hiding in Cambodia. The fugitives are said to be taking advantage of Cambodia's relatively lax legal system and the present inability of Royal Cambodian Government (RCG) law enforcement agencies to meaningfully fight crime. Interpol was further reported to be concerned that the apparent influx of criminals may signal a rise in organized crime activities in Cambodia—a country which has already seen an upsurge in international drug trafficking attributable, inter alia, to deficient law enforcement abilities.

In addition, police have launched a major investigation into the operations of a Phnom Penh-based company linked to Yoshimi Tanaka, a Japanese Red Army member, on charges of using counterfeit U.S. dollars. Police in Phnom Penh believe that Kodama International Trading (KIT), run by Tang Cheang Tong, a Japanese citizen of Khmer-Chinese origin, helped Tanaka launder fake U.S. currency through its export-import operations. Tanaka was arrested on the Cambodia-Vietnam border on March 24, 1996, by Cambodian police and Interpol officials after being accused of disposing of counterfeit dollars in the southeastern Thai resort of Pattaya. Cambodian customs officials and police were at various times offered up to US$40,000 in bribes to let him cross the border. One of Japan's most well known fugitives, Tanaka is also wanted for his role in the 1970 hijacking of a Japanese airliner to Pyongyang, North Korea.

Car- and Motorbike-jackings

There's been a surge in armed carjackings and forcible rip-offs of motorbikes in Phnom Penh. Even the police themselves are not immune to becoming victims. In many instances, the victims are shot.

Trains

Western tourists traveling by railroad have a better chance of being robbed and/or abducted than not. The Cambodian railway system may be the most lethal stretch of tracks in the world. In addition to the Westerners that have been abducted off trains by the Khmer Rouge, the guerrillas often target ethnic Vietnamese as well as other Cambodians. On New Year's day in 1995, KR guerrillas ambushed a train 60 km northwest of Phnom Penh, killing eight and injuring 36. Among the dead were four women. The rebels stopped the train by blowing up the tracks in front of it and then spraying the railway cars with machine-gun fire and B-40 rockets.

Buses

Western tourists are prohibited from traveling aboard local buses. Only the bus to Saigon is open to foreigners.

Farmers

Yes, even you have a price on your head. And some rice farmer with a sickle may cash in on it. Police arrested three farmers on charges of conspiring to abduct or kill foreigners for cash rewards from the Khmer Rouge. The Khmer Rouge tells us that Americans are worth $10,000, if you want to know. The three were arrested in the northwestern city of Battambang and charged with offenses under legislation passed in 1994 to outlaw the Khmer Rouge. The farmers were planning to abduct or kill foreigners who were exercising in the town along the river. Khmer Rouge rebels had told the sodbusters they would pay US$1600 for each foreigner abducted and US$800 for each one killed. Life's cheap. Nice to be wanted.

Timber

The Khmer Rouge make about $10 million a month in timber sales to Thailand, according to Global Witness. Depending on whom you talk to or what day it is, the Khmer Rouge control about 10 percent of Cambodia. Most of it is in rich in first-growth tropical hardwoods. The government of Cambodia has authorized soldiers to open fire on logging trucks or boats taking lumber out of Cambodia.

Getting Sick

Outside of the major cities, you are out of luck here. It would be best to fly to Singapore for treatment of serious wounds or diseases. You can expect malaria and other tropical bugs endemic to Southeast Asia. There is one doctor for every 27,000 people in Cambodia.

Nuts and Bolts

Americans can register at the U.S. embassy in Phnom Penh and obtain updated information on travel and security within Cambodia. *Fielding's Thailand, Cambodia, Laos and Myanmar* and *Southeast Asia* provide up-to-the-minute coverage of travel in Cambodia.

Plus Ça Change...

The Cambodian government invited DP to return to Cambodia in September 1995 to see for itself the country was no longer dangerous. It turns out the August 20, 1995 Agence France Presse article blasting Cambodia's inclusion in DP was a prophetic intro to an orgy of violence. On early Sunday morning, August 27, four foreigners were injured, two seriously, after government soldiers gunned them down in a case of mistaken identity,

Injured were two young Bulgarians—one the son of a diplomat—a Briton and an Australian in two separate incidents at the same roadblock around 1 a.m. in front of Second Prime Minister Hun Sen's Phnom Penh residence.

Australian Iain Howatson, 26, an employee of the local Land Rover dealership was shot at; the bullets hit his motorcycle, throwing him off. He also suffered a wound to his arm and a serious injury to his head when he hit the pavement.

Shortly afterwards, Bulgarians Dimitir Ivanov, 18, and Braiko Zahov, 17, and Briton Gregory James, 29, were fired on in the same area, again while passing by on a motorcycle. Ivanov, the son of Bulgarian embassy attaché Vasko Ivanov, suffered bullet wounds in the neck, back and right shoulder. His friend, Zahov, suffered a serious head injury when he tumbled from the motorcycle. The Brit, an English language teacher, was shot in the arm.

Three road blocks were erected Saturday night in the area around the towering monument in downtown Phnom Penh to control access to the house of Cambodia's Second Prime Minister Hun Sen after fears of a coup led by white mercenaries spread.

Plus Ça Change...

In a separate incident a few days later, the local journalist who had earlier interviewed DP contributor Wink Dulles regarding the security situation in Cambodia was robbed of his motorcycle and US$800 in cash at gunpoint by men in military uniforms the day the article ran in the Cambodia Daily.

Embassy Locations

U.S. Embassy
> *No. 20, Mongkol Iem Street (Street 228)*
> *Phnom Penh, Cambodia*
> ☎ *[855] (23) 26436 or (23) 26438; cellular: 018-810465; FAX: 855-23-27637*

The consular entrance to the U.S. embassy is located at *16 Street 228 (between Street 51 and Street 63).* The embassy is able to offer essential consular services.

Cambodian U.N. Section
> *866 U.N. Plaza, Suite 420*
> *New York, NY 10017*
> ☎ *(212) 421-7626*

Dangerous Days

01/15/1995	American Susan Hadden was killed by the Khmer Rouge near Banteay Srey temple.
07/26/1994	Three Western tourists bound for Sihanoukville by train taken hostage by the Khmer Rouge and subsequently executed.
04/11/1994	Three Westerners were taken hostage along Route 4 in southern Cambodia by the Khmer Rouge and subsequently executed.
01/07/1979	Vietnamese took Phnom Penh and installed Hun Sen as prime minister of Cambodia.
04/17/1975	Pol Pot and Khmer Rouge rolled into Phnom Penh and seized control of Cambodia.
10/09/1970	Cambodian monarchy abolished. The country subsequently was named the Khmer Republic.
11/09/1953	Independence Day
06/19/1951	Army-people solidarity day celebrates the founding of the Cambodian People's Armed Forces.
02/03/1930	Founding of the ICP, the Indochinese Communist Party.
05/19/1928	The birthdate of Pol Pot, the leader of the Khmer Rouge.
05/24	Birth of Buddha.

In a Dangerous Place

Cambodia, 1995: A Ride in the Country

Is travel in Cambodia safe for foreigners today? The government seems to think so and invited *DP* to see for itself.

In September 1995, in response to a Cambodian government protest over this chapter on Cambodia in the first edition of *DP*, we returned to Cambodia to reassess the country's safety for foreign travelers. Rather than simply take the beaten tourist cow path to Angkor, which—at press time—was secure for tourists (either by air or large speedboat), I journeyed by motorcycle down to Sihanoukville on National Highway 4, the route on which the three Westerners were traveling when they were taken captive and later killed by the Khmer Rouge in 1994. I did this despite being warned by many not to, including the government's tourism minister.

####

As planned, I telephoned Cambodian Tourism Minister Veng Sereyvuth to schedule dinner, and was told by his assistant to meet him the following night at 7:30 at the Cambodiana, Cambodia's queen of hotels and a good place to convince someone that land mines don't maim a thousand Cambodians a month or that Khmers' per-capita annual income isn't below 170 bucks a year.

I rented a Honda Rebel, the Tonka Toy of choppers, and headed back to the Capitol to find a guide. My Khmer is as fluent as my Swahili, and I didn't want to get stuck in the sticks trading my wallet and underwear for smiles with the locals.

I chose the guy who seemed most capable of talking his way out of a hole. He went by the name of "Tall Man". Appropriate, as he was over six-three, making him the King Kong of Khmers. Bony, with wavy, Waldo-like locks, and movie-star handsome, Tall Man had lost both his parents to Pol Pot during the four-year Khmer Rouge slaughter of the Cambodian people during the mid-1970s. His English was excellent.

I met with Sereyvuth the next night at the Cambodiana. He brought along with him a strapping, husky Australian, whose sneer couldn't be seen beneath mustache whiskers spilling over his mouth like stalagtite from the roof of a cave. His name was Trevor. He was introduced to me as an attorney. He looked more like a retired boxer.

"This *Dangerous Places* book has screwed this country," the Aussie said. "You have no idea how much you have pissed this man off." He nodded toward Veng, who seemed to be preoccupied looking at a floral arrangement at a distant table. "He won't tell you this stuff himself because he's Cambodian," Trevor continued. "He won't show his anger."

I was then informed that there were at least seven major projects that had been seriously jeopardized with the publication of *The World's Most Dangerous Places.* "What we need to know is what are you going to do right now to correct this matter?" Trevor demanded.

"I'm here to reevaluate Cambodia's security for tourists," I said. "If it's any safer than it was the last time I was here, I'll report it."

"Listen, my friend," Trevor said. "There's a way of doing things in this country, and there's a way of not doing them. Do not go to Sihanoukville."

"Tomorrow," Veng suddenly cut in, "go to Angkor Wat and have a good time."

The next day, I got a call from Pip Wood, national editor of the *Cambodia Daily*, who wanted an interview because he'd heard I might go to Kompot by train. Foreigners don't go to Kompot by train. Not possessing a death wish, I asked him if it was possible. He said we should ask the Khmers on the paper's staff if they'd make the journey by train.

"It's high in the sky," said Ek Madra, a Khmer journalist.

"What the hell does that mean?" I said.

"There's a chance you'll make it, and a chance you won't." he said.

Foreigners are still not permitted to purchase the discounted tickets for the first three cars of the train, which can only be had by Cambodians. At last check, clerks at Phnom Penh's train station refused to sell any tickets at all to foreigners on any of Cambodia's train routes.

"That's how those guys were hit last year," Martin Flitman, a longtime Phnom Penh-based photojournalist told me. "They were seen buying tickets at the station. Word goes down the line into KR territory. The KR knew those tourists were on the train before it got there. You might be able to make it today, but not if you buy your ticket at the station. Get aboard after Pochentong and you may make it."

I decided the train was out of the question. A death wish I have not.

Kompong Som—or Sihanoukville, the quaintly renamed port of the south—is 220 kilometers south of Phnom Penh. It's at the other end of a marvelously well paved ribbon of asphalt that cuts a swath through the flat rice fields around the Mekong River and winds its way through the Elephant Mountains, before descending into the sleepy seaside port town. Highway 4 is generally considered to be safe for 50 km out of Phnom Penh. The villages flanking its shoulders are large, and psychologically comforting, modern Western-style petrol stations spring from the rice fields every five kilometers or so. As the road cuts into the hills, the villages become fewer and farther between. The Shell stations cease. Rice fields cede the topography to rolling parcels of dense brush, much of the scrub blanketing many of the millions of land mines coated with soil in this Claymore-besieged country. This is Khmer Rouge territory. During daylight on most days, the guerrillas hide in the hills between five and 10 klicks off the highway. At night, they creep to the roadside and lay fresh mines and—along with other groups of thugs, bullies and bandits—stop vehicles and rob motorists.

As the route winds though KR turf, every half klick a small group of soldiers can be seen lounging by the roadside beneath makeshift lean-tos. The small bridges along Highway 4 are manned by troops 24 hours a day. They sleep beneath tarps strung in the trees just off the road. They have the special responsibility of preventing the KR from blowing up the bridges. A number will step into the road, attempting to halt cars for bribes. Few motorists pay them any heed, speeding past. They know they won't have such an escape opportunity at the larger, more fortified checkpoints. At these points, the line of cars and trucks waiting to pay the road "toll" can reach a kilometer long. Until recently, foreigners traveling in taxis were routinely hit up for kickbacks at the military roadblocks. Gratefully, such instances are rare these days.

About 50 klicks from Sihanoukville, Tall Man tapped my shoulder. He had to pee. I saw a bright red "DANGER! LAND MINES" sign off the road and parked the bike on the pavement next to it. Not on the soft road shoulder. There was a way to do things in Cambodia, and a way not to do them.

Three soldiers approached the bike, their automatic rifles slung like purses. They seemed friendly enough. I gave them cigarettes and Mr. DP stickers. Tall Man zipped himself back in and chirped with the soldiers in Khmer. Suddenly, his smile dropped. The soldiers trudged off.

"A child just stepped on a land mine," he said. "About an hour ago. Just up the road."

It started to rain again. I rolled the bike about 50 meters up the asphalt. A small compound of brightly painted hootches on stilts were on the right, just off the road. Tinny, reverbed Khmer mourning music blared from a small loudspeaker. Villagers huddled under one of the wooden dwellings. Beneath an overhang was a circle of people.

I was struck by the blood-soaked blanket covering the corpse, as the circle parted to let me through. An old man, on seeing my camera, removed the shroud and stripped the dead 12-year-old. The child had caught the blast in the groin. His eyes were milky, his tiny hands folded on his chest. He looked as if he had taken a while to die.

The old man was the child's grandfather. He said his grandson had been walking the family cow. The cow had stepped on the mine, then ran off into the forest on three legs. It explained why the boy's legs were fine. He said the mine was planted by some drunken government troops about a month ago.

INSIDER TIP

If you choose to go to Sihanoukville by road (there are also flights), be warned: Do not travel on National Highway 4 before 10 a.m. or after 3 p.m. The road is marginally (albeit decidedly) controlled by government troops during the daylight hours, and nighttime travel along this route is perilous, particularly south of Kampong Speu, 48 km west of Phnom Penh. Even the minesweeping teams covered by heavily armed government troops make a dash east to the safety of the capital environs starting in the late afternoon. Bandits and the Khmer Rouge prey the road at night.

We made it to Sihanoukville, escaping detainment, arrest, theft, abduction and execution. I got drunk on Thai whisky. The next morning, we headed back for Phnom Penh. I stopped to photograph the village where the youngster had died.

After another 60 kilometers, we came upon a unit of the Cambodian Mine Action Committee (CMAC) tiptoeing on Highway 4's shoulder with metal detectors. The team was led by a young Canadian army captain and supported by Royal Cambodian tanks and armored personnel carriers. A Khmer was slumped asleep behind the wheel of a Nissan pickup. In its bed, a huge Browning machine gun mounted on a turret was aimed toward the eastern mountains. It looked like the "technicals" used by the thugs and warlords in Somalia. Another soldier stooped by the side of the highway, wiping a pair of B-40 rockets. Steamrollers were pressing new asphalt. We had come upon the spot where the KR's diesel and fertilizer bombs had detonated a couple of days earlier. I reported our discovery to the Canadian.

"Thanks for the report," the officer said. "I didn't know there was any action down there. We'll report it to Phnom Penh, and they'll send a team down there to clean up the area soon."

"There's a lot of kids in the village," I said.

"They'll do it soon."

"The old man said government troops planted it about a month ago," I said.

"Unlikely. Probably old. But even we can't tell how long they've been under."

The Canadian had been in-country six months and was charged with clearing Highway 4 from Phnom Penh to Sihanoukville. He'd made it about halfway, saying his team had removed 1800 mines. The kid's mine made it 1801.

—**Wink Dulles**

In a Dangerous Place: Over the Line

We went to Cambodia on a lark. These days, Cambodia is not necessarily the most dangerous place in the world, or even a nasty place, but it is an exotic, very inexpensive stop that every traveler to Asia should make. Is it safe? Well, if you stay inside the tourist ruts (literally), don't venture outside the ill-defined "safety" zone and watch where you step, Cambodia can be safe. Cambodia can also be a brutal if you pass through the invisible safety barrier and end up in the hands of the Khmer Rouge. Just remember the advice of your first grade teacher, "Don't color outside the lines."

Cambodia has provided a safe corridor for tourists wanting to visit the great temple complexes around Angkor Wat. Depending on who you talk to, the Khmer Rouge is either a mighty Chinese backed juggernaut, complete with tanks, foot soldiers and tacit support from the Thai generals along the border, or as a ragtag band of starving anachronisms who have resorted to banditry just to eat. The truth is somewhere in the middle and at both ends of the spectrum.

One tourist can fly into Phnom Penh and Siem Reap on a modern jet, stay in a five-star hotel, and see the temple complex, complete with cold Pepsis, an air-conditioned car and a good meal, followed by an ice-cold beer at one of the many nightclubs the U.N. soldiers used to frequent. Another tourist can find himself kneeling at the edge of a shallow, hastily dug grave, waiting for the rifle butt that will slam into his cortex, ending his brief but adventurous life. The difference between the two scenarios might be 10 kms or lingering a few too many minutes along the road.

Despite the kidnapping, execution, injuring and shooting of a number of tourists over the last few years, the government of Cambodia considers its country safe...within certain limits. Those three ellipsis can be the difference between life and death here.

####

When we buy tickets, the Malaysian trained ticket agent for Royal Air Cambodge, a joint venture between Malaysian Airlines and the Cambodian government, is cordial and efficient. We ask whether many tourists come to Cambodia. He thinks we must be very stupid spies and points to the lack of tourists in the check-in area.

We ask, "Is it dangerous in Cambodia?" He looks up and says, "I would say it is a lot safer than Los Angeles," referring to the shooting of Hang Ngor, the Cambodian doctor turned actor who starred in *The Killing Fields*. He had managed to survive Cambodia, only to die on the mean streets of Los Angeles. Killed for a gold locket (that contained a picture of his dead wife) by a member of the Lazy Boys, a street gang made up of Chinese kids. That gold locket was what carried him through the horrors of captivity and his escape; it also killed him. Hang Ngor thought he had crossed over the line, but he never made it.

On the flight in, my sober thoughts about Cambodia are confirmed by the sight of the hard brown country below us. A visual shock after flying over the endless green carpets of Malaysia and Thailand. Cambodia has long been denuded and carved into a patchwork for wet season rice cultivation, interrupted by movie-prop-style sugar palms in random patterns.

When the monsoon arrives, the countryside floods, roads are impassable and the rice fields turn rich green. Food becomes plentiful. There is hope and happiness in the wet season. The dry season is a time of hardship and killing.

The dry season is when the government launches its tank and infantry attacks against the Khmer Rouge, who then retreat into their strongholds near Thailand and their jungle and hilltop hideouts. Slipping away like children chasing pigeons, the KR wait for the rainy season to regroup and infiltrate back to the south. The dry season is the most dangerous time for tourists. It is when food and supplies are at their scarcest for the wandering bands of KR and bandits. It is when the Khmer Rouge must rob and kidnap to raise money to buy supplies or just eat. Many say that members of the KR army simply take off their uniforms and dissolve into the general populace.

The wet season is the most dangerous time for the locals. This is when the KR enters villages to press gangs, farmers, kids, anyone who can carry a gun. Should the young people not be there, the KR promise to come back and kill the entire family if they do not supply a raw recruit. They also carry off rice, building materials and any possessions the villagers have not buried. The wet season is when it is easy to plant land mines and booby traps, which become invisible in the dry season. The villagers are constantly maimed and killed, as they go out to work their fields and paddies during the wet season.

Our flight is full of fat, middle-aged Chinese businessmen with bad haircuts who immediately start gambling and drinking as soon as the seat belt sign goes off. We ask why they are going to Phnom Penh. They all have clothing factories there, we are told. "Cambodia is just like Thailand was ten years ago. Cheap, very cheap."

As the plane comes in for the final approach, I notice the rows of rusty tanks and APCs. Studying the parched ground interrupted by wispy brown bushes and meandering vein-like footpaths, I can't help thinking that Cambodia looks like the skull of someone recovering from heavy chemotherapy.

Upon landing, formalities are brief—$20 in U.S. currency and a visa. The line, the crush of tourists, and the exotic-looking posters of Angkor Wat on the walls makes me feel like I am paying to get into a theme park. Another sick irony makes me laugh—it costs $38 dollars to get into EPCOT, and there are a whole lot less land mines there. On the simple forms we fill out, it seems the government wants to know if we are bringing in any gold bars, ammunition or firearms.

Pushing through the usual Third World crush of touts and taxi drivers, we pause again, these people are only asking for two and three dollars to drive us into town. Obviously, the supply is a lot higher than the demand here. Driving into town, the bullet holes, grass-filled craters and fading scorch marks have all been cleaned up. Phnom Penh is bustling, not a Bangkok bustle but still busy for a city that once looked like a scene from *Full Metal Jacket*. As if to provide a counterpoint to the death and destruction all around, our driver slows down as he passes a row of small shops with Vietnamese women sitting outside. He points, smiles and simply says, "fucking." This is obviously the standard route into town.

There is still something missing, though. There are very few, if any, people over the age of 45. More than 1 million people, some say more, were killed in here by Pol Pot and the Khmer Rouge in their attempt to re-engineer society. Today, like Saigon, the post-war generation is gregarious and eager to meet Westerners. The men above 30 are more reticent. Around town there are men and boys who have been maimed by land mines.They beg, politely repeating, *"Bapa Yam"* (or "please sir, rice"). I also notice that there are no flowers in Cambodia. Their tattered army uniforms and shiny plastic limbs make me think back to Afghanistan.

A few months earlier when we were at the headquarters of the *taliban*, their stairwells and courtyard were full of maimed fighters. The difference is that the tiny Russian mines only took off the foot at the ankle. Here, the legs are gone up to the knee and sometimes higher. Here, the men have prosthetic limbs; in Afghanistan, they gave the wounded a stick to walk with. Here, there has been a different kind of horror. In Afghanistan, the fighters and old men proudly wear their DP stickers and T-shirts. In Cambodia, if a soldier or civilian has been through the holocaust, he is more likely to politely hand back the image of the grinning skull of Mr. DP. There are far too many images of real skulls here. I notice something else. There are no birds or the singing of birds in Cambodia.

Walking down the main drag in Phnom Penh, we are followed by a Ray-Banned man in a yellow shirt and string tie. He doesn't do his job well, since we repeatedly sneak up behind him and give him a start. Paranoia and posttraumatic stress are just below the surface here.

As all good tourists must, we visit the killing fields as well as the police detention and torture center. It is hard to understand the methodical nature of the Khmer Rouges' killing, as we view black-and-white photos of every victim seated in a posing stool, their paperwork filled out in triplicate.

But then again, does anybody understand what motivates Turks to kill Armenians, Germans to kill Jews, Americans to kill Indians, Jews to kill Arabs, Arabs to kill Christians, Christians to kill Arabs and so on? There are so many skulls, they make murals, maps, monuments and whatever else they can think off. They try to be educational with their macabre building materials, but once again I can't help think what a great pavilion and "audio-anima-horrific" ride this would make. There are still hundreds of thousands of skulls left in the ground to make displays, office buildings or even entire pavilions.

Over 20,000 U.N. soldiers used to keep the lid on this country, but today just about the only remnants are the white Land Cruisers and Toyota pickup trucks of the U.N., repainted with various aid logos. You can see these vehicles parked outside the other remnants of the U.N.'s efforts. Upscale restaurants, air-conditioned massage parlors, cheap whorehouses and a surprisingly high-end discos keep Phnom Penh and Siam Reap hopping late in to the night. For a Westerner, a massage costs $5, a night of Cambodian passion, $25. In the bigger dance halls and restaurants, cheap beer is sold by attentive uniformed women who represent and get a commission from their sponsoring brewery. You can't slowly savor a beer here, as your glass is filled past the meniscus level by chatty beer ladies or impatient "go dancing" girls.

We hire a driver to tour the countryside, The hotel we stay in is run by a women who has hired her ex-husbands old army buddies. Not a difficult thing to do, since most Cambodian men are either in the army or have served in it. We ask the ex-army buddies who hang around the hotel if Cambodia is dangerous. They glibly reply, "Not so much anymore." We ask again, not happy with this pat answer. They pause and say it depends where you go. We ask our driver, who responds: "As long as you visit the temples, it is fine; if you go beyond...," His explanation trailing off, as he points to the hills and countryside.

Wink tells him of his trip north of Siem Reap. The driver thinks we are asking if this trip would be dangerous. He replies, shaking his head and laughing at our folly, "No, you cannot do that." Wink explains, that he has already done it. The driver says, "Then you are very lucky to be alive."

We stop at a Thai-owned bank to change money. The manager is equally impressed and amused, as he overhears Wink jabbering away in Thai. He has been here for three months. He cautions us that it is dangerous here. He says, "Do not go out after dark. There are many guns. Men dress up like police and stop foreigners at roadblocks. Do not drive outside of the city. It is dangerous." We ask if anyone has been robbed. He says, "Yes, many people." He warns us to be extra careful. The recent division between the two rulers sharing power is heating up, and he tells us that "the word is out on the street that there may be a coup soon."Aware that three foreigners were sprayed with machine-gun fire when they were mistaken for "white mercenaries," we thank him for the tip.

We ask around town if we can rent bikes or drive up to Siem Reap. Not possible, we are told, for the simple reason that at best you are guaranteed to run into Khmer Rouge roadblocks and be abducted, worst case is you will be shot and robbed. No cab drivers will take us. We book a flight instead.

Arriving in Siem Reap, we hire a driver and tell him we want to retrace the route of the American tourist who was injured in a rocket and machine-gun attack just north of the Angkor temple complex. He does not think that is a good idea. "It is too dangerous." He refused to take us there, so we content ourselves with visiting the temples in the company of reappearing chattering clusters of Japanese, Germans and Thai tourists.

Cambodia is happy. The bus tourists are finally coming back; the temples used to be silent with the occasional backpacker, expat or aid worker carefully avoiding the smaller paths and out-of-the-way complexes. Soon there will be a major development just outside the temples as well as in the nearby city of Siam Reap. This former battle zone is sprouting giant five-star hotels with room capacities in the hundreds, more appropriate for Las Vegas than this tiny county. The red skull signs that signaled areas still full of land mines are mostly gone. The soldiers no longer carry AK 47's (it scares the tourists they tell us). When we ask where the machine guns are, we are told don't worry—there are plenty at the army base. For now, Cambodia is one of the cheapest places to visit. A beer costs $2, a meal in a restaurant goes for about $3—steep, considering we are paying $3 a night for two people in a room. We get our laundry done for a buck. And all of this in U.S. greenbacks.

Hanging around the great man-made lake that surrounds Angkor Wat, we watch the sunset turn the temples' towers to a fiery red. It is hard to believe that the sun has been turning the temples this color for the last 700 years. There are a few bullet holes from where the Vietnamese army once camped out here. All the major statues have been stolen, destroyed or removed by Europeans, the Khmer Rouge or vandals, but there is still an awesome power of solemnity that holds visitors in its sway. The slightly bemused expressions of the great faces of the Bayon are a perfect contrast to the bloodthirsty scenes carved on the friezes that decorate the temple walls.

We strike up a conversation with a member of military intelligence for the Siam Reap provinces. He tells us that two Khmer Rouge generals have defected with military plans. One apparently wanted a Range Rover as part of his retirement package.

A British minesweeper and his assistant are kidnapped by the Khmer Rouge less than a half-day's drive from here. Surprisingly enough, our friend is quite pleased, since one of the goodies one of the generals dropped off at their office was a plan to kidnap a foreigner. The only snag is, they had to make do with a Brit.

Americans are the most favored kidnap victims, followed by British and then French. Yanks bring in an automatic $10,000 U.S. and provide the necessary publicity to give the government grief. We ask him how safe it is. He says, in town, at the temples and in daylight, there is no problem. But 20 kms away, there is a battle raging. We also tell him about DP's trip by motorcycle around the countryside. He also thinks we are talking in the future tense. He says that would not be a very good idea. We say, no, we already took the trip. He also says he was very lucky.

That night back in Siem Reap we go to a nightclub. The sign outside says "no guns or explosives." The music is pure sing song Khmer played at ear-damaging levels. The Khmers dance to the music in a circular line dance reminiscent of that on a bad TNN show. Wink decides to get up and jam with the band. The audience is dumbstruck and stares open-mouthed for two songs. The dance floor clears out, and the Cambodians don't know if they should clap or cover their ears. Wink finishes up to a round of applause. After Wink sits down, it seems not everyone is thrilled with his impromptu jam session. We are challenged to a fight in a less than sensitive manner. An elbow not once, not twice, but three times in the back—hard. We decide to split. This would not be a John Wayne punch 'em up, but probably a sloppy and quick burst of automatic weapons. As we change venues, the group of surly Cambodian men follows us out into the street. We face off, neither side wanting to be the first to start hostilities. Luckily, our driver pulls up and we drive off.

We stop at another place with the same bad music, same knife-edge tension. Wink sums it up by saying these people are very fucked up. The more genteel would say they suffer from posttraumatic stress, though they aren't even aware of the term here. There is a lot of rage. He echoes a sentiment a Malaysian friend expresses to me on hearing that I would be going to Cambodia: The people here are very quiet and angry—they have seen a lot of death.

We sit with three Cambodian girls, or rather three girls made a hurried grab for the empty chairs at our table. Westerners are big game for these bar girls. Wink keeps talking to them in Vietnamese. In Cambodia, most working girls are divided into "go dancing" girls, women who sit, talk and dance with and maybe sleep with you on request, and "taxi girls," who are simply sex girls. There are also houses where the function of intercourse is emotionally and financially comparable to the drive-through window at McDonald's. Most of the girls are Vietnamese, but these girls are Cambodian. To prove it, they mimic the ancient hand movements and music of the *apsara*, the temptresses seen on the temples at Angkor. Wink is surprised, since most girls who were trained dancers were killed by the Khmer Rouge. Aspiring to more intellectual entertainment, we teach one of the girls a few English words at her request. She tells us that if she learns English, she will get a better job. We find out that what she means is that she can sleep with more Westerners and therefore make more money. She tells us with some pride that one Japanese man actually paid her $40 for the whole night. A curious career ambition.

Wink keeps talking to one girl in Vietnamese, while another keeps on feeling the private parts of one of our party and encourages us to feel how big it is. All in all, a typical night in Siem Reap.

Sitting outside to avoid the chilling air conditioning and deafening noise inside, we are interrupted as a Cambodian cop comes flying out of the glass entry doors. The girls sitting with us immediately react, jump up, and drag us around the corner and down an alley. They plead with us to "Go, go, run! Please, before you are shot!" Not quite knowing what they are talking about, we walk back to the front, but the girls push us back, pleading with us to run away.

We push past them and are in time to watch the cop being kicked and beaten and then slammed unconscious into the back of a pickup truck. The girls explain that we are lucky (a term we are hearing a lot here). Usually, there is gun fire. They mimic the action of someone firing a machine-gun. They tell us that this week "a man fell down, went to sleep." I laugh. The expression on the girl's face tells me that she is not trying to be cute; she is trying to avoid saying the word "died." She halfheartedly repeats the machine-gun pantomime and tries to make me understand. The sad look in her eyes tells me that I am being far too casual about a very real threat. With a sense of resignation, she says, "This is a dangerous place. You should not be here."

—**RYP**

Bogotá

Colombia
★★★★★

Coca Loco Land

Each hour someone is killed in Bogota, the capital city of Colombia. The 8600 cadavers that pass through the morgue pile up every year at an average of 23 a day. Violent death is so ingrained in Colombian life that the health department has listed violence as the leading cause of death for individuals over 10 years old. To date, there isn't a known vaccine for a bullet to the head. The victims fit a neat pattern: male—one or more bullet holes and very dead; 61.2 percent are under 34. Firearms account for nearly 37 percent of the deaths (traffic accidents account for 14 percent of all deaths and 30 percent were from "unknown causes"). For those who don't want to spend an entire year in this beautiful land, it may be enough to know to that there are three kidnappings and three murders every day. A car is stolen every 24 minutes, and 142 houses are broken into every day.

The only saving grace in these morbid stats is that 75 percent of the 27,000 murder victims in Colombia in 1994 were classified as "common criminals." Colombia has a murder rate of 77.5 per 100,000 inhabitants (more than eight times higher than in the U.S.), making it among the most violent countries in the world for murders.

After soccer, murder seems to be the national pastime. After one Colombian soccer defeat to Venezuela a few years ago in Bogota, 27 people were killed and a police outpost was dynamited. You gotta just love these fans.

These National Statistics Office figures do little to reveal the entire story of what is happening in Colombia. Colombia is turning into a lawless nation that functions on the edge, barely keeping the lid on anarchy. Colombia's wealthy, its intellectuals, and the educated have fled to escape kidnapping, extortion and murder threats. The drug lords, criminals, revolutionaries and terrorists not only wage war against the government and infrastructure but among themselves.

In all, the price of the guerrilla war in Colombia since 1990 has cost upwards of a staggering US$20 billion, or 4 percent of the GDP yearly. Extortion, kidnapping, oil pipeline attacks and corpses inflicted by a 10,000-rebel-strong force (there were a mere 215 insurgents in 1964) have cost the state oil company, Ecopetrol, US$550 million—through lost royalties, pipeline attacks, repair and security costs, and ransoms. Between 1991 and 1994, 2300 hostages were taken, netting the kidnappers—i.e., guerrillas—US$350 million. Private-sector oil companies consider the loss of US$430 million due to death, destruction and mayhem as the cost of doing business here.

In Colombia, crisis management teams outnumber pipeline teams. Negotiations consultants are hired, not to strike deals on leveraged buyouts and drilling concessions from the government, but to procure the release of hostages. More than 800 people are being held captive in Colombia as this ink dries. One Colombian study estimates that, including extortion and drug trafficking, rebel income between 1991 and 1994 reached US$1.8 billion, providing the guerrillas an annual per-capita income of US$45,000, compared with Colombia's GNP per-capita income of US$1401.

Of more than 17,000 people killed since 1990, more than half of them were innocent bystanders. Colombia has spent $3.4 billion to fight rebels since 1990. One pipeline near the Venezuelan border was blown up 229 times during a 260-week period. That's almost as regular as the fireworks every night at Disney-World.

Although the government has extended an olive branch to Colombia's insurgents and promised the Colombian people they would make peace with the rebels, only one faction has stepped forward so far—the 250 guerrillas of the Jaime Bateman Cayon group, a breakaway coterie of the now-defunct M-19 insurgents.

Colombia may well be the butthole of South America. Don't believe us? You can actually receive updated security information about Colombia from the State Department by dialing ☎ 202-647-5225, and then enter the following letters: C-O-L-O-N.

The Scoop

Colombia is currently the most dangerous place in the Western Hemisphere. The druglords, terrorist groups, very active engagement by government forces against both these groups, and general lawlessness make Colombia a must-see for anyone planning a vacation in hell. If you travel to Colombia, you will be the target of thieves, kidnappers and murderers.

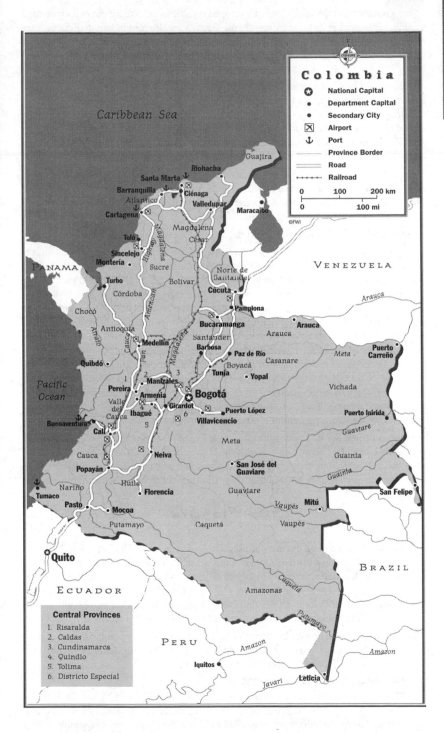

Colombia

- ⊛ National Capital
- • Department Capital
- • Secondary City
- ⊠ Airport
- ⚓ Port
- ┈┈ Province Border
- ─── Road
- ┼┼┼ Railroad

0   100   200 km
0   100 mi

©FWI

Caribbean Sea

Guajira

Ríohacha

Santa Marta ⚓
Barranquilla
Atlántico
Ciénaga
Valledupar
Cartagena

Maracaibo

PANAMA

Tolú
Sincelejo
Montería
Magdalena
César
Sucre
Bolívar
Norte de
Santander
Cúcuta

VENEZUELA

Turbo
Córdoba

Pamplona
Arauca

Chocó
Antioquia
Bucaramanga
Santander
Arauca
Arauca

Puerto
Carreño

Quibdó
Medellín
Barbosa
Paz de Río
Casanare
Meta

Vichada

Pacific
Ocean

Atrato
Cauca
Magdalena
Boyacá
Tunja
Yopal

1
2   3
Pereira
Manizales
Armenia
Ibagué
4
Bogotá
Girardot
6
Puerto López

Puerto Inírida

Valle
del
Cauca
5
Villavicencio

Guaviare

Buenaventura
Cali

Meta

Guainía

Cauca
Neiva

Guainía

San Felipe

Popayán
San José del
Guaviare

Guainía

Nariño
Huila
Florencia
Guaviare
Mitú

Tumaco
Pasto
Mocoa
Vaupés
Vaupés

Putumayo
Caquetá
Vaupés

Quito

BRAZIL

ECUADOR
Amazonas
Caquetá

Putumayo

PERU
Amazon

Iquitos
Amazon

Leticia

Javari

Central Provinces
1. Risaralda
2. Caldas
3. Cundinamarca
4. Quindío
5. Tolima
6. Distrito Especial

How bad is it? Civilians and soldiers are stopped at roadblocks, dragged out of their cars and summarily executed in Antioquia department. Tourists are drugged in bars and discos, then robbed and murdered. Expats, missionaries and other foreigners are favorite targets of terrorist groups, who kidnap them for outrageous ransom amounts that climb into the millions of dollars.

Wealthy rightwingers employ about 100 or so paid killers to systematically murder left-wingers. Left-wingers attempt to kidnap every freckle-faced foreigner they can get their hands on. Drug dealers are knocking off police at the rate of about one a day. The survivors are those who stay away from office buildings, bus stops, police stations and travel agents displaying American Express logos on their windows. However, tourists and other travelers are way down on the list of people who have any protection in this cocaine-fueled free-for-all.

Should you be victimized or seek revenge due to a misfortune, expect little comfort or sympathy from the police, military, and judicial or diplomatic folks; they're busy covering their own asses from the threat of terrorism, drug cartels and crime lords. Only 12 percent of the crimes committed in Colombia ever reach the judicial system.

If you get into trouble and can't afford the ransom, hire a death squad. The price is lower.

With the breakup in May 1992 of peace negotiations with the Colombian government, the country's remaining insurgency groups have focused on taking their war to the cities, using urban terrorism. Both the Colombian Revolutionary Armed Forces (FARC) and the National Liberation Army (ELN), united in the Simon Bolivar Guerrilla Coordinator (CGSB), have made efforts to increase their presence and infrastructure in urban areas, particularly in and around Bogota. The capital and other major Colombian cities (including Barranquilla, site of the U.S. consulate) have been hit by sporadic terrorist attacks, the most common of which have been bombings of financial institutions at night, apparently intended to cause damage but no injuries. But 1996 has seen a nationwide series of guerrilla attacks currently taking place. The FARC and ELN are staging the attacks in hopes of influencing a change in Colombia's government. As of April, 20 people had been killed and there were over 30 guerrilla attacks against public transportation, police stations and gas/oil pipelines. Guerrilla forces are also running a series of ambushes against government police and military forces.

Any good news? Some. The death squads have forced many drug traffickers to move into neighboring Brazil for "health" reasons. But the bottom line here, as one journalist commented, is this: "As many drug-trafficking countries fret about becoming another Colombia, with narcotics-dominated politics, Colombians worry that their country will become another Somalia, run by warlords."

The Players

The Government

Liberal Ernesto Samper Pizano squeaked into power June 19, 1993 in a dead heat with Conservative Andres Pastrana Arango. Considering that only one of every three Colombians voted, it doesn't seem to make any difference who runs the country. Samper has been accused as being a stooge of the Cali drug cartel, despite his public calls for the extermination of Colombia's drug problem. A recent investigation into his alleged ties with druglords concluded that he was offered backing but didn't accept it.

The government is actively but unsuccessfully trying to negotiate peace with various rebel factions, but for now is trying to figure out how to find jobs for the 5200 ex-guerrillas left over from the EPL and the M-19 groups.

The Simon Bolivar Guerrilla Coordinator (CGSB)

This is an unholy triumvirate of three terrorist groups: FARC, ELN, and the EPL/D. They claim about 8000 effective members among all three. The military has said that it managed to diminish that number in 1993 by killing 993 guerrillas and capturing another

1873. They also nabbed five tons of explosives and 1863 weapons in over 2000 armed engagements. Not as high a count as fowl during the duck hunting season in Minnesota, but not bad.

Bolivarian Movement for a New Colombia, or
Fuerzas Armadas Revolucionarias de Colombia (FARC)

FARC was founded in 1964 and is currently estimated to have between 12,000 and 17,000 combatants. Their stock in trade is kidnapping, extortion and protection of rural drug operations across Colombia. They have more of an entrepreneurial bent, considering they began as a Marxist, pro-Soviet revolutionary group. They are the largest and oldest of the three main rebel groups operating in Colombia.

The FARC rebels have decided to spruce up their image with a snapper name that will get them moved up in the Yellow Pages. They will now be known as the Bolivarian Movement for a New Colombia. Maybe Triple AAA Killing, Kidnapping and Narco Protection would get them more business.

The group specializes in armed attacks against Colombian targets, bombings of U.S. businesses, kidnappings of Colombians and foreigners for ransom, and assassinations. Their funding comes from extortion (ransom payments) and income from the trafficking of drugs (predominantly cocaine). FARC has well-documented ties to drug traffickers and Cuba. It is assumed that any drug transportation from Colombia to Cuba and beyond is controlled by FARC, and with the blessing of Fidel Castro. The dope bucks provide much needed hard currency for Cuba, whose economy has been in tatters since the collapse of the Soviet Union. Peace talks between the government of Colombia and FARC have proved unsuccessful.

There are an estimated 4500 to 5500 armed combatants and 10,000 supporters of FARC which likes to be cruel to be kind. They mainly target the wealthy, but off a couple of peasants once in awhile to keep them in line. The Patriotic Union (UP) is FARC's political arm, seeking change through old-fashioned rhetoric and arm twisting.

In a perfect world, FARC would overthrow established order in Colombia and replace it with a leftist and anti-American regime, in the process creating a broad antimonopoly, anti-imperialist front, while uniting left-wing parties and organizations into a single political movement.

On the scarier side, FARC is the largest, best-trained, best-equipped, and most effective insurgent organization in Colombia, and perhaps in all of South America—the one Western terrorist group voted "most likely to succeed" by U.S. intelligence services. Many consider FARC to be the "military" arm of the Communist Party of Colombia (PCC). The leadership of FARC is composed largely of disaffected middle- and upper-class intellectuals, although it recruits from the peasant population in an effort to maintain a popular base. FARC also draws support from traditional left-wingers, workers, students and radical priests. The popularity of FARC has been undermined by the questionable practice of kidnapping peasants and murdering them as "collaborators" and "traitors" if they're not cooperative.

FARC is the principal force behind National Simon Bolivar Guerrilla Coordinator (SBGC), which includes all major Colombian insurgent groups. FARC was able to muster this coalition due to its closer ties with Colombian narcotics traffickers than the other insurgent groups. The relationship appears to be the strongest in those areas where coca cultivation and production and FARC operational strongholds overlap. In exchange for FARC protection of narcotics interests, the guerrillas have received money to purchase weapons and supplies.

There is evidence that various FARC fronts have actually been involved in processing cocaine. Money from the narcotics trade has supplemented FARC revenues from kidnappings, extortion and robberies.

And on the military front, on April 16, 1996, FARC guerrillas killed 31 soldiers and wounded 18 others in a major ambush on an army patrol in the southwest province of Narino, highlighting a surge in rebel activity in 1996. The attack occurred at dawn in a remote area near Puerres, close to the Ecuadorian border. Troops were dispatched to the area, following a rebel sabotage of an oil pipeline that runs through the area. The patrol was attacked by 150 FARC rebels armed with automatic assault rifles and grenades. The attack was one of the worst to be suffered by the military this decade.

National Liberation Army (NLA), or Ejercito de Liberacion Nacional (ELN)

A rural-based, anti-U.S., Maoist-Marxist-Leninist guerrilla group formed in July 1964, the ELN raises funds by kidnapping foreign employees of large corporations and holding them for lofty ransom payments. The ELN conducts extortion and bombing operations against U.S. and other foreign businesses in Colombia, particularly the deep-pocketed petroleum industry. The group has inflicted major damage on oil pipelines since 1986.

They boast up to 2000 members, many of whom have been trained and armed by Nicaragua and Cuba. The ELN seeks "...the conquest of power for the popular classes..." along with nationalizations, expropriations, and agrarian reform.

The ELN is a political-military organization that draws its support from among students, intellectuals, peasants and, surprisingly, the middle-class workers of Colombia. Operations include the kidnapping of wealthy ranchers and industrialists, assassinations of military officers, offing of labor leaders and peasants, multiple armed robberies, various bombings, raids on isolated villages, weapons grabs on police posts and army patrols, and occupations of radio stations and newspaper offices. The ELN is currently perfecting attacks on petroleum pipelines and facilities, seeking to damage Colombia's economic infrastructure and investment climate.

Dignity for Cuba (DFC)

A twenty-year-old terrorist group called Dignity for Cuba bit the bullet in 1996. The three dozen members were an extra-pissed-off splinter group from the National Liberation Army led by former Spanish priest Manual Perez. The small group was composed of white collar workers who lived off the ransom money they made kidnapping politicians and wealthy Colombians. Their leader Hugo Toro, actually ran the group from his prison cell in La Picota prison where he was sentenced to 25 years for murder.

Their last hurrah was an attempt to force the Colombian congress to impeach President Samper for his association with drug cartels. To make their point more urgent they threatened not only to kill every person who didn't vote for impeachment but they kidnapped Juan Carlos Gaviria, the brother of the former president of Colombia, in April of '96.

Uncle Fidel interceded on behalf of the kidnap victim and even allowed the group to fly to Cuba where they will try to figure out what to do for a living.

Popular Liberation Army (EPL/D)

This dissident former affiliate of the Popular Liberation Army based primarily in Uraba can't seem to get ahead. The PLA signed a peace treaty several years ago with the government but these Maoist EPL/D sad sacks won't quit. The EPL/D leaders are followed and arrested on a regular basis (probably due to informants from the PLA). The 2800 armed troops demobilized in 1991 and the group changed its name to Esperanza, Paz y Libertad (Hope, Peace and Freedom), retaining the initials EPL. As the new group/party has had political success in the polls since making peace with the government, members have become favorite targets of disgruntled and jealous FARC fanatics, who moved into the areas the EPL abandoned. On January 23, 1994, FARC nasties ambushed an EPL fund-raiser, massacring 35 people.

Dignity for Colombia Movement (DCM)

This player on the scene seems to have a fairly simple agenda. Kill every member of the 165-member House of Representatives who votes to clear President Ernesto Samper of drug charges. A refreshingly direct change from our own political pressure groups.

Jame Bateman Front

About 250 members who split from M-19 group when the M-19 turned into a political group. They are based outside of Bogota.

The U.S. Military

The U.S. government has unofficially declared war on the drug trade in Colombia and, therefore, FARC. Currently, there are nine U.S. advisors in Colombia training troops; 62 military technicians are installing radar bases; 32 members of a navy construction battalion in Meta province are building a military base on the Meta River, a heavily used artery for drug transport; 156 U.S. Army engineers northwest of Cali are building a school, clinic and road. Although covert U.S. involvement in Colombia is low-key presently, further disintegration of Colombia's infrastructure would undoubtedly lead to an increased presence.

Death Squads

More than a hundred groups of teams made up of five to 10 members each are paid by wealthy and influential Colombians to kill former and current left-wingers and communists on an ongoing basis, and to act as a more effective deterrent to kidnapping, murder and extortion threat than the police or military. The death squads are primarily active in Medellin and Bogota, and around the Antioquia Department. One of the principal players is the Macetos paramilitary group, which is centered in the San Martin municipality. This group has performed numerous massacres against leftist guerrilla groups and their sympathizers.

Drug Lords

Pablo Escobar is gone; however, cocaine is still the biggest covert industry in Colombia. Coca is grown in the country, processed in labs and then shipped or flown out to various ports and other sites in the Caribbean and Mexico. The headquarters for the drug trade is in Cali and Medellin. The drug folks are very tight with both left- and right-wing terrorist groups. So be nice when you talk to anybody about drugs.

Fidel and Carlos Castano

Controlled by the drug lords, the Castanos run the northern seven of Uraba's 11 counties. They founded "The People Persecuted by Pablo Escobar," a group instrumental in the capture and death of the notorious leader of the Medellin cartel. Now they run a land-grabbing fiefdom in northern Colombia, executing any antagonistic peasants who get in the way

Getting In

A passport and a return/onward ticket are required for stays up to three months. Minors (under 18) traveling alone, with one parent, or with a third party must present written authorization from the absent parent(s) or legal guardian, specifically granting permission to travel alone, with one parent or with a third party. This authorization must be notarized, authenticated by a Colombian embassy or consulate, and translated into Spanish. For up-to-the-minute information regarding entry and customs requirements for Colombia, contact the nearest consulate in Los Angeles, Miami, Chicago, New Orleans, New York, Houston or San Juan, or the embassy in Washington D.C.: **Colombian Embassy** *2118 Leroy Place NW, Washington, D.C. 20008,* ☎ *(202) 387-8338.*

An onward ticket is not always requested at land crossings but you may be asked to prove that you have at least US$20 for each day of your stay in Colombia. Thirty-day extensions can be applied for at the DAS (security police) office in any city.

Entering Colombia by land usually presents no problems at the frontiers. But note that when leaving Colombia by land, you'll need to have an exit stamp from the DAS. You may not be able to get this stamp at the smaller frontier towns. Get the stamp in a city. Otherwise, you may be detained.

Getting Around

Cities within Colombia are served by Avianca, Aces, SAM, Intercontinental, Satena and Aires airlines. The bigger cities are reached on a daily basis, the smaller ones less frequently, sometimes once a week. By air, Avianca and American Airlines fly regularly to Bogota from the U.S., Cali and Barranquilla. There is an airport tax of US$18. Prices are higher in the high season (June–August, December). Purchase intra-Colombia tickets inside the country.

Buses are a great way to get around, but incidents of thefts are increasing. The air-conditioned buses are often quite frigid when the air conditioning is working. When it isn't they're quite hot, since the windows don't open. Bring your own food, as rest stops are infrequent. Additionally, expect the bus to be periodically stopped and boarded by police. Your identity will most likely be checked. Occasionally, a photocopy of your passport will be sufficient. Make one and have it notarized anyhow. Buses leave according to schedule, rather than when they are full. Colombia's VELOTAX minibuses are efficient. However, other buses experience frequent breakdowns (see "Dangerous Things").

Taxis are plentiful. Take only metered taxis. But if one cannot be found, bargain and set a fixed price before you enter the taxi. Women should not take taxis alone at night (see "Dangerous Things").

The roads in Colombia are often dilapidated and unmarked. Avoid driving at night; Colombian drivers are careless and often reckless.

Air Safety

In Colombia many radar and ground tracking stations are damaged by rebels and drug smugglers to protect illegal drug shipments. More than 1000 people have died in Colombian air accidents since 1986.

Dangerous Places

Where do we start? How about at the airport. Theft of hand luggage and travel documents at airports is common and should be expected. Use the well-marked taxis; do not share a ride or enter a cab with more than one person, even though many cabdrivers will tell you that your travel mate is for protection—you only need to be wrong once. Lock the doors, and be prepared to have Scopolamine sprayed in your face by keeping alert and a window cracked (not enough to let people reach in).

Taking the bus is worse. Here, taking a rural bus is asking for a close encounter of the wrong kind. Theft, druggings, extortion and kidnapping occur frequently on buses in both the city and rural areas.

If you survive the 7.5-mile ride into Bogota from the airport, be forewarned that crime is prevalent in cities, especially in the vicinity of hotels and airports. Large hotels, travel agencies, corporate headquarters and other institutions that display U.S. corporate IDs are targeted by terrorists for bombing attacks.

Santa Marta

The north end of town and the Rodadero Beach areas are extremely dangerous. Do not travel alone into these areas. Daylight armed robberies of tourists are commonplace. Thieves will often relieve their victims of their clothes as well as all other valuables.

The Darien

Pressed against the Panama border, Uraba is the murder capital of Colombia. The country's richest banana-growing region, it's also home to a myriad of drug runners, leftist guerrillas and paramilitary outfits. Uraba's annual murder rate of 254 per 100,000 people is the highest in Colombia. In 1995, 124 people—almost all peasants—were killed in 13 different massacres. A far greater number were gunned down singly or in pairs. On February 14, 1996, guerrillas massacred 10 banana farmers—and 10 more people were mowed down by AK-47 and R-15 gunfire in a billiards hall on April 4. How bad is Uraba? Local officials are pleading for U.N. intervention and for a peacekeeping force to be installed. The area around the Darien Peninsula is a major transit point for contraband goods and a center for drug processing. The FARC group provides protection for the drug labs.

Cartagena

Professional pickpockets abound, especially at the beaches. They especially like to strike in crowded areas. Cameras are a favorite trophy for thieves here. Scams in Cartagena are numerous. Other crooks pose as tour guides. Some of them can be rather touchy if you turn down their expensive excursion offers. If you're offered a job on a ship bound for the U.S. or other parts of South America, this is most assuredly a con.

Medellin

Despite being a major drug traffickers' center, the city is a remarkably friendly place. However, it's not the druglords you should be afraid of here. Rather, it's petty thieves and street thugs.

Valle Department

Everywhere off the main roads in Valle Department is extremely unsafe due to guerrilla activities. Beware particularly of Cauca Department E off the Pan-American Highway. Tourists should avoid this area entirely. Areas of Cra 6 are also extremely dangerous, including Parque Bolivar and the market. There has also been guerrilla activity in the Purace National Park area, particularly near the Popayan-La Plata Road. In Inza, women should not be on the streets unaccompanied.

Other Guerrilla Areas

The Departments of Boyaca, Norte de Santander, Casanare, Caqueta, Huila, Putumayo, Cesar, Guajira, Arauka, Meta, as well as the Turbo/Uraba region.

The Upper Magdalena

You'll constantly encounter riffraff here, touting everything from drugs, gold and emeralds to pre-Columbian art. The items are always fake, except for the drugs.

Antioquia Department and Medellin

Medellin was the focus of much of the shoot-outs and wars between Escobar and PEPES. There are roadblocks throughout the countryside, and there have been executions of military, civilians and locals without provocation. This is a very nasty area, and the most dangerous place in Colombia.

Bogota

Narco-traffickers/guerrillas have threatened and carried out terrorist attacks against Colombian officials, foreign embassies, and other targets. Expect to travel in fear of violent crime, particularly in the south of Bogota. Tourist areas are infested with thieves, pickpockets and opportunists. The richer, northern suburbs of Bogota have experienced a rash of car bombings.

Colombia East of the Andes

This area can be hazardous to your health, with the exception of the city of Leticia in the Amazonas Department and adjacent tourist areas in Amazonas.

North Coast/Barranquilla/Isla San Andres

Cali is the home of two of the major drug cartels. Expect plenty of fighting between the two rival groups. The island of San Andres is a major drug shipment area. Cartagena is considered somewhat safe, due to the increased presence of police protecting the lucrative tourist trade. Expect tourist crime.

Barranquilla is the site of guerilla attacks on businesses and government centers. The busy port is a major center for drug traffickers. Guerrillas like to regularly attack the Navy base near the airport at night. Outside the city limits is the domain of bad people, particularly at night.

Rural Valle de Cauca Department

As well as most of the Cauca River Valley, including the cities of Cali and Buenaventura, and the road between Cali and Buenaventura.

The Northern Half of Choco Department

Particularly the Uraba region, except for the tourist area of Capurgana.

The Magdelena Medio Region

The Magdelena River Valley south to Tolima, including western Boyaca, eastern Caldas, and northwestern Cundinamarca.

Tolima Department South of Espinal

Especially if traveling after dark.

Road Travel in Huila and Cauca Departments

The cities of Neiva and Popayan are considered to be safe if reached by air.

Dangerous Things

U.S. Companies

Several terrorist or guerrilla groups are active in Colombia; U.S. interests are among their targets. Kidnapping for ransom or political purposes, including U.S. citizens, is increasingly common in Colombia. In early 1994, bombs destroyed a Mormon temple in Medellin, damaged another in Bucaramanga, and damaged a Coca-Cola bottling plant in Bucaramanga. Additionally, two American missionaries were kidnapped for political reasons by guerrillas.

Kidnapping

Remember the last time you asked your boss how much you were really worth? Well, you may find out on your next trip to Colombia. In 1993 there were 121 kidnappings a month in Colombia, or about four a day. In 1994, there were 4000 for the year, or about 11 a day. Kidnapping has become a US$350 million industry in Colombia. Over 70 foreigners have been abducted in the last four years, each for huge ransoms. A Briton was killed in August of '95, while an American was released after being held for 11 months. It seems his captors just gave up on ever getting the $5 million they were asking for.

Fewer than one in 30 kidnappers are ever caught and sentenced. Although kidnappings in Colombia fell 23 percent between 1992 and 1993, in 1994 they shot up nearly 35 percent to 1378 abductions. Fewer than half the kidnappings that actually take place are ever reported. Luckily, Colombians make up the bulk of the victims. Most never report the abductions, fearing it would just advertise their culpability. There were believed to be 10 Americans being held captive in Colombia as of February 1995. A splinter group of the

Popular Liberation Army (EPL) took responsibility for the January 1995 abduction of Edward Gravowsky. Although the EPL was disbanded in March 1991, a group of about 150 diehards remains. Gravowski was the fourth foreigner kidnapped by Colombian guerrillas in a four-month period. In the past few years, only one in 10 of the reported victims has been rescued by security forces. Many others are murdered by the kidnappers, who often demand large ransoms and then return a corpse.

Murder

Think the U.S. is the murder capital of the world? Think again. Colombia has the highest murder rate in the world. For every 100,000 people, 77.5 are offed. That's more than eight times higher the rate in the U.S.

Oil Pipelines

Occidental Petroleum (Oxy) is the country's largest producer of oil. The Cano-Limon oil field (along the border of Venezuela and Colombia) yields Colombia's largest oil deposits. The 470-mile pipeline cost over a billion dollars and is the focal point for guerilla activity. Nasty men have blown up the pipeline over 400 times since it came on line in 1985. In 1988 an Oxy engineer was kidnapped and sprung for an impressive US$6 million dollars. To make things fair, the government of Colombia took responsibility for the repair of the pipeline every time the bad guys punched a hole in it. It takes about 36 hours to repair the bomb blasts. About 190,000 barrels of crude oil flow through the pipeline every day. The joke is that the rebels claim that the pipeline is robbing the Colombians of their natural resources. The real criminal seems to be the Colombian government, which skims 85 percent of every dollar generated by the oil. There is a $1.20 a barrel "war tax" to help fight the guerillas and a tax of 12 percent of all profits taken out of the country.

Scopolamine

Scopolamine (or Burundanga, as it is called locally) is a drug Colombian thugs use to incapacitate tourists in order to rob them. It's spiked into drinks in bars, and into cigarettes in taxis. The drug renders victims unconscious and causes serious medical problems. Colombian doctors report that hospitals receive an estimated 2000 Scopolamine victims every month in Bogota. One out of every three patients in the emergency room has been intoxicated with the drug. The druggings occur in all areas of the city throughout the day, but with more frequency at night. The most effective way to administer Scopolamine is in a liquid form, which can incapacitate the victim in two to three seconds. However, research has revealed that street tactics can involve the drug being utilized in a spray, dust or smoke form as well. Most drugging incidents take place in bars and discotheques. Some incidents occur when the server brings you a drink. On the way to the table, he/she will drug the drink or bottle. This usually occurs toward the end of the night, when most people are less observant. After being drugged, the server helps you to the door, where an accomplice is waiting. Another common tactic is through a casual conversation in a bar. During the course of the conversation or at a time when your drink is left unattended, the drug is administered. To defend against such tactics, avoid going to nightclubs alone. While inside such establishments, try to watch your drink being prepared and brought to the table. Do not leave your drink unattended. Street druggings are also common and may involve spray, dust or smoke. These scenarios typically involve being approached by a stranger on the street who initiates a conversation and then administers the drug. The best preventative measure is to try not to walk alone. Avoid stopping and talking to strangers or accepting anything to eat, drink or smoke from them. Druggings on public transportation are frequent, so buses should be avoided. Scropolomine symptoms include disorientation, incoherence, dilated pupils, mouth dryness, restlessness, fast heart rate, blurred vision and stupor. Victims of suspected Scopolamine druggings should be taken immediately to a hospital. And if that's not serious enough, the "high" isn't even any good, and you feel like hell the next day.

Power Blackouts

When the lights go out, make sure you are nowhere to be found by street criminals. Common street crime increases exponentially during blackouts in major cities.

Phony Cops

A common scam is an approach to an obvious tourist by an alleged "policeman" who says that he is checking for counterfeit U.S. dollars and wants to "check" the foreigner's money. The person gives the criminal his/her money, receives a receipt, and the "policeman" disappears. Others request that the victim accompany him "downtown." You have just been kidnapped.

Strolling Through the Country

You may want to save the rain forests, but coca growers and processing labs would prefer that you stay at the beach. Two French tourists were snatched by FARC in the La Macarena nature preserve south of Bogota. The countryside is effectively controlled by rebel groups who view you as a source of income.

Bombs

Bombs don't drop from the sky here. They are usually car bombs. Bombing is a deliberate attempt to capture publicity and strike fear into the populace. The victims are incidental. Car bombs are deliberately detonated in crowded central locations. Buses are bombed, as well as oil pipelines, refineries, hotels and office buildings.

Driving

Colombia's roads are in poor condition. Many routes aren't marked. Avoid driving at night. Many vehicles have dim headlights, if any at all. Other drivers are reckless. Cattle are unwitting, as they pause to pee in the middle of the road at midnight.

Taxis

Women should never travel alone at night in taxis. Both sexes are subject to popular scams where the driver feigns a mechanical breakdown. The passenger is asked to get out of the car and help push the taxi to a "jump-start," which separates passengers from their luggage. The driver will then start the car and drive off.

Buses

Bus travel in the south of Colombia can be hazardous. Thieves haunt buses in this area waiting for passengers to fall asleep. Then, guess what they do. Buses between Bogota and Ipiales and between San Augustin and Popayan are frequented by scam artists/ thieves who offer doped chewing gum, cigarettes, food and sweets before taking everything you've got.

Hotel Rooms

Hotel rooms of foreigners are not infrequently raided by the police looking for drugs. Having a witness around may prevent them from planting drugs in the room. But, then again, it may not.

Planes

In Colombia many radar and ground tracking stations are damaged by rebels and drug smugglers to protect illegal drug shipments. More than 1000 people have died in Colombian air accidents since 1986.

Rumors

A Spanish magazine, *Cambio 16*, published a report purporting to be from a DEA source, which claimed the U.S. government is attempting to bring about the resignation of President Ernesto Samper through attacks, blackmail and prison breakouts. The article cited the recent escape of Cali cartel leader Jose Santacruz Londono from prison as evidence of this plot. Colombian army commander General Harold Bedoya stated to the Colombian press that he had no knowledge of this plot and could not vouch for the veracity of the article. The apparently fabricated article appears to have risen out of recent tensions between the U.S. and Colombian governments. Nonetheless, the report appears to be raising anti-American sentiment in Colombia.

Booze

Beware of drinks poured from brand-label liquor, such as Johnnie Walker scotch, with broken seals. In many instances, the labels are fake and the booze is a potentially lethal spirit. Drink only beer if you need to catch a buzz.

Drugs

Despite what we said about the few criminals that get to justice in Colombia, if you get arrested for any drug-related crime expect at least threats of lifelong incarceration and spending a few thousand bucks bribing your way out of jail. The government will do little to help. Any foreigner who wants to cut out the middlemen and go into competition with the Colombian drug dealers should watch the movie *Scarface* a few times. Strangely enough, every year some yahoo ends up in a Colombian jail for doing exactly that.

Hassles with Police

Many police officers and soldiers will shake you down for doing everything from taking pictures to walking on the beach at night. The best bluff is to demand to see their supervisor and walk quickly in the direction that takes you farthest away from them. If the police really do arrest you, get on the horn to the consulate ASAP. They can't do much if you really screwed up, but they're all you've got.

Getting Sick

Medical care is adequate in major cities, but varies in quality elsewhere. Health problems in Colombia include the presence of cholera, though cholera is found largely in areas outside the cities and usual tourist areas. Visitors who follow proper precautions regarding food and drink are not generally at risk. Doctors and hospitals often expect immediate cash payment for health services. U.S. medical insurance is not always valid outside the United States. In some cases, supplemental medical insurance with specific overseas coverage is considered useful. If you are the victim of a Scopolamine attack, remember to seek medical assistance immediately. Scopolamine is usually mixed with other narcotics and can cause brain damage.

Nuts and Bolts

Spanish is the official language. English is common in major cities and tourist centers. The Colombians like to party, so expect massive crowds and price hikes during local holidays. Electricity is 110V/60hz. Local time is the same as New York. The local currency is the peso, about 837 to the U.S. dollar at press time.

Temperatures are fairly high throughout the year. It gets cooler and wetter the higher you go. Seaside areas are muggy. Heavy rain falls between April and October.

Business hours are from 8 a.m.–noon and from 2–6 p.m, Monday–Friday. Bank hours in Bogata are from 9 a.m.–3 p.m. Monday–Thursday, and from 9 a.m.–3:30 p.m. on Fridays, except the last Friday of the month, when they close at noon. In other major cities, they're open from 8 a.m.–11:30 a.m. and from 24 p.m. Monday–Thursday. On Friday, they're open until 4:30 p.m., except the last Friday of the month, when they close at 11:30 a.m.

Embassy Location/Registration

Upon arrival, U.S. citizens are urged to obtain updated information on travel and security within Colombia an to register with the following:

Consular Section, U.S. Embassy
Calle 38 No. 8–61
Bogota
☎ *[57] (1) 320-1300*

U.S. Consulate
Calle 77, Carrera 68
Centro Comercial Mayorista
Barranquilla
☎ *[57] (58) 45-8480 or 45-9067*

Dangerous Days

Anniversaries are bad days for a stroll in the country or shopping downtown in Colombia. Rebel groups like to remind people by blowing things up.

10/08/1987   The Simon Bolivar Guerrilla Coordinating Board (CNG) is an umbrella organization, under which the Revolutionary Armed Forces of Colombia (FARC), the National Liberation Army (ELN) and a dissident faction of the Popular Liberation Army (EPL) coordinate political positions and organize joint terrorist operations. It was founded on this date.

08/28/1985   April 19 movement (M-19) originated; leader Ivan Marino Ospina was killed in a clash with government troops.

11/20/1983   Legalization of the M-19. The April 19 movement (M-19), a leftist terrorist organization, was legalized by an amnesty law after the group had made peace with the government. The M-19 is now a legitimate political party.

04/29/1967   Founding of the EPL (Popular Liberation Army).

08/15/1964   The National Liberation Army (ELN) began its armed struggle.

05/27/1964   When government troops attacked the "independent republic" that communist peasant groups had set up at Marquetalia, Caldas Department.

11/11/1957   The Popular Liberation Army (EPL), a leftist terrorist organization, has since made peace with the government and become a legitimate political party. However, a dissident faction continues the armed struggle against the government.

07/17/1930   Communist Party founded.

08/07/1819   Battle Of Boyacas.

07/20/1810   Independence Day.

In a Dangerous Place

Colombia: Un Favorito, Por Favor

I had agreed to go out with the official's daughter. She was coming into San Andreas tomorrow from Cali for Holy Week. To decline the social request would not be a wise idea. I watched in amazement, as this distinguished gentleman was able to piss in the sink at the same time he was washing his hands. We were in his hotel suite, which served as his full-time home. He was a very high level government official on the island. Instead of wallpaper, he had cases of Mumm's stacked up from floor to ceiling, creating a pleasing but somewhat industrial pattern. His choice of music was limited to the one or two AM radio stations on the island— he used a state-of-the-art quadraphonic stereo system to blast out Julio Iglesias. Like most of his possessions, they were "gifts" or leftovers from customs inspections of travelers.

He explained how he makes his money. He has a group of three to five "beach boys" who sell coconut oil on the beach to tourists. Along with the golden fragrant oil in old beer bottles, they offer hash or marijuana to unsuspecting tourists. As the sun goes down, they turn in the money they've made and carefully point out each and every person who bought drugs that day. During the night, the doors of the surprised victims are crashed down and they're trotted off to jail at gunpoint. They then pay the judge, the lawyer, the DAS, the F2 and, of course, the Aduana dearly for their freedom. In fact, they even have to pay for meals while they are in jail. As he adjusted his evening clothes and carefully combed his hair, I thought he looked rather dashing for a thug.

—RYP

Djibouti
★★

Salt Pandemonium

You can be forgiven if you can't pinpoint this hot, arid place on a map. The only thing Djibouti is famous for is the French Foreign Legion and the mind-frying heat. When your neighbors are Ethiopia, Eritrea and Somalia, you know you live in a bad neighborhood. Djibouti is where sailors stop to fill up their ships, where even goats have a hard time staying alive and where some of the toughest nomads in the world live. It's the tiny armpit country that just happens to control the entrance to the Red Sea and the Suez Canal beyond.

That's why the French showed up in 1859 and paid 10,000 thalers to the Sultan of Obock (an Afar town on the north shore), much to the disgust of the Issas tribesmen, who were having fun killing each other over what little was worth killing for. Having a third party was going to make this complicated. The British sitting on the other side of the Red Sea in Aden made it necessary to garrison French soldiers for the next 200 years. When the French decided to slice up their little baked salt flat, they naturally screwed up any tribal, clan, linguistic, religious

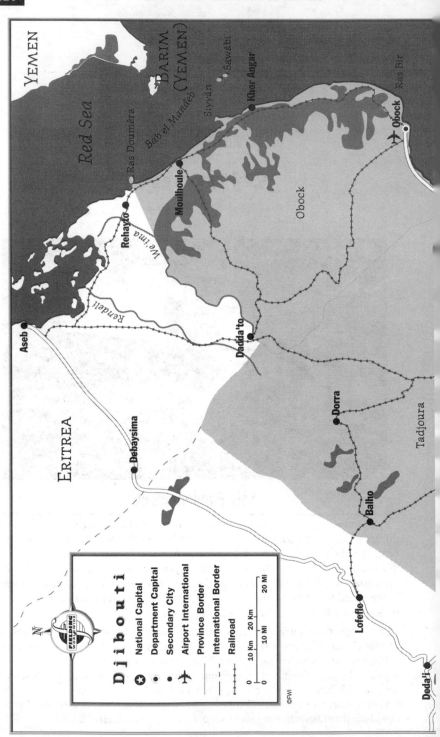

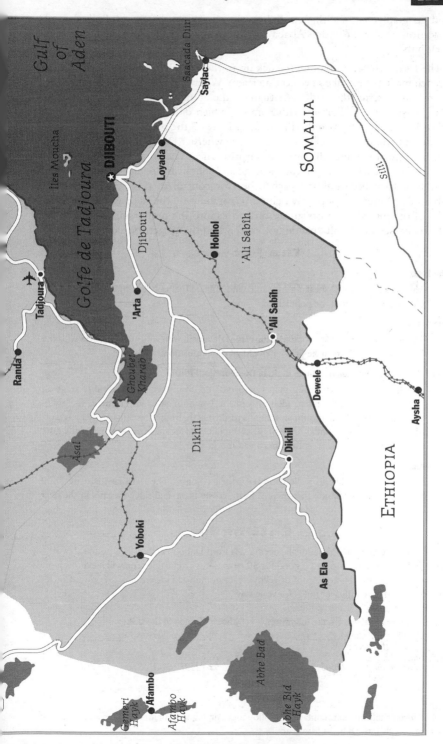

and geographic rational that existed previously. When the French built the railroad from Djibouti to Addis Ababa in Ethiopia, they truly drove the local tribesmen nuts.

The Issas were smart enough to suck up to the French from the get-go and the French made the mistake of educating them. When the Issas bit the hand that fed them and protested their colonial situation, the French became pals with the Afar. The Issas were also chummy with Somalis, which didn't go well with the Afars, who align themselves with the Ethiopians. In 1967 the French, with a little repatriation of ethnic Somalia, held a vote to see whether Djibouti should gain its independence or stay French. Surprise, surprise, the French won and the Issas were pissed. The French finally got the message and split in 1976. Since then, the Afars and Issas have been fighting each other for control of this flyspeck country. About 3500 French troops stay behind to catch up on their tan and shoot members of the FRUD terrorists group on sorties into the mountains. For now, the FRUD causes a little salt "pandemonium" when things get too slow.

The Players

The Issas

The Issas are Cushitic-speaking Muslims who affiliate themselves with the Somalis. The Issas are 38 percent of the population.

The Afars

The Afars are Cushitic-speaking Muslims from the north who affiliate themselves with the Ethiopians. The Afars make up 47 percent of the population.

Front Pour la Restauration de l'Unite´et de la Democratie (FRUD)

An offshoot of the Afar group that was formed in 1990, they have chosen to wage an armed struggle to gain independence from the Issa-dominated government. In July of 1993 they were forced into the mountains to the north, from where they carry on terrorist attacks. The Afars control most of the mountainous area south of Eritrea, and the government holds the towns of Tadjoura and Obock.

The French

The French never like to really hand back their colonies. The fact that there are 3500 troops here should ensure that there is fresh, crusty bread and sidewalk cafés in the next century.

Getting In

All visitors, except French nationals, need a visa from Djibouti embassies around the world. A single entry visa costs $15 and is good for 30 days and is extendable. You will need to supply two applications, two photos, proof of yellow fever immunization, proof of an onward or return ticket and have sufficient funds for your stay.

The U.S. representatives are the following:

Republic of Djibouti
1156 15th Street N.W.
Suite 515
Washington, D.C. 20005
☎ *(202) 331-0270*
or the

Djibouti Mission to the U.N.

866 United Nations Plaza
Suite 4011
New York, NY 10017
☎ *(212) 753-3163*

For further information, contact the following: Air France, Air Madagascar and a host of local airlines fly into Djibouti from Paris.

U.S. Embassy

Villa Plateau du Serpent
Boulevard Marechal Joffre
BP 185
☎ *35-39-95*

Tourist Office

L'Office de Developement du Tourism
Place Menelik
BP 1938
☎ *35-37-90*

Getting Around

There is the 782-km railroad to Ethiopia. Trains leave twice a day and the trip takes 24 hours. The train can be very full. Fares are about $60 for first class. Most roads are bumpy but passable year-round. The road to Addis Ababa is paved. Taxis are plentiful and the fare goes up 50 percent at night. Four-wheel-drives are available from Hertz (☎ *35-24-94).*

Getting Out

You can still buy passage on many of the ships that ply the Swahili coast. Many go south to Somalia and others visit ports in the Persian Gulf. Cargo ships are a little leery of the true career ambitions of strangers who sign on here.

Getting Sick

There is one doctor for every 4180 persons. Not bad for a sand-grain-sized country. In most cases, you are better off getting on a plane to Paris.

Nuts and Bolts

By now, you've guessed it's hot. Temperatures can easily hit 110°F. Much of the country is below sea level, which means salt is about the only thing of value here. There is less than 125 mm of rainfall a year, and June and August drive the Legionnaires crazy when the khamsin blows in from the desert. If you want to visit during the rainy season, pull up a chair and wait between October and April and don't blink.

Djibouti lives on what it can make from its port and on handouts from the French. The literacy rate of 19 percent means they don't sell too many John Grisham novels here. The life expectancy of 48 means they wouldn't be able to finish them, even if they could read them.

DJIBOUTI

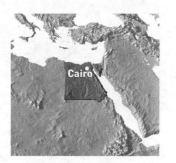

Cairo

Egypt
★★

The Temples of Doom

Egypt has long thrived on the income tourists spend to visit its ancient monuments, ever since Thomas Cook ran the first package tours to southern Egypt in the 1860s. Even during the most intense moments of the Arab-Israeli conflict, trips to the pyramids could be arranged for a minor fee for passengers in transit through Cairo. In fact, Cook used tourist boats to ferry troops up the Nile to Khartoum to rescue General Gordon. They arrived too late, and, no, the government of Britain didn't get a refund.

Today, Islamic fundamentalists furious over Egypt's pact with Israel and the Jewish state's April 1996 attacks on Lebanon, have decided to attack Egypt where it hurts most: the tourist industry. Sporadic attacks on tourist boats, buses and trains traveling to the Great Pyramids are designed to scare away Western tourists. For three years, tourism skidded as terrorists took pot shots at tour boats, placed bombs on trains and assassinated policemen in the area just south of

215

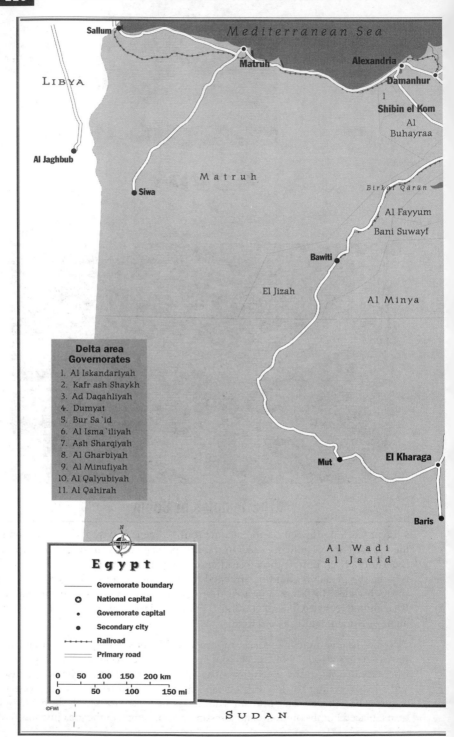

Delta area Governorates
1. Al Iskandariyah
2. Kafr ash Shaykh
3. Ad Daqahliyah
4. Dumyat
5. Bur Sa'id
6. Al Isma'iliyah
7. Ash Sharqiyah
8. Al Gharbiyah
9. Al Minufiyah
10. Al Qalyubiyah
11. Al Qahirah

Egypt

Governorate boundary
National capital
Governorate capital
Secondary city
Railroad
Primary road

0   50   100   150   200 km
0   50   100   150 mi

©FWI

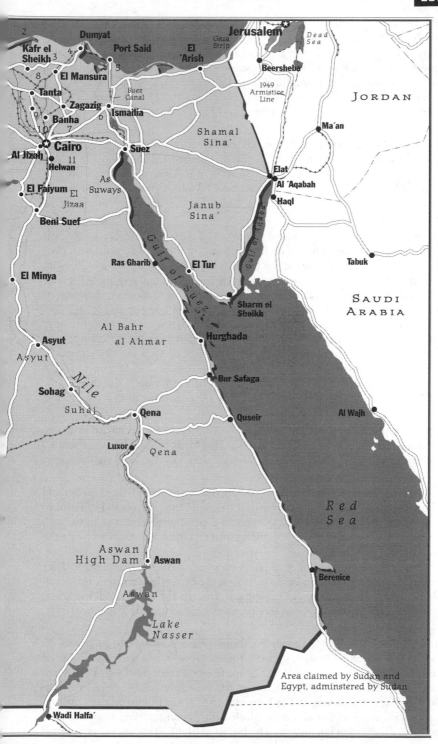

EGYPT

Cairo. Needless to say, the only person who might enjoy running this gauntlet could be Indiana Jones looking for the Temples of Doom.

About 150,000 Americans visit Egypt every year, eager to experience the newly discovered tombs of Ramses' sons and see some of the world's best-preserved antiquities. But the Islamic Group (al-Gama'a al-Islamiya), a fundamentalist army that wants to overthrow the government and set up a strict Islamic state, is doing its best to take away that chance. The group hides out in the dense sugarcane fields near the town of Farshut.

Naturally, the 121,000 beds Egypt has sheeted for tourists have stayed made up, and the 2.6 million tourists who formerly pumped US$2 billion a year into the economy faded. Tourism dropped 36 percent in 1993 and another 23 percent in 1994. Egypt estimates it has lost US$3 billion. A combination of heavily discounted prices, aggressive marketing and a full-out attack on the militants started to bring the tourists back.

In September 1995, Egypt hosted the World Tourism Organization and was happy to report that tourism was up for the year, by about 19 percent, with people staying longer. The chatter in the hotels is now more likely to be in Russian, Afrikaaner or Japanese, since Egypt gave up on Americans and now looks for people who don't read the small print in the international sections of newspapers. Egyptian tourism officials reported that there had not been an attack on a foreigner since 1994. And as if on cue, in November, trains carrying tourists were fired upon 300 miles south of Cairo. Twelve Egyptians were wounded as well as a Dutch man and French woman. Then, the stunner: On April 18, 1996, three Islamic Group terrorists mowed down 34 Greek tourists and an Egyptian parking attendant with machine-gun fire, killing 18, in front of a hotel less than a mile away from the pyramids. Next time you think *DP* is alarmist or that you believe government assurance, think again.

Egypt's response has been lethal and messy. Terrorists have been tried in absentia and tracked down as far away as Pakistan. Hundreds of suspects were rounded up after the killings of the Greeks. A number were killed in daylong shootouts with cops combing the sugarcane fields.

It is well known by *DP* that the al-Gama'a al-Islamiya is based out of Sudan and backed by Iran in their ongoing campaign to spread their own brand of Islam to the Arab world. Most of the attacks target Egyptian government officials, with the tourist attacks being more for PR reasons, and, as was the case with the Greeks, out of vengeance for Israel's April 1996 invasion of Lebanon. Unfortunately, no one knows why they chose Greeks to make their statement. They thought they were Israelis. In February 1994, the extremists threatened to accelerate their terrorist campaign against the government and called on all foreigners to leave Egypt. They declared that foreign investors and tourists would be the targets of this stepped-up effort.

Since February 16, 1994, 12 foreign tourists have been injured in attacks on trains. A Nile River cruise ship, with 17 tourists aboard, was fired upon with an assault rifle. On February 18, 1994, a southbound train from Cairo was fired upon, injuring four people. The attack on the overnight train occurred at about 1:30 a.m. just south of Assiyut. On February 23, 1994, a bomb placed in the luggage rack of the first-class section exploded on a train traveling from Cairo to Aswan, injuring six foreign tourists. The bomb went off 30 minutes after the train left the station in Assiyut and was placed onboard by a food vendor who hid the bomb in a Coca-Cola case. In March 1995, two Argentinians were wounded and six Egyptians were killed on a train. In 1996 18 tourists were shot near the Great Pyramids as they boarded a bus. Tourism will never be dull here.

The Scoop

The militant al-Gama'a al-Islamiyas seek to overthrow Egypt's government and turn the country into a strict Islamic state. Minya province has been the center of the conflict, which has seen about 850 people killed (mostly police and fundamentalists) in political violence in Egypt since the Gama'a began its guerrilla campaign of terror in 1992.

The Players

The Islamic Group (al-Gama'a al-Islamiya)

This Egyptian Islamic extremist group has been staging attacks against the government since the late 1970s. They began in 1928 with the Muslim Brotherhood. Gama'a leaders have a tight control on business and religion in the Assiyut region of Egypt. Their attacks on tourists began in 1992. Sheikh Omar Abdul Rahman (Abd al Rahman) is the group's spiritual leader and came to fame for his role in the bombing of New York's World Trade Center. The goal of the group is to overthrow the government of President Hosni Mubarak and replace it with an Islamic state. The group carries out armed attacks against Egyptian security forces and other government officials. Their targets are Coptic Christians, Western tourists and Egyptian opponents of Islamic extremism. The actual size of the group isn't known, but it's estimated to be several thousand hard-core members along with about an equal number of sympathizers. Recruiting is done around the mosques and poor neighborhoods in Cairo, Alexandria and other urban locations. They also recruit unemployed graduates and students. Activities are focused around the areas of al Minya, Assiyut, and Qina governorates of southern Egypt. There are recruiting and training bases in Pakistan. Financial and logistical support comes from Iran and Sudan. On January 11, 1995, a leading member of the group, Mahmud abd-al-Mahud, committed suicide when police raided his hideout. The group's worst atrocity on foreign tourists thus far came on April 18, 1996, when three of its members gunned down 18 Greek tourists in front of their hotel less than a mile from the Great Pyramids. Today, the group hides out in the bullrush-clogged fields and the sugarcane fields alongside the Nile to elude the police, who are making headway in their task of exterminating the group. Abdal Rahman will be guest of the U.S. government for the rest of his life.

President Hosni Mubarak

Moderate but change-resistant, Mubarak is seen by Iran and the terrorists it supports as being a U.S. puppet, and is attacked internally by socialists, conservatives and fundamentalists alike. Mubarak has ruled Egypt since the assassination of Anwar Sadat in 1981, and his National Democratic Party has imposed a national state of emergency since Sadat's death. The NDP has introduced severe measures to deal with the terrorist threat. He, along with Sadat before him, has been liberalizing the economy and promoting private enterprise, without bringing about similar changes in politics (the military-backed NDP essentially runs a one-party state), which is perhaps one reason for growing Islamic fundamentalism.

His Excellency
Muhammad Hosni Mubarak
President of the Arab Republic of Egypt
Abedine Palace
Cairo, Arabic Republic of Egypt
FAX: (+20) 2-260 5417

Mr. 'Amre Moussa
Minister of Foreign Affairs
Ministry of Foreign Affairs
Midan at-Tahrir
Cairo, Arabic Republic of Egypt
FAX: (+20) 2-723 173

Getting In

A passport and visa are required. For those arriving by air, a renewable 30-day tourist visa can be obtained at airport points of entry. Those arriving overland and by sea, or those previously experiencing difficulty with their visa status in Egypt, must obtain a visa prior to arrival. Military personnel arriving on commercial flights are not exempt from passport and visa requirements. Proof of yellow fever and cholera immunization is required if arriving from an infected area. Evidence of an AIDS test is required for everyone staying over 30 days. Tourists must register with local authorities (either through their hotels, at local police stations, or at the central passport office) within seven days of arrival. For additional entry information, U.S. citizens can contact the Egyptian consulates in San Francisco, Chicago, New York or Houston, or the Egyptian embassy in Washington D.C.:

Embassy of the Arab Republic of Egypt

3521 International Court, NW
Washington, D.C. 20008
☎ *(202) 895-5400*

Everyone entering Egypt must declare items such as jewelry, electronic equipment and other valuables. This requirement is strictly enforced. Any valuables not accounted for may be confiscated. For those staying in Egypt less than one month, there are no currency exchange requirements. For each month thereafter, U.S. citizens must present proof, in the form of bank receipts, that they have converted US$180 per month per person into Egyptian pounds. A maximum of 100 Egyptian pounds may be carried into or out of Egypt.

Getting Around

Egypt borders some of the world's most dangerous places. If you want to explore the remote border regions, including oases near Libya and off-road areas in the Sinai, you must obtain permission from the Travel Permits Department of the Ministry of the Interior, located at the corner of Sheikh Rihan and Nubar streets in downtown Cairo. Remember that the attraction of traveling by camel should be tempered by the reality of debilitating heat and the potential for injury; it makes this mode of transportation dicey at best. Attacks on tourists occur while traveling on buses, trains and riverboats between Cairo and Luxor. The attacks tend to be random.

Dangerous Places

Cairo

There have been attacks on obvious tourist facilities and tourist transportation vehicles. Avoid the large hotels and do not travel via tour bus.

The South (Minya, Assiyut, and Qina Governorates)

The center of Islamic fundamentalism in Egypt, Assiyut is the country's third-largest city, with 14,000 government troops trying to keep a lid on it. You can hire professional assassins here for pocket change. Anwar Sadat was a major supporter of the Muslim Brotherhood in an effort to keep out communist influences. It may not surprise some that Sadat was killed by a member of the Muslim Brotherhood and army officer, Khalid Islambuli, after he was enraged at what had happened to his brother, who was beaten and tortured in an Assiyut prison two months earlier. Most attacks on tourists have occurred in the southern governorates of Assiyut, Minya and Qena, which lie between Cairo and Luxor. Travel via tourist buses, Nile River boats, car and trains from Cairo (first-class sections) in this area through those southern governorates is considered dangerous.

The towns of Mallawi, Dayrut, Farshut, Assiyut and Abu Tig along the Nile River are centers for fundamentalists. The attacks are be targeted on the transportation links to the famous monuments of the south.

Dangerous Things

The Train

The train that heads south from Cairo just happens to pass through the papyrus-clogged banks along the Nile. An ideal hideout for bad people. The night train between Aswan and Cairo is a favorite target. Any north-south train that travels in this area is considered a target. Attacks are usually by men spraying the passenger compartments with automatic weapons fire. Other attacks have been with bombs placed in overhead luggage compartments. The night train usually passes through this area early in the morning when the passengers are asleep.

Crime

Crime is confined to pickpockets, purse snatching, and other petty crime. (U.S. visitors are rarely targeted because of nationality.)

Scams

Tourists are fair game in Egypt for scams. Travelers may find themselves being overcharged for everything from taxi rides to cheap *hookahs*. In many of the tourist areas, visitors can find special "tourist police" to assist them. The telephone numbers for the tourist police in Cairo are the following: ☎ *926-027, 984-750* and *847-611*. Outside of Cairo, tourists and business travelers should consult with their hotel for guidance.

Drugs

Travelers are subject to the laws and legal practices of the country in which they travel. Drug enforcement policies in Egypt are very strict. The death penalty may be imposed on anyone convicted of smuggling or selling marijuana, hashish, opium, LSD or other narcotics. Law enforcement authorities prosecute and seek fines and imprisonment in cases of possession of even small quantities of drugs.

Photography Hassles

Egypt has strict duties on the importation of expensive photographic and video equipment, including all video cameras, autofocus cameras, etc. They may try to charge you the standard duty for importing these items, so you can either have the equipment stored, an unlikely scenario, or you can ask that the Egyptian customs official inventory the equipment and list it by model and serial number in your passports. Your equipment will be checked upon your departure, in which case no duty will be collected. As in most African or Middle East countries, there are restrictions on photographing military personnel and sites, as well as bridges and canals.

Pigeons

Yeah, pigeons. In Egypt, these plump little feathered scroungers have a nasty tendency to make their coops near bread ovens, kilns and other flammable areas. After catching fire, they flee the coop in panic, lighting up the sky like fireballs, and then land on the roofs of neighboring structures, of course, igniting them as well. In Al Gharizat during April 1996, panicking pigeons, their feathers on fire, set light to the roofs of 20 neighboring houses. The fire boys got the bread oven fire out, but it took them a while to get to all the burning houses. Some of the villagers victim of the frying feathered fiends weren't complaining, however. Fast food had arrived in Al Gharizat. And it was free!

Getting Sick

Access to medical help and professionals is good in Cairo, Luxor and Aswan. The U.S. embassy in Cairo can provide a list of local hospitals and English-speaking physicians. Medical facilities are adequate for nonemergency matters, particularly in the areas where most tourists visit. Emergency and intensive care facilities are limited. Many Nile cruise boats employ a medical practitioner with the equivalent of a U.S. Bachelor's degree in medicine. The Nile and its canals are carriers of the bilharzia parasite. It'll get ya when swimming in the Nile or canals, walking barefoot along the river or drinking untreated river water. Bilharzia can cause extensive tissue damage, kidney failure and blindness. Rift Valley Fever (RVF) exists throughout Egypt, having spread from its original concentration along a 60-mile stretch of the Nile in the Kom Ombo area of the Aswan governorate. RVF is primarily a disease of domestic animals, but it can readily infect humans. The vast majority of cases of RVF in humans results in only fever and flu-like symptoms, with complete recovery in a few days. In 2–3 percent of cases, however, RVF leads to liver necrosis, encephalitis and blindness. Preventive measures include avoiding farm animals (particularly, those that appear ill), camels, freshly slaughtered meat, mosquitos, raw milk and locally prepared cheese products.

Nuts and Bolts

Egypt can be visited without many restrictions. Terrorists target trains and riverboats with little or no regularity to their attacks. The workweek in Egypt is Sunday through Thursday. The emergency number for local police assistance in Cairo is ☎ *122.*

Egypt has a mishmash of 600,000 laws derived from Islamic, Ottoman, French, British and Soviet laws, not including military laws or special presidential decrees. Judges have to handle up to 1000 cases a day.

Embassy Location

The American embassy in Cairo is on Lazoghli Street, Garden City, near downtown Cairo. The mailing address from the U.S. is as follows:

American Embassy Cairo
APO AE 09839-4900

In Egypt, contact the American embassy at:
8 Kamal El-Din Salah Street, Cairo
☎ *[20] (2) 355-7371 (24-hour switchboard)*
FAX [20] (2) 357-3200

The consular section of the American embassy is located at the embassy, but has a separate entrance on Lazoghli Street. From the U.S., contact the consular section at:

American Embassy Cairo
Consular Section, Unit 64900
Box 15, APO AE 09839-4900
☎ *[20] (2) 355-7371*
FAX [20] (2) 357-2472

Dangerous Days

04/18/1996   Gama'a terrorists gunned down 34 Greek tourists and an Egyptian parking attendant in front of their hotel near the Great Pyramids, killing 18 tourists.

01/07/1994   Coptic Christians in Egypt celebrate Christmas on January 7.

07/02/1993   Sheikh Omar Abdul Rahman, the radical Egyptian cleric, surrendered to U.S. Justice Department officials in Brooklyn, New York.

11/23/1985   An Egyptian jet was hijacked to Malta. Fifty-nine passengers, including one American, were killed when Egyptian troops stormed the plane in Malta on November 24.

10/07/1985   Hijacking of the *Achille Lauro.* Four Palestinian gunmen hijacked the Italian cruise ship *Achille Lauro* off Alexandria, Egypt. While off the Syrian port of Tartus, the terrorists killed a wheelchair-bound American. Egypt and Italy negotiated the return of the ship and the remaining passengers. U.S. fighters intercepted an Egyptian jet carrying the hijackers and forced it down at a NATO base in Italy.

Dangerous Days

09/15/1982 Black September terrorists seized the Egyptian embassy in Madrid, demanding that Egypt renounce the Sinai agreement with Israel. The ambassador signed a renunciation, which was later dismissed.

04/15/1982 The assassins of Anwar Sadat were publicly executed in Cairo.

10/06/1981 Anwar Sadat assassinated.

02/19/1980 Israel sends first ambassador.

03/26/1979 Egyptian-Israeli peace treaty.

09/17/1978 Camp David Accords signed.

06/05/1975 Suez Canal reopened.

10/06/1973 Armed Forces Day.

10/06/1973 Yom Kippur War begins.

03/09/1968 Day of the War Dead.

06/05/1967 Six Day War.

05/25/1963 OAU—Africa Freedom Day. The Organization of African Unity was founded on May 25, 1963. The day is celebrated as Africa Freedom Day. The OAU was organized to promote unity and cooperation among African states.

02/22/1958 Unity Day.

12/23/1956 Victory Day. Celebrates the withdrawal of British, French and Israeli Forces from Port Said and the Suez Canal Zone.

10/29/1956 Invasion of the Sinai. Israeli, French and British forces invaded the Sinai and seized control of the Suez Canal, following its nationalization by Egypt.

10/24/1956 Popular Resistance Day.

07/26/1956 Nationalization of Suez Canal.

06/18/1953 The monarchy was abolished and Egypt was declared a republic, following the coup led by Gamal Abdel Nasser.

07/23/1952 Egyptian Revolution celebrated.

01/07/1949 First Arab-Israeli war ended.

02/28/1922 Britain unilaterally declared Egypt independent in deference to growing nationalism.

01/15/1918 Former Egyptian President Gamel Abd el Nasser was born.

12/18/1914 Britain declared a formal protectorate over Egypt that lasted until February 28, 1922, when Britain unilaterally declared Egypt independent in deference to growing nationalist sentiment.

04/25 Sinai liberation day.

EGYPT

EGYPT

El Salvador
★★

U.N.der Fire

Ask most folks what comes to mind when they think of El Salvador and they'll say "contra." Nope, that was Nicaragua—but close. The second image is Gene Hackman getting his head blown off by some army thugs on a rutted bomb-scape street, while Nick Nolte records the atrocity with a Nikon.

Wrong again—it was Nicaragua. As far as Central American papaya republics go, Nicaragua has gotten most of the press, namely because it has a better journalism school and Mick Jagger's former wife happens to be a babe. While most of the breathy, puffy-lipped grads end up as news anchors at TV stations in San Diego, Tucson, El Paso and Santa Barbara, El Salvadorans mostly end up either as maids in Bel Air or dead trying to get there.

There was little romance and even less glory in El Salvador's nasty 12-year civil war, which claimed 75,000 lives.

It's hard to fathom how such a small place geographically is so prominent on the globe, and how so much killing has happened in such idyllic surroundings. El

225

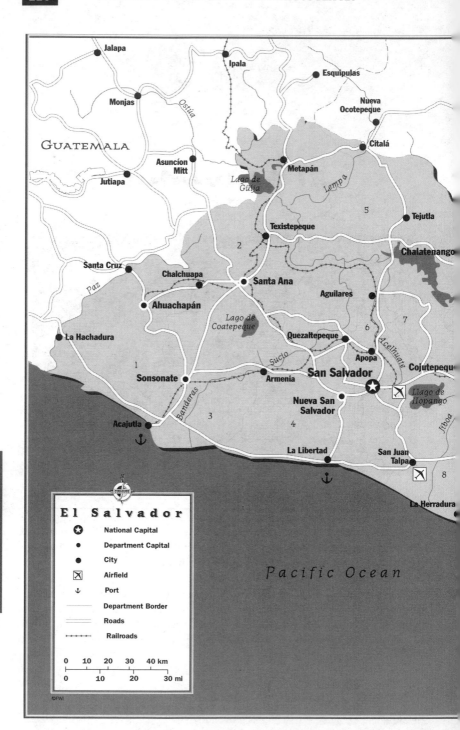

EL SALVADOR

El Salvador

- ⭐ National Capital
- ● Department Capital
- ● City
- ☒ Airfield
- ⚓ Port
- ········· Department Border
- ———— Roads
- ┝━━━━ Railroads

```
0    10   20   30   40 km
├────┼────┼────┼────┤
0    10        20        30 mi
```

©FWI

Jalapa
Ipala
Esquipulas
Monjas
Nueva Ocotepeque
Citalá
GUATEMALA
Ostúa
Asunción Mitt
Metapán
Lempa
Jutiapa
Lago de Güija
Tejutla
5
Texistepeque
2
Chalatenango
Santa Cruz
Chalchuapa
Santa Ana
Aguilares
Paz
Ahuachapán
7
Lago de Coatepeque
6
La Hachadura
Quezaltepeque
Acelhuate
1
Apopa
Cojutepequ
Sonsonate
Sucio
Armenia
San Salvador
Llago de Ilopango
Banderas
Nueva San Salvador
3
4
Acajutla
La Libertad
San Juan Talpa
8
Jiboa
La Herradura

Pacific Ocean

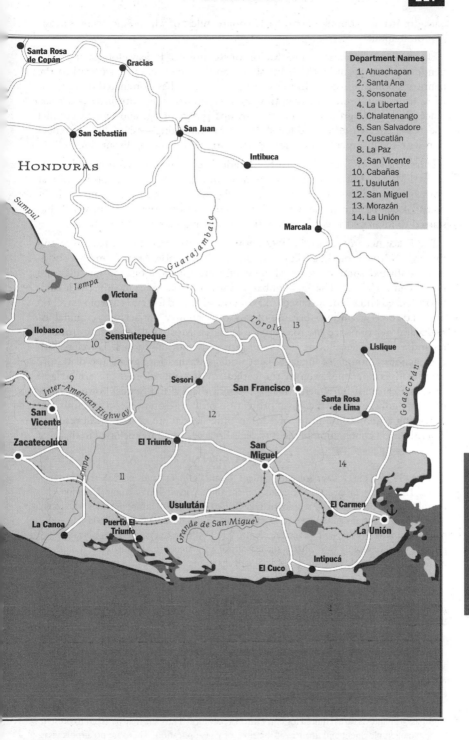

Department Names
1. Ahuachapan
2. Santa Ana
3. Sonsonate
4. La Libertad
5. Chalatenango
6. San Salvadore
7. Cuscatlán
8. La Paz
9. San Vicente
10. Cabañas
11. Usulután
12. San Miguel
13. Morazán
14. La Unión

HONDURAS

EL SALVADOR

Salvador is a tiny country of only 8124 square miles, of which 30 percent is mostly mountainous.

El Salvador (Republica de El Salvador, or Republic of El Salvador) gained independence from Spain in 1839. Instability and frequent coups have marked the country's political history. In this century, the army has dominated political affairs. From 1960 until recently, this domination was met with increased resistance, with underground opposition groups proliferating, and violent conflict and terrorism by rightist and leftist extremists escalating—especially in connection with the insurgent Farabundo Marti National Liberation Front (FMLN).

The most violent opposition to El Salvador's government was centered in the leftist FMLN. However, the group is now an active force in the post–civil war government. Its long fight against the ARENA-led government caused thousands of deaths, but finally resulted in major constitutional reform, which has started to improve the country's political, social and economic conditions.

The Peace Accords signed in 1992 between the government of El Salvador and the FMLN have brought a halt to fighting in El Salvador. Areas formerly considered conflicted zones or zones of concentration for demobilizing guerrillas are now open for travel. The U.S. embassy warns its personnel to drive with their doors locked and windows raised, to avoid travel after dark, and to avoid travel on unpaved roads at all times because of random banditry, carjackings, criminal assaults and lack of police and road service facilities. Most fatal accidents or robberies and assaults occur during the evening or early morning hours. Travelers with conspicuous amounts of luggage, late-model cars and foreign license plates are particularly vulnerable, even in the capital. Many Salvadorans are armed and shootouts are not infrequent. Travelers from the United States, however, may not carry guns, even for their own protection or for use on the road, without first procuring a gun license from Salvadoran officials. Failure to do so will result in detention and confiscation of the traveler's firearm even if it is licensed in the U.S.

The Scoop

After a 12-year-old civil war, some resentment toward "gringos" and anti-U.S. sentiment remains. The primary threat to U.S. citizens comes from the explosion of criminal activity. The consular section of the embassy sees approximately two to three Americans per week who claim to be victims of assaults and robberies. The theft of personal documents and effects, passports, money and vehicles is typical of these incidents. Within the past year, there have been no reports of violence against U.S. citizens for reasons of anti-American sentiment nor have there been organized acts of terrorism against U.S. citizens. A significant element of the rising crime rate is attributed to crimes of violence. There is great surfing on the west coast.

The Players

Death Squads

A number of rightwing terrorist groups and "death squads" continues to exist. The ruling Alianza Republicana Nacionalista (ARENA—National Republican Alliance) is an extreme rightwing party founded in 1981. It now works with the FMLN to preserve the integrity of the 1992 peace agreement that ended the long, bloody war between them.

Getting In

A passport and visa are required for entry into El Salvador. Travelers may be asked to present evidence of employment and finances at the time of visa application. There are no airport visas or tourist cards available for last-minute entry. Contact the nearest consulate in Houston, Los Angeles, San Francisco, New Orleans, Miami, New York or Chicago or:

Embassy of El Salvador
2308 California St., NW
Washington, D.C. 20008
☎ *(202) 265-9671*

Consular Affairs
1010 16th Street NW
Third Floor
Washington, D.C. 20036
☎ *(202) 331-4032.*

Getting Around

Of the country's 6214 miles of roads, only 932 are paved. There are 374 miles of railroad. Of the 105 airfields, only 74 are usable; five have a permanent surface, and only the major airport in San Salvador is serviceable for international flights.

Dangerous Places

Buses

The use of public transportation is not wise—taxis are safer. The road to and from the international airport is considered safe during the daytime, but traveling on it at night is strongly discouraged.

The Mountains

Travel to the northern and eastern parts of the country should be restricted to hard surface roads only. This physically comprises two-thirds of the country. Travel outside San Salvador between cities should be done during the day.

Eastern San Salvador

Travel to the eastern side of San Salvador should also not be attempted after sunset. Twenty-fifth Street (Calle 25) is the north/south line of demarcation used to make this distinction.

The following are emergency contact numbers for visitors to San Salvador. Travelers to other regions should note that the respective emergency telephone numbers are different and are encouraged to obtain them prior to departure from San Salvador.

National Police
☎ *[503] (271) 44-22*

Civilian National Police
☎ *[503] (298) 18-49 and (298) 18-56*

Ambulance Service from San Salvador's Diagnostico Hospital
☎ *[503] (226) 51-11 and (225) 05-19*

Dangerous Things

Robbery/Car-jacking

Violent as well as petty crimes are prevalent throughout El Salvador. There were 75 homicides in San Salvador in the first 15 days of January 1995 alone. This was nearly a 100 percent increase over the same period in 1994. Most of the murders in El Salvador are related to carjackings.

U.S. citizens are often victims. Visitors should avoid carrying valuables in public places. Armed assaults and carjackings take place both in San Salvador, the capital, and in the interior of the country, but are especially frequent on roads outside the capital, where police patrols are infrequent. Criminals have been known to follow travelers from the international airport to private residences, where they carry out assaults and robberies and other dirty deeds. Criminals often become violent quickly, especially when victims fail to cooperate immediately in surrendering valuables. Frequently, victims who argue with assailants or refuse to give up their valuables are shot.

Politics

The Salvadoran constitution prohibits foreigners from participating in domestic political activities, including public demonstrations. The government of El Salvador considers such involvement to be a violation of the participant's tourist visa status.

Land Mines

Mine removal efforts are underway, but land mines in back-country regions have caused numerous unintended casualties and pose a threat to off-road tourists, backpackers and campers.

The Maras

Gangs, known as maras, are extremely violent and employ weapons to commit their crimes. Using armed roadblocks, they rob victims and then carjack their vehicles. Due to the prevalence of combat weapons, the arms used in many of the assaults are M-16s, AK-47s and grenade launchers. The crimes take place in private residences, public streets, businesses, markets and the beach areas. Since it is generally accepted that many Salvadoran males are armed, a number of these crimes result in fatalities. The news media carry daily stories of gunfights and shootouts.

Given the prevailing violence, the people exercise their right to self-defense. Wealthy Salvadorans hire security guards to protect themselves, their families and personal property. All visitors are encouraged to cooperate and surrender personal effects in the event of a robbery. The legacy of the decade-long war has led many to place a low value on human life.

Getting Sick

Medical care is limited. There are about 12 hospital beds and four doctors per 10,000 people (1990). Doctors and hospitals often expect immediate cash payment for health services. U.S. medical insurance is not always valid, outside the United States. Most hospitals accept credit cards for hospital charges, but not for doctors fees. Tap water is generally not considered safe to drink in El Salvador. There have also been numerous incidents of cholera in recent months. The U.S. embassy advises its personnel to avoid shellfish and other food sold by streetside vendors or in establishments where hygiene may be questionable.

Nuts and Bolts

The Central American nation has a tropical climate on the coastal plain that changes to cooler and wetter weather in the mountainous inland regions. The average temperature for the city of San Salvador is 73° F. The rainy season is between May and November, and the average annual rainfall is 66 inches in San Salvador.

Currency is the colon, with 100 cents or centavos to the Salvadorean colon.

The people of El Salvador are predominantly Mestizo (94 percent) and Roman Catholic (88 percent). Indians comprise 5 percent of the population, while whites make up only one percent. Spanish is the predominant language, while some Indians speak Nahua.

Most people pass through El Salvador as they travel through Central America. The main reasons for stopping include beaches, volcanoes, lakes and Mayan ruins. El Salvador's 12-year civil war, which ended in 1992, continues to affect the country.

Embassy Location

Americans who register with the consular section of the U.S. embassy in San Salvador may obtain updated information on travel and security within El Salvador.

U.S. Embassy
Final Boulevard Station
Antigua Cuscatlan, Unit 3116
San Salvador, El Salvador
☎ *[503] (78) 4444*

Dangerous Days

10/10/1980   Founding of the Farabundo Marti National Liberation Front (FMLN), the umbrella organization of the five main leftist guerrilla groups in El Salvador.

03/02/1980   Archbishop Oscar Arnulfo Romero assassinated by a presumed right-wing death squad. The anniversary has been marked in succeeding years by leftist terrorist attacks, including attacks on American interests.

02/28/1977   Founding of the Popular League of 28 February (LP-28), a leftist guerrilla group.

06/14/1975   Founding of the Armed Forces of National Resistance (FARN), a leftist guerrilla group.

04/01/1970   Founding of the Popular Liberation Forces (FPL), a leftist guerrilla organization.

09/15/1821   Independence Day.

EL SALVADOR

Eritrea
★

Bitches' Brew

There's a new contestant for the inauspicious title of the world's most impoverished nation: Eritrea, an arid sliver of desert along the Red Sea, populated by Tigrinya-speaking peoples emerging from an ultimately successful 30-year independence struggle against Ethiopia.

Here a man cannot expect to live past his forty-fifth birthday and children are lucky to survive past the age of five. The GNP per capita, at US$120, is the second lowest in the world. More than 80 percent of Eritrea's inhabitants are subsistence farmers, and the economy is entirely dependent on foreign aid. Just another famine-stricken, war-torn, dirt poor republic in the bowels of the Sahara.

Eritrea started life as an Italian colony in the 19th century and came under British mandate in 1941. Addis Ababa took the reins in 1952, and the nearly two-generation-long struggle for independence started shortly thereafter.

Eritrea is famous for conducting one of the first wars of liberation fought in large part by women. Of the 100,000 freedom fighters who fought the Ethiopi-

233

ans, nearly a third were women. The Eritrean People's Liberation Front (EPLF), who shoved the Ethiopians out of the picture in 1991, accomplished what no other African liberation force had before it: It created the first African state on the dark continent carved out of another African state, not from a European colony.

In its mainly unheralded struggle for democracy—in which it is doing admirably well—the new nation waits for the world to realize its people are starving to death.

The Scoop

A revolution was fought here that would bring the SDS, Tom Hayden and even Jesse Jackson to tears. But few reach for their handkerchiefs, let alone their wallets. Eritrea patiently waits to be exploited for its mineral wealth, while its people starve in silence. This tiny country is staggering out of a 30-year war that obliterated both the infrastructure and the term decency. An independence referendum conducted in May 1993 featured a 98.2 percent turnout of eligible voters, 99.8 percent of whom voted for independence. Truly, the people have spoken here—and if they don't starve to death first, this could be the first working democracy to have come down the African pike in a long time. But the Eritreans have their spats, the latest one being a firefight with Yemen over the groundbreaking ceremonies of a whorehouse on the Hanish Islands to protect the investment in another carnal castle being built by the Eritreans in the Dahlak Archipelago.

The Players

Melawes Zenawi

President of Ethiopia since May 1991, Zenawi is the figurehead of the Tigre-led revolution that overthrew years of Amharic rule. Ethiopia's Tigre people are the namesake of the northern province of Tigre; there are a number of Tigre in Eritrea, as well. Neither the Tigre nor the Amhara are Ethiopia's largest ethnic group (the Oromo southwest of the capital of Addis Ababa claim that distinction), although these two groups have traditionally led the country.

The original Abyssinian empire of Axum was centered in what is today the Ethiopian province of Tigre and the newly independent state of Eritrea. Eritrea's Tigre never wanted to take over Ethiopia. They wanted the independence they have finally achieved. But once they began fighting the Amharic regime in Addis in the sixties, they had good reason to help the unhappy Tigre to their immediate south, who focused not on independence but on getting rid of the tyrants in Addis. Most obviously, trouble in Tigre would make it all the harder for Addis Ababa to fight the Eritreans. But there was also a less obvious, more important reason: The Eritreans came to insist on total independence as the only answer for them (a conviction that Addis faithfully fertilized by refusing them any real autonomy), but they knew that under any formula, they would be living in close quarters with Ethiopia, with a vital interest in who ran Ethiopia.

The Eritreans got what they wanted, and with a vengeance. They not only defeated the Ethiopians on the battlefield and secured the independence they wanted, but they were then able to sit back and watch their protégés from Tigre march on to Addis and take it.

Given the skills that these two groups—the diverse Eritreans and the much more homogenous Tigre—developed during their years of jointly organizing themselves against Addis, they could enjoy considerable regional power. Among the Somalis and others, the Eritreans have clearly won prestige as a dividend. Meantime, by sheer force of numbers, Ethiopia is a powerhouse. Eritrea has a population of 3.2 million. Ethiopia's is 58.7 million.

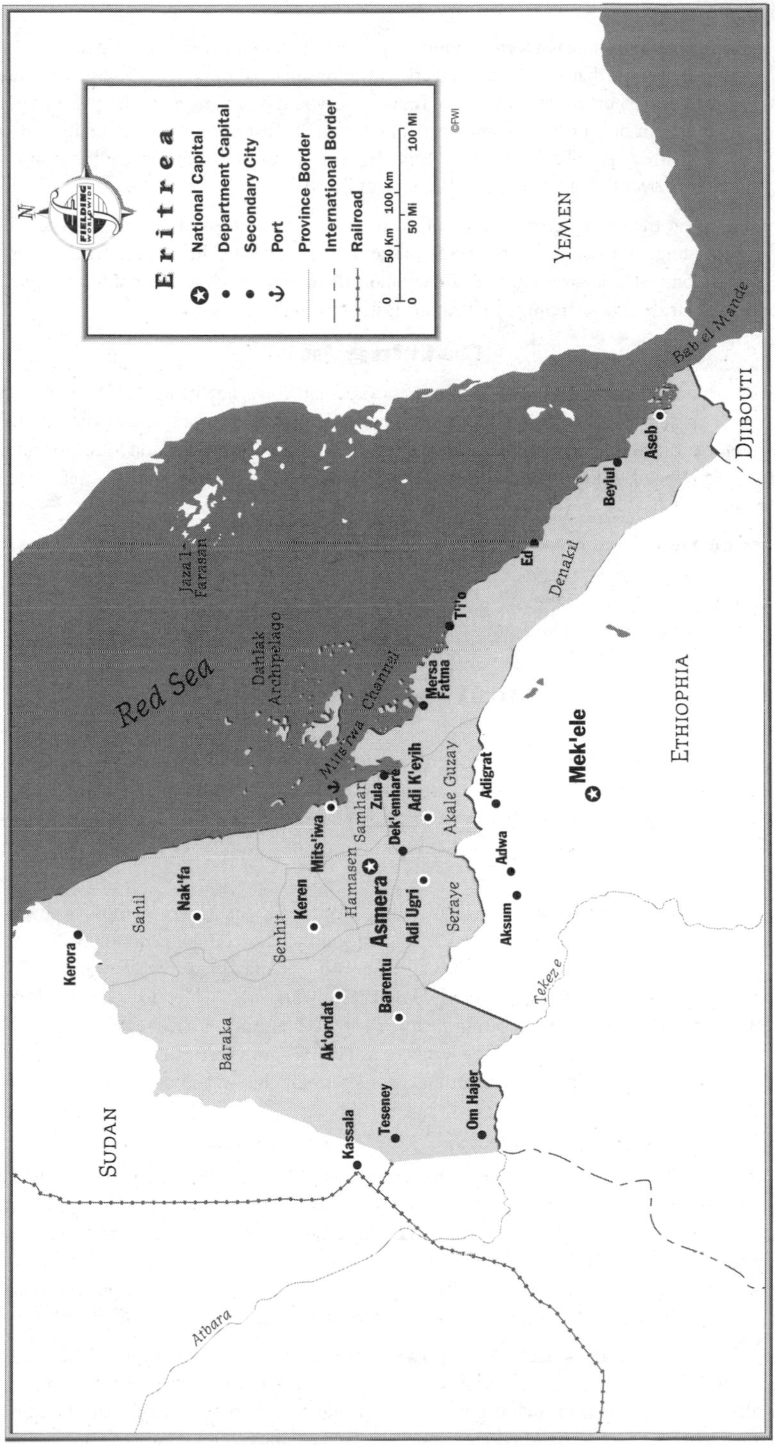
Eritrea
National Capital
Department Capital
Secondary City
Port
Province Border
International Border
Railroad
0 50 Km 100 Km
0 50 Mi 100 Mi
©FWI
Red Sea
Dahlak Archipelago
Mits'iwa Channel
YEMEN
DJIBOUTI
ETHIOPHIA
SUDAN
Bab el Mande
Denakil
Sahil
Senhit
Baraka
Hamasen
Samhar
Akale Guzay
Seraye
Tekeze
Atbara
Asmera
Mek'ele
Nak'fa
Kerora
Keren
Mits'iwa
Zula
Dek'emhare
Adi K'eyih
Adi Ugri
Barentu
Ak'ordat
Teseney
Kassala
Om Hajer
Aksum
Adwa
Adigrat
Mersa Fatma
Ti'o
Ed
Beylul
Aseb

Issaias Afwerki

Eritrea's head of state is a former military commander much in the mold of Museveni and Kagame, except that his Eritreans were in the business of building a disciplined grassroots force well before the other two. Indeed, he would be stage center rather than a godfather were it not for Eritrea's preoccupation with reconstruction and the limits that the size of Eritrea's population—just 3.2 million souls—puts on the influence it has won with its victory over the old Amharic regime in Addis Ababa.

However, the moral persuasion it won with that victory is considerable, reconstruction is proceeding, and just one thing seems to stand in the way of Eritrea becoming influential far beyond what its size suggests: the wave of Islamic fire sweeping the entire area and, in particular, Islamic extremists infiltrating Eritrea from the Sudan.

Getting In

Passport and visa required. Tourist/business visa valid for a stay of up to six months, requires one application, two photos, $25 fee (no personal checks). Business visa can be extended up to one year, and requires company letter stating purpose of travel. Include SASE for return of passport by mail. Allow three working days for processing. For more information, contact the embassy:

Embassy of Eritrea

910 17th Street., N.W.
Suite 400
Washington, D.C. 20006
☎ (202) 429-1991

Getting Around

Eritrea evokes exotic images, but there is little exotic about this capital. Many of the towns the Brits built in Africa during the late 19th and early 20th century have an uncanny way of looking and even feeling like sleepy midwestern towns built in America during the same period. Broad, clean streets laid out in grids, an agricultural economy, quiet sidewalks, a sense not of the Happy Valley high jinks that made Kenya notorious, but of solid, even stolid middle class prosperity.

There has always been a settlement here, but it was the Italians who built most of this efficient, cleanly plotted little city, and they built it around an agricultural economy which they also developed. Overflowing bougainvillea and espresso machines grace the sidewalks, making Asmara a good deal more pleasant than, say, Lusaka. Asmara, with its sidewalk cafes and flowers and clean streets, may be the most pleasant city in all of Africa. And with its population of lively, variegated Eritreans, it is hardly a sleepy Kansas town in midsummer. In fact, before World War II, Asmara's Italian population ran an annual sports car rally that was second only to Nairobi's East Africa Rally.

It is a city built on business and looks it. National Avenue is gracefully palm-lined, but it's pretty much a straight, broad avenue. It has an impressive grand Mosque and a Catholic Cathedral, but nothing to draw travelers; they're more visual cues that this quiet little place is no backwater. The nature of the war ruined much of the Eritrean countryside, but the war never really came to Asmara. It deteriorated some, but it never fell apart, and it always had an excellent infrastructure of sewers, water, phones. On top of that, it has a population whose skills don't need a lot more demonstration. It could become an efficient jumping-off point.

But it needs work, and what it doesn't have is money. It has a decent airport, but roads in and out are fair to poor to rotten. A rail line that the Turks built from the coast to Asmara to Agordat in the far west is in such disrepair that it may never be rebuilt...and that would be a true pity, as it cost a lot to build and traverses spectacular topography.

Getting Out

Cars can be rented. It's hard to say what difficulties might arise. There are a defunct railroad and a smattering of splattered roads. There is little reason to travel far and wide in this tiny country. Goat and camel trails abound in the hinterlands.

Dangerous Places

Hanish Islands

Israel, Yemen and Eritrea have been haggling over the Hanish Islands, in the lower Red Sea equidistant to Eritrea and Yemen—a potential hooker harem with zeal (some might say with a squeal). Yemen and Eritrea have come to blows over this barren cluster of desolate rocks in the sea. And what better player to have in a prostitute turf war in a border town in the Middle East than a Texan? Millionaire contractor B. K. Anderson signed a deal with the Eritrean government in December 1995 to build a giant US$210 million resort—complete with two casinos, a golf course, five-star hotel with 200 rooms, marina and holiday village—in an enclosed bay, not in the Hanish Islands, but in the Dahlak Islands off the coast of Massawa, Eritrea, about 420 km northwest of the Hanish chain. The purpose of the resort? To entice rich and bored Saudi Arabians seeking a little R&R from the Koran, by offering enough booze, broads, poker and boogey boards to keep a Hamas suicide bus bomber from pulling the pin. A place to go where upscale ground-sniffers can mothball Mohammed for a weekend. And if the Muslim Club Meders are forced to bring along their wives, a separate glass-domed complex staffed solely by former female Eritrean freedom fighters will suit their every veiled whim—as long as they keep their clothes on and their heads covered. At least that's what's advertised. Actually, the wives will be "preoccupied" by their EPLF captors until their humping husbands have played enough holes with the imported Russian pom-pom girls.

The government of Eritrea will receive an annual land rent of US$500 an acre and a whopping 40 percent of the casinos' gross revenues, enough dough to keep Eritreans facing Mecca for longer than they have to. B.K.'s pleasure palace should see its first hezbollah hedonists by 1999.

With Anderson's deal in the bag, it became known that an Italian financier was planning to set up a similar den of delights in the competitively close Hanish Islands. Would it be a sin shop for semites and horny Hebrews, or a Yemeni offshore oasis wooing the same oil-slickers the Eritreans and the Texan were trying to pump? The Eritreans didn't wait around to find out. In December 1995, Asmara sent troops out to Greater Hanish and threatened to go to war with Yemen over the islands' sovereignty, which the new nation first claimed in 1993 after independence from Ethiopia. Firefights and battles have been breaking out between the two foes on the islands. The Eritreans may not win their stake to the Hanishes, but they have enough troops (100,000-strong) to ensure a protracted battle—certainly one long enough to abort any Yemeni plans of building a high-rise whorehouse in the Hanishes in the near future.

Getting Sick

There is only one doctor for every 48,000 people. Doctors are likely to be found among the foreign-aid workers. Famine is a major problem and so is malaria.

Nuts and Bolts

Eritrea's constitution isn't even written yet. Many foreign governments are represented here, but the process of setting up embassies is still in flux. The U.S. used to have a huge presence here. There was even a U.S. military base, Kagnew Station, whose prime reason for being was a satellite dish which spied on telecommunications throughout this strategic region. U.S. advisors helping Haile Selassie fight the Eritreans were also based here, and U.S. Air Force pilots flew transport and training flights out of the air base. Kagnew is now a huge tank-park for war materiel, mostly Soviet gear captured from the Ethiopian army, that the Eritreans want to sell. Know anybody looking for a nice, low-mileage T-55 tank?

Banks are open 8:30 a.m. to noon, 3 to 6:30 p.m. The currency is the Egyptian Pound. Languages spoken are Arabic, Tigrinya and English. Governments are open on a casual basis. What do you say about the office hours of a government whose army still serves without pay? Somebody is always at work.

Women's Lib the Hard Way— or Why the Afro is Back

When the Eritrean Peoples Liberation Front (EPLF) won its hard-fought 30-year battle for independence in 1992, Mengistu Haile Mariam ran Ethiopia as a dictatorship with help from the Soviets. Hatred of him and his policies forged an alliance between Christian and Muslim, poor and wealthy, and men and women. The EPLF made use of women fighters and lifted them out of the Stone Age burden of dowry, circumcision and corn-row hairdos. When the women fighters marched into the capital of Asmara on May 24, 1991, the teenage girls were impressed by the Afros and men's trousers worn by the female freedom fighters and soon began to wear them themselves.

In a Dangerous Place

Eritrea: The Man Without a Gun

One evening, without prelude and so unexpectedly that for a minute I think he is joking, Kidane says, "Would you like to meet the freedom fighters in the mountains?" As if he is inviting me to dinner. "A squad could cross the border tomorrow night and be back in three days."

I say I'd really like to but unfortunately, I have this prior engagement....

Years later, considerable numbers of reporters, documentarians and writers are to go behind the lines with the Eritreans, not least the Australian novelist Thomas Kineally, who wrote *Schindler's List* and an emotional novel about Eritrea, *To Asmara*. But it will be years before that will happen, years in which the Eritreans will acquire not just tanks and heavy artillery, but much more importantly, jeeps in which to carry us frail vessels called journalists. Meantime, I have just arrived in this distant Sudanese town, barely aware there is a place called Eritrea, which in any case is most decidedly not my objective. Addis is my objective. If I am to go with these people at all, it can't just be across the border and back. Back in Kassala, I'd be in the same fix. It will have to be all the way across the territory to its capital, Asmara, from which I can then get to Addis on my own. Which is of course, a totally hypothetical notion: I am not about to disappear into some trackless hills with an off-the-wall band of African guerrillas.

Kassala is a backwater town on the Atbara River in the Sudan, a few dry miles from the Abyssinian frontier. By Kassala, the vegetation has begun to get thick. But the town is suffused with the atmosphere of the desert. The train station is out of town. I'd just dragged myself off the slow train from Haiya Junction, when suddenly a band of camel-mounted Bedj comes galloping at breakneck speed across the river and into the town.

In town, along with a clutch of Yoruba pilgrims bound for Mecca, I sleep on the floor of one of the outbuildings of the police post, a single-room building devoid of any appointment, save a few straw mats upon which duty officers sleep and pray. A single bald electric bulb burns constantly. Asleep in one corner is Yacoub, trustee and servant, a half-breed with a huge head, for which he was nicknamed, an Ethiopian, or at least, they tell me, in the pay of the Ethiopians. He is serving a sentence for bomb-tossing. "At whom?" I asked. "At the Eritreans," he later tells me. "At the Communists."

I am in no mood to understand. Eritrea is not my objective. My objective is Addis Ababa, and I have a headache: That goes with travel in these parts. It had been hard to get a visa for the Sudan. Americans were being turned down out of hand. Finally, I got a two-week overland permit. Now, it is virtually expired. In London, the Ethiopian embassy said I wouldn't need a visa for Ethiopia. They reminded me what an ally we had in Ethiopia; indeed, almost all the military aid we are sending to sub-Saharan Africa is going to the Emperor, commander of black Africa's largest standing army. "You're an American," they'd said, "a visa for Ethiopia is just a matter of picking one up at the border." Now I am at the border. My Sudanese visa is expiring. His Excellency's consul is hemming and hawing.

It is dangerous to cross here. "*Shiftas*," he says. "Bandits." But just to show what a good chap he is, he'll wire Addis.

It is Thursday. The next day, everything will be shut for the Muslim sabbath. I deal with the tension by pretending to create options should the answer come back as no.

I meet an Indian, a *Hendi*, in Arabic. Does he know the Eritreans? No, he says, over instant coffee at his radio shop, but will I photograph his infant daughter? We bicycle through Kassala's *suk* to his house on some suburban mud flats. I wait in the sitting room, as his mother prepares Japanese Kool-Aid and his wife prepares the baby. The sitting room is dominated by a single ornament: a blinking neon 'Sankyo' sign. As I wait, I see a young Bedj approach the yard with a wooden bowl of fresh milk. At the door, he glances about nervously, almost, it seems, like a wolf in a kennel, sets the bowl down, and hurries off without a word. The Hendi's wife appears with the infant. The child's face has been powdered almost geisha-white, her lips and cheeks are rouged and her eyes are made up like the eyes of houris in ancient illuminations from the Sind. I take the photos, drink the Kool-Aid, the Hendi says thank you, and, as I am leaving, he says that although he does not know the Eritreans, he does know Hassan mi Jack, and Hassan mi Jack knows the Eritreans.

Hassan mi Jack rents and repairs bicycles, refrigerators and Waring blenders. On the wall of his storefront office, which is also his repair shop, there are two pictures: one of Mao as a young scholar in Kiangsi, another of a female Chinese guerrilla about to pitch a grenade. The man is dark, imposing, heavy, gregarious. On his head, he wears a fake leopard turban.

"My name is Hassan mi Jack," he says. "They call me Jack Palance, the Man Without a Gun. Only I have a gun." And he pulls a.38 revolver from the top drawer of his desk.

Do I want to meet the Eritreans? I will meet the Eritreans. Unfortunately, he cannot be there to make the introductions, but if I take a table in the central gardens at about 9:30 in the evening, they will approach.

The central gardens of Kassala are an overgrown, ragged place, lit at night by lurid yellow neon bulbs, buzzing loudly with the electric hum and whine of nocturnal insects. The great Egyptian diva, Um Kalsoum, hoarse with static, moans soulfully over two loudspeakers. Small, circular metal tables are scattered about. A little stand serves fruit juices and tea. I come early and sit alone with a hot glass of tea. At 9:30 promptly, a young man in a crisp white shirt and black trousers approaches. I stand, we shake hands.

"I am Kidane Kiflu," he says in a clear but exotic English, the sort of English you hear from those who seldom hear our difficult language spoken but are especially intelligent and study hard, the English of a bright but provincial Japanese schoolboy. "I am of the Eritrean Liberation Front." Years later, when I learned he'd become more than something of a figure, it wasn't surprising.

We talk of this and that for most of that evening and most of several following evenings. He speaks of how Italian influence is heavier in Eritrea than it is in the rest of Ethiopia; his native province has been an Italian colony since the grab for Africa in the 19th century; the Italians hadn't marched into Ethiopia proper until the eve of World War II. On the question of independence, he offers the party line. He asks to see what I'd written.

During these days, the Eritrean insurgency is dominated by Muslim Bedouin like those camel-mounted Bedj I'd just seen galloping into Kassala. Kidane Kiflu is a Copt from the densely populated highlands. His native language is Tigrinya, but he also speaks the Amharic of Ethiopia's rulers in Addis Ababa, and well enough to have been accepted at the University in Addis on a scholarship. Like a fellow Copt and native speaker of Tigrinya, Meles Zenawi, who would become the president of Ethiopia, he'd dropped out to join the revolution. But Zenawi, the man who will lead all of Ethiopia in the nineties, is a native of Tigre province just south of Eritrea, and dropped out to fight for the overthrow of the government. Kidane was a native of Eritrea, and, for the sake of a distinct and independent Eritrea, this Tigrinya-speaking Copt had made common cause with Eritrea's Muslim tribes.

Six of us leave Kassala at dusk, squeezed with a driver and all our gear in an old Peugeot taxi that takes off straight out over the desert. There are three scouts—Ismail, Ibrahim and Ali—and two cadres—Abdullah and Abara. We all wear cheap muslin robes over khaki uniforms, the robes to be discarded when we cross the border. The robes of the scouts also cover AK 47s, what they call Kalatchnikovs.

The cadre Abdullah is slight, just seventeen, a quiet zealot. Abara is a heavy, 30-year-old Copt, a former schoolmaster, who seems to be leaving the meager comforts of Kassala with great reluctance. Neither carries a weapon, save a single suicide hand grenade apiece.

Soon enough, the old Peugeot can go no further and we get out and begin walking toward the barren mountains of the border. We walk well into the night. Eventually the sound of domestic animals (agitated at our approach, braying mules, bleating goats, the unloved yapping dogs of Islamic countries) indicates a Bedouin settlement ahead. The Bedouin feed us and we sleep in their huts. For several hours in the morning, we wait for someone to come with a camel, but he never comes. At 5 a.m., we leave the settlement and climb further into the foothills, until finally we come to a deep wadi. Here, we camp, still waiting for the camel. We wait all that day and all the next, changing camps only once, rough muslin robes still over our uniforms.

Abdullah, the young Muslim cadre, digs into the sand of the wadi for water, but finds none. Our supply, kept in goat hides and tasting of goat hide, is running low. He and Abara try to reassure me. They keep repeating the instructions I'd received from Kidane: If anybody asks me who I am, I'm to reply simply that I was a student: "*Ana talib.*"

I fall asleep in the heat, hallucinate a little, and wake-up disoriented, a face in my face asking, who are you?

"*Ana talib.*"

"Who are you!"

"*Ana talib.*"

The camel never comes. Finally, at dusk on the third day, we begin climbing on foot. It is hard. We have to rush. "Hurry," they keep saying. We have to get to the border before dawn. When at last we get to the border, it is just dawn. My

feet are swollen. Just over the crest of the last mountain of the border chain, Ibrahim takes out his binoculars and scans the great flat Eritrean plain spread beneath
us. At first, it looks greener than the Sudan behind us. It is studded with green
acacia trees. In the dawn light, it even looks cool. The dew is heavy. But on second glance, you can see how flattened the acacia trees are, as if bent to the desert
wind. Their branches are stiff and thorny. They are almost miniature trees growing close to the ground, and I am to discover beneath them more thorns, barbed
ones, that will pierce our shoes and stick to our legs as we walk, so that periodically we'll have to stop and pick them out. And beyond the plain, faint but evident even in the half-light of dawn, you can see another chain. And there will be
another, they told me, and another....

It takes a day and a half to reach the second chain; still we'd met no one. The
whole trip is to take seven days. Four and a half days have passed. We'd barely
penetrated Eritrea. The evening of the fifth day, the scout Ibrahim comes running back, gesturing, *"Yacoub. Wahid sanaf b'il Abu Shanab."*

Yacoub is what he calls me; *wahid sanaf* is one squad. Soon enough, from just
over a rise at the horizon, there they are—seven men, widely dispersed, at the extremities, uniformed riflemen with Enfields, just left of center a man with a Bren
gun, and slightly to the rear, a native leading a camel.

Neither group quickens pace, though we can see each other long before we
meet. In our group, only Ibrahim, the joker, is vibrant, the rest betray no emotion, though surely they are glad finally to have made contact. Nor does any sign
come from the advancing squad, no shouts, no waves. When we are within talking distance, Abara, the older cadre, says, *"Salaam alaiykum,"* "Peace be with
you" to which the leader of the advancing squad (older than the rest, middle-
aged, moustached, a.45 strapped to his hip, a camel crop in his hand) says,
"Alaiykum salaam" "With you be peace." When finally they reach each other,
they embrace in a long and formalistic ritual, and then we all do the same with
each member of the squad, in the same long and formalistic ritual we are to repeat
across the breadth of Eritrea, a ritual characteristic of all the Horn and Arabia
and, to a lesser extent, Arab and Islamic cities, asking questions about the well-
being of mothers, fathers, brothers, sisters, uncles, aunts and cousins, all of whom
we will hear are well (whether they are or not). And our mothers, fathers, brothers, sisters? Well indeed, we say. And theirs? Well indeed. And again, they ask of
ours. And again, we ask of theirs.

Little emotion is shown, but our collective sentiment is close to true joy. It is
evening. We build a fire and rest for the night, drinking rancid but wonderful
water from whole, untanned hides of goats.

The next morning we set out for the camp of Abu Shanab, this time with a
camel to share. As we move, the scouts fan out and come back with reports: Many
people, they say, have heard that a white man is coming. I can't imagine where in
this barren country "many people" might be, and the notion of a man uniquely
white rings as archaic as being called Mr. Jack by Abdullah and Abara. But the
next morning, two native runners catch up with us to find out if it is true. Abdullah tells me we will soon be in the camp of Abu Shanab, and the day after that,
just before we reach the camp, we pass through a Bedouin settlement, fenced by
thornbush against unseen predators: jackal, wild dog, leopard. From atop the

camel, I can just barely make out the forms of black-robed women as they peer out at us from the shadows of the doorways of their huts.

There are many more natives at the camp than uniformed guerrillas and many camels. Some of the natives wear crude muslin robes, but others are dressed like those wild Bedj back in the Sudan, Kipling's fuzzy-wuzzies, with elaborate gold, orange and turquoise robes with leather girdles, leather-sheathed sabres, knives and elaborately saddled camels. All wear their hair in those great fuzzy-wuzzy dos, all carry stout staves. The guerrillas wear uniforms like us, khaki shorts, khaki shirts. All mingle together, in assemblies under trees.

Abu Shanab is a big man with a sergeant-major moustache and a sergeant-major's booming voice. The natives argue loudly among themselves, and one has to be led from the meeting by a guerrilla sergeant-at-arms. At this, a nine- or ten-year-old boy in guerrilla uniform and carrying a small Italian carbine, jumps to his feet and begins shouting, apparently in defense of the native. Abu Shanab waves for him to be quiet, but he goes on. Abu Shanab waves again, and the same guerrilla sergeant-at-arms drags the young boy—screaming and in tears—from the assembly. The assembly, which has been laughing lightly, laughs aloud and goes back to its dispute.

The boy, it turns out, is Abu Shanab's recalcitrant son, sent to the field with his father by a mother who can't handle him.

The next day we leave Abu Shanab's camp with a fresh camel and fresh scouts, but things do not go well. We all get sick, and all around us is sickness and death. The twentieth day out of Kassala, thirteen days past schedule, it begins to seem we are traveling in broad circles. Abdullah is offended by the question. Abara rubs his feet and brushes his hair and says something about a battle somewhere, something about helicopters. It is hot.

####

There are many Ethiopians who honestly believe Eritrea is part of Ethiopia and Americans who see Haile Selassie as a heroic figure who was right to want Eritrea.

There were many knowledgeable Americans who saw the war here as the stuff of devious Levantine politics, clandestine factions, sinister games of cell versus cell. It was hard to argue with all that went on. In one nearly self-defeating episode of internecine killing, the original Eritrean Liberation Front, heavily Muslim, Arab-financed, was subsumed by the breakaway Eritrean People's Liberation Front, led primarily by Tigrinya-speaking Copts like Kidane—in fact, by Tigrinya-speaking Copts inspired by Kidane.

To Americans knowledgeable of all this, I was hopelessly naive. Exasperated, one once looked at me and asked, "Do you really think what you've got here is Emiliano Zapata and his boys?"

I didn't have anything to say, so he filled the awkward silence: "Of course, that's reducing it to the absurd, but do you really think..."

In fact, I hadn't taken it as a reduction to the absurd at all. Zapata and his boys were exactly how I saw them and never mind the Levantine moments.

####

On the evening of that twentieth day, as our latest complement of scouts (at each guerrilla encampment, a new set would take over) genuflects deeply in the evening prayer (a white spot of sand on their dark foreheads as they rise), it be-

ERITREA

comes suddenly and frighteningly clear: We have been traveling in circles. We are supposed to be traveling northeast, almost precisely in the direction of Mecca. But if the direction we are traveling is truly northeast, then Mecca will have to be due south, for the guerrillas are facing due south from the direction they have told me is northeast.

Abdullah, the zealot, himself suffering disease, refusing comfort, pushing himself, says nothing. Abara admits it. "Just trust us," he says.

Somewhere out there, something vague is happening, and then something not so vague, a battle we don't even hear, and then its backlash, forever and unexpectedly raking past us. We travel almost entirely by night.

One evening, they tell me a runner has brought orders for them to leave me. They introduce me to Hassan, an Arabic-speaking young cadre, who will take me to the other side of the town of Keren. Down the slope, by two wounded guerrillas, a female guerrilla, the only one I'd ever seen with them, is helping to pack and saddle a mule. They ask me to give them all my tape, all my 35mm film, all my notes. It is supposedly for my protection, and again they put me through the drill: If I am picked up and they ask me who I am, what am I to say?

"*Ana talib*, I'm a student."

"Just trust us," they say. But they don't watch closely, and it is possible to wrap one roll of 35 mm in a sock and to stick the sock in a hip pocket. Leaving the bivouac with Hassan, I turn in the saddle to wave good-bye. The pressure of the 35 mm cartridge in my hip pocket spikes any tendency toward excessive sentiment.

From then on, says Hassan, we will move exclusively by night. Hassan is a different sort of cadre than Abdullah and Abara. He speaks English hardly at all, only Tigre, a Sematic language close to Tigrinya but more characteristic of Eritrea's Muslims, and Arabic, long the *lingua franca* here, and that is how we use it. He is quiet, confident, and with the scouts (there are now three), much more the combat commander. And yet, for all that, he carries no weapon, only that single hand grenade.

The first morning out, Hassan leads the way up a short pass to an escarpment high above a valley. The valley is vast and much different from the valleys behind. The countryside is green, and I can see farms plotted out to a far horizon. From the hell behind, it looks like some fairyland ahead. The descent into the valley is very nearly precipitous. The mule is surefooted, but often I have to dismount as the trail winds down along ledges that keep disappearing into the face of the cliff.

At the bottom, we are in high grass country. We stop briefly by a village. The village structures are more permanent here. A delegation comes out, there is some nervous negotiation, and one of the village men comes along with us as a guide. He leads us at a quick pace to a wadi with high grass growing on either side, so that I cannot be seen, even atop the mule. We proceed single file down the wadi, one man behind me, Hassan just in front, the others in front of him, the point man way ahead. We move about half an hour, when suddenly shots crackle in the air. Hassan spins, waving me back, shouting "Ethiopi! Ethiopi!" Blood leaves my head; I wheel about on my mule and gallop back up the wadi. Then, just as suddenly, there are more shouts. "*Agif! Agif!*" ("Stop. Stop!") I pull up my mule and look back. Hassan, kneeling, is looking back as well. The shots have stopped. There are still shouts from back down the wadi. It turns out that it is not

Ethiopians at all, but another guerrilla squad that has mistaken us for Ethiopians as we have them, and opened fire. We have been approaching each other at the junction of two wadis. As I reach the junction, I see our point man genuflecting deeply in prayer. Each time he rises, I can see that white patch of sand on his dark forehead.

The night is cold. At the next village, there are more nervous negotiations and finally a new guide. As we are about to leave, the new guide refuses and we have to wait for another. At last he comes, there are some hurried whispers in the dark, and we take off so quickly that there is no time to explain, myself atop the mule, galloping up the wadi, while (to my total astonishment) the others run along on foot beside me, keeping right up. As I gallop, the black, thorny branches whip and cut my face. We are moving fast, too fast, it seems to me, for even these tough men to last. There is no actual panic, but the heavy breathing of the running men, and of my galloping mule, and the rushing slap of plastic sandals on the sand of the wadi strike a distinct note of hysteria held in hard check.

The branches whipping out from the embankment of the wadi get thicker, the shadows ever more black. There is no moon, hardly any sky to be seen above the suddenly dense vegetation in this near-desert country. Eventually, it crowds in so close that there is barely room to move single file, and at last we are forced to slow down. Just as I think the vegetation can get no thicker, we suddenly break into a large clearing which turns out to be the soggy bed of the Anseba River.

"Halhal," Hassan whispers, "Halhal min Anseba." It is all he needed to say, for he knows that I have learned well enough of Halhal, an Ethiopian combat base, and the name of a major battle that had been fought during the worst of the miseries with Abdullah and Abara, and aside from disease and infection, the reason for those miseries. As we move through country, the Ethiopian Second Division is scouring to find the guerrillas who have attacked Halhal. Though it is the dry season, in the middle of the bed the river still runs, black and deep.

Twice we follow promontories that seem to lead to the other side, wading up to our chests. It is cold, dark. Both times we have to turn back. The water rushes about my feet, as I ride the mule toward the other side. The guide, the guerrillas and Hassan cut in front of me, cross and scout up the river. Just over halfway, the mule suddenly begins sinking into the sandy bottom. She panics and throws me into the river. I am up and after her, but her panic is compounded as she struggles to pull herself free and sinks ever more deeply into the sucking bottom. I am into it myself nearly to my ankles, the water about my waist. She is down to her rear haunches. The others are in front of me, out of sight. I pull at the mule's saddle. Her eyes bulge. She heaves against the sucking sand. She seems to be coming out of it. In the cold I begin to sweat, and to sweat more. I feel somewhere near panic myself, but look at that panicked, stupid mule, eyes bulging, inviting disaster even as she is slowly coming free and think I can't be that stupid. In the midst of our mutual sweat and pulling, this mountain-nimble animal lurches free with an awkward heave and stumble. Afoot, I drag her up the Anseba, toward the men, remembering Hassan's whispered, "Halhal min Anseba..." and find relief from the fear and tension in anger: "The idiots!" I fume silently at my betters. All that noise. Then I discovered the reason for their slight commotion in the dark. They have discovered an orange grove and are delightedly picking oranges. Oranges! The first fresh thing I will have had in 21 days, a steady diet of sour milk and gruel finally broken. Sweating, soaking wet, shivering in the cold, we suck on oranges one after another.

Leaving Anseba and its little jungle, we begin once again to climb. Unlike Abdullah and Abara, they are able to tell me what is happening. Now, at last, we are due north of the town of Keren. We'd begun southwest of it. The plan was to circle the town, ending up southeast of it. We couldn't move directly from the point southwest to the point southeast, because the turf in between is securely in the hands of reinforced Ethiopian brigades, as is the town. A trip that might have taken a few minutes by car, a few hours by foot, is taking three or four days. Fatigue hits hard at three in the morning. Once again, we are very high up. Just before dawn one of the scouts pulls on my sleeve and bids me look back. I look back, twisting in the saddle. Beneath us, I can see, quite clearly, the lights of enemy-held Keren, the first electric light I will have seen in 21 days. Dawn is just breaking as we collapse, still soaked, on a cold mountain hillside.

The next day is pleasant. It is warm. We spend all day just lying about the hills, a lot like the foothills around San Francisco. We joke, eat some more Anseba oranges. A goat is brought up to us from one of the villages below, and we slaughter it. One of the guerrillas slings his Kalatchnikov over the branch of a tree, and, straight-faced, I pretend to reprimand him for something every recruit in every decent army is disciplined not to do; if we are surprised, he will have to stand up to get it. I never imagined myself their superior, but I'd put on their uniform and should have been. He takes me seriously. Hassan chews him out. They'd all been trained not to do that, he says and he tells me of his training in Syria, how fortunate he is to have been sent there, how much he'd learned. For example, he says, he'd never before known that 80 percent of the U.S. population is Jewish and that the war in Vietnam was being fought to make money for Jewish millionaires. "And I know it's true," he says. "I've seen pictures of their houses."

In the late afternoon, a headman, a Copt, comes up from one of the villages. We talk, eat another meal, and he offers me his daughter in marriage if I settle in his village.

In the evening, I go down to the village to prepare for the night's march. I'd taken off my uniform. I am to leave Hassan and his squad, the last of the guerrillas. From then on, the headman will lead me. From then on, Hassan reminds me, I can tell no one who I am or where I'd been. "Who are you?" he smiles.

"*Ana talib*. I'm a student."

The squad follows me down. All day we'd been joking. Now they are silent.

Near the edge of the village, the headman saddles my new mule. It is a nasty beast. It bucks and kicks as he rides it, but finally it settles down. He gets off, I get on, and again it begins to buck and kick. Finally, it settles down and I am about to ride around a hut when Hassan stops me.

"Not yet," he says. "The men are preparing."

I get down off the mule. Hassan looks around the corner of the hut. "OK. Now." I follow him around.

The squad is standing at attention, their ragged uniforms squared away to the best of all possible efforts. Hassan comes to position before them. He calls them to present-arms, and they bring their rifles up in snappy British manual. Hassan executes an about face and hand-salutes. Not knowing quite how to respond, awkwardly, I return his salute. He calls the men to port-arms. I shake his hand and thank him, and we embrace as we had in the desert. With each of the men I do the same. The headman come forward with the mule, I mount and we leave. Just once, I twist in the wooden saddle to wave back; it is a different wave than it had been a few days before, with that 35mm cartridge in my pocket. It is dusk. They are the last guerrillas I am to see.

As night comes, time begins alternately to rush at me and slow down to excruciatingly long hours. I lose all sense of it. He moves relentlessly, this old headman. We move upward through narrow corridors, dark cathedrals of rock that rise forever, echoing every pebble drop. I am barely able to stay awake. I keep slipping from the saddle, waking in rude starts. It is cold, silken webs spread from tree to tree, brushing across my face, and I am constantly hallucinating—old friends wait for me, perched in trees just ahead; old loves lie dead on the boulders beneath me; jackals bark accusations, howl of my guilt; Ethiopians lie in wait. We move on, slipping over rocks, through unseen thorned branches that whip at our faces, down gullies, over boulders, up narrow rock defiles that bruise our ribs as we smash against them. Up and up, again to high mountains. Finally, we stumble into a village. Dogs are yapping. The headman leads me to a hut and calls out by the thorn fence that surrounds the hut. Two adolescent boys come out. The headman speaks with them, and we enter the mud hut, warming ourselves at a small coal fire. The headman is exhausted. He speaks briefly with the boys, and then suddenly there is a fight. The headman springs at one of them and begins beating him with his fists. The second boy steps in, and we settle back down by the fire. I am confused, but without the strength to meet my confusion. I just want to sleep. For the first time, I notice how much this second boy looks like Kidane Kiflu.

In gentle textbook English, he asks me who I am, why I had come.

"I'm a student," I mumble, "*Ana talib.*"

"No," he said. "I know who you are. I know why you come. You come for freedom."

The headman disappears. Just before dawn this boy with the face of Kidane Kiflu wakes me up, leads me down to the Asmara road and says good-bye. I stick my thumb out. Within forty minutes I am atop a semi loaded with tractor tires. An easy hour after that, I am in Asmara—high, cool and Italian, where congenial Neapolitans prepare cappuccino with the latest machines.

True to their word, the Eritreans return all my tape, notes, film. They haven't even bothered to develop the film. Kidane sent the package, and with it a letter in long hand, in the same exotic English: "Allow me please to convey to you my heartfelt greetings. I hope you have had an enjoyable and not agonizing experience…due to the terranian nature of Eritrea and due to circumstances. I hope to write to you of the latest developments. I saw your article on a Lebanese Newspaper and our people here are startled by your presentation. Please convey Greetings to all members of your Family."

I have said that in the years after I met him in Kassala, Kidane Kiflu became something of a figure. I've also said that Eritrea never commanded much attention in the U.S. Kidane Kiflu became well known in the small world of the Eritreans, and I only learned of his prominence in the course of dry research.

Poring over a propaganda tract mimeographed on pink paper in which the Eritrean People's Liberation Front attempted to explain why it had been forced to move against the Muslim leadership of the Eritrean Liberation Front, I came at last to the middle of the last paragraph of the thirteenth page:

"...they placed six members in prison and subjected them to harsh treatment. Further, right in the heart of Kassala they murdered the two revolutionary fighters, comrades Kidane Kiflu and Welday Gidey, who for many years had energetically worked to redirect the course of the struggle. They were under the impression that if they killed these valiant and insightful leaders, the rest could hardly accomplish anything. The dead bodies were placed in sacks and put on a taxi to be transported to a trash dump called Hafera. On the way, however, as if to plead their case to the world-public, the corpses of the two martyrs fell out in the middle of the street."

—Jack Kramer

Addis Ababa

Ethiopia
★

Hungry for Peace

Beginning with the end of World War II, one Abyssinian tribe after another revolted against the ancient rule of the Amhara ensconced in Addis Ababa. Many of these revolts, if not most, eventually fashioned themselves after Marxists, but the victory of the Marxist Dergue over Haile Selassie in 1974 was no victory for these peoples. The Dergue was largely Amharic. It was a continuation of Amharic tyranny in Marxist garb.

Real victory didn't come until the Eritreans defeated the Ethiopian Army south of Asmara in 1991, sending their revolutionary protégés in the province of Tigre on a march to Addis that could have only one result. With their arrival at the city gates and the fall of the Dergue came a euphoria in which all things seemed possible...quickly followed by the frightened distrust of all the many peoples of this land, each deeply distinct, deeply traditional, anciently, rigidly structured.

For a true outsider, the human array is downright bewildering, but there is less chaos than first meets the eye. For a traveler in such dangerous parts, there's grief to be sidestepped and reward to be won in taking a closer look.

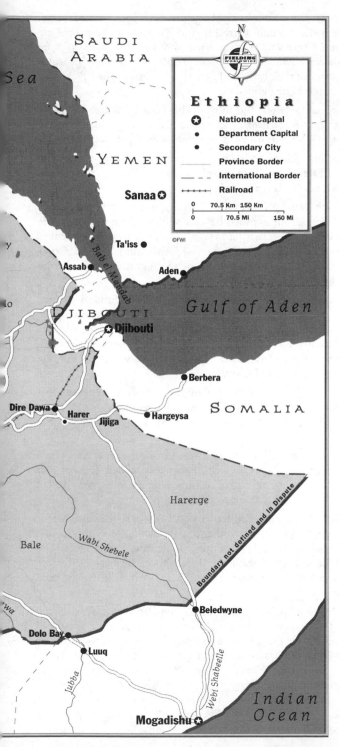

Ethiopia's Tigre people come from a northern province aptly named Tigre. There are many Tigre in Eritrea and Tigre province, as well. Tigre people are characteristically Coptic Christian. That in itself shouldn't be hard to keep straight, except that there's a wrinkle—the Tigre people of both Tigre province and Eritrea have a language of their own, and there is a language called Tigre, but it is not the language of the Tigre people.

The Tigre people of Tigre province and most of the Tigre of Eritrea are native speakers of a language called *Tigrinya*. Tigrinya's relative, Tigre, is the native tongue of most of Eritrea's Muslim tribes...and a few of its Tigre Copts.

It's only confusing at first. There are so many tribes, peoples and religions in Ethiopia, a gathering of Ethiopians in any one place is not unlike a meeting of the U.N. General Assembly, sans jackets and ties.

The panoply of nomadic Muslim tribes from Port Sudan through Eritrea, Djibouti and the Somali steppe share so much besides religion, from food to music to their handsome mocha features, that, at first, it's hard not to picture them as variations on a single people. Likewise, the customs of Abyssinia's highland Copts in Tigre and Eritrea are highly similar to those of the highland Copts further south around Addis, their Christian faith virtually identical.

The Afar language spoken by the fierce Afar Muslims of southern Eritrea, northeastern Ethiopia and Djibouti (which was once called the territory of the Afars and the Issas) belongs to the linguistic group called Hamitic. Likewise, the language of the Afars' enemy, the Somali Issa, and of all the other Somali tribes, and of the virtually Somali Galla of Ethiopia, is Hamitic. Likewise, the language spoken by the ancient Egyptians was Hamitic.

Those mellow, Somali-looking faces are carved on the walls deep within the pyramids of ancient Egypt, and the ancient Egyptian tales of Punt, a land which could have been either the Somali coast, the Eritrean coast, or both were in the "Hamitic" tongues.

Ham was the son of Noah; the Bible tells us it was Ham who begat the people of Africa. The most recent linguistic research challenges the old concept that Hamitic languages are strictly African; they're now lumped in a group called "Afro-Asiatic." But Africa is where you go to find Hamitic languages.

Noah's son Shem, by contrast, was the father of all Semites. Hebrew, Arabic and Amharic are all Sematic languages; Amharic is the language of the Coptic Christians, whose long rule of Ethiopia came to a momentous end in 1991. The Coptic Tigre who led the revolution also have ancient roots as rulers in Abyssinnia, but they are nonetheless distinct from the Amhara, with their own Semitic language, Tigrinya.

Meantime, among the seemingly similar Muslim nomads of Eritrea, only the Afar, sprawling across three countries, speak a Hamitic language. Only one small tribe claims Arabic (the Lingua Franca through much of the Horn) as its native tongue. A few share Tigrinya with the Coptic Christians of Eritrea and Tigre. And the first language of most of the rest of Eritrea's Muslims is Tigrinya's relative, Tigre. In short, these Semitic-speaking Muslim tribes have more in common with the Copts of Eritrea and Ethiopia than at first meets the eye and less in common with the Hamitic-speaking Muslims of Ethiopia and the Somali steppe. You drink deeply from the cup of history when you visit Ethiopia.

The Scoop

This is not combat as usual in Ethiopia. Landlocked Ethiopia (by Eritrea, Djibouti and Somalia) better be nice to its neighbors. If they don't figure things out, Ethiopia could actually come out worse, virtually destroyed as a nation by 76 ethnic groups and 286 languages. But there seems a genuine effort by almost everyone to arrive at a consensus for all Ethiopians (whatever an Ethiopian is), and, meantime, trouble has not gotten out of hand. Ethiopia today is a dangerous, exhilarating place, but hardly the most dangerous place in the Horn. If it survives the struggle, it will emerge a stronger nation than the brittle empire held together by Haile Selassie and the Dergue.

The Players

Mengistu Haile Mariam

Mengistu ruled Ethiopia for 17 years and is accused of killing hundreds of thousands during his communist regime. It seems he was reading the old Stalin political manual "How to Run a Country Into the Ground and Kill Most of Your People While Doing It." Right now, he is hiding out in Zimbabwe in Gunhill, an upscale suburb of Harare. It seems one of the most recent furors has been over his phone bills. The government picks up the tab for his massive phone charges, estimated at about $Z500,000 in 1994 alone. Some folks estimate that his phone bill is 38 percent of the total budget of the Ministry of Foreign Affairs.

A mild warning to *DP* wannabes, his bodyguards will rough up any journalists who try to interview him. The Ethiopian government is trying to extradite him to stand trial with the rest of his cronies.

Meles Zenawi

The man who led the revolution that overthrew centuries of Amharic rule in 1991, Meles Zenawi is Tigre. Tigreans, with the help of heavily Tigre Eritrea, had spearheaded the revolution. There was fear among other peoples that Amharic tyranny would simply be replaced with Tigrean tyranny.

The Amhara were especially apprehensive. To the outside world—indeed, to most Ethiopians—Tigreans and Amharas are a picture in similarities: both, anciently, the rulers of Abyssinnia, both Coptic, both speakers of Semitic tongues. The Amhara knew differently. Arabic and Hebrew are also Semitic tongues; after years of war, Ethiopians who spoke the Tigrinya of Tigre were getting along with those who spoke Amharic about as well as Arabs get along with Israelis.

Fortunately, Zenawi had credentials that impressed the other groups. He even managed to win the confidence of at least some Amharas.

Having been plucked from Tigre to board at the Brit's Wingate School in Addis, where he won honors both as a student and a card shark, he spoke Amharic. During the war in Tigre, he had challenged the dictatorial chief of his own Tigrinya-speaking front, took over the front, and eventually formed coalitions with other ethnic groups, especially the Oromo.

When Zenawi was a kid at the Wingate School, a volleyball game with Oromo students had turned into a brawl that didn't end until leftist students from Haile Selassie University rushed over, broke it up and delivered a stern lecture on the evils of tribal fighting. Zenawi was impressed, and, later, as a premed student at the university, he was impressed by Meles Tekle, the editor of the student journal, *Tigil*, in English, Struggle.

Before he could complete his studies, he was "in the field," as the Eritreans say, a guerrilla back home in Tigre province. He hadn't been there long before the leftist Dergue back in Addis killed his leftist hero, Meles Tekle. Until then, Zenawi's name had been Legesse Zenawi. From then on, it was Meles Zenawi.

Had he once fought side-by-side with Oromo? So what, say members of the Oromo Liberation Front, who feel he is not granting enough self-determination.

It has gotten so bad that under terms of a treaty penned by the winners after the revolution, the Eritreans (who desperately want to sell their war materiel to raise cash for reconstruction) have had to send armed brigades into Ethiopia to intervene as peacemakers in outbreaks of frustrated combat between the new Ethiopian Army and the Oromo. In a few instances, they have actually had to fire on the Oromo—a choice so uncomfortable for both parties that the Oromo leadership barely complained about it to the Eritreans.

Getting In

Passport and visa are required. Tourist and business visas are valid for a stay up to two years; the fee is US$50, or transit visa for 48 hours is US$20. One application, one photo and yellow fever immunization are required. A business visa requires a company letter stating the purpose of your trip. Send US$2 postage for return of passport, or US$15.30 for Federal Express and US$9.95 for Express Mail service (money orders only). Allow two weeks for processing. Exit visas are required of all visitors remaining in Ethiopia for more than 30 days. For longer stays and other information, contact the following:

Embassy of Ethiopia
2134 Kalorama Rd., N.W.
Washington, D.C. 20008
☎ *(202) 234-2281/2*

Ministry of Information
P.O. Box 1020
Addis Ababa
☎ *11-11-24.*
Journalists must obtain from here.

Ethiopian Airlines is one of the better airlines in Africa and maintains offices in 54 cities around the world. By land, depending on the level of internal tensions, it's possible to enter Ethiopia at Gambela from Malakal in Sudan; at Adua from Asmara, Eritrea, and at Dessie from Assab, Eritrea; from Kenya at Morale; and at Dire Dawa from Djibouti. The riskiest entrance is by river during the rainy season (June–September) aboard a boat from Khartoum to Gambela. However, anti-American sentiments in Sudan—and particularly the unrest in southern Sudan—make this journey potentially hazardous.

Getting Around

Life is simple here. Not because the Ethiopians want it that way but because they don't have a choice. The most popular method of travel is donkey or donkey cart. There is a mere 423-mile (681-km) railroad between Djibouti and Addis Ababa, and the only main thoroughfare is the Trans-East Africa Highway. Roads to the ports or Massawa and Assab in Eritrea are kept in decent condition. There are 24,534 miles (39,482 km) of roads in the country, most of them in poor condition. Travel by air is limited but preferred. The surfaced roads in Ethiopia are primarily found linking the capital Addis Ababa with the provincial capitals, although most are in poor shape due to the fighting. Travel times are also significantly slower during the rainy season. Other roads are mainly dirt and rock paths. There are bus and minibus service, and cars can be hired at National Tour Operation in Addis (*P.O. Box 5709, Ras Mekonin Avenue;* ☎ *15 29 55*). There are two trains a day in each direction along the Addis Ababa-Djibouti line.

Dangerous Places

The Ogaden

A hard place ruled by clans and bandits. The Ogaden is subject to the same whirling vortex of violence and predatory survival that rules Somalia. The Ogaden is inhabited mainly by Somali pastoralists and was occupied by the Italians from 1936 to 1941, and subsequently administered by the British until 1948, when it was returned to the Ethiopians. The Somalis could never accept Ethiopia's imperial governors and high livestock taxes, as well as border restrictions, and the region hasn't been the same since. A continued, low-intensity revolution has persisted since Somalia gained independence in 1960.

The Danakil

Another one of God's angry places inhabited by a fierce warlike tribe (must be the weather that makes these folks so ornery).

Dangerous Things

Land Mines

The Ethiopian government has defused more than 5000 land mines planted by troops of former communist leader Mengistu Haile Mariam, perhaps a fraction of those still buried in Ethiopian soil. Land mines and other antipersonnel devices can be encountered frequently in areas that suffered fighting during the war. Areas such as the route to Asebeteferi, the vicinity of Harar, the Ogaden region, and the roads north from Addis Ababa to Tigray province are known mined areas. Many persons, including foreigners, have been injured by these devices. Travel on paved roads generally is safer than travel on unpaved roads. Areas off the pavement around bridges or water crossings are also mined. Overland travel is especially dangerous in areas east and south of Harar, in Region 5 (formerly known as the Ogaden), due to land mines on the main road between Harar and Jijiga.

Crime

Pickpocketing is prevalent in urban areas, and there have been numerous reports of thieves snatching jewelry. Banditry occurs on roads outside major towns or cities, and may be accompanied by violence.

Drugs

Trafficking and consumption of illicit drugs have risen by more than 400 percent in Ethiopia in two years, according to the Ministry of Health. "Illegal trafficking and use of dangerous drugs has increased in Ethiopia, as a result of which a 470-percent growth has been registered during the past two years regarding the interception of hashish," the official Ethiopian News Agency (ENA) quoted the Ministry as saying. Meanwhile, a psychiatrist at the Emanuel Hospital in Addis Ababa has said that most of the patients undergoing mental treatment at the hospital were drug addicts who take cannabis or hashish, chew khat, or misuse medicines.

Getting Sick

Although there is one doctor for every 38,359 people in Ethiopia, about half the population lives within seven miles of a health facility. However, there are many rural areas with no medical facilities and the construction and staffing of new facilities is slow going. Some of the best health care in the country is found at church hospitals. Food is scarce, and skin and eye diseases are common. Chloroquine-resistant malaria is found throughout the country, and in all regions below 2000 meters—even the cities, although not in Addis Ababa. There is a 20 percent chance of p. vivax malaria exposure. In Ethiopia, dracunculiasis, rabies and typhus (endemic flea-borne and epidemic louse-borne) are prevalent. There are major risks of contracting diarrheal and respiratory diseases, as well as tuberculosis and malaria. The country is receptive to dengue fever. River blindness (onchocerciasis) affects more than 1.3 million Ethiopians and is endemic in the western part of the country. Louse-borne typhus poses a threat to people living or working (such as anthropologists, geoligists, archeologists, aid workers, etc.) in remote areas of the country.

Nuts and Bolts

Ethiopia is the world's second-poorest country, with a per-capita annual income of about US$400. Not much of a marketing position for tourism, but it says volumes for the problems travelers will encounter. Simple things like food, water and transportation can be elusive. Much of the country is run according to clan rules, not from a central government. Addis was always more colorful than efficient, and now it has a war to recover from, so it's not much of a competitor as a tourist mecca. Nor is it made more attractive by Khartoum's alcohol ban, or Asmara's tank-park. But Ethiopia remains the long-established tourist destination it's always been (with a few time-outs for combat). In the past, tourism has earned a lot for Ethiopia. The new regime does not want to lose it and knows that "no surprises" is key to keeping the goose laying its eggs.

The currency is the birr, which won't buy you much these days. About 5 birr is equal to 1 U.S. dollar. The country is known for its cool highlands and arid deserts to the south. Touristically, Ethiopia is known for its white-water rafting, the ancient Coptic churches, and as the rumored site of the Ark of the Covenant. Most tourists come in on expensive guided tours.

Only about 13 percent of the population live in urban areas. Muslims make up about 43 percent of the population and Ethiopian Orthodox Christians 37 percent, while those with indigenous beliefs comprise 17 percent. Ethnically, Tigrean and Amhara people comprise 32 percent of all Ethiopians, while the Oromo make up 40 percent. Another 9 percent are Sidamo.

Literacy in Ethiopia stands at a remarkably high 71 percent. The country's education system collapsed during the civil war. Because many students at Addis Ababa University are politically active and anti-EPRDF, the school is periodically closed and leading academics arrested.

Dangerous Days

03/16/1996	General Hayelom Araya, chief of operations of the Defense Ministry, was murdered.
06/25/1995	Gunmen sprayed Egyptian President Hosni Mubarak's bulletproof limousine with automatic rifle fire, as he arrived at the Organization of African Unity summit, but he was unhurt. As many a 12 bullets from an AK-47 assault rifle hit the car.
03/1994	Eighty thousand people demonstrated in Meskel Square in support of the opposition alliance, CAFPDE.
01/1993	Seventeen students were killed and 30 injured in a demonstration at Addis Ababa University, protesting Eritrean independence.
06/29/1992	Oromo Liberation Front rebels killed 50 government soldiers and wounded 30 others in two attacks on the Balé region.
05/21/1991	Mengistu Haile Mariam fled into exile after Soviet support dried up. Eritrea established provisional government in anticipation of independence.
10/27/1986	Goshu Wolde, Ethiopia's foreign minister, announced his defection to the U.S. in New York.
09/1984–03/1985	Seven thousand Ethiopian Falasha Jews were evacuated by the CIA to Sudan.
03/08/1978	Somalia announced the withdrawal of its troops from the Ogaden.
11/1977	Atnafu Abate, Mengistu's second-in-command and a potential rival, was executed.
09/12/1974	The Durge (Coordinating Committee of the Armed Forces) deposes Haile Selassie.
1972–1974	Famine killed an estimated 200,000 peasants.

In a Dangerous Place

Ethiopia: Sharifa's Story

The first time I heard of Sharifa, I wondered if she were real. Her tale was so perfect. She couldn't be. She had to be.

Then I heard the story again, and then again. Three sources—real story. And then months later, I heard it yet again. The ring of myth was beginning to attend Sharifa. Sometimes her name wasn't even Sharifa, and, with each telling, her beauty became more storied. As if the women of Abyssinnia are not beautiful enough as is, and as if her story would be any the less were she not beautiful.

Regardless, a story with a life of its own is a reality in its own right, and this one is Eritrea, through and through.

When I was there, way back in 1968, she must have been about three. Twelve years later, she was her father's pride, about 15, with an ability to maintain her modesty and flash her eyes at the same time, dressed always in the gauzy folds of white and brilliant color—turquoise, yellow, orange—colors characteristic of Muslim women's dress in this part of the world. Tattoos graced her forehead; she was laden always with hand-hammered jewelry, some of it washed in gold, some of it 14 karat.

Her father, a widower, was not a vastly wealthy man, but he was a merchant in a part of the world that is anciently mercantile and where women have been walking banks, wearing much of the family's wealth as jewelry. Of course, it's a man's world. Sons, especially first sons, are what count. But Sharifa's big brother had frustrated, even humiliated, their father. He'd rejected his family responsibilities, his inheritance, had run off to fight a war that was clearly unwinnable.

At least, he had Sharifa. Second only to a father's pride in his eldest son was his pride in a beautiful, marriageable daughter, bedecked in jewels that spoke of family status, of a father's accomplishment, of security.

Unmarried daughters may have been seen as burdens for some; for Sharifa's father, she represented security even more than her jewels. She stood for home and family, as much as impetuous young sons stood for the insecurity that was everywhere. Sharifa was a daughter of substance, exhibiting with schooled perfection the well-known modesty of Muslim women in public, exhibiting just as clearly (at least for her father) the less well known power a strong woman can wield within the family. His male world, after all, was itself largely one of competing, bargaining, feuding families. Fathers put themselves at the center of those families, but in each one, it is a woman who is the essential element.

Sharifa was an astute questioner of the details of her father's all-male palavers, having an active mind focused always on the family; she had in effect replaced her brother as her father's point of pride.

It was a scene full of timeless qualities, set in a part of the world that often seems timeless. The proud, well-to-do, but vulnerable merchant father, the almost predictably rebellious son, the female as an anchor in a sea of troubles.

The one element that isn't timeless, of course, is the specifics of the prodigal son's defection. There's nothing timeless about Soviet tanks.

Of course, he put it all in what he called "revolutionist" terms...which don't quite stand the test of time. The reader would recognize it for the propaganda it was and, likewise, my callow gullibility for what it was. In fact, it's probably best to leave the arguable details of their war with Ethiopia to the *Oxford Companion to World Politics,* whose entry on the subject was written by an Ethiopian scholar:

> *With its defeat in World War II, Italy relinquished its legal right to its colonies to...France, the United Kingdom, the United States and the Soviet Union [to] dispose of...by agreement, failing which they would submit the matter to the UN General Assembly. Libya's and Somalia's cases were determined without much ado at the UN; Eritrea proved to be difficult, principally because of Emperor Haile Selassie's interest in acquiring it, and U.S. strategic and geopolitical interest in the Red Sea region. The convergence of these two interests and the dominant U.S. position sealed the fate of Eritrean self-determination.*
>
> *Instead of gaining independence, as demanded by the majority of its inhabitants, Eritrea was joined with Ethiopia in a lopsided federation...imposed by a U.S.-engineered resolution. Eritrean protests were ignored by the UN, which bore responsibility for the integrity of the federation. Finally, emboldened by the impunity with which he had violated the UN arrangement, Emperor Haile Selassie abolished the federation in 1962....*

####

I've never seen a massacre, and with luck I'll never see one. In Vietnam, Eritrea, the western Sahara, Iran, Lebanon and the southern Sudan, I've seen mute evidence, heard stories, but I'm reluctant to repeat them. What can I really know of them? Talk is cheap. Suffice it to say that sometime near the end of the seventies, when Sharifa was 15 and her father's pride, her village suffered a massacre.

We don't know who they lost. We just know that while her father kept functioning, he apparently went days unable to talk. He must at some point have felt rage as well as grief, but when he did speak, he saw the war no differently. It was foolishness. This was Ethiopia. Even counting Eritrea's Christians, they were at best 3 million barely armed men, women and children against the tanks and bombers of a nation of 58 million.

And beautiful Sharifa? She witnessed her father's grief, but showed none, and then one day her father came home and she was gone. Where? "We're not sure," her sisters said. "She left most of her jewelry."

"Where?" her father repeated.

"To join the revolution."

In a rage, he gathered up two men and three camels and galloped into country he'd never dared enter and found her at a training camp, about to be inducted. He insisted she return. She refused. He raged that this was no fit enterprise for a woman; it was indecent. He grabbed her. She pulled back. He called her a whore. He said she was no longer any daughter of his. He demanded her remaining jewels. She ripped them off and threw them at him. For the past 15 years, they had spent every day of their lives together. They were not to see each other again for another 15 years.

By the time young Sharifa reached the field at the end of the seventies, a lot had happened. The Muslim-led Eritrean Liberation Front I found in Kassala had become the Eritrean People's Liberation Front. After barely surviving a spate of internecine bloodletting, it was now run primarily by Tigrinya-speaking revolutionaries like Kidane, but with Muslim recruits like Sharifa joining, as she would put it, "by the tens."

In the year after Haile Selassie was deposed, the Front had virtually won the war, with its troops occupying major towns and even entering the capital. Again it had suffered brutal losses, as the Soviets and Cubans intervened massively for the Dergue. Then came hunger, as the Ethiopians pursued a scorched-earth policy, which international aid agencies, in need of Ethiopian approval to move relief supplies, felt constrained to portray as "drought." Then came famine, as the Ethiopians used food as a weapon, refusing to let relief through to Eritrea.

But they survived, and now they were rebuilding, yet again, but this time they were building something more.

No longer heavily Muslim, the Front no longer had the appeal it once did for Arab backers, but it still had some. Meantime, the force it was fighting was fat with Soviet hardware, which meant that after most engagements, more Soviet hardware was carefully inventoried in the bush warehouses of the Eritrean Peoples Liberation Front.

The likes of Kidane Kiflu are now credited with enormous organizational and logistic talent. To Ethiopian pilots flying Northrup F5s, MiGs and Antonov bombers, the ground below looked barren, deserted by a population on the run. When I was with them, it was indeed barren. But this was Sharifa's time. Laboriously hidden from view in country with virtually none of Vietnam's notorious jungle cover were machine shops, munitions factories, motor works and fuel depots. There were truck yards for tractor-trailers and tanker trucks, whose drivers made routine nightly runs cross-country, off the road, over hostile turf, as well as hidden warehouses of stolen materiel, artfully inventoried for efficient access. In addition, there were hospitals in caves, staffed by young Eritrean surgeons and internists trained largely in the U.S. and Italy. Hospitals complete with operating theaters, intensive care wards, maternity wards, infectious disease wards, rehabilitation wards in which amputees were forever busy making artificial limbs, processing paperwork, issuing orders.

But more than all that, in a part of the world long maligned for its bloodymindedness, home of the baboon, the hyena, the cutthroat clan bandit, and after a trying contest that had pitted Muslim Eritrean against Christian Eritrean, they were forging some wildly diverse people into a unified nation.

Right through the war, Western intelligence experts who were convinced that Eritrea's Copts wanted to be part of Coptic Ethiopia and that its Muslims wanted to be part of the Sudan, simply refused to believe what was happening, and they couldn't be blamed. Here, indeed, was a people ready to die for their God, their tribe, their clan, their family, maybe even for the ancient Empire of Ethiopia. But for Eritrea? What was Eritrea besides a short-lived Italian colony, populated by dozens of tribes anciently antagonistic to each other, with virtually no national or religious coherence?

In fact, tiny Eritrea is so diverse that it may be more representative of the Horn of Africa than any other country. In the vastness of the Somali steppe and along the Somali coast, virtually everyone is Somali, save a few Bantu who are farmers...and, for that matter, can be found farming along the Red Sea coast of Arabia. The Sudan, of course, is richly diverse, and in the south has a large population of blue-black Nilotes, many of whom have given up their river gods for Christianity. But the Sudan's diversity is spread over yawning territories, and it is an indelibly Muslim state. Likewise, Ethiopia has many Muslims, but is an indelibly Christian place. Eritrea has all the variety of these much larger places, even a few Nilotes who worship river gods, and it sits perched between the Horn's Muslim and Christian worlds.

This makes for an interesting place to write about, but it does not make for a nation; some argue it makes for everything a nation is not.

Go tell it to the Eritreans.

They made Sharifa a forward observer for a mortar crew. It was a shock. She thought maybe she'd be a nurse. She didn't complain.

In all my time in Eritrea, nearly a month from west to east, I saw just one female guerrilla. But nearly a dozen years had passed since then, and Sharifa wasn't unique. There were thousands like her.

Part of the reason was the vision of leaders like Kidane Kiflu, who had made the revolution. Another reason was the men—the rank-and-file troops, the brothers, uncles, cousins, fathers of these young women—men who would ordinarily never tolerate such disgrace to their women, but now had a special reason not to protest.

They were dead.

This is not the United States, where every year feminists break new ground, but women still do not serve in combat. This is a part of the world where women are confined not just by ancient religious stricture, Christian and Muslim, but are often circumcised, which means considerably more for a young bride than a young boy; it means that her clitoris is cut off. It's a part of the world where it is not rare for a woman to be infibulated, which means her vaginal cleft is sewn tight—pleasure for her man, excruciating pain for her.

When Sharifa joined the Front, the Ethiopian Army was a quarter million strong. There were at best 90,000 Eritreans wearing the uniform of the Front, and so many men had died that almost 30,000 of those troops were young women like Sharifa.

Were most spared combat? Every guerrilla is a combat guerrilla. Every square foot of Eritrea was contested. She must have been stunned: all around her, women, pious young Muslim women, sweating with men, amputating limbs, loading trucks, loading shells into the breeches of heavy artillery, locking and loading in combat.

She was wounded, recovered in an underground hospital, was wounded again, married a guerrilla named Osman, the commander of a squadron of captured Soviet tanks, gave birth to a daughter in the same underground hospital, got a letter from her brother on another front, got a letter that her brother was dead.

Did her father know? She did not even try to write. The "field" was another world. For most of the guerrillas, there could be no communication with that world back in the villages. These boys and girls did not march off to war. They simply slipped away. In the hearts of their parents, each was given a funeral, and she knew that her father was no different. You do not send a child off to serve the duration of a 30-year guerrilla war and expect him to return; few did. After the war did finally end, there was story after story of elderly mothers and fathers suffering heart attacks when unannounced, their "long-dead" child showed up at the door. Sharifa knew that she was as much in the world of the dead as her brother.

Still, there were victories. Eritreans in tanks meant a war with front lines, trenches. Liberated zones. She dug trenches and helped administer liberated zones, and here she could see more clearly how the men were responding. There was no shame. They called their young women in uniform "our backbone."

But yet there was an undercurrent. She had lost her long beautiful hair, gone off to war, and everywhere, the men respected her, but it seemed much like the respect they paid the infirm who had gone off to war and lost a leg. In the villages, the beautiful young girls in their robes and jewelry looked up with awe at these young women with cropped hair. In this world where girls began losing their marriageability at 19, these young women were delaying marriage to serve. Some like Sharifa would marry guerrillas. More often the men with whom she fought would marry the pretty young things with long hair. Now and then, a guerrilla married to a female guerrilla would divorce her for the "genuine article." In one village, there was a father very proud of his short-haired daughter in uniform, but he would not let her near his other daughters.

The 3 million souls of Eritrea never enjoyed the support of a great, or even second-rank power. Ethiopia, a nation of 58 million, had the support first of the U.S. and then of the Soviet Union. As the Soviet Union imploded, the largest standing army in sub-Saharan Africa began to weave like a punch-drunk fighter.

Methodically, the Eritreans closed in. Again, Sharifa was wounded. Again, she was in a hospital in a cave, but this time her husband Osman was able to visit. It was spring, 1991. A huge Ethiopian garrison held both Asmara and its U.S.-built airbase, out of which the Ethiopian Air Force was now flying constant bombing runs. An Eritrean force swung around to the south of Asmara and cut the garrison off, virtually inviting the Ethiopians to commit yet more troops to relieve their men in Asmara.

The Ethiopians accepted the invitation. The full force of the Ethiopian Army—heavy artillery, self-propelled guns, troops in armored personnel carriers, tank brigades deployed on either side of the Asmara Road—rolled north, supported by Ethiopian fighter-bombers flying out of both Addis and Asmara.

Osman's squadron of captured, jealously maintained Soviet tanks was called to join the battle.

In May 1991, Ethiopian fighter-bombers out of Asmara and Addis hit the Eritrean force with air-to-ground missiles and napalm. The tanks closed in. Inside Asmara, the Ethiopian force deployed to break out and link up with the relief force. It was not to be. When it was finished, more than a battle was over. A 31-year war had come to an end.

ETHIOPIA

The Ethiopian Army was in the midst of a panicked retreat from which it would never recover. Eritrea was free. Osman was dead. Sharifa went home.

There was no way she could call ahead. Outside of Asmara, Eritrea still doesn't have much in the way of phone service. She could only show up, the prodigal daughter, old and tired, with short hair, a daughter and no husband. She told herself she had nothing to be ashamed of. If she was still disowned, so be it.

He was stunned, of course. He didn't say a thing. But as it began to get dark, he moved his belongings out of his bedroom and into the mud courtyard in the back. He said the house was hers. She was the head of the family now. "I was wrong," he said.

—Jack Kramer

Georgia

★

Rebel Yell

Georgia seems to suffer more from the spillover of the Armenian-Azeri conflict than it does from its own internal problems, which, in their own right, are profound.

Georgia came into existence on July 24, 1783, when the kingdom of Kartli-Kakheti sought protection from Catherine the Great. It is actually not called Georgia, but Sa-kartvel-o, and the people are known as Kartvel-ebi. Some say the word Georgia comes from the Persian word *Gurj*. There was also a succession of rulers in the Middle Ages named Giorgi who expanded the Georgian Christian empire. So, take your pick. The area was annexed by the Red Army in 1921. Nothing new, since the region had been raped, pillaged and abused by Hittites, Assyrians, Scythians, Cimmerians, Greeks, Romans, Byzantines, Persians, Turks and Mongols. The Georgians may not have even noticed the change of landlords, since folks in this area will tell you that the Georgians do like their liquor. In fact, the origin of the country harks back to an old drinking story they like to tell.

It seems that when the good Lord was working on creation, he was handing out chunks of real estate to the world's peoples. Well, wouldn't you know that the Georgians were having a party and showed up too late to get anything. The Georgians quickly regrouped, and, despite their aching heads, went back and told God that the reason they were late was because they were drinking toasts to him. God was so pleased at their explanation that he gave the Georgians a chunk of the world he had actually put aside for himself.

Whether this means that the Georgians are incorrigible drunkards and liars or the quickest thinking, most charming folks on this planet is best left to the reader's imagination. Georgia's rugged topography still makes it an excellent hideout for rogues and revolutionaries. As for any other romantic connections, Georgia was said to be ruled by Jason of Jason and the Argonauts and to be the birthplace of Joseph Stalin (born in the village of Gori on December 21, 1879) and his chief of secret police, Beria.

In the 1920s and '30s, Georgia was not spared Stalin's cruelty. Over 5000 Mensheviks were executed after a failed uprising, and in 1936 and 1939 most of Georgia's writers, scientists and intellectuals were killed, sent to prison camps or fled the region.

The Scoop

When Stalin pissed off all of his homeboys as he carved out countries, oblasts and autonomous regions that sliced right through homelands, the idea was to divide and conquer. It worked. Today, Russia is not happy that Georgia gave them a dear John letter and started their own country. So now Russia needles away and incites the ethnics at Georgia's borders and generally raises hell.

The Worst Place to Sell Life Insurance

You knew there was something famous about this remote region, didn't you? There has to be something other than hardship, warfare and Russian politics in Georgia. Does yogurt ring a bell? Back in the '80s, Dannon did a commercial on the staggering number of centenarians (people over 100 years old, for those of you who failed Latin). In Tbilisi there are just a little less than 100 people who were born at the turn of the century. Abkhazia has the highest incidence of geezers over 100. There is even one person 130 years old. The average rate is 51 centenarians for every 100,000 people.

The Players

Although things have quieted down in Georgia, there still is a simmering discontent among special-interest groups who want to take advantage of Georgia's poverty and confusion.

The Mkhedrioni (Knights)

The personal militia loyal to Jaba Iosseliani, president of the Georgian Emergency Committee. This militia contains some criminal elements. The current Georgian government has been trying to disband the mkhedrioni and absorb them into regular army units.

Zviadists

These rebels are fighting for former President Zviad Gamsakhurdi, who returned from exile and is fighting to regain control of Georgia. They are in cahoots with the Confederation of Mountain Peoples. The Zviadists are also opposed to the stationing of Russian troops at three military bases in Georgia. The Zviadists are engaged in a low-key civil war with the Shevardnadze government.

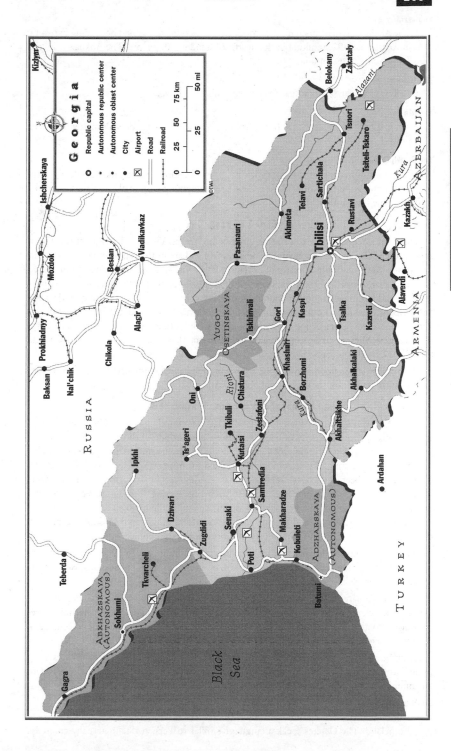

Georgia

○ Republic capital
★ Autonomous republic center
• Autonomous oblast center
• City
⊠ Airport
— Road
—— Railroad

50 mi
75 km

0 25 50

0 25 50

GEORGIA

Abkhazians

The Abkhazians demanded more autonomy, and Georgia responded by sending in troops in August of 1992, resulting in the deaths of hundreds of people. The Abkhazians were supported by Russian units.

The Government

Led by Georgian leader Eduard Shevardnadze.

The Mafia

There is little the Mafia does not control in Georgia, so it really doesn't matter who is in power.

The South Ossetians

The south Ossetians want to join their neighbors in north Ossetia; the trouble is Russia doesn't want them. Meanwhile, the Ossetians are fighting a war with their Ingush neighbors, the Ingush Republic.

Getting In

A passport is required. A visa is not required before arrival. Visitors who enter at the Tbilisi airport receive a temporary stamp at passport control and are instructed to obtain a visa from the consular division of the Ministry of Foreign Affairs. Visas are usually granted within three days. Fees vary from US$30 to US$90, depending on the duration of the visa. Travelers arriving from and returning to another country of the former Soviet Union are not required to obtain a Georgian visa. Those arriving from the former Soviet Union and departing to countries outside the former Soviet Union must obtain a visa in order to leave. On an exceptional basis, the Georgian Ministry of Foreign Affairs can assist travelers in obtaining visas for Georgia through the checkpoint at Sarpi on the border with Turkey.

Visitors get a stamp upon arrival at the airport in Tbilisi and are instructed to get a visit from the Consular Division of the Ministry of Foreign Affairs.

Dangerous Places

The U.S. government has prohibited U.S. officials from traveling overland between Georgia and Armenia due to the activity of bandits on the Georgian side of the border. Sporadic violence occurs in the western regions of Georgia and south Ossetia. In Abkhazia, extensive fighting has occurred. Georgia has become the battlefield for Armenian and Azerbaijani terrorists. There have also been numerous bombings of trains destined for both Armenian and Azerbaijani territory. Oil and gas pipelines have also been sabotaged. The prime suspects are Armenian terrorists. The railway line between Tbilisi and Yerevan is the frequent target of Azeri and Armenian saboteurs. The oil and gas pipelines in the area have also been hit some 12 times in the last year. All this is "spillover" from the Nagorno-Karabakh conflict.

Recently, a bomb was detonated in an Armenian drama theatre in Tbilisi. As long as the conflict over Nagorno-Karabakh continues, there will be ongoing terrorist attacks against both Armenian and Azerbaijani-related targets in Georgia.

Between February 25 and March 3, 1995, 38 people were killed and 138 wounded in fighting in Ochamchire Rayon. As of March 1993, the number of people killed in the Abkhaz region alone stood at 781 and the number of wounded totaled 2565. A significant percentage of this figure were civilian casualties.

A number of aircraft have been lost in the fighting, including civilian airliners, also resulting in numerous civilian deaths and injuries. The U.S. government has prohibited any travel to Sukhumi by U.S. officials for the foreseeable future.

Southern Ossetia

Although they make up three percent of the population of Georgia, they want their own homeland. The Ossetes speak a language similar to Persian. Stalin actually created a "homeland" for the Ossetes on Georgian soil, although they already had a homeland in northern Ossetia. The Ossetians had migrated south in the 18th and 20th centuries and now comprise 66 percent of the region's 98,000 peoples.

Abkhazia

The Abkhazian Autonomous Republic is a mountainous area of 3359 square miles with 535,634 inhabitants that borders the Black Sea to the west of Georgia. Abkhazians are an even smaller splinter of the ethnic mix in Georgia, about 1.8 percent at last count. The Georgians believe that the Russians are backing the Abkhazians just to keep Georgia on their toes. Their capital is Sokhumi.

Meskheti

Meskheti is a tiny 420-square-mile enclave in the south of Georgia bordering Turkey with a group of Moslem Georgians (whom Stalin deported to Uzbekistan in 1945) who want their homes back. The problem is the Armenians and Georgians (both Christian) live there now. They are called Meskhetian Turks, even though they live in Uzbekistan and do not speak Georgian.

Nighttime

Georgia has a high rate of crime; the risk is especially high at night. Georgian citizens in uniform or civilian clothes openly carry firearms. Criminals are often armed. Gunfire in the capital city of Tbilisi is fairly common. Outside Tbilisi, unescorted travel is difficult and dangerous. Police authority in many cities in western and central Georgia has collapsed. Foreigners have been the targets of criminal activity.

Dangerous Things

Having a Good Time, Part I

Remember how we told you that Georgians like to drink? Well, the cautious among us should be aware of the dangers of this liquid sport. When the bottles stop clinking and the men folk are done drinking, you will find many young men staggering through the dark streets. Chances are they will do nothing worse than puke on your shoes, but many people are beaten or get into fights. Some will mistake you for whichever group they hate and set upon you. Stay inside after dark.

Having a Good Time, Part II

OK, we told you to stay in at night, which means that you have a choice of watching badly dubbed soap operas or, hey, you guessed right, drinking. Georgians will invite you share whatever they're drinking, whether its after shave or glycol for their car's radiator. The best way to reduce your intake of alcohol is to tip your glass with gusto but do not drain it. Toasts are a big part of drinking and even though your hosts will slam back drink after drink, you can point to your head and simulate being woozy. The key is to have a good time and minimize your alcohol intake.

Getting Sick

Medical care in Georgia is limited. The U.S. embassy maintains a list of English-speaking physicians in the area. There is a severe shortage of basic medical supplies, including disposable needles, anesthetics and antibiotics. Elderly travelers and those with existing health problems may be at risk due to inadequate medical facilities.

Nuts and Bolts

According to Pliny, the Romans estimated it required 130 interpreters just to figure out what the heck the Georgian tribes were complaining about. Although the current language is supposed be Indo-European in origin, it is incomprehensible to most travelers. The language piles up the alphabet to create words seemingly devoid of vowels and then uses Cryllic to totally baffle outsiders. The Georgians are the only Caucasian peoples other than the Armenians to have had a written language before the Russians. For example, hello is *gamarjobat*, thank you is *gmadlobt*, and only the expert or lucky will be able to discern the difference between left (*martskhniv*) and right (*martzhvniv*).

It just doesn't sound right to order an egg for breakfast by saying *kvertsxi, inebit* (egg please).

Ethnically the region is about 70 percent Georgian with Armenians making up 7.7 percent, Russians 6.6 percent Azerbaijanis 4.6 percent, Ossetians are 3 percent, Greeks 1.8 percent and Abkhazians 1.8 percent. The Georgians have been Christians since 330 A.D.

Georgia is a "cash-only" economy. Traveler's checks and credit cards are rarely accepted.

Embassy Locations

In Georgia:

The U.S. Embassy
25 Atoneli Street
Tbilisi, Georgia
☎ *[7] (8832) 98-99-67 or 93-38-03*
Telex: 212210 AMEMB SU
FAX [7] (8832) 93-37-59

In the U.S.:

Embassy of the Republic of Georgia
1511 K Street, N.W., Suite 424
Washington, D.C. 20005
☎ *(202) 393-5959*
FAX (202) 393-6060

Dangerous Days

12/25/1991   U.S. Recognition of Georgia. President George Bush formally recognized Georgia and other former Soviet republics on this date; he also stated that formal diplomatic relations would be established with six of the republics as soon as possible and that diplomatic relations would be established with the other six (Georgia was one of them) when certain political conditions were met.

12/21/1991   Commonwealth formed at a meeting in Alma-Ata, Kazakhstan. On this date, 11 former republics of the Soviet Union (which ceased to exist on December 25, 1991) established the Commonwealth of Independent States (CIS). Georgia sent an observer but did not join the CIS.

Delhi

India
★★★★

Kashmir Sweat

INDIA

It is a miracle that India even exists. Being a nation of so many ethnicities and religions, it should have ripped itself into a bunch of dinky fiefdoms long ago, each with hundreds of years of history, separate religions, dialects and customs. Instead, 866 million Indians and their government hobble painfully forward—burdened not only with poverty, skin-and-bones hunger and sickness, but also with an alarming birthrate and a potential nuclear conflict with neighboring Pakistan.

Like a terminally ill patient, India deals with the ugliest boils and rashes first. Its big problems are in the extreme south with the Tamil Tigers, and in the north with Sikh separatists. The Hindu majority can't get along with the Muslim minority. If simmering disdain for each other wasn't enough, on December 6, 1992, militant Hindus, intent on aggravating the Muslims, demolished a mosque in Ayodha in Uttar Pradesh state. They then intended to build their own temple on the grounds, but the government wisely stepped in and stopped them. By the

269

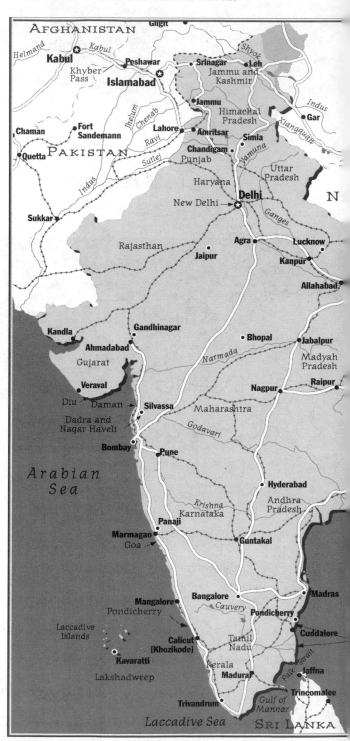

India

- ⊗ National Capital
- • State or Union Territory Capital
- • City
- Disputed Territory

- State or Union Territory Border
- Primary Road
- ⊢•⊣•⊣ Railroad
- ▪ ▪ ▪ ▪ Disputed Border

0 100 200 300 400 km
0 100 200 300 mi

©FWI

CHINA

Tongtran (Yangtze)

Mekong

PAL

Kathmandu

Arunachal Pradesh

Sikkim
Itanagar
Ledo

Gangtok
BHUTAN
Assam
Nagaland

Siliguri

Sillong
Kohima

Meghalaya

Imphal

Varanasi

BANGLADESH
Manipur

Ganges
Agartala
Aizawl

Bihar
West Bengal
Dhaka
Tripura

Jamshedpur
Calcutta
Jessore
Mizoram

Irrawaddy

Mouths of the Ganges

Mandalay

Mahanadi
Cuttack

MYANMAR
(BURMA)

Bhubaneshwar
Orissa

Puri

Irrawaddy

Vishakhapatnam

Yangon
(Rangoon)

Pondicherry

Bay of Bengal

Mouths of the Irrawaddy

Andaman Islands
(India)

Port Blair

Andaman Sea

Pondicherry

Andaman and Nicobar Island

Nicobar Islands
(India)

INDIA

time the dust had settled, 1200 people had died throughout India. This gave the Islamic fundamentalist nasties in Iran and Pakistan a good reason to stir things up in India. The fallout has been felt as far away as Great Britain, where a large Indian community lives. Every time a bomb goes off, and they go off a lot, the suspects include Indians, Pakistani agents, Kashmiri separatists, Sikh terrorists, Maoist rebels, Sri Lankan Liberation Tigers of Tamil Eelam guerrillas, Muslim militants, drug traffickers and even gangsters. Mother Theresa is the only one exempt from suspicion.

India is rattling its sabre at Pakistan and Sri Lanka and having a go-at-it with Bangladesh, who they've also charged with providing aid to Indian rebels, including allowing Pakistan to instigate terrorist activities on Bangladeshi soil.

But inarguably, the ugliest mushroom on the horizon is India's nuke race with Pakistan. While the world ignores the global consequences of what is perceived as a Hatfield-and-McCoy stick-fight in the boonies, the CIA quietly announced recently that Pakistan and India are two of the planet's top choices for potential serious instability.

Being on each other's borders means both nations don't require the technology to blast intercontinental ballistic rockets 10,000 miles able to strike a dime. India is believed to have the capability of lobbing a nuclear warhead within 1000 feet of a target 150 miles away. In fact, India is now capable of striking most major Pakistani cities within five minutes after launch. (See "Dangerous Things.") In this part of the world, that's close enough. In January 1996, a mosque in the Pakistani-held portion of Kashmir was turned into mush by a conventional rocket; it killed 20 worshipers. Each side blamed the other, and an artillery and small arms squash match ensued.

India and Pakistan, in their relatively embryonic relationship, have already fought three wars. Firefights on the disputed border occur regularly between the two sides. Both countries aid separatist extremists—Pakistan funds the nasties in the Indian-controlled region of Kashmir, while India fans the flames of hatred in Pakistan's Sind area. Nepal is another nasty neighbor. India can't seem to get along with anyone. However, it's trade and transit issues that dominate relations between India and Nepal.

Not one to miss out on ideological rocket attacks, China is also part of India's multi-front diplomatic fray. Just to keep China honest, India fought a brief border war with the Sinos back in 1962. Since then, though, the two countries' relations have improved—if for no other reason than their mutual respect for the size of each others' populations, and the realization that a conventional ground war might take a few hundred years to fight, and still leave each country with populations the size of the U.S. Although India is furious over closer Sino-Pakistani ties, it has withdrawn most of the troops deployed to the border area with China.

With so many enemies, who do you call? Why Russia, of course. Everyone else who needs arms does. Motherlode Russia, the Office Depot of weapons systems.

India actually enjoyed smooth relations with the U.S. when George Bush called the shots, literally—but they've deteriorated since President Bill Clinton took office. Time will only tell if the Republicans' new Contract with America will include a new contract with India as well.

The Scoop

The beheading of a Norwegian tourist in August 1995 by the group calling itself Al-Faran (comprised of Afghan mercenaries) in Kashmir sent chills up and down the spines of Patagonia-clad yuppie trekkers worldwide. Although Hans Christian Ostrow was the first tourist to be killed in five years in Kashmir, it only brought attention to the ongoing state of war in India. A hefty 249 terrorist incidents have put India at the top of the list for individuals injured in terrorist attacks—2546 people. Their tiny teardrop neighbor to the south, Sri Lanka, still has the record for terrorist-related fatalities. Its interconnected agony with India gives Sri Lanka the dubious *DP* Award for being the World's Most Dangerous Place—Terrorism Category (WMDP—TC)—with 1268 deaths. The get-tough policy of the Indian army and police has been somewhat effective combating Sikh militants in the Punjab. The rising incidents of rape, torture and murder attributed to the Indian security forces are creating a furor with human rights groups outside of India.

Meanwhile, the Islami Harkat-ul-Momineen and the Khalistan Liberation Force separatist groups have been bombing foreigners in an effort to stop elections from taking place in Jammu and Kashmir, predominantly Hindu India's only Muslim-majority state, where more than 20,000 people have been killed in the six-year separatist insurgency. More than a dozen militant groups fighting New Delhi's rule in Kashmir tried to stop India's efforts to hold parliamentary elections in May 1996 in Jammu and Kashmir.

On July 8 of 1996 Muslim guerillas Ikwhan Jammu and Kashmir kidnapped 19 journalists for 10 hours. It was a year after the kidnapping of German Dirk Hasert. The journalists were on their way to a press conference held by the Muslim Mujahedin in Achabal (40 miles from Srinagar) another guerilla group. Ikwhan held the journalists because their editors refused to stop publication of their newspapers after they refused to publish one of the group's press releases.

Each Kashmiri rebel is offered 5000 rupees (US$145) to surrender with his gun. Just part of the 7.9 bilion the government spends on defense to fight insurgent wars.

The Players

There are over 100 different rebel factions, with 10 being militarily significant, and about 60 intergroup clashes a year. Thousands of Kashmiri youths have received rudimentary training in Afghanistan and Azad Kashmir that takes two weeks to three months. Although there are plenty of weapons supplied by Pakistan, there is little organized fighting. Typically a mine will be laid across a road and a military convoy will be under attack by small arms fire from a group of 5 to 10 insurgents. The insurgents then run away and do not press their advantage. The ratio of deaths for insurgents to military is about five to one. There are also about 1000 volunteers, primarily from Afghanistan (500), Saudi Arabia (80) and Sudan (200) fighting in Kashmir.

For now there are two main players: the JKLF and the HM

The Jammu and Kashmir Liberation Front (JKLF)

The leader of the JKLF is Halil Hyder and their headquarters is in Anantnag, 44 miles from Srinagar. They have been fighting since 1990. Founded in 1977 and led by President Yasin Malik, the JKLF wants to make Muslim Kashmir independent from Hindu India. The ball got rolling in 1988 when one of the leaders, Amanullah Khan, got together with the Srinager-based Islamic Students League. They typically plant bombs and engage in antigovernment activities

Hizbul Mujahedin (Fighters for the Party of God)

The new players and leaders of Kashmir's struggle for independence are now the largest military force against the Indian government.

In 1989, the Muslims became violent in opposing Indian rule. There are 6 million people in Kashmir; 4 million of them are Muslim. Since 1989, about 25,000 people, mostly

Muslims, have been killed. Half the toll has been civilians. Most of the casualties have been in the Kashmir Valley area around Srinagar. Kashmir is currently divided, with some parts under the control of Pakistan rebels and others under the auspices of the Indian army.

Syeed Salahuddin, whose real name is Syeed Mohammed Yusuf Shah, is the commander of the Hizbul Mujahedin. It receives financial backing and support from Pakistan. Pakistan's Prime Minister Benazir Bhutto wants the Muslim majority states of Jammu and Kashmir out of Hindu-dominated India and aligned with Pakistan. The rebels claim they are fighting for *azad* Kashmir, or free Kashmir. Currently, there are about 15,000 active rebel fighters with several subfactions among them. The rebels operate in small hit-and-run groups in cities like Srinagar, or from remote bases in Kashmir. Pakistan has fought two out of three of its last wars over Kashmir, and the situation is expected to remain tense for years to come. The geopolitical volleyball started when Britain sliced up India and Pakistan in 1947, based on geographic divisions rather than religious ones. At the time, India promised to hold a plebiscite among all Kashmiris to determine whether the territory should be part of India or Pakistan. They backed down, and the conflict has been going on ever since.

Al-Faran

Nobody that *DP* has talked to had ever heard of Al-Faran before the kidnapping. The Pakistanis are convinced it is a sick plot by the Indian Secret Police to discredit Muslim freedom fighters, and the rest of the world writes it off to fundamentalist terrorism. On July 4, 1995, two Brits and two Yanks were nabbed by Al-Faran, reputedly a shadowy Kashmiri separatist group but actually Afghan mercenaries hired to spring captured fighters out of jail. Kashmir is a Muslim area occupied by India, according to Pakistan. One of the Americans escaped, and the remaining hostages were joined with a German and a Norwegian seized in a separate incident. The Norwegian, Hans Christian Ostrow, was beheaded while still alive and left in the village of Seer. The group demanded the release of 15 prisoners in exchange for the hostages. Although the group has been visited by a doctor and sent faxes and telephone messages, the Indian government says this murky group is holding the Westerners in a remote mountain area.

Inter Services Intelligence (ISI)

Members of the Pakistani Secret Service, or ISI, are busy boys. Besides being accused of supplying money and arms to the *taliban* in Afghanistan and the Kashmiris, they are also busy looking for nuclear parts for Pakistan's nuclear program. They also are interested in any info that might embarrass India.

Mohajir Qaumi Movement (MQM)

The bustling port of Karachi is a war zone, thanks to the MQM. The name means Refugees National Movement and is led by Altaf Hussain (who conveniently lives in sedate London). The Urdu-speaking Mohajirs feel they are discriminated against (which they are) by the Sinhis. There is also a lot of banditry, drug feuds and Sunni/Shiite violence that is blamed on the MQM. There is even a splinter group called the MQM Haqiqi—or the real MQM.

Every day this dirty, sprawling metropolis of 13 million people tosses five or six bodies into the back of a police van for ID. In 1995 there were 2100 people killed in Karachi, strikes crippled the economy, and people feared for their lives. The government's reaction was to declare open season on the MQM. In many cases suspects are rounded up (many with a price on their head) and simply shot later. Most are shot when police open fire first and ask questions later.

The Government and the Indian Army

Governor K. V. Krishna Rao, the aging former chief of staff of the Indian Army, has about 400,000 soldiers, border troops and police at his service to keep the peace in Kashmir. It is the largest force India has ever fielded against a secessionist rebellion. Governor Rao subscribes to the Domino Theory: If Kashmir is allowed to break away from India, other parts of the country with separatist groups would follow and India would exist no longer.

The Honourable
Prime Minister of India
South Block
New Delhi, India 100 001
Fax: 91-11-301-0700

All-Party Hurriyat Conference

This is an alliance formed by the numerous guerrillas who use secession from India as a common rallying point. Maulvi Omar Farooq, 22, is chairman of the All-Party Hurriyat Conference, the umbrella group formed of 32 rebel organizations. Farooq is also the hereditary Mir Waiz of Kashmir, the religious leader of the region's Muslims. The losers seem to be the Hindus of the region. At last count, there were about 400,000 Hindu refugees from the Kashmir Valley in refugee camps around the state's winter capital of Jammu.

United Liberation Front of Assam (ULFA)

The ULFA was supposed to cede their fight for a socialist state in Assam when they signed a peace deal with the government in January 1992. The hard-liners said "screw that" and began a campaign of kidnapping and extortion against the rich tea growers. The Indian Tea Association quickly put together a 7000-man private army to protect themselves from ULFA thugs.

There have been reports of large-scale extortion and attacks on police stations throughout Assam by both ULFA and the Bodo Security Force (BSF). ULFA murdered the chairman of Assam Frontier Tea in 1990 and continued gunning for more high-level executives. Another tea executive, working for the Tata Tea Company, has been held for ransom by militants since April 1993. His kidnappers are demanding a US$5 million ransom. The executives are Indian nationals. Security forces have stepped up their operations against the militants and rounded up large numbers of both suspects and weapons. Assam state officials, however, are hoping that the government in New Delhi will send in a paramilitary force to end the rebels' kidnappings. For now, Assam is an especially dangerous place if you grow tea. Crumpets, anyone?

The Sikhs

The Sikhs want their own turf, and India doesn't want them to have it. They are led by Sohan Singh, a 77-year-old doctor who was captured by the Indian government in November of 1993. Typically proud and bellicose, a small segment of Sikhs wants to establish an independent homeland called Khalistan, or Land of the Pure. The Sikhs target security forces and other government symbols in their bomb attacks. The problem is that the bombs, although they may lean left or right, don't have political affiliations—and kill a lot of innocent people. Sikhs comprise only 2 percent of India's population, but they are a majority in Punjab state. The center of the Sikh terrorist movement is in the capital of Punjab, Chandigarh. Pakistan is sympathetic to the Sikh movement. Although the Indian government claims that the movement has been shrinking since its leader was captured, there are still a lot of angry bad boys in turbans with the last name of Singh (all Sikhs carry the name Singh, meaning "lion"). Journalist Peter Hillmore described the Sikhs: "Let us get one thing clear. The bands of Sikh gunmen who rampage around here regularly and randomly shooting people in cold-blood are not, repeat not, a bunch of mean and vicious terrorists. They are in fact dedicated and idealistic militants who are simply misunderstood. Actually, that is a load of nonsense. Of course, they are terrorists; they certainly seem to enjoy creating terror. They are barbaric and vicious killers, murdering at random. They appear to be totally without moral scruples and, by now, are devoid of even political logic. Too many people are being killed every week for there to be any restraining influence at work. There are too many different gangs at work for there to be any grand scheme. Punjab, quite simply, is out of control."

Sri Lankan Liberation Tigers of Tamil Eelam (LTTE)

The Tigers bagged their biggest victim when a suicide bomber killed former Indian Prime Minister Rajiv Ghandi. Ghandi sent 50,000 troops to put down the Tamil insurrection in 1987. These guys know how to carry a grudge. The Tamil Tigers may be too effective; India's Tamil population provides little sympathy or support to the overly violent Tigers.

Naxalites

This group is also called the Peoples War Guerrillas, a Maoist insurgent group that continues the plight of the Naxalites, a 1960s revolutionary group. They operate out of Andrah Pradesh.

Getting In

A passport and visa (which must be obtained in advance) are required for entry into India for tourism or business. Evidence of yellow fever immunization is needed if the traveler is arriving from an infected area. Convicted drug offenders in India can expect a minimum jail sentence of 10 years and heavy fines. Indian customs authorities strictly enforce the laws and regulations governing the declaration, importation or possession of gold and gold objects. Travelers have sometimes been detained for possession of undeclared gold objects. For further entry information, the traveler can contact the following:

Embassy of India

2536 Massachusetts Avenue
NW, Washington, D.C. 20008
☎ *(202) 939-9849 or (202) 939-9806*

Or contact the Indian consulates in Chicago, New York and San Francisco.

Bombay International Airport is a 45- to 60-minute ride from Bombay and about 23 miles northwest of the city. There is a departure tax of 100 rupees for international flights, 50 rupees for Southwest Asian flights.

Getting Around

A taxi from the airport to the center of New Delhi runs about Rs150. In Bombay it will cost you Rs170 and takes about an hour; in Calcutta, about Rs120. You can prepay in New Delhi and Bombay, but drivers will haggle a fixed price with tourists.

There are about 2 million km (1.2 million miles) of roads in India, 33,112 km of which are the national highways. While this constitutes only 2 percent of total road length, these arteries carry about 35 percent of the traffic. According to the National Transportation Research Centre, Indian roads are the most dangerous in the world. With one percent of the total vehicles in the world, India accounted for 6 percent of total road accidents and has the highest accident rate in the world at 34.6 per 100,000 people. See "Dangerous Things."

The size of the railway network was estimated at approximately 63,900 km (37,850 miles) in 1990. India's railway network is the largest in Asia and the second largest in the world. India has four major international airports—Bombay, Calcutta, Madras and Delhi—and 115 other airports serving domestic routes.

Travel by road after dark is not recommended, and train passengers have been subjected to robberies and schedule disruptions due to protest actions.

Restricted Areas

Permission from the Indian government (from Indian diplomatic missions abroad, or in some cases, from the Ministry of Home Affairs) is required to visit the states of Mizoram, Manipur, Nagaland, Meghalaya, Assam, Tripura, Arunachal Pradesh, Sikkim, parts of Kulu district and Spiti district of Himachal Pradesh, border areas of Jammu and Kashmir, areas of Uttar Pradesh, the area west of National Highway 15 running from Ganganagar to Sanchar in Rajasthan, the Andaman and Nicobar islands and the Union Territory of the Laccadive Islands.

Dangerous Places

Countrywide

Serious communal violence and riots erupted in India following the destruction of an Ayodhya mosque in December 1992. There continue to be major civil disturbances. These riots pose risks to a traveler's personal safety and can disrupt transportation systems and city services. In response to communal violence, Indian authorities may occasionally impose curfews. In addition, political rallies and demonstrations in India have the potential for violence and bomb attacks.

Kashmir

Each week about 50 people lose their lives in Kashmir due to violence. It is even more frightening to know that the executed Norwegian tourist contacted three Indian government tourist offices to inquire about the danger and was told that there were no risks. Terrorist activities and violent civil disturbances continue in the Kashmir Valley in the states of Jammu and Kashmir. There have been incidents in which terrorists have threatened and kidnapped foreigners.Undoubtedly, though, Pakistan is the biggest influence on India's foreign relations. India and Pakistan have duked it out on the battlefield three times since World War II— in 1947, 1965 and 1971. Relations between the two became less strained only after Rajiv Gandhi replaced his mother as India's prime minister. In December 1985, Rajiv Gandhi and Pakistan President Mohammed Zia ul-Haq each pledged not to throw the first punch, particularly jabs aimed at the nations' nuke sites. But the increased violence in Kashmir, the one Indian state where Muslims comprise a majority, has brought about a greater likelihood that the two countries will again go to war. India claims that Pakistan is fueling the flames by encouraging and supporting Kashmir secession from India. Of course, rather than Kashmir becoming an independent entity, Pakistan would like to be the sponge that absorbs it. In December 1992, Hindu extremists turned the Muslim mosque at Ayodhya into rubble. The Indian governor of Kashmir charged Pakistan in January 1994 with hiring more than 10,000 Afghan mercenaries to help Kashmiri rebels in their efforts against the government. The kidnapping and executing of a Western hostage has made this area very dangerous. In July 1994 an American tourist was fatally shot in Srinagar, and in June 1994 militants held two British hikers hostage for 18 days before releasing them. These and even more recent events demonstrate that the Kashmir Valley in the states of Jammu and Kashmir remains a dangerous place where terrorist activities and violent civil disturbances continue.

India-Pakistan Border/Kashmir

Pakistan wants Kashmir and India won't let them have it. Some groups want to glue together the Indian- and Pakistani-controlled sections of Kashmir and create a separate country; other militants want Kashmir to annex with Pakistan. You can guess which group is backed by the government of Pakistan. All groups have managed to cause the deaths of about 17,000 people since January of 1990 when the tiff began.The Kashmiri separatist groups keep their squabbling and killing confined to the predominantly Muslim states of Jammu and Kashmir.

Tensions run high between India and Pakistan, particularly over Kashmir, resulting in frequent clashes. There are stringent security checks, travel restrictions and curfews. The only official India-Pakistan border crossing point for foreigners is at Attari, Punjab/ Wagah, Pakistan. A Pakistani visa is required.

Karakoram Mountain Range

Both India and Pakistan claim an area of the Karakoram mountain range that includes the Siachen glacier. The two countries have established military outposts in the region and armed clashes have occurred. Because of this situation, U.S. citizens traveling to or climbing peaks anywhere in the disputed area face significant risk of injury and death. The disputed area includes the following peaks: Rimo Peak, Apsarasas I, II and III, Tegam Kangri I, II, and III, Suingri Kangri, Ghaint I and II, Indira Col and Sia Kangri.

Assam

Terrorist groups in Assam have bombed trains, buses and bridges. The government of India has declared Assam to be a "disturbed area."

Punjab and Uttar Pradesh

Significant separatist violence continues in the Punjab and nearby regions outside Punjab state. Gangs have kidnapped and held for ransom foreign company executives. Militants and robber gangs operate in the area in and around Jim Corbett National Park and Dudhwa National Park, as well as on roads leading to Hardwar, Rishikesh, Dehra Dun and Mussoorie. There are violent encounters between police and activists for a separate state for the hill districts of Uttar Pradesh.

Delhi and Northern India

In Delhi, there have been several bombings that have resulted in casualties and property damage. The targets are areas of public access, such as public transportation facilities, bazaars and shopping areas, and restaurants. In the states of Jammu and Kashmir, and Punjab in northern India, the terrorist threat is considerably higher. Bombings, kidnappings and assassinations are common occurrences in these regions. The State Department is advising American citizens not to travel to Kashmir and to avoid nonessential travel to Punjab.

Foreign residents throughout India usually employ *chawkidars* (residential guards) outside their homes. Police assistance throughout northern India can be requested by dialing 100 from any public phone; 100 connects to the nearest police control room, which can usually dispatch a patrol vehicle. Civil unrest pervades the Northeast States. Terrorist groups in Assam have bombed trains, buses and bridges. The government of India has declared Assam to be a "disturbed area." Numerous political killings have occurred in Nagaland and Manipur.

Kashmir and Sikh separatists set off a bomb that destroyed a lodging house in the Indian capital on April 19, 1996, killing at least 14 people, five of them foreigners, and injuring 37. A joint statement from the Islami Harkat-ul-Momineen and the Khalistan Liberation Force distributed to newspapers in Srinigar, summer capital of the northern states of Jammu and Kashmir, said the bomb in the crowded district of Paharganj had been triggered by remote control. Also killed in the blast were three Nigerian men, a Dutchman, and a European woman whose nationality is not known. A Briton, a Dutchman, and a Nigerian were also injured.

Bombay

There has been a dramatic increase in the number of organized criminal gangs operating in Bombay, and police confirm that the problem exists throughout Maharashtra state. Drug gangs have proliferated in the larger cities, and police report these gangs have moved into some of the most affluent areas of Bombay. In 1994, there were three drive-by shootings in the Malabar hill area of Bombay. Home burglary still remains the most prevalent crime in Bombay, often committed by servants or other persons with easy access to the residence involved.

Restricted Areas

Permission from the Indian government (from Indian diplomatic missions abroad or, in some cases, from the Ministry of Home Affairs) is required to visit the states of Mizoram, Manipur, Nagaland, Meghalaya, Assam, Tripura, Arunachal Pradesh, Sikkim, parts of Kulu District and Spiti District of Himachal Pradesh, border areas of Jammu and Kashmir, areas of Uttar Pradesh, the area west of National Highway No. 15 running from Ganganagar to Sanchar in Rajasthan, the Andaman and Nicobar Islands and the Union Territory of the Laccadive Islands.

Calcutta

Insurgent activities, including killings and kidnappings by the United Liberation Front of Assam (ULFA) continue in the northeast. Despite army intervention, violent dissidence continues in parts of Assam. Local ULFA militants have carried out coordinated kidnappings throughout the state. A Soviet mining engineer was killed and a number of Indian hostages taken, including several high-ranking officials. Political clashes occur sporadically in different parts of west Bengal and Bihar. Americans who are members of the Ananda Marg have been victims of mob violence in some areas of west Bengal and Bihar states (especially Calcutta and Purulia district) and are not welcome by state government authorities, who, upon locating such individuals, usually detain and deport them.

The crime situation in west Bengal and Orissa relates to petty thefts, etc. However, in Bihar, there have been killings and other violence stemming from caste and tribal differences. Travel by road after dark is not recommended, and train passengers have been subjected to robberies and schedule disruptions due to protest actions.

Emergency numbers:

Police Headquarters in Calcutta
☎ *25-5900, 25-5762*
Control Room (24 hours)
25-3340

The South

Sri Lanka is a thorn in India's side because of the ethnic conflict between Sri Lanka's Sinhalese majority and the island's Tamil minority.

In May 1994, Prime Minister Rajiv Gandhi was killed in Tamil Nadu by a suicide bomber. Members of the Sri Lankan Tamil terrorist group, Liberation Tigers of Tamil Eelam (LTTE), commit acts of terrorism and violence throughout southern India. To the north in Andhra Pradesh, the Peoples' War Group, popularly known as Naxalites, kidnaps and/or murders politicians and bureaucrats.

Dangerous Things

Prithvi Rockets

Ironically, the name "Prithvi" means "Earth." Realistically, the name means "Death." The latest models of these nuke-capable projectiles, first tested in January 1996, have a range of 150 miles and can strike most major Pakistani cities within only a few minutes after launch. The short-range version can carry a 1000-kilogram payload. Although the Indians have some fine tuning to do on their accuracy, these little puppies are quite capable of mass death and destruction. It simply remains a matter of on whom and what they fall.

The Roads

According to the National Transportation Research Centre in Trivendrum, Indian roads are the most dangerous in the world. With one percent of the total vehicles in the world, India accounted for 6 percent of total road accidents and had the highest accident rate in the world at 34.6 per 100,000 people in 1988/89. In October 1989 there were about 2 million km of roads in India, 33,112 km of which were National Highway. While this constitutes only 2 percent of total road length, it carries around 35 percent of the traffic.

Bombay Train Stations

There have been many bombs defused or detonated at Bombay's crowded rail stations. It is not known exactly who the perpetrators are, but it is a safe guess that you wouldn't care who blew you up. A rash of 13 car and suitcase bombs in Bombay caused almost half the injuries in one day, March 12, 1992. Luckily, police defused three more bombs.

When Bombay police filed charges against 189 people in connection with the bombings they had to use canvas sacks to haul in the 9392 criminal charges. Bombay's chief of police claims the Pakistani Government was behind the attacks and that they provided cash and arms for the bomb attacks.

Political Rallies

Various separatist groups love to blow up politicians using suicide bombers. These bombs usually contain way too much explosive material and nasty things like ball bearings. Needless to say, they bury what's left of the politician in a sandwich bag and a lot of people die. Political rallies in India are much safer on TV.

Crackdowns

The army likes to talk to folks early in the morning. Between 3 and 4 a.m. they will seal an area off, roust folks from their beds and take them to a open area. They are divided into young, middle-aged and old. Women are allowed to return to their homes. Then the men are paraded in front of "cats," hooded informers who point out Kashmir insurgents.(The term "cats" comes from Concealed Apprehension Technique.) Anyone who looks like a bad guy is taken away for further interrogation. Some of the men never return home.

While the male population plays "What's My Line," soldiers go through the houses making searches for weapons. In many cases, the unprotected women have been raped and the homes looted.

AIDS

There are 3.8 million Indians with HIV and 200,000 with AIDS. India is predicted to have the highest incidence of AIDS in the world by the year 2000.

Mountain Climbing

Both India and Pakistan claim an area of the Karakoram mountain range which includes the Siachen Glacier. The two countries have established military outposts in the region, and armed clashes have occurred. Because of this situation, U.S. citizens traveling to or climbing peaks anywhere in the disputed area face significant risk of injury and death. The disputed area includes the following peaks: Rimo Peak, Apsarasas I, II, and III, Tegam Kangri I, II, and III, Suingri Kangri, Ghaint I and II, Indira Col, and Sia Kangri.

Piloting Civil Aircraft

In past years, there have been a number of incidents in which civil aircraft have been detained for deviating from approved flight plans. U.S. citizens piloting civil aircraft in India must file any changes to previous flight plans and may not overfly restricted airspace.

Malaria

Calcutta, West Bengal and northeastern India are once again suffering from serious outbreaks of malaria. Calcutta is reported to be the worst hit of the country's major metropolitan cities. Initial reports suggest that this is a continuation of a longer trend of higher incidences of malaria in general and of malignant and chloroquine-resistant strains in particular.

Getting Sick

Adequate medical care is available in the major population centers but limited in the rural areas of the country. Travelers to India should take preventive measures against malaria, hepatitis, meningitis and Japanese encephalitis (if arriving during the monsoon season). Travelers arriving from countries where outbreaks of yellow fever have occurred will be required to furnish a certificate for yellow fever vaccination. Cholera and gastroenteritis occur during the summer monsoon months, mostly in the poorer areas of India. The best protection includes eating only at better-quality restaurants or hotels, drinking only boiled or bottled mineral water and avoiding ice.

Nuts and Bolts

India has three main regions: the mountainous Himalayas in the north; the Indo-Gangetic Plain, a flat, hot plain south of the Himalayas; and the Peninsular Shield in the south, where India's neighbors Sri Lanka and the Maldives are located. The coldest months are January and February, with sweltering heat between March and May. The southwestern monsoon is from June to September. The post monsoon, or northeast monsoon, in the southern peninsula occurs from October to December.

India is hot, dirty and humid throughout most of the year. If you are looking to latch onto some bacteria, India is the place to do it. A 1994 outbreak of pneumonic (not bubonic) plague, a deadly disease spread by breathing, didn't help the tourist business much. Bombay may be the dirtiest city on earth. The hottest months are April to July, the wettest months from June to August.

There are more than 900 million people crammed into India's 3.3 million square kilometers (1.3 million square miles). About 40 percent of India's people live below the poverty line, defined as the resources needed to provide 2100 to 2400 calories per person per day. About 70 percent of the population lives in the countryside. The official language is Hindi, but English is the second language and is widely spoken. All official documents are in English. In keeping with India's diverse makeup, there are 18 languages recognized for official use in regional areas, of which the most widely spoken are Telugu, Bengali, Marathi, Tamil, Urdu and Gujarati, each with its own script. Hindus do not eat beef. Muslims avoid pork. Sikhs do not smoke. Strict Hindus are also vegetarian and do not drink.

Vegetarian dishes and rice are popular in the south. In the north, meat dishes with unleavened breads are the standard. Popular dishes are *rogan josh* (curried lamb), *gushtaba* (spiced meatballs in yogurt) and *biryani* (chicken or lamb in orange-flavored rice, sprinkled with rose water). *Tandoori*, a marinated meat or fish cooked in a clay tandoori oven, is a northern speciality.

Banking hours: 10:30 a.m.–2:30 p.m., Monday to Friday; 10:30 a.m.–12:30 p.m., Saturday. Business hours: 9 a.m.–noon, 1–5 p.m., Monday to Friday. Stores are open 9:30 a.m.–6 p.m., Monday to Saturday. The workweek is Monday through Friday.

The Rupee (about 31 to the U.S. dollar) is the currency and should be changed only through banks and authorized money changers. Electricity is 220v/50hz.

Embassy Location

U.S. Embassy
   Shanti Path, Chanakyapuri 110 021
   New Delhi
   ☎ *[91] (11) 600651*

U.S. Consulates General

In Bombay:

U.S. Consulate General
Lincoln House
78 Bhulabhai Desai Road, Bombay 400026
☎ [91] (22) 363-3611

In Madras:

U.S. Consulate General
220 Mount Road, Madras 600006
☎ [91] (44) 827-3040, 827-7542

In Calcutta:

U.S. Consulate General
5/1 Ho Chi Minh Sarani, Calcutta 700071
☎ [91] (33) 242-3611, 242-2336, 242-2337

Other Useful Numbers

Ministry of Communications

Sanchar Bhawan, New Delhi 110 003
☎ 383600

Ministry of External Affairs

South Block, New Delhi 110 011
☎ 301-1813

Ministry of Tourism and Civil Aviation

Parivahan Bhavan, Sansad Marg, New Delhi 100 001
☎ 351700

Dangerous Days

08/13/1995	Norwegian Hans Christina Ostroe is found beheaded near Anantnag, 37 miles from Srinagar.
07/04/1995	Al-Faran guerillas kidnap two Britons, and two Americans near Pahalgam, 55 miles from Srinagar.
10/1994	Rebel leader Shabir Shah released from prison
06/1994	Two Brits are kidnapped and released unharmed 17 days later
03/1993	Three hostages are swapped for seven guerillas
12/06/1992	Hindu extremists destroyed the 16th-century Muslim mosque at Ayodhya in India's Uttar Pradesh state. The subsequent rioting and Muslim-Hindu clashes that engulfed India, Pakistan, Bangladesh and other nations resulted in over 1000 deaths. Hindus claim the mosque was built on the birth site of the Hindu god Rama, a claim disputed by Muslims.
12/06/1992	Dr. B. R. Ambedkar, revered leader of India's Dalits (Untouchables), died and was cremated in Bombay.
08/1992	Two army engineers are kidnapped and killed after the government refuses to release 17 jailed rebels
02/1992	India plants mines along border with Pakistan to stop traffic of insurgents between countries.
12/1991	A bank officer is swapped for a guerilla.
11/1991	The manager of the state run radio station is kidnapped and exchanged for a guerilla.

Dangerous Days

09/1991	Former Kashmiri minister and her husband are kidnapped and freed in a raid one month later. The brother-in-law of an Indian minister, a policeman, an insurance worker, and a bank employee are kidnapped the same month. They are exchanged for rebels but not until a hostages severed thumb is sent as proof.
07/1991	Four government officers are kidnapped and executed three months later.
06/1991	Eight Israeli tourists are kidnapped. Six escape and one dies in the attempt. An oil executive is kidnapped and released 53 days later.
05/21/1991	Former Prime Minister Rajiv Gandhi was assassinated during a campaign rally in Tamil Nadu state.
03/1991	Two Swedish engineers as well as a daughter and wife are kidnapped. The wife and child are released but the men are not released until 97 days later
02/1991	A pregnant 29-year-old is kidnapped and swapped for five rebels
04/1990	University vice chancellor and two businessmen are abducted and killed.
03/1990	Kashmiri political leader, Mir Ghulum Mustafa is kidnapped and killed.
12/1990	Indian army fires on demonstrators killing 38 in Srinagar. Separatists begin a military campaign for independence.
12/1989	Guerillas kidnap daughter of Indian Home minister and swap for five insurgents.
01/06/1989	Two of Prime Minister Indira Gandhi's Sikh bodyguards were hanged for her assassination on October 31, 1984.
01/03/1989	Muslim Kashmiri militants began their campaign for independence from India.
07/06/1987	Seventy-two Hindus were killed in an attack by Sikh militants on a bus in the Punjab.
04/29/1986	Sikh militants seized the Golden Temple of Amritsar in Punjab and declared the independent state of Khalistan. Expelled by government of India forces the next day.
06/23/1985	A bomb exploded on an Air India flight over the North Atlantic following its departure from Canada, killing all 329 passengers on board. A second bomb exploded at Narita airport in Japan, killing two people. Sikh extremists claimed responsibility for both bombings.
12/03/1984	A chemical leak at Union Carbide's Bhopal plant resulted in 2000 deaths and nearly 150,000 injuries.
10/31/1984	Indian Prime Minister Indira Gandhi was assassinated by her Sikh bodyguards. Anti-Sikh rioting following the assassination resulted in thousands of Sikh deaths throughout India.
08/09/1984	The head of the Indian security forces that stormed the Sikh golden temple of Amritsar was assassinated by Sikh terrorists.

Dangerous Days

06/06/1984   Indian troops stormed the golden temple of Amritsar, killing 300 Sikhs in the attack.

02/11/1984   Maqbool Butt, founder of the Jammu-Kashmir Liberation Front, was hanged in a New Delhi jail for the 1965 murder of an Indian intelligence agent in Kashmir. Militant Muslims have marked the anniversary of his death with sometimes violent demonstrations in Jammu and Kashmir.

01/26/1950   India's constitution was promulgated and India became a republic within the Commonwealth. (Republic Day is also called Constitution Day.)

01/30/1948   Mahatma Gandhi was assassinated.

08/15/1947   Independence Day.

04/13/1699   Sikh religion was founded in 1699 by Guru Gobind Singh.

07/13   Martyr's day in Kashmir. It commemorates the deaths of Kashmiri nationalists during the British raj.

05/24/563 B.C.   Birth of Buddha.

Jerusalem

Israel
★★★★

Eye For an Eye

On November 4, 1995, the blood spilled from the top of the ladder. Israeli Prime Minister Yitzhak Rabin was gunned down at point-blank range by an unrepentant 25-year-old Jewish extremist, Yigal Amir. The Jewish-Palestinian struggle came full circle, as Israel discovered the biggest threat to the peace accord may not be Hamas, the Palestinian terrorist group bent on Israel's destruction, but from right-wing Jewish extremists within its own precarious borders.

The leader of Shin Bet (the General Security Service, or GSS—Israel's secret service apparatus), known only as "K" under Israeli law, resigned after taking responsibility for a dearth of GSS precautions in preventing the assassination of Rabin. But it's interesting to note that "K" was well aware of the kinetic dangers posed by the enemy within; his Master's thesis had been on the need of Israel's security forces to be prepared not only for the Palestinian threat, but also that from Israel's own hard-core religious right.

Reach Out and Kill Someone

Israel paid a Gaza businessman a million dollars and a false passport to deliver the booby-trapped cellphone to 30-year-old Yehiya Ayash in the Gaza Strip. The phone was a loaner while Ayash's phone was being repaired. Yehiya Ayash was from the West Bank and is credited with the string of suicide attacks and bombings. He did not know that the phone had high explosives in the earpiece set up to be detonated by audio signal. The security people made a call to Ayasha and then triggered the explosion. It is not known whether the call made to Ayash was collect or not. The businessman is suspected to be in hiding in the States where his son lives.

Despite the Israelis' need and demand for a homeland, their Arab brethren don't see eye to eye, more like eye for an eye. Despite the peace agreement reached with the PLO, the trading of eyes and teeth between Israel and its numerous enemies continues at unprecedented levels. The increase in terrorist threats against Israel, particularly in the wake of the historic Israeli-Palestinian pact, has turned out to be more than merely the holy smoke of bored car bombers. Since 1988, there has been an upward trend in the number of terrorist incidents: 50 in 1988; 203 in 1989; 197 in 1990; 152 in 1991; 215 in 1992; 240 in 1993; 142 in the first half of 1994. The 1994 quarterly average of 71 incidents is 54 percent higher than the average of 46 incidents per quarter compiled since 1988.

America's checkbook diplomacy convinced Israel and the Palestine Liberation Organization (PLO) to recognize each other's right to exist on September 9, 1994, with the historic signing of a Declaration of Principles by Rabin and PLO Chairman Yasir Arafat. It would be fair to say that the increase in attacks, deaths and political violence is escalating due to the intense opposition to the agreement by extremist Palestinian groups such as Hamas and right-wing Jewish groups.

While most of the world has lauded the pact as the most significant peace agreement in decades, enemies of Israel and Israeli settlers in the Occupied Territories, believing they'd been bought out by the U.S.—which essentially they were— have nothing but revenge in mind for Arafat. These "enemies" include some heavy hitters. Both Abu Nidal of the Fatah Revolutionary Council and Ahmed Jibril, leader of the Popular Front for the Liberation of Palestine–General Command (PFLP-GC), have threatened to assassinate Arafat for treason. George Habash, head of the Damascus-based Popular Front for the Liberation of Palestine (PFLP), said the agreement would, ironically, increase *intifada*, the uprising on the West Bank and the Gaza Strip. He was right. Right-wing Jewish settlers and Hamas alike have launched terrorist attacks in an attempt to discredit and dissolve the agreement.

Earlier that year, on May 4, 1994, Rabin and Arafat signed a long-awaited pact allowing Palestinians limited self-rule in the Gaza Strip and Jericho. Under the agreement, Israeli forces were withdrawn from designated areas, turning enforcement over to a Palestinian police force. A week later, the first contingent of nearly 150 Palestinian police officers entered the Gaza Strip from Egypt. (The agreement calls for an eventual force of 9000 officers to police what is to become Palestine.) The new cops were greeted with flowers by inhabitants in the Strip. Not so by Hamas and other radical factions.

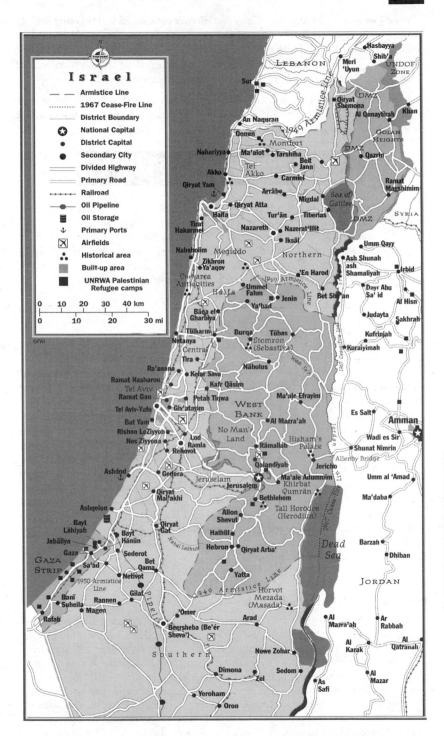

Israel

- — — Armistice Line
- .... 1967 Cease-Fire Line
- ——— District Boundary
- ⊛ National Capital
- • District Capital
- ● Secondary City
- ═══ Divided Highway
- ═══ Primary Road
- ┅┅┅ Railroad
- ●━ Oil Pipeline
- ▤ Oil Storage
- ↓ Primary Ports
- ☒ Airfields
- ⁞ Historical area
- Built-up area
- ■ UNRWA Palestinian Refugee camps

0   10   20   30   40 km
0   10   20   30 mi

While I was doing a radio interview, one listener phoned in and was surprised to hear me include Israel in *DP*'s list of war zones. Then, on April 10, 1996, Israel responded to an April 9 Hezbollah rocket salvo in northern Israel—which injured 40 people—by invading Lebanon. Hezbollah continued to launch hundreds of Katyusha rockets into northern Israel despite the invasion.

Despite the recent peace accords, Israel is still at war within and without. The assassination of Rabin by a right-wing Jew is sad proof that Israel is under attack by even its own people, in addition to Hamas and Hezbollah.

Gee, I wonder why they're so mad...

It seems that their friends, the Israelis, like to make life miserable for their former landlords. Palestinians must carry ID cards. Sixty thousand in Gaza and the West Bank need magnetic-striped ID cards to cross into Israel. There are literally hundreds of Israeli checkpoints that range from minor ID checks to complete strip searches. Over 25,000 Palestinians in Gaza must go through checkpoints every day to their jobs in Israel. Electric fences are being built, license plates are color-coded, and life is generally miserable for these folks concentrated in the areas forcibly occupied by Israel.

The Scoop

Israel was carved out of Palestine by the British after World War II to provide a home for the Jews. The Arabs who had inhabited the region for hundreds of years were not happy. Not happy at all. Like most colonial border carvings, both sides are still arguing about it. What complicates the situation is that Jerusalem is a holy site for Christians, Jews and Muslims. It's a stew pot, filled with just the right spices and garnishes for one helluva long war. The Israelis' land grabs in Egypt, Jordan, Syria and Lebanon have not made them very popular with their neighbors. Peace agreements with their once bellicose neighbors have cooled things down, but Hamas, Hezbollah and their hometown supporters of Iran, Syria and Lebanon aren't just going to forgive and forget. It's been a helluva year for Israel. Yitzhak was assassinated, Hamas launched a series of bus bombings in 1995 and 1996, and Israel invaded Lebanon in April 1996 in an attempt to oust Hezbollah, who continued to pound northern Israel with rockets. The recent spat with Lebanon displaced 10 percent of the population of Lebanon, destroyed 200 homes and caused $600,000 in damage. Israel fired 11,000 shells and launched 1000 aircraft sorties. Despite the cultural and scenic attractions of the Holy Land you could end your vacation as a puff of holy smoke. You stand a better chance of being caught in a terrorist attack in Tel Aviv than in most cities of the world.

The Players

Prime Minister Benjamin Netanyahu

American packaged to the max, Netanyahu is the consummate baby-kissing politician—apple pie style with kosher twist. Maybe a little too kosher. His Likud Party lists so far to the right, soon the Mediterranean will be lapping at the West Bank. His supporters include ultra-orthodox Jews who would blow away Yasir Arafat at the drop of his towel. Netanyahu may represent the biggest threat to Middle East peace since Saddam's scuds rained down upon Jerusalem. The problem is he's just such a likeable guy—and he speaks English with a McDonald's accent. Consequently, everything he says seems as if it were written by White House staffers, or scriptwriters in Hollywood penning a pilot for the night soap, "Golan Heights."

ISRAEL

The Israeli Military

Without the Israeli army, Israel would cease to exist. A tiny nation with a reputation for striking first, Israel has been on the offensive rather than the defensive for most of its short life. The armed forces total 141,000 personnel including 110,000 conscripts. The army consists of 104,000 personnel, including 88,000 conscripts and 598,000 reservists. The navy has 9000 personnel, including 3000 conscripts and 300 naval commandos and a further 10,000 reservists. Naval bases are at Haifa, Ashdod and Eilat. The air force totals 28,000, including 19,000 conscripts and a further 37,000 reservists.

The Israelis spend about 20 percent of their entire budget on defense. Uncle Sam kicks in another US$1.8 billion a year. Troops are stationed in the occupied zones, throughout the country and along the border with Lebanon, where a security zone is controlled by the South Lebanese Army (SLA), a militia funded by Israel. The military is a big part of any Israeli's life in Israel (unless you are an Arab, Christian or Circassian). Military service is four years for officers, three years for men and two years for unmarried women. Annual compulsory reserve duty continues up to the age of 54 for men, 24 for single women. Because of the Palestinian *intifada*, or uprising, annual compulsory reserve duty was increased to 62 days from 42 days in 1988. Jewish and Druze citizens are conscripted, but Christian, Circassian and Muslim citizens are exempt. However, they're permitted to volunteer.

The military budget was US$6.9 billion in 1994, US$4.7 billion in 1990 and US$4.3 billion in 1989. This includes an allocation to cover the Palestinian *intifada* in the Occupied Territories. Troops are also stationed along the border with Lebanon, where a security zone is controlled by the South Lebanese Army. The security zone is designed to prevent guerrilla attacks on the country. In addition, troops are stationed on the Golan Heights. The navy patrols the eastern Mediterranean and the Red Sea. Israel has a strategic cooperation agreement with the U.S.A., signed in 1982.

The fear of an Arab chemical or missile attack has prompted the Israeli government to research and develop increasingly sophisticated weapons. It was the largest foreign participant in the U.S.A.'s Strategic Defence Initiative (SDI). The U.S. paid 80 percent of the cost of the Arrow antimissile system, which Israel can use for its own defense. In addition, the navy is developing an interceptor system capable of destroying missiles, ships and aircraft within a 12-km range. An intelligence gathering satellite is being developed. It's aim is to reduce dependence on U.S. intelligence sources. Although it has never been confirmed, Israel is believed to have the capacity to manufacture nuclear weapons.

Hezbollah

The most dangerous thorn in Israel's side is Hezbollah, the Iranian-backed Shia group that continually battles Israel on their northern border. Under the religious guidance of Sheikh Fadlallah, the most senior cleric in Lebanon, Hezbollah members are typically Shiites recruited from the various Palestinian refugee camps. The Israelis conduct numerous retaliatory attacks against these camps in revenge for Hezbollah's shelling and rocketing of Israel.

Shortly after the revolution in Iran, the country began recruiting the most fanatical Shiites to set up its first major military base outside Iran, at Zabadani in Syria. The Iranians sent in about 5000 Pasadaran to Lebanon to help the fight against Israel. A thousand of these troops fought the Israelis in the Shouf mountains. After the fighting ended, 500 Iranians stayed behind in the Bekáa (or Biqáa) Valley under the protection of Syrian forces. The Baalbak area became something of a Silicon Valley for terrorism, where a number of special-interest groups lived and trained, from Abu Nidal's headhunters to the Libyans. The Bekáa Valley became the world headquarters for terrorism in 1982. Supplied from Damascus and supported by Iran, these Iranians quickly consolidated their dominance of

Hezbollah. Soon, Hezbollah would become a federation of 13 Islamic terrorist movements (11 Shiite and two Sunni). Decisions are made by a religious council. Although Sheikh Sayyid Muhammad Hussein Fadlallah says he is not the movement's leader, it's known that his authority is absolute, even if not secured with a title. He was born in 1943 or 1944 in Najaf, Iraq, to a family originally from Lebanon. He rose to prominence after the Iranian revolution. He is an author of two books on Islam: *Islam and the Concept of Power* and *Dialogue in the Koran*. His religious preachings and his political beliefs are one and the same: Jihad is absolute and all encompassing and the war must be fought by whatever means necessary.

Hezbollah's Sayyid Abbas al-Mussawi has vowed that the terrorist group will continue its struggle until the city of Quds (Jerusalem) is liberated.

For more information, see "The Players" section in the Southern Lebanon chapter.

Islamic Jihad

Islamic Jihad sprang from the Muslim Brotherhood in Cairo. It was founded by Dr. Shakaki, a medical student from Gaza when he felt that the Brotherhood would not take direct action against Israel. He inspired the *intifada* in December of 1987, pulling in the support of the Brotherhood, which then formed Hamas, to become a militant arm. The headquarters of the movement is in Damascus, Syria.

The leader of the Palestinian Islamic Jihad, Fathi Shakaki, 43, was assassinated in Malta in October of '95 by Israel's covert agency, the Mossad. The new leader is Ramadan Abadallah Shallah, a British educated teacher who has been living in hiding since the mid'80s. His last job was teaching Islamic studies in Tampa, Florida.

Hamas

Hamas was formed in 1987 in the West Bank as competition to al-Fatah (Arafat's group) for political leadership of the 1.8 million Palestinians in the occupied zones. Currently the group is supported by about 30 percent of the Palestinians in the Gaza Strip and is the second most powerful organization behind Fatah, the PLO's military wing. The *intifada* (which began in the summer of 1988) hardened Hamas into the most ardent and powerful group defending the Palestinians' perceived right to not only self-determination, but to the destruction of Israel. Part of their success strategy is a decentralized structure based on the Muslim Brotherhood, a popular Islamic fundamentalist group.Hamas has been having its lunch handed to it by Shin Bet (the Israeli Secret Police). In August of '95, Shin Bet held a news conference to gloat over the capture of Abdel Nasser Issa, 27, and his apprentice, considered to be the head bomb-maker for Hamas. Both men credited Yehiya Ayash—aka "The Engineer"—as the man who taught them their bomb-making skills in the Gaza Strip. Issa is accused of recruiting and transporting suicide bombers. The arrest also confirmed that the group's spiritual mentor, Sheik Izzadine Khalil, is now in Damascus. Khalil was deported from Israel in 1992.

But in a turn of events for Hamas, Ayash was assassinated by Shin Bet in January 1996 in a daring cellular phone explosion in Gaza City. Most Israelis rejoiced, while others pondered how many Palestinians Ayash had taught his trade to and how many of those would employ their new skills to avenge their mentor's death.

The head of the political wing of Hamas is Mousa Abu Marzuk, 45, who has lived in New York for 14 years and has a permanent resident visa. He was captured in New York, evading a shoot-to-kill order issued by Israel after the Tel Aviv bus bombing. He is a guest of the U.S. government, prisoner #42665054 in the New York Correctional Facility. Israel is currently seeking his extradition. Oddly enough, the political wing wants to make peace with Israel, but the military wing, Issedine al-Qassam, wants to completely eliminate both the state and people of Israel. Not a wise opening bid for successful negotiation. For now, Hamas was left without a chair when the music stopped. When the peace was forged, it was the ever-smiling bad boy Yassar Arafat who got the seat and the dubious distinction of forging the Palestinian's future. Now Arafat, once the most reviled terrorist leader, is viewed as a lackey with little chance of demanding reforms from the hard-line government of Israel. Hamas, on the other hand, has a strange luster now that its members are hunted downed and killed by Israeli spooks. In Gaza, where 65 percent of the Palestinian population is under 18 and 30 percent have spent time in an Israeli jail, it is akin to voting for Ringo Starr or Johnny Rotten to represent you.

For now, there are plenty of angry 14 to 20-year-olds to toss rocks, pull triggers and vaporize themselves for Hamas. The only university these kids have a chance of attending is the ultra-radical Islamic University of Gaza.

Hamas is short for *Harakat al-Muqaama al-Islamiya* (Islamic Resistance Movement), but also means zeal or enthusiasm in Arabic. Hamas members are not the well-trained military terrorists of al-Fatah but a youthful cadre of young Palestinians mostly enlisted from the poorest parts of the Occupied Territories. Most believe that they will find salvation and martyrdom by destroying Israel. Every member is sworn to destroy Israel and to create a new Islamic state based on the Koran. Initially, their campaign of rock throwing turned to stabbing Israeli citizens, including teenage schoolchildren. After Hamas killed five Israeli Defense Force members, 415 Hamas members were exiled to southern Lebanon by the Israelis, provoking an international outcry. In the seven years of *intifada*, Israelis have killed more than 2000 Palestinians. Hamas has slain more than 575 collaborators and more than 160 Israelis. The attacks have escalated in their frequency and nature, including the recent bombing of a Tel Aviv bus. Hamas is expected to continue to terrorize Israelis into the foreseeable future, and Yasir Arafat and his Palestinian police will be expected to control Hamas, thereby pitting Muslim against Muslim to maintain peace with the Jews. The Jordanian chapter seems to be the most hawkish of the bunch and was credited with the July 1995 bombing in Ramat Gan.

Hamas is loosing its support amongst the Palestinians and looking to mend fences with the PLO.

Izz ad-Din al Qassam Brigade

The military wing of Hamas is the smallest section of the group, numbering only a few hundred young men. But the group's political followers number in the tens of thousands. Hamas, like Hezbollah, has created schools, clinics, mosques and financial support systems for the poor, widows and orphans. The group even sponsors a soccer team.

It is important to note that the Qassam Brigade and militant Palestinians will continue to attack, murder and terrorize Israelis while the political structuring continues. Volunteers to the Qassam Brigade are trained in Sudanese camps and in Southern Lebanon by Hezbollah. The Iranians provide over US$30 million a year, including use of a radio station in southern Lebanon that broadcasts messages of revolution into Israel. The Hamas base of power is in the West Bank and Gaza Strip. They have managed to create an alliance of the 10 Palestinian groups including the PLFP and the DFLP. The leadership of Hamas is young and highly educated. Hamas runs information offices out of Amman, Jordan (Ibrahim Ghosha and Mohammed Nazzal); Teheran; Lebanon (Mustapha Kanua), and Khartoum (Mohammed Siam). Their U.S. rep (Moussa Abu Marzouk) operates out of Damascus.

Because of Hamas' political strength and the support it receives from Palestinians, it finds a ready source of financing from Muslim and non-Muslim wallets alike. America is an important source of funding for Hamas. It is alleged by the Israelis that the leadership and central control of Hamas is actually in the United States, an accusation once dismissed by the FBI but now being studied very seriously.

Organizations considered supportive of Hamas in the U.S. are the following:

The United Association for Studies and Research in Springfield, Virginia
The Islamic Association for Palestine in Dallas, Texas
The Monitor and the Al-Zaituni (Olive Tree in Arabic)
The Islamic Committee for Palestine
Muslim Youth League
Mostazafan Foundation in New York
Muslim Students' Association in U.S. and Canada
Al-Da'wa (the Call)

Yasir Arafat and the PLO (Palestine Liberation Organization)

The PLO began in 1964 as a Palestinian nationalist umbrella organization dedicated to the establishment of an independent Palestinian state. After the 1967 Arab-Israeli war, control of the PLO went to the most dominant of the various *fedayeen* militia groups, the most dominant of which was Yasir Arafat's al-Fatah. In 1969, Arafat became chairman of the PLO's executive committee, a position he still holds. In the early 1980s, the PLO became fragmented into several contending groups but remains the preeminent Palestinian organization. The United States considers the Palestine Liberation Organization to be an umbrella organization that includes several constituent groups and individuals holding differing views on terrorism. At the same time, U.S. policy accepts that elements of the PLO have advocated, carried out, or accepted responsibility for acts of terrorism. PLO chairman Arafat publicly renounced terrorism in December 1988 on behalf of the PLO. The United States considers that all PLO groups, including al-Fatah, Force 17, Hawari Group, PLF and the PFLP, are bound by Arafat's renunciation of terrorism. The U.S.-PLO dialogue was suspended after the PLO failed to condemn the May 30, 1990, PLF attack on Israeli beaches. PLF head Abu Abbas left the PLO executive committee in September 1991; his seat was filled by another PLF member.

In the early 1970s several groups affiliated with the PLO carried out numerous international terrorist attacks. By the mid-1970s, under international pressure, the PLO claimed it would restrict attacks to Israel and the Occupied Territories. Several terrorist attacks were later performed by groups affiliated with the PLO/al-Fatah—including the Hawari group, the Palestine Liberation Front (PLF) and Force 17—against targets inside and outside of Israel.

Formerly the number-one bad boy of terrorism, Yasir Arafat and his fashion-conscious wife have gone mainstream. It remains to be seen whether he can be as powerful in peace as he was in war. Arafat's administrative skills are primitive at best, and his handling of economic issues in the autonomous zones of Jericho and the Gaza Strip particularly have come under fire—the protests fueled by Arafat's own assertions that the peace accords would bring greater prosperity to Palestinians. Skeptical investors are staying away from the Gaza Strip, at least until the former terrorist charts an economic course for the newly liberated Palestine.

Arafat's group al-Fatah trained more terrorists and freedom fighters than any other group in the 1960s and 1970s. Running the government of the West Bank, Gaza and Jericho may be more of a challenge than the terrorist battle he fought to get to this position. As Israel withdraws its occupying troops, it will be up to Arafat's group to provide security and management of these impoverished, undeveloped and primitive areas. More importantly, he will be expected to protect the Jewish settlers (or occupiers, from the Palestinian point of view) from Hamas.

Perhaps wishful thinking, but Arafat feels that economic aid will undermine the Hamas' zeal and build a lasting peace. He doesn't have much choice; a forceful attempt to restrain Hamas will plunge Gaza and Jericho into civil war. Now he must battle two enemies instead of one. In the meantime, Arafat continues to tiptoe around continued Hamas bus bombings in Tel Aviv and Shin Bet assassinations of Palestinians in his own new backyard.

Popular Front for the Liberation of Palestine (PFLP)

George Habash's group of about 800 Palestinians follows a Marxist-Leninist doctrine and disagrees with Arafat's deal with the Israelis. The PFLP lost a lot of steam when Wadi-Haddad was taken out in 1978. Qaddafi and Assad provide most of the green for this hard-line group. For more information, see "The Players" section in the Lebanon chapter.

Popular Front for the Liberation of Palestine-General Command (PFLP-GC)

PFLP-GC's leader Ahmad Jabril regarded, and still does, Habash's PFLP as a bunch of wimps, so he and his men split in 1968 to focus on killing and maiming, while Habash employed just a little less violence to achieve his ends. Because Jabril was a captain in the Syrian army when Assad was minister of defense at the time Israel took the Golan Heights, it's understandable why the PFLP-GC is tighter with Syria than latex on an aerobics instructor. The PFLP-GC is headquartered in Damascus. Iran chips in when they run short of funds.

The group's sensationalist suicide attacks, employing everything from hang gliders to hot-air balloons, has given its "airline" the fewest number of members of any frequent flyer program found in Palestine. Although not as large as the vanilla-flavored PFLP, the PFLP-GC is still a major threat to Israelis. For more information, see "The Players" section in the Lebanon chapter.

Palestine Liberation Front (PLF)

This is a break-away faction of the PFLP-GC (which is a break away faction of the PFLP, which is a break-away faction of the PLO). If this sounds like a scene from Monty Python's *Life of Brian*, you're not far off. The PLF is led by Abu Abbas, or Muhammad Abbas, who usually hangs out in Libya with his buddy Qaddafi or in the Bekaa Valley. Abbas' group is tiny, possibly nonexistent. Their most famous job was the attack on the *Achille Lauro* and the less than admirable killing of wheelchair-bound Leon Klinghoffer. For more information, see "The Players" section in the Southern Lebanon chapter.

Democratic Front for the Liberation of Palestine (DFLP)

The Hawatmeh faction does not go along with the Arafat-brokered peace and continues their opportunistic attacks and raids. For more information, see "The Players" section in the Lebanon chapter.

Israeli Extremists

There are random incidents of far right-wing Israelis and external Jewish groups such as the Kahane Chai and Kach, as well as individuals striking against Palestinians and moderate Jews. These groups present little danger to Americans.

JDL

About 150 hotheads who were implicated in a number of bombings in the U.S. back in the early '80s and late '70s.

Getting In

Ben Gurion International Airport is 20 km from the center of Tel Aviv. Taxis are common and a bus service runs every 15 minutes. A passport, an onward or return ticket and proof of sufficient funds are required. A three-month visa may be issued for no charge upon arrival and may be renewed. Anyone who has been refused entry or experienced difficulties with his/her visa status during a previous visit can obtain information from the Israeli embassy or nearest consulate regarding the advisability of attempting to return to Israel. Arab-Americans who have overstayed their tourist visas during previous visits to Israel or in the Occupied Territories can expect, at a minimum, delays at ports of entry (including Ben Gurion Airport) and the possibility of being denied entry. To avoid these problems, such persons may apply for permission

ISRAEL

to enter at the nearest Israeli embassy or consulate before traveling. For further entry information, travelers may contact the following:

Embassy of Israel

> *3514 International Drive, N.W.*
> *Washington, D.C. 20008*
> ☎ *(202) 364-5500*

Or contact the nearest Israeli consulate general in Los Angeles, San Francisco, Miami, Atlanta, Chicago, New Orleans, Boston, New York, Philadelphia or Houston.

Getting Around

The major airport is Ben Gurion International Airport with a smaller civilian airport in Tel Aviv. There are also airports in Jerusalem, Haifa, Eilat, Herzlya, Mahanayim and Sodom. A new airport at Eilat is under construction and will replace the old one. National airline El Al operates international flights to Europe, North America and some African countries.

Israel has a modern road system, although it abounds with crazy drivers. In 1988 the paved road network was 12,980 km, including 3995 km of intercity roads of which 284 km were motorways. Road accidents have been on the increase in the last decade, due mainly to deteriorating road conditions. The Israeli cabinet has, on several occasions, pledged to improve road safety. There are approximately three fatalities for every 100 million km traveled.

The rail system is operated by Israel State Railways under the supervision of the Israel Ports and Railways Authority. The length of the main lines is 528 km and secondary lines and sidings total 337 km. The main passenger service is between Tel Aviv and Haifa, with some trains continuing to Nahariya in the north. The government has been building a rapid railway service between Netanya and Tel Aviv to solve the traffic congestion in northern Tel Aviv. In addition, the railway line south is being extended to the Red Sea port of Eilat.

Hassles with Police

Israel has strict security measures that may affect visitors. Prolonged questioning and detailed searches may take place at the time of entry and/or departure at all points of entry to Israel or the Occupied Territories. American citizens with Arab surnames may expect close scrutiny at Ben Gurion Airport and the Allenby Bridge from Jordan. For security reasons, delays or obstacles in bringing in or departing with cameras or electronics equipment are not unusual. Items commonly carried by travelers such as toothpaste, shaving cream and cosmetics may be confiscated or destroyed for security reasons, especially at the Allenby Bridge. During searches and questioning, access may be denied to U.S. consular officers, lawyers or family members. Should questions arise at the Allenby Bridge, U.S. citizens can telephone the U.S. Consulate General in Jerusalem for assistance at ☎ *[972] (02) 253-288*. If questions arise at Ben Gurion Airport, U.S. citizens can phone the U.S. embassy in Tel Aviv at ☎ *[972] (03) 517-4338*.

Broadcasting and the Press

Under the military censorship system covering defense and security matters, journalists are required at all times to submit all relevant items to the censor's office for approval before transmitting them abroad or issuing them in the local media. The occupied territories are officially open to media coverage, except that local commanders may close specific areas for a limited period "for operational reasons." Since the *intifada* began in the occupied West Bank and Gaza Strip in 1988, censorship, closures, arrests, detentions and distribution restrictions have muzzled Palestinian newspapers; those that can still publish are virtually unable to use original material. Various measures were also enforced on newspapers in Israel and on foreign media correspondents, most of whom are Israeli citizens. The army has sometimes imposed a virtual news blackout. The media has regularly complained about security forces personnel impersonating journalists in order to obtain information about the Palestinian *intifada*, and journalists claim it puts their lives at risk.

Israel Television and Israel Radio are owned by the government and run by the Israel Broadcasting Authority (IBA). Its central committee members oversee programming. Israel TV broadcasts on one national channel in Hebrew and Arabic, funded by viewer license fees and, more recently, by commercial sponsorship. The government plans to set up an independent commercial second channel. The IBA is a member of the European Broadcasting Union (EBU) and receives its satellite feeds. There were 1.18 million television sets and 2.07 million radio receivers in use in 1988.

Israel Radio broadcasts nationally on five stations, one of which is in Arabic. External Services broadcast in Hebrew, easy Hebrew, Arabic, Moghrabi, English, French, Russian, Spanish, Portuguese, Amharic, Bukharian, Georgian, Persian, Hungarian, Romanian, Yiddish and Ladino. The Soviet Union used to jam Israel Radio's international broadcasts, especially the Russian language service, but this stopped in November 1988.

Dangerous Places

The Occupied Territories

Following the killings of Palestinians in Hebron on February 25, 1994, the Israeli government closed the West Bank and Gaza Strip. The West Bank has since been partially reopened. Travel restrictions may be reimposed with little or no advance notification, and curfews placed on cities or towns in the Occupied Territories may be extended or, if lifted, reimposed. Palestinian demonstrations in the West Bank and the Gaza Strip have led to violent confrontations between the demonstrators and Israeli authorities, resulting in the wounding or death of some participants. Demonstrations and similar incidents can occur without warning. Stone-throwing and other forms of protest can escalate. Violent incidents such as stabbings have occurred. Vehicles are regularly damaged.

Northern Israel

See "Southern Lebanon."

East Jerusalem

Although the Department of State had warned all U.S. citizens against traveling to East Jerusalem, the West Bank and Gaza, the consular section of the U.S. consulate general at *27 Nablus Road, East Jerusalem*, remains open. Traveling by public or private transportation in parts of East Jerusalem less frequented by tourists, however, remains dangerous. If persons must travel to other areas of East Jerusalem, including the Old City, or to the West Bank, they may consult with the U.S. consulate general in Jerusalem, and in the case of travel to the Gaza Strip, with the U.S. embassy in Tel Aviv, for current information on the advisability of such travel.

Suicide Bombers' homes

Two months after "The Engineer" was cellphone whacked by the Israelis, the Israeli army blew up his family home in the West Bank village of Rafat in March 1996, sending a clear message to suicide bombers and other Hamas volunteers that anyone considering blowing their own viscera into the heavens in the name of Allah may want to consider the fate of their families before pulling the pin. Would-be Jihad martyrs, take note: After you kiss your own good-bye, the Mossad will make quite certain your kids, mom and pop, and other relatives quickly join you in Mohammed's tent in the sky. Or at least the Israelis will blow up their houses.

Dangerous Things

Buses

One and a half million Israelis use the bus every day, almost 25 percent of the population. There have been nine suicide attacks on buses since April of 1994, resulting in 67 people killed. Injuries run at two to three times the death rate. One American tourist was among the dead. Violent incidents also involved bus stops. The U.S. embassy is advising its employees and American citizens in Israel to avoid use of public transportation, especially buses and bus stops. This restriction does not apply to tour buses. Although Israelis must take the bus, only thrill seekers and cheapskates need expose themselves to what is Israel's most dangerous form of transportation.

Driving

Traffic fatalities increased from 387 in 1985 to 415 in 1986 and to about 500 in 1987. In 1986 there were 1.5 motor vehicles involved in road accidents per 1 million km traveled. There are 3.2 fatalities for every 100 million km traveled.

Rocket Attacks

Rocket attacks from Hezbollah positions in Lebanese territory can occur without warning close to the northern border of Israel.

Land Mines

In the Golan Heights, there are live land mines in many areas and some minefields have not been clearly marked or fenced. Visitors who walk only on established roads or trails reduce the risk of injury from mines.

Being arrested in the West Bank and Gaza Strip

U.S. citizens arrested or detained in the West Bank or Gaza Strip on suspicion of security offenses often are not permitted to communicate with consular officials, lawyers or family members in a timely manner during the interrogation period of their case. Youths who are over the age of 14 have been detained and tried as adults. The U.S. embassy is not normally notified of the arrests of Americans in the West Bank by Israeli authorities and access to detainees is frequently delayed.

Getting Sick

Medical care and facilities throughout Israel are generally excellent. In 1987, there were 153 hospitals, including 60 private hospitals, with 27,500 beds. Israel has one of the highest doctor-patient ratios in the world, about one doctor for every 339 patients. Travelers can find information in English about emergency medical facilities and after-hours pharmacies in the *Jerusalem Post* newspaper. Water is normally safe to drink, but bottled water is a better choice for the cautious. Tap water outside the main towns is not safe for drinking.

Nuts and Bolts

Israel is a small country, about 20,700 square km (7992 square mi.), that forcibly occupies the Golan Heights (annexed from Syria in 1981; 1150 square km, 444 square mi.), the West Bank (annexed from Jordan; 5878 square km, 2270 square mi.) and the Gaza Strip (363 square km, 140 square mi.). The territories currently occupied and administered by Israel are the West Bank, Gaza Strip, Golan Heights and East Jerusalem. The Israeli Ministry of Defense administers the Occupied Territories of the West Bank and Gaza Strip. In 1993, 65 Israelis were killed and 390 wounded; 14 Palestinians were killed by Israeli citizens; 83 Palestinians were killed by other Palestinians. In 1992, Fatah and Hamas were going at it and managed to kill 200 Palestinians between them.

The population includes 635,000 Muslims, 105,000 Christians (almost all Arabs) and 78,000 Druze. Mass immigration of Jews from the former Soviet Union since late 1989 has swelled the population. Although Israel claims Jerusalem as its capital, the claim—especially to East Jerusalem, annexed in 1967—is disputed by most countries. The currency is the new *shekel* (IS), with 100 *agorot* to the *shekel*. The weather is arid, warm and mild most of the year with hot days and cool evenings. Because of its higher elevation, Jerusalem is quite cool, and even cold in the winter. In Tel Aviv and along the coast, the weather is more humid with warmer nights.

The Jewish Sabbath, from Friday dusk until Saturday dusk, is rigorously observed. Stores close on Friday by 2 p.m. and do not open again until Sunday morning. Most cinemas and restaurants are closed on Friday night. In most cities during the Sabbath there is no public transport (except for taxis), postal service or banking service. It is considered a violation of the Sabbath (Saturdays) to smoke in public places, such as restaurants and hotels. The same is true on the six main Jewish religious holidays.

Jewish religious laws (*Kashrut*) prohibit the mixing of milk products and meat at the same meal. Kashrut is strictly enforced in hotels. Because of this, some restaurants serve only fish and dairy dishes while others serve only meat dishes. Pork is banned under religious laws, but some restaurants serve it, listing it euphemistically as white steak.

Banks are open from 8:30 a.m. to 12:30 p.m., and from 2 p.m. to 6:30 p.m. on Sunday, Tuesday and Thursday, and from 8:30 a.m. to 12:30 p.m. on Monday, Wednesday and Friday. Businesses are open from 8:30 a.m. to 7:30 p.m. Sunday to Thursday; some are open 8:30 a.m. to 2:30 p.m. on Fridays. Government offices are open from 7:30 a.m. to 4 p.m. Sunday through Thursday.

Registration

U.S. citizens who register at the U.S. embassy in Tel Aviv or the U.S. consulate general in Jerusalem can obtain updated information on travel and security within Israel and the Occupied Territories.

Embassy and Consulate Locations

U.S. Embassy
71 Hayarkon Street
Tel Aviv, Israel
U.S. mailing address
PSC 98, Box 100
APO AE 09830
☎ *[972] (3) 517-4338*

U.S. Consulate General
27 Nablus Road
Jerusalem
U.S. mailing address
PSC 98, Box 100
APO AE 09830
☎ *[972] (2) 253-288 (via Israel)*
☎ *[972] (2) 253-201 (after hours)*

U.S. Consular Agent,
Jonathan Friedland, in Haifa
12 Jerusalem Street
Haifa 33132
☎ *[972] (4) 670-615*

Useful Addresses

Central Bureau of Statistics
Hakirya, Romema, Jerusalem
☎ *[972] (2) 553553*
FAX [972] (2) 553325

Federation of Israeli Chambers of Commerce
P.O. Box 20027, 84 Hahashmonaim Street
Tel Aviv 67011
☎ *[972] (2) 5612444*
FAX [972] (2) 5612614

Ministry of Communications
P.O. Box 29515
Tel Aviv
☎ *[972] (3) 5198247*
FAX [972] (2) 5198109

Ministry of Trade and Industry
Palace Buildings
P.O. Box 299, 30 Agron Boulevard
Jerusalem 91002
☎ *2-750111*
FAX 2-253407

Ministry of Tourism
24 King George Street
P.O. Box 1018
Jerusalem 91000
☎ *[972] (2) 754811*
FAX [972] (2) 253407 or (2) 250890

Dangerous Days

04/10/1996 Israel invaded Hamas positions and cities within Lebanon after a Hezbollah rocket attack on northern Israel injured 40 people.

11/04/1996 Prime Minister Yitzhak Rabin assassinated by right-wing extremist.

10/11/1994 The Palestine Liberation Organization (PLO) Central Council approved Chairman Yasir Arafat's peace deal with Israel by a vote of 63 to eight, with 11 members abstaining or absent.

09/23 Yom Kippur.

09/13/1994 Israel and the Palestinian Liberation Organization signed a peace agreement in Washington, D.C., outlining a plan for Palestinian self-rule in the Israeli Occupied Territories.

09/09/1993 The PLO and Israel signed a mutual recognition agreement.

12/17/1992 More than 400 suspected members of Hamas were forcibly expelled from Israel into Lebanon, following the kidnap-murder of an Israeli border policeman. The expellees were refused entry into Lebanon and forced to camp in the Israeli-controlled security zone in south Lebanon.

12/16/1991 The United Nations General Assembly repealed the 1975 resolution which said Zionism is a form of racism.

10/30/1991 The first round of Arab-Israeli peace talks began in Madrid, Spain.

05/15/1991 Palestinian Struggle Day.

01/15/1991 Abu Iyad, the second-ranking PLO leader, and two other high-ranking PLO officials were assassinated by a guard suspected of working for the Abu Nidal Organization (ANO).

10/08/1990 Eighteen Arabs died during clashes with police at the Temple Mount religious site.

05/20/1990 A lone Israeli gunman killed eight Arab laborers in Rishon le Ziyyon, south of Tel Aviv. Nine workers were injured. The gunman was identified as a discharged Israeli soldier.

07/28/1989 Israeli commandos seized Shaykh Obeid from a village in southern Lebanon and detained him in Israel on allegations of involvement in terrorist activity on behalf of Hezbollah.

12/09/1987 Date used to mark the beginning of the *intifada*, or uprising on the West Bank and the Gaza Strip.

10/01/1985 The Israeli Air Force bombed the headquarters of the Palestinian Liberation Organization (PLO) in Tunis.

05/17/1983 Israel signed an accord with Lebanon for the withdrawal of Israeli troops from most of south Lebanon.

06/06/1982 Israel invaded Lebanon.

06/04/1982 Israeli planes bombed Beirut.

ISRAEL

Dangerous Days

06/03/1982   Abu Nidal terrorists critically injured the Israeli ambassador to the United Kingdom in an attack in London. The government of Israel used the incident as a pretext for launching the invasion of Lebanon in the "Peace for Galilee" operation.

06/06/1981   Israeli warplanes attacked an Iraqi nuclear power plant near Baghdad.

02/19/1980   Egypt sends first ambassador to Israel.

05/15/1979   The Arab 15 May Organization under Muhammad al-Umari was founded from the remnants of Wadi Haddad's Popular Front for the Liberation of Palestine—Special Operations Group (PFLP-SOG). The group was headquartered in Baghdad until it disbanded in 1984–1985.

03/26/1979   Egyptian-Israeli peace treaty.

09/17/1978   Camp David accords signed.

03/16/1978   Israel forces invade Lebanon.

07/04/1976   The Israeli raid on Entebbe airport in Uganda freeing 103 hostages from a hijacked Israeli airliner.

03/30/1976   Land day protests by Israeli Arabs against alleged expropriation of Arab property.

12/21/1973   Geneva Peace Conference opens.

10/06/1973   The Yom Kippur War begins.

12/28/1972   Black September terrorists took hostages after seizing the Israeli embassy in Bangkok. The hostages were released in exchange for safe conduct.

09/06/1972   Palestinian Black September terrorists massacred Israeli athletes at the Munich Olympics.

05/30/1972   Members of the Japanese Red Army (JRA) killed 26 people in a massacre at Lod Airport.

02/21/1970   Suspected members of the PFLP-GC placed a bomb on a Swissair passenger jet enroute from Zurich to Tel Aviv, resulting in the death of all 47 passengers.

07/22/1968   Members of the Popular Front for the Liberation of Palestine (PFLP) hijacked an El Al flight enroute to Tel Aviv and forced it to land in Algiers. The attack marked the first aircraft hijacking by a Palestinian group. The hijackers were said to have believed Israeli General Ariel Sharon was on the flight. The passengers and crew were detained by Algeria for six weeks.

06/05/1967   The Six Day War ends.

05/31/1967   Israeli troops captured East Jerusalem in the Six Day War.

01/01/1964   Fatah Day. The Palestine Liberation Organization (PLO) was founded at a meeting in Jerusalem.

04/14/1949   Holocaust Memorial Day.

Dangerous Days

03/21/1949   Palestinian Solidarity Day. Arab solidarity day with the Palestinian people against Israel.

01/07/1949   A cease-fire was signed by the major combatants, ending the first Arab-Israeli war.

05/14/1948   Israel was proclaimed a state, as the British mandate in Palestine expired. Arab armies launched attacks on Israel immediately following the proclamation.

05/14/1948   The first Arab-Israeli war began shortly after the State of Israel was proclaimed.

05/07/1948   Israeli Independence Day, as observed by Arabs in the Occupied Territories.

11/02/1917   Anniversary of the Balfour Declaration, which promised a Jewish homeland in Palestine. Demonstrations in the Occupied Territories and the Gaza Strip area have occurred on this date.

Monrovia

Liberia
★★★★

Smell No Taste

In Liberia, there's a small town called Smell No Taste. One legend has it the town was named because of its proximity to the former Robertsfield International Airport. Locals gazed longingly at well-heeled passengers hopping on planes bound for Paris, London and New York. The Liberians could only fantasize about such a way of life. They were close enough to smell, but not close enough to taste. The same can be said of peace in Liberia. Peace has been a carrot dangled in front of Liberians' noses more than 12 times during the seven-year-old civil war here. "Close" only matters in horseshoes and hand grenades.

Founded in 1822, Liberia was an attempt—an experiment, really—by the American Colonization Society to create a homeland in West Africa for freed slaves from the United States. It became the Free and Independent Republic of Liberia in 1847.

It's interesting that a group of individuals so jaded by the racial strata system of 19th-century America chose to re-create the United States constitution on the other side of the Atlantic. As Africa's first "republic," Liberia's debut government

SIERRA
LEONE

Gueckedou
Voinjama
Kailahun
Panguma
Pendembu
Zorzor
Kenema
Moa
Joru
Gbeya
Lofa
Lola
Via
Zimmi
Noway Camp
Saint Paul
Bong
Gbarnga
Grand
Cape
Mount
Bomi Hills
Sulima
Tubmanburg
Bong
Town
Totota
Robertsport
Bomi
Margibi
Kle
Kakata
Montserrado
Grand
Bassa
Monrovia
Gardnersville
Harbel
Saint John
Paynesville
Buchanan

Liberia

- National Capital
- County Seat
- Secondary City
- Airport
- County Border
- Road
- Railroad

| 0 | 25 | 50 | 75 km |
| 0 | 25 | | 50 mi |

River Cess

Atlantic Ocean

©FWI

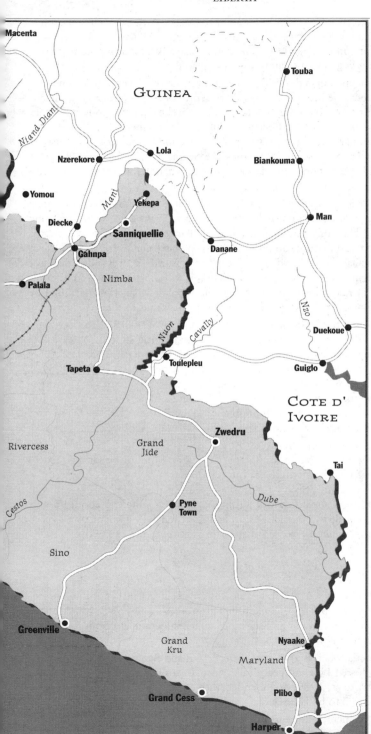

was modeled directly after the one it sought to escape. With names like Joseph J. Roberts, William V.S. Tubman, Charles Taylor and William R. Tolbert, Jr., prominent figures in Liberian history read more like a Palm Beach polo team roster than a struggling ragtag community of displaced slaves.

The attempt at creating a duplicate America in Africa, however, never came full-circle, namely because more than a century's worth of efforts at bringing the aboriginal population onto the same "playing field" as the emigrants proved unsuccessful. Instead of democracy, liberty and all that stuff, Liberia's course became marred by factional fighting, civil war, partitioning and bloody coups led not by men with sinister, nasty-sounding names like Stalin, Arafat, Noriega, Hitler or Amin, but with such innocuous, landed-gentryish handles as Doe, Taylor and Johnson. Sounds like a Savannah law firm.

Instead of freedom for all, Liberia has become a free-for-all, reduced to primal clashes among rival clans, randomly slaughtering each other with old machine guns from the back of ancient, dented jeeps. Bands of marauders cut swaths across the rain forest plateau, donning Halloween masks and bolt-action rifles, as they rape and pillage in small villages before finally razing them. Calling the situation in modern Liberia a "civil war" is giving it too much status—crediting it with too much organization and purpose. The reality is villagers slaughtered by tribal-based militias that mark their territory with the skulls of their victims.

One of the few Liberian leaders with any longevity was William V.S. Tubman, who was in his sixth term as president when he died during surgery in 1971. He was replaced by his longtime associate, William R. Tolbert, Jr. Tolbert actually lasted nine years in office, before he was ousted by a mere master sergeant, Samuel Doe, in 1980. Yet another coup attempt was borne by Charles Taylor, a senior official in Doe's government, in 1989. Leaving a bloody wake in capturing most of the nation's economic and population centers, Taylor failed by a whisker to wrestle power from Doe by mid-July 1990.

Shortly afterwards, a six-nation West African peacekeeping force called the Economic Community of West African States Cease-Fire Monitoring Group (ECOMOG) essentially partitioned Liberia into two zones. The first encompassed the capital of Monrovia and was led by President Amos Sawyer. The other half, run by Taylor and his National Patriotic Front (NPFL), amounted to about 95 percent of Liberian territory (World support had been generally enjoyed by Sawyer's marginal slice of the apple pie until the latest peace accords signed in August 1995.)

Reconciliation and peace agreements were signed like journalists' bar tabs. A March 1991 conference failed to get anything accomplished but the reelection of Sawyer as interim president. Despite a peace agreement in 1991, fighting continued to flare. Another peace agreement and cease-fire in July 1993, which established an interim government and set up general democratic elections, crumbled a short time later in November.

Gambia, Nigeria, Mali, Ivory Coast, Switzerland and Benin are among the venues that have hosted Liberian peace talks since Taylor launched the civil war the day before Christmas, 1989. Some ended with agreements hailed at the time as historic. All proved to be failures.

The 12th agreement, signed in Benin with U.N. guarantees, seemed the most likely to succeed. It ended up in tatters. Only 3000 of Liberia's estimated 60,000 fighters—many of them teenagers addicted to drugs along with killing and raping civilians—have been disarmed.

In August 1994, there were accusations by ECOMOG in Liberia that Cote d'Ivoire (Ivory Coast) was supplying arms and ammunition to Taylor's NPFL in violation of a United Nations embargo. The embargo on shipping arms to Liberia was imposed by the United Nations in August 1992, following repeated accusations by ECOMOG and the former Liberian Interim Government that Cote d'Ivoire (Ivory Coast) and neighboring Burkina Faso (formerly Upper Volta) were openly supporting Taylor's forces.

ECOMOG's COS General Femi Williams claimed that a dozen lorries from Cote d'Ivoire had delivered arms and ammunition to the headquarters of the NPFL in Gbarnga 120 kilometers (75 miles) west of the Liberian-Cote d'Ivoire border. A charge the Cote d'Ivoire Foreign Ministry vehemently denied, citing that its 340-mile border with Liberia isn't entirely manageable and part of ECOMOG's responsibility to monitor it. ECOMOG has also claimed links in arms trafficking between Burkina Faso and the NPFL. In July 1994, the Liberian transition government charged that 3000 Burkinabe as well as Gambian mercenaries were operating in the ranks of the NPFL troops.

Regardless, Taylor continued to put up a fight. In 1990, his forces sat opposite the presidential mansion in Monrovia for a month, but were never able to take the city because ECOMOG arrived and put an end to the fighting.

At least a third of Liberia's prewar population of 2.5 million fled the country after fighting broke out on December 24, 1989, when Taylor invaded Liberia from the Ivory Coast. Forty percent of the population is living in accessible areas, reflecting the huge number displaced. In 1993, the U.N. estimated 150,000 have died, but stopped counting after that. It has become nearly impossible for relief workers to operate in rebel-controlled areas. Military structure and law and order are a bad joke. A peace accord signed in August, 1995 called for countrywide ECOMOG deployment and disarmament of factional fighters, but 10 months later neither of these processes had gotten off the ground.

Liberia is currently run by a six member interim council of state, sometimes erroneously referred to as a collective presidency. Taylor is one of three warlords sitting on the council, which is led by a civilian, Wilton Sankawulo—admittedly something of a Taylor stooge.

Peace in 1996 wouldn't last long. In April 1996, Monrovia was again launched into lawlessness. Fighting resumed in earnest between the rival factions. In only three days, Monrovia toppled into anarchy. Thousands fled the capital city in panic. As many as 20,000 Liberians descended upon the residential annex of the U.S. Embassy. U.S. military commandos evacuated about 2000 frightened American citizens and other foreigners by chopper to the Sierra Leone capital of Freetown, starting in the middle of the night on April 8, as Monrovia's airport was destroyed in the fighting. Evacuations continued for at least two months.

And what about Smell No Taste? Today, as many as 200 people flee from battles in central Liberia to Smell No Taste every day, bringing the number of displaced people living here to more than 40,000. However, they're no longer drooling over arriving and departing jet-setters—too busy trying to find something to eat.

Fly the Friendly Flag

Ever notice that small type after those cool cruise ads? It usually says Liberian Registry. Yes, you read right, Liberia, the country without a postal system, phone network or even a government sells a lot of flags and registrations. Over 1600 ships totalling 59.8 million gross tons fly the Liberian flag. In fact, the $50 million in fees paid to the Liberian government comprises 90 percent of the revenue to the government in tough times. It is called a flag of convenience, and shipping lines escape many of the taxes and restrictions imposed by more sedate countries. Liberia maintains that it spends 10 percent of its earnings training ship inspectors and says they are second to none in safety. The government of Liberia is run by a six-member council that includes tribal chiefs, warlords and politicians. Charles Taylor, a former civil servant and now lead member in the council, started the civil war in 1989, now says that none of the funds is used for the military but instead go towards schools, travel and payroll.

The checks are cashed by an American company called International Trust Company, which manages the registration business for the government of Liberia. The International Maritime Organization is permanently based in London, England.

The second most popular country to register ships? Why the conflict-, crime- and drug-free country of Panama, of course.

The Scoop

Liberia was once the most Americanized country in Africa. Created by former slaves who brought American surnames and American-style politics to Africa, Liberia no longer functions as a country. Prolonged civil war has reduced the country to a subsistence economy.

The country is terrorized by up to 60,000 mostly young (sometimes under 15), but always brutal, armed thugs who dress up in masks, wigs and ballroom gowns and use rusty guns and vicious tempers to steal food, rape and butcher people. Anarchy prevails. Bandits and terrorists continue to wax and dismember each other in the countryside, and the capital Monrovia exists at all only because it is surrounded by ECOMOG peacekeepers. And even ECOMOG loses control. In April 1996, any sense of stability that existed in Monrovia at all was shattered by seven weeks of rioting and looting, which forced the American military to evacuate more than 1500 Americans and other foreigners from the U.S. embassy in Monrovia. More than 20,000 frightened civilians took refuge inside the embassy residential complex during the fighting. Inside the city itself, there remains a dawn-to-dusk curfew that has been in place since 1992. Foreigners, when they can be found, are targeted for violent crime. Violent, armed residential break-ins are common. The capital's two airports are closed to commercial airliners; one's closed, period. The other was badly damaged in factional fighting in April 1996. The nearest airports are in Freetown, Sierra Leone and Abidjan, Ivory Coast. But what difference does it make? Cholera is on the rise, and has been killing the people in Monrovia that Taylor's and Roosevelt's boys haven't.

The Players

The Ruling Party

An uneasy alliance between:

Charles Taylor, National Patriotic Front of Liberia (NPFL), Alhaji Kromah, the ULIMO-K faction, George Boley, Liberia Peace Council, Oscar Quiah, Liberia National Conference, and Ruth Perry, new head of state.

The idea is that if you put all the bad boys in one room they won't fight; then the 2.5 million people displaced by the war will come home and work in the rubber plantations. After 12 failed peace accords and more than 50 chin wags among the leaders, we doubt there will be much future in this round. Others say the rest of West Africa is sick and tired of what is going on, because it is hurting their pockets in lost investment. For now this is the only shred of normal government left with a tenuous grip on Monrovia. These folks are keeping their bags packed and cashing their checks before the ink dries.

Ruth Perry

Perry, 57, is the first woman to be named head of state in modern Africa. She was sworn in on September 3, 1996. She is faced with the challenge of guiding the country's armed factions to disarmament and elections scheduled for May, 1997. Perry was a senator during the 1980s under late president Samuel Doe, and has urged Liberians to reconcile and unite.During talks to set a new timetable for disarmament, West African leaders chose Perry to replace former council chairman Wilton Sankawulo. The other four members of the Council of State attended Perry's swearing-in ceremony. Also in attendance was ethnic Krahn leader Roosevelt Johnson, who most Liberians blame for the gunbattles that wrecked the capital in April and May. In her inaugural address Perry said: "The time has come to put the past behind us and move our country forward. I will play the role of stabilizer and the Council of State must be seen as one united force speaking with one voice." The U.N. Security Council plans to keep its 10 military observers in Liberia for a a few more months and U.S. ambassador William Milam said the U.S. would assist with demobilization of the country's estimated 60,000 gunmen, along with restructuring the police and former national army.

Mu'ammar Qaddafi

Ole Mu'ammar has been stirring things up here and in Sierra Leone for a while now. Seems like if he can't have these countries then at least he makes them unlivable for others. His main man is Blaise Compaore, the president of Burkina Faso, who funnels arms from Libya to Taylor in Liberia and Sankoh in Sierra Leone.

Charles Taylor and the National Patriotic Front of Liberia (NPFL)

The leader of the National Patriotic Front of Liberia (NPFL). Charles Taylor, 48, who started the miserable war in Liberia back in 1989, is pegged to be the next leader of Liberia. He has an interesting resume. In 1984 he was accused of embezzling $900,000 from the Liberian coffers and then fled to the U.S., where he was captured for extradition back to Liberia. He bragged about how he sawed through the bars of his cell after bribing his jailors with $30,000. He went to live in the Ivory Coast, where he assembled an army with the help of the Ivorian president, whose brother-in-law, William Tolbert, was executed by Samuel Doe. He gathered together about 4000 soldiers from the Gio and Mano tribes from eastern Liberia and invaded in 1989.

He has taken up wearing suits instead of his military outfit. He makes no secret of his presidential ambitions and feels sure he can realize them through democratic elections. Now it is time to play statesman. Taylor is a descendant of freed American slaves, and his enemy is the Krahn tribe (about 2 percent of the population) led by warlord Roosevelt Johnson. Taylor unsuccessfully tried to take Monrovia in 1990 and 1992. When politics did what bullets couldn't, Taylor was made part of a ruling committee, but he overstepped his authority when he tried to arrest Johnson, who still controls the Barclay Training Centre barracks in downtown Monrovia. (Since many blame Taylor for the spring mayhem in the capital, his chances of winning an election have diminished.) All hell broke loose, and the U.S. had to send in the marines to evacuate the embassy and foreigners stuck in the crossfire. Taylor's choice of media is the KISS FM radio station in Monrovia. His troops are ill-equipped and he is famous for his groups of teenage soldiers, one of which is called the Butt Naked, a group of brutal young kids who fight wearing only tennis shoes.

Alhaji Kromah, Roosevelt Johnson and the United Liberation Movement of Liberia for Democracy (ULIMO)

Warlord Kromah leads one wing of the ethnically divided United Liberation Movement (ULIMO), and is a member of the six-member collective presidency called the Interim Council of State. Kromah is Taylor's former enemy and now part of the ruling committee that babysits what is left of Liberia. His boys, although they haven't laid down their arms, are at relative peace with the other two main factions—the Liberian Peace Council and the NPFL—and control the western portion of the country. The ULIMO-J faction, led by Chief of Staff Roosevelt Johnson, likes to war with the ULIMO Mandingos when things get slow. Johnson usually wins. But Johnson can't see the forest for the trees and is now content to trade lead with ECOMOG and the forces of Charles Taylor over a diamond mining concession dispute. He certainly wasn't happy with his former cabinet post of minister of rural development. To show his countrymen and the world how seriously he took his job, he kept his hacker bush boys fed by hijacking food aid convoys moving through his territory on their way to the thousands of displaced Liberians and refugees from Sierra Leone's smouldering civil war in the north. He was seemingly out of the peace process and the inner circle of Liberian political power until Taylor tried to have him arrested in April 1996. The fighting lasted two weeks between the rival factions, and Johnson negotiated directly with the U.S. government for a cease-fire.

Samuel Doe and the United Liberation Movement of Liberia for Democracy (ULIMO) and Armed Forces of Liberia (AFL)

Samuel Doe, a Krahn, was a 28-year-old master sergeant who put an end to the line of wealthy coffee-colored descendants of freed black slaves from America when he overthrew and executed Tolbert and 13 ministers. The fact that he televised the death of the 13 ministers set the tone for Liberia's future. When a coup was attempted, Doe's soldiers drove around Monrovia, publicly displaying the offenders' severed testicles. Doe persecuted the Gio and Mano tribes along with anyone else he didn't like and laid the groundwork for Taylor's emergence. Charles Taylor, then head of the new government's procurement, first came to prominence when he pocketed almost a million dollars and fled to the U.S. When he was not busy killing and torturing people for fun, Sam Doe was applying his newfound financial genius. He managed to plunge the country deeper into debt, print new money to pay bills that came due and still keep the treasury empty, while bumming millions of dollars in foreign aid. He did manage to cut all government workers' salaries by $10.

He was offered safe passage out of Liberia by the U.S. government but turned it down. Probably because Doe lived in luxury on the fifth floor of the Executive Mansion, with his two pet lions (which he fed with his many victims) and protected by his Israeli-trained bodyguards. Until one day in September of 1990, when he went to visit the ECOWAS headquarters. (See "Prince Johnson"). His memory lives on with the Krahn tribe and the highfalutin-sounding ULIMO group who control small pockets near the Sierra Leone border (from their base in Freetown) and Tubmanburg. The Armed Forces of Liberia (AFL) is a splinter group loyal to the dead Doe and responsible for the slaughter of hundreds of people at Harbel in 1994.

Prince Yormie Johnson and the Independant Patriotic Front (IPF)

Johnson originally was allied to Taylor when he first attacked Doe in 1989. He then broke away with 1000 of his better-trained troops from the Gio tribe, leaving Taylor with the larger but less effective Mano tribal troops. In 1990 when Taylor controlled the countryside, Johnson controlled most of Monrovia, killing and torturing at random. About

200 of Johnson's men captured Doe when he went to the ECOWAS headquarters. They later cut off his ears and tortured him to death while videotaping the festivities. His dismembered body was paraded around Monrovia. Johnson and Taylor both claimed the presidency and set off another round of bloodshed. The fighting lasted seven weeks between the rival factions and as it raged Johnson was flown by U.S. marines to Accra, Ghana to attend peace talks. None of the other warlords showed up and Johnson complained bitterly when both the Americans and ECOMOG refused to take him back to Monrovia.

Armed Forces of Liberia (AFL)

Formerly the national army under the Doe regime, and largely comprising ethnic Krahns-Doe was a Krahn. By 1992, as a result of the war...another faction. By 1992, as a result of the civil war, the AFL maintained only limited authority and most of its equipment had been destroyed or rendered useless. The army these days is essentially just another faction.

During the April and May clashes in the capital, Krahn fighters loyal to Johnson were based in an AFL barracks downtown. Although its high command said the AFL was not involved in the conflict, many of its soldiers were thought to be fighting alongside fellow Krahns loyal to Johnson and Boley against the forces of Charles Taylor and Alhaji Kromah. Two men claim to be the AFL's chief of staff. Abraham Kromah was "appointed" to the position by the virulently anti-Krahn NPFL while Brigadier General Phillip Karmah inherited it when his predecessor was killed early on in the spring clashes in the capital.

Economic Community of West African States Cease-Fire Monitoring Group (ECOMOG)

The six-nation peacekeeping force sent in by the Economic Community of West African States (ECOWAS) was supposed to be keeping Liberia cool and calm but spent most of their time hiding in their camps during the '96 flare-up. Leader General John Mark Inienger bravely returned to tour the looted capital and pledged "to do everything possible to protect the city" and, we are sure, his hide. Their most shining moment was back in 1990 when then leader Doe went to negotiate at ECOWAS headquarters; Johnson's troops broke in, shot him and cut his ears off while the peacekeeping troops sat and watched.

"General" Butt Naked

Krahn fighter who leads the Butt Naked Brigade, which, as you might expect, goes into battle in the altogether as a sign of defiance and invincibility. Now a celebrity in Monrovia, young boys cheer him when he cruises through the capital on his motorbike.

"General" Julue (A.K.A Rock One)

He was once the security chief for President Samuel Doe and now claims to be the leader of Liberia with a pathetic army of about 100 men. Brutal, cruel and imprisoned for his brief attempt at wresting power Julue was sprung from jail in April '96 and hasn't been seen since.

Liberia Peace Council (LPC)

A Krahn-dominated faction led by George Boley, who left Liberia before the latest round of fighting in Monrovia. The LPC used to control the key port of Buchanan, but this has since fallen into the hand of the NPFL. Skirmishes between the two factions continue in the southeast.

The Lofa Defence Force

A small group based along the border with Sierra Leone who is opposed to the current government and Charles Taylor.

LIBERIA

Political Parties

Founded in 1878, the True Whig Party ran the country until the 1980 coup, after which it was banned. It was revived in 1991. The National Patriotic Party (NPP), formed in December 1991, is the political wing of the National Patriotic Front of Liberia. The Independent Democratic Party was created as the political branch of the breakaway Independent National Patriotic Front of Liberia (INPFL) in 1991. Also formed in 1991, the United Liberation Movement of Liberia for Democracy (ULIMO) was organized by supporters of the late President Samuel Doe. It split into two factions in November 1992, one being based in Tubmanburg, Liberia, and the other in Freetown, Sierra Leone. Former members of the pan-African Movement for Justice in Africa founded the Liberian People's Party (LPP), a significant factor prior to the 1980 coup that brought Doe to power. The party's leader is former interim President Amos Sawyer.

Rubber

There is little left in Liberia, except for rubber. The Firestone company owns the largest rubber plantation in the world, about one million acres that it originally leased for 6 cents an acre back in 1926. The world's largest rubber estate, about 30 miles east of the capital, is now better known as a battlefield.

Wilton Sankawulo

Member and former chairman of the Interim Council of State, Liberia's six-member ruling body. Appears to be comfortably ensconced in Charles Taylor's pocket.

George Weah

International award-winning AC Milan striker. Liberia's favorite son, a national hero.

Getting In

The roads leading from Monrovia are passable for limited preapproved travel, but they are extremely dangerous. Liberia is accessible by road from Danane, Ivory Coast. This road leads to NPFL stronghold Gbarnga, from there is a road to Monrovia. U.S. embassy employees are not allowed to travel outside Monrovia, except for official business. Roberts International Airport outside of Monrovia is closed. Spriggs Payne International Airport reopened in June, 1996. West Coast Airlines, WESWUA and Air Ivoire have resumed Monrovia service. Belview may be next if the city remains calm. Overland routes to other West African countries are not open. Travelers who plan a trip to Liberia are required to have a passport and a visa prior to arrival. Additionally, in order to be granted a visa, you must present to a Liberian embassy a letter stating the purpose of your visit and another from a doctor confirming you have no communicable diseases. Evidence of yellow fever vaccination is required. An exit permit must be obtained from Liberian immigration authorities upon arrival. There is no charge for a tourist visa. Gee, we wonder why?

The embassy tells us that the only area traditionally considered "safe" is inside the capital of Monrovia, since the Liberian National Transitional Government does not control areas outside of town. But even Monrovia occasionally erupts into mass, deadly violence. If you are caught entering illegally, you will be arrested and tried, at which point you will be imprisoned or deported.

Further information on entry requirements for Liberia can be obtained from the following:

Embassy of the Republic of Liberia

5201 16th Street, N.W.
Washington, D.C. 20011
☎ *(202) 723-0437 to 723-0440*

This building is currently closed because of fire. The temporary address is the following:

5303 Colorado Avenue, N.W.
Washington, D.C. 20011

Getting Around

Total road mileage in Liberia is 6268; 1818 miles are paved. Total railroad track miles are 298. There are four ports, the three major ones at Buchanan, Greenville and Monrovia. There are 66 total airfields in Liberia, 49 with a permanent surface. (One of them was built as a backup landing site for the space shuttle.)

Roads leading out from Monrovia are dangerous but passable. Travelers to the interior of Liberia may be in danger of being detained, harassed, delayed, injured or killed. Travel to most parts of the country is not a good idea. If you have US$12,000 you can hire a Russian helicopter to take you in from Freetown.

When traveling by road in Liberia, extreme caution is urged even when roads are open, motorists are frequently hassled at checkpoints manned by stoned gunmen. Cigarette rolling papers, indeed any kind of paper to make joints with, will increase your popularity immensely, as will booze, cigarettes, etc. But not a good idea to travel by road without someone who has done so before, and who knows how to deal with the fighters. As far as payoffs go, there is no rule of thumb—as little as you can get away with. Flashy watches, jewelry, sunglasses, etc....should be kept well out of sight.

In June 1996, all aid agencies (or NGOs- nongovernmental organizations) working in Liberia said they would limit their operations to emergencies only. When fighting broke out in the capital in April, most aid workers pulled out of the country. Only a few NGOs left a core staff behind. The agencies said looting of their stuff was so bad, they thought their presence only helped the factions, i.e. prolonged the war and did more harm than good to the civilians they were trying to help. They said full-scale operations would only resume once security improved and faction leaders demonstrated a commitment to humanitarian principles. (That should be around the same time hell freezes over.) The U.N. had 489 vehicles stolen (worth $8.3 million). Only 11 have been returned.

Dangerous Places

Monrovia

A curfew is strictly enforced in Monrovia. Monrovia's crime rate is high, regardless of the level of tensions. Foreigners, including U.S. citizens, have been targets of street crime. Residential break-ins are common. The police are largely incapable of providing effective protection.

In April 1996, Monrovia plunged into seven weeks of fierce factional fighting after Charles Taylor tried to arrest rebel leader Roosevelt Johnson. The streets were littered with corpses and the American government ordered the evacuation of the Embassy— nearly 2000 people in all, including other foreigners. Things have cooled down, but the conflict is far from over.

Anywhere Outside of Monrovia

Essentially, the entire country is a free fire zone. The situation in Liberia can change daily. Although a very scant security buffer exists around Monrovia, tensions remain high in much of the country. There have been incidents of violence against civilians by partisans of Liberia's several warring factions. Armed bandits continue to spread panic among the city's civilians.

Are We Having Fun Yet?

I remember the look of disgust on the war photographer's face at an all-night party in Paris. He would start to tell stories of what he had seen in Liberia and then stop himself and change the subject. His photographs of the atrocities had been published around the world, yet these photos paled when compared to the horror of the others in his private collection. In the last few years the stories coming out of Liberia strain the credulity of even the most seasoned reporters. A typical day with Sam Doe was sleeping in, drinking American beer and then jumping in jeeps wearing Halloween costumes. People would be shot for fun from the speeding jeeps, and some hapless victims were dragged back to the Executive Mansion to be tortured to death and then fed to Doe's two pet lions. Rapes and torture were common. Not too many journalists were sad when Doe was tortured to death on video tape.

Dangerous Things

Peace Accords

There have been no fewer than 14 peace accords in Liberia since 1989, each of them brutally shattered before even the ink could dry. The current agreement signed in August 1995 seems in danger of unraveling as well, as ULIMO-J militia warlord Roosevelt Johnson has said his faction will not disarm and will not abide by the August peace agreement, alleging that ECOMOG was no longer neutral in the national dispute. ULIMO-J forces have been fighting sporadically with the ECOMOG peacekeepers since the signing of the treaty.

Costumes

In Liberia, if you see anyone dressed in a wig, a Batman mask or a ballgown—run like hell. In a macabre twist to the killing and maiming, tribal militiamen don the clothing of clowns and women while razing villages and slaughtering and raping their inhabitants. The costumes provide protection from bullets.

Cholera

In April 1996, Monrovia experienced an outbreak of cholera. The disease, which is endemic in Liberia, struck 3000 people in 1995, killing about 100.

Embassy Locations and Useful Telephone numbers

U.S Embassy
111 United Nations Drive
P.O. Box 10-0098
Monrovia
☎ *(231) 226370/226154*

Maddison Weon
Ulimo-J deputy chairman. Good contact for Ulimo-J leader Roosevelt Johnson
☎ *(231) 226763/8 or 225804*

Liberian National Police Force
☎ *225825 or 222113*

National Security Agency
☎ *221099*

European Union
☎ *(231) 226516 or 227468*

Nigerian Embassy
☎ *(231) 224658*

Mamba Point Hotel
United Nations Drive (100 yards from U.S. Embassy)
☎ *(231) 226050*

Victoria Reffell
Information Minister and good place to start if seeking Charles Taylor
☎ *(231) 227007, FAX 227006*

ECOMOG HQ
Freezone, P.O. Box 10-9033, 100 Monrovia
☎ */FAX (231) 226244*

Emergency
☎ *115 (Don't hold your breath!)*

Getting Sick

All visitors more than one year old must have a yellow fever vaccination certificate. Malaria and Hepatitis B are widespread, and such arthropod-borne diseases as river blindness and sleeping sickness can also be a hazard. There are 15 hospital beds and one doctor for every 10,000 people. Medical facilities have been disrupted. Medicines are scarce. Information on health matters may be obtained from the Centers for Disease Control's international travelers hotline at ☎ *(404) 332-4559*. Expect a laundry list of nasties.

Nuts and Bolts

Liberia, 37,743 square miles, is situated on the west coast of Africa, bounded by Guinea and Sierra Leone on the north and Cote d'Ivoire on the east. Monrovia, with a population of about half a million, is the capital. Liberia's total population is estimated at 2,839,000, with about half the inhabitants living in urban areas. Currency is the Liberian dollar. Officially there is parity between the U.S. and Liberian dollars but ubiquitous money changers will give around 50 Liberian dollars to the greenback. (Take a bag instead of a wallet—the notes only come in five dollar denominations.)

Liberia has a tropical climate, with temperatures ranging from 65° F to 120° F. The rainy period extends from May through November and is characterized by frequent, prolonged and often torrential rainfall. Humidity is high, usually between 70 and 80 percent.

Indigenous Africans (including Kpelle, Bassa, Gio, Kru, Grebo, Mano, Krahn, Gola, Gbandi, Loma, Kissi, Vai and Bella) make up 95 percent of the population; Americo-Liberians (descendants of black American settlers) account for 5 percent. Liberia is officially a Christian state, although indigenous beliefs are held by 70 percent of the population. Muslims comprise 20 percent and Christians only 10 percent of the population. English is the official language. There are close to 20 local languages derived from the Niger-Congo language. About 20 percent of the population uses English. Illiteracy stands at about 60 percent.

Lodging, water, electricity, fuel, transportation, and telephone and postal services continue to be uneven in Monrovia. Such services are nonexistent or severely limited in rural areas. All electrical power is supplied by generators. Mail delivery is erratic. Parcel delivery service is available to Monrovia. Courier mail services are available in Monrovia.

U.S. citizens who register at the U.S. embassy in Monrovia may obtain updated information on travel and security in Liberia. Don't be surprised if you meet them at the departure lounge at the airport.

Embassy Locations

U.S. Embassy (in the capital of Monrovia)
111 United Nations Drive, Mamba Point
☎ *[231] (2) 222-991 through 222-994*
FAX [231] (2) 223-710
The U.S. embassy's mailing address:

P.O. Box 10-0098
Mamba Point, Monrovia
or APO AE 09813
or P.O. Box 98.

Liberian Consulate (in Canada)
1080 Beaver Hall Hill, Suite 1720
Montreal, Quebec, Canada H2Z 1S8
☎ *(514) 871-4741*
FAX (514) 397-0816

Dangerous Days

04/06–5/26/1996	Monrovia and Liberia again were plunged into civil war. Corpses littered the capital's streets, and perhaps 2000 Americans and other foreigners were airlifted from the American Embassy.
12/14/1989	Charles Taylor launches his rebellion from neighboring Ivory Coast.
01/06/1986	New constitution inaugurated.
04/12/1980	President William Tolbert was overthrown in a coup led by Staff Sergeant Samuel K. Doe, who subsequently suspended the constitution and imposed martial law.
05/25/1963	OAU—Africa Freedom Day.
07/26/1847	Independence Day.
02/11	Armed Forces Day.

LIBERIA

In a Dangerous Place

Liberia: Theme Park of the Macabre

Getting into Monrovia is cheap, getting out is not. The Russian Hind ferried journalists into the war zone at no charge (we find out later that it costs $5000 to get 11 people out). When we arrive we find out that the new economy is driven by journalists, $12 for french fries, $4 for a beer or a half a gallon of water. We take a ride with the U.S. Marines who are evacuating terrified expats and civilians. Considering that we are being dropped into a confused fire fight, we find it funny that they explain how our life jacket works and give us ear plugs to avoid hearing loss.

The Sea Knights fly in a group of three, it seems to be overkill against the freaked out kids with broken rifles and sticks below. Shots are fired up at us from the ground. The Marines respond with devastating firepower from all three helicopters. The choppers land in the huge compound in the U.S. Embassy. We sign a release form absolving the Americans from any blame. A strange formality after watching the machine guns blast away at the fighters on the ground. This is a land with no laws, no higher court and nobody to protect us. It is truly the law of the jungle. As the throbbing Sea Knights lift off we are keenly aware that there is no way out know. We have arrived in Hell without a return ticket.

The size of the compound is roughly ten football fields and there are about 2000 Liberians camped out. At one end is the loot market. Here everything from escargot to computers are for sale. All the material has been looted and there is a definite shortage of buyers.

We stay at a Lebanese run hotel. It is supposedly safe here because the two Lebanese brothers (who fought with the Falangists in Lebanon) pay off the warring groups. It has the curious distinction of being used by the factions as the marker for the end of the fighting since it is about 200 meters from the well-protected U.S. embassy. It costs $200 a night but they fulfill the two main needs of all combat journalists: a satellite phone and a bar.

The fighting rages on at night but it is quiet in the morning. We walk out and meet with Roosevelt's group, the Krahns. It looks like a nursery school, children as young as 6 or 7 are among the fighters. I guess it's not much different than playing GI Joe except this is the real thing and you get killed when you lose instead of crying to your mother. The morning is the time when the soldiers scrounge for food and booze, clean their weapons and play a little football. They also smoke weed which grows wild here. As the drugs and alcohol take over the insults will begin and the fighting will begin.

We decide to see what the government forces are up to. It's a long walk, since there are few private cars and only scrounged gas. To use a silly but appropriate cliche, it is hot as hell.

The fighters like journalists. They think they will be famous if we take their picture. In fact many will do things they would not normally do because they think they might be on the cover of *Time*. Beheadings and mutilations are offered but refused. It is almost a design your own atrocity place for the bang bang folks.

The situation is understandably confused. Roosevelt's troops control the suburbs and Taylor's troops control the center. It is important to keep in mind that Taylor's forces are not thrilled with the idea of journalists documenting their activities. The peacekeepers called ECOMOG are rarely keeping the peace. For now Taylor's forces have rockets and mortars and usually win any pitched battle. The battles start with a charge. One side (usually Roosevelt's) will break and run, drawing Taylor's troops deeper into the suburbs and unfamiliar areas. Then the Roosevelt troops will circle around and attack the attackers from behind and the sides. The government troops will break and run to the safety of their lines. Along the way a few people are left dead or dying. The dead ones are the lucky ones since now the blood lust and adrenaline take over and the atrocities begin. The fighters invite us to watch what will happen. We put our cameras away.

We go to visit the hospital. All they have is prayer. There is about one doctor for 10,000 people here. As we leave the hospital we bump into a tough group of Roosevelt's men. These fighters have been trained and carry AK-47's. They are surrounded by children who carry anything that even looks like a gun. They wear bizarre items like wigs and life jackets that they say protect them from the bullets. They are here for the thrill, the smell of blood and the exhilaration of escaping death. They dance, sing songs, yell insults and wiggle their private parts at the opposing side to incite a battle. One kid fires his rifle in time to the music playing on his Walkman. It is common to see a small child beat an older person senseless with his rifle just for fun. The leaders give the children drugs making them even more savage.

The one place that no one trifles with is the U.S. Embassy. Snipers shoot to kill and they don't miss. Marines with machine guns have no qualms about wiping out any foolhardy warriors who shoot at them. The dead are like a macabre theme park. Each side uses a totem or fetish to show their territory. Monrovia is decorated with severed heads put on tables as warnings, children with deep knife wounds and bloated corpses. I get some other journalists to help me drag an old man who is wounded in the face by shrapnel to the hospital. It seems to be a trivial symbol of decency in this godforsaken place. We know that he will not make it but we feel better for helping him.

Running low on money and getting weary of the brutality, we buy places on one of the Hind helicopters back to Freetown in Sierra Leone. There is a huge fuel tank and a large Coca Cola sign inside the worn Russian helicopter. Like the end of a bad nihilistic science fiction movie we are leaving a social experiment gone badly wrong and can't wait for the lights to come up and the darkness to end.

—**Coskun Aral**

LIBERIA

In a Dangerous Place

Monrovia, May 1996: My First War Zone

At least the dogs had a good time of it. From the balcony of the Mamba Point Hotel I could see a small pack of mongrels, perhaps half a dozen, gathered on a beach where huge Atlantic rollers crashed incessantly, ignorant of the mayhem that had brought these shores to international headlines. Food had become very scarce so I was surprised to see the dogs gorging themselves, tails wagging contentedly. Most people could hardly afford the inflated cost of feeding themselves, so it seemed unlikely anyone would think of the welfare of animals.

They hadn't. A convenient telescope revealed the largest and fiercest of the dogs chewing on something I couldn't quite make out. A slight adjustment brought into focus five swollen brown figures, then an arm, then my first ever human corpse.

"Welcome to Monrovia," said a war-junkie photographer, handing me a beer.

####

I arrived in the Liberian capital in early May, three weeks after the city exploded into an orgy of factional clashes and violent looting. U.S. Marines were still evacuating American citizens and other "friendly nationals," a massive operation that promoted this hitherto neglected corner of West Africa to the number one media event across the globe.

Back in April, ashen-faced evacuees landing in Freetown—the capital of neighboring Sierra Leone—had spoken of being robbed in their homes at gunpoint, often by children carrying automatic weapons as tall as themselves. Hundreds of fighters, many making their first visit to the capital after battling in the bush since civil war broke out in December 1989, roamed the streets of Monrovia, exhilarated by the freedom to help themselves with impunity. Little of the cash generated by Liberia's rich resources of diamonds, timber, and scrap metal had gone

LIBERIA

much further than the faction leaders during the war. Pay day for the foot soldiers had arrived at last.

The West African peacekeeping force, known as ECOMOG, sent to Liberia in 1990, and in charge of security in the "safe haven" of Monrovia, seemed powerless to prevent either the looting or the battles raging downtown. Some witnesses saw ECOMOG troops joining in the pillage.

The first journalists to land at the U.S. embassy, courtesy of the Marine Corps, were greeted by an exasperated Ambassador William Milam.

"What the hell do you want to come here for? Everyone else is trying to leave!"

####

Liberian civilians certainly were not having a good time of it. The million residents of a capital whose population had doubled since the start of the war because of its "safe haven" status did not get much airtime on the networks. A few thousand, however, were granted their fifteen minutes of fame by virtue of being crushed for ten days into a leaky, rusting Nigerian freighter with little food or water, let alone sanitary facilities, as Liberia's West African neighbors, one after the other, refused to let it dock.

Did the hundreds of paid-up wanna-be Bulk Challenge passengers left behind in Monrovia's port feel lucky to have been spared such a nightmare odyssey? No. Living in freight containers neatly arranged in rows on the port's football pitch, sometimes more than a dozen to a container, their unanimous sentiment was: "We've had enough. We want to leave now."

####

If Monrovia was a mess before the spring clashes—with no power lines, little running water and that tired look of a city in dire need of several thousand gallons of fresh paint—by the time the fighters had made their mark, with rockets, bullets, spray paint and a burglar's disregard for the personally sacred, downtown areas of the capital became uninhabitable. Most of the time the city was deserted by all except a few uniformed and armed peacekeepers and Lebanese traders busy welding closed the steel shutters of their supermarkets and electrical goods stores. Occasionally, when calm broke out, civilians would venture out in search of water, food, and lost relatives. Sticking close to the side of buildings, they would snake in single file only to scatter in seconds when gunfire erupted.

The streets were strewn with a bewildering variety of refuse. Rubble from shelled houses, rotting corpses, ragged clothes, passports (boxes of unused ones had been stolen from the foreign ministry) and other documents. I could hardly take a step without sending shell casings clattering or treading on somebody's cherished collection of family photographs, rejected as worthless by the looters—who, incidentally, emerged from the ranks of all of the factions. Jimmy, for example, a 27-year-old Libero-Lebanese, was at home when the frontline moved past his house. Ethnic Krahn fighters swarmed in, put one gun to his head, another to his belly and told him: "we're gonna steal everything and then we're gonna kill you." They were halfway done with the first part of their promise when the frontline changed again and the Krahns swarmed back out to do battle, giving Jimmy a chance to flee to the building next door...the Mamba Point Hotel. From the balcony, Jimmy had a clear view of so-called government forces (in reality fighters loyal to Charles Taylor and Alhaji Kromah, but what's important is they were

fighting the Krahns) taking over from where the others had left off. By the time
they were through, Jimmy's house looked like it had been derelict for years.

####

The only vehicles that moved were ECOMOG's armored personnel carriers,
looted aid agency 4-by-4's, and windowless and often doorless jalopies, spilling
over with heavily armed youths, their factional allegiance displayed in messy graffiti. One group had installed an antiaircraft gun in the well of a stolen pickup
truck.

When fighting broke out in early April, thousands of civilians fled the city center
for makeshift camps for the displaced, such as the Greystone compound, a 27-
acre site once housing just seven U.S. diplomats and their families. It quickly became the temporary home to 20,000 Monrovians. As if the threat of cholera and
other diseases were not enough, Greystone's residents had to put up with a daily
diet of gunfire and explosions as factions battled just outside the compound's
walls. Stray bullets ended their trajectories in tragedy on several occasions.

####

At least the kids with the guns had a good time of it, even when doing their ut-
most to kill each other. Perhaps it was fortunate that this was an activity carried

out with staggering incompetence. Most of those involved in direct combat were very young teenagers already veterans of a war that by 1993 had claimed the lives of 150,000, mainly civilian, Liberians. Only commanders were beyond their twenties. They had adopted a bizarre variety of *noms de guerre*. Among the "senior officers" I met were Generals No Mother No Father, Housebreaker, Fuck Me Quick and Butt Naked.

Those without guns, a good half, made do with what they could find to justify sticking with the gang. Waterpistols, broomsticks, garden rakes, rolling pins, air filters, Coke bottles and powerless power drills were among the makeshift weapons at hand. Those with guns often had no idea of how to use them. On the first day I dared to leave the relative safety of the hotel, I found myself chatting with a group of fighters. Suddenly there was a loud explosion and a blast of hot air rushed up my leg. I looked down to see a small crater in the tarmac and the teenaged gunmen next to me looking sheepishly guilty. He had fired his rifle accidentally, almost with tragic consequences for my left foot. The gun's magazine, like many in the city, was held together by adhesive tape printed with the logo of the aid agency Save the Children Fund.

Much of the fighting itself was also chaotic, a tragic parody of cowboys and Indians, cops and robbers —with real bullets. From our ringside seats on the hotel balcony we watched battles conducted with Kalashnikovs held high above the heads of the young warriors, who screamed obscenities in Liberian English at their enemies. A favorite war-cry was "Yo ma pussy-oh," a genital insult also daubed on many of Monrovia's walls.

It was not uncommon to see boys of nine or ten on the frontlines, the bravest or most brainwashed of them all. Looking into the eyes of these boys, self-assured arrogant eyes, long-robbed of anything resembling childhood innocence, was a chilling experience. One morning such a child got into an argument with a comrade fighter some ten years his senior. They shouted at each other at the gates of the Mamba Point Hotel, neither willing to back down in front of the rest of the gang. The older boy calmly removed a rifle from his shoulder, passed it to a friend and squared up to the child, whose nose reached no higher than the gunman's chest. Undaunted by the other's size, the child continued to remonstrate and the argument grew more heated. The child then fished in the pocket of his shorts and pulled out a hand-grenade, held it to the face of his adversary, fingering the pin. I was no more than a couple of yards away.

"Shut up, man, or I'll pull it!. I tell you man, you don't shut up I'll fucking pull the pin!"

Despite my presence and my appeals to wait until I had made myself scarce, I believe that pin would have been pulled had the gang's leader not intervened.

Ray Benedict, a lanky, befreckled twentysomething (he was unsure of his age) with implausibly ginger hair, was not a typical Liberian fighter in that he was adept at using his weapon, a cherished rocket propelled grenade launcher. Recruited into Charles Taylor's National Patriotic Front of Liberia at the age of 14 to "defend his country," Ray had become something of a hero among both his comrades and his foes, even the media. Although it had rendered him near-deaf, Ray was at his happiest when firing his rockets, and never more downhearted than when his daily allowance was used up. In the ecstatic moments following each explosion, he wore the triumphant expression of an Olympic sprinter about to break the tape. One photographer had captured such a moment, Ray almost in silhouette running towards the camera from a large cloud of smoke produced just seconds earlier by his RPG. The picture appeared on the cover of a special supplement on Liberia published in a Madrid newspaper, brought to Monrovia by a Spanish journalist. Ray probably doesn't receive gifts very often, and I'm sure this testimony to his unsolicited international fame is now among his most treasured possessions.

He hadn't spent much time analyzing his role in the war: "The people I killed, I killed'cause they wanted to take Monrovia. The people I killed, plenty-oh."

Out of this modern conflict conducted with medium-tech weapons emerged much older aspects of Africa: magic, nudity, mutilation, even cannibalism. Fighters wore a variety of "protective" talismans such as cowrie shells and strips of animal skin. Since the beginning of the civil conflict Liberia's warlords had taken advantage of the widespread faith in such bullet-proofing trinkets to encourage children as young as eight into the frontline. The Butt Naked Brigade, whose leader elicited cheers when seen in public, regularly disrobed in the face of enemy fire as a sign of defiance and invincibility. Other men went into battle decked out in women's dresses, wigs and floral hats. Some said this practice was rooted in the inability of young recruits in the bush to distinguish between female and male attire when attacking the first town in which they had ever set foot.

Juju gear and cross-dressers notwithstanding, there was little to distinguish battle-dress from ordinary street clothes. Combat boots and camouflage fatigues were rare. Charity-donated tee-shirts (Malcolm X was a favorite design), cutoff jeans and flip-flops were more the order of the day.

The prisoner's ordeal was a vicious one. Having been stripped, punched and kicked, his arms would be tied at the elbow behind his back—"to stop him flying away" one captor explained. Not only is this position excruciatingly painful (just try it), it also leads to slow suffocation. But there is rarely time for that process to take its deadly effect.

Looking at the victims it wasn't always clear whether it was the machete cuts or the bullet to the head that finished the job but it was often evident that vital organs had been removed before the moment of death. The eating of enemies' innards was a common, if discreet, practice said to imbue the consumer with the strength of the consumed.

"Hey, man, you want some meat?," one fighter asked me at a checkpoint. He held out his hand to reveal half a fresh heart. I couldn't swear it was human, but then again I hadn't seen many pigs around the city. I wondered where the other half was.

Decapitation was also prevalent and dozens of heads in various states of decomposition littered the streets. Fresher ones were prominently displayed at battlefronts, while others were left to rot away in gutters. When fighters from opposed factions called a temporary truce one day in mid-May they put down their weapons and decided to play soccer. Since no football was available, they kicked around a fleshless skull found nearby.

####

At least the media had a good time of it. The Mamba Point Hotel was among the very few establishments still functioning in Monrovia. Thanks to some judicious palm-greasing it had barely been looted. The world's press enjoyed intermittent electricity, fine wines and excellent food prepared by Ming, a Chinese chef who, when asked, as we took cover under a table during a shootout, why he was still in town, said "No money go home."

Among the regulars at the bar were our armed factional protectors, eager to see themselves on CNN.

We felt safe there, even when battles raged just yards away, occasionally sending bullets into the hotel. One of these projectiles entered the owner's bedroom, passing through a closet containing his wife's dresses and leaving a coin-sized souvenir hole in the left shoulder of each.

Of the dozens of journalists who came to Monrovia during the seven weeks of fighting, only one, a French photographer, was injured. A rocket-propelled grenade exploded twenty yards away and its shrapnel broke his leg.

Most of the fighters treated the media with respect and often offered advice as to the safety of crossing roads or venturing down alleys. War-zone veterans said it was the only conflict they had covered where they could cross frontlines in a matter of minutes, often by staying in the same place.

In retrospect it seems foolish to have refused armed demands for money or cigarettes, but at the time, lies such as "I'm broke" or "I don't smoke" came easy. A joke was always enough to defuse tense situations. Of course it took a while to get used to the liberties one could take. A radio correspondent, on his first day out, eagerly handed over his watch to an appreciative militiaman.

"Yeah, that looks good, man," said the young fighter, admiring his new acquisition. "But tell me, man, what time does it say?"

—**Anthony Morland**

Nigeria
★★★
Formula 419

Four-one-nine.

That's Nigeria's code for criminal fraud. Travelers know that tripping to corrupt, impoverished Nigeria can make even the hardened swear off travel to Africa entirely. For nearly two-thirds of its 35-year history, Africa's most populated country has been bullied by military despots who promise elections and then spend more time shopping at Harrods than running the country.

So it is not surprising that, despite current leader General Sani Abacha's promise to set up a democratically elected government, the current scenario in Nigeria seems like a precursor to another coup or civil war. In the meantime, what do the enterprising Nigerians do to bolster their economy? In keeping with its tainted image as one of the most corrupt nations in Africa, there are a number of quasi-sanctioned, clever scams that sucker in dozens of unsuspecting foreigners every year (see below).

Nigeria's biggest export is oil (with Uncle Sam slurping up about half). Yet that darn oil money keeps getting lost. Former President (and, of course, Army General) Babangida managed to misplace US$12.2 billion dollars worth. A black hole if there ever was one.

Shell Oil Co. has sucked from the floor about US$30 billion worth of Nigerian oil since its discovery in 1958, yet the Ogoni tribe still lives in poverty in the swamps. When they tested the trickle-down theory, their leaders (including Ken Sarowiwa) were hung in November 1995 and the Ogonis chased into the swamps. Another black hole.

As one would expect, even though the Christian south is where the oil riches are coffered, the government has always been from the Muslim north.

Grow Hair, Pick Up Chicks and Make Big Money in Nigerian Oil Deals!

Nigerians have finally figured out how to bring corruption and misery straight to you without your leaving the comfort of your office. Nigerian business scams are confidence schemes, designed to exploit the trust you develop in your Nige-

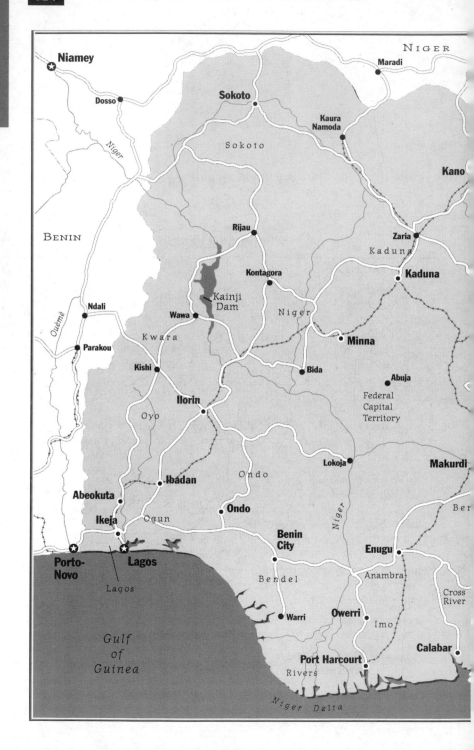

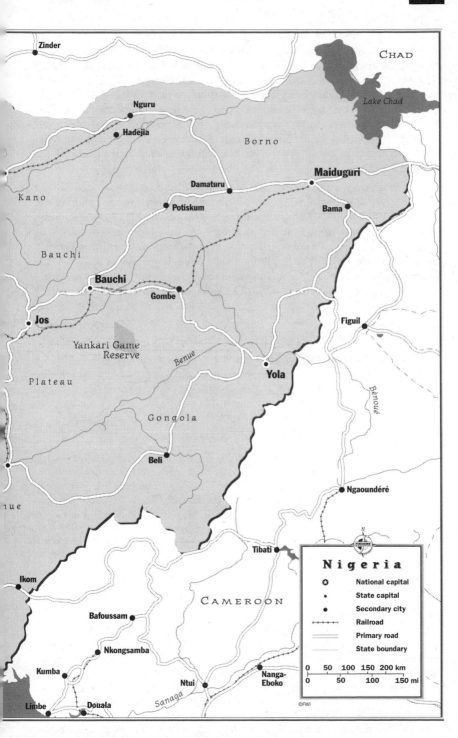

rian partner and to bilk you of goods, services or money. The scams are flexible, and operators adapt them to take the greatest advantage of the target—you.

Every week the U.S. embassy in Lagos tries to console victims of these scams where businesspeople have lost sums ranging from a few thousand to upwards of one million dollars. Patsies who have traveled all the way to Nigeria to clinch these "lucrative"deals have been threatened, assaulted or even killed. Local police couldn't care less, and Nigerian officials find the whole thing funny. The U.S. embassy can't do much more than lend you a toothbrush and a quarter to call your mother for airfare. Some Nigerian immigration officials have begun to warn folks upon arrival at Lagos airport, but the lemmings keep arriving to pick up their pot of gold.

Scams range from attempts to engage American businesspeople in fictitious money-transfer schemes to fraudulent solicitations to supply goods in fulfillment of nonexistent Nigerian government contracts. Most scam operators are sophisticated and may take victims to staged meetings, often held in borrowed offices at Nigerian government ministries. They do their research and can often provide plausible, but nonexistent, orders written on seemingly genuine Ministerial stationery, replete with official stamps and seals. Nigerian business scams are not always easy to recognize, and any unsolicited business proposal should be carefully scrutinized.

It is not possible to describe here how each of several hundred different scams works but they all center on greed (yours), gullibility (yours) and money (yours).

This scam stuff is so much fun that we won't even dwell on the conflict (Muslim north versus Christian south) that ripped the country apart during the Biafran war, the billions of oil dollars that go straight into the pockets of the select few, or the overall poverty and population growth that plague this large country. For now, we just keep seeing how many suckers will travel here to make their fortune.

The Scoop

As OPEC's fourth-largest oil producer, Nigeria is oil-rich and human-rights poor, the scam capital of the world, a boot camp for fatigue-clad banana dictators, and the Bermuda Triangle of currency. For all but nine of its 36 years of independence, Nigeria has been ruled by the military. The current bunch of boys chomping on stogies behind Ray Bans work for General Sani Abacha, perhaps the most iron-fisted despot of them all. He recently ruled out the reinstatement of 1993's annulled elections and has swindled the Nigeria's treasury to such an extent, the entire country is on the brink of total collapse. The regime is repressive, stone-blind and violent. In addition to the countless billions siphoned by the government from international oil contracts, Nigeria Airways reported in February 1996 that the US$100 million paid by the government in 1992 to create an international airline had vanished without a trace. Just disappeared like magic. Gone. Another black hole. The principal activities of the Nigerian government are swindling, fraud, graft and execution.

Unlike other African dictatorships, there is no government-in-waiting in Nigeria—nor in exile elsewhere—ready to play the white knight role when Nigeria finally implodes. Try telling that to the government. Starting in February 1996, there was a renewed crackdown on the few dissidents with the nuts even to make a soupy verbal challenge to Sani Abacha's supremacy. Nine political activists were executed for their antigovernment views in November 1995. Meanwhile, the government continues its grabbing of the Ogonis' land for oil. There are more than 250 different ethnic groups in Nigeria's population of 100 million that have been manhandled by seven different military rulers since 1960. And the situation looks only bleaker. Nigeria's civilian politicians are extremely weak and divided like an Arizona chasm. The general keeps them in his coop with enough hush money for hookers and Johnny Walker's. The government recently admitted that fully two-thirds of the 55,000 people in Nigerian jails have never had a trial.

Will Nigeria self-destruct? Undoubtedly. And what will happen? Well, it happened once before—in 1967–1970, when the east split apart from Nigeria and became Biafra. And that was stopped only after a brutal civil war that—along with famine—killed more than a million people.

When You Gotta Go, You Gotta Go

A group of chanting, dancing and shouting youths were seen parading down the streets of Kano with an unusual object on the end of a long stick. It was the head of a Gideon Akaluka, an automotive spare parts dealer who had been accused of using the Koran for toilet paper. He was originally arrested and detained for the charges, but a group of Islamic youths broke into the jail, beheaded him and presented his head to their traditional leader, the Emir of Kano. The Emir sent a messenger to tell the crowd that they had acted in a barbaric manner and that he was shocked. The crowd reacted by caning the courier with 100 strokes. There was never any proof of the victim's guilt brought forward.

The Players

General Sani Abacha

As Nigeria's seventh military dictator, Sani Abacha takes destitution, murder, repression, corruption and greed to a new stratosphere. This guy makes Idi Amin look like a bonafide Berkeley philanthropist. The fat man is unscrupulous, power-mad and paranoid. He rarely leaves Nigeria (who the hell would have him over for a state dinner anyhow?) and was involved in the last three coup attempts before finally taking the government's reigns on November 17, 1993. His first act was to abolish all democratic institutions, including the senate, national assembly and state councils. As well, he banned all political parties. He swept in military rule and purged the government of all civilians and the army of officers loyal to former President Major General Ibrahim Babangida, who himself seized power through a coup in August 1985. Without any political or ideological agenda at all, Abacha busies himself these days stuffing his pockets with embezzled cash—and lining those of the brown-nosing northern primroses—and executing dissidents.

Shell Oil Company

Shell's been catching a lot of flack from bleeding hearts groups—from human rights lobbies to environmentalists. Some of it's deserved, some isn't. Nigeria sits atop a confirmed 20 billion barrels of oil. Shell (Nigeria Shell) accounts for half of the government's income. So what's the big deal about the unexplained loss of a few billion dollars here or there? On the other hand, the oil giant has started a US$3.6 billion liquefied natural gas project that's gotten a clean slate from the green crowd and can only be for the welfare of all Nigerians.

The Ogonis

The Ogoni people are a small minority in Nigeria—perhaps numbering 500,000—but Abacha has been systematically raping their oil-rich land, and, of course, the Ogonis have nothing to show for it. So when Ken Saro-Wiwa decided to champion the group's rights, he and eight of his buddies were promptly executed by the government. Nigeria was suspended from the Commonwealth (which is like getting a bimonthly bye in the weekly bridge club), and Britain—in protest—recalled its ambassador, who was back in his Lagos digs by the middle of January 1996, only a couple of months after Saro-Wiwa was hanged and Abacha had his wrists slapped by the West. Now, it's back to the business of pumping for petro-bucks. Hey, life goes on.

United Front for Nigeria's Liberation (UFNL)

This previously unknown faction (in Nigeria, all rebel factions are unknown) claimed responsibility for the plane crash on January 19, 1996, that killed the son of military dictator Abacha. The UFNL then blasted a bomb at the airport where the plane had taken off. Given the West's aloofness in supporting an overt democracy movement in Nigeria, something scary's happening: a murderous African terrorist group endorsed by Middle America.

The United Democratic Front of Nigeria

Composed of 13 exiled democracy groups, the UDFN was formed on April 1, 1996. This fledgling body is more identifiable than UFNL, which the government claims doesn't even exist.

Getting In

A passport and visa required. Visas, at no charge, are valid for one entry within 12 months of issue. You'll need one photo, a yellow fever vaccination, proof of onward/return transportation, and for a tourist visa, a letter of invitation. Business visas require a letter from counterpart in Nigeria and a letter of introduction from a U.S. company. For further information, contact the following:

Embassy of the Republic of Nigeria

2201 M Street, N.W.
Washington, D.C. 20037
☎ *(202) 822-1500 or 1522*

Consulate General (in New York)

☎ *(212) 715-7200*

If you think you are going to save money by flying Nigeria Airlines from Europe, think again. Remember, NA flights are banned from entering the U.S., and one of its new Airbus A310s was nabbed by the Belgians for nonpayment of debt. Another NA plane had to make an emergency landing in Algiers and has been sitting there for months waiting for spare parts. Many flights are cancelled because politicians borrow the planes to go shopping in Europe or just feel like visiting their money in Saudi Arabia.

Getting Around

Nigeria is mainly dependent on road transportation. During the oil boom in the mid-1970s, a number of long-distance roads were built—but arteries have become dilapidated in recent years due to the civil war and shrinking government revenues. And the accident rate in Nigeria is nearly the worst in the world. There is a nominal railway system, but even this has fallen into disrepair.

Dangerous Places

Lagos

The capital is a free-for-all, plagued by acute crime. Violent crime committed in broad daylight is the norm, and foreigners are particularly targeted and sometimes murdered for no reason. Shakedowns, muggings, carjackings, robberies, assaults, armed break-ins and even murders are frequently committed by uniformed police and soldiers in the capital. The Nigerian government has not heeded urgent U.S. embassy requests for the perpetrators to be disciplined. Unlike other coconut coalitions in the Third World, Nigeria possesses a capital city that is every bit as dangerous as the countryside.

The Rest of the Country

Factional fighting continues in Nigeria. Areas of noted danger include the border region in the northeast near Lake Chad—where outbursts of communal violence are common— usually involving clashes between Muslim fundamentalists and Christian proselytizers, southern Nigeria along the Niger River and regions in and outside Lagos in the southwest. Armed break-ins, muggings and carjackings are especially prevalent in the north.

There has been an increase in the number of unauthorized automobile checkpoints. These checkpoints are operated by bands of police, soldiers, or bandits posing as or operating with police or soldiers, whose personnel should be considered armed and dangerous. Many incidents, including murder, illustrate the increasing risks of road travel in Nigeria. Reports of threats against firms and foreign workers in the petroleum sector recur from time to time. Chadian troop incursions have reportedly occurred at the border area in the far northeast, near Lake Chad.

Bakassi Peninsula

Nigeria and Cameroon have been duking it out in the disputed Bakassi Peninsula, where the two nations have long been at odds. Since February 1994, the armed forces of the two nations have frequently clashed in the peninsula, a series of impoverished islands in the oil-rich Gulf of Guinea, which each claims to be its territory. Elf-Sarepca, the Cameroonian unit of France's Elf Aquitaine and several other oil firms are exploring for crude oil there, and just south of the islands.

Dangerous Things

Politics

Chief K. O. Abiola won the 1993 democratic elections fair and square. When he was imprisoned and charged with treason by Abacha for declaring himself president, it sent a clear message that politics is not a healthy career choice in Nigeria. Former President General Olusegun Obasanjo is cooling his heels in the clink for his two coup attempts against Abacha, and there are an estimated 43 dissidents sharing his cell. On March 16, 1996, Nigeria held elections for 593 local councils, but the government prohibited members of the Movement for the Survival of the Ogoni Peoples—the antigovernment group Ken Saro-Wiwa championed—from running. On March 21, Abacha signed a law permitting the military junta to dismiss any local councilman without cause.

Crime

Nigeria has one of highest crime rates in the world. There are 94 murders for every 100,000 people and 1256 thefts. Murder often accompanies even the simplest burglaries.

Organized Crime

In April 1996, German police uncovered a Nigerian organized crime ring that was operating throughout Europe, who were allegedly involved in counterfeiting, drug running, and credit card fraud. Over the past few years, German police investigations of these crimes have inevitably led them to Nigeria. Since 1990, the Nigerians have worked the following fraudulent trick: Offers were made to private individuals and medium-sized companies via letters or fax that they should help with the transfer of millions of dollars from Nigeria to Germany. In return, between 30 and 40 percent of the amounts were promised. In reality, however, the gangsters were interested in collecting high amounts for alleged charges in Nigeria from those whom they were cheating. By investigating these scams, the Germans were able to uncover that the Nigerians suspected of the crimes obviously were part of well-organized, internationally active groups.

Uniforms

Many both petty and violent crimes committed against foreigners are performed by bandits dressed in police or military uniforms. Bandits regularly murder foreigners without provocation. As well, foreigners are frequently robbed, assaulted and/or killed by legitimate police officers and soldiers, and never reprimanded or punished by the government. Pickpockets and confidence artists, some posing as local immigration and other government officials, are especially common at Murtala Muhammad Airport. In addition to harassment and shakedowns of American citizens by officials at airports and throughout Nigeria, there have been reports of violent attacks by purported government officials on Americans and other foreigners.

Road Travel

Road travel is extremely dangerous throughout Nigeria, but particularly in the south and the northeastern border near Lake Chad. Unauthorized automobile checkpoints are set up regularly in rural areas and manned by armed bandits or police/military personnel with the sole purpose of hijacking, assaulting and/or robbing motorists. U.S. citizens are targets for carjackings, robberies and violence.

Flying

The U.S. FAA has prohibited aircraft from Nigerian Airlines from landing in the U.S. due to the unsafe upkeep of the airline's fleet. Additionally, the quality of fuel used in the airliners doesn't meet international minimum requirements—it's low-grade, often dirty and spiked with other ingredients that don't help planes stay off the ground.

Getting Sick

Health services are generally limited to the cities, and only affordable for wealthy Nigerians. Modern medicine is nonexistent in rural areas. Public health has crashed with the government's pilfering of anything of value sent into the country. Yellow fever, chloroquine-resistant malaria, trachoma and yaws are the biggest medical threats in Nigeria. Malaria is found in all parts of the country, including all urban areas, and the risk is present all year. There is a 17 percent risk of p. vivax malaria exposure. Dracunculiasis, meningitis, lassa fever, leishmaniasis (both cutaneous and visceral), rabies, relapsing fever, African sleeping sickness and typhus (endemic flea-borne, epidemic louse-borne and scrub) are prevalent. Muslim northern Nigeria is the area worst affected by the meningitis scourge that has killed thousands of people in the Sahal belt of West Africa. Nigeria is also receptive to dengue fever, and schistosomiasis may be found throughout the country. There is one doctor for every 6134 people in Nigeria.

Outbreaks of meningitis, cholera, measles and gastroenteritis swept across the arid areas of West Africa in March and April 1996, particularly in Nigeria. Around 70,000 people in 17 African countries have been afflicted by meningitis alone, and nearly 9000 have died, more than half of them in Nigeria. The health problem is seen as so grave by Saudi Arabia that it banned all Nigerians from entering the Kingdom to perform the annual pilgrimage, or Haj, to the Islamic world's two holiest shrines. Meningitis is inflammation of the brain and spinal cord. If treated in time, its victims can be saved, although complications can bring deafness or loss of the fingers.

Nuts and Bolts

The Federal Republic of Nigeria is a tropical country (356,668 square miles, or 923,770 square kilometers) with two different climatic zones. The south is hot, rainy and humid for much of the year, while the north is equally hot but dry from October through April.

Nigeria is a federation of 30 states under the control of a military dictatorship and marred by corruption and instability. Muslims comprise 50 percent of the population, while Christians make up 40 percent. The Hausa-Fulani, Yoruba and Ibo ethnic groups total 65 percent of the population, and the estimated 250 ethnic comprise the other 35 percent. The official language of Nigeria's 100 million people is English.

There are more than 20 English-language newspapers in the country, but they are heavily monitored and supervised by the military junta. Foreign journalists are routinely expelled for citing corruption in the government.

The literacy rate is 51 percent. Less than 20 percent of the population graduates from secondary school. The official currency is the naira, divided into 100 kobo.

Dangerous Days

03/1996	Nigeria moved troops into Cameroon.
03/21/1996	Abacha signed a law permitting the military junta to dismiss any local councilman without cause.
01/19/1996	UFNL claimed responsibility for a plane crash that killed the son of military dictator Abacha.
11/1995	Writer and Ogoni rights champion Ken Saro-Wiwa and eight colleagues were executed by the Abacha government.
11/17/1993	General Sani Abacha's coup made him Nigeria's seventh military ruler.
06/23/1993	General Ibrahim Babangida annulled elections; military remained in power.
06/18/1993	It was leaked that Moshood Abiola won the presidential elections comfortably over Bashir Tofa.
05/1992	Two hundred people were killed in ethnic clashes.
07/03/1986	Former President Shehu Shagari and former Vice President Alex Ekwueme were released after spending 30 months in detention.
05/23/1986	Fifteen students were killed in clash with police.
08/27/1985	Major General Ibrahim Babangida takes over the government in a military coup.
01/15/1966	A group of army majors (mainly Ibo) failed in Nigeria's first coup attempt.
10/01/1960	Independence declared.

Islamabad

Pakistan
★★★★

Dodge City with Skiing

Some parts of Pakistan, like its neighbor Afghanistan, have been surprisingly effective in resisting the influences of the outside world. Even though planeloads of trekkers, hippies, and hard-core mountain climbers travel here to explore some of the world's most rugged scenery, there are still many wild and dangerous areas. The tribal areas of Pakistan have never felt the presence of their own government, let alone tourists. Pashto-speaking tribes and warlike clans maintain their own social, political and military structures, free from politics, taxes and MTV. Many of the more entrepreneurial tribes view travelers and visitors as walking CARE packages. British adventurers, such as Rudyard Kipling and Sir Richard Burton, maintained a healthy respect for the "wily Pathans," who have always controlled the remote mountainous regions of northwest Pakistan.

Today, Pakistan is an angry jigsaw puzzle of four semiautonomous provinces—Punjab, Sind, North-West Frontier Province (NWFP) and Baluchistan. It also encompasses federally administered tribal and northern areas (FATA/FANA) and

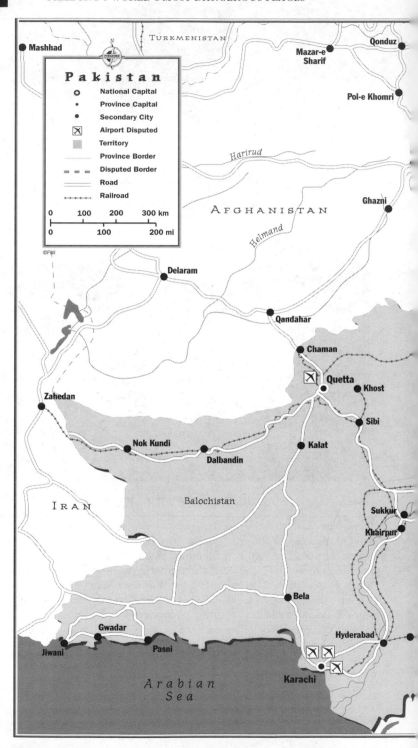

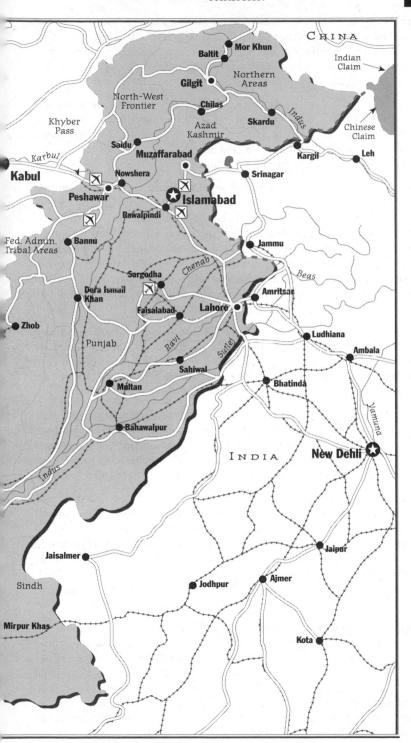

lays claim to the Indian-occupied but mostly Muslim states of Azad Jammu and Kashmir. The teeming population of Pakistan is as diverse as it is large. Its 115.59 million people are comprised of Punjabi (56 percent), Sindi (23 percent), Pashtun (13 percent), Baluchi (5 percent) and others, including Mohajirs, or Urdu-speaking Muslim emigres from India.

Pakistan is dirt-poor, even by African standards. The per-capita annual income in 1992 was US$410. Thirty percent of the population lives below the poverty line, and only 35 percent of the population can read and write. Only 20 percent of Pakistani females can read and write, and barely 40 percent of children of primary school age were actually enrolled in schools.

Pakistan was the first country created as an Islamic state. By law, the country's president must be a Muslim. The legal system follows both the Islamic code of justice, or *Sharia*, and old British laws. Even the banking system must abide by Koran dictates that say it is improper to charge or pay interest. Bank customers actually share the profits and losses with the institutions where they do business. However, fiscal common sense still supercedes religious zeal, when, every year, just prior to Ramadan, customers withdraw their entire bank accounts to avoid the Zakat tax, a 2.5 percent levy on certain bank accounts charged annually on the eve of Ramadan.

Even a minor discussion with a Pakistani will evoke a long devotional treatise on the joys of Islam and the power of Allah. Pakistanis may not be entirely supportive of their government (I heard the phrase, "Benazir is a bitch," numerous times to describe the contempt many Pakistanis have for their female leader), but they are certainly wild about Allah.

And just to throw a little more mayhem into the picture, there's this nasty little nuclear arms race going on with India. Being on each other's borders means both nations don't require the technology to blast intercontinental ballistic rockets 10,000 miles able to strike a dime. India, for instance, is believed to have the capability of lobbing a nuclear warhead within 1000 feet of a target 150 miles away.

In this part of the world, that's close enough. India and Pakistan, in their relatively embryonic relationship, have already fought three wars. Firefights on the disputed border occur regularly between the two sides. And both countries aid separatist extremists—Pakistan funds the nasties in the Indian-controlled region of Kashmir, while India fans the flames of hatred in Pakistan's Sind area. While the world ignores the global consequences of this seemingly Hatfield-and-McCoy stick-fight in the boonies, the CIA quietly announced recently that Pakistan and India are two of the planet's top choices for potential serious instability.

Pakistan (Islami Jamhuria-e-Pakistan, or the Islamic Republic of Pakistan) became independent on August 15, 1947, when Britain sliced up India in response to public pressure to create a separate Muslim state. East Pakistan seceded and became the separate country of Bangladesh in March 1971. Pakistan aligns itself with the U.S. and was a vital supply line for anti-Communist Afghan insurgents. Population growth is among the world's highest, the literacy rate is low and deteriorating, and the unofficial unemployment rate is greater than 25 percent. Agriculture still accounts for about 70 percent of total exports.

Good For What Ails You

Travelers to Muslim countries are used to getting goofy on too sweet tea and whooping it up on watery yogurt. Ingesters of the fermented liquid form of the hop, grape and grain will be happy to learn that alcohol in Pakistan can be prescribed for medicinal purposes. Although alcohol is banned in Pakistan under Islamic law, you can order hard liquor and beer by the bottle through room service at the swank hotels in the large cities. You must fill out a form (for non-Muslims only), pay a small fee (about a dollar), and then sit in the quiet solitude of your room feeling like a junkie on methadone treatment. Malt beverages (beer without alcohol) are commonly available, and some remote areas feature homemade brews.

The Scoop

Pakistan is still the classic adventurer's paradise, a wild mountainous region (to the north) and an arid wasteland (to the south), inhabited by fierce warring tribes and squabbling minorities. The isolation and poverty are positively biblical in the smaller towns. The big cities make *Bladerunner* look like a Caribbean resort. Sensory-numbing amounts of noise, dirt, poverty, temperature extremes, crime and general mayhem send most travelers fleeing to New York seeking peace and quiet. But as many Pakistanis point out, don't forget India is worse. Pakistan offers natural, archaeological and historical sites, as well as a wealth of interesting backwaters. Amazingly, amongst this Third World developmental disaster, the Pakistani people are some of the most handsome, generous and engaging to be met on this planet...despite their constant warfare and banditry.

There have been major ethnic tensions in Pakistan since the country became independent. Pakistan has been pushed closer to the edge by the massive influx of weapons and refugees caused by wars in Afghanistan and conflict with India. There are a lot of guns in Pakistan with a lot of people who use them on a regular basis. Tourists are kidnapped for ransom but have not been harmed or executed.(Though a Swede was killed in 1991 in a messy government rescue attempt.) Your health is definitely at risk; everything from cobras to dengue-carrying mosquitoes can end it all rather suddenly. Mountainous highways and insane drivers make Pakistan's roads a killing ground. Much of the country is not under the control of the government but ruled by tribes. Professional bandits prey on poor and rich alike. What better place for a stroll through the countryside?

The Players

The Army/Government

You have to give Pakistan an A for effort when it comes to defending their Muslim state. Even though Pakistan has lost every war they have started, they still love to rattle their rusty colonial-era sabers at the huge Indian army to their east and watch their backs as Afghanistan descends into the apocalypse. Warring tribes in Baluchistan, Sind, the North West Frontier and the tribal areas keep the army's bullets from corroding in their clips, while criminals and ethnic terrorists in Karachi, Quetta and Hyderabad make soldiers sleep with one eye open. Having China as a neighbor to the north and Iran to the west does not make flower power high on the political agenda either.

The government, bolstered by total armed forces of 580,000 (513,000 reservists), is actively stirring up revolt in what they consider to be occupied (by India) Jammu and

Kashmir. In June 1990, the Pakistan army had a total strength of over 500,000 soldiers. The navy has a total force of 20,000 men (including naval air personnel). The Pakistan air force (PAF) has 30,000 servicemen. Pakistan supplies much of the Middle East's cheap labor and is the world's prime low-cost supplier of military troops. About 30,000 military contract personnel from Pakistan were serving with the U.N. in Saudi Arabia, Libya, Oman, the United Arab Emirates and Kuwait in mid-1989, mainly in an advisory capacity. There have been complaints that the government actually makes money by renting out its poorly paid troops to serve in U.N. peacekeeping missions. The U.N. compensates Pakistan at a higher rate of pay, and the government allegedly pockets the difference. The government of Benazir Bhutto is consistently criticized for the plight of the poor Pakistanis, but considering that Ali Bhutto was strung up—his son was killed mysteriously in France, and General Zia Ul-Haq died in a mysterious plane crash—it's a wonder anybody wants to run this country. If you'd like to, it's a fax away.

Prime Minister Benazir Bhutto

Office of the Prime Minister
Islamabad, Pakistan
FAX: (+92)-51 821 835 (with remark: please forward to Prime Minister)
Telex: 082 5742; telegrams: Prime Minister Bhutto, Islamabad, Pakistan

Or:

Foreign Minister Assef Ahmad Ali

Office of the Foreign Minister
Islamabad, Pakistan
FAX: (+92)-51 821 835 (with remark: please forward to Foreign Minister)
Telex: 082 5742; telegrams: Foreign Minister Assef Ahmad Ali, Islamabad, Pakistan

The "Afghans"

There are 3 million "Afghan" refugees in Pakistan, most of them live in squalid mud-walled refugee camps outside of Peshawar and Quetta. Many others live in UNHR tents in small mountainous villages and deserts. There is little chance for education or economic future, but most prefer Pakistan to returning to war-wasted Afghanistan. There are also hundreds of "Afghans" from Libya, Egypt, Yemen, Jordan, Palestine, Algeria and Tunisia based, recruited and trained in Peshawar, and the border regions between Pakistan and Afghanistan.

The inner circle of the "Afghans" consists of 300 Egyptians. The "Afghan" branch of the Islamic Jihad is directed by Mohammed Shawky Islambuli, brother of the assassin of President Anar el-Sadat. Some 30 Egyptian "Afghans" work directly with the Iranian Pasdarans. Eight of these Egyptians constitute the central command of the Islamic Legion, a terrorist and political group active in Egypt, Eritrea, Kenya, Tanzania, Sudan, Algeria, Libya and Lebanon.

Some of the "Afghan" leaders have fled to Jalalabad from Peshawar. The Arab "Afghans" have ties with fundamentalist Muslims in the United States. Ramzi Ahmed Yussef, a suspect in the bombing of the World Trade Center in New York, is an "Afghan." Yussef was trained from 1987 to 1990 in Peshawar camps in the ranks of the Islamic Jihad groups under the orders of Dr. Ayman al-Zawahiri.

The Mohajirs

As of the beginning of 1995, the Mohajirs are the principal disturbers in the Karachi area. The Mohajirs are Urdu-speaking Muslim immigrants who came here from India after the partition between Pakistan and India in 1947. Their political/military group, the Mohajir National Movement (MQM), is directly battling police and strongarming locals. There are six major political and religious groups in Karachi. In total, they have 1000 armed guerrillas and snipers operating at any one time.

Getting In

A passport and visa are required. The visa must be obtained from a Pakistani embassy or consulate before arrival at the point of entry. Information on entry requirements can be obtained from the embassy of Pakistan or the Pakistani consulate general.There is a $20 fee for the visa and a $10 fee for rush delivery. Business visitors and tourists are required to carry a valid Pakistan visa in their passports that must be obtained prior to entry. Pakistani requirements to legally cross the country's borders are different for each nationality. U.S. citizens must have a visa issued by a Pakistani consulate as well as a valid U.S. passport. Make sure you apply for your visa in the country of your residence, since you will be told that only the embassy in your home city or country can issue visas.

Embassy of Pakistan

2315 Massachusetts Avenue, N.W.
Washington, D.C. 20008
☎ *(202) 939-6200*

Pakistani Consulate General

12 East 65th Street
New York, New York 10021
☎ *(212) 879-5800*

Do not bring in alcohol; it will be confiscated and given back to you upon your departure. Crossing from Afghanistan officially is forbidden for foreigners, although many of the remote tribal areas do not observe any immigration formalities. Currently, the Afghanistan-Pakistan border is closed, but it is easy to streak across. Only U.N. personnel and locals are allowed to cross the border officially. The Iranian border can be crossed using weekly train service (Zahedan–Quetta), or by a painfully slow 22-hour bus trip (Taftan–Quetta). Folks who like avoiding those messy passport stamps can expect to be arrested and tried in court, which can result in deportation, fines and/or imprisonment.

You can enter from China via the efficient, but weather-sensitive Karakoram Highway. The road is open from May 1–November 30 if Mother Nature obliges. The route continues to the famous trading town of Kashgar, but the bus ride will test the stamina and intestines of any traveler. Coming in from India is via train (Lahore–Wagh) or a four-hour bus ride (Lahore–Amritsar) but subject to closure due to Sikh attacks. Check with the government or the embassy for exact restrictions and closures. The only land border crossing with India is Amritsar.

Getting Around

Safe travel inside Pakistan is subject to weather, regional idiosyncracies and plain luck. Bandits prey on buses and trains; the roads are makeshift, and if the robbers don't get you, the dilapidated buses might. Pakistan is a patchwork of tribal- and government-controlled areas, sprinkled liberally with bandits who couldn't care less who "rules" the area. Most travelers have a great time, despite the chaos.

Substantial areas within North-West Frontier Province are designated tribal areas, outside the normal jurisdiction of government law enforcement authorities. Travel within these areas is particularly hazardous. Tribal feuds or conflicts between smuggling factions may incidentally involve foreigners. Even in the settled areas, ethnic, political or sectarian violence may target foreigners. Car hijackings and the abduction of foreigners are occasionally reported from the tribal areas. If visitors must enter the tribal areas, a permit must be obtained from the Home Department, which may require that an armed escort accompany the visitor. *DP* was in the market in Peshawar when a man was shot dead trying to take off with a stolen car. Three bullets in the neck. They did not ask for ID before they shot.

Driving

PAKISTAN

Today, Pakistan is busy spending the millions appropriated to it by the World Bank to upgrade its highways. Unfortunately, no one has been taught to drive. The white lines on those freshly made highways are an old colonial anachronism. Drivers weave, honk, squeeze, yell, wave, swerve and do everything except brake when faced with an oncoming car.

Considering the Pakistanis' creative use of their roadways, it is not surprising that, despite all the press about *dacoits* (local bandits) and civil unrest, the greatest potential for injury while traveling through Pakistan is the chance of being involved in a crash or being smacked like a cricket ball when crossing the street. To give pedestrians and other drivers a chance, Pakistanis decorate their vehicles with as many bright and shiny objects as possible

The aging Bedfords, three-wheeled rickshaws and "Suzukis" are adorned with loud horns, extensive murals, miniature disco systems, tassels and other bric-a-brac. Prayers to Allah, bucolic scenes, dingleberries, doodads and mascots glued like African fetishes are just some of the advanced safety techniques designed to ensure the longevity of the driver (but not necessarily the passengers). The decorations are supposed to ward off danger but, apparently, are ineffective in stopping the carnage.

Of a total 35,258 miles of roads in Pakistan, 24,952 (a generous 70 percent) are paved. The torturous terrain requires major engineering feats to put in roads. Most of the country can only be traversed via pack-trails and footpaths. The main highway is the Grand Trunk Road between Karachi and Peshawar. The multilane highway linking Karachi with Hyderabad is also a major route, permitting crazed drivers to get more out of their sheet-metal buckets than Isaac Newton would ever advise. The Indus Highway, the other north-south artery, is being improved, and there will eventually be a highway connecting Peshawar with Karachi, via Islamabad and Lahore.

The most impressive highway is the 1200-km Karakoram Highway, built over a 20-year period to link the remote Chinese market town of Kashgar with Peshawar to the south. The road is a mind-blower for its mountainous scenery and is frequently closed due to landslides, snowstorms, floods and other topographical afflictions. Various adventure groups offer bicycling tours for the eco-adventurous. Obviously, the hundreds of ever smiling drivers would think nothing of adding one more shiny decoration to the side of their overloaded trucks.

On paper, Pakistan borrows the British rule of driving on the left. In reality, driving is a death-defying blend of the German habit of operating motor vehicles with the pedal to the floor, the Italian habit of talking with their hands, and the Asian custom of ignoring mirrors, or side and rear windows. The fact that most Pakistani roads are designed for Alexander's (the Great) camels keeps it interesting. If you want less control over your destiny, you might want to hire your own talkative driver and deathtrap car from the Pakistan Tourism folks. A 4-WD jeep is preferable for more rugged trips in the north. Suzukis and Jeeps are popular. You will need a large security deposit and will be dinged about eight rupees per km and 200 rupees per day. Or, you can negotiate a fixed rate if you know your itinerary.

In the cities, yellow taxis are cheap and should be hired round-trip, since they tend to gravitate to hotels and are hard to find elsewhere. Wildly decorated buses are cheaper, but remember they expect you to jump on (and off) while they are moving. Don't forget the seats by the driver are for women and don't be shy about yelling before your stop.

The taxi fare from the airport to the centers of both Islamabad and Karachi is approximately 150 rupees. Peshawar is about 50 to 80 rupees. As you exit the terminal you will be mobbed by hundreds of official and nonofficial cabdrivers. It doesn't matter who you choose. Negotiate the fare with at least three drivers, since foreigners have traditionally been charged what the market will bear (about twice to three times the correct rate). Serious cheapskates will walk out past the airport and catch the sardine-can-like rickshaws who will ding you about 20 to 30 rupees. If you want to see the country by bus, stick to the more comfortable "Flying Coach" buses rather than the brightly decorated but deadly local buses. For brief amusement but not long-distance touring, try the horse-drawn *tonga* carriages and cheap three-wheeled motorized rickshaws. Big Westerners may not fit in the back of a rickshaw.

By Rail

As with many other former British colonies, Pakistan was built around its aging railway system. The country is linked by the north-south railway between the southern port of Karachi and the city of Peshawar in the North-West Frontier Province. The line runs through most major population centers.

Pakistan Railways offers 8775 km of track, 907 stations, 78 train stops, 714 locomotives, 2926 passenger coaches and 32,440 freight wagons. Sixty percent of Pakistan's track and 30 percent of its rolling stock are supposed to be scrapped, but are in use every day. Express trains have been held up by *dacoits* on the link between Karachi port and Lahore. You'll have a choice between 2nd, Economy, 1st, and Air-Conditioned classes. Go for the Air-Con class, since rail travel is cheap, slow and nostalgic in this class. The other classes are just torture. Bedding, toilet paper, soap and towels are not supplied on first-class couchettes but can be rented from the reservations office. The train between the Afghan border and Peshawar is the most interesting, as two steam trains (one at each end of the train) labors up and back down the Khyber Pass every Friday. Currently, Westerners are not allowed on this train, since it goes through the locked-down Khyber area.

By Air

Air travel is the recommended means of transportation between the major cities in Pakistan. Air travel, particularly to the northern areas, is often disrupted due to weather conditions. Regional airlines in the north have to fly *below* some of the world's tallest mountaintops.

Islamabad/Rawalpindi International Airport is five miles northwest of Islamabad and a 20-minute drive by taxi. State-run Pakistan International Airlines (PIA) maintains tardy but vital service to 41 international and 33 domestic destinations. There are 112 airfields, of which 104 are usable, 75 have a permanent surface. There are 31 runways over 8000 feet. Domestic tickets are cheaper when bought inside Pakistan. Pakistanis pay about half what you will pay. Airfares are laughably cheap (about $10–$80US for any internal leg). You must pay in rupees. International flights to Karachi or Islamabad should be bought in major European or Asian bucket shops. Security is very tight. On nearly every flight, I had to go through X-ray, metal detector, tag, stamp tag, punch tag, rip tag, claim luggage and scrotum-squeezing personal searches. My film and luggage were X-rayed so much I am sure they glow in the dark.

Pakistan International Airways has the dubious task of flying very used equipment around the world's most hostile flying environments. Soaring mountains, dust, high winds, turbulence, down- and updrafts and the extra maintenance required to keep planes airborne may be the reasons why the landing announcement is a Muslim prayer: "Ladies and Gentlemen, *Inshallah* (God willing), we will be shortly landing." The feeling of flying heavily loaded turboprops well below many of the world's highest mountains is, quite frankly, a thrill. The turboprops can be very bumpy, and don't be surprised to find passengers praying fervently on rough flights. Despite the white-knuckle flights, air travel is still the recommended means of transportation between major cities in Pakistan. Keep in mind that many flights are overbooked, but seats on these flights can be bought by sweet-talking (and, of course, bribing) an airport porter.

Insider Tip

Pakistan is a land of frustrating red tape but there are many ways to cut through it. For example, you can be told that a flight is overbooked, only to find out that a flight with one connection to the same destination is available. You can be stopped from entering a region by an emphatic border guard, only to walk 20 yards further along the border and walk right through. There is little that cannot be bought, solved, rented or fixed in Pakistan for a moderate fee. In fact, getting around problems is a major source of income for enterprising Pakistanis and "Afghans." There was little DP could not do or make happen in Pakistan with a little financial lubrication. So, when in doubt, whip it out (your rupees). A case in point.

A newly made friend asked me if I could get him a visa to America. I said, "It's not like Pakistan, you can't just pay people off."

"Surely you can pay the police 2000–3000 rupees (about $US100) to get me in? I could be your gardener."

"Sorry, no way."

"What kind of country is that?" he said in disgust.

Trekking

Since many of the major historical sites have been pounded to rubble by invading armies, and the vast deserts to the south do not inspire too many nature photographers, Pakistan realizes that most of the tourism is related to its spectacular northern mountain scenery. You will find this area of Pakistani tourism well run and efficient. In a country where you would have a hard time finding a decent motor-coach tour, you can climb a major mountain with great ease (or at least make the preparations). To facilitate understanding and access, tourism officials have divided the country into open, restricted, and closed zones for trekkers. Open zones go up to only 6000 meters. Travel above that point is classified as mountaineering and requires a separate permit. The best source for information and permits is through the various trekking packagers well in advance of your trip (permits can take months). Good sources for information, permits, guides and porters are the following:

Pakistan Tours
Flashman's Hotel
The Mall
Rawalpindi
☎ 64811

Adventure Pakistan
10 Kahayaban-e-Suharawardy
Aapara Market
Islamabad
☎ 28324

A *DP* money-saver tip: There are literally hundreds of expensive European hiking boots for sale in the bazaars of Pakistan. These $100–$300 leather mountaineering boots can be bought for $4 to $7. Where do they come from? Simple! They are stolen from trekkers in hotels and shipped to Karachi.

Climbing

Although Everest is number one on the list of climbers, K2 (8611 m, 28251ft) really is the tougher climb. It is also one of the world's most dangerous climbs. Only 119 people have made it to the top of K2, compared to the 600 that have planted a flag on Mt. Everest. What makes K2 the most dangerous mountain in the world is its annual death toll. When *DP* was in northern Pakistan, there was a reward to find the bodies of two climbers who had disappeared in an avalanche. Seven died in 1995 and 13 were killed in 1986. Everest is on the border with Nepal and Tibet and costs a staggering $50,000 for six climbing permits. K2 is a bargain at $10,000 for six climbers. These are just the climbing fees, and with supplies, porters and excess baggage fees, climbing the big peaks is a sport for not only the brave—but also the rich.

Getting Out

You will need an exit visa to leave the country. Although you may adhere to the paper chain faithfully, expect to get a quizzical look if the immigration official notes certain "irregularities" and requires additional funds to let you catch your plane out. If you are carrying anything that can be interpreted as being an antiquity, you are in trouble again. You'll need an export permit for rugs, and don't think for a moment that nifty pen gun you bought in Darra Adam Khel is not going to be spotted and confiscated. If you're bringing some smoking green back with you, expect it to be discovered by sniffer dogs at Karachi and Lahore airports. Also, you will get dinged for the carpet export license scam. Every carpet must have an export permit, and every rug dealer claims you don't need one. Regardless of the value of the carpet, demand an export receipt. Please note that although hashish and heroin are as easy to buy in Peshawar as Snickers bars in Pacoima, there is much money to be made (5000 rupees last we checked) turning frugal hippies in to police. The naive stoners will then have to pay up to 5000 US *dollars* to the concerned but financially adept police to save their skin.

Remember, you will need to keep your exchange receipts to change your grubby rupees into more stable currencies. Most people take care of exchanging their money in the bazaar (watch out for bogus US 100 bills printed in Syria, Iran and Lebanon before 1989). Remember to keep enough for your taxi, something to eat at the airport, 200 rupees for your departure tax. Everything else can be paid for in dollars. Some banks only cash traveler's checks and do not take foreign cash. The border with Afghanistan is technically closed, but *DP* found plenty of folks who will take you by camel, truck, foot or private car. This is illegal, of course. You can exit using the Karakoram Highway north into China, but you will need the correct paperwork before you get there. The only land crossing to India is from Lahore to Amritsar. If you have *cojones* and strong legs, you could walk across the Hindu bush through Afghanistan into Tajikistan. Iran requires a visa that is double-checked in Teheran. The best place to get creative about your country of exit is in your home country with a double-check with the embassies in Islamabad.

Dangerous Places

Karachi

About five to 10 people die every day as a result of political violence in Karachi. Karachi is a dirty, bustling port town, with a population of more than 5 million people. Like most large cities, it has a serious problem with crime, strikes and demonstrations, as well as ongoing incidents of ethnic and sectarian violence. Robbery and kidnapping are often carried out with the distinct intention of creating terror and instability among the populace. Bombings have occurred at Pakistan government facilities and public utility sites. Vehicular hijacking and theft by armed individuals are common occurrences. Persons resisting have very often been shot and killed. Overly detailed and gory reports of murders, bombings, robberies and assassinations fill the papers every day.

Sectarian violence killed more than 1000 people in 1994, compared to 75 in 1993; '96 was worse. Even the army left in December '94, saying it was too "hot" for them. In 1993, 88 soldiers and police officers were killed in ambushes and shootings. No one has been convicted or even charged with the murders. More than 170 people were killed in sectarian and ethnic violence in December 1994 alone in this steamy southern port. Even Pakistanis stay out of Karachi. If you get bored waiting around to be shot or kidnapped, you can spend a few hours crabbing or rent a camel on the beach.

The North-West Frontier Province

An area created in 1901 by the British who could never figure how to "civilize" the many tribes and clans, the NWFP is still the land of *badal*, or revenge. It is the oldest continuously lawless area in the world. Home to the "wily Pathans," this rugged land of green valleys and snowcapped valleys has never been fully conquered by Alexander, Moghuls, Sikhs, Brits or even the Russians. The North-West Frontier Province has an affinity with Afghanistan in the west and is known for its well-armed populace. Weapons are carried and sold openly on the streets. Peshawar, the largest city and capital of the province, could be accurately described as Dodge City without Wyatt Earp. Peshawar is the home of over 1 million Afghan refugees who live in three large mud cities. Western travelers and well-heeled residents are frequently kidnapped to bring attention to their causes and to get some quick folding money. Expect to pay about $20,000 to $35,000 if you know someone in Peshawar or a lot more if you are working for a Western company in Peshawar. Backpackers are usually cleaned out and sent running to the American Express office in Islamabad.

Khyber Pass

It would be an understatement to say that it is dangerous to travel overland through the tribal areas along the Khyber Pass to Kabul. The North-West Frontier areas are ruled by the Afridi tribes and are not under the control of the Pakistani government or police. Many, if not most, make money smuggling hashish, heroin and contraband into Pakistan. If you can get past the checkpoint at the smuggler's market (just walk through the gate in the north market square into the Afridi bodyguard complex) expect eight more Pakistani army checkpoints until you reach Afghanistan. Once you are in Afghanistan, you are on your own. There are many deadly tribal feuds over things as important as stolen goats or errant wives, so lightening some dumb foreigner of his vehicle or belongings does not even appear on their list of "things not to do." Car-hijackings and the abduction of foreigners are occasionally reported from the tribal areas. If visitors must enter the tribal areas, a permit must be obtained from the Home Department, which may require that an armed escort accompany the visitor. As of late, permits are not being issued due to the war in Afghanistan.

Sind Province

Hundreds of years ago, travelers called Sind the "Unhappy Valley," because of its burning deserts, freezing mountain peaks, dust, lack of water and general fear of the predatory tribes. Today in rural Sind Province, neither the weather nor the emotional tone have improved, and the security situation is still hazardous, especially for overland travelers. Foreigners have occasionally been kidnapped, and in one incident in 1991, a Swedish kidnap victim was killed in a rescue attempt that turned into a battle between police and bandits. The home of the ancient Indus culture was known for its total lack of warfare or warlike activity. Naturally, that civilization completely disappeared in 1700 B.C. Today, Sind province is in turmoil due to friction between the political factions based out of Karachi. Drug smugglers and *dacoits* (local bandits) also make the rural areas unsafe for travel. Smugglers use the local beaches of Karachi to move drugs and contraband at night. Sinds, Pathans and Mohajirs are jostling for political supremacy in the region. The result is frequent assassinations, firefights, bomb attacks, murders and overall mayhem. Travel outside of Karachi into the Sind interior must have prior approval of the government of Pakistan.

Dacoits are well armed and will attack travelers even with trusty police escort. They have been known to stop entire trains or vehicle caravans, often kidnapping and killing passengers. Anyone contemplating travel into the Sind interior should first contact the American Consulate (*8 Abdullah Haroon Road, Karachi,* ☎ *515081)* for advisability. If travel is subsequently approved, a Pakistan police escort would normally be provided.

The Pakistan government requests that travelers inform police authorities well in advance of the trip so that necessary police security arrangements can be made. Bodyguards can be hired from travel groups or on the street (not advised) for about 4000 rupees a day. You will have to pay for your bodyguards' room and board. The best place to start planning your own death trip is the U.S. embassy in Karachi. Sind province still has a fairly healthy kidnappings-for-ransom business: 45 in 1990 to 79 in 1991, to 16 in 1992. The drop is supposed to be because of the increased military presence in the area. It might have more to do with the shortage of travelers who are into kidnapping.

Hyderabad

In Hyderabad, there have been recurring outbreaks of ethnic and sectarian violence which have been characterized by random bombings, shootings and mass demonstrations. Recent incidents have resulted in several deaths and the unofficial imposition of curfews. There have also been numerous incidents of kidnapping for ransom.

Islamabad and Rawalpindi

Welcome to the Twin Cities: Dirty Rawalpindi and squeaky-clean Islamabad, the capital of Pakistan, are only 10 kilometers and two worlds apart. Islamabad is the showcase city for the embassy folks, and Rawalpindi is where all the real people live. The crime rate in Islamabad is lower than in many parts of Pakistan, but it is on the rise. In the recent past, Americans have been the victim of armed robberies and assaults, although these types of incidents are not frequent. Thefts from the massive walled residences are common. As usual, they are typically inside jobs. Most incidents experienced by the American community are committed by servants employed in the household. Rawalpindi has experienced some bombings in public areas, such as markets, cinemas and parks.

Lahore/Punjab Province

The Punjab Province has been the site of numerous bomb blasts occurring at cinemas, marketplaces and other public areas. A professional criminal element exists in the Punjab (operating mainly in the interior), with kidnapping for ransom, robbery and burglaries all being carried out by gangs of professional criminals. There are frequent armed clashes between Pakistani and Indian army groups along the border area and in east Punjab and particularly in the disputed territory of Kashmir. Travel to the border areas of eastern Punjab is not recommended. Lahore is famous for rip-offs of tourists in cheap hotels, bogus traveler's checks and other tourist crime.

Kashmir

The biggest hornet's nest in Pakistan is Kashmir. Called "Occupied Kashmir" by the Pakistani, the area should have been part of Muslim Pakistan. In 1947 the princes who ran the "princely states" cut a quick deal with India instead and screwed the Muslims. The Kashmir dispute, which caused the 1948 and 1965 wars with India (Pakistan got whipped both times), remains unresolved. Kashmir has turned into a war zone with both sides owning large chunks of land. The Simla Agreement after the 1971 Bangladesh war adjusted the boundary between the Indian state of Jammu and Kashmir and the Pakistani state of Azad and Kashmir. The Muslims in the Indian state of Jammu and Kashmir demand, greater autonomy from Hindu and somewhat colonial India. Since an active insurgency began in January 1990, estimates of the numbers who have died range from a low of 7000 to a high of 13,000. The Indian Secret Police is very busy in the area and is reputedly assassinating vocal Muslims and has even been blamed for creating bogus political/terrorist groups (who then conveniently surrender on demand). The kidnapping of the Western trekkers has been rumored to be a bizarre PR plot. The terrorist group regularly sends faxes and telephone messages, yet the Indian government insists they are high up in the mountains. *DP* understands that they are dead.

The separatist elements within Jammu and Kashmir, particularly the Jammu and Kashmir Liberation Front (JKLF), openly receive training and military equipment from Pakistan. China is also aligning itself with Pakistan against India. Both sides agree a solution must be reached, but both are intractable. For now, Kashmir joins the ranks of Chechnya, Afghanistan, and Bosnia for long-running, messy and deadly Jihad worlds with admission to only the unwise or committed.

Baluchistan/Quetta

The province of Baluchistan that borders both Iran and Afghanistan is notorious for cross- border smuggling operations. It should actually be in our "Forbidden Places," since few if any permits are given and you must have the permission of the tribal chief to move in relative safety. Why anyone would want to travel to Quetta, southern Afghanistan, eastern Iran or the bleak Pakistani coast is a good question. We say relative safety, because kidnapping for money is as popular here as it is in the tribal regions up north. You would actually be safer if you were kidnapped than if you stumbled upon a drug caravan or wandered into war-torn Afghanistan. Any student of geography will quickly figure out that the fastest way from landlocked Afghanistan is through remote Baluchistan. The major drug smugglers (actually smuggling may be too ludicrous a term to apply here) run large truck and even camel caravans from Afghanistan to the coast.

This region also has a high occurrence of armed robberies, probably because just about everybody carries a gun. Terrorist bombings have occurred frequently in the region, primarily concentrated among those districts along the Afghanistan border. There is limited to no provincial police. Those hardy persons considering travel into the interior should first notify the province's home secretary, travel in a group and limit travel to daylight hours and see a psychiatrist. Although the Pakistani government tells *DP* that permission from the provincial authorities is required for travel into some interior locations, I couldn't help but wonder which government folks would be around to check.

Quetta, the capital city of the province, has experienced outbreaks of serious ethnic violence. Police have in the past used deadly force and imposed curfews in response to these ethnic clashes. Information regarding current conditions may be obtained by contacting either the American Consulate in Karachi or the U.S. embassy in Islamabad. Crimes such as robbery and vehicular hijacking have also been on the rise in Quetta. Western organizations have been targeted, and travelers should be alert as to what areas of the city to avoid.

Refugee Camps

Pakistan is home to 3 million Afghan refugees as a result of the ongoing war in Afghanistan, millions of Mojahair from partition days, and Kashmiri escaping persecution from clashes with India in the west. These camps are populated by hundreds of thousands of destitute, displaced people, many of them widows and orphans. They are not criminals per se and indulge in every possible business and service to eke out a living. However, the sight of rubbernecking tourists will send even the least scrupulous heart fluttering with dreams of riches. If you find yourself a victim of theft or robbery, consider yourself lucky.

Police will not bother to recover your items or even find the perpetrator. Many of these camps can be visited with an armed guard, and you may see many Westerners working as aid workers, but do not be fooled into thinking that these are safe places. Most of these people will welcome you into their humble homes and offer you what little food they have. Just hope you don't meet the one who doesn't.

Bogus Boogie

When the International Federation of the Phonographic Industry, the global cop for pirate CDs, comes to town, music store owners will want to run for the hills. In 1994, 92 percent of all CD and tape sales in Pakistan were bootlegged copies.

Dangerous Things

Crime

Pakistan is a special place when it comes to crime. There are three levels of crime. The first is the friendly constant pressure to relieve the unwitting of their possessions. Just as the wind and rain can erode granite mountains, the traveler to Pakistan will find his money slowly slipping from him. Perhaps this is not a crime, since the victim is consensual, but it nevertheless is not an honest transfer of funds.

The second level is petty crime, the fingers rummaging through your baggage, the wallet that leaves your pocket or the camera that disappears from the chair next to you. Everyone will caution you on petty theft. Here, theft is an art, almost a learned skill. These crimes happen to the unwary and unprepared. Lock your zippers, do not leave anything of value in your hotel room, and do not tell people your schedule. The luggage of most airline and bus passengers looks like a Houdini act with locks, rope, sewn-up sacks, and even steel boxes used to keep out curious fingers. Mail must be sent in a sewn-up sack to prevent theft. Naturally, thieves love the many zippered, unlocked backpacks of foreign trekkers. The best solution is to put your luggage in a canvas or vinyl duffel bag, and keep all valuables on your person. Do not carry any money in pockets, and use money belts as well as decoy wallets when traveling. (Decoy wallets are cheap wallets with old credit cards, pictures and addresses of your worst enemy, and Iraqi dinars.)

The third level is where Pakistan outshines many other areas: The cold calculated art of kidnapping, extortion and robbery. There is little any traveler can do to prevent this crime in certain areas. People who have regular schedules and who travel to crowded markets, along well-known paths, or do not have good security are at risk. Check State Department reports and contact the local embassy for the latest horror stories. All large cities have Security agencies that can provide advice, drivers and bodyguards for reasonable daily rates.

Terrorist Training Camps

The teeming, long-term refugee camps of Peshawar and Quetta provide the raw recruits for a number of terrorist training camps and Islamic universities that train Mujahedin for Jihad. Here not only do young "Afghans", but Algerians, Tunisians, Yemenis, Jordanians and others train for Holy War. There are no tours, and visitors are not welcome. The blindly curious (like *DP*) may eventually wangle an invitation, but you may be followed by Pakistani secret police and detained for questioning. Most camps have been moved into Afghanistan around Jallalabad, but even they may be shut down with the arrival of the *taliban*. The famous university in Peshawar was shut down (in July 1995) due to pressure from the U.S. government.

Dacoits

Possibly the most lucrative night job in Pakistan. Many *dacoits* are professional bandits aligned along tribal lines who hold normal day jobs and then head out into the country for a little extra cash at night. Unlike the greasy thugs of Russia or the gold-toothed banditos of Mexico, *dacoits* are usually bad guys for hire led by educated or civil service level young men. They cannot find employment, so they use their organizing and planning skills to support political parties, back up rebel units, raise operating funds and expand operations areas. Despite the genteel background of the leaders, the actions of their members are bloody and crude. *Dacoits* will stop buses and trains, rob, rape and murder, and generally create a bloody mess. They also use kidnapping as a way to generate funds and "flip the bird" to the local government. Expect to be a well-treated but powerless pawn, as the *dacoits* negotiate with the strapped local government (not your fat, rich home government) for payment for your release. Your biggest problem may be a heavy-handed (but fiscally efficient) rescue attempt staged by the government on your behalf. Stay out of remote tribal areas or areas known for *dacoitry*.

Ethnic Clashes

Pakistan is the botched result of seven weeks of planning by Sir Cyril Radcliffe in 1947 in an effort to separate warring Muslims from the Hindus. The hastily created border caused instant riots and violence, sending 6 million people from each region fleeing across the new border. It is estimated that up to a million people were killed. Today, with 60 million Muslims in India and more than 10 million Hindus in Pakistan, there is little hope for peace. Demonstrations often get ugly in Karachi and Hyderabad, where Sindhis and immigrant groups in Karachi and Hyderabad duke it out. Between January 1990 and October 1992, Pakistan-trained militants killed 1585 men and women, including 981 Muslims, 218 Hindus, 23 Sikhs, and 363 security men. In three years, over 7000 Kalashnikov rifles, 400 machine guns, 400 rocket launchers, 1000 rockets, 7000 grenades, 2000 pistols and revolvers, and thousands of mines were seized. One of the keys to staying alive in heavily armed areas is to not bring a knife to a gunfight. If you visit Pakistan, you might want to bring your own army. (see "Cheap Guns.")

Cheap Guns

The border regions of Pakistan are (and traditionally have been) a Wild West region with most tribal, ethnic and criminal groups being well armed with cheap weapons brought in from Afghanistan or manufactured on demand. There are few tribes that don't possess large arsenals and have fierce rivalries against one another. The code of a *badal*, or revenge, requires tribes to extract vengeance no matter how long ago the insult was committed. Crime is becoming a problem in Karachi and other areas where theft, burglary and kidnappings of businessmen are becoming endemic. Most urban residents employ *chowkidaars*, or private guards, for protection. If you are not caught in the middle of a firefight, you may be worse off at a wedding or party. In the tribal areas, Pathans have a bad habit of celebrating weddings using their AK-47s as firecrackers and shoot bursts into the air, ignorant of Newtonian physics.

The Pathans (Pahktuns)

Pakistan's Pathan community still wants to unite with the Pathans in Afghanistan to create Pahktunistan.

Mountain Climbing

Bandits, bugs and break-ins may be the least of your worries as you wait out a sudden blizzard, clinging to the icy face of one of the world's highest mountains. Make sure you are hooked up with an experienced guide and spend some time getting acclimatized to the thin air. The world's second-highest mountain, the famed 8611-meter-high K-2

(Mount Godwin Austen), is the star of the Karakoram Range: K-2 has been the site of several notable climbing expeditions since 1909.

Getting Sick

There are good medical facilities in all the major towns in Pakistan. You may need it after you see how the food is prepared and stored. Pakistan may not be the dirtiest place in the world, but it is enough to make some Siberian mining towns look positively bucolic. Expect to get the runs, unless you have a PVC gastrointestinal tract. Some folks go gaga over the spicy food, and other folks end up crouched over a grubby pit toilet learning the hard way that fiery spices and peppers burn as bad going out as they do going down. Take the normal precautions you would take in any Third World country, and carry medicine for diarrhea.

You need proof of a cholera vaccination if arriving from infected areas. You should get a typhoid shot and take malaria prophylaxis. Yellow fever vaccination and certificate are required if you have visited a country in the endemic zone recently.

Inoculations against yellow fever and cholera are required for visitors arriving in Pakistan within five days after leaving or transiting infected areas. In addition, immunizations against typhoid, polio and meningitis are recommended, as are prophylactic antimalarial drugs. Malaria is present throughout Pakistan at altitudes below 2000 meters. Remember, even if you are heading straight for the mountains, you can still get bitten in the airport waiting lounge in Karachi. Hepatitis and tetanus are further health risks in Pakistan, as are amoebic dysentery and worms. Bilharzia (schistosomiasis) and elephantiasis (filariasis) are also endemic diseases, although not widespread. Follow the usual precautions for countries with poor sanitation. Military hospitals, frequently open to fee-paying local civilians and foreigners, often provide the best facilities.

Nuts and Bolts

Pakistan is a land of hard extremes. The climate is generally arid and very hot (very, very hot), except in the northern mountains, where the summers are hot and winters are very (very) cold. The best time to visit Pakistan is between October and April. Karachi and Lahore are pleasant; Islamabad can get cool. The average annual temperatures in the southern city of Karachi are between 55° F and 93° F. Summer brings the monsoon season, but rainfall is negligible at other times of the year. After April, the temperatures climb from mid-July through September during the monsoon season, which can dump up to 16 cm of rain. North of Islamabad is mountainous, with a temperate climate. Summers are cool, winters cold, and the average annual rainfall is 120 cm.

The currency is the rupee; about 32 rupees to the U.S.dollar. You can only bring into Pakistan up to 100 rupees. The rupee is best purchased at a bank, not at your hotel. Many money changers will try to foist off the faded dirty notes, but don't take them. They will be tough to exchange back. You will need to carry around the paperwork you get when you swap dollars for rupees. Most folks change their money at the market. Credit cards are worthless outside the major cities, but good old AMEX has offices in Islamabad, Rawalpindi, Lahore and Karachi. Don't expect much help from Amex, other than cashing a personal check up to $500 or replacing your card. The best exchange rates are on the black market. Merchants will give you a slightly better exchange rate if you pay in U.S. dollars. You will not get a receipt for the transaction, since the transaction is illegal. *Baksheesh* is the Pakistani version of tipping. When people help you, it's normal and expected that you will drop a few rupees (about 10 percent) in their palm. Don't forget to haggle, haggle, haggle. Having a local guide do your haggling (shopping, bus, hotel, air fares, taxis, bribes, souvenirs) for you can easily save you his fee. You can bring in as much foreign currency as you want, but it must be declared upon arrival.

Electricity is 220V/50Hz. The electrical system can only be described as deadly, and shorts and blowouts are common. Be careful plugging in appliances around wet areas. Many water heaters are electric. Do not turn lights or appliances off with bare feet or in the shower.

If you hate crowds and crave danger, Pakistan provides excellent opportunities for winter sports, including mountaineering and hiking in the Himalayan hill stations. Folks who like to ski will be glad to know that there are absolutely no downhill ski facilities in this mountainous paradise. Pakistan features the longest continuous drops on the planet (heli-boarding anyone?) as well as breathtaking scenery. The AK-47s, pistols and 50-caliber machine guns are dirt-cheap in Peshawar but a bitch to bring home as hand luggage. Down below, where the Indus River makes the Punjab and Sind fertile, temperatures are more moderate, with an average of 60° F in January to an average of 95° F in the summer. Baluchistan consists of deserts and low bare hills. Here and in northern Sind, temperatures can climb over 120° F in the summer.

Normal office hours from Saturday to Wednesday are from 9 a.m. to 2 p.m., with at least one hour for lunch. Offices close earlier on Thursdays, usually at lunchtime. Friday is the weekly Muslim holiday. Banks are open from 9 a.m. to 1:30 p.m. from Saturday to Wednesday, and until 11 a.m. on Thursday. Urdu (the national language) and English are the official languages of Pakistan. Punjabi, Sindi, Pashtu, Baluchi, Seraiki and other languages and dialects are also spoken. Most children and older adults speak English.

Many people confuse Pakistani cuisine with Indian food. Kebabs, *tikkas* (spiced grilled meats) and curries are the staples; they're served with *naan* (flat bread). The most popular drinks are tea (black or green), *lassi* (a milk drink) and Western-style soft drinks, which are widely available.

Polo

One of Pakistan's most famous exports (besides drugs and terrorists) is polo. Afghans and Pakistanis love polo, a violent spirited game that is as close to horse-mounted warfare as one can get. The British picked it up while stationed here, and it quickly became the upper-class macho sport of Britain. You can still see polo games played by soldiers, cops and just regular folks in Chitral and Gilgit. Today, the best polo players in the world are from Argentina. The Argentinian gaucho put back a lot of the violence and death-defying elements of the game. Before polo, the Argentinians played puto, *a tamer form of the Afghan game of* buzkashi, *instead of a headless goat being manhandled around a huge field, the Argentinians would whack a duck with sticks. The most violent form of polo in Argentina is the Creole style. Ponies are ridden hard, bones are broken, and each seven-minute* chukka, *or period, is guaranteed to be full of action.*

Useful Addresses

Associated Press of Pakistan (APP)
House 1, Street 56
F 6/3 POB 1258, Istanbul
☎ *[51] (8) 26158*
FAX [51] (8) 13225

Pakistan International Airlines Corp. (PIA)
Head Office Building, Quaid-i-Azam International Airport
Karachi
☎ *(21) 4572011*
FAX (21) 4572754

Canadian Embassy in Pakistan
Diplomatic Enclave, Sector G-5
P.O. Box 1042
Islamabad
☎ *[92] (51) 211101*

U.S. Embassy in Pakistan
Diplomatic Enclave, Ramna 5
P.O. Box 1048
Islamabad
☎ *[92] (51) 826161*
FAX [92] (51) 214222

Pakistan Tourism Development Corp. Ltd.
House No. 2, St. 61, F-7/4
Islamabad
☎ *811001*

UK Embassy
Diplomatic Enclave, Ramna 5
P.O. Box 1122
Islamabad
☎ *822131*
FAX 823439

Pakistani Embassy in Canada
151 Slater Street, Suite 608
Ottawa, ONT. K1P 5H3
☎ *(613) 238-7881*
FAX (613) 238-7296

Pakistani Embassy in United States
2315 Massachusetts Avenue, N.W.
Washington, D.C. 20008
☎ *(202) 939-6200*
FAX (202) 387-0484

Embassy Location

The U.S. Embassy
Diplomatic Enclave, Ramna 5
Islamabad
☎ *826 161*

The Consular Section
Located separately in the USAID building
18 Sixth Avenue
Ramna 5

The Consulate General
8 Abdullah Haroon Road
Karachi
☎ *568-5170*

The U.S. Consulate General
Sharah-E-Abdul Hamid Bin Badees
50 Empress Road
New Simla Hills
Lahore
☎ *636-5530*

The U.S. Consulate
11 Hospital Road
Peshawar Cantonment
Peshawar
☎ *279-801, 279-802, 279-803*

Dangerous Days

04/07/1991 Shia Muslims mark the death of Hazrat Ali, fourth caliph of Islam.

08/05/1988 Arif Hussain al-Hussaini, a leading Shiite religious and political leader in Pakistan, was shot to death in Peshawar.

07/17/1988 An airplane carrying President Zia Ul-Haq and U.S. Ambassador Arnold Raphel crashed, killing everyone aboard.

09/05/1986 Twenty-one persons, including two Americans, were killed in an abortive hijacking of Pan Am flight 73 by four Arab gunmen.

04/10/1986 The daughter of former President Bhutto, Benazir Bhutto, returned from exile in Europe.

07/18/1985 Shahnawaz Bhutto, son of executed President Zulfikar Bhutto and older brother of Pakistani People's Party Leader Benazir Bhutto, died under mysterious circumstances in France.

07/14/1985 Bombing of Pan Am office.

11/22/1979 The U.S. embassy in Islamabad was attacked and burned by Islamic militants, following rumors that the U.S. was involved in the violent takeover of the Grand Mosque in Mecca, Saudi Arabia.

04/04/1979 Former president of Pakistan Zulfikar 'Ali Bhutto was executed by the Pakistani government under President Zia. The terrorist group al-Zulfikar, founded by his two sons, is named after him.

Dangerous Days

07/05/1977   Army Chief of Staff Mohammad Zia led an army coup to seize power and became chief martial law administrator.

06/08/1962   Martial law, which was imposed in 1958, was lifted and the national assembly convened.

03/23/1962   A new constitution was promulgated by President Ayub Khan.

10/07/1958   President Iskander Mirza, supported by senior military officers, seized power and imposed martial law.

09/06/1957   Defense of Pakistan Day.

03/23/1956   The national assembly adopted a new constitution that rejected Pakistan's status as a dominion and became an "Islamic Republic" within the commonwealth. Also known as "Pakistan Day."

08/14/1947   Independence Day. Pakistan became a self-governing dominion within the British commonwealth.

In a Dangerous Place

Pakistan: Along the Northwest Frontier

The Northwest Frontier of Pakistan is adventure defined. Men in turbans and robes stroll hand in hand down dusty streets carrying machine guns. *Mujahedin*, spy, separatist and smuggler are considered normal occupations in this high risk border area. Shootouts, bombings, kidnapping and violence are common. This is also the land of the Pukhtun (or Pathan) who live by the code of Pukhtunwali, an unwritten code of revenge against your enemies, hospitality to strangers and refuge to friends (*badal*, *melmastia* and *nanwata*). The trick is knowing whether you are friend, stranger or enemy. I will travel to Peshawar, in Northwest Pakistan, then travel onward to Afghanistan to meet with the *taliban* army.

I arrive at Green's hotel in Peshawar. Not upscale, but definitely Western. Walking down the streets of Peshawar it becomes quite apparent that I am the only pigeon in town. I smile and wave, and within 20 minutes shopkeepers, touts, gawking loiterers and an entourage of kids know me as Mr. Robert. Peshawar is an interesting city for those looking for adventure. For years this was the gateway to Afghanistan through the Khyber Pass by train, road or air. Now the war in Afghanistan between the *taliban* and the government of Rabbiani has closed the pass. Although not reported in most Western papers there are kidnappings, murders, robberies and other violent acts as life goes on in this dusty, bustling border town.

Any Westerner in Peshawar is automatically affiliated with aid organizations, journalism, arms, drugs or spying. Most yuppies head straight to the mountains and hippies head straight to the drug markets. The heat has turned up a little too high for itinerant adventurers because of the kidnappings and robberies.

Since I do not speak Arabic or Pahktun (Pathan or Pashto depending on your translation) I will need a guide. Since I naively assume I will have to travel over the Khyber Pass into Kabul, I will need a member of the Afridi clan. The wily

Pathans are actually three main groups: the Sarbanni, the Bitanni and the Ghurghush. The Afridi tribe is a member of the last—the typical stereotype of the "wily Pathan" proud, noble as well as treacherous and cruel. The Afridis look like throwbacks to the old testament with their long flowing robes, turbans and long magnificent beards. They are the same men that bedeviled conquerors from Alexander to the Russians along the Khyber pass.

If I am to enter Afghanistan I will also need to find someone who works with another Afridi. Yaqub Afridi is "the man" around here—the largest drug and gun smuggler in Northern Pakistan. His people control all the illicit trade between Kabul, Jallallabad and Peshawar.

Jawing with Jabba

After a few discreet inquiries, I am directed to ascend a rickety spiral staircase above a dusty tourist shop. Here I wait for my host who ascends after I am uncomfortably seated cross legged on a dirt-filled rug and given sweet tea in a dirty glass. My host who shall remain nameless reminds me immediately of Jabba the Hut. The rotund, grubby alien of *Star Wars* fame. When my host smiles he reveals a set of black and brown teeth and breath that forces me to sit back a few more inches.

I make it clear why I am here but he is determined to unload some of his faded trinkets before granting my wish. He instructs his sons to bring out Russian bayonets, Russian uniforms, Russian money, Russian field glasses, and then with a conspiratorial wink, a Russian AK-47.

Nope, not interested.

Then a parade of ancient coins, ethnic bric-a-brac, tattered rugs and rusty knives follow.

Nope, don't need it.

Then my host leans toward me and looks around as if the crowd of grubby cross eyed children blocking the stairs have never heard the word and whispers "hashish?"

His breath is painful, but I wheeze back. Nope.

He sits back and scratches his scrotum under his dirty white shalwar. Frustrated and pensive, he picks his rotten teeth and then burps while he figures out how he will make a little money from me. He puts on a squeaky Tom Waits tape in a stolen Walkman to make me feel at home.

Temporarily freed from reviewing the piles of war surplus and cheap clothing, I restate my need is only for a trustworthy guide who can take me into the Afghan camps and around the Khyber Pass beyond. Trying to figure how much to gouge me, he probes my intentions (or backers). He asks me if I am a journalist and smiles conspiratorially. Nope. Are you a diplomat? Nope. A spy? I think that this guy has been watching too many Sidney Greenstreet movies. I tell him that I want to meet the *taliban* and he gives me a pained look. "This can be difficult."

He says something to one of his sons who scuttles down the staircase and out into the street. The other sons continue to stare as if they paid admission and want to get their money's worth.

Finally eyeing me after a pregnant pause and flicking something off his toothpick, he says "I have the man but it will cost you 100 rupees. He will not make trouble for you if you do not make trouble for him."

Not agreeing or disagreeing, I thank him and then figure I should loosen up a little cash so that he will have a vested interest in keeping me alive for further plucking. I tell him that I am traveling but I will come back to buy souvenirs of my trip. Invigorated he pushes the pile of rusty weapons, smelly caps and trinkets towards me again. I ask him at what generous price would he sell me these fine ancient coins. We haggle for about 20 minutes until what looks like a bearded gopher sticks its head up the stairwell and introduces himself as Papa. He is introduced to me by my Jabba the Hut like friend as "my man." I quickly pay him an outrageous sum of $50 for the counterfeit Greek coins and Russian rubles and push my way down the stairs with my new guide in tow.

A well fed but sprightly man of about 60, Papa is wearing the white Chitrali cap and white robes of the region. He is a Pahktun and he speaks perfect but imprecise English. He worked at the U.S. base in Pakistan and learned his English while being the house *wallah*. He has forgotten much of his English but I promise him I will teach it back to him. Papa struggles to keep up with my stride. He has a long white beard, glasses, a pot belly and a nervous, happy personality that reminds me of one of the Seven Dwarfs. Then I decide it's not a Disney character he reminds me of, Papa looks exactly like the R. Crumb character who keeps on trucking. So we set off down the street with Papa hustling to keep up with me. Papa tugs at my sleeve:

"We have made a bargain, my friend?"

Puzzled as to why he is starting the negotiations anew I ask him what he means

"I have been sent to you to guide you, yes"

"There are many things I can show you."

"Like?"

He rattles off the list of bazaars and tourist sights and I stop him midsentence.

"I am not here for these things" I am interested in meeting the *taliban*."

After a brief silence and a cinematic look around to see who is listening, he says: "There are many things to see in Pakistan, my friend."

Sensing that my aims are not strictly touristic, he launches into another hushed spiel. " I can take you to a place where we can find hashish, heroin, marijuana.

"Papa, I am here to meet with the *taliban*."

Finally I figure out why he doesn't understand me. *Taliban* means religious student here. It is not directly associated with the Afghan group called the *taliban*.

"You want guns? I can take you to where we can fire many guns, even rockets, many, many rockets. Hand grenades, anti-aircraft, boom boom."

"No Papa."

I wait for the women or young boys pitch but it doesn't come. Papa, who I find out later is devoutly religious, sticks to clean stuff; drugs and weapons. It dawns on me that there will be much to discuss in the days ahead.

We get back to his original topic of discussion, his rate. He explains that he must pay his friend for the referral and asks to borrow 10 ruppees to pay his commission. He runs back and conspiratorially mentions that our deal is now between us and that I should not mention anything to our friend if he asks what we did. The impression is that Papa was to continue the *baksheeh* until we are through.

He asks me what I would like to do. Thinking that I had already failed in explaining exactly what I wanted to do, I say, "Let's go to the Afghan refugee camps." At least Papa would come in handy as an interpreter. He explains that we can go to the market but I cannot go into the camps because I would be kidnapped. There are three camps outside of town. Actually small cities complete with mud huts, phone, electricity and a smattering of services. There are about 3 million Afghan refugees who live in Pakistan in camps like these and they are here to stay, something the financially beleaguered Pakistanis don't like. The Afghans handle all the transportation in Peshawar. They also evoke the wild west feel of men strolling around with machine guns. Shootouts enforce *badal* or revenge, and a host of entreprenurial efforts include kidnapping people for ransom.

We jump on a bus to the market and Papa is very nervous. Although the people are cheerful and glad to see me, there is a dark curious look in many of the men's faces. We push past the money changers and kabob houses to the depths of the market. We stop in a simple *chai* house for tea and cakes. Not much to look at. Just a large tent with three wide carpeted tables running the full length. Men sit and sleep on the tables in the midday heat. None are particularly thrilled to see us. I finally figure out what I am looking at. We are surrounded by out of work *mujahedin*. Tough 30 and 40 something men with hard gaunt faces, many of them scarred or limping. They all stare directly and impassively at us. Papa is nervous. I ask Papa who these men are. He replies these are the fighters. I ask them if I can take their pictures. He says no. I acknowledge some of the men. Some nod back, others continue to stare. Papa and I talk about the fighters. He tells me that many men came during the war with Russia for money but now there is not much work.

After our tea I ask him to take me to the Smugglers Bazaar. Once it was in Landi Kotal at the end of the rail line. Now it has moved to the outskirts of Peshawar. I can tell that Papa is not entirely thrilled with my choice of tourist spots. He asks me if I want to see where they paint the buses. Once again I tell him my purpose. He, once again, is suddenly hard of hearing.

The Walking Dead

We jump off the bus, just before a military checkpoint and end up in a carpet of trash in an area of shade trees. Among the trash are what look like piles of dirty rags. Upon closer inspection they are people. Bearded and blackened with the hard core soot of derelicts, it is hard to tell if they are dead or alive. Since they are not bloated I assume they are alive. Other men with frizzed hair and beards stagger in slow motion. Papa warns me away. These are the walking dead—heroin addicts left to wander and then die in the boulevard facing the market. A sobering sight and not one inclined to induce anyone to buy drugs at this, one of the largest drug markets in the world.

It would be unfair to characterize this place as all seedy and depressing. Here shoppers can also buy gold Rolexes, Panasonic radios, and cameras. The fact that you can also buy heroin, hashish, machine guns and rocket launchers is more a result of an enthusiastic retail strategy than anything sinister. At one shop I intimate that maybe his Rolex watches are the same ones found on the streets of New York—tinny, Chinese made with $5 workings. Insulted, he pulls out an entire tray of solid gold GMT Masters and Datemasters. I shut up. He even offers to buy my battered and faded 25-year-old steel GMT master for US$800. Not a bad deal, but I decline. I give him a DP sticker for his door and we are friends again.

I mention to Papa that I wish to travel on to Afghanistan and meet with the *taliban* army. He smiles and says "Come with me." We go to the far end of the bazaar and Papa cautions me to walk quickly and not get lost. He also stops and tells me that when we cross into the other side he cannot help me if I am kidnapped or killed. I ask him how much it would cost to pay my ransom. Without pausing he tells me $35,000 U.S.

Through the Door

Papa drops his guard and takes me into a quiet corner. He looks me straight in the eye and asks me: "Are you CIA?" I say no. He asks me: Are you a journalist? I say no, but I write a travel guide to dangerous places. He then asks me if I will make trouble for him. I say no.

Papa satisfied for now says "Come with me."

We wait until the soldiers at the military checkpoint are occupied with a heavily laden truck than we walk quickly but purposely into a compound of shops. Papa smiles conspiratorially and points at the large red on white sign "No Foreigners Past this Point." After a couple of lefts and rights through the shops we walk through a large gate in the high wall. Thinking that this has been far too easy, we turn the corner and run smack into a group of armed men pointing machine guns at us.

Having been asked many times what was my most dangerous moment, I always answer that I really have no idea of when I am in danger or not. But considering that I am surrounded by unsmiling machine gun-carrying Afghans and escorted by a total stranger who for some strange reason, seems to know exactly what kidnapped foreigners are worth, the first few seconds of this experience would rank up there.

Papa pauses briefly and then makes the introductions. It turns out that these are some of Afridi's men. A group of about 10 out of 100 heavily armed men who make about 2000 rupees a month to make sure the drug and contraband business runs nice and smooth. And who should be their long lost friend (or best customer) but Papa. I don't know why, but it seems in this part of the world you always get kissed (twice) by men who were pointing machine guns at you a few moments before.

Welcomed into their simple barracks I am introduced to my brigand friends. Not only are the men carrying well-used SKS's and AK 47's but there are machine guns and ammunition cases lying around the wire cots. They thrust weapons into my hands and urge Papa to take pictures of me. They pose with me and bring me tea.

They chat in Pashto while I smile and hand out *DP* stickers. I run out of stickers as they paste them on their rifle butts. They ask me if I would like to fire the gun. I decline thinking of the armed police not more than 200 yards away behind the sandbagged checkpoint.

We talk about getting into Afghanistan and Kabul. Everyone is coming out of Kabul. Kabul is under siege. No one is going in. They will definitely not let foreigners in. The *taliban* is camped above the hills waiting to attack. I ask if can go in disguise. They laugh and tell me "You can take the bus right from here for only 50 rupees but there are eight checkpoints from here to Jalalabad and one of them is sure to find you. Another development is that Afridi has been asked to get out of Pakistan because of the heat the U.S. government is putting on him. He graciously has moved out of his mansion to another one high in the hills of Jalalabad. He is not about to get into more trouble by inviting some foreigner for dinner and a ride into Kabul. Although his bodyguards are eager, they know I'll be arrested and turned back.They also explain that the *taliban* execute drug dealers and it might not be wise for me to arrive under their protection. It looks like the Khyber is not the way to go.

Papa shows me around the market where piles of sickly looking hashish and heroin are on display. There are piles of well-used weapons and even lethal pen guns that fire one bullet. The merchants watch me with some remorse as I jot down the going rates. Two kilos of hash goes for 5000 rupees, 10 grams is 80 rupees, one gram of injection heroin for 100 rupees and one gram of smoking heroin is 50 rupees. In this market weapons are to drugs as shovels are to farming. I can pick up a slighty used rocket launcher for 30,000 rupees (Rockets are 400 rupees each) hand grenades are 100 rupees, Russian AK's go for 6000, a beat up AK-47 goes for 8000, a "short" Chinese-made assault version of the Kalshnikov is 30,000, 30 bullets go for 300 rupees. A helpful salesman reminds me that the barrel of the Chinese AK doesn't get as hot as the home made versions.

Thinking of the wasted humans outside on the boulevard, I pass on buying anything even after Papa explains the profits to be made once we cross back inside the gate. Papa excuses himself to do a little shopping while we wander through stacks of hashish and marijuana.

On the way back to town Papa loosens up. He says he does a little bit of this and that to make ends meet. Besides drugs, (he prefers to buy his drugs directly in Afghanistan, in the region of Mazar-i-Sharif, he also buys stamps for stamp collectors, takes the occaisional tourist around Peshawar but mostly he directs foreigners to where they can buy drugs. He warms to the fact that I have no interest in drugs and seem to be comfortable around his well-armed friends. I tell him that I would like to look around the border areas until I can figure out how to get into Afghanistan. It seems getting to Afghanistan through Peshawar is a bust. There is a Red Cross plane that flies into Kabul now and then but I am told it is always full with supplies. I figure it might be worth trying the more scenic and wild northern borders. I ask him if he wants to go visit the remote mountain areas of Gilgit and the Kalash valley and he agrees.

The North West Frontier

The next day Papa shows up with just a single blanket and a plastic shopping bag with his toiletries. I thought I traveled light but Papa puts me to shame. We take the postal bus north to Mingora. He mentions in an offhand way that the bodyguards we met yesterday were asked by the Pakistani police to help show the U.S. that they were cracking down on drugs, so Afridi's bodyguards offered Papa 10,000 rupees to bring them people to turn over to the police. I ask if he would have set me up. He smiles in a hurt way and says "But you are my friend."

It is important to remember that the Afghans are a complex result of their code of honor. They are hospitable to strangers, will invite you into their house, and if you become their friend they will deny you nothing. In fact Pathans hate haggling or coyness and are much happier when you simply state your purpose no matter how far from the legal path it strays.You just never want to be on the wrong side of a Pathan because they will kill you even for the slightest wrong.

Along the way we talk about many things. Papa is amazed at the strange places I have been and I am equally intrigued with his stories about his home in Afghanistan. He grew up in a small town along the Khyber Pass in a fortresslike house where the only profession was smuggling. Every member of the family must post guard duty in the tower and every house is heavily armed. The tower has peepholes to allow the defenders to shoot back when attacked and the thick mud and stone walls make it cool in the summer and warm in the winter. They fight over goats, women, past wrongs and anything else they find worth killing for. Many villages and clans have been warring for years simply because every new generation must carry on the revenge or *badal* for the continuing seesaw of bloodshed. Papa looks into my eyes and says dramatically: "Mr. Robert, if you kill someone, you come to my village, I will give you house, bodyguard, no problem." I keep that in mind.

As we come out of the hot arid valley we head up the Grand Trunk line into the rugged mountains. We pass the old British forts and wind up and down the tortuous passes. Papa tells me stories of how one Australian named Keith came to his village to make a hollowed out Samsonite briefcase so he could smuggle hashish back home. The trick worked once and the second time he was caught. Keith's girlfriend flew in to get him out of jail and lived with Papa in his house helping him cook and even posting guard duty. An Afghan chief from another town took a fancy to her and one day gave her a black Afghan horse worth about $30,000 rupees. Meanwhile Keith liked it in jail because he got to smoke cheap hash with the other inmates. Finally the girlfriend saved up enough money (Papa wouldn't tell me how she made it) and she bribed his way out of jail and flew back to Australia.

Papa sees the pictures of my twin daughters and exclaims; "I must have these for the chief of the Kyhber's son." He is a fine man and his father feeds 50 people a day! I don't know how I will break the news to my daughters that they have not only both been betrothed to one of the world's largest drug smugglers.

I Read the News Today... Oh Boy

The Northwest Frontier is a land with bad endings. The Peshawar paper has a story about a young Afghan couple, each from a different village, who were spotted kissing by one of the boy's relatives. The father of the boy kidnaps the girl and a cousin ties them up and pumps 75 bullets into them. Just yesterday in the Smugglers Bazaar a man was shot in the neck three times as he tried to run the checkpoint we had so deftly sidestepped. He was trying to take a stolen car into Afghanistan. The newspaper fills up five pages of murders, shootings and crime. Just another day in Pakistan.

I ask Papa how old he is. He tells me that only rich people pay attention to paper and since he cannot write he has no idea how old he is.

####

We are back on the road in the back of a battered Toyota pickup truck I hired. We talk to pass the time. I tell him I like to cook. He tells me that is women's work. He has no idea how to cook. I joke and tell him that he would starve if he did not have a woman to cook for him. "I cook tea" he replies indignantly. Papa's main interest for coming with me seems to be the disparity between the prices of weapons in the north versus Peshawar. In his village in Afghanistan he can get AK-47's for around 6–8000 rupees. He figures he can unload them in the northern town of Dir for 12,000–15,000 rupees each. All he needs to do is find a buyer on this trip and he'll be back in a week.

We arrive at Dir that night. The evening air is frigid. I check into a room for 300 rupees. Papa takes the cheap one for 200. I get a straight razor shave for 5 rupees. That night I have a warm shower by plugging in a heating element directly into a bucket of cold water. The lights in the hotel dim and I wonder how may people are electrocuted like this. I shiver all night. Dir is a dirty frontier town. Severed goat heads neatly laid out in rows and all business from tailoring to tinkering is conducted while you wait. Overly decorated and loaded trucks blast through town. The blasting of their air horns and jangling of the steel chains that decorate the bumpers are the only things that interest me.

At breakfast the next day we sit next to a stubbly old man with a pure white beard. Both he and Papa extoll the virtues of Allah and the Koran as they drink their tea. They are shocked when they find out that I have read the Koran and drag me into the conversation. Proselytized to the point of pain, I try to change the subject and mention that the short man has a nice beard. He blushes deeply. Papa tells me that with Allah all things are possible and that it will only be a matter of time before I am converted.

He warns me about the tough going ahead, the cold, the lack of food and even the danger of traveling in this area. I reassure him that I enjoy wild mountainous places and that bathing in an ice cold stream by moonlight is one of my favorite things. I realize that it is Papa who doesn't like the cold and the moutains.

It is October and as we climb higher and higher into the mountains we are getting cold. Papa is shivering and I give him my black Goretex jacket newly bought in Frankfurt. He praises Allah for creating such a marvelous garment. Knowing full well that it is a custom to give something that is so lavishly praised as a gift, I say "No Papa, you can't have it." We climb to the summit of the pass at 10,500 feet. Far down below we can see the overloaded diesel trucks that grind and groan up the switchbacks at less than five miles an hour. It is actually faster walking than taking one these trucks. They will continue northward into China along the Karkoram pass loaded with everything from rice to brake pads. Heading down the other side of the pass is unsettling. We descend across 45 switchbacks down to the river below. An armed policeman appears out of nowhere and flags us down. No, we are not in trouble. It seems the government has just put in electricity and the minister will be coming along the other direction. Could we please tell the policemen stationed along the road not to smoke or drink tea? Pakistan is a polite place.

On the truck is a man from the village of Bahrain. He invites us to stay at his home. Although there are a number of new and reasonable hotels in Bahrain we take him up on his offer. His house is a 20' by 20' room with large security bars on the doors. He has a spectacular view of the valley and rushing river that carves through the town. We buy food and fruit and he is embarrassed. He invites his relatives from around the valley to meet me. We eat a large but simple dinner. While his son entertains us by reading out of a primary school English book he confesses that he is a Pahktun separatist and is eager to fight for a separate homeland for the Pahktuns. After seeing the difference between the dark-skinned leather jacketed Punjabi tourists from Lahore and the light haired Afghans it is understandable.

That night something hit me like a train. Lying shivering I had to go to the bathroom, and fast. Maybe it was the fly covered kebab I had in Mingora or the dinner that night but I jumped up and realized I was in a pitch black room with no windows and no idea how to get out. I frantically searched for the heavy bolts that sealed the top and bottom of the doors. Rushing outside the night was brilliant with stars. I couldn't get my pants down in time and for the first time in my life felt like a three-year-old who wasn't diaper-trained.

The panic over, I took my clothes off in the freezing night air and decided to clean myself in a stream or river. As I walked through the orchids along the side of the hill, I punctured my feet with the sharp thorns from the trees. Finally I found an ice cold stream tumbling down the mountain. I began the painful process of washing myself and my clothes. As I shiver and shake under the stars I can't help thinking how funny this is. Papa and my guest find me and they are frantic. I tell them relax, I just came out for a bath. Papa points to me in my nakedness and says "I didn't believe when you told me you like to bathe in mountain streams but now I see that you are made of steel. Allah be praised." My host is less poetic. He tells me that the villagers shoot anyone found walking around at night. And that if I had gone down to the river I would have been killed.

In the morning I tell Papa the real reason I went for a walk in the middle of the night. He doesn't believe me and thinks I am being modest. My host apologizes thinking it is food that has caused it and I feel like an idiot. I don't eat for the next four days.

The Valley of Swat

Shivering from the high altitude we pull into the valley of the Kalash. The Kalash (which means black because of the black garments they wear) are an animist tribe who live in a region sometimes called Kafiristan. The Kalash are considered to be descendants of Alexander's army but have no recorded history. They are known for their colorful festivals, the fact that they leave their dead in exposed coffins and they are in an anthropological timewarp.

It is hard to imagine such a beautiful place in the middle of such desolation. The valleys are lush and green and the people who live in this valley are either touted as the lost tribe of Israel or descendants of Alexander the Great. In any case they are mentioned in many guidebooks as a lost race of peoples rarely seen or visited. Yeah sure.

We make the tortuous trip into the valley along a road that is smashed out of a sheer rock cliff. Coming down from the valleys and moutains beyond are Indian Jeeps with a single 2–3 foot diameter log tied like a battering ram over the cab and hood of the truck. Places where the road has caved in are patched with rubble. Even Papa exclaims "hacha!" as we veer out over the edge of the cliff.

Naturally when we pull up to the main junction there is no primitive scene but instead a huge billboard with all the rules that tourists must follow when taking pictures of the Kalash. Just like a low budget amusement park there is a fee for everything. It seems that the Punjabis come up here in the summer to escape the heat and gawk at the diminuitive white-skinned Kalash. Not only do we pay an admission fee to get in, we pay to bring in my camera. Hard to believe that this valley was just opened up to road traffic in the 70's.

Once inside there are tiny hotels with names like the "Hayatt Hotel" and restaurants that serve "meshed potatoes" or even spagetti. Here we are just a few yards from the Afghan border. As we finally meet the famed Kalash, an old lady not only tells us how much we must pay for their photos (20 rupees), but adds up the fee for every time she hears the shutter click. I assign them to the other Kodak cultures who make their living wearing "authentic garments and pose for tourists wearing Tilley hats. The dark-haired Kalash were look like ethnic Greeks, Macedonians or even Armenians. Now they have the cultural relevance of a cigar store Indian. There is one Punjabi group in the valley who direct the Kalash to perform for their massive VHS recorders. They look like they are having a day at the zoo. Papa mentions that we could take a six hour trip to Afghanistan from here on mules for 80–150 rupees but there are no mules for rent. I see the heavy snow cover in upper valley and remember how cold it was coming over the pass in our thin clothes. I say no thanks, let's try somewhere else. As a bizarre footnote there is a solar eclipse and I can't help but think of Kipling's *The Man Who Would be King*. This time the Kafirs or kalash do not fall down and worship me, they just want more money because I am using a "big" lens to take their picture.

The Foothills of the Hindu Kush

We head into the mountain town of Gilgit, beneath the snow-capped mountains of the Hindu Kush. Within a 60 mile radius there are 20 peaks that rise above 20,000 feet. Nearby K2 is the most dangerous mountain in the world. The 28,250 ft. high peak has killed an average of every second person who attempts its summit. It is very cold and usually by now the snow in the high passes has cut off Gilgit from the rest of the world. Fokkers can fly out of the 4000 foot high valley by just scraping the tops of the passes but bad weather can lock people in for weeks and once the runway is snowed in you are in for the duration. Gilgit is a one horse town with the spectacular backdrop of Tirich Mir towering above its main street. In the simple hotel there is a Pakistani quiz show on the United Nations.

We walk around the town. In one stall I watch a tailor patiently work on fixing a torn button hole for 20 minutes. He charged his customer 2 rupees or .8 of a penny.

Hob Nobing with the Nawab

Gilgit is the home of two things. One is polo, the other is the Sultan of Swat. Not Babe Ruth but a dynasty that has ruled this remote kingdom for centuries. Technically the Sultan or Nawaab was removed from his position of authority in 1969.

I check out the red brick British fort by the river. Despite the Do Not Enter signs, I poke around over the protestations of Papa. The fort looks as if it was abandoned by the British last week with coal fireplaces, rose gardens and hunting trophies of antelope, snow leopard and mountain sheep adorning the balcony. British cannons from 1913 and 1898 still point across the river. Earthquakes have destroyed some parts yet other parts are definitely nostalgic. Turning a corner I am caught trespassing by security guards. I find myself in the presence of a small dapper man in an Eddie Bauer blazer with a small cocker spaniel. It seems I am in the presence of Saif -ul-Mulk-Nasir the Nawab or Mehthar of Swat.

Instead of chastising me, the Nawab (or Nabob in its English form) is pleased to find a Westerner here. He invites me to have coffee at his former home, now a hotel. As we sit on the lawn with bodyguards and aides, he tells me his story.

The kingdom of Gilgit used to control the trade along the ancient Silk Road. It has been overrun and occupied by everyone from the Chinese to the British. The Nawab says his family has ruled the valley since the 15th century. In 1969 Pakistan declared the sultanate dissolved. His father was the last to hold official power and his job is strictly ceremonial. (20% of the people in the valley are direct descendants of his dynasty.) His father was one of 16 children. His oldest brother was killed in a plane crash so it is now his turn to be the Wali.

The hotel is run by a bearded lanky German and I can't help but comment on it. The Wali mentions that his manager was a truck driver from Germany who had studied hotel management. He stayed in Pakistan and has now become a Pakistani national and runs his hotel. He slyly comments that he found out that his trusted hotel manager has local interests of the smoking kind. I noted on the path into the hotel grounds that marijuana plants grew wild along the road.

We spoke of many things. The Nawab likes to hunt and with some sadness pointed to his hunting lodge high up on the mountain behind us. We set up a game preserve to protect the wildlife and now the goverment wardens can be bribed for $10 U.S. and use .22cal rifles to hunt deer (which only wounds them).

He is trying to breed cocker spaniels to be bird dogs but is not having much luck. I comment on the fact that the fort looks good in its coat of red paint. He says he painted it that color because it was the cheapest paint he could find. Things will change—the Nawab travels every year to San Francisco to the University of California for medical treatment and he has four daughters. When he goes the dynasty will end.

Polo, With or Without Headless Goats

Since I am in Gilgit I can't skip the polo game. I hang out in the fields by the river with the Afghans who have come to play *buzkashi*. Although polo has been played here for 400 years, *buzkashi* is the real thing. Buzkashi is a very violent game played with a headless goat. It is rough and it is violent and it packs the spectatorsin. Naturally there were none when I was there but during the summer people fly in from the South to watch both *buzkashi* and polo being played.

An Afghan tribe has set up camp and welcomes me. The horses have the skin rubbed down to the muscle in some places and there are scabby bull mastiffs tied to trees. It seems the Afghans get paid the equivalent of 1000 rupees for each game they play. The dog fights are a way of entertaining themselves and making some extra money. The chief offers to let me ride a horse all day for 200 rupees. As we hang around the camp of 20 people I watch the men take the horses out in the field. They ride fearlessly through trees, over broken ground and over brush. They treat their horses brutally yet they never make a false move. Even when the horse rears up in fear they keep pushing it to ride faster.

We talk to the Afghans. They ask us if we want to see a dog fight between their massive Kochi dogs (traveling dogs). They are from Mazaar i Shariff and will gladly take us to Kabul.

We can can hire pack horses for 300 rupees a day and walk across the pass. We say we want to leave now, but they say we are too late. It will be too cold, the snow will be too deep and the horses will starve or freeze. Why not wait until spring they ask? I don't bother to explain my Western impatience.

Later that day we watch the polo matches. Polo is from 2 p.m. to 6 p.m., timed more by the narrow band of light that the mountains allow into the valley than by a clock. The long field slopes downward and is bordered on the long sides by six foot cement walls. The spectators squat and sit along the wall cheering and yelling. When the horses and riders crash into the wall, mallets flailing, the spectators are ejected like ducks in a shooting gallery. The only thing I could compare it to was the sight of an Indy car going into the railing flicking off spectators in a long ragged rooster tail. When a team charges the open ends of the fields to score a goal, the crowd simply gets run over by the stampeding horses. Finally, a sport that is as dangerous for the specators as the particpants.

The long nose Chitralis are not only good at polo but they play each game like it is the world championship. Few wear protective gear and many are limping or bleeding afterwards. The ones that do wear gear wear plastic construction helmets tied with string, others wear just the padded Chitrali wool cap. A band plays exotic whiney music to keep the spectators pumped up. When I climb up on the wall to take a picture of the band they suddenly stop. I motion with two fingers towards my mouth to communicate that I want the band to play again. The audience explodes with laughter and the flute player laughs so hard he can't play for five minutes. I had used the symbol for "give me a blow job" to indicate I wanted him to play his horn. So much for cultural literacy.

The game is full of chills and spills. One player hits the goal post so hard it falls over. Horses limp off the field and players are knocked unconscious. Mallets fly and hit both horses and riders. The white wooden ball bounced off the heads of more than a few myopic spectators. Horses were crushed against the rough stone walls and after a while it becomes painful to watch.

Stymied with any attempt to get to Afghanistan, we decide to avoid the tortuous trip back to Peshawar and fly out. We join the crush at the PIA ticket counter. In Pakistan all flights are full but then magically have seats. I pay 650 rupees for myself and 300 for Papa on the exact same flight. It is actually cheaper to fly in Pakistan than drive. Waiting at the airport I gather two oddly striped stones from the river as souvenirs. As he waits for the plane Papa is nervous. I find out it will be the second time he has ever flown.

As the twin engine plane strains to get off the ground I notice that we never actually clear the mountain tops. We are flying in between the peaks. Down below I recognize the long winding mountian passes, ridged fieldings and small villages that took so long to drive through. Despite the spectacular scenery outside, Papa stares straight ahead and prays for the entire flight.

Back in Peshawar

Back in Peshawar, Papa asks to go home to see his daughter and I set out to find the *taliban*. I visit the local newspaper to ask the editor where I can find the *taliban*. He says they have a headquarters in the Afghan market. Stunned by this simple truth I realize I have come full circle. Peshawar, along with Damascus and Beirut is a major center for revolutionary Islamic groups. There was even a university for terrorists here until three months ago. The *New Yorker* had featured them much to the displeasure of the U.S. government who politely asked the Pakistanis to shut it down. The editor rummages through his Rolodex and gives me a local number. He says there should be somebody there who speaks English. Good Luck.

I call the number and ask if anyone can speak English. There is a pause as the person at the other end yells out something in Pashto.

"Hello," an educated voice answers.

"Is this the *taliban*? I ask.

"Who is this?"

I explained who I was and asked if I could ask them some questions to better understand what their goals are.

"Are you a journalist?"

"No. I came here to meet you because no one else in the world seems to know who you are.

"We are in the Afghan market. Just ask anybody and they will bring you to us," he says.

Pleased with my detective work, I go back to the hotel to get Papa to act as translator. Papa is not pleased. It seems that he heard me just fine when I asked him about the *taliban* before.

Papa was dead serious. "You understand that we are going to a place where they can kill you?"

"Yes, but I don't think they will."

"Do you realize we are going to a place where they may kill me?

"Then don't go."

"I cannot let you go alone because then they will kill you and I will be to blame."

"Then come and we will visit the fighters."

We get on a bus and I grab my cameras. I am elated. Papa is quiet.

As I stride through the market past the money changers we ask where the office of the *taliban* is. The men point in a general direction but do not take us there.

As we come across the tracks of the train that goes into Afghanistan, the muezzin calls the people to prayer. "It is time for me to pray," Papa says. "Please wait here."

As I plunk myself down in the shade, I notice two sun-browned men with black turbans sitting eating in the open. Black turbans with long tails and white stripes—the symbol of the religious student. I couldn't believe how blind I'd been—this was the uniform of the feared *taliban*. I nodded in their direction and they just stared back grimly.

Papa comes from washing up and praying and nods towards the fighters. "*Taliban*." I wave as I walk by and ask if should take their picture. Papa says "Please, no." I notice that besides praying, Papa has fortified himself with hashish.

A young boy directs us to a nondescript house with heavy green metal gates. Outside two men with machine guns sit in the shade. I walk past the men and push through the lower half of the green gates. I startle a man behind the gate. I am staring into the face from the first century. The man is dressed in white robes with a white turban. His eyes are piercing and ringed with black eyeliner, a custom rural Afghanis have to keep evil souls from entering their eyes. He just stares. Behind him are a group of men with vicious wounds, some with missing legs others with gashes and bandages. They sit on a pile of dirty blankets 3–4 feet high. Papa is about 8 feet behind me and I motion him forward to make the introductions.

In the courtyard we walk past a battered ambulance and the *taliban's* troop carrier of choice, a well-used white Toyota pickup truck. Black headdresses are hung up to dry. They are over 20 feet long and look like odd mourning flags hanging horizonatally in the sun. The men in the courtyard just stare as we walk up the dusty steps. There are wounded men lining the staircase. At the head of the stairs are piles of cheap plastic sandals. My hiking boots look odd among the piles of dirty brown sandals. I am met by a young man named Abdul Ghafoor Afghani. He is 23 and when asked for his title calls himself the "information person." We are taken into a dingy green room to wait. We sit on the scabby yellow and red plastic mat and take in our surroundings. A ceiling fan is motionless. There is no electricity but the light switches are grubby from many hands.

In various other rooms are badly dressed turbaned men in shalwars who huddle in deep discussions. They do not have the hard look of killers but rather of unwashed country bumpkins. By the hard brown look of their hands and faces many of the men look like farmers not like soldiers. Our host invites us into the main room in to chat with the leader. He is wearing a fully packed bandolier containing an ancient revolver, the white turban of the mullah, and he looks a little pissed at us for interupting his meetings. He asks our host to apologize for the pistol but the market is a stronghold of Hekmatyar and somebody tried to assassinate him yesterday. So he is wearing it just in case they try it again. They also apologize for the armed men outside the door, saying they were put there by the government to make sure nothing got out of hand.

They tell me that this is a staging area for volunteers and bringing out wounded for treatment in the hospitals of Peshawar. Recruits are gathered from the religious schools and the wounded are dropped off at the Chinese hospital. The recruits are sent via 3rd class mini bus to Quetta and then onward to the front by pickup truck. The Pakistanis do not stop the recruits or ask for papers. When the volunteers get to the front they will be given a weapon, ammunition and food supplies. In the double talk of killing, our host explains that there is no recruiting, the men come for *jihad*. This is definitely a low budget war. The dirty faded blankets outside are testament to the fact that the refugees donated their own blankets so that the men would not freeze this winter. He said that during the haj people donated the sales of animal skins slaughtered in the festival and raised 8000 rupees (about $250US) and that even the dingy office we were in was donated by local businessman at 7000 rupees a month. Occasionally they would get 100,000 and 200,000 rupee donations from businessmen to the cause.

He apologized for having no "propaganda" to give me but he said that the *taliban* was in its formative stages and only a year old.

PAKISTAN

"We the *taliban* wish to rid Afghanistan of robbers, rapists, killers and militia and to create a new Islamic country." He tells stories of how the movement started in October of 1994. In Kandahar there was a brutal warlord who stopped everyone at roadblocks (most of these people would be robbed). But when he began stopping men, having them put makeup on, sodomizing them and killing them, it infuriated the people. The religious students at the mosque got the people together and hung the leader and the gunmen from the barrels of their tanks. From that point on the revolution was in motion. They now have a radio and television station in Kandahar but it cannot broadcast very far. So far they have sent in a BBC crew and an independant TV crew but that is it. I am the first person from North America they have met.

I ask him if I can journey to Kandahar and the front lines or send in film crew to interview the leaders and cover the war. He would like that and I ask him again to make sure he is not just being polite. There is one catch—the leaders of the *taliban* do not allow their photographs to be taken because of the Koran. I explain very carefully that only cowards do not show their faces and that in my culture a man who does not wish to be seen cannot be trusted. He said this is not his decision but I can discuss it with them.

I ask him if they are supported by the Pakistani Secret Police. He looks puzzled. A man from the back of the room booms back in an educated English public school voice.

"Do you see any foreign backing in this room?"

He is an orthopaedic surgeon trained in Britain and volunteering his time to repair the damage of mine blasts. He is mildly pissed since it is obvious even to the blind that the *taliban* are running this operation with one Panasonic phone and little else.

Throughout our conversation my host is painstakingly polite and takes great pains to give full details to my questions. When I ask him how many men they have or other sensistive questions he replies with an embarassed look. "That is a secret. I cannot tell you or our enemies might find out."

He goes on to tell me that they have no designs on neighboring countries and that "after they win the war they have expressed their desire to communicate with all peace loving countries of the world. " As for foreign policy, economics and other items, they will get to that after they win the war. I ask him where all those shiny new tanks and weapons come from if they are just simple students. He smiles and says that when they captured Herat from Hektmatyar they found enough new weapons, vehicles and ammunition to fight Rabbiani for 25 years. I did not get into the fact that all those shiny new toys were actually courtesy of Uncle Sam vs. the Russians via Pakistan. When asked about training he said they have enough people who were trained during the war with Russia. Many were trained by Pakistan with U.S. help. He complained that Rabbiani now has planes and pilots from India and ammunition and weapons from Russia and military advisors from Iran. He said his backers were Saudi and Pakistani businessmen.

There is no trace of artifice, no haraunging, no pat answers. When I ask him to show me what parts of the country the taliban control he pulls out the only reference book in the room. The six inch stack of reports turns out to be copies of the same document. (A well-thumbed 1991 UN report on Kandahar with maps and statistics.) During our conversation there is a constant coming and going of men who wait patiently outside. The bandoliered mullah excuses himself, goes out and then rejoins us. We drink tea while along the back of the wall about 20 men watch us in silence as we talk. The phone rings throughout our conversation and my host apologizes every time. It seems they are arranging for a Danish Red Cross shipment and are trying to figure out how much to charge them. They are waiting for a fax with the bill of lading which must be sent to a copy shop down the street. The field commanders use a wireless radio to keep in touch.

He invites me to share lunch and as we eat red beans and flat bread I am amazed at being in a place where a group of rag tag students are taking over a country. As we share lunch it is obvious that he is hoping to convince me that they are sincere in their goal. He does not understand why I ask some of the questions. I tell him that it helps me understand the world better and hopefully I can help other people understand as well.

He and some fighters that have joined us insist that I finish the last of the watery broth as a courtesy. It is a humbling experience. After lunch he shows me around the compound and says I cannot take pictures of the men upstairs but that maybe the men downstairs won't mind. He explains they had trouble before with the Russians using pictures to identify and kill people. The men are lounging on the blankets recovering from various wounds. As I lift my camera a man with a deep face wound begins swearing at me. He says that Allah does not like photographs and that I should get a better job than being a thief. I click away while my host and Papa get nervous. Trying to ease the tension, I ask my host to take my picture. He holds my camera up backwards with the lens facing his nose.

The haranguing continues as I tour the compound. I point to the black clothing and ask him if this is the uniform of the *taliban*. He laughs and points to all the men ands says "He is *taliban*, he is *taliban* and he is *taliban*. We do not have a uniform."

He excuses himself and I thank him for his time. I remind him that I will be sending in a film crew. That night in the hotel I will call Coskun in Istanbul and tell him that we can have the world's first filmed interview of the *taliban* leaders. They will pass a special fatwah for us to allow us to film them. I tell Coskun of the route I have set up and give him my contact's name. He thinks I'm crazy but he says he will be here as soon as he can.

Out in the bright light of the market, people stare at me. I have my picture taken by an old man with an ancient wooden camera. A crowd of Afghans press around him and never take their eyes off me during the long process. Someone plunks an Afghan chitrali cap on my head. He uses the lens cap as a shutter and then develops the paper negative inside the camera. He then photographs the negative to give me a blurred 2" paper portrait. He hands me the crude, orthochromatic picture. I am a pale eyed afghan from the 18th century. I am in a time machine and I am holding the proof in my hand.

I sit in the shade while Papa goes to pray in the simple mosque across the tracks. A fighter comes up to me to practice his English. We watch a young boy is walking around with a white plastic garbage bag and a handful of wooden splinters and sticks. My new friend sees me looking at the young boy and says "He does this every day. He will take these things and make a beautiful kite." As I look around at the dirty ancient scene peopled with the hard-faced, turbaned mujahadeen all I see is the result of centuries of warfare.

My new friend pauses and then says proudly;

"He will fly this beautiful kite very high."

—RYP

Lima

Peru
★

Shadow and Light

When Francisco Pizarro and the Spaniards "discovered" Peru in 1531, the Incan empire was already past its zenith. The Incas were licking the wounds of a nasty civil war and were easily thumped by their uninvited guests.

The Spanish weren't the first or the last conquerors to impose a military dictatorship on Peru. But the nation's destiny was reflected in a historical strobe light as it vacillated between despotism and democracy, continuing to this day, nearly 500 years later.

After almost 300 years of Spanish rule, it took more outsiders—Jose de San Martin of Argentina and Simon Bolivar of Venezuela—to finally break Spain's grip on the country. Peru announced its independence in 1821, but it took a few more years to purge the Spanish. In December 1824, General Antonio Jose de Sucre defeated the Spanish troops at Ayacucho, ending Spanish rule in South America. Spain recognized Peru's independence in 1879 after yet another war with Peru between 1864 and 1866.

Today, the ruling class is a tossed salad of predominantly white-bread landed gentry hailing from families of global origins, with a sizable garnishing of East Asians. It's quite the norm in Peru to have a surname of German, Spanish, English, Japanese or French lineage. But that hasn't enhanced the "civility" of Peru. Modern Peru is the world's leading producer of coca and perhaps its largest concealer of citizens killed, tortured or abducted. In 1993, a Peruvian human rights group estimated that 28,809 people had been killed in 12 years of political violence. The government fessed up to only 53 of the deaths (leaving at least 2660 people unaccounted for). The Maoist rebel group Shining Path (SL) seems proud to admit that nearly half the body count came at their hands.

In 1992, 3101 people were killed in violent actions; 60 percent died in battles, 30 percent were murdered. Two hundred and eighty-six people were abducted in the same year; 178 weren't heard from again. The balance were summarily executed. Torture is the favored method, and a routine, mode of interrogation employed by Peru's armed forces, and used even during investigations of petty crime.

The U.N., the Red Cross and the U.S. Department of State all agree that, in Peru, human rights are human wrongs. Executions by the military, the disappearance and murder of students and the torture of arrested persons and missing people are simply everyday life in Peru. The only good news is that deaths by terrorism were down in 1993 and 1994—almost by half. Only 1692 people died in guerrilla wars in 1993, compared to 3101 in 1992. Things are getting better.

The country has been under emergency rule permitting President Alberto Fujimori to put some heavy-duty dents into terrorist itineraries. And, he did some serious name-dropping. Literally, the names dropped. Victor Polay Campos, head of the Tupac Amaru Revolutionary Movement (MRTA), was recaptured (he had escaped from custody in 1990) after he was recognized in a Lima bar. Peter Cardenas Shulze, MRTA's second-in-command, was busted in a raid by security forces on a safe house in Lima. Government forces snatched Abimael Guzman Reynoso, the SL founder, along with seven other SL members. His personal diary and plans for an upcoming SL offensive were also found.

Now that Fujimori has Guzman and Campos wearing stripes and is singing for peace like a lonely finch (with a little prodding from the head of the secret police), you'd think he could relax. Fujimori also brags that he has convicted more than 1000 terrorists, reformed another 1500 and captured thousands. The fact that he thinks he's David Copperfield by making students, political opponents and journalists disappear doesn't seem to bother hardworking Peruvians, who are sick and tired of the terrorist actions.

Well, dictators can never relax.

Fujimori fled his Lima palace the night of November 13, 1992, after being tipped-off about a coup attempt. Not to a television station did he dash to plead for calm or reassure a frightened nation, nor to a military base to bravely lead his troops on a counterassault. Instead, Fujimori high-tailed it to the Japanese embassy to save his own butt. Safe, sound and sushi-satiated, he then directed his crush against the insurrection by calling coup leader General Jaime Salinas from his cellular phone. Finally, after a predawn shoot-out with Salinas' rogues, the coup was put down; thank Vladimiro Montesinos for saving his bacon. Montesinos is the man who runs the military; he's got direct connections to the CIA and

PERU

Peru

⊙ National Capital
• Department Capital
• Secondary City
― Department Border
═ Primary Road
＋-＋-＋ Railroad

| 0 | 100 | 200 | 300 km |
| 0 | | 100 | 200 mi |

©FWi

the drug mafia. Montesinos is allegedly the man who directs death squads, bullies the military with his secret files and put Fujimori into power. He apparently intends to keep him there. Fujimoro seemed to be taking care of business. Inflation was down from an amazing 7650 percent in 1990 to a modest 12 percent. Investors were attracted by Peru's new fiscal health, and the government continued to annihilate terrorists with impunity. In January 1995 fighting broke out again along the disputed border with Ecuador, claiming nine lives. Peru declared a unilateral cease fire in mid-February. In the April elections that followed, Fujimori was reelected president. So far, his efforts to improve the economy and control Shining Path seem to be working but there is still a great disparity in the distribution of wealth.

The Scoop

Among the more than 6 million dispossessed, homeless and impoverished souls in Lima hides, arguably, the most apocalyptic group of terrorists on earth. The squalid, nameless shantytowns dotted across the Peruvian landscape are where the Shining Path (Sendero Luminoso) recruits its legions.

With the exception of certain tourist areas (Arequipa, Cuzco, Ica, Iquitos, Paracas, Puerto Maldonado, Puno and Trujillo), many regions of the country are designated as "emergency zone" areas. These are areas under terrorist threat and governed under martial law by well-armed soldiers who rip off a couple of clips on full automatic first and ask questions later. Despite the arrest of key leaders in 1992, two insurgent organizations—the Shining Path (SL) and the Tupac Amaru Revolutionary Movement (MRTA)—continue to carry out bombings and other terrorist attacks against a range of targets in Peru, principally Peruvian nationals, government installations, banks and foreign interests.

The unofficial headquarters of terrorism is the city of Lima, a designated "emergency zone." Bombings and terrorist incidents have been frequent in the city, and violent crime is common. There are power outages during the day, due to the drought conditions affecting the hydro-electric plants. This is important to know when choosing a high-rise hotel. Ask if the hotel has its own generator. Hotel rooms are favorite targets of burglars. The lack of tourists means that you will be particularly conspicuous.

Banks do not normally cash traveler's checks, but money changers will come to your room to exchange soles into U.S. dollars. Credit cards are accepted. There is a black market in soles, but don't be scammed by trading U.S. dollars for old notes.

Police augment their meager paychecks by setting up checkpoints on Thursday and Friday evenings to finance their weekends. Use air transportation when possible, and don't trust reports claiming that certain areas are safe.

Junkyard locos, like the Shining Path, have deliberately killed governors, mayors, tourists, schoolteachers, civil servants, hundreds of campesinos, entire villages, journalists, elderly people, children, presidential candidates, British ornithologists, Mormon missionaries, an agronomist, nuns and priests from various countries, mine workers and their wives, American helicopter crew members and a helluva lot more. They have bombed embassies, power lines, police vans, police stations, even public parks.

If, by some miracle, you don't run into the military or terrorists, there are always the hardworking farmers who live off the land. The fruits of their labor generate about US$1 billion in sales. What is the favorite cash crop of Peru? Why coca, of course.

The Players

Alberto Fujimori

The current ruler is President Alberto Fujimori. Fujimori is Peruvian of Japanese descent. In two years, he managed to dissolve parliament and assume the role of dictator. His stated goal was to deal with political corruption, and he bestowed upon himself absolute, unimpeachable authority in destroying the terrorist elements within Peru. Fujimori deftly constructed a new congress completely under his control, albeit behind a facade of democracy.

A tough-talking leader who is criticized for his abuses of human rights, Fujimori was elected in July of 1990 and took absolute power in an *auto-golpe*, or self-coup, in April 1992. He was reelected in April, 1995. He is also applauded by the ruling classes for his success against the two main terrorist groups, the MRTA and the SL, but despised by others for his brutality toward opposition groups and elimination of human rights and the democratic process. The first acts of Fujimori's new government were to have the army spend two days and nights destroying over 10,000 judicial files on active cases in the Palace of Justice. Not only did the most incriminating evidence disappear on all legal files on Fujimori and his family; those of his trusted confidant Vladimiro Montesinos magically disappeared, as well. This act took place the same day Fujimori dissolved parliament and became a dictator.

Vladimiro Montesinos

Presidential advisor and unofficial director of the National Intelligence Service. Montesinos has had ill-defined connections with the drug kingpins, Peruvian military, intelligence community and, since 1990, the direct support of the CIA. Called Rasputin by one local paper, Montesinos is considered the power behind the throne. Born in Arequipa, the same neighborhood as the SL's Guzman, he has had a rocky and convoluted climb to the top. A former court-martialed soldier, fugitive and legal fixer for the corrupt members of the Peruvian military, Montesinos is considered instrumental in helping Fujimori climb to his position of power. Montesinos is accused of directing death squads and being responsible for ordering various massacres and disappearances. He is also in charge of the eradication of drugs in Peru, using Peruvians trained and equipped by the CIA. Much like similar programs in Haiti, their efforts were diverted from drug eradication into private activities that helped overthrow the democratic leadership.

In August of '96 one of Peru's top drug runners testified that he paid Montesinos $50,000 a month for protection of drug flights into Colombia.

Coca

Coca is at the root of most of the killings—it's the base for the "white stuff," nose candy, rails, speedballs and crack. The Upper Huallaga Valley near the provincial city of Tingo Maria is one of the world's biggest coca-producing centers. In May 1991, Peru was the producer of 60 percent of the world's supply of raw coca leaf.

The Military

Emergency legislation has permitted the military special autonomous powers in fighting terrorist and politically subversive elements. The military administers and tightly controls emergency zones comprising over one-quarter of the country's territory. People arrested by the military are subject to the dreaded military courts. Many are not seen again afterwards.

The military appreciates its new power, but continues to be antagonistic toward the government. Fujimori still does a lot of personal promoting of buddies and demoting of fast-trackers. Any soldier opposed to his policies is relieved of duty, sometimes of bodily functions as well.

In 1992, 286 people were reported abducted, 178 of whom were subsequently reported missing. Responsibility for almost 90 percent of missing detainees was believed attributable to the armed forces. The same year, there were 114 extrajudicial executions, including 50 people who were captured by security forces and later found dead.

Since 1983, Peru has managed to win the grand prize or at least the runner-up trophy for the "Country with the Highest Number of Missing Detainees," a dubious and oft-sought distinction awarded by the United Nations work group on missing people. In 1992, the Red Cross counted 3330 arbitrary arrests; the State Department counted 654 bodies attributed to the Sendero Luminoso and 95 as the work of the government, the result of victims being executed without trial. In that same year, 30 students disappeared, 11 of whom turned up dead.

Armed forces personnel number about 80,000 conscripts in the army, 25,000 in the navy and 22,000 in the air force.

At least 300 military men have been investigated and charged with drug connections since 1990.

Sendero Luminoso (Shining Path, or SL)

Oscar Ramirez Durand (or Comrade Feliciano) has taken over leadership from the jailed Abimael Guzman (#1509) also known as Presidente Gonzalo and is working hard to keep the group's reputation for badness and cruelty they once possessed. The name came from Jose Carlos Mariategui, the founder of the first communist party in Peru, who called Marxism "a shining path to the future." The group was led by Manuel Ruben Abimael Guzman Reynoso, a pudgy, Ray-Banned, bearded ex-philosophy professor, who now will spend the rest of his life in San Lorenzo naval base on an island just off Callao. Guzman follows the teaching of Mao and was a student in the Chinese Communist Party's cadre school. The Shining Path began its armed struggle in 1980 and has been responsible for numerous bombings and assassinations. It has vowed to pursue "total war" until the government is overthrown. The group hopes to create a peasant-worker state along Maoist lines. The group's ideology is a strange hybrid of Maoism, Marxist-Leninism and the religious beliefs of the highland Quechua Indians of Peru. What began as a rural following in the remote highlands around Ayacucho spread along the mountainous rural areas toward the south and the east, until the Shining Path included rural revolutionaries, urban terrorists and the coca-growing farmers of Upper Huallaga Valley.

The Shining Path became famous for its Viet Cong tactics of intimidation of villagers. Villagers would be tried, the victims publicly tortured, mutilated, executed and left on display.

In urban areas, car bombs have been another successful terror weapon. Using a simple mixture of ammonium nitrate, diesel and dynamite, these car bombs had the strength of hundreds of pounds of explosives.

Most of the SL leaders are college-educated, middle-class Peruvians from Lima, who command Indian peasant armies. The approximately 10,000 attacks since 1980 against the government and innocent villagers have killed 30,000 people and cost the country more than US$24 billion. The SL likes to bomb symbols of bourgeois power: banks, police stations, political party headquarters and factories in Lima. Before the arrest of their leaders, the SL was estimated to comprise 5000 to 10,000 armed members. Now their numbers are dwindling to about 1000.

Shining Path leader Guzman has issued a number of government-sponsored communiques from prison that call for an end to the guerrilla war, alienating about half its membership in the year following his bust. Prior to Guzman's arrest, the SL controlled an impressive 40 percent of Peru's territory.

The group is self-sustaining, with some fund-raising done in Europe. It gets cash from the lucrative drug trade, which it uses to procure weapons and supplies. The group controls large portions of the Upper Huallaga Valley, the center of Peru's coca plantations, and taxes drug traffickers near their base in the southern highlands around Ayacucho.

Movimiento Revolucionario Nuevo Peru
(New Peru Revolutionary Movement)

These boys don't like holidays. The movement is a new, hard-line group of radicals once part of the Shining Path and based in the highland provinces of Huancavelica and Puno. The group has carried out attacks in the highlands and detonated bombs in the capital over holiday weekends, including an attack on an army post late one Christmas day that wounded eight people in Lima's impoverished El Agustino section. The group apparently split from Shining Path after its jailed leader, Abimael Guzman, called for peace. The leader is Oscar Ramirez, or "Comrade Feliciano." Comrade Feliciano says those who support any peace process with Fujimori's government are servants of Yankee imperialism and terms such pacts as "revisionist bitches' excrement." The man's got a way with words.

Tupac Amaru Revolutionary Movement (MRTA)

The current MRTA groups are the ragged remnants of a traditional Marxist-Leninist revolutionary movement formed in 1983 in Peru. The MRTA, led by Nestor Serpa and Victor Polay—now in prison—and its objective is to rid Peru of its imperialist influence and establish a Marxist regime. Their chances are slim at this point, but, in their heyday, they were responsible for more anti-U.S. attacks than any other group in Latin America. Originally 1000 to 2000 combatants strong, it has dwindled to less than a hundred, which have split into unorganized criminal bands. But they aren't simple thugs. Most have received training in Cuba. And, at one time, the MRTA enjoyed close ties to Libya but now gets its only support from Cuba.

If you are detained by MRTA cadres, remember that most are former college students who may have lived in Russia or Cuba in the 1970s who like to kick Yankees' asses. So you may get a lecture and a whipping and be told to go on your way. If you are stopped by a xenophobic Maoist of the SL, bend over and kiss it adios.

The MRTA is not as violent or unpredictable as the Shining Path. Founded in 1984 and based in Lima, the MRTA has links to Colombia's M-19 guerrillas, Ecuador's Alfaro Vive and the Cuban government. Using publicity as its major weapon, the MRTA likes to attack the news media and U.S.-related businesses.

The MRTA tried to wrest control of the coca traffic from the SL but lost. And their battles with the government ended with the capture of their leader. With most of their leaders behind bars (Victor Polay Campos studied in France and Spain in the 1970s, was captured in 1989, escaped and then was recaptured in 1992), the MRTA has broken down into small bands of criminals with little or no coordinated political agenda. They continue their financially (if not politically) successful M.O. of kidnapping and extortion.

The Alianza Popular Revolucionaria Americana
(APRA–American Popular Revolutionary Alliance)

A democratic left-wing, middle-class party with strong worker support and led by former President Alan Garcia Perez, the APRA did not get along with the military during the party's rule of Peru.

The Frente Democratico (FREDEMO–Democratic Front)

A right-of-center coalition with three main partners: the liberal, pro-U.S. Accion Popular (AP–Popular Action); the Partido Liberal (Liberal Party), a right-wing group led by former presidential candidate Mario Vargas Lhosa; and the conservative Partido Popular Cristiano (PPC– Christian Popular Party).

Izquierda Unida (IU–United Left)

A mishmash of left-wing groups including the Partido Comunista Peruano (PCP–Peruvian Communist Party), the Frente Obrero, Campesino, Estudantil y Popular (FOCEP–PopularFront of Workers, Peasants and Students), the Partido Comunista Revolucionario (PCR –Revolutionary Communist Party), the Partido Integracion Nacional (PADIN–National Integration Party), the Partido Socialista Revolucionario (PSR–Revolutionary Socialist Party), and the Partido Unificado Mariatequista (PUM–Unified Marietaguista Party).

The Izquierda Socialista (IS–Socialist Left)

Way, way left. Toward the dateline. A coalition of left-wing groups that broke away from the IU before the April 1990 elections.

Getting In

A passport is required. For U.S. citizens, a visa is not required for tourist stays up to 90 days, extendable after arrival. Tourists may need an onward/return ticket. For official or diplomatic passport and other travel, visas are required and must be obtained in advance. A business visa requires a company letter stating purpose of trip and US$27 fee. For current information concerning entry and customs requirements for Peru, travelers can contact the following:

Embassy of Peru

1700 Massachusetts Avenue, N.W.
Washington, D.C. 20036
☎ *(202) 833-9860*

For further information, contact the embassy of Peru or nearest consulate:

Los Angeles, California
  ☎ *(213) 383-9896/5*

New York, New York
  ☎ *(212) 481-7410*

San Francisco, California
  ☎ *(415) 362-5185 or 7136/2716*

San Juan, Puerto Rico
  ☎ *(809) 250-0391*

Miami, Florida
  ☎ *(305) 374-1407*

Houston, Texas
  ☎ *(713) 781-6145/5000*

Chicago, Illinois
  ☎ *(312) 853-6173*

U.S. Embassy
  Corner Avenidas Inca Garcilaso de la Vega
  and Espana
  Box 1995, Lima 1
  ☎ *(51) (14) 33-8000*

Consular Section
  Grimaldo del Solar 346
  Miraflores, Lima 18
  ☎ *[51] (14) 44-3621 or 44-312*

Getting Around

Peru is a tough place to get around via land. Internal air services link a number of cities that are difficult to get to by land. A number of new airlines have sprung up in recent years, causing domestic prices to go down somewhat. The four principal carriers are AeroPerú, Cia de Aviacion Faucett, Aero Continente and Americana. The two most dangerous airlines are Expreso Aéreo, which connects with some of the isolated burgs in the jungles and the mountains, and Aero Tumi, which hauls a few passengers aboard its cargo routes. Schedule changes and delays are frequent. Cancellations are common during the rainy season. The main airport is Jorge Chavez International, about 10 miles northwest of Lima, about 35 minutes by cab. A trip between the center of Lima and the airport costs about US$5.

Arrange to be met at the airport by someone you can identify. Hire only taxis from inside the airport. Unlicensed taxi drivers have been known to drive victims into the barrios and rob them.

The streets are not safe at night, despite vehicle curfews. Inside major hotels, there is a generally decent level of security. Hotels are usually empty so don't be shy about negotiating a good rate.

Very few roads in Peru are paved, the major routes of the Pan-American and Central Highways being the exceptions. The roads connecting Pacasmayo with Cajamarca and Pativilca with Caraz and Huaraz are also paved. The road to Bolivia from Puno-Desaguadero has been completed. There are also numerous toll roads in Peru. Outside the cities, travel can be a mess. Roads are dusty when they're dry and impassable when they're wet. The roads have been falling apart since 1985, when the government stopped maintaining them. Some work has begun rebuilding the south section of the Pan-American Highway. The South American Explorers Club is a good source for maps, as well as the Touring y Automóvil Club del Peru (Av César Vallejo 699, Lince, Lima; ☎ *403270; FAX: 419652*). As throughout most of the world, green and red are merely pretty colors, hardly incentives to brake or accelerate. Be wary of drivers everywhere in Peru.

Trains are more comfortable than buses, although many routes are cut back or even cancelled in the rainy season. Trains link virtually all the major cities in Peru. There are two major rail lines. One runs inland from the capital, Lima, and reaches the highest point of any standard gauge railway in the world at 4780 meters. The other major line runs inland from the port of Matarani in the south, linking the Altiplano to the sea. This line stretches in the Altiplano from Puno on Lake Titicaca to Cuzco, and extends from Cuzco to the Quillabamba on the Urubamba River, the main waterway to the jungle region. It passes the Inca city of Machu Picchu, Peru's most famous tourist attraction. The Cuzco–Machu Picchu route accounts for about 30 percent of all rail traffic.

Bus service is generally good, but exceedingly uncomfortable. Avoid bus travel at night. Bandits prey on tourists dozing on nighttime bus rides.

Taxis, identified by a small red-and-white windshield sticker, are plentiful and cheap. Taxis have no meters and fares are negotiated in advance. A map is useful, as few drivers know specific streets in the sprawling suburbs where many businesses and ministries are located.

Dangerous Places

Military areas, or "Emergency Zones"

More than 25 percent of Peru's land and 50 percent of its population are situated in "emergency zones;" areas where terrorist groups still control large parts of the country. Here, the "military-political commander," usually an army general, is the supreme authority. Elected civilian representatives have little or no real roles in local affairs. The military has also acquired wide powers in the administration of justice. Leading terrorists charged with "treason to the fatherland" are tried by secret military courts. They regularly receive summary life prison sentences from what critics describe as "faceless" judges. Travel to, and within, emergency zones outside Lima subjects one to extraordinary risk. These zones are extremely dangerous regions where both terrorism and violent crime are common. Overland travel to, or through, the emergency zones outside the capital city of Lima is particularly dangerous.

The following departments have been designated as "emergency zones" by the Peruvian government: Apurimac, Ayacucho, Huancavelica, Huanuco, Junin, Lima (except the city of Lima). Also the areas of Pasco, San Martin, Ucayali (except for air travel to the city of Pucallpa), as well as La Convencion and Calco Provinces within Cuzco Ucayali and Alto Amazonas Provinces within Loreto Department. The military has started arming peasants in an effort to make the SL's job of intimidation a little more risky. This, in turn, prompts the SL to execute entire villages as punishment for bearing arms. Guerrillas can expect speedy and one-sided military trials, and there are plenty of stool pigeons fluttering about to put away their former cohorts. Villagers can look forward to a few more centuries of oppression and brutality.

Cuzco and Iquitos

Pickpocketing and armed robbery in or near hotels is common. Foreigners, unarmed and cash rich, are sitting ducks for thieves. The police are too busy sniffing out terrorists, so don't expect a team of detectives to be put on the trail of your missing camera case or AMEX card.

Police or Military Facilities

If you haven't guessed by now that the Peruvian zanies have a thing for bombs and government facilities, hang around and find out for yourself.

Lima

Despite the setbacks suffered by Sendero Luminoso during 1993, the terrorism that occurred in the capital in 1994 helped certify Lima as one of the most violent cities in the hemisphere. While the number of attacks and deaths in Lima during 1993 were down significantly compared to 1992, nearly 60 percent of the total number of attacks nationwide were carried out in the capital in 1994, comprising 20 percent of the total number of deaths. According to statistics issued by a political violence monitoring group, at least 153 persons were killed in some 639 terrorist-related incidents in Lima's metropolitan area in 1994. Lima's central district (where the U.S. embassy is located) accounted for some 25 percent of all incidents and close to 40 percent of related deaths in Lima, making it decidedly the most dangerous part of the city. (Incidents in the outlying shantytowns are sometimes underreported.)

The western districts, including Lima's port city of Callao and the international airport sector, were the next most dangerous areas, with some 16 percent of Lima's terrorist incidents and deaths reported in these areas. Residential districts accounted for only 12 percent of the incidents and 5 percent of the deaths, but were the target of 13 of Sendero's 33 car bombs in 1993. At least 12 bystanders were killed by car bombs in 1993, a brutal example of being in the wrong place at the wrong time. The 33 Lima car bombs in 1995, however, do not include at least eight other car bombs (three in residential districts) that were defused or did not explode. For a brief comparison, there were 62 car bombs in Lima during 1992, with 19 in the residential districts. While the overall number of car bombs dropped by almost half in 1993 (33 versus 62), it is important to note that the number of car bombs in the residential districts remained almost the same (13 in 1993 versus 19 in 1992).

The city of Lima is located in Lima department, a designated emergency zone. Bombings and terrorist incidents have been frequent in the city, and violent crime is common. Most acts of terrorism occur in Lima. The targets are police stations, banks and commercial areas. Terrorist activities are shifting from the rural areas (which require money to support) to urban areas (which make money). Although many of the threats are for extortion, some robberies result in goods being confiscated and then distributed in the shantytowns. The SL continues to murder villagers and assassinate high-level government and military officials.

The group known as "Los Destructores" are knocking off banks and armored cars with continued success. There are problems with petty theft of auto parts taken from parked cars. Lima's airport and American Airlines have been the targets of terrorist attacks. On January 22, 1993, an AA flight from Miami was hit by three bullets while taxiing shortly after landing. The shots were assumed to have come from the Villa El Salvador shantytowns bordering the airport. No one was hurt. Four days later, a small bomb went off in the duty-free shop. Again, no injuries were reported.

If you need police assistance in Lima (don't hold your breath), contact the following:

Policia de Turismo (Tourism Police)

Avenida Salavarry 1158
Jesus Maria
☎ *71-4313 or 71- 4579*

American Businesses

The SL continues to target high-profile American businesses, such as IBM, Coca-Cola and American Airlines, and to bomb the U.S. embassy. Japanese interests have also been targeted.

The Border with Ecuador

Why these people fight over their northern border is a mystery to most civilized folks. Dense jungle, monkeys and mud are the spoils that will go the victor. Ecuador and Peru fought a war over this 1000-mile-long swamp in the Amazon basin back in 1941. In 1942, the Protocol of Rio de Janeiro was signed and Peru ended up gaining 77,220 square miles. Because the border was defined as "the river flowing into the Santiago River," it didn't take long for Ecuador to figure out there were two rivers flowing into the Santiago and they changed course every rainy season. So they fought again in 1981 and called each other nasty names in 1991.

Now they are squabbling over a 50-mile stretch in the lush, jungle-covered mountains of Cordillera del Condor, which would give Equador access to the Amazon and Maranon rivers, an area that is supposedly rich in gold. Naturally, any heavily armed visitors posing as ecotourists with metal detectors are highly suspect.

Dangerous Things

Drugs

In January 1995, three tons of pure cocaine and 500 kg of cocaine paste were seized and 20 traffickers were busted in northern Peru in what was to date the greatest amount of hydrochloride confiscated in the 1990s. Among those arrested were the leaders of the notorious Los Nortenos cartel. The cocaine empire covers one-fifth of Peru's territory and affects the lives and activities of 1.2 million people inhabiting 60 percent of the Peruvian Amazon. The "empire" handles nearly 300 tons of cocaine per year and receives US$1 billion annually. Additionally, the cartel controls 241 clandestine airstrips.

Money Changers

Tourists have been ripped off while changing money with street money exchangers called *cambistas*. Counterfeit U.S. dollars are exchanged or slipped in during the transaction. These counterfeit bills are of very high quality, and most people do not realize they are counterfeit until they try to pass them, or compare them to real bills in bright sunlight.

Power Outages

When the towns go black, the crooks grow hair on their palms and howl at the moon. Get inside a hotel or business during a power outage. Ahooooooo!

Getting Sick

Medical care does not meet U.S. standards. Cholera is present in Peru. However, visitors who follow proper precautions about food and drink are not generally at risk. U.S. medical insurance is not always valid outside the United States. In some instances, supplemental medical insurance with specific overseas coverage has proved useful. Malaria and yellow fever are present in Peru.

Nuts and Bolts

The official language is Spanish, the mother tongue of around 70 percent of the population. Quechua and Aymara are also official in some regions. Numerous other languages are spoken by Indian tribes in the Amazon basin.

Peru's three distinct geographic regions present significant difficulties for economic development. Offshore and coastal areas in the northwest contain oil deposits, but the width of the arid Pacific coast that runs the length of the country averages less than 160 kilometers, and rivers flowing from the Andes irrigate only a few valleys. Major traditional exports include fish products, cotton and fruit grown on the coast, and coffee grown in the Andean foothills.

The Andean highlands rise sharply from the coast to a height of more than 4000 meters, and much of the country's mineral wealth comes from mines in the Andes. Coffee and coca are the major cash crops of the foothills of the east Andes. The real agricultural export is coca, the United States being the biggest customer with more than US$1 billion generated in coca sales. Half the country lies in tropical lowlands. The northern jungle is a wealthy oil-producing area that used to cause friction with Peru's neighbors.

The coastal population is primarily mestizo, with a small percentage of whites of European descent. The Quechuan highlanders are direct descendants of the Incas, and the Amerinds are related to the jungle tribes of the Amazon.

The currency is the Nuevo Sol, which fetches about 2.1 to the U.S. dollar. Electricity is 220V/60Hz. Any time of the year is best to visit Lima, since it's dry with temperatures ranging from an average high of 82° F in January to lows of 66° F in August. Lima is arid with an annual rainfall around 48 mm; the marine layer is a common factor, with long periods of overcast skies, *garua* between June and September. Higher up in the Andes and the Amazon, the rainy season is from December to March. Remember, the summer and winter are reversed. There are also fertile valleys, such as those of Cuzco and Cajamarca. Lake Titicaca in the south, at an altitude of 3815 meters, is the highest navigable lake in the world. About 60 percent of Peru's area is covered by the triple-canopy rain forest in the Amazon basin. The Andes, of course, with some peaks as high as 7000 meters, can get quite frigid.

The informal "*tu*" form is commonly used with younger Spanish-speaking business visitors. While Peruvians are sometimes inclined to be late for appointments, visitors are expected to be punctual. Phone calls are very expensive from the hotels in Lima.

Useful Addresses and Phone Numbers

Aeroperu
Avda Jose Pardo 601
Miraflores, Lima 18
☎ [51] (14) 322995

Aeropuerto Internacional Jorge Chavez
Avda Elmer Faucett
Lima
☎ [51] (14) 529570

Empresa Nacional de Ferrocarriles, del Peru
Ancash 207
Apdo 1379, Lima
☎ [51] (14) 289440

Ministry of Industry, Commerce, Tourism and Integration
Calle 1 Oeste, Corpac
San Isidro, Lima 27
☎ [51] (14) 407120

UK Embassy
Edif El Pacifico Washington
Piso 12, Plaza Washington
Esq Avda Arequipa
Casilla 854, Lima 100
☎ [51] (14) 334738
FAX [51] (14) 334735

U.S. Embassy
Avda Garcilaso de la Vega 1400
Apdo 1995, Lima 100
☎ [51] (14) 338000
FAX [51] (14) 316682

Foptur (Tourist Promotion)
> *Jiron de la Union 1066*
> *Belen, Lima*
> ☎ *[51] (14) 323559*
> *FAX [51] (14) 429280*

Embassy Location/Registration

Upon arrival, U.S. citizens are requested to register with the consular section of the U.S. embassy in Lima to obtain the latest travel and security information within Peru.

U.S. Embassy, Consular Section
> *Grimaldo del Solar 346*
> *Miraflores*
> ☎ *[51] (14) 44-3621 or 44-3121*

Dangerous Days

10/07/1992 Abimael Guzman, the founder and leader of Sendero Luminoso, was sentenced to life imprisonment by a military court.

04/05/1992 President Alberto Fujimori, with military cooperation, closed the congress and courts and set aside portions of the constitution in an action that concentrated extraordinary powers in his hands. The Organization of American States (OAS) demanded that Fujimori restore the constitution. Opposition parties and leftist insurgents oppose Fujimori's takeover.

06/18/1986 Security forces killed more than 200 jailed members of the Sendero Luminoso (SL) guerrilla organization during a riot at Lima's Canto Grande prison. The event is marked by the guerrillas as "Heroes Day."

07/28/1985 President Alan Garcia Perez succeeded Fernando Belaunde Terry as president, the first transfer of power from one democratically elected Peruvian president to another in forty years.

11/04/1982 MRTA founded the Tupac Amaru Revolutionary Movement (MRTA), a Cuban-inspired Marxist guerrilla organization.

05/18/1980 The Maoist Sendero Luminoso (Shining Path) guerrilla organization began its armed struggle 12 years ago with an attack on a rural polling station; it has since grown into the largest and most active insurgent group in the country.

12/03/1934 Birthday of Abimael Guzman, also known as "President Gonzalo," the founder and leader of the Sendero Luminoso guerrilla organization. Guzman's followers often "celebrate" his birthday by carrying out attacks or murdering soldiers, public servants and municipal authorities.

12/26/1893 The birthday of Chinese communist leader Mao Zedong has been "celebrated" by the Sendero Luminoso (SL) guerrilla organization reveling in terrorist attacks.

07/28/1821 Independence Day.

10/07 Communist Party founded.

02/21 Birthday of Haya de la Torre Victor, the founder of the American Popular Revolutionary Alliance (APRA), the former ruling party of Peru. Date is also celebrated in Peru as the "Day of Fraternity."

PERU

Manila

The Philippines
★ ★

The Crescent and the Cross

The Philippines seems to get bypassed on most travelers' Southeast Asia itineraries. The world's second largest archipelago after Indonesia, the Philippines comprise some 7100 idyllic islands; only 4600 are named and a mere 1000 are inhabited. The islands are in three main groups: the Luzon group, the Mindanao group and the Sulu and Visayan group. Earthquakes pound the islands when Muslim guerrillas aren't. Throw in a bunch of active volcanos and a couple of abandoned U.S. military bases—Subic Bay and Clark—and it can be partly gleaned why tourism to the islands has dropped. Most tourists to the Philippines these days seem to be horny Australians on sex junkets, despite the Australian government ban on sex tourism.

In the 1950s, the Philippines had the strongest economy in Southeast Asia, if not all of Asia, surpassing even those of South Korea, Japan, Thailand and Malaysia. However, today, nearly half of all Filipinos live on the poverty line But it's not only the rudimentary infrastructure that's keeping the charter jets away. See, there's a nasty little problem with imported terrorism. All that money from Saudi Arabia and the United States that was funneled into Afghanistan to stave off the Soviets has found its way not only to the World Trade Center in New York but to a brutal and strengthening Muslim insurgency on Mindanao.

The Muslim separatists of Mindanao have been around for a while. Their quest for autonomy from the Roman Catholic Philippines isn't one of those Johnny-come-lately bus bombings or rocket attack parties. The Spanish had 300 years to snuff these guys; they couldn't. Neither could the Americans during their 50-year rule of the islands; nor could the Japanese during their occupation of the country during World War II. Although various Philippine governments have negotiated with the principal Muslim extremist group, the Moro National Liberation Front (MNLF)—with varying degrees of success—an even nastier, deadlier faction has come on the scene, the Moro Islamic Liberation Front (MILF). Not to be confused with moderate Moros or morons, these Hezbollah-backed fundamentalists have been quietly proliferating and arming themselves, while Manila busies itself hosing down a Libyan-brokered autonomy agreement with the MNLF reached in Tripoli in 1976.

The government claims the MILF is only about 8000 guerrillas strong, yet it deploys nearly two-thirds of its 70,000-soldier army on Mindanao to contain the separatists. The MILF itself claims 120,000 troops, but Western analysts believe the group numbers about 40,000 combatants, only about a third of which are on "active duty" at any given time. Even at that number, the MILF is far stronger than the communist New People's Army of the mid-1980s. And just to give the movement a little international flavor, there may be as many as 1000 MILF members who went to fight in Afghanistan.

And, unlike the MNLF, the MILF is unlikely to cave in. Whereas a number of MNLF leaders have been co-opted into the mainstream Philippine social and business fabric since the diluted and still unimplemented 1976 autonomy plan, the MILF is hard-core Islamic fundamentalism at its nastiest, a downright Jihad, Southeast Asian style. As a case in point, the MILF has received at least 29 arms shipments from Hezbollah and other extremist groups in the Middle East since 1994. They're packing Russian-made AKs and rocket-propelled grenade launchers, the same equipment with which their buddies in the sand are blasting each other. And they haven't had a lot of opposition, as they've been largely ignored by Manila since their inception in 1978, particularly because of the government's concern with the communist threat. Consequently, Muslim extremism and separatism in the Philippines has been put on the back burner.

Manila has its reasons for ignoring the Muslim threat. First of all, Muslims comprise only about 5 percent of the Philippine population, and they are even greatly outnumbered by government supporters on Mindanao itself. Secondly, since the 1987 constitution was ratified, any successional or autonomy move must be approved by a plebiscite, and both Moro groups would lose handily on Mindanao.

So, for now, the Muslim insurgents are content to be left alone in the mountains of the central Philippines, occasionally terrorizing towns and villages. They lay in waiting. The MILF couldn't win a head-to-head war with the Philippine army, and the group admits as much. But they'd make it a bloody enough battle to be marginally victorious at the negotiating table. Instead, the Front is waiting for the collapse of the Philippine government, as did the fundamentalists in Iran

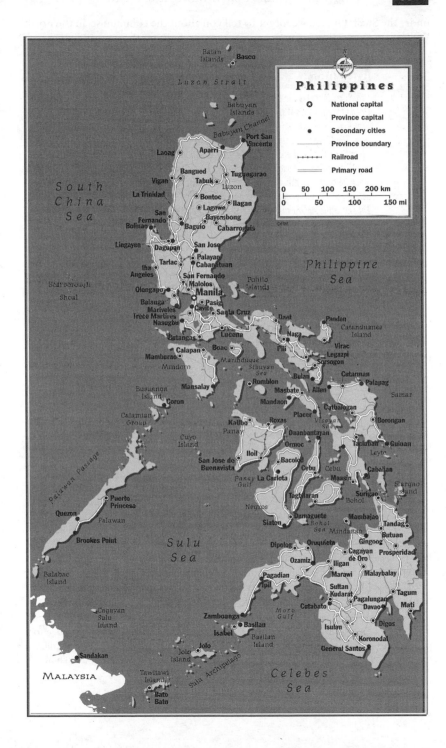

under the Shah. Oh, did we forget to tell you about the communists in the north? Well, there is an active, aging group of commies fighting the government as well.

The Hours Suck
But Think of The Accrued Holidays

Hiroo Onada makes the Energizer Bunny look like a piker. Second Lieutenant Onada fought World War II for 30 years. The fact that nobody bothered to tell him that Japan surrendered in 1945 didn't stop him from hanging on until 1974. The 73-year-old Onada hid out on the island of Lubang in the Philippines, living off wild animals and plants. A Japanese journalist found Onada in 1952, but Onada thought he was a U.S. spy. In a way you can't blame him since he could see the activity at Subic Bay and the constant U.S. military activity made him believe that the war raged on. His orders were to stay in Lubang if the Americans captured it and to wage a guerrilla campaign. His only companion, Private Kinshinchi Kozuka, was shot by Philippine police after 19 years on the island.

He was finally convinced to give up his fight when Norio Suzuki, a Japanese adventurer, conveyed a direct order by his commander to surrender. He now teaches at an outdoor survival school in the Fukushima prefecture of Japan.

The Scoop

Muslim and communist separatists have been battling various Manila governments for nearly 30 years, resulting in more than 10,000 firefights between insurgents and government troops during that time. More than 50,000 people have been killed. The government kept a relative lid on the extremist problem—in the interests of promoting tourism—until the recent terrorist plot to kill the Pope and blow up numerous airliners simultaneously. Meanwhile, army rebels are busy plotting the next coup of the month. In all, the mayhem keeps the hotel rates down.

There are perhaps 4 million Muslims in the Philippines—which is 83 percent Catholic and the only Christian state in Southeast Asia. Mindanao has become a virtual battlefield, as MILF guerrillas and government troops shoot bullets at each other and trade camps. Further south still and nearly 1000 kilometers from Manila—yet only a short boat ride from the mainly Muslim Malaysian and Indonesian island of Borneo—secessionists on the two principal islands in the Sulu Archipelago, Basilan and Jolo, continue to fight for their independence, a fight that's lasted the better part of 300 years. Many of the Muslim people who inhabit the Sulu Archipelago have been split by modern national borders and, as a result, travel frequently and freely between neighboring countries. Numerous radical Muslim groups have emerged from the poor fishing villages scattered across the islands, but most have evaporated over the years, taking a more conciliatory path or becoming entangled with more radical factions. As the Mindanao-based Moros (the Moro National Liberation Front, or MNLF) work out a peace agreement with the Philippine government, a new, more radical group has emerged, the MILF.

The southern Philippines always was predominately Muslim but immigration from the north has increased the Christians to a majority. That's why the Muslim groups will not agree to a plebescite to determine who should rule the south. It is estimated that communist guerillas in the northern Philippines has dwindled from a high of 25,000 in 1987 to about 5000 now.

The Players

The Big Blast

Project Bojinka, or "the Explosion," was supposed to be the biggest terrorist attack in history. The idea was to blow up 11 U.S. airliners over the Pacific on the same day. Five Muslim terrorists would plant bombs aboard 747 aircraft. The plotters, Pakistani nationals, Ramzi Ahmed Yousef and Abdul Hakim Murad, were arrested. Both men were also accused of trying to assassinate the pope in January of '96. The plot was discovered when the men were mixing up chemicals to make explosives in their sixth-floor apartment's sink. The mixture began smoking and the firemen were called. The men hid out in a karaoke bar down the street, and, when Murad was sent back to get the incriminating evidence, he was nabbed by the cops. The smoking gun? Their computer's hard drive had been erased but when restored, contained complete details on the plot.

The scary part is that the two men successfully carried out a dry run when they placed a small bomb under the seat of a Tokyo-bound Philippines Airlines Flight 434 on Dec 11, 1994. The bomb killed a Japanese tourist and wounded 10 others. Yousef had placed the bomb under the seat when he flew the same airliner. The difference is, he got off at Cebu and then the ill-fated flight continued on to Tokyo.

Yousef actually made the bomb in the toilet of the airliner from liquid nitroglycerine and other inert chemicals. He hid the clear nitroglycerin in a bottle of contact lens wetting fluid.

The Moro National Liberation Front (MNLF)

Filipino Muslims have been called Moros since Spanish colonial times. The word "Moro" means Moor, or Muslim in Spanish. A strange bit of gun trivia is that the U.S. Army's 1911 Colt .45-caliber pistol was actually developed because the smaller-caliber bullets wouldn't knock down the drug-crazed Moros. The recent uprising of the Moros began in 1972 with the MNLF, which, with Arab support, was unsuccessful in liberating the large Islamic community of the southern Philippines. Libya stepped in to broker a cease-fire, and, today, the Moros are essentially a mainstream political entity. The current MNLF chairman, Nur Misuari is opposed to Abu Sayyaf's attacks on clerics and has publicly asked the group to release its hostages. The radical Abu Sayyaf Group has divorced itself from the Moros, who are now working with the army to free hostages and turn in Abu Sayyaf members. The government puts their strength at about 17,500 men. Commander Ting Ting, leader of the Lost Command, a splinter group of the MNLF, was captured on January 19, 1996.

Hashim Salamat & the Moro Islamic Liberation Front (MILF)

An offshoot of the MNLF that sprang up in 1978 in the wake of the Tripoli-brokered autonomy agreement between Manila and the Moros, the MILF has no word for "compromise" in its Islamic dictionary. MILF troop strength is estimated at between 20,000 and 40,000 by independent analysts, but no one seems to know for sure. The MILF itself claims a force of 120,000 members, 80,000 of them armed—while the Philippine government says the group numbers no more than 8000. The Front's leaders claim that as many as 1000 Filipino Muslims in its ranks fought against the Soviets during the war in Afghanistan (Philippine military intelligence says no more than 300 did). Highly disciplined and equally as radical, the MILF doesn't simply seek autonomy (as the more moderate MNLF has sought) but complete succession of Mindanao from the Philippines and the creation of a fundamentalist Islamic state—and will settle for no less. The Front's military commander, Al-haj Murad, boasts of possessing six full divisions of soldiers; however, it seems to be a rotating army, with only two divisions on duty at any given time. This may explain the massive gap in estimates of the group's strength. MILF leader Hashim Salamat is a tough guy to get a hold of—military commanders and many of the Front's other bellwethers have never set eyes on him—but does give regular religious sermons on radio broadcasts in Mindanao. *DP* had no problem setting a chin wag and a guided tour at his base camp. Salamat received his religious training in Egypt and Pakistan in the 1960s (he was heavily influenced by Syed Abul Ala Mau'dudi of Pakistan's Jamaat i Islami Party and Syed Outh of Egypt's Muslim Brotherhood) and formed the Moro National Liberation Front in 1970. His training in the Middle East made him a lot of bearded buddies with bombs, so he had no problem arming his spin-off gangsters when he founded the MILF. These days, the MILF is busy funding itself through the kidnapping of Taiwanese diplomats and by attacking Philippine military detachments and burning schools.

The Abu Sayyaf Group (ASG)

The Abu Sayyaf Group (ASG) is an Islamic fundamentalist faction with zero tolerance for the Christian government that first appeared in August 1991. The ASG began as Tabligh (Spread the Word), an organization founded in 1972 by Iranian missionaries who came to the Philippines to spread the doctrines of Ayatollah Ruhollah Khomeini. The ASG figured the Philippines was a good place to wage a secessionist Jihad, or Holy War.

Tabligh's military arm became known as the Mujahedin Commando Freedom Fighters (MCFF), and later tagged as the Abu Sayyaf Group—named after charismatic leader Abdurajak Janjalani Abubakar, who goes by the handle of Abu Sayyaf (Father of the Sword). The group is based in Darayan, Patikul and Sulu and can muster only about 120 armed combatants. But these boys are fierce, namely because they can afford to be. They're supported by Libya and Iran and generate their own income by kidnapping businesspeople. On January 23, 1995, Muslim rebels kidnapped a businesswoman and her companion in the southern Philippines and demanded one million pesos and 100 cattle for their safe return. The Abu Sayyaf group also held five journalists for four days before releasing them unharmed on January 23, 1995. Scores of people, including foreign missionaries, have been kidnapped in the southern Philippines.

Since August 1992, the rebels have been targeting members of the Roman Catholic Church. They kidnap priests, missionaries and nuns, usually releasing them after a lengthy captivity. The MCFF also provides protection for the numerous smugglers and pirates who prowl the Sulu Sea. There have been reports of Mujahedin veterans from the Afghan war providing training to MCFF members in guerrilla tactics and explosives.

The ASG is at least partially financed by Iran and Pakistan, as evidenced by the recent arrest of four Middle Easterners for visa irregularities. The men were from Jordan, Pakistan and Iran, one of whom was carrying a large amount of cash. One of the Jordanians arrested was Mahmoud Abdel-Jalil, the Jordanian regional director of the International Islamic Relief Organization. Although Abdel-Jalil is a 10-year resident of the Philippines, it is suspected that he has ties to Islamic extremists in Pakistan and Iran.

Abu Sayyaf has also been allegedly behind a number of bomb blasts, assassinations, grenade attacks and ambushes. The group's first attack came in August 1991 when a grenade was thrown into a crowd of people in Zamboanga, killing two missionaries and wounding 40 others. In February 1993, 22 marines and four rebels were killed in an ambush.

Since then, government officials have attributed more than 15 violent incidents to the group, including another reprisal attack for the Jolo assault in June that killed three people and injured 28 in a shopping center in General Santos City on the southern island of Mindanao.

Abdurajak Janjalani Abubakar is a Filipino trained in Libya and fluent in Arabic. He was reported killed in combat with government troops on January 13, but *DP* has heard that he is still very much alive. Janjalani is the son of a poor fisherman. He studied Islam and Arabic in Saudi Arabia in the 1980s and continued his studies in Libya. He returned to the Philippines, where he traveled throughout the Muslim regions giving lectures and preaching Islamic fundamentalism, its ultimate goal being the creation of an independent fundamentalist state in the southern Philippines. On January 17, 1995, the government sent in 200 additional soldiers to the remote southern island of Basilan to "neutralize" the Abu Sayyaf group, adding to the strength of more than 2000 soldiers already deployed in the area, who face perhaps 200 guerrilla soldiers. Basilan has been the group's base of operations. On January 13, 33 guerrillas and seven soldiers were killed and 15 other rebels and eight troopers were wounded in a major firefight between the two forces.

A large shipment of arms from Afghanistan arrived in Cotabatu in January 1995 for the MCFF. Estimates put the shipment at some 3500 high-powered guns. There were reports the cache included surface-to-air missiles.

A major government offensive against the Abu Sayyaf was launched on Basilan in January 1995. Philippines president Ramos declared Basilan Island under a "state of calamity." He also whined about the $38,000 a day it was costing him to chase down the fanatics. Meanwhile, the legislature authorizes the purchase of 2 billion dollars-worth of arms over the next five years.

The New People's Army (NPA)

The communist NPA was, until recently, the most powerful insurgent group in the Philippines, but is now fading out of the picture. One of President Fidel Ramos' principal objectives after he was elected in 1992 was to pursue peace with the NPA, which has been largely accomplished. The NPA has now split into a number of relatively impotent factions; its leader, José María Sison, is now in exile in the Netherlands. Ramos scored a success when he was able to persuade another NPA leader, Leopoldo Mabilangan, to leave the group. Mabilangan was later assassinated by NPA operatives.

The Alex Boncayao Brigade (ABB)

The ABB is a lethal leftist death squad led by Sergio Romero that has taken scores of lives in its 10-year history. These guys are the assassin branch of the Communist Party of the Philippines. Most recently, the group has been active offing Chinese businessmen in sort of an ethnic cleansing of the ranks of the Philippines' industrialists. In December 1995, President Fidel Ramos "declared war" on the group, which Romero responded to with an announcement that the death squad would expand its arenas of operation beyond Manila to throughout the country. The government has drawn up a list of more than 160 ABB members targeted for arrest.

Wanna Buy Baby Gang (WBBG)

Yeah, you read it right. Philippine security forces are hunting a gang that snatches babies and children and sells them to childless Filipino and foreign couples. The group, called Wanna Buy Baby Gang, preys on babies and children aged eight months to two years. The going price per child is US$20,000 if the buyer is a foreigner and 20,000 pesos (US$785) if the client is a Filipino. The chief of the antikidnapping unit of the National Bureau of Investigation (NBI) said the existence of the gang was reported by parents who had been victimized. Women gang members carry out the abductions by applying to work as maids. After gaining the trust of their employers, they disappear with the babies. The gang has reportedly taken over 30 babies and small children in recent years. (We couldn't make this stuff up if we tried).

The Pirates of Zamboanga

Zamboanga is a colorful, dangerous place and home to pirates, smugglers, terrorists and the most charming people *DP* has met. The name Zamboanga is derived from the Samal word *samboangan*, meaning "anchorage." The Samals live in stilt houses built over the shallow waters. The children play in the "front yards," just like children play on grass, but in the water. They travel to market and to visit neighbors in tiny dugout canoes. They find it quite exciting when foreigners visit; they wave and hold up their children for a picture when strangers are in town.

Zamboanga is a city of half a million people and is the center for the export of copra timber and other natural products. The population is 75 percent Christian and 25 percent Muslim. Originally a Christian outpost surrounded by Muslims, the city was occupied by American troops in 1899. They believe that Sabah, the oil- and timber-rich state of Malaysia, should be part of the Philippines. They base their claim on the historic rights, going back to the 16th century, belonging to the Sultanate of Sulu. One of the sultans leased Sabah to a private firm, the British North Borneo Company, in 1878, even though the boundaries were ill-defined and disputed by other rulers in the region.

In 1946, the company handed Sabah over to the British government, which, in turn, ceded it to Malaysia in 1963. But Manila claims that the Sultan of Sulu had already transferred his rights to the Philippines in 1962. The ancient 16th-century document is considered a gimmick by Manila, similar to selling a tourist the Brooklyn Bridge, as both the Sultan of Sulu (or Sooloo) and the Sultan of Brunei grandly claimed all the islands in the region, even though they had little idea of just how large Borneo really was.

Even now, the Philippines has never renounced its formal claims to Sabah, principally because the Philippines congress would have to ratify such a step.

The Muslims living in southwestern Mindanao and on the Sulu islands have been trading for centuries with their fellow Muslims in Sabah to the west and Sulawesi (Indonesia) to the south without considering that anyone would create a demarcation line between them. There are between 300,000 and 700,000 illegal immigrants from the southern Philippines living in Sabah, as well as Timorese from the Indonesian island of Timor. They work cheaply, but are a growing concern for the Sabahans because the Sabahans are outnumbered.

Zamboanga is a historic trading center, where luxury goods from Indonesia, Malaysia, Singapore and China are as plentiful as the raw materials from the sea and jungles that surround the city. The goods are brought in on *tora-toras*, flat-bottom boats, that are usually loaded to the gunnels with cheap TVs, beer, cigarettes and other prized items.

The "pirate" ships are an assortment of rusting freighters, aging ferries, modern speedboats, *basligs*—the large boats with outriggers to avoid capsizing in the heavy seas—and speedy canoelike *vintas* with their colorful sails.

The amount of trade in high-ticket items from duty-free ports, such as Labuan in Brunei, make legitimate traders easy targets for pirates who employ everything from *parangs* (machetes) to machine guns to kill their victims.

Ouch...

A former communist rebel in the Zamboanga del Norte region of Datangan who believed his life was being threatened was killed when a grenade he was carrying for protection detonated while he was sleeping. The blast also killed the man's son and a relative, as well as injuring his wife and daughter and four other relatives. The man was sleeping with the grenade in his trousers pocket. Meanwhile, airport security officers in Manila were seizing aerosol sprays, perfumes and lotions from passengers bound for the U.S. No word on whether officials were seeking to prevent these items from blowing up in the pockets of passenger's trousers at 37,000 feet.

Getting In

A passport and onward/return ticket required. For entry by Manila International Airport, a visa is not required for a transit/tourist stay up to 21 days. Visas are required for longer stays; the maximum is 59 days. You'll need to fill out an application and provide one photo, at no charge. Company letter needed for business visa. AIDS test required for permanent residency; a U.S. test is accepted. For more information contact the following:

Embassy of the Philippines

1600 Mass. Ave., N.W.
Washington, D.C. 20036
☎ *(202) 467-9300*

Or nearest consulate general at:

Hawaii, ☎ *(808) 595-6316*   *New York,* ☎ *(212) 764-1330*

Illinois, ☎ *(312) 332-6458*   *Texas,* ☎ *(713) 621-8609*

California, ☎ *(213) 387-5321 and (415)*   *Washington,* ☎ *(206) 441-1640*
433-6666

Arrival into the Philippines from abroad is primarily through Manila's Ninoy Aquino International Airport, a modern facility with 14 jetways. Located in nearby Pasay City, the airport is less than 30 minutes away by car to any major hotel and services an average of 170 international flights weekly. Manila is just over an hour by air from Hong Kong, three hours from Singapore, five from Tokyo, 17 hours from San Francisco and 22 hours from New York.

Several Southeast Asian regional carriers have direct flights into Zamboanga, Mindanao, and proposed international airports are due for Cebu City and Zamboanga.

PTICs are located at Ninoy Aquino International Airport (☎ *828-4791/828-1511*), Nayong Pilipino Complex, Airport Road (☎ *828-2219*) and on the ground floor, Philippine Ministry of Tourism (Ermita) building near Rizal Park in Metro Manila (☎ *501-703, 501-928*). Field offices are situated in Pampanga, Baguio, Legazpi, La Union, Bacolod, Cebu, Iloilo, Tacloban, Cagayan de Oro City Davao, Marawi and Zamboanga. The Department of Tourism hotline is ☎ *501-660/728*.

In North America, the Philippine Tourist Office has the following locations:

Philippine Center

556 Fifth Avenue   *Suite 1212, 3460 Wilshire Boulevard*
New York, NY 10036   *Los Angeles, CA 90010*
☎ *212-575-7915*   ☎ *213-487-4525*

THE PHILIPPINES

Suite 1111, 30 North Michigan Avenue
Chicago, IL 60602
☎ *312-782-1707*

Getting Around

Accommodations, food and travel in the Philippines offer some of the best bargains found in Asia. The National Railway serves the island of Luzon, from Lagaspi in the south to San Fernando, La Union, in the north. Car rentals are available in the major cities, with or without a driver. Jeepneys are cheap and plentiful in Manila and other large towns. Domestic flights connect Manila daily with about 50 other towns, cities and rural areas. Where scheduled flights do not serve, there are aircraft for charter. Local service is bare-bones basic, with nothing offered but plastic cups of water. Allow plenty of time before departure for security inspection. Around the archipelago there are inter-island sea vessels with first-class accommodations that sail between several different ports daily.

Getting Out

If you find yourself in a pinch, or need quick transport out of the Philippines, you can charter a boat from Sitangkai for the 40-km trip to Semporna in the Malaysian state of Sabah. This, of course, is completely illegal. However, there are a slew of boats that make the trip from the Philippines to the busy market in Semporna. Keep in mind that Sabah has its own customs and immigration requirements, so you'll need a separate stamp when you move back and forth from Sabah to peninsular Malaysia. These waters are also home to Sulu pirates, actually a combination of minor smugglers and armed thugs who prey on large commercial vessels. Pirates have also been known to rob banks and terrorize entire towns in coastal Sabah. Just inquire at any fishing village or dockside hangout in Sitangkai. Usually, you'll have to cross at night, and don't be surprised to pay two to three times the normal rate of P$150. Going the other way is also easy; there are boatmen who can hook you up with the many speedboats that are for rent in Semporna. Be careful dealing with the Ray-Banned entrepreneurs you meet along the docks. They might turn you in for the reward money and simply pocket the sizeable fee you paid them to get you across.

Leaving from Ninoy Aquino International or Domestic Airport can be a drag due to the tight and zealous security inspections. The airport taxes are P$500 for international flights and P$25 for domestic flights.

Dangerous Places

Mindanao

More than 10,000 firefights between government soldiers and rebel separatists as well as countless bombings and other politically motivated slayings have left 50,000 people dead over the last 30 years in the Philippines, most of them on the island of Mindanao. Sultan Kudarat is particularly dangerous. Government soldiers are regularly attacked by MILF guerrillas in this area, and surrounding parcels of land change hands regularly. Dangerous as well is the city of Zamboanga, where a wave of bombing attacks by ASG terrorists rattled the city for six days in March 1996.

Basilan

This island, just southeast of Mindanao in the Moro Gulf, has been the scene of separatist activity for decades, if not centuries. Muslim separatists here prefer blowing up schools— as there is little else here to watch go kaboom.

Dangerous Things

Crime

Crime is high throughout the Philippines, particularly in urban areas. Many stores employ armed guards. There are 30 murders and three rapes per 100,000 people. There are 72 thefts for every 100,000 people.

Kidnapping

If you're a Chinese businessman living and/or working in the Philippines, consider wearing a mask or seeing a plastic surgeon, as you're the favorite target of kidnappers. Kidnappers like snatching Chinese guys for ransom, because their companies/embassies/families invariably will pay up. Filipino body snatchers aren't stupid. Kidnappers realize that if they take a Westerner, they'll have to feed the poor SOB for a couple of months, only then to get stormed by police commandos. In one recent incident, on March 13, 1996, the son of a Taiwanese diplomat was kidnapped and then released five days later after a ransom of US$38,500 was paid to his abductors. In 1995, more than 160 people were abducted in the Philippines—many of them belonging to rich ethnic Chinese families—hauling in more than a US$3.6 million booty for the kidnappers. That's positive cash flow.

Do You Also Need a Picture ID?

Kidnapping has become such a way of life in the Philippines that gangs now accept checks to cover their ransom demands. At least three Filipino-Chinese businessmen were quickly freed by kidnappers after they issued checks ranging from US$11,500 to US$38,000. One anticrime watch official stated that he doubts "if they gave stop payment instructions because the kidnappers would certainly have gotten back to them."

Being President

Corazón Aquino's administration from 1986 to 1992 survived no fewer than seven different coup attempts.

Getting Sick

Shots for smallpox and cholera are not required for entry, but cholera shots are suggested when the Philippines appears on a weekly summary of areas infected (according to the World Health Organization). Yellow fever vaccinations are required of all travelers arriving from infected areas. There is one doctor for every 6413 people in the Philippines. Medical care in the Philippines outside of Manila can be below Western standards, with some shortages of basic medical supplies. Access to the quality facilities that exist in major cities sometimes requires cash dollar payment upon admission. Most of the general hospitals are run privately. Malaria, once a big problem in the Philippines, has been eradicated in all but the most rural regions. Tuberculosis, respiratory and diarrheal diseases pose the biggest threats to travelers. The U.S. embassy and consulates maintain lists of health facilities and of English-speaking doctors. Drinking only boiled or bottled water will help to guard against cholera, which has been reported, as well as other diseases. More complete and updated information on health matters can be obtained from the Centers for Disease Control's international travelers' hotline, ☎ (404) 332-4559.

Nuts and Bolts

The Republic of the Philippines comprises 300,000 square kilometers (777,001 square miles) on 7107 islands in the South China Sea between Borneo to the southwest and Taiwan to the north. Its 65.2 million inhabitants speak Tagalog and English. Roman Catholics comprise 83 percent of the population, Protestants, nine percent, Muslim, five percent; and Buddhists three percent. There are more than 100 different ethnic groups in the country. The

Philippines has one of the developing world's highest literacy rates. Nearly every child in the country finishes primary school and nearly three-quarters of the population completes secondary school. The education system is based on the U.S. model. Although relatively highly educated, about 50 percent of Filipinos live at or below the poverty line, namely because economic expansion falls short of the country's population growth rate. The official currency is the Philippine peso. Approximately 26 pesos equal US$1. Hard foreign currency and traveler's checks are easily exchanged at banks, hotels and authorized money changers throughout the country. Credit cards are also now widely accepted.

Local time in the Philippines is GMT plus eight hours, i.e., exactly 13 hours ahead of Eastern Standard Time, 14 hours in advance of Eastern Daylight Time. Add another hour for each mainland U.S. time zone (add five for Hawaii). Manila is in the same time zone as Beijing, Taipei, Macau, Kuala Lumpur, Singapore and Hong Kong, but one hour ahead of Seoul and Tokyo. It is one hour ahead of Bangkok, Jakarta, and 1-1/2 hours ahead of Yangon.

The local current is 220 volts/50 cycles—when there is power. Electric razors can be used in major hotel multifitting bathroom plugs, but most hair dryers will need converters.

The local water is generally potable, except for remote rural areas. Those with delicate stomachs should stick with bottled water at all times, not use any ice and avoid all fresh, raw vegetables. Fruits that you peel yourself are always considered safe. Drink only bottled beverages that are opened in your presence.

Hours of business in the Philippines are from 8 a.m. to 5 p.m. Monday through Friday, with most offices closed from noon to 1 p.m. or so. Banks open from 9 a.m. to 4 p.m. Monday through Friday. Shops in major tourist centers open at 9 or 10 a.m. until at least 7 p.m. daily. The smaller, family-owned shops outside Metro Manila are open whenever and for as long as the spirit prevails. There are also three stock exchanges (Manila, Makati, Metropolitan) that trade in the Philippine market from 9:30 a.m.–1:30 p.m. Monday through Friday.

Telephone, telex and fax services in the Philippines are surprisingly poor, and communication with the outside world is slower than you'll find in other parts of the Far East. Overseas calls take from 30 minutes to an hour to put through, although IDD is coming to some of the better hotels. Overseas calls can be costly and frustrating from this country because hotels add a 20 percent or more surcharge and you must pay even though no connection was made. Local calls are about P$5 for three minutes from your hotel room, about P$10 from a red public phone. However, connections are not always clear and phone lines have a habit of breaking down. It's easier to make an international call than get a local connection.

One of the biggest infrastructural problems in the Philippines is electricity. The Corazón Aquino Administration did little to improve the power situation in the country. There was little investment in power stations; consequently, the country experiences frequent and lengthy power outages on 258 out of the 297 working days each year. This unreliability has deterred foreign investment.

Although the Philippines exports copper and is the world's largest supplier of refractory chrome, perhaps 90 percent of the country's natural resources have yet to be tapped, as the Philippines haven't been largely surveyed.

The weather is hot and humid year-round; the rainy season runs from May through October.

Embassy Locations

United States Embassy

Roxas Boulevard, near the Manila Hotel
☎ *598-011.*

The Canadian Consulate

4th floor, Philippine Air Lines Building
Ayala Avenue
Makati
☎ *876-536.*

Rwanda
★★★

Walking Backwards

How can one of the tiniest, lushest countries in Africa become one of the largest killing fields in the world? Tribalism. Rwanda, like neighboring Burundi, is a rather simple (for most African countries) hybrid of two tribes: the Hutus and the Tutsis (plus a small indigenous Pygmy population). A four-year uprising made minor headlines every time Tutsi guerrillas would infringe on the territory of Rwanda's famous silverback gorilla families. When full-scale war broke out after the death of Burundi's and Rwanda's leaders in a plane crash, the majority Hutu tribe blamed the minority Tutsis and began indiscriminately slaughtering them. But the surprise success of the ragtag Tutsi rebels transformed them from freedom fighters into outright butchers. The Hutu-controlled government has been replaced by Tutsi rebels, and the wholesale massacre is now being directed at the Hutus.

Now massive waves of refugees are making their first tentative explorations homeward. They find strange people living in their houses and will never know what happened to their missing family members. They don't need to know—be-

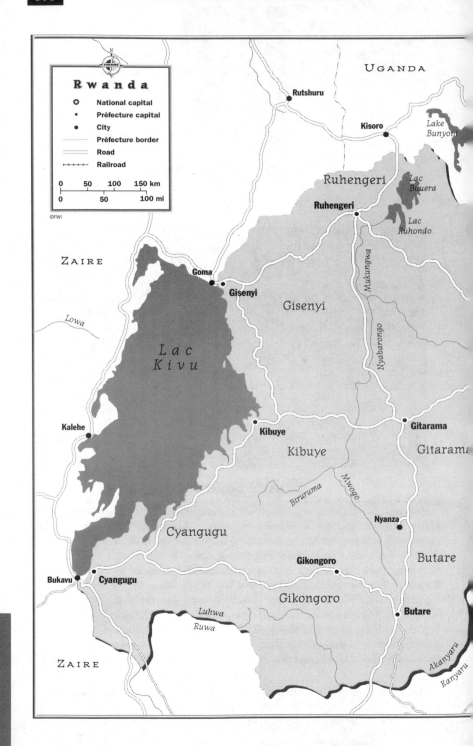

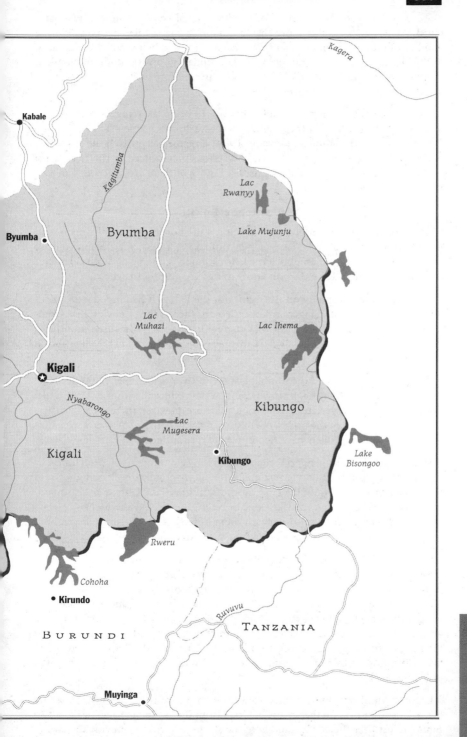

cause they are dead. The number of dead and displaced is countless. Estimates put the Tutsi fatality toll at more than a million in the last few decades, and the number of refugees at more than twice that figure. It is being called the greatest exodus in modern history. Almost half of Rwanda's population of 8 million fled during the hostilities in April 1993; 10,000 per minute at its peak crossed the borders.

Major-General Paul Kagame is doing his best to bring the refugees back, particularly the Hutus, who fled the country en masse after Kagame's Tutsi Rwandan Patriotic Front (RPF) came to power in 1994. Kagame has ordered the execution of any soldier who kills a civilian. That he's serious is evidenced by the 1116 Tutsi soldiers now jailed in four military prisons. Eighty of them are officers—and 125 face murder charges.

Three Roads South

Maps don't often show Merama Hill, but it's the border post on the main road from Uganda to Kigali. The land (scrub, candelabra trees), what game you can see (fine impala) and the longhorn cattle look much the same on both sides. But the minute you're in Rwanda, you know things are getting treacherous.

Traffic, for one, is running on the right, not the left, as it had in Uganda, and if it takes more profound dangers to unsettle you, there's the genocide that seems to have stopped at a million, but may merely have paused. In three months of 1994, the Hutu hard-liners killed as many people as the Khmer Rouge did in three years.

Here is where you'll find the tumbling Kagera River, a.k.a., the Alexander Nile, rushing on to Lake Victoria, from where its waters will spill into the Albert Nile, from where they will find the Mediterranean. It tumbles fast, there are white caps, and you can almost see the bodies of children rushing with the river down to Tanzania, to which their killers have fled in fear of retribution.

Across the border, Ruhengeri is charming as only a mountain town anchored by a grass air strip can be. But what haunts Ruhengeri are fully developed ghosts, in particular a group of about 100 Tutsi mothers caught in the Christmas season pogroms of 1962–63. On a road just out of town, they found themselves trapped between two mobs of Bahutu. Beneath them flowed the Nywarungu River, alive with crocodiles. They threw their children in, then jumped in after them.

This was not an isolated incident. It echoed from the past, it echoed again in 1994, and, even as those women jumped, it was echoing throughout Rwanda. Another 100 Tutsi women in the town of Shgira jumped into the river after their husbands were rounded up and they knew they'd never see them again. Children were skewered alive and left to die, buried alive, thrown into rivers, heads tied to knees. Tutsi men were left to bleed to death after having had their legs cut off at the knees, "to bring them down to our size." After 10,000 Watutsi were killed near Gikongoro, a thousand women and children there gathered and committed collective suicide.

There's a third way into Rwanda from Uganda. Halfway between Merama Hill in the east and Kisoro in the west is the road from the Ugandan town of Kabale to Biumba, just over the border, and here the story turns from genocide to war.

On the Horns of a Dilemma

Paul Kagame, head of a force of 5000 mostly Tutsi insurgents, was watching a soccer video in a tent near Biumba when a runner came with the news that a burst of shellfire had brought down the president's plane as it took off from Kigali airport, killing the president, the chief of staff of the armed forces, plus Burundi's president. This confronted him with a dilemma. He could concentrate his forces, as sound doctrine dictates for outnumbered forces, or he could split his men up in an attempt to stop the genocide, which was now beginning in earnest. Hutu hard-liners blamed the Watutsi for the attack, and the Hutu Radio Des Milles Collines explicitly incited the population to slaughter Watutsi. But this was only one aspect of his bind.

Under the cease-fire that preceded the outburst, he was permitted to barrack 600 troops in Kigali; now they were stranded and under heavy attack. More fundamental was the strategic position of his main force in the north. As the press put it, his forces "controlled" this corner of Rwanda. It would be accurate to say that the heavily armed, French-trained, 25,000-man Rwandan Army, backed by Guarde Nationale troops everywhere, had him cornered here. When the news of the crash came, he was in a tent near Biumba, not in the town. Based in Biumba were seven battalions of the Rwandan Army, backed up with heavy weapons, armored personnel carriers, paratroops, and helicopter gunships. Kagame's troops, with no such weaponry, were scattered out of harm's way, entirely afoot, carrying all their materiel on their backs. Now that was something of a blessing. He immediately sent orders for them to gather at preplanned assembly points, but it would take them a little time, which gave him a chance to think what to do with them when they got there.

Reporters didn't write much about the war itself. It was not easily accessible, and at that point, the French-Canadian officers running the United Nations contingent in Rwanda had little to say about what little they knew. Off the record, there was speculation aplenty. All agreed that whatever Kagame's numbers, he must and will take the offensive, and to be successful in any way, he must concentrate his limited forces for a focused attack. But beyond that, they split into two camps.

Camp one kept it simple: Find a weak spot, concentrate forces, attack it for a doable big victory in one battle, certainly no more than a few, then use the Hutu pogroms to call for a cease-fire that the United Nations might actually enforce, then negotiate.

Camp two said negotiations with the less extreme government of the late president were barely working. Negotiations with the extremists who killed him just weren't really promising. Concentrate, yes, they said, but in a bold strike at Kigali.

Camp one said impossible, since a major force was defending the capital. Assuming he could get around the major force cornering him in Biumba, Kagame's small, ill-equipped force would be ground up in a frontal assault on Kigali, even if it won. Meantime, on its rear would be the heavily armed Biumba force it had earlier bypassed. There would be virtually no Watutsi left to negotiate anything.

Kagame knew camp one was right. Both the force cornering him in the northwest and the force defending Kigali were too strong to attack frontally. Meantime, all over the country, Watutsi were being slaughtered, a powerful

inducement to split up his forces rather than concentrate them to win a significant battle. For years, he had planned for this moment, but now that it was at
hand, and his forces were assembling, he didn't know what to do.

Reporters strive for economy, but digging into the making of this fight, and the
danger that hangs over Central Africa, a quick telling of the Watutsi's swift victory over the Bahutu can make what must have been a monumentally difficult and
dangerous undertaking seem downright easy. Kagame's strategy pivoted on mobility. Without vehicles, that meant moving at night—fast. If you caught a
glimpse of them, it would be in those same hours that Africa's great predators are
about, amid the fog and smoke of dusk and dawn. Maybe it's them, maybe it
isn't.

To this day, there are a few of the pygmoid Batwa living amidst the smoke and
mist of the forests around Lake Kivu west of Biumba, but mostly the country to
the west is heavily cultivated and thick with Bahutu. In fact, in early '94 it was a
stronghold of hard-line Bahutu, and with Kagame unlikely to strike in this inhospitable direction, the strong blocking force of the Hutu based in Biumba was positioned to keep him from slipping to the east in an attempt to bypass the
blocking force and strike at Kigali, due south.

Not long after the president's plane crashed, the Presidential Guard assassinated
Prime Minister Agathe Uwilingiyimana, Kagame struck, and every observer who
knew about the assassination (no news reports) was nonplussed. First surprise: He
struck west into that inhospitable country thick with Bahutu, which caused some
terror, even though he had no designs here at all. The strike to the west finessed
the Hutu force deployed mostly to block an attempt to bypass them on the east.
Having passed them on the west, he moved south toward Kigali. That surprise,
however, seemed almost natural in retrospect. The second surprise didn't. Having bypassed the blocking force in Biumba, Kagame split his forces in two, sending one in a wide sweeping arc to the savannas of the east, and sending barely half
his men, now doubly vulnerable, to strike at Kigali.

The Importance of Focus

Afoot, Kagame's Kigali-bound force cut through 40 miles of enemy-held turf in
four days in April. As they approached the city, U.N. staffers in town were reporting widespread slaughter of noncombatant Watutsi by the Army and the Guarde
Nationale, both of which often fired large volumes of ammunition wildly. But
Kagame didn't attack. The city was defended all around by heavily armed Hutu
forces with ambushes prepared along street after street.

Instead, Kagame focused on three more modest objectives. First, he organized
an advance to link up with his force of 600 men in Kigali as they tried to break out
of their compound that was under heavy attack. The Bahutu were intent on those
600, and many showed exceptional courage attacking the compound. But the
Watutsi inside were at least as intent; they broke out, joined up with Kagame's Kigali force, and Hutu morale was hit hard.

Then, as the Hutu generals redeployed to defend a city Kagame had no intention of taking at that point, the Tutsi leader wheeled his strengthened Kigali force
on his second objective, the airport. By mid-April, his mortar fire had shut it
down, and hard fighting for limited targets filled the next month, with no sign of
a concerted attack on the city whose streets were seeing the slaughter of more and
more Watutsi civilians. Then, on May 22, these tactics paid off. Both the airport

and Kagame's third limited objective, the Rwandan Army's Kanombe barracks, fell to the Watutsi.

Reporters and the Hutu population were stunned. But military observers knew Kagame had still not won a major pitched battle with a heavily armed Hutu force. His enemy in Kigali was still more numerous and better armed, and his force was split, with half of it off somewhere to the east. But those were just military observations. Everyone else expected Kagame to join a battle for Kigali, and as days passed without an attack, reporters wondered in print why he was taking so long, as Watutsi in Kigali were butchered. Kagame answered, "We have to do this methodically; we can't rush in."

What reporters didn't know—but the Hutu military did—was that even as Kagame was explaining why he was proceeding so slowly, his Kigali force was wheeling rapidly away from Kigali and toward a new target: the heartland of the hard-line Bahutu in the hills to the west. Their core constituency threatened, the Hutu generals moved reinforcements to defend this heartland.

What they didn't know is that Kagame had no intention of seeing his troops chewed up in this Hutu heartland, where the largely untouched Biumba force was still based. Instead, he turned again, all the way around to the east, again ignoring Kigali, even though some of its defenders had been drawn off for the defense of the western heartland. He left just enough forces to keep the Hutu generals pinned down and wondering, and linked up with the eastern spearhead he had launched at the beginning of April. Now at last, his forces were rejoined and concentrated, as they swept around Kigali from the north to the south and then to the west, nearly enveloping the capital, but carefully leaving the government one avenue of escape, and an attractive one at that: west to the Hutu heartland.

Panicked, the Hutu leadership took the bait and quit the capital for the town of Gisenyi. At the time, it sounded much more like a retreat to the bush, with a government representing the vast majority fighting with its people from the countryside. But Gisenyi is a resort on Lake Kivu, a lighthearted place where steep lawns sweep in extravagant expanse around equally extravagant villas. Nonetheless, it was surrounded by heavily Hutu country, and now the Hutu armed forces, still unhurt by any major defeat in battle, were deployed to defend a much more compact area, backed by a friendly border with Zaire. When Kagame's force first invaded in 1990, Zairois troops had joined the French and Belgians to fight the Watutsi. In an arc from Biumba to Ruhengeri to Gisenyi, strong points were set up. On high ground dominating all three key towns, paratroops, regular army troops and militiamen from the Guarde Nationale manned armored personnel carriers, heavy artillery, and an array of other weapons Kagame didn't have.

A Face-off with the Bahutu

Thanks to a U.N. weapons boycott, the Hutu forces were running low on ammunition, lower than that of the Watutsi, who had greater fire discipline. But the Bahutu still had heavy weapons, armor and aircraft, none of which Kagame had, and its forces still had not lost a major pitched battle. The way the elusive Watutsi had fought, there had been no major pitched battles. But now, at last, that day was at hand, and the Hutu hard-liners had the weapons.

Come the end of the day, who would be the victor? That was the question, as Kagame's force headed from southeast to northwest. But it was never really answered. The rulers of Hutu Rwanda's rump government in carefree Gisenyi took one look at the Watutsi headed their way, and they were out of there.

The French Connection

As France publicly deliberated putting together a force to rescue civilian Watutsi from slaughter, belligerent members of Kagame's front charged that France was actually planning to join the war on behalf of the Bahutu. True, the Bahutu were still French clients, and true, the French had fought against the Watutsi. But it was clear this time that with the slaughter of the Watutsi so horrible, no French government could survive actually going to war for the Bahutu against the Watutsi. This was surely clear to Kagame, as well. But that was just his dilemma. With the French public aware that the government would not possibly fly in to fight the Watutsi, the government could comfortably fly in to rescue civilian Watutsi, and in so doing, secure strategic ground for their Hutu clients. In short, unless Kagame played this dangerous game just right, the French could again defeat the Watutsi, this time without firing a shot.

Specifically, the French could fly in to the uncaptured south of Rwanda in order to stop the slaughter there, and not incidentally, to keep the south out of Kagame's hands. And that's pretty much how it developed. With the world calling for an end to the butchery, French President Francois Mitterand announced "Operation Turquoise," a short-term rescue mission to demilitarize the south and southwest. On July 3, as the world heard of Kagame's troops moving into a largely deserted Kigali, France choppered paratroops and naval commandos to a lower profile, political prize— Rwanda's second-largest city, Butare, far to the south on the Burundi border, a city bursting with Bahutu who had chosen French protection in the south to protection by their own army in the north. France would not battle Kagame for turf. Having proclaimed neutrality, they couldn't. But they would occupy turf like Butare in the far south that he had not yet reached. What they didn't realize as they flew in was how fast Kagame's foot soldiers were moving, and now there were nearly 25,000 of them.

What the French found as they landed in far southern Butare July 4 was Kagame's army just 500 yards from the city line. They pulled out, and Bahutu driving everything from Peugeots to backhoes followed them. Their license plates were from all over Rwanda, not just the "CB" plates of Butare, but "ABs" from Kigali, and even "IBs" and "HBs" from Ruhengeri and Biumba.

The French had to make a deal, and after the hot words of his cohorts, Kagame proposed one that was very tough for them to refuse. Essentially, it was a deal that would make certain that the French "rescue mission" was indeed just that, terms confining the French to a small refuge they would briefly protect on Zaire's border.

On paper—and in the papers—this looked like no big deal; basically, it was just getting the French to affirm their benign intent. But a big deal it was. France's deputy commander in Rwanda, Colonel Jacques Rosier, frankly acknowledged that the agreement amounted to a retreat. "This is not what we thought two days ago," he said as he pulled his force back, virtually *hors de combat*, to positions along the edge of the Nyungwa Forest (a primeval place where the forest elephant, with its small, hard tusks, has long dwelled, and where six of them may yet dwell).

As the Bahutu in Gisenyi watched the French pull back, they knew the French wouldn't be choppering here and there as a "humanitarian" blocking force between them and the Watutsi. Meantime, Kagame could ignore the far southwest, temporarily secured for him by his French friends, and drive his entire concentrated, strengthened force to a foregone conclusion in Gisenyi.

The Scoop

In 1959, a faction intent on maintaining Tutsi privilege in Rwanda assassinated several Hutu leaders. Hutu rage slaughtered 100,000 Rwandan Watutsi, and the carnage was on—a 22-year program that, in 1994 alone, would wipe out half a million Watutsi in Rwanda.

When the Belgians pulled out of the two countries in 1962, Bahutu ruled Rwanda. In Burundi, Watutsi were hanging on to power and still were, a decade later, when Hutu frustration exploded in Burundi's landmark revolt of 1972. A thousand Watutsi died in the outburst. Having witnessed the 1962 killing of 100,000 Watutsi in Rwanda, this 1972 rampage by Burundi's Bahutu was all Burundi's ruling Watutsi needed. They killed 100,000 Bahutu and chased out another 200,000. Then the pickings got a little less abundant for the vultures. As the rest of the world saw it, an equilibrium, of sorts, had been struck. In Burundi, where the mass murderers were Watutsi, the Watutsi ruled. In Rwanda, where the mass murderers were Bahutu, Bahutu ruled. But the equation was inherently volatile. For one thing, the Bahutu remained the overwhelming majority in both countries. For another, if the Watutsi were to rule anywhere, it made more sense in Rwanda since, historically, Rwanda's Watutsi were a stronger group than Burundi's. In a way, this was the reason they had become the victims of genocide, the failed preemptive strike by one of their clans.

But this hardly justified the genocide, and it hardly made the quarter-million Rwandan Watutsi in exile any less talented or disciplined a people. Amidst the horror of Idi Amin's Uganda, they hung on. When Uganda's agony was finally brought to an end, it was the work of an obscure, disciplined guerrilla army made up in good part of adolescent orphans of the horror, very much a latter-day children's crusade, with a "security chief" still in his twenties. His name was Paul Kagame, a Rwandan Tutsi.

Inevitably, Paul Kagame went home with about 8000 of his friends. In front of them was a Hutu army 30,000-strong, but like Idi Amin's army, it was corrupt. Unfortunately, what French and Belgian papers saw as all this unfolded in the fall of 1990 was not resistance against an army that had committed genocide. What it saw was an evil bouillabaisse boiling over, a stew in the creation of which France and Belgium had been no mere sous-chefs. It saw the minority Tutsi overlords, already in power in Burundi, about to regain power in Rwanda. They were beginning to feel guilty. Some, also saw opportunity. The tide, through Africa, has been with the majority. In any case, it's always easier to find room in a European budget for financing neocolonial clients who are "democratic" (read: a majority). France, Belgium and Zaire rushed in to stop Kagame's army.

Nowadays, air safaris are becoming especially popular. The planes can soar above the tangled geography, the volcanic Virungas, the snow-dashed Mountains of the Moon, whose lakes and foaming white waters are the source of both of Africa's two great rivers: the Zaire and the Nile. Beneath them is all the wonder that spreads below the soaring buzzard, whose grim acuity must see so much more.

The Players

Paul Kagame and the Rwandan Patriotic Front (RPF)

The man is a Rwandan Tutsi, born in Rwanda, and residing there today. He is the most powerful man in the Tutsi homelands of Rwanda and Burundi and probably the most powerful man that either of those two precarious states have known since they both became independent in 1962. But most of his life he lived in Uganda, during that country's most wretched years—and there's the twist. The very wretchedness of that period helped bring the Watutsi and their son Kagame back to Rwanda.

The Uganda in which Kagame matured was a nether world, a place of attenuated pain, both psychological and physical. This, the Watutsi shared with their Ugandan hosts and helped them bear, first the nightmare of Amin, then two more nightmares, as bad or worse, of which we'll learn more later. With little more outside help than refugee Watutsi could provide, the people of Uganda finally ended those nightmare years, and when they did, the Watutsi were not without influence.

First among these influentials was young Paul Kagame, Rwandan refugee, intelligence chief for all of Uganda...and a key organizer of the RPF. The Tutsi front was formed by the guerrilla years its leadership had spent with Museveni's National Resistance Army, which drew its strength from popular support. This meant, above all, discipline. Rape was punishable by death, and a summary execution for just such an offense was meted out to a Tutsi fighter in the midst of 1994's 14-week war for Rwanda. The front demanded no privileges for the Watutsi, though there was little rhetorical nonsense, either: It was clear that majority rule would be balanced by minority rights. And there was clearly a danger that with meager resources, it could not control the climate of terror.

As a member of Uganda's military, Kagame was able to apply for a course in tactics given by the U.S. Army Command and General Staff College at Fort Leavenworth, Kansas. In fact (and reflecting in part Tutsi chutzpah), Kagame was in Kansas in October 1990, the very month he and a close comrade-in-arms, Fred Rwigyema, had planned to invade Rwanda. The invasion went ahead anyway, and it went well, until France put together a combined force of French troops, Zairois troops, Belgian troops and French-trained Hutu paras. The Watutsi were thrown back, Kagame's old friend Fred Rwigyema was killed in combat, and like many a college student with trouble at home, Kagame had to drop out.

In 1991, his movement launched its last frustrated invasion. Again, it went well, but with the prospect of intervention again hanging on the horizon, he stopped short in the north and agreed to talks. These were to drag on for two years in the Tanzanian town of Arusha at the foot of Mt. Kilimanjaro. At last, late in 1993, Rwanda's hard-line president agreed in prinicple to terms that called for a moderate Hutu to be installed as president and another as prime minister. The hard-line president signed a formal cease-fire, Rwanda's even harder-line military was enraged, and a large question began to loom as to whether Rwanda's government would or could fulfill the terms to which it had agreed. As he watched from his camps along the Biumba road, this was the chessboard upon which Kagame had to focus all his strategic faculties: French armor in Hutu hands, French heavy weapons, a Hutu military for which France and Belgium had successfully bought time for a huge buildup—Hutu airborne troops and 30,000 regulars, all trained by the French. Against this, he had no armor and no heavy weapons, just mortars and rocket-propelled grenades that Uganda had to pretend it didn't supply. As for training, it's basically the homegrown discipline of Museveni's children's crusade, plus Kagame's course, which was in tactics, not strategy, as American reporters were wont to boast.

Mwalimu Julius Nyerere

A great teacher of lessons, not all of which should be taught. Tanzania's soft-spoken leader, now retired, is influential still: For Africans, he remains *mwalimu*, the teacher. In fact, without portfolio, he is more influential than most African heads of state. His power has declined distinctly, but this has little to do with his retirement. What he retired from, the presidency of backward, resource-poor Tanzania, was never the prime source of his influence. The decline is due almost entirely to the failure of his most ambitious ideas.

They are powerfully attractive ideas, even after their failure, and he is an attractive figure: the very image of intelligence, unblemished by greed, stirred by the responsibilities of leadership, an intellectual who did not merely adopt ideas, but tried to craft them to fit Africa. Alas, for all the shrewd pragmatism that implies, he is not a practical man. He is known, will long be known, for a magnificent idea that has failed magnificently. Nyerere tried to craft, from the Swahili word for family, *ujamaa*, something between a voluntary Israeli kibbutz and a compulsory Chinese commune.

It rarely worked. It cost millions. Whole villages were uprooted. Labor was forced. It never came close to paying its way. Today, the effort is largely abandoned.

Regardless, he is a man of integrity, remains a powerful teacher of integrity, and many believe Africa needs more leaders like him. For a while, they saw Nyerere's Ugandan protegé, Apollo Milton Obote, a schoolteacher who became prime minister, as a good example. We'll see how he became an example of something much different.

General de Divison/Augustin Bizimungu

The Hutu general, now a Hutu renegade, is not to be confused with Hutu moderate Pasteur Bizimungu, who was slated to become Rwanda's president under terms of a peace agreement signed by Kagame's Tutsi front and Rwanda's Hutu government. The agreement was violently resisted by military leaders like Augustin Bizimungu, who itched to turn their French heavy weapons on the Watutsi in a military showdown. Augustin Bizimungu thus became, quite unintentionally, the man most responsible for the success of Pasteur Bizimungu. When the showdown came and the Watutsi licked the Rwandan Army, Kagame's front simply let the previously signed peace treaty kick in and Pasteur Bizimungu became president.

When Rwanda's military collapsed, Augustin Bizimungu was its chief of staff. As he sees it, he's still its chief of staff, and a chief he most certainly is. He's ensconced at this resort hotel or that, commander of an army without a country, at large in Zaire.

According to various sources, it is speculated that Bizimungu and his cronies blew up at Rwanda's longtime, hard-line Hutu president, Juvenal Habyarimana, for not being hardline enough when he initialed the agreement with the Watutsi calling for Hutu moderates as president and prime minister. Also, if you found it irritating to read, in the background graph of one Rwandan news item after another, that the country's president had been "killed in a suspicious plane crash," Bizimungu and his buddies are the suspects.

It's been widely reported that the president of Burundi was also on that plane; less widely reported was news that Rwanda's chief of staff was aboard, which is how Bizimungu became chief of staff. (Chew on that, Tom Peters.) But the promotion didn't come right away. The prime minister didn't want Bizimungu in the slot, and he was under the protection of the Presidential Guard. As jockeying for the leadership of the military went on, Bizimungu and his cronies told the rank and file that their president had been shot down by the Watutsi. The military (army and militia) then went on its infamous *pogrom*, and, in the meantime, Bizimungu's appointment as chief of staff was iced by the Presidential Guard killing the prime minister it was supposed to be protecting.

The Parti Liberation du Peuple Hutu (PALIPHUTU)

This is the Hutu People's Liberation Party, formed in 1980 as a tiny Hutu opposition group of exiles in Rwanda and Tanzania.

Getting In

Diplomatic ties were severed with Rwanda in July 1993. Diplomats were expelled and the embassy closed. Passport and visa are required. Multiple-entry visa for a stay of up to three months requires a US$30 fee (cash, check or money order), two application forms, two photos and immunization for yellow fever. Exact date of entry into Rwanda is required with application. Include prepaid envelope or $1.50 postage for return of passport by certified mail.

Although President Clinton has declared that the Rwandans are not welcome on our soil, the embassy staff does not know exactly when they will be leaving. Embassy staff recommends applying at Brussels, Belgium, for visa information:

Embassade du Rwanda

> *1 Avenue de Fleurs*
> *(coin Avenue de Terzuren)*
> *1150 Bruxelles, Belgium*
> ☎ *[32] (2) 763 07 21 or 763 07 02*
> *FAX [32] (2) 763-0753*

At the height of the hostilities, when *DP* asked about entry permission, a spokesperson replied, "We know nothing." Later, after things had calmed down, it seemed the embassy staff had developed a sense of bureaucratic humor. When we asked if there were any Americans currently in jail in Rwanda, we were told, "We have none; they have been behaving so far." You should know the first of the 12 conditions for entry and stay in Rwanda is that "proper attire and conduct are required of persons staying in Rwanda." The embassy maintains that it is safe to travel in Rwanda.

Embassy Locations

U.S. Embassy in Rwanda
> *Boulevard de la Revolution*
> *BP 28, Kigali*
> ☎ *[250] (7) 5601/2/3*
> *FAX [250] (7) 2128*

Embassy of the Republic of Rwanda
> *1714 New Hampshire Avenue, N.W.*
> *Washington, D.C. 20009*
> ☎ *(202) 232-2882*

Canadian Embassy in Rwanda
> *Rue Akagera, BP 1177*
> *Kigali*
> ☎ *73210*
> *FAX 72719*

Rwandan Embassy in Canada
> *121 Sherwood Drive*
> *Ottawa, Ontario, Canada K1Y 3V1*
> ☎ *(613) 722-5835/722-7921*
> *FAX (613) 729-3291*

Permanent Mission of Rwanda to the U.N.
> *336 East 45th Street*
> *New York, NY 10017*
> ☎ *(212) 808-9330*

Consulate General in Chicago
> ☎ *(708) 205-1188*

Consulate General in Denver
> ☎ *(303) 321-2400*

Getting Around

Rwanda has a total road length of 3036 miles; 286 of them are paved. There are neither railways nor ports. There are eight airfields in the country, three of them with a permanent surface.

Air Rwanda flies internally from Kigali to Gisenyi and Kamembe. Occasionally, you can fly between Gisenyi and Kamembe. Due to the amount of foreign aid into the country, Rwanda's road system isn't too bad. As in neighboring Burundi, the roadways are served by a fleet of relatively late-model Japanese minibuses. The buses leave most towns when they are full. Larger government buses also traverse Rwanda's roads, although they are fewer and farther between. They cost less than the minibuses, but take longer to get to their destinations.

RWANDA

Dangerous Places

The Entire Country

The entire country of Rwanda can be considered unsafe. Travelers are regularly the victims of theft, petty crime and murder. Sporadic violence is a problem in Kigali as well as in the interior. Fighting caused thousands of refugees to flee into neighboring Burundi as well as other countries in the region. In 1996, Paul Kagame ensured the safety of returning refugees and a trickle began returning to Rwanda, many to find their land and dwellings seized by squatters. Travelers should use extreme caution everywhere in Rwanda. Do not travel into the troubled areas of Kigali or anywhere in or near Gisenyi. Do not travel after dark.

Dangerous Things

Volcanoes

Near Goma, Zaire, two active volcanoes threaten more than 800,000 refugees. The two volcanoes, Nyamuragira and Nyiragongo, have been leaking lava toward a massive camp at Mugunga, home to 200,000 refugees.

The Lakes

There are very large man-eating crocodiles and an abundance of germs to be found in all lakes and large rivers in Rwanda.

Getting Sick

Medical facilities, doctors and supplies are dangerously scarce in Rwanda. There is one doctor for every 33,170 people under normal conditions and 15 hospital beds for every 10,000 people in the country. There are 34 hospitals and 188 health centers in this tiny country, so the traveler has some access to treatment. Cholera and yellow fever inoculations are required. Tetanus, polio, typhoid and gamma globulin vaccines are advised, as are antimalarial prophylaxes: DPT, measles and mumps vaccines are recommended for children. Tap water is not potable.

Nuts and Bolts

About the size of Vermont and located in east central Africa, Rwanda (the capital is Kigali) is a landlocked country just south of the Equator bordering Uganda to the north, Burundi to the south, Tanzania to the east, and Zaire to the west. There were estimated to be over 8 million people in Rwanda before the holocaust. They live packed in 789 per square mile: 90 percent are Hutu, 9 percent Tutsi. Today, almost half of the Tutsi have been murdered.

Rwanda (Republika y'u Rwanda—Republique Rwandaise—Republic of Rwanda) was originally a feudal monarchy ruled by the Tutsi tribes. From 1899–1916, the country was a German protectorate, before it came under the administration of Belgium in 1920 as part of Ruanda-Urundi. Rwanda became an independent state on July 1, 1962. Strife between the majority Hutu tribe and the Tutsi resulted in a bloodless coup on July 5, 1973, led by the head of the National Guard and Minister of Defense, Major General Juvenal Habyarimana. A civilian-military government was established. All legislative processes were banned until 1975, when the Mouvement Revolutionnaire National pour le Developement (MRND—National Revolutionary Movement for Development) was formed and later recognized in the December 17, 1978, Constitution as the sole legal party. Recognizing the need for reform, on June 2, 1991, Habyarimana announced the legalization of multiparty politics, and on June 10, 1991, a revised Constitution was adopted.

In 1988, 36,000 tourists made the trek to Rwanda. Many went to visit its population of rare mountain gorillas and the bizarre topography and plant life of its forests found in Parc National des Volcans. Visitors to Rwanda are attracted to the country's beautiful mountain scenery, national parks, and recreation offerings at Lake Kivu. Tourism provides Rwanda with its second-largest source of foreign funds. Found in Parc National des Volcans, as of July 1994, the gorillas have been unharmed due to their remoteness and that the Rwandan park guards have remained on duty. The World Wildlife Fund reports that foreign researchers and scientists were evacuated in April. At last count, there were only 650 mountain gorillas left on the planet, of which 320 live in the 125-sq.-kilometer Parc National des Volcans in Rwanda's northern mountains.

The 1991 Constitution introduced a multiparty system and a separation of powers between the executive, legislative and judiciary. It also mandates that although political party formations may be established along tribal or ethnic lines, they must remain open to all. The Constitution also guarantees freedom of the press and awards civil servants the right to strike.

The currency is the Rwanda franc (RFr). There are 100 centimes to the RFr. Local time is two hours later than GMT, seven hours later than U.S. EST. Hutu comprise 90 percent of the population; the Tutsi account for 9 percent. Sixty-five percent of the population is Roman Catholic. Protestants make up 9 percent, Muslim 1 percent and indigenous beliefs 25 percent.

Kinyarwanda and French are the official languages, and Kiswahili is used commercially. Illiteracy stands at 50 percent (1990). In 1989, there were 1671 primary schools with 1,058,529 students, 65,323 students enrolled at secondary schools, and 3389 students enrolled at institutions of higher education.

Rwanda has a tropical climate that varies slightly with altitude. The major rainy seasons are February through May and November through December, with an average annual rainfall of 31 inches.

Total armed forces number 5200. Rwanda also maintains a 200-member parachute company. Military service is voluntary in Rwanda.

Dangerous Days

08/12/1994	Thousands of Rwandan refugees began moving toward Zaire from southwest Rwanda.
08/03/1994	Rwandan President Pasteur Bizimungu warned that his government was prepared to go to war if France refused to grant access to its self-declared safety zone in the southwest of the country.
07/19/1994	Pasteur Bizimungu was sworn in as president at a ceremony at the parliament building in the capital of Kigali. Rebel commander Major General Paul Kagame was named vice president and defense minister.
07/18/1994	The rebel Rwandan Patriotic Front (RPF) claimed it had won Rwanda's civil war.
07/15/1994	A tidal wave of Rwandan refugees poured into neighboring Zaire.
07/04/1994	Rwandan rebels captured the capital of Kigali and the last major government-held southern town of Butare.
04/06/1994	President Juvenal Habyarimana was killed in a plane crash, sparking nationwide fighting.
01/28	Democracy Day.
07/01	Anniversary of Independence.
07/05	National Peace and Unity Day.
10/26	Armed Forces Day.

In a Dangerous Place

Rwanda, 1994: The Slaughter

The apocalypse in Rwanda is too dark and compelling to ignore. In the 20th century an entire nation is being murdered, while the world sits by and refuses to believe it. If any story needs to be captured, it is this one. We fly to Nairobi. On our arrival, we discover that the jeep we have reserved is not available. It is the height of safari season, and they have rented out four-wheel-drive vehicles for the $250 to $500 a day they can get.

For $20 a head, we take a five-hour minibus ride to Arusha just south of Nairobi. Seeing our massive professional camera, the locals just assume we are tourists. For $5, we can take still photos and, for $20, all the video we want. We pass. We find a 4x4 and driver that will take us on the 13-hour trip to Nyanza, a major staging area for the relief effort in Rwanda. The price is $100, but we have to squeeze in all the locals who want to go along as well. We go through some of the more dramatic scenery of East Africa, but the rough road and long trip make it an ordeal.

We treat ourselves to a three-star hotel when we arrive in Nyanza. There is a U.N. crew, and, wherever there are U.N. people, there are usually pilots around. Naturally, we go straight to the hotel bar to find them. Strangely, not a pilot to be found. The next day we find the pilots eating breakfast. I go to the oldest and ask him if he will fly us to the Ngara Refugee camp. The answer is a definite no. We work on them until finally they agree to take us on. When we let people know that our footage and coverage will support the relief effort, they have a greater desire to help us. As we climb into the Spanish-built *CASA*, we make ourselves comfortable among the crates of medicine and food destined for the refugees.

The 90-minute flight is uneventful, except for the trip over Lake Victoria. From our altitude, I can see tiny islands floating in the turquoise water—they are clumps of bloated bodies. We land on the dusty runway surrounded by a tent city that seems to stretch for miles. A fleet of Land Rovers arrives to collect the supplies and take us to the U.N. headquarters for the camp. There is a veritable United Nations of relief organizations here—the U.N., the Red Cross, MSF, CARE and the Red Crescent. All of them tell us that they have no room for us. The Tanzanian branch of the Red Cross gives us some simple mats to sleep on and a hot meal.

There are endless lines of Hutus and Tutsi waiting for their daily handout of milk, flour and rice. We shoot some photos and interview the people. There are clusters of children, newly orphaned and wandering around with blank expressions on their faces. There is not much to capture here, other than a sea of gaunt faces. We find a Tutsi chauffeur who, for $100, will take us as far as the headquarters of the "Rwandese Patriotic Front" about 10–15 km inside the border. We don't bother with a visa, since we doubt there is much of a government left. It takes us an hour to get as far as the Tanzanian border post on the eastern shore of the Kagera River. It should only take 15 minutes, but we are like salmon swimming upstream as we try to make our way through the river of refugees streaming out of Rwanda. The people are carrying the last of their possessions; even the children carry bundles. Old men carry firewood, now a valuable commodity. At this rate, it will take us all day just to get to the headquarters in Rwanda where there are no basic commodities and terror reigns at night.

We decide to try to cross the border the next morning. Our hunch is right. All the refugees are sleeping by the side of the road and the going is easy. We are waved across the Tanzanian border with little fuss. Our exit visas are simply gifts of pens and Camel Trophy stickers, strangely powerful international currency. As we cross the bridge high above the Kagera River, we can see bodies floating downstream. It is strange how their dark skin turns white. One cadaver is caught between two rocks and bobs up and down in the fast moving water.

At the other side, there is no one manning the border posts. Our relief is short-lived. About 50 meters past the bridge, we are stopped by armed members of the RPF. They ask for ID, question our purpose here, and treat us like celebrities when they see our press cards.

Our Tutsi driver does not fare as well. The guards treat him as a deserter and question his ownership of the vehicle. They take him away to a nearby building, despite our desperate protests. We never see him again. Distraught, we come across two old friends—fellow journalists Luc Delahey and James Natchway. We hug each other and exchange information. They have come from Kigali to report on the recently discovered massacre in the village of Nyarubuye 115 kms away. They never got there, having all the tires on their vehicles blown when they ran over sabotage spikes laid across the road. They had spent two days trying to find a way out. They had flown in from Uganda, and then were stuck in Kigali by the fierce fighting. They had seen our vehicle and are disappointed that it is no longer here.

We hang around the bridge pondering our situation. When a truck crosses the border, we flag it down and cut a deal on the spot. For $400, we now have wheels. A guard from the RPF rides shotgun in the front with Jim Natchway. Our first dramatic sight is thousands and thousands of rusty, bloodstained machetes confiscated by the RPF from captured Hutus. I immediately think of the piles of glasses, shoes and clothing photographed in the concentration camps in WW II. We drive through burned-out villages and by rows of bodies—most killed with machetes. Among the bodies are stunned survivors searching for relatives. I am struck by the look in these people's eyes. I have seen many, many wars but never one that created so much fear and horror.

The 115 km of horror brings us to Nyarubuye, site of a dark tale we had heard from the refugees inside Tanzania. They told us of hundreds of men, women and children herded into a church and slaughtered like pigs. We smell the heavy stench of rotting flesh long before we come upon the scene. We try to inhale the scent of the eucalyptus trees, but all we can smell is the revolting odor of decay. There are pieces of humans strewn everywhere. Wild dogs had probably been feasting on the corpses. None of us have ever seen anything like this before. Even Luc, Jim and I, who have seen so much, cannot comprehend the horror that we behold. The monastery is surrounded by a brick wall. Inside the wall is a flower-filled garden. Among the flowers are the rotting bodies of hundreds of women and children. The building is a low brick structure built during the Belgian colonial period. There is a simple church adjoining the monastery.

We had all emptied our stomachs when the stench first hit us—a natural and healthy reaction to human decay—but I continue to wretch as nausea comes over me in waves. The people had fled to the church afraid for their lives. They had been taught that the church was the place of last refuge. They were wrong. Men armed with machetes ordered them into the garden and began to slash and cut them. Some tried to escape. One man's upper torso is halfway up the metal ladder on the church steeple. His lower torso and legs hang half a meter below.

Inside the church, a man lies hacked to death at the altar. Piles of bodies lie among the pews. I stare at the dead bodies in the bushes, probably dragged there by the dogs, at the strange grimacing expressions of the contorted faces, as they putrefy.

We return the way we came, knowing that we have captured mankind at its most base. The perverse irony of this sin being committed in a church makes it even more tragic and surreal.

—**Coskun Aral**

In a Dangerous Place

Rwanda: Spilt Milk

I well remember our friend, Gupta, as we sat in this gray light, sipping piping-hot tea from chipped enamelware cups on the Tanzania side of the Kagera. Peering into the mists, he would wonder not just about the identity of the shifting shadows they shrouded, but at the nature of the shroud itself: fog, mist, smoke from a cooking fire, from a land-clearing fire, from a dry-season fire set by lightening, from fire set by poachers to flush game.

This is Karagwe country; it had been a long day, we'd had a decent meal, and, as we pass the plastic Listerine bottle full of *waraki* among us, we feel the spell of the old empires hereabouts. Karagwe, Ankole, Tutsi, have Gupta conjuring punch-drunkenly, straining to glimpse Lord knows what through the mists, as he tells us that an ancient Iron Age city has recently been excavated on the flanks of the Ngorongoro crater on the Serengeti Plain, a highly developed place whose people and whose collapse remains a mystery. He says they had buildings made of brick, which required firing in kilns, which in turn required charcoal. "That mist over there," he says, gesturing toward a cloud that looks like fog to me, "I'm reckoning it's a charcoal mound. What they're doing, you see, is they're digging a pit, lining the bottom with damp leaves and hot coals, filling it with timber, then covering it with dirt, and you're walking about and you're seeing this mound of earth with smoke rising from it, as if the earth itself were smouldering. Well, soon enough they're coming along and uncovering it all, and there you have your charcoal."

He tells us it was also done that way in an ancient empire on the Indian subcontinent called Mohenjo-Davo, and apropos of nothing charcoal, he tells us one of the primal legends of the Watutsi. "As Rwanda's first king lay dying, he summoned his sons, Gatwa, Gahutu and Gatusi. Here's a jug of milk for each of you, he told them. Guard it all night. But Gatwa drank all his, and Gahutu fell asleep, spilling half his jug as he rolled over. Only Gatusi sat up the night, presenting his father with the full jug, and thus Watutsi came to rule the land, Bahutu became serfs, and Batwa were driven from mankind to live in the forests."

—Jack Kramer

Freetown

Sierra Leone
★★★★

Guess Who's Coming to Dinner

The trail of coups and corpses continues in Sierra Leone. In January 1996, yet another military dictator, Captain Valentine Strasser, was ousted by...you guessed it...another military leader, whose new junta announced that Strasser's continued leadership "would have been a recipe for chaos." But what isn't in this tiny West African nation?

The former British colony of Sierra Leone gets its sustenance from diamonds. It also yanks enough bauxite, gold and iron ore out of the ground to keep it mildly solvent. But diamonds are the lifeblood of this sweaty little backwater.

Britain ceded independence to Sierra Leone in 1961, and the country formed a republic in 1971. In 1992 the people overwhelmingly voted to have democratic elections, which was a cue to the folks that were draining the diamond coffers that it was time for a coup. In April 1992, Captain Valentine Strasser seized control of the government and ruled whichever pieces of the pie he could govern.

The problem with the word "democratic" in Africa is that it is an antonym of the word "tribal." In Sierra Leone, where 52 percent of the population are animists, 39 percent are Muslim and 8 percent are Christian, it didn't make for a recipe for democracy. Soon a rebel group of Muslim blacks were formed by a former army photographer, Foday Sankoh. Libya trained the motley, human flesh–eating Revolutionary United Front (RUF) as best it could, and mayhem has served as Sierra Leone's constitution ever since.

The rebels were at the doorstep of the capital Freetown until Strasser rented a group of mercenaries under the command of well-known American merc Bob MacKenzie. MacKenzie had fought in Vietnam, with the SAS in Rhodesia, and in El Salvador, and he had trained Muslim fighters in Bosnia. The British government (unofficially, of course) asked him to head a group of Ghurkas from Nepal to safeguard the diamond mines in Sierra Leone and push back the rebels. When MacKenzie was killed two months later (and cannibalized by the rebels!), the Ghurkas flew home to Nepal. Pretoria, South Africa–based Executive Outcomes saw an opportunity and put together a small army of 200 South African mercenaries, complete with an air force and supply jets. They began training the Sierra Leone army and got to work liberating the diamond fields. The army was pumped up to about 14,000 men (and children).

Battles mainly consisted of brief encounters, with both sides discharging only a single clip before running like hell in the opposite direction. Both the army and the RUF rebels were whacked out of their brains on ganja and booze, which made for low casualties. Executive Outcomes had been determined to carve disciplined killers out of the government army ranks, and the face of the war was changing. The body count was rising (thanks in part to EO's very own Russian Hind Mi-24 helicopter gunship air force flown by Russian mercenary pilots), and the rebels were in retreat. Sierra Leone soldiers were no longer selling their weapons and uniforms to the RUF rogues, and the diamond fields were back in the hands of Strasser and De Beers. The diamond mines were the first targets for repossession, as Strasser hired the mercs on credit, with a promise of US$500,000 a month payment in diamonds. Hardly surprising, as Executive Outcomes is reportedly owned by a mining company with close ties to key British politicians.

The rebels took great pleasure in not only killing folks but taking Western hostages. Seven foreigners were grabbed in two days by RUF rebels and then released. Then the insurgents snatched seven nuns, who were at least spared from becoming Sunday night meatloaf. Because the drug-crazed rebels enjoy their victims as meals, most foreigners split Sierra Leone and the government mobilized all available troops to prevent the insurgents from getting any closer to Freetown. To date, more than 24,000 Sierra Leonians have fled into Guinea and 50,000 have been killed in the five years of fighting since 1991. Some hospitals report that up to 100 people a day die from starvation. The eastern areas of Sierra Leone are especially volatile. The country's population of 4 million is suffering from food shortages and a general disintegration of society.

It seems that when the youthful Captain Valentine Strasser—who doesn't look old enough to have gotten a merit badge in the Cub Scouts—seized power from General Joseph Momoh in 1992 he didn't quite have the undying loyalty of the people or the military. Only four of the seven army battalions were loyal to Strasser, and the battalions that were fighting the rebels were mostly kids press-ganged

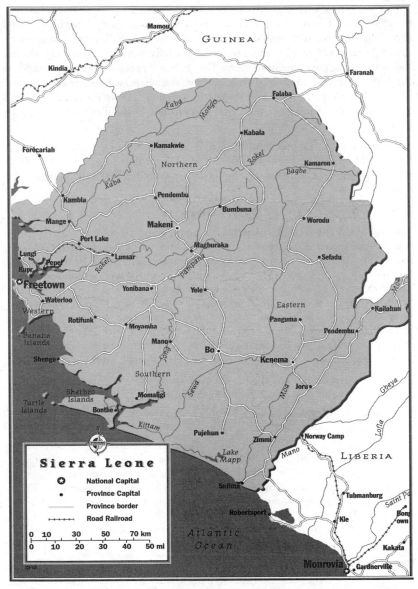

into slowing down the rebel's advances. Consequently, white mercenaries from Britain, America, South Africa and Russia were busy fighting alongside Nigerian and Guinean troops against the rebels. The RUF was led by Foday Sankoh, whose first demand was that all foreign soldiers be expelled from the country. Strasser, who was personally guarded by Guinean soldiers, didn't see a good reason for it. Apparently, neither did Sankoh himself when the cards were dealt. He and his irregulars were backed by Liberian guerrilla—and soon-to-be president—Charles Taylor, who invaded Sierra Leone in April of 1991 because West African peacekeeping forces were using the country as a base for fighter planes.

With Sierra Leone having turned into a veritable Summer Olympics for international soldiers of fortune, the West seems to be looking away. After being asked about the presence of British mercenaries in Sierra Leone's internal struggle, a British Foreign Office spokesman replied, "We have not been giving any military assistance to the government of Sierra Leone, but if people who are no longer in the British Army decide to sell their services elsewhere, we cannot stop them." The rebels are slowly pressing in on the major cities and are expected to fight a guerilla war of attrition if the mercs are successful in pushing them back into the jungle.

Anyone looking to supplement his unemployment check might also make a try for the US$75,000 in diamonds offered by RUF for downing one of the Mi-24 Hinds used against the insurgency by Executive Outcomes' Ukrainian mercenary pilots.

The Scoop

Sierra Leone is a tin-pot dictatorship that lives off the largess of outside mining companies. It is the world's second-largest producer of titanium oxide (an ingredient for paint pigment) and a major source of diamonds. Captain Valentine Strasser—known as "The Redeemer"—wasn't the first military dictator to run this former British colony. Strasser was disposed in January 1996 by Julius Maada Bio, who was himself replaced by Ahmad Tejan Kabbah two months later. The number of ex-presidents in this country reads like a UCLA alumni directory. Sierra Leone may become the world's first privately owned nation, as South Africa–based merc firm Executive Outcomes seems to be winning the war here. The mercs are rented by wealthy mine owners with the tacit backing of the British government. But expect "Execute Outcomes" to reign for a long time to come. More than 50,000 people have been slaughtered in the war since 1992, and a full quarter of the population has been displaced.

The Players

Spooks, Spectres and Other Adventurers

People always ask me, "Who travels to these lousy places?" Well, Sierra Leone was one example of what *DP* calls the "side show." When the stuff hits the fan as it did when the Italian nuns were killed, the main hotels in Freetown were full of all sorts of interesting types. Here is a partial list of who could be found at the bars in Freetown over the last year: white mercenaries from the United States and South Africa, former soldiers from Unita, Ghurka trainers, bankers from the World Bank, bureaucrats from the International Monetary Fund, do-gooders from aid organizations, U.N. advance men, Italian intelligence agents, reporters from British newspapers and, of course, the usual assortment of hookers, touts and hangers-on.

The Mercenaries (Executive Outcomes, GSG, et al)

The Sierra Leone government has been using mercenaries to fight against the Libyan-trained and Liberian-backed RUF rebels since 1991. The government army was an anemic 1000 men back in '91 but is now estimated at 10,000–14,000 men, consisting mainly of press-ganged youths with about a week of training. Colonel Bob McKenzie, a well-known mercenary and former U.S. Special Forces officer, was killed and eaten by rebels in Sierra Leone in 1995. The government of Sierra Leone maintains that all the foreigners in the country are being utilized as "advisors," but it ain't so. The white mercenary stereotype is fading; the 150–200 Executive Outcomes (EO)-hired mercenaries are predominantly black (about an 8–1 ratio of black to white) and are recruited from the ranks of former warriors with extensive bush warfare experience in South Africa, Namibia and Angola.

Drug and alcohol abuse are considered to be a major obstacle to training Sierra Leone government soldiers. EO is no fly-by-night merc group. For US$500,000 a month, they supply 150 men (who earn about US$2000 a month), a 20-chopper-strong air force (all Russian Mi-24s and Mi-17s), nationwide radio communications, a full-time doctor and two evacuation aircraft on 24-hour standby (one based in Freetown and another in Luanda). They can supply as many experienced men as needed. EO also charters two Boeing 727s to run supplies in and out of the country to South Africa. The EO training camp in Sierra Leone is at Waterloo, about 32 km east of the capital of Freetown. Troops go through a three-week boot camp.

In Sierra Leone, EO is fighting for diamonds in payment, but has diversified from simple soldiering in recent months. EO mines for gold in Uganda and drills boreholes in Ethiopia. In all, EO is part of a family of 32 companies, ranging from adult education to computer software, in countries such as Angola, South Africa, Zambia, Botswana and Lesotho. In September of '96, President Kabbah managed to get a discount on the $18.5 million they owed to EO for their security work. *DP* wonders if EO could foreclose?

Executive Outcomes

Recruitment Officer
PVT. BAG X-105
Hennopsmeer 0046
South Africa
☎ *011-27-12-666-8429/7005*

Gurkha Security Guards (GSG)

In February of '95, sixty former Ghurkas from Nepal were flown to Sierra Leone to train the Sierra Leonan army. Nick Bell, one of the directors of Gurkha Security Guards (GSG), thought that this would motivate the underpaid and anemic army, but the British government pulled the plug when they realized that even bad students of history can connect the Ghurkas with the British Government. Fearing that British troops would have to be flown in to rescue any wiry little Ghurkas, they decided to let South Africa take the heat.

Captain Valentine Strasser

Known lionheartedly as "The Redeemer," Strasser—then only 28, with the face of Bart Simpson—seized the helm of the government in April 1992, when President Momoh misinterpreted a group of disgruntled soldiers angry over late paychecks as a coup attempt and fled to Britain. Strasser, who was deposed in a January 1996 coup, promised free elections and a return to civilian rule, without delivering. Yeah, he made some gains against the RUF insurgents, but not without having to cede half of Sierra Leone's diamond reserves to Executive Outcomes. His efforts to place a tax on imports by overseas charities working in the country is seen as progressive only by the generals with broken VCRs. Strasser, who pledged to weed out corruption in the government, has been involved in diamond trafficking. He personally took 435 carats of diamonds worth US$43 million to Belgium and sold them, buying a house in London with the profits. Must've been a helluva house. Strasser was overthrown in a "peaceful coup" by his second-in-command, General Julius Maada Bio.

"The Polite Man" General Julius Maada Bio

Julius Maada Bio overthrew Strasser in a palace coup January 16, 1996. Hailed as the "Polite Man" by the Freetown Press, Maada Bio pledged to follow through with the February 26 elections and a return to civilian rule in Sierra Leone. Strasser contended from his exile at the Sierra Leone embassy in Conakry, Guinea, that Maada Bio's pledge was anything but what the new leader had in mind for Sierra Leone. Bio stepped down with the election of Tejan Kabbah.

Ahmad Tejan Kabbah

Sierra Leone's newly elected president has, like his predecessors, promised to make peace with the RUF rebels. And he may be close to achieving it. On April 23, 1996, Tejan Kabbah and rebel leader Foday Sankoh met in the Ivory Coast and announced a truce in order to detail peace and disarmament accords.

The Rebels: Revolutionary United Front (RUF)

The 3000-man Revolutionary United Front is predominately Muslim and consists mainly of ragtag adolescents and villagers forced into fighting. The group has an office near the Liberian border and a press office in Abidjan (run by RUF leader Alfred Foday Sankoh's brother Alimany Sankoh) on the Ivory Coast. RUF offers US$2000 reward to anyone who can capture a mercenary alive.

RUF rebels commit atrocities on a regular basis. The eating of victims is not uncommon. The most favored entrées are the liver and heart. Another nasty trick the guerrillas employ on the captured is the slashing of ankle tendons and neck muscles.

The guerillas forced into service are under the constant threat of torture and execution, as are their family members. Besides the rebels getting support from Charles Taylor, there is also backing from the Ivory Coast and Guinea. Libya is a major supplier of arms and money to RUF.

Alfred Foday Sankoh is a former army corporal and photographer. A member of the Jemme tribe, he joined the Royal West African forces in 1956 and was trained as a wireless operator by the British. In 1961 Sankoh was sentenced to 15 years in jail for taking part in an attempted coup against Joseph Momoh. Pardoned in 1980, he traveled to the U.S. to meet with black Muslim groups. Returning to Sierra Leone, he put together a cadre of like-minded revolutionaries and knocked on Qaddafi's door for some bullets and bucks. While there, he was introduced to Charles Taylor, the chief antagonist in Liberia's misery. Taylor used the border areas of Sierra Leone for his bases, and Sankoh received guns and support from Taylor during the late '80s and early '90s. In April of '92, a group of peach-fuzz army officers calling themselves the National Provisional Ruling Council (NPRC) overthrew the government of Momah, and 28-year-old Valentine Strasser took over, only to be bounced by another soldier who then set up democratic elections. All of this transpired without Sankoh even being invited to the inauguration or getting to threaten the boss. Strasser did bring in Executive Outcomes, who pushed Sankoh's 300-strong Revolutionary United Front even further into the bush and obscurity.

Foday Sankoh and his tweaked warriors are sucking wind now that Executive Outcomes has tossed them out of the major towns and reopened the bauxite, rutile and diamond mines. The Libyan-backed RUF invaded Sierra Leone from neighboring Liberia in 1991 and don't have much future. For now, they are sulking in Abidjan, Ivory Coast, after leaving his jungle hideout.

Meanwhile, the war has killed 20,000 people, displaced a third of Sierra Leone's 4.5 million people and destroyed the economy.

The Army

Apparently, the soldiers in the 12,000 man Sierra Leonean army would rather make love than war on their two bags of rice a month and 15 leo.

Getting In

Visas can be had for a stay of 30–90 days and can be obtained at Sierra Leone embassies and consulates. The country maintains embassies in the U.S., Great Britain, Germany, Belgium, Sweden, the Netherlands, Egypt, Austria, Switzerland, Spain and Italy—to mention the major sources of visas. In countries where Sierra Leone does not maintain an embassy, it may be possible to obtain a visa through the British High Commission. The Sierra Leone embassy in the U.S.:

Sierra Leone Embassy
1701 19th Street N.W.
Washington, D.C. 20009
☎ *202-939-9261*

If you are a U.S. citizen applying for a visa through the Washington embassy, you will most likely be required to provide a letter from both your employer, stating that you've indeed got a job to which you must return, and your bank, stating that you've got enough funds to motivate you to return. Officials at the embassy may require you to first send a self-addressed stamped envelope for a list of visa requirements. A 90-day single-entry visa costs US$20. You'll need two passport-sized photos and quite possibly proof of your round-trip airline ticket. Allow two weeks for processing.

Although entry permits for Sierra Leone can be obtained in West African states, visas and entry permits cannot be had at the border.

Getting Around

The single 52-mile (84-km) railroad line was abandoned in 1971. Most roads are hellish; the airlines bring in ammunition and supplies for mercenaries and whisk the wealthy away for shopping sprees in Paris. Freetown, once besieged, is relatively sedate now—and the countryside is slowly being upgraded from absolutely deadly to very dangerous. It will be a long time yet before travelers can wander through the rain forests in Sierra Leone looking for rare orchids. Currently, the safest way of getting around is by hitching a ride aboard one of Executive Outcomes' Mi-17s or Mi-24 helicopter gunships.

Dangerous Places

The Entire Country
Most of the country is still pretty touchy, with rebel activity taking place primarily in the eastern areas.

The Liberian Border
The border with Liberia is the main staging area for the Charles Taylor–supported rebels.

Diamond Mines
Diamond mines are considered off-limits to all outsiders, and, if bumbling travelers happen to stumble upon them, they will be extremely lucky if they are merely detained and lectured on their stupidity. If you come across diamond smugglers, you'll likely end up in a shallow, hastily dug grave.

Dangerous Things

Being a Journalist
Journalists are routinely rounded up, arrested and beaten by government thugs. The French-based reporters' rights group, Reporters Sans Frontieres, occasionally sends in lawyers from Brussels to Freetown to bail out and defend busted reporters. They, too, are usually beaten up and busted.

Being a Mercenary
RUF has put a bounty of US$2000 on every mercenary captured alive.

Getting Sick

Malaria in the severe falciparum (malignant) form occurs throughout the entire country and is chloroquine-resistant. Tungiasis is widespread. Many viral diseases, some causing severe hemorrhagic fevers, are transmitted by ticks, fleas, mosquitoes, sandflies, etc. Relapsing fever and tick-, louse- and flea-borne typhus occur. Sleeping sickness (human trypanosomiasis) is regularly reported. Foodborne and waterborne diseases are highly endemic. Bilharziasis is present and widespread throughout the country, as are alimentary helminthic infections, the dysenteries and diarrheal diseases, including cholera, giardiasis, typhoid fever, and hepatitis A and E. Hepatitis B is hyperendemic; poliomyelitis is endemic, and trachoma widespread. Frequently fatal are navirus hemorrhagic fevers which have attained notoriety. Rats pose a special hazard; lassa fever has a virus reservoir in the commonly found multimammate rat. Use all precautions to avoid rat-contaminated food and food containers. Ebola and Marburg hemorrhagic fevers are present but reported infrequently. Epidemics of meningococcal meningitis can occur. Echinococcosis (hydatrid disease) is widespread in animal breeding areas. One atlas of the world lists even childbirth as a communicable disease in Sierra Leone. So be careful—there is only one doctor for every 13,153 people in the country. Witch doctors provide the only "health care" available outside the capital.

Nuts and Bolts

Sierra Leone was founded in the late 18th century by the British as a settlement for Africans freed from slavery. The country's nasty brother to the south, Liberia, was established by the Americans for the same purpose. In retrospect, even the snowiest of doves has conceded this was a bad idea. So, for now, the British content themselves with relieving the country of its natural resources (mainly diamonds and bauxite) and meddling into the questionable affairs of a questionable government.

Sierra Leone can proudly boast the lowest life expectancy of any country in the world (41.5 years). It also has the second-highest infant mortality rate on the globe, and leads the human race in overall destitution and despair in other key categories as well. Zany and paranoid, the government executed 26 people in December 1992 for plotting to topple the regime—while most were in jail at the time!

Sierra Leonians bathe in rain water, and they have plenty of opportunities for showers. It rains about 195 inches a year in Freetown and on the coast, making the country the steamiest and wettest in coastal West Africa. During the *harmattan* season from November to April, it can be hot and dry. Most of Sierra Leone is fetid lowlands with scenic mountains in the northeast.

The currency is the *Leone*, which is worth nothing, perhaps due to the country's 81 percent inflation rate. Unemployment is endemic and Sierra Leonians make an average of US$145 a year, making it the sixth most impoverished nation on Earth. The official language is English.

Embassy Location

The U.S. Embassy is located in the capital of Freetown

Corner Walpole and Siaka Stevens Street
Freetown
☎ *26481*

Dangerous Days

01/16/1996	Captain Valentine Strasser deposed in a military coup.
9/1992	Liberian-backed RUF rebels began offensive against the NPRC.
6/20/1992	Government announced the arrest of three British mercenaries accused of plotting to overthrow the government.
5/29/1992	President Joseph Momoh deposed by Captain Valentine Strasser.
1991	ULIMO rebels from Liberia set up camp in Sierra Leone.

In a Dangerous Place

Sierra Leone 1996: RUFing It with the Guerillas

The taxi driver wanted $40 for the journey. From Gueckedou, the largest and closest Guinean town to Sierra Leone, to the border was a tricky road, he explained. There are military checkpoints all along the road, not to mention that the road is likely to ruin his precious car with its vast and numerous potholes. I cave in, reflecting as we cruise past the numerous refugee camps en route, that it's a small price to pay if it gets me to my destination without any hassles. Doma refugee camp is right on the border with Sierra Leone and that's where I'm heading to join guerrillas of the Revolutionary United Front (RUF) in one of the nastiest low intensity wars around.

The checkpoints are a breeze, until the dreaded question comes. "Do you have a permit to be in the area," a soldier asks. I try to dodge the issue of permits by telling the driver to say that we're just going to a village up the road and will be back in a couple of hours. That and about $5 seems to satisfy the soldier and we move off, eventually reaching the sprawling mass of mud huts and thatched roofs that Doma refugee camp consists of. Now is the moment of truth. According to my briefing by RUF officials, barely 48 hours earlier in the Ivory Coast, I will be approached in the camp by the RUF contact man who will arrange my passage across the border.

For some time, the only people who surround me are a group of curious, raggedly clad children, who find seeing a white man something of an exotic spectacle. They are soon joined by adults of the camp. Just as my faith in the RUF organizational ability begins to fade completely, I am approached by a young man named Christopher. "Welcome to my Moa," he says, which are the words I have been waiting to hear from my contact since my arrival. In his hut we discuss how I will cross the border. He speaks in barely comprehensible pidgin English and I struggle to understand his words. He explains that we will leave the camp in the early morning but before we can cross the border I will have to give some money to the Guinean border guards. They supposedly have the key to a small boat that will take me across the river to Sierra Leone.

Even reaching the border poses problems. Some of the villages are inhabited by Guineans, Christopher explains, and if they see us, the alarm will be raised, dashing any hopes of crossing the border. The next hour is chaotic as we run through villages only to find that even at this late hour there are people colliding with each other in the darkness in their attempts to backtrack and hide before the oncoming invasion. It's like a scene out of "The Keystone Cops" and would be comical except that I am overdosing on adrenaline.

Finally we reach the compound housing the border guards, and by torch light I count out the equivalent of $100 for the captain, who after a cursory examination of my bag, allows us to proceed to the riverbank. It is dark and moonless as my boat sets out from the Guinean side of the border. At the rear of the dug-out tree that serves as our canoe, a Guinean soldier paddles us across the river Moa, which separates Guinea from Sierra Leone. This part of Sierra Leone is currently under control of guerrillas of the RUF, who have waged a five-year war against successive governments, and they are the guerrillas I am clandestinely crossing the border to meet.

There is something surreal about the presence of the Guinean soldier. Just across the border his compatriots are doing their incompetent best to help the Sierra Leone government defeat the rebels, but he appears indifferent to the contradiction of ferrying a journalist into rebel territory. He gratefully takes the $5 I offer him in local currency. From the far riverbank, a torch suddenly flashes three times and I reply with two short dashes from my own torch.

Three teenage guerrillas are waiting for me on the riverbank. They are dressed in what I will come to recognize as the standard guerrilla uniform of jeans, T-shirts and plastic flip-flops on their feet. Additionally, of course, there are three AK-47s slung casually over the shoulders. It is an hour walk through the jungle before we arrive at the first village. The cacophony of noise the jungle emits is alternately hypnotic and disconcerting. Bar the handful of guerrillas billeted there, the village is deserted. In one of the houses a group of guerrillas listens to raucous reggae music. A bowl of cold, unappetizing rice is provided for me to eat. Wagging his head from side to side to the beat of the music, a guerrilla shouts, "Power to the people!" A little inappropriate, perhaps, as all the locals seem to have taken a rather permanent vacation.

At dawn, I stroll around the village with the commander, Lt. Stanley. The guerrillas, like almost all their ilk, are eager for me to take their photographs, as they hope for a fleeting moment of fame on the inside cover of a magazine. The village is smeared with graffiti: crude drawings of AK47s grace the walls as well as the usual misspelled slogans, such as "RUF is fighting for [sic] di people." Another building has "Agriculture Committes Office–Dia" written on the wall, but the office is an empty wreck and has probably never been anything other than a few words on the wall.

The following day I receive word that the RUF leader, Foday Sankoh, wants to see me at his headquarters. It will take several days to walk through the bush to reach the leader's camp, says Lt. Marba, into whose care I am entrusted. The daily 30 kilometer trek is exhausting, the breaks infrequent and the fear of government troops constant. During a break, as we sit eating oranges in one of the innumerable burned-out villages, a guerrilla, under the *nom de guerre* of "rebel 245," rolls up a cigarette with a page from the Bible. I ask if he can read the paper he is using. "Small, small," he says with a contrite grin. "When I smoke through the Bible I become very strong...all the words go up to my head and I become invincible," he boasts. "The Bible is very good."

Others apparently prefer more traditional methods of increasing their strength, or making sure their insurance premium stays at a reasonable level. Noticing that another guerrilla has a series of rectangular cuts on his upper arm, I inquire about their significance. "Bulletproof" comes the slightly embarrassed reply, as if he is fearful (quite rightly) that I won't believe a word of it. "They (the cuts) protect me from bullets," he says, jabbing at his chest with his fingers, then flinging his arms away in imitation of the imaginary bullets bouncing off his body. My suggestion that a proper bulletproof jacket would probably be more effective is met with horrified denials. "No, no, it's African culture...very powerful," he says emphatically. I suspect he means African magic or voodoo but he can't find the right words. Despite such protestations of faith, however, he churlishly refuses to let me put the power of his protection to the test.

As I join the march again, the Lieutenant hands me lunch, which proves to be lumpy, cold lamb. Gesturing to the jungle path, which has already consumed most of the column, and between mouthfuls of lamb, he asks if I know about antipersonnel mines. With a sinking heart, I admit some knowledge. "Well, then," he says, "the whole of this area is mined and you must make sure you follow exactly in the footsteps of the man in front of you." Amazingly, after two days of jungle trekking, we reach the first of the base camps without incident. The camp is constructed almost entirely from roofing zinc, and now I begin to realize why so many of the deserted villages that we have passed through have no roofs.

The camp mascot is a Strasser, a dog irreverently named for the former military ruler of Sierra Leone, Captain Valentine Strasser, who had recently been deposed by his second in command, Brigadier Julius Maada Bio. Like almost every rebel camp I visit, it resounds to the sound of reggae music as guerrillas relax, confident that the previous day's declaration of a cease-fire will spare them shelling. The strains of Bob Marley and "Buffalo Soldier" emanate from ghetto blasters attached to looted car batteries that have been recharged courtesy of equally looted British Petroleum solar panels.

A guerrilla turns up the music and begins to dance. He is no older than nine or ten, but he handles the Kalasnikov hanging from his shoulder with the confidence of a veteran. In his hand he is holding a book, "Elementary English for Beginners." It is the kind of surreal contradiction that has become all too familiar in Africa—children whose only real schooling in life are lessons in dispensing death. He is joined on the earthy "dance floor" by a woman who loosely holds a Russian-made Tokarov pistol in her hand as she sways, rather fittingly, to the rhythm of "I Shot the Sheriff."

Some days later I set off again to the headquarters in the southeast of the country. By now Foday Sankoh has left the bush for negotiations with the government of newly elected President Ahmd Tejan Kabbah. As we enter one of the many camps en route to the headquarters, I notice a human skull impaled on a stick rising above a cluster of undergrowth. "Enemy's head," says Corporal Chinese Pepper by way of explanation, with a grin. Corpses and skeletons become a gruesome but common sight amongst the shattered remnants of the rural villages. The body of a semidecomposed man, huddled on a pathway, still clad in what looks like a sports jacket, is ignored as we pass by. It is only as I move downwind and the stench of death catches up with me that I, like the guerrillas escorting me, move faster.

In the early evening we arrive at a village where we are met by a platoon that will take me on the final leg of the journey to the headquarters. The senior NCO is decked out in camouflage and white Adidas sneakers—he seems to be the equivalent of a richer cousin to his colleagues from the north. A party is dispatched to find food, a euphemism, I later learn, for raiding a village. If they are unsuccessful, we will eat the standard bush meal of raw boiled bananas and snails. In the meantime, the two platoons relax and chatter in the ruins of the village. Dried tobacco leaves are torn up, and with a piece of paper from notebook, rolled into cigarettes that are passed around. A fire is quickly lit and wet clothes are hung around the flames to dry.

Some hours later, flushed with success, the food team returns carrying large quantities of rice and fried fish. Their leader, improbably named High Firing, confirms that they paid a social call to one of the local villages. They told the villagers that running away is bad form, gave them a lecture about the war and convinced them that the RUF is fighting on their behalf. In turn, the villagers donated food, cigarettes and money to them. It's amazing what an AK-47 does for good PR and mutual understanding.

In the morning we set off again. Trooping through open swamps, we can hear the sound of throbbing in the distance. It is almost certainly a helicopter, but the crucial question is what kind. A guerrilla column caught in the open by one of the newly acquired Mi-24 Hind gunships might, despite the ceasefire, prove too tempting a target for the gunners, and it was with an added urgency in his voice that the commander told us to head quickly for cover. Running toward the closest dense bush, I can hear the click-clacks of weapons cocking, and by the time we reach the bush, the sound of the helicopter is deafening. The density of the foliage around us means that we cannot see the helicopter flying over, and more importantly neither can it see us. Eventually the sound fades into the distance.

On arrival at the Zagoda headquarters I am greeted by the commander in Sankoh's absence, Lt. Col. Mohammed Tarrawally. He is resplendent in a pair of American military jungle boots, combat trousers and Nike-emblazoned sweatshirt.The green beret worn jauntily on his head, courtesy of the Sierra Leonean army, is as good an indicator of his status as anything else. Soft-spoken and small, he is the replica of a little Napoleon as he escorts me to my new quarters. In comparison to the other camps, my accommodation is five star—even including the rare luxury of Lipton's teabags, which like cigarettes, are regularly smuggled in from Guinea.

But even here, far from the front line, the war is never far away. The sound of a jet fighter through the roof of the forest canopy galvanizes guerrillas into frantic action. While they rush to turn over the solar panels that might give away the exact position of the camp, others forlornly seek cover as the jet screams overhead leaving sound waves in its wake, but thankfully, no bombs. "It's just their means of letting us know that they're still around," says Lieutenant Colonel Tarrawally, with a smile, as the camp returns to normal. "The war is not over yet."

—Roddy Scott

In A Dangerous Place

Sierra Leone: Diamonds Are a Guerrilla's Best Friend

It's amazing the number of wars I've covered in Africa where there just happen to be diamonds. Of course, the side that's dressed in rags and running around in the bush with guns invariably has an earnest Columbia graduate doing the Washington cocktail circuit telling any dimwit prepared to listen that his side is only fighting for democracy and the rights of the common man. What he doesn't mention is that there just happen to be oodles of diamonds where he comes from. Or that his side would really like to get their hands on those babies. And the gold deposits. And the...well, you get the picture.

Speaking of pictures, if there is ever one made about Sierra Leone it will be a surefire hit. Imagine the opening scene as a 4X4 filled with black and white soldiers and one journalist (that's me, played by Robert Redford for the *gravitas*) noses into the shabby African village. Cut to: close-ups of narrowed eyes following its progress along the potholed streets. Above the buzz of flies, whispers of "South Africans" ripple ahead. The jeep bumps into the market square and the gathered throng freezes, then approaches timidly, surrounding the car in silence. One woman suddenly shrieks, "South A-fri-ca!" the words becoming a mantra picked up by the others. Children dart in to touch their heroes, racing away in giggling triumph. A woman grabs my arm. "They saved us. They are saints!" These special forces veterans of the Namibian and Angolan wars, case-hardened tools of the old apartheid regime, cast shy looks at the dancers, then at me. "This happens every time we come here," mumbles the driver. He ducks his head in embarrassment as the wails gather strength. "They really like us."

Now as a serious war tourist you might be thinking, "So far, so good. Might be fun, but how the hell do I go about getting there?" Okay, imagine it's the middle of the night and your KLM or Sabena flight has just landed in Sierra Leone after a six hour flight from Amsterdam or Brussels. The good thing is, even if you're at the back of the line, you won't wait long to get through immigration. Not many people get off in Sierra Leone.

Immigration may be a breeze, but customs can be a little tricky. Before the officer tells you about his ailing mother and crippled children and asks for a small contribution, say that you're here to interview the Prez and what is the nice customs officer's name so you can mention it to the Big Fella. This will get you a quick and remarkably obsequious "Welcome to Sierra Leone, sir."

Be aware that Lungi airport is separated from Freetown by ten very dark miles of potholes punctuated by kerosene-lit check points, followed by a rust bucket ferry ride, then another 10 miles to your hotel. Outside the terminal, about two dozen shouting taxi drivers will dive for your luggage. Once someone grabs it, you're not getting it back until you're at the hotel and he's demanding 100 bucks, so keep a grip. Your few fellow travelers will be heading in the same direction, so suggest sharing a taxi. Sharing or solo, however, the bone-jarring ride will carry a tariff of at least $50, plus another tenner each for the rust bucket. The best thing about the ferry is the open upper deck and the opportunity to rehydrate yourself with cold beer. Take the opportunity. The flight from Europe may have spanned 1500 miles and six hours, but the 25 mile journey from Lungi to your hotel is likely to take three more.

If you're on an expense account, the only place to stay is the Cape Sierra. The rooms are air-conditioned and, critically important for a hack, there is a well-appointed bar. In the event you're moved to actually file a story, the telephones do work. If your editor is prepared to spring for a C-note a night you're laughing. If you're a freelancer and can't convince any of your various editors to cough up ("We'll be happy to take a look at what you've got when you get back."), then it's down the road to the charmingly named Mammy Yoko. Just across the road from a stunning beach, the rooms were cleanish when I was there, there wasn't too much fungus in the showers, and the air-conditioning worked— sometimes. Although I negotiated down to $50 a night, Mammy Yoko's recently undertook a major refurbishment and may now be less inclined to accommodate journos on a budget.

If you're hoping to be snapping bang-bang photos from your beachside balcony, by the way, you're out of luck; the war's in the interior and you're going to have to get over to army headquarters for an introduction to the South Africans of Executive Outcomes. Bribing your way in isn't desperately difficult, but it may take a while, in which case hire a taxi to wait for you. You should be able to negotiate a daily rate of about $30.

Bribes are definitely part of Sierra Leone's cultural fabric. The aforementioned customs officer, for example, could have been bought off for a couple of dollars. There may well be other instances where the demand will be substantially inflated. An acquaintance found himself under arrest for taking photos of Freetown's landmark baobab tree. For a mere 100,000 Leones ($1000), however, the police were prepared to overlook this open and shut case of espionage. After much haggling, they meekly accepted five dollars. Bribe money should be carried in bills of $1 and $5 denominations. (But never in one wad.)

So what's all the palaver about Sierra Leone, anyway? Unless you picked up this book because you thought it was about public toilets in Brooklyn, you'll already have guessed they have one of those dinky little wars going on. And guess what?

It's all about diamonds. Mountains of diamonds. Not to mention the biggest rutile (titanium ore) mine in the world, serious bauxite and gold deposits, and a good chance of platinum and oil. But it's the same old story: there are a few folks who have it all, and few folks who'd like to have it all. Naturally. The screwy thing is that since independence the haves have turned Sierra Leone into the world's sixth poorest country. Officially. And they were about to lose the whole shebang to the have-nots, until they dialled 911 for outside help.

At the South Africans' base overlooking the Koidu diamond fields a Mi-24 gunship settles noisily. I snap a few photos and fall in with the Belarussian crew, offering to send copies to their families in Minsk. Volodya and Valerii, grizzled veterans of Afghanistan, growl an unmistakable "Nyet!" Valerii slaps a mosquito. "Look, our wives think we're flying cargo. here. If they knew what we're really doing, they'd kill us." He stops alongside Colonel Rudolph van Heerden, the South African commander for the Kono District, and takes the offered beer. "But you can send them to Rudolph and he'll make sure we get them," he says as the former mortal enemies turn to discuss tomorrow's joint operation against the rebels.

The side without the goodies are the rebels of the Revolutionary United Front. Their idea of a good time is a bit of ritual cannibalism in between lopping parts off innocent bystanders. Their head dude is Alfred Foday Sankoh, a 62- year-old former corporal, who a couple of decades ago ended up in the slammer for trying to overthrow the government. Eventually granted amnesty, but still sore at everyone, he headed to Libya for some counseling. A pal at Qaddafi's college for aspiring revolutionaries was warlord Charles Taylor from Liberia, which happens to be right next door to Sierra Leone. Taylor went on to overthrow Liberian President Samuel Doe. Between capturing Doe and putting him out of his misery, Taylor sliced off poor Sam's ears, then sauteed and fed them back to him. One of those cultural things, I guess. I mean, who are we to judge? (Besides, Sam ate his predecessor's liver and inherited his vote at the U.N.) Anyway, when Al Sankoh's time came, Charlie gave him a start with a few guns and thugs to keep the standards up. Oh, and they're fighting for democracy and the rights of the common man. I almost forgot to mention that.

Until recently the side that did have the goodies was led by Captain Valentine Strasser and his four best chums. Back in 1992 the Boyz From the Barracks, all grumpy lieutenants and captains, marched up to the presidential mansion one day to complain about not being paid for months. Seeing them coming, President Joseph Momoh, ever mindful of his neighbor Mr. Doe's fate, was out the back door like a flash and making tracks for the airport. When the last of the lads' "Hellos?" echoed through the empty mansion, they propped their boots on Momoh's desk and discussed the latest in job opportunities. After flipping coins, 25-year-old Strasser ended up as chairman of the new National Provisional Ruling Council. The others gave themselves the inspired, if not actually prescient, titles of S.O.S., for Secretary of State it's said, and P.L.O., for permanent liaison officer, then shot craps for S.O.S. for Mines, S.O.S. for Treasury, for Defense, for Tourism, Fisheries, Trade and Industry... you name it, then divvied up all the P.L.O. positions. It was tough, but they knew where their duty lay and accepted the heavy burdens of responsibility.

Back in the jungle, the rebel attacks were low key at first: a village for food, a clinic for medical supplies, an everyone-asleep-at-the-wheel army convoy for more guns and ammunition. All straight out of Al's favorite course at Goofy Qaddafi's University, How to Get Your Start in Revolutionary Warfare 101. But with a twist: instead of being nice to the people to get them on side, which every guerrilla leader since Mao has preached, Al Sankoh preferred chopping off arms and legs and heads. This, according to a RUF defector, was Uncle Al's way of suggesting the survivors join up. As recruiting programs go, it was said to be rather persuasive.

As the rebel attacks moved closer to Freetown a stressed out Strasser & Co. began grabbing kids off the streets, giving them a gun, a uniform and a few words on their sacred duty to Sierra Leone, then shoving them into the jungle. The intermittent salaries of $20 and two bags of rice a month, coupled with the prospect of the RUF pouncing on them, convinced a fair number to do a bit of looting, murdering and amputeeing themselves.

There was a certain ebb and flow to the business until Sankoh's Neanderthals grabbed the mines. Suddenly there were no millions flowing into the treasury. Almost as bad was that the diamond smugglers, who paid certain folks good money not to have their bags examined too closely at the airport, had nothing to pay anyone not to look for. And to top it all, the pesky rebels were threatening Freetown itself. It was a vexing moment. Were the boys to do a Momoh and hightail it for the tall and uncut, or bring in some muscle?

In April 1995 Pretoria-based Executive Outcomes, a private security company staffed by black and white former special forces soldiers, signed a contract to sort things out. To the astonished relief of the Boyz, it took less than a week to eliminate the RUF threat around the capital. Before the even more astonished rebels could ask, "Who was that masked man?" EO roared off to recover the diamond fields. That two day operation barely worked up a sweat. As soon as rumors of this reached London, I wangled an invitation, got myself a visa and sprinted for the airport.

Hours after arriving I was sitting on the tailgate of an Mi-17 surrounded by black and white South Africans in all their feathers and warpaint as we skimmed the trees. At Koidu they dragged me off on a jolly op to mortar the bejeezus out of the bad guys. Our nights were spent either under monsoon rains or running back and forth to escape columns of enormous army ants. Two choppers eventually picked us up, then dropped down to a town just captured. Dripping with cameras, I was out the door and down on one knee in my best Hollywood pose, looking for action. I blinked at the sight of the wheel struts lengthening on my helicopter. That means it's taking off, I choked. This is not good. Deafened by the whop-shriek of blades and turbines, I next saw the gunner frantically motioning me to return. Are the bad guys coming? Is someone shooting at us? When the wheels actually left the ground, the determined expression of the professional poser dissolved into near—well, total, actually—panic at the prospect of being left to the mercies of the RUF. (You won't say anything about this to Bob Redford, will you?) This was followed by a leap that left me clinging catlike to the bottom of the door. Hands grabbed my wrists and hauled me inside 100 feet above the jungle. "That'll teach you to get out of my helicopter without telling me," the

South African pilot said over a few beers that night. "If you had just stayed there, you silly twit, I'd have come back for you."

Back at Executive Outcomes' headquarters, I leap aside as a shiny 4X4 skids to a stop. Two Sierra Leonean soldiers stagger out under the weight of chromed pistols, shotguns, Bowie knives and hand grenades. One also carries a machine gun and about 50 yards of ammunition belt wrapped around him. The mere weight of it all has this metallic mummy pop-eyed and sweating buckets. The ear protectors perched atop his head are a particularly fetching touch. They are followed by their boss, Colonel Tom Nyuma, universally loved as one of the five coup d'etat-ers back in '92. To the everlasting joy of all Sierra Leoneans, he was recently promoted from captain to colonel, skipping the tiresome ranks in between, and added S.O.S. of Defence of the NPRC of Sierra Leone to his other S.O.S.s. He held on to all his P.L.O.s for old time's sake. It's rumored that the main requirements for holding the high octane titles are being able to say them without a crib sheet or taking a breath. You probably think I'm joking.

Colonel Tom struts past his bodyguards, the patches on his vest proclaiming him "Ranger," "Airborne," and "Special Forces." Tom is not known to have attended any such courses anywhere in the world. Ever. His clear favorite is a skull and crossbones with the warning, "Mess With the Best, Die with the Rest." Tom, who went from being an impecunious captain with an attitude to a senior government minister with property in England and monthly trips to the U.S., is said to have purchased the patches through *Soldier of Fortune* magazine. Tom is 26 years old. The reader will sleep better knowing he is also in charge of the war.

Inside the operations room Colonel Renier Hugo, EO's operations officer, is briefing the Belarussian gunship pilots and Colonel Tom on another attack. Next to Tom is a Sierra Leonean major whose men have been guarding the diamond fields for Tom since the South Africans chased out the rebels. It should be stated here and now that even though he's keeping a very close eye on the diamond fields, it has nothing to do with him being tight with Tom's sister, or that Tom might have one or two ideas about what to do with those diamonds.

Hugo's pointer taps the map, his tone crisp and professional: The infantry company will advance to this point, another company will be landed here by helicopter, support elements will be placed there, the gunship will orbit over here until.... The pilots listen intently, making notes on their own maps. The major, whose men are integral to the operation, is content with the plan; so content that he's snoring gently. A blinding flash fills the room. Duck! It's Tom's official photographer. Tom bobbies up to the map to explain how the attack should be conducted. Volodya and Valerii's eyebrows lift then meet in bewilderment. The South Africans smile fixedly. Two more flashes for the Freetown newspapers and Tom takes his seat. Hugo carries on as if nothing has happened.

The attack was successful. Of course, Tom and his sister's boyfriend really didn't think it important enough to be at the sharp end with their troops. It was too small an operation for them to be involved, they told me hastily when reports of six wounded were radioed from the advancing soldiers. Consummate professionals, they spent their time studying tactics as revealed in their complete collection of Rambo videos. And no, I'm really not joking this time. But if there ever is a film made, by God you'll split your sides laughing.

—Jim Hooper

Mogadishu

Somalia

★★★★★

SOMALIA

Clan Bake

Blood is thicker than water, and in Somalia there is a whole lot more blood spilt than water. The different blood-related groups, or clans, have been drilling holes in each other ever since the first Somalis decided to marry someone other than their sister. How long will this clan-banging go on? Well, until they run out of bullets and somebody ties down every rock in this parched, godforsaken country.

First, you must know that there are really two but equally lawless Somalias.

The dodgy Republic of Somalialand in the northwest with the capital of Hargeisa; Somali, the land that makes up the long southern coastal section and the home of the Digila and Rahanweyne clans, and the northeast with Bosaso as its hub. The capital of the south is the hotly contested city of Mogadishu. To further complicate the divisions, Djibouti is actually half-Somali. Beirut was easy to figure out compared to Somali. The breakaway republics are not recognized by any international body, although perhaps they should be.

Only the southern part makes the news—the southern half, which is to say that section of Siyad Barre's defunct Somali Republic, which was formerly Italian Somaliland. The south is simply lawless territory inhabited by Somalis and ruled by clans. The northern part, formerly British Somaliland, barely makes the news and is sometimes portrayed as considerably more peaceful. Unlike the south, the north has had something of a government—the government of Somaliland— since the fall of Barre's republic, and even, at times, a head-of-state. But even Somalia has a hold out area called Sonaay.

Yet overall, it's been an orgy of blood feuds in Somalia. After the rebel United Somali Congress (USC) captured Mogadishu during the last week of 1990 and toppled Barre's despotic regime (although it at least was a regime), Somalia watched its last government—or anything resembling it—go down the drain. Siyad fled and the USC installed Ali Mahdi Mohamed as temporary president. But the USC was marred by internal bickering and bloodshed within its ranks, and from them rose General Mohamed Farah Aidid. Aidid and Mohamed signed a U.N.-bullied peace agreement in March 1992, but it broke down as perhaps a million Somalis fled the country's famine and clan warfare. Soldiers looted U.N. food supplies, the world body was unable to protect.

Somali Warranty

As you approach the compound's high white walls, a teenager's eyes challenge, demand and insult all at once. A rifle slips from his shoulder, then slips back.

Nowhere in the world have I felt the predatory menace you feel on these streets.

On paper, the property in the particular neighborhood I was visiting belonged to a once-privileged clan, the Murusade. By the terms of force majeure, it belongs to a heavily bandoleered clan named the Habr Gedir. A couple of weeks before I approached the compound on this street, a gunman had slipped in the gate, pulled a mechanic out from under the Land Cruiser on which he was working, and shot the man in the head, then calmly walked out. Now a visitor must bang on the heavy steel plate of the gate to enter. A peephole slides open, and you slip through a small gate within the gate. Such is Somalia.

Enter the U.S. and Operation Restore Hope. Eighteen hundred American marines landed in Mogadishu on December 9, 1992, the first of nearly 30,000 troops to arrive here with the mission of restoring some semblance of order. (Hussein Aidid, the general's son, was one of the U.S. Marines. See "The Players.") Aidid and Ali Mahdi grudgingly shook hands. On January 11, 1993, a general cease-fire was agreed to. But it, like the dozens before it, hadn't a prayer. After Somalis became used to the strange aliens called Americans, they decided to off a couple and even dragged one corpse through the streets of Mogadishu. Of course, CNN was there, and, of course, Americans back home hadn't the stomach to watch their sons being killed in some muddy African hell-hole of no interest to Exxon, Occidental or Caltex. So, Uncle Sam did what it's done in virtually every banana-bash since Vietnam—it sent most of the boys home, in this instance in April 1993. The U.N. troops that replaced the GIs came under fire big time: 26 Pakistani peacekeepers and 50 Somalis were killed on June 5, 1993, when the

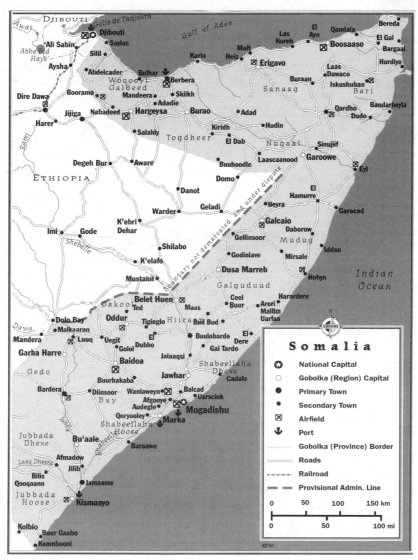

U.N. went up against Aidid's thugs. The U.S. went after Aidid, without success, and decided to get out of Somali affairs altogether in November of that year.

With the Americans gone, Somalians were again permitted to resume killing, raping and maiming each other. And this time, they had more U.N leftover toys to play with. This is a tragic story of a labyrinth of clans and subclans, of split militias and drug-crazed bullies blowing themselves away on the streets with recoilless rifles and antiaircraft missiles.

The Scoop

It's tough running a country by selling camels, and collecting taxes from roadblocks, license plates, port duties and whatever spare change is left in the sand. But Somalialand manages to keep the northern chunk of what we call Somalia together, er well sort of. The eastern half of this tiny area is called Sanaag and is controlled by a clan who does not agree with Egal's presidential ambitions. Self-elected "President" Mohammed Ibrahim Egal has put the lid on half of his new country. The country of Somalialand (not to be confused with Somalia or Disneyland) prints its own money in Britain, has a funky homemade flag and is protected by a ragtag army of about 15,000 kids and unemployed. The main airport is closed, and its ill-defined border with Ethiopia to the south is a free fire zone ruled by rejects from a Mad Max movie. Heavily armed clans dodge land mines in the rocky wastelands in their technicals, rusty tanks and camels. Its main exports are goats, sheep and camels to Saudi Arabia and the Gulf States.

Somaliland was created in 1980, thanks to Egal's efforts, but his domain was merged into Somalia. Military man Mohamed Siad Barre tossed Egal into prison after he grabbed power, even though Egal was the prime minister at the time. There was plenty of fighting, killing, bombing and persecution, as the north fought against the south. When the Northerner returned, there was not much left with which to put together a country.

Strangely, Somaliland has yet to be recognized by any other country. While the war-torn south is considered to be the real McCoy. Party on dudes.

Son of Sam

The Somalias are related to the Oromo of Ethiopia and Afar of Djibouti. This group is called Hamitic or Cushites. Their original home was along the Omo and Tana rivers. The Somalis are a subgroup called the Sam, named for the father of the tribe who split from the Cushites in the first century BC. The Somalis inhabited the Somali peninsula and became known as Samaale or Somaal. The word Somali first appeared in written form in a song about the defeat of the Somalis in 1415. Mogadishu is either a mispronunciation of the Swahili words Mwyu Wa (Last Northern City) or the Arabic Maqad Sha (Seat of the Shah).

In any case the historians among us can take comfort in the fact that the Somalis have always been wanderers and their capital Mogadishu has been turned into a pile of rubble many times before.

As many as 30,000 Somalis have been killed—300,000 have died due to war-induced starvation. There has been no central government since 1991.

Ali Mahdi Mohamed controls the relatively sedate northern area of Mogadishu. He is allied with Osman Ali Atto, who formerly bankrolled Aidid's fight for power. Atto and Aidid battled it out in the south, with casualties per day that could be up to 60–100 people killed and 10 times as many wounded. With the elder Gen. Aidid dead and his son Hussein, now in power, it remains to be seen if things will change.

The front line in Somalia runs along The Green Line, a southeast axis down Afgoye Road with Atto controlling the area around the former U.S. embassy and Somali National University. Aidid controls the south and the port of Merca. Atto's area borders on the Medina district, where he is backed up by Mussa Sudi, an ally of Mahdi.

The groups want to establish a fundamentalistic government that would adopt the *sharia*, or Islamic law. The north is now called Somaliland and is run by Mohammed Ibrahim Egal but has not received any diplomatic recognition.

The Players

Hussein Mohammed Aidid

Ironically, Somalia's new warlord, Hussein Mohammed Aidid, is a corporal in the United States Marine Reserve, who has been conspicuously absent from his Pico Rivera, California artillery unit. Hussein Aidid, 34, is the son of the slain General Aidid, and had been working as a $9-an-hour municipal clerk for the city of West Covina, California. While working part time, Aidid was taking civil engineering classes at Cal Poly Pomona. He joined the Marine Corps Reserves in 1987, last reporting for duty in July, 1995. He failed to report for duty last September because he had quit his job and returned to Somalia. Aidid was first brought to the United States as a teenager by his mother, Asli Dhubat, Gen. Aidid's first wife. He graduated from Covina High School in 1981. While the warlord role is new to Hussein Aidid, he previously walked Somalian soil in 1992 as a U.S. Marine and served as an interpreter until January, 1993. Recently interviewed by the Associated Press in Somalia, Aidid said he valued his Marine experience: "I'm proud of my background and military discipline," he said. "Once a Marine, always a Marine." Aidid's top foreign policy advisor also spent time in the U.S.—he was a Washington cab driver for three years. (As a side note, the name Aidid means "rejector of insults." The young Aidid may soon find he has to live up to his name.)

Mohamed Farah Aidid and the Somalia National Alliance

"President" Mohamed Farah Aidid was killed in factional fighting in late July, 1996. According to his enemies, he died "while killing people." Aidid led troops that killed 18 U.S. soldiers in 1993. That action resulted in the U.S. withdrawing its forces and blocking the U.N. effort to reconstruct the country. His Somalia National Alliance had been duking it out with Ali Mahdi's Somali Salvation Alliance. In reality, the chance of either side actually controlling all of Somalia is nonexistent. Aidid collected taxes from—or shot—anyone who crossed his "green line." The alliance of Ali Atto and Ali Mahdi controlled the other side of the green line.

Mohamed Siyad Barre, the ex-president of the Somali Republic, whose excesses finally undid him, was cozy with Egypt and a buddy of Boutros Ghali's when Ghali was with Egypt's Foreign Ministry. When Barre's man Aidid became Barre's enemy Aidid, Boutros Ghali, understanding the exercise of power, targeted Aidid. He worked against him before the U.N. intervention, and it was during his tenure as secretary general, with his men ensconced in Mogadishu, that he allowed the U.S. functionaries to get so worked up over Aidid that they shifted the focus of the U.N. mission there. As Boutros Ghali looked on, the U.S. went after Aidid.

The U.N. Security Council issued an arrest warrant for Aidid but he managed to elude both U.N. forces and U.S. troops. The U.S. never got Aidid. (Strangely enough while all this was going on *DP* saw Aidid attending a rubber chicken dinner in Nairobi on the front page of the local newspaper.) Despite the price on his head and the number of spooks who I assume can read a newspaper, nothing ever happened and the military continued its search-and-destroy mission at great cost in both money and, later on, lives.

Aidid was weakened by the defection of his sugar daddy, the wealthy Osman Ato. Ato stepped on a land mine, and he lost most of his left foot. His dissatisfaction with Aidid split the Habir Gedirs.

Ali Mahdi Mohamed

The other "president" of Somalia is backed by the Somali Salvation Alliance and supported by the Saad and Abgal clans. Ali Mahdi presents himself as a moderate and is in favor of alignment with the West. His brand of Islamic justice has led to amputations, stonings and floggings in the northern Mogadishu areas he controls. In the last year, the SSA has judged at least 500 cases and ordered five executions, 21 amputations and 421 floggings. In one case, a court of 12 religious leaders sentenced a man to stoning for rape. He was shackled to the ground and stoned to death with cinder blocks hurled by an enthusiastic crowd. Naturally, the media was invited to film the festivities.

The Habr Gedir Clan

Aidid's Habr Gedir clan (actually a subclan of the Hawiye) comes from the Mudug region. The hot, dry and destitute condition of the Mudug region ensures that only the strong survive. Aidid's driving ambition is to forge a Somali state. When his U.S. pursuers boasted of getting so close to catching him that his bed was still warm, reporters invited into that "still warm" sanctum found a book on Thomas Jefferson on the bedside table. But this is not merely a man who as head of the Habr Gedir clan is unable to accommodate other clans. Within his own Habr Gedir, vicious infighting has erupted between extended families.

Ethiopia

The Ethiopians are getting a little tired of the "Kids from Hell" next door. They killed 232 "terrorists" last year.

Al Hahad

The Saudis are backing a small group of Islamic fundamentalists based along the Juba River on the Ethiopia border. They have also been attacking Ethiopia which simply sends in troops to the lawless area of Somalia and kills as many as they can (see "Ethiopia").

Everybody Else

In this clan war, if your mama's from a different family tree than Aidid's, you are the enemy. There are over 500 clans and 20 political groups in Somalia. The Lisan subclan clashes with Aidid as does the forces of Ali Atto and Ali Mahdi. The Yaalahow militia controls the Mecca and Medina districts of Mogadishu, depending on what day it is. Break out those phonebooks and history books if you want to figure this one out.

Getting In

Visas are not available at either the airport in Mogadishu nor at any of the border crossings. From the U.S., unless you're an aid worker or have been specifically invited by whomever's in charge at the time, forget it. However, it may be possible to obtain a visa from Somalia's embassies maintained in Kenya, Egypt, Djibouti and Tanzania. In Nairobi, try the International House (Mama Ngina Street). For a three-month visa, you'll need three photographs and a letter of introduction, preferably from your embassy. You should be able to pick up your visa the next day. In Cairo, try the Somali mission on Dokki Street. Here, you'll definitely need a letter from your embassy stating the purpose of your journey, as well as proof of onward travel by air. There are no land crossing visas issued. Here, you'll also need three photos. Processing takes a day. In Tanzania, Somali visas are issued at the Italian embassy:

Italian Embassy

Lugalo Road
P.O. Box 2106
☎ *46352/4*

Somalia has a consulate in Djibouti and this may be the easiest place to get a Somali visa:

Somalia Consulate

Boulevard del Republique
BP 549
☎ *353521*

From Kenya, you might chance a land crossing from Liboi, Kenya, to Kisimayo in Somalia, or from Mandera, Kenya, to Luuq in Somalia.

Getting Around

The road network in Somalia is thoroughly dilapidated. There are surfaced roads between Mogadishu, Kisimayo and Baidoa in the south, and between Hargeisa, Berbera and Burao in the north. There is the skeleton of a bus network in the south and no public transportation in the north. Fifty percent of the Somali people are nomads, and the camel is the principal form of transportation in the country. The IDA agreed to repair the road network in Somalia but has yet to get started on the work, for obvious reasons. The only way to get around, at present, is to hitch a ride with one of the few aid agencies remaining in the country. In the past, lifts have been available with United Nations High Commission for Refugees vehicles in Mogadishu and other areas. In Mogadishu, you can try hiring a cab or motorbike driver, but you'll probably be abducted or shot, or both. The twice-weekly Somali Airlines flights between Mogadishu and Berbera and the weekly flights to Hargeisa and Kisimayo from Mogadishu have been suspended.

If you do attempt to travel by road, make sure you bring along some friends. Technicals (ideally, with 50-caliber guns) come in very handy at the many roadblocks, which are just a way for the locals to make money. A show of force or a short burst above their heads will force them to ponder the relative value of dying for a few dollars. There are no fixed prices for renting a technical with *mooryaan*, or teenage gunmen, but there will be plenty of offers. It is estimated by the U.N. that there are 2 million assault rifles in Mogadishu alone.

Dangerous Places

The South

The guerrilla force that overthrew Siyad Barre in Mogadishu—the Somali National Movement—got its start in the north, and having seen to Barre's overthrow, it has long since gone back to the north. The problem in the north is that the victorious guerrillas turned the government over to an interim president—Abdirahman Tour—who at worst was bent on destroying his own government because he wanted to see a reunited Somali Republic (he has ties to the old Barre regime and to Egypt, which supported Barre) and at best was simply unable to contain clan warfare. In fact, clan warfare began in the north when the president sent armed men from his own clan, the Habre Younis, to seize Berbera, the north's chief port and the turf of the Issa Musa. Already ensconced in the capital at Hargeisa, it now appeared as if he were set. At least for a few months.

Along came an old man now commonly acknowledged to be brilliant, Ibrahim Dhega Weyne. Under his direction, the Issa regrouped and took Berbera back. With that, the two clans repaired to a mountain village, where for 17 days they argued fiercely.

The North

In October 1994, fighting broke out between President Mohamed Ibrahim Egal, who is supported by the Habir Awal, Gadabursi and Saad Musi clans, and the Idegale militia, who are aligned with the Habir Younis. Normally, a peaceful area, the fighting quickly sent 150,000 refugees fleeing from the capital of Hargeisa. The Idegale make a little folding money by controlling the airport and charging a tax on all who use it. The government muscled in, and that's when the fighting started.

The Habir Younis (now remember, they support the Idegale Militia) appealed to Aidid and were sent a plane full of rifles and ammo. Egal (the guy who runs the country) called Ali Mahdi Mohamed (Aidid's enemy in the south) and received a nice letter in return but no guns. So Egal hit up his buddies the North Koreans, and then got busy fighting. The fighting spread to the Garhadjis (a subclan of the Idegale and Egal in Burca, Sheikh and Burao). The government forces didn't do so well, so now the Garhadji militias have most of the government weapons in their possession. To make things more complicated, Egal does not have support from the majority of people but is pushing for an independent Somaliland. His opponents want to join up with Somalia. His predecessor, President Abdurahman Tur of the Habir Younis clan, was voted out and is now hanging out in Mogadishu under the protection of Aidid.

Even though Egal has done a good job of whipping Somialaland (not Somalia) into fiscal and governmental shape, not one Western country will recognize its sovereignty. Go figure.

Dangerous Things

Bandits and Clans

Most of the factions are simply extended families engaged in blood feuds. They take no prisoners, and, if you stumble onto anybody's turf, expect to be treated accordingly—i.e., shot or macheted. Where clans don't rule, bandits do. Bandits control large rural areas and snipe around in the cities, as well. Police forces are present in some cities, but are essentially impotent and refuse to stand up to the clans and bands of thugs. They have few resources and are as likely to be targeted for death as anyone else. Muslim *sharia* law, which has replaced any form of institutional legal system in Somalia, is enforced in a non-cohesive fashion by clan elders.

Kidnapping

Kidnapping of foreign-aid workers is on the rise, as the rival clans strive for control of a single Somali government and subsequent international recognition. The good news here is that hostages are rarely harmed and often released quickly. The bad news is that more of them are being taken, as they make convenient political bargaining chips. On December 18, 1995, Italian aid worker Marco Lorenzetti was taken hostage by a gang loyal to Aidid. On December 26, Aidid ordered the man turned over to his own custody, after which he "arrested" and "deported" the Italian for entering Somalia without a valid visa issued by the "legitimate" government (Aidid's). By releasing the hostage, Aidid was seeking to be seen in a good light by the Italians. On March 23, 1996, an American aid worker was kidnapped but released the next day. On March 21, five U.N. workers were abducted from Balidogle airport by gunmen and rescued on the 22nd by a Somali militia that recognized them on a BBC broadcast.

Khat

Although not dangerous, it is one of the underpinnings of the economy here. Those who don't fight battles or raise camels grow khat, an amphetamine-like stimulant that, when chewed, provides a mild high. Khat is preferred fresh, and Federal Express would be green with envy to watch the bundles of Khat being airfreighted out of Mogadishu to Yemen and the Gulf States. Khat can also be used as a form of currency.

Technicals

Every American teenage kid's fantasy is to drop a big 454 into an old Chevy Nova and terrorize the neighborhood. Here every Somali's fantasy is to drop an antiaircraft gun onto the back of a Toyota pickup truck and terrorize the country. Actually, a technical might be a great way to get through the morning commute. Technicals are essentially anything with wheels to which Somalis can bolt a belt-fed machine gun. Homemade technicals were invented in Lebanon in the'80s when warring groups wanted to hit and run (and make a lot of noise). Technicals became the ride of choice when the locals found out that the U.N. workers would hire them as security. Needless to say it was harder to find a Toyota Land Cruiser with a roof after that. Thank goodness it only rains bullets here.

Journalists

No need for nasty letters to the editor here. The Somali warlords are a well-read bunch, and if they take issue with something you've written, they send a *mooryaan* to knock on your door and deliver their response. Four Somali journalists were executed by followers of Aidid for offending him in an article they wrote in a U.N.-sponsored paper. An Italian journalist was executed after being mistaken for an executive of an Italian banana exporter. Most journalists do not sign their name on local articles for fear of reprisals.

Killing People

With all these guns and hair-trigger tempers, it doesn't take more than a few minutes for a clan fight to break out and people to get killed. The only consolation we can offer you if you are convicted of killing someone is that the *sharia*, or Islamic law, mandates that you must pay 100 camels. If you are a woman the penalty is 50 camels.

Getting Sick

The state-run medical system has collapsed in Somalia, and only rudimentary care is available through NGOs. There is one doctor for every 4640 people in Somalia. Diarrheal, communicable and parasitic diseases are rampant in the country. Chloroquine-resistant malaria is present in all parts of the country. Larium should be used for chemical prophylaxis. Cholera, dracunculiasis (Guinea worm), cutaneous and visceral leishmaniasis, rabies, relapsing fever and typhus (endemic flea-borne, epidemic louse-borne and scrub) are prevalent. Somalia is also receptive to dengue fever, as there have been intermittent epidemics in the past. Meningitis is a risk during the dry season in the savanna portion of the country, from December through March. Schistosomiasis may also be found in the country and contracted through contact with contaminated freshwater lakes, streams or ponds. A yellow fever vaccination certificate is required for all travelers coming from infected areas. If you become ill in Somalia, or have an accident, get the hell out ASAP. The best place to be evacuated to is Riyadh, Saudi Arabia.

Nuts and Bolts

Located in the Horn of Africa, British Somaliland and Italian Somaliland formed independent Somalia in 1960. The population is 9.3 million with a 12-percent mortality rate. Somalia covers 637,655 square kilometers (246,199 square miles).

Somalia is not really set up to be the next big tourist attrition in Africa. Its long coastline has some of the nicest sand beaches, but the waters are infested with sharks and there is little shade. March to June and September through December are the rainy seasons. Nomadic grazing is the name of the game here, with temperatures hot and landscape arid. The country is 100 percent Sunni Muslim; the entire population is ethnic Somali. English is widely spoken, and Italian is popular in the south. Somali is a difficult language and uses the Roman alphabet. Somali has been a written language only since 1972, and just 24 percent of the country is literate. Money is the Somali shilling broken down into 100 centesimi. The money is surprisingly stable since there is no government to print more. Oh, did we forget to tell you that there is no government.

Somalis like to be called by their nicknames. The slender Somali frame creates a lot of nicknames like *Ato*, or thin, or *Dheere* which means tall.

Dangerous Days

03/21/1996	Five U.N. aid workers were taken hostage at the Balidogie airport.
06/05/1993	Twenty-six Pakistani peacekeepers and 50 Somalis were killed in a battle with Aidid's men.
12/09/1992	In Mogadishu, 1800 U.S. marines arrived prior to 28,000 other American troops—for the start of Operation Restore Hope.
03/03/1992	Under U.N. pressure, Ali Mahdi and Aidid signed a cease fire.
01/25-31/ 1992	United Somali Congress rebels captured Mogadishu.
1991–1992	Massive famine. Seventy-five percent of the country's 6 million people were at risk from starvation.
10/31/1980	President Siyad Barre declared a state of emergency.

Dangerous Days

10/21/1969   Bloodless coup brought Siyad Barre to power.

07/1960   British Somaliland and Italian Somaliland united to become independent Somalia.

SOMALIA

Beirut

Southern Lebanon
★★★★

Hell's Boot Camp

If God created a training ground for the Armageddon, Southern Lebanon would be the stage. Once called the Paris of the Mediterranean, it is more like bullet-riddled plaster of Paris. No longer vibrant but tired, the shattered ruins of Western development and Eastern tradition stand broken, sad and dead.

The realities of Beirut would challenge even the most creative scriptwriter. Religion, drugs, war, love and death all have interacted in this biblical epic of destruction. Southern Lebanon has been incinerated by the heat of Judeo-Arabic hate. The one true god has surfaced and has remained unshakable: the U.S. dollar, now the formal currency of this land. Beirut is trying to shake itself off and evolve from its 12th-century feudalism into the 20th century. Someone, though, needs to inform the fanatics.

For 15 years, from 1975 to 1990, Lebanon was plunged into a civil war that violently divided the country into regions controlled by religious and ethnic factions, including Sunni, Shiite and Druse Muslims and Maronite Christians. A central government in Lebanon was one in name only.

The war was fueled by the belief that the 1943 National Pact, which had determined the distribution of power between Christians and Muslims and among the different Muslim sects, no longer reflected the nation's ethnic and religious demographics.

Introduced by Muslim leaders and Syrian officials and approved by the surviving members of the legislature, the 1989 Taif Agreement reestablished a central and legitimate government in Lebanon. The larger Muslim population was reflected in an increased number of seats in the National Assembly. De-facto leader General Michel Aoun, however, refused to accept the Taif Agreement and remained in power until he was ousted by factional Lebanese Army units and Syrian forces in October 1990.

Although a number of Maronite Christians boycotted the polls, Lebanon conducted its first legislative elections in 20 years in the fall of 1992. The assembly

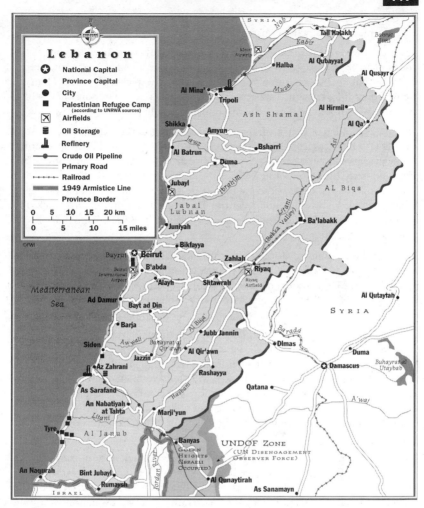

has 128 members. The Taif accord stipulated that half the membership of the National Assembly chamber should be Muslim and the other half Christian, altering the 5:6 ratio that had existed previously.

The majority of Lebanon's political parties have traditionally been based on ethnic and denominational differences, namely because seats in the National Assembly are distributed on the basis of religion as opposed to politics. The AMAL (Movement of the Deprived) is a Shiite party that was at vicious odds with left-wing Palestinian forces during the civil war. It now spends a good portion of its time protecting the position of Shiite Muslims forced out of their homes by fighting among rival pro-Palestinian forces and between those forces and Israeli-backed forces in the south. And Hizb al-Ahrar al-Watani—Parti National Liberal (NLP, or National Liberal Party)—refuses to join with any Muslim groups that are linked to Palestinians or Palestinian independence. Of course, the militant Shiite group, al Jihad al-Islami (Islamic Jihad, or Holy War—a.k.a. Hezbollah) has claimed responsibility for a number of kidnappings of foreigners in Lebanon, as well as other terrorist acts, including the 1983 Beirut bombings in which 300 U.S. Marines and French troops were killed.

In all, there were 330 attacks on Israeli and the Southern Lebanese Army (SLA) troops in 1993, compared to 170 in 1992. Iran, especially, likes to recruit terrorists from among the Lebanese camps. Prime for the picking are the Hamade, Tleiss, Bdreddine, Kassem, Yazbeck, Berjaoui and Ammar. They are then sent to the Iman Ali school north of Teheran, Sudan and other training camps.

Beirut, as is much of Lebanon, is again reaching out to the world—and Western tourists and businesspeople are beginning to trickle back in. Lebanon's rebirth can be evidenced by the trickle of requests made to tourist offices in London and other Western European capital cities. Some estimates reveal that more than US$400 million has been raised by billionaire businessman and Lebanese Prime Minister Rafik Hariri to rebuild central Beirut. Major hotel chains, including Marriott and Inter-Continental, are running hotels in Beirut. Things looked as sunny as the Mediterranean sky.

Despite the continuing gloom, Lebanon has made progress toward rebuilding since the civil war. In Beirut, armed militias are gone and the dreaded Hezbollah now limit their activities mainly to the southern part of the country. Under the Taif accord, the Lebanese have created a more equitable political scheme, particularly by giving Muslims a greater say in the political process.

Nearly 30,000 Syrian troops still refuse to move from Beirut. Damascus says this is due to the weakness of the LAF. Israel continues to support a proxy militia, the SLA (Southern Lebanese Army), near its border. About 1000 Israeli soldiers and 3000 SLA militiamen patrol the 15-km-wide security zone established in 1985 against anti-Israeli guerrillas, as Israel withdrew the bulk of its 1982 Lebanon invasion force. But they're still playing rocket volleyball in the south on a weekly basis. Syrian troops are based principally in Beirut, North Lebanon and the Bekaa Valley.

The fright began all over again in April 1996 when Israel, in response to what it claimed was an unprovoked Hezbollah rocket attack on northern Israeli settlements that killed 40, viciously pounded both Beirut and the southern city of Tyre in what was called "Operation Grapes of Wrath." A rapid escalation of a long-standing eye-for-eye policy of attacks turned the area into a war zone, surprising both tourists and politicians. Election time was near.

The Scoop

Until April 1996, the Republic of Lebanon had been getting back to normal, although the south has remained a war zone since the civil war. During that month, hell started all over again for the Lebanese people. This was when Israel, in retaliation to Hezbollah rocket attacks on northern Israeli settlements pounded Beirut and the southern city of Tyre in "Operation Grapes of Wrath." The world saw images of an Israeli helicopter gunship take out an ambulance in Amiriyya in Southern Lebanon near Tyre, killing four children and two women. More than 400,000 civilians fled Southern Lebanon in a scene of biblical connotations; most of them ended up as refugees in Beirut with nowhere to go. Despite the "Wrath," Hezbollah continued to hurl Katyusha rockets at northern Israel. Lebanon is trying to emerge from two decades of civil war, which has seriously damaged the economy and the social fabric. The population is composed of both Christians and Muslims from a variety of sects. Hezbollah still controls the south, while the north is still safe.

History has never been kind to Lebanon, a country that has been conquered, sacked, pillaged, rebuilt, demolished and then rebuilt by everyone from the French to the Babylonians. Come on now, everyone likes a beach vacation, don't they?

The most recent misery began when a busload of Palestinian guerrillas traveling through a Christian suburb was ambushed in April of 1975. In retrospect, we should have known that anytime Christians and Moslems live in a Mediterranean state, you are asking for trouble. After all the outside meddlers (Syria, Iran, Israel, Russia, America, France), religious fanatics and other players had left, Lebanon looked like a frat house on Saturday morning. All that was left to do was the cleaning up and paying the bills. The problem is that when everybody was supposed to go home, there were still the Ayatollah, Assad and Israel fighting over the last keg. *DP* is thankful it doesn't have to explain the characters who created Lebanon of the '70s and '80s. They ranged from the Phalange, started by Pierre Gemayel who founded his group in the '30s after being impressed with what the Nazis were doing in Germany, to Yassar Arafat, who went from reviled terrorist to Nobel peace prize winner. Read Coskun's account "In a Dangerous Place" to understand how senseless the whole thing was.

What is important is what Lebanon is today. The Lebanese are known for being, along with the Chinese and Indians, the merchants of the world. Between 500,000 and 800,00 people left Lebanon during the war. Which war you might ask. The war that destroyed $15 billion worth of infrastructure and countless futures. Today the people who remain baby-sit about 640,000 registered refugees who are not allowed to work at professional or skilled jobs. They have an occupied southern area that is an active war zone, and they have bully neighbors to the east (Syria and Iran) who use Lebanon in the finest of puppet traditions to smack Israel so that they don't get smacked back. Lebanon always loses. Israeli planes do not streak into Teheran or Damascus but into the shell-shocked refugee camps to deal out punishment.

Back before "the war," tourism used to be 20 percent of Lebanon's gross national product. Hezbollah is running tours and even providing security for historic areas. In 1992, 177,503 people visited Lebanon. In 1995, 409,755 arrived. Today, folks in Beirut ignore the fact that the airport is guarded with antiaircraft guns and that the south is a free fire zone and look forward to the big tourism boom. The fact that the States is known as the Great Satan might have something to do with the anemic tourism figures. The only boom they get in Lebanon is the sound of incoming artillery shells from Israeli troops. The most popular poster boy is not Mickey Mouse but the Ayatollah Khomeini. The ruins at Baalbeck are also famous for being the main headquarters of Hezbollah, a university and training center for terrorists, the place where the U.S. hostages were kept and the future site of a music festival. For now, Lebanon rebuilds and awaits its tourists to deliver it from the Stone Age.

The Players

Few playwrights could create a cast of characters and dramas as dark and complex as the terrorist groups in Lebanon. Forged by desperation, nurtured by Syria and Iran, supported by oil money and hardened by Israeli intolerance, the terrorist factions in Lebanon have worldwide reach and are responsible for much of the pain, death and suffering since the early '80s.

Hezbollah (Party of God)

Founded in Lebanon in 1982, Hezbollah means Party of God or Army of God, depending on how militant you are. The name comes from the torture and murder of a young mullah in Qom, Iran, in 1973. His last words were that there is only one party, the party of God. Hezbollah is an Iranian-backed organization that polarizes the plight of Muslims into Muslim versus the Great Satan. The Great Satan can be Israel or America, depending on expediency. Hezbollah is a political machine as well as a terrorist organization. This group has been responsible for some of the most well known acts of terrorism in the last 15 years, including the bombing of the U.S. Marine barracks in 1983, the hijacking of the

TWA flights, the kidnapping of Western hostages in Beirut and the car bombing of the Israeli embassy in Buenos Aires, Argentina, in 1992 that killed 56 people.

Hezbollah is a political, social and military organization that seeks to achieve in Lebanon what the Muslims achieved in Iran. It espouses an intense hatred of any influence that does not support its views of Shi'a ideology. The movement was born from the merger of Sheikh Husayn Musawi's Islamic Amal and the Lebanese branch of the Da'wa party in 1982–'83. It should be noted that Sheikh Musawi was killed in early 1992 in Southern Lebanon in an Israeli attack on his motorcade. Three area councils—Beirut, the Bekáa Valley, and Southern Lebanon—oversee activities in their respective regions. A series of functional committees play roles in policy recommendation and execution. A consultative council *(shura)* functions as the principal governing body on day-to-day matters but actually exists to advise Iran on the unique situation of the Islamic movement in Lebanon. Hezbollah elements receive training in the Bekáa Valley of eastern Lebanon. Through this connection, Iranian revolutionary guardsmen provide political indoctrination, financing and material support. The Hezbollah and the revolutionary guards work together on terrorist operations. The group itself seldom claims responsibility for specific acts, but does so under a variety of aliases.

Hezbollah is probably the most dangerous and committed terrorist organization in the world. Under the direct control of Teheran Hezbollah, the group seems to be the most successful in following in the steps of Mohammed by combining religious, political and military fanaticism to spread the cause of fundamentalist Islamic belief.

Not content with waging war with the world, Hezbollah is undergoing some serious infighting. In February 1995, two rival Hezbollah clans shot it out in the Baalbeck, reflecting the differing beliefs of hard-liner Nasrallah and pro-Syrian Sobhi el-Tufaili. The Syrian army intervened before they could kill each other off. There is a move to replace the Secretary General Hassan Nasrallah with Hezbollah's spiritual leader, Mohammed Hussein Fadlallah who works to support and train other fundamentalist groups.

Today, Hezbollah conducts its most visible campaign of terror in the very southern part of Lebanon. But recent events in Brazil and Argentina and recruitment drives among Algerians in Europe indicate that they are expanding their activities toward a more global scale reducing the risk of direct retaliation.

Hezbollah has been involved in numerous anti-U.S. terrorist attacks, including the suicide truck bombing of the U.S. Marine barracks in Beirut in October 1983 and the U.S. embassy annex in September 1984. Elements of the group are responsible for the kidnapping of most, if not all, U.S. and other Western hostages in Lebanon. The military wing is estimated to have 5000 members.

Hezbollah operates in the Bekáa Valley, the southern suburbs of Beirut and in southern Lebanon and has established cells in Western Europe, Africa and elsewhere. The group has claimed responsibility for attacks as far afield as Argentina. It receives substantial amounts of training, financial aid, weapons and explosives, as well as political, diplomatic and organizational assistance from the Islamic Republic of Iran. Iran provides an estimated $50 to $100 million to Hezbollah every year. It also furnishes funds to Hamas, Islamic Jihad and the PFLP-GC. Libya kicks in some dollars and safe haven, and Sudan provides training bases and freedom from arrest.

They want to establish a revolutionary Shi'a state in Lebanon, modeled after Iran, eliminate non-Islamic influences, force Western interests out of the region and, of course, become Lebanon's principal Islamic movement with close ties to Iran.

The following chart shows the religious groups in Lebanon and the seats they hold in Parliament.

Religious Group	Number of Seats
Maronite Christians	34
Sunni Muslims	27
Shia Muslims	27
Greek Orthodox Christians	14
Druze	8
Greek-Melkite Catholics	6
Armenian Orthodox	5
Alawite Muslims	2
Armenian Catholics	1
Protestant Christians	1
Other	3

Source: UNDP

Hamas (Islamic Resistance Movement)

Hamas was formed in late 1987 as an outgrowth of the Palestinian branch of the Muslim Brotherhood and has become Fatah's principal political rival in the Occupied Territories. Various elements of Hamas have used both political and violent means, including terrorism, to pursue the goal of establishing an Islamic Palestinian state in place of Israel. Hamas is loosely structured, with some elements working openly through mosques and social service institutions to recruit members, raise money, organize activities and distribute propaganda. Other elements, operating clandestinely, have advocated and used violence to advance their goals. Hamas' strength is concentrated in the Gaza Strip and in a few areas of the West Bank. It has also engaged in peaceful political activity, such as running candidates in West Bank chamber of commerce elections.

Hamas activists—especially those in the Izz Al-Din Al-Qassem forces—have conducted many attacks against Israeli military and civilian targets, suspected Palestinian collaborators and Fatah rivals. During 1992, elements of Hamas were responsible for several prominent anti-Israeli attacks, including ambushes of military units in the West Bank and the murder of a member of the Israeli border police in December 1992. Hamas elements increasingly use lethal weapons and tactics—such as firearms, roadside explosive charges and car bombs—in their operations.

It is estimated that there are tens of thousands of supporters and sympathizers. Funding is received from Palestinian expatriates, Iran and private benefactors in Saudi Arabia and other moderate Arab states. Some fund-raising and propaganda activity takes place in Western Europe and North America.

Harakat Al-Muqawama Al-Islamiya, Islamic Resistance Movement, (HAMAS)

AKA: Abdallah Azzam Units (operational cell units of Qassam, formerly known as Azzedine al-Kassam Units, reorganized after 12/92 deportations; active in and around Napulse, Jenin, and Tulkarem in the northern occupied territories)

The Islamic Association for Palestine is a religious association based in Dallas,Texas and are associated with HAMAS. They published the group's charter in English and distribute the communiqués, Al-Zaytuna, and other publications. Dallas is also home to the Holy Land Foundation for Relief and Development a charity organization. The United Association for Studies and Research based in Springfield, VA is also linked to HAMAS.

Hamas was formed in December 14, 1987 and is headquartered in the Sheikh Radwan district of Gaza City. They have a training camp at a farm outside of Khartoum in the Sudan. They also have offices in Amman, Jordan and support groups in Britain and the U.S. with offices in Chicago, New Jersey, and Virginia, Washington DC, Detroit, and Kansas City.

They believe that there is no solution to the Palestinian problem except through Jihad. There are at least 15–20 special operatives active in Gaza (HAMAS claims 28) and 20 in the West Bank and between 750 and 1200 active fighters. Their most famous member was Yehiya (Yaki) Ayyash aka 'the Engineer' or 'the man with seven souls' an explosives expert who was behind a number of bombings in Tel Aviv.

Hamas' budget is about $30 million a year about with about a third coming from the U.S. and Europe. The rest comes from Iran, Jordan, Sudan, and the Gulf States. They publish Al-Thabat (Perseverance) and Al-Zaytuna, the pro-HAMAS publication published in the United States).

Palestine Liberation Front (PLF)

The PLF is a terrorist group that broke away from the Popular Front for the Liberation of Palestine–General Command (PFLP-GC), in the mid-1970s. It later split again into three factions: one pro-PLO, another pro-Syrian, and the last pro-Libyan. The pro-PLO faction is led by Mohammed Abbas (Abu Abbas), who became a member of the PLO executive committee in 1984, but left the executive committee in 1991.

The PLF was established under Mohammed Abu al Abbas in opposition to PFLP-GC leader Ahmed Jibril's support for the Syrian incursion into Lebanon in June 1976. After unsuccessfully attempting to gain control of the PFLP-GC in September 1976, the PLF was split from the PFLP-GC officially by PLO chairman Yasir Arafat in April 1977. The PLF was established with Iraqi support, and its existence as an independent group was recognized when it obtained seats on the Palestine National Council in 1981 with its headquarters in Damascus. Near the end of 1983, the PLF itself split into factions, when Abu Abbas felt that his organization had become too close to Syria. Leaving Damascus, along with many supporters, Abu Abbas went to Tunis to align himself with Arafat and the mainstream Fatah organization. Following the *Achille Lauro* incident, the Abu Abbas faction relocated to Baghdad at the request of the government of Tunisia.The parts of the PLF remaining in Damascus were further split in January 1984, when Abd al-Fatah Ghanem attempted a takeover of the PLF offices and held Tal'at Yaqub, secretary general of the PLF, hostage. Through Syrian intervention, Yaqub was released and Ghanem formed his own faction with ties to Libya. Yaqub's faction joined the Palestine National Salvation Front and is generally aligned with Syria.Operationally, the Abu Abbas faction of the PLF has demonstrated creativity and technical acumen. The group has employed hot-air balloons and hang gliders for airborne operations, and a civilian passenger ship for mounting a seaborne infiltration operation.The *Achille Lauro* hijacking in October 1985—followed by the murder of an elderly American citizen, Leon Klinghoffer—contributed to the international condemnation of Abu Abbas and the PLF. In 1988, the PLF and Yasir Arafat feuded over the PLO's moderating stance on Israel and on the use of terror against Israel. The differences appear to have been overcome when the PLO refused to condemn an attempted attack by the PLF on a Tel Aviv beach.

The Abu Abbas faction of the PLF carried out an abortive seaborne attack staged from Libya against Israel on May 30, 1990. The same group was also responsible for the October 1985 attack on the cruise ship *Achille Lauro* and the murder of U.S. citizen Leon Klinghoffer. A warrant for the arrest of Abu Abbas is outstanding in Italy. The PLF openly supported Iraq during the Persian Gulf War.

There are at least 50 members within the Abu Abbas faction. The other two factions have between 200–250 members. They receive logistic and military support mainly from the PLO, but also from Libya and Iraq. They are working to destroy Israel.

Popular Front for the Liberation of Palestine–General Command (PFLP-GC)

The PFLP-GC receives logistic and military support from Syria and Iran as well as financial support from Libya. The group is given safe haven in Syria.

Ahmed Jibril formed the Popular Front for the Liberation of Palestine-General Command in 1968 when he became disenchanted with George Habash's leadership of the Popular Front for the Liberation of Palestine (PFLP). An officer in the Syrian army, Jibril was initially interested in developing conventional military capabilities to complement PFLP-GC terrorist activities. As a result, the PFLP-GC has always been known for its military expertise. In addition to ground infiltration capabilities, the PFLP-GC has worked toward developing air and naval striking capabilities as well. PFLP-GC terrorist activities have included the use of letter bombs and conducting major cross-border operations directed at Israeli targets. The PFLP-GC has also shared its terrorist expertise with other international terrorist groups, such as the Armenian Secret Army for the Liberation of Armenia (ASALA), as well as European groups that have sent members to Lebanon for training. The PFLP-GC arsenal includes sophisticated weaponry, such as Soviet SA-7 anti-aircraft missiles, heavy artillery and light aircraft, such as motorized hang gliders and ultralights. The Communist Bloc countries provided small arms, such as Kalashnikov assault rifles and RPG-7 antitank rockets, but Syria and Libya may have served as conduits for such support. The PFLP-GC actively participated in the Lebanese conflict, including sniping attacks that injured U.S. marines who were members of the peacekeeping forces in Beirut in 1982–'83. In addition, the group attacked Israeli citizens and interests through operations launched from Lebanon. The PFLP-GC has also occasionally recruited West Bank Palestinians to conduct terrorist operations inside Israel.

The group specializes in suicide operations and has carried out numerous cross-border attacks into Israel, using unusual means, such as hot-air balloons and motorized hang gliders. It is not known how many current members there are, but the more radical factions tend to attract young volunteers at a greater rate than the more moderate.

Popular Front for the Liberation of Palestine (PFLP)

Marxist-Leninist group that was a member of the Palestine Liberation Organization (PLO). Founded in 1967 by George Habash. After Fatah, the PFLP is the most important political and military organization in the Palestinian movement. The PFLP has spawned several dangerous terrorist groups.

The group committed numerous acts of international terrorism between 1970 and 1977. Since the death in 1978 of Wadi Haddad, the PFLP's operational planner of terrorism, the group has carried out less frequent but continued attacks against Israeli and moderate Arab targets.

The group of about 800 men receives most of its financial and military aid from Syria and Libya. The PFLP is trying to create a Palestine in the manner of a Marxist-Leninist revolution. The PFLP was formed after the Arab defeat in the 1967 Arab-Israeli war. George Habash created the PFLP as a merger of three formerly autonomous groups—the Arab Nationalist Movement's Heroes of the Return, the National Front for the Liberation of Palestine and the Independent Palestine Liberation Front (to be distinguished from the present Palestine Liberation Front—PLF). Referred to by his followers as *al-Hakim* ("The Wise One" or "The Physician"), Habash has remained consistent in his position towards solving the Palestinian problem—the total liberation of Palestine. The PFLP established itself early as one of the most violent Palestinian terrorist groups. It concurrently sought to establish strong ties to other Marxist revolutionary organizations. Those links facilitated PFLP operations in Europe, which gave the group much of its notoriety. Habash strongly favors well-publicized attacks on civilian targets, and the PFLP reputation for ruthlessness was built on that strategy. As a result of ideological inflexibility, internal disputes and personality conflicts, the PFLP has spawned several splinter groups, including the PFLP–General Command (PFLP-GC) and the Democratic Front for the Liberation of Palestine (DFLP). The PFLP was one of the most active terrorist organizations in the early 1970s. As a result of publicity that attracted condemnation even from Communist Bloc countries, the PFLP curtailed international operations and concentrated on developing conventional and guerrilla forces for use against targets in Israel.

South Lebanese Army (SLA)

The SLA has been Israel's early warning system since 1978. After the Israelis were pushed out of the country by Syrian- and Iranian-backed militia in 1985, they left behind a little pocket protected by Lebanese General Antoine Lahd.

The SLA controls about 8 percent of Lebanese territory. Although no one believes that the moniker Lebanese is correct, these are occupation forces paid for and trained and supported by Israel. The SLA is about 2500 strong and manned by Christians and Shiites. They also have backup from about a thousand Israeli Defence Forces (IDF). The SLA occupies a string of hilltop bunkers that parallel the Israeli-Lebanese border. They are well armed but no match for the hardened Hezbollah fighters who control the region. Many of the SLA soldiers are inducted without their consent and the constant boredom and stress have taken their toll on discipline. There are about 160,000 Palestinian refugees in Southern Lebanon. They provide a fertile recruiting ground for Hezbollah. The various Palestinian groups, such as the PFLP, PRLP-PC, DFLP and Abu Nidal's FRC, also recruit from these camps. True to Middle East politics though, the refugee camps have their own small cliques and groups that often create violent confrontations without outside agitation. Hezbollah's main source of support comes from the Bekáa valley and squalid camps in southern Beirut.

The United Nations Peacekeeping Mission (UNIFIL)

The United Nations Interim Force in Lebanon is kept away from the border, so its 4500-person task force gets to twiddle its thumbs in Naquoura on the coast. They operate checkpoints inland from Tyre and throughout the area. They can only try to keep carloads of machine gun– toting Palestinians from wiping each other out. They also create a human barrier that Israel has to think about if they roll tanks back into Lebanon.

The Lebanese Army

The Lebanese army prefers to let the Israelis and Palestinians duke it out while they look the other way. Since the Lebanese army is under the direct influence of Syria, they are not about to fire on Islamic elements to please their bellicose neighbor to the south. On the other hand, they feel a slight obligation to bring some law and order to the south, but so far there is little indication that they will replace the SLA or the United Nations.

The Syrians

Lebanon is a vassal state of Syria. Syria has 35,000 troops deployed in eastern Lebanon. Syria uses Hezbollah to carry out its dirty work against Israel: a charge that Israel has always echoed. That's why Israel considers Lebanon to be merely a buffer zone between itself and Syria. Syria is still angered that the Israelis stole the strategically important Golan Heights from them during the 1967 Arab-Israeli war.

The Israelis

The Israelis had 21 killed and 18 wounded in Southern Lebanon in 1994. Although the number seems low, it is a constant reminder that Israel is still at war with Hezbollah, which is backed and directed by Syria and Iran. Israel is not foolish enough to take on Syria or Iran directly, therefore each side has created its pawns to judge the strength and commitment of the other without resorting to total warfare. Israel has the SLA, and Syria has Hezbollah. Israel may decide to invade Lebanon again to push back Hezbollah fighters and clear out the Palestinian refugee camps, but each side remembers the lingering and vicious war that was triggered by Israel's invasion of Lebanon in June of 1982, which has lasted in various forms to this day.

For now, Israel is content to wage an eye for an eye war. When Hezbollah sends shells and rockets into Israeli outposts, the Israelis are content to send in their Cobra gunships and take out preannounced villages, cars or buildings. In response to what it claimed was an unprovoked Hezbollah rocket attack on northern Israeli settlements that injured 40 during April 1996, Israel pounded both Beirut and the southern city of Tyre in "Operation Grapes of Wrath."

Getting In

IF you want to travel to Southern Lebanon some folks suggest trying the Rosh Haniqra border crossing from Israel on the coast but you will immediately be on Mossads list for the rest of your life. Others drive south from Beirut and hope to God they don't run over a freshly laid mine. The entire northern border is ringed with mine, concertina wire, electric fences and is patrolled by motion detectors and video cameras. It is because of this "creative containment" that terrorists have resorted to using ultralight aircraft, balloons, jet skis and single engine planes packed with high explosives.

Passports and visas are required. Without the requisite validation, use of a U.S. passport for travel to, in or through Lebanon may constitute a violation of U.S. law and may be punishable by a fine and/or imprisonment.

The categories of individuals eligible for consideration for a special passport validation are set forth in 22 C.F.R. 51.74. Passport validation requests for Lebanon should be forwarded in writing to the following address:

U.S. Department of State
> *11 19th Street, N.W., Suite 300*
> *Washington, D.C. 20522*
> ☎ *(202) 955-0518*

The request must be accompanied by supporting documentation, according to the category under which validation is sought. Currently, the four categories of persons specified as being eligible for consideration for passport validation are as follows:

Professional reporters: Includes full-time members of the reporting or writing staff of a newspaper, magazine or broadcasting network whose purpose for travel is to gather information about Lebanon for dissemination to the general public.

American Red Cross: Applicant establishes that he or she is a representative of the American Red Cross or International Red Cross traveling pursuant to an officially sponsored Red Cross mission.

Humanitarian considerations: Applicant must establish that his or her trip is justified by compelling humanitarian considerations or for family unification. At this time, "compelling humanitarian considerations" include situations where the applicant can document that an immediate family member is critically ill in Lebanon. Documentation concerning family illness must include the name and address of the relative, and be from that relative's physician attesting to the nature and gravity of the illness. "Family unification" situations may include cases in which spouses or minor children are residing in Lebanon, with and dependent on a Lebanese national spouse or parent for their support.

National interest: The applicant's request is otherwise found to be in the national interest.

In all requests for passport validation for travel to Lebanon, the name, date and place of birth for all concerned persons must be given, as well as the U.S. passport numbers. Documentation as outlined above should accompany all requests. Additional information may be obtained by writing to the Department of State (see above) or by calling the Office of Citizenship Appeals and Legal Assistance at ☎ *(202) 326-6168* or *326-6182*.

Getting Around

Kidnapping was a fine art in Beirut. The most dangerous place used to be the airport and the road leading into town. These areas were easy pickings for Americans during the glory days of hostage-taking. If you are still nervous, have a driver meet you at the airport with a prearranged signal or sign. If not, take the official airport taxis. If you take a taxi, officials will write down your name and destination so that the news media can get it right after you're abducted. The many bombed, shelled and abandoned buildings are being reclaimed by squatters. The U.S. embassy, destroyed in a 1983 suicide attack, is a modest but comfortable home for a few ragged families. Most of the downtown area is being bulldozed and rebuilt. Many corporations have set up headquarters in Jouneih (Juniyah), about 45 minutes north of Beirut. The south is dangerous, even with an armed escort from Hezbollah.

Dangerous Places

Southern Lebanon

Southern Lebanon was the base for the PLO in the early '70s, and now it is Hezbollah and SLA territory. It is a no man's land, 850 kilometers square, that protects Israel's border. The area south of the Awwali River is known as Southern Lebanon. To the east is Mount Hermon and the Syrian-Lebanese border and to the west are the ancient cities of Tyre and Sidon. The landscape is rough, with small villages and wadis connected by poorly maintained roads. The area has predominately Shiite Muslims, who eke out a living growing oranges and olives.

The best way to find out what the hot zone of the day is, is to listen to Voice of the South Radio operated by the SLA, which will broadcast areas to be attacked by Israeli jets or helicopters.

The entire area is under curfew at night and few SLA or IDF soldiers venture out after dark. It is at night that Hezbollah will mine the roads with remote-control bombs. The terrorists will also use rockets against bases and missiles, usually Saggers or SA-7s, against helicopters. Hezbollah strongholds are at Mlita, Jebel Safi, Ain Busswar, Mach Gara and Saghbine.

Dangerous Things

Prisons

Israeli-controlled prisons in Lebanon are notorious for torture and brutality. A young Lebanese prisoner, held for 10 years without a trial, died in January 1995 of torture. He was the third prisoner from the Khiam Detention Camp in Israel's Southern Lebanon occupation zone to die in less than two months. Israel and the Southern Lebanese Army have refused to allow prisoners' families to visit them, as well as refusing international humanitarian agencies access. Perhaps 250 Lebanese and 100 Palestinians are held at Khiam. One human rights agency estimates that 80 percent of the inmate population has heart, pulmonary or nervous disorders due to the extreme dampness of their cells. It is also believed the prisoners are allowed outside only once every three days.

Embassy Locations

U.S. Embassy
> P.O. Box 70-840
> Antelias
> Beirut, Lebanon
> ☎ [961] (1) 402-200, 416-502, 426-183,
> 417-774

Embassy of Lebanon
> 2560 28th Street, NW
> Washington, D.C. 20008
> ☎ (202) 939-6300

Getting Sick

In Beirut and the surrounding areas, basic modern medical care and medicines are widely available. Such facilities are not always available in outlying areas.

And You Thought "Cops" and "Rescue 911" Were Reality TV

What is the hottest TV station in Lebanon (well, actually number 4 in the ratings)? If you are a fan of reality shows, you might want to check out **al Manar** *(the Beacon), the new TV station sponsored by your local purveyor of fine terrorist activities and mayhem: Hezbollah.*

Al Manar is probably the strangest of the 50 odd new TV stations in Lebanon. They feature live action shots of rocket attacks against Israelis and other bang-bang news reports. Just so things don't get too exciting, there is also daily news dished out by glum-looking, chador-wrapped female newscasters. And the long (and we mean long) three- to four-hour interviews with the leaders of Hezbollah are guaranteed to make sure you sleep right through retaliatory raids by the Israelis. DP did an interview with Hezbollah leader Sheikh Hassan Nasrallah and Fadlallah; they make the Unabomber's 30,000-page manifesto seem absolutely terse and well organized.

Al Manar is owned by well-heeled Shia Muslims, and programming content has to be "blessed" by a senior cleric who OKs what is selected by a committee. No Showgirls NC17 programming here. The station broadcasts movies, sports and documentaries. But you won't see a lot of women in strong roles—i.e., cussing and drinking. Those who wish to reach this militant demographic can buy 30-second spots for as little as US$400.

Useful Addresses

Hezbollah
> Mekteb-1 Hezbollah
> South Suburb
> Bir-al Abed
> Beirut, Lebanon

PKK (Kurdish Workers Party)
> Mekte-Bi Amele-1 Kurdistan
> Barelias-Chotura
> West Bekaa, Lebanon

Dangerous Days

04/10/1996   In retaliation to what it claimed was an unprovoked Hezbollah rocket attack on northern Israeli settlements that injured 40 after Passover week, Israel viciously pounded both Beirut and the southern city of Tyre in what was called "Operation Grapes of Wrath."

Dangerous Days

04/20/1993	Russia and the United States issued invitations to Israel, Lebanon, Jordan, Syria and the Palestinians to meet in Washington, D.C., to resume peace talks stalled by the Israeli's expulsion of 400 suspected Hamas activists to Lebanon.
12/17/1992	The government of Israel deported more than 400 suspected members of Hamas; however, the government of Lebanon refused to allow the deportees to enter and they were sent "camping" in the Israeli "security zone" in Southern Lebanon.
02/16/1992	General Secretary Abbas Musawi was killed in an Israeli helicopter ambush near the village of Jibsheet in southern Lebanon.
10/30/1991	The first round of Arab-Israeli peace talks began in Madrid, Spain.
07/28/1989	Israeli commandos seized Shaykh Obeid from a village in Southern Lebanon and detained him in Israel on allegations of involvement in terrorist activity on behalf of Hezbollah.
02/28/1987	Georges Ibrahim Abdallah, a principal figure in the Lebanese Armed Revolutionary Faction, was sentenced to life in prison for murder.
01/28/1987	U.S. bans travel to Lebanon.
06/14/1985	TWA flight 847 was hijacked from Athens to Lebanon. The hijackers shot and killed U.S. Navy diver Robert Stetham in Beirut on June 16 and dispersed the remaining passengers throughout the city. Thirty-nine American citizens were released on June 30 in Damascus, Syria.
09/20/1984	Fourteen people were killed and 70 were wounded when a van loaded with 400 pounds of explosives drove past the checkpoint in front of the U.S. Embassy annex in Awkar and exploded. The driver of the van was shot and killed by British security guards. Islamic Jihad claimed responsibility for the bombing in a call to the media.
02/06/1984	West Beirut fell to Muslim militias.
10/23/1983	Islamic Jihad (read that as Hezbollah) bombings in Beirut killed more than 200 U.S. Marines and more than 50 French paratroopers.
04/18/1983	A car bomb exploded in front of the U.S. embassy in Beirut, killing 63 people, including 17 Americans. More than 100 others were wounded. Islamic Jihad claimed responsibility, calling the bombing "part of the Islamic Revolution." Iran subsequently denied having any role in the attack.
09/15/1982	Israel invaded West Beirut.
09/15/1982	Lebanese Christian Phalangists killed hundreds of Palestinian refugees in a camp near Beirut.
09/14/1982	President-elect Bashir Gemayel was assassinated.
07/19/1982	David Dodge, president of the American University of Beirut, was kidnapped. He was subsequently released on July 19, 1983.
06/06/1982	Israel invaded Lebanon.
06/04/1982	Israeli planes bombed Beirut.

Dangerous Days

03/16/1978	Invasion by Israeli forces.
06/01/1976	During this month, Syria entered the civil war in Lebanon on the side of the Christian Phalange and against the Palestinians and their Muslim allies. In response, Abu Nidal renamed his terrorist group, then based in Iraq, the Black June Organization and began attacking Syrian targets.
04/13/1975	Phalangist militiamen attacked Shia Muslim targets, sparking the first round of fighting in the Lebanese civil war.
04/11/1968	The Popular Front for the Liberation of Palestine (PFLP-GC) split from the PFLP under the leadership of Ahmad Jabril.
07/15/1958	U.S. Marines were sent to Lebanon in order to thwart the overthrow of the government.
11/22/1943	Independence Day.
05/06/1915	Martyr's Day.

In a Dangerous Place

Lebanon, 1980–1986: Living with Death

For more than 15 years, the war in Lebanon was the compulsory and compulsive topic of headlines and television news throughout the world—a hopeless quagmire of death and destruction. A place where we could never figure out who was killing whom or why.

With its 17 different religious communities and an obsolete political system, Lebanon was, and still is, the ideal battlefield for warlords who have wanted control of this ancient region. Lebanon also became the best place for marketing and testing weaponry coming from all corners of the planet.

The war began in Ayn er-Remmane (a suburb east of Beirut), on April 13, 1975, with a massacre: During the inauguration of a church, by the leader of the Katayeb party, four people were shot dead from an unidentified car. The retaliation was immediate. A few hours later, in the same place, Christian militants machine-gunned a coach transporting Palestinians from the camp of Sabra to the one at Tall ez-Zatar. Twenty-seven people died in this coach and three more in the crowd. The answer was prompt: One hundred Christians were killed the very next day. Massacres and revenge had become a common feature of this war.

Unlike the wars that make good movies or backdrops for spy novels, Lebanon was not black and white, good and bad. Lebanon was and still is a nest of wars. It is a civil war between several of the 17 religious communities. It is a national war in which Lebanese fight Palestinians, Lebanese (or at least some of them) fight against Syrians, Lebanese (or the majority of them) fight against Israelis. It is a religious war between Christians—the majority group when the state was created in 1920. It is a war of sects between Sunnites and Shiites, the latter of whom constituted the majority, and within the Shiite community, between Amal, pro-Syrian, and Hezbollah, pro-Iranian. It is a war between militias of all factions, but more particularly, from the Christian group. It is a social war pitching the poor (Christians and Muslims) against the rich (Christians and Muslims).

What made this new medieval hierarchy so bizarre was that a few months prior, Lebanon was called the Switzerland of the East. With an affluent population of just under 3 million in 1975, it was a comfortable, tolerant, harmonious and beautiful place, and was an important seaport, banking center and holiday resort.

The war in Lebanon was my "home" for many years. I became acquainted with a lot of different people, learned about their difficulties, saw many of them wounded or dead. I saw history firsthand. The new war of terror was fraught with booby-trapped vehicles, suicide commandos, kidnappings, and so on. I would like to think that in later years, people will look at my photos, examine the faces of the people who fought this war, and try to understand why humans can do these things. I flew in and out, depending on the level of activity at the time. Like drifting in and out of a bad dream, there are certain incidents that capture the war in Lebanon and will explain the unique people, places and activities that have shaped this turbulent region.

1980—Poppies and Missiles

The history of Lebanon is best left to scholars and philosophers, since, like the rest of the Middle East, it is like a mass of knots that once untied, bears no resemblance to the original structure. When I first came to Lebanon, the war had been raging for five years. Eager to earn my spurs as a war correspondent, I went to visit the Druses, an ancient heretic sect born in Egypt around the year A.D. 986, and later classified as Muslim. I was there on a short assignment to take photos of SAM-106 missiles being secretly deployed in the Bekáa Valley by the Syrians who (at that time) backed and actually controlled the Druses. Along the road, I saw hashish plantations that kept the militiamen loyal and well paid. Drugs were an important source of income for all the militiamen controlled by the Syrians.

It is not surprising that in a war-torn country with a dismembered economy, the people try to make the quickest profits possible. The missiles were there all right, amidst the hashish fields.

1982—A View to a Kill

I flew into Cyprus (the Greek side) from Paris because the airport in Lebanon was closed. We then waited for two days before taking a cargo boat transporting wood to the Lebanese port of Jounieh. The Israelis had crossed their common frontier with Lebanon and were moving forward toward West Beirut. Their ultimate target was to be the headquarters of the Feddayins of the Palestinian Liberation Organization (PLO), led by the ever elusive Yasir Arafat, and other Palestinian groups. Around the same time, the Israeli Air Force launched heavy bombing raids using American-made fighters and Israeli-made *Kfirs*.

It is hot and sunny out, but the black smoke has turned everything to grey. From time to time, I can hear small explosions accompanied by bursts of flames.

The journalists are all staying at the Hotel Commodore off Hamra Street. This is where the journalists usually gather to watch the war. Today, I have decided to set up my observation from the terrace of the Hotel Carlton, a cheaper place but affording an equally cinematic vista of Beirut under the bombs. The Carlton Hotel is situated in the residential quarter of West Beirut in Raoucheh, by the coast. I spend time with an Algerian journalist named Sadri. The streets below are empty. Everybody is seeking refuge underground. For the first time in my life, I am watching the heavy bombing of a modern city. We stare in amazement at the jets hurling down dangerously close to the ground (100 to 200 meters). At the same time, warships launch their shells from the Mediterranean sea, shooting missiles of 150- to 240-mm caliber. The noise and destruction are overwhelming—30,000 people die during those terrible days, most of them civilians buried in the rubble of collapsing and burning buildings. I am struck by the Israelis deliberately killing innocent people—people who are not attacking them but who are easy to kill. I do not know whether to be angry or appalled.

We decide to climb down from our "watchtower," on the 13th story's terrace, to take pictures of the destruction. There are two armed men ahead of us. Suddenly, the two of them turn toward Sadri and myself, abruptly asking us to hand over our cameras. I think at first they are going to take all the cameras, but I soon understand that they only want mine because I have got the latest Nikons whereas Sadri has only got old Leicas. Our two aggressors then shoot around our feet and start shouting at us to freeze. Then they frantically run away, holding our cameras tightly in their hands. A young Palestinian man, wearing a *keffieh* and a sash, who has been watching from a nearby balcony, comes down to the street and asks us for details, then starts making a call on his walkie-talkie. Soon men in jeeps and military vehicles arrive on the scene. They ask us, "Where did the thieves run?" After indicating the way, I am told that direction leads to the headquarters of the Panarab party, the Mourabitoun, which follows Nasser's ideology.

The bombing is still going on, but the Palestinians seem to ignore it; they surround the Mourabitoun building, and one of them, using a megaphone, requests the cameras as well as the surrender of the thieves. Their answer does not come in words but in bullets. The Palestinians reply in kind. During the shoot-out we take cover under a car. The car explodes from a grenade thrown by a Mourabitoun, and we are dragged out by a Palestinian fighter. The shoot-out lasts about 30 minutes. Finally, the men inside the building send out our cameras. The cost for their return has been three men killed and 10 people wounded.

1982—Through a Glass Darkly

I knew a young man, a Christian Maronite, during those turbulent days in Lebanon. He had told me about his education at the Sorbonne (he spoke perfect French) and revealed his refined taste for arts and culture. He was involved in a shoot-out against another faction, and I was there to cover the event, confident in my friend's desire to protect me from harm. But under fire, the blood lust comes. He becomes another person, shouting, firing, demonstrating his joy at killing people. In the massacre that ensues, it is obvious that he is deriving great pleasure at cutting off the heads and ears of his victims. He even tries to kill me, after having declared his friendship the very day before, when he sees me taking pictures of what he is doing.

I had planned to go to Khalde, near the front, with my friend Reza, an Iranian photographer working, like me, for SIPA, a photo agency. We decide to leave in the very early morning and on foot, since nobody wants to take the risk of driving us there due to the intense gunfire. We want to see for ourselves how far the Israelis have advanced and to take some pictures.

Khalde is a small town facing the Mediterranean Sea about 10 kilometers away from Beirut and about eight kilometers from Baabda, the inland town where the Lebanese presidential palace stands. The Israelis had been progressing very quickly over the past few days, using the coastal highway across Israel and Lebanon. Baabda is about to fall, and soon afterwards so will Beirut.

We walk in the rising heat toward the white smoke in the distance and listen to the sound of the gunnery; we are also aware of the brisk clattering noise made by the bursts of machine guns and the isolated shots of automatic weapons. We come across two soldiers walking slowly in the heat. One is helping the other, who is obviously terminally wounded. They do not utter a word as we pass them and do not even acknowledge our presence when I take their picture.

Nothing unusual perhaps, but enough to force us to breathe a little faster and to feel a little edgy.

The tension and mounting fear get to us, and Reza stops and says he will not go any further because it is too trying to do anything in such adverse conditions.

For some reason, I decide to carry on alone, and there I am walking and getting tired when I see a group of people near a petrol station. It is on the front. I am stopped by one of them who is carrying a Kalashnikov. He asks who I am, listening carefully to my answer. Then he tells me that he and his friends belong to the

SAIKA, a pro-Syrian organization fighting against the Israelis. As soon as he understands I am Turkish and I speak a little Arabic, he befriends me, telling me his name, Saleh, and offering me some tea and sandwiches.

We all sit around an improvised table made from an oil drum. I take some pictures of him. One photo is still my favorite, a portrait in classic warrior pose; he's ready to shoot on sight, looking through the hole left by a shell in the inner wall of an abandoned house. All the while, the bombardment is going on around us.

Then it happens: First a giant flash of white light, followed by a shock... around me everything seems to be rocking, and I lose consciousness for a minute....When I wake-up again, I can see nothing but dust. I think that it must have been the explosion of a shell. Everything is so silent that I think I have lost my sense of hearing.

The dust settles and I realize that I am surrounded by the pieces of hacked bodies. I panic. The next thing I remember is that I can hear again; people are shouting and running in every direction. Around me nothing is the same anymore: tables upturned, glass broken, dust, rubble...blood, torn limbs...and so on. I look at myself frantically. I have been lucky. I am complete, without even a bruise, but I am trembling. Then I see them: Saleh's eyes, wide open, transfixed, staring at me. The explosion had instantly killed most of the people who were drinking tea around us. Only Saleh, the Syrians and I have been spared.

All of a sudden, a man comes to the scene from the burning petrol station, brandishing his Kalashnikov. He starts yelling that I am a spy, responsible for the bombings, and that I ought to die. He shoots in my direction. For a second, I am petrified. Saleh understands the danger faster than I, and he shouts at me to run away to a safer place. Thanks to his intervention, I realize that my life is at stake and I start running away as fast as I can, leaving the burning petrol station behind me.

Nobody has followed me. I shut myself in a bath cabin. And I cry and cry and cry....

I stay in the bath cabin for a few hours, till the end of the bombardment. In the evening, I go out and walk back to Beirut. I am still in a state of shock when I meet a fellow photographer, Patrick Chauvel, who works for Sygma.

As I tell him my story, I realize that in the panic, I have left all my cameras behind near the petrol station. Chauvel cheers me up and tells me not to worry. His words cannot calm me, since I realize that without my cameras I am just an idiot wandering through a war zone.

The next morning, I start asking everybody how I can go back to Khalde to fetch my cameras.

I find an Italian nurse working, like Saleh, for the SAIKA organization. She drives me in her ambulance to look for the leaders of the SAIKA. We find them just as the bombardment is resuming.

We go inside a grocery store to feel the illusory but comforting presence of a ceiling above our heads. The gunnery is intense. We have nothing to do but wait anxiously. I feel useless without my cameras. Suddenly, as if answering my silent prayers, one of the combatants comes smiling like a politician, proudly handing me a video camera. I explain to him that it is not mine since I only work with still cameras; he says I can have that one as a replacement. I agree to take it anyway to prevent an argument. I can tell by the stickers that it belongs to the CBC (Canadian Broadcasting Company) who are staying at the same hotel as I am.

Back at the hotel, I return the videocamera to the Canadian television crew who had lost it the day before.

I feel anguished not to be able to take pictures. Luckily, Robin Moyer, a *Time* correspondent, lets me borrow one of his cameras.

Two days later, the Italian nurse comes to tell me that my cameras have been found among the corpses of Palestinians in the morgue of Sabra in West Beirut. One of my cameras is broken, but the other one is still usable. I am happy to retrieve them but sad to do so on corpses. I cannot help thinking that a piece of these people is inside my bashed cameras, along with their joy when they took pictures of each other with my cameras and how their happiness had been halted so stupidly and so suddenly.

SIPA covers only half of my expenses while I am in Lebanon. To stay one night in Beirut costs as much as US$400 in a big hotel, so I decide to stay in a hotel inside a refugee camp opposite the Hotel Commodore. The other journalists can afford to be driven around in armored vehicles and stay in the Commodore. A Palestinian named Mahmud has become my driver, and he provides me with all sorts of information and help.

I take an interesting shot, in East Beirut, of a woman carrying a child in her arms running away from the explosions. She is surrounded by soldiers carrying machine guns who seem to protect her amidst cars and rubble and smoke. One can see how the people had to move from house to house during the bombing in order to avoid getting killed. This picture has been taken with a broken camera (that's why it is blurry) because of the bombings.

The other journalists cannot go out of their hotel. I manage to snap this shot and others, because I am close to the action. But it is impossible to send my film out because of the siege. The American television crews organize "shippings," but the print journalists who want to use this system have to pay $10,000 per package. I only have $100, but my friend Reza proposes to put my film with his own in an envelope to be given to the American newspapermen.

I am most surprised when I get a telegram of congratulations a few days later. The pictures had reached Paris via New York, and I am told that one of my pictures had been chosen to become the cover of *Time* magazine, *Paris Match, VSD* (French) and other magazines around the world.

Being a war correspondent, I can say that I was there when it happened. My photos are silent witnesses to war. Most people see these scenes on TV during their evening meal, are very moved for a short while, and then flip the channel to something else. But a magazine photo can haunt you for a long time.

I am in a street not far from the Hotel Commodore, the general headquarters for the Red Cross, when a booby-trapped car explodes. Usually journalists arrive with the police and the military too late to capture anything but the confusion and wet blood.

For once, I am there right on time and I have the reflexes to take photos during the panic scene which follows the explosion. Everybody is running, desperately looking for shelter or just to get away.

I notice a young man start running who is wearing only a white singlet and carrying his pajama-clad son. He is followed by his wife. He is holding a silver pistol in his right hand. I start taking pictures of the three, rapidly running along with them as they rush in my direction. I am quite excited with my eye glued to the viewfinder, and so the pictures will come out a little blurry. I see him leveling his pistol at me, taking aim and shooting, but I don't connect his actions with reality. And he keeps shooting as he runs by me. All around me, everyone is screaming and yelling. The explosion has blown out all the windowpanes around us, and the noise of the glass crunching and shattering under the feet of the passersby adds to the cacophony. Then the sirens take over, first those of the ambulances, very quickly and on the spot, as usual in Beirut, then those of the vehicles of the civil protection.

After the scene has calmed down I walk back to my hotel, and it is only then, in the lobby, that I realize what had happened. The hotel attendants and the clients are all watching me with a look half disgusted, half concerned. I looked at my clothes, trying to understand what is wrong; then I put my hand on my head. When I remove my hand, I see that it is smeared with blood. The man's bullet had grazed my scalp.

1985—The Show Must Go On

In Beirut, a massacre always follows another massacre. The chain is impeccable and implacable. This time, it is the Druzes who are responsible for the deaths of some 300 Christian combatants of the Kataeb party and of the Lebanese forces. The Druzes have lived for centuries in the mountains of the Shuf and been considered to be ferocious warriors. Their leader is Wallid Jumblatt (the son of Kamal Jumblatt, founder of the PSP, Progressive Socialist Party).

The Druzes have just finished a merciless battle in the mountains overlooking Beirut, in the southeast of the city, which they won against the Phalangists. Once their victory was assured, they immediately perpetrated a massacre in order to avenge another massacre perpetrated against them (so they claim) by the Christian Phalangists.

I go to Bhamdoun, about 20 kilometers southeast of Beirut with two other journalists to visit Wallid Jumblatt and see the situation. The two other journalists are Samy Ketz of the AFP (*Agence France Presse*, French Press Agency) and David Hirst of the *Guardian*. We have been blindfolded to prevent us from seeing the exact location of the headquarters.

We meet with Wallid Jumblatt; then we go to see firsthand the extent of the damage inflicted upon Bhamdoun and its defenders. Although we are forbidden from taking pictures, we are not blindfolded and I am able to take some photos with an autofocus camera. I count approximately 300 dead. Most of them had been killed, after having been captured, hanged with electrical wires, and dragged through the streets, where they were abandoned like trash. It is hard to understand how killing, and killing cruelly can be such a joyful activity.

I am able to photograph the gaiety of the Muslim combatants after they have massacred their enemies. Some of them had discovered some mannequins in a shop and amused themselves with one of these, transporting it to the street in front of me, and then hanging it with a cable. A placard was attached under its strangled neck on which they hastily wrote the name: Amin Gemaye (the Christian president of Lebanon). One of the Muslim militia kisses a dummy dressed in a grey flannel three-piece suit. The whole scene is surrealistic. They do it because they are aware I am recording their actions. It is not much different from what soccer supporters do after a match or what happens during a carnival. The camera is a tease.

The Muslim militiamen of the AMAL movement had asked some photojournalists to accompany them. The sky, usually bright blue, is evenly grey-white, very shiny, and quite disturbing for the eyes—not very good for pictures either. The militants want us to come to the vicinity of an ancient well situated 10 kilometers north of Sidon. It's in a region that was recently under the control of the Lebanese forces and has fallen into the hands of the Shiites of the AMAL movement and the Druses of Wallid Jumblatt's PSP. They had just made a horrible discovery.

Hunters had signaled to the militiamen the presence of corpses in the bottom of an ancient well. The militiamen had to go down wearing gas masks. When we arrive, they show us the decomposed bodies of Muslim militants killed a year before on a beach near Sidon during a massacre by the Christians.

Later, I learn that there is some doubt about the identity of the corpses I had photographed near Sidon. Some people claim that they are not Shiite Muslims but perhaps even Christians. A small voice awakens in my head:

> *Like a bullet, I pride myself on my lack of alignment or cause, but I am becoming a tool for killers, a weapon to be used by whomever wants to create damage.*

Some time later, I take a photo-souvenir of a very special sort. It is in Jieh, a Christian village set along the road to Sidon. This village has been besieged by Wallid Jumblatt forces. They eventually managed to break the resistance of the villagers, and on their victory, they allowed the photographers to take pictures of their rejoicing. They look like the famous hunters of the safari days in the African savanna, proudly posing with one foot on the slaughtered lion. The difference is that the lion has been replaced this time by an unlucky and very dead enemy soldier.

The men are proudly posing, lifting their weapons high above their heads in a victory gesture, while stepping joyfully on the corpse of their enemy, as if they were walking on a carpet.

Without this picture, the world might seem saner, cleaner and fairer, but now that this picture is recorded, people will know how low humanity can sink.

Weapons and soldiers. That's what the war is about, no? I have taken countless shots of both. It is always a surprise for me to see how the soldier identifies himself with his weapon. Everybody knows that there is something sensual about holding a weapon. In the case of men holding a gun or a machine gun, it also has something to do with male pride. I have never encountered a soldier who refused to be photographed, and in every case the rifle or gun is raised upward like an erection.

In Lebanon, stereotypes are falling apart. There is a clash of cultures and images. In past wars, soldiers were like football players. One red, one green. One good, one bad. Here, everyone is evil, everyone is righteous. There is no regular army to speak of. The militiamen are usually dressed in a hodgepodge of half-civilian, half-military clothing. They choose freely the fashion they want to follow after their favorite mythology, revealing an incredible mixture of Western and Oriental influences. Some of these men wear big cowboy hats, or T-shirts with the picture of Ayatollah Ruhollah Khomeini on them, or hairbands and ammunition bands crossed on their chest like Mexican revolutionaries in Zapata's time.

All the world's a stage and we are just actors upon it.

These past days, I have accompanied the Druses militia close to the demarcation line in the Shuf mountains in southeast Beirut. They are fighting against the Christian Phalangists, using Soviet-built tanks that they received from their Syrian allies. With these weapons, the fight will be fierce and not likely to last very long. I manage to get close to what is happening. I always have to remember that I only have a still camera, not a movie camera. I have to take shots with continuity, so as to make my "story" understandable. Sometimes I wish I could just watch and direct what is happening to tell the story. I am allowed 36 pictures for each camera I carry; then I must reload.

I try to capture the essential moments even though I have no idea of the outcome of each battle. The dust flying, the oblique light of the sun contrasting with the silhouettes of the soldiers, the sudden movement of a tank, the bursting of a shell, the assault of the infantry, the last moments of a soldier brought on a stretcher to an ambulance. I am able to take these pictures because I follow the militiamen everywhere instead of staying in a downtown hotel with the rest of the journalists.

SOUTHERN LEBANON

I am becoming biased because I am learning too much.

1986—I Am the Piano Player

Snipers get their kicks shooting at isolated and unarmed people. Many snipers are mercenaries hiding out in apartments on top of buildings.

I meet a sniper today, a Frenchman, who uses a rifle specially designed for his line of work, made in the U.S.A. He would shoot people, then play the piano, mostly Mozart, then resume his watch, waiting for the next target to come along. He killed children or old ladies without remorse or hesitation. Dozens of deaths have been attributed to him, but he has never expressed the slightest regret, because, as he explained to me, he was on the demarcation line, the line that separates Beirut into two parts, East and West, and it was not to be crossed. Therefore, he had every right to do what he did.

Special rifles are available for conscientious snipers. For example, the American M-16 with a field glass and the Soviet-made Brejnev. I took many pictures of people trying to pass the demarcation line; very few of them made it.

My advice about snipers is to never be number three. The first one across the street has a 90 percent chance, the second has a 50 percent chance, but the third has no chance at all, because the sniper has had ample time to adjust his aim and tracking.

I am beginning to remember rules that should never be needed.

The main contradiction of a war is its perpetual vacillating between lawlessness and obeyance to strict and strange rules. To kill at random whatever comes in front of your rifle does not mean there are no situations where some sort of rules are followed. In the past, for example, the soldiers were not supposed to go about killing each other during certain periods of the day, at night, and on Sundays.

In Beirut, there is an unwritten tradition, somewhat bizarre, probably inherited from the Middle Ages, and respected by all parties: Shoot from 5 a.m. till 8 a.m., then stop for breakfast, and resume shooting up to lunch time, stop again for lunch and a siesta, and resume shooting until sundown.

1986

The influence of Muslim fundamentalism is felt more and more in Lebanon. It comes from Iran whose leaders have always said they wanted to export their Islamic Revolution to all the Arab countries first and then to the rest of the world. As Islam is the second most important religion in Lebanon, it was normal that the new ideology would provoke a tremor in the diverse Muslim communities. Things would have been complicated enough that way, but the Iranians infiltrated the country and trained the people to the new ideas so that many turned to Iran as a model to follow. A movement was born that was soon going to be well known throughout the world for the expediency of its methods and for its extremism. This movement is the Hezbollah, the Party of God.

The Shiites have been influenced by the Khomeini-like AMAL militia. I have taken many photos that show the extent of the personality cult to which the famous Ayatollah is subjected in the various Muslim communities and factions.

Fanaticism is an indispensable feature of many wars, especially those fought for religious reasons. Everybody remembers the kamikaze of the Second World War who gladly gave their lives for their Emperor-God. The same thing happened in Iran during its eight-year-long war against Iraq, and in Lebanon. Sana, the young Palestinian girl who blew herself up in the explosion of a truck she had loaded with explosives, was a modern kamikaze. She took the time to explain her gesture to journalists (including myself) and had taped a message that was distributed to the press after the success of the operation.

####

Looting and robbing became very commonplace in Lebanon. People actually went shopping with a weapon.

I come across the body of an old man who has been murdered for the plastic bags full of goods he had just bought in Beirut.

I can imagine him, just moments before, walking peacefully under the bright blue sky, feeling the warm sun on his back and the heat bouncing off the hot road. The shining light is difficult to bear, so he lowers his head. Suddenly, everything seems to blur, the world around him stops, the light diminishes, and a pain digs into his belly. He has dropped his bags; blood is gushing out of his bowels. He dies wondering what he has done to deserve such an ending....

Why am I taking a picture of this?

####

I have heard that the young Lebanese militants have taken up Russian roulette as a badge of courage. I introduce myself to a group of militants averaging 19 years of age. I gain their trust slowly, and I eventually ask them how they feel about the war and how they cope with anxiety, fear of death, and the like. I also talk to them about my own fear of death; then I switch from this topic to war being a big lottery, and what do they think of games, gambling, etc. At last, I am able to ask them about Russian roulette, saying only that I have been told it is common practice for the militants but that I have never seen proof.

They remain mute for a while; then one of them nods in a silent acquiescence. He explains to me that almost all the militants, whatever the party, play this game, that he himself has played it often and that it is quite an enthralling experience, quite addictive in fact. I then ask him to permit me to photograph them during a game, but they quickly reply that it is not possible because all this is done clandestinely and that if their chiefs hear about it they will be punished. I eventually manage to photograph them, but due to my subjects' suspicion of being jinxed I am barred from taking pictures of the real game of death.

The table is set with a white tablecloth. The bets have already been taken. The game is for money and for the thrill. The rules of the game are simple and well known. Everybody bets on the chances of the shooter surviving and the game starts. The game must be played with a six-shot revolver, usually a small Smith & Wesson or Colt Detective. One bullet is loaded into the chamber, and the cylinder is spun around. Without looking, the player must hold the pistol to his temple and pull the trigger.

If he survives, the gun is passed, the barrel spun and the trigger pulled again.

The game can stop at any time or start anew. In Lebanon, some men have taken to playing this game alone.

This nihilistic game is perfect for Lebanon, where life is worth little and drugs and death provide the entertainment. In the beginning of the war, they were content with smoking hashish or marijuana to pass the time. Now it is cocaine and heroin. Death is the ultimate high.

The young bearded man has put a gun on his right temple. He is now facing his possible imminent death. The others watch him in awe. For a brief moment, he is a superior being, a true hero; in a second he might become a true zero....Like a powerful drug, every drop of adrenaline surges to his brain, he pulls the trigger slowly, his testicles tighten, and then...click. Today he is lucky—after all, it was but a mock game.

Two days after having posed for these photos, he tried his luck once more, with a loaded pistol this time (the very one in my pictures), and died. There was no click.

How can young men kill themselves for no reason? Russians invented this game when they were bored on the battlefield. These photos were taken 10 years after the beginning of the war. These young men have known nothing but war, death and violence during the crucial years of their adolescence.

I have heard that sound before. Click is the sound my shutter makes when I push the button. With that click comes the same rush of adrenaline, the feeling of omnipotence. As long as I click that shutter, I am immortal, free from death, separated from the horror on the other side of my lens. But someday I will not hear the click.

####

The incident happened during Terry Waite's press conference at the Hotel Commodore, the headquarters for the French press. An Anglican minister from England, Waite had come to Beirut to help find a solution to free the hostages and ended up kidnapped and remaining as a hostage for more than three years himself.

A car with three passengers inside is the target of a shoot-out probably just aimed at scaring Terry Waite. When the car stops in the middle of the street, I realize that the driver has been hit by a bullet. I rush to help the driver, forgetting about taking pictures, and try pulling him out. An American journalist (working for *U.S. News*) comes to our rescue, but we both arrive too late. The driver of the car is dead.

Later on, the driver is considered a hero by the militiamen and other witnesses of the simple violent event. The shooting is filmed by the cameramen who have come for the press conference and is shown around the world by the TV networks.

Just another death, no pictures, another nameless victim.

####

I am traveling in and out of the main Palestinian camps of Beirut, Sabra and Chatila and Borj el Barajneh. They are all situated in the south of Beirut, not far from the City of Sports. The war is more violent than ever. The leader of Shiite militia AMAL, Nabih Berri, who is also the minister of state for South Lebanon and who proclaimed himself minister of national resistance to fight against the Israelis, receives his orders from Syria and has the camps attacked.

The AMAL and the Lebanese forces militiamen can be organized like search-and-destroy teams and go from one house to the other to accomplish their task, or they surround a quarter and wait patiently for the end, cutting all the roads and blockading the supply of food and water. The people inside are starving, and some have already died of hunger and thirst. Those who are daring enough to get out are killed instantly by the militiamen standing outside.

The women and the children are, of course, suffering more than the men, because they cannot fight and must wait anxiously for the outcome of all this. They already know by instinct that the worst is always guaranteed. I also try to record their suffering for their history. Sometimes the women come to me, begging me to stop this nightmare, as if I can do something about it. My so-called "neutral position" makes everybody believe I can be a go-between.

Some Palestinians manage to sneak out of the camps, but the militiamen are waiting outside, and whenever they have a doubt about the identity of one person or another, they apply what is known around here as the "tomato test." It consists of asking the person caught to pronounce the Arabic word for "tomato." A Palestinian will denounce himself immediately by pronouncing this word as *panadora* instead of *ponadora*, which is the way the other Arabs pronounce it around here. Once a Palestinian is found, he is usually taken aside and executed. Hundreds of people have already died that way, or another, since the reawakening of intercommunal feuds.

#####

Today, I follow and photograph a child who has probably become half-crazy because of the bombings. He is hanging around in the camp of Sabra, wearing only his underwear and a pair of grotesque pink slippers, far too big for him. As soon as he sees me, he starts behaving like a clown, dancing, chanting, making faces amidst the rubble and the ruins of the camp. I take many pictures of him, because he seems to me the epitome of what has happened to the people here. Being very young, he represents the future of this world without a future. His hopeless behavior reminds us of the hopeless world that humankind is proposing for the young generation of this country who were born with the war. Next to him is a young man wearing a funny straw hat, his face covered by a yellow handkerchief like a bandit set out to attack the stagecoach in the western movies, but this one has given it a personal touch—he has poked three holes in his mask in order to breathe and see. This young man was following the kid; he is probably his brother or a relative. I found the contrast between the two very weird.

####

I did something unusual, even for me, a few days ago. Something which has left a bitter taste in my mouth. Photojournalists are sometimes like vultures hovering above and around those who are going to die or who have already met their demise, in the vulgar expectation of a spectacular shot.

The light is bright as usual in this "blessed" country, but the sky is uniformly white. I go to a Palestinian camp near Sidon during a heavy attack. The camp has been bombed nonstop for many days. The shells keep exploding around us, damaging only the walls of the houses, until one, guided by I don't know which force, bursts out very close to a group of people. A child happens to be there....badly injured in the chest and belly, he dies almost immediately.

I then see his father, a man in his late twenties, coming to his side, in a very dignified way. He covers the frail dead body, still dripping blood, with a white sheet in the false hope to stop the draining and to resuscitate his son.

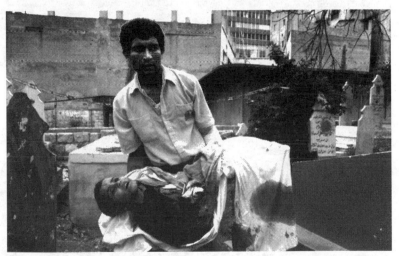

He quickly understands that the task is beyond his limited powers and he lifts his child in his arms, unaware of his weight, and directs his steps toward the cemetery. I decide to follow him. We are alone. No one else has come. I am taking photos all the while. I will never forget the gaze in his eyes.

In a universal gesture of love, devotion and pity, he is looking for the proper place to bury his child.

There are still human feelings in Lebanon. I am thankful I still have mine.

—**Coskun Aral**

SOUTHERN LEBANON

Colombo

Sri Lanka
★★

Tamil Tear

The bitter, 14-year-old conflict in Sri Lanka has left 50,000 Sri Lankans dead, including the president, the Navy commander, the government's opposition leader and the husband of new President Chandrika Kumaratunga, not to mention India's Prime Minister, Rajiv Gandhi. The major conflict is centered in the north and eastern Jaffna Peninsula, and is slowly being compressed to the north.

Just when things seem to be going the government's way, the pesky Liberation Tigers of Tamil Eelam (LTTE) blow a few Sri Lankan navy ships out of the water and lay siege to major army bases. Or, of course, they revert to their time-tested tradition of car-bombing Colombo skyscrapers into tiny glass shards, shredding a couple of hundred innocents in the process. These guys make Northern Ireland's IRA look like a bunch of schoolkids with scraped knees pounding caps with a couple of rocks. Perhaps even more ingrained into our memories than tattered duchesses staggering half-naked and bloodied out of Harrods—than body parts twitching on the street in front of a blown-out Sarajevo supermarket—are scenes of downtown Colombo, ripe with screaming Sinhalese, fresh from amputations they hadn't paid for. The glass is falling like a hard rain, unheard by the hundreds whose eardrums have exploded like an aerosol can tossed into a fire.

Known as Serindip in ancient times and then as Ceylon, Sri Lanka is made up of a teardrop-shaped main island and groups of smaller islands 50 miles off the southern coast of India. Sri Lanka, with its lush jungles and dramatic interior, has been called one of the most beautiful islands in the world. Thirty-one percent of the island is mountainous jungle nestling ancient cities such as Polonnaruwa and Anuradhapura. The 833 miles of coastline are primarily pristine, coral-fringed beaches, basking in the sun beneath towering and jutting coconut palms, caressed by the lapping azure waters of the Indian Ocean and the Bay of Bengal—a beautiful destination for you to put on your island-hopping itinerary. Unfortunately, the Liberation Tigers of Tamil Eelam (LTTE) have put this enchanted isle on their island-popping itinerary. And they take no prisoners.

The majority of the island's population are Sinhalese Buddhists, the troublesome minority being the ethnic Tamil, who comprise about 20 percent of the population. The ethnic Tamils, virtually indistinguishable from the Sinhalese, save for different languages, are seeking independence. Muslims make up the difference at about 7 percent.

Although the Sinhalese and Tamils have been at odds with each other for more than 2000 years, much of the tension and fighting that has gripped the island has occurred only in recent years. The fighting began in earnest after a Tamil Tiger ambush of an army patrol in the Jaffna area in 1983. Sinhalese all over the island then went on a rampage for the next three days, murdering and looting Tamils and burning down their villages. Perhaps 2000 Tamils were killed in the uprising.

The north and the east of the island have been war zones for the better part of 10 years. Although fighting and terrorism cooled around 1990, and tourists had written Sri Lanka off as a battlefield in the mid-1980s, tourism surged once again until the government's offensive against the Tamils beginning in October 1995. Although areas in the south are still relatively safe, nowhere on the island is 100 percent secure. The former Tiger "capital" of Jaffna was taken by government

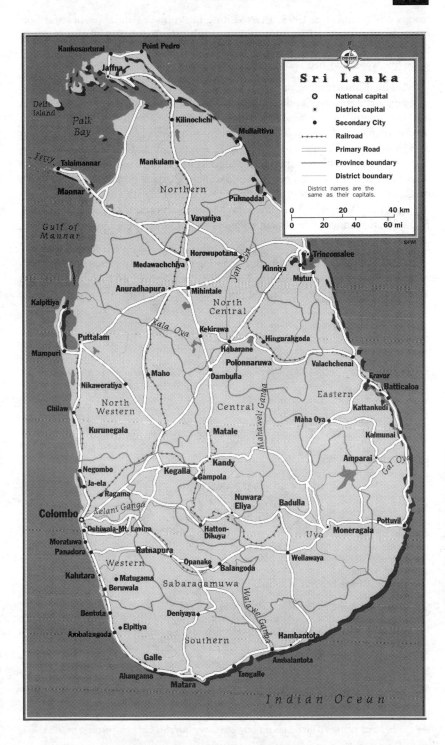

troops on December 5, 1995. Even visiting the ruins at Anuradhapura and Pol-onnaruwa is risky. The Batticaloa region remains the Tamil Tigers' principal area for staging operations in the south. In July 1992, a train on the Colombo-Batti-caloa line was ambushed and some 40 people were killed.

President Kumaratunga, during her election campaign in 1994, promised to find a peaceful means of ending the war, and the government offered a proposal for "devolution" to the Tigers, granting Tamil provinces in the north and east nearly complete autonomy. The government move was lauded both internation-ally, by moderate Tamils, and by Sri Lanka's imposing and Tiger-backing neigh-bor, India. But a restless military persuaded Kumaratunga, whose ruling coalition party had a majority of only one vote, to launch an attack on Jaffna and the north on October 17, 1995. Government forces were spectacularly successful in captur-ing Jaffna in December, but took heavy losses. According to the government, 500 soldiers died while nearly 2000 Tigers were killed. The guerrillas, of course, claimed the reverse figures.

But the LTTE wasn't vanquished, remaining in control of a vast area of the Jaff-na peninsula known as the Vanni. From their stronghold of Kilinochchi in the Vanni, the Tigers have been regrouping as a bickering parliament trades insults over the devolution legislation—which has not yet been approved.

The Scoop

The Sinhalese Buddhists are the majority. The minority Tamils want independence. The two groups have been massacring each other since 1983. By 1988, the entire country was in turmoil and the economy was crippled. The tourist doors began opening up again in 1990. But the hatches were battened down soon afterwards, as terrorism and renewed fighting resumed again. The government army doubled in size to 75,000 from 1983 to 1992 in order to fight the Liberation Tigers of Tamil Eelam (Tamil Tigers, or LTTE). More than 50,000 people have died since 1983. The Tigers have been pushed back into the jungle where leader Velupillai Prabhakaran vows to continue their fight. President Kumaratunga claimed in January 1996 that the war would be won in 12 months. In 1995, more than 6 percent of Sri Lanka's gross domestic product was shoveled into the 13-year-old civil war. To put that in perspective, if the U.S. were to do likewise, fully a third of a trillion dollars would be spent. In December 1995, government forces took the rebel capital of Jaffna in the north. But it hardly silenced the Ti-gers. On January 31, 1996, LTTE guerrillas crashed a truck packed with explosives into Sri Lanka's central bank in Colombo. The blast killed 53 people and wounded more than 1400.

And the Tigers didn't lick their wounds simply by trashing a few buildings in the capital. They've continued to be a formidable military force in the field. In July 1996, LTTE forces be-sieged the key northern military base of Mullaittivu about 170 miles north of Colombo. They took the base on July 22 after a five-day siege. Although the government claimed the base was still in government hands, Tamil Tiger spokeswoman Helen Whitehead told *DP* in London a rather different story, one in which the results were the loss of 1208 government soldiers and 241 guerrillas (including 68 women fighters). "We have taken the base at Mullaittivu," White-head said. Sri Lanka claimed its forces killed 400 rebels, while suffering only 300 casualties of its own. A couple of days later, government forces retook Mullaittivu, finding alive only 11 of the 1200 troops stationed there. The siege marked the bloodiest fighting of the 14-year-old conflict. And just to keep Colombo on its toes, two LTTE bombs aboard a commuter train in the capital killed nearly 70 innocents on July 24. Obviously, Sri Lanka is partying on.

The Players

Velupillai Prabhakaran and The Liberation Tigers of Tamil Eelam (LTTE)

The LTTE began in 1972, and today it is the largest Tamil separatist guerrilla group. The Tigers have maintained their hard-line position on separatism and conducted numerous military and terrorist acts to further their cause. They are most famous for their suicide attacks on prominent politicians. These attacks not only snuff their intended victims, but, because of the type of bomb employed (usually a very powerful explosive unleashing a volley of shrapnel or metal pellets), they usually take out a couple of dozen innocents as well. It is believed that LTTE members were responsible for the 1993 assassination of President Ranasinghe Premadasa. The Tigers are experiencing an internal rift between leader Velupillai Prabhakaran and his top deputy Gopalaswamy Mahendrarajah. (Mahendrarajah was accused by Prabhakaran of plotting with the Indian government against him. Prabhakaran fled into the jungle to avoid reprisals after trying to arrest Mahendrarajah in a surprise raid on April 23, 1994.)

The LTTE maintains its own navy, called the "Sea Tigers." Operating in the Jaffna Lagoon, each light boat carries five or six guerrillas who attack Indian Navy ships or make landings to attack Sri Lankan army units. Sea Tigers also are suicide frogmen who blow up navy ships with self-detonated explosives.

Bombs are the favored method of Tamil suicide guerrillas. One does not know if this is due to the lack of timing devices or just old-fashioned bravado. In any case, the suicide bombers are revered among the Tamils. Their pictures are defiantly and proudly displayed along the road and in the houses of their families. Their families are accorded a distinction equal to the mothers of saints. How do you spot a suicide bomber or Black Tiger? Despite the fact that an average Tamil lives until he is over 70, most suicide bombers are young, in their early 20s; they wear a pendant around their necks with a cyanide capsule dangling from the end. The cyanide will kill in 5 minutes when bitten.

A favorite mode of assassination is for the bomber to drive right up to the victim on a scooter and detonate the bomb.

The LTTE lost its "capital" of Jaffna in the final weeks of 1995 and is on the run from a major offensive by the government. The Tamils have retaliated by slaughtering innocent villagers to slow the government offensive. Prabhakaran, widely believed responsible for the 1991 assassination of Indian Prime Minister Rajiv Gandhi and the 1993 snuffing of Sri Lankan President Ranasinghe Premadasa as well as a wave of other suicide bombings, is hiding out in the Vanni forests plotting his next target.

The Tamil Tigers have a seaborne arm called the Sea Tigers and a suicide division called the Black Tigers. They have used microlight aircraft and submarines in their attacks. They even have all-women units.

Don't be fooled. These petite-elite squads aren't the island's Olympic crewing team, an audition for American Gladiators, nor a shoot for a Sri Lanka tourism board ad. These ladies are nasty, and they don't cook. The only cleaning they do is ethnic. In fact, the Tigers as a whole take a certain pride in their scrub jobs of ethnic Sinhalese, butchering entire villages. The 3000 lasses who help make up the Tamil Tigresses don't seem to mind taking a bullet or two, either. Some 68 female LTTE guerrillas were whacked during the siege of Mullaittivu. And on July 4, 1996, a female suicide bomber adorned in designer explosive devices crashed into a Jaffna motorcade on her scooter trying to assassinate the minister of construction. He survived, but 23 people were killed and 60 others were injured by the blast. Tamil Tiger strength is estimated to be between 6000 and 10,000. If you want to talk to some of the Tamil Tigers and get the scoop for yourself, you can—but you better have a good reason. They talked to *DP*, but only after "checking us out."

Liberation Tigers of Tamil Eelam
211 Katherine Rd.
London E6 1BU
United Kingdom
☎/FAX 011-44-181-470-8593
Speak with Helen Whitehead, but she may have more questions for you than you have for her.

The Government

The current president and daughter of two former Sri Lankan prime ministers, Chandrika Kumaratunga, 50, is not letting the assassination of her husband by the LTTE get in the way of the peace process. In November 1994, she sent delegates to begin discussions on ending the 12-year-old civil war. The protracted talks ended up with the government's proposed offer of autonomy for Tamil provinces in the north and east.

The Sri Lankan military is small and has required help from the Indian Army to control the LTTE. The total strength of the armed forces is 105,900, including recalled reservists. The breakdown is 89,000 army, 8900 navy and 8000 air force (including 2000 active reservists). To hasten the fight against the LTTE, the government has been on a shopping binge. Added to the arsenal in early 1996 were three Israeli-made Kfir fighters, three Soviet-model attack helicopters, and a Chinese-made antisubmarine vessel to pick off swimming suicide bombers.

The Tamil United Liberation Front (TULF)

The Tamil Unite ' Liberation Front (TULF) is an alliance of a number of Tamil groups. It was formed shortly after the LTTE (1974). Originally named the Tamil Liberation Front, the TULF is working for (as opposed to killing for) the creation of an autonomous Tamil region. They are moderates and criticized by other Tamil groups for being too complacent in light of the Indian Army militant crackdown on Tamils.

Eelam Revolutionary Organization of Students (EROS)

Organized in 1985, the Eelam Revolutionary Organization of Students (EROS) is a smaller Tamil separatist group that became the third-largest group in Parliament following the 1989 elections. In 1990, all 13 of the EROS members in Parliament resigned their seats, stating that they "do not want to be dormant spectators who witness the torment of our people."

The little-known group Ellalan Force of Tamil rebels has threatened to attack tourist hotels in southern Sri Lanka. There are also other groups, like the Maoist JVP, who want all foreign-owned estates returned to the people. Sri Lanka's return to normalcy, which followed the apparent decimation of the JVP and the ensuing negotiations with the LTTE, was short-lived, when, on June 11, 1990, the LTTE initiated hostilities against the GSL in the eastern district of Amparai and Batticaloa; the fighting quickly spread to the north.

Getting In

A passport, onward/return ticket and proof of sufficient funds (US$15 per day) are required. A tourist visa can be granted at the time of entry into Sri Lanka, and may be valid for a maximum period of 90 days. For business travel or travel on an official or diplomatic passport, visas are required and must be obtained in advance.

Business visas are valid for one month and require an application form, two photos, a company letter, a letter from a sponsoring agency in Sri Lanka, a copy of an onward/return ticket, and a US$5 fee. Include US$6 postage for return of your passport by registered mail.

Yellow fever and cholera immunizations are needed if arriving from an infected area.

For further information, contact the following:

Embassy of the Democratic Socialist Republic of Sri Lanka
2148 Wyoming Ave., N.W.
Washington, D.C. 20008
☎ *(202) 483-4025*
or nearest consulate:

California
☎ *(805) 873-7224*

Hawaii
☎ *(808) 735-1622*

New Jersey
☎ *(201) 627-7855*

New York
☎ *(212) 986-7040*

or the Sri Lankan consulate in New York. There are also honorary Sri Lankan consulates in Los Angeles, Honolulu, New Orleans and Newark.

Getting Around

About a third of Sri Lanka's 47,070 miles of road are paved. There are 1210 miles of heavily traveled railroad and 14 airfields; the only major airport is in Colombo. There aren't any internal flights in Sri Lanka, so the traveler is limited to buses and trains. Trains are arguably more comfortable than buses, but are slower and don't service as many areas of the island as do buses. The train stations, although dilapidated, aren't nearly as crowded as those in India, where rail travel is the lifeblood of Indians. However, don't fall asleep on the trains. You'll more than likely get ripped off by a thief.

Dangerous Places

There is a long-standing armed conflict between the Sri Lankan government and the Tamil extremist group, the Liberation Tigers of Tamil Eelam (LTTE). Fighting between government security forces and the LTTE continues in northern and eastern areas of the island. Sri Lankan defense regulations forbid travel in much of the island's northern area.

National Parks
Remote forested areas, such as Wilpattu and Galoya national parks, are considered especially unsafe. Rebels like the peace and quiet and may take exception to your need to explore and save their rain forest. They're doing just fine beneath their blanket of triple-canopy forest hidden in deep bunkers—excellent cover from air force helicopter and bomb attacks.

Jaffna
In retreating from their stronghold at Jaffna in November 1995, LTTE Tigers booby-trapped virtually the entire city with trip-wired antitank and antipersonnel mines. Anything that could be picked up—from books to cooking utensils to clothes on the floor—were booby-trapped by the fleeing rebels. The city's population plummeted from 120,000 to a mere 6000 in just a few short weeks. Like Paris in August—with land mines.

Jaffna Lagoon
The lagoon has been declared a shoot-on-sight zone by the Sri Lankan government. The Sea Tigers (the marine version of the LTTE) operate small gunboats to conduct naval- and marine-style raids. Each boat usually carries five or six guerrillas. When *DP* used these boats to visit the Tigers, the boat in front of us was blown from the water by a naval shell. Usually, though, the high-speed boats manage to outrun the slower naval gunners.

North and East
Currently, fighting between the government forces and the LTTE continues in much of the north and east. Although the current situation appears to be contained in these

regions, security checkpoints have become the norm along major crossroads in and around Colombo, as a result of the March 1991 bombing assassination of Deputy Defense Minister Ranjan Wijertaine, the June 1991 bombing of the Ministry of Defense's Joint Operations Command and the January 1996 bombing of the Central Bank of Sri Lanka in Colombo—just a few hundred yards from President Chandrika Kumaratunga's office. (The LTTE is believed to be responsible for al three incidents.) Travelers should be alert to the continuing threat of terrorism in Colombo.

Colombo

The LTTE bombings here are just plain scary. On January 31, 1996, a blast took at least 53 lives and wounded 1400 others. However, in general, the level of criminal activity in Colombo is moderate in relation to other cities of the world. Nonetheless, visitors should be aware that petty "street" crimes are not uncommon. Although pickpocketing and purse snatchings do occur with some frequency, violent crimes such as armed robberies are rare, particularly among the expatriot and tourist population. Residential crime, historically a problem in the city, has been on the decline. The Sri Lankan police, though limited in resources, generally make every effort to provide assistance to foreign visitors. This is particularly so within the confines of Colombo. Police coverage tends to be less reliable outside of the city. Important police emergency telephone numbers for the greater Colombo area:

Police Emergency (24 hours daily)
☎ 433333

Cinnamon Gardens Police Station
☎ 693377

Colpetty Police Station
☎ 20131

Bambalapitiya Police Station
☎ 593208

Dangerous Things

Political Rallies

The Black Tigers, or suicide bombers, cast their votes and reduce the pool of voters by blowing themselves and anyone else in a 50-yard radius into small fleshy pieces. Using massive explosives packed around ball bearings, pellets and other homemade shrapnel, they can kill up to 60 people at a time. Prominent national leaders and senior military personnel have been targets and/or victims of terrorist violence, which, of course, makes anyone else in the neighborhood a target, as well.

Road Blocks

Travelers who encounter roadblocks staffed by security personnel are wise to listen closely and heed any instructions given.

Dudes with Amulets Around Their Necks in Colombo

At least 60 LTTE suicide bombers are combing the streets of Colombo searching for somebody important to blow up. Because security is so tight around President Kumaratunga and other high-ranking government officials, the bombers have started stalking anyone with a title or who's gotten his or her name in a newspaper—even leaders of the opposition. Assisted suicide has never been easier.

Getting Sick

Medical facilities are limited—you'll find one doctor and 27 hospital beds for every 10,000 people. Doctors and hospitals often expect immediate cash payment for health services. Malaria is prevalent in many areas outside of Colombo. Visitors must take precautions against malaria, hepatitis and yellow fever prior to arriving in Sri Lanka. Rabies is common in many animals in

Sri Lanka; take some comfort that the painful injections against rabies can be obtained locally. Tap water is laced with everything from amoebas to horses and should not be ingested unless boiled for a couple of decades, strained through an offset press and carpet-bombed with iodine.

Nuts and Bolts

The major ethnic group is the Sinhalese (74 percent) followed by the Tamils (18 percent) and Moors (7 percent). Burghers, Malays and Veddhas comprise the last 1 percent. The Sinhalese are predominantly Buddhist and the Tamils are Hindu. Christians and Muslims make up only about 8 percent of the religious pie.

English is widely spoken in this former British colony. Sinhala is the official language, but Tamil is recognized as a national language. As one would expect in the Indian Ocean, the heat and humidity can wring you out like a wet sponge in a boxing match. Since the British were fond of colonizing tropical destinations with cooler hill stations, you can expect cool, moist weather up high. The average temperature along the coast is a sweltering 80° F with little change all year.There are two cooling monsoon seasons, the southwest and the northeast monsoons, which dump about 100 inches of rain every year.

Embassy Location and Registration

Updated information on travel and security within Sri Lanka is available at the U.S. embassy:

U.S. Embassy
> *P.O. Box 106*
> *210 Galle Road*
> *Colombo*
> ☎ *[94] (1) 448007*
> *FAX [94] (1) 437345*

U.S. citizens are encouraged to register at the U.S. embassy upon arrival in Sri Lanka.

Embassy Locations

Canadian Embassy in Sri Lanka
> *6 Gregory's Road*
> *Cinnamon Gardens*
> *Colombo 7*
> ☎ *[94] (1) 695841*

Postal address:

> *P.O. Box 1006*
> *Columbo, Sri Lanka*

Sri Lankan Embassy in Canada
> *85 Range Road, Suites 102–104*
> *Ottawa, Ontario, Canada K1N 8J6*
> ☎ *(613) 233-8440/8449*
> *FAX (613) 238-8448*

Dangerous Days

01/31/1996	Colombo blast killed 53, injure 1400. LTTE believed responsible.
12/05/1995	Jaffna fell to government forces.
10/17/1995	Government offensive of the north began.
05/01/1993	Assassination of President Ranasinghe Premadasa.
09/04/1992	Dasain (Hindu) Festival.
06/13/1990	The Liberation Tigers of Tamil Eelam (LTTE) launched a renewed offensive against Sri Lankan government forces by storming at least 24 police stations in northern and eastern Sri Lanka. Several hundred police officers were taken hostage and a number of them later killed.

Dangerous Days

08/18/1987	Grenade attack on Sri Lankan parliament. One legislator was killed.
07/29/1987	Indo-Sri Lankan peace accords.
07/20/1986	Sinhalese rioting.
05/14/1985	Tamil separatists killed more than 150 people in an attack on a Buddhist shrine at Anuradhapura.
07/23/1983	The killing of 13 Sri Lankan soldiers in an ambush by Tamil militants touched off widespread anti-Tamil violence that left as many as 2000 Tamils dead and 100,000 homeless.
05/22/1972	Republic Day. Also known as National Heroes' Day.
11/24/1954	LTTE founder's birthday. Prabhakaran birthday is marked by the LTTE as "Heroes Week," which also commemorates LTTE members who have died in battle.
02/04/1948	Independence Day.
05/24	Birth of Buddha.
01/14	Tamil Thai Pongal Day.

Khartoum

Sudan
★★★

The Cauldron of Hate

There is a great seething cauldron of hate fired by the two-headed monster—love of Allah and hatred of the Great Satan (the West). Its nexus is in Sudan. Here, young men and women from Third World countries learn how to love the purity of Allah and how to further the cause of Islam by killing, maiming and terrorizing the corrupted servants of Satan. What that means is the moment you decide to get on a plane to Sudan, you've become the enemy and are taking a vacation behind enemy lines.

Sudan is cursed not only by poverty (a per-capita income of only US$330), its size (it is the largest country in Africa) and a history of fundamentalist leaders who declare Holy War on the West, but it is also crippled by its dubious distinction of straddling the uneasy and unmarked border between the arid Islamic Arab north and the lush, animistic black south. These two cultures have never dwelled in harmony, and, in Sudan, they never will. The two tribes continue to battle, as the north persists in imposing its political will on the tribal south. The U.N. estimates that the war has caused 5 million refugees, of which one million have starved to death.

Sudan is 70 percent Muslim, 20 percent animist and 5 percent Christian—a bad mix on any continent. Ethnically, it's an even nastier brew: Sudan is 52 percent black, 39 percent Arab and 6 percent Beja. The hatred between the north and south has killed more than 500,000 people and driven 4.5 million others from their homes. Even the rebel factions are known for their intolerance of each other. They wage warfare against each other, using starvation and terror as weapons of war. The SPLA (Sudan People's Liberation Army) rebel factions have been known to murder international aid workers and will not even guarantee safe passage for relief aircraft in case they may be providing food or medicine for the enemy. The north, with its equally zealous adherence to Islam, threw every Christian missionary out of the southern city of Juba in 1992.

Since Iran has 23 years left on its leases of bases in Port Sudan and Suakin, there are thousands of Iranian soldiers stationed and training in Sudan. There is also an Iranian-funded radio station based in Port Sudan that broadcasts Islamic and Iranian propaganda to Egypt and other Arab countries. Sudan's strategic position and its holy alliance with Iran give it a powerful presence in the Red Sea and the Horn of Africa. Iran's recent meddling, and the resultant civil war in nearby Yemen, might provide a good reason to dust off the domino theory formerly applied to Southeast Asia. Iran pays its new friend with oil and military supplies, while it receives strategic real estate and full cooperation from Sudan. Sudan also has new lethal exports to pay its militant friend: murder and mayhem.

Some side effects of this new export business include the terrorist attack on the World Trade Center in New York, the murders of more than 210 of the Algerian defense forces by Algerian fundamentalist groups and the continuing attacks on tourists and officials in Egypt. Although a Muslim country, Egypt is considered too soft on Israel and becoming too Westernized.

Sudan is a country known for its unrelenting heat and sandstorms, and its inability to create a stable government or a unified country. Sudan (Jamhuryat es-Sudan—the Republic of the Sudan) was conquered by Egypt in 1820–'21 and was ruled from Cairo until 1881, when a revolt led by the Mahdi, a charismatic self-proclaimed prophet, began. The Mahdist revolt succeeded in 1885, and its leaders controlled the region until an Anglo-Egyptian force invaded in 1898. The nation was ruled jointly by Britain and Egypt until 1954, when it became an independent state.

Since then, there has been a succession of military leaders and little relief from overwhelming poverty. In 1972, the Addis Ababa accord gave the south limited autonomy (an oxymoron) that ended the war against the Anyana guerrilla movement. But in the early 1980s, the SPLA (Sudan People's Liberation Army) came into being to fight the same battle. In 1984, Islamic law was introduced and the SPLA began fighting in earnest. The SPLA was supported by Cuba, Ethiopia, Libya and, strangely, by Israel. In 1985 Nimeiri's regime was overthrown in a coup and democratic elections were held. "Democracy" lasted until yet another coup in 1989 brought in the current ruler, General Omar Hassan Ahmad Al-Bashir, in June of that year.

The Ethiopians have had their hands in the pie since November of 1987. Khartoum has also sought the assistance of Iran and Libya, including MIG-25s flown

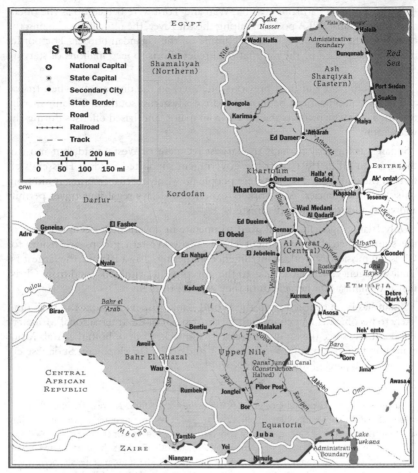

by Libyans. Even Iraqi and the PLO (Palestine Liberation Organization) lent a hand by flying bombing missions over the south.

Ethiopia hasn't meddled in Sudan's affairs since the ouster of Mengistu, allowing the SPLA to go on a roll. They almost took the city of Juba in the spring of 1989, when a factional group led by Garang's second in command, Riek Machar, created SPLA/United. The two southern factions began to battle each other. In 1993, the two southern SPLA groups called a truce after killing thousands of each other's members. The CIA is busy working to get the two sides to kiss and make up.

Today, the Southern Sudan is controlled by the SPLA, with the exception of the city of Juba, which is still a garrison town. The Islamic fundamentalist military government of General Omar al-Bashir finally launched its long-awaited offensive against the rebel Sudan People's Liberation Army in February 1994 in an effort to end the 25- year civil war. Tens of thousands of refugees have fled to the Ugandan border.

The government garrisons at Juba, Wau and Torit were beefed up as the offensive began against SPLA positions along the Kit River, the ultimate goal being the capture of the rebel supply base of Nimule on the Ugandan border. The border routes are also used by the international relief efforts to feed millions of starving Sudanese.

The government launched previous offensives in the dry season, when troops and heavy equipment can be moved more easily across southern Sudan's marshy terrain. This tactic protects the rebels from major land-based offenses during the wet season.

Sudan was formerly perhaps the largest recipient of Western aid, but most of that was cut off in 1991, after the government supported Saddam Hussein's efforts in the Gulf War. The Sudanese people now only receive emergency aid from outside relief agencies. Aid workers experience delays regarding travel permits and visas, and sometimes are arrested.

Only Islamic agencies are allowed to operate in government-occupied areas of the south, since the government claims many Western groups are fronts for Christian missionary work or intelligence-gathering. Dawa Islamia, the largest Islamic aid agency, with close links to the government, withholds food from Christian and animist Southerners until they convert to Islam.

Sudan has been expelled from the World Bank, suspended from the IMF (and likely to become the first country to be thrown out of the International Monetary Fund entirely since the fund was created) and kicked out of both the Arab Monetary Fund and Arab Fund for Economic and Social Development. Sudanese experience 300 percent inflation per year.

The Scoop

Sudan is a large, underdeveloped country in northeastern Africa. Tourism facilities are minimal. U.S. citizens are warned against all travel to Sudan because of potential violence within the country. Due to continuing security concerns, the U.S. Department of State closed the U.S. embassy in Khartoum in the beginning of 1996, although Sudan still maintains an embassy in Washington. Travel anywhere outside the capital city of Khartoum requires the permission of the government of Sudan. In March 1996, President Omar Hassan al-Bashir was reelected with a claimed 75 percent of the vote. Although the government stated that there was a 72 percent turnout at the polls, only 5 percent of those eligible voted in the election. Sudan is also known as a terrorist's sanctuary, harboring nasties from Egypt, Morocco, Nigeria, Kenya and other countries. Three men who were involved in the plot to assassinate Egyptian President Mubarak are in Sudan getting their hair cut and nails done and watching the V Channel, despite an OAU call for the government to hand over the thugs. There are land mines on the main road on the Sudanese side of the border with Eritrea. There are an estimated 15,000 militants living or training in Sudan.

Sudan's conflict is unique, because it is the first time that black Africans had told an Arab power to get stuffed. On the downside, they have been waging this war since 1955 and decimated their people, so it may not have been such a wise idea.

The original bad boys in the south were called the Anya-Nya, which means Snake Poison or, more specifically, the Venom of the Gabon Viper in the Madi, Moru and Lotuko languages. They even had a snappy logo that showed two snakes bordering a charging buffalo with an arrow down the middle. The first real warfare began in 1963 and ended up with their leaders and soldiers being captured and hung. So much for T-shirt sales. The next tactic was to create incidents that would attract the U.N. and create a separation of north and south. There were about 2000 active combatants in 1964. From then on, it was a steady diet of attack against attack and reprisal against reprisal until the north by its brutality had managed to create a real civil war.

The only curious incident was in July of 1969, when 39-year-old Rolf Steiner, a former SS Hitler Youth Group member, Legionnaire and veteran of Indochina, Algeria, the Congo and Biafra, showed up. Steiner was rebuffed by the Anya-Nya and then tried to create the tiny Anyidi Revolutionary Government in a small area in southern Equatoria region near the Zaire and Ugandan border. He applied for citizenship in his own little kingdom but was kicked out in November. When he crossed over to Uganda, he was arrested and put on trial in Khartoum. He was convicted of inciting war against the government, illegally entering the Sudan and distributing medical drugs, and was sentenced to death, which was commuted to 20 years in prison.

The early years also brought in the Russians, who traded guns for the cotton in the north (and made a handsome profit), and the Israelis to the south (who deny any involvement).

Garang's SPLA faction comprises about 80 percent of the rebels. The other two factions are the SSIM and the al-Ghazal faction of the SPLA.

The Players

Lieutenant General Omar Hassan Ahmad al-Bashir

This is the leader of the 15-member National Salvation Revolutionary Council, a junta comprised entirely of military officers. Reigning in a state of emergency and with a suspending constitution, al-Bashir has brought Sudan into the swelling ranks of despot-ruled countries in Africa. The people get their news from the daily newspaper of the armed forces. There have been only three periods of civilian rule since 1955. He continues to appoint National Islamic Front (NIF) loyalists, though more for their religious zeal than political skills. The NIF leader Dr. Hassan Abdullah al-Turabi was the minister of justice and attorney general under Nimeiri and was the architect of both the 1983 and 1991 versions of *Sharia* (or Islamic law). Before the new federal structure was introduced, *Sharia* only applied to administrative and civil cases and not to criminal cases. The first victim of the new *Sharia* was a Christian southern Sudanese petty thief, whose punishment was the "cross-amputation" of his right hand and left foot. Nimeira was said to have fainted while attending his first amputation. Al-Bashir is not so squeamish about carrying out the wishes of al-Turabi's NIF. He is busy battling the 55,000 or so armed Southerners with his 68,000 soldiers. Al-Bashir was reelected as president in a fraud-tainted, "supervised" election March 23, 1996.

Dr. Hassan Abdullah al-Turabi

The man pulling the strings. Intelligent, well educated and determined to be the first fundamentalist on his block to have his own fundamentalist state. He has described himself as being the symbol of a new movement that will change the history of humanity. His goal is to unify the billion or so Muslims under one guiding theocratic government. He was educated in London and earned his doctorate at Sorbonne in 1964. Five years later, he became leader of what was then a small and fanatical group of religious nuts. Turabi became the head of the Muslim Brotherhood, only to be banished from Sudan less than a month later, when General Nimeiri's Marxist coup made Turabi's style of religion out of style. Saudi Arabia took him in and the Brotherhood took hold among the 350,000 professional Sudanese working in oil-rich but skills-poor Saudia Arabia. They provided a source of funds, which Turabi used to send the brightest Sudanese to Western universities to get their Ph.D.s. The Brotherhood was busy turning out doctors, lawyers, writers and teachers, who would then take the message of Islam back to other Muslim countries. They created the Islamic African Relief Fund (now the Islamic Relief Association) to help with the millions of African refugees in sub-Saharan Africa. In the mid-1970s, they created Faisal Islamic Bank to handle the deposits of expat workers in the Gulf States. Islamic banks charge no interest, pay no interest and share profits with their depositors. The bank made loans to small businessmen, taxi drivers and shopkeepers.

After building a strong financial and political base from Saudi Arabia, Turabi returned to Sudan in 1977 as attorney general under Nimeiri's program of national reconciliation with former enemies. In 1983, Nimeiri declared *Sharia*, or Islamic law, after a particularly vivid dream. Turabi was not the force behind the change. Although Turabi is extreme in his long-term plans, he is a moderate in affecting change.

The dramatic changeover did not affect the political climate as much as it influenced the financial health of Sudan. Nimeiri instituted the 354-day year, and taxes were abolished and replaced with voluntary tithing. Interest was abolished, and the resultant loss of revenue and fiscal chaos plunged Sudan into bankruptcy. Sudan was US$8 billion in the hole and sinking fast. When the government couldn't cut a check for US$250 million, they went into default with the IMF. By March of 1985, Nimeiri blamed the country's slide into debt on the Islamic laws now ostensibly enforced by Turabi. Leaders of the Muslim Brotherhood were removed from political office, and Turabi was put in jail. Three months later, Nimeiri was ousted in a coup, and the first thing General Siwar el-Dahab did was dispatch a plane to fly Turabi back from prison to Khartoum. By then, Turabi was head of the National Islamic Front, originally an opposition party. But Turabi, once again, became attorney general. The Muslim Brotherhood was welcomed back into politics. It ran most of the newspapers and businesses and began to build a strong base in the military.

In 1989, the end of the war in Afghanistan released upon the world thousands of hardened war veterans. The Mujahedin were well-trained volunteers from various Muslim countries who had little chance of employment but were well armed and tempered to a hard fanatic edge by years of hardship in Afghanistan. The warehouses of Afghanistan and Pakistan overflowed white containers of weapons and ammunition that the U.S. had sent in to be used against the Russians.

This surplus of Muslim warriors was ready-made for the Muslim Brotherhood. Turabi realized that God had sent him the tools of his next great project. Sudan became a provisioning and training point for the Mujahedin. In August and September of 1993 alone, four planeloads of weapons were flown in from Kabul. The Arab-Sunni Muslim Brothers even bit the bullet and forged a link with their traditional enemies, the Shia Muslims of Iran. The Brothers began sending men to Iran for training as security officers, even though they had sent men to fight Iran in the Iran-Iraq war. Turabi also invited Iran to play in his backyard. This includes use of seaports and training bases for terrorists.

Sudan, like Iraq and Libya, is now an outcast, not only financially (Sudan was removed from the support of the IMF in 1987). Western pressure is actually strengthening the fundamentalist movement. Meanwhile, Turabi has taken up the mantle of the Ayatollah Khomeini; he continues to give lectures, write books and spread the concept of a world Islamic union free from Western corruption. Today, the Muslim Brotherhood has strong membership in Algeria, Egypt, the Israeli Occupied Territories, Jordan, Tunisia and Yemen. It has members in all Islamic countries. Total armed forces in mid-1990 numbered more than 75,700 men in active service.

The Sudanese

Sudanese heads-of-state come and go. You'd think that in the midst of the current Islamic tide, at least Sadiq el Mahdi, leader of the Umma Party (in Arabic, *Umma* means the Muslim community) and grandson of the zealot who took Khartoum from Gordon, could maintain power. He could not. The state seems inherently unstable.

But short of violent revolution in Khartoum, Hassan Turabi and his National Islamic Front will be the Sudan's most focused, coherent power. Not the most popular. Turabi's currency is popular will and public sentiment, but he is not the master of a majority, and if he represents anything it is this: The fact, often lost in the West, that Islamic fundamentalism has many faces, and the fact that the Sudan is far from the simple place it is thought to be.

Politics goes back a long way here. The Sudanese were among the first pharaohs. The Sudanese were among the first Christians. The Sudanese were among the first Muslims, and, to this day, they adhere to such a pure and fundamental Islam, and speak its language with such pure distinction (an Arabic that may be closer to Muhammad's than the Arabic spoken in Arabia) that they are commonly reckoned to be Arabs. Indeed, they are an immensely handsome people, tall and grand in their deliberately simple white *jelabas*. But to this imperfect eye, they look less Arab, with darker skin and heavier features, than the Bedj tribes of the Red Sea Hills, Kipling's forbidding fuzzie-wuzzies. They regard themselves as Arab and they're recognized as Arab, this pleases them to no end, and, in the complexity of their feelings toward the *kaffir* (there's another Arabic word; in South Africa today the equivalent of nigger, but coined by the Arabs) can perhaps be found their predisposition for complex politics.

Not long ago in the Sudan, there were basically three parties, two of which were religious. Followers of the Khatmiya sect made up the one that demanded independence most insistently from the Brits and Egyptians. Followers of the Mahdi made up the other—Sudanese just as eager for independence, but with baggage that made foreign governments a little nervous. The secular party was simply a creature of the army that took over the government by force in 1956, because the two Islamic parties were locked in what amounted to Islamic gridlock. Eventually, they were overthrown, but not punished, so in a few years they took over again, yielded again, took over again....

During the sixties, as Marxism swept the Third World and often toppled military dictatorships, in the Sudan it was the other way around. Military governments, swayed by Nasser, moved steadily left, and, meantime, in command of the state's propaganda apparatus, they set about cultivating a new generation of Sudanese leaders in their own leftist image.

Often on the outside looking in, the two Islamic parties continued to command electorates, but, once elected, they just couldn't govern. The last time around, it was a coalition of the two Islamic parties, star-crossed from the beginning, and, once again, the military took over.

This time, though, the military is taking over in the name of rising Islamic sentiment, and backed by a civilian party, the new, highly focused Islamic Front, so militantly religious that Turabi has been virtually able to position the two Islamic parties as secular. This is not an outlandish notion. The Front is militantly Islamic, and, though Sadiq el Mahdi is a Muslim through and through, and the grandson of the greatest firebrand of them all, he is nonetheless a couple of comfortable generations removed from the Khalifa's backcountry fervor—and an Oxbridge man, to boot.

But this is the Sudan, and anything this complicated is bound to get even more complicated. While Turabi's Muslim credentials go way back, those of many in his Islamic Front are a lot more suspect than Sadiq el Mahdi's. The reason is that more than a few of these guys are simply the constituency developed by the old military governments, Islamic partisans who were not so long ago leftist, Arab-Socialist, the most secular of Muslim Sudanese, Jerry Rubin in drag as Jerry Falwell.

The Sudan could provide a great case in point for proponents of displacement theories. Denied alcohol, constrained to behave with great dignity in the male world, and with even greater reserve should he find himself among proper females, the devout Muslim seems to have developed an incomparable sweet tooth (*helweh, helweh,* sweet, is among the finest of compliments) and, along with it, a considerable appetite, sanctioned by Islam, for buying concubines, or seizing them as a prize of Holy War. Among the Baggara of Kordofan and the Bedouin tribes of Darfur, raids on the south have always been and still are part of the year's rhythm—like calving and harvest. The Khedive (as if he cared, it was Britain calling the shots) sent Chinese Gordon, fresh from the Boxer Rebellion, to stop it and to raise some taxes while he was at it. With heroic effort, he had some modest success, which is to say he made a hell on earth for the Sudanese, who love their harems. Throughout history, whenever hell has descended upon the Islamic world, a *mahdi* would come to redeem the faithful, and so he did, killing Gordon and restoring slavery while he was at it.

The Iqhwan

The Muslim Brothers, the Iqhwan, in conversation simply *aqhi*, "brothers," the Arab world's oldest Islamic party, was founded in Egypt in 1928 and today is a force in Syria, Jordan, the Sudan. Trying to use his riveting personality to transform Egypt, Nasser banned them as reactionary. Under fire from the Nasserite left, Sadat brought it back to legal life as a counterweight. Today, Hosni Mubarak uses them as a foil to parry the Islamic radicals bearing down on his regime; he pressures them to renounce terror, and he makes sure the favors due Islam either go their way or the way they favor.

SPLA (Sudanese People's Liberation Army)

Like the Shilluk and the Nuer, the Dinka are Nilotes, perhaps the tallest, blackest people in the world. For centuries, the Muslim north raided them for slaves, concubines, wives. For decades, they have been so ravaged by venereal disease that many clans are almost totally barren. When we drove overland from Malakal to the heart of the Sudd at Bor in 1979, warriors from a barren Nuer village raided a Shilluk village, carrying off several girls.

The minimum demands of the SPLA are for the abolition of Islamic Sharia law, introduced by Bashir, and the creation of a new constitution. The breakaway faction of the SPLA is calling for the complete independence of southern Sudan. The SPLA is headed by Dr. John Garang de Mabior, a former Sudanese army colonel. He is a graduate of the Infantry Officers Advanced Course at Fort Benning, Georgia, and has a Ph.D. earned while Stateside.

Garang's original job was to fight the rebels, but he ended up joining them instead. He worked his way to the top of the SPLA, mostly because he was on very close terms with Ethiopia's Lieutenant General Haile Mengistu Mariam. He feels that the simplistic principle of Muslim against Christian and black against Arab is too Western in concept. It is simply a matter of discrimination, which gets in the way of economic development and political power—a raison d'etre echoed by German mercenary Rolf Steiner, who helped the Anya in the 1970s and was tortured, tried and imprisoned for his troubles. The current war is about life for the south not about death for the north. Iran is pushing Sudan relentlessly to create a fundamentalist Islamic state. The fact that the black Africans of the south predate the Muslims of the north is immaterial. The SPLA armed forces are estimated to number 55,000. Support, even clandestine training in the bush, came from Israel and Ethiopia.

The SPLA currently controls five regions in the south where it maintains civil authority. They get weapons and support from Ethiopia and Eritrea.

Sudanese rebels train in Eritrea.

Nuba Mountains Central Committee of the SPLA (NMCC/SPLA)

Another splinter group of the southern Dinka dominated SPLA formed in June of 1996. Only three out of the 58 senior SPLA positions were filled by Dinka. The NMCC/SPLA is led by chairman Mohamed Haroun Kafi Aburas

Southern Sudan Independence Movement of Riek Machar (SSIM)

A spin-off of the SPLA is fighting the SPLA and has captured Akobo and Nyandit. Some say it is a front for the northern government and signed a peace treaty in April of 96. The group is led by Kerubino Kwanyin Bol who was imprisoned by Garang from 1987 to 1992.

South Sudan Independence Movement (SSIM)

The SSIM is a small splinter group of the SPLA, which has been wreaking havoc. However, the government accepted a cease-fire offer by the SSIM in March 1996, which led the larger SPLA to accuse the SSIM of complicity with the government.

Nafi Osman Nafeh

The powerful intelligence chief of the National Islamic Front (NIF), directed by Hassan al-Turabi. He was trained in intelligence in Pakistan and the United States after becoming a member of the fundamentalist movement in the 1960s. Using Saudi money, he created a clandestine fundamentalist intelligence network inside the Sudanese army. He was one of the brains behind the June 1989 military coup that brought al-Bashir to power.

General al-Fateh Orawa

Security advisor to the Sudanese president, Orawa is a member of the powerful Orawa clan. Trained in the United States, Turkey and Pakistan, he worked closely with the CIA in 1985 during the Nimeiri regime to organize the transfer of Falashas from Ethiopia to Israel via Sudan.

General Hachim Abu Said

The director of Sudan's foreign intelligence service. CIA-trained, Abu Said served as a senior Sudanese intelligence officer during the regime of Gaafar Nimeiri. He was later employed by Saudi intelligence, before taking up service with the new fundamentalist government of Sudan.

Spies

The Horn of Africa is buzzing with spies from the French DGSE, the American Defense Intelligence Agency (DIA) and the British MI6. Regardless of the latest political makeover of this war, there is no denying that a war for liberation between the south and the north has been fought since 1956, when Sudan gained its independence. The SPLA is the latest name under which the south has been fighting. It has undergone a power struggle, and the north is content to let the two subfactions try to kill each other.

The government of the north has little jurisdiction in the south. The provinces of Upper Nile, Equatoria and Bahr el Ghazal are controlled by the SPLA.

Sudan is trying to distance itself from Iran. With the recent serving up of Carlos and the flurry of media interviews that al-Turabi has given, things may be changing.

Charles Pasqua and the Deuzieme Bureau in the Horn of Africa

This back-slapping Corsican has made good use of his aggressive cultivation of contacts in the Arab and African world. Even before nabbing Carlos, Pasqua was riding a wave of popularity for ordering nightly ID checks of the immigrants surging into France from dangerous places throughout the community, and especially from Algeria. There was even talk of him succeeding Francois Mitterrand as president, and even if that was a long shot for a one-time salesman for the Marseille pastis, Ricard, it was clear he was boosting the presidential stock of his boss, Premier Edouard Balladur.

Pasqua is most famous for nabbing Carlos. The press hinted that this was a swap—the Jackal for the passage of northern armored units to the south. Drawing on deep French influence in two of the most corrupt states in Africa, Zaire and the Central African Republic (where de Gaulle's "noble idiot" practiced cannibalism in the Presidential Palace), Pasqua persuaded these governments to permit the Sudanese Army to cross into their territory with entirely mechanized brigades.

The move permitted the Sudanese to deploy for a climactic push on the beleaguered Southerners, and it promised to internationalize the war even beyond Zaire and the Central African Republic. Squeezed from these two directions, many of the Southerners would be cornered in the Nimule theatre at the Sudan's far southern extremity, thus making a player of a man who didn't need the headache, but to whom France was glad to give it.

The French have a charming capacity to be as frank about politics as they are about sex. We find it hard to believe that in the post–Cold War world, something as craven and pointless as the grab for Africa is on again. Who needs the Sudan? *Beau geste* imperialists out of French West Africa once faced-off against Edwardian Brits down from Cairo over these badlands that neither could ever control, bring peace to, or make any decent use of. Are we still that nuts?

In a dictated memoir published late in the winter of 1995, Pasqua confirmed everyone's worst fears about the French in Africa: Indeed, when Felix Mumie, a leader of the opposition in Cameroon, was assassinated in Geneva, it was on French orders. Indeed, many French ambassadors to many a state in France's African sphere have a hotline to the head of state's bedroom. Yes, many such heads of state have signed blank communiques authorizing French intervention. Yes, Omar Bongo, president of Gabon, literally had to audition for the job before he got it; in fact, Foccart conducted the interview. Yes, America is as much a predator in Africa as the leopard. Indeed, France installed Jean-Bedel Bokassa as dictator of the Central African Republic. Indeed, Bokassa called Charles de Gaulle, "papa." Yes, de Gaulle called Bokassa, "a noble idiot."

Is Foccart the last of his kind? Is that sort of thinking gone from the French Foreign Office? From the Deuzieme Bureau? Have the French spent all these years cultivating that Gallic shrug for nothing? But to be fair, this cynicism is not totally unrelieved. Sometimes they even insist they value common decency, and to demonstrate theirs, they participate when they feel we're doing something right.

The Non-Players

The tall and muscular Nuba people of Sudan used to number nearly 1.5 million. The latest and best estimates say only 200,000 remain. Is it because of disease and pestilence? Hardly. Rather they've been banished to "peace camps" by the government to keep them fighting in support of the separatists in the south—and evidently from propagating, as well.

Getting In

A passport and a visa are required to enter Sudan. The visa will cost Americans $50 and is good for eight days to three months. The Sudanese government recommends that malarial suppressants be taken and that yellow fever, cholera and meningitis vaccinations be administered. Visas are not issued to those who have previously traveled to Israel. Business visas require a letter from a sponsoring company in Sudan with full details on length of stay, financial responsibility and references in Sudan. All borders are open, but questionable people who enter in the South may experience problems. Expect three to four weeks to process your visa.

SUDAN

Journalists have been known to enter Sudan from the village of Periang, 500 miles northwest of the Kenyan border. From there, it is about 100 miles into the Nuba Mountains and SPLA-controlled territory.

Others enter from Uganda to interview pro-SPLA groups and leaders without a passport or visa. Rides can be hitched for little or no money. Bring cigarettes and small gifts, and be prepared to meet starvation and disease head-on. There is little to help you tell the difference between freedom fighters and bandits. Both may happily shoot you for your boots or supplies. The trip to the center of Khartoum from the airport is about 4 km. Negotiate and write down the agreed-upon taxi fare on a piece of paper before you get into the cab. There is a surcharge after 10 p.m. Remember, before you use our taxi tip, that 73 percent of the population is illiterate, according to the World Bank.

Those travelers who enter illegally will be prosecuted under Sudanese laws.

Contact the Sudanese embassy for more information:

Embassy of the Republic of the Sudan

2210 Massachusetts Avenue N.W.
Washington, D.C. 20008
☎ *(202) 338-8565*

Getting Around

Unforeseen circumstances, such as sandstorms (April and September) and electrical outages, may cause flight delays. The Khartoum Airport arrival and departure procedures are lengthy. Passengers should allow three hours for predeparture security and other processing procedures at the airport.

Only 994 of Sudan's 12,428 miles of roads are paved. The main paved routes are from Port Sudan through Kassala to Shavak, and from Khartoum through Sennar to Malakal. Most rural roads are simple tracks. In the northern part of the country, most of the roads are impassable during the July to September rainy season.There is an ancient rail system (with only 40 out of 150 locomotives working) with 3418 miles of track. The rail system links Khartoum with Port Sudan, Kassala, Wau, Nyala, and Wadi Halfa. The Sudan Railways Corporation operates a three-class service, including air-conditioned cars as well as sleeping and dining cars. There are 66 airfields, eight with permanent surfaces and four runways over 8000 feet. The main international airport is Khartoum International Airport.

Major airlines flying to Khartoum include Aeroflot, Air France, British Airways, Egypt Air, Ethiopian Airways, Gulf Air, KLM, Kuwait Airways, Lufthansa, and Saudia. Other less attractive carriers include Iraqi Airways, Libyan Arab Airlines, Kenya Airways, Middle East Airlines, Tunis Air and Yemenia. The national airline is Sudan Airways.

In the north, the major attractions are ancient temples and pyramids, and the ruins at Shendi and Karima.

Dangerous Places

Travel in all parts of Sudan is considered hazardous.

The South

Civil war persists in southern Sudan in the three provinces of Upper Nile, Bahr El Ghazal and Equatoria. The most recent phase of the civil war has killed 259,000 people and driven 3 million from their homes. In 1988, 250,000 died and over 4 million fled their homes. Sudan is anti-Christian and Zionophobic to the point of psychosis. Iran and Sudan have joined together in declaring Jihad on the Great Satan, so consider yourself Satan's Fuller Brush salesman.

The West

Banditry and incursions by southern Sudanese rebels are common in western Sudan, particularly in Darfur province along the Chadian and Libyan borders, and in southern Kordofan province.

Khartoum

Western interests in Khartoum have been the target of terrorist acts several times in recent years.

Iraqi Military Sites

Iraqi missiles and fighter planes were positioned in Sudan to threaten the Saudi Arabian Port of Jeddah and Egypt's Aswan High Dam.

Dangerous Things

Fighting

Renewed fighting between Sudanese and rebel forces in southern Sudan is sending 500 refugees a day into Uganda. The bombing and firefights between the Sudanese forces and members of the SPLA can be heard well into northern Uganda.

Terrorist Training Camps

Sudan is considered very dangerous for Western travelers because of the large number of terrorist training bases here. There are Islamic fundamentalist and terrorist training camps outside Khartoum, along the coast and in other nameless places.

Curfews

The government of Sudan has ordered a curfew that is strictly enforced. Persons who are outside during curfew hours without authorization are subject to arrest. Curfew hours change frequently.

Dinner Parties

It is against the law in Sudan to have a gathering of more than four people at one time.

Hassles with Local Police

Travelers are required to register with police headquarters within three days of arrival. Travelers must obtain police permission before moving to another location in Sudan and register with police within 24 hours of arrival at the new location. These regulations are strictly enforced. Even with proper documentation, travelers in Sudan have been subjected to delays and detentions by Sudan's security forces, especially when traveling outside Khartoum. Authorities expect roadblocks to be heeded.

Getting Sick

Medical facilities are as scarce as literate Sudanese outside Khartoum. In 1981, the country had 158 hospitals with a total capacity of 17,205 beds. There were 220 health centers, 887 dispensaries, 1619 dressing stations and 1095 primary health care units. Although there were 2122 physicians and 12,871 nurses working in the country, you can expect less than one doctor and nine hospital beds per 10,000 people. Don't expect squat in the rebel-held south. Some health care is provided free of charge, but your best bet is to have repatriation insurance should you get truly ill. Visitors traveling to the south of the country will need a valid certificate of vaccination against yellow fever. Travelers entering Egypt from Sudan will need to produce either a certificate of vaccination against yellow fever or a location certificate showing that they have not been in a yellow fever area. A valid cholera certificate is required of travelers arriving from infected areas. Malaria, typhoid, rabies and polio are endemic. Bilharzia is also present, and visitors should stay out of slow-moving freshwater.

Nuts and Bolts

The arid north of Sudan is mainly desert with greener, agricultural areas on the banks of the Nile. Crops can only be grown during the rainy season (July to September). The south is mainly swamp and tropical jungle. The most important features are the White and the Blue Nile. The Blue Nile is prone to severe flooding. Mid-April to the end of June is the hot, dry season with temperatures above 110°F.

The official language is Arabic, but English is widely understood. The government is trying to eradicate the use of colonial-tainted English as part of its Islamification. Ta Bedawie and Nubian are also spoken, as are dialects of the Nilotic, Nilo-Hamitic and Sudanic languages. Evening meals are served around 10 p.m. The staple diet is *fool* (beans, or *dura*) eaten with vegetables.

Disruptions of water and electricity are frequent. Telecommunications are slow and often impossible.

Banks are open from 8:30 a.m. to noon Sunday to Thursday. Businesses are open 8:30 a.m. until 2.30 p.m. Government offices are open in Khartoum 8 a.m. to 2 p.m. Sunday to Thursday, and other centers are open 6:30 a.m. to 2 p.m. with a break for breakfast. Shops are open 8:30 a.m. to 1:30 p.m., then 5:30 p.m. to 8 p.m. Saturday through Thursday. Note: Government offices and businesses have been closing on Sundays since 1991 in an effort to conserve energy.

The strict Islamic code (the Sharia) has been in force since 1991. There is no gambling or alcohol allowed in the north. Individuals who exchange money anywhere other than an authorized banking institution risk arrest and loss of funds through unscrupulous black marketeers. The dinar is the official currency. The new dinar (introduced May 18, 1992) is equal to 10 Sudanese pounds.

Photography Restrictions

A permit must be obtained before taking photographs anywhere in Khartoum, as well as in the interior of the country. Photographing military areas, bridges, drainage stations, broadcast stations, public utilities, slum areas and beggars is prohibited. Sudanese are reluctant to be photographed without their permission.

Registration

U.S. citizens who visit or remain in Sudan, despite the warning, cannot, at press time, register at the U.S. embassy to obtain updated information on travel and security, as the embassy was closed in 1996.

Embassy Locations

The U.S. Embassy is located at *Sharia Ali Abdul Latif* in the capital city of Khartoum. The mailing address is *P.O. Box 699, or APO AE 09829.* ☎ *74700 and 74611.* The work week is Sunday through Thursday. However, at press time, the embassy was closed due to the continuing turmoil.

U.S. Embassy in Sudan (temporarily closed)
P.O. Box 699
Sharia Ali Abdul Latif
Khartoum
☎ *[249] (11) 74700/74611*

UK Embassy
St 10, off Baladia Street
P.O. Box 801
Khartoum
☎ *[249] (11) 70760*
FAX 873-1445 605 ext. 239

Sudanese Embassy in Canada
85 Range Road, Suite 407
Ottawa, Ontario, Canada K1N 8J6
☎ *(613) 235-4000*
FAX (613) 235-6880

Embassy of the Republic of Sudan
2210 Massachusetts Avenue, N.W.
Washington, D.C. 20008
☎ *(202) 338-8565/6/7/8*

Other Addresses

Bank of Sudan
Gamaa Avenue
P.O. Box 313
Khartoum
☎ *[249] (11) 78064*

Ministry of Trade, Cooperation and Finance
Khartoum
☎ *[249] (11) 730030*

Sudan Airways Co. Ltd.
SDC Building Complex, Amarat Street 19
P.O. Box 253
Khartoum
☎ *[249] (11) 47953*

Sudan Chamber of Commerce
P.O. Box 81
Khartoum

Dangerous Days

The following days are good days to stay inside, due to the proclivity of terrorist groups to generate lethal publicity on media spin days (i.e., anniversary dates).

06/30/1989   A group of officers led by general Omar al-Bashir overthrew the government of Sadiq Mahdi.

04/15/1986   A U.S. embassy communicator was shot and wounded while riding home from the embassy in Khartoum. The shooting was believed to be in retaliation for U.S. air raids on Libya earlier in the day.

05/16/1983   Founding of the SPLM/SPLA (The Sudanese People's Liberation Movement/Army).

03/01/1973   U.S. Ambassador Cleo Noel and Deputy Chief of Mission George Moore were assassinated in Khartoum during the seizure of the Saudi embassy.

03/03/1972   Anniversary of the Addis Ababa accords that ended the insurgency against the central government and granted southern Sudan wide regional autonomy on internal matters.

07/22/1971   Anti-Communist military elements loyal to Gaafar Nimeiri led a successful countercoup and brought him to power several days after a coup by the Sudan Communist Party.

06/09/1969   The south declared independence.

05/25/1963   The Organization of African Unity was founded on May 25, 1963. The day is celebrated as Africa Freedom Day. The OAU is organized to promote unity and cooperation among African states.

01/01/1956   Independence Day.

SUDAN

Dushanbe

Tajikistan
★ ★ ★

Persian Rogues

Tajikistan is one of those "stan" places we skip over in geography lessons. The word stan means two things. First "stan" means it is a Muslim homeland and second it is named after the tribe or peoples (Afghan, Pak, Turkmeni, Kazak Uzbek etc.) who claim it as their homeland. The problem here is that the Tajik forgot to put together a country. There is a civil war raging that at press time threatened to turn the tables against the Russians. This mountainous sparsely populated country has many parallels to Afghanistan. Its hard, ugly, deadly and ruled by tribes and clans. Another main feature of Tajikistan is the almost impassable mountain range called the Pamirs. The Pamirs act as a physical barrier between southern Asia and Russia.

If you thought the Russians just started killing Tajiks in the last few years you need to brush up on your history. China, Russia and Afghanistan have been using the area called Tajikistan as a battleground ever since the Mongols under Tamerlane came cruising through. The first known local terrorist groups were the "wily

Pathans" that Kipling chronicled in his stories of Afghanistan and the Pamirs. (Pathans are actually Pahktuns who live in Western Pakistan and Eastern Afghanistan). Even in 1917 there was a group of terrorists called the basmachis who fought the Bolsheviks for an independent Muslim homeland. They were defeated after four years and fled to Northern Afghanistan.

The Russians created a Tajikistan to be an autonomous satellite of Uzbekistan in 1924 and then changed to a full union republic in 1929. In the Russian tradition of totally screwing up ethnic and indigenous history, they left 475,000 Tajiks in Uzbekistan and all important government positions were run by round-faced, hard drinking Soviets from the north. Things were relatively calm under the iron fist of Mother Russia. A fundamentalist group called the Islamic Resistance Party began pushing for Tajik nationalism and began raising hell in the 80's. They really didn't come into their own until 1990 when the Russians threatened to resettle Christian Armenians in Dushanbe. In 1991 when the rest of central Asia declared independence, Tajikistan became an independent republic and magically voted in a corrupt communist government. When the locals decided to take matters into their own hands they took over the presidential palace and installed a coalition government run by Akbarshah Iskandarov. Having neglected to make Politics 101 a required course under Soviet rule, the whole system went to hell and the various factions started using bullets instead of stern memos to get their point across. The lines broke down as the Moscow friendly old liners from the North battled the Kulyabis from the south.

The civil war erupted in a very nasty shoot-out until 1993. Over 40,000 people lost their lives in this flare-up and not too many folks in the west even heard of the massacre. Plenty of ethnic cleansing and revolving political structures opened the door to the Russian army who then stepped in to babysit their puppet ruler Imamali Rakhmanov (from the Kulyab district) and to spank all the various warring factions. Russia still views Tajikistan as a buffer zone and does not want nasty Islamic fundamentalists messing up their nice subway in Moscow. As of July, 1996 rebels had taken and then lost the key town of Tavildara that links the capital of Dushanbe with the Pamir mountains.

The Scoop

The Russians are still playing the Great Game and using Tajikistan as a no man's land in its bid to keep their sworn enemies the Afghans out of Moscow. The ruling clan is simply government de jour but the Russians call the shots (and the range) here. A ring of forts and bombing raids into the rebel camps inside Afghanistan can't stop the onslaught. Check which flag is flying next time you land in Dushanbe and give us a call.

The Players

The Tajiks

Muslim Tajiks are originally from northern Afghanistan. They descended from Persia and consider themselves a superior race and have a millennium of culture achievements to back it up. Their capital was Bukhara where some of Islam's brightest stars held court. Poets, philosophers, artists and calligraphers spread their skills throughout the Muslim world from here. There are about 5000 Tajik fighters based in Northern Afghanistan. DP's pal Ahmed Shah Massoud (the Tajik warlord who is defending Kabul and the Afghan government of Rabbiani and Hektmatyar) is a hero to these folks. The Tajiks are very Southern European looking due to Alexander's randy army and political agenda.

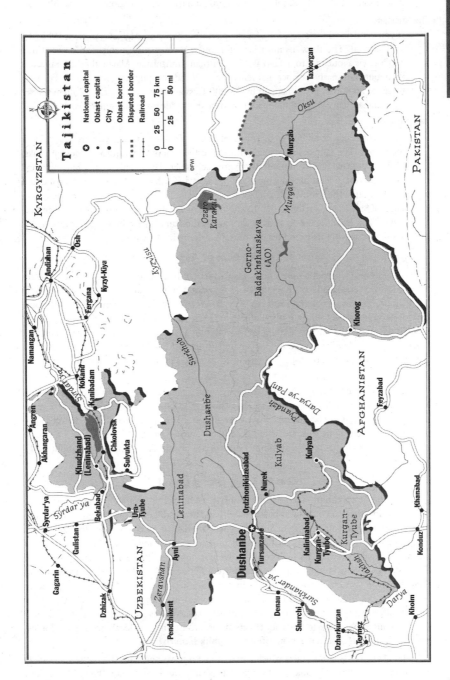

Tajiks are primarily Sunni Muslims with the Pamirs being Shia's. You can also find Tajiks in Uzebistan (860,000), Kazakstan (100,000) and the Xiajang region of China (30,000).

The Russians

If you get deja vu for disco, long lapels, platform shoes and Afghanistan circa 1985 you aren't far off. The Russians must have forgotten their history lessons and decided that Tajikistan is a lot easier to defend as a border than Afghanistan. Maybe they didn't notice the mountains, nasty weather, hardened fighters and silly puppet government. For now there are 50 border posts manned by 25,000 Russian soldiers along the 1200km border with Afghanistan. Many of them are bored or shot to death on a regular basis.

The Pamirs

To be considered a hillbilly in a remote place like Tajikistan means you are way back in the woods. The Pamirs live in high altitude fertile valleys between the imposing peaks. Most have a hard time communicating with each other. The people are poor and in many cases destitute. Seems like just the place for a playboy who was born in Switzerland and jet sets around the world to be a religious leader. The Pamirs are Ismailists who believe in a sect of Shia Islam, a religion that has no house of worship, icons, holy men or even holidays. Their leader is the Aga Khan who keeps the Pamiris alive by his generosity. He is considered a living deity and his photograph is hung in every home.

Getting In

You can fly into Dushanbe from London via Tajikistan International Airlines. Where else do you get to fly on creaky 60's era Boeing 707's? Aeroflot won't guarantee but they will try to fly you in from Moscow for about $300 one way. There are a variety of charter fleets with outbound space. Just head to the airport and haggle. There is a train from Moscow. Don't be surprised if the person sharing the sleeping compartment is a female. The trains are coed here. You haven't lived until you've slept in the same compartment with a snoring flatulent Russian with BO. Trains are popular spots for thieves and you can also get shaken down for a few bucks by border agents.

You can fly directly from London to Dushanbe via Tajikistan Airlines on Sunday and from Moscow about every second day. There are also flights to Delhi. Due to a lack of fuel, there are not many taxis. Taxis can be called by dialing ☎ 24-66-29 or catching one at the Hotel Tajikistan. Negotiate and agree to a fare first. Take the bus into and around town. There are private buses that cruise Dushanbe. DP recommends hiring a private driver and car for about $30 - $50 a day.

Getting Around

Tajikistan is not a country designed for leisurely touring. The mountains make most of the country an adventure. The civil war makes the driving interesting, and the general lack of infrastructure means you come in or you go out. There are daily train connections to Uzbekistan, trucks going through the northern mountains into Kyrgyzstan and Uzbekistan (has anybody ever seen a Tajik drivers license?). The alpine scenery along the Pamir Highway into or from Kyrgyzstan is supposed to be worth the life-shortening ride, bad food and lack of accommodations. The road to Afghanistan is used only by Russian military vehicles. There are supposed to be regular flights to Khojand, Khorog and most major towns in Tajikistan. Naturally the reality is quite different so check when you get in country. Reservations are not taken until 3–7 days before the flight. You have to buy your tickets at the airport since the locals get to pay a lot less at the airline offices. You can get the latest from **Tajik Intourist** ☎ 21-68-92.

You must be very specific about which cities you wish to visit and make sure they are clearly written in. The militia will look for any reason to shake you down for a bribe. If you do not have the proper paperwork you will be sent back on the plane you came in. If you arrive by land you risk being detained and fined.

NOTE: The "rebels" are making serious headway at press time so obviously you will need to call the embassy (if its still there) and find out the latest.

Getting Out

You can't take any antiques out of the country. That of course is the least of your worries. Antiques could be anything from the phone system to the political philosophy of the current rulers. You also are not allowed to take any local currency out. Once again not too much of a problem since there is not much call for Tajik rubles. The only place you might run into a customs person would be the border with Kyrgyzstan. Needless to say the border with Afghanistan is more concerned about folks trying to sneak in at night with rocket launchers and trucks full of opium. The only thing you have to think about is when the airlines stop flying and you have to figure out how to get out of this godforsaken place with Afghan fighters to the south, mountains to the north and a whole lot of Central Asia to the north and west. Tajikistan is a long way from anywhere. The only thing your credit cards will be good for is scraping the ice off the dilapidated truck's windshield and your travelers checks will make good kindling on those nights in the mountain passes.

Dangerous Places

The M-41 Highway

There is a road that heads east from Dushanbe and then winds south along the Afghan border that is off limits to even locals. You will be turned back at any one of the military checkpoints or even find yourself front and center at a Tajik attack on your Russian border stop. Many sections of the road are regularly mined. Some people take the daily flight from Dushanbe to Khorog ($60) and then take a bus through the mountains into Osh.

Dushanbe

The capital city of Dushanbe (Tajik for Monday, the day of the weekly market) is a dangerous place due to street crime and violence after dark. Westerners are targeted not only in public but in their hotel rooms.

Dangerous Things

Flying

The chances of crashing are good in Tajikistan. The Russians pay their pilots an additional sum to make the 45 minute flight between Dushanbe and Khorog white knuckle flying at its finest. The high altitude prevents the aircraft from passing gracefully over some of the highest mountains in Russia. So the pilots simply fly in around, and by the peaks. You should know that you are flying over (or rather through) an active war zone and one unlucky flight was downed by Tajik rebels using a surface to air missile.

Opium

The general lack of government or law enforcement means that the opium poppy is grown in great abundance in the valley areas. Although the farmers don't have any axe to grind with foreigners you will be in an area controlled by smugglers.

The Yeti

Somewhere on the "Roof of the World" exists a large white hairy creature who has been tracked but never seen. The creature emits a bloodcurdling scream and usually runs when tracked. It is said that it will attack pack animals. There has been no proof the Yeti exists except in folklore. There are, however, snow leopards who emit screams when mating and have been known to attack pack animals.

Money Hassles

Tajikistan started printing its own version of the ruble in 1995. Remember that the Tajik ruble is worth 100 Russian rubles. You get about 300 rubles for a U.S. dollar. Needless to say, napkins and coasters might retain their value longer than this creative solution to insolvency.

You can't take money out of the country. Credit cards are useless. Banks have no idea what a traveler's check is. Needless to say the almighty dollar is good as gold here. Don't take or accept 100 dollar bills because of the high amount of bogus Iranian printed C notes. It is a good habit to only carry new or post 1990 American bills to avoid having them handed back to you. Worst case is that money changers will discount your raggedly greenbacks for up to 25% of their value. The locals pay a much lower price for just about everything and if you get caught hiring a local to buy your tickets you will get dunned for the difference or a bribe.

Getting Sick

Tajikistan has malaria in the southern and lower regions. The water supply is not potable and bottled water should be your only source. Hepatitis A is a risk. Ticks are found in higher elevations in grassy and wooded areas. Rabies is a significant risk from local dogs, many of whom are trained to attack strangers.

There has been a significant deterioration in the medical infrastructure in Tajikistan with many trained personnel having fled the country. Tajikistan has a general scarcity of medical equipment and medicines. The potential exists for significant disease outbreaks, because of massive population displacement and a partial breakdown in immunization activities. U.S. medical insurance is not always valid outside the United States. Travelers have found that supplemental medical insurance with specific overseas coverage has proved to be useful. Further information on health matters can be obtained from the Centers for Disease Control's international travelers hotline: ☎ *(404) 332-4559.*

Nuts and Bolts

The best times for masochists to visit hardy Tajikistan would be between October and May to experience the blizzards or between June and October to be sandblasted by the dust storms. Since most of Tajikistan is above 3000 meters, it is freezing cold in the winter and hot and arid in the summer. March and May bring the most rain, the heat in June to August will fuse your Airwalks to the pavement with temperatures reaching well over 100 degrees. Only 7% of the land is arable and the rest is comprised of "hidey holes" for folks with guns.

Almost the entire country is mountainous and earthquake-prone; its rivers are sourced in mountain glaciers. But not a lot of helicopter skiing here, folks. More like helicopter gunships. Tajikistan, about the size of Illinois, is bordered by Afghanistan to the south, China to the east, and by Uzbekistan and Kirghizia to the west and north.

Tajikistan has a population of 5.6 million. Dushanbe, with a population of slightly more than half a million, is the capital. Sunni Muslims comprise perhaps 80 percent of the population. The official and most widely spoken language is Tajik.

Tajikistan is a cash-only economy. International banking services are not available. Major credit cards and traveler's checks are rarely accepted. Traveling in Tajikistan with large amounts of cash can be dangerous.

Embassy Location

The U.S. embassy resumed operation in April 1995, but is providing only emergency consular services.

U.S. Embassy

Oktyabrskaya Hotel
#39 Ainii Street
☎ *[7] (3712) 21-03-56*

Dangerous Days

09/10/1992   Declaration of Independence.

09/07/1992   President Rakhmon Nabiyev resigned after Islamic rebels forcefully took control of the government. The Islamic Party was overturned in a bloody coup late in October 1992. September 10 is recognized as the date of Tajikistan's declaration of independence. Islamic rebels have continued fighting since early September 1992.

12/25/1991   President Bush formally recognized Tajikistan and 11 other former Soviet republics. On that occasion, he also stated that formal diplomatic relations would be established with six of the republics as soon as possible and that diplomatic relations would be established with the other six (Tajikistan was one of them) when they met certain political conditions.

12/21/1991   Tajikistan joined with 10 other former republics of the Soviet Union (which ceased to exist on December 25, 1991) in establishing the Commonwealth of Independent States.

02/12/1990   Twenty-five persons died as Interior Ministry troops fired on demonstrators massed outside the Tajikistan Communist Party headquarters in Dushanbe, the capital of Tajikistan. February 12 now is celebrated as "Memory Day," and an obelisk was unveiled on February 12, 1992, to commemorate the persons who died in February 1990.

Turkey
★★★

Muddle East

Here is where East meets West. Turkey can be as cosmopolitan as Paris and as depressingly medieval as Iran. Americans know little about this country. Most of our impressions have been formed through Hollywood, particularly by the dark, disturbing movie *Midnight Express,* the harrowing story of a young American arrested for drugs and tortured by his Turkish captors. To many others, Turkey is simply some godforsaken, giant landing strip for American F-18s—a land-based aircraft carrier—a convenient place for allowing us to periodically blow the hell out of Baghdad. It's a country where, within 100 miles of each other, you can find stealth fighters and people who live in caves.

Although Turkey is as civilized as Paris, France it can get as wild as Paris, Texas. Turkey is waging an all-out war against the terrorist Kurdistan Workers Party (PKK), the stated representatives of the ethnic Kurds and the unstated representatives of the grim reaper. These boys are bad; they make Hezbollah look like the Fort Lee Kiwanis Club shooting Roman candles off at a Fourth of July picnic.

509

Many think these nasties are the most vicious assemblage of zanies since the Peloponnesian Wars. Turkey's Marxist guerrillas of the PKK have declared war on the country and attack tourist targets as well as teachers, government workers and other innocent bystanders. They believe that by destroying the infrastructure and hard currency earners of Turkey, they will be ceded their own homeland. The PKK operates primarily in Turkey and Western Europe. Its targets also include civilians and government forces in the eastern portion of the country. For some variety, they began taking Western hostages in 1991.

Perhaps Turkey's biggest problem has been its long denial of even the existence of the Kurds. The Kurds' demands as recently as the 1970s had been limited to the government's recognition of their language in culture, but rising Kurdish pride and a recognition of their resources turned into vehement nationalism and moves toward independence. Although the Kurdish political parties that formed in the late '70s were illegal, they nonetheless brought huge parcels of Kurdistan under their own control, until another period of assimilation began after the Turkish military coup of 1980. Enter the PKK, which, in 1984, not only forced the government to open its eyes to the Kurdish problem, but also the eyes of innocent people who began finding themselves staring down the barrels of AKs.

But not for long.

The war against the Kurds costs the Turkish government about $7 billion a year and keeps about 75 percent of its 500,000-man army busy. On the other side, the PKK has a fairly backwoods army of between 8000 and 15,000 soldiers recruited from the refugee camps and trained in Syria and eastern Turkey. Many of the PKK are women. In the nine-year period between 1987 and March of '96 the government figures that it knocked off about 10,663 terrorists while they only lost 3400. Oh yeah, about 3938 civilians got aced in the cross-fire and about 1200 villages (give or take a few) have been razed to the ground by the Turkish army. The 12 to 15 million Kurds make up about 15 - 20 percent of Turkey's 62 million population. More than 80 Turkish journalists, academics and writers have been imprisoned for speaking out on the Kurdish issue.

What is Syria's beef with Turkey? Well, it doesn't like Turkey siphoning off water from the Tigris and Euphrates rivers. So it continues to support the PKK and its leader, Abdullah Ocalan, who lives in Damascus and the Bekaa valley. Despite the 17,500 number offered by the government, other sources estimate that well over 19,000 people have been killed since 1984—many more in northern Iraq.

Incest?

An enraged mob of 200 Alawite demonstrators attacked the Istanbul headquarters of a private Turkish television channel, Interstar, with stones, sticks and shovels after a game show host had suggested that Alawites—an esoteric branch of Islam—practiced incest regularly. The host later apologized and admitted his allegation was merely an uneducated guess.

The Scoop

Although you hear about "terrorist" activity in Turkey, it would be more accurate to say that—with 19,000 people killed since 1984 in violent encounters with the PKK and the Dev Sol—the situation is better summed up as a civil war. The problem is figuring out who's killing

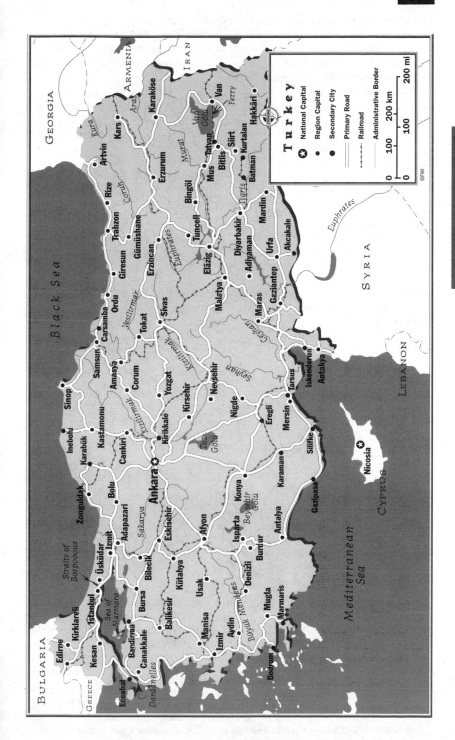

TURKEY

whom. First with a bullet is the PKK (Kurdistan Workers Party), perhaps the most ruthless terrorist group in the world after the FIS in Algeria and the Khmer Rouge in Cambodia. In one five-month period, the army killed more than 1700 Kurdistan Workers Party members and captured 2000 others. In southeastern Turkey, the government troops used to quell the Kurd uprising numbered more than 150,000.

There has essentially been a state of war in southeastern Turkey since the PKK opted for a guerrilla war in early 1984. The conflict became agitated even further by other players getting involved in the fray: The Iranians, Iraqis, Syrians, Armenians, regional warlords, police, private militias and the military joined in the fun. Southeastern Turkey may be the most dangerous place in the world, because of its warring neighbors and attempts by the government to portray the problem as less significant than it is.

Although the source of discontent is in the east of Turkey, the most visible terrorist acts have been in the west. The PKK likes to target tourist sites and tourist-oriented facilities in western and Aegean Turkey in an effort to scare away tourists. In 1993, there were seven attacks against tourist facilities by the PKK, injuring 27 tourists. The PKK also kidnapped 19 foreigners (one American) in southeast and eastern Turkey in 1993. During the summer of 1993, a series of bomb attacks in Antalya wounded 26 persons; in Istanbul, a grenade was thrown under a tour bus, injuring eight persons, and a bomb was thrown at a group of tourists as they were sightseeing around the city walls, resulting in six injuries. A hand grenade was found buried on a beach southeast of Izmir, and there were reports of similar incidents in other areas along the west coast. In 1994, PKK bomb attacks were conducted on some of Istanbul's most popular tourist attractions, including St. Sophia and the Covered Bazaar, resulting in the deaths of two foreign tourists. Intermittent terrorist bombings have also occurred elsewhere, including Ankara, the state capital, causing damage to property and loss of life. Some parts of Turkey are currently under the control of the PKK.

In addition, the Dev Sol has been up to its old nasty ways. Early in 1996, the leftist guerrillas executed two prominent Turkish businessmen and a secretary in their offices on the 25th floor of the swanky Sabanci Center in downtown Istanbul. Each was killed with a single bullet to the head—a left-wing flag was left behind as a calling card. The attack was to avenge the deaths of three prison inmates at Istanbul's Umraniye prison, when security forces brutally quelled a riot there. The inmates' deaths ignited five days of riots in 10 different Turkish prisons, which ended only after the government suspended two top officials at the Umraniye facility. Under pressure from the leftist member of Turkey's ruling coalition government, new Prime Minister Yilmaz extended emergency rule for four months, beginning at the end of March 1996, and promised he would lighten up the government's stand on the PKK.

The Players

Kurdistan Workers Party (PKK)

The Kurds want their own homeland. Turkey says the Kurds will enjoy the same rights as any other ethnic minority in the country. So the PKK has taken it upon itself to blow people to bits until it gets its dream home. But, considering that Turkey is proud of its long record of assimilating diverse cultures into the Turkish social and political mainstream, Ed McMahon is unlikely to be knocking on the PKK's door anytime soon. Out of this endless philosophical quagmire comes the largest, best organized and most active terrorist group in Turkey, the PKK. Founded in 1978, the PKK does not represent all 20 million Kurds in the Middle East, but is the best-known and most violent advocate of Kurdish independence. Many nonsupporters are marginal sympathizers, though; most Kurds are still miffed that their language was once outlawed in Turkey, and that many were displaced from their traditional homelands in the east to new settlements in the west.

The PKK has declared war on a formidable foe—tourists—since it feels that income from tourism (US$7 billion a year) funds the Turkish government's war against the Kurds.

Despite their tough talk, the 20 or so tourists that have been kidnapped have all been released unharmed. Why? Because frightened tourists make for better interviews on CNN than dead ones.

In southeast Turkey, the PKK is very active, setting up roadblocks, placing land mines and kidnapping foreign tourists. Although, geographically, the PKK should be fighting in Iraq, Iran and Syria, it does most of its warring in eastern Turkey and carries out most of its terrorist activities along the Aegean resort towns and in Europe. In Germany alone, there are more than 450,000 Kurds, about a quarter of the total Turkish population in Germany. The PKK, along with 35 other organizations, was banned by the German government in November 1993.

Westerners can relax slightly because, unlike the Algerian fundamentalists, most assassination victims of the PKK are locals—typically Kurds—suspected of informing on the organization or of not complying with PKK decrees. The PKK has also reportedly extorted money from businesses and professionals not only in Turkey, but from Turkish businesses in Europe. They threaten to kill those who do not contribute "taxes" to their cause. The PKK is a Marxist group now controlled from Syria, where its leader, Abdullah Ocalan, a former law student from the University of Ankara, fled when the PKK was outlawed in 1980. Their major source of income is from extorting money from Turkish expats in Europe and fees for safeguarding drug shipments from Lebanon into Afghanistan, Iran and Russia.

There are an estimated 5000 female Peshmerga in the Free Womens Movement of Kurdistan; 30 are operative commanders in the PKK.

There are estimated to be about 8000 armed PKK members. They currently control areas of Eastern Turkey, 3000 of them in mountainous Tunceli province. There is a US$94,000 reward for information leading to the arrest of "Fingerless Zeki," whose real name is Semdin Sakik. Zeki is a rebel commander who is in charge of the PKK troops in eastern Turkey. (*DP* will give you a head start: He can be found in Tunceli province.) If you want to collect, give Prime Minister Mesut Yilmaz a call.

The PKK doesn't maintain any high- (or even low-) profile press or media offices ("That would be pretty stupid, don't you think?" Estella Schmidt of the Kurdistan Solidarity Committee told *DP*, however, the guerrillas use a number of Kurdish political action organizations (i.e., front groups) in London as conduits for disseminating information. These activist cells are semilegal in Great Britain and often used by the PKK for entirely illegal activities. Many of their members are kicked out of the country and deported to Germany, which will then send the nastiest of the lot back to Turkey. The one with the closest ties to the PKK is the London-based Kurdistan Information Centre. London also seems to be a safe house for these other nasties' front operations.

Kurdistan Information Centre
10 Glasshouse Yard
London EC1A4JN
United Kingdom
☎ *011-44-171-250-1315*
Att: Mizgin Sen

Kurdistan Solidarity Committee
☎ *011-44-171-586-5892*
Att: Estella Schmidt

Kurdistan Workers Association
☎ *011-44-181-809-0743*

PKK (Kurdish Workers Party)
Mekte-Bi Amele-1 Kurdistan
Barelias-Chotura
West Bekaa, Lebanon

Patriotic Union of Kurdistan
☎ *011-44-181-642-4518*
Att: Latif Rashid

Also see Kurdistan in "Coming Attractions."

Dev Sol (Devrimci Sol, or Revolutionary Left)

This isn't a retro surf reverb rock group out of California, but a splinter faction of the Turkish People's Liberation Party/Front formed in 1978. They espouse a Marxist ideology and are intensely xenophobic, virulently anti-U.S. and anti-NATO. Dev Sol seeks to unify the proletariat to stage a national revolution. The group finances its activities largely through armed robberies and extortion. Their symbol is a yellow star with hammer and sickle against a red background.

Dev Sol has conducted attacks against U.S., Turkish and NATO targets but was weakened by massive arrests from 1981–'83. In the early 1990s, the group killed several foreigners, including two Americans. Five members, including one of its leaders, were shot and killed in Istanbul on March 6, 1993. Types of attacks include handgun assassinations and bombings, including execution of informers and collaborators. Since its reemergence during the late 1980s, it has concentrated its strikes against current and retired Turkish security and military officials and was responsible for the murders of four generals and nearly 30 police officers in 1991. The police are usually shot while sitting in their patrol cars. Dev Sol also claims responsibility for assassinating two American contractors and one British businessman, an attempt to murder a U.S. Air Force officer, and conducting over 30 bombings against Western diplomatic, cultural and commercial facilities.

Dev Sol is down to several hundred hard-core radicals with several dozen armed militants. Its support comes from Lebanon, with training and logistical support from Palestinian radicals.

While other groups have concentrated their actions in Adana in recent years, only Dev Sol has attacked Americans. In February 1991, the group assassinated an American employee of a Department of Defense contractor outside his home in downtown Adana. The same year, the group bombed the American consulate and other U.S.-affiliated organizations.

Despite these attacks, the main targets of these groups are Turkish officials and Turkish government property. In a recent attack in Adana in August 1993, Dev Sol assassinated the former medical director of a state hospital. Early in 1996, Dev Sol guerrillas murdered two prominent Turkish businessmen and a secretary in their offices in downtown Istanbul, to avenge the deaths of three prison inmates at Istanbul's Umraniye prison. Local state banks are a favorite target and have been bombed numerous times. Dev Sol is led by Karatas.

IBDA-C/IKK (Islamic Great East Raiders-Front/Islamic Retaliation Detachments)

This is the Iranian-backed fundamentalist group that attacks the PKK as well as the Turkish establishment. Their goal is to create a more rigid Islamic state.

Hezbollah

This is where things get complicated. Iranian-supported Hezbollah (based in the Bekáa Valley in southern Lebanon) has unleashed a scourge on the Marxist PKK. Imagine a terrorist group that preys on another terrorist group. You would think the Turkish government would be ecstatic, but Hezbollah is gunning down Islamic fundamentalists as fast as the Marxist rebels. Thirty-five Hezbollah are on trial in a state security court in the southeast on charges ranging from supporting separatism to killing 25 people and wounding 32 others in 39 attacks in recent years around Diyarbakir and Batman. The Hezbollah calls on its followers to kill PKK members on sight and is believed to be behind many street murders in the southeast. For a more complete description, see "The Players" section in the Lebanon chapter.

Turkish Workers Peasants Liberation Party (TIKKO)

A small group with a fetish for blowing up automatic teller machines (everyone's enemy) and banks in major cities. What fun.

Kawa

Kawa is a legendary folk hero among the Kurds. The Kawa group was established in 1976 after breaking away from the Revolutionary Culture Association (DDKD), a pro-Soviet Kurdish group advocating uniting all the Kurdish people under the Marxist banner. Kawa's anti-Soviet stance was the reason for the break with the DDKD. Kawa also fell victim to dissension within its own ranks over the teachings of Mao Zedong.

Alawites

The Alawites are a Muslim minority who live in Turkey but are unrelated to both the Shiites, who worship Ali, or to the Syrian ruling faction, which is also called Alawite. They adhere to a moderate branch of Islam started in the 13th century by philosopher Bektas Veli. Occasionally, there are violent demonstrations and riots in the Istanbul and Ankara areas. In March 1995, 16 people were killed in two days of riots.

The Army

Turkish military forces (there are over 150,000 troops in the southeastern region) have killed 1700 Kurdish rebels and captured 2000. A special ops unit under the control of the local governor conducts raids against the PKK. Their utilization of the latest American military hardware (i.e., Cobra helicopter gunships) against the PKK's guerrilla tactics and small arms (AK-47 rifles) gives the conflict a neo-Vietnam aura.

Getting In

A passport is required. A visa is not required for tourist or business visits of up to three months. For information on entry requirements to Turkey, travelers can contact the nearest Turkish Consulate in Chicago, Houston, Los Angeles or New York, or the embassy in Washington, D.C.:

Embassy of the Republic of Turkey

1714 Massachusetts Avenue, N.W.
Washington, D.C. 20036
☎ *(202) 659-8200*

When you get off the plane in Istanbul, you need to proceed to the line to the left of the longer lines. You'll know what we're talking about.

If you wish to travel to eastern Turkey, your request may be refused. There are numerous police, militia, army and special ops roadblocks in the area. *DP* visited the area and can confirm that Turkey is indeed at war with the PKK and conducting major operations on an almost daily basis. Do not believe any tourism hype about a minor problem with rebels. Certain areas and roads around southeast Turkey are under the control of the PKK.

Getting Around

The authors have traveled extensively in eastern Turkey, both alone and with an armed military escort consisting of armored personnel carriers and commandos using Land Rovers. We consider traveling with a military escort to be the most dangerous way to travel, since the PKK regularly ambushes the military. Travel by road after dark is hazardous throughout Turkey. There are currently four groups fighting at night, and any one of them will shoot you dead without asking a question. When we were staying in a small village, we were told about a man who set out to fetch his cow on a recent evening. Hearing noises in the dark, the entire town militia began firing their AK-47s and G3s into the dark on full automatic. Luckily, the man was only injured. Road and driving conditions off the main highways and in remote areas are particularly dangerous. A curfew exists from dusk to dawn, so plan your itinerary accordingly. Turkish drivers drive fast but are generally considerate. Buses are common but are subject to lengthy searches at all checkpoints. Turkish authorities expect travelers to cooperate with travel restrictions and other security measures imposed in the east—which means you should get plenty of permission and paperwork before you go.

Ataturk Airport, near Istanbul, is the main international entry and exit point. Turkish air carriers are modern and safe. Ankara's airport is the hub for domestic flights and about 20 miles from downtown.

Dangerous Places

Eastern Provinces

With the exception of the Mediterranean and Black Sea coasts, travel in Turkey can be hazardous—particularly eastern Turkey. Terrorist acts by the PKK continue throughout the eastern provinces. These attacks are not only against Turkish police and military installations, but also against civilian targets, including public ground transportation. While most attacks have been at night, daytime attacks are increasingly frequent. Over the past 10 years, several thousand Turkish civilians and security personnel have been killed in terrorist attacks. In 1991, the PKK began kidnapping foreigners in eastern Turkey to generate media attention for their separatist cause. Over the past three years, a number of foreigners, including Americans, have been held by the PKK and eventually released. On October 9, 1993, an American tourist was abducted by the PKK while traveling by bus on the main highway between Erzurum and Erzincan. Due to the tense security situation, the climbing of Mt. Ararat in eastern Turkey is extremely dangerous, even with the required Turkish government permits. In light of these dangerous security conditions for travelers in eastern Turkey, the U.S. military has advised its personnel to avoid all tourist travel to this region. U.S. embassy and consulate personnel travel to eastern Turkey only for essential U.S. government business, and only with prior approval. In instances where travel to cities in eastern Turkey is essential, air travel is considered safer than other forms of public transportation. As stated above, travel to this part of Turkey should not be undertaken without first consulting the American embassy in Ankara, ☎ *[90] (312) 468-6110*, or the American consulate in Adana, ☎ *[90] (322) 454-3774*.

The Hills Are Alive with the Sound of Gunships

Travel to east Turkey is most dangerous in the spring and summer. That's when the government offensives get going. In other countries, like Cambodia, the dry seasons herald the sound of rockets and mortars. Keep this in mind when making your travel plans.

Istanbul

Police presence is heavy at historic sites to guard against any major terrorist incidents. However, during August 1994, there were two incidents of terrorism directed at tourists in Istanbul. One group of German tourists was attacked by a young man with a small incendiary device. The other attack involved a hand grenade being tossed under a parked Hungarian tourist bus. In both cases, tourists suffered minor injuries. Istanbul does not have a major crime problem. Typical street crimes (i.e., purse snatchings, pickpocketings and thefts) have been reported in the major shopping areas, tourist sites and around many hotels. The U.S. consulate warns visitors to stay away from nightclubs in the Beyoglu section of the city. Frequently, visitors to these clubs have been subjected to scams that have resulted in a loss of money and, in some instances, physical assault.

Ankara

While Americans living in Ankara on a permanent basis are at some risk of being involved in a terrorist incident, visiting Americans are at significantly less risk. Some minor bomb attacks have occurred at American business offices in Ankara, and a U.S. military member was killed in late October 1991 by a car bomb. The locals' attitude toward Americans in Ankara is generally positive. Heavily armed police are a common sight throughout the city. Young Turkish males like to hassle American women. Americans living in Ankara on a permanent basis are more at risk from crime; burglaries to some American residences have been reported.

Western Turkey/Mediterranean and Aegean Areas

Expats are at some risk of being involved in a terrorist incident, although visiting Americans are at significantly less risk. However, during the summer of 1994, the PKK conducted a series of hand grenade attacks against establishments frequented by tourists in Antalya and planted at least six hand grenades in beaches around Izmir and Kusdasi. The Antalya attacks injured both Turkish nationals and tourists, as well as causing extensive property damage. These attacks apparently were directed at financially damaging Turkey's tourist industry rather than causing tourist casualties. Crime against Americans is rare in western Turkey. However, there are continuing reports of pickpocketing and petty theft occurring among the large number of European tourists visiting the Turkish coast every summer.

Dangerous Things

Crime, Muggings and Bar Brawls

There is the usual petty crime against tourists, including pickpocketing, purse snatching and mugging. In Istanbul, incidents have been reported of tourists who have been drugged and robbed in nightclubs and bars, usually by other foreigners who speak English and French. Americans have been involved in fights at discos, and bar scams involving girls ordering drinks at inflated costs have been reported.

Pavions

There is a certain style of clipjoint in Istanbul and Ankara called a glitter bar, or *pavion*. Many are found around Taksim Square in Istanbul. The pretty ladies you meet will order enough drinks to melt your VISA card. Even if you drink yourself into a coma without the help of a local lass, your eyeballs will roll back in your head when you see the bill. Owners of pavions do not take kindly to debt restructuring or threats of recrimination. Many patrons have been robbed of watches or rings to meet payment with little sympathy from the local cops.

Newspaper Publishing

Don't publish anything advocating separatism or the Kurds in Turkey. Turkish police seized two days' editions of the pro-Kurdish journal *Ozgur Ulke* and accused it of publishing separatist propaganda. On orders from an antiterrorism court, police seized about 13,000 copies of the daily. Turkey maintains strict laws against advocating separatism.

Drugs

In Turkey, the penalties for possession, use, and dealing in illegal drugs are extremely strict, and convicted offenders can expect lengthy jail sentences and fines. Turkey is subject to smuggling of drugs due to its proximity to Syria and activity in the eastern states. Do not get involved.

Police Hassles

Dual U.S.-Turkish citizens may be subject to compulsory military service and other aspects of Turkish law while in Turkey. Those who may be affected can inquire at a Turkish embassy or consulate to determine status. In some instances, dual nationality may hamper U.S. government efforts to provide protection abroad.

Unauthorized purchase or removal from Turkey of antiquities or other important cultural artifacts is strictly forbidden. Violation of this law may result in imprisonment. At the time of departure, travelers who purchase such items may be asked to present a receipt from the seller as well as the official museum export certificate required by law.

Ankara

Police presence throughout Ankara is high. The Turkish National Police is headquartered in Ankara, and the quality of service it provides is adequate by American standards. However, response time in some cases can be significantly slower than that of its U.S. counterparts. Plainclothes policemen are used extensively. Although responsive, few Turkish policemen speak English, and communicating with them can be difficult. American citizens having a need to communicate with the police should contact the U.S. Embassy for assistance. The U.S. embassy security office can be reached at ☎ *[90] (312) 426-5470, extension 354* and the Air Force Office of Special Investigations at ☎ *[90] (312) 287-9957.*

Western Turkey/Mediterranean and Aegean Areas

Turkish National Police response to accidents and crime scenes in this part of Turkey is similar to that found in Ankara, except the uniformed police presence is not as heavy.

Istanbul

There are numerous police stations throughout the city, along with a large uniformed police presence around the major tourist areas. Police assistance is generally good. All Americans involved in a criminal incident are urged to contact the consulate at ☎ *[90] (212) 251-3602* for immediate assistance.

In Istanbul, street crime occurs more often due to the large number of tourists. Travelers should exercise caution and beware of pickpockets while shopping and sightseeing.

Some tourists have been drugged and robbed in Istanbul. Normally this occurs to persons traveling alone. Again, if at all possible, travel with a companion and avoid overly friendly tour guides or people offering free drinks or assistance.

There have been incidents reported where tourists, usually traveling alone, have been drugged and robbed by criminals, some posing as taxi drivers. Visitors must only ride in taxis with meters and should note the license plate in case there is a problem.

Getting Sick

Medical facilities are available, but may be limited outside urban areas. Doctors and hospitals often expect immediate cash payment for health services. In the southeastern city of Diyarbakir, there are recurring outbreaks of dysentery, typhoid fever, meningitis and other contagious diseases.

Nuts and Bolts

The local currency is the Turkish lira, a limp currency that makes you an instant millionaire each time you change about 15 bucks. Turkey has high plateaus and Mediterranean coastal areas. The plateau areas in the east get very cold in the winter and very hot in the summer. The fall and spring are quite pleasant. Istanbul has moderate temperatures year-round, with summer temps in the 80s (F) and winter lows in the mid 40s (F). Istanbul gets about four inches of rain a month in the winter.

The bulk of tourists in Turkey are Russians, attracted by the proximity, beaches and cheap goods. Germans comprise the second-largest block, followed by tourists from England, Romania and Israel.

The world's first town was Catalhoywk in central Anatoylia; it was founded in 6500 B.C.

Registration

U.S. citizens who register at the consular section of the U.S. embassy or consulate may obtain updated information on travel and security in Turkey.

Embassy and Consulate Locations

U.S. Embassy in Ankara
110 Ataturk Boulevard
☎ *[90] (312) 468-6110*

U.S. Consulate in Istanbul
104–108 Mesrutiyet Caddesi
Tepebasl
☎ *[90] (212) 251-3602*

U.S. Consulate in Adana
At the corner of Vali Yolu and AtaTurk Caddesi
☎ *[90] (322) 453-9106*

Adana local police emergency number
☎ *(322) 435-3195*

Americans who are victims of crimes may also call the consulate
☎ *(322) 454-2145*

Dangerous Days

04/17/1992	Turkish police killed 11 suspected Kurdish guerrillas in a series of raids in Istanbul. Kurds undertook several terrorist attacks in 1992 in Germany and Turkey citing this date.
08/30/1991	August 30, 1991, was celebrated as Victory Day and made an official Turkish holiday.
05/27/1991	May 27, 1991, was celebrated as Constitution Day and made an official Turkish holiday.
04/25/1988	Hagop Hagopian, leader of the Armenian Secret Army for the Liberation of Armenia (ASALA)—aka the Orly group, 3rd October Organization—was shot dead in his home in Athens by two gunmen. No group claimed responsibility for his murder.
09/06/1986	Twenty-one Jewish worshippers were killed in Istanbul during an attack on a synagogue by an Abu Nidal terrorist team.
08/15/1986	Turkish troops raided Kurdish rebel camps in Iraq.
08/15/1984	The day that Kurdish Workers Party (PKK) elements first launched an attack against Turkish government installations.

TURKEY

Dangerous Days

08/27/1982	The Turkish military attache in Canada was assassinated by Armenian extremists.
08/07/1982	Nine people, including one American, were killed, and more than 70 were wounded in an attack on the Ankara airport by the Armenian Secret Army for the Liberation of Armenia.
01/28/1982	The Turkish consul general to the U.S. was assassinated in Los Angeles by members of a group calling itself the Justice Commandos for the Armenian Genocide.
03/10/1979	The death of Kurdish leader Mullah Mustafa Barzani (Kurdish regions only).
11/27/1978	Considered to be the date on which the Kurdish Workers Party (PKK) was founded. PKK guerrillas may engage in terrorist attacks in connection with this date.
05/01/1977	More than 30 leftists were killed during clashes with security forces in Istanbul.
10/24/1975	The Turkish ambassador to France and his driver were shot and killed in Paris by members of the Armenian Secret Army for the Liberation of Armenia (ASALA).
01/22/1946	Kurdish Republic Day.
11/10/1938	Death of Kemal Ataturk.
10/29/1923	Turkish National Day. The date commemorates the declaration of Turkey as a republic by Mustafa Kemal Ataturk and his inauguration as its first president.
03/16/1921	Signing of the Soviet-Turkish border treaty that ended Armenian hopes of establishing an independent state.
04/24/1915	Armenians observe this date as the anniversary of the alleged 1915 Turkish genocide of Armenians.
03/12/1880	Birthday of Kemal Ataturk, founder of the modern Turkish state.
06/16	June 16 is the anniversary date of the founding of the Turkish leftist terrorist group, 16 June. Until 1987, the group acted under the name Partisan Yolu. Since 1987, the group has claimed responsibility for numerous acts of terrorism, including the December 1989 firebombing in Istanbul of the Hiawatha, a U.S. Government–owned yacht.
03/21	Kurdish New Year.

TURKEY

In a Dangerous Place

East Turkey: Rocking the Cradle of Civilization

The road is full of vehicles—tractors, horse carts, sawed-off buses with sagging rear ends, yellow taxis, overloaded motorcycles with sidecars—some carrying entire families with their goats. Everything is square and grey. The road and sidewalks are broken, dirty and patched. Unlike the deathly grey of the towns, the hills beyond are a rich chocolate-brown. The water is a sickly green-blue-black. The sky is the color of slate, with one enormous white cloud stretching off toward the hills in the distance. Acres of cheap boxlike housing sprout from the plains.

DP has come to the cradle of civilization, the uppermost tip of the fertile crescent, now torn apart by ethnic, political, tribal and religious strife. We are determined to get at the heart of this land, in order to understand why so much of the world is a dangerous place.

We stop to buy gas at a new petrol station. The attendant is baffled by our credit card. I run the card and sign the bill for him.

We drive past scattered groves of figs and pistachios. Trucks carry giant pomegranates. We are following the Iraqi pipeline on a highway originally built by the U.S., formally known as the "Silk Road."

Cheap Iraqi diesel, or *masot,* sells for 10,000 TL (Turkish lira or lire) a liter. It is brought from Iraq by trucks fitted with crude, rusty tanks.

As we go east, the fertile soil becomes fields of boulders and sharp rocks. The hills are ribbed and worn by the constant foraging of goats. Not much has changed here in 1000 years.

At Play in the Fields of the Warlords

We drive through the nameless streets of Sevirek, a small town that serves as the center of the Bucak fiefdom. In this age of enlightenment, there are still dark corners in the world where ancient traditions persist. We are in the domain of the Bucaks, an age-old feudal area in war-torn southeastern Turkey.

As we drive along the cobblestones, we notice that there are no doors or windows in the stone houses, only steel shutters and gates. We ask the way to the warlord's house. Men pause and then point vaguely in the general direction.

We pull up to the Turkish version of a pizza joint. From inside, two men in white smocks eye us apprehensively. The fat one recognizes Coskun and walks out to our car when we call out for directions.

We drive up a narrow cobblestone alleyway just wide enough for a car to pass. There's a Renault blocking the way. Getting out of the car, we notice for the first time that there is a man behind a wall of sandbags pointing an AK-47 in our direction. The large house was built 200 years ago and is lost in the maze of medieval streets and stone walls.

We politely explain who we are and why we have come. We had telephoned earlier and were told that no one was at home—an appropriate response for someone who has survived frequent assassination attempts from terrorists, bandits and the army.

Out from a side door comes a large man with a pistol stuffed into his ammunition-heavy utility vest. He flicks his head at me and looks at Coskun inquisitively. He hears our story. He recognizes Coskun from a year ago, when the photojournalist stayed with the warlord for three days. He smiles and gives Coskun the double-buss kiss, the traditional greeting for men in Turkey. He then grabs me by the shoulders, does the same, and then welcomes us inside. We walk up one flight of stairs and find ourselves in an outside courtyard. We are joined by two more bodyguards. They're older, more grooved, hard looking. Most of one man's chin has been blown off his face; it tells us that we should probably just sit and smile until we get to know each other a little better. We sit on the typical tiny wooden stools men use in Turkey. These have the letters DYP branded into them, the name of the political party with which the warlord has aligned himself.

The bodyguards stare into our eyes, say nothing and watch our hands when we reach for a cigarette. It seems that Sedat Bucak, the clan leader, is out in the fields, but his brother Ali is here. We are offered *chai*, or tea, and cigarettes. The bodyguards do not drink tea, or move, but they light cigarettes. One of the bodyguards sucks on his cigarette as if to suffocate it.

When Ali finally emerges, he is not at all what one would expect a warlord to look like. The men rise and bow. Ali is dressed in shiny black loafers, blue slacks, a plum-colored striped shirt and a dapper windbreaker. He looks like an Iranian USC grad. That he and his brother are the absolute rulers of 100,000 people and in control of an army of 10,000 very tough men is hard to imagine.

A Drive in the Country

Not quite sure why we're here, he offers to show us a gazelle that he was given as a gift by one of his villages. The gazelle is kept in a stone enclosure and flies around the pen, leaping through doors and windows. We ask if we can visit with Sedat. Ali says, "Sure," and repeats that he is out in the fields.

Realizing they would be embarking outside of their compound, they bring out an arsenal of automatic weapons from another room. Ali and his bodyguards get in the Renault and drive down the streets with the barrels of their guns sticking out the windows. Strangely, nobody seems to mind or notice. Even the soldiers and police wave as they drive by.

Following close behind, we are brought to their fortress, an imposing black stone compound that dominates the countryside. It is a simple square structure, each wall about 100 feet long. A central house rises to about 40 feet. The walls are made from *kaaba*, or black stone and are hand-chiseled from the surrounding boulders into squares, filled with special cement to make them bulletproof. One wall is over 20 feet tall.

The men appear nervous when I photograph the compound. This building is intended for combat. For now, it serves as a simple storage place for tractors and grain. From the top, one feels like a king overlooking his land and his subjects, which is exactly what the Bucaks do when they are up here. From this point, we can only see 50 miles to the mountains in the north, but we cannot see the rest of their 200 miles of land to the south and west of us.

We continue our caravan along a dusty road past simple villages and houses. The people here are dirt-poor. They subsist off the arid land. The children run out into the road to wave at us as we drive by.

Ali stops near a field where men, women and children are picking cotton. Cotton needs water, and there's plenty of it. It also needs cheap labor, another commodity of which the Bucaks have plenty.

The people stand still, as we get out of our cars. Ali tells them to continue working, while we take pictures. They resume picking, but their eyes never leave us.

The men decide this would be an opportune time to show off the capability of their arsenal. For one nauseating moment, I have the impression they intend to gun down this entire village. Yet it is target practice that Ali has in mind. Boys will be boys. So we then start plinking away at rocks, using all sorts of automatic weapons. We aim for a pile of rocks about 400 yards away. We are only aware of little puffs of smoke, as we hear the sound of ricochets as the bullets hit the black boulders. Ali is more interested in our video camera, so he plays with that while we play with his weapons.

When boredom sets in, we continue our journey in search of Sedat. We finally locate him about three miles away. We know it's him because of the small army that surrounds the man. His bodyguards are not happy at all to see us. We are instantly engulfed by his men poised in combat stances. Ali introduces us, but we still have to state our case. Sedat recognizes Coskun, but instead of the kiss, we get a Western-style handshake. We introduce ourselves to his dozen or so bodyguards. They do not come forward, so we reach for their hands and shake them. It's awkward, unnerving. They never let their eyes stray from ours.

Ahmed, a chiseled sunburned man who wears green camouflage fatigues, seems to be the chief bodyguard. He appears to like us the least. He wanders over to our car and starts rummaging through the luggage and junk on the backseat. I deliberately put my stuff there so that it would be easy to confirm that I am a writer. He picks up a Fielding catalog and starts flipping through the pages. When he sees my picture next to one of my books, he points and then looks at me.

The Feudal Lord

We chat with Sedat. He is eager to present a positive image to the outside world. We have brought a copy of an interview he had just done with a Turkish magazine. In it, he proposes linking up with the right-wing nationalist party and, together he says, they could end the Kurdish problem. Coskun suggests that such a comment could be taken as a bid for civil war. Sedat says, "Hey, it's only an interview. But I'm still learning." We suggest getting some shots of him driving his tractor. He is happy driving his tractor. But out here there are few other farmers who drive a tractor with an AK-47-armed bodyguard riding behind on the spreader.

Turkey has been at war with the PKK, or Kurdish Workers Party, since 1984. The Kurds want a separate homeland within Turkey, but Turkey insists they possess all the rights they need for now. The Turkish government is correct, but it doesn't stop the PKK from killing, maiming, executing and torturing their own people. The Bucaks are Kurds and the sworn enemies of the PKK, who are also Kurds. The difference is that the Bucaks have essentially carved out their own kingdom and even managed to integrate themselves into the political process in an effective, albeit primitive, way. They use votes rather than bullets to curry favor. They are also left alone by the government. They pay no taxes and have complete control over what goes on in their ancestral lands.

The Bucak family has been in Sevirek for more than 400 years. They are Kurds, but more specifically, they're from the Zaza as opposed to the Commange branch of the Kurds. They also speak a different language from the Commange. They have always controlled a large part of southeastern Turkey by force and eminent domain. Their subjects give them 25 percent of the crops they grow, and, in return, they receive services and are protected by a private army of about 10,000 men. Many other groups have tried unsuccessfully to force them off their land. In times of all-out warfare, all the subjects are expected to chip in and grab their rifles. The Bucaks have wisely aligned themselves with the current ruling political party, the DYP. Realizing that the Bucaks can deliver 100,000 votes goes a long way toward successful lobbying and handshaking in Ankara, the capital of Turkey. Sedat Bucak is head of the clan, at the age of 40. A warrior and farmer by trade, he is now a sharp and shrewd politician. If he's killed, his younger brother Ali will take the helm. Ali is only 24.

Sevirek has long been a battleground. The city was completely closed to all outsiders, including the army, between 1970 and 1980. During this period, there was intense street-to-street fighting between the Bucaks and the PKK. Thousands of people were killed; the PKK moved on to choose easier victims. The Bucaks cannot stray eastward into PKK-held territory without facing instant death.

The countryside the Bucaks rule consists of rolling plains, similar to Montana or Alberta. This is to the benefit of the Ataturk dam project, the fifth-largest dam project in the world.

Sedat can never travel without his bodyguards; neither can Ali. The bodyguards match the personalities of the brothers. Sedat's bodyguards are cold, ruthless killers. They're picked for the bravery and ferocity they showed in the last 10 years of warfare. Ali's bodyguards are younger, friendlier, but just as lethal.

They pack automatic weapons: German G-3s, M-15s and AK-47s. They each also carry at least one handgun as well as four to six clips for the machine guns and three to four clips for their pistols. Ali and Sedat also carry weapons at all times. Their choice of weapons also reflects their personalities. Ali packs a decorative stainless steel 9mm Ruger, and Sedat carries a drab businesslike Glock 17.

Some of the bodyguards, such as Nouri, wear the traditional Kurdish garb of checkered headpiece and baggy wool pants. The *salvars* appear to be too hot to wear on the sunburned plains. One of the guards explains that they work like a bellows and pump air when you walk, an example of something that works. Others wear cheap suits. Some wear golf shirts; still others wear military apparel.

While we are taking pictures of Sedat on his Massey Ferguson, the guards bring out the *gnass*, or sniper rifle (*gnass* is Arabic for sniper). It is an old Russian weapon designed to kill men at 4000 meters. When I walk down to take pictures, Ahmed, the cagey one, slides the rifle into the car and shakes his head. He knows that a sniper rifle is not for self-defense but is used for one thing only, as they explain to us, "With this rifle, you can kill a man before he knows he is dead."

Many of the men have a Turkish flag on the butts of their clips. One bodyguard offers me a rolled cigarette from an old silver tin. It tastes of the sweet, mild tobacco from Ferat. We both have a smoke. I open my khaki shirt and show him my Black Dog T-shirt, a picture of a dog doing his thing. He laughs: Seems as if we're finally warming up this crowd.

The younger brother of Ali's bodyguard asks me if I am licensed to use guns. He likes the way I shoot. I try to explain that, in America, you need a permit to own a gun and that people are trained or licensed. He looks at me quizzically. It's no use. I doubt they would understand a society that lets you own a gun without knowing how to use it.

We blast off some more rounds. Ali's bodyguards are having fun. We then bring out the handguns. We are all bad shots. Trying to hit a Pepsi can, no one comes close. Then one of the bodyguards marches to the can and "executes" it with a smile. It is a chilling scene, and I'm glad it's only an aluminum can.

While Ali's bodyguards clown around with us, Sedat's bodyguards never move, or even take their hands off their guns. Nouri has his AK-47 tucked so perfectly into the crook of his arm, it is hard to imagine him not sleeping with it.

After chatting with Sedat and nervously entertaining his bodyguards, we head back into town. There, we're taken to lunch at Ali Bucaks restaurant and gas station. We eat in Ali's office. The bodyguards act as waiters, serving us shepherd's salads and kabobs with yogurt to drink. They serve us quietly and respectfully. They eat with one hand on their guns. The SSB radio crackles nonstop, as various people check in. We talk to Ali about life in general. Can he go anywhere without his guards? No. What about when he goes to Ankara on the plane? They have to put their guns in plastic bags and pick them up when they land. What about in Ankara? They change cars a lot. Does he like his role? He doesn't have a choice. Does he like feudalism? No, but he doesn't have a choice. The government does not provide services or protect their people, so they must do it themselves. Who would take the sick to the hospitals? Who would take care of the widows? Since power is passed along family lines, it is his duty.

As we eat, a storm comes in from Iraq. Lightning flashes and thunder cracks. We talk about politics, baseball cards and America. They are all familiar with America because every Turkish home and business has a television blaring most of the day and night. The number-one show is the soap, "The Young and the Restless," which comes on at 6:15 every night.

Sedat is a soft-spoken man—about 5 feet 6 inches tall, sunburned and suffering from a mild thyroid condition. He wears a faded green camouflage baseball hat, Levis and running shoes, as your neighbor might. He also carries a Glock 17 in a hand-rubbed leather holster. It is unsnapped for a quicker draw. Maybe not quite like your neighbor! He is never more than 15 feet from his bodyguards. Men drawn from his army as personal bodyguards have the lean, sunburned look of cowboys. He comes from an immediate family of 500 Bucaks. They make their money by growing cotton and other crops they sell in Adana.

It is hard to believe that this gentle, slightly nervous man and his forces are the only ones in Turkey who here been able to beat the PKK at their own game.

For now, everything is well in the kingdom. The dam will bring water for crops; the PKK is now concentrating on other areas; the people are happy, and Sedat is now a big-wheel politician. There is much to be said for feudalism. I offer to send him some of my books so that he can read about the rest of the world. He thinks this is a great idea. But he doesn't speak or read English.

TURKEY

DP Fashion Tip

Mekap is the brand of sneakers preferred by the PKK. They can be identified by the red star on a yellow badge. If you ask at a shoe store for Mekaps, you will get a very strange reaction; the merchant will assume you're from the police and testing him.

We drive from Sevirek to Diyarbakir. We will pass from a feudal kingdom to a large, bustling city that is the flashpoint for much of the violence that grips Turkey. We realize as we drive down the lonely roads that we are leaving the protection of the Bucaks and will soon be in PKK territory. If we were to be caught with Ali's address, we'd be killed. If the PKK had any knowledge of our contact with the Bucaks, we'd be instant enemies.

The PKK control the countryside and, it is said, the whole of eastern Turkey at night. It is not a particularly large group, perhaps some 8000 soldiers trained in small camps, but they're armed with small weapons—AK-47s and RPGs and a few grenade launchers. They travel in groups of 12 men and can muster a sizable force of about 200 soldiers for major ambushes. Their leader lives in the Bekáa Valley in southern Lebanon, under the protection of the Syrian government. He calls for an independent Kurdistan, which Saddam Hussein has given him by default in northern Iraq. But he wants more. He wants a sizable chunk of Iran and Turkey as well.

Despite the numerous checkpoints and military presence in the area, there has been little success in defeating the PKK. The Turkish Army has set up large special ops teams and commando units that specialize in ambushes, foot patrols and other harassment activities. But once you see the topography of eastern Turkey, you realize that you could hide an army 1000 times the size of the PKK. The terrain is riddled with caves, redoubt-shaped cliffs, boulders, canyons and every conceivable type of nook and cranny. It is easy terrain to move in, with few natural or man-made obstructions.

The PKK go into the villages at night to demand cooperation. If villagers do not cooperate, they are shot. In some cases, entire families, including babies, are executed. The PKK follow a Marxist-Leninist doctrine and play out their guerrilla tactics similar to the former Viet Cong or the Khmer Rouge. The PKK also likes to kidnap foreigners for money and publicity, and they like to execute schoolteachers and government officials. Special ops teams report to the civil authorities and to the military. Turkey considers the PKK as criminals and is reluctant to use civil law and superficial civilian forces against it.

Turkey has been in a state of war for 10 years now—that being the war the military is waging within its own borders.

The Test Pilot

We decide to spend an evening with a former leader and trainer of special ops teams. Hakan is now Turkey's only test pilot. In Turkey, this doesn't mean flying new prototype planes; it means flying out to helicopters downed by the rebels, making repairs and then flying or sling-loading them out.

Hakan lives in a high-rise building, guarded by three soldiers, barbed wire and fortifications against attack. His apartment is modern and well furnished. There are no traditional rugs, just black lacquer furniture complete with a fully stocked bar. Except for the barbed wire, we could be in Florida, which is where he trained as a Sikorsky Blackhawk pilot.

He has a two-month-old baby and is looking forward to being transferred back to western Turkey. His contempt for the PKK is obvious, having killed many of its members and having many PKK rounds aimed at him. He feels that the PKK is winning in this part of the country, but there will be no victory. The PKK problem cannot be solved militarily. It must be solved economically, by making the Kurds the beneficiaries of government help and giving them a stronger political voice. Killing terrorists is merely his job. He can't wait to get transferred out of Dyabakir. His wife plays with their baby on the floor. The baby never stops smiling and laughing. I think of the barbed wire and nervous soldiers downstairs. He can offer no political insights: PKK are people who he is paid to fight. When he is in Ankara, he will occupy himself with other things.

Eastern Turkey is the poorest and least developed part of the nation. Most educated people come from western Turkey. Most of the soldiers, politicians and professional classes are from western Turkey. The government sends these people to eastern Turkey for a minimum of two years of service. Most can't wait to get back to Istanbul or Ankara. Eastern Turkey has much closer affiliations with Armenia, Iran, Iraq, Azerbaijan, Syria and Georgia. Western Turkey has the ocean as a border. Eastern Turkey is rife with dissension and must deal with its warlike and poor neighbors. Iraqi, Iranian, Armenian and Syrian terrorists actively fight the government and each other. Hezbollah, the Iranian-backed fundamentalist group, hates the PKK. The PKK hates the government. The militia hates all rebel agitators, and the army and police clean up the messes left behind.

The Governor

I decide that we need another point of view. We go to Siirt about 40 km from the Syrian border and directly in the heart of PKK territory. We are definitely in harm's way, since the PKK travel from Syria into the mountains behind us. Just down the road is the military outpost of Erub, designed to control a critical mountain road that leads down toward the Syrian border. There is another reason why we have chosen this tiny town. Coskun was born and raised in Siirt. I suggest that we go and chat up the governor and get his point of view.

Coskun is somewhat hesitant about meeting with the governor of Siirt province, because he has a natural (and well-founded) aversion to politicians. But since we will be traveling directly into and through the war zone, we want to be sure that when we get stopped by the military we can drop names, flash the governor's card and ensure at least a moment of hesitation before we are shot as spies or terrorists.

As we pass the heavy security of the Siirt administration building, it seems that the governor is in. His bodyguards are quite perturbed that these strangers have walked right in and asked for an audience. They quietly talk into their walkie-talkies and stand between us and the soundproofed door that leads into the governor's office. The governor takes his time to put on his game face and finally invites us in. It is kisses all around, chocolates, tea and cigarettes. We thank him and tell him our business. We are here to see what is going on in Turkey. He is proud to have us in his region. Two of his aids sit politely on the couch. The governor speaks in long, melodious, booming soliloquies that, when translated into English, come out as "We are maligned by the press" or "There is no danger here." Finally, they ask me what I have seen and what I think of their country. I tell them the truth. The people here are extraordinary in their friendship and warmth but we are in a war zone. He launches into a response that boils down to "It's safe here, and we want you to tell your readers to come to Turkey and Siirt province." He then tells us of the attractions that await the lucky traveler: canyons as deep as the Grand Canyon, white-water rafting, hiking, culture, history, etc. We say great, give us a helicopter and we'll go for a spin tomorrow.

He goes one further. He invites us to dinner that night so that he can spend more time with us. Coskun wants to kick me, as I accept. Later that night we go to the government building for dinner. Joining us will be the head of police, the head of the military, three subgovernors and a couple of aides.

We pass through security and are ushered into the dining room. Sitting uncomfortably, we make small talk while a television blares away against the wall. As we sit down to dinner, we indicate that we are curious and ask the military commander just what is going on. Everyone is dressed in a suit and tie or uniform. Coskun and I do the best we can with our dusty khakis. Either because the room is hot or they are just being polite, they take their jackets off for dinner. The governor carries a silver 45 tucked into his waistband. His formal gun? As the men sit down to dinner, something strikes me as funny. Coskun and I are the only ones not packing a gun for dinner.

The dinner is excellent: course after course of shish kebob, salads and other delicacies washed down with *raki* (a strong anisette liquor) and water. The taste of the *raki* brings back memories of the hard crisp taste of Cristal aquadiente, the preferred drink of the Colombian drug trade. Throughout dinner, the head of police is interrupted by a walkie-talkie-carrying messenger who hands him a piece of paper. He makes a few comments to the side, and the man disappears. Every five to 10 minutes the man returns, the police chief makes a quiet comment, and he goes away.

Meanwhile, the governor continues to extol the beauty of his country—nonstop. He is the center of attention, simply because no one else is speaking. The others nod, smile or laugh. Most of their attention is on the television blaring in the corner. Suddenly, the red phone next to the television begins ringing. The call is answered by the attendant. It is for the colonel. The colonel excuses the interruption and speaks in low tones. The police chief puts his walkie-talkie on the table. It becomes apparent that the base is under attack by a group of PKK of unknown size. Throughout dinner, the conversation steers toward politics as it must. Like many countries, there are two parallel worlds here: the world of administrators, occupiers and government, then the world of the dispossessed—the people who till the soil, who build their houses with their own hands, who bury their dead in the same ground that yields them their crops. Tonight and every night, that world is ruled by the PKK, Dev Sol, Armenian terrorists, Hezbollah and bandits. At dusk, the world is plunged into fear, ruled by armed bands of men that are neither chosen nor wanted by the ordinary people. At dawn, the country is back in the hands of the government, the people and the light. During our conversation, there is no right and no wrong, only an affirmation that each side believes it is in the right.

The red phone continues to ring, and the little pieces of paper continue to be brought up to the police chief. The police chief is now speaking directly into his walkie-talkie. Meanwhile, the governor continues to regale us with stories about Siirt. As we eat course after course, I am offered cigarettes by at least three to four people at a time. Doing my best to accommodate my hosts, I eat, smoke and drink the sharp *raki,* all the time keeping one ear on the governor's conversation and the constant mumbled conversations being carried out on the phone and the walkie-talkie.

The governor is very proud of the tie he wore especially for me—a pattern of Coca-Cola bottles. He brings in his young daughters to meet me. They are shy, pretty and very proud of their English. We chat about life in Siirt, and I realize that they are virtually prisoners in the governor's compound. The governor tells us of a road we should take to enjoy the scenery, a winding scenic road to Lice via Kocakoy. Finally, the colonel is spending so much time on the phone that he excuses himself. The police chief is visibly agitated but is now speaking nonstop on the walkie-talkie. Messages continue to arrive.

The television is now featuring swimsuit-clad lovelies and has captured the attention of the governor's aides and his subgovernors. As the dinner winds down, we retire outside to have coffee. I am presented with a soft wool blanket woven in Siirt. We have a brief exchange of speeches, and I notice that the colonel and police chief have now joined us. I ask them what all the commotion was about, and they mention that it was a minor incident that has been handled. The governor reminds us to tell people of the beauty of this place, the friendliness of the Turkish people and the people of Siirt.

As we prepare to go, they wrap my blanket in today's newspaper. Smack dead center is a full-color photograph of a blood-soaked corpse of a man who has been executed by the Dev Sol terrorist group for being an informer.

The next day, there is no helicopter waiting for us. When we inquire as to its whereabouts, we are told that it was needed to do a body count from the attack the night before. We ask the blue-bereted special ops soldier what the best way is to see the countryside. He assumes that we must be important, and, instead of telling us to get lost, he carefully reviews our options. As for the road we want to take into the mountains, he informs us that it is heavily mined and would have to be cleared before we could attempt a crossing. In any case, we would need an armored car and an escort of soldiers and probably a tank. We ask about the helicopter, which would be safer, but we will need to wait until he can get a gunship to accompany us.

A Place in Time

We figure the only sightseeing we are going to do today is on foot. Coskun reminisces with his first employer, a gentle man who puts out a tiny newspaper with a 19th-century offset press and block type. He has broken his arm, so he apologizes on the back page for the paper being so small. Everyday he laboriously pecks out the local news with one finger using an old Remington typewriter; he then reads his copy, marks it up, and hands it to the eager teenagers who sort through the dirty trays of lead type. He has a choice between two photoengraved pictures that sit in a worn old tray. One is the governor, the other is the president of Turkey. When the type is hand-set, they laboriously run off a couple of hundred copies for the dwindling number of loyal readers. I leave Coskun with his old friend.

Siirt is a dusty, poor Kurdish town, with a history of being occupied by everyone from Alexander to the Seljuks to the Ottomans. Some of the people are fair-skinned, blonde and blue-eyed. Others have the hard Arabic look of the south; while still others have the round heads and bald spots of the Turks. Siirt is a happy town, with the children contentedly playing in the muddy streets. As I walk around the town, the children begin to tag along with me. All are eager to try out their words of English. I urge them to teach me Kurdish. They point at houses, dogs, people, and chatter away, "Where come you from?" and "Hello mister, what eeze your name?" I wonder where I would ever need to use Kurdish. Some visitors say Siirt looks like a poorly costumed bible story. Here and there along the broken streets are ancient houses with tapered walls; many people still use the streets as sewers. Goats, cows and chickens wander the streets. Near the mosque, the less fortunate goats are sold and then slaughtered on the spot. Donkeys sit patiently. Men physically pull me over to where they are sitting and demand that we have tea. I realize it would take me years if I stopped and had tea with everyone who wanted to chat. I begin to respect the delicate but strong social web that holds this country together. Soldiers, fighters, rebels, farmers, politicians, police all offer us hospitality, tea and a cigarette. The tiny parcels of information and face-to-face encounters transmit and build an understanding of what is going on, who is going where and why.

In every shop a television blares. Western programs and news shows constantly bombard these people with images that do not fit into their current world. At 6:10 "The Young and the Restless," dubbed in Turkish, captures the entire population. It is typically Turkish that they would treat the TV like a visitor, never shutting it up and quietly waiting for their turn to speak. I can only imagine that the blatant American and Western European images are as familiar and comforting to the older generation as MTV's "The Grind" is to us. As with all small rural towns around the world, the young people are moving to the big cities. The future is colliding with the past.

They're Your Modern Stone Age Family

We decide not to hang around and wait for the helicopter and the helicopter gunship to be arranged. Instead, we decide to drive into the countryside, where the army has little control. Along the way, we stop in a little-known troglodyte village called Hassankeyf. Here, Coskun knows an old lady who lives in a cave. In three years, this historic area will be underwater when the massive hydroelectric dam is completed. Hassankeyf could be a set from "The Flintstones." The winding canyon is full of caves that go up either side, creating a cave-dwellers high-rise development. Far up in the highest cave is the last resident of this area. The lady claims to be 110-years-old. I guess she is closer to 80. But it probably doesn't matter, since in this land, she could be older than Methuselah and have seen nothing change. We climb up to chat with her, while down below the golden rays of the sun illuminate the Sassouk mosque. Across the canyon are the ruins of a Roman-era monastery. This was once a remote outpost for the Romans.

She doesn't seem pleased to see us. In a grouchy manner, she invites us into her cave. The lady lives alone with a cat and her donkey. The donkey has his own cave carved cleanly and laboriously out of the soft limestone.

The cave where the old woman lives leads back into a rear cave, where she makes her bed on straw and carpets. The roof is covered with a thick greasy layer of soot from the small fire she uses for cooking. She says she is ill and needs medicine. We have brought her a bar of chocolate but we do not have any medicine with us. We give her some money but realize she is days away from any drugstore and her only method of transport is her donkey or a ride from one of the villagers.

People from across the steep valley yell and wave at us. They do not get many visitors. We take pictures of the lady. She seems happy to have someone to talk to, and, after her initial grumpiness, she offers us some flat bread. It crunches with the dirt and gravel baked into it. We smile and say it is good.

As the sun sets further, the ancient ambience is broken by the loud thumping and hoarse whistling scream of a Cobra gunship returning to Siirt. This was probably our escort, but we are glad to be sitting here in the cool golden dusk in a cave, in a place that will soon be erased off the map.

We have to leave. Travel at night is not safe. The PKK control this area and the military will fire at anything that moves on the roads at night. We must make it to the Christian town of Mardil, or as the locals call it Asyriac, before it gets completely dark. The old lady wishes us well. The Christians who live in the town of Mardil speak the language of Jesus: Aramaic. Strange that we are also in the land of the Yezidi, the religion that prays to Satan. We are told the PKK do not attack Asyriac because of their ties to Assad. Here, we will spend the night with some people who hold the honor of having the most dangerous profession in east Turkey: schoolteachers.

The Most Dangerous Job

Schoolteachers are part of the colonial oppression against which the PKK is fighting. Kurdish children are not allowed to speak the native tongue in school. Teachers in Turkey are assigned to work for four years in East Turkey before they can work in the more lucrative eastern cities of Istanbul and Ankara. Here, they are paid 8 million Turkish lira a month, about $220 U.S. and about 30 percent more than they would usually make. About 30 percent never do their time in east Turkey and buy their way out of the dangerous assignment. By comparison, soldiers get paid 35–40 million Turkish lira a month.

The teachers live in simple stone houses—one room for living and one room for sleeping. There is no plumbing; the bathroom is an outhouse about 20 yards from the house. But these conditions are not what make this job dangerous. Over the last three years, 75 schoolteachers have been executed by the PKK. Schoolteachers in east Turkey are not raving political stooges of the government who spread torment and hate.They are bright college-educated people who teach reading, writing and math. Many are just starting families and enjoy the work they do. The few who are dragged out of their houses at night, sentenced, and shot in the chest probably wonder what they did to deserve such a cold and uncelebrated death.

We spend the evening with two young teachers, a husband and wife, and their two young girls. They share their simple food and are good company. There is little to do here once the sun goes down.The inside of the simple stone house reminds me of a bomb shelter: whitewashed, cold and damp. The house is lit with a single bare lightbulb hanging down from the ceiling. After dinner, we walk to the homes of the other teachers in this small village. Each family of teachers is happy to meet outsiders. There are two young female teachers who bring us cookies and tea, and there are two married couples, each with a small child. We gather together in their simple homes and talk about life in the war zone. Three days ago, three teachers just northwest of here were rounded up, tied hand and foot, and shot the same way you would kill an old dog.

Many people feel that the teachers were shot because they had weapons in their houses. After the shootings, the teachers from this village traveled to town to talk to the region's military commander and protest the arming of teachers as militia. The colonel instead greeted them as the protectors of the village. Taken aback, they explained that they thought he was the protector of the village. "No," he smiled and said, "it is much too dangerous to have troops out there at night." The colonel offered them rifles and ammunition to give them peace of mind. "After all," he said, "I am surrounded by hundreds of soldiers, barbed wire and fortifications as well as over a hundred trained antiterrorist commandos for backup." He offered the teachers one of each: a "big gun" (a German G-3) for the men and a little gun (AK-47s) for the women. Not knowing how to react, the teachers abandoned their first line of attack and glumly accepted the weapons and boxes of ammunition. They admitted to us they had no idea how to use them and were terrified that the children would find the rifles under their beds. So they kept them unloaded.

As I walked back under a brilliant star-filled sky, I marveled at the ridiculousness of it all. Here we were with eager, youthful young men and women—educated, enthusiastically discussing life and politics, sharing what little they have and trying to make sense of it all, while a few miles down the road was the PKK training base of Eruh and the Syrian border only 50 km away. The town has been the scene of heavy fighting between the PKK and the Turkish special forces. No one dares go out of the village at night for fear of being shot as a terrorist by the nervous militia.

The people are thankful for their stone houses, as they cower below windows during the heaviest shooting. Here, there is no doctor, no store, no transportation, no facilities of any kind. To think that a beautiful night like this could be interrupted by sudden death is unimaginable.

Tearing Down the Silk Road

Despite our token flirtation with death, we spend a sunny morning playing with the children and then continue on our way to the Iraqi border. I am curious. Just before we leave the village, we are stopped by a group of people. They point to a stinking swamp in the center of the village. They complain that the government came in to build a pond and now it is a sewer. They seem to think that we have some way to restore it. We listen, shrug our shoulders and sadly drive off.

Winding our way down to the main road, we inhale the clean mountain air and stop to take pictures of the sparkling brooks and lush scenery. This can't be a war zone. Down on the main road, the military checkpoints begin. At the first checkpoint 14 km from Cizre, we are quite bluntly asked, "What the hell are you doing here?" The appropriate answer seems to be the most absurd: "Just looking around." Cooling our heels and drinking tea in the commander's bunker, we are given our passports back and smugly told that we have been scooped. A television news crew from "32 GUN" (a Turkish news show) had already made it into Iraq. The commander assumes that we are journalists trying to cover Saddam's big military push to the south. Apparently, the television crew got special permission from the Iraqi embassy in Ankara and is the only news crew in Iraq. Not too bothered by this revelation, we share a cigarette with the sergeant, and more tea is brought out. It appears that our time with the governor and the military commander of Siirt province has paid off. We ask the officer in charge if he could radio ahead and let the trigger-happy soldiers know we are coming.

We should be in the cradle of civilization, between the fertile thighs of the Tigris and the Euphrates. Instead, we are in a hair-trigger war zone, where every man is a potential killer and every move might be your last.

We take a few Polaroids for the officer and we hit the road again. At each blown bridge and sandbagged checkpoint, we stop and chat with the soldiers. Up ahead of us is Mount Kadur, where the Koran says the ark of Noah rests: It sits like a forbidden beacon 3500 meters high. We drive along the Syrian border clearly defined by eight-foot high barbed wire and 30-foot guard towers every 500 meters. We are on a beautiful piece of smooth two-lane blacktop built right smack on top of the "Silk Road." We are not traveling by camel today. I keep the Fiat's gas pedal pressed to the floor, the speedometer spinning like a slot machine. The only time we have to slow down is at a checkpoint or when a bridge has been blown up. The heavy trucks labor toward the west, as we pass burned-out hulks of gas stations. We stop in Silapi, the last Turkish town before the Iraqi border, to get something to eat. Silapi is one of the dirtiest, drabbest holes I have ever visited. Row after row of truck repair shops, dusty streets, and grease-smeared people watching as we drive by.

We pick a restaurant where the secret police eat. You can tell the secret police by their bull necks, gold chains and walkie-talkies. The hotel next door is decorated with stickers from the world's press and relief agencies. The food is good. Outside our restaurant, a retarded man with no legs sits on his stumps. Using blocks to get around, he is black from the soot and grime of the street. He uses an old inner tube to prevent the hot road from burning his stumps. He watches us eat. The people pass him by as he grimaces and grunts, his hand extended. I marvel that this man is still alive in this godforsaken outpost. I go outside and give him some lira. He begins to cry and tug at my leg, thanking me in his tortured way. When I leave him, children begin to crowd around and start to beat him for his money. I go back outside, and another man chases the children away. We tuck the money away, since his spastic hands keep flailing around. When I go back into the restaurant, one of the men at a table next to ours tells us that the beggar will probably be dead tonight, killed for the money he now has. I feel very sad and want to leave this place.

As we blast down the road toward the Iraqi border, I notice that the big guns in the Turkish bunkers are not facing south across the road to Syria, but toward Turkey to the north and the rebel-held hills beyond.

The Angels

Much later, back in Istanbul, I stand in front of the massive Hagia Sophia Mosque. Inside, it is quiet. Two men make their prayers in the serious, hurried style of Islam. The worn carpets and the vast ceiling absorb the whispering and rustling like a sponge.

Outside, it is dark and the rain is cold and heavy, pushed by the sharp wind. The brilliant floodlights cut tunnels of light upward into the low clouds above the softly sculpted building. It is as if the prayers of centuries power this energy, sending the shafts of pure blue light through the clouds and to the stars. High above, I think I see angels. A mysterious low chorus seems to pervade the atmosphere. But alas, the angels are just seagulls and the chorus is a distinct ship horn. And the prayers of a thousand years are lost and rubbed to dust in the aging carpets inside the mosque.

For a brief moment, it was calm and peaceful. The angels had come to answer those prayers. Instead, I know that out in the rolling fields of the east, there will be more death under the Turkish stars tonight.

—**RYP**

TURKEY

Kampala

Uganda
★★★

Where Danger Still Hangs Out

Until Rwanda became the new symbol of man's descent into his dark soul, Uganda typified our stereotype of fear. But that was 10 years ago, and seventy-something Idi Amin is now retired (sort of) in Saudi Arabia, Obote is gone, and the 13 main ethnic groups are supposed to be working in harmony to restore this beautiful land. Return to Central Africa after four or five years and you court disorientation. This place, once decent, is deadly again.

Back in January '71, correspondents came out of State Department backgrounders in more than one capital reporting, "This new guy Amin might be okay." ("Establishment military," authoritative sources had said; "we've dealt with him.") They were wrong.

Alas, when Yoweri Museveni's outlaw army began showing up on a distant bush horizon 15 years later, it wasn't so easy to get the scoop. He just wasn't the State Department's type. All we could tell was that authoritative sources were uneasy. So we were uneasy, too.

We fancied ourselves detached and independent, but after all, that was the news. Without putting it in so many words, important sources were uneasy, and absent of much more to go on, what else could we write? In our correctly objective voice, correctly throwing in easily missed qualifiers like "unconfirmed," we speculated about Museveni, the radical, about reports he'd been with FRELIMO in Mozambique, among Maoist Chinese on the Tanzanian island of Pemba. We heard reports that this renegade off in the shadows of the bush was even sending children into battle...and, hey, the reports checked out. He was. Now he runs the place.

We pictured a gang of bush-hard cultural revolutionaries, armed with AKs and simpleminded slogans, about to drag Uganda right back into chaos, just as new and moderate leaders were at last in place to nurse that sorry realm back to life.

During his long march on Kampala through a shell-shattered free-fire zone in Buganda known as the "Lowery Triangle" (shattered largely by the government's North Korean shells), Museveni had slipped out to London. In fact, he was there during a period when any practical leader (and he is a practical man) could see his cause was lost. He had virtually no financial resources, no trained military re-

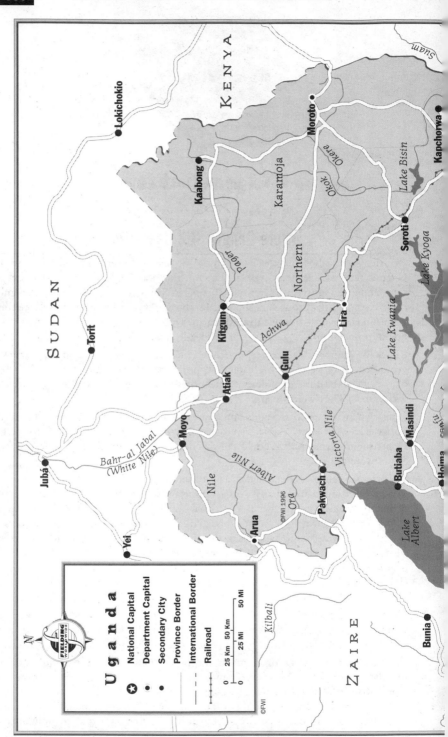

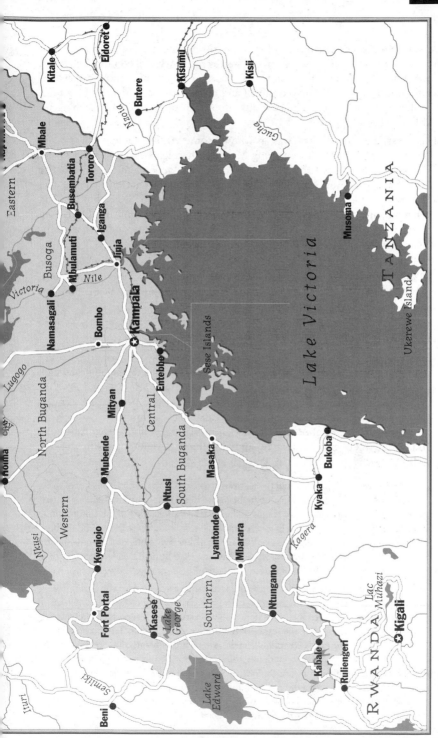

sources. The triangle was hamburger, it was over, and guile with reporters was pointless.

Alas, we paid slight attention to him then, just as we failed fully to appreciate until too late that Uganda's "moderates" were crooks who killed more Ugandans than Amin. A little more attention to quiet voices and we might not have evoked such foolish dismay as we relayed third-hand reports about a bullet-riddled beast (so rudely subhuman in its ability to live after such punishment), slouching toward Kampala.

This beast, as we now know, was an army of some 20,000 adolescents and kids in their twenties—those the despairing Museveni had left behind. On their own, they had hung on, and at last, slowly, pushed on. Less dependent on authoritative sources, we might even have provided some modest inspiration in dispatches about a true children's crusade, about orphans left with no choice but combat, their families and their lands having been trashed first by Amin, then by the undisciplined, unpaid and rapaciously angry soldiers of Tanzania, and then again by Amin's old military, now led by corrupt "moderates."

We didn't deliver that story until Museveni's kids were on the cusp of victory in mid-'85. To this day, many are surprised to learn that Julius Nyerere's protégé, the school teacher Apollo Milton Obote, killed more Ugandans than Amin.

All this matters now because all of Central Africa is dangerous. Danger here is almost always tied to danger there, and, wherever you land, sooner or later somebody shows up to say don't count on the news to keep you out of trouble.

Museveni had almost succeeded in removing most of Uganda from the world's most dangerous places. The State Department reports that snatch and grabs from cars stalled in Kampala traffic are common, but security in Kampala and Entebbe is by no stretch frightful. Uganda's frontier with Rwanda is notably less dangerous than the refugee-ridden frontiers that Tanzania, Burundi and Zaire share with Rwanda. But throughout East and Central Africa, you hear that we ignore Uganda at the risk of getting taken by surprise yet again…and not just in Uganda.

The Scoop

Even after a fairly brief safari through the towns and lore of Central Africa, the likes of these three monsters, Mutesa, Amin and Bizimungu, begins to hint at a monumental lending library of malevolence accumulated in the old realms of the great lakes. Like the English Constitution, it's an unwritten inheritance. Like the English Constitution, its influence is felt beyond the borders of the mother country. And a little like England, Uganda is something of a mother country, home to all the great lake kingdoms, save Rwanda and Burundi, and something of a cultural home to their shared brand of statecraft, whose most distinctive feature is terror.

Amin is from Uganda's primitive far north, and General de Division Augustin Bizimungu is neither princely nor Ugandan. A Rwandan Hutu, he was chief of staff of Rwanda's military in early '94 when the military there began its pogrom. Mutesa, by sharp contrast, represents the unalloyed essence of the tradition, the source of the trouble. After killing 60 of his brothers to win power, he carried Buganda's centuries-old tradition of brutality into the modern age, exercising the power to kill (casually, randomly, often) for both enjoyment and statecraft, to frighten subservience from his court. As the Watutsi sang the praises of an ancient emperor who roasted a Hutu serf alive, Mutesa thought nothing of executing a dozen subjects to celebrate some middling event, who minced about in tiptoe imitation of a lion, and never bothered to look where he sat because he knew implicitly that a peon would be on hands and knees to receive his backside.

In a narrow but important sense, Paul Kagame, the "parfit gentle knight" of the Rwandan Watutsi, a man with a largely unblemished record, is closer to Mutesa, a brutal creature from another country and another century, than he is to his countryman and contemporary, Bizimungu. Unlike Bizimungu and Amin, both Kagame and Mutesa were spawned by the ruling classes that cultivated statecraft by terror. Two more quick and random examples of how interwoven the people of Central Africa are, regardless of today's borders:

First, the word *saza*. On both sides of what is today the Rwanda, Uganda border, it meant one of the king's subchiefs, and on both sides of the border today, the word is still used as an official title for someone resembling a district commissioner. And then there is Kagame's recent past: Before he led the Watutsi back to their homeland from Uganda, he was not simply a refugee there, totally out of his element, but Uganda's chief of intelligence.

The Players

President Yoweri Museveni and Uganda's National Resistance Army (NRA)

The new president of Uganda is former guerrilla chief Yoweri Museveni. Museveni was born in 1944, raises about 1500 head of cattle and became a guerrilla fighter in 1971. With the help of Tanzanian troops, he ousted Idi Amin in 1979. He married Janet Kataha in 1973 and has four children.

When word of Museveni and his guerrillas began popping up in the mid-80's, they were the most obscure of players. In Kampala, moderates of various stripes had been at work trying to pull Uganda from the pit into which Amin had shoved it. At most, this reputed Maoist with no visible Mao for support (indeed, North Korea was helping Kampala's moderates deal with him) would be a spoiler, making Uganda's slow recovery all the slower.

Uganda, under Yoweri Museveni as its president, is today still struggling to recover. Large portions remain insecure. Its military (still the NRA, now with a political wing, the National Resistance Movement) is poorly armed and underpaid (they make about US$30–160 per month). But Museveni, without seeking the role, has become the most powerful man in Central and East Africa today, more powerful inside and outside Uganda than the well-armed, well-financed (though ultimately bankrupt) Amin could ever have hoped to be.

Lord's Resistance Army

An armed faction, led by a former altar boy, that's been pouring guerrillas into Uganda from Sudan in recent months, the LRA is—get this—a Christian fundamentalist group bent on wreaking havoc through fierce hit-and-run raids. Five hundred LRA guerrillas from Sudan hooked up with another Ugandan faction and cut the road off between Kampala and the northern regional capital of Gulu in mid-February 1996. There are daily occurrences of looting of convoys and hit-and-run firefights with the army, usually leaving scores of government soldiers and civilians dead. Joseph Kony leads this savage group—armed and uniformed by Sudan—whose members believe their bodies will deflect bullets when smeared with tree oils. The group claims to have killed 130 army soldiers during an attack on Pabor Palocwan on February 17, 1996. Kony was wounded in a clash with soldiers at Pacilo, which left 12 dead. In the beginning of March 1996, the LRA ambushed a convoy of 17 buses, cars and trucks that had a military escort. The armed escort fled, and more than 100 civilians were killed.

The strength of the LRA has been estimated by the government at 600 men, but Kony says he has 6500 men in three brigades that operate in groups of 30 or less. They have warned villagers that anyone within six miles of a road, riding a bicycle or motorcycle, and anyone keeping ducks or sheep will be killed. The LRA considers ducks and sheep to be unclean animals. If they prevail, they say, they will rule Uganda following the Bible's Ten

Commandments. (What will they do about expired parking meters or noisy rock concerts?).

The LRA has experienced a number of setbacks at the hands of Clabe Akandwanaho the brother of Museveni. Another reason for their dismal performance in combat could be their use of rocks that they think will explode like bombs and smearing themselves with oil to make themselves bulletproof. Sudan is providing them with weapons and training in an attempt to even the odds.

West Nile Bank Front (WNBF)

Former aide to Idi Amin, Juma Oris leads about 2000 WNBF rebels against the Ugandan government. Based in Sudan (who isn't these days?), they make sporadic attacks on the Ugandan army in the Arua area along the Ugandan Sudanese border. They began their insurgency in May of 1995. The rebels are loyal to former dictator Idi Amin and are supported by Zaire and the Islamic government of Sudan. Sudanese troops even provide covering artillery fire for the WNBF incursions into Uganda. Amin, living in relative luxury in Saudi Arabia and now 71 years old, was bounced by the Tanzanians and current president Museveni in 1979, after causing the deaths of over half a million of his own people.

Ronald Mutebi and the Kingdom of Buganda

A king named Ronald? Yes, Buganda's back and Ronald is king. The ancient kingdom of Buganda was symbolically restored in July of 1993, and the tourists still stay away.

Hezbollah

Yeah, even Hezbollah is a player here. In the middle of January 1996, the Lebanon-based, Iran-backed terrorist group threatened to overthrow the Ugandan government. Did they get off at the wrong airport perhaps?

Getting In

A passport is required. Immunization certificates for yellow fever and cholera are required (typhoid and malaria suppressants recommended). For a business visa and other information, contact the following:

Embassy of the Republic of Uganda
5909 16th St., N.W.
Washington, D.C. 20011
☎ *(202) 726-7100-02*

Permanent Mission to the U.N.
☎ *(212) 949-0110.*

Getting Around

There is something to be said for the third-class train. There is a branch line to Gulu, and if it is running, it could be a reasonably safe way to get to Gulu and see the country. Driving to Gulu is discouraged; there have been numerous incidents. Hitching is even less advisable, but you may end up hitching if you decide to drive.

Dangerous Places

Mbarara and Ankole Country

The maxim for most dangerous places is, don't go unless you have to. That's not what you hear about the town of Mbarara and Ankole country just north of Rwanda and Tanzania, where you still find, after years of the white man's devastating rinderpest, longhorn Ankole cattle. Not unlike Tutsi cattle, they are owned by a tall, dark aristocracy, descended like the Watutsi from northern invaders who seized a Bantu-speaking kingdom. Here, the serfs are the Hima people, the aristocrats, the Ankole.

This is the region through which Henry Morton Stanley (the explorer who presumed to discover Dr. Livingstone) passed in 1875 on his way to meet Mutesa, king of Buganda, and what you hear about it, is don't let the danger keep you away.

For one, it's beautiful, often the spare, dry beauty of the savanna rather than the ever-lush beauty of Buganda just to the north. (Buganda's deep green light filtering through banana groves colors the Uganda of our imagination.) For another, there is both the human and animal population. Mbarara is not an unusual African town, but then you begin to realize how combat tore the place up, and how other towns, similarly battered, still languish in a decrepit state. It's bracing to experience the resilience of this much patched place. Gusty *jambos* in a town with cheap hotels sporting names like The Super Tip Top Lodge Bar & Restaurant; this is Africa? Wildlife is devastated, but just when you think it is utterly gone, there it is, and seeing it in such circumstances, the sudden appearance, for example, of a bull eland, big and blue, brings a melancholy rush.

Gulu and the North

Kampala, Entebbe, the Uganda of repute, is a place of enveloping warmth, lush-green, coffee-rich, a jacaranda breeze. The far north of Uganda is nothing like this. The country north of the Victoria Nile and Lake Kyoga is drier than the savanna in the far south—wide open land, often trackless, which even before the days of Idi Amin, travelers were warned to enter with no less than two four-wheel-drive vehicles. Today, you're warned to shun it altogether, unless you can rent a light plane to get in and out of secure redoubts like the army base on the Kidepo River frontier with the Sudan, a region whose land, people and animals are so close to the Pleistocene, and so palpably distant from the rest of the world, that you find yourself hypnotized.

This is Nilote country. Amin came from the Nilotic tribes that populate this harsh country; likewise, Obote. Meantime, Museveni's crusade came from the green south and west, the heartland of the old Bantu kingdoms.

The far north has always been a rough place, a place where men can still be seen with chest scars toting their kills (left breast for women, right for men), and cattle rustling has long been both a routine way of life and a routine way of death. Today, it's especially dangerous. Remnants of Amin's army are about along with the Lords Resistance, as well as outright *shiftas*. In this territory the term *shifta*, meaning bandit, is likely to be used honestly, and not as a euphemism for guerrillas.

One expedient in spots like this is to travel with army or U.N. convoys, but the government doesn't have resources to patrol the north frequently, and in recent months, even U.N. convoys have been hit. The LRA feeds on Gulu and the far north, with continuous raids on government positions and the sacking of entire villages and towns. Twelve villagers were killed when 200 LRA guerrillas looted the town of Purongo on February 14, 1996.

Dangerous Things

Travel Outside Kampala

Kampala is relatively safe, but outside the capital is a war zone. LRA guerrillas control the roads north of Kampala at night, and bandits those to the southwest. Teams of LRA rebels regularly ambush convoys to the north and have even tried to take the key northern city of Gulu. A convoy of 140 vehicles, complete with armed escort, was ambushed by LRA zanies on April 6, 1996. The guerrillas like to burn dwellings in their hasty retreats as a calling card.

Safaris

In the best of times, driving into the country north of the Victoria Nile has entailed the sense of entering country so open and vacant that once you're off the track and in trouble, it could be weeks before you're found. Kampala safari operators maintain radio contact with safaris. Should things get hot, they'd likely get their clients out fast; there's a chance they could get you out aboard a light plane with an extra seat. A minor problem is that you might have to kiss your gear good-bye. Depending on distance and danger, count on paying anywhere from US$750 to $10,000. If there is anyone flying out of Entebbe or any other field, the best way to find out would be through Wilson Airport (not Embakazi, out of which the commercial airlines fly) north of Nairobi. **Z. Boskovic Air Charters** (☎ *501210*) is one possibility; **Air Kenya Aviation** (☎ *501421*) is another. Whether or not they are flying, they are in as good a position as anyone to know who might be. If you can't get through, and even if you can, you should either have a car and driver available or be looking for one. The best bet is a group of two or three who hire a four-wheel-drive vehicle and a driver. Self-drive rental cars are not easily available in Kampala.

Getting Sick

You're on your own, friend. Any number of Western embassies in Kampala can, of course, advise where to get competent medical attention in Kampala, but Kampala isn't a dangerous place, nor for that matter are the actual towns of Gulu and Moroto, where there are also adequate (and, of course, inadequate) medical facilities. Yet, when a country has an average of one doctor for every 22,291 people, your chances of getting one are slim to none. AIDS is a big killer here, along with the usual Central African lineup of malaria, intestinal bugs, respiratory ailments and other tropical killers. Malaria is present throughout the country and chloroquine-resistant. Louse-borne typhus is especially prevalent where groups of people congregate together.

Nuts and Bolts

There is an eerie quiet in this once bustling country—akin to the sound of waiting for another boot to drop. Uganda can be seen as an inherently civilized country surrounded by nasty neighbors: Sudan to the north, Zaire to the west, Rwanda to the south. The white minority in Kenya to the east are betting on prosperity as a ravaged economy begs for outside investment. There are only about 85,000 or so visitors every year compared to Kenya's 800,000, but it is growing at about 10 percent each year.

Crime is common in Uganda, with violent crime being more common than not. Roadblocks around the country are just as likely to be thugs. Taking pictures of the military is considered a crime. Border areas are not safe.

There are 17,605 miles (28,322 kms) of roads, and 764 miles (1230 kms) of railroad. Getting around is still dodgy, but the countryside is free from the thugs who once worked for Amin. The north is dangerous for any kind of travel. We can only vouch for two towns, Gulu and Moroto, and one outpost, the National Resistance Army Camp on the Kidepo River frontier with the Sudan. Moroto is a lovely place in this sere wilderness. There are even some decaying colonial structures surrounded by green, and a huge green mountain rises due east of the town. But as far as we know, this has always been the sort of African town where you sleep on the floor of the police post.

Gulu, on the road to the Sudanese frontier town of Nimule to the north, and the rail line to Pakwach on the Albert Nile to the west, offers considerably more, but outside of town, this country is just as dangerous. There are the proper, if faded, Acholi Inn (a reminder that this is the country of the Acholi, many of whom were killed en masse by Amin) and, a notch down, the Luxxor Lodge (a reminder, perhaps, that the Khedive, through his agents in the Sudan, once claimed all Uganda as Egyptian territory). These days it's unlikely that either of these hotels would require reservations, but even if they do, it's not a police-post town: Both the Church of Uganda and the Red Cross Society are said to offer accommodations.

Dangerous Days

07/27/1985	Milton Obote was ousted as president for the second time in a military coup.
05/27/1981	Obote returned as president after nine years in exile.
04/10/1979	Tanzanian and UNLF forces entered Kampala after driving out Idi Amin's forces.
10/1978	Idi Amin's forces invaded Tanzania.
06/1976	Israel launched commando raid on Entebbe airport.
01/25/1971	Idi Amin became president.

UGANDA

CRIMINAL PLACES

Brasília

Brazil
★★

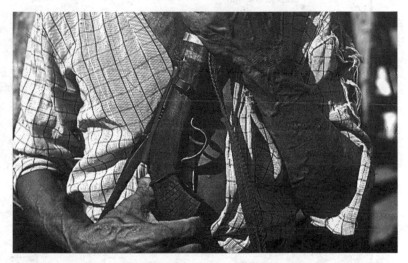

Street Kids Named Desire

Brazil is a bad place even for its own people. And the guys Brazilians watch out for are the cops, anyone who ever was a cop, and anyone who's ever thought of becoming a cop—not to mention all off-duty cops. Four policemen and the brother-in-law of one of the officers, were arrested in August 1994 for the murders of eight young boys (the youngest was eight) outside the Candelaria Church, a popular Rio tourist attraction.

Rio de Janeiro is a continuing source of petty crimes committed by street kids barely out of pajamas. Most people believe shopkeepers pay the police to pick off the toddler thieves like coyotes on a Wyoming sheep farm. About five street children are murdered a day, according to the University of São Paulo. Treated like vermin, most street urchins have a short life span. Many work for drug dealers; they sniff glue and gasoline to kill their hunger pangs. There is little sympathy on behalf of Rio's citizenry for these prepubescent dope peddlers, and it's unlikely that the police who knock them off will be convicted for what is generally viewed as a socially beneficial act.

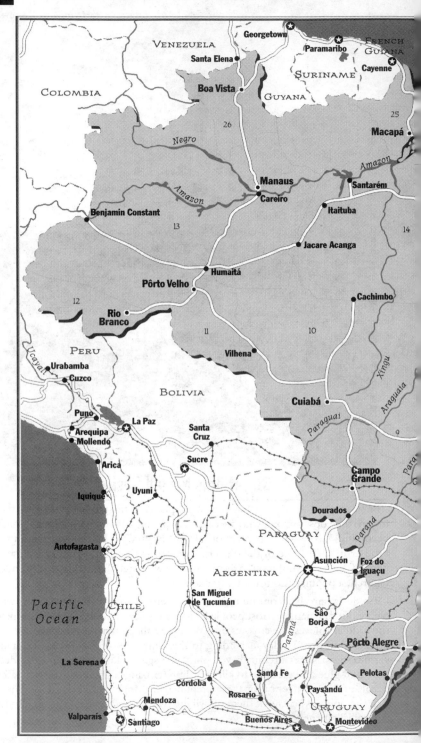

Brazil

- ✪ National Capital
- • State Capital
- • Secondary City
- State Border
- Primary Road
- Secondary Road
- ┼─┼─┼ Railroad

0   250   500   750 km
0   250   500 mi

©FWi

Atlantic Ocean

Belém
São Luís
Santa Inês
24
Fortaleza
Teresina
Pôrto Franco
22
21
Natal
20
Picos
João Pessoa
23
19
Recife
Miracema do Norte
Juàzeiro
18
Maceió
17
Gurupi
15
16
Aracaju
Barreiras
Ibotirama
Salvador
Brasilia
São Francisco
Vitória de Conquista
Goiânia
Pirapora
Montes Claros
Pôrto Seguro
Uberlândia
8
7
Belo Horizonte
Vitória
5
Volta Redonda
Niterói
São Paulo
Rio de Janeiro
Curitiba
Santos
Florianópolis
sório
Tocantins

States of Brazil

1. Rio Grande do Sul
2. Santa Catarina
3. Paraná
4. Mato Grosso do Sul
5. São Paulo
6. Rio de Janeiro
7. Espírito Santo
8. Minas Gerais
9. Goiás
10. Mato Grosso
11. Rondônia
12. Acre
13. Amazonas
14. Pará
15. Tocantins
16. Bahia
17. Sergipe
18. Alagoas
19. Pernambuco
20. Paraíba
21. Rio Grande do Norte
22. Ceara
23. Piauí
24. Marnahão
25. Amapá
26. Roraima

Note: Brasilia is surrounded by a federal district

Is is estimated that there are 7 million kids living on the streets in Brazil. Hunted by death squads like rats in a sewer, they subsist by begging, stealing and deionizing themselves on petrol-based solvents. Are they a threat? You bet.

Other criminals in Brazil fall under the umbrella of nebulous quasi-terrorists. Since 1988, nearly 100 incidents of terrorism and other forms of political violence have been reported. No indigenous terrorist group is known to operate within the country, although leftist guerrillas from Peru and Colombia occasionally cross Brazil's western frontier. A street gang with visions of sugarplums and Abu Nidal menacingly calls itself the Commando Vermelho (Red Command). The "terrorist" group strikes from time to time, but its actions are essentially criminal activities, such as the January 2, 1994, brief armed abduction and robbery of an American business executive and his wife in Rio de Janeiro. The Red Command may be no more than a gang operating under a *nom de guerre*. And the absence of any identifiable pattern in the crimes suggests most are the work of individuals rather than any organized group.

There's a huge difference in living standards between the developed south of Brazil and the northeast. Consequently, there has been massive migration to Rio's slums. This has caused a sharp increase in urban violence. The poverty-stricken lower classes have essentially seen zero benefits from the past growth of the economy. About half of Brazilians are black, and they make, on average, about half of what whites make. In Brazil, nearly one-fifth of the population is illiterate. The country can be embarrassed by having one of the world's most disparate income distributions: 60 percent of the national wealth is possessed by one percent of the population. Perhaps 50 percent of the population lives in poverty. Since World War II, the purchasing power of Brazil's minimum wage has been cut in half. Because of widespread inefficiency and corruption, only eight percent of the government's social spending reaches the poorest of the population. In Rio, poor families have become squatters on empty lots and in abandoned and partially completed housing complexes. Brazil's underbelly is also being corroded by the spread of drug abuse and such diseases as AIDS, bubonic plague and cholera—a few good reasons for a lot of crime.

The Scoop

In the first nine months of 1995, there were 6012 murders in Rio alone—a 10 percent rise over the same period in 1994. On the city's "Day of Peace" in November 1995, there were 24 murders in greater Rio, a city of 6 million—one an hour. About 90 percent of all the violent crimes in the city are committed against or by minors. Most of the violence can be linked to drugs and theft. Teenage drug bosses have set up their narco shops in the *favelas*, the slums in Rio's surrounding hillsides, and loaf around in sandals toting automatic rifles. Auto thefts average a staggering 3000 per month in Rio.

Between 1990 and 1995, there were 568 kidnappings in Rio, something prepubescent dope peddlers like to do when cash and stash run low. Although it is improving in both efficiency and honesty, Rio's 18,000-man police force is so corrupt that the families of kidnap victims rarely report the crime and privately pay off the ransoms themselves.

The Players

Hit Squads

Despite their reputation for tardiness and diffidence in daytime law enforcement, the Military Police are famous for off-hours overzealousness. Human rights groups estimate there are two police-committed killings a day on average in Brazil. About 200 police officers are fired every year for their participation in organized kidnapping, corruption and death squads. The Vigario Geral shantytown massacre on August 30, 1994, is probably the most famous example of their devotion to cleaning up the streets. That night 21 men, women and children were murdered by at least 30 masked gunmen believed to be police officers acting in vengeance for four officers killed two days earlier in the shantytown.

But while the Policia Militar (usually retired or off-duty police officers) spend their off-hours in hit squads eliminating street kids, the hit squads are being hunted by other less violent but equally eager hit squads. In August 1994, Brazil's justice minister announced the creation of a force to police the police force, a federal police unit that would investigate and eliminate death squads all over the country.

Death squads and drug traffickers are considered major contributors to Rio's murder rate of more than 60 per every 100,000 people. In 1993, 3255 individuals were murdered in Rio alone. Instances of multiple executions and murders are not uncommon here.

Rather then retaining attorneys to handle legal matters, Brazilians prefer hit men. The tab reads like the a restaurant menu. Want to off an impoverished peasant? This week's special is only US$70. But if you want to take out a prominent politician, expect to pay for the caviar: about US$20,000. Although foreigners are rarely targeted, about 10 killings a day in São Paulo—half the daily total—are contract killings. Read that as nearly 4000 assassinations every year executed by hired executioners.

Teenage Drug Gangs

Prepubescent drug gangs in Rio are involved in an estimated 90 percent of all the city's violent crimes. Hundreds of drug dealers operate in the hillside slums ringing the city.

Getting In

A passport and visa are required. Tourist visas are valid for 90 days, must be obtained in advance, and are free of charge. Minors (under 18) traveling alone, with one parent or with a third party, must present written authorization by the absent parent(s) or legal guardian, specifically granting permission to travel alone, with one parent or a third party. This authorization must be notarized, authenticated by the Brazilian embassy or consulate, and translated into Portuguese. If you are caught entering illegally, you must leave the country voluntarily within three to eight days.The Ministry of Justice can hold you for 90 days before deporting you.

For current information concerning entry and customs requirements for Brazil, travelers can contact the following:

Brazilian Embassy

3006 Massachusetts Avenue N.W.
Washington, D.C. 20008
☎ *(202) 745-2700*
FAX (202) 745-2827

Brazil also has consulates in Los Angeles, San Francisco, Houston, Miami, New York, Chicago and San Juan.

Dangerous Places

Rio

Rio likes to party, so it's no surprise that the areas surrounding beaches, discos, bars, nightclubs and other similar establishments are dangerous, especially at dusk and during the evening hours. Prime targets in Rio are the popular beaches and neighborhoods of Copacabana and Leme.

São Paulo

On the weekend of June 11–12, 1994, 42 people were murdered in the city, 21 of them shot execution-style. However, crimes of opportunity, such as larceny, purse snatching, armed street robbery, car theft and carjackings, pose the greatest threat to foreign visitors in São Paulo. Most foreign visitors dress differently and do not speak the local language, increasing their chance of being recognized as a foreigner and, therefore, perceived as an easier target for criminals.

Ciudad del Este, Paraguay

This smugglers' boomtown is technically in Paraguay along the border with Brazil and Argentina, but may as well be in Brazil. This is a major base for drug traffickers smuggling Bolivian cocaine via hidden landing strips cut out of the jungle. More than US$12 billion moves through here a year. As the Brazilian drug lords have been pushed out of the shantytowns of Rio, they've found a convenient base in Ciudad del Este. In fact, this place has it all—murder, mayhem and even Islamic fundamentalist guerrillas, who are suspected of using the city to launch bombing attacks against Israeli and Jewish targets in Argentina. In 1994, 200 people were murdered in this city of 100,000, most of the executions identical in appearance with Brazilian gangland slayings. It costs US$500 to bribe a customs official in Ciudad del Este, and a bogus passport can be had for US$5000. The city is also a channel for smuggled electronics goods and computers from Miami and stolen cars from Brazil. It's estimated that half the cars on Paraguay's roads were stolen in Brazil.

Ciudad del Este is a tax-free center and popular with Paraguayans for its bargains on consumer goods. The 400-yard bridge is usually packed with trucks and passenger cars stuffed with brand-new goods bought in Brazil. It is also a great place to pick up bogus U.S. dollars, antiaircraft guns, rare and endangered animals, weapons, and drugs. The area is also called the "Triangle"—the frontier area between Argentina, Brazil and Paraguay—a South American Barbary Coast rough-and-ready area with a Shia Muslim community of about 6000 people. Lebanese, Syrians and Iranians came here in the early 1980s and brought with them a New World cell of Hezbollah. Hezbollah trains local recruits in the jungles around the main city of Foz do Iguacu and gets its support from both the local merchants and Iran.

Dangerous Things

Kidnapping

Kidnapping in Rio and São Paulo has become a pastime in the last few years. And it's as easy as stealing an apple off a produce cart. More than 150 people were kidnapped in Rio in 1992. That figure is almost double what it had been the year before. Both figures were records. Authorities believe the actual number was far greater. Many in Brazil have no faith in the police to handle kidnapping situations competently and successfully. It's part of a vicious cycle, giving kidnappers the confidence for carrying out their activities.

Carnival

About US$24 million gets injected into Rio's economy during Carnival week. In addition, the 80,000 tourists who attended the Carnival (a new record) in 1994 represented an increase of 20 percent over the last year, boosting hotel occupancy rates to 90–100 percent. Most revelers come to Rio from São Paulo and from around Brazil; many also come from Argentina.

Getting Sick

Medical care varies in quality, particularly in remote areas. Cholera has been reported in the Amazon Basin region and northeastern Brazil. Some cholera outbreaks have also been reported in major cities. However, visitors who follow proper precautions about food and drink are not usually at risk.

Nuts and Bolts

Emergency Numbers

Local "911-type" police numbers include the following:

Rio tourist police
☎ *511-5112*

Fire
☎ *193*

Military police (patrol)
☎ *190*

Civil police (investigations)
☎ *147*

The U.S. embassy is located in Brasilia:
Avenida das Nacoes, Lote 3
☎ *[55] (61) 321-7272*

There are consulates in the following:

Rio de Janeiro
Avenida Presidente Wilson 147
☎ *[55] (21) 292-7117*

Porto Alegre
Rua Coronel Genuino 421 (9th floor)
☎ *[55] (51) 226-4288*

São Paulo
Rua Padre Joao Manoel 933
☎ *[55] (11) 881-6511*

Recife
Rua Goncalves Maia 163
☎ *[55] (81) 221-1412*

There are also consular agencies in the following:

Belem
Avenida Oswaldo Cruz 165
☎ *[55] (91) 223-0800/0413*

Manaus
Rua Recife 1010, Adrianopolis
☎ *[55] (92) 234-4546*

Salvador de Bahia
Avenida Antonio Carlos Magalhaes S/N
Edificio Cidadella Center, Suite 410
Candeal
☎ *[55] (71) 358-9195*

Fortaleza
Instituto Brasil-Estados Unidos (IBEU)
Rua Nogueira Acioly, 891
Aldeota
☎ *[55] (85) 252-1539.*

Chechnya
★★

Boris Badenough

It seemed only a matter of time before the fiercely independent Chechen people would rise up against "Mother Moscow." Banished to northern Kazakhstan (along with the Tartars) by Stalin for being German collaborators, accordingly, the Chechens have a mean streak as wide as the mountainous border that divides their country. After they were repatriated, the Chechens, hardened and without any means of earning a living, set about forming the largest criminal gangs in the former Soviet Union. They were as far from the socialist, there-is-no-god, one-size-fits all Soviet model as one could be. First, Chechens are Muslim; second, they are more entrepreneurial than Donald Trump, and their loyalties are to one of the over 100 *teips,* or clans, that constitute Chechen society. For centuries, they have been considered by Russians as the toughest, baddest people in the former Soviet Union. Their image certainly isn't enhanced by the Chechen tendency to raise money through hijacking airliners and school buses and then hotfooting it back to Chechnya to hide out in their inaccessible mountain villages.

Some folks might even call them hillbillies, and Ned Beatty wouldn't be alive long enough to just squeal like a pig if he went eco-touristing through Chechnya.

It is strange that the news media were so quick to recast the ornery Chechens as the underdog/heroic-defenders-of-their-homeland in the West. Outnumbered by five (some say 10) to one, the Chechen irregulars, along with volunteers and mercenaries (some brag they get paid the equivalent of $2000 a day, but the reality is about one-tenth of that), resigned themselves to waging a guerrilla war from the mountains. The Russians seemed happy to oblige, as they hid in their newly built forts along the major highways. In Grozny, nervous Russian troops stopped and checked papers endlessly and regularly arrested any male Chechens they found hiding in their homes just to be sure.

It was a story the Western media loved—peasants armed with sticks and shovels defiantly dancing around bonfires in central Grozny, seemingly holding off the entire might of the Russian army and air force. Chechen fighters, unshaven and dirty, waving their flag while strafing fighters soar overhead and turn their parliament into Swiss cheese. Meanwhile, the most feared army in the world turned out to be shivering, underfed, confused and mostly prepubescent.

Just prior to Russia's intercession into the rebellion, Russian Defense Minister Pavel S. Grachev bombastically boasted that a single paratroop regiment would need only a couple of hours to wipe out the rebellion. Boy, was he wrong. Two months later, Russia could say it had taken the rubble that once had been Grozny—but there was little of which to be proud.

Although the vastly superior Russian forces eventually took the Chechen capital in January 1995, they have faced a low-budget Afghanistan since. The Chechen insurgents—many of them former Soviet soldiers trained in mountain guerrilla fighting—have dug into the hills, and waged a long and fierce battle of attrition against an undisciplined, underaged band of Boris' best. And, in true Afghanistan form, the Russian army set up a puppet government, while the rebels regrouped in the hills. Since the Russians have decided to exterminate any and all Chechen fighters, there is little for the Chechens to lose. Although the daytime is ruled by Russian APCs and soldiers, the night belongs to the Chechens.

By most estimates there are about 1500 to 3000 Chechen fighters in three groups still fighting this pocket gazavat, or Holy War. Dazhokhar Dudayev ran his tiny rebel army from his "secret" base in Roshni-Chu, about 45 minutes south of Grozny until he was wounded by a Russian missile, which finally homed in on his satellite phone in a clearing 20 miles southeast of Grozny in April 1996 (see "The Scoop"). Reportedly, he was smuggled out through Azerbaijan via Turkey and hidden in a NATO hospital in southern Germany.

In February 1995, the Russian army needed 38,000 troops just to keep the lid on Chechnya, and the Interior Ministry had deployed an additional 15,500. Russian sources insist Chechen strength is far greater than what's being reported in the media. There continue to be gunfights, ambushes and massacres, as both sides side nervously finger their triggers. Just to make things interesting, Chechen military commander Shamil Basayev boasts that he will use nuclear materials to poison Moscow.

Yeltsin expected a quick victory when he first sent troops into Chechnya but the ill-trained Russian infantry has found the Chechens' desire for independence has made them formidable opponents. An aggressive drive by the Chechen fighters

The Republic
of Chechnya

⭐ National Capital
● City
── Primary Road
── Administrative Border
── International Border

0   25 Km
0   25 Mi

©FWI

on August 6, 1996 (Yeltsin's inauguration day) reversed the war driving thousands of Russian troops and civilians out of Grozny. When Alexander Lebed was sent in by Yeltsin to work out a ceasefire, he found Russian soldiers had become weaklings due to being underfed, underclothed and lice-ridden. After the ceasefire went into effect, sporadic firing continued and Chechen refugees were bombed by the Russians as they fled the city. The Chechens want nothing short of outright independence while the Russians would like them to accept autonomy within the Russian Federation much like that negotiated with Tatarstan. As of September '96, Lebed and the Chechens had hammered out a peace process that should end major hostilities. Now where do they send the royalty checks for that oil flowing through Grozny?

The Scoop

Chechnya is not a country but a mountainous region that Russia has to pump oil from Azerbaijan through. It's about a thousand miles south of Moscow in Russia and controlled by perhaps 30 large clans whose major concern is lining their pockets before Mother Russia or the other clans can line theirs. The typical career path offered to a Chechen is smuggler, rebel, gangster or corpse. Chechen clans are famous for smuggling, extortion, kidnapping, pimping, gambling and just all-around gangstering. Lately, the Chechens have given Moscow the ultimate headache: another Afghanistan. Chechnya proclaimed its independence in 1991. Boris let 'em alone for a while (not a bad idea, considering the Chechen *mafyia* seem to have a tight grip on Moscow) but sent in the heat in December 1994. (For more information on the Chechen organized crime presence in Moscow, see the chapter on Russia.)

How'd the war start? The best reason we've heard was that the conflict was ignited by a big oil deal struck by Azerbaijan, which needed to export the oil through Russian pipelines that pass through Chechnya. Both Grozny and Moscow wanted a piece of the action, in terms of transport fees. Moscow and Grozny had been rhetorically duking it out for three years over the Moscow control of Chechen oil exports. Since Yeltsin pays the military by the week, he constructed a meaner deal.

The death toll in the war is at least 80,000 people (90 percent of them civilians) and the toll is climbing. More than 500 Russian soldiers had been killed in 1996 through May. In March 1996, Boris Yeltsin outlined a peace plan that was supposed to "officially" end the 15-month-old war. It didn't. Then Lebed stepped in with a major rout and said enough is enough. The Chechens have taken a liking to killing Russians or other Chechen tribes, so don't expect peace soon.

The Players

Boris Yeltsin

Boris was mad as hell, and he wasn't going to take it anymore. Boris forgot that the massive army of Stalin and Breshnev is long gone. When Boris pushed the button, all he got was a bunch of sparks and fizzles. Finally, when he sent in the few generals who would obey him, the entire world saw the ineptitude and deceit on television every night. An early 1995 poll gleaned that fully 72 percent of the Russian people do not trust Boris Yeltsin, although his popularity has increased dramatically since—especially since the announced death of Dudayev in April 1996. The Chechens celebrated his inauguration by defeating the Russian army in Grozny and killing over 2000 people.

Alexander Lebed

When Lebed ran for president last spring, one of his campaign promises was that he could bring the war in Chechnya to an end. He demanded that Yeltsin fire Interior Minister Anatoli Kulikov, whom he blamed for the disaster that returned Grozny to rebel control. After Lebed lost the election he was surprised when Yeltsin appointed him special representative to find a settlement to the Chechnya mess. Lebed is described by government colleagues as a bull let loose in the Kremlin corridors, but if he can find a way for Russia to save face in the war that has cost it US$5 billion, he stands to become a formidable political figure at a time when Yeltsin's health is declining. At press time he had negotiated a ceasefire, called for Russian troops to be withdrawn for "humanitarian reasons," and bullied Yeltsin into giving him authority over all armed forces and intelligence services in Chechnya. He claimed to be working on a "radical plan" that might offer hope for peace. Lebed is quickly racking up points with the Russians and the Chechens.

The Chechens

Mountain-bred and mean as polecats, the Chechens are an unaligned assortment of 30 clans that are constantly fighting for influence and shifting alliances with other clans. Each clan is led by a spiritual mystic. They adhere to a Sufi mysticism branch of Sunni Islam called Muridism. This branch of Islam divides its followers into sects led by local feudal leaders. They are united only in their opposition of domination by Christians. In fact, they break all the fundamentalist Islamic laws. The men smoke and booze it up, while the women do not cover their heads, as they're required to do in stricter branches of the religion. Instead of praying five times a day, Chechens may pray only once or twice a day.

Militarily, the Chechens' chain of command is like a pickup basketball game. If units of irregulars meet up with each other, it's purely by happenstance. They go out and fight, then come back to eat and sleep. They're about as coordinated as a demolition derby, but equally as destructive. As of mid-1996, Chechen fighters numbered between 1500 and 3000.

Russia has supported the Terkh-hu Clan, which is usually in power, for almost a century. The Nadterechny faction of the Terkhhu Clan still receives direct aid (in the form of tanks and weapons) to fight the Myalkhi Hill Clan.

Of the three Chechen factions, Shamil Basayev and his Lone Wolf are the most powerful. Basayev operates from mountainous southern Chechnya and wears a silver ring with the lone wolf symbol of the country.

Tartars

Not the stuff the dentist scrapes off your teeth, but a group of about 180,000 people who were shipped off along with the Chechens by Stalin. The Tartars are fighting alongside Chechen rebels against the Russian government. Of the current community of 6 million Tartars, 250,000 are found in the Crimean, but their sympathies lie with the Chechens.

Dzhokhar Dudayev

Dudayev was wounded and left for dead but he reportedly was smuggled out of the country to a German hospital to recuperate in April 1996. Looking and acting surprisingly like Boris Badenov of "Rocky & Bullwinkle" fame, Dzhokhar (pronounced Jokar) Dudayev is a Muslim and a former general in the Soviet air force. He was a member of the Myalkhi Hill Clan, a very unpopular clan amongst other Chechens. The Myalkhir Hill Clan is poor, feisty and treacherous, sort of the Chechen equivalent of our white trash without the mobile homes.

Dudayev delivered on his promise of a gazavat, or Holy War, when Moscow invaded his tiny gangster kingdom. Dudayev hated Russians (who weren't too fond of him, either— even those opposed to the war and Boris Yeltsin alike).

Dudayev's men were veterans of the war in Abkhazia, where they are mildly related and supportive of the 20-odd clans that are fighting the Russians there. Dudayev's son was killed during the Russian assault on Grozny.

Dead or In Bed

DP was told that Dudayev is in a NATO hospital in southern Germany. Supposedly he was seriously wounded by a Russian rocket attack on April 20 and then smuggled by Russian OMON troops through Azerbaijan, then Turkey and by plane to the NATO base. The vacation was supposed to be arranged by Uncle Sam, Turkey and Moscow to let Yeltsin get his job again.

Iman Shamil did the same Jesus act back in the 19th century when he fought off the Russians. This would all be conjecture had not Salman Raduyev suddenly appeared from the dead and also said Dudayev is alive. Raduyev was shot in the face by a Russian sniper and was assumed dead. Raduyev underwent plastic surgery and reappeared on July 18. Talk about comebacks.

Zelimkhan Yanderbiyev

After the Russian Army decided to reach out and touch Dudayev with a guided missile while he was making a satellite call, *DP* scrambled to get some background on his replacement. Within a day of Dudayev getting his April 21 airmail present from Yeltsin, a bogus story placed by the Russian puppet government said he had been shot dead in a quarrel.

Yanderbiyev, 44, is a former writer and had been Dudayev's vice president since 1993. He is married with two daughters and was the founder of the Vainakh Democratic Party in 1990. He helped form the Congress of the Chechen movement that brought Dudayev to power in 1991.

He went to Moscow to sign a peace treaty, but Yeltsin actually snuck off to Yanderbiyev's turf and did a surprise inspection of the troops in Chechnya. The idea was that Yeltsin wouldn't return a package from the Chechens while he held their leader hostage in Moscow. Sneaky guys, these Russians. Within hours of the peace treaty being signed, Chechen rebels were blasting away at Russian soldiers. Yanderbiyev may have kept to the shadows while Dudayev was boss, but he is actually the main ideologist behind the Chechens move for freedom. It seems that Mother Russia wants those pipelines to go through real bad and is looking to strike a deal.

Doku Zavgayev

By now the title "Russian puppet ruler" may even be on a list of short-term occupations back in Moscow. Doku probably hasn't unpacked yet and is keeping his resume up to date.

Asian Maskhadov and Shamil Basaev

Maskhadov is the prime contender to be Yanderbiyev's successor. Maskhadov is a brilliant military strategist but has the personality of a piece of cardboard. The other likely candidate is Basaev, the charismatic field commander. Though full of tough rhetoric, he lacks the former leader's diplomatic skills. He is also more extreme than the moderate Maskhadov, whom the Russians have apparently targeted for peace talks—more intensively since Dudayev's death.

Ruslan Khasbulatov

Chechen home boy, former speaker of the Russian Parliament and leader of the October coup against Yeltsin, Khasbulatov was originally Moscow's favorite pick for puppet leader. Khasbulatov has powerful friends in Chechnya, and the village of Tolstoy-Yurt is his base of support. Apparently some 40 percent of all Chechens favor his election as Russian president.

The Russian Army

The Russian army, since the czarist era and through the Soviet period, has always relied on brute force and sheer numbers to win wars—which they haven't been doing a lot of recently. Tactically deficient and technologically marginal, the army has always relied on overpowering numbers of untrained troops to take home battlefield trophies. Even during the Soviet era, there was little need to train elite commando units, as there weren't any uprisings for them to put down. As one observer stated: "They have probably a far greater willingness to use massive force than surgical force."

Since Christmas of 1994, the Russian army claims it has lost 2483 soldiers but managed to kill 16,843 rebels. They lost four planes, 18 helicopters and 80 tanks. The rebels are supposed to have lost 119 tanks. Early in 1996, the Russian government said that about 30,000 people (including civilians) had been killed in the conflict and then changed it to 80,000 or 90,000 "give or take 10,000."

Getting In

Chechnya is a state within Russia. The official line is that there has been a peace accord, but that doesn't stop both sides from killing each other or you. A passport and Russian visa are required for all U.S. citizens traveling to or transiting through Russia by any means of transportation, including train, car or airplane. While under certain circumstances travelers who hold valid visas to some countries of the former Soviet Union may not need a visa to transit Russia, such exceptions are inconsistently applied. Travelers who arrive without an entry visa may be subject to large fines, days of processing requirements by Russian officials, and/or immediate departure by route of entry (at the traveler's expense). Carrying a photocopy of your passport and visas will facilitate replacement should either be stolen.

All Russian visas, except transit visas, are issued on the basis of support from a Russian individual or organization, known as the sponsor. It is important to know who your sponsor is and how they can be contacted, as Russian law requires that your sponsor apply on your behalf for replacement and extension of and changes to your visa. The U.S. embassy cannot act as your sponsor. Tourists should contact, in advance, their tour company or hotel for information on visa sponsorship.

For current information on visa requirements, U.S. citizens can contact the Russian consulates in New York, San Francisco or Seattle, or the Russian embassy in Washington D.C.:

Russian Embassy

Consular Division
1825 Phelps Place N.W.
Washington, D.C. 20008
☎ *(202) 939-8918, 939-8907, or 939-8913*

All foreigners must have an exit visa in order to depart Russia. For short stays, the exit visa is issued together with the entry visa; for longer stays, the exit visa must be obtained by the sponsor after the traveler's arrival. Russian law requires that all travelers who spend more than three days in Russia register their visas through their hotel or sponsor. Visitors who stay in Russia for a period of weeks may be prevented from leaving if they have not registered their visas. Errors in the dates or other information on the visa can occur, and it is helpful to have someone who reads Russian check the visa before departing the United States.

The southern borders are not manned, and checkpoints are only on main roads. Most Russian soldiers can be bribed due to their low pay and acceptance of side income. Do not expect any assistance if you are detained by soldiers or Chechens. A well-known American aid worker was executed by the Chechens when Russians incorrectly leaked information that he was a spy.

Entry into Chechnya should only be attempted by journalists or aid groups. Journalists can enter Chechnya on the ground with the Russian Army after flying from Moscow to Ordzonikidze. Journalists covering the conflict from the rebel side can either contact Chechen elements in Moscow or fly from Moscow to Kizljar in Dagestan and make their way to the mountains near Gudermes to make contact with the insurgents. It may take hanging around for a while, but you'll get in. *DP* arranged for the Chechen Mafia to transport us into Grozny. The Dagestanis can be used as well. It included a meeting in Istanbul with a Chechen representative, a flight to Moscow to meet with the Chechen Mafia and then a long flight into Dagestan. From there we were met by fighters and hiked into the area around Grozny. (See "In a Dangerous Place.") It is not recommended that our readers duplicate this method, since Russian troops shoot first and ask questions later. Secondly, the Chechens do not hold any specific part of Chechnya and are subject to air and ground attacks at all times.

Getting Around

There is no way to safely get around Chechnya. The only mechanized means of getting around the republic are via military convoys and occasionally by passenger cars. Fighting is still going on sporadically in the southwest area.

Dangerous Places

The Entire Country

The Russians have claimed they control all of provincial Chechnya. Most military activity is in the southwest. Most of the 400 villages are heavily armed and very jumpy. The area is under martial law. For those who like political subtlety, the area north of the Terek river is pro-Russian and does not grumble, the lowland middle of Chechnya is under heavy occupation, and the mountainous southwest is still happy fighting the war that was supposed to be ended by the peace agreement.

Grozny

The Chechens control Grozny while the battered Russians are pulling out. The situation seems to be stable during the day, with sporadic small arms fire and shelling during the night. Grozny would make a great film set, since only Kabul in Afghanistan has been more obliterated in recent years. A Turkish company has been awarded a $284 million contract to rebuild downtown Grozny. We wonder if they can find enough Chechens to inhabit it.

Dangerous Things

Being a Civilian

So far, over 80,000 civilians have been killed or are missing. Another 450,000 or so are refugees. Either Russian pilots are bad shots or they feel the odds are better at snuffing unarmed civilians. Markets (bazaars), medical facilities and civilian cars on the roadways— some sites hit multiple times—seem to be the Russians' favorite targets. The Russians even attacked a funeral procession in Samashki, killing three.

Being a Russian Civilian

Chechen terrorists took 255 hostages aboard a ferry in the Black Sea in January 1996. Chechen fighters also took a Russian hospital in Budyonnovsk in June 1995 and another one in Kizlyar in January 1996. Russian forces killed perhaps hundreds in their efforts to win them back.

Smaller Cities

The Chechens like to fight in the towns and cities, terrain they know and the Russians don't. If the Chechen fighters possess any fear, it is fear of open fields and the countryside. Chechen rebels even intentionally left the way into the strategic town of Argun open, hoping to lure Russian soldiers into an urban front. Evidently, Grozny taught them a lesson and they stayed away.

Getting Sick

Not much to speak of here. Chechnya is a fairly healthy place, but with very limited medical resources.

Dangerous Days

1817–1864 Imperial Russia fought a 40-year war to conquer mountainous lands between itself and newly acquired Georgia, defeating the Chechens and other Muslim peoples.

1859 Chechnya was incorporated into Russia.

1921 Chechnya became part of Russia's Mountain Republic, which was formally incorporated into the Soviet Union in 1924.

1934 Chechnya merged with neighboring Ingushetia in Checheno-Ingushetia.

1944 Hundreds of thousands of Chechens were deported by Soviet dictator Josef Stalin with other Caucasus peoples to Soviet Central Asia. Many died during the journey or in exile. After Stalin's death, they were allowed to return home in 1957.

09/05/1991 The government of Checheno-Ingushetia, which supported the August hard-line coup against Mikhail Gorbachev, resigned. Soviet Air Force General Dzhokhar Dudayev left Estonia and was installed as national leader.

10/1991 Dudayev launched a campaign to topple Moscow's temporary administration, attacking government offices and holding mass rallies. He won 80 percent backing in presidential polls and unilaterally declared Chechnya independent.

11/1991 Yeltsin declared a state of emergency in Checheno-Ingushetia and sent troops to Grozny. Troops were blocked at the airport, parliament overruled his declaration, and Yeltsin pulled them out after three days.

06/1992 Chechnya and Ingushetia split, Ingushetia remaining in the Russian Federation.

04–08/1994 Kidnappers from Chechnya carried out a series of hostage seizures of civilians in southern Russia. Russia blames Dudayev, and called on Chechens to topple him.

11/25/1994 Moscow-backed rebels attacked Grozny with tanks and artillery but pulled back a day later. Dudayev claimed victory.

11/29/1994 Yeltsin threatened to impose a state of emergency. Russian planes bombed Grozny.

11/30/1994 Russia sent troops to Chechen borders.

12/14/1994 New peace talks were held and broken off.

12/22/1994 Russian warplanes launched bombing raids.

02/09/1995 Former Soviet leader Mikhail Gorbachev described the campaign as a huge mistake that would cost the country dear.

Dangerous Days

06/14–20/ 1995   Chechen fighters took the southern Russian town of Budyonnovsk and 1500 hostages in a hospital. Russian forces freed 200 people on the 17th, but at least 150 were killed. Talks were held between Chernomyrdin and the Chechen leader of the hostage-taking Shamyl Basayev. Agreement was reached freeing the remaining hostages in return for a halt in fighting in Chechnya and negotiations for the withdrawal of Russian troops in Chechnya.

01/09-24/ 1996   Chechen commandos, led by Salman Raduyev, took 2000 people hostage at a hospital in Kizliar in the republic of Dagestan.

01/17/1996   Russian troops attacked Chechen fighters and their hostages dug in the village of Pervomaiskaya on the Chechnya/Dagestan border. Eighteen hostages were reported missing by Moscow, which also claimed killing 153 Chechens and taking 28 prisoner.

01/16–19/ 1996   Pro-Chechen commandos hijacked a Black Sea ferry at the Turkish port of Trabzon, taking 150 hostages, most Russian tourists. Hostages were later released after the hijackers claimed their aim of drawing worldwide attention to Russian atrocities in Chechnya was achieved.

03/31/1996   Yeltsin announced peace plan and that all Russian military operations will be suspended.

08/06/1996   Chechen fighters reversed the war driving Russian troops out of Grozny.

In a Dangerous Place

Chechnya, 1995: Front Row Seats

One can never lead a normal life as a war photographer. As soon as the words "hostilities have broken out in…" are heard on CNN, it is expected that there will be a flow of videotapes and photographs that cover and explain the conflict. Most journalists are dispatched in a hurry and get in-country before the borders are closed. Others must make their way in by whatever means necessary. *DP* is part of the latter.

The large networks and news gathering organizations pay extraordinary amounts of money not only to send in news teams but also to charter airplanes, couriers and even military planes to get their dispatches out of the country. Satellite telephones and transmitters make it easy to send reports now, but the units are expensive and heavy to pack.

When Russia sent its troops into Grozny, there were plenty of journalists and reporters. As the situation became embarrassing, the Russians began to simply round up and send journalists out of the country. Previously, Dudayev had expelled all Russian reporters because of their inflammatory articles. When the Russian and Western press began to highlight the Russian incompetence and division, the Russians rounded up the Western press. Unlike major conflicts where the press are carefully clothed, fed, housed and "spun" by briefings, press releases and carefully prepared interviews, Chechnya was the opposite. Russian troops couldn't care less if they shot at the glint of a camera lens or a sniper's telescopic sight. Mortars, bombs and shells dropped by the Russians cared even less.

We wanted to see for ourselves, so we sent in a correspondent to try to understand the situation firsthand. The story of just what it takes to get into a war zone like Chechnya will give you some idea of the new face of reporting war.

We made our preliminary arrangements before leaving Istanbul with the "Caucasus Peoples Federation," a group that was supporting Dudayev's fight in Chechnya, or Chechenstan as it is locally known. The plan was to allow us to go in with a group of "volunteers," or mercenaries, via Baku in Azerbaijan through Dagestan and then on to Grozny. Although they could provide some forms of transportation to the border, from Hasalyurt we would have to walk for about three days through the mountains in the middle of winter to reach Grozny. Although we were being sent in under the protection of the Chechen forces, there was no guarantee who would be in charge once we arrived.

We set off the day before Christmas with minimal survival gear: our cameras, a stove, some tins of fish and warm clothing. We fly to Baku, in Azerbaijan, to meet the people who will take us into Grozny. The "friends" turn out to be members of the Lezgi Mafia, one of the toughest groups in Russia and the Transcaucasus region. The Lezgi number about 1.5 million and live in the north of Azerbaijan and in south and central Dagestan. Our goal is to fly 1800 kms east to Baku and then travel 400 kms north along the Caspian Sea through Dagestan and then west 50 kms over the border into Grozny.

These entrepreneurial bandits have decided that since things are heating up (and as they don't know the difference between *DP* and NBC), they will need a $5000 transportation fee. Now normally when you make a business transaction in any country, you have some basic understanding of the value of money, and the intentions and general cost of a service. When you are dealing with the Mafia in Azerbaijan, however, there is no guarantee that you will not end up a frozen cadaver with a slit throat two miles out of Baku.

Seeing how we have a plan "B," we have nothing to lose by negotiating this fee down to a paltry $1000 which included transportation, food, lodging but no cable TV.

Plan "B" was the official Russian tour of Chechnya. Most Westerners are not aware of Moscow's new entrepreneurial spirit. Journalists who are accepted can arrange a $4000 junket into Chechnya from Moscow via military transport. We opt for the lower-priced, more adventurous ground operator version via the locals.

We make our deal over tea and cigarettes, and, once accepted, we are as good as kinfolk with these tough characters. Although we are kissing cousins, we also agree to pay our fee once we are over the border in Hasalyurt. The man who is to take us there tells us we will have company. He is bringing in 10 mercenaries and volunteers from Iran, Uzbekistan and Tadjikistan who will be joining us 10 kms short of the Azerbaijan-Dagestan border. Oh, he mentions casually, a load of antitank missiles as well. We don't ask him how much money this one trip will clear but it is obvious that war is good for business in these parts.

One of his men drives us two hours north to Quba in a Lada, complete with reflective tinted windows. The Mafia may have money, but they sure don't have taste. We stay at an old Russian farmhouse surrounded by apple orchards as far as the eye can see. Now abandoned, it was a way station and safe house for the Lezgi Mafia. In the courtyard are two tractors with the antitank rockets. The men are packing oranges, apples, flour and other agrarian items to camouflage the clearly labeled crates.

We are awakened early the next morning and set off north toward Qusar, a town about 25 kms short of the Dagestan border. We are now traveling in three groups. The first group consists of two Lezgi, who would travel ahead of us to meet with the local officials, grease the border guards, and ensure our safe passage into Dagestan. Behind us come the volunteers, now happy farmers bringing in foodstuffs. The border is officially closed, but the guards just stare dispassionately at us and never bother to even wave us down or check our passports. We thought the mirrored windows were bad taste; now we know their function. Inside Dagestan, we stay in the car until we reach an old Lenin Pioneer Camp, a relic of the Russian regime, where primary and high school kids learned the ways of the revolution. It is the Soviet version of our Boy Scout Camps.

That night we have a typical Azeri meal—smoked meat, and smoked fish, washed down with homemade vodka strong enough to remove paint. Tonight will be cold, but the fire from the vodka will warm us up.

After our feast, we set off down a small side road that leads to the official checkpoint at the border. The cart track is used by the local farmers and is too bumpy to allow large trucks. There is little reason for a 24-hour border patrol, and, by "coincidence," there is no border patrol that night. As we travel along the grey Caspian sea into Derbent, we learn some unsettling news. Moscow has replaced the local police and border guards with special security team members known as "Omon." This is indeed a bad "omen." Security is tight because one of Dudayev's assistants has made a visit to Turkey and asked for the Turks to send assistance to Chechnya via Azerbaijan. The sudden heavy presence of the Russian military is to cut off any aid coming to the embattled capital of Grozny.

We are told this by a Lezgi mafia customs official. The fellow who holds this oxymoronic post advises us that in order for us to continue through Dagestan, we will need to become citizens of the Dagestan Autonomous Region.

That night, a man from the local police force brings two blank passports and we become Dagestanis for $300 each. It is a busy night as we fill out forms, and complete the passports. Before dawn the next morning, it seems that our new status is to be rewarded. Our transport is a brand-new BMW bought (or stolen) in Germany. We leave our old passports behind as partial payment and to avoid being searched and arrested as spies. Dagestan is a war zone with a penalty of two years in jail for crossing the border illegally. The Russian soldiers are also empowered to detain and/or execute people whom they suspect as volunteers or spies.

I wonder who Sefail Musayev is, but I carry his passport thankfully. The fact that we cannot speak a word of Russian makes every border crossing a gut wrencher. The Russians are not in any mood for levity, but our Azeri driver/guide manages to chat and joke our way through a total of seven checkpoints. At each tense checkpoint my hair turns a little greyer, the lines on my face are etched deeper and I wonder what the hell I am doing here. When we reach the bustling city of Mohachkale (or Makhachkala), we finally can breathe. From here it is 170 kms to the border of Chechnya. From this point on, our driver knows nothing of the conditions ahead.

We drive on in our beautiful new BMW, feeling like royalty, although we are the last people the Russians want in this area. We come to Kizlar, and our driver stops to talk with a Chechen contact family, who works as a link between the Chechen Mafia and the Lezgi. We ask about the Reuters journalists who are based in Hasalyurt. We have made an earlier deal to use their transmitter and satellite phone. The news is not good. The day before, the Russians severely bombed the Hasalyurt-Grozny road, knocking out a number of bridges. The journalists who were staying in the local sports stadium and using it as a base for their forays into Grozny were rounded up and sent back to Moscow.

After coming this far we have no way to send out our information and no one to take us across the border; all that lies ahead of us is a bombed-out wasteland.

After much discussion with the Chechen family, we learn there is one chance. If we can make it to Babayurt, another border town, we can try to contact a group of Chechen volunteers who are to cross the border soon. They mention that we will be safer in Chechnya, since the Russians are increasing their crackdown on foreigners and volunteers in Dagestan daily.

Kizlar is about 40 kms north of Hasalyurt, and Babayurt is halfway in between. One of the refugees from Kizlar staying in the house offers to come with us to help us get into Chechnya and to ease our way past the checkpoints that await us. Our luck holds, because the Russians have concentrated their Omon special forces south of Hasalyurt and the checkpoints to the north are manned by local Dagestanis. We meet up with a group of 20–30 Chechen volunteers who are preparing to cross the border that night. We discuss the various ways into the country. Most agree that to try to walk over the mountains into Grozny is futile since the snow is now 4 to 5 meters deep. The 130-km trip will take at least a full week, with an excellent chance of being attacked by jets or helicopters during the day.

We decide to tag along with the heavily armed volunteers. We begin our trip in a convoy of cars and cross the empty border post. At around midnight, the drivers of the cars drop us off and return. We will continue on foot. We walk for six or seven hours, covering 20 km of frozen lowland impeded only by a slight snow cover. We let the main group of armed volunteers go on ahead of us. Our group was not armed, but if they meet up with the Russians, we are close enough to hear the sound of gunfire before we stumble into the same trap.

The cold is numbing, and we plod on through the night like zombies. The wind whips and slaps our faces making icicles on my mustache. The moon is our only light. After a while, we come upon a dirt track that leads to the village ahead. The wind not only brings cold and pain; it now brings the sound of heavy gunfire, alternately fading and building. Our temperatures begin to rise, as we go through the fields leading down to the village. Rockets and automatic weapons crack and thump in the crystal-clear night. As we crunch our way down to the village, the light of the dull blue sky begins to rise like a curtain at the start of a movie. The sound of the Russian helicopters increases from a muted drumroll to a thunderous chorus.

My cold hands reach for my frozen cameras in anticipation. This is the play for which we have come, the drama to which we have fought so hard for admission. Now on with the show.

—**Sedat Aral**

Haiti
★★

Voodoo Doodoo

American troops ironically referred to their 1994 occupation of this island as their "Haitian Vacation." It may rhyme but the real key is probably in the name Haiti. There is a lot of hate, suffering, misery, poverty and despair. That can't be fixed with gunboat politics. Although the troops are now gone and there is supposed to be law and order,there will always be a genus of Central African fear and dark sorcery in this wasted island. It says something about the condition of Haiti that three American soldiers on assignment committed suicide.The fact that Haitians are caught stealing topsoil from neighboring Dominican Republic will tell you how poor this land is.

The nation held free elections in June 1995; while the country was fraught with chaos and fraud, it still was a baby step toward democracy. "Whether it is a step forward or sideways remains to be seen," said the Council of Freely Elected Heads of Government, an international group that observed the elections. Throughout the Caribbean, tourism has been the engine of growth but having every major news organization in the world cover marines landing and people being beaten and burned to death doesn't make for attractive tourist brochures.

Haiti could blame its present agony on its dysfunctional upbringing. Columbus left the first Europeans there in 1492 and all ended up dying within a year. In 1617 the French were given control of the western part of Hispaniola (called Saint Domingue then by the Spanish) and turned it into an extremely wealthy colony, exporting sugar, coffee and indigo. Years of torture and subjugation followed for the imported African slaves who tilled the lands for rich European gentry. Finally, at the end of the 18th century the slaves conducted a massive rebellion, led by Toussaint l'Ouverture. (At that time, U.S. plantation owners were terrified that the Caribbean revolutionary wave would inspire their slave population.) In 1804, the country of Haiti declared itself independent and Jean Jacques Dessalines emerged as the world's first black emperor. He was assassinated in 1806 and the country became divided again. Ever since then, strife has marked the country's nature: the mulattos of the south waged fierce civil war against the blacks in the north, only to be followed by a succession of tyrannical dictators and an American invasion in 1915. (The 1915 U.S. takeover of Haiti was led by a Virginian-born commander who boasted that he knew all about handling black people, and during their 19 years the "blans" (foreigners, literally "whites" in Creole) smashed an insurgency, imposed Jim Crow rules in Haiti's best clubs, and set up a Haitian army whose brutality, greed and incompetence decades later set the stage for a new intervention. By 1934 the Americans had returned. In 1957, the country was taken over by Francois Duvalier, known as Papa Doc, who wielded a reign of terror through the help of sadistic secret police. Until the mid-1980s his son Baby Doc (Jean-Claude) continued in his father's bloody footsteps, until a political movement called Operation Deschoukay drove him out of the country. Elections were held, but coup after coup shook the stability of the country. In the last eight years, there have been three coups.

In 1990, in the first genuinely public elections, a black charismatic priest, Father Jean-Bertrand Aristide, won the presidency with about 67 percent of the vote, only to be overthrown in a military coup led by Lt. General Raul Cédras. For the next three years, Cédras and his "attaches" (a Haitian term for what amounts to paramilitary thugs), introduced a new reign of terror, killing over 3000 people and committing untold human rights abuses from the killing of children to the raping of women. Since 1991, the country has been faced with great economic and social crisis largely due to the trade embargoes (enforced by the U.S. out of protest) and a lack of viable opportunities that have always plagued Haiti. In the fall of 1994, the sparring of threats between the Clinton administration and the military junta escalated beyond endurance for both sides. Cédras, who is white and sports a Jay Leno chin, held onto a diplomacy-of-defiance as the U.S. began threats to invade. The U.S. goal was to reinstate Aristide as president, whose power over the masses was singular in Haiti's history. Many poor Haitians (though considered fanatics) considered Aristide as some sort of prophet, or messiah, who could create miracles that would instantly solve the people's problems (Aristide himself advised against such ideology). Nevertheless, even before his ousting, Aristide was used to making strong impressions without bearing much responsibility for the political consequences, with his sermons often bringing the people out to the streets, only to be gunned down by the army.

The final denouement of the conflict became dramatic. On the eve of an American invasion, former President Jimmy Carter with General Colin Powell and Sen-

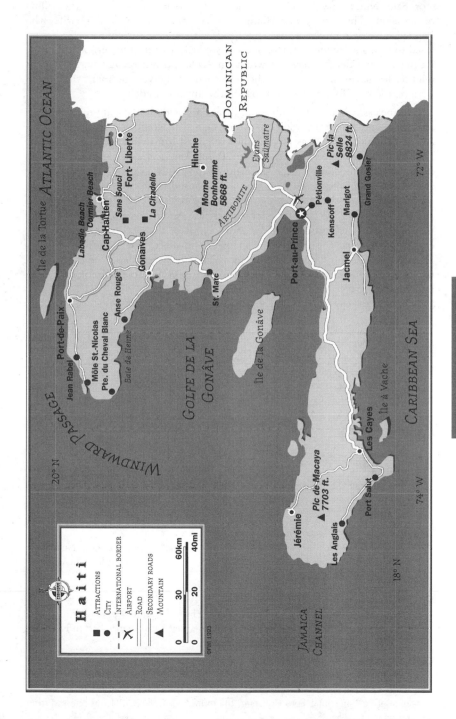

Haiti

- ■ ATTRACTIONS
- ● CITY
- –·– INTERNATIONAL BORDER
- ✈ AIRPORT
- ━━ ROAD
- ═══ SECONDARY ROADS
- ▲ MOUNTAIN

| 0 | 30 | 60km |
| 0 | 20 | 40mi |

ATLANTIC OCEAN

DOMINICAN REPUBLIC

WINDWARD PASSAGE

20° N

Île de la Tortue

Fort-Liberté

Sans Souci

Labadie Beach

Cormier Beach

La Citadelle

Cap-Haïtien

Gonaïves

Anse Rouge

Port-de-Paix

Jean Rabel

Môle St.-Nicolas

Pte. du Cheval Blanc

Baie de Henne

Hinche

▲ Morne Bonhomme 5668 ft.

ARTIBONITE

St. Marc

Étang Saumâtre

Port-au-Prince

Pétionville

Kenscoff

Marigot

Jacmel

Grand Gosier

▲ Pic la Selle 8824 ft.

GOLFE DE LA GONÂVE

Île de la Gonâve

CARIBBEAN SEA

72° W

74° W

18° N

Les Cayes

Port Salut

Île à Vache

▲ Pic de Macaya 7703 ft.

Jérémie

Les Anglais

JAMAICA CHANNEL

HAITI

ator Sam Nunn flew to Haiti to negotiate a surrender among the ruling dictatorship. The last-minute drama was complicated by Cédras' wife who claimed she would rather die with her children than leave the country. Cédras refused to sign a surrender, on risk of court-martial, without the permission of the incumbent president Jonaissant, whom the U.S. did not recognize. At the last minute, Jonaissant finally signed the agreement at the very moment that planes were on the way, forcing Clinton to stop the invasion midair.

Nevertheless, what started out as an invasion was diplomatically renamed "intervasion" and American soldiers were instructed to come ashore and "cooperate" with Haitian police as long as they refrained from violence and abuse.The Haitian army looked on sullenly as over 20,000 American troops fanned through the country in full combat gear, dismantling their only arsenal of heavy weapons and their few armored cars. American tanks turned their tanks on FRAPH, the paramilitary thugs who did the regime's dirty work, built barbed wire around the airport, and locked up 75 of the worst attaches. Americans also took control of the state-controlled radio and TV station, and gave the city its first dependable electricity in years. Casualties were incurred, however, when Marines engaged Haitieds in a firefight in Cap Hatien, in which nine were killed. The irony is that the agreement provided for a general amnesty and honorable retirement for dictators.

The Scoop

Haiti is an errant child that is spanked by Uncle Sam when things get too nasty. The people are sharply divided between a tiny, light-skinned French-speaking elite and the desperately poor, black Creole-speaking masses. Some days you would swear you were in Liberia. Haiti's history of self abuse has left it virtually without law or even vegetation. The elite, the army, and their thugs have pillaged the country for their own benefit. The elite of Pétitionville, in the words of one businessman, look at who ever is running their country as their servant.

For now Haiti is a hot stinking place where the rich have stepped up private patrols of their flower-fringed villas and sleep with pistols beneath their beds.

The Players

The Good Guys

The 100 or so U.S. trained presidential security units have been using their newly found skills to assassinate right wing political opponents. Seems oddly familiar. Isn't this where we came in?

The President

The current President has his hands full running a bankrupt, central African Hellhole in the middle of the Caribbean. For now Rene Preval is president. Good Luck Rene.

The Bad Guys:

EX- FADH (Former members of the Haitian Military)

These folks are busy trying to spring old drinking buddies, get back pay and trying to get back into power. It is not known what the difference is between members of FADH or FRAPH.

EX-FRAPH

A right wing military group that is supposed to be disbanded but now seems to be very much alive and just waiting until the U.S. and the U.N. are looking the other way. In June of 96 Emmanuel Toto Constant, the former head of FRAPH was released from prison in the U.S.

Getting In

U.S. and Canadian citizens need a tourist card to enter Haiti (about US$10) purchased from consulates, tourist offices, airlines on departure or at the airport on arrival. Do not wait to obtain it in Haiti because the airport is usually a vision of pandemonium and you will be needlessly tied up for hours. The limit time on tourist cards is two months; extensions may be obtained from the Immigration Department. All visitors should have an ongoing or return ticket.

There are direct flights from Miami to Cap Haitien Monday to Friday on **Gulfstream International**. **American Airlines** and **Haiti Trans Air** fly from New York. American Airlines, Haiti Trans Air and **ALM** fly direct from Miami. Fort-Lauderdale-Cap Haitien link is provided by **Lynx Air**. **ALM** flies from Curaçao to Cap Haitien. Once a week **Air France** flies from Santo Domingo to Cap Haitien. **Cairbintaxi**, a Haitian air taxi service, flies three times a week from Santo Domingo. Do check your reservation several times from Miami since they tend to be overbooked. Sometimes credit vouchers are given if you want to give up your confirmed seat to someone else.

The airport at Port-au-Prince is located at the northern edge of Delmas, 13 kilometers outside the capital. It would help facilitate you through customs if you have a working knowledge of French; the scene can get crazy, crowded and hot if more than one flight has landed. Baggage inspection is rigorous and thorough, with a strict drug law enforcement (whatever you do, don't carry drugs—life in a Haitian prison is the definition of hell). It' s best just to keep your head about you, your eye on your luggage and documents, and your goal fixed on getting to your hotel. Once you get outside, you are pushed into another mass of humanity waiting for taxis and families to pick them up. You can either take a taxi to town (about U.S.$10 or sit in the back of a tap-tap, an open-backed truck, which costs about 10 cents (probably the cheapest transportation in the Caribbean, if not the most colorful); throw in another ten cents per bag.

Getting Around

Taxis in Port-au-Prince are usually shared vehicles, called *Publiques*, which you flag down in the street. There is usually a standard fare (about 20 American cents) which is multiplied according to the length of the destination. There is also a minibus called a *camionette* and open-backed pickup trucks, called taptaps which run fixed routes and charge about 15 American cents. They do not carry luggage well and rarely travel after 10:30 p.m. There are few radio taxis at present, although democracy may have changed all that. Sometimes you may have to wait an hour for one to arrive. Try **Nick's Taxis** (☎ *57-7777*). Sometimes a Publique that has no customers can sometimes be persuaded to act as a private taxi, with the right monetary incentive.

Chauffeurs-guides cater to the foreign trade, usually waiting outside the finest hotels or at the airport; you can hire them as regular taxis or for a portion of the day. To make a reservation, call ☎ *22-0330.*, or go to the office of the Association des Chauffeurs-Guides at *18 Blvd. Harry Truman*. This is a more expensive, but more comfortable way to go to outlying beaches.

To reach other cities, take buses or colorful converted pickup trucks, leaving from what is called a station, most of them somewhere along the Blvd. Jean-Jacques Dessalines and the waterfront. There is no regular schedule, and buses depart when they have enough passengers (usually they are required to be full). You may, therefore, have a long wait. The trip can be torturous, since roads are incredibly poor and the conditions hot and dirty. You will be safer to pay a little extra to sit closer to the driver, especially if you have any valuables. (Do your best to carry only essential goods with you. It goes without saying that you should not wear any jewelry, watches should be kept out of sight, and it's best to carry your money, credit cards, etc., inside your clothes in a body pouch. Simply, whatever you do, do not call attention to any personal wealth.)

Car rentals are available, though gas supplies are so iffy that you probably should think twice about renting one. Avis, Budget, and Hertz all have offices. Airplane flights are sometimes available to Jeremie, Cap, and Hinche, but schedules are not reliable, since fuel has been a problem. Only time will tell as the democratic regime take what supplies are available.

Getting Out

There is a US$25 departure tax and a US$2 security fee, payable in U.S. currency.

Dangerous Things

Politics

There are flareups against the former Duvalierists and rousted Tonton Macoutes. These demonstrations usually result in the victim's house being looted and destroyed and can end in a gruesome public murder. Haitians continue to whack other Haitians for their political leanings. DP's advice is don't get involved in these brutal confrontations since many lead to death and mutilation.

Used Tires

Many victims are beaten senseless, garlanded with an old tire (cutely called Pere LeBrun) by the locals, doused with gasoline and then left to burn alive. It's hard to say how many miles you get on a tire in Haiti but we do know that it is a fairly effective and painful way to murder people. A nasty sport picked up from their South African brothers.

Zenglendo

The local name for armed thugs (not always with a gun) that prowl Port au Prince looking for victims. They arise during the many power blackouts that occur at night. Since the cops are useless and the court system nonexistent, it is probably not even worth calling for help.

AIDS

For a while Haiti was supposed to be the home of AIDS, a place where gay men went on wildly lustful holidays and paid the ultimate price. Haiti remains a highly infected area for AIDS. Prostitution is not illegal in Haiti, but foreigners are targeted. All precautions should be taken as the country suffers from a very high AIDS epidemic, among both sexes and sexual orientations.

Port au Prince

The capital city is the most dangerous spot in Haiti with about 70 - 80% of the violent incidents reported. During some periods there is an average of a murder a day.

Driving

In Haiti thieves actually practice the old Woody Allen joke about stealing hubcaps from a moving car. Many U.N. vehicles are stripped or stolen while they are moving. The port road at night, La Saline and Cite Soleil roads are considered dangerous.

Parades

If there is a parade, it is usually filled with *bandes-a-pieds*, roving bands on foot who attract large crowds with their chanting and circular dancing. Most of the lyrics are highly satirical and often erotic. (Do avoid being crushed by crowds since fights tend to break out easily; you might find the safest perch near the Holiday Inn.) During the three or four weekends prior to Carnival, there may be open-air concerts. Most of the upper-class head to Jacmel for Carnival, where you will find a more sophisticated costume party; the downside is that the music tends to be less than thrilling.

Voodoo

More fascinating is the peasant carnival called Rara, which follows on its heels, a ritual of voodoo societies. During every weekend of Lent (including the Easter weekend), flamboyantly dressed bands wander the countryside, asking for donations while singing and dancing. Some bands have up to a thousand members. One of the most important voodoo festivals is the Gede on November 1 and 2 (All Saints Days and the Day of the Dead), where spirit-filled participants dress up as dead people and prowl through cemeteries as a reminder that eros is the source of life. During this celebration, the dance movements become quite vulgarized, and hangers-on are pulled in to participate.

Who Do Voodoo?

To attend a voodoo ritual is not easy for a foreign visitor. They are not publicized and you will have to have an introduction from an insider. Most of the worship happens in lower-class neighborhoods. Most of the time an enormous sum of money is asked for the privilege of attending; don't be bribed but understand that your income level is probably heads beyond that of the average Haitian. Some offering should be made, at the very least a bottle or two of local whiskey or rum. On the western side of Port-au-Prince is a voodoo dancehall run by Max Baeuvoir ☎ 34-2818/3723, who can provide you introductions into the cult.

Nuts and Bolts

And you thought you had to go all the way to Africa or Asia to visit the world's poorest country. Well Haiti has the lowest per capita income in the world—$250, about the same as Rwanda, a life expectancy of 55-years-old, a 35 percent adult literacy rate, and safe drinking water for only 41 percent of the population. The country has been so black, so isolated, and so racially polarized that the cheering throngs welcoming the American troops addressed black Americans as "blans," a Creole term (meaning white) that signifies any foreigner.

In coastal areas temperatures range from 68 degrees F to 95 degrees F. Further inland, it is generally hot, but offshore trade winds keep the air endurable. It is hotter between April and September. The drier months are December-March. As you go further up the hill, where several resorts are situated, you will find the air gets cooler.

The current runs 110 volts, 60 cycles, AC. Power cuts are regular occurrences in Port-au-Prince for half a day at a time, although American troops have tried to solve the problem. One reason to stay at the best hotels is that they have their own private generators. Do take a flashlight for emergency blackouts.

All Haitians understand Creole and speak it part of the time. Only the elite and middle-class use French. Eighty-five percent of the population can't even understand French. The 1987 constitution, however, gave Creole equal status with French, and popular music is increasingly being written in Creole as a sign of national identity. It's been said that Aristide's charisma with the masses was his ability to speak Creole.

The official currency unit is the gourde, divided into 100 centimes. What makes things confusing is that, at least in the past, Haitians have referred to some of their own money as the dollar, so be dead-sure when exchanging money, that you know which dollars—American or Haitian—is being quoted. The best exchange rate is obtained from money changers. American dollars get the best rate of all currencies. Credits cards, such as American Express, Visa and Mastercard are all widely accepted. However, do call your car d company before going since conditions in Haiti are ever-changing.

The telephone system is a nightmare in Haiti. It's been said that fewer than 33 percent ever make their connection.The international operators in Haiti seem to be sleeping, or else they don't like to answer—you can give a hero's try by dialing the number 09. If you are staying at the Holiday Inn, Montana, El Rancho and Oloffson hotels, you will have AT&T, USA Direct telephones for easy collect calls to the USA or anywhere else in the world with an AT&T credit card.

HAITI

Getting Sick

Community sanitation is very poor. You should never drink the tap water in Haiti, and you should carefully choose your food. Avoid eating food that has not been properly washed or cooked; do not eat food cooked on the streets, and avoid anything raw or unpeeled. Stomach troubles are best soothed by a local herb tea. Prophylaxis against malaria is essential; ask your family physician for the proper medication, which he can receive by calling the Centers for Disease Control in Atlanta, Georgia. You can call yourself and listen to the latest up-to-date reports on Haitian conditions *(☎ (404) 332-4557)*. You will need a push-button phone to proceed through the menu.

Take all medicines and prescriptions that you will need. Shortages frequently occur, although pharmacists/chemists can fill prescriptions if they have supplies. Always bring a letter from your doctor explaining your need for certain medication and also several copies of the prescription itself.

The best hospitals are **Canapé Vert**, *on rue Canapé Vert;* ☎ *(404) 45-1052/3/0984*, and **Adventistse de Diquini** *on Carrefour Road;* ☎ *(404) 34-2000/0521*. However medical care is not up to U.S. standards and you will be expected to pay doctors and hospitals in cash.

Useful Addresses

The tourist office in Cap Haitien is located at Ruse, 24, Esplanade. ☎ *57-4647* or in the U.S. ☎ *(212) 697-9767.*

U.S. Embassy
Harry Truman Boulevard
P.O. Box 1761
Port-au-Prince
☎ *(509) 22-0200, 22-0354, or 22-0612*
FAX (509) 23-1641.
Open 7:30 a.m. to 4 p.m.

The Consular Section
Rue Oswald Durand
Port-au-Prince
☎ *(509) 23-7011, FAX (509) 23-9665.*

Emergency Police/Fire Numbers

Port-au-Prince: ☎ *22-2744*

Petionville: ☎ *57-0019*

Police Headquarters: ☎ *21017*

Delmas: ☎ *46-2859*

Carrefour: ☎ *34-1815*

Dangerous Days

09/30/1991	Overthrow of Aristide. President Jean-Bertrand Aristide was overthrown by the military and replaced by a military-backed government that the Organization of American States (OAS) declared illegitimate.
12/16/1990	Election of President Aristide. Father Jean-Bertrand Aristide was overwhelmingly chosen as Haiti's first popularly-elected president.
01/01/1804	Independence Day. The slave revolt that began in 1801 under the leadership of Pierre Dominique Toussaint L'Ouverture triumphed with the establishment of an independent haiti under Jean-Jacques Dessalines.
11/02/0000	All Souls Day. Schools, stores and businesses are closed.
11/01/0000	All Saints Day. Schools, stores and businesses are closed.

HAITI

Mexico
★★

Run for the Border

Walking through the barrios of Tijuana overlooking the suburban sprawl of the United States, it is hard to imagine that half a mile could make such a difference. Here is where the Third World runs smack into the First World—like putting Mogadishu next to Santa Barbara. Stick any red-blooded American here for more than a week, and they'd be scrambling over the chain-link fence and dashing for the promised land. Although the contrast between these two countries is obvious, Mexico itself is a land of contrasts and turmoil. Even in the far south where Mexico blends seamlessly into Guatemala there is turmoil.

Imagine a bunch of armed Texans in ski masks in 100° heat rallying around a statue of Sam Houston and declaring the state an "autonomous region." On second thought, it isn't that difficult to imagine at all. On New Year's Day 1994, hundreds of armed peasants in ski masks—brandishing bolt-action rifles and sticks—declared their autonomy. They called themselves the Zapatista Army of National Liberation, after Emilio Zapata, one of the leaders of the 1910 Mexican

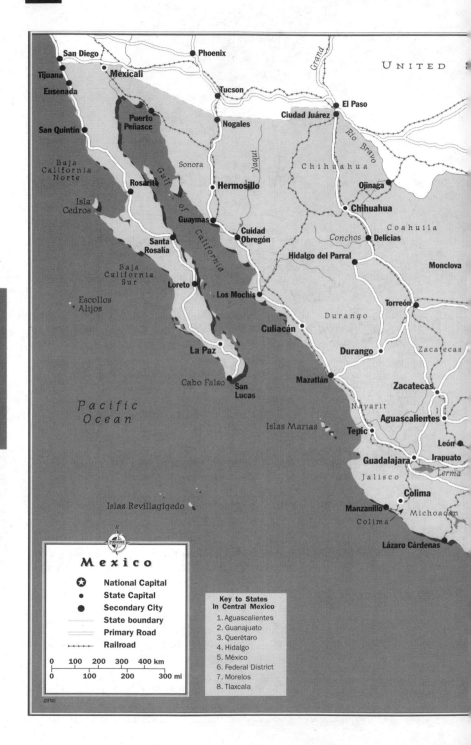

Mexico

- ⊛ National Capital
- • State Capital
- ● Secondary City
- —— State boundary
- ········· Primary Road
- ┝╾┿╾┥ Railroad

| 0 | 100 | 200 | 300 | 400 km |
| 0 | 100 | 200 | 300 mi |

©FWI

Key to States in Central Mexico

1. Aguascalientes
2. Guanajuato
3. Querétaro
4. Hidalgo
5. México
6. Federal District
7. Morelos
8. Tlaxcala

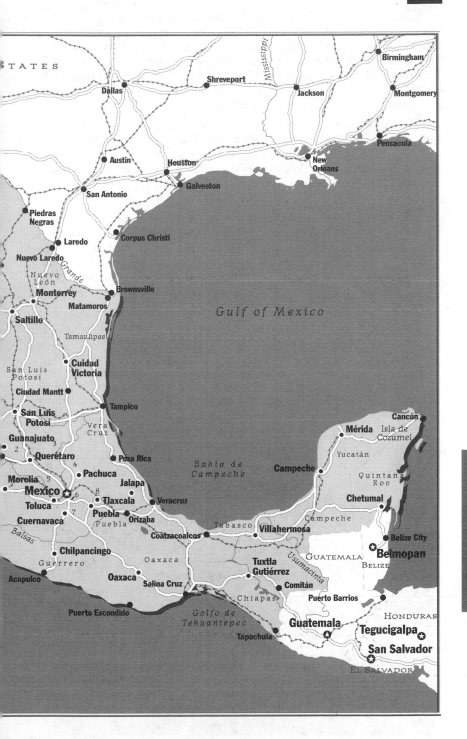

Revolution. They stormed a number of Chiapas communities, including San Cristobal, Ocosingo, Altamira and Las Margaritas. The uprising came with the January 1, 1994, implementation of the North American Free Trade Agreement. The Zapatistas said, and continue to say, that the agreement will essentially strip the *indigenes* of claims to their ancestral land. The tour buses that usually descended upon San Cristobal and the surrounding indigenous Indian villages in droves slammed on their brakes and stayed away.

After a lengthy cease-fire, the rascals were back at it. Armed Zapatista rebels set up countless roadblocks and checkpoints across Chiapas in a surprise "military action" in December 1994. They virtually doubled the amount of territory they seized during the January 1994 insurrection. But, as with the last occupation, once confronted by the superior forces of the Mexican army, the rebels melted into the rain forest ahead of advancing troops, leaving 145 people dead.

Adventure nuts, "daredevil" tourists and *DP* readers have been visiting the town of La Realidad in Chiapas since February 1994, including high-profile visits in 1996 to Subcommander Marcos by filmmaker Oliver Stone and former-French President Francois Mitterand's jetsetting PC wife. Zapatpurists who want to follow in the footsteps of MTV and greying left wingers can now make the pilgrimage down the muddy path to the Zapatista camps deep in the jungle near Toluca.

Mexico has been faced with a triple-whammy. Not only have the Chiapas rebels been a thorn in the country's side, and the PRA is threatening the discos at Acapulco, but, while they weren't looking, the peso crashed. Investors began makin' a run for the border in droves in January 1995. The national solvency continues to dissolve, with the peso so low against the dollar that Mexicans may stop robbing other Mexicans entirely. With armed insurgent highlanders brandishing black flags emblazoned with a red star stalking the southern rain forests, it's a wonder so many still venture to this part of the world.

One thing is for sure—for the traveler, Mexico is filled with extremes. Whether you want the coke-dusted lifestyle of the rich and famous on the Mexican Riviera, or like to shop for .45 caliber ammo behind the saloon in Sonora, Mexico has a little danger for everyone.

The Scoop

Mexico has one foot in the First World and the other in the Third World. Depending on where you are, you can be perfectly safe or in mortal danger. Sounds like America.

The Players

Popular Revolutionary Army (EPR, PRA, PROCUP-PDLP)

When you're number two you try harder. Or kill faster. Unlike the laid back, college, Internet savvy methods of the Zapatistas, the PRA are some mean dudes. Marxist/Leninist/Maoist mean like the Shining Path and the PKK.

The PRA first showed up in new uniforms with shiny new guns at a funeral in 1994. They say they are made up of 14 organizations. Their 45 point wish list includes canceling foreign debt and nationalizing any U.S-held interests. They did not discuss back end points and credit type size on movie deals. The government wrote them off as one shots, the press scrambled (unsuccessfully) for witticisms and the people thought they were army stooges sent in to provide an excuse to send in the government troops. Meanwhile the tourists on the beach in Acapulco and shopping for silver in Oaxaca thought they might be in 1950's Cuba, but Club Med in Huatulco is a lot further than 90 miles to safety

In September of 96 the PRA officially started a second uprising in Mexico by launching coordinated attacks in five of Mexico's 32 states. When it was over, 16 people were dead and the army got to use all the nice new U.S. issue military toys. The PRA are Marxist-Leninist *and* Maoist which means their leader must be a throwback to the '70s. Who is the shadowy leader of this new/old group? Well it's a long story so we'll make it short. PROCUP was formed by students at the Autonomous University of Benito Juarez in Oaxaca and the University of Guadalajara in 1964. The Party of the Poor began in 1967 by Lucio Cabanas, a schoolteacher from Atoyac de Alvarez in Guerrero state. Cabanas put together a group of about 400 men and raised hell in the mountains of Guerrero until he was killed by the army in 1974. He managed to kill 50 soldiers and the police chief of Acapulco and to elude about 16,000 soldiers before he passed into legend and worm food. He is now viewed as a hero in the remote untouristed regions east of Acapulco.

The PDLP then joined up with PROCUP and became PROCUP-PDLP and has been bombing, killing, robbing and kidnapping off and on since then. They have also aligned themselves with the Zapatistas and in 1994 blew up a car bomb in a Mexico City mall just to make sure their press release got ample coverage. Their alleged leader, Felipe Martinez Soriano, a former rector of Oaxaca university, is sitting in a high security prison outside Mexico City. Unlike the media and movie friendly Sub Commandante Marcos, the PRA and its leaders are up to some serious stuff. Like other Marxist Leninist Groups in Peru and Colombia, they do some serious bloodletting using their chunky ransoms (the family of a Mexican bank executive paid $30 million as a ransom in 1994).

For now the PRA attacks government, military and police installations and although their attacks take place in heavily touristed areas, they do not focus on attacking Americans or travelers, they just want to scare off the touristas. Enterprising journalists beware, the PRA did kill two security guards at a newspaper that refused to run their press release.

Rafael Sebastin Guillen Vicente (a.k.a. Subcommander Marcos)

(Starring in *Che for a Day*, or *The Adventures of Subcomedian Marcos*)

Although the image of the intellectual revolutionary is an appealing one in Latin America, there are few Latinos who are willing to lead a heroic group. Che Guevara did, and now it seems like the son of a furniture store owner in Tampico is going for it. Rafael Guillen, er, sorry Marcos, is a former college professor (with a degree in sociology) from a well-off family in the state of Tamaulipas.

Alas, his revolution will never match "Uncle Fidel's" nor Mao's nor even that of his real ideal, Sandino. Vincente was born on June 19, 1957, and educated at the National Autonomous University of Mexico. He left in 1980 with a degree in sociology, earned a graduate degree, and became an associate professor at Xochimilco south of Mexico City.

In 1984 he left for Managua, where he taught and learned about revolution. He returned to Mexico in the late '80s to start up the Zapatista National Liberation Army.

The pipe-smoking, balaclava-wearing Marcos appeared on January 1, 1994, when the rebels suddenly said they were mad as hell and not going to take it anymore. What attracted the world's press was the'60s aura of a group of peasants led by a charming, wisecracking mystery man who never appeared without his trademark disguise, shotgun bandoleer, pistol and pipe. He communicated with the press via video press release, satellite phone, fax machine and word processor. Adventurous types, including filmmaker Oliver Stone, beat a path to his jungle doorway for an in-depth interview. He was long on rhetoric and short on results. His methodology was to "capture" a town with his ragtag army (some armed with sticks carved to look like rifles), then hightail back into the bush before the troops arrived. Most of the victims were innocent villagers killed by bombs or wild crossfire when the rebels didn't move fast enough. He is now making the transition to political respectability.

President Ernesto Zedillo

Accused of being weak and indecisive and smarting from his recent trashing of the peso, Zedillo ordered the Boris Yeltsin manual, "How to Stamp Out Insurrections." He initially bombed the hell out of Chiapas and ended up with truckloads of dead peasants. He then adopted a conciliatory stance, and, after the peso was lower than a cucaracha's belly button, he sent the troops in again. This time, the stock market went up and the white ruling class applauded, while the working class protested. The bottom line is that Zedillo has the tanks, men and helicopters; Marcos doesn't.

Juan García Abrego (El Muñeco) and the Gulf Cartel

As the reputed supplier of a third of the cocaine that reaches the United States, Abrego ("The Doll") was the first international drug trafficker to get his name pasted to post office walls as an elite member of the FBI's Ten Most Wanted list. He joked to his captors after he was busted by the FBI in January 1996 that "I never thought you'd get me." And he probably had a good reason to think they wouldn't. You see, "The Doll" was cozy with former Mexican President Carlos Salinas de Gortari's brother Raúl. In fact, Raúl used to party regularly with the boys of the cartel, one of Mexico's big four, and stashed some US$84 million into frozen Swiss bank accounts. The stinger was Raúl Salinas de Gortari's alleged trip to Colombia to pick up US$10 million from the Cali drug cartel, which he then tried to use to fund Luis Donaldo Colosio's bid for the presidency. When Colosio turned down the contribution, he was wasted by the Gulf cartel in March 1994. Raúl is now in prison for plotting the September 1994 murder of one of Mexico's top politicians. One thing for sure, while Carlos Salinas de Gortari was in office, the Gulf cartel rose to the top rank among Mexico's drug syndicates. Now this conglomerate of traffickers is on the downslide; 70 of its members have already been convicted in three U.S. states.

Amado Carrillo Fuentes ("Lord of the Heavens") and the Juárez Cartel

With the capture of Abrego and other gold-chained fat dudes of the Gulf cartel, the Juárez cartel has emerged as Mexico's strongest dope alliance. Cartel kingpin Amado Carrillo Fuentes, under indictment in Dallas and Miami, is chummy with the Cali cartel and is accused of facilitating huge jet-loads of dope into Mexico from Colombia, thus his moniker. From Ciudad Juárez, the coke moves to American cities like Los Angeles, Dallas, Houston and New York.

Miguel Caro Quintero and the Sonora Cartel

Quintero's northwest Mexico-based gang mostly runs ganja into Nogales, Arizona and the western United States but also dabbles in the white stuff. Quintero, 32, assumed the helm of the cartel after his brother Rafael was busted for the murder of DEA agent Enrique "Kiki" Camarena. The softspoken Quintero is under indictment in Denver and Tucson.

The Arellano Felix Brothers and the Tijuana Cartel

Ruthless and territorial, Benjamin Arellano Felix is supposedly running the most violent dope syndicate in Mexico (his brother is wasting away in a Mexican jail cell). The cartel is behind the massive quantities of methamphetamine that have been flooding into San Diego, L.A. and points east. Arellano Felix's enforcers are thought to have been the trigger men in the 1993 assassination in Guadalajara of Catholic Cardinal Juan Jesus Posadas-Ocampo. That is a lot of Hail Mary's if he wants to go to heaven.

The DEA and the FBI

The DEA and the FBI have considered each other deadbeat Princeton flatfoots for years. The DEA guys think they're cool because they're above politics and can meddle in the sovereignty of every banana and bongo junta with MFN status on the globe, not to mention MFN wannabes, centuries' old monarchies, Mother Russia and Uncle Sam. The fibbies are making a run at catching the splinters of the disintegrating CIA's turf, having never been content with hanging out in step vans and tapping phones in Peoria and Tyler, Texas, motels. The two have kissed and made up for the purpose of nailing Mexican narco-monarchs and *contrabandistas* who, for decades, have been ponying guns, liquor, flake, smack and blue jeans across the Rio Grande. Together, they scored a coup with the García Abrego bust. Maybe a bigger one than they think. García Abrego may know enough mud in the Mexican government to cause the country's greatest crisis since the 1910 revolution.

Getting In

All U.S. citizens visiting Mexico for tourism or study for up to 180 days need a tourist card to enter and leave the country. The tourist card is free and may be obtained from Mexican consulates, Mexican tourism offices, Mexican border crossing points and from most airlines serving Mexico. If you fly to Mexico, you must obtain your tourist card before boarding your flight; it cannot be obtained upon arrival at an airport in Mexico. The tourist card is issued upon presentation of proof of citizenship such as a U.S. passport or a U.S. birth certificate, plus a photo I.D. such as a driver's license. Tourist cards are issued for up to 90 days with a single entry, or if you present proof of sufficient funds, for 180 days with multiple entries. Upon entering Mexico, retain and safeguard the pink copy of your tourist card so that you may surrender it to Mexican immigration when you depart. You must leave Mexico before your tourist card expires, or you are subject to a fine. A tourist card for less than 180 days may be revalidated in Mexico by the Mexican immigration service.

If you wish to stay longer than 180 days, or if you wish to do business or perform religious work in Mexico, contact the Mexican embassy or the nearest Mexican consulate to obtain a visa or permit. Persons performing religious work on a tourist card are subject to deportation.

Travel Requirements for Persons Under 18

A person under age 18 traveling with only one parent must have written, notarized consent from the other parent to travel, or must carry, if applicable, a decree of sole custody for the accompanying parent or a death certificate for the other parent. A child traveling alone or in someone else's custody must have notarized consent from both parents to travel, or if applicable, notarized consent from a single parent plus documentation that parent is the only custodial parent.

Short Stays Near the Border

U.S. citizens visiting Mexico for no more than 72 hours and remaining within 20 kilometers of the border do not need a permit to enter. Those transiting Mexico to another country need a transit visa that costs a nominal fee and is valid for up to 30 days.

Driving Your Car to Mexico

Once you cross the border, things change dramatically. When you drive to Mexico, you must obtain a temporary vehicle import permit. You must show your proof of ownership or notarized authorization from the owner to bring the car into Mexico, a valid driver's license, proof of auto liability insurance, and current registration and plates. The permit is issued free at border entry points and is generally valid for the same period of time as your tourist card (up to 180 days). You must remove your motor vehicle from Mexico before the permit expires or have the permit extended by the Temporary Importation Department of a Mexican customs office. If you do not do so, your motor vehicle may be confiscated. You may not sell, transfer or otherwise dispose of a motor vehicle brought into Mexico on a temporary importation permit, nor may you leave Mexico without the vehicle. In case of emergency, or following an accident where the vehicle cannot be removed, the owner may request permission to depart Mexico without the vehicle from the Mexican Customs Office in Mexico City, or the local office of the Treasury Department (Hacienda) in other cities.

If you bring spare auto parts to Mexico, declare them when you enter the country. When you leave, be prepared to show that you are taking the unused parts with you or that you have had them installed in Mexico. Save your repair receipts for this purpose. If you wish to authorize another person to drive your car, record the authorization with Mexican officials when you enter Mexico—even if you expect to be a passenger when the other person drives. Do not, under any circumstances, allow an unauthorized person to drive your vehicle when you are not in the car. Such a person could have to pay a fine amounting to a substantial percentage of the vehicle's value, or your vehicle could be confiscated.

Car Insurance

Mexican auto insurance is sold in most cities and towns on both sides of the border. U.S. automobile liability insurance is not valid in Mexico nor is most collision and comprehensive coverage issued by U.S. companies. Purchase auto insurance adequate for your needs in Mexico when you cross the border. Motor vehicle insurance is invalid in Mexico if the driver is found to be under the influence of alcohol or drugs if you are involved in an accident. Regardless of whether you have insurance, , you will be taken into police custody until it can be determined who is liable and whether you have the ability to pay any judgment. If you do not have Mexican liability insurance, you are almost certain to cool your heels in jail until everyone is paid off.

Bringing in Expensive Items

Tourists should enter Mexico with only the items needed for their trip. Entering with large quantities of an item a tourist might not normally be expected to have, particularly expensive appliances, such as televisions, stereos or other items, may lead to suspicion of smuggling and possible confiscation of the items and arrest of the individual.

You may have difficulty bringing computers or other expensive electronic equipment into Mexico for your personal use. To prevent being charged an import tax, write a statement about your intention to use the equipment for personal use and to remove it from Mexico when you leave. Have this statement signed and certified at a Mexican consulate in the United States and present it to Mexican customs as you enter Mexico. You will be subject to a second immigration and customs inspection south of the Mexican border where unlawful items may be seized, and you could be prosecuted regardless of whether or not the items passed through the initial customs inspection.

Firearms

Do not bring firearms or ammunition into Mexico without first obtaining a permit from a Mexican consulate in the United States.

Illegal Entry

If you are caught entering Mexico illegally, you will typically be expelled to your point of entry. The Mexican authorities can fine you between 300 and 5000 pesos and put you in jail for up to two years. For some reason, this is not a major problem for Americans.

For further information concerning entry requirements, travelers may contact any of the Mexican consulates in major U.S. cities or the embassy:

Embassy of Mexico

1911 Pennsylvania Avenue N.W.
Washington, D.C. 20006
☎ *(202) 728-1600*

Getting Around

Mexico has an extensive road, rail and air system. Travelers in the remote areas should be very careful at night or when stopped outside of town. Robbery is common in these areas. Roads may seem well paved but huge potholes, animals, people and large objects can be found around blind corners.

During heavy seasonal rains (January–March), road conditions can become difficult and travelers can become stranded. For current Mexican road conditions between Ensenada and El Rosario, travelers can contact the nearest Mexican consulate or tourism office or the U.S. consulate general in Tijuana.

Between 4 and 6 million U.S. citizens visit Mexico each year, while more than 300,000 Americans reside there. Although Mexico is "just across the border," it cannot be compared to Canada in terms of safety, health and crime threats. Remember that you are entering a country struggling to leave its Third World status. All tourists (both Mexican and American) are the best targets for criminal acts simply because they routinely carry cash and expensive goods. Expect to be viewed as an easy mark for robbery whenever you travel to major cities and tourist areas in Mexico. There are an average of 35 homicides yearly in Baja, 40 percent of which are connected to the drug trade. Most of the murders are inTijuana and most of these executions occur in daylight.

Many car rental companies in the U.S. have clauses in their contracts that prohibit drivers from traveling out of the country. The Mexican police are aware of these regulations, and will sometimes impound rental vehicles driven from the United States. When renting a vehicle in the United States, check with the company to see if your contract allows you to drive it into Mexico.

Getting Out

Residents of the U.S. returning to the U.S can expect long lines and waits in Tijuana and other major gateways. You must present the pink copy of your tourist card at your point of departure from Mexico.

Exporting Gold or Silver Currency

There are no restrictions on the import or export of bank notes and none on the export of reasonable quantities of ordinary Mexican coins. However, gold or silver Mexican coins may not be exported. Take traveler's checks with you because personal U.S. checks are rarely accepted by Mexican hotels or banks. Major credit cards are accepted in many hotels, shops and restaurants. An exchange office (*casa de cambios*) usually gives a better rate of exchange than do stores, hotels or restaurants.

Wildlife or Products Made from Wild Animals

You risk confiscation and a possible fine by U.S. Customs if you attempt to import virtually any wildlife or products made from wild animals from Mexico. In particular, watch out for and avoid all products made from sea turtles, including such items as turtle leather boots, tortoiseshell jewelry and sea turtle oil cosmetics; fur from spotted cats; Mexican birds, stuffed or alive, such as parrots, parakeets or birds of prey; crocodile and caiman leather; black coral jewelry; and wildlife curios, such as stuffed iguanas. When driving across state lines within Mexico, you can expect to be stopped at agricultural livestock inspection stations.

Antiques

Mexico considers all pre-Columbian objects to be the "inalienable property of the Nation" and the unauthorized export of such objects as theft that is punishable by arrest, detention and judicial prosecution. Under U.S. law, to import pre-Columbian monumental and architectural sculpture and murals, you must present proof that they were legally exported from the country of origin. U.S. law does not prohibit the import of nonmonumental or nonarchitectural artifacts from Mexico.

Dangerous Places

Chiapas

Travel throughout Chiapas, Mexico's southernmost state, may be delayed due to security checks. Chances of meeting a rebel roadblock are reduced after the recent military crackdown. Sometimes you may run into a roadblock put up by locals. Roadblocks in the Chiapas region can be as simple as a piece of string held up across the road. Many times rebels or locals will ask for articles of clothing. There have been no reports of attacks on travelers in this region. Travelers should exercise caution, and obey requests by Mexican military personnel. Journalists are also restricted in their movements. Interviews with Subcommander Marcos, although fairly easy to obtain, frequently involved long waits (up to a week or more) and a late night rendezvous in a remote location.

The town of San Cristobal in the state of Chiapas is relatively quiet after the disturbances in early January and December of 1994. The situation could become unstable in areas of Chiapas state outside of San Cristobal. U.S. citizens residing or traveling in Mexico may contact the U.S. embassy or consulates for further security information.

Highways 15, 40 and 1

Beware of Highway 15 in the state of Sinaloa and of Highway 40 between the city of Durango and the Pacific coast areas. These are particularly dangerous and are where a number of criminal assaults have occurred. Avoid express Highway 1 (limited access) in Sinaloa altogether—even in daytime—because it is remote and subject to bandits.

To avoid highway crime, try not to drive at night and never drive alone at night. Never sleep in vehicles along the road. If your vehicle breaks down, stay with it and wait for the police or the "Green Angels." Do not, under any circumstances, pick up hitchhikers; not only do they pose a threat to your physical safety, but they also put you in danger of being arrested for unwittingly transporting narcotics or narcotics traffickers in your vehicle. Your vehicle can be confiscated if you are transporting marijuana or other narcotics. There are checkpoints and temporary roadblocks where vehicles are examined.

Persons driving on some Mexican roads, particularly in isolated regions, have been targeted by bandits who operate primarily after dark. Criminals, particularly in Sinaloa, sometimes represent themselves as Mexican police or other local officials.

On the Road

The U.S. embassy advises its personnel not to travel on Mexican highways after dark. Highway 15 and Express Highway 1 (limited access) in the state of Sinaloa are particularly dangerous areas where criminal assaults and murders have occurred during the day and at night.

Tijuana

What you have thought or read about Mexican border towns is true. Tequila-happy gringos looking to break every rule in the book, senoritas with hearts of gold, hardened and impoverished immigrants all controlled by a police force that makes the Keystone cops look like our Delta Force. Don't blame the cops for all the raucous bloodletting and bad times. Just in the last two years, 19 Tijuana cops have been gunned down, so forgive them if they are a little trigger-happy or are looking for a handout. Cops in Tijuana must not only supply their own uniforms, but they drive beat-up cop cars that U.S. citizens have dumped, they buy their own bullets and they do this on a salary of about US$179 a month. (Stateside cops start at $3100 a month.) One of the 19 victims was a former police chief who was gunned own when he refused a US$100,000 bribe from a drug cartel.

Dangerous Things

Being Drunk

Despite every stereotype of the unshaven drunken *muchachos* firing their rusty guns into the air on Friday nights, drunkenness is a no-no south of the border. Certain border towns have become impatient with teenaged (and older) Americans who cross the border to drink and carouse. This behavior usually leads to fights, arrests, traffic accidents and even death, not to mention those nasty mescal hangovers. Cops do crack down on drunks, and the chances of you retaining your wallet and your teeth are not high.

Dining and Dashing

Failure to pay hotel bills or failure to pay for other services rendered is considered fraud under Mexican law. Those accused of these offenses are subject to arrest and conviction with stiff fines and jail sentences.

Driving

Poor roads, infrequent repairs and lack of repair stations make motoring in Mexico a true adventure. It is not uncommon to be driving for 50 miles along a newly paved highway only to find a four-foot-wide chasm marked by a single branch. You have more to fear from cows than rattlesnakes, since livestock like to sleep on the warm asphalt at night. Many routes have heavy truck and bus traffic, some have poor or nonexistent shoulders, and many have animals on the loose. Also, some of the newer roads have very few restaurants, motels, gas stations or auto repair shops. If you have an accident, you will be assumed to be guilty, and, since you are a "wealthy foreigner," all efforts will be made to detain you until satisfaction for the victim is received.

For your safety, have your vehicle serviced and in optimum condition before you leave for Mexico. Pack a basic first-aid kit and carry an emergency water supply in your vehicle.

Zapatista or Blast-ta-Piece-a-s? The DP guide to Revolutionaries.

Before you run off to La Realidad to hang with the latest poster boys of the revolution you should know the difference between the EZLN (who don't kidnap, torture and kill people) and the EPR. (who do)

The EPR are hard core terrorists and criminals. Although they wear cute green camouflage and wear brown face masks for the press, the EPR usually operates in 12 man cels in urban areas in plainclothes. If in uniform, the EPR have red and green arm patches and assault rifles. They are very heavily armed, politically indoctrinated and will go out of their way to protect their identity if stumbled upon.

They have bombed U.S and Japanese corporate offices, robbed dozens of banks and kidnapped prominent businessmen in Mexico. Tourists are not specifically targeted but the EPR uses plenty of ammo in their attacks. A tourist was hit by the crossfire at Huatulco Club Med.

Their training bases are deep in the Sierra Madre mountains. They practice hit and run raids and shoot to kill. They are closer to terrorists, have little grass roots support and are in the DP dictionary under "bad guys."

The Zapatistas is a ten-year-old homegrown Indian group led by poorly trained but laid-back commanders. Most cels are village-based with no real distinction between the military arm and the political arm. There was only one actual clash in January of 94. They wear a yellow and red star patch and favor balaclavas. Chances are some will be carrying sticks and their guns will be rusty. The Zapatistas welcome foreigners as insurance policy against military excesses and the government does turn back people at checkpoints in the area. In August of 96 over 2000 people visited five Chiapas villages in a weeklong convention (called the Intercontinental Encounter for Humanity Against Neo-Liberalism) to hear Marcos crack a few jokes and tell a few stories. By the way trivia fans, Oliver Stone is a DP reader and Marcos turned down his chance to star in his own feature-length movie. Stay tuned for RevolutionaryLand coming to Orlando soon.

Do not drive at night. Loose livestock and mufflers can appear at any time. Mexicans not only drive fast but seem to be unfazed by the lack of lights or sobriety at night. Construction sites or stranded vehicles are often unmarked by flares or other warning signals. Major dropoffs are sometimes marked with bent tires and other resultant pieces of detritus. Sometimes cars have only one headlight; bicycles seldom have lights or reflectors. Be prepared for a sudden stop at any time. Mexican driving conditions are such that, for your safety, you must drive more slowly than you do at home. In Mexico, a blinking left-turn signal on the vehicle in front of you could mean that it is clear ahead and you may pass, or it could mean the driver is making a left turn. An outstretched left arm may mean an invitation for you to pass. When in doubt, do not pass. An oncoming vehicle flashing its headlights is a warning for you to slow down or pull over because you are both approaching a narrow bridge or place in the road. The custom is that the first vehicle to flash has the right of way and the other must yield. Freshly wet roads are dangerous because oil and road dust mix with water and form a lubricant. Until this mixture washes away, driving is extremely hazardous. Beware of sudden rains. Stop, or go extremely slowly, until conditions improve.

Sport-utility vehicles are in demand by Mexican thieves. Some even display California license plates long after they are pinched. About 10 percent of the stolen vehicles in San

Diego county end up in Mexico. The recovery rate for sport-utilities is only 20 percent compared to 82 percent for stolen cars. Ideal for the rough roads of Tijuana and the Baja peninsula, the sturdy, swiped vehicles are also the favorites of Mexican officials, who keep the trucks once they are recovered from *aspirinas*, or paid enforcers, who control the theft rings in California. In San Diego, thefts of Jeeps jumped to 88 during May 1994 alone, up from an average of 34 a month. The explanation was that officials who were sent in to investigate the death of Luis Donaldo Colosio were taking advantage of the situation to place their own orders for the shiny but stolen California cars.

Drugs

Sentences for possession of drugs in Mexico can be as long as 25 years plus fines. Just as in the U.S., purchase of controlled medication requires a doctor's prescription. The Mexican list of controlled medication differs from the U.S. list, and Mexican public health laws concerning controlled medication are unclear. Possession of excessive amounts of a psychotropic drugs such as Valium can result in arrest if the authorities suspect abuse.

Drugs are a major part of Mexican life. Some areas are considered to be run by narcotics dealers. Drug dealers can be spotted by their love for Chevy Suburbans and Jeep Cherokees, Ray Bans and AK-47s.

Mexico rigorously prosecutes drug cases. Under Mexican law, possession of and trafficking in illegal drugs are federal offenses. For drug trafficking, bail does not exist. Mexican law does not differentiate between types of narcotics: Heroin, marijuana and amphetamines, for example, are treated the same. Offenders found guilty of possessing more than a token amount of any narcotic substance are subject to a minimum sentence of seven years, and it is not uncommon for persons charged with drug offenses to be detained for up to one year before a verdict is reached. Remember, if narcotics are found in your vehicle, you are subject to arrest and your vehicle can be confiscated.

Earthquakes

Earthquakes pose a major danger in Mexico, due to the lack of earthquake standards in buildings and the frequency of earthquakes and tremors.

Emergencies

It's best if you avoid them, because it may take awhile to be assisted. (If you think 911 is a sports car, you're not alone. For Mexicans, it may as well be.) In Mexico, "rapid response" is a bumpy canoe ride. During the first six months of 1996, there were 72,548 emergency calls received in Mexico City. In more than four percent of those requiring emergency police, fire or ambulance assistance, no one bothered to show up. In many other instances, it took more than an hour for a response. The situation is so bad, the city has contracted with a private "08" service to help handle the flood of calls. The catch? You have to be a paid subscriber. Sort of like cable for hypochondriacs.

Firearms

Do not bring firearms or ammunition of any kind into Mexico, unless you have first obtained a consular firearms certificate from a Mexican consulate. To hunt in Mexico, you must obtain a hunting permit, also available from the consulate. Travelers carrying guns or ammunition into Mexico without a Mexican certificate have been arrested, detained and sentenced to stiff fines and lengthy prison terms. The sentence for clandestine importation of firearms is from six months to six years. If the weapon is greater than .38 caliber, it is considered of military type, and the sentence is from five to 30 years. When you enter Mexico, make certain that Mexican customs officials check both the firearms and your certificate. When you reach your destination, register your firearms with the appropriate military zone headquarters. If you enter Mexican waters on a private boat, you are still subject to the ban on importing firearms. Remember that before you leave the States, you must also register your firearms and ammunition with U.S. Customs or they will assume you picked them up from a kid in a bar. In some areas of Mexico, it is not wise to carry anything that might be construed as a weapon. Some cities, such as Nuevo Laredo, have ordinances prohibiting the possession of knives and similar weapons. Tourists have even been arrested for possessing souvenir knives. Most arrests for knife possession occur in connection with some other infraction, such as drunk and disorderly behavior. Strangely enough Mexicans are allowed to bring in to the United States three weapons and a whopping 1000 rounds of ammo.

Mexican Jails

The Mexican judicial system is based on Roman and Napoleonic law and presumes a person accused of a crime to be guilty until proven innocent. There is no trial by jury nor writ of habeas corpus in the AngloAmerican sense. Trial under the Mexican system is a prolonged process based largely on documents examined on a fixed date in court by prosecution and defense counsel. Sentencing usually takes six to 10 months. Bail can be granted after sentencing if the sentence is less than five years. Pretrial bail exists but is never granted when the possible sentence upon conviction is greater than five years.

Mexico has the highest number of arrests of Americans abroad—over 2000 per year—and the highest prison population of U.S. citizens outside of the United States—about 425 at any one time. If you find yourself in serious difficulty while in Mexico, contact a consular officer at the U.S. embassy or the nearest U.S. consulate for assistance. U.S. consular officers cannot serve as attorneys or give legal assistance. They can, however, provide lists of local attorneys and advise you of your rights under Mexican law. If you are arrested, ask permission to notify the U.S. embassy or nearest U.S. consulate. Under international agreements and practice, you have the right to contact an American consul. Although U.S. consuls are restricted by Mexican law as to what they can do to assist you in legal difficulties, they can monitor the status of detained U.S. citizens and make sure they are treated fairly under local laws. They will also notify your relatives or friends upon request. An individual is guaranteed certain rights under the Mexican constitution, but those rights differ significantly from U.S. constitutional guarantees.

Phony Cops

Be aware of persons representing themselves as Mexican police or other local officials. Some Americans have been the victims of harassment, mistreatment and extortion by criminals masquerading as officials. You must have the officer's name, badge number and patrol car number to pursue a complaint. Make a note of this information if you are ever involved with police or other officials. Do not be surprised if you encounter several types of police in Mexico. The Preventive Police, the Transit Police and the Federal Highway Police all wear uniforms. The Judicial Police who work for the public prosecutor are not uniformed.

Volcanos

Popocatepetl volcano, about 40 miles south of Mexico City, has been active. Villages in the area were evacuated in December 1994, and travelers in the region should avoid areas near the mountain's base. Popocatepetl, which means "Smoking Mountain" in the local Nahuatl language, had its last major eruption in 1921. Mexico City is not considered to be in danger.

Watersports

Many people are injured having fun in Mexico. Sports equipment that you rent or buy may not meet the safety standards to which you are accustomed. Critical equipment used for scuba diving or parasailing, jet-skis or motorboats may not be properly maintained and be defective. Inexperienced scuba divers should beware of dive shops that promise to "certify" you after a few hours of instruction. On a recent trip to Acapulco we were separated into two groups: experienced divers and people who had never been underwater.

The neophytes had their equipment strapped on, a brief explanation about how to breathe using the regulator, a warning not to go too deep, and within five minutes they had become certified scuba divers.

Getting Sick

Good medical care can be found in all major cities, and many U.S. prescription drugs are available over the counter. Most major hotels have a doctor on call who can treat everything from venereal diseases to drug addiction. Health facilities in Mexico City are excellent, and are generally quite good in the major tourist and expat cities, including Cancun, Acapulco, Puerto Vallarta, Mazatlan, Merida, Manzanillo and Guadalajara. Care in more remote areas is limited.

In some places, particularly at resorts, medical costs can be as high as or higher than in the United States. If your health insurance policy does not cover you in Mexico, it is strongly recommended that you purchase a policy that does. There are short-term health policies designed specifically to cover travel.

Immunizations are recommended against diphtheria, tetanus, polio, typhoid, and hepatitis A. For visitors coming directly from the United States, no vaccinations are required to enter Mexico. If you are traveling from an area known to be infected with yellow fever, a vaccination certificate is required. *Malaria* is found in some rural areas of Mexico, particularly those near the southwest coast. Travelers to malarial areas should consult their physician or the U.S. Public Health Service and take the recommended dosage of chloroquine. Although chloroquine is not considered necessary for travelers to the major resort areas on the Pacific and Gulf coasts, travelers to those areas should use insect repellent and take other personal protection measures to reduce contact with mosquitoes, particularly from dusk to dawn when malaria transmission is most likely.

Montezuma's revenge is as sure as hangovers from cheap tequila. Drink only bottled water or water that has been boiled for 20 minutes. Avoid ice cubes. Vegetables and fruits should be peeled or washed in a purifying solution. A good rule of thumb is, if you can't peel it or cook it, don't eat it. Medication to prevent travelers' diarrhea is not recommended. If symptoms present themselves and persist, seek medical attention, because diarrhea is potentially dangerous. Air pollution in Mexico City is severe. It is the most dangerous during thermal inversions, which occur the most from December to May. Air pollution plus Mexico City's high altitude are a particular health risk for the elderly and persons with high blood pressure, anemia, or respiratory or cardiac problems. If this applies to you, consult your doctor before traveling to Mexico City. In areas, such as Mexico City, most people need a short adjustment period. Spend the first few days in a leisurely manner, with a light diet and reduced intake of alcohol. Avoid strenuous activity— this includes everything from sports to rushing up the stairs. Reaction signs to high altitude are lack of energy, a tendency to tire easily, shortness of breath, occasional dizziness and insomnia.

Nuts and Bolts

Emergency Help

In an emergency, call ☎ *[91] (5) 250-0123*, the 24-hour hotline of the Mexican Ministry of Tourism. The hotline is for immediate assistance, but it can give you general, nonemergency guidance as well. In Mexico City, dial ☎ *06* for police assistance.

If you have problems filling out a police report or in filing a report, you can call the "Silver Angels." This group helps tourists who are victims of crime file a police report.

If you have an emergency while driving, call the Ministry of Tourism's hotline to obtain help from the "Green Angels," a fleet of radio-dispatched trucks with bilingual crews that operate daily. Services include protection, medical first aid, mechanical aid for your car and basic supplies. You will not be charged for services, only for parts, gas and oil. The Green Angels patrol daily, from dawn until sunset. If you are unable to call them, pull well off the road and lift the hood of your car; chances are good that they will find you.

Embassy and Consulate Locations

American Embassy

> Paseo de la Reforma 305
> Mexico 06500, D.F.
> ☎ [52] (5) 211-0042
> FAX [52] (5) 511-9980U

U.S. Export Development Office/
U.S. Trade Center

> 31 Liverpool
> Mexico 06600, D.F.
> ☎ [52] (5) 591-0155

American Consulate General

> Avenue Lopez Mateos 924-N
> Ciudad Juarez, Chihuahua
> ☎ [52] (16) 134-048
> After Hours (emergencies) ☎ (915) 525-6066
> FAX [52] (161) 34048 ext. 210 or [52] (161) 34050 ext. 210

American Consulate General

> Progreso 175
> Guadalajara, Jalisco
> ☎ [52] (36) 25-2998, [52] (36) 25-2700
> FAX [52] (36) 26-6549

American Consulate

> Calle Monterrey 141, Poniente
> Hermosillo, Sonora
> ☎ [52] (621) 723-75
> After Hours (emergencies) ☎ [52] (621) 725-85
> FAX [52] (62) 172375 ext. 49

American Consulate

> Avenue Primera No. 2002
> Matamoros, Tamaulipas
> ☎ [52] (891) 2-52-50 or [52] (891) 2-52-51
> FAX [52] (89) 138048

American Consulate

> Circunvalacion No. 120 Centro
> Mazatlan, Sinaloa
> ☎ [52] (678) 5-22-05
> FAX [52] (678) 2-1775

American Consulate

> Paseo Montejo 453
> Merida, Yucatan
> ☎ [52] (99) 25-5011
> After Hours (emergencies) ☎ [52] (99) 25-5409
> FAX [52] (99) 25-6219

American Consulate General

> Avenida Constitucion 411 Poniente
> Monterrey, Nuevo Leon
> ☎ [52] (83) 45-2120
> FAX [52] (83) 42-0177

American Consulate

> Avenida Allende 3330, Col. Jardin
> Nuevo Laredo, Tamaulipas
> ☎ [52] (871) 4-0696 or [52] (871) 4-9616
> After Hours (emergencies) ☎ (512) 727-9661
> FAX [52] (871) 4-0696 ext. 128

American Consulate General

> Tapachula 96
> Tijuana, Baja California
> ☎ [52] (66) 81-7400 or (706) 681-7400
> After Hours (emergencies) ☎ (619) 585-2000
> FAX [52] (66) 81-8016

Dangerous Days

05/05/1867   Archduke Maximilian of Austria, who was established as emperor of Mexico in 1864 by Napolean III of France, was deposed by Benito Juarez and executed in 1867.

12/06/1822   Establishment of the Republic.

09/16/1810   Independence from Spain was declared by Father Miguel Hidalgo. The war for independence continued until 1822, when the Mexican Republic was established.

MEXICO

Moscow

Russia
★★★

Big Red

Russia has an affinity for red. If it isn't the red blood of its people that is being spilled it is the red ink that Russia seems to be drowning in. Their flag is too cute-sy to really represent the bloody and financial woes this country is going through. Strangely enough, the red blood and red ink seem to go hand in hand, as Russia tries to rebuild its economy while rebuilding its empire. The brutal crackdown on Chechnya and its resultant costs (in lives, bad PR and money) derailed Russia's attempt to revive its economy. Suddenly communism doesn't look so bad anymore. Poverty was a lot easier when you could blame it on the U.S. imperialist aggressors.

The bricks that hold Russia together are the stoic, proud people who seem to endure any injustice, survive any hardship and still maintain a sense of cynical humor throughout their Draconian trials. Russia is a tough place, but then again its people have always been tough and are getting tougher.

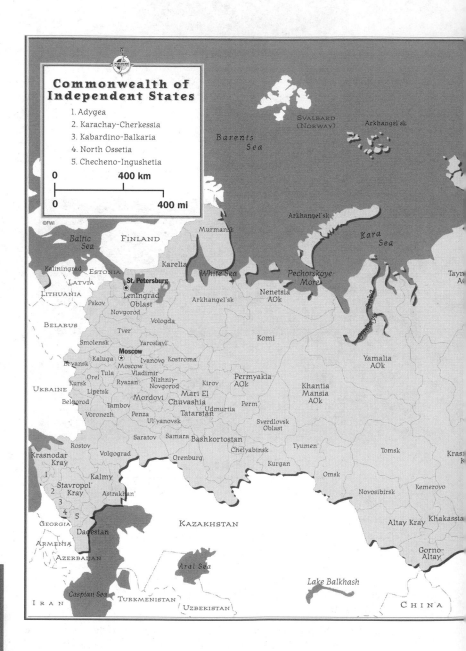

Commonwealth of Independent States

1. Adygea
2. Karachay-Cherkessia
3. Kabardino-Balkaria
4. North Ossetia
5. Checheno-Ingushetia

0   400 km

0   400 mi

©FWI

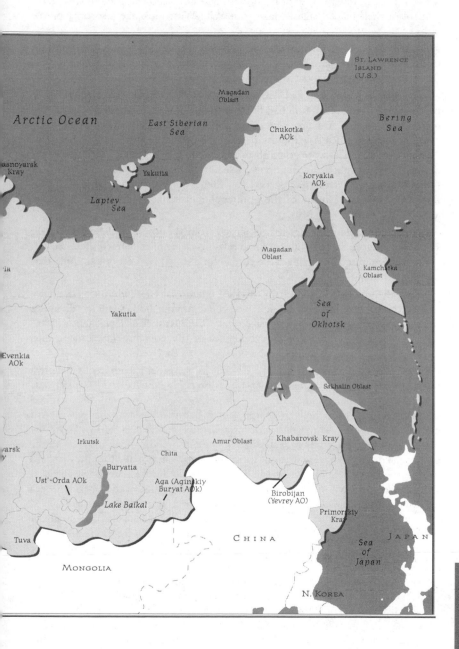

How tough is it? In the grubby town of Nizhini Tagil in the Ural Mountains, Russian criminals hijacked (or rented) a T-90 tank from the local military base, drove it back to town, and shot it out with Muslims who had tried to strongarm control of their market stalls. Makes our Wild West look like a sorority pillow fight.

Russians are famous for their bullheaded achievement of objectives against all odds. When the Russians lose, as in Eastern Europe and Afghanistan, there is little for the other side to gloat about owning.

In December 1991, the Cold War ended when the Soviet Union collapsed. The high-flying Russian revolution had finally run out of gas and crashed. The jagged pieces totalled 12: Armenia, Azerbaijan, Belarus, Georgia, Kazakhstan, Kyrgyzstan, Moldova, Russia, Tajikistan, Turkmenistan, Ukraine and Uzbekistan. And most of these states are going through a secondary breakup, as ethnic and religious factions fight for sovereignty, usually with the help or antagonism of "Mother Russia," Iran or gangsters. After their brief taste of independence (and financial insolvency), many of these independent states are thinking about realigning themselves with Moscow.

Russia is the largest country that emerged from the former U.S.S.R. In 1992, Russia introduced an array of economic reforms that not only freed the prices on most goods and services, but set the course for a downward economic spiral that continues today.

Although President Boris Yeltsin survived a national referendum on his ability to lead the country in 1993, he dissolved the legislative bodies still left dangling from the Soviet era and signed a peace treaty. On October 3, 1993, tensions between the executive and legislative branches of the government escalated into armed conflict. With the help of the military, Boris survived.

A December 1994 attempt to take Grozny in the rebel Republic of Chechnya revealed in a rebel rout of the Russian forces precisely how weak the Russian war machine had become, and subsequent events showed even greater disorganization. Yeltsin may think he is in charge, but it became apparent that when push comes to shove, the army will decide. Renegade commanders refused to follow orders or never received them. Russian soldiers captured by the insurgent Chechens revealed that they were without food and maps—essentially that they had no direction nor any idea of what the hell they were doing. Russian corpses littered Grozny like dead worms after a heavy rain. Although the vastly superior forces eventually took the Chechen capital in 1995 only to retreat in August of 1996, they've faced a repeat of Afghanistan since. The Chechen insurgents—many of them former Soviet soldiers trained in mountain guerrilla fighting—have dug into the hills, waging a fierce battle of attrition against an undisciplined, underage band of Boris' best.

However, crime may be Russia's biggest export in the next decade. The brutal control of a central government has been reborn in the form of Russian Mafias. In the first five months of 1994, there were 664 crimes committed with firearms and explosives, 118 cases of hostage-taking, and an average of 84 murders a day. The ominous part is that the majority of the murders were contract killings, according to the Ministry of the Interior. Compare the rate of 16 murders per 100,000 in Russia to the U.S. rate of nine per 100,000, and you can see why even triggerhappy Americans look like Buddhist monks next to the Russians.

There is more afoot than just thuggery in Russia. Tired of polishing their ICBMs and rotating their nuclear weapons, some army units have decided to strip them down into more economically attractive components and, by doing so, generate a little cash. In 1993, there were 6430 cases of stolen weapons, ranging from assault rifles to tanks. To date, there have been over 700 cases of nuclear material being sold to various buyers outside and inside Russia. On the black market, a kilo of chromium-50 can go for US$25,000, cesium-137 for US$1 million and lithium-6 for US$10 million. Prospective customers for these goodies are Iran, North Korea, Libya and other nations looking for a big bang for their money.

Future civil disturbances and uprisings are inevitable, as the economy continues its slippery slide and the standard of living continues to drop.

The good news is that there's not a lot of anti-American sentiment in Russia, although some Russians despise foreigners, particularly Americans and Western Europeans, who remind them of all they don't and will never possess. Occasionally, there are protests against U.S. policy. Americans aren't targets because of their nationality, but because Russians perceive all Americans as rich. Americans aren't hard to spot in their Levis and Nikes, toting camcorders and wearing bulging fanny packs. As social and economic conditions in Russia deteriorate and there are more unemployed and low-salaried workers, crimes against monied foreigners will rise. Americans who possess hard currency and imported goods have increasingly become attractive targets.

Instability in the social-political sphere, deteriorating economic processes, a falling standard of living and an absence of specific programs to combat crime are all contributing to a general and steady increase in crime. The entire former Soviet region is a patchwork of government and private organizations that may or may not be functioning when you get there. Some are being replaced by new governments or are withering away without replacement. **Intourist** (☎ *212-757-3884*) is a good source of local information for prospective visitors to this beleaguered land. Intourist is now a nongovernmental body and still the largest tour operator in Russia and the former Soviet republics.

The Scoop

Russia is still red, blood red. Someone is murdered in Russia every 18 minutes. Sixty percent of the murders are for material gain, and 20 percent are thought to be murders of gangsters by rival gangs. In fact, there are more gangsters than there are police in Russia. Less than half of all perpetrators are ever brought to justice. Russians based in Moscow put much of the blame for this crime wave on southern foreigners, people who come from Armenia, Azerbaijan, Chechnya and Georgia. Crimes against foreigners jumped 44 percent in 1993 and continue to rise.

The Players

The Russian Mafia (*Organizatsiya* or Mafyia)

The Russian Interior Ministry says that in 1993, police uncovered 5700 organized crime groups and brought charges against 11,400 people. One-sixth of these groups were working in more than one region, while 300 were operating outside Russia's borders. The report also claimed that 150 major criminal societies controlled 35,000 enterprises. Most crime in Russia is controlled by eight "families," such as the Chechens, the most powerful group and descendants of a centuries-old tribe who still control the Caucasus Mountains. The Chechens specialize in bank fraud and extortion.

The Government

What government?

The Army

The army is slowly building back its power base in Russia and the CIS. The army finds itself the target of organized criminals. In some areas, army commanders rent out weapons and men are hired out as mercenaries to the highest bidder. The army is not firmly under the control of the government.

Perestrelka

No, not *perestroika*, a word used by Mikhail Gorbachev to symbolize reforms. *Perestrelka* means "shoot-out" in Russian and is a better description of what is going on in Russia today.

The military vacuum in Russia has allowed the rise of the *vory v zzakone*, or thieves in law. A class of thugs created before the revolution and toughened in Soviet gulags, these gangsters are enamored with pomp and circumstance and even possess private jets. The government estimates that there are 289 "thieves in law" operating in Russia and 28 other countries around the world. Below these very wealthy and powerful Mafia figures are the gangs. There are about 20 criminal brigades, or gangs, that control Moscow with L.A.-style monikers for their neighborhoods. There are estimated to be 5800 gang members in Russia. The gangs aren't quick or smart enough to control the country, so it's left to the *vory v zzakone* to reap the profits of absolute control.

There are four levels of Mafia in Russia. The lowest stratum consists of shopkeepers who sell goods at inflated prices to afford protection money. The enforcers are burly, loud men with a fancy for imported cars (usually stolen). They'll also double as pimps, gunrunners and drug dealers. The businessmen are unfettered capitalists who steer most of the lucrative deals the Mafia's way.

Finally, at the top of the food chain, is the "state Mafia." They are the controllers of a large percentage of the money earned by the lesser Mafia. These politicians/gangsters allow the lower echelons to operate in peace and without fear of prosecution. They have driven away a lot of Western investment and businessmen who find themselves forced to retain a local "partner" in their enterprises.

Getting In

A passport and Russian visa are required for all U.S. citizens traveling to or transiting through Russia by any means of transportation, including train, car or airplane. While under certain circumstances travelers who hold valid visas to some countries of the former Soviet Union may not need a visa to transit Russia, such exceptions are inconsistently applied. Travelers who arrive without an entry visa may be subject to large fines, days of processing requirements by Russian officials and/or immediate departure by route of entry (at the traveler's expense). Carrying a photocopy of passports and visas will facilitate replacement should either be stolen.

All Russian visas, except transit visas, are issued on the basis of support from a Russian individual or organization, known as the sponsor. It is important to know who your sponsor is and how they can be contacted, as Russian law requires that your sponsor apply on your behalf for replacement and extension of or changes to your visa. The U.S. embassy cannot act as your sponsor. Tourists should contact their tour company or hotel in advance for information on visa sponsorship.

For current information on visa requirements, U.S. citizens can contact the Russian consulates in New York, San Francisco or Seattle or the embassy:

Russian Embassy

Consular Division

1825 Phelps Place, N.W.
Washington, D.C. 20008
☎ *(202) 939-8918, 939-8907, or 939-8913*

All foreigners must have an exit visa in order to depart Russia. For short stays, the exit visa is issued together with the entry visa; for longer stays, the exit visa must be obtained by the sponsor after the traveler's arrival. Russian law requires that all travelers who spend more than three days in Russia register their visas through their hotel or sponsor. Visitors who stay in Russia for a period of weeks may be prevented from leaving if they have not registered their visas. Errors in the dates or other information on the visa can occur, and it is helpful to have someone who reads Russian check the visa before you depart the United States.

Many areas along Russia's southern borders are not manned, and checkpoints are only on main roads. Russian soldiers can be bribed due to their low pay and acceptance of side income.

Getting Around

Internal travel, especially by air, can be erratic and may be disrupted by fuel shortages, overcrowding of flights and various other problems. Travelers may need to cross great distances, especially in Siberia and the Far East, to obtain services from Russian government organizations or from the U.S. embassy or its consulates. Russia stretches over 6000 miles east to west and 2500 miles north to south. Winter can last a long time.

Unlike the old days, you can go just about anywhere you want these days. You don't even need to use Intourist to get around. The cheapest way into Moscow from the airport is via the regular bus. You can use rubles. Taxis usually require long waits and cost about 1000 rubles. You can also pick up a private car from one of the many people who will try to offer you one. Expect to pay US$50 in real money (not rubles) or the equivalent amount in cigarettes. You run the risk of getting waylaid or robbed if you take the wrong car. For about the same price, you can arrange a car in the arrivals section. You must use a credit card. In Moscow most taxis demand U.S. dollars, or one to three packs of cigarettes, or R10 to R20.

About half the roads in Russia are paved. The worst time to traverse Russian roads is during the spring, when the rural roads become muddy rivers. About 20 percent of the roads are simple tracks. The railways are the major means of transport, with most routes spreading out from Moscow on 11 major trunk lines. There are 32 railway subsystems within the Soviet Union. The main route is the passenger artery through Russia along the Trans-Siberian Railway, which travels east from Moscow across Siberia to the Pacific and China, Mongolia and Korea.

The main entry rail route to the West is the Moscow-Smolensk-Minsk-Brest-Warsaw and Berlin line. The new Baikal-Amur Mainline (BAM) follows a more northerly route than the Trans-Siberian route. The lines south from Moscow run through Kharkov to the Caucasus and the Crimea.

Traveling by sea is also an efficient way to get around Russia, particularly in the Baltic. Twenty-seven former Soviet passenger ships form the largest such fleet in the world.

Russian airlines service 3600 population centers inside Russia. The severe winters affect schedules.

Keep in mind that many Russian airlines have dubious safety records; you may prefer to go by rail.

The telecommunications infrastructure remains underdeveloped. Only 30 percent of urban and 9 percent of rural families have telephones. More than 17 million customers have ordered telephones, but are still waiting (sometimes for years) to have them installed.

Dangerous Places

The situation remains unsettled in Russia's north Caucasus area, which is located in southern Russia along its border with Georgia. Travel to this area is considered dangerous. The regions of the Chechen Republic, the Ingush Republic and the North Ossetian Republic have experienced continued armed violence and have a state of emergency and curfew in effect.

The Caucasus

In Nagorno-Karabakh, Armenians have been fighting for independence from Azerbaijan since 1988. Over 3000 people have died, according to a count in 1992. Things are quiet now, but *DP* wouldn't recommend buying any real estate any time soon. See "Armenia" on page 111.

Georgia

In Georgia, fighting in the south Ossetia region and the Mingrelia area has killed hundreds since 1989. In May of 1991, Zvaid Gamsakhurdia was elected president of Georgia with an overwhelming majority of the popular vote (86.5 percent). Not content with popular support, Zvaid began to conceive and implement very undemocratic statutes, such as "making fun of the president gets you six years in the slammer." He also put his money on the wrong ponies when he backed the coup plotters who failed to overthrow Yeltsin. He cracked down on the southern Muslim state of Ossetia, which instigated a revolt effective enough to force him to flee on January 6, 1992. The opposition, which consisted of his prime minister and foreign minister (who had backed Yeltsin), invited Eduard Shevardnadze, the former Soviet foreign minister and first secretary of the Georgian Communist Party, to be chairman of the state council.

The return of old hard-line communist hacks did not satisfy the Muslim Abkhazian separatists, who, feeling their oats, had taken over the Abkhazian region along the Black Sea.

The Russians meddled and brokered a cease-fire, which was quickly broken on September 16, 1993. Despite a pistol-waving Shevardnadze, the rebels took over the strategic Black Sea port of Sukhumi. The bizarre twist is that Shevardnadze blames the Russians for setting him up by brokering a phony cease-fire and then letting the rebels take over the country. The fact that the "rebels" were using Russian-supplied weapons and equipment confirmed the perception that the Russians were backing the Abkhazians.

Additionally, there is the continual threat of Zvaid Gamsakhurdia and his efforts to set up his own republic in Mingrelia.

(See "Georgia" on page 263.)

Moscow

In Moscow alone, in 1993, there were 5000 murders and 20,000 incidents of violent crime. The local population easily recognizes U.S. tourists and business travelers as foreigners because of their clothing, accessories and behavior. American visitors tend to experience a relatively high incidence of certain types of crime, such as physical assaults and pickpocketing of wallets, money traveler's checks, passports and cameras on the street, in hotels, in restaurants and in high-density tourist areas.

St. Petersburg

St. Petersburg has a crime rate 30 percent higher than Moscow's. The area around Gostiniy Dvor and the underground passage on Nevsky Prospekt, as well as train stations, the food markets, the flea markets and the so-called "art park" are frequent stages for street crime against foreigners. It is estimated that 20 percent of the foreign businesses are controlled by the Russian Mafia. Most groups who try to set up businesses in the city find they are hit up for a US$10,000 fee to arrange the "necessary contacts." If you are edgy, bodyguards can be hired for about $600 a month (U.S. dollars only). Not bad, when you figure that the average monthly wage is about US$20. Most crimes are committed in broad daylight, since the police will do little, if anything, to help or track down your assailants. If you are staying in one of the better hotels in St. Petersburg, have them send a car for you at the airport. If not, you can take a taxi into town for about US$30. If you want a car for the entire day, figure on spending about double that.

Emergency Numbers

Fire	**Hard Currency Taxi**
☎ *01*	☎ *298-6804, 298-3648*
Police	**Western-Style Medical Care**
☎ *02*	☎ *310-9611*
Ambulance	**American Express**
☎ *03*	☎ *311-5215*
U.S. Consulate	**Delta Airlines**
☎ *274-8692*	☎ *311-5819/20/22*
Taxi	
☎ *312-0022*	

Chechnya and the "Chechens"

A remote Trans-Caucasian region just north of Georgia, the Republic of Chechnya is home to Russia's largest and most powerful crime families. In fact, they have a friendly neighborhood branch in what may be your own hometown (Boston, Philadelphia, Chicago, Los Angeles and New York). The Chechens told Yeltsin to get stuffed during the winter of 1991, and Boris must have thought they meant snuffed. Boris turned his eyes away for a while, but then launched one of the most bloody military attacks in Russian history that has so far killed more than 80,000 people.

There were, at last report, about 1500 Chechens living in Moscow. Many came back to Chechnya after the outbreak of hostilities to fight Yeltsin's army. The "Chechens" in Moscow are really an old-line crime family originally from Chechnya or Chechestan, one extremely difficult to infiltrate or join, unless you are a member of the family.

The Chechens are split into three main criminal factions. The most powerful is the "Central," followed by the "Ostankinsky" and the "Automobile." Finding these groups used to be easy, as they operated from plush Moscow hotels until the war. The Centrals could be found in the Hotel Belgrade, the Golden Ring and the Russia Hotel. Here, they controlled drugs, prostitution, restaurants, Moscow markets and the retail trade. The Ostankinsky takes its name from the Ostankinsky Hotel. The group is also headquartered in the Voskhod and Baikal hotels. Their specialty is the transfer and shipment of all types of goods (including drugs) between Moscow and their home base of Chechnya. The "Automobile" group brings in cars from Western Europe and looks after seven gas stations.

The transport and sale of drugs are a major source of income for the Chechens. They also employ the time-honored method of extortion to supplement their income. Everyone from street vendors to major international corporations have to cough up about 10 percent of their gross or face the music. The Chechens are linked to the three main Italian Mafia families as well as members of the former Soviet government, the KGB and former Soviet Communist Party members. See "Chechnya" page 557.

Tajikistan

Afghanistan-based Tajik guerrillas continue their attacks against Russian border posts and inside the country. Russian planes have been bombing rebel positions inside Afghanistan. The Russians have tracked dozens of Arab mercenaries on their way to aid the insurgents, armed with Stinger missiles and mines. See Tajikistan page 501

Train and Metro Stations

Many attacks against tourists take place on trains (both city and national) and in the subways. The Trans-Siberian Railway is a common target of organized gangs of criminals who rob, rape and murder passengers. Russian businesses have stopped sending any valuable commodities through Chechnya.

Dangerous Things

Airlines

Airline passengers are more likely to be killed in Russia than anywhere else in the world. The number of fatalities per million passengers has risen from one in 1990 to 5.5 in 1993. The breakup of Aeroflot into hundreds of regional carriers that cannot afford to properly maintain their planes has a lot to do with it. Pilots, who make an average of $21 a month, have even spoken out.

Americans

Yep, you read that right. There have been reports of Americans creating a distraction while a local rips you off.

Banking

The second most dangerous job in Russia may be that of a banker. Banks are the most common target of the Mafia. In 1993, 30 bankers were murdered across Russia, 10 in Moscow.

Business Partners

More than 90 people classified as entrepreneurs were murdered in Russia in 1994—a very convincing reason why 80 percent of the businesses pay protection money to the Russian Mafia. It ranges between 10 and 20 percent of gross revenues. It is estimated that 40,000 private and state-run businesses are already controlled by the Mafia.

DP'S Eastern European Shopping Tips, or Capitalism Comes to Russia

Forget the cubic zirconia, its nuclear materials that are hot now. If you're shopping in the CIS or Eastern Europe why not pick a kilo (2.2lbs) or two of something special for those banana republic dictators who have everything. Confused by all those high tech names? Just remember uranium is a radioactive element. When enriched as Uranium-235 it is used to produce nuclear fission reactions. Plutonium is a by-product of nuclear reactors used in making nuclear weapons. Cessium-137 is a radioactive isotope used in cancer research and radiation therapy and don't forget that Strontium-90 is a deadly radioactive isotope of strontium. So bring those lead lined Baggies. and no peeking.

Between 1991 and 1994 the University of Pittsburgh found 140 attempts to sell stolen nuclear material on the other hand Germany's BND intelligence agency found that the only potential buyers for underground bomb-making ingredients were undercover government investigators. But if you've got glowing goodies for sale, DP would bet that Muammar or Benazir would still take your call.

1991–1992   *An employee of the Research Institute of Podolsk near Moscow systematically stole 45 percent enriched Uranium-235 by cheating the scales he used at work. He stored the 1.5 kilograms he accumulated on his balcony. His neighbors wondered why he never needed charcoal to BBQ.*

DP'S Eastern European Shopping Tips, or Capitalism Comes to Russia

1991–1992 *In an Italian raid on a plutonium deal involving Libyan buyers, authorities arrested an Austrian electronics engineer who implicated 15 others, including nine KGB officers and five Russian military officers as being part of a smuggling ring. The engineer told a judge that in addition to plutonium and uranium, heavy arms were being moved by the group, all with the help of authorities in Moscow. He was arrested when he ordered the material from the new Russian military catalog called Nukes 'n More.*

June 3, 1992 *In a parking lot near Vienna, two Czechs and four Hungarians were arrested and metal discs weighing 1.2 kilograms were seized from a traveling bag. The material included 261 uranium oxide pellets containing 4.4% uranium-235 and another 55 grams of pure uranium-235. The people involved were described as simple criminals, and it was believed that they had obtained access to former Soviet nuclear storage sites through the Russian Mafia. Police stopped them to ask why they were glowing in the dark.*

October 1992 *Authorities in Germany discovered a container of Cesium-137 weighing 17 kilograms in Frankfurt station, and a container with three capsules of Strontium-90 in the trunk of a car. Three Poles and a German were detained when they complained of hernias and couldn't carry their bags.*

March 1993 *A Lithuanian was arrested for smuggling around 10 kilograms of uranium from Russia to Lithuania to be sold in Poland. The smuggler threw two rods of the radioacitive uranium into a river when he heard that his colleagues had been arrested. Local residents noticed the taste of the water improved but their hair fell out.*

April 1993 *The Ukrainian customs service discovered about 80 tons of nuclear fuel accompanied only by railroad waybills and lacking export papers. The fuel was sent from Russia. It is thought that the freight was scheduled for shipment to Bulgaria, then Libya. They were tipped off by the label that said only "Muammar, Libya"*

July 4, 1994 *The police arrested a Czech man at a gas station near Munich. In a black briefcase he was carrying they found 120 uranium pellets (weakly enriched) weighing 600 grams. It had been smuggled from Slovakia, via Prague, to Germany. The man said the pellets were vitamins and that his skin had always peeled off in large sheets.*

Aug. 4, 1994 *It was reported that Romanian police seized three kilograms of enriched uranium in the form of 583 tablets from a private company. The uranium had entered the country from Ukraine. Five persons were arrested. The company said "Uranium tablets? I thought they ordered Geranium tablets!"*

October, 1995 *In October, authorities arrested 12 uranium smugglers in Moscow who police said tried to get $1.5 million for almost 60 pounds of Uranium-238. The thieves said if that's too much OK we'll take a dozen Laker tickers, behind Jack Nicholson.*

Crime

In a place where hiring a hit man to kill someone costs only US$200, you had better watch your step. Foreigners are targets of crime in Russia, especially in major cities. Pickpocketing and muggings occur both day and night. Street crimes are most frequent in train stations, airports and open markets; on the Moscow-St. Petersburg overnight train; and when hailing taxis or traveling by the Metro late at night. Groups of children who beg for money sometimes pickpocket and assault tourists. Foreigners' hotel rooms and residences have also been targeted. Some victims have been seriously assaulted during robberies. If you receive a replacement for your lost or stolen U.S. passport from the U.S. Embassy or a consulate in Russia, your exit visa must also be replaced, with assistance from your sponsor, so that the passport number written on the visa matches your new passport. This normally requires a Russian police report.

Older people are also targets of crime in Russia. In addition, there has been a sharp rise in the number of taxi drivers killed while on duty. Policemen have been killed at their posts. And, to make matters worse, Russian jails are becoming overcrowded. An expected 40,000 prisoners in Russian jails have been, or are expected to be, released earlier than scheduled, much earlier. The government has been calling it amnesty. Keep up your guard.

Extortion

Apart from the street muggings, which are the most dangerous thing in Russia, extortion is number two. If you're lucky, you'll get mugged and hit up for a bribe. Russians say that 70 to 80 percent of businesses pay extortion demands to criminal groups. Only about 10 to 15 foreigners file extortion charges each year.

Kidnapping

Foreigners are routinely kidnapped because they bring higher ransoms than locals.Seven foreigners were kidnapped in Moscow, St. Petersburg and Irkutsk in the first six months of 1994. One American kidnapped in St. Petersburg in March 1994 was killed.

Deaf Mutes

There are scams in Russia where deaf mutes feign illness and seek the aid of an American. While you're helping the ailing, a bunch of his buddies will rip you off.

Drinking, Eating and Smoking

If murder doesn't take out most Russians, vodka will. Russian deaths as a result of disease caused by toxins such as alcohol and nicotine are rising at an alarming rate. There was a 20 percent increase in alcohol poisoning between 1993 and 1994, and a 17.9 percent increase in infectious disease in the same period. Russians are famous for their love of vodka, heavy, greasy foods and smoking. Stress, leading to cardiovascular disease, is another big killer. One disease not commonly reported as a cause of death is cancer. Russia produces 75 million *tonnes* of toxic waste each year. It also does not have a single toxic waste treatment center.

Kids

Crimes by kids pose a unique threat to the population. Adolescents, often unemployed, travel and operate criminally in groups. One may also find younger boys of ages 10 to 12 operating in small groups or as individuals. The groups may have an adult ringleader for whom the kids work. If you're a victim of youth crime in Russia, especially in the cities, contact the police and fill out a report. In many instances, youths strike in the same place, employing similar methods, making them easier to catch. Some foreigners have also reported successes in catching thieves by advertising on local TV stations.

Overnight Trains

Thieves routinely rob the sleeping berths in overnight trains throughout Russia. The problem is most acute along the Moscow-St. Petersburg route. The common M.O. is for the thief to drug victims before robbing them.

Police

An alarming trend in Russia is the growing police involvement in crimes against fellow Russians and foreigners. This is particularly worrisome in Moscow and St. Petersburg. In other instances, the police may not come to the aid of a crime victim, even if the crime is being committed in their presence.

Some Helpful Hints from the Locals

A booklet entitled *How Not to Become a Crime Victim/Advice of Professionals*, published by the Leningrad Association of Workers, offers advice to citizens on avoiding crime. Here's some of it:

- Make purchases at reputable outlets.

- Count your change carefully before leaving the cashier or the seller. Recount your change if the seller has recounted it a second time because of a problem, to make sure you have not been tricked during the recounting.

- Check to make sure that the article you believe you have purchased is the one that is packed for you.

- Do not invite people you do not know well into your living quarters, or drink alcohol with them to avoid the possibility of being drugged.

- Do not open the door to your quarters to unknown individuals.

- If you feel you are being followed, apply to the police for help.

- Do not get into an elevator alone with a stranger.

- If you are in trouble, yell *pozhar* (fire) to attract attention for aid.

- Be constantly aware and on the alert.

St. Petersburg security office recommendations:

- Dress down and do not flash cash or jewelry.

- Do not tell strangers where you are staying or your travel plans.

- Avoid crowds. Although this is difficult to do, do not let your curiosity get the better of you. Leave the area as soon as you can.

- When deciding when and where to make your purchases or to change money do not place convenience over your personal security. Street vendors are certainly more convenient, but dealing with them necessitates that you subject yourself to the scrutiny of bystanders who will make note of the location of your passport, money and other valuables. In many instances shortly after making a purchase, the customer falls victim to street thieves.

- Do not purchase drinks from already-opened bottles; i.e., in bars.

- When out on the town, leave hard-to-replace, nonessential items, such as passports, credit cards, driver's licenses and family pictures, with the hotel security office or at home. Disperse your money throughout your garments. Remember the amounts in each location and when making purchases retrieve only the amount of money needed for that purchase. Never display large sums of money.

- Do not believe that you are getting a bargain. When you believe this, watch out; chances are that you are being set up. Thieves understand and utilize human emotions such as greed and lust. Situations in which these emotions are most commonly played upon include dealings with vendors of so-called "antiquities," with prostitutes and in currency exchanges.

Some Helpful Hints from the Locals

- Never patronize unmarked taxis or enter any taxi carrying unfamiliar passengers. Agree upon the price and destination prior to entering the vehicle.

- If you have a car with you, do not leave any items inside the vehicle when it is parked. These items will be attractive to thieves and will encourage break-ins. Also remove windshield wiper blades when parked. Do not park in dark and isolated places.

- Never drink alcoholic beverages without having a trusted friend along who has agreed to remain sober. Even slight intoxication is noted by professional thieves.

- When a victim of a crime, be it a violent act or general trickery, do not let your vanity or apathy prevent you from immediately making a report to the police and U.S. embassy or consulate. Others will benefit. In addition, stolen items are routinely retrieved.

Getting Sick

Medical care in Russia is usually far below Western standards, with severe shortages of basic medical supplies. Access to the few quality facilities that exist in major cities usually requires cash dollar payment at Western rates upon admission. The U.S. embassy and consulates has a list of good facilities and of English-speaking doctors. Many expats travel outside of Russia for most of their medical needs. Travelers may wish to check their insurance coverage and consider supplemental coverage for medical evacuation.

An outbreak of diphtheria continues in Moscow, St. Petersburg, and other parts of Russia. Although only a small number of cases have been reported, up-to-date diphtheria immunizations are recommended. Typhoid can be a concern for those who plan to travel extensively in Russia. Drinking only boiled or bottled water will help to guard against cholera, which has been reported, as well as other diseases. More complete and updated information on health matters can be obtained from the Centers for Disease Control's international travelers' hotline, ☎ *(404) 332-4559.*

Nuts and Bolts

The Russian Federation is the largest republic of the CIS; it's almost twice the size of the United States. Moscow, with nearly 9 million residents, is the largest city.

The Russian Federation officially came into existence in December 1991. Russia is a presidential republic, containing 22 autonomous republics that maintain an uneasy balance between the Russian president and the Congress of People's Deputies (parliament). In practice, the power base is much more complex. Russia's vast size (10.5 million square km) and small population (148 million) could make the region ripe for exploitation by Western investors; but the corrupt infrastructure, however, makes business profits unlikely for years to come.

Russian is the official language, although there are many local ethnic tongues. English is widely read but not yet fluently spoken. Translators, of varying abilities, will be found in all sizeable organizations. The country boasts a nearly 100 percent literacy rate.

Business hours are from 9 a.m. to 1 p.m., with a break for the typical heavy Russian lunch between 1 and 2 p.m. Some stores close from 2 to 3 p.m. Banks are open from 9:30 a.m. to 12:30 p.m., with currency exchanges open longer. You can change money at Sheremeytevo II International Airport in Moscow 24 hours a day. Also, the American Express office in Moscow can cash your Amex traveler's checks into dollars.

Russia is US$80 billion in debt but still manages to keep finding major oil fields, such as the Tenghiz field in Kazakhstan. The field is estimated to contain between 7 and 25 billion barrels of oil. The Azeri oil field in the Caspian Sea and the Timan Pechora basin in the north Russian

Archangels province will help to pay off that debt.The former U.S.S.R. had about 6.4 percent of the world's oil reserves and was the world's largest producer and exporter of natural gas. However, poor management has led to annual decreases each year since the 1980s.

Gas comes from western Siberia; the largest areas are Urengoi and Yamburg. New fields on the Yamal peninsula are waiting for development. The former U.S.S.R. was the world's third-largest coal producer in 1990 (after China and the United States). Russia possesses the world's largest explored reserves of copper, lead, zinc, nickel, mercury and tungsten.It also has about 40 percent of the world's reserves of iron ore and manganese. Figures released in September 1990 show confirmed iron reserves of 33.1 billion *tonnes*. The world's largest gold deposits at the Sukhoi Log reserves are estimated at more than 1000 *tonnes*, much of which is smuggled out of Russia through the Baltic States. Russia is also trying to retain more control over its diamond reserves. The government created the Federal Diamond Centre, granting parliament more control over the industry. The intent is to weaken control over Russia's diamonds by De-Beers, which has operated a supply cartel and maintained Russia's output at 7,500,000 carats per year.

Russia will be a net food importer for some time to come. In 1990, though, there were record harvests, but despite this wealth, a shortage of labor caused the crops to rot in the fields.

Arms sales continue to be an important part of Russia's exports, although there is worldwide concern that a lot of high-tech systems are getting into the wrong hands. In 1992, Russia sold more than US$2 billion worth of weapons through contracts with China, India, Iran and Syria.

In 1992, the former Soviet Union had more than 3 million men in its armed forces, over 60 percent of them conscripted for a two-year period. About 1 million conscripts perform essentially civilian jobs, such as construction. All men are subject to conscription, although in the past, many students have received exemption. There were between 2 and 2.5 million members of the military by 1994. Today, there is a reserve force numbering about 55 million.

Useful Addresses and Phone Numbers

British-Russian Chamber of Commerce
60a Pembroke Road
London W8 6NX
☎ *[44] (71) 602-7692*
Services for members: (Moscow office) group visits to Russia, seminars in conjunction with Oxford University scholars and others

Consulate of Russia
Kensington Palace Gardens
London W8 4QS
☎ *[44] (71) 229-3215/6*

Department of Trade and Industry, Russia Desk
Overseas Trade Division
1 Victoria Street
London SW1 0ET
☎ *[44] (71) 215-5265/4268*
FAX [44] (71) 222-2531/2629

East European Trade Council
Suite 10, Westminster Palace Gardens
Artillery Row
London SW1P 1RL
☎ *[44] (71) 222-7522*
Telex: [44] (71) 290-1018

EETC GUS-Russia Trade and Economic Council
805 Third Avenue
New York, New York 10022
☎ *(212) 644 4550*

The official currency is the ruble; it's pointless to post its rate against the U.S. dollar, since it changes as frequently as most people change their underwear. There are 100 kopeks to the ruble.

Goods that are purchased from street vendors can be problematic and expensive to export. Russian customs laws state that any item for export valued at more than 300 rubles (value is established by customs officials at the time of export—for example, just prior to a traveler's departing flight) is subject to a 600 percent export tax. Items purchased from government-licensed shops, where prices are openly marked in hard currency, are not subject to the tax. Request a receipt when making any purchase.

Money Hassles

Traveler's checks and credit cards are not widely accepted in Russia; in many cities, credit cards are only accepted at establishments catering to Westerners. Old, or very worn, dollar bills are often not accepted, even at banks. Major hotels or the American Express offices in Moscow or St. Petersburg may be able to suggest locations for cashing traveler's checks or obtaining cash advances on credit cards. Western Union has agents in Moscow, St. Petersburg and some other large cities that can disburse money wired from the United States.

Getting Out

Russian customs laws and regulations are in a state of flux and not consistently enforced. A 600 percent duty is required to export any item with a value greater than 300,000 rubles. All items which may appear to have historical or cultural value—icons, art, rugs, antiques, etc.—may be taken out of Russia only with prior written approval of the Ministry of Culture and payment of a 100 percent duty. Caviar may only be taken out of Russia with a receipt indicating it was bought in a store licensed to sell to foreigners. Failure to follow the customs regulations may result in temporary or permanent confiscation of the property in question.

Embassy and Consulate Locations and Phone Numbers

Moscow

Novinskiy Bulvar 19/23
☎ *[7] (095) 252-2451.*
After-hours duty officer: ☎ *[7] (095) 230-2001/2601.*

U.S. Consulate General in St. Petersburg

Ulitsa Furshtadskaya 15
☎ *[7] (812) 275-1701.*
After-hours duty officer: ☎ *[7] (812) 274-8692.*

U.S. Consulate General in Vladivostok

12 Mordovtseva
☎ *[7] (4232) 268-458/554 or 266-820.*

Consulate General in Yekaterinburg

☎ *[7] (3432) 601-143*
FAX [7] (3432) 601-181
Provides emergency services for American citizens

Better Living Through Chemistry

Russia's drug addicts number 1.5 million (or 1 percent of the entire population), and the figure keeps growing. Illegal hemp fields in Russia cover an area exceeding 40 million hectares. In an eight-month period in 1994, Russian law enforcement bodies made arrests in connection with 40,000 drug-related crimes, seizing 13.3 tons of various drugs. Police have busted 3300 gangs engaged in drug trafficking and sale. From 30 to 35 percent of the drugs are imported. In Moscow and St. Petersburg, however, the figure reaches 80 to 90 percent.

Better Living Through Chemistry

The price of one gram of cocaine in Moscow is from 400 to 900 percent higher than in New York, for which reason the Russian drug market looks very attractive to the international Mafia. Nearly US$100 million were involved in the drug trade in Russia in late 1993. The police force fighting drug dealers today numbers as few as 3500 men. Police are especially concerned that a new synthetic drug–trinisilsyntholin–is being produced in Russia. It had formerly only been produced in the U.S. The substance is so strong that one gram of it is enough to make 10 liters of narcotics more powerful than heroin or cocaine. Imported drugs, such as heroin and cocaine, are now sold everywhere in this country. In Moscow, for instance, the price of one gram of heroin ranges from US$200 to US$300. The government is taking urgent measures to stamp out the social malady. A comprehensive federal antidrug program for 1995–1997 is being worked out by a special government commission.

Dangerous Days

07/02/1996   Soviet election.

12/31/1991   President Bush recognized the independence of all 12 former Soviet republics and proposed the establishment of full diplomatic relations with six of them, including Russia. Russian President Yeltsin responded formally and positively on December 31, 1991, the date officially considered to be when the U.S. established formal diplomatic relations with Russia.

12/25/1991   Mikhail Gorbachev resigned as president of the Soviet Union and transferred control of the Soviet nuclear arsenal to Russian President Boris Yeltsin. A few hours later, the United States recognized Russia as the successor state to the Soviet Union. These actions marked the end of the Soviet Union, 74 years after the Bolshevik revolution.

12/21/1991   Russia joined with 10 other former republics of the Soviet Union (which ceased to exist on December 25, 1991) in establishing the Commonwealth of Independent States. The Commonwealth was expected to have military and economic coordinating functions and would be headquartered in Mensk, Byelarus.

08/19/1991   Failed coup attempt that symbolized the end of communism in Russia and the breakup of the Soviet Union. Violent demonstrations occurred in Moscow in August 1992, resulting in several deaths.

05/02/1945   Berlin fell to the Soviets.

02/01/1943   Germany's 6th Army surrendered to Soviet forces in Stalingrad.

06/22/1941   German invasion of U.S.S.R.

11/07/1917   Revolution Day, considered the most sacred day by Russian communists.

Washington D.C.

The United States

How the West Was Stunned

Land of the free and home of the brave. You'd better be damned brave here, because people are free to do pretty much anything they feel like. Behind white picket fences and two-car garages, husbands clobber their wives silly while their kids make crack deals over the phone with *Scarface* on the tube.

In L.A., inner-city toddlers catch stray bullets from drive-by shooters, while, in New York, Islamic whackos use a rented van full of fertilizer makings to blow up the World Trade Center. In San Diego, a despondent plumber hot-wires a tank, flattens some cars, and is shot to death after high-centering on a freeway divider. What would Ozzie and Harriet Nelson say?

Doctors kiss their wives good-bye and later lose their lives outside burning abortion clinics in Massachusetts, Virginia, Florida, Oregon, Ohio, Minnesota and California—the victims of preachers, former altar boys, and women who look more like manicurists than terrorists.

United States

⊗ National capital
• State capital
• Secondary city
── Primary road
┼┼┼┼ Railroad
┈┈┈ State border

0 ────────── 800 km
0 ────────── 500 mi

In Idaho, Montana, Alabama, Louisiana, Georgia and Utah, young white-trash punks, parading as "Freemen" under the lofty and pontifical banner of white supremacy, stash a couple of years' worth of Spam into a cave in the hills, run around in the forest with paint guns, and plot the demise of every "nigger" and "kike" west of Bethesda. Fear not, because in this land of equality and free speech, the JDL and Nation of Islam do their part to keep the hate at a fever pitch.

In Florida, penniless, HIV-positive heroin addicts from Haiti stalk the streets near Miami Airport, looking for Chrysler convertible Lebarons and Ford Aerostars sporting Hertz stickers, whose occupants they strip-rob before perforating them with 9-mm blobs of molten lead and tossing the corpses into a drainage ditch.

Throughout the U.S., selected business executives and university professors open up packages that come in the mail, only to be blown into orbit.

In Wisconsin and Illinois, deranged cannibals lure teenage gay hookers into their homes, decapitate and disembowel them, boil their heads and consume their viscera for dinner. In jail, they get stuck by nasties who can't live with a guy who's munched on some dead dude's brains.

A recent Gallup poll discovered that 40 percent of the American people think that "the federal government has become so large and powerful that it poses an immediate threat to rights and freedoms of ordinary citizens."

In Oklahoma City, the Alfred P. Murrah Building is blown up. The nondescript building has no significance other than being the headquarters for the DEA, Secret Service and the ATF. The aftermath is a nine story-hole, a crater 30 feet wide by 8 feet deep, and 168 innocent people killed. The methodology is very similar to that used in the World Trade Center bombing: a 1000 to 1200-pound fertilizer- and diesel-based bomb packed into a rented Ryder truck and detonated by remote control or timer.

The press is quick to blame "Muslim fundamentalists," but the real horror starts to sink in. According to the FBI, the worst terrorist attack on American soil is the reputed handiwork of two pissed-off rednecks. Trained by Uncle Sam, fired up by hatred of the government, they provide a singularly unproductive and deadly solution. The message is clear: The dispossessed are amongst us. We no longer have to worry about Egyptian clerics, Sudanese cabdrivers or Palestinian tourists.

Farther south, some 300 miles away in Waco, Texas, the site of the Branch Davidian compound is becoming a popular local tourist attraction. The bomb blast in Oklahoma City occurred two years to the day after the attack by the ATF on the cult's compound. During the ATF raid, a brainwashed prophet with an arms cache the size of the Serbs' had his followers blow their brains out as he torched his compound—and their children.

The 1996 Olympic Summer Games bring American terrorism to international headlines when a pipe bomb explodes during a concert resulting in two deaths and hundreds injured.

And across the South, African American churches are being destroyed by fire—apparently the result of racially motivated arson. As of June 1996, more than 30 churches had been hit within the past 18 months.

Mayhem, Tabloid Style

We used to chuckle at the tabloids, as we bought our groceries. Now we can't figure out if it's the news we're watching or promos for sick B movies.

Hey, America... what time is it?

Every 2 seconds	a criminal offense
Every 12 seconds	a burglary
Every 17 seconds	a violent crime
Every 20 seconds	a vehicle is stolen
Every 51 seconds	a robbery
Every 5 minutes	a rape
Every 23 minutes	a murder
Every 28 seconds	an aggregated assault
Every 30 minutes	news, sports and weather

Sources: F.B.I. Uniform Crime Report, DP

In all 50 states, plumbers, carpenters, politicians, real estate agents, movie moguls and cops get into their cars after a fifth of gin at Sam's Bar and later plow into and kill a family on the interstate while they end up with just some scratches.

In America everywhere, 12-year-old kids playing on the railroad tracks stumble across one of their classmates—who was sodomized and strangled to death...a month ago.

In California, fires ravage the hills of Berkeley and Malibu. Tremors, measuring 7.1 on the Richter scale, rattle hills that later disappear entirely—along with the houses on them—after 10 inches of rain fall in a 14-hour period.

And the corpses of Central American would-be illegal immigrants float like logs down the Rio Grande. Those who make it to the other side of the river are looted, beaten and raped by sinister "coyotes."

Criminals as Superstars

Hard times breed strange heroes. The hardscrabble days of early America bred the outlaws of the Wild West. Jesse James and Billy the Kid were popularized in East Coast dime novels. The Great Depression gave us Dillinger and Al Capone. Today, in down-on-its-luck L.A., we are hatching a new breed of famous ne'er do wells. In Los Angeles, the land of "three strikes you're out" has become "do a crime, do the prime time." Here, random violence and thoughtless pain take on plot, character and movie deals, as two rich kids splatter their parents' brains against a wall with a 12-gauge for a couple of Rolexes. In Los Angeles, a former football hero and movie star is accused of nearly severing his ex-wife's head and brutally stabbing to death her acquaintance. Meanwhile, during his "getaway," traffic on plagued L.A. freeways comes to a halt; motorists emerge from their cars waving banners urging, "Go O.J.!" and "Save the Juice!" After the most publicized trial in history, the jury lets him go free.

Here, crime needs a subplot and linkage. A mother tosses her kids off a bridge and jumps in afterward. The news media immediately connects it to a woman in the South who rolled her two kids to their watery end—a woman who played the media like a fiddle in her search for her "kidnapped" children.

Crime also needs a surprise ending, a payback. Rodney King gets the crap beaten out of him, sues and gets millions. Reginald Denny gets the crap beaten out of him and hugs and kisses the mother of one of his attackers. The Unabomber's big demand is that he have his antitechnology manifesto published. We like our crime. Just keep it fresh, surprising and very brutal.

Crime Statistics

In 1965, 91 percent of homicides were solved. Today, only 65.5 percent get figured out. One reason is the high percentage of murders committed by family members and acquaintances against each other. The chances that you will get killed by a stranger are only two out of 10, if you take into account just solved murders. When unsolved murders are tallied, the FBI estimates that 53 percent of all homicides are being committed by strangers and that only 12 percent of homicides take place within a family. Eighty percent of crimes are committed by same-race perpetrators. Robbery is committed by strangers 75 percent of the time, and aggravated assault is committed by a stranger 58 percent of the time. Eighty-seven-percent of all violent crimes are committed against whites and Hispanics. Lone white offenders select white victims 96 percent of the time, and lone black offenders select white victims 62 percent of the time. White rapists select white victims 97 percent of the time, and black rapists select white victims 48 percent of the time.

Although 51 percent of prison inmates are black, the balance is out of whack, since African Americans make up about 12.3 percent of the U.S. population. The number of black males in prison between the ages of 25 and 29 is 7210 per 100,000. According to the Department of Justice, the homicide rate for whites is 5.2 per 100,000 and for blacks about 44.7 per 100,000. Urban killers tend to be male (90 percent) and young (15–29). Something is very wrong.

In 1960 12 percent of the population reported owning one or more handguns. In 1976, 21 percent owned a handgun. Today there are well over 200 million handguns, with 4 million new guns being manufactured each year. Professor Gary Kleck of Florida State University estimates that 1500 citizens used guns to kill criminals in 1980. Police only kill about 500 criminals each year.

In America one in every 175 people is in jail. Prison populations have doubled in the last 15 years. Major crime was down 17.5 percent in New York. The decrease in violent crimes in the nine U.S. cities with populations of more than one million was down 8 percent. Hallelujah, the streets are safe, or are they? Those figures were 1994 numbers. What they didn't tell you was that the '95 and '96 numbers put violent crime right back on track again. The major reason for the drop was the reduction of kids in the crime-prone ages of 15–19. The bad news is that the next wave of kids is meaner, badder and more prone to kill.

U.S. Incarceration Rate (per 100,000 people)	
States with Highest Incarceration Rate	
Texas	**659**
Louisiana	**573**

U.S. Incarceration Rate (per 100,000 people)	
Oklahoma	536
Arizona	473
States with Lowest Incarceration Rate	
Vermont	135
W. Virginia	134
Maine	112
Minnesota	103
North Dakota	90

Clearance rate is the number of crimes that result in an arrest or conviction. In America it is wise to know when local law enforcement is on the case. Criminals may find it very convenient to commit crimes since there is little threat that they will do the time. A brief look at the top five cities makes one wonder if the word "mob" might have something to do with it.

Violence in the Media

Rocky Mountain Media Watch estimates that crime disaster and war coverage make up an average of 42 percent of all newscasts. UCLA researchers say that even though murders make up 2 percent of all felonies in Los Angeles, the news devotes 27 percent of its coverage to them. In the same study, it was disclosed that 50 percent of crimes committed by blacks in L.A. are violent and that 47 percent of crimes committed by whites are violent. There were about 30 percent more stories on black crimes involving violence than white crimes.

Top-10 Talk Show Subjects	
Parent-child relations	48%
Dating	36%
Marital relations	35%
Sexual activity	34%
Reconciliations	25%
Physical health	24%
Abuse	23%
Alienation	23%
Physical appearance	23%
Criminal acts	22%

Entertainment is no family affair. A cable industry–sponsored report says that 57 percent of shows feature violence. In 1995 the three major networks ran 2574 stories on crime, four times the number they ran in 1991.

Two Hundred Grand, Free Housing and All the Bullets You Can Dodge

In Washington, D.C., a convicted crack freak is reelected mayor. In Louisiana, an admitted KKK leader and affirmed racist nearly gets elected to the U.S. Senate.

In South Carolina, an already elected and longtime U.S. senator warns the president of the United States that he had better have a lot of bodyguards if he's going to visit a military base in that state. America is the land of the tough guy, people who don't take any crap, and will gun you down if you give them any lip. In New York, Bernard Goetz gets slammed in a $41 million lawsuit for gunning down thugs (while Bronson makes millions in movies doing the same thing). Meanwhile, on the other coast, prosecutors won't file murder charges against a white man who guns down Latino taggers. Go figure.

Being the boss man of the land of the free is no picnic. In America, four presidents have been assassinated. Two others have been shot. There have been nearly successful assassination attempts on three others. Three serious contenders for the presidency have been critically shot, two dead.

The White House should consider opening up a shooting range to give irate voters an outlet for their violent tendencies. The venerable building has been riddled with the bullets of drive-by shootings, bad snipers, even a crashed airplane. America is not a Pepsi commercial or the "Brady Bunch." America is a dangerous place.

President Bill Clinton has called crime "the great crisis of the spirit that is gripping America today." The number of crimes recorded by police in the U.S. has risen by more than 60 percent since 1973. Violent crime, by the most conservative estimates, has risen by nearly 25 percent during that same period. The Statue of Liberty may well want to pull her arm down and take in the welcoming mat. Four out of 10 violent crimes in the U.S. are committed by relations or acquaintances of the victims. In the U.S. nearly 10 of every 100,000 people are the victims of a homicide. In 1900, only one person in every 100,000 could expect to become a murder victim.

Fear of Islam, People Who Wear Bedsheets and Other Bad Folks

And if crime isn't enough, there's a new bad guy in town—the terrorist. Islamic terrorism is on the rise. Right-wingers are blowing up government buildings, left-wingers mailing bombs, and Right to Lifers are taking lives to save lives. Overseas, Libya, Iran, Iraq, Syria and the Sudan are cutting backroom deals and mailing checks to keep us on our toes. The U.S. is the Great Satan, whose demise is the ultimate objective and goal of all Islamic terrorism movements. For eternally pissed off countries, such as Syria, Iran and Libya, terrorism is state policy (they can't finance a real war), and the obese, limpwristed and pantywaisted U.S. of A. is the kid these bullies like to pick on.

The U.S. is more vulnerable than it's ever been. We can't follow rules of engagement with terrorism, because then we would look like the bullies. We can't send America's sons and daughters to patrol the mean streets of the world, because their parents back in Iowa want to know why they keep coming back dead, murdered by people they have never heard of and for reasons that are as alien to them as the IRS's taxation laws.

When acts of foreign terrorism creep onto American shores, as with the World Trade Center bombing, the heartland calls out for revenge against the "ragheads, sand niggers, A-rabs, Eye-raqis" and every other xenophobic and naive stereotype. Our new enemy does not have a face or even a good press agent. We now cast the entire Muslim, Arab and red world, trying to remember if the Arabs were our friends (the Gulf War) or our enemies (the fuel crisis). When we get tired of figuring out the difference between Hamas and Hezbollah, Shiite and Sunni, or Khomeini and Khameini, we simply flip the channel or change the subject. Nuke 'em all into the Stone Age seems like a good foreign policy, as we settle in for another busty episode of "Baywatch."

What Your Eyewitness, Action Cam News Reports Don't Tell You

Acts of terrorism in the United States are not the same as freeway pileups, gang murders or even a local bank robbery. Even though the acts seem random and opportunistic, terrorism in the United States can be compared to a low-level war.

Qadaffi, with the help of North Korea and Cuba, is busy establishing a terrorist infrastructure in the U.S. It's no secret. One only has to go back to the 1982 International Conference of the World Center for Resistance of Imperialism, Zionism, Racism, Reaction and Facism (we wonder how they got all that on the hotel's marquee) held in Tripoli to glean that Libya, Iran, Syria, Cuba and Benin established an executive committee to organize concerted efforts at exporting terrorism inside U.S. borders. In 1983, Qadaffi sponsored another symposium to devise a coordinated effort to bring the Islamic struggle into the U.S. In attendance was a U.S. delegation, comprised of elements from the American Indian Movement, the Nation of Islam, Black Argus and the Afro-Arab Foundation, among other groups. The Colonel must have been impressed by what he saw. The Americans met privately with the Libyan leader at least twice, while he assessed their capabilities of fermenting torment among the dispossessed of America. Flash to 1996 and Farrakhan is all aflutter about getting a silk sash and a promise of a billion dollars (and some folding money for himself). The beat goes on.

The export of terrorism into the U.S. is running along two other channels: drugs and arms.

The drug trade is helping to bring terrorism to America. Terrorist organizations, such as Hezbollah and M-19, have been establishing closer ties with drug lords in an effort to get into America's veins. A deal was struck between Syria and Pablo Escobar's Medellin cartel in the mid-1980s. It called for the Colombians to help establish Syria's fledgling Lebanon cocaine factories in exchange for terrorist training and military supplies that would be (and still are) used to fight local governments and drug enforcement agencies in Colombia and elsewhere. Coca paste is sent to Syrian labs in Lebanon's Shouf mountains, processed and then moved into Western Europe.

In 1992, the weapons really began moving into Colombia, with some US$20 million worth in one shipment alone that reached the eager paws of the Colombian insurgent groups FARC and the ELN. Guns are being gobbled up by Syrian and Iranian purchasers in Eastern Europe and funneled into the Colombian cartels. And if that's not enough, they're being bought with devastatingly authentic counterfeit U.S. bills printed at Iran's state currency mint in Tehran.

Tehran is the suspected instigator behind the Pan Am explosion over Lockerbie, Scotland, on December 21, 1988, killing 270. On March 10, 1989, pro-Iranian terrorists exploded a pipe bomb in the van of Sharon Lee Rogers in San Diego, California. Rogers was the wife of the captain of the U.S.S. *Vincennes*, which had accidentally shot an Iranian airliner from the sky on July 3, 1988. On March 26, 1992, in Franklin Lakes, New Jersey, Mrs. Parivash Rafizadeh, the wife of a senior officer in the Shah's SAVAK, was shot at close range in the stomach and died. Her assailants vanished without a trace. On January 25, 1993, an Iranian-planted Pakistani terrorist blew away two CIA employees and injured three more with an AK-47 outside the agency's headquarters in Langley, Virginia. Although the shootings took place in broad daylight, in front of dozens of witnesses on a crowded street, the shooter, 28-year-old Mir Aimal Kansi, turned up a week later munching *mughlai* with his mom in Pakistan. It was subsequently learned that Kansi's uncle was assassinated in 1984, in all likelihood by the CIA.

The Rogers' bombing in particular revealed that Iran had established a viable terrorist infrastructure within the U.S. Among the 30,000 Iranian students in the U.S., at least 1000 can be counted upon by Tehran to carry out some form of terrorism. In 1991, Iran sent assassination teams into Canada, one of which is believed to have been responsible for the Rafizadeh attack. These teams remain buried in both Canada and the U.S.

The explosion of TWA Flight 800 over Long Island, New York that killed all 230 onboard is another wakeup call for America that terrorism is an ever-present threat. The beat goes on.

It is only through extraordinary efforts on the part of industrialized countries that terrorism is contained. Just catching a plane now requires the same security as entering a maximum security prison. Millions of dollars are spent studying and infiltrating these small terrorist groups, and the assassination of Islamic Jihad's leader in Malta by the Mossad shows that the world is at war with terrorists.

Which Is Meaner? Our Army of God or Their Army of God?

Have we scared you yet? Don't be—at least not of these bad boys. Because it's Betty Boop next door, an accountant's secretary married to her high school halfback sweetheart, who is more likely to be versed in hexogene and combustible fuses than taxi drivers who go by Mohammed, Ahmad or Abdul.

Take Shelley Shannon, for instance. She's a regular Betty Boop, but a Betty Boop who's shot a man and allegedly injected toxic acid into or burned to the ground nine abortion clinics in four states. A Florida jury needed less than 30 minutes to convict Paul Hill of the murders of an abortionist and his aide. The list goes on. There is an ongoing investigation into pro-life (save a baby, kill a doctor) groups to see if there is a national conspiracy going on.

Between 1985 and 1995 in the U.S., there were at least 154 attacks on abortion clinics (not including another 21 in 1995), including bombings and arson, costing more than $14 million. The National Right to Life Committee, to which most of these homebred terrorists belong, has 3000 chapters in all 50 states. Although this "pro-life" organization doesn't sanction the violence, its numbers suggest that a significant percentage of its zany membership does. The offshoots sound like delegations at a Middle Eastern terrorism conference: the Pro-Life Action League, Defensive Action, Christian Action Group, Operation Rescue, Rescue America and the American Coalition of Life Activists. And these folks are about as likely to abandon their bombs as the Libyans are to serve cocktails at the end of a symposium.

To pin the correlation further between these American terrorists and the Middle Eastern groups they so emulate, radical antiabortionists adhere to a doctrine spelled out in their bible, *The Army of God*. Now, if we're not mistaken, in Arabic, that translates into Hezbollah. Seems to me we might have some trademark or copyright infringement here.

Some samplings from *The Army of God* (U.S. version) manual:

- If terminally ill, use your final months to torch clinics; by the time the authorities identify you, you will have gone to your reward.

- Use a high-powered rifle to fire bullets into the engine block of a doctor's car.

- Never make a bomb threat from anywhere but a pay phone.

- Hot-wire a bulldozer at a construction site, drive it to a clinic, jump off and let the bulldozer crash through the clinic wall.

- Drop butyric acid into dumpsters or boxes of trash when people are in the building.

- Put holes through clinic windows. The problem with .22-caliber weapons is the noise—the Fourth of July and New Year's Eve are great times for gunshots.

- Why get out of the way of an abortionist's car? The current lawsuit-crazy attitude can be used against baby-killers, and many awards have been received.

- Look up magazines such as *Soldier of Fortune* or *Survivalist*. Guaranteed that you'll be amazed, if not shocked, by the materials available.

We live in the land of the free, the home of the brave, where everyone has a right to do something, to speak his mind, to 15 minutes of fame, to a guest appearance on the "Ricki Lake Show." What is wrong with this picture? It seems that Americans are punctuating their angry sentences with bullets. The beat goes on.

The Scoop

The United States is a large modern country with devolving inner cities. There are more than 200 million guns in the possession of Americans. Most violent acts in the States are the result of robberies and drug-related violence. Terrorist acts, ranging from killing of abortionist doctors to the bombing of the World Trade Center, are highly publicized but not considered a real threat to travelers. The threat of robbery or violent crime in inner cities and some tourist areas is real and should be taken seriously. Travel in America is considered safe, and danger is confined to random violence and inner cities. Those seeking adventure can find it in a New Orleans bar at five in the morning or strolling through South Central L.A. after midnight.

The Players

Whackos

In most dangerous places, the players have a sense of purpose—through lineage or frustrated political or theological ambition. Here in America, we possess a bunch of whackos whose motivations make the "Pee Wee Herman Show" look intellectual. And most of these folks wouldn't know what to do with this country even if we gave it to them. Even Ross Perot looks like a puppet with a bad haircut when he takes on presidential trappings. Bottom line is, there are no more Ben Franklins or George Washingtons vying for political power.

Aryan Nation, the KKK and Hate Groups

These are right-wing belligerent groups that specialize in pipe bombs and the intimidation of blacks, Jews and immigrants. Although not considered a threat to the social structure, they constitute a growing menace. On July 30, 1994, two skinhead thugs of the white supremacist group Aryan Nations Brotherhood were busted on charges that they offered to kill a federal drug agent in exchange for $120,000 in cash, weapons and cocaine. One of the men allegedly said he would kill a Drug Enforcement Agency (DEA) agent by bombing his home. On July 29, 1994, two zanies from Washington—members of the white supremacist group known as the American Front—who were in possession of three metal pipe bombs, four rifles, military-type clothing, wigs and white supremacist literature, were busted by the FBI in Salinas, California. The men were allegedly behind a pipe bomb explosion on July 20, 1994, at the Tacoma chapter of the National Association for the Advancement of Colored People (NAACP). In a twist on the hate thing, a black male shot 23 whites and Asians, killing five and wounding 18, on a Long Island commuter train in mid-December 1993. Klanwatch Project, the rights group, called the incident a "shocking reversal" in the pattern of hate crime.

Another terrorist goon squad to hit the scene in 1996 was the Aryan Republican Army. On April 2, 1996, a pipe bomb tore through the offices of a Spokane, Washington, newspaper, followed by two men who ripped the paper off for $50,000, who then set off another explosion. They left a letter behind announcing the end of "Babylon," a popular buzz term white supremacists use to call the federal government. These guys get off using the names of federal agents when they rent getaway cars.

Rights Groups

Activities by rights groups are centered around the abortion issue, but certainly aren't confined to it. Animal rights activists have been out doing dirty deeds, but their acts go largely unnoticed. The Animal Liberation Front (ALF), an underground animal rights group, claimed responsibility for a number of fires that caused damage in downtown Chicago department stores in November 1993. Five of eight incendiary devices ignited, causing fires in Marshall Field's, Carson Pirie Scott and Saks Fifth Avenue stores. While death is not an objective in the actions of most rights groups—as it undermines their causes—each possesses its crazies, and terror and death are the tools. In August 1994, an antiabortion activist tried to kill Dr. George Tiller in Wichita, Kansas, and in March of the same year, Dr. David Gunn was killed in Florida.

Islamic Terrorists

Despite the seriousness given Islamic terrorists by American journalists, they tend to resemble the gang that couldn't shoot straight. True, Islamic terrorists were behind the February 26, 1993, bombing of the New York World Trade Center (WTC), which killed six and wounded more than 1000 others. The FBI and local authorities busted nine suspected Islamic terrorists associated with the bombing as well as other plots to bomb targets in New York, including the U.N. building and the Lincoln and Holland tunnels beneath the Hudson River. They also are alleged to have put plans together to assassinate both prominent American and Egyptian politicians. FBI agents and immigration authorities nabbed a blind Egyptian cleric named Sheikh Omar Abdel-Rahman (famous for allegedly issuing the *fatwa* that led to the assassination of Egyptian President Anwar Sadat in 1981) on felony charges in connection with the WTC bombing and the other proposed terrorist activities. Rahman and his nine followers were convicted in October 1995 of seditious conspiracy and will be guests of Uncle Sam (using your tax dollars, of course) for a long time.

However, on closer inspection, it seems that the sheik's bodyguard, Emad Salem, a former Egyptian army colonel, was an FBI informant who supplied 150 hours of audio- and videotapes of the entire plot. The videotapes even include shots of the men mixing their homemade fertilizer bombs. Many experts agree that it was a miracle that any of the crudely made bombs could go off at all. Some defendants turned the table on Salem, accusing him of selecting the bombing targets, renting the safe house and having the only key to the garage that held the explosives. Salem stands to make almost a million dollars for his work in turning in the one hit wonders, who will never make anything more complicated than licence plates.

Additionally, the indictment named El Sayyid Nosair as aiding in the planning of the bombings. Nosair, a close associate of Abdel-Rahman, had been in prison on a weapons possession conviction at the time and an assault rap in connection with the killing of Rabbi Meir Kahane in New York City in 1990. The charges also accused the group of planning to bomb bridges and U.S. military facilities.

The Rugged Mountain Folk of Montana

This remote, rugged and mountainous state breeds individualism, for sure, but it also produces a disproportionate share of mental cases and whackos. Some of these folks have just been in the woods too long and eaten too many squirrels. Montana is the home of the suspected Unabomber, Theodore Kaczynski, who was busted by the feds April 3, 1996, in his Montana remote cabin. The Unabomber killed three people and injured 23 during a 17-year mail bombing spree. Montana is also the home of extremist militiaman John Trochmann (see "Militia of Montana" below), as well as Terry Nichols of Oklahoma City blast fame. And the state is the base for a bunch of zanies who go by the handle "Freemen" (they're not free any longer). These guys, devout white supremacist Christians who reject government authority, refuse to pay taxes and like to write bad checks. On March 25, 1996, a standoff began in Jordan, Montana, between 20 armed Freemen and more than 100 FBI agents after two of the Freemen's leaders were jailed over a $1.8 million fraudulent check scheme, the theft of television equipment and for threatening a federal judge. Even former Green Beret and borderline fascist James "Bo" Gritz couldn't negotiate this wolfpack's surrender. Toss in another chunk of meat.

Office Workers

There's an alarming trend of murder in the workplace. More than 1000 Americans are murdered on the job every year. The U.S. Postal Service has had 34 employees gunned down since 1986. In 1994, there were 214 assaults at post offices. Ask nicely for those stamps.

Gangs

America's willingness to absorb large masses of refugees resulted in the growth of some of the nastiest and hardest groups of street gangs in any Western country. In New York, rival gangs of Puerto Ricans, Irish or blacks don't actually break out into spontaneous choreography when they want to settle a dispute. *West Side Story* has become *Apocalypse Now*. In L.A., fast cars and even faster weapons have elevated gangs into small armies. The weapons of choice are full-automatic weapons with semiautomatics reserved for rookies. Assault weapons, like the AK-47, Tec 9, MAC, UZI or shotguns are preferred. Most gangs are created along ethnic and neighborhood lines. Bloods and Crips are the new Hatfields and McCoys. The *gangsta* look has become big business now. Baggy pants, work shirts, short hair, and that unique gangsta *lean* have all been adopted by freckle-faced kids from Iowa. Gangsta music has towheaded kids reciting tales of inner-city woes, just as their parents were able to recite *Ittsy Bittsy Teeny Weenie Yellow Polka Dot Bikini*. The new proponents of this violent/hip misogynistic culture seem to live life a little too close to their lyrics. Rappers Tupac Shakur and Snoop Doggy Dog both probably wish they were singing Barney's theme of *I love you, you love me*. In Los Angeles, there are over 800 gangs with 30,000 members. There are at least 1000 homicides every year and well over 1000 drive-by shootings. In 1993 L.A. officers were involved in 700 officer-involved shootings, 21 of them fatal.

According to figures presented to the White House, there are 500,000 gang members in 16,000 gangs in the U.S. Eight hundred American cities are home to these gangs, compared to 100 in 1970. Fifty-seven percent of towns with over 25,000 residents have reported gang-related incidents.

But gangsterism in America is not black, white and Hispanic. Gang members come in all flavors. The most dangerous gangs in America are the new Asian gangs, groups of Cambodian, Vietnamese, Laotian and Filipino youths whose families came from the refugee camps, killing fields and dung heaps of Southeast Asia. Chinese-American gang members are being blamed for the March 1996 murder of Cambodian actor Dr. Haing Ngor, a former refugee of the Khmer Rouge and the star of the 1984 movie *The Killing Fields*. After enduring four years of savage brutality under the Khmer Rouge during the guerrilla group's reign of terror between 1975 and 1979, the Academy Award-winning doctor was ironically slain in the land of the free, for a Buddhist amulet.

Your Next Door Neighbor

Four out of 10 violent crimes in the U.S. are committed by relations or acquaintances of the victims.

Militias

Militias were once social centers for good 'ole boys with a strong sense of gun love. Ignored by the mainstream press until the Oklahoma bombing, they were free to dress in army surplus gear and shoot off guns in the swamps of Florida or the mountains of Colorado. The Branch Davidians created a dangerous mix of Jesus, gunpowder and news attention and became targets for their insolence.

Now militias are in the spotlight, and they don't quite know what to do with their political notoriety. Given a few more longnecks and a couple of pinches of Skoal, it won't be long before they come up with a coherent political agenda.

The Southern Poverty Law Center has identified 440 self-proclaimed antigovernment militias. And they've infested every state in the union. The government calls them "Internet commandos," but is taking them quite seriously (see "The Babylonians"). Currently, there are 24 states where the higher-profile militias are in operation. California, Arizona, Nevada and Colorado make up the South/Western area while the Southeastern area includes Florida, Alabama, Georgia, Tennessee, Arkansas, Missouri, North Carolina and Virginia. There is also a Northeastern area that is composed of New York, New Hampshire, Ohio, Pennsylvania, Indiana and Wisconsin.

It is interesting to note that many of the militia groups are growing in popularity, thanks to Janet Reno and the massive television coverage of the immolation of the Branch Davidians. The most well-known militias in the good 'ole U.S.A. are the following:

Florida State Militia

A right-wing Christian group with about 500 members led by Robert Pummer.

Guardians of American Liberties (GOAL)

This Colorado-based group wants to be the mouthpiece for militias everywhere (probably in direct competition with the Unorganized Militia based in Indianapolis).

James "Bo" Gritz

Although Gritz is not a militiaman, he is very active in the militia business, giving commando training and survival courses. James "Bo" Gritz, an icon to the right-wing set and former Green Beret "bring 'em back alive" war hero, has done much to advance the MIA cause, because he was convinced that there were still live POWs in Southeast Asia. None ever were brought back alive or positively identified. He does so well as the poster boy and role model for the ultra right wing that he ran as vice presidential candidate in 1988 with David Duke. Gritz alleges there is a "parallel government," through which top American officials utilize arms smuggling and drug trafficking to support covert operations. At one speaking engagement in 1995 at a Holiday Inn in Visalia, California, Gritz burned a large U.N. flag onstage. He got back into the newspapers in April 1996, when he mediated the surrender of the "Freemen" holed up for a month in a shack in Montana during a standoff with the FBI.

Lone Star Militia

Leader Robert Spence (who bills himself as an Imperial Wizard of the True Knights of the Ku Klux Klan) says he heads up 11,000 militia members.

Militia of Montana (MOM)

John Trochman heads a little family-run militia in the wide-open, "Negro free" lands of Montana. This white supremacy group is reported to be working closely with the Aryan Nations Church in Hayden Lake, Idaho.

Northern Michigan Militia

It's cold in Michigan, so cold that it can freeze the rational parts of most folks brains. Considering the inclement weather and "band together or freeze" syndrome, it seems that joining a militia is the next favorite activity after ice fishing. Commander Norm Olsen manages to combine his skills as minister, gun store owner and former air force officer to lead his flock of 12,000 NMMS (Numbs?).

Police Against the New World Order

Although we couldn't find a *Yellow Pages* listing for the New World Order (we couldn't figure out if it was a Chinese restaurant or a church), apparently this group thinks "it's" out there. Probably the most famous and visible of the groups, PANWO(?) is captained by former Phoenix police officer Jack McLamb. McLamb was last seen nationally doing some expostulating and mugging for the camera with Bo Gritz at the ill-fated Waco compound.

Texas Constitutional Militia

Once headed by Jon Roland, the group claims 1500 members in 30 separate groups.

Unorganized Militia of the United States

Created by Linda Thompson, a lawyer from Indianapolis whose specialty seems to be suing the Federal government. The only nationally organized militia with far, far less members than the 3 million their PR claims.

The Babylonians

President Bill Clinton

Not a whacko, but the current rash of domestic terrorism—not seen since the bombings by radical students in the 1960s and early 1970s—has gotta be driving the man nuts. Responding to what Clinton termed "a wave of crime and violence" in America, the Senate passed a modified version of the president's crime bill in September 1994. It's difficult to say whether politicians are echoing public anger over crime or fueling it. Although most Americans believe the levels of crime have increased in recent years, some statistics say that they have indeed dropped. Whereas police statistics show that violent crime affects more than 180 Americans for every 100,000—up from 100 people in 1973—a recent National Crime Victimization Survey has shown the actual level to be slightly lower than 100 people per every 100,000.

Executive Working Group on Domestic Terrorism

This secret task force meets at the Justice Department every couple of weeks and plots strategy against the burgeoning number of boy scouts-turned-Abu Nidals. How much damage they're doing isn't certain, but since its inception in late 1995, the number of FBI investigations into militias around the country has increased 300 percent. The group is privately being called instrumental in stopping a Texas terrorist from blowing up Austin's IRS office in 1995.

The Mob

The Russians

The Russians started coming in the late 1970s and early 1980s—300,000 in all—when the Soviet government temporarily lifted immigration barriers allowing persecuted Soviet Jews to emigrate. Included in this batch was what the FBI terms as "second-echelon" criminals, who settled in Brighton Beach in Brooklyn. They basically beat up on each other, and the Feds stayed out of it. The second wave arrived after the collapse of the Soviet Union, when Russia upped the number of visas to the U.S. from 3000 a year to nearly 33,000—a more than 10-fold increase. Savage and unrepentant, the Russian mob counts on fear to scare its enemies—and doesn't think twice about wasting cops. In 1994, the FBI—with the help of the Russian Ministry of Internal Affairs (MVD)—got a tip on a top Moscow crime boss, Vyacheslav Ivankov, who was coming to New York to oversee the gang's U.S. operations. Ivankov was under surveillance once he got to the States and then made the mistake of extorting a couple of Russian emigrés who owned a Wall Street investment consulting firm. To show he was serious, Ivankov had one of the targets' father show up dead in a Moscow train station. Ivankov was later busted and ended up spitting at and kicking reporters after he was fingerprinted. The Feds have a lot more to learn about the Russian gangsters, who one MVD official categorized as "very tough, very smart, very educated and very violent."

The Triads and Tongs

The FBI knows quite a bit more about the Chinese *triads*, *tongs* and street gangs than they do about the Russians. The Chinese population in the U.S. has been spiraling for decades and have provided a far more penetrable profile for the Feds. They're well aware of the three tiers: the Hong Kong–based *triads*, the secretive criminal families that were on the scene well before the Sicilian mafia; the *tongs*, which are ostensibly Chinese-American business associations, but in reality crafty overseers of devious doings; and the Chinese-American street gangs brought in as enforcers. The *triads* and *tongs* do their biggest business bringing China white heroin into the U.S., but also dabble in the smuggling of Chinese illegal aliens. The *triads* get them to Mexico, or somewhere else knockin' on Uncle Sam's door, where the *tongs* take over and put the illegals to work at slave wages in sweat shops and whorehouses, where they have to pay off the *tongs* from US$30,000–50,000 for their freedom.

Cosa Nostra

See "In a Dangerous Place: New York City."

Right Wing Groups

There is a movement afoot in America, distrust of big government and a need to push back. There are two dispossessed groups in America. The first is the large groups of racial minorities who live in the inner cities; the other is the much larger group of whites who for whatever reason cannot avail themselves of the American Dream. Most of these folks are content to listen to Rush Limbaugh and throw empty beer cans at Bill Clinton on TV. Others gather together and create groups that commiserate and plot. Few ever do anything meaningful, but they do exist.

Luckily none of the right wing whacko groups are under the players sections. Although the names sound interesting, even a brief review of their political agenda or beliefs will convince you that many of these folks aren't firing on all cylinders. Most groups are poorly financed, loosely organized, like guns, think small, have few members, drink a lot of beer, live in the woods and usually have a pot bellied leader who likes to go by a goofy name as exalted something or grand poobah.

Klu Klux Klan

The Klan is probably the most well known hate group in the U.S. Known for decorating the south with flaming crosses, they now are more of a parody of the old guard right wing in America. Some people jokingly estimate that most remaining Klan members are actually FBI plants. (It could also be those dorky bed sheets they have to wear.) The Klan in North America has some proponents like Louis Beam (leader of the Fifth Era Klan) of Texas and Dennis Mahon (who leans more towards Tom Metzger's WAR movement) of Oklahoma who demand revolutionary violence. There are Klan-lite groups like the one led by Arkansas-based Thomas Robb who portray the Klan as the white man's nonviolent NAACP. For now they are targets of the FBI and left wing groups who prosecute the group on behalf of its victims for any hate crime.

White Aryan Resistance (WAR)

WAR is a group led by Tom Metzger, a television repairman who lives in rural Fallbrook California. He lost everything he had in a landmark lawsuit which determined he and the activities of his group were responsible for the beating and death of a man in the Pacific Northwest.

Christian Identity Groups

It's hard to believe that you could get enough people for a cocktail party under the premise that the most egregious "theft of culture" in human history was perpetrated by Satan and the Jews to dispossess the Anglo-Saxon and kindred peoples of their birthright but there are Christian Identity groups that use this basic pretext at their core. These folks also believe that the world is heading into an apocalypse soon. These folks blame the Jews for making them live in trailer parks and shanties and say that it will be payback time when the millennium rolls around.

National Alliance

The National Alliance is a Neo-Nazi group begun after leader William Pierce wrote a book called the *Turner Diaries* (under the pen name of Andrew McDonald). The radical right wing adopted the book about a Neo-Nazi underground group that kills Jews, blacks, and those whites guilty of "racemixing," as part of an effort to overthrow a Jewish-dominated government. The *Turner Diaries* is one of Timothy McVeigh's favorite books.

Odinism

Odinism is a Christian-based type religion that also includes ritual magic, anti-Semitism, and a desire to get back to the good old days when the Aryan race (Nordic/Germanic) was cool. Fellowship, Wiccan witchcraft, and a supremacist bent make this religion popular with white groups. Odinism has followers in Scandinavia, Germany, South Africa and America. Asatru is a belief much like Odinism, except for the racist part.

Mountain Kirk

The Mountain Kirk is Robert Miles' take on a medieval French sect called the Cathari. Miles passed on in 1992.

The Order

Robert Mathews' group known as the Order is a scrambled omelette made up of skinheads and National Socialists who are also Odinists.

Church of the Creator

Church of the Creator was created by a charismatic and highly authoritarian leader Ben Klausen who ministers via mail order. The COC centers on the belief that all religions are false since Christianity was built on a Jewish fable. Reverend Ben (he called himself "Pontifex Maximus") said that "creativity" is the thing, a blend of militant atheism, health faddism and racism is where it's at. The problem is that Ben offed himself and his followers can still be found primarily in Europe and the U.S.

Posse Comitatus

Posse Comitatus founded by William Potter Gale fights the idea of income tax.

Skinheads

The Anti-Defamation League estimates that there are a minimum of 3500 skinheads in the U.S. DP does not know how many prematurely bald men there are.

Getting In

Passport required. The United States has over 20 different types of visas indicating different reasons for travel. Visa type and length varies by country. Travelers from selected countries can stay for up to 90 days without a visa. New Zealand and Australian nationals need visas, not necessary for British citizens. Contact the nearest U.S. embassy or consulate to obtain visa information and requirements.

Getting Around

However you want to. The United States possesses perhaps the most modern and comprehensive transportation systems in the world, both private and public. As public transportation in the U.S. is not nationalized, you can expect different levels of service in different areas. Whereas New York City possesses an intricate public transit infrastructure, public transit in Los Angeles is still in the development stage. However, intercity and interstate transportation links in the U.S. are considered excellent. Problem areas are principally inner-city areas at night. Avoid late-night trips in these areas, due to the increased probability of crime.

Dangerous Places

Miami

Florida has the highest crime rate of all 50 states and Miami is now America's most dangerous city. In 1995, 41.3 million tourists flowed through Florida, so it may not seem like a big deal when one or two of them are offed. A Dutch tourist couple on their way to a shopping center in west Dade was robbed and murdered on February 23rd. After a brief respite of two years, it seems that the tourist death toll is beginning to climb again. The Dutch tourists were lost in the seedy area of Liberty City in Dade County in the mid-morning. They pulled into a gas station at the corner of 79th Street and 22nd Avenue to ask for directions. The husband went in to ask for directions, while the wife waited in the car with the doors locked and windows rolled up. Obviously, the three perpetrators could not believe their good luck when they went over and asked for the woman's earthly possessions. Frustrated by her lack of charity, they simply shot her through the window.

In Daytona Beach, a Canadian teenager was shot on March 15th while yakking on a pay phone around midnight. Seven youths ganged up on the kid, and he was shot during the robbery. Over 200,000 visitors descend on Daytona Beach during Spring Break.

Many tourists are victims of bump-and-rob scams in which the perpetrator rear-ends the victims on the highway and then robs them as they pull over to exchange info. Miami is home to thieves who like to create confusion by spilling food, asking directions or bumping into you while their accomplice grabs your belongings. These folks tend to be from South America.

Atlanta

This southern city has the dubious distinction of possessing one of the highest crime rates in North America. The F.B.I. headed a counterterrorism network to neutralize any terrorist threats at the 1996 Olympic Summer Games in Atlanta. Then a pipe bomb planted by a "good ole boy" killed two innocent people and injured nearly 200 other attendees.

Los Angeles

The men (and women) in blue that patrol the home of the cop show and home of gangsta' rap are proud to announce that crime is actually down in L.A. Whether it is our videotaped beating of traffic offenders, turning thugs into music stars or putting on top-rated trials of former football stars, L.A. must be doing something right. Total crimes fell from 312,415 in 1993 to 278,352 in 1994. Murders were down from 1076 to 846. It would appear that no one has notified the 1140 street gangs that rule the night in L.A.'s poor neighborhoods. There are an estimated 142,000 gang members in L.A.'s South Central—10,000 make their livings simply by selling crack—and the strip that connects downtown to the harbor like a digestive tract is still the most dangerous place in L.A. Apart from the 230 black and Latino gangs identified by the L.A.P.D., there are some 80 Asian gangs that specialize in burglary and carjackings. The L.A.P.D. has started issuing shotguns to its motorcycle officers to meet "the firepower carried by many criminals."

New Orleans

It's not the bad guys here that make "The Big Easy" so damn uneasy. It's the cops. The New Orleans Police Department is considered the most corrupt and brutal major city force in the U.S. Currently, an FBI investigation is ongoing into police abuses of civil liberties and overall corruption in the department. A few years ago, the week before Rodney King was clobbered by the cops in L.A., a DP contributor was arrested and beaten by the police in New Orleans—he was hauled in on drug trafficking and prostitution charges after he had been seen giving an impoverished black guy (he's white) a few dollars for directing him to an ATM in the French Quarter. But the good-ole-boy attorney network in N.O. went to work for him. His attorney played golf with a prominent judge a few days later and got the charges dropped—and it only cost him five grand. During a subsequent attempt to sue the department and the city, he was informed that the highest damages he would receive would total no more than $3000, that the city was bankrupt and that any damage award would be paid over 18 years.

The murder rate dropped 14 percent in New Orleans in 1995. Still in the French Quarter, it is best to stay south of North Rampart Street and keep to the center of the street. Do not stop if someone asks you for the time. The housing projects are rife with crime—Desire, Florida and B.W. Cooper are the worst. Do not visit the cemeteries after dark.

Anchorage, Alaska

Yeah, Anchorage, we hate to say it. This city of 260,000 has finally caught up to the 20th century. There are drivebys, crack houses, handguns and Uzis—in the hands of teenagers.

There were more than 25 homicides in Anchorage in 1995, tying a record. The Crips and the Bloods are here. Even the Mexican and Asian gangstas have arrived, all wearing colors. And the legal climate in Alaska offers a warm welcome to young criminals and thugs, if the weather doesn't. Under Alaskan law, first- and second-time juvenile offenders are typically punished with a letter that is sent to their parents from authorities. "We still have laws from the 'Leave it to Beaver' era," Alaska Governor Tony Knowles said, "for thugs from the 'Terminator' age."

Schools

School used to be a simple red building with a bell on top and belle inside. Today, some high schools use metal detectors and armed security guards to keep the peace. Recently in Los Angeles, a five-year study proved once and for all that schools are safer than the neighborhoods around them. For example, gun use was down from 391 reported incidents in 1990–'91 to 291 in 1994. Assaults were down to a paltry 99, battery almost disappeared at 686, and assault with a deadly weapon was a nonevent with only 291 incidents of students, teachers or school employees being attacked or threatened with knives, pipes and guns. Child molestation and rape was edging up to 477 incidents, and robbery (to buy more guns?) was up at 461. Incidents of marijuana usage at school were exploding from 185 in 1990–'91 to 729, and burglaries were almost nonexistent at 946. If you want to know which age group was responsible for all this raping, shooting, burning, stealing, beating and doping, it was 14-year-olds. Remember these are the crime statistics just for L.A. *schools.*

The South

The southern states lead the U.S. in per-capita murder rates. Seven of the 10 states with the highest murder rates are in the South. The U.S. is the most murder-prone country in the developed world.

Minnesota During the Winter

A Minnesota home is the most dangerous place in the state to be when it comes to fire. There were 40 residential fire deaths in the state in 1994. By November 1995, that year's death toll had swelled to 62—still early in the home heating season. The most dangerous time of the year? The week between Christmas and New Year's Day, when winter heating, decorative lights, holiday cooking and too much booze make Minnesota such a kinetic kettle of embers that the state fathers are considering flying in B-17s from California and placing Red Adair on 24-hour call at the Wisconsin border. Ouch.

Minneapolis

It's not just home heating killings making the news in Minnesota. While murders are going down in some major U.S. cities, the rate is soaring in Minneapolis (pop. 368,383)—approaching even those found in New York and Washington, D.C. By the middle of August 1995, Minneapolis had already topped its yearly record for homicides; there were 67 killings by mid-August, four more than the total for all of 1991, previously the city's deadliest year. Nearly three-quarters of the victims were black, although blacks make up only 13 percent of the population.

The Most Dangerous Cities in the U.S.

Although Uniform Crime Report (UCR) statistics released by the FBI show a slight decrease in overall crime, the report found that minorities remain in the grasp of a major crime wave. Black teens between 16 and 19 years old are becoming victims of serious crimes at nearly seven times the national rate. Blacks in America are three times more likely than whites to be victims of violent crimes. Cities with the highest populations do not necessarily possess the highest crime rates.

	Most Dangerous	Safest
1.	Miami, FL	Johnstown, PA
2.	New York, NY	Wheeling, WV
3.	Tallahassee, FL	Parkersburg, Marietta, WV/OH
4.	Baton Rouge, LA	Williamsport, PA
5.	Jacksonville, FL	Altoona, PA
6.	Dallas, TX	Scranton, Wilkes-Burre, PA
7.	Los Angeles, CA	Sharon, PA
8.	Gainesville, FL	Danville, VA
9.	West Palm Beach/Boca Raton, FL	Lancaster, PA
10.	New Orleans, LA	Danbury, CT
11.	Fayetteville, NC	Utica, Rome, NY
12.	St. Petersburg, Clearwater, FL	Wausau, WI

Source: Places Rated Almanac, based on F.B.I. and city crime statistics

Dangerous Things

Murder

About 70 people are murdered each day in the U.S. The U.S. homicide rate is 17 times greater than Japan's, and 10 times the rate in Germany, France and Greece. Louisiana has the highest homicide rate in the country, with 18.5 murders per every 100,000 people. Anywhere in the South is dangerous; the southern states possess the highest rates in the country. But the place where you're most likely to be snuffed is in the nation's capital; a whopping 66.5 people are murdered in Washington, D.C., for every 100,000 people. Males between the ages 15 and 24 are most likely to commit murder. Men commit 91 percent of the murders in the U.S.

Being Black

African-Americans make up about half of the murder victims in the U.S. Young African-Americans are more likely to be killed than any other segment in the country.

Being an Immigrant in California

Immigrants are more likely to be wasted than people born in the United States. Between 1970 and 1972, immigrants were the victims in about 23 percent of the homicides in California, even though they represented only 17 percent of the population. Non-Latino white immigrants, most of whom emigrate from European countries, are more than twice as likely to be the victim of a homicide than U.S.-born whites.

Terrorism

The number of terrorist incidents in the United States had declined each year from 1982 through 1994 (except for 1986), according to an FBI intelligence division report issued in late August 1995. From a high point of 51 incidents in 1982, the count had dropped to four in 1992, for a total of 165 over the entire 11-year period, according to the division's counterterrorism section. In addition, there were 44 suspected terrorist incidents in the U.S. during the same period, with most in 1989. The 165 incidents included 77 involving Puerto Rico, 23 by left-wing groups, 16 by Jewish extremists, 12 by anti-Castro Cubans, six by right-wing groups, and 31 by various other groups. The preferred targets were commercial establishments (60 incidents), followed by military targets (33), state and federal property (31), private property (18) and diplomatic establishments (17). The preferred regions were Puerto Rico (65), northeastern U.S. (53), western states (20) and southern states (19). Also according to the FBI, 74 terrorist incidents were prevented in the U.S. during the same period.

Although the State Department's annual report on incidents of "international" terrorism (as distinct from the "domestic" U.S. terrorism as described by the FBI) showed a 17-year low (361 incidents), officials spoke of "ominous signs" of escalation. Boy, were they right.

In 1995, there were more incidents of terrorism on U.S. soil than there were in Lebanon. For the first time, the U.S. jumped into the Top 20 list of nations experiencing the highest levels of terrorism and other forms of political violence. The U.S. placed 19th on the terrorism list for 1995, one place behind 18th-place Spain and one spot ahead of number-20 Lebanon.

The most deadly act was the April 19th bombing of the Federal Building in Oklahoma City. Only five days later, the Unabomber struck, killing the president of the California Forestry Association in Sacramento with a parcel bomb.

Twenty-one incidents were directed at abortion clinics and doctors involved in performing abortions, and other incidents were motivated by opposition to the U.S. government.

A TWA 747 was blown out of the sky in July of 1996 killing 230 people over Long Island. It fell from 8000 feet and many watched its fatal descent. At press time the F.B.I. was piercing the plane back together seeking clues to the perpetrator.

AIDS

According to the U.S. Centers for Disease Control, in 1993, AIDS surpassed accidents as the leading cause of death for Americans between 24 and 44 years old. For every 100,000 people, about 35 die of AIDS, about 32 die in accidents.

Methamphetamine

Meth has become the drug of the '90s, and the deadly high is taking its toll. Methamphetamine-related deaths nearly tripled between 1991 and 1994, from 151 to 433. In places like L.A., San Francisco, San Diego and Phoenix, methamphetamine-induced emergency rooms cases showed triple-digit increases during those same years. With the heat on and the decreasing popularity of cocaine, the Mexican drug cartels have started turning to meth, the biggest being the Amezcua cartel. The group operates clandestine labs in Guadalajara and Tijuana and cells in California. One lab that was seized by the DEA in Guadalajara by Mexican police in February 1995 could produce 2640 pounds of meth a month. Hundreds of metric tons of ephedrine, the principal ingredient in meth, are being shipped to Mexican front companies from India, Switzerland, China and the Czech Republic. Even with a 1994 seizure of 3.4 metric tons of ephedrine at Dallas/Ft. Worth Airport, the DEA has yet to scratch the surface.

Small Aircraft

Over the past five years, regional airlines, flying mostly turboprops, have averaged 5.1 accidents per million departures. Commuter carriers, flying planes with 30 seats or fewer, have averaged 6.6 accidents. The big carriers, flying jets, have averaged 2.9 accidents for the same number of departures.

Driving or Owning a Car

Driving a car is 20 times more dangerous than flying, the statistics say. Half of all traffic-related fatalities involve alcohol. Car theft is considered the number-two crime problem after drugs. Over 80,000 cars are stolen every year in America. Many of them end up in Central America and the Caribbean. For example, when officials sent back a list of cars registered in Belize, they found that 80 percent were stolen. El Salvador is said to have at least 20,000 hot cars with equal numbers in Guatemala, Honduras, and Colombia and Argentina has twice as many.

Fatal Crash Rates per 100 Million Miles Traveled	
Alaska	2.077
Nevada	1.757
Montana	1.603
New Mexico	1.481
Wyoming	1.309
Idaho	1.221
Arizona	1.210
Mississippi	1.194
Utah	1.156
Colorado	1.104

Car-jacking is the simple act of stealing a car while someone is still in it. This new form of theft is an outcome of all the many safety devices created to foil thefts once a car is parked. Carjackings usually occur in the right lane at a stop light or in parking lots where the thief has an exit.

Most carjackers never get caught. Out of the 1.7 million vehicles stolen last year, only 17 percent of the perpetrators were caught. Some tips are to keep your windows rolled up and locked and do not give directions to young males who approach you from the street. Watch for people waiting by your car, as you walk up to it. Also, turn off and lock your car when you use ATM machines.

Slowing down makes for better fuel economy. It also bores the hell out of people in the West. As you can see by the death rates in the chart below, it is hard to tell whether it is high speeds or pure boredom that kills folks faster in the wide open spaces. Lowering speeds has reduced the fatality rate in America. Now that the speed limit has jumped up to 65m.p.h., the death rate jumped 21 percent from 1.4 deaths per 100 million miles to 1.7. The only good news is that the death rate way back in pre-air-bag 1973 was a whopping 2.3 deaths per 100 million miles traveled.

America's Most Dangerous Highways (Fatalities per 100 Million Miles Traveled)		
1.	I-90 (Silver Bow, Montana)	6.206
2.	I-70 (Emery, Utah)	4.136
3.	I-15 (Beaverhead, Montana)	4.031
4.	I-25 (San Miguel, New Mexico)	3.749
5.	I-10 (Crockett, Texas)	3.511
6.	I-59 (Lamar, Mississippi)	3.342
7.	I-15 (Millard, Utah)	3.250
8.	I-27 (Lubbock, Texas)	3.233
9.	I-80 (Churchill, Nevada)	3.197

THE UNITED STATES

America's Most Dangerous Highways (Fatalities per 100 Million Miles Traveled)	
10. I-20 (Ector, Texas)	**3.108**
U.S. Average	**0.645**

Rental Cars

Tourists driving rental cars are easy marks for thieves, muggers, rapists and murderers. Although the car rental firms have pulled their identifying badges off their cars in most areas of the country, cunning criminals can still ascertain a vehicle belonging to a rental firm through its license plate numbers. Confused tourists doing circles around the airport looking for the beach or the hotel are plum pickin's for carjackings and other crimes. Particularly dangerous areas are the urban sunspots, such as Miami, Ft. Lauderdale and Los Angeles.

Handguns

Americans own more than 6.7 million handguns (200 million of all types of guns), and aren't afraid to use them. Firearms send almost 40,000 Americans to their graves each year.

Murder One

Fifty-six murderers were put to death in 1995 in the U.S., nearly twice as many as the year before. It was the largest number in four decades. Texas led the bandwagon of the 16 states that executed prisoners in 1995, putting to death 19 inmates.

Teenagers with Guns

Juvenile killings with guns rose fourfold between 1984 and 1994; the number of pubescent offenders rose from 500 in 1984 to nearly 2400 in 1994. Handguns were the choice in 66 percent of all juvenile killings involving guns over a recent 15-year span.

Getting Sick

Excellent health care is available throughout the U.S. Medical facilities and supplies, including medicines, are in abundance. The level of medical training of U.S. doctors is considered excellent. Foreign visitors without medical insurance will be expected to pay in cash or by credit card where accepted. No special precautions are required.

Hassles with the Police

The U.S. features one of the most disciplined and honest police structures in the world. However, there are the bad apples. Prejudiced detainment of travelers is frequent. Use of excessive force, particularly in the inner cities, occurs frequently. False arrest occurs less frequently but is also common in the inner cities. Police response time in most areas of the U.S. is considered excellent. Police in rural areas are known to stop speeders and demand immediate payment for traffic violations. Refusal to pay will result in free room and board.

Dangerous Days	
03/25/1996	Standoff began in Jordan, Montana, between 20 armed "Freemen" and more than 100 FBI agents after two of the Freemen's leaders were jailed over a $1.8 million fraudulent check scheme.
04/19/1995	Bombing of the Alfred P. Murrah Federal Building in Oklahoma City, which killed 167 and injured more than 400.
03/04/1994	Four convicted in the bombing of the World Trade Center.
03/01/1993	Law agents besieged Texas Davidian religious cult, after six were killed in raid at Waco.

Dangerous Days

02/26/1993   New York's World Trade Center was bombed by Islamic extremists.

06/05/1968   Robert F. Kennedy assassinated.

04/05/1968   Martin Luther King assassinated.

11/22/1963   President John F. Kennedy assassinated.

09/06/1901   President William McKinley assassinated.

07/02/1881   President James A. Garfield assassinated.

04/14/1865   President Abraham Lincoln assassinated.

In a Dangerous Place

Los Angeles: Having a Riot

Above Los Angeles, aboard a Delta jetliner that's had to deviate from its approach due to zero visibility, the result of thick black plumes of smoke billowing into the sky, the captain announces to the passenger cabin: "Ladies and gentlemen, the city of Los Angeles is in a state of civil unrest. We will be landing. However, we must urge you in no uncertain terms to use extreme caution in reaching your final destination. Lawlessness and violence exist in many areas of the metropolitan region. A Delta representative will be at the gate to advise you about which sections of the city should not be traveled through under any circumstances."

A petite dental hygienist in 26B turns and says to a long-haired record store manager from Van Nuys in 26A: "So? What else is new?"

The scene here is pure Beirut. Pillars of thick black smoke rise straight up in the hot windless afternoon. Looking down from the hill where I live, I see dozens (I counted at least 120) of puffy dark columns rising up from Long Beach in the south to the Valley to the north. Down there, people are looting, burning, killing, maiming and beating each other up. In the air over 20 helicopters circle and swoop like hawks. Onboard are video cameras with new image stabilizers that make your living room feel like the cockpit of a Huey going into a hot LZ. The cameras are in tight. Kids look up and make victory signs as they hustle six-packs, clothes, backyard toys, 19-inch televisions and even mattresses out of shattered storefront windows. Ostensibly, the black community is angered at the "not guilty" verdict in the Rodney King trial. King, a known criminal, was stopped, detained and beaten into submission. Had a neighbor not captured the scene on videotape, Rodney would have been just like any one of L.A.'s petty hoodlums. Today, he is a lucky man. His violated civil rights have elevated him to the level of celebrity and wealthy icon of America's need to punish itself for not doing the right thing.

Because the television viewers can see the expressions of joy on the faces of the looters, we know this is shopping time. These folks are tired of paying retail for the American Dream, and they are going straight for that Friday night Smith & Wesson discount. This isn't necessarily about race nor is it necessarily about anger; it's about maximizing the one benefit of being forced to live in the foul, wasted bowels of one of America's wealthiest cities. It's payback time. Poverty means not being able to buy all the things they sell incessantly on TV. Well, now every looter in South Central L.A. is rich.

Normally, the merchants of the inner city have iron bars, security guards, video cameras, buzzers, 911 autodialers, shotguns taped under counters and fast-draw waist holsters to enforce compliance with their usurious prices. Anyone who tries for a five-finger discount (a stickup) is either gunned down, picked up, or chased down with police helicopters, dogs and car patrols. This day, the balance is out of whack, big time.

Although the police try to put a lid on the initial drunken violence, they are quickly outnumbered. Fearing for their safety, the police try driving by to scare off the first malcontents. When the spectators start throwing beer cans and rocks at the cop cars, they beat a hasty retreat. The police are reigned in by politics and overly sensitive to the violence that must be dealt out to contain the looters. They are prisoners in their stations. When the word goes out over the news that the police are not going in, all hell breaks loose. For the first time since the '60s, America looks straight into the face of its dispossessed and blinks.

Business stops; people dash to their cars and head home. Along with most residents of L.A., the police watch the mayhem live on television and wonder how it will end.

On the street, looters are methodically knocking off first liquor stores, then the big chain stores. The Koreans, the only people tough enough to run the inner-city five-and-dimes, waited a long time for this day. They finally have a chance to use all that German and American firepower they have been practicing with and oiling for years.

Any visitor to L.A.'s shooting ranges can't help but notice the Asian shooters with their black Cordura bags full of expensive and well-oiled weapons. They range from shotguns to 9mm handguns to MAC 10s and AKs, many with full-automatic capability.

As the riot rages, the Koreans luckily never get to use all their ammo and those weapons. The looters think twice and focus on the national chain electronics and camera stores.

The 911 lines are jammed with terrified people who have spotted cars full of "black" men or "Hispanics" in their white neighborhoods. The police inform the people that they are responsible for the safety of their neighborhood, not for the safety of individuals or their private property. Suddenly, people start rummaging in the attic for their old WWII-era Garands, hunting rifles, even BB guns. Gun stores quickly sell out of ammunition, and the city works fast to ban gun sales as they hit record highs. People now sit in their Barca Loungers, watching the news, waiting for the first sign of looters heading into their neighborhood.

As in *War of the Worlds*, people sit glued to their television screens and radios tracking the spread of the violence. Reports come in from Beverly Hills, Orange County and Newport Beach—some false, all inflated, but ominous just the same. The rioters move to the north like locusts. Along the way, some business owners, tired of eking out a miserable existence, clean out their cash registers and torch their own businesses.

Coskun calls me from Istanbul. Always the photographer, he asks, What's it like, are you getting pictures? The world has learned that L.A is in flames and its black population has risen up. I tell him that years of hard knocks have taught me that driving my nice new car into a maelstrom of fire, smoke, bullets, looters and thugs is probably not a wise idea.

Into the night, coverage from helicopters gives us all the amazing sight of hundreds of glowing fires over the Los Angeles Basin.

Once the drinking lets up and the National Guard rolls in, the riots subside. Many proud new owners of ironing boards, car stereos and toasters can't wait to try them out. Driving through the worst hit area is no different from visiting Groxny, Beirut or any other burned-out war zone, except there are no bodies on the street and the curious splatter marks from RPGs and 50-caliber bullets are absent. In the aftermath, the civic leaders pledge to rebuild L.A and a committee is formed to do absolutely nothing. Most inner-city business owners decide that the snow in Iowa looks a lot more inviting than the white soot that gently falls on their burned-out lot.

When it was all over, there were 52 people dead, 2383 injured, 10,000 arrested, 4500 buildings or homes destroyed and $735 million in property damage.

In a Dangerous Place

New York City: All in the Family

There are Americans who have never heard of either Fort Apache or the Bronx. Even more draw a blank when they hear the conceit that forever links the two in Paul Newman's faded hit, *Fort Apache, the Bronx*, now too dated for the late, late movie.

As it happens, there really is a precinct house in the Bronx dubbed, for good reason, Fort Apache. Nor has the movie faded without leaving a trace. However unfamiliar they are with either the Bronx or Fort Apache, the image linking the two seems to have become part of America's shared image of New York City.

Badlands of broken glass, rats, smack and crack cocaine. Cars stripped and abandoned, buildings abandoned, decaying blocks of ten-story tenements yawning on, block after grey, treeless block—police besieged.

Entering the zone now, we find ourselves cruising into a vision of life as we know it falling apart. Rotting garbage, gangs, men, women too, passed out on the street (junkies or just winos?), resurgent TB, methadone clinics reeking of urine, dank subways, death by AIDs, hepatitis, mugging. There have been attempts at rehabilitation, and one going on right now has done a lot, but the South Bronx is still the South Bronx.

In better neighborhoods, steel bars and clanking tambours protect bodegas and botanicas. Here, they protect nothing. The bodegas and botanicas are gone. There used to be do-wop and salsa groups on the corners. In other neighborhoods, street corners showcase salsa and rap. Here, it's just sullen kids with baggy shorts pulled low. They give you directions in New Yorican, that vibrant patois of Rosie Perez, with vowels sometimes Brooklyn, sometimes Latin. Here, the Spanish accent is especially heavy, but when you ask directions in Spanish, you realize that New Yorican is their native language. They can't speak Spanish.

As for the South Bronx, yesterday's bad memory is today's bad trip. A bad place, with little reason to linger. But by itself, it's not what makes New York a dangerous place. Badlands as grim as this are not exactly rare, but neither do they blanket the city.

In a way, what makes New York dangerous is what makes it one of the world's great places.

Fort Apache No More

All news is not bad news in the Big Apple, but the latest doesn't bode well for New York's street scum. The cops have started to crack their whips and are tossing slime into the slammer. In 1990, there were 2245 murders committed in the city. In 1995, there were fewer than 1200—for the first time since 1973.

The Players

The Thugs

Akbar Community Services has been around for a while. Now it has offices in a storefront on Livonia Avenue in the Bedford-Stuyvesant section of Brooklyn. Next year it could be gone. But the likes of Akbar Community Services are unlikely to be gone. It's the right time and the right place for playing the Akbar game.

It goes like this: For years, the skilled construction trades were a tough nut to crack for minority workers. To some extent, they still are. While mid-level white-collar jobs, and especially government jobs, have enormously increased minority staff, progress has been real but slower in the skilled blue-collar trades, which should be a more practical rung up for populations trapped in poverty. But mix residual (and often not so residual) blue-collar prejudice, along with the modest hiring progress their skilled trade unions have made, with the fact that many minorities don't have the skills, and the bottom line has been that while middle-class minorities have leaped ahead, the skilled trades have not offered nearly the same opportunity for the minorities. And it's the minorities who have by far the most critical need for help...and who make for the danger in New York's most dangerous places.

Enter Akbar Community Services. Any major construction contract, and they organize the community to make sure minorities are hired. Makes perfect sense. Makes a perfect scam. For one thing, big contractors in New York City have been filling their unskilled ranks with minority labor for years. For another, unless he's got a sweetheart deal, which is not unheard of, the contractor is in a competitive business. When it comes to skilled jobs, he can't afford to hire more less-qualified minorities than the competition does, which is to say what the law makes them hire, and they do hire, not out of the goodness of their hearts but because they can't offer competitive bids if they have to figure the cost of going to court into the price.

In fact, court is what Akbar, for the record, threatens; lots of minority hiring suits have been brought, and with some success. But these suits, at least not the successful ones, weren't brought by Akbar or the outfits like Akbar spread out among the boroughs. In fact, court is not their real threat. Their real threat, as their front man hands the manager of the construction site his business card, is the van full of guys looking bored, some with boom boxes, some with ball bats, some with box-cutters and foot-long lengths of 3/4 inch galvanized pipe. Likewise, jobs are not what they really want. They have to insist on a few, but what they really want, and not just a few, are dollars.

It's such a lucrative business that there are between 55 and 65 outfits like Akbar heavily represented in virtually every borough except Staten Island.

In early '95, a major brawl broke out at a construction site in the center of Manhattan, just a few blocks from the New York Police Department's Midtown South Precinct. Major rehabilitation work was being done to the Times Square area, and at first it seemed the brawl was between workers at the site and one of the minority coalitions demanding work. And not just a little dust-up. As tourists and businesspeople looked on, men jumped out of vans, rushing up 42nd Street, pipes raised. Then as tourists and business-people dove for cover, shots cracked through the normal din of traffic, followed by sirens, and bleeding men were carried away in ambulances, one of them from a gunshot wound.

In fact, workers at the site weren't involved at all. The battle was between two of the minority coalitions, in open combat in mid-Manhattan over which one got the payoff.

In the Bronx, East Harlem and sections of Brooklyn like Crown Heights, Bedford-Stuyvesant and Red Hook, it's distinctly worse. Here, the contractors are often minority, and negotiations with minority contractors in particular can be especially short, running something like this:

"We don't think enough of your work force is minority."

"My work force is a hundred percent minority."

And that's it. For those who pay up, the cost on a small to medium-size contract is $4000 to $7000 a week. Those who don't pay up come home each day, check their answering machines for messages, listen to the death threats, and then, like you and me, they routinely erase them.

Both local and federal prosecutors are doing what they can, but this business has become so common that, for cops, listening to yet another series of death threats on a yet another contractor's answering machine is not altogether unlike wasting time on paperwork for a fender bender.

The Organizations

On their own, tough New York cops like Robert Morgenthau, Rudolph Giuliani and William Bratton have put the squeeze on crime. Meantime, the Medelin cartel's Jaime Escobar has been smoked, a boon to the Cali cartel. But even as they reap this windfall, it proves too much for their most crucial staffers, i.e., the ones who do the laundry. One after another, compromised U.S. bankers and businessmen, a couple of them Chassidic rabbis, have been caught by the Maytag repairmen of the FBI. And above all, the RICO statutes, which permit the Feds to go after criminal organizations rather than individual criminals, have been acting a little like the Sherman antitrust act of the criminal world. This is what makes the drug trade these days such a dangerous one: None of the events just recited has done a thing to dampen the market for drugs, but as it corners the big boys, it opens worlds of dangerous opportunity for upstarts.

This does not mean that one-time street dealers in Manhattan's notorious Washington Heights are the capos of the future. Nor does it mean that the *organizatsiyas*, the new mobs from the Ukraine and Russia, are going to take over. Drugs are in fact among their rackets, but they have many more going, from running bootleg gasoline to bootleg cigarettes to insurance fraud to murder for hire, and, in any case, they do not have the easiest access to the drug market.

The Brighton Beach Bath and Racquet Club will close soon and that has more than nostalgic meaning. The *organizatsiyas* really sort of liked Brighton Beach and put their stamp on it. Where else in America can you sit down in a restaurant where they serve vodka by the carafe? But they were starting to get around anyway, looking at the bigger picture, and with the baths closing, that just puts the clincher on it. New York City's Russian Mafia is already going nationwide.

Specifically, the New York *organizatsiya* is now operating in Boston, Philadelphia and Los Angeles. A Los Angeles grand jury has already indicted one *kapusta*, Michael Smushkevich, for a billion dollar insurance fraud in which Americans were offered free medical exams over the phone. Those who took up the offer ended up signing forms that surrendered their medical benefits to the *organizatsiya*, which then collected from insurance companies for the "free exams."

We can only hope the restaurants last. The carafes of vodka are the least of it. Where else can you get an assortment of cold cuts that includes smoked chubb, jellied beef feet, fat veal and that *basterma* advertised by halal butchers over on Eighth Avenue? Where else can you enjoy all this while the band goes wild and the patrons jump up in spontaneous dance? Even if you come early, they'll have "Family Feud" on TV, and for dessert there's something only a Russian could come up with: Chocolate Potatoes.

To go with it, a full cup of Turkish coffee. Brighton Beach is the only place in the world where I've seen Turkish coffee served in an American-sized cup.

The Odessa Mafia has made Brighton Beach their new-world neighborhood. There are occasional shootouts in its string of new restaurants, where fastidiously prepared Georgian, Ukrainean and Russian delights are served beneath those decorative basketball-sized balls of bluish cut-glass that were popular in the fifties. As you get off the subway, a blond-haired man once Soviet and now drunk stumbles on in a Roadrunner T-shirt.

Brighton Beach and its boardwalk show every sign of seedy health, a Georgian Black Sea resort transported to the Atlantic, with girls, comely girls, beefy and true *babushkas*, which is what Russians call their doughy little grandmothers, after the scarves, the *babushkas*, they forever wrap around their heads.

Only these *babushkas* wouldn't be caught dead in a *babushka*. One was wearing a tight Calvin Klein T-shirt that said "Paris." Behind her, on the landward side of the boardwalk, was a big sign, nicely executed, with the professional gloss of the '40s.

But that's just what you can see. What's out of sight is the *organizatsiya* with ties to the Columbo and Lucchese families. These boys call their capo *kapusta*, and their core business is bootleg gasoline, jewel robberies, and murder for hire. Needless to say, in this sort of world, no one is created equal, least of all *kapustas*. Vyacheslav Lyubarsky was a *kapusta* of sorts, making pretty good money, they say. In fact, his son Alexei was something of a *kapusta* himself. Until January 12, 1992, when they were both murdered.

Right now two *organizatsiyas* are jockeying for power in Brighton Beach. The Brooklyn DA's office says they're importing hit men from Russia, which is having its own crime boom. Hit men from Russia work cheap—contracts run in the $2000 to $3000 range. On the black market back home that can bring a half million rubles, which for now is a fortune.

That's a problem, but the fundamental problem is the U.S.-based *organizatsiyas* that put out the contracts. Just one in Brighton Beach, known on the street as Monya's Brigada, has handled volume drug traffic and extortion rackets, but they have competition, and some other headaches, too.

In mid-March of '95, in the Adriatic town of Fano, Italian police arrested Monya Elson, the Brigada's 44-year-old *kapusta*. In Manhattan, he was indicted on a laundry list of charges, among them, contracting the murders of Vyacheslav Lyubarsky and his son Alexander.

The Mob

No metaphorical pun intended. In the dangerous places of the New York of lore, the mob is stage center. The New York of lore, however, does not exist. What exists is a reality both less sensational and less pat. New York is unfathomable.

Right now the mob is tired. Some strong prosecutors, federal and local, lawyers like Robert Morgenthau and Rudolf Giuliani, have put the squeeze on outfits whose vaunted traditions of silence and honor have commanded so much frightened respect, thereby winning such notoriety, that notoriety has led to familiarity, which, as we all know, breeds contempt. What better targets. Dapper John Gotti is dapper as ever in prison (that kind of dapper is more than threads), but Gotti had been untouchable. The direction in which he had been trying to move, some 20 years ago, was that of rackets run with such businesslike skill that fronts wouldn't be just fronts; they'd be smart, conservative investments, at once more credible as generators of income that really came from rackets, but with greater opportunity for deception in their books. On top of that, they spent more money for good accountants and good lawyers. And on top of that, RICO.

Where do you find the silk-suited vipers with the razor-cut hairdo? Along with similarly isolated neighborhoods like Bensonhurst in Brooklyn, Arthur Avenue has a reputation of being more the redoubt these days of the mob than shrinking Little Italy. Umberto's Clam House in Little Italy used to draw mobsters with its reputation for seafood oreganato; it now draws tourists with its reputation as the place where Joey Gallo met his maker in a tabloid burst of small arms fire.

The salumerias are moving to Arthur Avenue, as are the osterias and the mob.

On Arthur Avenue, you can even get *pasta fazool*. Only that's not what they'll call it on the menu. Physically, Arthur Avenue is vintage Italian-American. A lot more salumerias and osterias than you'd find in your average Italian-American neighborhood, but neither is this Gore Vidal's Rome. It's restaurants are dark and ornate, with floral carpets, gold leaf, dark paneling (don't look too close—it's four-by-eight sheets of Masonite), a foam-cast replica of Michelangelo's *David* staring over your shoulder as you stuff your face. Or maybe it's the master's rendering of Perseus holding up the head of Medusa by the snakes that grow out of her scalp; from his perch on top of the cigarette machine, he stares down at the perfectly prepared calamari before you.

However, as those robustly stocked salumerias suggest, Arthur Avenue is more than spaghetti and meatballs. Never mind the kitsch; white-coated waiters speak real Italian, and if it's a steaming bowl of pasta fazool you want on a frigid winter day, you'll find it on the menu as *pasta e fagiole*. (An echo of America's dangerous places past, when Sicilians were sometimes called A-rabs by seemingly ignorant American rubes. For six hundred years, Sicily was, in fact, Arab; the Mafia has roots in Arab resistance to the conquering Papacy, and to this day, what Italians call beans—*fagiole*—both Sicilians and Arabs call *fazooli*. Pasta fazool!)

Given the direction organized crime was going when they were enacted, the RICO statutes may be working better than the wizards who mixed this brew ever hoped. In being able to go after a bad guy just because he can be proven to be a member of a criminal enterprise, rather than for committing any individual crime, prosecutors were handed one wicked weapon. Meantime, dovetailing with RICO, the FBI has shifted from a focus on tracing crimes back to criminals to a focus on criminal organizations.

For years, New York's Coliseum on Columbus Circle at the southwest corner of Central Park was famous as the venue for a national convention, and then, for years it was infamous as the place not to book a convention. The mob had seized control of its union, turning it into such a craven patronage mill that the Coliseum priced itself out of the market.

Then along with RICO came New York State with the Javits Center, purposely-built to upstage the Coliseum and its mob-controlled union. Then aggressive prosecutors. Competition from the Cali and Medellin drug cartels. Gotti put away. Bloody noses as they tried to hang onto the Fulton Street Fish Market.

But then they haven't exactly retreated to Bensonhurst and Arthur Avenue.

While all this was going on, mob interests were taking control of the Teamsters local at—you guessed it—the Javits Center, which had virtually priced itself, and New York, out of the convention market. In February 1995, under fire for rank corruption at its local, the International seized control.

But nobody claims the last chapter has been written. Meantime, the mob is working out relationships with the likes of New York's Columbian drug traffickers, Chinese *tongs* and Russian racketeers that focus more on a role as godfather than competition. The FBI has formed special Chinese and Russian organized crime squads along the same lines as the one developed to fight the Cosa Nostra.

Dangerous Places

The Subway

Much of the best of hidden New York is outside Manhattan, and even Manhattan is gridlocked most of the day. Moreover, the subway *is* New York. Not too pretty, this isn't the Moscow underground. Nor does it have that fast, almost silent whoosh of the Paris Metro with its rubber wheels. High-decibel squeals is all you get here, the screech and whine of metal against metal, a perfect complement to the headache the city has already given you, and those things are dangerous to boot.

Real improvements have been made over the past few years. The subways aren't as dirty as they used to be. But things could get worse. Every day the city's books look worse. And anyway, at its best, the subway has never been a joy ride.

But then what did you come to New York for? This is not a pretty city. It's big, powerful, rich in just about every category you can think of, but pretty it's not. Least of all, the subway. There is not a more extensive system in the world, and its combination of express trains and locals (way too ambitious for Paris or London) can make for some nimble block-hopping. It also makes for a complex system, so complex it seems designed to madden; it's a maze with treasures at the end of the ride...and, like a maze, it's designed with such complexity that its true purpose can only be to protect those treasures rather than get you to them.

Ticket to Safety

Most first-timers to New York refuse to ride in the subway, citing the perceived 100-percent probability that they'll be raped, mugged, knifed and thrown on the tracks. Actually, in New York City, you're more likely to get blown away in a Subway sandwich store than on the subway system.

More than 3.5 million people ride the subway every day in the Big Apple. While, in 1991, there were 9374 crimes committed in the city's subway system, the number dropped nearly 50 percent to 4720 in 1994. Still, think it's safer on the street? Of the 1561 murders in New York City in 1994, only 11 of them were in the subways.

Uptown

Vast stretches of New York City are turf that prudent strangers simply don't wander into, and in most cases, there's not much reason to wander in anyway.

Rolling into the city toward Grand Central Station on the old York Central tracks, you can see great dismal stretches of backstreet Harlem and East Harlem that fall thus beyond the pale.

La Marqueta, the Latin market in East Harlem, has long been a cynosure for Puerto Ricans from up and down the coast, and East Harlem is still the place to find Santeria. Of course, any of the tiny New York shops Latinos call botanicas will have the requisite candles, oils, spiritual unguents and plastic figurines. Some may even dispense advice on how, why, when and where to stick the needles. But Santeria is one of those things you encounter on successive levels, as nerve, inclination and access permit.

Should you be of a mind, when the bars close, to go sit on the floor of a half-lit basement apartment, on the walls of which hang black velvet tapestries of Jesus, Mary, Joseph and Jack Kennedy, and in the air of which *cannabis sativa* hangs thickly sweet, and should you happen to have a hard-to-get fifth of Ron Jave (harsh stuff, but the rum closest to Puerto Rican hearts), *and* you know where to go, then your hostess just might take the Ron Jave as a sign you understand that she can't be bought for the $75 you offer. You'll trade a few shots, she'll invite you back, you'll proffer another bottle, another $75, and there will be a ceremony, during which the fuller lore of Santeria is brought to bear.

Spirits consulted, spirits shouted down, spirits invited, spirits most certainly consumed— eventually a spirit invades the body of the chubby lady puffing a cigar with a gaze that penetrates right through you, the basement wall and whatever lies beyond that, until at last with a suddenly violent flapping of wings, raking of claws, squawks and spurting blood, a living ovenstuffer roaster looses her life in this effort to reach the spirits controlling your destiny as a midtown lawyer, uptown gambler, aspiring beautician or besieged publisher.

For this, East Harlem is as good a place as any. But there aren't a lot of Puerto Rican (or as they often describe themselves, from a relict Indian tribe, "Borinquen") restaurants in New York generally. Back home, they say, there was a long tradition of street chefs who delivered if you didn't want to cook. On top of this, many New York Puerto Ricans are working-class people without the business skills to run restaurants. And moreover, the gaunt, grey, bombed-out "alleys" of East Harlem do not invite.

Washington Heights

Washington Heights, the Dominican barrio north of Harlem, has had an even worse rep. Here danger doesn't merely lurk; it attacks. In 1994, this nethermost tip of Manhattan north of 155th Street registered 8608 arrests (20 percent jump from '93), 81 rapes, 56 murders, 1330 robberies, 794 felony assaults. Drug dealing on the street has been so blatant that in 1986, Al D'Amato (then as now New York's Republican senator) and Rudy Giuliani (then the U.S. attorney for Manhattan) donned sunglasses, leather vests and old army caps, went up to 160th Street and quickly scored crack cocaine on the street.

In fact, dealers in Washington Heights come as young as 12; a free clinic run by Columbia-Presbyterian Hospital, which sits in the middle of all this, draws long lines of teenagers seeking treatment for VD, and at night gunfire echoes through alabaster caverns.

But Dominicans seem an immensely complex people, and as with all such people, all is not what it seems.

Take even the neighborhood's worst feature: assertive crime, unwilling merely to lurk. These are indeed assertive people. But that doesn't mean raw brutality; it means a real skill for political assertion. When a politically active young Dominican named Jose Garcia—"Kiko" to the community—was shot to death by a cop one July night in 1990, there were five days of riots, angry editorials, sermons on brutality, and with some dispatch, the cop, one Michael O'Keefe, was relieved of duty and hauled before a grand jury.

Which made some interesting findings:

Kiko Garcia, to whatever extent he might have been a community organizer, spent a lot more time pushing drugs. Because they simply couldn't control the drug traffic, Washington Heights' 34th Precinct had instead focused on controlling the mayhem. Cops on patrol learned how to spot men with concealed weapons. O'Keefe and his partner had spotted Garcia, Garcia had noticed, and he had run. Anticipating the sort of slip they expected Garcia to give them, they split up, but it didn't work and O'Keefe found himself trapped in a dark hallway with this known, armed drug dealer, unable to radio his location to his partner. Garcia pulled his weapon; so did O'Keefe.

It turned out that the entire flap was a hustle by Dominican drug dealers trying to pressure the cops off their turf. They had almost destroyed the careers of young Michael O'Keefe, sitting dazed at home with his wife and kids.

So now you know the worst. It's time for the reason it's worth the danger:

For one, a *media noche*. In fact, this sandwich, called the middle of the night, is Cuban, but consumed in a Dominican restaurant, with Dominican Broadway still alive in the *media noche*, it's a great little meal.

And *mofongo*, which is really Puerto Rican, a ball of mashed pork and plantains, but Dominicans eat it *con queso* for breakfast, which makes for a breakfast as substantial as American ones.

And *mondongo*; whoever can make something this tasty out of tripe has to know how to cook.

And *merengue, merengue, merengue,* which is not something they put on your pie for dessert. It's the beat to which Dominican Broadway jumps, both a style of Latin music and a dance. Before it was a Dominican neighborhood, Washington Heights was populated heavily by Greeks and German Jews who came over after World War II, and remnants remain on the street, a Kosher butcher, a Greek diner, and other living, resonant echoes: the Audobon Ballroom; St. Nick's Arena. Everywhere there are signs touting international phone calls, "*Pronto Telefonica.*" It's a sign that hints of more going on: Dominican families are tight. Money raised in Washington Heights often courses straight back to the island, where peasants then live like dukes.

You gotta make a living somehow. Ask some residents of neighborhoods where drugs are rife what it's like and they draw their thumbs across their throats. Ask a Dominican about Washington Heights and he's more likely to rub his fingers together. Money. About the same time Jellybean Benitez struck his deal, the U.S. attorney arraigned a 64 year-old gambler called Spanish Raymond whose business does $30 million a year.

Yes, that's in the present tense. Do you really think that kind of volume goes away just because the boss gets arraigned? Sold maybe. Or franchised. Or merged. But go away? In fact, this was the second time in a few months the heat had come down on Spanish Raymond. Released on bail on condition he refrained from gambling, Raymondo tried to go the merger route, but the deal doesn't seem to have had nearly the finesse it needed. For one, the other half of this merger was run by a gaming entrepreneur named Spanish Bob, who the police were bound to be watching pretty closely because of the relationship the two already had. (In fact, Roberto is Raymond's nephew.) For another, he did a lot of his business on a cellular phone, which $30 million a year doesn't seem to have taught him isn't exactly a secure means of communication. The NYPD was listening and the U.S. attorney was real peeved.

As for drugs, police can boast that the mayhem on the street is down. Those crime figures, the stuff of Washington Heights' image, are especially misleading. Compared to the 56 murders in 1994, there were 119 in 1995. A prime reason for the drop is that drug dealing has moved off the street.

But not out of Washington Heights. Nowadays, customers from Jersey still drive across the George Washington Bridge, which carries drivers to the heart of the Washington Heights barrio. But they don't make many buys on the street anymore. Instead, they get steered to a bare apartment with little but a desk, scales, video cameras trained on the street outside, and young men with CBs talking to other young men on the street with CBs.

Harlem Heights and Harlem Hollows

A few blocks south of this bridge, on high ground overlooking the Apollo Theater down on 125 Street, George Washington challenged the British camped down in Harlem Hollows. When it was over, George had won what became known as "The Battle of Harlem Heights and Harlem Hollows."

The whiff of cordite seems never to have gone away, though Harlem is not and never has been the South Bronx or Red Hook, or for that matter, largely Puerto Rican East Harlem. Even during its days as a step up for immigrant Jews and Italians, East Harlem didn't boast buildings as solidly substantial as those of Harlem proper. The elegant brownstones of Harlem Heights still stand—still elegant.

Early in 1995, New Yorkers were enjoying a film made about a single photograph taken in front of one of those brownstones. It was taken for the January 1959 issue of *Esquire* and it featured on the stoop of that Harlem brownstone, Sonny Rollins, Dizzy Gillespie, Maxine Sullivan, Coleman Hawkins (in his trademark porkpie hat), Gene Krupa, Lou Williams, Charlie Mingus, Jimmy Rushing, Mary Lou Williams, Lester Young, Gerry

Mulligan, Count Basie and Thelonious Monk, most of whom are now dead and only the last of whom I ever heard in person, at a club in San Francisco that same year, 1959, about the only place an 18 year-old college kid could get into without an ID. Harlem today is known more for crime than for the days of the Harlem Renaissance and the Cotton Club, but the charm of those days is at least painted in part with the air brush of nostalgia while today's crime obscures resilient talent. New York watched the film with some nostalgia, but the music they made was notably intellectual and unsentimental, and just as the brownstones are still there, the music is still there, with good young musicians like the Marsalis brothers playing jazz not because it's a nostalgic kick but because they love it and have chosen it as their profession.

The dashing old Hotel Theresa is now an office building. At the indelibly Harlem Theresa, notables from Adam Clayton Powell to Fidel Castro let the Scotch flow. Nkita Khruschev once made a great show of visiting Castro there, and, when he came to New York immediately after his release from prison in 1990, Nelson Mandela chose the street in front of the Theresa to give his speech. But the Apollo is still alive, and not all the changes are for the worse. Up where the best brownstones are clustered, that one-time bastion of poor, determined Jewish students, CCNY now has a heavily black student body, and throughout Harlem are stories that defy the stereotype.

For example, just a few blocks away from where that *Esquire* photo was being taken, a single mother was just beginning the upbringing of two young sons, who would spend virtually all of their years in or near Harlem until the eldest, Jonah, went off to Cornell, and his younger brother Eddie went off to Phillips Exeter Academy, where he graduated with honors in 1985.

Sadly, they must appear again in this picture of the dangerous place that is New York City, but the fact is, they did it. (See "Just Another Mugging.")

The Upper East and West Sides: The Happy Hunting Grounds

These neighborhoods have distinctly different personalities. The East Side matron would sniff at the sight of them lumped together. The West Side TV producer would implore, "Pleeeze."

Tailored WASPS, whose breeding over the generations has tended to lock their jaws ever more rigidly, still set the tone on the Upper East Side. In their way, these quiet, wealthy blocks are as variegated as the rest of New York. There aren't many poor Jewish tailors, but plenty of tailored Jews; their jaws, too, have begun to lock over the generations. And now there are the tailored, connected expats, Hong Kong Chinese, Japanese, Brits, French, Northern Italians, and at expensive private primary schools like Dalton, the lock jaw children of Bombay bankers, Arab diplomats, tribal Arabian dealseekers and wealthy Persians chased out by the mullahs.

On the West Side, pretensions are more ambitious, more intellectual, more artistic.

For the thief, there's not a lot of difference. More furs on the East Side, but otherwise.... Out to eat on an East Side evening, you wear worn jeans with your well-cut blazer; it shows you're not as stuffy as the rest. On the West Side, you wear a well-cut blazer with your worn jeans; it shows you're civilized. The West Side producer is the only child of the East Side matron.

East Side, West Side and all across the park, this is rich game country for those sportsmen whose gear of choice is a four-inch, flat-bladed screwdriver whose short shafts they bend to a nearly precise 30° angle in a bench vise.

This is all they need for their prey, which sits enticingly within East Side BMWs and West Side VWs, the last of whose drivers, they know, are anything but just plain folks. Just plain folks don't park with baggies full of dried herbs and powdered chemicals in the glove compartment.

On the city's many drug markets, a stash ripped off from a glove compartment, or from under the dash, or the passenger seat, or the rug, is fungible, like cash.

For the thief, this is where the money is. Here, the prey is abundant, secure in its wealth. The prey here does not show nearly the caution of other New York quarry. In Washington Heights, the block watches the block, or at least it watches a lot closer than the blocks do on the East and West sides. A junkie breaks into a car in Washington Heights, he runs a bigger risk for a smaller reward.

Upscale New Yorkers are a little like high-strung wildebeest. As danger lurks, there is a general unease, but once the jackal picks its prey and runs it down, the herd goes on browsing.

It's not quite the Kitty Genovese scene—that infamous case in which a young woman was murdered on a New York street even as her neighbors heard her scream for help and did nothing. It's more like this: The well-schooled are educated to question everything. The West Side gent's no fool. He sees a stranger fiddling with a car, then nosing inside, and he does question whether this is legit…and then he questions the easy conclusion that it's a break-in. If he opens his mouth, it's likely to be something along the lines of, "Excuse me…"

Stop! Or I'll Try to Shoot!

New York City cops discharged their firearms at an amazing range of targets. They missed an even larger number.

TARGET	SHOTS FIRED	HITS	MISSES
Suspected criminals	928	173	755
Dogs	155	111	44
Accidental discharge	43	17	26
Protecting another officer	18	10	8
While officer intoxicated	10	N/A	N/A
Suicide	8	8	0
Inside locker	6	N/A	N/A
Vehicle	5	0	5
Girlfriend	3	3	0
Attempted suicide	3	2	1

Source: Police Magazine

In a Dangerous Place

New York: A Night in the Life of Midtown South

Midtown South at 357 West 35th Street, near Eighth Avenue, is the largest precinct house in New York City. For officers Gene Giogio and Charlie Edmond, on the four to midnight shift, the routine this summer night starts with a swing right up Eighth. Both are young and trim, Edmond with light hair, Giorgio, dark.

Some heavy real estate money is betting on Eighth Avenue and the entire Times Square area, which, in fits and starts, is improving. Forty-second street has drifted upward from total decrepitude marked by child pornography, to moderate decrepitude, marked by sex shops that provide shopping carts for men in suits to push through aisles marked "Tickling," "Shoes," "Spanking," "Slaves"....

Eighth Avenue has never been pretty, but beneath its grime there's always been real life and still is. As Giorgio and Edmond cruise north, they pass an Italian pork store with a 62-cent-a-pound special on pig's toes, a kosher meat market featuring the world's best pastrami, a halal meat market featuring the world's best *basterma* (which not only sounds but tastes like a distant cousin of pastrami), and further up, some totally different meat markets, lounges with three-gold-chain minimums where wise guys from the union go to pick up broads.

At 44th and Eighth is Smith's Restaurant, one of those long-established operations that's open 24 hours for a neighborhood that works 24 hours: a takeout counter, a bar the length of a bowling alley, booths, the kind of place where you can get your pleasure at 4 a.m., breakfast or a tumbler of Irish whiskey and a steak. They get a lot of trade from Midtown South.

"You see those prostitutes over there," says Charlie Edmond to his backseat guest.

"Men," says Giorgio. "Over here on Eighth, most of the prostitutes are men."

The Seventh and Eighth avenues corridor is not the most dangerous in New York, but it is periodically plagued, and will be so in the weeks ahead. Rapper Tupac Shakur will be shot in a lobby on Seventh, and as summer fades to autumn, a rash of knifings will overtake Eighth Avenue. A victim will be knifed, a few hours later a uniform just coming on duty will scan the report, look into space a second, then inform himself out loud: "I think we got a prior aggrieved party." Finally in October, a rookie cop, Timothy Torres, will make a collar.

As they cruise slowly past what might be a nascent game of three-card monte, an order in the indecipherable language called static breaks over the radio and suddenly we're shooting east across town on 42nd Street a lot faster than I'm used to. The siren wails on, and I look around to see where it's coming from.

"Mugging," says Edmond. "Grand Central. Right in front." By then, we're there. Another squad car had squealed up even earlier, and a large, muscular man, so dirty you can't tell what color he is, wearing hardly any clothes, is lying face-down on the sidewalk, handcuffed. The cops from the other car had just finished stringing their yellow tape, outside of which a crowd is gathering and inside of which there are just "the perp," the other two cops, and two college kids in shorts, looking like they're on the wrong side of the yellow tape. But nobody's asking them to leave.

The victim, an elderly woman who only spoke Spanish, has just been taken away, shivering, they say, in the heat.

The kids look mildly stunned. The front of Grand Central Station, just after dark on a pleasant summer evening, right on Park Avenue, should not be among New York's most dangerous places.

Just like that, it is over, the street is returning to normal, and, as we are getting back into the squad car, through the New York cacophony of honks, shouts and distant sirens, I catch snatches of a conversation a black man in a smartly tailored business suit is having with a liveried black doorman. *"Le probleme aujourd'hui est..."* Haitien, I think to myself, then wonder why this incidental detail in a brutal picture has stood out and induced me to jump to a conclusion. To impress on myself that this is New York? Haitians are in the news, and Haitien refugees are everywhere. But here, these men could be from Martinique, Senegal, the Ivory Coast....

Thus mulling as the lights twinkle by, there's a sudden lurch and I realize we're violating the speed limit again. Back to the West Side. A silent alarm on an office building in one of the side streets between Eighth and Seventh.

"This time of day over there, or I should better put it, this time of night over there, it's real closed up. Dark." It's the driver, Edmond, talking, as we shoot toward the intersection of 42nd Street and Sixth Avenue; the light's red ahead, and I'm hoping that at this time of night up there, drivers pay attention to sirens. "Not long ago, we're just driving around, checking things out, and up ahead we see bales of dresses getting thrown out of a window, maybe six, seven stories up, must have been thousands of 'em. Later we hear it's been going on. Perps ran, but two weeks later, they're collared."

"Thing is, you never know what you're going to run into there," says Giorgio. By now, we're coming up on the block and the siren goes off; we roll down the narrow, deserted side street. In a city where a parking place is a valued commodity, there are more dumpsters strewn along the curb than parked cars. Way ahead, a homeless guy is rooting through one of them. We pull to a stop. One light is on in the lobby, but that's it. We get out. I make a point to stay out of the way (or if you prefer, harm's way.) "Generally, it's a false alarm," says Giorgio, "and, generally, perps in this line of business don't give you trouble."

"Unless sometimes. When they get surprised," says Edmond. It comes back to me: This was a silent alarm.

"Problem building," says Giorgio.

They already have keys. They draw their.38s. After the first floor, the building is dark. At a control panel, they snap on lights, push the elevator button. From above, there's a noise. Floor to floor, along the corridor walls—if there's no one there, it's faintly ridiculous, but then how do you know when it's for real?

False alarm. No actual danger. Just the daily drumbeat of tension.

There are homeless wherever we go, not in great droves, but they're here, thanks to a byzantine system of aid that parks some of New York's poorest people on some of New York's most expensive real estate. In the theater district, they come because the pickings are good. Virtually next door to the Algonquin Hotel where the legendary round table once regularly held forth, a 300-pound woman with an amputated foot now regularly holds forth with her sweet eight-year-old son who lives there with her. They've got an address at the distant end of some subway line, but it's clearly not much, it's hard for her to get around, and this is where the money is. The conversation with Edmond and Giorgio is professional. They're just checking. She knows they can't move her. They know they can't either.

One of the homeless of Midtown South, Carlos Sam, by name, is a computer repairman. Not a former computer repairman fallen on hard times, but a computer repairman now, on the street, with no prior training beyond electronics picked up in an uncle's TV repair shop. He's illiterate, periodically delusional, crippled. He owns a jealously guarded tool box and three canvas mail carts. From discarded computer parts rummaged out of dumpsters, he's taught himself computer repair. Nowadays, he's not only a repairman, but he's in the business. For $15 to $45, you can get a repaired monitor or keyboard. His shop is on the 43rd Street sidewalk between Seventh and Eighth.

By this hour, Carlos Sam is off the street, but this is when the porn shops, now run largely by Indians and Pakistanis, bring in their biggest bucks. "Stuff they sell isn't as rank as it used to be, and on top of that, they're mostly cheap copies, but these guys rake it in," Giorgio informs me.

The porn store is, above all, a business struggle. Landlords who rent to porn shops between 40th and 53rd get $90 to $125 a square foot. If it isn't porn, it only commands $60 to $90. Meantime other landlords are trying to light a fire under the redevelopment that slowly proceeds, anticipating a boom that may already be getting underway...if they can finally get rid of the porn. Disney is spending $34 million to renovate the extravagant, dilapidated New Amsterdam Theatre on 42nd, a 92-year-old landmark that was home to the Ziegfeld Follies. But still there's those rents that can be had from the porn shops. They say one group of landlords actually went to the rabbi of a wavering colleague to help him resist.

There are other ways in which this midtown corridor is less impersonal than it seems. Timothy Torres, the Midtown South cop who collared the Eighth Avenue stabber a couple of months after our cruise through the precinct, was a college dropout, on the force barely two years, wearing the same badge, No. 4049, that his dad, Cesar, had worn as a New York cop before he resigned. Young Torres was on foot patrol the October night he saw the suspect racing up Eighth Avenue on a bike, knife in hand. He jumped the guy, and came out of it bloodied, but with considerable pride for father and son.

Smith's again. Another rapid-fire set of directions over the radio, again indecipherable to me.

"A heavy bleeder," Giorgio translates. "Group therapy session at this hotel, a welfare hotel, a welfare hotel for guys with AIDS actually. Terminal cases. Looks like the group therapy got out of hand, and we got a heavy bleeder."

The dispatcher's voice cracks over the radio again: "All units. Stay off the air unless you have priority. All units."

We brake to a stop, with squad cars from every direction. Cops are all over the place. They're up there for 15 minutes, a half hour. Gaunt, unshaven men in stocking caps stand about in the grim light; beefy young men in stocking caps, also unshaven, come out, an undercover team. There's tension, but when Giorgio and Edmond return, they don't make a big deal out of it.

"If it was serious, they would have had a sergeant over here."

A few minutes later, cruising up Seventh Avenue, we're flagged by a cabbie, Indian or Pakistani. His fare won't pay. Fare is out of the cab by now, a little stocky, substantial, middle-aged guy in a suit, maybe a little tight but not obviously drunk, and meantime he's quiet, even sort of fatherly with the cops, who ask him what the trouble is. He doesn't have the money? Come on, he says. A wad is discreetly flashed. He's getting a little more fatherly. So what's the trouble, sir? Again, fatherly, but no direct answer.

It was going nowhere, except from fatherly to patronizing to abusive. Once they got him to pay, they let it be, but of everything that happened—the mugging, the silent alarm, the 300-pound amputee living on the street with her eight-year-old son, the heavy bleeder at the AIDS hotel—this seemed to get under their skin the most. Perhaps because of its ordinariness—and that it was so unnecessary.

Across the country, about 300 cops killed themselves in 1994; that's more than twice as many as the 137 who died in the line of duty. Over the past decade in New York City, more than 20 cops have been killed in the line of duty; 64 killed themselves.

Columbia University released a study in '94 that showed NYPD officers killing themselves at a rate of 29 for every 100,000. Among the general population the rate is 12. The cops are almost always young, with clean records. The study notes that a virtually standard feature of every suicide is a statement from the department or the family or both that the suicide was personal, the job had nothing to do with it.

Christmas Eve, Timothy Torres, who had brought down the stabber in October and wore his father's badge, pulled the midnight to eight in the morning shift at Midtown South, foot patrol. A little after midnight, he responded to a call on West 43rd, where a man was distraught and raving in the lobby. Torres got him to Bellevue for treatment.

At four, he met up with another cop on foot patrol, and they went to Smith's, the landmark on Eighth Avenue, for breakfast. It was now Christmas Day. Torres shot himself in the head in a booth.

"My understanding was that he went through a divorce six months ago," said a police spokesman.

On the same street that Torres responded to the call about the man raving in a lobby, Carlos Sam is still doing business. He melts plastic spoons to solder the innards of keyboards and monitors. If you want to know if he's really fixed the thing, he uses the swivel chair, which is among his few possessions, to squeak over to a light pole, at the base of which is an electrical outlet. In fact, every light pole in New York City has an outlet at its base, usually sealed. Carlos Sam swears he only uses the ones that are already open.

—Jack Kramer

• Kinshasa

Zaire

★★★★

Heart of Darkness

There is no other country on the continent that more typifies the deep, festering core of darkest Africa. Joseph Conrad based his famous tale of depravity and corruption on this dying, diseased land, formerly the Belgian Congo. It is hot, violent and dark.

Zaire, a little larger than the size of a quarter of the U.S., is mostly a vast drainage pan for its mountains in the east. Its neighbors are no shining examples of humanitarianism. Sudan, Uganda, Tanzania, Angola, Burundi, Rwanda, the Central African Republic and the Congo all compete for the title of "Horror Capital of Africa." Like the decay that quickly turns vegetation and animals into rot, the economy and social structure of Zaire has disintegrated. The local currency has lost all value. Most families live off subsistence farming. A barter economy has returned—all this while, Zaire sits on some of the world's largest reserves of mineral and agricultural resources.

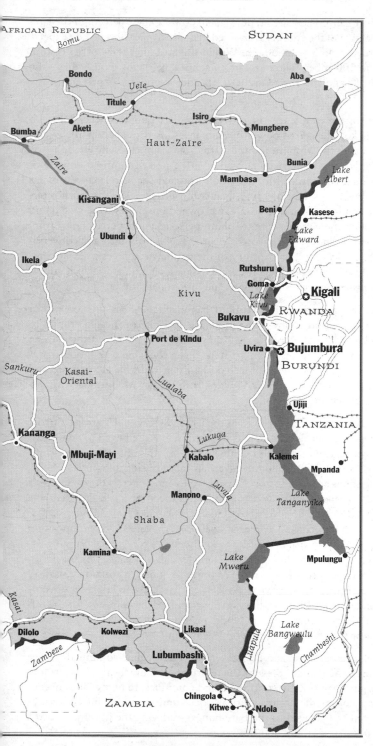

Life is tough in Zaire. There are no permanent crops. Only 3 percent of the land is arable; 78 percent of the country is covered in dense tropical forest. Life expectancy is a depressing 45.5 years of age. Within this steaming bowl of vegetation exist more than 200 tribes. The most prominent is the Bantu. Four tribes—the Mongo, Luba, Kongo and the Mangbetu Azande—comprise 47 percent of the population.

Blame much of the pestilence on the CIA and its puppet, General Joseph Mobutu Sese Seko, who seized power in Zaire in a CIA-backed coup in November 1965. Although the Mobutu regime started out democratically enough—by African standards—as a military dictatorship with a junta comprised entirely of the military's high command, Mobutu soon assumed the standard role of his neighboring compatriots: that of a one-man-controlled, single-party, authoritarian dictatorship. All small and medium expat-owned businesses were seized and distributed among the nation's elite. Mobutu personally plundered the treasury and state-owned businesses. The word "kleptocracy" sneaks into any conversation about Zaire. However, his banditry of the nation's resources pales in comparison with Mobutu's record for murder, assassination, extrajudicial executions, kidnapping, torture, massacres of civilians and unfounded arrests.

In line with the dictator motif, Mobutu has maintained his grip on power through brutal repression of any opposition. He appointed educated cronies to key ministerial positions. To keep them happy, they were made board chairmen of seized companies, allowing them to milk these companies as Mobutu was doing Zaire. He reshuffled the cabinet constantly in order to allow more and more lackeys the opportunity to pick cookies from the jar. Mobutu had five different prime ministers in 1991 alone.

With the breakup of the Eastern Bloc in the late 1980s, the CIA saw no further reason to support Mobutu's crimes, and opposition in Zaire began to take a recognizable shape. In 1990, Mobutu began a series of "political reforms," including abolishing the one-party system. Given an inch, dissidents wanted a mile. Mass demonstrations against the government led to another crackdown. On May 11–12, 1990, Mobutu's personal commandos, Division Spéciale Présidentielle (DSP), massacred unarmed university students, provoking a world outcry. The Union Sacrée was formed in 1991 as a coalition of Zaire's major opposition groups. The group's principal demand was to organize a conference bringing together representatives from all sectors of Zaire's society. Because this would do nothing more then expose the horrors of Mobutu's regime, the president used all of his might to crush the conference. At least 30 people were killed by government troops in February 1992, as they were peacefully demonstrating for the reformation of the conference. Again, world revulsion to the brutal act forced Mobutu to allow the conference to reconvene in April 1992.

But good 'ole George Bush and France's Mitterrand regime continued to give enough support to Mobutu to prevent the reformers in Zaire from achieving anything but marginal gains. Zaire continued, and continues, to plunge into deeper and deeper squalor, as the entire political, social and economic infrastructures have been looted and pillaged to the bare bones—reducing the government to a loose clan of petty street thugs and thieves.

The Scoop

Zaire is the largest sub-Saharan African country. It has substantial human and natural resources, but for the past several years the country has suffered a profound political and economic crisis, which has resulted in the dramatic deterioration of the physical infrastructure of the country; insecurity and an increase in crime in urban areas (including occasional episodes of looting and murder in Kinshasa's streets); occasional official hostility to U.S. citizens and nationals of European countries; periodic shortages of basic needs such as gasoline; chronic shortages of medicine and supplies for some basic medical care; hyperinflation; corruption; and, in some urban areas, malnutrition of the local population to the point of starvation. Tourism facilities are minimal.

Zaire has closed its border with Burundi. The border was closed in April of '96 because Burundi believes that Hutu rebels use eastern Zaire to launch their attacks against Burundi's Tutsi-dominated army. It is expected to be reopened soon.

Goma and Bukavu are the main arms centers for Hutu rebels. There are still about a million refugees in the area, about half of the 2 million Rwandan and Burundian refugees from the 1994 war.

Hey, Who Said Third World Politics, Mercenaries and the Ecology Can't Work Hand In Hand?

Now follow this closely. In order to get funding to protect national game parks in Zaire, President Mobutu hired his old friend, Belgian mercenary Christian Tavernier (who commanded the 14th Battalion against the Simba rebels in the '60s) to do a study on wildlife preservation and find out why his troops were turning freelance in northern Zaire.

Northern Zaire is the area choked with refugees from Rwanda that borders on Uganda and Sudan. Well, it seems that Tavernier found out that some of Mobutu's troops were pulling down two paychecks and being bad boys. Not only were they fighting for the Sudanese army, but they were fighting with the SPLA (the southern Christians fighting the Muslim north) over who gets to poach the remaining elephants and rhinos in the national parks. Officers of the Zairian army battalion actually got into a firefight with SPLA soldiers while on a poaching trip in the Garumba National Park. In order to have a little weekend money, the army was also forwarding weapons and supplies from Khartoum through Bunia airstrip and then on to the 5000 Sudanese troops in military camps across the Sudanese border. Tavernier also found that several hundred Zairian soldiers were fighting for the Sudanese inside Sudan. Oh yes, in case you wondered, Garumba National Park is a World Heritage Site and the last natural habitat of the white rhino. Tavernier's final report mentioned that it may soon become a battleground for the SPLA and the Sudanese troops and that he declined to look further into the matter without the instruction of Zairian authorities.

The Players

General Joseph Mobutu Sese Seko

Yet another "president-for-life," Mobutu is really the only player in Zaire. Mobutu is the Idi Amin of Zaire and a stooge of Uncle Sam. He's known best for his massacres, executions and assassinations of political opponents. His brutal, despotic regime has weakened in recent years, but, as all of Zaire has crumbled, so have his opponents.

By what reasoning, you may well ask, is a man who puts together a US$5 billion fortune, safely socked away in Switzerland, a stooge?

Well, maybe Mobutu isn't a stooge at home. But there's no need to invade the poor man's privacy. We're talking about the role he plays on the Central African stage. Larry, Curly and Moe probably weren't stooges at home either. It was a role they were paid to play. Likewise Mobutu, and you've got to say this for the guy: However overpaid he might be, he gives that role all he's got, throwing around hundreds of millions on palaces and Swiss dairy farms re-created in the jungle, even as his mineral-rich nation slips more deeply into squalor, with streets so heavy with desperation that you drive through them with every window of your vehicle tightly rolled. Overhead, banners proclaim: *MOBUTU POUR TOUS, TOUS POUR MOBUTU.*

Meantime, a private Disneyland goes up in his distant hometown, and even as such outrages to social justice are played out, one after another, he instructs his people to address each other, in the egalitarian tones of the French Revolution, as *citoyen*, which, incredibly, they do, even though they consider him (as does much of Central Africa) a stooge. More specifically, he's considered a stooge for the West, and is paid to frustrate their aspirations whenever they conflict with Western interests. For this reason, paying him is getting to be an increasingly dangerous game, yielding a short-term advantage at the cost of trouble down the pike.

Union Sacrée

The opposition coalition Union Sacrée was formed in July 1991 under the leadership of the Union pour la Démocratie et le Progrés Social (UDPS) and Joseph Ileo's Parti Démocrate Social Chrétien. The UDPS was formed in 1982 after a 1980 rebellion by 13 parliamentarians. This "Group of 13" was tormented and brutally treated by the government. They formed the UDPS in response to Mobutu's outlawing of opposition parties. Also in the coalition is the former Parti Lumumbiste Unifé (PALU), led by the "Iron Lady of Zaire," Thérèse Pakasa. The PALU also was able to organize mass demonstrations against Mobutu's regime.

Getting In

A passport, visa and vaccination certificate showing valid yellow fever and cholera immunizations are required for entry into Zaire. Travelers are advised that the government of Zaire announced in 1993 that visas would not be issued to nationals of countries practicing "discriminatory" visa policies toward Zairians. Although the government did not name the countries to which this edict would be applied, it is presumed that Zairian visas will become more difficult for U.S. citizens to obtain. In addition, some travelers are currently obliged to transit the Congo to reach Kinshasa, which means a Congo visa may also be necessary. U.S. citizens may not be able to obtain a visa at Zairian embassies in neighboring countries; it is suggested that travelers apply at the Zairian embassy in Washington, D.C., well in advance of any planned trip. Visa fees range from US$45 for a transit visa to US$360 for a six-month multiple-entry visa. Most visitors will opt for the one-entry, one-month visa for US$75, or US$125 for multiple entries for the same period.

You will need a valid passport, proof of inoculation against yellow fever, a copy of your return ticket as well as application forms and passport photos in triplicate. If you show up in person, it takes 48 hours for a visa to be issued or 24 hours if you are a diplomat.

For more information, the traveler may contact the following:

Embassy of the Republic of Zaire

1800 New Hampshire Avenue N.W.
Washington, D.C. 20009
☎ *(202) 234-7690, 91*

Zaire's Permanent Mission to the U.N.
747 Third Avenue
New York, NY 10017
☎ *(212) 754-1966.*

Air Zaire flies into Kinshasa and, within Zaire, to Goma and Kinsangani. Within Zaire, the plane may be appropriated by Mobutu on a whim for his own purposes, so schedules are not always maintained. By land, from Burundi, you can get into Bukavu via Cyangugu in Rwanda, and into Bakavu via Uvira. From Uganda, the two routes are from Kasese to Rotshuru and from Kisoro to Rotshuru. From Rwanda, the two main arteries are between Gisenyi and Goma and Cyangugu to Bakavu. See "Getting Around" for more details.

Getting Around

Of the 146,500 km of local roads, only 2800 km are paved. Most intercity roads are difficult or impassable in the rainy season. When driving in cities, individuals often keep windows rolled up and doors locked. At roadblocks or checkpoints, documents are displayed through closed windows. A government "mining permit" may be required to travel to large areas of the country, regardless of the visitor's purpose in going there. This permit must be obtained before entering the "mining zone."

Border Crossings

A special exit permit from Zaire's immigration department and a visa from an embassy of the Congo are required to cross the Congo River from Kinshasa to Brazzaville, in the Congo.

There are three ferry crossing points for overland traffic between Zaire and the Central African Republic. They are located at Bangui, Mobaye and Bangassou. Beginning in the summer of 1993, the crossing points at Bangui and Mobaye have been closed to overland tourist traffic on the direct order of President Mobutu of Zaire for security reasons. The ferry crossing point at Bangassou is not affected and remains open. The ferry serving that crossing point has, however, a history of breaking and can be down for weeks at a time, waiting for someone to pay for repairs. In the event it is not functioning, overland groups will be stranded on either side of the border, unable to use the other working, but restricted ferry crossing points. Local citizens are not affected by these orders, but may also be temporarily stranded at times.

Taxis

There is a fixed rate for taxis from the airport, posted at the airport. In town it is wise to agree on the price prior to getting into the taxi, or you may be overcharged.

Dangerous Places

The Entire Country

Although there are several flights each week between Kinshasa and European cities, schedules are often disrupted by security problems in Kinshasa or neighboring Brazzaville. There have been instances of shooting into Kinshasa from Brazzaville and of shell fragments falling on Kinshasa from fighting in Brazzaville. In the past, during these occasions, the U.S. embassy in Kinshasa has alerted U.S. citizens to the precautions to be observed. In September 1991 and January 1993, there were major episodes of military mutiny in Kinshasa, resulting in many deaths and major property theft, damage and destruction. Similar events occurred in late November 1993 in the provincial capital of Kananga. The underlying cause of these mutinies—the inability of the government to pay the military sufficiently to enable them to support themselves and their families—has not been resolved. Civil disturbances, including looting and the possibility of physical harm, can occur without warning in all urban areas of Zaire. Zairian security personnel are increasingly suspicious of foreigners and sometimes stop them on the street for proof of immigration status. Some foreigners, especially journalists, have been arrested for contacting members of the Zairian opposition parties. Border control personnel scrutinize passports, visas, and vaccination certificates for any possible irregularity and sometimes seek bribes to perform their official functions. Travelers are requested to be cautious and polite if confronted with these situations.

Dangerous Things

Crime

In a country where there is little law or the police are the major criminals, you have to park your moral indignation when visiting. Morality, legality and right or wrong issues have been sidelined in the interest of survival. It is estimated that customs officials have an unwritten law of extracting about US$100 from all Western travelers that enter Zaire. All border officials will hit you up for some type of *cadeau*, or bribe. Once inside, you may wish you were being jacked up by a uniformed border guard rather than the street criminals who will continually hit on you. The continued deterioration of Zaire's economy has led to an increase in armed street crime, especially in Kinshasa, where violent crime is commonplace. Vehicle thefts, including hijackings at gunpoint, are on the increase.

Zaire is quickly reverting to an agrarian or barter economy. Most visitors will tell you that it is a predatory environment where the use of deadly weapons has led to the deaths or serious injury of several expatriate citizens. As the economy continues to collapse, crimes such as armed robbery, vehicle theft and house break-ins increase accordingly, with the foreign community and travelers expected to become more frequent targets. If you look to the police for help, you may find yourself in worse hands. Police officials are often corrupt and demand bribes for their services.

Walking

Walking through Serrekunda and Half-Die in Banjul is not considered safe day or night. You should not walk alone at night, or on the beach, day or night.

Taking Photos

Photography of public buildings and military installations is forbidden, as is photography of the banks of the Congo River. Offenders can expect to be arrested, held for a minimum of several hours and fined.

Carrying Money

The Foreign Exchange Office at N'djili Airport in Kinshasa closed in September 1991. While U.S. dollars and traveler's checks can, in theory, be exchanged for local currency *(zaires)* at banks in Kinshasa, banks often do not have sufficient Zaire cash on hand to make transactions. Visitors may be given an unfavorable rate of exchange, making any daily necessities extremely expensive. Participating in the unofficial, "parallel" money exchanges that flourish in some areas is illegal. Some foreigners have been picked up for infractions of this type and had their money confiscated. Credit cards are accepted at a few major hotels and restaurants. It is illegal to take Zairian currency out of the country. When you consider that you need 2 million zaire to buy one U.S. dollar, there is little incentive to smuggle the local currency for anything but gerbil nesting.

The Police

Zaire's Gendarme force fired nearly 100 patrolmen in January 1995 and said it would reorganize itself after a public outcry over police corruption and abuse. The complaints were made to Prime Minister Kengo Wa Dondo about the Gendarme patrols who demand money to let drivers pass. The police and government soldiers are responsible for much of the crime in Zaire, especially violent crime—from street holdups to periodic mass rampages of looting, rape and murder.

Getting Sick

Getting sick in Zaire is as inevitable as it is debilitating. Zaire is famous for being the incubator of some of the world's nastiest diseases. If you come down with anything, try to get on the next plane out to Europe. Medical facilities are extremely limited.

Nuts and Bolts

Zaire was formerly called the Belgian Congo until 1971 and was inhabited principally by the Pygmies, until they were driven into the mountains by the Bantus and the Nilotics. Zaire is located in west Central Africa. The main rivers are the Ubangi, the Bomu (both in the north) and the Congo in the west. Lake Tanganyika forms Zaire's eastern border.

Zaire is hot and fetid, with little relief except in the southern and eastern highlands. The wet season north of the equator is from April to October; the dry season is December to February. Below the equator the wet season is November to March, with the dry season April to October.

The influence of the former Belgian colonists is evident in Zaire, as half the population is Roman Catholic. Protestants make up 20 percent, Kimbanguist 10 percent, Muslim 10 percent, and indigenous 10 percent. The official language of Zaire is French. However, English is also spoken, as is Swahili, Lingala, Ishiluba and Kikongo. Zaire is made up primarily of Bantu, Sudanese, Nilotics, Hamites and Pygmies. The literacy rate stands at about 72 percent.

The official worthless currency in Zaire is called the *zaire*.

Embassy Location

U.S. Embassy in Zaire
310 Avenue des Aviateurs, Unit 31550
APO 09828
☎ *[243] (12) 21532/21628*

Dangerous Days

11/24/1965	Revolution Day commemorates the establishment of the Second Congolese Republic by General Joseph Mobutu (now Mobutu Sese Seko) following his seizure of control of the government on this date.
05/25/1963	The Organization of African Unity (OAU) was founded on this date. The day is celebrated as Africa Freedom Day. The OAU was organized to promote unity and cooperation among African states.
06/30/1960	Independence Day.
10/14/1930	Birthday of President Mobutu.

FORBIDDEN PLACES

Tirane

Albania

Oil and Water

What do you get when you throw into a bowl a bunch of Albanians and a garnish of fanatical separatist Greeks? Oil and water. Add in some nasty drug traffickers using Albania as a transshipment point for Southwest Asian heroin transiting the Balkan route, and you've got a regular lead salad.

A battlefield during World War II, Albania has been one of the poorest countries in Europe and has vacillated between communism, democracy and anarchy since it proclaimed independence on November 28, 1912 after a history of Roman, Byzantine and Turkish domination. Located in southeastern Europe on the Balkan Peninsula, Albania has some nasty neighbors, the likes of Serbia and Greece.

March 1991 elections gave the communists in Albania a decisive victory. But soon after, strikes and demonstrations broke out, and the entire communist government hightailed it out of the capital of Tirana in the spring of that year. The Communist Party of Labor was reborn as the Socialist Party and abandoned its former communist principles. However, the opposition Democratic Party won a landslide victory in elections held in 1992. The economy improved slightly, but relations with Greece continued to be the bane of Albania. And Albania continues to get its tentacles caught up in the Bosnia-Herzegovina conflict. Its two primary disputes are the Kosovo question with Serbia and Montenegro and the Northern Epirus question with Greece.

On May 20, 1994, Albanian authorities charged six ethnic Greek Albanians with espionage, fomenting separatism, possessing weapons without a license and maintaining links with the Greek secret service. The six were all ranking members of the ethnic Greek organization Omonia. The accused were residents of an area some ethnic Greeks claim as Northern Epirus—linking it by name to a neighboring Greek province. Greece cancelled ministerial talks with Albania in protest of the detention of six ethnic Greeks, severing hopes that the two Balkan countries could patch up their shaky relations, caused by the killing of two Albanian soldiers on April 10, 1994, by what Albania believed were ethnic Greek separatist gunmen.

On that day, six or seven gunmen, wearing Greek military uniforms and shouting "This is for Vorio Epirus (Northern Epirus)! Don't think we have forgotten!" opened fire on sleeping Albanian border guards in their dormitory. One was killed and three seriously injured. The gunmen had previously killed another border guard before reaching the dormitory. A group calling itself the Northern Epirus Liberation Front (MAVI) claimed responsibility for the attack. Vorio Epirus is a term used by Greeks to refer to southern Albania, and seen by Albanians as a foundless territorial claim to the region, which borders Greece's province of Southern Epirus and contains either a large or small ethnic Greek minority, depending on who you talk to. Many ethnic Greek leaders in southern Albania have called for autonomy or unification with Greece, which has been the basis of poor and heated relations between the two countries. Albania maintains some 60,000 ethnic Greeks live in the south, while Greece claims there are 400,000 ethnic Greeks there.

No matter the number, Albania is ethnically quite pure, as 90 percent of all Albanians are of Albanian descent. Greeks comprise 8 percent of the population, while the Vlach, Serbs, Gypsies and Bulgarians make up the last 2 percent. The country is 70 percent Muslim. Greek Orthodox make up 20 percent of the population and Roman Catholic 10 percent. The official Albanian dialect is Tosk. Greek is also widely spoken, but, obviously, not understood very well.

Getting In

The Albanian government no longer requires visas of U.S. citizens for stays up to 30 days. A passport is required. A US$10 airport fee must be paid to Albanian customs officials upon departure. For specific entry/exit requirements, travelers can contact the following:

Embassy of the Republic of Albania
> *1150 18th Street, N.W.*
> *Washington, D.C. 20005*
> ☎ *(202) 223-4942*
> *FAX (202) 628-7342*

Getting Around

Facilities for tourism are not highly developed, and many of the goods and services taken for granted in other European countries are not yet available.

Albania has a low rate of crime. However, crimes against tourists (robbery, mugging and pickpocketing) do occur, especially on city streets after dark. Credit cards, personal checks and

ALBANIA

BOSNIA-
HERZEGOVINA

SERBIA

Valbonë

2
Bajram
Curri

Drin

Han i Hotit

1

Laq i
Koman

Bajzë
Koplik

Lake
Scutari

Ligeni i
Fierzës

Shkodër

4

Kukës

Laq i të
Dejës

Pukë

3

Buenë

6

Drini zt

Shëngjin

Lezhë

Krrëshen

Zall-Reç

Adriatic
Sea

Rubik

Milot

7

Peshkopi

Laç

Burrel

8

Klos

9

5

Krujë

Mat

Shijak

10

Mat

Durrës

Tiranë

11

MACEDONIA

Kavajë

12

Librazhd

Rrogozhinë

Elbasan

Shkumbin

Cërrik

Lake
Ohrid

13

Lushnjë

Pogradec

Lake
Prespa

Seman

Qyteti
Stalin
(Kuçovë)

Gramsh

16

Fier

Berat

Devoll

Maliq

14

15

Osum

19

18

Korçë

Ballësh

Vjosë

Selenicë

Çorovodë

Strait of
Otranto

Vlorë

21

25

Mavrovë

Këlcyrë

Ersekë

2

22

Tepelenë

Përmet

24

Gjirokastër

Delvinë

GREECE

Sarandë

23

Disricts (rreth)
of Albanli

1. Shkodër
2. Tropojë
3. Kukës
4. Pukë
5. Krujë
6. Mirditë
7. Mat
8. Dibrë
9. Durrës
10. Tiranë
11. Librazhd
12. Elbasan
13. Lushnjë
14. Fier
15. Berat
16. Gramsh
17. Pogradec
18. Korçë
19. Skrapar
20. Përmet
21. Tepelenë
22. Vlorë
23. Sarandë
24. Gjirokastër
25. Kolonjë

Albania

⭐ National Capital
● Region Capital
● Secondary City
— Primary Road
+—+ Railroad
— Administrative Border

0   25 km
0   25 mi

traveler's checks are rarely accepted in Albania. In addition, hotel accommodations outside Tirana are very limited, and even confirmed reservations are sometimes not honored.

The U.S. embassy in Tirana, Albania, is located at *Rruga E Elbasanit 103;* ☎ *(355-42) 32875.* Although the U.S. embassy in Tirana is open, routine consular assistance to U.S. citizens in Albania is limited by the difficult environment and a small staff. U.S. citizens who register at the U.S. embassy can obtain updated information on travel and security within Albania. Medical facilities are limited and medicine is in short supply. Several Albanian citizens were killed in a car bombing in February 1996. Following that incident, a number of widely scattered bombings occurred. No one has claimed responsibility, and no Americans have been affected or targeted thus far.

Cuba

The Sinking Island

Fidel Castro is still *numero uno* in Cuba. After 37 years of socialism and dicta-torship—a dictatorship that itself replaced the seven-year, brutal authoritarian reign of Fulgencio Baptista—Castro retains an undaunted defiance against the United States, an antagonism that seems to grow ever more resolved with each act by the U.S to choke Cuba into democracy.The U.S. aircraft shot down for fly-ing into Cuban airspace and distributing anti-Castro pamphlets in early 1996 has escalated tensions between the two countries.

However, the 37-year U.S. embargo on Cuba, tightened with the Cuban De-mocracy Act of 1992 and again by President Bill Clinton in August 1994, is now taking its toll on the island nation. The Cuban economy is in tatters, and the signs are visible everywhere. The cars are gone—the result of the reduced availability of oil—having been replaced by Chinese-made bicycles. Everything from shampoo and paper to medicine and eyeglasses is in short supply. There are few medical supplies. Sutures, syringes and even surgical gloves are in such demand that those that exist are reused time and time again. The shortage of eyeglasses has ham-pered the ability of schoolchildren to learn.

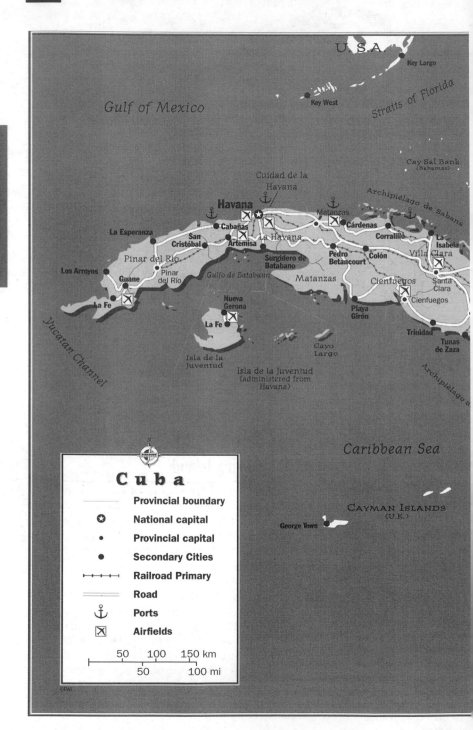

Cuba

·············	Provincial boundary
✪	National capital
•	Provincial capital
●	Secondary Cities
├──┼──┼──┤	Railroad Primary
────────	Road
⚓	Ports
⊠	Airfields

50   100   150 km

50   100 mi

There is little food. With the U.S. embargo, Cuba simply doesn't have access to food as it once did. U.S. foreign subsidy trade with Cuba is now prohibited with the passage of the Cuban Democracy Act. Ninety percent of this trade included food, medicines and medical supplies. Before the act, Cuba had virtually purged itself of the communicable diseases so endemic to developing countries and was primarily plagued with those found in advanced countries, such as chronic diseases like cancer, diabetes and heart disease. Cuba's infant and child mortality rates rivaled those of any industrialized nation. New diseases, such as neuropathy—a debilitating eye disease—have mushroomed all over the country. Venereal diseases, hepatitis A, anemia in young children and pregnant women, and stomach disorders are on a marked rise. Much of Cuba's diagnostic equipment is under U.S. patent, making the procuring of replacement parts virtually impossible. With a decrease in access to such vital minerals as iron, as well as protein-rich food, malnutrition is also on the rise.

Yet, the embargo has still failed to bring democracy to Cuba. Castro remains in power, despite suffering the loss of Soviet subsidies and enduring Cuba's worst sugar harvest and most destructive tropical storm in years (the March 1993 storm caused more than US$1 billion in damage). Defenders of the embargo have argued that by cutting Castro off from the rest of the world and by strangling the Cuban economy, the U.S. will eventually force Castro to capitulate—or at least incite a deprived Cuban people to stage an uprising to overthrow the dictator.

But, to date, the embargo has yet to accomplish either goal and has essentially only reinforced nationalism in Cuba and provided a common anti-U.S. stand that all Cubans can rally behind. Castro's continued resiliency in defying U.S. pressure seems to only strengthen with each tightening of the noose around his neck.

Another of the reasons for the continued U.S. embargo on trade with Cuba surrounds the human rights issue. Whereas the U.S. policy has been designed to champion the human rights cause on the island, it's apparently backfiring and, instead, creating a justification for Cuba's silencing of political opponents. A 1994 U.N. report to the U.N. commissioner on human rights stated that the embargo is "totally counterproductive" to improving human rights. The embargo, rather than unifying the masses against the regime, has permitted the suppression of anyone advocating reform.

In the post–Cold War world, Fidel Castro's near bankrupt island is no longer a security threat to the U.S. The prospects for a peaceful transition to democracy through the embargo are diminishing, many experts argue. If anything arises from the economic sanctions, it will be such hardship as to incite mass political violence on the island, resulting in an unparalleled mass exodus of the nation and the consequent intervention by the U.S. military—on a scale that will make the Haiti intervention seem like running down a purse snatcher on the Bonneville Salt Flats.

Cuba is no longer exporting liberation and Marxism because it cannot afford to. Cuba used to import US$8 billion worth of goods during its Soviet marriage. Now it has a hard time exporting US$1.7 billion to anywhere.

Tourism has been generating hard dollars and creating jobs. According to a March 1993 report by Cuba's Tourism Group, the number of visitors per year more than doubled from 289,000 in 1987 to more than 600,000 in 1993. The industry generated US$530 million in gross hard currency in 1992 and directly accounted for 62,000 jobs.

The downside? Economists say Cuban tourism would be four or five times more profitable if it had access to the U.S. market, which traditionally accounted for 60 percent of Caribbean tourism. Due to the U.S. economic embargo, American tourists cannot legally visit the island. Yet many still do by way of Canada or Mexico, and return back home to Peoria and Fresno to tell their friends about it. Want to be a pioneer?

The Scoop

More than 5000 Cuban boat people were picked up by U.S. Coast Guard boats in 1994, far exceeding the total of 3656 picked up in 1993. The 1993 total was the highest since Mariel. The recent tightening of the 30-year-old U.S. embargo, which Cuba claims has cost it US$40 billion, also is contributing to the country's economic crisis. In a major speech on July 26, 1993, President Fidel Castro spoke of the need to postpone the construction of socialism and to take some steps leading to a market economy, making "concessions" because of the extremely grave economic situation the nation was facing. He announced plans to legalize the possession of foreign currency and create an alternative market to the present hard currency market. Authorities disclosed the country closed 1993 with foreign currency revenues of only $1.719 billion in comparison with US$2.236 billion in 1992 and US$8.139 billion in 1989, before the collapse of the Eastern European socialist community, with which the country carried out 85 percent of its foreign trade.

The Players

Uncle Fidel

After a bitter and often heroic three-year struggle against the government of dictator Fulgencio Batista (at one point Castro's guerrilla force had been whittled down to a dozen or so men), Fidel Castro came to power in 1959 and led Cuba down the path of communism. As he experienced increased hostility to his new regime from the U.S. Castro's government seized all farms greater than 67 hectares, and all American businesses, including banks, were nationalized. The subsequent U.S. embargo and severing of diplomatic ties with Cuba only began to choke the island nation after the fall of the Soviet Union and Eastern Bloc. Castro maintains a Stalinistic grip on Cuba's people, although the economy is in tatters.

Uncle Sam

After the revolution, the United States slapped a trade embargo on Cuba, despite U.S. interests having an estimated US$1 billion invested in the island nation, primarily in agriculture, oil and mining. The U.S. had been the recipient of more than 65 percent of Cuba's exports and responsible for more than 70 percent of the nation's imports. The embargo had relatively minimal impact until the collapse of the Eastern Bloc and the Soviet Union in the late 1980s and early 1990s. Although trade between Cuba and the former U.S.S.R. continued and continues today, the U.S. has put pressure on the Russian government to end oil shipments to the island as a means of receiving U.S. aid. President George Bush, prior to the 1992 elections, signed the Torricelli Bill (the Cuban Democracy Act), which further tightened the embargo by prohibiting all U.S. subsidiary firms in other countries from doing business with the Castro government. Another recent tightening of the embargo, which Cuba claims has cost it US$40 billion, was enacted by President Bill Clinton in August 1994.

Half of Miami

Almost half the population of Miami today is Hispanic, the vast majority Cubans, or families of Cubans, who fled their homeland after the communist takeover in 1959. Virtually the entire Miami Cuban community is ardently anti-Castro. In 1980 alone, more than 125,000 Cubans fled Cuba, most ending up in Miami.

Getting In

According to a recent consular information sheet, travel to Cuba in the form of "tourist and business travel is not licensable. This restriction includes tourist or business travel from or through a third country such as Mexico and Canada. Visitors who attempt to enter Cuba without the proper documentation are subject to detention and arrest.Transactions are authorized by general license for the following categories of travelers: U.S. and foreign government officials, including representatives of international organizations of which the United States is a member, traveling on official business; persons gathering news or making news or documentary films; persons visiting close relatives residing in Cuba, allowed visits once a year for extreme humanitarian reasons; and full-time professionals engaging in full-time research in their professional areas where the research is specifically related to Cuba, is largely academic in nature, and there is substantial likelihood the product of research will be disseminated."

In August 1994, President Clinton further tightened restrictions on travel by Americans to Cuba, by essentially saying "forget about it" unless you have a direct relative in Cuba in a "grave emergency" situation and can prove it. A *DP* call to the U.S. Treasury Department gleaned that a letter of request to the Office of Foreign Assets Control isn't enough. The letter must clearly describe the relative's condition and be accompanied by a medical certificate describing in detail the medical condition.

"It is absolutely illegal for an American tourist to visit Cuba," a representative of New York– and Miami-based Marazul tours told *DP* from Miami. "How about from Mexico?" we asked. "I'm not in position to answer that," she said. "How about from Canada?" "I cannot comment on that either," she said and hung up. A representative of the company's New York office echoed much the same but added that an American tourist in Cuba "would be in defiance of the U.S. Trading with the Enemy Act." Those actually permitted to travel to Cuba on a visa must report to the immigration office at the corner of Calle 22 and Avenue 3 within 24 hours of arrival in Havana.

So is it impossible to get into Cuba without meeting the above criteria? "Of course not," said a representative with Bureau de Tourisme de Cuba in Montreal who gave her name only as Veronica. "U.S. tourists are not refused in Cuba. There aren't any flights from the U.S., but the Cubans haven't been stamping passports since 1990, regardless of your nationality. As an American tourist, you can get to Cuba either on a package tour or independently from either Canada or Mexico."

The key is obtaining a tourist card. These can be had through a number of travel wholesalers, including Cuban Holidays in Montreal, ☎ *(514) 272-8080*, perhaps the best-contacted wholesaler in the Americas regarding tourism to Cuba. The wholesalers can provide American tourists with Cuban tourist cards without any questions asked by the Cuban embassy or consulate issuing the cards. If you attempt to procure the card yourself through a Cuban embassy or consulate, there's a good chance you'll be turned down for being an American. But no such problems have been reported through the wholesalers. You can obtain a tourist card for either package or independent travel in Cuba for US$15.40 (CAN$20). You must first have a reservation for at least three nights in a Cuban hotel and an airline ticket showing your departure date. A U.S. citizen cannot enter Cuba with an open airline ticket. And when making your hotel reservations, do so from either Mexico or Canada. Do not place the call to Cuba from the U.S. "If, by chance, you're an American and have arrived in Havana without a hotel reservation, you'll be required to immediately make one before you'll be permitted to leave the airport," Veronica said. "If a Canadian is in the same predicament, he'll be given preference over an American, especially if there is a shortage of hotel space. It's a nationalism thing."

Round-trip airline fares on Cubana from Montreal to Havana range from approximately US$300 during the low tourist season to US$400 during the high season. The tourist card is actually valid for one month and can be renewed twice, for a stay of up to three months.

Although entry by Americans into Cuba can be handled in a similar way from Mexico, it's more easily accomplished from Canada, where travel wholesalers have better connections in Havana regarding accommodations, tour packages, and—yes—food (tough to find in the island country). "We simply have better contacts in Cuba," said a rep from Cuban Holidays. "We get travelers into the better hotels than our Mexican counterparts. A lot more people come to Cuba from Canada than from Mexico. There's much more of a demand from Montreal than from Cancun. The biggest reason is the climate. Hell, Mexico has the same climate as Cuba." Entry into Cuba, according to San Francisco–based Freedom to Travel Campaign, is possible from any nation outside the U.S. where travel to Cuba is possible. The major springboards for Americans are Montreal, Mexico City and Cancun, Mexico and Nassau, and the Bahamas.

"Although it's tempting to go to Cuba as an independent tourist, especially since you can travel the country relatively freely once inside, we suggest going in as part of a package tour," Veronica said. "The main reason is food, or a lack of it. On a package tour, you're guaranteed at least three international-standard meals a day. On your own, it will be quite difficult to find food and keep yourself properly nourished. Additionally, accommodations are more difficult to procure. If you travel independently, bring food."

For more information, to book tours or to acquire a tourist card, contact the following:

Freedom to Travel Campaign
P.O. Box 40116
San Francisco, California 94140
☎ *(415) 558-9490*

Global Exchange
2017 Mission Street, Suite 303
San Francisco, California 94110
☎ *(415) 255-7296*

Cuban Information Project
198 Broadway, Suite 800
New York, New York 10038
☎ *(212) 227-3422, FAX (212) 227-4859*

Getting Around

Getting around Cuba is remarkably cheap. Cubana de Aviación offers fares as low as US$38 to Camagüey, US$44 to Holguín, US$58 to Baracoa, US$44 to Manzanillo, US$54 to Guantánamo, US$54 to Moa, US$44 to Bayamo, US$50 to Santiago, US$42 to Las Tunas, US$32 to Ciego de Avila and US$12 to Nueva Gerona/Isla de Juventud. Cubana is located at the seaward end of Calle 23. Payment is usually preferred, if not required, in U.S. dollars.

Trains offer the best way to get around Cuba. Buses often won't accept foreigners and, when they do, usually require payment in U.S. dollars. Rail tickets will also have to be paid for in U.S. dollars. Car rentals are scarce, but are available at the Capri, Triton and Riviera hotels in Havana, as well as at the airport. The minimum fee is US$40 per day (US$45 for air conditioning) and US$.30 for every kilometer after 100. You'll need to purchase petrol coupons in 20-liter amounts. Tack on another US$5 a day for insurance, and you're looking at a US$70-a-day range.

Getting Out

Getting out of Cuba is as simple as getting in—as long as you get back to the point where you left before returning to the States. Certainly, do not attempt to return directly to the U.S. from Cuba. Since your passport hasn't been stamped by the Cuban authorities, getting back into the U.S. will pose no problem from either Mexico or Canada, as you've left behind no "passport trail." Expect to pay a US$11 airport departure tax. Many American visitors to Cuba go in protest of the travel ban and have their passports stamped as badges of crusade. Some go in groups that leave and return through Mexico. American customs and other authorities will know who you are, no matter where you arrive back in the States. If you get your passport stamped, expect some trouble once Stateside.

Dangerous Places

Tourists frequenting beaches, hotels and historic sites are prime targets for petty theft and other crimes. Some of the beaches include Miramar, Playa de Marianao, El Mégano, Santa María del Mar, Bacuranao, Arena Blanca and Bahía Honda. Areas around museums are also frequented by muggers.

Dangerous Things

Crime

Crime is rising steadily and tourists increasingly are targeted. Robberies, including those resulting in injuries, are increasing. Even low-budget travelers find they have many items, including currency, that are attractive to thieves. The country's worsening shortages and living conditions are attributable to an economic crisis reaching critical proportions. The government of Cuba does not publish crime statistics. However, according to informal reports, thefts and burglaries are high in the diplomatic community and among tourists. Clothing, passports and food items are most likely to be stolen. Robberies, especially purse snatching, are frequently accompanied by assault. Visitors, in general, are easily identifiable in this environment, with all tourists being especially attractive targets. Since U.S. credit cards are not valid in Cuba and most expenses must be paid in dollars, American visitors can be counted on to have large amounts of cash on hand. Police and security forces are visible throughout the country. However, criminal investigations are often slow. Police seldom capture criminals or recover stolen goods. At the Havanauto car rental office at Havana's international airport, the company offers two insurance policies to cope with the theft of car tires used ultimately for raft-building. The cheaper US$10-a-day policy provides no coverage against tire theft, while for US$18 a day partial coverage can be obtained. Even backpackers and other low-budget tourists have become targets in recent years—simply because even they possess more of value than would-be assailants and most other Cubans, for that matter. Many tour packagers and travel agents have reported a surge in cancellations to Cuba. There have been reports of tourists discovering the corpses of rafters on Cuba's beaches, although this is rare. Many women have been forced into prostitution, making the island a burgeoning destination for sex tourists.

Terrorism

There is no specific threat to Americans traveling to or doing business in Cuba. There is no known terrorist organization operating on a continuing basis within the country, although it suffers from occasional forays by anti-Castro emigres based in Florida. Only 11 incidents of terrorism and other forms of political violence have been reported since 1988, but the trend is up as all but one of the 11 incidents occurred during the past 30 months. This increase is most likely tied to the deteriorating state of the economy that has befallen the country since the disintegration of its major trading partners. In early November 1993, Andres Nazario Sargen, head of the paramilitary anti-Castro group Alpha 66, affirmed threats to kidnap foreigners in Cuba beginning November 27 of that year. He acknowledged such kidnappings would "constitute a terrorist action," but vehemently denied characterization of Alpha 66 as a terrorist group. In addition, he averred, Alpha 66 "cannot be accused in Miami of what occurs in Cuba." According to Nazario, one of the 66 Cuban exiles who founded the organization in 1961, its membership totaled approximately 6000 members in the U.S., plus a network of 45,000 "collaborators" in Cuba. He stated that for the past 20 years, Alpha 66 had "underground cells" in place that were "now preparing for an irregular struggle" by staging attacks against tourism centers, government enterprises and sugar plantations in Cuba. The U.S. Government subsequently strongly urged the Cuban community in the United States to discard the use of violence against Cuba and threatened legal action against those who attacked or conspired to attack U.S. citizens with links to Cuba. To date, no such attacks have occurred.

Government Harassment

Private U.S. citizens whom the Cuban government judges to oppose the regime have been harassed and followed, but since so few come to Cuba, it is difficult to make a general statement.

Anti-U.S. Demonstrations

In the past, the government has encouraged anti-U.S. demonstrations, sometimes staged at the U.S. interests section. In addition, U.S. diplomats have previously been targeted for harassment. While there is significant in-country opposition to the Castro regime, the growing economic stress leads some observers to predict an end to the communist system once the charismatic but aging leader passes from the scene.

Blackouts

Nighttime blackouts in Havana (and other locations) have increased vandalism and anger against Cuba's communist government. Cubans, already putting up with drastic cutbacks in public transport and entertainment facilities and severe consumer shortages of everything from fresh meat to toothpaste, now are enduring daily electricity cuts lasting between 12 and 20 hours. The blackouts plunge whole sectors of Havana into darkness at night, leaving pedestrians, cyclists and property vulnerable to attack and robbery. Numerous apparently spontaneous and unrelated incidents have occurred in which individuals or groups have damaged state and private property and shouted antigovernment slogans. Foreign diplomats and local residents say crime and vandalism, especially at night, have reached unprecedented levels in a city previously known for safe streets. Although major tourist hotels and hospitals are spared power cuts, foreign consular officials in Havana have reported an upsurge in muggings and purse snatchings against foreign visitors, even in daylight.

Getting Sick

Despite being only 90 miles from the U.S., Cuba is not where you'll want to become ill enough to have to enter a hospital. Once having been a showcase of socialized medical care—on par with Sweden's system—the loss of billions of rubles for health care in the wake of the collapse of the Eastern Bloc has left Cuban hospitals unsanitized and suffering from a severe shortage of even the most rudimentary medical supplies and medicines. For example, in Havana itself, syringes and needles are in such demand that they are routinely reused on multiple patients. They're supposed to be sterilized, but it's a crap shoot if you have to be injected with anything. Antibiotics and other medicines and vaccines imported from the former Soviet Union are all but nonexistent. The only medicines available are those that are produced in Cuba itself—and these consist of only a limited number of vaccines. And Americans will not receive preferential treatment in Cuban hospitals. In other words: Get sick, get out.

Dangerous Days

10/08/1967   Che Guevara was killed by security forces in eastern Bolivia while trying, unsuccessfully, to spark an uprising. Celebrated as "Heroic Guerrilla" day.

01/08/1959   President Fulgencio Batista flew to exile in the Dominican Republic and Fidel Castro marched into the capital of Havana to take power on this date.

Dangerous Days

12/04/1956   Revolutionary Armed Forces Day.

07/26/1953   Castro led a group of revolutionaries in an attack on the Moncada army
barracks in Santiago de Cuba on this date. The attack failed and Castro
was imprisoned for two years before being allowed to go into exile in
Mexico. Castro slipped back into Cuba in 1956 to begin his final drive
for power.

08/13/1927   Fidel Castro's birthday.

05/10/1902   Independence Day. Cuba achieved independence as a U.S. Protectorate
in 1899. This date marks the end of U.S. Protection.

10/28/1492   Discovery of Cuba by Columbus.

Tehran

Iran
★ ★

Terror's Backbone

Ronald Reagan had it easy. When he thought the world was being overrun by zealots, controlled by subversives, bullied by foreign-controlled thugs or just getting too full of fanatics, lunatics, heretics, zombies, crazed clerics, guerrillas, psychotics and brainwashed bandits, all he had to do was call up Moscow and threaten to push the button, drop the "big one" or send in the Marines. The former Soviet Union policy of guns for butter demanded that countries like Libya, Cuba, Bulgaria and East Germany export death and fear to feed their people. Today, there is a new sugar daddy who asks only that its people strike at the heart of the Great Satan in exchange for a paycheck.

Their M.O. is surprisingly similar to the old-fashioned brand of communism: Find the oppressed, teach them to respect themselves, give them pride, and then give them a gun. The commies screwed up by tossing out religion. The Iranians know that adding their interpretation of the Koran to this classic revolutionary format is like adding nitro to gasoline. It burns brighter and goes faster.

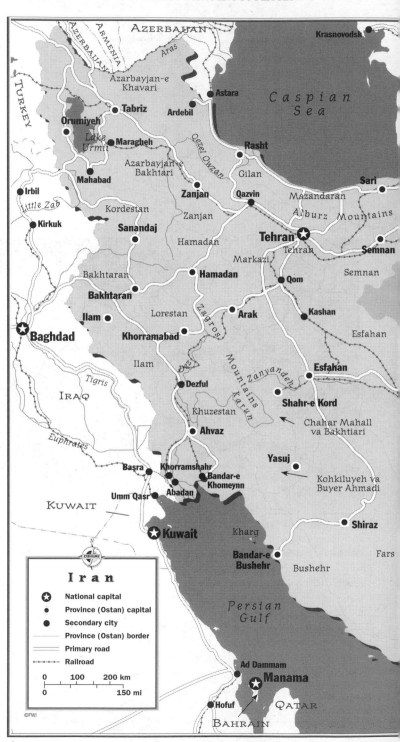

Iran

National capital
Province (Ostan) capital
Secondary city
Province (Ostan) border
Primary road
Railroad

0   100   200 km
0   150 mi

©FWI

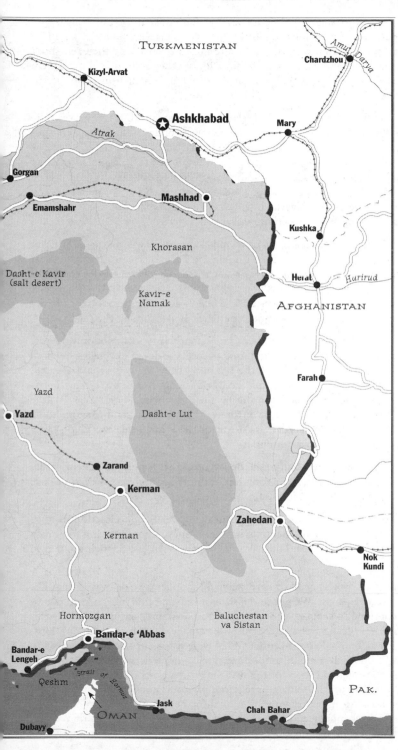

How do we as the Great Satan fight back? We can't nuke it, we can't buy it, and we can't pay our worst enemies to bleed Iran to death (as we tried by backing Iraq during the eight-year war with Iran). We arrest terrorists here and there, we shoot one now and then, and we pay the bill for a lot of other countries to hunt them down, but you can't use a gun against a virus. Fundamentalism continues to spread.

How do we fight the new sword of Islam? We scream at Libya to turn over the alleged destroyers of the Lockerbie disaster, only to find out that they were simply filling out an evil Purchase Order from Iran to pay us back for downing one of *their* flights. We snatch one evil henchman from his bed in Pakistan and charge him with the World Trade Center bombing, only to find out that even though he was trained by Iran, it was Iraq who actually wrote the check. We dare not even get involved in the Sudan, Algeria, Egypt, the Philippines, Bosnia, Turkey and India. Jihad is coming soon to a country near you.

Jihad or Holy War, has many eager recruits. The poor, war-hardened Muslim teenagers from the dusty cities of the Middle and Far East see jihad as their great war. They sign up with the same fervor that cleared out the iron mines and dead-end towns in World War I. It was not surprising in December of '94 when they slipped out that Iran had spent over US$10 billion dollars on weapons just in the last five years—all that money and not one B1 or ICBM among the purchases.

Pity poor Bill Clinton and his southern Judeo-Christian roots. Not only does he not have a red phone to call or a big button to push; he doesn't even know whom to call. Worse yet, this just may be the big one—truly the war to end all wars. From New York City to Zamboanga, the world is under siege by Islamic fundamentalists. Bill may be at the helm during the apocalypse, World War III, the 21st-century crusade, the final showdown in the land of Gog and Magog, home of the Antichrist, the fomentors of Armageddon. Whew, this was a lot easier when it was just commies or dominoes.

To Iran, we are the Great Satan, the defiler of all that is pure, the enemy of Islam. The U.S., despite its recent roundup of the WTC bombers, wouldn't have enough jail space to house every Iranian-trained terrorist.

Who is to blame for the rise of this fanatical empire? Is our addiction to fossil fuels to blame? Like a junkie spending his rent money, are we pouring too much hard currency into dirt-poor Third World countries? Are we financing our own downfall?

In our (and Europe's) need to have stable oil supplies , we dealt with Iran like an overprotective parent. We put in the shah of Iran and told him to keep pumping. We continue to support a tribal clan in Saudi Arabia, and we are willing to send in one less Stealth bomber, because we actually don't mind mad dog Hussien barking at Iran's Western border. What we got for our trouble was close to the second coming. Khomeini, a dour and intelligent cleric, made the Pope look like Rodney Dangerfield. Iran for the first time had a charismatic, devout leader. It didn't take long for the *fatwas*, or religious pronouncements, to start shooting off like missiles. More importantly, Iran used the new power vacuum created by the loss of Soviet money and began to harness the seething hatred of Western "corruption" beyond its borders.

Muslims, once content with being misunderstood but never bellicose, were told to strike down the Great Satan. Some laughed at Khomeini's return to the biblical era. But when jihad was on CNN, we stopped laughing.

Iran was the principal supporter of Somali warlord Mohammad Aidid. Iran sent 10,000 troops into Azerbaijan against the Armenians. Iran sent 60 tons of weapons and 400 Revolutionary Guards into Bosnia. Iran supports fundamentalist insurgent groups in Algeria and Egypt. Iran caused the Yemeni civil war by creating the fundamentalist party in northern Yemen that unbalanced the ruling coalition. Iran supplies 19,000 barrels of oil a day to North Korea and receives Scud missiles and weapons in exchange, which they exchange with all the above for their souls. Iran has disputes over no fewer than three islands—Abu Musa and the Greater and Lesser Tumb islands.

The list of killings, subversive activities, insurrection and general mayhem attributed to Iran is impressive. Intelligence agencies keep monstrous dossiers on the convoluted connections between the religious leaders in Iran and the skinny, badly shaven men who pull the trigger. The problem is that the religious leaders are not politicians, and wield absolute control over their military and political leaders. The Koran spells out very clearly what is right and what is wrong. If Western leaders do so much as affront the Iranian view of Islam, it won't take much more than a brief discussion and a nod of the head for the next terrorist attack to be launched. They will go so far as to issue a *fatwa*, identifying someone as an enemy of Islam, to make him a target for life. Salmon Rushdie has switched to children's tales, but there is no court of appeals for him.

Like showbiz agents from hell, the Iranians orchestrate the creation and success of some very scary groups. To cover its tracks, Tehran is using members of the Lebanese Hezbollah, of Army of God, to do its dirty deeds. The Iranians have enlisted dozens, perhaps hundreds, of Lebanese Shiites in Beirut, in the Baalbeck region, and particularly among specific clans, such as the Hamade, Tleiss, Bdreddine, Kassem, Yazbeck, Berjaoui and Ammar. The recruits are trained at the Imam Ali school north of Tehran. Using Turkey as a base, Iranian intelligence and terrorist "services" have extended their reaches into Germany, where a significant Turkish community lives. In a land where many young teens have known nothing but war and killing. Hezbollah is a well-funded political group that seeks to lift up the social and mental status of all its members. Their tone is a bit strident to Western ears, but anyone who has spent his or her childhood in Afghanistan or Palestine could do with a bit of uplifting. These are dangerous times and these are dangerous people.

Since the Islamic Republic was formed in 1979, Iran has had two goals: to become the dominant power in the Persian Gulf and to further the efforts of Islamic fundamentalism around the world. Because bullet-buddy Saddam Hussein in Iraq has sort of the same idea in mind for his crumbling "fiefdom," it became "all Muslims for themselves," as Iran became embroiled with Iraq in a lengthy and bloody eight-year war in the 1980s. Relations are still hair-triggered at best. After Iraq's withdrawal from Kuwait in 1991, Iran backed the failed effort of Iraqi Shiites to dump Saddam. Iran has also refused to return Iraqi warplanes that fled to Iran during the Persian Gulf war.

Iran has seemed to make partial amends with some of its other neighbors, though. Iran and Saudi Arabia normalized their relations in 1991 (perhaps because of their mutual disdain for Hussein). Tehran's support of the return to power of the Kuwaiti government after the Iraqi invasion of Kuwait in August 1990 has led to improved relations with Kuwait, but the United Arab Emirates continues to be pesky. Iran claims total sovereignty over the small Persian Gulf island of Abu Musa, but the UAE has been like a tick you just can't pull off.

You got the wrong one baby, uh huh

In January 1995, the Ayatollah Ali Khamenei issued a religious decree apparently banning the consumption of both Coca-Cola and Pepsi-Cola, American soft drinks that had recently been reintroduced into Iran. Khamenei was asked by a local paper, "Assuming drinking Coca-Cola and Pepsi politically strengthens world arrogance and financially helps Zionist circles, what would the Islamic decree on the issue be?" Khamenei replied: "Anything that strengthens world arrogance and Zionist circles in itself is forbidden." Only time will tell which real thing Iranians consume, Islamic dogma or the right one, baby.

You probably won't be surprised to learn that satellite dishes are also banned.

Iranian relations with some other Islamic countries have gone to hell in a handbasket, because of well-founded allegations that Iran is supporting Islamic terrorists. In March 1993, Algeria broke diplomatic relations with Iran, citing Tehran's aid to over-the-edge fundamentalist rebels. This has forced Iran to seek closer ties with more xenophobic Islamic states, although it periodically makes conciliatory overtures to the West, especially concerning the reform of its economy. Iran is also sticking its nose in the new breakaway Islamic states that helped comprise the former Soviet Union in Central Asia. Iran has offered to aid Azerbaijan in its conflict with Armenia over the Nagorno-Karabakh enclave. Even though Iran has criticized Russia for helping Tajikistan battle Islamic fundamentalist insurgents, no reactionary Third World country in its right mind puts too much distance between itself and the "Moscow Machine Gun & Missile Market's" weekly specials. In March 1993, Iran and Russia reached an agreement for economic and military cooperation.

What does the future hold for better relations between Magog (the home of the biblical Antichrist) and the Great Satan (me and you)? Iran doesn't like our opposition to the established fundamentalist states, especially those backed by Iran. We haven't got a hope in hell of infiltrating them or buying them off, so we just have to chase them around the world like international Keystone cops. When we catch 'em, they have to have done something pretty direct (like pulled a trigger) or preached violence (we have to tape them) or tried to sell or buy something nasty from a government informant. Bottom line is, we don't get around enough to figure out who's who and chances are slim we will send in the Marines again after they scared us off with just two car bombs in Beirut. We hauled ass out of Somalia, when we ended up looking like bad guys, and I doubt you will see America's youth in Algeria, Pakistan, Sudan or any other place where they don't have McDonald's. So Iran will be out stalking us. They're still incensed that we supported Saddam in the Iran-Iraq war, and they are not happy that we are sitting on US$5 billion in Iranian assets that we froze in 1979. Our efforts to prevent the ayatollah from buying anything deadlier than firecrackers or muskets keeps a lot of their Shah-era hardware in mothballs.

Terrorism on a Budget

The lower-budget but far more terrible arm of Iran is Hezbollah. The foreign operations sections of the Lebanese Hezbollah is busy recruiting, training and arming the world's dispossessed. Nobody joins Hezbollah to see the world and have an expense account—probably one good reason why CIA operatives are not lining up to infiltrate this group. Hezbollah stirs it up in the world's cesspools— the destitute and war-torn regions of Iraq, Turkey, Afghanistan, Pakistan and the occupied territories in Israel.

They are busy recruiting folks to beef up their opposition party in Iraq (definitely a short-tenure, high-risk political profession). Hezbollah's goal is to combine all the fundamentalist groups in Iraq and set up a single Supreme Council for the Islamic Revolution in Iraq.

The Scoop

Iran is hurting because of the long drop in world oil prices. The *rial* fluctuates on the free market as much as 15 percent a day. Inflation is between 60–100 percent a year, and a thriving black market takes advantage of outrageous official rates. Government employees make the equivalent of US$60 a month, and many Iranians are forced to take two jobs to get by. Iran is home to more refugees than any other country in the world. There are an estimated 2.2 million Afghans, 1.2 million Iraqis and 1.2 million others who have fled the strife in Pakistan, Azerbaijan and Tajikistan. The country is held together by a wide net of informers. But give Iran credit, like most exporters of terror, it's a peaceful country. In December of '95 the CIA was given a budget of $20 million to overthrow the government of Iran. Anybody wear the same size crown as the Shah?

The Players

The National Liberation Army (NLA)

The NLA is the military wing of the National Council of Resistance (NCR). It was first created in 1987, arming itself with captured Iranian hardware and Iraqi equipment. Because of the windfall of abandoned and captured equipment during the long war between Iran and Iraq, the NLA is one the few armored liberation groups. The NLA can field 15,000 soldiers, 160 T-54/55 tanks and dozens of rocket launchers, APCs, towed howitzers and even attack helicopters.

They maintain that they do not receive any direct aid from Iraq but keep bases inside Iraq. They are constantly under siege by scud missile and air attacks.

Mujahedin Khalq Organization (MKO)

The MKO is officially branded a terrorist group by the U.S. government and its claims to be the Iranian government in exile are disputed.

Khomeini Money

In 1989 the Iranian government used its official government currency presses to print the first of about $10 billion in counterfeit U.S. currency. The U.S. bills or 100-dollar denominations were originally used to finance terrorists in the Bekaa valley. There were little if any clues to the bills origin (some say the zero's have flattened tops).

Khomeini Money

The U.S. government estimates that there is around $400 billion in U.S. currency outside of the country. The paper used is the same paper used by the U.S. mint ,and, in many cases, the bills cannot be detected even by optical scanners. The bills continue to appear, and have been spotted most recently in North Korea. In dangerous places where U.S. currency is the standard, DP has taken to carrying only $20s and not accepting any $100 bills printed in the '80s. The new $100 bill should solve this problem for now.

Ayatollah Mohammed Ali Khamenei

The ayatollah is Iran's spiritual leader and commander in chief. A hard-liner and a fundamentalist to the max, he is viewed as the most likely successor to Rafsanjani.

President Ali Akbar Hashemi Rafsanjani

The president has tried to resign three times, and three times has been told no. The fact that he has narrowly escaped seven assassination attempts might be the source of his on-the-job dissatisfaction. He is viewed as a moderate, and has the support of the middle class. He gathered 63 percent of the 1993 presidential election vote and 94 percent a year later. Regarded as the most pragmatic of the Iranian leaders, Rafsanjani is credited with persuading Khomeini to finally agree to a cease-fire in the war with Iraq in August 1988.

Rafsanjani has attended primarily to the economy and repairing the damage left by the war with Iraq. He has strived to get Iran reacquainted with the international community by expanding world ties and by arranging the release of hostages held by terrorist groups with ties to Iran. The defeat of the Muslim extremists in the 1992 parliamentary elections strengthened Rafsanjani's stance in his pursuit of moderate policies. However, Rafsanjani's position has weakened because he has been blamed by hard-liners for the country's continuing economic struggle. Additionally, Rafsanjani's grip on the country's economic and foreign policies has also been loosened by Khamenei's pronouncement that he was taking more personal responsibility in those areas. Rafsanjani may be replaced by the parliamentary speaker Ali Akbar Nateq-Nouri, a conservative mullah favored by local businessmen because he wants to return to a centrally controlled economy.

Ali Akbar Mohtashemi

The leading Islamic fundamentalist critic of the Rafsanjani government. The leader of the Muslim extremists in the previous Majlis, Mohtashemi could play a critical role as an ally of Khamenei, should Khamenei try to oust Rafsanjani. It's agreed Mohtashemi has enough political support to become president or supreme ayatollah if the Muslim extremists pick up some steam in Iran. After the start of the war with Iraq, Khomeini made him ambassador to Syria. He helped obtain Syrian support for Iran and strengthened Iranian ties with sympathetic terrorist groups in Lebanon. His service in the key post of minister of the interior ended when Rafsanjani was elected president. More than 100 members of the Majlis asked Rafsanjani to retain Mohtashemi. Nonetheless, the president excluded him during the reorganization of the Cabinet. Politically, Mohtashemi has become stronger as Rafsanjani has weakened.

Ali Mohammed Besharati

He's the influential interior minister. A former student and Revolutionary Guard, Besharati was one of the students who seized the American embassy in 1979. His latest action was to unsuccessfully ban Iran's embarrassingly popular satellite dishes—which he views as instruments of Western filth—when he learned that "Star Trek" and "Baywatch" were getting better ratings than "Modern Muslim! Live From Mahabad!" and "Good Morning, Tehran—with Ali Mohammed Besharati."

The Mujahedin-e-Khalq

Founded in 1980, this is an armed group based in Iraq. Its ideology is a combination of Islam and Marxist babbling. The group is headed by Masud Rajavi. The Iranian government insists that the Mujahedin is supported by England and France. The government may be looking for an excuse to conduct a full-scale attack on Mujahedin forces in Iraq, where the time seems appropriate for Saddam Hussein to look the other way. Iran's top judge accused the Mujahedin-e-Khalq of conducting a campaign of bombings and assassinations aimed at igniting sectarian tensions. Although government repression has significantly curtailed the effectiveness of the Mujahedin-e-Khalq, the guerrillas still conduct operations inside Iran and remain vocal in the opposition to the government of Iran. The organization was 50,000 strong after the Islamic revolution, with nearly half a million supporters. About 5000 activists have been executed in the government's crackdown, and more than 25,000 imprisoned. After the cease-fire in the Iran-Iraq war, the Mujahedin invaded Iran but were crushed by the Iranian armed forces.

The organization abandoned much of its leftist diatribe in order to gain support from the U.S. and stepped up attacks on government targets, including a February 1994 attack at the tomb of the Ayatollah Khomeini on the anniversary of the establishment of the Islamic government. There was also an unsuccessful assassination attempt against the ayatollah during the Friday sermon at the Meshad mosque.

The Iranian Military

Rafsanjani has raised the prestige of the regular army, navy and air force since becoming president. The military's support could be decisive in determining which political faction gains control should economic and political conditions deteriorate. The military is a large player, despite desertions, the imprisonment or execution of a number of soldiers who had served under the shah, and the huge losses it suffered in the Iran-Iraq war. The balance of the purging occurred during the war. The army is the most important branch of the military. However, the Revolutionary Guards Corps, numbering 250,000 soldiers, is considered more reliable by the government, as it is dedicated to the Islamic Republic.

Iran continues to spend a large percentage of its budget on defense (or offense, some might argue), mostly in the search and procurement of expensive weapons systems. Iran still doesn't trust Iraq. And what would a Middle East superpower be without some Scuds and Sidewinders?

The Sunnis

The Sunni Muslims comprise only about 4 percent of Iran's population and are regularly gunned down by their enemies, the Shiites.

Getting In

The U.S. government does not currently have diplomatic or consular relations with the Islamic Republic of Iran. The Swiss government, acting through its embassy in Tehran, serves as the protecting power for U.S. interests in Iran and provides only very limited consular services. Neither U.S. passports nor visas to the U.S. are issued in Tehran.

Visa and passport are required. The Iranian government maintains an interests section through its embassy in Washington, D.C.:

Embassy of Pakistan

2209 Wisconsin Avenue, N.W.
Washington, D.C. 20007
☎ *(202) 965-4990*

U.S. passports are valid for travel to Iran. However, U.S./Iranian dual nationals have often had their U.S. passports confiscated upon arrival and have been denied permission to depart the country documented as U.S. citizens. To prevent the confiscation of U.S. passports, the Department of State suggests that Americans leave their U.S. passports at a U.S. embassy or consulate overseas for safekeeping before entering Iran. To facilitate their travel in the event of the confiscation of a U.S. passport, dual nationals may obtain in their Iranian passports the necessary visas for countries that they will transit on their return to the U.S., and where they may apply for a new U.S. passport. Dual nationals must enter and leave the United States on U.S. passports.

Getting Around

Mehrabad International Airport is seven miles west of Tehran, about a 30-minute drive. Airport facilities include a 24-hour bank, 24-hour post office, 24-hour restaurant, snack bar, 24-hour duty- free shop, gift shops, 24-hour tourist information and first aid/vaccination facilities. Airline buses are available to the city for a fare of RL10 (travel time: 30 minutes). Taxis also are available to the city center for approximately RL1200–1500. There is a departure tax of RL1500. Transiting passengers remaining in the airport are exempt from the departure tax.

Once inside Iran, transportation by private car (with driver) or with a guide (who will be assigned to keep tabs on you) is recommended.

Dangerous Places

Travel throughout Iran continues to be dangerous because of the generally anti-American atmosphere and Iranian government hostility toward the U.S. government. U.S. citizens traveling in Iran have been detained without charge, arrested and harassed by Iranian authorities. Persons in Iran who violate Iranian laws, including laws that are unfamiliar to Westerners (such as laws regarding proper attire), may face penalties that can be severe.

The eastern and southern portions of Iran are major weapons and drug smuggling routes from Pakistan and Afghanistan. Drug and arms smuggling convoys may include columns with tanks, armored personnel carriers and heavily armed soldiers. "Miami Vice" doesn't have a prayer against these guys.

Dangerous Things

The Iranian people, being an American, the Vavak and Savama (secret police), disease, pestilence, drugs, Washington Redskins ballcaps, your opinion, speaking at all, getting off the plane, trying to get back on.

Drugs

Three pieces of advice: Don't do 'em, don't bring 'em in, and don't bring 'em out. Iran has executed well over 1000 people since 1989, when it made possession of 30 grammes (slightly over an ounce) of heroin or five kg (11 lbs.) of opium a capital crime. Read that as death. The Golden Crescent—Pakistan and Afghanistan—has become the world's second-biggest source of heroin after the Golden Triangle of Southeast Asia. Opium is grown mostly in Afghanistan, processed in the tribal areas of Pakistan where Pakistani law doesn't reach, and smuggled to Iran for shipment to the West. About 10 percent of the drugs that enter Iran are destined for consumption in Iran and the rest for other world destinations, including London, Paris and New York. There are approximately one million addicts among Iran's 60 million people.

Dual Citizenship

U.S. citizens who were born in Iran or who were at one time citizens of Iran, and the children of such persons, may be considered Iranian nationals by Iranian authorities, and may be subject to Iranian laws that impose special obligations upon Iranian nationals, such as military service or taxes. Exit permits for departure from Iran for such persons may be denied until such obligations are met. Dual nationals often have their U.S. passports confiscated and may be denied permission to leave Iran, or encounter other problems with Iranian authorities. Specific questions on dual nationality may be directed to the following:

IRAN

Office of Citizens Consular Services, Department of State
Washington, D.C. 20520
☎ *(202) 647-7899*

Imported Goods

On May 6, 1995, President Clinton signed an executive order prohibiting exporting goods or services to Iran, re-exporting certain goods to Iran, new investments in Iran or in property owned or controlled by the government of Iran and brokering or other transactions involving goods or services of Iranian origin or owned or controlled by the government of Iran. These restrictions have been added to those already contained in the Iranian Transactions Regulations that prohibited unauthorized importation of Iranian-origin goods or services into the United States. For information regarding the issuance of licenses, contact the Licensing Division, The Treasury Department's Office of Foreign Assets Control ("FAC") at ☎ *(202) 622 2480).*

FAC issues licenses only for goods that were located outside of Iran prior to imposition of these sanctions on October 29, 1987. Goods in Iran after that do not qualify for authorization from Customs criteria for authorization. Iranian-origin goods, including those that were in Iran after October 29, 1987, may enter the United States if they qualify for entry under the following provisions administered solely by Customs:

(1) gifts valued at US$100 or less,

(2) goods for personal use contained in the accompanied baggage of persons traveling from Iran valued at US$400 or less, or

(3) goods qualifying for duty-free treatment as "household goods" or "personal effects" (as defined by U.S. law and subject to quantity limitations).

Inquiries about these provisions should be directed to Customs in the U.S. port where the goods would arrive.

Getting Sick

A yellow fever vaccination is required for travelers over the age of one year coming from infected areas. Arthropod-borne diseases and Hepatitis B are endemic. Malaria is a risk in some provinces from March through November. Food- and waterborne diseases, including cholera, are common, as is trachoma. (Snakes and rabid animals can also pose a threat.) Basic medical care and medicines are available in the principal cities of Iran, but may not be available in outlying areas. There are three doctors and 14 hospital beds for every 10,000 people. The international travelers' hotline at the Centers for Disease Control, ☎ *(404) 332-4559*, has additional useful health information.

Nuts and Bolts

Iran, about three times the size of Arizona, is a constitutional Islamic Republic, governed by executive and legislative branches that derive national leadership primarily through the Muslim clergy. Shia Islam is the official religion of Iran, and Islamic law is the basis of the authority of the state. Islamic ideals and beliefs provide the conservative foundation of the country's customs, laws and practices. Shiites comprise about 95 percent of the country. Sunnis make up about 4 percent. The literacy rate is at about 75 percent. Iran is a developing country.

The workweek in Iran is Sunday through Thursday. The rial is about 1800 to the dollar. Electricity is 220V/50hz. Languages are Farsi, Turkish, Kurdish Arabic and scattered English.

Temperatures for Tehran can be very hot in the summer and just above freezing in the winter. The northern part of the country can experience quite bitter winters. Iran has a mostly desert climate with unusual extremes in temperature. Temperatures exceeding 130° F occasionally occur in the summer, while in the winter the high elevation of most of the country often results in temperatures of zero° F and lower.

There is no U.S. embassy or consulate in Iran. The U.S. does have an interests section at the **Swiss embassy** in Tehran:

Swiss Embassy, U.S. Interests Section
Bucharest Avenue
Argentine Square
17th street, No. 5
Tehran
☎ *[98] (21) 625-223/224 and 626-906.*

Dangerous Days

07/03/1989   Day the Ayatollah Khomeini died.

02/14/1989   Khomeini announced a death decree on *Satanic Verses* author Salman Rushdie, an Indian national, resident in the United Kingdom.

07/03/1988   The U.S.S. *Vincennes* mistakenly shot down an Iranian Airbus airliner over the Persian Gulf.

12/04/1984   Four Islamic Jihad terrorists hijacked a Kuwaiti airliner bound for Pakistan from Kuwait and ordered it flown to Tehran. Two U.S. aid personnel were killed during the hijacking, while two others, another U.S. aid official and an American businessman, were tortured during the ordeal. Iranian troops stormed the aircraft on December 9, retaking it from the hijackers.

06/28/1981   The prime minister and 74 others were killed in the bombing of the legislature.

01/20/1981   U.S. embassy hostages released. Fifty-two American hostages were freed after 444 days in captivity, following an agreement between the U.S. and Iran arranged by Algeria.

09/19/1980   Iran-Iraq war began.

07/27/1980   Death of the shah of Iran.

04/25/1980   The day operations to rescue American hostages failed in the desert of Iran, due to operational shortfalls and an aircraft accident. The hostages remained in captivity until released by the government of Iran.

11/04/1979   The U.S. embassy was seized and 63 people were taken hostage.

04/01/1979   Islamic Republic Day commemorating riots by Islamic fundamentalists in Isfahan.

03/10/1979   Death of Kurdish leader Mullah Mustafa Barzani. (Kurdish regions.)

02/11/1979   Revolution Day. Celebration of the victory of the Islamic revolution.

02/04/1979   Iranian revolution began. Iran's Shiite clerics started their takeover of the government.

02/01/1979   Khomeini returned from exile and called the start of the "Ten Days of Dawn," commemorating the 10 days of unrest, ending with Khomeini taking power on February 11 (the "Day of Victory").

01/16/1979   The shah departed Iran.

11/04/1978   Student uprising against the shah.

09/09/1978   The shah's troops opened fire on protesters in Tehran, killing several hundred demonstrators.

Dangerous Days

11/04/1964	The Ayatollah Khomeini was exiled to Turkey.
06/05/1963	The arrest of the Ayatollah Khomeini by the shah's police. Also the Day of Mourning and Revolution Day.
01/22/1946	Kurdish Republic Day.
02/07/1902	Birth date of the Ayatollah Ruhollah Khomeini.
06/28	Revolutionary Guard's Day.
03/21	Persian New Year. Kurdish New Year celebrated.

Islam

Islam is the religion of more than a billion people on this planet. Long viewed as the Arab religion, it is just as likely that a Muslim is Indonesian, Chinese, Russian or even an American black.

Islam is based on some very simple premises. It could be said it is a shade more intolerant (regarding the hatred of Jews and nonbelievers) and a shade more merciful (in charity toward orphans and widows) than Christianity. Muslims have dietary and health laws (no pork or alcohol), have a period of fasting (the ninth Muslim month of Ramadan) and are encouraged to make a pilgrimage to Mecca at least once in their lifetime (the hajj).

Muslims' adherence to the Koran (a holy book revealed to Mohammed by God) and the tenets of Islam range from tolerant to fanatic. The two main sects of Islam are the mostly Arab Sunnis (85 percent) and the mostly Persian Shi'ites (15 percent). The Iranian Shi'ites are the most evangelistic of the two branches.

Are there really any major differences between Christianity and Islam? First, Muslims believe that both Christians and Jews have it all wrong since they worship untrue gods. Second, Muslims see decadence as a sign of Westerners being infidels.

Terrorism has been linked with Islam—an unfair connection since Christian antiabortion groups are just as reprehensible in this practice as Islamic fundamentalists from a legal sense. There is no denying that Iran has encouraged the development and activities of fundamentalist groups around the world. The one area where Islam scares Westerners is that there is no promise of material happiness or personal gain from terrorist activities. More important, Islam has not lost a war since the Crusades. The real enemy of Islam is factionalism. Warring Islamic groups in Afghanistan, Iraq, Turkey and Iran show that any ideology loses its momentum once a common enemy (in this case, Russia) is removed.

IRAN

In a Dangerous Place

Iran: Hijacked

In October of 1980 I was 23 and a beginning war correspondent. I was return-ing from my first trip to Iran, where Iraq had just launched what was to be a long, deadly war of attrition. I went to the front, but my film was developed and the best shots confiscated by Iranian censors. I was left with useless shots of people, smiling soldiers and not much else. After I checked in with SIPA, my photo agen-cy in Paris, I was told to try the other side—Iraq. On my way, I decide to cover the military maneuvers of the Turkish army near Diyarbakir in the southeast of Turkey. First, I would stop in at Ankara to get my visa for Iraq.

Our Turkish Airlines *Boeing 727* took off as scheduled around 5:30 p.m. for its 35-minute-long flight. But one hour later we still had not landed. The other pas-sengers and I start feeling uneasy. I wonder if the wheels of the plane are blocked. Suddenly, the voice of the pilot breaks through the tension: "Ladies and gentle-men, we might be obliged to land in Diyarbakir. Otherwise, we will head toward Iran. I now give the microphone to a Muslim brother." Instantly, the entire plane knows we have been hijacked.

Yilmaz Yalciner, the leader of the hijackers, carries on with his statement, given in the most imperative intonation:

"Islam takes over the plane. Long live the Divine Ayatollah Ruhollah Khomeini…. *Shariat*, the unique sure way to bring happiness to the entire human race, is the name of our mission. We are changing the route of this plane so as to go to Teheran, the cradle of the Islamic Revolution. Then, my three Mus-lim brothers and I will proceed to Afghanistan, where we will fight alongside the brothers who are leading the Jihad [Holy War] against the Russian atheists. For this reason, I am now going to pass around the hat. Whatever you give, make sure to give with your heart."

The passengers, in a state of shock after this announcement, search their pockets for some money. The collection begins. The passengers, afraid of the reprisals, give as much as they can to the militant who is passing a bag. Yilmaz Yalciner counts the money and gets back to the microphone: "Eighty-nine Turkish Lira [US$100]," he says, "it's really too little for people like you, but thanks anyway. Don't forget that we are going to fight with this money against the atheist Soviets."

For the passengers, the unbearable wait starts.

Nobody moves anymore; there is little to talk about, and everyone knows the gravity of the situation. All of us are probably thinking the same thing—fanatics are unpredictable. All we can do is wait anxiously for their next move. Once more, the voice of the hijacker breaks the heavy silence: "All women onboard must cover their hair—it is a rule of Islam. And Islam only constrains you to do good things." The 28 female passengers quickly cover their hair with whatever is available, including the white cotton cloth of the headrests of their seats. Some women, short of anything looking like a *chador,* shroud themselves under their husband's jackets.

Being a photojournalist first and a terrified passenger second, I pull out my camera and start taking photos. I am more concerned about running out of film since I do not know how long the ordeal will last. I found myself elated that I am at the center of what will be an international story, but scared out of my wits that the usual *laissez passer* accorded to the press will not be observed by the Muslim fanatics. The hijackers seem just as terrified as the passengers but apparently find comfort in carrying out this simpleminded and dangerous act.

At first, I photograph the passengers clandestinely, but this is not the story. Then I have an idea. I inform my friend Osman, a radio journalist, sitting next to me about my intentions to talk to the hijackers and ask their permission to take photos of the whole event. He quickly dismisses the idea as insane and advises me to adopt a low profile instead, so as not to attract their attention.

My hunch is that the hijackers are Iranian. I figure that if I show them the recent stamps in my passport and some of the recent Iranian photos I have with me they might allow me to document the hijacking. I head toward the first-class compartment where three of the militants have gathered, and tell them I am a journalist and ask permission to take photos. One of them, Omer Yorulmaz (I learned his name later), calmly tells me to wait and he will check with the leader in the cockpit. In the meantime, I go back to my seat to get my cameras. He comes out and tells me I can enter. I am elated.

As I quickly take photos of the crowded cockpit, I notice the contrast between the tense but efficient crew, and the theatrical laughter of the hijacker (Yilmaz Yalciner) as he holds a gun close to the right temple of someone sitting behind the pilot. I am even more elated with the fact that this is the first time a hijacking has ever been photographed in the air.

Suddenly, Yalciner commands me to stop. I realize his smile is a natural schoolboy's reaction to the camera and not indicative of the tension in the cockpit. Ignoring me, he resumes his negotiations with the pilot. I am being watched carefully by another hijacker. The pilot, Ilhan Akdeniz, is trying to convince Yalciner once and for all: "It is impossible," he says, "to violate Iran's airspace. There is a war going on! They are going to shoot us down with missiles! They won't want to know whether we've been hijacked."

Yalciner's answer surprises everyone, "Don't worry, the Muslim world knows me very well. Khomeini knows me too. Stop worrying—we'll make it to Teheran.

The pilot explains there would not be enough fuel. He asks if the plane can land in Dyabakir to refuel. The hijackers, convinced, agree. That issue resolved, the lead hijacker seems to relax and resume his casual demeanor.

He turns toward me and tells me abruptly, "I am not a mean terrorist. I am a good terrorist. So you're a journalist?" "Yes." "So am I, and the three brothers, too," he explains. "You can take more pictures of me, you know, but I must admit, I don't know how to pose," he adds before bursting out laughing.

They are all working for a banned publication called *Shariat*. Hence, the name of the "mission" they are undertaking. They are religious terrorists belonging to the "Akincilar group" (independent Sunni Muslims linked with the National Salvation Party).

I resume taking pictures of the scene, and of the passengers. The passengers still have no idea what fate has in store for them. These hijackers appear unusually calm. They are obviously fanatics to the point of candidness; they seem to be absolutely confident that they are going to get to Teheran. But I can feel their tension. I lie to them pretending I understand their motivation and want to provide them oodles of publicity. They are quite willing to talk. I ask them how they managed to smuggle their guns onto the Boeing in spite of the tight security control. Yalciner pulls out a book, which he opens to show me that it had been hollowed to make room for a pistol. He laughs heartily about the clever trick he has played on the security guards. Another shows me an attaché case filled with Turkish lires so that they can survive in their new country, Iran. It is hard to tell whether I am in the presence of childish stupidity or enormous confidence.

We make small talk until the plane lands at Diyarbakir. The passengers don't know what city or country they are landing in. Most passengers know that bad things start to happen once hijacked planes touch down.

I become self-conscious realizing that I am the only one who does not seem afraid. The passengers look at me with hatred and fear. Am I a hijacker? The confusion makes them suspicious. I find myself in a no man's land, between the passengers and the terrorists. Because of my decision to document this criminal act, the terrorists have made me part of their drama. By not intervening against the hijackers, I have become a coconspirator in the minds of the passengers. The camera has given me a special passport.

The hijackers also treat the cowering passengers differently. The burning light in the hijackers' eyes looks nothing but ominous.

We wait on the ground. The stewardesses attend to the people quietly and efficiently. The air in the plane is hot and stale. There is no more water or food. The plane feels like a tomb or a submarine that had sunk to the bottom of the ocean. Outside our plastic windows the ground crews, the vehicles and the world seem a thousand miles away. Time is irrelevant.

It is not hard to figure out what is going through the minds of the 148 people aboard. The hijackers are also getting tense, and I sense it is time to stop taking pictures.

It is now 8:30 p.m. We have only been on the plane for three hours but no one aboard would forget this day. Given the time for reflection, I remember why I am going to Diyarbakir in the first place. I realize that the hijackers have made a fatal mistake: They have landed in the center of a major military base and smack in the middle of preparations for showy military maneuvers. I was supposed to cover the strength and power of the Turkish Army. I was about to be center stage. To make matters worse, the Turkish and European press are there in full force. Faced with the tedious coverage of a nonevent, they were delighted to be at the scene of a hijacking. The worst part is that the new hard-liner president of Turkey himself, Kevan Evren, is at the airport and has taken charge of the event. He declares, "No concessions."

The negotiations between the hijackers and the Airport Authority are going on with no apparent progress. The hijackers make a concession—they will free the women and the children. But it really doesn't matter what they agree to, since their fate is being decided for them in the smoke-filled meeting rooms inside the airport.

At 10 p.m., 19 *Celik Kuvvet* (Steel Force) commandos take off from Ankara and Adana. Their planes land at Diyarbakir at 11 p.m. At midnight the airport is blacked out and the plane is by itself on the tarmac. The fear aboard is palpable.

It is now Tuesday. We have lived another day. At 1 a.m., electronic listening devices are installed on the body of the plane to locate the hijackers. Four more hours are necessary to prepare the rescue operation. Inside the grounded plane the passengers are aware of, and can see, nothing.

At 5 a.m., the commandos split into two groups. One group silently cuts open the rear door, while the front group creates a minor diversion near the cockpit. The commandos burst through the back of the plane, yelling, "Lie down everybody," followed by a shoot-out. The sound of the firefight in the small enclosed space is deafening.

The passenger I photographed in the cockpit is wounded and later dies in the hospital. I duck under my seat, afraid that my camera might be mistaken for a gun. I regret not taking pictures, but realistically I know I would be killed instantly.

Crowded below the seat, I have just enough time to hide some film in my underwear and to give some rolls to Osman, the radio journalist sitting next to me. The three surviving hijackers surrender quite easily as if all was in good fun.

The passengers are asked to lie down on the tarmac and later we will be driven to an army barracks. I am pointed out by some of the passengers as one of the hijackers. In fact, the news wire reports include me in the list of hijackers arrested in the assault. I am taken into custody for interrogation.

After some minutes, most of the passengers are freed and brought to the barracks. Five passengers and I are kept behind. The three hijackers are taken away in a truck. Then the police throw the six of us in a second truck, which follows the first one. My cameras have been confiscated. I still feel confident that the whole situation will soon be clarified.

There are six of us crammed into the same jail cell. We are tired, dirty and thirsty from the 12-hour ordeal. Two engineers, one Italian and two Turkish customs officers who usually control the passports on board, Osman, the radio-journalist, and myself are detained. The police suspect the customs officers of complicity. They want to confirm the identities of the foreign engineers. Osman is detained because he is a journalist, and I, because I am a suspected terrorist. The hijackers are put in another cell not far from ours.

My interrogation is a lot tougher than I anticipated. I am bullied by the policemen when they discover that I work for SIPA Press (SIPA means donkey in Turkish). When I tell them that I was born in Siirt, they realize that I am a Kurd. They find my story hard to believe—that I would simply ask permission to take photos because it is my job. They do not believe I am only a journalist, and I am sent back to my cell. During the entire night, we can't sleep very much, as we are disturbed by the comings and goings of our jailkeepers accompanying the hijackers to their interrogations. We can hear a lot of their yells. We are very uneasy about all this. We can also hear the news on a radio set. I gather that everybody believes I am the fifth terrorist and I therefore should not expect any mercy.

The next day, Osman is freed and I have time to give him some more film to take to SIPA. I am left alone in the cell. Later on, the terrorists and I are sent to another jail well known as a torture center for prisoners captured by the military.

Luckily, this time my interrogation is shorter. I am told I will be released because they checked my identity and they understand I have told the truth. It seems also that some people (journalists and politicians) have vouched for me. Never underestimate the usefulness of political contacts.

I am very surprised and elated when I am finally released. I rush back to SIPA's headquarters in Istanbul, just in time to learn that only a handful of my photos have been published in Turkey as well as around the world. Most of them had been lost due to Osman's mishandling of the developing process. But there were more rolls of film that I had hidden under the aircraft seats that had still not been recovered.

1985: Hijacking No. 2

Five years later (1985) I was involved in another hijacking. This time I am not inside the plane, a TWA *Boeing 727*, but on the tarmac in Beirut.

The plane is coming from Athens, Greece, and going to Rome, Italy. Two Shiite Lebanese order the pilot to divert the flight to Beirut. Other hijackers join them at Beirut. They demand the discharge of more than 700 Shiite prisoners and others detained in Israel. One passenger, a member of the Mexican Navy, is killed. Between June 14 and 26, 111 passengers are released, as well as five crewmen. The 36 other passengers and three other crewmen are detained until June 30. The plane is prevented from leaving Beirut by the Lebanese authorities.

So it becomes a long wait with pictures few and far between.

The hijacking is a comic opera. The hijackers are able to roam about outside the plane and even go back home to sleep at night, thanks to the complicity of the AMAL militia. I am a little wiser, tougher, and cynical. I decide to leave the dull, monotony of the airport and cover the more saleable action in town. I negotiate a deal with one of the hijackers for him to cover the event from inside the plane. The hijacker agrees and I give him an automatic camera. The reward for my ingenuity is that I am run over by an armored vehicle, which crushes one of my legs. I assume the hijacker showed up with the film to get his payment, but he didn't know that I was in the hospital with an injured leg. So I could not get the photos. *C'est la guerre.*

—Coskun Aral

IRAN

Baghdad

Iraq
★ ★ ★

Let's Make a Deal

After Saddam Hussein's recent efforts to turn the Persian Gulf deserts into Mr. Boffo's hell, people were surprised to learn that not only did Saddam still have an army, but he was willing to use it and lose it. Saddam doesn't have a whole lot of options these days. His people are hungry, the country is in shambles, and he still eludes one or two assassination attempts a year. His next door neighbor, Iran, is busy destabilizing his country and organizing the disparate opposition groups into one central party. Iran's long-term goal is to erase the border between the two countries.

Iraq's plummet into the depths began in earnest in 1980. That year, Saddam launched the war against Iran, which lasted until August 1988. Iraq had long-standing border disputes with Iran and Kuwait and a fierce animosity toward Israel. In addition to this, the ruling Iraqi Ba'ath Party had a 20-year rivalry with the ruling Ba'ath Party of Syria. After the August 1988 cease-fire with Iran, Iraq supplied arms and money to the Christian forces in Lebanon to relaunch the war

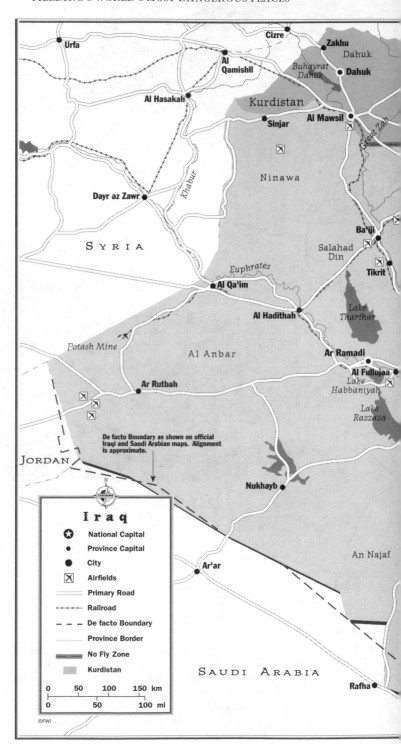

IRAQ

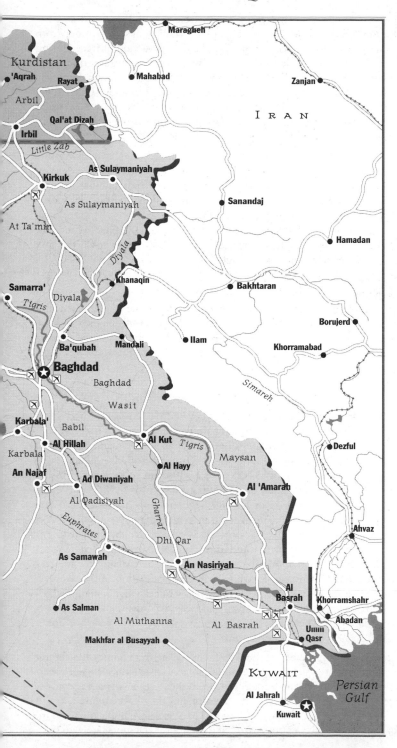

there against the Syrian army and Islamic Lebanese forces. It invaded and annexed Kuwait in August 1990, with the apparent intention of seizing funds from Kuwait's banks and investment companies for the reconstruction of Iraq. During the Iran-Iraq war, many countries supplied Iraq with arms in contravention of international conventions that preclude arms supply to countries at war. Suppliers included the U.S.A., the former Soviet Union, France, Germany, U.K., Italy, China, Chile, Brazil and East European countries. Iraq was accused of using chemical weapons against Iranian forces and subsequently against the Kurds in northern Iraq.

For now, Iraq is one of the world's great travel bargains. You'd have a hard time finding things to buy, however, no matter what budget you're on. But if you want to top your tank off, you're in luck. The collapse of the Iraqi dinar from its official rate at about US$3.20 to its real rate of about a thousand times less means that when you buy a full tank of gas using dinars, you pay less than an Uncle Sam's penny. Gasoline costs .0009 cents a gallon and costs 0.07 dinars a liter. But if you make other transactions at the official rate, beware. Don't reach out and touch someone. Telephone calls from Baghdad to the U.S. can cost US$158 a minute.

The embargo on Iraq imposed after Iraq's invasion of Kuwait, and a scarcity of U.S. dollars, is pulling the value of Iraq's currency to the value of used Charmin. In a country where educated people make about 2000–3000 dinars a month, there is little to buy and even less to buy with it. Just imagine a country where a crisp U.S. 100-dollar bill will bring you a thousand 25-dinar notes. It's positively retro! The currency is worth so little that people pay for goods, where they can find them, in wads of a hundred 25-dinar bills wrapped with rubber bands. Shopkeepers don't even bother counting the notes.

After the Gulf War, Allied forces had destroyed, neutralized or captured 41 of the 42 Iraqi army divisions in the war zone of Kuwait and southern Iraq. The coalition estimated the number of Iraqi prisoners of war at 175,000 and the number of Iraqi casualties at 85,000–100,000, out of an estimated 500,000 soldiers positioned in the combat area. Iraq lost 3700 of its 5500 main battle tanks, 1857 of its 7500 armored vehicles and 2140 of its 3500 artillery pieces. Ninety-seven of Iraq's 689 combat aircraft and six of its 489 helicopters were destroyed. One-hundred-sixty combat aircraft were flown to Iran, where they were impounded as war reparations. Nine airfields were destroyed, as well as 16 chemical weapons plants, 10 biological weapons plants and three nuclear weapons facilities. Yet Baghdad continues holding onto thousands of pieces of civilian and military equipment that it had stolen from Kuwait during its occupation of the country. Iraq currently possesses approximately 9000 pieces of military equipment, including trucks, jeeps, armored personnel carriers and Grog-7 missiles, as well as perhaps 6000 civilian items. These items were supposed to have been returned under the 1991 U.N. Security Council Resolution.

Since Iraq's devastating defeat in the 1991 Gulf War, the country has rebuilt much of its infrastructure, including the phone system, electrical plants, government buildings and bridges. The Iraqi people have shown themselves to be a very resilient people. Saddam's is not the first dictatorship they have endured, and it won't be the last. Economic embargoes tend to have greater ramifications on innocent citizens than on the dictators who led them into it. Despots rarely go hungry. They're occasionally assassinated, but usually with full stomachs. Saddam still sports that tire around his waist, while his people are being starved to death by the West. Just a single well-aimed cruise missile could dramatically change things for the better in what used to be the cradle of civilization. Saddam's effectiveness in eliminating successors and the West's fear of a more belligerent successor are the main reasons he is still in power. He seems to be somewhat confident of a long reign, despite the U.S.'s claim that its embargo will ensure his demise. Why do we know he is confident? Well, since the Gulf War, he has spent $1.2 billion building or rebuilding more than 40 palaces in Iraq. In April 1995, Saddam threw a big 58th birthday bash to remind everyone he was still alive. Meanwhile, things get worse for the common folk.

The U.N. reports that most of Iraq's population is experiencing mass deprivation, chronic hunger and endemic malnutrition, along with the collapse of personal incomes and a rapidly increasing number of destitute, jobless and homeless people. Sounds like a great place for a bargain vacation. For now the Iraqis can sell oil for food.

In 1996 President Clinton sent a Labor Day present to Saddam in response to his sending the Republican Guard north. (About 44 cruise missiles, half from B52's from Guam and half from the navy.) The goal was to take out radar and air defense installations in the south. C'mon Bill, we sent you a copy of DP. What we got was a very expensive pre-election Labor Day fireworks show. Later we found out that Bill had spent $20 million on a CIA operation to overthrow Saddam using a base outside Irbil. As usual it didn't work and most of the agents were rounded up and shot. (Their Yank supervisors escaped.)

The Scoop

Considering that Baghdad used to be the Garden of Eden, the breadbasket of the ancient world and part of the fertile crescent, the boys from Baghdad have done a good job of screwing it up—despite having enough oil to make Saudi Arabia look like a dry sump in Lubbock. Instead of basking in its riches, Iraq is poor, the consequence of Saddam's maniacal insistence on becoming the superpower of the Middle East. The Gulf War was a laughable attempt by Hussein to shun international diplomacy and snatch back oil-rich Kuwait. Either Saddam didn't pay attention during history class or he just likes expensive fireworks, because he plunged his country into the Third World club in a mere three months.

There are lots of reasons to travel to Iraq—its history, people, culture, etc. But you can't if you are an American. You can if you are a journalist or aid worker, but that's it.

The Players

President Saddam Hussein al-Tikriti

He's still the man. Hussein has managed to remain in power since 1979, despite questionable and ill-fated foreign policy moves that have caused the impoverishment of his country and the deaths of more than 100,000 Iraqis in the Gulf War. But the man still retains a respectable following. He is president and chairman of the Revolutionary Command Council (RCC), regional secretary of the ruling Ba'ath Party and head of the 100,000-strong Popular Militia. When he needs help running the country, he hires good old boys from his hometown of Tikrit, north of Baghdad.

Hussein's absolute rule rests with his status in the RCC. The chairman of the RCC is, ex-officio, president of the republic. The president appoints ministers and judges, and laws are enacted by presidential decree. Routine governing of the country is carried out by an appointed council of ministers.

Saddam is swiftly using up his nine lives. He survived a failed military coup in May 1991, and he offed 18 senior army officers just to make sure he could get a good night's sleep. It isn't known how many times the U.S. tried to take him out during the Gulf War. In June 1991, he fired 1500 senior army officers and 180 senior police officers as a reward for following his orders during the Gulf War. Since then, there have been at least three coup attempts against Saddam's rule. More than 200 current and former officers and civilians were arrested, including the commander of the Republican Guard's tank battalion Brig Sufiyan al-Ghurairi and former parliamentarian Jasser al-Tikriti. All the plotters hailed from Saddam's hometown of Tikrit, as well as from Mosul and Ramadi. The attempt appears to have been the first in which members of the Tikrit clan played an important role in removing the despot. There were at least two unsuccessful assassination attempts against Saddam in late December 1993 and January 1994. Hussein's recent misguided saber rattling in the fall of 1994 managed to anger more troops just itching to deliver some high-priced ballistics directly into his place of residence.

Hussein also leans on the loyalty of his security services and the Republican Guard divisions of the army to put down any uprisings. The Republican Guard suppressed the Shiite uprising in the south of the country and the Kurdish rebellion in the north. Saddam's paranoia is well founded.

Saddam is one heck of guy. In fact, he is like Gaddafi with *cojones*. A guy who takes on the entire Western world, his own people, his relatives and just about anybody who isn't him has to be either real smart or real stupid. Whatever you believe, Saddam Hussein still calls the shots in Iraq. In fact, he has a new economic incentive package where he offers US$10,000 (who would want Iraqi money?) to anyone who kills a foreigner in northern Iraq. The goal is to force out aid workers from the area known as Kurdistan. AFP reporter Lisle Schmidt and her bodyguard probably made somebody 20 grand richer in April of 1994 when they were murdered.

The Kurds

Only a few days after the Gulf War ended, major insurrections broke out in both the south of Iran and particularly in Kurdistan, where Kurd rebels seized large areas of territory by the first week of March 1991. Iraq's "elite" Republican Guards used repugnant brutality in suppressing the Kurd rebellion. Kurd refugees fleeing the wrath of the Republican Guard numbered 2 million or more along the Iraqi borders with both Turkey and

Iran. The U.S. and Great Britain dispatched troops to northern Iraq on a short-lived effort to entice the Kurds to return home.

When the Iraqi army pulled out of the north they left a political vacuum. The U.S.-controlled area is now called Kurdistan. Of the 19.2 million people in Iraq, 21.6 percent are Kurds (73.5 percent are Arabs). There is a legitimate argument for the state of Kurdistan since the Kurds were left out of any postcolonial country-carving. The Iraqi army has been doing bad things to the Kurds while away from the scrutiny of the world. They have been engaged in using a variety of methods to exterminate the Kurds, including bombing, starvation and even employing chemical weapons in an effort to reduce the population. Hussein is less interested in being nasty to the Kurdish people than he is in keeping the oil their new country would sit on—especially the oil fields in the Kirkuk area.

The Marsh Arabs (the Ma'dan)

It seems every country makes fun of whoever lives in the south—Spain, Italy, the U.S. Russia and even Iraq have their hillbillies and country folk who just want to be left alone. In Iraq there are about 50,000 Shiites who live in the areas once considered to be the Garden of Eden. Some are Sabeans who predate Islam. The government of Hussein is Sunni, even though 55 percent of Iraq are Shiites.

This area between the Tigris and the Euphrates has been home to the Ma'dan for over 5000 years. Today, the people live in rural simplicity and survive by raising water buffalo and sheep, growing rice, and selling reeds which are used to make mats. The people live on islands and travel using ancient dugout canoes. Many of their villages are actually man-made floating islands. There is also a group of about 10,000 insurgents who fight against the government of Iraq. Although the people allude to it as the Garden of Eden, it is a hot, humid place infested with mosquitoes, fleas and ticks. Winters are cold, with gales coming from the mountains of Kurdistan to the north or Iran to the east.

For now, Saddam is building dams, draining the marshes and pouring poison into the rivers (he loves to play with chemicals, doesn't he?) in an effort to simply eliminate every living thing in the marshes. When he gets bored of poisoning the people, crops and animals, he has his army pound on them with artillery, strafe them with gunships and drop large bombs on them. If things are a little slow, he has his soldiers burn hundreds of acres of weeds just to give them something to do.

The Army

Despite all the smart bombs we dropped on Iraq, there are still 400,000 soldiers that have 2200 tanks,, 2500 APC's, and 1650 artillery pieces. There are about 300 combat aircraft left that are hampered by the two no-fly zones monitored by the West. Why didn't we leave Saddam with a slingshot and two rocks? Well, seems that George Bush was more worried about Iran, so he whittled Saddam's toys to Third World size. We think we got all of his scuds, but the CIA still insists he's hiding a few. He also has about 7000 nuclear scientists and a fairly covert biological warfare program.

Supreme Council of the Islamic Resistance in Iraq (SCIRI)

There were about 40,000 rebels in southern Iraq called the Supreme Council for the Islamic Revolution in Iraq. Most have reformed in the north. Many were killed in 1991 by Saddam Hussein during the aborted uprising. They have joined with the Iraqi National Congress (INS).

Potatoes for diesel

Despite the embargo on Iraq, when DP visited northern Iraq in October of 1994 during Hussein's military feint to the south, we passed a line of trucks three kms long and in rows of three waiting to bring basic foodstuffs into northern Iraq. The truckdrivers were rewarded for their three-day waits with homemade rusty tanks bolted below the trucks full of crude diesel fuel, which would later sell in Turkish gas stations for around 10,000 Turkish lira a liter.

Money Hassles

The Iraqi dinar is virtually worthless. The shortage of foreign currency has created a thriving black market, although the penalties for its use are severe, with heavy fines and possible imprisonment. The difference in exchange rates is vast between the black market and the official rates. The official exchange rate to the U.S. dollar has remained unchanged at US$3.2169:ID1 since 1982, but the real rate is about 8000 to the dollar. You must declare your funds on entry, but few people do. It is legal to bring only ID25 into Iraq and take out ID5. Any amount of hard currency may be imported, but this must be declared on entry, and receipts must be obtained for any expenditure in Iraq. The balance and receipts must be shown upon leaving the country. Credit cards are not generally accepted, and traveler's checks are virtually useless. Iraqis traveling abroad may take out ID100.

Getting In

Travel Warning

The Department of State warns all U.S. citizens against traveling to Iraq. Conditions within the country remain unsettled and dangerous. The United States does not maintain diplomatic relations with Iraq and cannot provide normal consular protective services to U.S. citizens. U.S. passports are not valid for travel to, in or through Iraq, unless they are specially endorsed by the U.S. Government. There is a U.S. trade embargo that severely restricts financial and economic activities with Iraq, including travel-related transactions.

The Iraqi embassy considers Iraq safe for travel, and they are probably about 80 percent right. It's the 20 percent you have to worry about. Border crossings between Jordan and Iraq are closed; all others are open. Crossings from Turkey are backed up but are orderly and efficient.

You have to be a reporter or use a foreign passport. Passports and visas are required. On February 8, 1991, U.S. passports ceased to be valid for travel to, in or through Iraq and may not be used for that purpose unless a special validation has been obtained. Without the requisite validation, use of a U.S. passport for travel to, in or through Iraq may constitute a violation of 18 U.S.C. 1544, and may be punishable by a fine and/or imprisonment. An exemption to the above restriction is granted to Americans residing in Iraq as of February 8, 1991, who continue to reside there, and to American professional reporters or journalists on assignment there.

In addition, the Department of the Treasury prohibits all travel-related transactions by U.S. persons intending to visit Iraq, unless specifically licensed by the Office of Foreign Assets Control. The only exceptions to this licensing requirement are for journalistic activity or for U.S. government or United Nations business. The categories of individuals eligible for consideration for a special passport validation are set forth in 22 C.F.R. 51.74. Passport validation requests for Iraq should be forwarded in writing to either of the following addresses:

Iraqi Embassy

1801 P Street, N.W.
Washington, D.C. 20036
☎ *(202) 483-7500*

Deputy Assistant Secretary for Passport Services

U.S. Department of State
1111 19th Street, N.W., Suite 260
Washington, D.C. 20522-1705
Attn: Office of Passport Policy and Advisory Services
☎ *(202) 955-0231 or 955-0232; FAX (202) 955-0230.*

The request must be accompanied by supporting documentation according to the category under which validation is sought. Currently, the four categories of persons specified in 22 C.F.R. 51.74 as being eligible for consideration for passport validation are as follows:

[1] Professional reporters: Includes full-time members of the reporting or writing staff of a newspaper, magazine or broadcasting network whose purpose for travel is to gather information about Iraq for dissemination to the general public.

[2] American Red Cross: Applicant establishes that he or she is a representative of the American Red Cross or International Red Cross traveling pursuant to an officially sponsored Red Cross mission.

[3] Humanitarian considerations: Applicant must establish that his or her trip is justified by compelling humanitarian considerations or for family unification. At this time, "compelling humanitarian considerations" include situations where the applicant can document that an immediate family member is critically ill in Iraq. Documentation concerning family illness must include the name and address of the relative, and be from that relative's physician attesting to the nature and gravity of the illness. "Family unification" situations may include cases in which spouses or minor children are residing in Iraq, with and dependent on, an Iraqi national spouse or parent for their support.

[4] National interest: The applicant's request is otherwise found to be in the national interest.

In all requests for passport validation for travel to Iraq, the name, date and place of birth for all concerned persons must be given, as well as the U.S. passport numbers. Documentation as outlined above should accompany all requests. Additional information may be obtained by writing to the above addresses or by calling the Office of Passport Policy and Advisory Services at ☎ *(202) 326-0231 or 955-0232.*

U.S. Treasury Restrictions

In August 1990 President Bush issued Executive Orders 12722 and 12724, imposing economic sanctions against Iraq, including a complete trade embargo. The U.S. Treasury Department's Office of Foreign Assets Control administers the regulations related to these sanctions, which include restrictions on all financial transactions related to travel to Iraq. These regulations prohibit all travel-related transactions, except as specifically licensed. The only exceptions to this licensing requirement are for persons engaged in journalism or in official U.S. government or U.N. business. Questions concerning these restrictions should be directed to:

Chief of Licensing Section, Office of Foreign Assets Control

U.S. Department of the Treasury
Washington, D.C. 20220
☎ *(202) 622-2480*
FAX (202) 622-1657

In the past year, most foreigners detained at the Kuwait-Iraq border, regardless of nationality, have been sentenced to jail terms of seven to 10 years for illegally entering Iraq.

During 1992 and 1993, Iraq detained nine Westerners—three Swedes, three Britons, a U.S. national, a German and a Frenchman—on charges of illegally entering Iraq. They were released by late 1993 after much diplomatic energy. In March 1995, two Americans were held and sentenced to eight years in prison. Tom Jerrold and an ABC news crew were also detained but were released after the U.N. intervened. Brent Sadler, who interviewed the two Americans in the Iraq jail, was asked for his written permission to be in the jail, even when accompanied by a Polish diplomat negotiating the release on behalf of the U.S. State department!

There have been attacks against foreigners, and antagonism is still high in the Western world. Many Egyptians and other Arab expatriates were killed by disgruntled, unemployed Iraqi ex-soldiers. Don't forget that expats were held hostage by Hussein from mid- to late-1990 during the Mexican standoff between Iraqi and Allied forces over the Iraqi annexation of Kuwait. All travelers and foreigners in Iraq run the risk of being detained, harassed and questioned, particularly in the south near the Kuwaiti border. The Iraqi embassy referred us to Mr. Ganji at Babylon Travel ☎ *(312) 478-9000*, for readers who want more details about travel to Iraq.

AIDS Test

Iraqi government officials have seemingly watched so many soap operas and pay-for-view dirty movies while out of the country that they think all Westerners are sex-crazed adulterers, fornicators and deviants.

Therefore, all visitors aged over 12 and under 65 who plan to stay in Iraq for longer than five days (official visitors have 15 days) must call on the Central Public Health Laboratory in Al Tayhariyat al Fennia Square between 8 a.m. and 2 p.m. to either present HIV and Syphilis (VDRL) certificates or arrange for a local test at a cost of ID100. HIV and VDRL certificates valid for Iraq may be obtained in the U.K. by arranging a blood test with a general practitioner. The sample should then be tested by a Public Health Laboratory Service listed on the blank certificate and attested by the Foreign Office and the Iraqi embassy in London. Failing to comply with these requirements carries a fine of ID500 or six-months imprisonment. A yellow fever vaccination certificate is required for all visitors arriving from an infected area.

Getting Around

Iraq has 33,238 km of roads, most of them improved during the 1980s. Expressway No. 1 (a 1200-km, six-lane freeway connecting Baghdad to Kuwait in the south and to Jordan and Syria in the west) was damaged by the bombing raids during the Gulf War. A 630-km freeway (Expressway No. 2) is being built to run north from Baghdad to the Turkish border, where it will link up with the modern freeway connecting southeast Turkey to Ankara and Istanbul. Another Baghdad-Basra route is planned via Kut and Amarah and will be known as Expressway No. 3.

There are 2035 kms of rail network, including the 461-km Baghdad-Kirkuk-Arbil line, the 528-km Baghdad-Mosul-Yurubiyah standard line and the 582-km Baghdad-Maaqal-Umm Qasr standard line. The 516-km line between Baghdad and al-Qaim and Qusaybah on the Syrian border was opened last year. The 252-km northern line between Kirkuk, Baiji and Haditha,which connects the Baiji oil refinery with the al-Qaim fertilizer plant, was opened in 1988.

Iraq's main port of Basra is inoperative, because of the closure of the Shatt al-Arab waterway during the war with Iran. Several Iraqi naval vessels were sunk in the waterway during the Gulf War.

Iraq has one functioning international airport, at Bamerni, 17 km south of Baghdad. The airport at Basra reopened in May 1991, following repairs. A third international airport was planned for Mosul, with a 4000-meter runway capable of handling 30 landings and takeoffs a day. Domestic regional airports at Arbil (3000-meter runway), Amara and Najaf (for small 50-seater aircraft) were also planned. Iraqi Airways has a fleet of four Boeing 747s, two Boeing 737s, six Boeing 727s and two Boeing 707s.

You can rent a car from the airport. You will need both national and international driving licences. You can also take the bus service for the 17-km trip from the city center to the airport. In Baghdad, the double-decker buses are cheap and can take you just about anywhere you want to go; don't forget to buy your tickets at the kiosks first. There are also private minibuses and shared taxis. A train service operates three times a day from Baghdad to Basra; don't plan on comfort or air conditioning unless you're lucky. You can choose from three class services with sleeping accommodations, restaurant cars and air conditioning. You can take the train between most of Iraq's major centers (Baghdad-Mosul, Baghdad-Arbil and Baghdad-Basra).There is also regular bus service from Baghdad to other major cities and regular flights between Baghdad, Basra and Mosul. Domestic airports are at Mosul, Kirkuk and Basra, as well as Bagdad.

Taxis must be negotiated in advance. During the war, *DP* paid US$1200 to get out of Baghdad, but we didn't have to tip. Taxis have meters, but it is legal to charge twice the amount shown on the meter. After 10 p.m. there is a surcharge.

Dangerous Places

Baghdad

Baghdad is the location for periodic bombings against state targets and occasional unsuccessful coup attempts against the regime of Saddam Hussein. Passersby occasionally sustain injuries in such incidents.

Family Reunions

Fruit doesn't fall too far from tree in Iraq, especially if it's rotten. By now, we all know that Saddam's son Udai makes Arnold Schwarzenegger look like Bambi in his lust to kill as many people as he can (including members of his own family). But did you know that Qusai commands the special forces that protect *el jefe* and that son-in-law Hussein Kamel Hassan takes care of making the factories work?

We also know that being a member of Saddam's family can lead to early retirement. In 1995 not only did Saddam blow away his homecoming son-in-law but he also fired his cousin Ali Hassan Majid, known affectionately as Chemical Ali for his gassing of Kurdish villagers in 1988–'89. Saddam also blew out his half-brother Watban, who used to be interior minister. Not much call for used politicians in Iraq these days, but at least he can cash his retirement checks. Bad vibes abound if you aren't a family member. A recent mutiny in the army resulted in the leader being executed and mutilated and the pieces sent back to his family.

The North (Kurdistan)

There have been uprisings against the government by Kurds in the north as well as fighting between Kurdish factions. Since May 1991, Kurdistan has been a semiautonomous state, home to large numbers of Kurdish refugees in Iran and Turkey in the north. In September '96 Iran sent troops to help the PUK. The Iraqis have withdrawn but the fighting continues.

The South

Shia refugees have fled to the marshlands bordering Iran, to Iran itself and to Kuwait and Saudi Arabia. The Iraqi government is currently busy draining the marshes to deprive the Shias of their homeland.There have been uprisings against the government by Shias in the south.

The Kuwaiti Border

U.S. citizens and other foreigners working near the Kuwait-Iraq border have been detained by Iraqi authorities for lengthy periods under harsh conditions. Travelers to that area, whether in Kuwait or not, are in immediate jeopardy of detention by Iraqi security personnel.

Everywhere Else

Hostilities in the Gulf region ceased on February 27, 1991. United Nations Security Council Resolution 687, adopted on April 3, 1991, set terms for a permanent cease-fire, but conditions in Iraq remain unsettled. Travel in Iraq is extremely hazardous for U.S.

citizens. Iraq is crawling with informants who report any movements of foreigners and dealings with locals. Because of Iraq's "Big Brother" environment, do not try to bribe police or military personnel.

Getting Sick

The diseases you should be vaccinated against are typhoid, cholera and hepatitis. Tap water should be sterilized before drinking, and visitors should avoid consuming ice. Milk is unpasteurized and should be boiled. Comprehensive medical insurance covering repatriation is essential, unless you want to get even sicker in an Iraqi hospital. Health and sanitary conditions weren't too good before the war, and they are worse now in all the major cities. Water, refuse and sanitation services are nonexistent, especially in the south, where outbreaks of typhoid, hepatitis, meningitis and gastroenteritis had reached epidemic proportions by late 1993. An outbreak of cholera was contained. Hospitals and other medical facilities were also damaged during the war and vital electricity supplies disrupted. Many expatriate doctors and hospital staff left the country. Stocks of pharmaceuticals have been depleted, and there are severe shortages of even nonprescription drugs. Essential drugs are almost nonexistent. If you need or think you may need medication or drugs, bring plenty with you. You can always donate or sell what you don't need on your way out.

Nuts and Bolts

The Iraqi currency, for what little it's worth, is the Iraqi dinar (ID). One ID=1000 files. Banks are open from 8 a.m.–noon (Saturday–Wednesday); 8 a.m.–11 a.m. (Thursday); 8 a.m.–10 a.m. during Ramadan. Government offices are open 8:30 a.m.–2:30 p.m. (Saturday–Wednesday); 8:30 a.m.–1:30 p.m. (Thursday, winter); 8 a.m.–noon (Saturday–Wednesday); 8 a.m.–11 a.m. (Thursday, summer). Businesses are open 8 a.m.–2 p.m. (Saturday–Wednesday); 8 a.m.–1 p.m. (Thursday). Shops, when they have anything to sell, don't follow the clock, opening at dawn, closing for lunch when the sun is high, and reopening when the day cools off around 4 p.m. Small shops tend to open very early, close during the middle of the day, and then reopen from around 4 p.m. till 7 p.m. or later. Food markets open around 9 a.m. and close at midday, or when supplies are exhausted. The Islamic year contains 354 or 355 days, meaning that Muslim feasts advance by 10 to 12 days against the Gregorian calendar each year. Dates of feasts vary according to the sighting of the new moon, so they cannot be forecast precisely.

There is a neutral zone between Iraq and Saudi Arabia, administered jointly by the two countries, with Iraq's portion covering 3522 square km. The country's most fertile area is the centuries-old flood plain of the Tigris and Euphrates rivers, from Turkey and Syria to the Gulf. The northeast of Iraq is mountainous, while the large western desert area is sparsely populated and undeveloped. The northern mountainous region experiences severe winters, but the southern plains have warm winters with little rain and very hot, dry summers. The temperatures in Baghdad are between 40°F and 60°F in January, and between 75°F and 90°F in July and August. The average annual rainfall is 28 mm.

Iraqi dishes provide the usual range of Middle Eastern and Turkish offerings: *tikka* (shish ke bab) *kubba* (cracked wheat mixed with minced meat and molded around nuts, sultanas, spices, parsley and onion); *dolma* (vine leaves or other vegetables stuffed with rice, meat and spices); *quozi* (small lamb stuffed with rice, minced meat and spices and served on rice); and *masgouf* (fish from the Tigris cooked on the riverbank). Alcohol is available only in international hotels.During the Ramadan fasting month, both smoking and drinking in public are forbidden.

Although 53.5 percent of the population are Shia Muslims, the minority Sunni Muslims (41.5 percent) are politically dominant.

Embassy Location

There is no U.S. embassy or consulate in Iraq. The U.S. government is not in a position to accord normal consular protective services to U.S. citizens who are in Iraq. U.S. government interests are represented by the government of Poland, which, as a protecting power, is able to provide only limited emergency services to U.S. citizens. The U.S. interests section of the embassy of Poland is located opposite the Foreign Ministry Club (Masbah Quarter):

U.S. Interests Section,
Embassy of Poland

> *P.O. Box 2447 Alwiyah*
> *Baghdad, Iraq*
> ☎ *(964-1) 719-6138, 719-6139, 719-3791, 718-1840*

Dangerous Days

04/16/1991	U.S. President George Bush announced that U.S. Troops would enter northern Iraq to create a safe haven for displaced Kurds around Zakhu.
03/02/1991	Iraq signed a cease-fire agreement with allied forces ending the Persian Gulf War.
02/27/1991	Allied forces in Kuwait and Iraq suspended military operations against Iraq.
02/24/1991	Allied forces launched the ground assault against Iraqi forces occupying Kuwait.
01/30/1991	Iraqi and multinational force elements had their first combat engagement in Khafji in the Persian Gulf War.
01/17/1991	The start of hostilities between the multinational forces and Iraqi forces. The beginning of Operation Desert Storm.
08/02/1990	Iraqi forces invaded Kuwait and seized control of the country.
08/15/1986	Turkish troops raided Kurdish rebel camps in Iraq.
11/26/1984	Relations with the U.S. restored.
06/07/1981	Israeli warplanes attacked an Iraqi nuclear power plant near Baghdad.
09/19/1980	Iran-Iraq war began.
03/10/1979	Death of Kurdish leader Mullah Mustafa Barzani (Kurdish regions).
06/01/1976	During this month, Syria entered the civil war in Lebanon on the side of the Christian Phalange and against the Palestinians and their Muslim allies. In response, Abu Nidal renamed his terrorist group then based in Iraq the Black June Organization and began attacking Syrian targets.
07/17/1968	Ba'ath Party seized power.
02/08/1963	Revolution Day.
02/03/1963	The Ba'ath Party took power in a popular revolt.
07/14/1958	Republic Day. Celebrates the coup by General Abdul Karim Qasim during which King Faysal iI and Prime Minister Nuri as-Said were killed.
04/08/1947	Iraqi Ba'ath Party was founded.
01/22/1946	Kurdish Republic Day.
04/28/1937	Saddam Hussein's birthday.
03/21	Kurdish New Year celebrated.

IRAQ

In a Dangerous Place

Iraq: On the Wrong Side of the Crusaders

The Gulf War, as it was known even during the six months of its preparation by the Allied forces (led by the U.S.A.), began on August 2, 1990. I was on holiday and by chance was headed back to Istanbul just before the beginning of the war. I was told to go to Habur in Turkey, the gateway to Iraq, a very important entrance during the eight-year-long Iran-Iraq war. I was being sent there to take photos of people fleeing the country. The Kerkuk-Yumurtalik pipeline had just been closed by the Turks at the request of the international community for a boycott of Iraqi oil. The boycott was imposed by the U.N. as retaliation against the invasion of Kuwait by Saddam Hussein's Iraq.

The frontier was only open to the refugees during the preparation of the war.

After the ultimatum of the UN to Iraq, I went to Amman in Jordan in order to get a visa to go to Baghdad. I was not alone; 1500 journalists came from all over the world for the same reason. Everybody was anxious to be the first and only ones, and the street in front of the embassy of Iraq was vibrant with rumors and stories of the "media circus." The Iraqis were not willing to allow such a mass of people into their country, and they wanted to use them if possible for their own propaganda.

There is a real battle to get the precious visas. The Iraqi authorities allow the first batch of 15 journalists to get in. I am not taken in at first, but get accepted in the second batch.

I soon discover that it is a mistake to try and get in, because we will be trapped in the world-famous hotel Al Rachid, where all the journalists are to stay under heavy surveillance and without any opportunity to get out. We are like prisoners, but prisoners who have to pay tremendous amounts in U.S. dollars…for everything.

I am to stay in this hotel for two and a half weeks prior to being expelled like the others. Food is scarce. Electricity is soon cut because of the American bombs. Water is not readily available. We have to climb seven stories by foot, because the lifts are no longer working.

We have little to do, apart from listening to the radio. The Iraqis are not allowed to listen to Western radios, but some do so anyway. The journalists do too, of course, and make interesting comparisons between the propaganda from Iraq and the absence of concrete news from the West. The Iraqis begin feeling that they have been fooled, but none will dare say so. The soldiers coming back from the front look exhausted, and the triumphant communiqués of near-complete victory against the "forces of evil" sound increasingly dubious to more and more people.

But the society is too much under the tight control of agents faithful to Saddam Hussein, so that nothing can really happen inside the country. It does happen, though, with the rebellion of the Kurds and of the Shiite Muslims.

####

Saddam Hussein is still in power; most of his ministers are too. The same old system rules the country. Saddam Hussein managed to defeat two rebellions (the

Kurds and the Shiites) in his usual bloody way, after having officially lost the war against the U.N. coalition.

There is not much to be said about the effect of the Gulf War. The U.S. did an infomercial for its new military technology. Saddam Hussein, the dictator, runs the country exactly as he did before the war. The only difference is that the Kuwaitis can now continue to dance in their discos and fly back and forth to London to go shopping.

Barbie Jihad

Kuwait issued a fatwah against the Barbie doll. Insisting that it would affect the cultural stereotype of Kuwaiti women, a religious cleric has asked that all Barbie toys and accessories be banned from the country of Kuwait. It is not known whether all Barbies must go into hiding or whether Mattel is coming up with a chador to pacify the Islamic world.

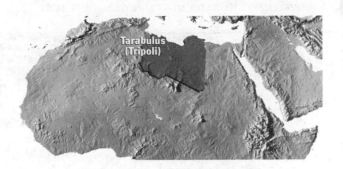

Libya

The Future's So Bright I Gotta Wear Shades

Libya, or as the locals abbreviate it, al-Jamahiriya al-'Arabiyah al-Libiya al-Sha'biya al-Ishtirakiya (The Great Socialist People's Libyan Arab Jamahiriya), has a bright future.

In fact, it's so bright that Libyan leader Colonel Muammar Qaddafi needs shades—even at night. And with that toothy, earlobe-to-earlobe grin, the man could get a job on the side of a Close Up toothpaste box (most in the West would like to see him close up to a Tomahawk). In fact, times are so good in that garden oasis of his that he threw a big Marxist bash in the fall of 1994 to celebrate the 25th anniversary of the military coup that plopped him into Tripoli's driver's seat. The evening's feature: all brand-new, uncensored, anti-Western rhetoric! Must've been one hell of a party.

He gassed up about a thousand of his rusty old Soviet-era tanks, greased up a whole parade-load of mechanized vehicles, and had an old-time, Marxist-style dictator birthday bash for the benefit of his North African guests.

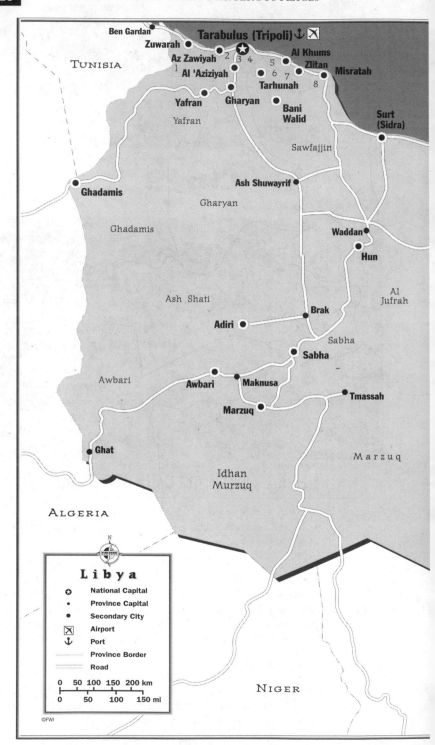

TUNISIA

Ben Gardan
Zuwarah
Tarabulus (Tripoli) ⚓ ✕
Az Zawiyah
Al 'Aziziyah
2
3 4
5
Al Khums
Zlitan
Misratah
1
6 7
8
Yafran
Gharyan
Tarhunah
Yafran
Bani
Walid
Surt
(Sidra)

Sawfajjin

Ghadamis

Ash Shuwayrif

Gharyan
Gharyan

Ghadamis

Waddan
Hun

Ash Shati

Adiri
Brak

Al
Jufrah

Sabha
Sabha

Awbari

Awbari
Maknusa
Tmassah

Marzuq

Ghat

Idhan
Murzuq

Marzuq

ALGERIA

L i b y a

⊕   National Capital
•   Province Capital
●   Secondary City
✕   Airport
⚓   Port
  Province Border
  Road

0   50   100   150   200 km
0   50   100   150 mi

©FWI

NIGER

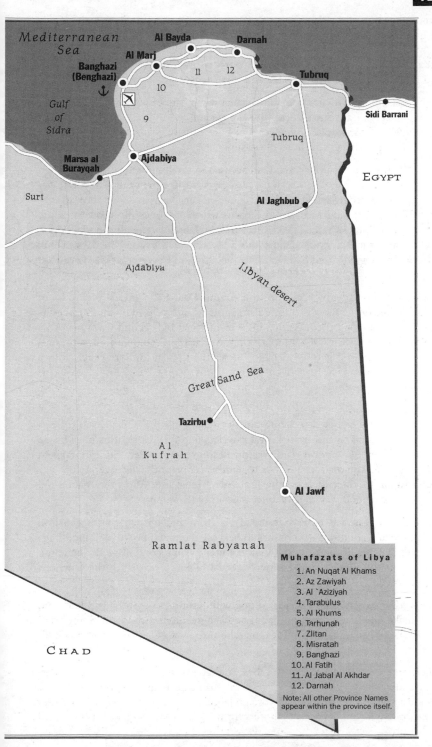

Mediterranean Sea

Al Bayda

Darnah

Al Marj

Banghazi (Benghazi)

11   12

Tubruq

10

Sidi Barrani

Gulf of Sidra

9

Tubruq

EGYPT

Marsa al Burayqah

Ajdabiya

Surt

Al Jaghbub

Ajdabiya

Libyan desert

Great Sand Sea

Tazirbu

Al Kufrah

Al Jawf

Ramlat Rabyanah

Muhafazats of Libya

1. An Nuqat Al Khams
2. Az Zawiyah
3. Al `Aziziyah
4. Tarabulus
5. Al Khums
6. Tarhunah
7. Zlitan
8. Misratah
9. Banghazi
10. Al Fatih
11. Al Jabal Al Akhdar
12. Darnah

Note: All other Province Names appear within the province itself.

CHAD

Among the honored visitors was a former enemy, Chad's President Debi. (Qaddafi invaded Chad's Aouzou Strip in 1987.) Other folks, seemingly in need of a free meal and the chance to wear their dime store medals, were the presidents of Algeria, Sudan, Tunisia, Maurtania and Morocco and the secretary-general of the Arab League. A regular terrorist tea and toast party.

In his self-imposed quarantine and chicken wire chain of command, Qaddafi is still a colonel—it's anyone's guess who the general is—and he's truly focused on the goodwill of his people. Three years of U.N. sanctions and isolation from the rest of the world doesn't seem to phase him.

He still refuses to surrender two men accused in the bombing of the 1988 Pan Am jet over Lockerbie. The U.S. and Europe don't like the shades or the smile. Qaddafi's assets are frozen abroad; travel imports are restricted. Inflation runs at about 100 percent, and the Libyan dinar is worth 10 times more on the black market than its official rate. The chances of a McDonald's opening up in Tripoli are slim since the sanctions against Libya are reviewed every 120 days. Think Uncle Sam's worried about Saddam? The sanctions on Iraq are reviewed every 60 days.

What are you missing by not being able to tour Qaddafi's Corner? Well, a lot of sand and some of the most exquisite Roman ruins in the world, including the ancient Roman city of Leptis Magna, built in the first and second centuries A.D. and the once-buried city of Sabratha—preserved by entombment in desert sands for a millennium. But getting a chance to see the sites in the foreseeable future will be tough. The U.S. State Department warns against travel for all U.S. citizens, and U.S. passports are not valid in Libya unless special authorization has been obtained from the U.S. government.

The Libyans are resigned to being out of circulation for a while. Even though air travel is banned to and from Libya, travelers find few restrictions once inside the country. There is a good road system. Resourceful travelers can hire taxis to nearby Tunisia. The road from Libya to Tunisia is one of the few overland routes those wishing to enter or leave the Jamahariya must use. And the ferry to and from Malta is a good way to slide into and out of the country.

Education in Libya is now widespread. The tiny but propagating population (4,212,000 and counting—there should be a big digital billboard at Tripoli's airport) still benefits from the US$8 billion a year in oil income. But the embargo has taken its toll. Oil revenue is down US$23 billion a year since the sanctions were imposed.

The *mukhabarat* (security police), along with hundreds of paid informants and thugs, make sure that everyone is happy and in agreement with Qaddafi's policies. The media, or Muammar's Minions, march in step with Qaddafi's bombastic diatribes.

There aren't many decent jobs in Libya, so that leaves a lot of time for idle chatter in coffee shops (chatter more cerebral than idle is illegal), praying in the mosque and watching the cheaper foreign labor do most of the dirty work. Libya is a major employer of contract laborers from Egypt, Mali, Sudan, Morocco and South Korea.

Despite the tight controls on speech, printed communications and politics, Libyans can watch European and American television shows on their satellite dishes and there are few restrictions on communications by fax and telephone.

Libya was an independent monarchy until 1969. Qaddafi and some army buddies changed that by turfing out the anachronistic government and setting up a Revolutionary Command Council (RCC), with Qaddafi as chairperson. He proclaimed Libya the Libyan Arab Republic. In March 1977, he fine-tuned the country's name by calling it the more popular word Jamahiriya, or State of the Masses.

He also took the title of "revolutionary leader." He continues to be Libya's dominant political force, wielding final and total authority. The government is based on Islamic law derived from the Koran, and local authority rests with a variety of socialist groups: people's committees, trade unions, vocational syndicates and people's congresses.

Qaddafi permits the Arab Socialist Union (ASU) to exist as Libya's sole political party. The ASU began in Sudan in 1981. The National Front for the Salvation of Libya (NFSL) was the country's principal opposition group, but is now in exile. The NFSL's modest goal is to establish a democratically elected government. There are a number of political parties outside the tent, so to speak. Other exiled political parties include the Libyan National Democratic Front, the Libyan National Association, the Libyan Democratic Movement and the Libyan Liberation Organization.

Libya is 91 percent desert, with only 1 percent usable for growing food. Qaddafi's 2000 miles of coastline once attracted European tourists (about 100,000 of them every year used to pump money into the economy in better days), and his oil once allowed him to buy secondhand Russian and East German weapons. In fact, he made so much money, he spent a lot of it on terrorist groups and picking fights with his neighbor to the south.

But Libya got its butt kicked by the Chadians and the French between November 1986 and March 1987, when the Chadian army evicted Libyan and pro-Libyan forces from their strongholds of Fada, Ouadi Doum and Faya Largeau. The Libyans retreated to the Aouzou Strip, basing its ownership of the area on a 1935 treaty between Italy (which controlled Libya) and France (which controlled Chad).

A cease-fire was signed with Chad on September 11, 1987, and it was agreed that the border dispute would be arbitrated. Libya had also settled previous disputes with Tunisia and Malta through arbitration. In October 1988, Libya and Chad restored diplomatic relations. Historically, Libya has shied away from full-blown hostilities and settled its disputes amiably. But that hasn't stopped the U.S. from taunting its enemy and periodically teasing it into cat-and-mouse exchanges of rockets. In January 1989, the U.S. concocted a silly story alleging Qaddafi had built a chemical weapons (mustard gas) factory at Rabta. After enough finger poking and name calling, Libya threw the first punch when one of its Mig-23s attacked a U.S. Navy task force mockingly positioned off the Libyan coast. The aircraft was blasted from the sky. The U.S. bombing of Tripoli and Benghazi in April 1986 didn't do much for Uncle Sam's image, either.

U.S. economic sanctions introduced in June 1986 forced five U.S. oil companies out of Libya, forcing them to kiss away US$4 billion in equipment and oil. The companies lose an estimated US$120 million a year in revenue.

Libya provided military supplies to the Islamic fundamentalist military junta in Khartoum, Sudan, in its civil war against the rebel SPLA, but denied responsibility for the bombing raids against SPLA positions. During the Gulf War, Libya did not support President Saddam Hussein. Qaddafi insisted upon a complete Iraqi withdrawal from Kuwait and the return of its legitimate government. He wasn't pulling for Western forces; he just hated Saddam Hussien more than George Bush.

The Egyptian government imposed new travel restrictions on Egyptians crossing the border into and from Libya and Sudan in 1993. Egyptians are now required to show passports rather than identity cards (which are easily forged). The new rules were imposed to make it harder for militant fundamentalists to cross the borders. The opening of the border with Egypt has, however, led to a boom in the smuggling of electrical goods, clothing and other merchandise. Egyptians travel to Libya to procure goods because of the cheap Libyan dinar on the black market. Libyan customs officials no longer make vigorous inspections at the border.

Although Qaddafi relies on foreign workers, he is still xenophobic. Between two and four years of military service is mandatory for men and women between the ages of 18 and 35. Qaddafi is a fan of Rommel, Patton and Stalin and owns more than 2300 Russian tanks (mostly T-54s, 55s and 62s). He boasts 38 tank battalions and 54 mechanized infantry battalions, as well as more than 1000 military aircraft, if he wants to pick a fight again. Currently, most of the equipment is gathering dust in storage.

Libya's biggest wrench in the spokes of global acceptance is not coming clean on the December 1988 bombing of Pan Am flight 103 over Lockerbie, Scotland. It still refuses to hand over two members of its security force accused by the U.S. of carrying out the catastrophic deed. The strongest evidence suggests that nongovernment elements in Iran hired the Palestinian Syrian-based PFLP General Command to blow up an American aircraft in revenge for an earlier accidental U.S. downing of an Iranian passenger aircraft. The Libyan Security Service is assumed to have acted as the hired guns; however, the real culprits are still in Tehran. The U.S., having little or no intelligence capabilities in Iran, apparently prefers the bird-in-the-hand solution to the bird-in-the-bush problem.

Not that the Libyans are completely innocent. Tripoli was also accused of blowing up a UTA flight over the Sahara in 1989, killing 171 people. The plane exploded over Niger after making a stopover in Chad during a flight from Brazzaville to Paris. The French had warrants out on four Libyans, including the deputy head of Libya's Security Service, Abdullah Senoussi, who is Qaddafi's brother-in-law.

Qaddafi, in a PR effort to mend his ways, cut off support for the IRA. He told the Chief of Intelligence Services, Colonel Youssef Abdel-Qader al-Dabri, to work on cleaning up his image abroad. Although the 1986 freezing of Libyan assets in the U.S. (estimated to be from US$1–$2.5 billion) hurt Qaddafi, Tripoli has plenty of liquid money (about US$6 billion) in Switzerland and the Gulf States as well as significant holdings in other European countries.

To show how bright the future is for Libya, Qaddafi is blowing US$25 billion on the Great Manmade River, a program designed to suck water from the deep underground in the Sahara and carry it to irrigate coastal farmlands.

The Great Manmade River (GMR) project alone employs 10,000 Asian workers. It's estimated that there are about 6000 Americans, 4500 Britons, 4000 Italians, 2000 Germans, 25,000 Eastern Europeans and around 10,000 South Koreans in the country working on the project.The GMR is considered to be the Middle East's largest irrigation project, providing a flow rate of 2 million cubic meters a day and enough water for 400 years.

Qaddafi has pledged up to 25 percent of all Libyan oil sales to debt repayment and barter deals. So the country has about US$6 billion left to subsist on. Senators in Washington, D.C., thought that the oil companies should be compensated by divvying up Libya's frozen assets in the U.S. About US$2 billion—leaving enough left for a postage stamp and a letter to let Muammar know where his money went.

The future looks bright though since oil exploration experts believe that the barren sands of Libya will be one of the top-three oil discovery sites in the world. It seems Qaddafi has some interesting ways to spend that money. In August of 1996 he pledged $1 billion (to form joint ventures) to Louis Farrakhan and kicked in another $250,000 to the eternally pissed off Farrakhan as the first prize in Qaddafi Human Rights Award (we are not making this up!). Uncle Sam quickly stepped in and shattered any dreams of Bentley Turbos and silk suits when they reminded Louis of the embargo. Louis did get to keep the pretty green sash and bouquet of flowers.

The Scoop

The Socialist People's Libyan Arab Jamahiriya considers itself an Islamic Arab Socialist "Mass-State" (i.e., a state run by the masses). Libya has a developing economy. Islamic ideals and beliefs provide the conservative foundation of the country's customs, laws and practices. The country is virtually ethnically pure. Berber, Arab and Sunni Muslim comprise 97 percent of the population. Arabic is the official language, but Italian and English are spoken in the main urban centers. About half the people are illiterate, although the situation is improving rapidly.

The Players

Colonel Muammar abu Minyar al-Qaddafi

After losing his crown as the "West's most despised Arabic ruler" to Saddam (who inherited it from Yassir Arafat), Qaddafi still refuses to hand over the two Libyan intelligence officers who are accused of being responsible for the bombing of two aircraft. Former U.S. President Ronald Reagan's April 1986 attempt to "wax his ass" while he was sleeping has toned down Qaddafi's troublemaking.

Internally, he has lost little popularity. There is no denying who is in charge of the Jamahiriyya. The People's Committees and General People's Congress know that the equally powerful and less democratic Revolutionary Committees call the shots.

There has not been and is unlikely to be a viable alternative to Qaddafi in the foreseeable future. A member of the Qadhafa tribe and born in 1941, Muammar was an early Arab activist when he joined the Army after being educated in Britain. He formed the Free Officers Movement, a group of military officers who believed in Arab nationalism. He made it as far as captain. When King Idris was away on vacation in September 1969, the Free Officers Movement took control of the government of Libya. Qaddafi became head of state in 1970. Born in Arab nationalist times, and influenced by communist successes, he created the Green Book, a three-volume collection of his personal ideology. Portrayed as a comical figure and buffoon in the Western press, he has managed to shape the political and ideological future of Libya over the last 25 years through both good and bad times—a feat his Western political counterparts cannot claim. Only Fidel Castro can claim more longevity.

Libyan National Salvation Committee

In 1987, the dissident groups merged to form the Libyan National Salvation Committee under the leadership of Abdel Moneim al-Houni, a former Revolutionary Command Council member and interior minister. The group has accomplished little.

National Front for the Salvation of Libya (Inqat)

The largest opposition group, formed in 1980 by Mohamed Megharief, the former auditor-general and Libyan ambassador to India. They have found support from the Saudis and the U.S., but there is a slim chance of any power changes soon.

The CIA and Israel

Who else are you gonna call to train hundreds of anti-Qaddafi Libyans in an effort to insert a "contra" army designed to infiltrate southern Libya and start a general uprising?

The Muslim Brotherhood (Ikhwan)

This and other fundamentalist groups do not support the Qaddafi regime since Qaddafi has suppressed fundamentalist groups like the puritan Wahabis (an ancient sect that once dominated Saudi Arabian society for more than 100 years).

Abu Nidal

Kicked out of Syria in March 1994, terrorist-for-hire Abu Nidal returned to Libya via Sudan and is now living in Suk Sabat in the Tripoli suburbs near the airport. Even after his recent tear-jerking news conference, no one wants him living in the neighborhood.

Islamic Fundamentalists

Although the Colonel waves his little green book, there are at least six fundamentalist groups looking to overthrow Gaddafi. They include al-Jihad, al-Dawa, al-Takfir, the Islamic Liberation Party, the Islamic Group and the Muslim Brotherhood. Believe it or not, he thinks that they are backed by the CIA.

The Inner Circle

If Gaddafi gets tossed, it will be probably from the inside out. His former Putsch friends have been demoted, and *Janes Intelligence Review* says put your money on Musa Kousa, Abdullah Senoussi, Khalifa Huneish and Ahmad Gaddfdam to be the next boss.

Islamic Movement of Martyrs

Just one of the many groups who is trying to knock Qaddafi from power. Their nemesis is the comically named Anti-Heresy Department based in Benghazi.

Getting In

Warning: The United States Department of State warns all U.S. citizens to avoid travel to Libya and to depart the country immediately if residing or visiting there. The U.S. Government has determined that due to Libya's long history of flouting international law and directing terrorist attacks against U.S. citizens, it is unsafe for Americans to travel there. U.S. passports are not valid for travel to, in or through Libya, unless a special validation is obtained from the Department of State. All financial and commercial transactions with Libya are prohibited, unless licensed by the U.S. Treasury Department. There is no U.S. embassy in Libya. U.S. Government interests are represented by the Government of Belgium, which as a protecting power can provide only limited emergency services to U.S. citizens.

Passports and visas are required. On December 11, 1981, U.S. passports ceased to be valid for travel to, in or through Libya and may not be used for that purpose without a special validation. Without this requisite validation, use of a U.S. passport for travel to, in or through Libya may constitute a violation of 18 U.S.C. 1544, and may be punishable by a fine and/or imprisonment. In addition, the Department of the Treasury prohibits all travel-related transactions by U.S. persons intending to visit Libya, unless specifically licensed by the Office of Foreign Assets Control. There are limited exceptions to this licensing requirement for Libyan nationals' family members and for journalists. The categories of individuals eligible for consideration for a special passport validation are set forth in 22 C.F.R. 51.74. Passport validation requests for Libya can be forwarded in writing to the following address:

Deputy Assistant Secretary for Passport Services

U.S. Department of State
1111 19th Street, N.W., Suite 260
Washington, D.C. 20522-1705
Attn: Office of Citizenship Appeals and Legal Assistance
☎ *(202) 955-0232*

The request must be accompanied by supporting documentation according to the category under which validation is sought. Currently, the four categories of persons specified in 22 C.F.R. 51.74 as being eligible for consideration for passport validation are as follows:

[1] Professional reporters: Includes full-time members of the reporting or writing staff of a newspaper, magazine or broadcasting network whose purpose for travel is to gather information about Libya for dissemination to the general public.

[2] American Red Cross: Applicant establishes that he or she is a representative of the American Red Cross or International Red Cross traveling pursuant to an officially sponsored Red Cross mission.

[3] Humanitarian considerations: Applicant must establish that his or her trip is justified by compelling humanitarian considerations or for family unification. At this time, "compelling humanitarian considerations" include situations where the applicant can document that an immediate family member is critically ill in Libya. Documentation concerning family illness must include the name and address of the relative, and be from that relative's physician attesting to the nature and gravity of the illness. "Family unification" situations may include cases in which spouses or minor children are residing in Libya, with and dependent on, a Libyan national spouse or parent for their support.

[4] National interest: The applicant's request is otherwise found to be in the national interest.

In all requests for passport validation for travel to Libya, the name, date and place of birth for all concerned persons must be given, as well as the U.S. passport numbers. Documentation as outlined above should accompany all requests. Additional information may be obtained by writing to the above address or by calling the Office of Citizenship Appeals and Legal Assistance at ☎ *(202) 663-1184*.

U.S. Treasury Restrictions

In addition to the passport validation, U.S. Treasury requirements must be met. Travelers may contact the Treasury Department at the following address and phone number:

Chief of Licensing Office of Foreign Assets Control

U.S. Department of the Treasury
1500 Pennsylvania Avenue, N.W.
Washington, D.C. 20220
☎ *(202) 622-2480*
FAX (202) 622-1657

U.S. Treasury Sanctions

On January 7, 1986, the United States imposed sanctions against Libya, which are administered by the U.S. Treasury Department, prohibiting all travel-related transactions with respect to Libya for U.S. citizens and permanent resident aliens. There are limited exceptions for Libyan nationals' family members who register with the Treasury Department's Office of Foreign Assets Control or with the embassy of Belgium in Tripoli, and for full-time journalists. As of February 1, 1986, the president further prohibited transactions by U.S. persons relating to transportation to or from Libya. Additionally, all financial and commercial transactions by U.S. persons anywhere in the world with Libya are prohibited. This includes working in Libya, providing a service of any nature to Libya, or participating in an unauthorized transaction of any kind involving property in which Libya has an interest. Violations of the Libyan sanctions may result in penalties, fines and/or imprisonment.

Under the Libyan Sanctions Regulations and in addition to any passport validation issued by the Department of State, the U.S. Treasury Department requires that U.S. citizens and legal permanent residents who wish to travel to Libya to visit immediate family members in Libya are authorized to visit Libya only if they file a registration letter prior to their trip with the Office of Foreign Assets Control or with the embassy of Belgium in Tripoli. The registration must contain the following information:

(1) Name, date and place of birth of the person registering (including the name under which a registrant's most recent U.S. passport was issued, if that is different).

(2) If applicable, place and date of the registrant's naturalization as a U.S. citizen, and the number of the registrant's naturalization certificate, or, for permanent resident aliens, the alien registration number of the registrant's alien registration receipt card.

(3) The name, relationship, and address of the immediate family member in Libya whose relationship forms the basis for the registrant's eligibility.

(4) The number and issue date of the registrant's current U.S. passport, and the most recent date on which the passport was validated by the U.S. Department of State for travel to Libya.

U.N. Sanctions

U.N. Security Council sanctions against Libya, including an air embargo, took effect on April 15, 1992. U.N. Security Council Resolution 748, passed on March 31, 1992, imposed sanctions on Libya until Libya fully complies with the provisions of U.N. Resolution 731 and 748, adopted on January 21, 1992. U.N. Security Council Resolutions 731 and 748 were adopted in response to Libya's alleged responsibility for the bombings of Pan Am flight 103 and UTA flight 772. The U.S. cannot predict if or when Libya will comply with the U.N. demands. Since April 15, 1992, when air links were discontinued, it has become difficult to leave Libya. The sale in the United States of air transportation including any stop in Libya became illegal under the International Emergency Economic Powers Act, 50 U.S.C. 1701.

Getting Sick

Basic modern medical care and medicines may not be available in Libya. There are 14 doctors and 53 hospital beds per 10,000 population.

Nuts and Bolts

Needless to say Libya is hot, cooler along the coast, and hot enough to melt the treads on your Nikes down south. Temperatures normally range from 55°F to 100°F. Bus and taxi services are quite good, and the road system excellent (14,914 miles out of Libya's 20,195 miles of road are paved). Local air transportation is also good and airfields are in abundance (122 at last count, with 53 paved and 37 over 8000 ft.). Don't expect to fly anywhere outside of Libya's borders. Just to show how tough Libyans are, a group of pilgrims to Mecca rode camels to protest Libya's lack of an international air transportation system. In May 1994, 110 pilgrims rode 60 camels from the Libyan border to Suez where they took a ship to Jeddah.

The currency value is 1000 dirhams = 1 Libyan dinar. There are no Canadian or American embassies in Libya. The U.S. Government is not in a position to accord normal consular protective services to U.S. citizens in Libya. U.S. Government interests are represented by the

Government of Belgium, which as a protecting power can provide only limited emergency services to U.S. citizens.The U.S. interests section of the embassy of Belgium is located at Tower 4, That al Imad complex, in the capital city of Tripoli. The Belgian embassy's mailing address and phone number are as follows:

Embassy of Belgium
> *P.O. 91650*
> *Tripoli, Libya*
> ☎ *[218] (21) 37797, FAX (218-21) 75618.*

Dangerous Days

04/15/1992   United Nations security council sanctions, approved on March 31, 1992, went into effect. The sanctions sever air links, ban arms sales and significantly reduce the staffs of Libyan embassies and consulates abroad.

03/31/1992   The United Nations Security Council voted to impose wide-sweeping sanctions on Libya for its refusal to surrender two suspects in the 1988 bombing of Pan American flight 103. Under the sanctions, all countries must bar flights to or from Libya, prohibit any arms deals and significantly reduce the staff of Libyan embassies and consulates. The sanctions took effect on 4/15/92.

11/14/1991   The United Kingdom issued indictments against two Libyans for the bombing of Pan Am flight 103 in December 1988.

08/13/1987   Libyan forces routed by Chad.

04/15/1986   U.S. bombed Tripoli and Benghazi in retaliation for terrorist attacks against American targets. Several terrorist operations commemorating the raid have occurred on this date.

03/24/1986   U.S. sunk Libyan patrol boats. The U.S. Navy forces crossed the "line of death" in the Gulf of Sidra and engaged Libyan patrol boats. Four Libyan vessels were sunk or damaged and an SA-5 radar site was crippled.

01/04/1986   U.S. warplanes shot down two Libyan warplanes over the Gulf of Sidra.

08/13/1984   Temporary union with Morocco.

08/19/1981   U.S. shot down two Libyan jet fighters over the Gulf of Sidra.

03/02/1977   People's state established. The official name of Libya was changed to the Socialist People's Libyan Arab Jamahiriya.

10/07/1970   Fascist Evacuation Day. Celebrates the departure of the last Italian settlers from Libya. (Also called Revenge Day.)

06/11/1970   U.S. bases were turned over to Libya. Also known as Evacuation Day.

09/01/1969   Qaddafi seized power in a coup.

05/25/1963   The Organization of African Unity (OAU) was founded on this date. The day is celebrated as Africa Freedom Day. The OAU is organized to promote unity and cooperation among African states.

12/24/1951   Independence Day.

11/21/1949   Proclamation Day. Commemorates the United Nations resolution on Libyan independence.

10/26/1943   Day of Mourning. Day to commemorate Libyan suffering and the deportation of Libyans to Italy during Italian colonial rule.

LIBYA

In a Dangerous Place

Chad, June 1983: Wrong Place, Wrong Time

In 1979 Chad plunged into a civil war pitting Goukkouni Oueddei and Hissène Habré, the two northern leaders, against each other. In 1982, Hissène Habré seized power and installed his government in N'djamenah, but Goukkouni Oueddei signed a pact with Lybia's leader, Muammar Qaddafi, who sent an army to Chad.

Lybia occupied the north of the country in 1983, causing France to intervene. The country was neatly split in two: the Islamic north (above the 19th parallel) was placed under the control of the GUNT of Goukkouni Oueddei and Lybia, while the animist south was placed under the control of Hissène Habré supported by France and the U.S.A.

In 1986, the rallying of Goukkouni Oueddei helped Hissène Habré fight against the Lybians. In 1987 a cease-fire was decided, and in May 1988 the Lybians officially recognized Hissène Habré's government. Diplomatic relations were restored in October, and Libya agreed with Chad to evacuate the Aouzou Strip, a piece of land between the two countries that it had occupied since 1972. Are you with us so far?

The political situation was not stable for long, though, because of the rebellion of Idriss Deby, former commander-in-chief of the armed forces, and companion of Hissène Habré, in 1990. One more time France was asked to intervene. On December 2, 1990, Idriss Deby, at the head of his FPS (Forces Patriotiques du Salut-Salvation Patriotic Forces), entered N'Djamenah and forced Hissène Habré's National Army (FANT) out. Habré took refuge in Senegal. France eventually decided to let things go and intervene less in Chad.

####

I am flying into Chad from Tripoli. I have negotiated a trip into the combat zone, and we are taken aboard a C-130 plane along with other journalists and military. We take off from Faya-Largeau and head toward Oumchalloulah and

Abeche, where the battle is raging. The heat on the ground had been intolerable, but the unpressurized, unheated plane soon drops below freezing as we gain in altitude.

As we are on final approach into the airport at Abeche, the cold is the least of my worries. There are strange movements on the tarmac. I climb up to the cockpit to grab some photos in case anything happens. While in the cockpit, the pilots figure out that Hissene Habre's troops have taken the town and the airport, and we are landing in enemy territory.

The strange movements we see are men shooting up at the plane. In the clear air, I can see the bullets and rockets arc toward our plane.

The pilots pull the nose up and give it full power. Slipping and sliding, they try to dodge the bullets, as they make the long trip out of range of the soldiers on the ground.

We land without any damage 20 minutes later, not far from Abeche.

Once on the ground, we realize that we hadn't planned to spend more than an hour in the desert and here we are in the middle of the Sahara with only some soup, rotten camel meat that we bought from a local and dirty water.

We spend the night hoping the enemy soldiers will not find us. The next morning, a Libyan picks us up and returns us to Faya Largeau.

Five years later in Kuwait for a summit of African heads of state, I told this story to a soldier from Chad. He recognized the incident and told me he was the leader of the soldiers on the ground that were trying to shoot down the plane. *C'ést la guerre.*

—**Coskun Aral**

LIBYA

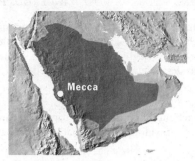

Mecca

Mecca and
the Impenetrables

Olé

If you're afraid of bulls, but still love a good stampede, this is your place. In 1990, 1426 people were killed in a stampede inside the al-Muaissem tunnel leading from Mecca to Mina in Saudi Arabia. In May 1994, 270 died in a stampede in Mina.

The pilgrims were trampled to death during a ritual known as "stoning the devil." It takes place in Mina, a town 10 km east of Mecca. It's the Middle East's version of the Ickey Shuffle, the Sack Dance, Australian Rules football and the Iditarod thrown into one. The hell with Barcelona. Forget Cuba. Tecate's boring. Mina is where the real action is.

During the ritual, the pilgrims throw pebbles at three stone pillars surrounded by low walls to symbolize man purging himself of evil. The ritual must be performed at specific times of the day. The tragedies usually occur when large crowds surge toward the pillars.

Stoning the devil can be performed at two levels, from an overhead bridge and from a tunnel beneath the bridge. The slightly less devout (in other words, the more practical) perform the ritual within the tunnel, where there are fewer people, and where you are less likely to end up covered with Nike and Timberland treadmarks.

Religious leaders and hajj travel agents (known particularly for their economy desert-crossing packages and discount round-trip camel fares) have even gone so far as to offer pamphlets providing tips on what hajj pilgrims should do in a stampede.

In the event of a stampede, they suggest, stay calm and head straight for the nearest post of your nationality. The posts are set up at prominent places by general sales agents for the hajj and can be spotted flying the flag of your nationality. People who are lost should also head for one of these posts.

Try not to panic. Remaining calm will help in such a situation, say the travel agents. That's authoritative.

But there's plenty of reason for panic. Each year, enough hajji converge on Mecca to make the Super Bowl seem like a cockfight in a bookie's basement. More than 2 million of them show up every year. In 1994, 2.5 million Muslim pilgrims descended upon Mecca during hajj in May—certainly the largest annual gathering where beer isn't on the agenda.

The stampedes happen mainly on the bridge, where masses of pilgrims hang out and camp out, setting themselves up to become pancakes during the *zuhur*, the midday peak period for performing the ritual. The crushes begin for a number of reasons. In some instances, people fall from overhead bridges, sparking panic and, ultimately, a human *sunami*. At any rate, Saudi authorities have spent millions of dollars to widen roads and build tunnels and overhead passes so that the large crowds can be handled more easily.

The pilgrims who travel to Mecca for hajj every year number more than 2 million. They come from all over the world, but, mainly from the Middle East, Asia and Africa. Most, today, travel via modern conveniences such as planes, trains and automobiles. Others caravan through baking deserts astride camels. In 1994, a number of Libyan hajjis traveled by these "ships of the desert" to Mecca in protest of the U.N. embargo on Libya. At least two of the Libyans died en route due to the scorching conditions. Others, as well, use hajj as a vehicle to voice their discontent of and hatred for the West, especially the U.S. In 1993, Libyan pilgrims took a detour from Mecca, where they ended up in Israel in an attempt to encourage Israel to put pressure on the U.S. to drop the embargo against Qaddafi. Iranian pilgrims use hajj as a stage for anti-American protests.

After Iran's Islamic revolution of 1979, the Ayatollah Khomeini began utilizing the hajj as a venue to stage anti-U.S., anti-Western, anti-Israel and sometimes anti-Saudi protests. Saudi security forces and Iranian pilgrims clashed in 1987, resulting in 250 Iranian deaths, a breaking of diplomatic relations between the two countries and a three-year Iranian boycott of the pilgrimage. In the last few years, the Saudi government has tolerated the Iranian protests, but has insisted they only take place in segregated areas. But they put the clamp down in 1994. In the early 1990s, the scene was circuslike, or resembled some type of surreal consumer electronics convention. In one booth, you'd find a Jordanian exhibiting his footwear, and in another, yapping Iranians torching American flags.

Hajj, indeed, is the religious Disney World of the Middle East. Surrounding the mosques and the perimeter of the Mecca itself, vendors pack the alleys and streets, hawking everything, it seems, from Ayatollah Khomeini T-shirts to Qaddafi Cream for Younger Skin. Attendees are arbitrarily pulled aside by security personnel and hussled into makeshift booths, where they are demanded to recite passages from the Koran to prove they're truly Muslim and not Marge and Bill Smith on a bus tour from Wisconsin.

Camels have been largely replaced by beat-up automobiles as the principal means of getting to Mecca. In the past, travelers often lost their way because of a lack of road signs, or they became incapacitated in narrow mountain passes or on boulder-strewn routes. Travelers have been known to show up for hajj as late as Christmas, which isn't good.

In the past, in Mina, Arafat and Muzdalifah, water was generally unavailable and food in short supply. There was a scarcity of hospitals, doctors, hotels and bathrooms. Pilgrims wrote down their wills before going on hajj, quite sure they wouldn't be coming back. Today, residents of the Eastern Province of Saudi Arabia can complete the pilgrimage in five days, whereas it used to take nearly a month.

These days, pilgrims travel in comfortable vehicles on sweeping expressways and stay in air-conditioned tents. They're even known to rush out for 99-cent Big Macs.

The Impenetrables: Or
Countries We'll Get to After We Visit Disney World
One More Time

Who are the richest people on earth, and what will they pay the most for? Time's up! The answer is, of course: the Saudi Royal Family and water. Having a country all to yourself and being king makes for some very unusual dress codes (head to toe) and tourism policies (no, no).

Of course, the people of the desert regions do not suffer from "Oprah" reruns, drive-by shootings, "Beavis and Butthead" marathons and other cultural treasures. They take their guardianship of Mecca and Medina very seriously and are, on the one hand, the most welcoming country to the true believers and, on the other, the most forbidding to the rest of us. If you truly want to visit Saudi Arabia, it pays to know a member of the Saudi Royal Family, convert to Islam, work in the oil patch, be a journalist or join the air force during the next Gulf War. Otherwise, a couple of weeks in northern Mexico or Namibia will produce the same experience.

Saudi Arabia

It was bound to happen sooner or later.

In November 1995, as scores of Americans were munching on lunch at the U.S.-run military training center for the Saudi National Guard in Riyadh, an explosives-laden van parked outside the building blasted into the sky, taking six people with it and injuring another 60, virtually all of them Americans.

Americans were shocked that such an act could take place in this U.S.-friendly powerful king/oildom, which has been spared from the political violence that has ripped apart the rest of the Middle East.

The Saudis weren't.

The House of Saud has been playing a dangerous hand of diplo-religious poker since the Soviet invasion of Afghanistan. In one suit, the Saudis need the Americans to counter challenges from Iran and Iraq, as Riyadh moves further from Baghdad and Teheran and closer to Washington and the West—particularly in the wake of the Gulf War. In the other, powerful Saudi businessmen and politicians were chiefly responsible for funding the Washington- and King Faud–backed Islamic militants in the Afghan war, and have continued to pipe perhaps hundreds of millions of dollars to Islamic extremists and terrorists across the Middle East and Asia, in order to preserve internal peace and appease hard-line Muslim elements both at home and abroad.

This double standard was bound to blow up in someone's face. It did, and it was in Uncle Sam's. Fueled with Saudi cash, American know-how and Afghan combat experience, these nasties now have access to every part of the globe (including Saudi Arabia)—and it would no longer be a surprise to discover a deeper, albeit unwitting, connection between the World Trade Center bombing and Saudi deep pockets. Saudi Arabia is fanning the flames of a fire that it only rhetorically is trying to put out. Or maybe Riyadh is just simply shooting from the hip, buying time for the short haul. Oil, after all, is a finite resource.

The Saudis have also been active in supporting the Muslim-led government in Bosnia—an estimated US$300 million covert weapons-funneling operation with alleged tacit cooperation from the United States, despite it being a violation of the U.N. arms embargo on the former Yugoslav federation that Uncle Sam pledged to enforce. The action was similar to the aid the Saudis gave to Afghan guerillas in the 1980s during the *mujahedin's* war against the Soviet Union. That operation also was supported by former U.S. military and intelligence personnel. However, in the Bosnia scenario, Saudi funds were not matched by the U.S. government, as they were during the war in Afghanistan. The Saudis also provided the Bosnian Muslims with about US$500 million in humanitarian aid.

One suspects the Saudis announced the military aid to the Bosnian government in an effort to derail the illusion that the crux of the aid to the Bosnian military was coming from Iran and former Muslim fundamentalist guerrilla fighters who fought in Afghanistan.

Getting In

The Saudi government does not issue tourist visas. It issues two types of entry visas: one for temporary business visits or to visit relatives, the other for individuals entering Saudi Arabia on an employment contract.

One problem—the Saudis don't like tourists. Can't stand them. Even though the Saudis are the Americans' buddies, the country has banned tourists, even satellite dishes. They don't want any part of the West. Neither do pilgrims to Mecca. Anti-West and particularly anti-U.S. demonstrations break out like a high school kid with a skin problem. With no Americans around to kill, the gatherings usually end up as—yeah, you got it—stampedes. Saudi Arabia possesses the two holiest sites in Islam: Mecca and Medina. It features public beheadings and perhaps the most breathtaking deserts on earth—two great reasons for making the country your family's next vacation destination. Forget about exploring the lore of the Bedouin. Saudi Arabia is closed. The country does not issue visas for tourism. The only way to get in is to have bonafide business in the country and a Saudi sponsor.

Customs Clearance

Customs clearance procedures in Saudi Arabia are formal, thorough and lengthy and may involve a full search of every piece of luggage. Transit passengers who wish to leave the transit area of the airport are subject to the same strict searches as arriving passengers.

Vaccinations

Travelers to Saudi Arabia may wish to get a meningococcal vaccine prior to departure. Before traveling, consult the Centers for Disease Control for updated recommendations on this and other vaccines.

AIDS Clearance

All persons going to Saudi Arabia for purposes of employment are required to present a certificate stating that they are free of the Acquired Immune Deficiency Syndrome virus. The test should be included as part of the global medical examination that is given to those who enter Saudi Arabia on a work permit. It is not required of travelers entering Saudi Arabia on a temporary visitor visa.

Temporary Visits

All applicants for temporary visitor visas for the purpose of business consultations must have a Saudi company or individual sponsor their applications. Individuals who wish to visit non-Saudi relatives must have their relatives or a Saudi sponsor request authorization of their applications through the Saudi Foreign Ministry. Persons present in Saudi Arabia on temporary visitor visas should not surrender their passports to the Saudi sponsor. The passport and visa are the only evidence of the bearer's legal right to be present in the country. If an individual is present in the kingdom on a temporary visitor visa and has obtained Saudi sponsorship for employment, he or she must exit Saudi Arabia to obtain an entry visa for employment. This visa need not be issued in the individual's country of origin, but the applicant must be physically present to apply for the visa.

Employment and Residence

Visas for employment and residence are obtained the same way as visas for temporary visits. Documentation, such as a letter from the sponsoring company, a copy of your signed contract or a notarized copy of your university degree, may also be required.

Before you sign a contract with a Saudi company, it is extremely important for you to obtain an independent English translation of the contract. The official and binding version of the contract that you sign is the Arabic text. Some Americans have signed contracts that in fact did not include all of the benefits they believed they were acquiring. The employee's dependents (spouse and children under the age of 18) may be brought into Saudi Arabia only with the concurrence of the Saudi sponsor and authorization of the Foreign Ministry. Ordinarily, only managers and professionals (holders of college degrees) may bring their families. Children over age 18 are likely to be refused residence.

Visas

Persons entering Saudi Arabia for the purpose of employment are issued residence permits *(iqamas)*. These permits are evidence of legal residence in Saudi Arabia and must be retained at all times. Foreign residents are not permitted to travel between different major regions of Saudi Arabia, unless permission is noted in their permits.

Getting Around

The passport offices have introduced a new law controlling the travel of foreigners within Saudi Arabia. The new law requires sponsors to provide reasons for their employees' travel within the country. They may also be asked to submit details or documents of commercial registration or contracts of the sponsor's establishment in the city or cities where the employee is traveling. Previously, sponsors could get travel permits without specifying reasons for the movement of their employees within Saudi Arabia. The residential permit *(iqama)* rules in

Saudi Arabia require expat workers to stick to the area where they work. When they travel within the kingdom, they have to carry a letter from the sponsor certified by the passport authority.

If an employer doesn't possess commercial registration or a contract in the city where his employee is visiting, the employer is required to submit an application specifying the reasons for the employee's travel. The only exceptions are for travel to Mecca or Medina. Visits are not to last longer than 10 days. Additionally, employees may be permitted to visit family and relatives within Saudi Arabia if they can substantiate their existence and provide proof of the relationship. Travel within Saudi Arabia by expat workers has dropped significantly since the implementation of the new regulation, according to Saudi sources.

Getting Out

A resident in Saudi Arabia may not depart the country under any circumstances, however exigent, without obtaining an exit visa. Exit visas are issued only upon request of the Saudi sponsor. U.S. consular officials are not able to "sponsor" exit visas for Americans resident in Saudi Arabia under any circumstances. In a genuine emergency, however, consular officials will attempt to facilitate the Saudi sponsor's request for the exit visa. Residents in Saudi Arabia are almost always required to surrender their passports and those of their dependents to the Saudi sponsor. This practice is specifically authorized in the Saudi employment law. If an urgent need for travel exists and if the Saudi sponsor will not release the first passport, the U.S. embassy or consulate can issue a replacement passport. The issuance of a replacement passport does not guarantee, however, that a person will be able to depart, since the replacement passport would not contain a Saudi residence permit or exit visa.

A woman married to a Muslim should be aware that she must have her husband's permission to depart or have their children depart from Saudi Arabia. This is true even if the woman or children are U.S. citizens. The husband is the sponsor of his foreign wife and of his children, and is, as such, the only individual who can request an exit visa for the wife or children.

Dangerous Things

Booze

Import, manufacture, possession and consumption of alcoholic beverages are strictly forbidden. Saudi officials make no exceptions. Americans have spent up to a year in Saudi prisons for alcohol-related offenses. Americans have also been sentenced to receive 75 lashes in lieu of prison for failing a blood test for alcohol. Travelers should also exercise extreme care and discretion when consuming alcohol on flights landing in the kingdom. Persons obviously inebriated are subject to arrest or deportation.

Drugs

Laws regarding the importation, manufacture, possession and consumption of drugs are just as nasty. Many drugs sold with or without prescription in other countries may be illegal in Saudi Arabia. For instance, Captagon (fenetylline hydrochloride), a drug used to treat exhaustion that is available without a prescription in some countries in Asia, is considered an illegal substance in Saudi Arabia. Americans in Saudi Arabia have received prison sentences of up to two and a half months and 70 lashes for possession of Captagon. The attempted importation of drugs or controlled substances, even in very small amounts, is a serious offense under Saudi law. The traveler will be arrested and tried for carrying drugs into the country. Some Americans are currently in Saudi prisons serving sentences for drug possession or use. The death penalty for drug smugglers and traffickers convicted of a second offense underscores the gravity with which authorities treat drug offenses in the kingdom. Customs authorities are now using dogs to detect drugs at Saudi airports. Prescription drugs in small quantities, clearly labeled with the traveler's name, doctor's name, pharmacy, and contents on the original container, should cause no problem. It is wise to carry a copy of the prescription as well. The importation of drugs in large amounts, however, can be done legally only through the Ministry of Health.

Being a Woman (or Just Dressing Like One)

Females are prohibited from driving vehicles or riding bicycles on public roads or in places where they might be observed. Males and females beyond childhood are not free to congregate together in most public places, and a man may be arrested for being seen with, walking with, traveling with, or driving a woman other than his wife or immediate relative. In Saudi Arabia, playing of music or dancing in public, mixed bathing, public showing of movies and consumption of alcoholic beverages are forbidden. Saudi religious police, know as *Mutawwa*, enforce female dress standards in public places and may rebuke or harass women who do not cover their heads or whose clothing is insufficiently concealing. In addition, in more conservative areas, there have been incidents of private Saudi citizens stoning, accosting, or pursuing foreigners, including U.S. citizens, for perceived dress code or other infractions. While most such incidents have resulted in little more than inconvenience or embarrassment for the individual targeted, the potential exists for persons to be physically harmed. U.S. citizens in Saudi Arabia should be aware of Saudi social practices, and that any infractions may be dealt with aggressively. If you are accosted by Saudi authorities, cooperate fully in accordance with local customs and regulations. U.S. citizens who are harassed by private Saudi citizens should report the incidents immediately to the U.S. embassy in Riyadh or the U.S. consulate general either in Dhahran or in Jeddah.

Pornography, Etc.

Items considered pornographic by Saudi standards, including magazines and videocassettes, are strictly forbidden. It is also illegal to import firearms of any type, ammunition, related items such as gunsights and gun magazines, food items and banned books. Personal religious items such as a Bible or a rosary are usually permitted, but travelers should be aware that, on occasion, these items have been seized at entry and not returned to the traveler.

Commercial and Business Disputes

If you get into a tiff, don't plan on leaving anytime soon. Disputes between parties who do not have a signed formal contract must be settled through mutual agreement or through an appeal to the local governor (*amir*) for judgment. Such disputes usually involve business representatives on temporary visit visas. Some Saudi business sponsors have gained possession of the passports of their visitors to use as leverage in disputes, but this is not authorized under Saudi law. Commercial disputes between parties who have a formal contract can be brought to the Commercial Arbitration Board of the Saudi Chamber of Commerce or to the Committee for the Settlement of Commercial Disputes in the Ministry of Commerce. Disputes involving a government agency may be brought before the Grievance Board, an autonomous court body under the Office of the King. Employer/employee disputes may be brought before the Committee for the Settlement of Labor Disputes in the Ministry of Labor. An amicable out-of-court settlement is always the best and least expensive way to resolve a dispute, since referring matters to commercial or labor tribunals can be costly and time-consuming. Ultimate responsibility for obtaining private legal counsel and resolving a dispute through the Saudi legal system lies with the parties involved. Consular officers will offer lists of local attorneys to help settle such disputes. Business visitors should be aware that if the Saudi party in a commercial dispute files a complaint with the authorities, Saudi law permits barring the exit of the foreign party until the dispute is completely settled, including payment of any damages. Saudi law is applied exclusively in all commercial and contract dispute cases, even if the contract was drawn up and/or signed outside Saudi Arabia. Remember that the Arabic text of the contract or agreement is the text that is considered binding.

Photography

Visitors should not photograph mosques, people who are praying, military or government installations and key industrial, communications or transportation facilities. If you have any doubts about what you may photograph, request permission first.

Dogs

Most pets, except dogs, may be brought into the country, provided they are accompanied by a health certificate authenticated by the Saudi consulate in the country of origin. Dogs are banned, with the exception of guard dogs, hunting dogs and seeing-eye dogs. Dogs in these excepted categories must be accompanied by a health certificate and a certificate authenticated by the Saudi consulate in the country of origin that attests that the dog fits into one of the exempt categories.

Nuts and Bolts

Nearly 36 percent of the inhabitants of Saudi Arabia are resident foreigners. This includes approximately 30,000 American citizens. English is acknowledged as a second language and is taught in the secondary schools. Islam dominates all aspects of life in Saudi Arabia, including government policy, cultural norms and social behavior. Islam is the only official religion of the country, and public observance of any other religion is forbidden. The Saudi government considers it a sacred duty to safeguard the holy mosques located in the cities of Mecca and Medina. Travel to Mecca and Medina is forbidden to non-Muslims. Muslims throughout the world turn to Mecca five times a day for prayer. Restaurants, stores and other public places close for approximately a half-hour upon hearing the call to prayer, and Muslims stop their activities to pray during that time. Government and business activities are noticeably curtailed during the month of Ramadan, during the celebrations at the end of Ramadan, and during the time of the annual pilgrimage to Mecca, the hajj. Travel facilities into, out of and within Saudi Arabia are crowded during these periods.

Saudi Arabian Social Norms

U.S. citizens are advised that Saudi Arabia is a conservative country with a rigorous code of public behavior that everyone, including foreigners, is fully expected to observe. In particular, Westerners need to be aware of the standards of appropriate attire and the prohibition of mingling of the sexes.

Other Middle Eastern Countries Not Likely to Be Chosen as a Site by the Walt Disney Corporation for a Major Theme Park

OK, so a trip to Saudi Arabia or a job with Aramco is out of the question. Just where can you go to get your fill of sand dunes, camels, cold starry nights and all the lamb you can eat? Well, how's this for spiffy ad copy for tourist ads straight from the State Department and *DP*:

Bahrain

Bahrain is getting a little miffed at all the fundamentalists Iran keeps sending in to stir things up. Tourism is still possible with some fairly major restrictions. Business representatives, conference and exhibition delegates, and holders of diplomatic and official passports may obtain a visitors visa, valid for up to three months, from the Bahrain Embassy in Washington, D.C. or the U.N. Mission for Bahrain in New York. Persons in the above categories may also be able to obtain either a seven-day visa or a 72-hour transit visa at the Bahrain airport upon arrival if they present a confirmed return or onward air ticket.

Single women who have no sponsor or family ties in Bahrain may have difficulty in obtaining an airport visa. In addition to an onward ticket, they may need to secure in advance a sponsorship from a hotel that will arrange to have an airport visa waiting for them. The 72-hour airport visa can be extended, on a case by case basis, for up to one week if a Bahraini sponsor applies to the Immigration Director stating the purpose for the extension.

A seven day visa is possible for members of tourist groups, provided arrangements are made with the Directorate of Tourism and Archaeology in the Ministry of Information or through a private agency in Bahrain, such as a hotel, travel agent or tour group organizer. Journalists planning travel to Bahrain should contact the Ministry of Information, providing travel details at least one week in advance of arrival. The Ministry will then authorize airport officials to issue a 72-hour or a seven-day visa upon arrival. Failure to notify the Ministry may result in delay at the airport or denial of permission to enter the country. The Ministry is open from 7 a.m.–2 p.m. Saturday through Wednesday.

Ministry of Information
> P.O. Box 253
> State of Bahrain
> ☎ (973) 689-099
> FAX (973) 780-345
> Telex: 8399

Water is drinkable though often highly saline. Conservative dress is recommended. Bahrain prohibits the import of pornography, firearms, ammunition or of items such as knives, swords or daggers that are capable of being used as weapons. Videotapes may be screened by customs in Bahrain and either confiscated or held until the traveler departs the country. Consumption of alcohol is allowed in most bars and restaurants, except during the month of Ramadan. If there is any indication that a driver has consumed alcohol, authorities will regard that as evidence of driving under the influence of alcohol. The penalty for drunken driving may be incarceration or a fine of 500 Bahraini dinars, the equivalent of US$1300. This fine can be increased up to double that amount, depending on the circumstances of the case and the judge's decision. Under Bahraini law, convicted drug traffickers may receive the death penalty.

Kuwait

Visitors to Kuwait should be aware of the danger of unexploded land mines, bombs and shells throughout the country, courtesy of the Iraqi Tourist Bureau. We couldn't come up with many tourist attractions, so we assume that if you want to retrace the road to victory you'd better watch where you step.

Stay on main roads, do not travel on unpaved roads, and avoid open areas and beaches. A large amount of weaponry left in Kuwait by the Iraqis after the August 1990 invasion remains in private hands and may be used in committing crimes. The crime rate in Kuwait has increased from prewar levels. Women have been the object of an unusual amount of harassment and should take precautions as they would in any large city. Women should be alert to the possibility of being followed, should not respond to the approaches of strangers and should avoid travel alone in unfamiliar or isolated parts of the city, especially at night. Conservative dress is recommended, particularly for women. Garments should cover elbows and knees. No alcohol may be imported or consumed in Kuwait. If customs officials discover alcoholic beverages in a traveler's personal effects, the traveler may be arrested and prosecuted for smuggling. U.S. citizens should avoid the Iraq border and surrounding areas because of the risk of detention by Iraqi authorities. Be extremely careful when traveling north of Kuwait City because the border is not well marked. Persons near the border have been taken into custody by Iraqi officials and convicted of violations of Iraqi law. Some have received lengthy prison sentences. Anyone who must travel near the demilitarized zone is strongly advised to notify family, friends, colleagues and the U.S. embassy in Kuwait of their intention.

Morocco

U.S. citizens do not require a visa for a tourist or business visit of up to three months. The regular route in for visitors is via ferry from Malta.

Syria

Syria being the eye of the storm is a very calm, quiet place. Damascus also provides one-stop shopping for people who like to collect brochures on terrorist organizations from the PKK to Hezbollah. Syrian law does not recognize the U.S. citizenship of a naturalized Syrian, unless the Syrian government has given that person permission to renounce Syrian nationality. U.S. Syrian dual nationals who have not received that permission are considered Syrian when they enter Syria, even when they enter on their U.S. passports. A Syrian male cannot leave the country until he has satisfied the requirement for military service. This does not apply to a man who is the only son in a family, but it applies to all other men of normal military service age or older. Any person, male or female, who is considered Syrian may take no more than US$2000 worth of convertible currency out of Syria, no matter how much they may have brought into the country. U.S. citizens of Syrian origin may experience difficulties if they remain in Syria after the expiration of their visas. If you are a dual national, check with the Syrian embassy on the obligations of Syrian citizenship before you visit Syria. Travelers may bring any amount of currency into Syria. Syrian law does not require currency to be declared unless the total is more than US$5000. It is wise, however, to declare any currency you have, because you cannot take currency out of Syria unless it has been declared upon arrival. There are two rates of exchange in Syria. In addition to the official rate, Syrian pounds may be purchased at the more favorable "neighboring country rate" at the Syrian Commercial Bank or at a major hotel if you have convertible currency in cash or traveler's checks. Hotel bills must be paid in convertible currency or with Syrian pounds obtained at the official rate from the Commercial Bank of Syria (receipt required). Meals and all other purchases can be paid for with Syrian pounds and do not require official rate certification. Credit card charges are figured at the official rate. Syrian pounds cannot be taken out of Syria. Travelers cannot convert Syrian pounds back into convertible currency, and should therefore not purchase more of the currency than they expect to spend in Syria. Conservative dress is recommended for Syria. Travelers should exercise caution when photographing historic sites. Photographs may be taken of regular tourist attractions, such as ancient ruins and temples, but warnings are issued against photographing anything other than tourist sites.

United Arab Emirates

The United Arab Emirates (U.A.E.) is a federation of seven independent emirates. Visitors to the U.A.E. must obtain a sponsored visa before arrival. The sponsor can be a business associate, a relative or friend, or the hotel where the visitor has a reservation. Non-Muslims may consume alcohol in licensed bars or restaurants.

Yemen

U.S. citizens should exercise caution in Yemen and avoid travel in remote areas. Local tribal disputes in remote parts of Yemen have occasionally led to violence. Westerners, including U.S. citizens, have been kidnapped as a result of such local disputes, and vehicles have been hijacked. Because of the 7200-foot altitude of Sanaa and the lack of adequate medical facilities, travelers may wish to consult their physicians before visiting Yemen. Independent travel in Yemen is difficult; it is advisable to arrange your trip though a travel agent. Specific written permission from the Yemen General Tourism Corporation must be obtained for any travel outside the cities of Sanaa and Aden. Specific permission is also required to use a video camera. Photography of military installations, equipment or troops is forbidden. Although the civil war is over, there are rumblings of new hostilities between the Saudis and the Yemenis. There is little, if any, fixed border between the two countries, leading each country to do a little "fudge" on where to build a nice picket fence.

Oman

There are no tourist visas to Oman, and visa requirements for business travelers are stringent. Anyone arriving in Oman without a visa is subject to arrest. A business visitor must contact an Omani sponsor, either a businessman or firm, for assistance in procuring a nonobjection certificate (NOC). The sponsor should begin application procedures several weeks ahead of expected travel. American firms new to Oman may receive guidance on Omani sponsorship from the commercial office of the U.S. embassy in Muscat. They should send a telex (TLX 3785 AMEMBMUS ON) describing their company's activities and what they expect to accomplish in Oman. Relatives of Omanis may be sponsored for a short visit using the NOC procedure. Although Oman imposes stringent entry requirements for all visitors, it does not require exit permits. Conservative dress is recommended for Oman. No alcohol, firearms, pornography or fresh food may be imported.

Qatar

Visitors to Qatar must have a business or personal sponsor. Passengers may transit Qatar without a visa if they continue their journey within 24 hours, have confirmed reservations on the same or the next available flight, and do not leave the transit lounge of Doha Airport. Conservative dress is recommended for Qatar. No alcohol may be imported.

####

For information on other Middle Eastern countries, see individual chapters on Algeria (page 93), Egypt (page 215), Israel (page 285), Iran (page 681), Iraq (page 701), Lebanon (page 445) and Libya (page 717).

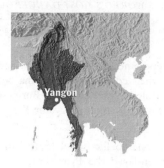

Yangon

Myanmar

Politically Incorrect

Watching tourism surge (and hard currency) in its Southeast Asia neighbors such as Thailand, Malaysia, Vietnam and Indonesia, good old SLORC (the State Law and Order Restoration Council) has said, "Why the hell not?"

The most politically incorrect destination on earth has to be Myanmar. While its buddies along the Pacific Rim sponsor tourism years and award lucrative contracts to companies to build up the infrastructure and create tourist attractions, Myanmar saves a few bucks by having its general population do it—at gunpoint.

Then there are the drug lords. The most famous, the notorious Khun Sa, now supplements his income with a line of ladies' shoes. It's not Payless, but we certainly hope the business is feeding him, because it'll have to now that the Rangoon generals have overrun his headquarters camp deep in the jungle at Ho Mong.

Between SLORC, the Karl Lagerfeld of opium and Aung San Suu Kyi—the Nobel prize–winning activist who was released after five years of house arrest and

743

behaves as if she's still under it—Myanmar makes for a bad soap opera. But let's go back a bit.

In keeping with the trend among developing and newly independent states to throw off the stigma of their colonial past, Burma became Myanmar in 1989. (Burma has always been called Myanmar in the Burmese language.) Rudyard Kipling turned in his grave when Rangoon became Yangon and the Irrawaddy became Ayeyarwady.

Myanmar has been a nation of bellicose rulers and brutal suppression since 2500 B.C., when the Yunnan enslaved the Pyus along the upper Ayeyarwady river. Throughout its various occupations by the Mons, the Arakanese, the British and the Japanese, there have been tales of ruthless excess and exotic splendor. Unlike the nepotistic concept of royal hierarchy in Western countries, it was considered normal for Burmese rulers to exterminate heirs, rivals or the offspring of rivals. Up until the mid-1800s, Burmese rulers burned, beat and drowned not only any potential claimants to the throne but also their children and servants. Hey, so what's the big deal about enslaving a few thousand peasants to build a road?

Today, the despotism continues. It's called something right out of a "Get Smart" episode: SLORC. A foreboding name in a forbidding land.

Myanmar was cocooned from the world by General Ne Win, who seized power in 1962. His 26-year reign plunged Myanmar backwards. He ruled until 1988, when pro-democracy demonstrators won and Ne Win stepped down. But the military refused to honor the results of an election it itself organized. Over 3000 Burmese protestors were killed when SLORC wrestled control of the government in a military crackdown. The 80-something Ne Win lives in the shadows and is a close friend of current intelligence chief Major-General Khin Nyunt.

Although the 21-member military junta of General Than Shwe (Saw Maung was removed due to mental problems, according to the new regime) continues to violently suppress any dissidents or uprisings, it controls only about 35 to 50 percent of the country at any one time. There are about 1000 political prisoners in about 20 "detention" centers around the country.

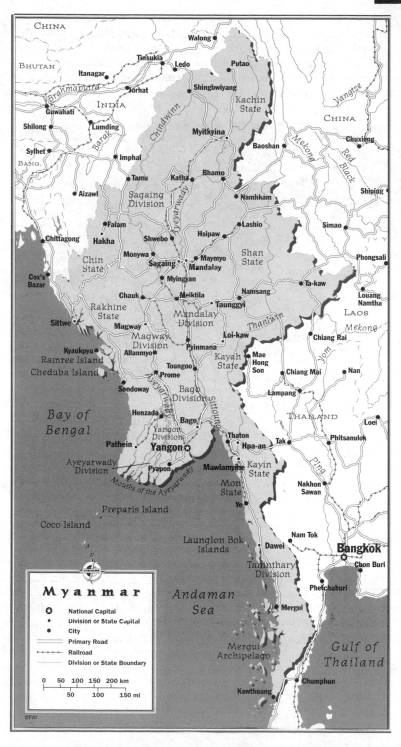

MYANMAR

CHINA

BHUTAN

Walong

Tinsukia   Ledo

Itanagar   Putao

Jorhat   Shingbwiyang

Brahmaputra   Kachin
State

Guwahati   INDIA

CHINA

Shilong   Lumding   Myitkyina   *Mekong*   Chuxiong

Barak   Baoshan   *Red*   *Black*

Sylhet   Imphal   Shiping

BANG.   Tamu   Katha   Bhamo   Simao

Aizawl   *Chindwin*   Sagaing   Namhkam

Chittagong   Hakha   Falam   Shwebo   Hsipaw   Lashio   Simao   Phongsali

Chin
State   Monywa   Sagaing   Maymyo   Shan
State

Cox's
Bazar   Sagaing   Mandalay   Ta-kaw   Louang
Namtha

Chauk   Myingyan   Namsang   LAOS

Rakhine
State   Meiktila   Taunggyi   *Mekong*

Sittwe   Magway   Mandalay
Division   Loi-kaw   Chiang Rai

Kyaukpyu   Magway
Division   Pyinmana   Kayah
State   Mae
Hong
Son   Chiang Mai   Nan

Ramree Island
Cheduba Island   Allanmyo   Toungoo
Prome   Lampang

Sandoway   *Ayeyarwady*   Bago
Division   *Sittoung*   THAILAND   Loei

*Bay of
Bengal*   Henzada   Yangon
Division   Bago   Thaton   Tak   Phitsanulok

Pathein   Yangon   Hpa-an

Ayeyarwady
Division   Pyapon   Mawlamyine   Kayin
State   Nakhon
Sawan

Mouths of the Ayeyarwady   Mon
State   Ye

Preparis Island

Coco Island   Nam Tok   Bangkok

Launglon Bok
Islands   Dawei   Chon Buri

*Taninthary
Division*   Phetchaburi

*Andaman
Sea*   Mergui

*Mergui
Archipelago*   Chumphon   *Gulf of
Thailand*

Kawthuang

Myanmar

⊛ National Capital
• Division or State Capital
• City
   Primary Road
⊢⊢⊢⊢ Railroad
   Division or State Boundary

0   50 100 150 200 km
    50   100   150 mi

©FWI

Whether by blowing up a student union building the day after a large student protest or executing members of its own army for insurrections, the government continues to keep a tight grip on this dirt-poor but culturally rich land. The current boy's club government hasn't lured a steady stream of eager investors, so the bulk of the 42 million Myanmarese are condemned to exist on an average per-capita income of US$200. Even the normally idealistic causes of insurgent groups have been replaced by the need for profits from opium production.

In getting ready for Visit Myanmar Year 1996, and true to form, the government—to prepare for the jumbo jet–loads of camcording Honshu islanders—chain-ganged not only criminals and dissidents, but regular folks to help rebuild monuments, palaces, temples and attractions. In Mandalay, the junta ordered that each family must contribute at least three days of free labor. Mandalayans could pay US$6 a month to be exempted from this drudgery. The average wage is about $6 a week in Mandalay.

The military regularly abducts villagers in rural areas to serve as porters in their wars against the insurgents, and to build roads to get there.

Sixty-eight percent of the population is Burmese; however, there are five major ethnic groups (Shan, 11 percent; Karen, 7 percent; Kachin, 6 percent; Arakanese, 4 percent; and Chin, 2 percent.). There are an estimated 26,000 insurgents in Myanmar fighting for various causes at any one time. But figuring out who's fighting whom is like unraveling an urchin stuck in a gill net. The Shans, found also in China, Laos and Thailand, have been waging a battle with China. The Karen straddle northern Thailand and eastern Burma and pay little attention to the border between the two countries. The Burmese live primarily in the central plains along the Ayeyarwady River and are the builders of the great monuments at Bagan. The Shan are found in the north of Myanmar and along the Myanmar/Thai border. They are fiercely independent, speak Tai and are represented by the Shan State Progress Party. The Mon populate the same fertile area as the Karen and are ethnically related to both the Khmers and Burmese.

Burma is unique for its multitude of worn but largely intact historical monuments. The country is famous for its Buddhist pagodas, especially the huge

Shwedagon Pagoda, as well as the plains of Bagan, its gentle people and colonial ambience. It is one of the best countries in the world to visit hill tribes and bask in unvarnished history.

The forbidden zones and the Golden Triangle may lure adventurers, but there is little to see or do in these mostly rural and deforested areas. As the government creates an uneasy but profitable peace with rebel groups, more and more areas will open up to tour bus–bottomed "adventurers." In all cases you are expected to have an MTT guide, who's very disinterested in anything adventurous.

The Players

Everyone

In Burma (whoops, Myanmar) you can't tell the bit players without a program. Even *DP* dares not dive too deeply into the various military, political, narco, ethnic, regional and ideological groups that want a piece of Myanmar for themselves. There are estimated to be at least 35 insurgency groups fighting or operating inside Myanmar. Depending on who's counting, they range in size from a handful of overeducated hotheads living in refugee camps, bad-ass shoot-to-kill drug smugglers, archaic political parties, regional warlords, and well-meaning but poorly equipped tribes to large, well-equipped armies of over 25,000 soldiers, complete with armored divisions. There are four major ethnic divisions, with 67 recognized tribal groups, with the majority Burman (67 percent) living along the fertile center. Keep in mind as you travel around the country that most border and northern areas have some sort of grudge match going on at any one time. The Karen Nationals have been fighting for independence since 1949. The various groups fighting the SLORC are united under the name Democratic Alliance of Burma

Ksar el Hirane, SLORC and the Generals

With a 265,000-man army, the 21-member junta comprised of the ruling families and selected investors holds most of the marbles here, at least in the majority of the country. However, the real and future wealth of the country is in the rich but remote regions ruled by ethnic tribes. Timber, jade, precious stones and, of course, opium are all under the control of the ethnic minorities, many of whom are wealthy enough to support affluent civic centers, tax collectors, customs, public services and their own private armies.

Recent announcements of peace between insurgents and the government are assumed to be "live and let live" agreements, which allow the rebels to concentrate on the more lucrative business of raising and exporting opium rather than vying for political power.

Although vast parcels of Myanmar are controlled by insurgent groups, there exist tacit agreements between SLORC generals and Thai logging companies permitting rebel factions to smuggle hardwood and gems out of the country into Thailand. In turn, the logging roads created by this lucrative trade provide the government an expedient route to send in troops during the dry season to pressure-play the insurgents. Myanmar possesses about of 75 percent of the tropical teak left in the world. The government, the Karens and the Shans, along with about 20 Thai logging companies, are rapidly sawing everything down before the political winds shift direction. According to some estimates, in 10 to 15 years, there won't be enough teak left to put together a decent deck chair.

Karen National Liberation Army (KNLA)

The largest insurgent group is the Karen National Liberation Army of the Karen National Union (KNU), based in Manerplaw and headed by Saw Bo Mya. Converted to Christianity by missionaries at the turn of the century and allied with the British during WWII, they have been fighting for their own independence since Burma was granted its independence without provision for a Karen homeland. The Karen battle for sovereignty has been ongoing since 1948, one of the longest struggles for freedom in Asia. They are funded through their control of the smuggling routes between Myanmar and Thailand. About 5000 government troops supported by ethnic Wa militia are slowly squeezing the life out of the Karen rebels.

The Karens are divided by religion, with Buddhist and Christian factions. The Buddhist faction has aligned itself with the Myanmarese government, weakening the Karen's chance for an independent homeland. The government is currently "cleaning house" by killing all remaining Karenni fighters.

They still control many smuggling routes and border crossing between Myanmar into Thailand. They impose a 5 percent tax on all items smuggled into Thailand. Their big cash cow used to be the mountainous border crossing at Payathonzu. But they still control the northern smuggling points. The Karens have the dubious distinction of being Asia's longest-running insurgency group.

The Arakan Rohingya Islamic Front and the Rohingya Solidarity Organization

The Arakan Rohingya Islamic Front and the smaller Rohingya Solidarity Organization represent the Rohingyas, Muslim refugees from Arakan state now based in camps in eastern Bangladesh. About 280,000 Myanmarese Muslims fled from Arakan state to southern Bangladesh in early 1992. In a century-old tradition since the days of King Bodawpaya, the refugees are persecuted by the Myanmarese military. In the past, the Rohingyas have been armed and trained by Afghan *mujahedin* and Filipino Moros.

The Kachin Independent Organization

This is a group of 5000 rebels also known as the Kachin Independence Army (KIA). The Kachins are animists and Christians of Tibeto-Burman descent who originally migrated from China. Found in northern Myanmar, they are funded in part through the mining of rich jade deposits in the area. The jade is then sold to China. At one time this group was the primary organizer of opium transportation to the Thai border.

The National League for Democracy

The National League for Democracy is an opposition party, whose rarely seen dissidents have allegedly hidden in the jungle since 1988, when the Myanmarese military suppressed a nationwide uprising for democracy. They've come out of the closet recently with the 1995 release from house arrest of NLD leader Aung San Suu Kyi, but may have to step back into it after walking out on SLORC's late-1995 constitution convention.

Aung San Suu Kyi

The charismatic and brave figurehead of the NLD. She stood in front of SCORC's rifles during the student riots of '88, was busted by the evil generals and got a Nobel prize for her efforts. Placed under house arrest in 1989, she wasn't heard from until her release in the summer of 1995. She's chosen not to leave Burma, but instead to engage in "constructive dialogue" with SLORC and to consult with her NLD colleagues to find a way of bruising the SLORC bullies without getting her behind back in the slammer. SLORC sees her as more of a nuisance (albeit a major one) than a threat, as Euro and ASEAN conglomo-cash is beginning to flow into Myanmar like fleeing Iraqis, ensuring the generals a lasting reign. But the foreign investment well may dry up suddenly if they bounce Suu Kyi's butt back into her bathroom again. She and some supporters were rousted by Khin Nyunt's Ray-Ban cops at a dissident's New Year's Eve bash on January 1, 1996. She was asked a couple of questions by the guys in sunglasses and told to go home and have a nice day. Her buddies we won't hear from again. Final score: SLORC: 10, NLD 9 (in overtime).

SLORC Bullies Hurl Tomatoes in Bid to Get Drafted into the Majors

Los Angeles Dodger manager Tommy Lasorda has found pitchers everywhere from the jungles of Mexico to the base of Mount Fuji. He may want to start sending some scouts to Rangoon for a new generation of hurlers. SLORC figures if they start gunning down NLDers like they did in 1988 with real bullets, the world will back out of oil and pipeline deals and half-finished hotels. So, through sheer political genius, they've resorted to hiring thugs to lob tomatoes at Suu Kyi and her supporters. The generals figure a few tomatoes and a few messed-up hairdos won't make the pages of the New York Times. So they've enlisted the services of the Union Solidarity and Development Association (USDA)—ostensibly a government-sponsored social welfare association, but in reality a gang of shock troops and a Cleveland Indians farm team—to practice their pitching skills at NLD demonstrations. In one instance, in February 1996, as Suu Kyi was speaking at a memorial ceremony for former Burmese Prime Minister U Nu, a Toyota pickup filled with crates of tomatoes rolled up; the tomatoes were intended to be lobbed at the participants by USDA fledging Florida Marlins. They refused to fire the tomatoes at the crowd, thinking that crates of jackfruit (a much larger fruit) were to be supplied instead.

The Shan State Army

Another group, the Shan State Army, was given large timber concessions along the Thai border and also benefit from trade in gemstones and opium. Their relationship with the Thai military has led to massive deforestation of the region.

The Shan United Army, or Mong Tai

The Shan United Army was the private play-toy of ruthless drug lord Chang Chi Fu, also known by the thespian title Khun Sa (the Prince of Death), until it broke up into factions in mid-1995. The U.S. government credits Khun Sa with providing a full two-thirds of the world's heroin supply. Khun Sa "officially" stepped down from "power" at the end of 1995.

Khun Sa

Khun Sa is a self-styled "freedom fighter" who's been duking it out with the government as well as his equally notorious enemy, drug lord Chao Yelaiin, an ethnic Wa. A peace agreement the two signed in October 1993 resulted in an unabated surge of heroin flowing through the Golden Triangle area. Khun Sa, who's wanted by the U.S. government on narcotics smuggling charges, agreed to the settlement with his traditional rival, as it became more apparent that the heroin factories in the Shan state were becoming increasingly dependent on raw opium produced in Wa-controlled areas. The Myanmar government accuses Khun Sa of dozens of massacres, including the slaughter of 122 villagers in Shan state in March 1993.

Khun Sa and his Mong Tai army has not been faring that well; the ranks defected into three factions in June 1995, charging that their leader was spending too much time tinkering with his dope business and not enough fighting for freedom. (Khun Sa theatrically claimed the defections occurred because he is half Chinese.) And government troops seized the drug warlord's mountain stronghold at Ho Mong in January 1996. Many think the cagey guerrilla commander cut a deal with SLORC in which he turned over his territory and what was left of his army to the government in exchange for amnesty. Problem is, it seems he didn't tell his guerrillas. One Mong Tai army officer who made it into

Thailand shortly before SLORC took the base said, "We were told our commanders were negotiating with SLORC for a cease-fire—but it turned out they were allowing the Burmese troops to take over our bases." Oh, well. Khun Sa has maintained all along that he was never an opium trader but a freedom fighter, and that he taxed drug runners moving through his territory to help fund the Shan liberation cause. The great one has gone into hiding for now, but if you're interested in finding out where he's at, call 66-53-612007 and talk to the man who answers the phone. Don't dare say you got the number here. Hey, did you DEA guys know this?

All Burma Students Democratic Front (ABSDF)

Burmese Communist Party (BCP)

Chin National Front (CNF)

Democratic Alliance of Burma (DAB)

Karenni Liberation Army (KLA)

Karenni Peoples United Liberation Front (KPULF)

Kayah New Land Revolution Council (KNLRC)

Kuomintang (KMT)

Ma Ha Faction of the Wa Army

Mon Liberation Front (MLF)

National Democratic Front (NDF)

National Coalition Government of the Union of Burma (NCGUB)

Pa-O Shan State Independence Party (PSSIP)

Palaung State Liberation Organization (PSLO)

Tai National Army (TNA)

Shan United Revolutionary Army (SURA)

Shan United Army (SUA)

United Pa-O Organization (UPO)

Khun Sa's Boy Soldiers

Khun Sa had hundreds of kids with guns whacking SLORC troops and rival drug armies, most of them between 10 and 14 years old. With the drug warlord's army now defunct, at least 500 of the kids don't have a home. SLORC's policy? They've asked that local families adopt the kids as farm laborers. Most won't take the kids in. Who knows, they may become the next rage in the States, like pet rocks and Vietnamese pygmy pigs. Want to adopt one of Khun Sa's boy guerrillas? Check with the Myanmar embassy in Bangkok or Washington, D.C. (see addresses and phone numbers on following page).

Getting In

Visas are required of all travelers to Myanmar, ages seven years and above, for a stay of up to 30 days (formerly, you couldn't stay in the country for more than two weeks). From Bangkok, visas now only take about two to three days to be processed and cost 800 Thai baht (US$32). Tour operators process visas for travelers on their organized tours, although it is no longer mandatory to be in Myanmar on an organized tour. Tourists can travel independently in Myanmar, but aren't permitted to stray from the "approved" tourist sites. Tourist visas are not extendable except in rare circumstances (i.e., you want to become a monk). Once inside Myanmar, a business visitor may possibly apply for an extended visa with the invitation and recommendation of a state enterprise. For a tourist visa, you'll need three passport-sized photographs. Keep in mind that visa regulations have a habit of changing regularly with this country. Check with:

Myanmar Embassy

132 Sathon Neua Road
Bangkok
☎ *66-2-233-2237*
or

Myanmar Embassy

2300 S St., N.W.
Washington, D.C. 20008
☎ *202-332-9044*

The only downside to the new lengthened visa is that you will be required to exchange US$300 into Foreign Exchange Certificates at the government's absurd exchange rate of 6 kyats to the U.S. dollar. (This is changing, as SLORC is revaluing its currency to the more realistic level of 120 kyats to the dollar for Visit Myanmar Year 1996.)

Sneaking into Myanmar can be easily done by hiking over land or along logging roads into the country from Thailand. Troubles you encounter won't be with the government but with the various ethnic and rebel groups, who will have no qualms about shooting you and leaving you to rot. You can try contacting the various groups through expat sympathizers; however, don't try this from inside the country. Another alternative is having a couple of 13-year-old schoolkids-turned-commandos sneak you across the border for a nominal fee (call warlord Khun Sa at ☎ *66-53-612007*).

The northern and eastern border areas are technically closed. But since the government has been in control of so few of these areas (it now controls the former Mong Tai border stronghold of Doi Lang), it raises the question of who will stop you first, the government or the rebels. If you are a caught, you will be deported and may magically lose most of your valuables.

Arakan province is technically closed, but there are flights to Sittwe and two attractive beach resorts in Ngapali. This is the favorite getaway of the rich and famous, and the area is sprinkled with their homes away from home.

You have a choice of seven air carriers into Myanmar, the best choice being Silk Air (an arm of Singapore Airlines), and the worst being Myanmar Airways. You can buy a ticket outside the country, but you will not be guaranteed a seat. Even if you make a reservation inside Myanmar, there still is no guarantee that the plane will leave, or that an unsmiling gentleman with a military uniform and Louis Vuitton luggage won't be given your seat.

You won't find the usual crush of touts when arriving in Yangon's airport, since they are not allowed in. Buses into town cost about US$4; taxis should be no more than US$6.

When you leave, you will need US$6 for the airport tax. They never have change.

Getting Around

The 100,000 to 200,000 or so tourists who will visit Myanmar each year don't put too big a strain on the country's infrastructure. The locals tend to push the existing airline, train and bus lines to bursting anyway. The major sights of Myanmar are easy to get to if you choose from any one of the 23 major airports (66 strips in total) serviced by the two flying museum Air Myanmar or the shiny new planes of Air Mandalay. Try not to fly at night or in bad weather, since they are just getting around to installing IFR, or all-weather capability. Rail service, as in any former British colony, is aged but efficient. There are 4684 km of track, 550 railway stops, 318 locomotives and 1130 passenger coaches. There are daily trips between Yangon and Mandalay. Train service (with the exception of the express runs) tends to be slow, deadly and crowded. As many as 120 people were killed in one incident in 1995 due to a derailment. Buses would be our third choice with the new air conditioned express buses being a comfortable second as opposed to a second-class train. Other forms of vehicular transportation are typically Third World: crowded, dangerous, cheap and requiring lots of pushing in the wet season.

Private cars with drivers go for about $50 a day, and motorcycles and bikes can be rented for $25 and pennies a day, respectively.

Up the Lazy River

Myanmar not only has about 50 steam engines still in service; they still operate hundreds of ancient riverboats that go back as far as the 1880's. These paddle wheelers (now converted to diesel) chug up the 8000 km of navigable rivers in Myanmar, carrying passengers and freight. Many are used as ferryboats. There are now newer luxury versions, but the hard core can still read their Rudyard Kipling poems on the deck of a slow-moving 19th-century paddle boat.

You will need permits to travel outside the a standard tourist rut (Yangon, Mandalay, Bagan, Inle Lake, Taunggyi). Permits are letters generated from MTT and approved by the Military. MTT or Yangon-based travel agencies will arrange for these. You will need to have a guide or driver and a pretty clear idea of where you want to go. You will not know which areas are specifically out of bounds until you apply to go to them. You can try to travel without a permit (many do) but be prepared to be turned back at any one of the military checkpoints throughout the county. Soldiers at checkpoints in partially controlled zones, like the Chin, Mon, Kayin or Shan states, will rarely bend the rules. You can, however, enter from Thailand illegally and take your chances with the insurgent checkpoints. You can fly into some areas much easier than by road. In many cases, the roads are controlled by insurgent armies. The need for permits and the areas that are considered dangerous or hot change daily, so check with the local embassy.

Most tours start in Bangkok, and most tour companies are based there as well. You can fly in from Chiang Mai to Mandalay and Bagan. Pwin Ol Lwin, or Maymyo as it was formerly known, is an old British hill station that still has 153 horse-drawn carriages left over from colonial times. The Burma Road in the Shan hills is the major trade route with Yunnan in China.

The Golden Triangle area in Myanmar can be reached by train from Mandalay. You can also make the arduous 160-km trip from Kengtung to Tachileik. Additionally, travelers have been able to get from Kengtung to Mai Sai in Thailand's Chiang Rai province. But the border is shut, and you'd probably get popped anyway.

Lashio is a mecca for adventurers, for this is where the Burma Road begins its long, winding path into China. Mogok is 115 km from Mandalay and is the site of jade and ruby mines controlled by rebels on odd days, and the government on even days. You can see (and purchase) the fruits of their labors by posing as a buyer at the annual gem auction each February in Yangon.

Good maps are not available. Bartholomew, Nelles and Hildebrand are the best brands for maps of the country. The local MTT office in Athenian and Mandalay can provide street maps.

DP likes to group Myanmar in a group of countries that includes Turkey, Egypt, Cambodia, Russia, the Philippines, Israel and Colombia—countries that aggressively seek tourists even though they are, uh, well, kind of having a few problems in the hinterlands. Myanmar has a basketful of troubles, and the official word is that they have signed truces with almost all the major players. (See "The Players" for an eye opener.) The problem is there are over 35 independence groups and we haven't seen any democratic elections (at least ones Jimmy Carter was invited to).

So is Myanmar dangerous? In a word, no. Like Cambodia, if you stay on your leash and visit all the nice monuments, you will be fine. But if you head into the boonies, you are guaranteed to meet a lot of pissed-off folks. Those won't be rolled up election posters they're pointing at you.

Shan State (The Far North and Southeast)

So, where do you stay away from (or run to, depending on your taste in travel)? Well, start with any hilly, northern area bordering Thailand, China and Laos. This is where drugs are grown, sold and refined. (See "Drugs" for more than you ever wanted to know about the opium trade.) Shan state is home to the Shan, Kachin, Karen, Wa and other ethnic groups, all of whom have armies and control movement inside and across the borders. The mountainous areas are ideal for growing opium poppies. This region is headed by a narco government run by warlords with large armies. There are frequent clashes for turf and with government troops.

Mon State (Southern Area)

The Mon and the Karen insurgents hide out in this strip of land that parallels the Thai border. Although there was a cease-fire in 1995 between the government and the Mon National Liberation Front, the Mon still duke it out with the Karen over control of the smuggling checkpoints into Thailand. Banditry along the highways by armed groups is prevalent in daylight.

Chin State

The ethnic Chin want their own remote mountainous country, and guess what they want to call it? Yep, Chinland. These folks need a little better feel for Marketing 101. The Chin are Tibeto-Burmese who are primarily animists. Of course, where there are happy animists, there are Christian missionaries handing out faded Ninja Turtle shirts and Addidas shorts. The government has also sent in Buddhists missionaries to tug their souls in another direction.

There are many people with Indian or Bengali ties, so the government is also actively persecuting the Muslims, forcing many to flee to neighboring India or Bangladesh.

Rahkine State

Rahkine state is stirred up by the activities of the Arakan Rohingya Islamic Front and the Rohingya Solidarity Organization, extra-agitated folks from among the quarter of a million Muslim refugees who live across the border (not by choice) in scenic, affluent Bangladesh.

The Name Game

Despite all the PC babble about Myanmar being the bad guys name for Burma, don't believe it. Myanmar is the name of the country, and Burma is the name of the people and language found around the capital city of Yangon. The region has been called Myanmar even as far back as the 13th century, when Marco Polo called it that. It makes more sense to call the country a name other than just one of the many ethnic groups. Imagine if America was called India after what was our largest ethnic group. All the generals were doing was a little colonial house cleaning when they renamed the country and many of its cities.

Nuts and Bolts

Myanmar experiences the typically Southeast Asian tropical monsoon climate, with hot, humid lowlands and cool highlands. The wet monsoon season is from June through September, the cool dry season from November to April.

The official language of Myanmar is Burmese; a number of ethnic languages are also spoken. Burmese is a completely indecipherable script for most casual visitors. English signs have been removed so bring a phrase book if you want to do anything more than eat or sleep. It is helpful to know that Burmese have one given name between one to three syllables, usually preceded with a form of address. In Burmese, use *Oo* (uncle) for adult males, *Ko* (elder brother) for males of the same age, *Bo* for leader, *Ma* (sister) for young girls, *Daw* (aunt) for older women, and *Saya* (master) for teachers or employers. Other ethnic groups use variations on this theme. Buddhists comprise 85 percent of the population, while animists, Muslims, Christians and other indigenous religion followers comprise the rest. The literacy rate stands at 81 percent. The monetary unit is the kyat. Officially, the exchange rate is six kyats to the dollar. However, on the black market, a buck will get you 120 kyats

Big Brother

The military rulers of Myanmar keep a very close watch on their own people and particularly hnakaung shays or long noses. That probably means you. Do not converse freely with strangers. It can be safely assumed that anyone who loiters near you or reappears often in your travels is a paid intelligence operative.

Telephone calls can be made from hotels and the Central Telegraph office in Yangon. International calls go through operators (watch what you say and whom you call). There is no guarantee of a phone line being available or even usable. Telexes can be sent from major hotels as well as the telegraph office.

It costs six kyats to post an airmail letter, but don't count on it getting there anytime soon. Buy the stamps and mail your postcards or letters from Bangkok. MTT, *77-79 Sule Pagoda Road*, is the main source for travel info in Yangon. There are also offices in Mandalay, Bagan and Taunggyi.

Voltage is 220/50 cycles when it works.

Note: February and March are bad times to visit due to the influx of gem buyers into Yangon for the annual auction.

Embassies/Consulates

American Embassy

> 581 Merchant Street
> Box B
> Yangon
> ☎ [95] (1) 82055 or 82181

Embassy of the Union of Myanmar

> 2300 S Street, N.W.
> Washington, D.C. 20008
> ☎ (202) 332-9044-5

Permanent Mission of Myanmar to the U.N.

> 10 East 77th Street
> New York, NY 10021
> ☎ (212) 535-1311/0/1716
> FAX (212) 737-2421

Money Hassles

If you thought straight currency conversion was a pain, wait until you get to Myanmar. The kyat (pronounced chat and made up of 100 pyas) or Myanmar's version of Monopoly money is worth about 20 times more than the official rate on the black market. Wait until you try to decide whether you should pay for something in the 45, 50 and 90 or 100 denomination bills. Upon arrival, foreign visitors are required to exchange US$300 (or the equivalent in British pounds) into Foreign Exchange Certificates. They are funny money in denominations of $5, $10 and $20 notes equivalent to the value of U.S. currency. You can swap your FECs for kyat or pay for your hotel or transportation inside Myanmar. Guess who controls FECs? The government charges 10 percent to convert FECs to kyat and only government-owned banks get to do so. Also, items in high demand can only be bought with foreign currency. Once you are out of the country, they are only good for rolling cigarettes and souvenirs.

Most locals ask for and horde U.S. greenbacks in case they need to get out of town fast or the generals decide to leave first. US. dollars can legally be accepted by establishments permitted to do so. Most folks will gladly swap dollars for kyat at a much better rate. Be warned this is considered illegal.

DP TIP

Make sure your kyat says "Central Bank of Myanmar" instead of "Central Bank of Burma." Hawkers like to pawn off the worthless Burma bills on tourists.

Don't be surprised if you get hit up for a "present," the English form of Africa's "cadeaux." Government workers will be quite direct about their desire for a little extra incentive to process paperwork. Don't get too generous, since they want a minor item that can be resold. Cigarette lighters, pens or a T-shirt will do fine. Sold-out airlines are less sold out if a U.S. 10 spot magically appears.

In the north people actually use unprocessed opium as a form of currency, since it is worth a lot more than the kyat. The good news is that Myanmar is still cheap (there is a 30 percent inflation rate); Arthur Frommer could still legitimately do a book called "Myanmar on $5 a Day."

Internet Sites

http://www.freeburma.org
http://danenet.wicip.org/fbc
Two places to find information on Aung San Suu Kyi and contact other people interested in a democratic Burma (Calling the country Myanmar is *tres outre* for these folks). There is also an electronic service called BurmaNet which will distribute information on the going's on inside Myanmar (whoops, Burma). You might want to let all your boycott tuna, save the whales and Body Shop pals join in what is the 90's most in protest. To be politically correct, you're not supposed to visit Myanmar so that your dollars don't fall into the evil hands of the Generals. DP takes no sides but you might actually want to visit Myanmar and form your own opinion. You might actually do something about it instead of driving the economy into the stone age.

MYANMAR

Pyongyang

North Korea

Il or Illin?

At Pyongyang's Mansudae Hill, a line of street cleaners who look more like housewives (which, of course, they actually double as), armed with straw brooms, march stooped over like a bad ensemble at Pasadena's DooDah Parade. Like a 17th-century Zamboni machine, they clear what little soil has accumulated on the walkway in front of the Korean Revolution Museum before a giant bronze statue of the late North Korean leader Kim Il Sung. Kim's massive right arm is eternally locked forward in a handshake with the clouds, which was about all he was able to shake hands with during his neurotically xenophobic, despotic and frequently brutal 46 years of rule of a country that may as well be on Mars.

Shaking hands with nothing. The image lingers with you, even after reading the romantic, campy description in the city's official guidebook: "The statue of Kim portrays his sublime figure looking far ahead, with his left hand akimbo and his right raised to indicate the road for the people to advance."

Oh.

That's what he's doing.

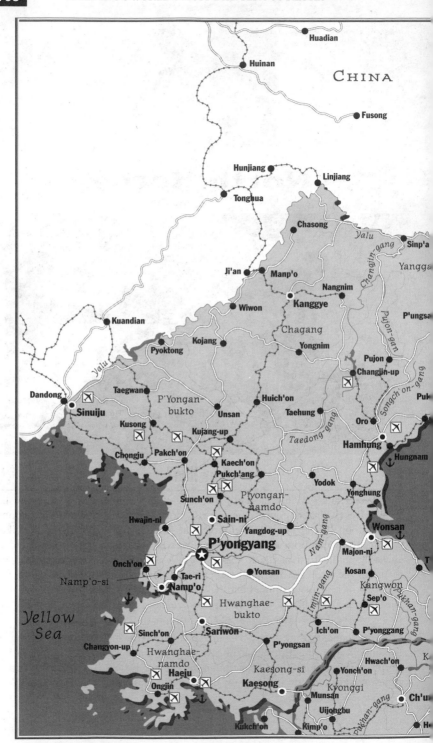

The road to the 38th parallel, no doubt.

The Great Leader departed for the Great Unknown on July 18, 1994, succumbing to illness that he tried vainly to thwart with a combination of meteorology and herbs. Millions of North Koreans have made pilgrimages to the statue and other shrines, openly weeping for a man who they were taught since birth created the dawn of each new day. Literally. It must have come as quite a shock when the sun rose that next morning. Myth and legend shrouded Kim Il Sung. His legendary heroics against the Japanese during World War II, by all historical accounts, never occurred. His greatest victory was a stalemate in the Korean War, at the cost of a half million North Korean lives. He might also claim a victory of sorts in the arrest of more than 20 million people.

North Koreans are taught that Kim was the inventor of everything from centuries-old scientific and physics theories to such modern conveniences as the automobile and the toaster. Some believe he's walked on the moon. By law, every North Korean household must possess at least two portraits of the Great One. Not Gretsky, but of Kim. That's overachievement.

Certainly not overachieving is Kim's son, 54-year-old Kim Jong Il, the Great Leader's heir apparent, who hasn't quite yet assumed the duties of president or leader of the Communist Party due to his extended grieving for his dead dad, despite being tagged the Supreme Leader (or Dear Leader). More than likely, some of the military boys put a rifle to his head and ordered him to grieve for a while. Perhaps for a couple of hundred years. Cry, baby, cry.

And they may have a good reason. Reclusive, cognac-guzzling Kim Jong Il is both a reported lush and an alleged terrorist. He's been implicated as the mastermind behind a number of terrorist attacks, including a Korean Air jetliner explosion that took 115 lives in 1987. He is believed responsible for North Korea's nuclear program (the bomb part, anyway), as well as the foiled assassination attempt on the South Korean president in Myanmar that instead blew away 17 high-level South Korean officials.

But the mythmaking continues. Kim Jong Il was actually born in Siberia, but because most North Koreans have never heard of Siberia, Jong Il was reborn near North Korea's Mount Paektu. He is reputed to have written hundreds of books, all epic masterpieces. His face fills the television screens every night, at all times and on every channel. The man who claims "socialism is not administrative and commanding" may have a different relationship with communism and alcohol. He is reported to spend nearly three-quarters of a million dollars a year on Hennessy cognac, specifically the Paradis line. That's commanding. Yet, he remains the subject of adulation. Normally bright, responsible scholars and educators from North Korea and abroad reduce themselves to writing driveling, soppy odes to this inglorious, silver-spooned papa's boy. Sample this, written by a doctor at Delhi University in India:

Dear leader Kim Jong Il
Friend of masses, savior of
humanity
Increased efforts of yours inspired
the masses
You have awakened them

To build modern DPRK
Brick by brick
Made them independent and masters
of their own destiny
Dear leader Kim Jong Il
A rising star on the horizon
Shown the path of salvation
Of realism
Removed flunkeyism in the face of
Severe odds
Dear leader Kim Jong Il
A versatile personality
I salute you

Removed flunkeyism? Whoa.

The "My Automatic Rifle" Dance

In North Korea, propaganda has become an art form. Perhaps the most entertaining reading we've come across at *DP* is the "consumer" magazine that comes out of Pyongyang—*Korea Today*, of the DPRK (Democratic Peoples Republic of Korea). There are magnificent book reviews, all on Kim Jong Il's hundreds of books. No room for anything else. And no comments such as "The plot is frayed; the characters develop like a fungus. The author has talent, but should have restricted it to flyer writing for the PTA." Nope, nothing like that. You'd end up in the gulag for a few centuries.

The harshest criticism we spotted was surprisingly scathing, though: "Many of the world's people call Kim Jong Il the giant of our times. This means that he is unique and distinguished in all aspects—wisdom, leadership, ability, personality and achievements." (*Korea Today*, No. 3, 1992.). The writer was anonymous, fearing for his life if his byline were to be published. There's coverage of some great plays and performing arts shows. One particularly caught our attention, a tear-jerking rendition of the "My Automatic Rifle Dance," performed by two voluptuous actresses prancing about the stage with their AKs.

Korea Today publishes cutting-edge, bohemian poetry that mainstream periodicals wouldn't have the balls to print:

My song, echo all the way home from the trenches.
When I smash the American robbers of happiness,
And I return home with glittering medals on my chest,
All my beloved family will be in my arms.

Cool stuff. Want to subscribe? Write: The Foreign Language Magazines, Pyongyang, DPRK.

For more laughs, write The Korean People's Army Publishing House (Pyongyang, DPRK) for a copy of their enormously popular *Panmunjom*, a chronicle of North Korea's innumerable military accomplishments. There are some great combat shots, with captions like "U.S. imperialist troops of aggression training south Korean puppet soldiers to become cannon fodder in their aggressive war against the northern half of Korea." Another innocuous shot of a group of soldiers is depicted as "A U.S. military advisor and the south Korean stooges are on the spot to organize the armed invasion of the northern half of Korea." Another photo shows a 1953 armistice meeting between North Korean and U.N. officials breaking up, and is appropriately captioned: "The U.S. imperialist troops of aggression hastily leave after their crimes have been exposed at a meeting held at the scene of the crime."

But the *DP* runner-up in the book goes to a 1976 shot of an American soldier using a chain saw to cut down a tree. The caption: "The U.S. imperialist troops of aggression committed a grave provocation, cutting down a tree."

And the winner? A fuzzy shot of a letter from Secretary of State John Foster Dulles to a South Korean colonel, dated June 20, 1950. The caption reads: "Secret messages exchanged between the south Korean puppets and the U.S. imperialists to invade the north, and Dulles' secret letter instigating the puppets to start a war." It took a magnifying glass, but we read the letter:

The dinner which you gave in our honor last night was something I shall always remember. The setting was really glorious, the company distinguished, the entertainment most interesting to us and last, but not least, the food was delicious. The antique vase (you gave us) will grace Mrs. Dulles' living room in New York and always keep fresh the memory of our visit with you.

The Scoop

No one's quite sure. North Korea is perhaps the most closed society on the globe. It is also perhaps the most lobotomized. Obtaining information from abroad is illegal, as is picking up hitchhikers (who might reveal contaminating Western secrets, such as John Travolta actually is a decent actor). North Koreans can't even visit many areas in their own country. Talking to a foreigner is grounds for arrest.

For sure, the pawns of Pyongyang have nuke capabilities, scaring the hell out of the U.S. puppet imperialists to the south and, of course, Japan. So much so, that Uncle Sam has gone to the brink of (dread!) normalizing relations with Pyongyang. When a U.S. military chopper strayed over North Korean airspace toward the end of 1994 and was shot down, killing one of the two pilots, Bill and Hillary didn't get back the remains for 10 days, and the live one for another week after that, but curiously, there wasn't significant protest from Washington. The Clintons are taking them seriously, at least for the moment.

North Korea's a damn difficult place to get around. Number one, there aren't any cars (bicycles were even illegal in many areas until the early 1990s). Western tourists can only visit selected areas of the country and only under the chaperoned and watchful eye of a government guide.

The Players

Kim Il Sung

Yeah, he's dead. But long live the Kim. The effects of playing God for 46 years don't go away overnight. The North Koreans still show, and will continue to show for years, blinding adoration of their beloved pinko deity, except for, perhaps, the estimated 20,000 political prisoners held in the country. But, remember, in North Korea, you're a political prisoner if you don't turn on your television in the morning.

Kim Jong Il

The Dear Leader isn't seen around a lot. Rumor has it he's in Il health. But more likely he's at a Blockbuster somewhere in L.A., either stocking up on copies of *Rambo*, *Godzilla*, and *Goodfellas* or abducting waitress/actresses. Jong's a movie freak; he owns perhaps 20,000 videotapes. It's also widely believed that Jong once kidnapped a South Korean actress and director and held them captive for nearly a decade while he played Dino de Laurentis. He shot a series of anti-Japanese films that make Crichton's *Rising Sun* look like the Meiji Constitution.

Kim Pyong Il

Half-brother of Kim Jong Il. A January 1995 shoot-out occurred in the streets of Pyongyang between followers of Kim Jong Il and Kim Pyong Il, suggesting a power struggle between the two. Jong's response? He banished his half-brother to one place on earth more miserable to live in than North Korea. He made him ambassador to Finland.

Jimmy Carter

Jimmy goes where no Bill dares. Carter was instrumental in brokering the October 1994 nuclear agreement between Pyongyang and Washington. Carter was born to be an ex-president. Enjoying the now popular and strong credentials of having been weak in office, this ex has been globe trotting to the nastiest places on earth, meeting face-to-face with bullies, warlords, pranksters and gangsters and washing his hands later. For the most part, it's worked.

The Military

North Korea has approximately 1.2 million troops, most of them massed along the border with South Korea. Fortunately, for the time being, Jong has their support. The biggest reason is that the Dear Leader apparently has no plans to socialize the military, whose elite members enjoy such Western luxuries as Mercedes, Marlboros and mint-flavored Crest.

Getting In

Passport and visa are required. Visas must be arranged prior to arrival in Pyongyang, usually through a tour packager. The best places to procure North Korean visas are in Bangkok and Macau. You must pay for your entire trip before you depart, as you will be part of a government-organized tour. The North Korean Visa Office is a better bet than the North Korean embassy in Beijing. Perhaps even a better bet is through M.K. Ways in Bangkok *(57/11 Wireless Road, Bangkok 10330;* ☎ *[66](2) 254-4765, 255-3390, 254-7770, 255-2892).* The company specializes in tour packages to Indochina, but has introduced packages to North Korea in an exclusive agreement with the government.

Tours of North Korea vary in length, but most are for 14 days. You'll need three passport photos and approximately US$15 for the visa. If you are asked if you are a journalist, it would help facilitate the process to say no. Inside the country, you may be able to extend your visa, but, again, you'll have to pay in advance for accommodations and guide services. Your guide should be able to make the necessary arrangements.

By air, you can get to Pyongyang via Beijing on Air China or Korean Airways. By train, you can enter North Korea from Beijing via Tianjin, Tangshan, Dandong and Shinuiju. You'll be met at the Pyongyang station by your guide. By boat, you may want to try the ship that runs from Nagasaki, Japan, to Wonsan on North Korea's east coast.

It would be foolish to try and enter North Korea illegally. You won't get back out.

Getting Around

You won't have much choice in the matter. Most likely, you'll be with a government guide in a government vehicle and you'll go where the government wants you to go. U.S. citizens may spend money in North Korea only to purchase ordinary travel necessities such as hotel accommodations, meals and goods for immediate personal consumption in North Korea. There is no longer any per-diem restriction on these expenses, and the use of credit cards for these transactions is also authorized. Because the sanctions system prohibits business dealings with North Korea, unless licensed by the U.S. Treasury Department, purchases of goods or services unrelated to travel are prohibited. There exists only the skeleton of a public transit system in North Korea: very few buses, virtually no cars and no domestic flights. Travel by train is your best bet if you're not traveling by car. Again, you'll have no say. But trains are usually used to visit some of the more popular tourist sites (which sites aren't?).

Dangerous Places

The entire country if you are an American: The North Koreans think all Westerners who visit the country are spies. North Korea is host to few foreign tourists, and those who do get in will only see areas of the country targeted by the government for them to see. All visitors are accompanied by a government guide. You will be subjected to intense propaganda wherever you go. And you will never be permitted to stray off the beaten path unattended, although you might be occasionally permitted an unattended evening stroll around Pyongyang. Crime is not a problem in North Korea. There is wide speculation that thieves and criminals get the death penalty. In this regard, no area of North Korea can be catgorized as unsafe. There is no U.S. embassy in North Korea. The U.S. government is not in a position to offer normal consular protective services to U.S. citizens in North Korea. U.S. government interests are represented on an interim basis by the government of Sweden, which, as a protecting power, is able to provide only limited emergency services to U.S. citizens.

Dangerous Things

Insulting the Great Leader, or the Dear Leader

Want to end up in the slammer fast? Here's how: Tell your guide that Kim Jong Il wears his mother's (Kim Jong-suk) army boots. Or, perhaps, mention you believe that the U.S. would kick North Korea's ass in soccer or in a ground war. Or mutter your suspicion that Kim Il Sung was gay. You get the point.

Giving Gifts

Never give North Koreans whom you meet gifts of any nature, especially Western items, foreign currency or any currency. Although the individual might gracefully accept your generosity (most won't), you're setting that person up for trouble. Remember, you're a spy. Anyone you come into contact with will be assumed to be collaborating with your efforts to pass information and gather intelligence. Silly, but true.

Touching a North Korean Woman

Regardless of how she might come on to you (she won't, by the way), never touch a North Korean woman. Do not even shake hands. This will be construed as an immoral act and will undoubtedly get you both in trouble.

Getting Sick

North Korea has a shortage of medical supplies, facilities and doctors. Western medicines and remedies are even more rare. On the plus side, the water is potable, and the hygiene and sanitation very good. Also, you won't find the food stalls that are seen throughout the rest of Asia. North Korea is squeaky clean.

Nuts and Bolts

After the Japanese surrender of 1945, Korea was divided into two directorates: The U.S.S.R. occupied the north, while the U.S. controlled the south below the 38th parallel. In 1948, the division between the two zones was made permanent. Trade was cut off between the two zones at the advent of the Cold War in the late 1940s.

The Democratic Peoples Republic of Korea (DPRK) is very much a communist nation. Before the demise of the Soviet Union, the DPRK imported nearly three-quarters of a million tons of oil from the U.S.S.R. per year. These supplies have been essentially cut off. North Korea is nearly US$6 billion in debt.

The country is covered almost entirely by north-south mountain ranges and is about the size of Pennsylvania.

The language in North Korea is Korean, with indigenous elements in the vocabulary. Religions in North Korea include Buddhism and Confucianism. However, religious activities within the country basically don't exist. There is no public worshiping of deities in the DPRK. The currency is the won. The won=100 jon. Per-capita income is US$1000.

The time in North Korea is GMT plus nine hours. Electricity is 220 V/60 Hz. Overseas phone calls can be made from the major hotels, and IDD is available in certain establishments. Mail can be received at some hotels and the Korea International Tourist Bureau. But it will be read by the government. Fax services are readily available.

The climate in North Korea is cold and dry in the winter with warm summers. More than 60 percent of the annual rainfall occurs from June through September.

The capital of North Korea is Pyongyang.

Dangerous Days

11/12/1994 An American army helicopter was shot down in North Korean airspace. One pilot died in the crash, and the other repatriated more than two weeks later.

07/18/1994 The death of the Great Leader, Kim Il Sung.

07/27/1953 The armistice ending the Korean War was signed.

09/15/1950 U.N. Commander General Douglas MacArthur made an amphibious landing at Inchon, behind North Korean lines, and routed the North Korean army.

06/27/1950 U.S. President Harry Truman ordered U.S. combat units into action to enforce the U.N. condemnation of North Korea's invasion of South Korea.

06/27/1950 The United Nations condemned North Korea's attack of South Korea and decreed a withdrawal of the invading forces.

06/25/1950 North Korea mounted a surprise invasion of South Korea.

05/01/1948 The establishment of the Democratic Peoples Republic of Korea.

NORTH KOREA

Coming Attractions

Over the last 10 years, there have been more than 100 wars with 20 million fatalities. So it would take a moronically optimistic person to assume that the next millennium will bring love, peace and happiness to this planet. For those who travel in harm's way, we have shoved all the Little League wars, nasty places and brewing discontents into this overly cute chapter.

As you probably have guessed, this book became out of date the second the ink hit the paper. When I started this edition, Chechnya and Rwanda were my favorite picks for coming attractions. Since then, half a million Tutsis were turned into worm food and Chechnya went from a cocky little gangster land to little Afghanistan, and then to a wasteland. So with some trepidation and a roll of the dice, we open ourselves to possible ridicule as we present our low-budget trailer of things to come in the next *The World's Most Dangerous Places*.

Bangladesh

Head for the Hills

The Shanti Bahani and the government of Bangladesh are working under the 24th extension of the 1992 ceasefire. The rebels have been fighting for control of a 5500 sq ft. area in the Hill Tracts. They want 300,000 Bengalis expelled from the region. Since 1973, 3500 people have been killed as a result of the uprising. The government said they cannot give the Shanti Bahini self rule or expel the settlers.

The Basque Country

There's No Place Like Home

Straddling the border of France and Spain, the seven provinces of the Basque Country—three on the French side, four in Espana—stretch across both sides of the Pyrenees mountain chain all the way over to the Atlantic Coast and the Bay of Biscay. Boundaries that harbor ethereal mists, snowcapped peaks, ancient monasteries, world-class surf spots, and semi-naked-Beautiful People resorts. Toss in an abundance of ambrosia-like food and wine. Ah—but even Shangri-La was an illusion and Euzkadi also exudes some tricky shadow play.

The fiercely independent Basques—about 2.5 million of them—have for decades been trying to gain autonomy from both Spain and France. Simply, they'd like to establish their own homeland, an exclusive turf on which to preserve their much-older-than-the-hills traditions and language (Euskal). And, just as simply, both the Spanish and French governments would as soon see those feisty and troublesome Basques either shut the hell up or disappear off the face of *their* respective lands. The result? The usual unpleasant loop of rebel/underdog strategies versus powerful-government-and-police tactics—i.e., terrorism.

The players have been at each other's throats and other body parts in earnest since the 1960s. Franco and his not-famous-for-humanitarianism regime had sought to crush the Basque political presence (if not the entire population) back in 1937. The Generalissimo and His Boys may have quashed the movement for the short-term but—come the '60s—the Basques' big itch for freedom reared up with a vengeance. Vengeance at least for the ETA (*Euskadi Ta Askatasuna*, or "Basque Homeland and Freedom"), the *muy* energetic militant extremist movement with a commitment to violence. The ETA advocated armed struggle for the independence of Euskadi, and its inaugural pranks included bombings, grenade attacks, and an all-out ferocious war—aimed mainly at the Spanish government down in Madrid, its power mongers and henchmen. The ETA's blockbuster wake-up call was the 1973 assassination of Francoist Prime Minister Luis Carrero Blanco. Spain, obviously, could forget about *this* unwanted bunch just disappearing into the paella.

In a seemingly good-faith attempt to appease the ETA, Euzkadi was granted semi-autonomy in 1979, four years after Franco's death. Basically this translated to permitting signs in the native Euskal language to be erected along roadsides and on public buildings, along with the usual lip service about "official talks" and "future concessions." Meanwhile—lest the peasants became a little too impatient or semiautonomous, the Spanish government immediately installed its own particular brand of "safeguards" in the region, i.e., a sizable "special" police force and a veritable military occupation—plus all the predictable perks: blatant abuses of power, unfounded arrests, police brutality, and, everybody's favorite antiguerrilla cure—death squads.

Prime Minister Felipe Gonzalez, who in the 1980s claimed to be oh-so-sensitive to the Basques' plight and desire for home rule, is alleged to have had knowledge of the death squads (G.A.L.) which were in full swing at the same time of his heartfelt outpourings. Another finger is pointed at Julian Sancristobal, Spain's former Director of State Security and head of the antiterrorist unit in one of the Basque provinces—directly linking him to G.A.L. snuffing of suspected Basque separatists.

But, hey, the ETA wasn't falling for all that semi-autonomy fluff-stuff anyway. No G.A.L. death squads were going to make them run for the hills. They simply went elsewhere for support—purportedly Libya, Iran, Syria, and the Irish Republican Army—collecting explosives, arms, and post-Rambo training. Anyway, the ETA wants full autonomy. Consequently, the past two-and-a-half decades have added up to one miserable cycle of attack and retaliation. And while tourists to the Basque Country come to "take the waters"—for some of the locals and their enemies, the big soak has been one long blood bath.

What makes the Basques so damned special? They profess to be the oldest people—with the oldest language—in all of Europe. And no one can refute the claim that their origins are a mystery, their language a linguistic oddity. Scholars refer to them as "Europe's mystery people."

Long isolated in the Pyrenees border region, they are so secretive that many of their accomplishments have either been overlooked or credited to others. The Basques claim—and evidence agrees—that their fishers and whalers cruised to the New World at least a century before Columbus and his *Nina*, *Pinta*, and *Santa Maria menage a trois* ever hit the shores. Historians believe the early Basques were far more sophisticated than even the rich and shapely sunbathers over at Biarritz. Among the findings are intricate navigational aids, a fanatical precision in recording topography, a base-7 numerical system, and a whole lot of Stonehenge-era fancies.

The contemporary Basques are jovial, spirited, fun-loving and strong. Very few are members of the ETA and most deplore the violence—however, the death squads and military presence quickly turned a lot of the "can't-be-bothereds" into sympathizers (albeit silent ones). They continue to practice their culture no matter what any government entity decrees, going about their business in the mountain villages—dancing, singing, producing crafts, drinking local wine and cooking hearty meals. Most of the men play a mean game of *pelota* (a sport they invented) as well as the unique "Basque lifting"—weight-lifting with 200-kilogram-plus stones. They love contests of strength—tossing poles, dragging boulders and oxen. To prepare their famous "mountain oyster stew," specially trained shepherds simply gnaw off a sheep's testicles with one deft bite.

Originally, ETA attacks were launched on the Spanish side of the border, after which the guerrillas would head over to the French side for refuge. (The Basques refer to themselves as *Zaspiakbat*, or "the seven make only one"—united without regard to any "artificial" borders.) Since 1992, however, the French police have stepped up their crackdown on suspected terrorists—encored by France's rightwing government breathing down their necks. The ETA, to its credit, has tried to keep innocent bystanders out of its scope, predominately targeting politicians, industrialists, and civil guardsmen. Some of the larger railway stations and banks, however, have been sporadically hit by bombs. Cars with French license plates are also red-flagged. As for the police and military in the region—anyone can qualify for their brand of fun and games.

You're about as safe in the Basque Country as in most other places in Western Europe. Beach resorts, ski areas, spas, and the Tour de France route are visitor-friendly. Searches at border crossings are occasional inconveniences—and it's probably best not to linger around any railway stations or public buildings.

Bougainville

Jungle Boogie

Bougainville is a lush jungle covered island 800 miles to the east of Papua New Guinea. The uprising started in 1988 when the Aussie managers of a copper mine refused to fill in a hole they left behind. The locals believed the place was holy (in a religious sense) and the bickering escalated into an armed conflict. This further evolved into a liberation movement from Papua New Guinea. The Bougainville Revolutionary Army made chummed up with the Solomon Islands, their true geographic kin a few miles to the east. There have been military offensives but it is unlikely that the PNG army will flush out the rebels, who operate from remote, inaccessible bases and camps as well as the Solomons.

Central African Republic

CAR Cesspool

We'd like to warn you that it is getting more dangerous, but then it never has been safe in this pocket-sized cesspool. The only thing that keeps it from turning into Liberia or Zaire is the French Paratroopers that baby-sit the potentate for a day. There are about 2500 French citizens in the country.

In May of '96 the streets were slippery with blood as the French put down another weeklong mutiny attempt. The French use CAR as a staging ground to defend Chad against Libya.

Ceuta and Mellia

It's a Small, Small War

DP can never be accused of painting the world with too broad a brushstroke. In these two minuscule Spanish enclaves on the north coast of Africa, it seems they have enough room for an insurgency group. The two areas were kept by Spain when they handed over Morocco in the 16th century. It has taken this long for a coalition called the "August 21" group, led by Moslem activist Mohamed Abdou, to threaten Spain with further armed attacks. The August 21 group claimed responsibility for two car-bomb attacks in April of 1995; no one was hurt. In a recent visit by the Spanish prime minister with the king of Morocco, they forgot to bring up the issue. It appears Spain shut Morocco up back in 1974, when they handed them their colony of Spanish Sahara. The August 21 group sent a threatening fax and asserted that their cause was "as holy and noble... as other nationalist groups."

Chad

Pieces in Our Time

A litany of coups, failures, factionalism and failed peace, Chad is perpetually embroiled in the same tensions its volatile neighbors share. What kind of chance does a country that's bordered by Libya, the Sudan and Nigeria have? Not much of one.

Chad, though, has had the dubious distinction of kicking Qaddaffi's butt on the battlefield. It was back in 1987 and had the tacit support of the French, but it had a lot of mercenaries licking their chops.

Qaddaffi may talk as if he can take on the Great Satan, but he has more than he can chew with the Little Chadian.

How bad is it here? Chad's in pieces. Political tension is high in both N'Djamena and the countryside, especially in the southern and eastern portions of Chad, as well as north of Lake Chad. Armed conflicts between government and opposition groups occur regularly. Ethnic and religious demonstrations in the major cities usually result in violent outbreaks. Chad's northern provinces bordering Libya constitute a military zone and remain heavily mined. Travel to this area is ex-

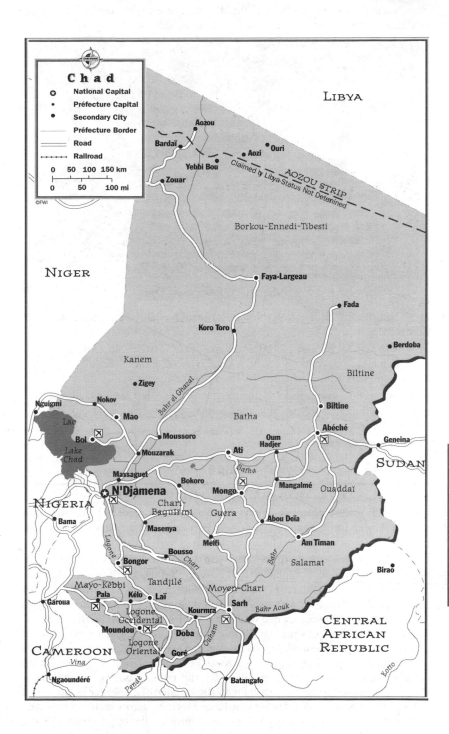

tremely dangerous and may be prohibited. Travel across the southwestern border by Cameroon is hazardous because of continuing bloodshed.

As a result of the anarchy in Chad, extraordinary security precautions are in effect. You'll definitely run into a number of nasty roadblocks—if you get that far—in N'Djamena and elsewhere in the countryside. Overland travel undertaken after dark is a death wish.

And where there isn't war, pickpockets and purse snatchers are endemic, particularly in market and commercial areas. Vehicle thefts and the breaking and entering of homes are commensurate with the rise in temperature.

The only bright spot is that rebel leader Moise Kette has accepted amnesty and has promised to use only political means to fight for an autonomous Christian state in the South.

Helluva place Chad is.

China

Breaking Up is Hard To Do

A secret Pentagon report (China in the Near Term) predicted that when the Chinese leader Deng Xiaoping dies—which is expected any day—there's a 50 percent chance that China will break up like the USSR did.

China has its problems. In the next five years it is estimated that the current 100 million people who have migrated to the city to find work will swell to 200 million. Beijing has over 3 million who cannot find steady work. Forty million are unemployed. Inflation runs about 25%. 100 million people are underemployed. Half of the 100,000 state owned business lose money and will be shut down or sold off. 800 million peasants live a subsistence life and resent the new city based economic growth. There are serious doubts that China will be able to feed itself without importing massive amounts of food. For now the nest rung down of the corrupt alienated government get ready for the coming power struggle. Jiang Zemin is supposed to be the successor to the doddering, wheel chair bound 91 year old Deng Xiaping.Word is out that Jiang a former factory manager and Minister of the Electronics Industry will be eaten alive by the other power brokers, wealthy and others waiting in the wings. There are enough power hungry leaders, criminal gangs, guns, backers and definitely enough people to create hundreds of new countries, city states, ethnic enclaves or republics.

If all of China's 1.2 billion people were to do anything at once, let alone jump off a wall, it would paralyse the country.

This isn't good news for tourists and even worse news for the government because tourism to China has been surging in recent years. About 1.74 million foreign tourists visited Beijing alone in 1992, compared with less than 300,000 in 1978. In the first six months of 1993, 882,600 foreigners visited the capital city, up 13 percent over the corresponding period the preceding year. Throughout China, tourism brought in a whopping US$1.69 billion in the first five months of 1993, up 22.2 percent over the same period in 1992. That figure is a record.

China possesses no known terrorist groups, but a ride on one of their domestic airliners may make you wish they did—so the plane could be hijacked to a country with decent air traffic control. Unlike in other parts of the world, hijackers in China aren't trying to draw world attention to a cause (they wouldn't get it, anyway). They're not likely to make ransom demands. And it's not done for the love of God. They're simply trying to get the hell out. Taiwan is the favored destination. There were 10 hijackings to Taipei in 1993 and three other foiled attempts. However, the hijacking problem may be more serious than these figures reflect. A May 25, 1994 report carried by the Beijing-controlled Hong Kong China News Agency said that airport police in Shenzhen, the Special Economic Zone near Hong Kong, claimed to have successfully prevented 16 hijacking attempts to that date in 1994.

Safety on China's roads, railways, boats and aircraft is also questionable. In 1993, 73 people were killed in three separate air crashes. Hundreds of other people have been killed in road, rail and boating accidents and China now has a growing reputation with foreign tourists as one of the least safe places to travel in the world, although this isn't entirely justified.

There is no real terrorist threat to Americans traveling to, or doing business in, the People's Republic of China (PRC). An insignificant 39 terrorist incidents and other forms of political violence have been reported since 1988, however; 21 of these occurred in 1993. Americans as a specific group are not targeted by the Chinese but will, as all foreigners to this relatively closed society, continue to receive the usual close scrutiny of the native inhabitants.

Although the crime rate is rising, it is lower than those rates found in the West. Crimes are generally nonviolent; thefts form the crux of them. However, some analysts forecast that the thrusting of the Chinese economy in recent years is creating an environment that may breed disorder in the future. They cite burgeoning social conflicts, including racial and religious disputes, which may endanger stability. Indicators include a surge in major crimes, gang activities, social evils, fraud, violence and industrial accidents. Major crime incidents have risen by nearly 20 percent annually in the past four years.

White-collar crime seems to have arrived in China. Some of these S&L wannabes give bribes to banking officials to launder and move tremendous amounts of foreign exchange out of the country. The number of assaults on public security officers has also risen. The number of injuries rose from about 600 in 1985 to more than 8000 in 1993; 275 officers were killed.

As China becomes more stratified, the lower classes are becoming more prone to commit crimes. China is not a dangerous place if you stay in the tourist ruts. However, you may find yourself in trouble in some of the out-of-way places. The most dangerous places for highway robbery are in the remote mountainous regions. Other dangers include organized raids on passenger trains and simple thefts from hotels. There was a 36-hour orgy of rioting in Guangdong Province when the Ling Xiao Yan resort came under attack by locals. The resort caters to Chinese visitors from Hong Kong and Macau. In March, 1994, 24 Taiwanese tourists were killed on Qiandao Lake.

In Henan province police broke up 300 organized gangs and arrested over 1800 gang members. 135 were sentenced to die.

The Chinese Public Security Ministry has admitted the country does not have the resources to protect tourists from the rising rate of crime across the mainland. The Qiandao Lake incident may be a precursor of what's to come.There have been numerous recent incidents where tourists have been robbed, beaten and even murdered. There was one occasion in Zhejiang involving 70 participants and 80 police where local residents battled with a tour group.

The U.S. Department of State published the following general crime report on February 3, 1994. It includes coverage for Beijing, Chengdu, Guangzhou, and Shenyang Consular Districts.

"China continues to enjoy economic prosperity though it has been somewhat tempered in recent months by inflationary trends. Its political structure continues to exert strong control over all sectors of Chinese society with only minor disruptions in the countryside over payment of taxes and loss of some government subsidies. Americans are not specifically targeted as a distinct subgroup of foreigners, but do experience the same degree of scrutiny that all other classes of non-ethnic Chinese receive.

"China experiences a low, but gradually rising crime rate. Crime has increased principally in the major cities where economic progress is most evident. Most crime is nonviolent in nature, with pickpockets and purse snatchers accounting for the bulk of petty thefts.

"Police are only moderately effective in providing assistance throughout the country. Most police have only a little formal education and their equipment and training are below those standards set by American enforcement agencies. Response to an emergency may take between 15 and 30 minutes. Police generally speak little English; in Beijing, foreigners may call the police foreign control unit at ☎ 552729 for an English speaker.

"Americans and other foreign visitors to China are occasionally victims of criminals. Most crime remains nonviolent, with the victim's lack of awareness of his/her surroundings being the major contributor to incidents. Crowded public areas such as hotel lobbies, bars and restaurants, or public transportation and tourist sites are major risk areas that account for almost all of the reported crime scenes where thefts have occurred. Travelers should avoid using unmarked taxis. Legal taxis are clearly marked, are metered, and should have the driver's identification clearly displayed.

"Travelers must protect all their valuables assiduously. All identification media and travel documents, such as passports and airline tickets, need to be safeguarded. Hotel safe deposits can be used for this purpose. Travelers should limit the items they carry on the street to a minimum. They should carry identification and utilize a money belt or concealed abdominal pack in which to secure it."

The following constitutes Shanghai's 1993 report on crime and safety information:

"Major civil disturbances, by Western standards, are rare in Shanghai. However, even mundane situations such as traffic accidents or arguments can draw a large crowd almost instantly. Though these situations seldom get out of control, visitors should not attempt to photograph or videotape the incident. Involved parties or police authorities may take exception to having their photo taken without prior approval and the photographer may suddenly find himself at the center of attention. Americans are not specifically targeted as a distinct subgroup of foreigners, but do experience the same degree of scrutiny that all other classes of non-ethnic Chinese receive.

"Shanghai experiences a low, but steadily rising crime rate. Most crime is nonviolent in nature, with pickpockets, purse snatchings, and bicycle thefts accounting for the bulk of criminal incidents. Burglaries of residences and thefts from hotel rooms are on the rise.

"Police are moderately effective in providing assistance, considering the low crime threat environment. Levels of authority and functional responsibilities are more specialized among Shanghai police authorities in comparison to American counterparts. Shanghai police officers often have a specific function, i.e. traffic control, and are generally not trained to deal with situations beyond the scope of their specialty. The training and equipment they do receive is below those standards set by American law enforcement agencies. Response to an emergency may take between 15 and 30 minutes. Police generally do not speak English, but will generally attempt to overcome language barriers to help foreigners requiring assistance. Foreigners may call the police foreign control unit at ☎ *321-1997* for an English speaker.

"Americans and other foreign visitors to Shanghai are occasionally victims of criminals. Most crime remains nonviolent, with the victim's lack of awareness of his/her surroundings being the major contributor to incidents. Crowded public areas such as shopping areas, bars, public transportation and tourist sites are major risk areas that account for almost all of the reported thefts. Travelers should avoid using unmarked taxis. Legal taxis are clearly marked and metered and should have the driver's identification clearly displayed.

"Travelers must protect their valuables assiduously. All identification, media and travel documents, such as passports and airline tickets, need to be safeguarded. Hotel safe deposits can be used for this purpose. Travelers should limit the items they carry on the street to the minimum. They should carry identification and utilize a money belt or concealed abdominal pack in which to secure it."

Getting In

Passports and visas are required. Most tourist visas are valid for only one entry. Travelers are required to obtain new visas for additional entries into China. Those who arrive without a visa will be fined a minimum of $400 at the port of entry and might not be allowed to enter China (or get out!). A transit visa is required for any stop (even if one does not exit the plane or train) in China. Specific information is available through the Embassy of the People's Republic of

China or from one of the consulates general in Chicago, Houston, Los Angeles, New York or San Francisco.

Chinese Embassy in the U.S.

2300 Connecticut Avenue, NW
Washington, DC 20008
☎ *(202) 328-2500.*

U.S. Embassy in China

Xiu Shui Dong Jie 3
Beijing -100600
☎ *[86] (1) 532-3831*

Corsica

The Tourist War

Petru Pogglii, born in 1940, is the leader of the Corsican Nationalist Alliance. The CNA is an offshoot of the Corsican National Liberation Front/Front Liberation National Corsican (NLNC) founded in 1976. Their headquarters is in Carbuccia.

There are about a 1000 separatist rebels in a number of small gangs, most of whom are aligned with a liberation front. The gangs spend as much time fighting among each other as they do the French. Over the last 20 years there have been 8400 terrorist attacks and 100 deaths A poll in 1996 showed that 86 percent of Corsicans are against independence. On July 2 a car bomb exploded in daylight in the middle of Ajaccio, killing one of leaders of the Corsican FLNC and injuring another leader seriously. About 2 million tourists visit the island each year.

Cyprus

U (N) Can Never Go Home Again

The oldest U.N. mission in the world is living testament to the fact that you can keep the kids from squabbling but you will never make them kiss and make up. Its the Greeks versus the Turks. Both sides will tell you horror stories of what will happen once you cross the U.N. border. As usual, both sides are charming, hospitable people. Meanwhile, gangsters from Eastern Europe fight amongst each other for control of nightclubs and entertainers.

Ecuador

Rumble in the Jungle

What do you get when you have a border that no one can see and that changes like a baking loaf of bread? And with hot heads baking it? Why, Equador and Peru, of course. Ecuador and Peru fought a war over this 1000-mile-long swamp in the Amazon basin back in 1941 and they haven't forgotten about it. In fact, they duked it out again in 1981 and almost came to blows yet another time in 1991. There was even a bullet pinball game in early 1994.

This time it's over a 50-mile stretch in the lush, jungle-covered mountains of Cordillera del Condor that would give Equador access to the Amazon and Maranon rivers—if they had it. Although no one seems to be able to prove it, the area is supposedly rich in gold deposits. Just the rumor alone is apparently enough to raise rifles.

The Protocol of Rio de Janeiro was signed in 1942 to end that first war, but Ecuador later said "screw you" after getting their hands on one of the world's first portable calculators and realizing the ramifications of losing half their territory—nearly 77,220 square miles, to Peru. The problem with the Rio Pact was that it defined part of the border between the two countries as "the river flowing into the Santiago River." Well, there are two rivers flowing into the Santiago River. Sprinkle some gold between the two and you've got a good fight. Even though Pope John Paul II has issued a call to both countries to stop the fighting, no one's listening.

Equatorial Guinea

Dictator of the Week

Coups could become a weekly event replacing soccer in this forgotten armpit of Africa. Back in 1969, Macias Nguema took over this oversized cocoa plantation and began systematically killing all his fellow politicians. By the time he was done, he had killed 50,000 of his own people, including every senior politician and civil servant, and 100,000 people, a third of the population, had fled.

When he was finally tried and executed in 1979, he had managed to spend the entire $105 million treasury. Since then, the remaining residents have been playing dictator for a week. One coup in 1986 only took 30 people to overthrow the government. Why not invite your church choir, and you too could be dictator for a day. The one good outcome is that there have been so few tourists that there technically is no tourist crime.

The Gambia

'No Elections for the Next 1000 years'

Gambia, a small nail-hole in the snout of West Africa, was once a bastion of democracy, as stable as any in the West. And tourists—the mainstay of the economy—formerly came here in large numbers; here was the only place to see more of West Africa than a muzzle flash.

Then, in July 1994, Sir Dawda Jawara was overthrown by a bush punk army captain named Yahya Jammeh. Great Britain, the former colonial ruler, demanded that democracy be restored and cut off aid, which totaled US$90 million a year, or 20 percent of the country's GNP. Tourism dropped 60 percent. Finally, in August 1995, the youthful Jammeh relented and promised to restore Gambia to democracy—by December 1988. A slap in the face to the West, and aid continued to be suspended until Jammeh could schedule something a little sooner than a period shorter than the nation's average life expectancy.

Jammeh's love of democracy has been well-documented. At the end of 1995 he was quoted as saying: "If we don't want elections in the next 1000 years, there will be no elections. We will make sure that those who want elections will go six feet deep, and there's nothing anyone can do about it."

Journalists and others who make comments about the baby brigadiers in fatigues are rounded up and imprisoned. Political parties are banned, as is free speech. Although Jammeh has since promised elections for July 1996, no voter registration has begun and it looks unlikely that it will. It seems Jammeh is quite willing to direct the Gambia down the road to the anarchy of its neighbors.

Greece

November 17; a Good Day to Die

The November 17 group is the most feared terrorist group in Greece and perhaps the most ruthless in Europe. The terrorist ring got its start with the December 1975 assassination of Athens CIA station chief Richard Welch while he was on his way home from a Christmas party, zapping him with what would become its signature grim reaper: a.45-caliber pistol.

Since then a.45 has been used in six more of its subsequent 20 executions, including of four Americans, 13 Greeks and couple of Turkish diplomats. It doesn't sound like a particularly huge body count in these days of *Hezbollah*, GAI and Chechen whackos, but considering that a not a single member of this shadowy group has been identified—much less arrested—it is. And the group has also conducted at least 35 other attacks on multinational companies and Greek tax offices, employing bombs that suggest their construction techniques were learned in the Middle East in the early 1970s.

Of all of Europe's homegrown radical assassins, only the November 17 group remains entirely an enigma. Italy's Red Brigades and the German arm of the Red Army Faction have been snuffed. Rebel Basque, Irish and Corsican separatists have been picked off like flies by INTERPOL. Action Direct in France was similarly destroyed. But November 17's 10-25 members continue to allude all attempts to expose and drain them.

The terrorists named themselves for the day in 1973 when a student uprising at Athens Polytechnic University was crushed by soldiers and tanks sent in by the ruling military junta. These guys don't work on a single agenda. When the U.S. was supporting the military junta in Greece during the first decade of the terrorists' existence, the group blew away Americans. When Turkey occupied Cyprus in 1974, Turkish diplomats became the targets. For sure, November 17 is a Marxist outfit, professing hatred for both the U.S. and NATO, as well as the European Union. It's thought that its founding members belonged to a resistance group created by Socialist Premier Andreas Papandreou during the 1965-1975 military dictatorship. And there has been some indication that Papandreou knows who they are. But he's not talking.

The former East German police are believed to have been chummy with November 17, however attempts to retrieve information from their files have been futile. In the meantime, suspicions of connections with Middle East terror clans continue—as do.45 slugs to the head.

Germany

The Fourth Reich?

Once the brightest of Europe's economies, Germany now suffers from rising unemployment and a deep ethnic malaise, turning the pride of European capitalism into a melting pot of hatred.

Officially, more than 4.2 million Germans are out of work. Unemployment has hit a postwar high of 11.1 percent. Since 1990, 1.2 million jobs have been lost in the manufacturing sector alone. Germany's gross domestic product plummeted.5 percent during the fourth quarter of 1995 and is expected to slide even further.

Combine this with an immigration policy that has permitted millions of Third World refugees to settle in the country and you've got a stew of steel-toed boots, Molotov cocktails, K-bar knives and shaved heads.

Enter the Kurdistan Workers' Party (PKK), a violent rebel group battling anyone in the way for Kurdish independence and autonomy southeastern Turkey. Germany has become fertile ground for PKK firebomb attacks on Turkish properties in Germany. In March 1996, about 1500 angry Kurds—many waving PKK flags—battled police in Dortmund, using brutal force against the cops and blocking two major German motorways. The violence was so intense that police from the Netherlands crossed the border to aid their beaten and outnumbered German colleagues. Another 1500 protesting Kurds blocked A44 motorway near Aachen for nearly a day.

This is only the start.

Guatemala

Body Parts

Guatemala's 33-year-old insurgency was supposedly put to rest by a covert war organized, financed and efficiently run by Uncle Sam in eastern Guatemala in 1968. It then blossomed to include a western highlands uprising in the 1970s after 500,000 Indians took their cue from the success of the Sandinistas in Nicaragua and revolted against the Guatemalan government.

Of a total Guatemala population of 9.5 million, some 150,000 were killed in the ensuing fighting. More than 440 villages were entirely destroyed and 45,000 people fled to Mexico and the United States. Since then, the government has kept Guatemalans on a short leash by militarizing the country. Today, there are only 45,000 soldiers holding that leash. Although 50 percent of Guatemala's population is Indian, its government remains nothing more than a penny arcade parade of military strongmen backed by the U.S. government.

BOXING MAGDELENA

Small babies are a big thing in Guatemala. A lot of Americans like to go down there to pick one up and raise it at home. The problem is, most Guatemalans think that Yankees are buying the babies for body parts. Stranger than fiction, but true. The Guatemalan newspaper Prensa Libre *recently published a story showing the prices for human organs. Shortly afterward, a group of farmers beat an American woman to death.*

Janice Vogel adopted a young Guatemalan girl. Four days later she was trapped by an angry mob who assumed she was going to sell her adopted child for body parts. Babies do get stolen in Guatemala for illegal adoptions—young boys for about US$500—but not for body parts. Try telling that to the Guatemalans, who can't tell the difference between a stolen Blazer and a little boy.

The Players

The Guatemalan National Revolutionary Unit (Unidad Revolucionaria Nacional Guatemalteca or, URNG)

The URNG is what remains of previous rebel groups. Although the government believes only 800 members of the URNG still exist, the actual figure and its sphere of influence may be much larger. In September1993, an arms cache of more than 750 machine guns, 310 kilos of explosives, and rocket and grenade launchers was discovered in Nicaragua en route to the URNG in Guatemala. Nonetheless, the core of the URNG has been forced back into the highlands of the northwest, northern Peten province and along the Pacific coast in the volcanic regions.

Although the URNG has been in peace negotiations with the government, the group has been busy blowing up bridges, tossing bombs and engaging in spirited firefights with the Guatemalan army. In the fall of 1993, in San Marcos province, three soldiers were killed and 27 wounded in a 100-hour-long firefight. There were approximately 300 soldiers killed in 1992, up from 27 killed in 1991. The military claimed it killed 125 guerrillas in that period.

With the URNG receiving support from Fidel Castro, Nicaragua and income derived from drug trafficking, and because of the government's continued hard-line stance with the guerrillas, there appears little chance of a breakthrough in the peace process.

In 1993, the URNG staged three hit-and-run attacks on the military, laid numerous mines and destroyed power lines and generators in Quiche, Huehuetenango, Alto Verapaz and the outskirts of Guatemala City.

The URNG has also been engaged in ecoterrorism made popular by Saddam Hussein during the Gulf War. Near the end of 1993, rebels began striking oil tanker convoys in the Peten and Alta Verapaz regions, spilling 400,000 gallons of fuel and crude oil into the countryside.

THE BIRDS OF WAR

One sign that there may be cloak and daggery afoot is the sight of the ungainly aircraft with the equally ungainly name of Pilatus Porter. Designed for Short Takeoff and Landing, or STOL, operations in remote regions, these planes are the favorite attack plane of low-budget air forces. Although the Swiss government has banned sale of the PC-P and PC-7 Pilatus plane to countries at war, the Third World has made the aircraft a familiar sight in Myanmar, Guatemala, Iraq, Angola and South Africa. Sold as trainers, they are quickly converted to fighter bombers by using the six hard points under the wing to attach weapons (usually four 68mm rocket pods or 7.72mm machine guns) or extra fuel tanks. In recent operations by Executive Outcomes pilots against UNITA in northern Angola near Zaire, the PC-7 was more functional than the Russian-built Mi-24 Hind helicopter gunships. The Pilatus could stay up longer (4–5 hours), could cruise lower, required less maintenance and was more accurate firing its arsenal.

The Swiss government has banned the sale of the aircraft with more than two mounting points. Frustrated armies that don't have the time, budget or expertise to convert the newly pacified plane are said to be switching to Tucano trainers.

Guinea

Eeny Meeny Miney Mo

The wettest country in Africa has one of the nastiest cities in Africa. Conrakry can just about guarantee you will be picked, thumped, attacked or robbed. Even the customs officials will try to bilk you before you have even technically entered the country. So it's no surprise that tourism is just behind snowshoe manufacturing in contributing to Guinea's paltry income. Recently, the military felt they needed a pay raise. To add exclamation points to their request, they fired a few rockets at the Presidential Palace and killed over 50 civilians. At the first shots, President Lansara Conte hid out in his bunker for 36 hours while the mutineers tried to find someone to complain to that wasn't hiding in the bunker. Suddenly realizing they had effectively overthrown the government, they couldn't find anyone to replace the president.

It didn't help that the government stiffed the soldiers when they came back from peacekeeping duty in Sierra Leone and Liberia. Oh, did we mention that Guinea is the source of the Niger river and has nice scenery?

Hong Kong

Red Dawn

At the stroke of midnight on June 30, 1997, Hong Kong—Asia's bastion of pure, raw capitalism—will come under Chinese rule. And although the British colony will technically be ruled as a Special Administrative Region (SAR), with promised "high autonomy" for the next 50 years, the prospects of a smooth tran sition from British to Chinese rule are somber indeed.

If China's military maneuvers off the Taiwan coast in March 1996 and its vow to replace Hong Kong's elected legislature with its own provisional body are any indication, expect the increasingly hard-lining gopher cheeks of Beijing to quickly bring Hong Kong into the fold.

First of all, virtually all of the British colony's 6.3 million residents disdain China. Witness the 200,000 people who rushed for British overseas passports during March 1996. On the last day of the passport offer—which grants Hong Kong residents the right to travel abroad on British passports (but which doesn't permit citizenship)—54,000 people flooded Hong Kong's immigration office to apply for naturalization papers that pave the way for getting the passports.

Anti-Chinese protests by pro-democracy groups and others have increased both in size and intensity. Usually staid newspaper columns have begun ripping into Beijing. Even Hong Kong's neutral head of the civil service has started lashing out the anticipated communist bohunks who will be administering the SAR. Beijing has made it quite clear that it intends to reverse all of Hong Kong's democratic reforms of the last 15 years. In fact, it's even set a target date for tearing apart Hong Kong democracy—mid-1997. That's when Hong Kong's legislature (LEGCO) will be sloughed and civil servants will be replaced with eager Party cadres. That includes the police, many of whom are applying for work as London bobbies or LAPD Rampart Division motorcycle cops. As one analyst surmised: "The rockets aimed at Taiwan [in March 1996] landed on Hong Kong."

Meanwhile, ticktock.

Indonesia

Timor Bomb

Indonesia is an archipelago of more than 13,000 islands, the largest of which are Kalimantan (Indonesian Borneo), Sumatra, Irian Jaya (West Irian), Sulawesi and Java. Nearly two-thirds of the population lives on Java, one of the most densely populated areas in the world. Sumatra contains 25 percent of Indonesia's land area and 20 percent of its population.

But it's on the far flung island of Timor where a lingering insurgency festers. The Timorese are not fond of their Indonesian rulers and continue to battle for their independence. More than 100,000 people are believed to have died in the Indonesian invasion of east Timor in 1975. The Indonesian government is reticent to admit the problem exists, much less the gravity of it. Nonetheless, at least 450 armed Timorese insurgents continue to wreak havoc among the occupying Indonesian forces.

The biggest hotel in Dili was formerly the headquarters of the Indonesian Army Intelligence Group. East Timorese prisoners were regularly tortured in the basement here and then taken away for execution. Some estimates say that one-third of the population of east Timor has been killed and the remaining rebels are hiding out in the most remote areas of the island. The Indonesian military's reputation for brutal suppression of this 16-year uprising has not deterred efforts, however, of the Jakarta government to develop tourism facilities in the area.

On the other end of the archipelago, the rebels of Aceh, on the northern tip of Sumatra, have all but ceded their war of independence.

The Portuguese were the first Europeans to arrive in Indonesia; they controlled the eastern half of the island of Timor until it was occupied by Indonesia in 1975. Slowly, the Dutch gained control of most of the islands and occupied them until Indonesia was granted independence in 1949. As the Netherlands East Indies, Indonesia became one of the world's most lucrative colonial outposts, providing tea, rubber, rice, sugar and petroleum.

The Indonesian independence movement began early in the 20th century, but it really didn't get a head of steam until World War II. Japanese forces occupying the islands in 1942 induced in the natives hostility toward the Dutch, making it easier for them to control the region. In this case, it made a great ingredient to successful freedom fighting. After the Japanese lost the war and were no longer around, the Indonesians decided they weren't into any outside domination. In 1945, Indonesian nationalists proclaimed their independence and said "Get lost" to the Dutch, who failed in their opportunistic efforts to retake what they thought was theirs. The Dutch caved in and granted Indonesia independence in 1949.

Apparently, there is progress. The Indonesian government actually fessed up to having tortured and murdered six Timorese protesters in January 1994. Australia praised the Indonesian government for "admitting its own errors." The U.N. condemned Indonesia for repression in Timor on the same day. But the idea of someone actually being held accountable is a long way off. By the way, the Aussies are brown-nosing the Indonesian government because they want to drill for oil near Timor.

Timor isn't the only place in the archipelago with guerrillas in the midst. Often entirely forgotten are the ragtag rebels of the Free Papua Movement (OPM), who have been fighting the Indonesian government for the independence of Irian Jaya with sticks, stones and rusty flintlocks for the last 30 years. These guys don't get into the news that much and are often called the "T-shirt" army because they're about as trained and equipped as a Connecticut cub scout den.

But for a group of seven unlucky foreigners, the rebels may as well be the charge of the Light Brigade. In January 1996, two Dutch researchers, four British students and a German stumbled into a solitary OPM unit, probably out gathering nuts and berries; the guerrillas found the juicy, plump, white-skinned Westerners a godsend. Just think, real live hostages—frightened Anglo pussycats—just like the kind we pick up on our satellite dish! The world, and CNN, had discovered the OPM.

Now known by the outside world, they and their supporters have taken to the streets. On March 18, 1996, thousands rioted in the Irian Jaya provincial capital of Jayapura, torching vehicles, shops and other buildings. Three demonstrators were shot dead, one a policeman who joined the rioters and was blown away by a shopowner protecting his investment. Don't expect a Visit Irian Jaya Year anytime soon.

President Suharto

Istana Negara, Jalan Veteran
Jakarta, Indonesia
Fax: (+62) 2136 0517, (+62) 2136 7781, (+62) 2136 7782 (all via Ministry of Foreign Affairs)

Kenya

A Rift in the Valley

Tourism to Africa's most "civilized" country has declined due to attacks in game parks, lawlessness in the major cities and continuing tribal clashes in areas such as the Rift Valley. Tourism revenue plummeted from US$400 million in 1991 to US$295 million in 1992. The Gulf War and Somalia were a couple of good reasons. Somali bandits crossed the border and attacked U.N. relief workers in Wajir province. At least 35 security officers and 50 civilians have been killed in Wajir, Garissa and Mandera provinces. The Red Cross has suspended selected relief operations in the northern provinces due to bandit attacks and the theft of materials.

In Nairobi, armed robbers ambush expensive vehicles as they drive in exclusive neighborhoods: Mercedes Gelandwagons, Land Rover Defenders, Discoveries, Range Rovers, Toyota Land Cruisers and Isuzu Troopers are their favorite targets. In Nairobi, 1224 cars were stolen in the first six months of 1992. Twenty-five were stolen from the U.N. High Commission for Refugees alone. The M.O.: Carjackers cut off the intended victim, occasionally utilizing an accomplice to prevent a rear escape. Most carjackings take place after 7 p.m., but there have been incidents during daylight hours in populated places.

With more than half of the population of Kenya under the age of 15 and unemployment at over 60 percent, there is ample motivation for criminal behavior. Average per-capita income in Kenya is below US$450 a year. Add to the soup bloodthirsty cops and more than 330,000 refugees and thousands of automatic weapons from Somalia, and the continent becomes darker indeed. Displaced by the war in Somalia, rugged hardy bands of desperate Somali men go south in search of anything of value. Just hope you don't have what they want.

Kenyan police enjoy bragging that they've killed (not apprehended) 70 percent of the bandits operating in the game park regions. But that's little solace. There's no guarantee you won't run into elements of the other 30 percent.

No unraveling republic would be complete without a little religious clan violence. Although religion-based political parties are banned in Kenya, there are outlaws who love to whoop it up. The Mombasa-based Islamic Party of Kenya gets involved in frequent clashes with the pro-government United Muslims of Africa party. In the Rift Valley, it's everyone for themselves, as Daniel Arap Moi's Kalenjin tribe battles with the dominant Kikuyu tribe in the valley. More than 1000 people have been killed in such violence since 1991.

Kurdistan

Blowing Your Kurds Away

There are 25 to 28 million Kurds in the world. The area of Kurdistan is over an area of 74,000 square miles and typically mountainous with fertile valleys. The Kurds were a warring people who never really had a means to group together for a common cause. But now the increasing persecution is forcing the Kurds into a polar stance against their oppressors in Turkey and Iraq.

The Kurds are mostly Sunni Muslims and are descended from the Medes. Their language is a form of Persian but centuries of isolation have created many dialects and tribal schisms. They are still aligned along tribal loyalties with the KDP being led by the Barzini tribe under Massud Barzini. His grandfather Ahmad Barzini led the initial uprising against Iraq in 1931, which was continued by his son Mustafa Barzini in 1961. In 1992, after the U.S. created a safe haven, the two opposing Kurdish parties finished in a dead heat creating the constant back and forth balking that continues to this day.

When the Ottoman empire broke up, the Western Allies created the country of Kurdistan in 1920 with the Treaty of Sevres. They changed their minds in 1923, when they decided it was more expedient to suck up to Turkey and make it an anticommunist buffer zone against Russia. The 1923 treaty of Lausanne did provide for basic recognition and rights, which have been ignored by Turkey and Iraq.

As many as 12 to 15 million Kurds live in Turkey (a third of Turkey's members of parliament and foreign ministers have a Kurdish background), 5 to 7 million live in Iran, 1. 5 million live in Syria and 4 million live in Iraq. There are approximately a million Kurds in Russia. There are also Kurds in the Caucasus region.

After waging 10 years of all-out warfare with the PKK, someone in the Turkish government decided to add up the cost: $179 billion dollars and 22,000 people dead. That radically changes the previous estimate of only 12,500 dead.

Although there has been ongoing war between Turkey and the PKK, the Kurds as a people do not necessarily condone or even care about the terrorist group's actions. The actions of the PKK do little to help the Kurds gain political and financial clout. The possibility of creating a new country carved out of Iran, Iraq, Turkey and Syria is as likely as Saddam taking a military planning job at the Pentagon. In the meantime, warfare and fear grip eastern Turkey. The army and the PKK have demolished over 2000 villages during the last seven years in an attempt to erase their presence. After former President Bush gallantly came to the aid of Kuwait, a country weakened by too many late nights at the disco, the Kurds thought they were next in line to be liberated from big bad Saddam. Obviously, the Iraqi Kurds never studied postwar Eastern European history or oil exploration. The U.S. did send them bread. We save the military stuff for rich backward people; until they get that oil out of the ground, they will have to be poor backward people.

For now, the Kurds have possession of a frozen, windswept mountainous country. The capital of Kurdistan is Arbil, a hellish limbo with little chance of being granted independence.

On August 31, 1996 40,000 Republican Guards rolled up to the gates of Arbil (also called Irbel and Erbil in Western reports). Arbil was controlled by the Patriotic Union of Kurdistan, and since this time Saddam's elite soldiers were issued bullets, they left in a hurry. Saddam's folks got busy blowing up the Iraqi National Congress, rounding up and shooting CIA-trained flunkies and leaving behind a number of Iraqis who changed into KDP uniforms.

Clinton's electionmeisters scrambled to see how they could spin this confrontation, after Bill hadn't figured out whether whomping Saddam was good or bad. They vaguely remembered that footage of cruise missiles, stealth bombers and a stern president were good for public opinion polls. What they forgot was back then Saddam was choking off our oil supply and Bush had Swartzkopf in the field with a multinational army instead of Dick Morris in bed with a hooker.

About 69% of Americans supported Clinton's decision; 0% of Americans know how many people the cost of a cruise missile could feed. (DP figured that 44 cruise missles at $1.5 million each translate to $113.20 per Kurd in Iraq. That doesn't include building or delivery costs. A mild exaggeration, but appropriate, considering the UN had just allowed a $50 per Kurd allowance to feed the destitute Kurds in northern Iraq.) Now they can sell Tomahawk parts for salvage to scrape together the $3500 per family smugglers are charging Kurdish families to escape from their mountainous hell to Germany. Darn, it worked so well for the Republicans.

Saddam wasn't fazed a bit. It didn't take long for Iraq to do the dirty deed and they were soon parked out on the desert waiting for whatever newfangled gizmos Uncle Sam was going to throw at them. They could have kept on killing and plundering since Clinton sent his cruise missiles to the south knocking out unrelated Iraqi radar and air defense sites as an expensive IOU to the Saudis and Kuwait. This time the rest of the world was not drinking Pepsi and cheering from the bleachers. With Slick Willie's finger on the trigger, they did not want to get caught in the crossfire (political or military) so most European, Asian and Arab neighbors publically dissed Bill while checking to make sure their Swiss bank accounts were OK. Meanwhile the U.S. spent a lot of taxpayers money by launching B-52's from Louisiana to Guam and then to the Persian Gulf to launch 13 cruise missiles. They matched another 14 Tomahawks from U.S. warships in the Persian Gulf. The next day the military used the bizarre term of "mopping up" to justify the launching of another 17 Tomahawks to take out the 15 air defense centers in the south.

The U.S. did not do anything to protect the Kurds or to defend the "safe haven" they created for Kurds after the Gulf War. A few days later Saddam and his new Kurdish buddies captured the rest of Kurdistan.

The intrigue came to light when the papers revealed that Saddam had blown up a 6 year, $20 million CIA operation to back Barzini and his KDP. The goal was to support a grass roots uprising against Saddam run by a handful of CIA agents with dozens of trained (yes you guessed it) terrorists to overthrow or assissinate Saddam Barzani decided to ditch Uncle Sam and called in Uncle Saddam instead, with much more effective results.

The Players

The United States

Bill Clinton OK'd a $20 million covert action to overthrow Saddam from the north. Saddam outfoxed Slick Willie and killed or captured most of the U.S. Kurdish operatives in his September raid on Arbil.

Patriotic Union of Kurdistan (PUK)

Led by Jalal Talbani, who lives in Damascus, Syria. Supported by the Turkish Army and Iran. They say they have 20,000 armed men. In September of 1996 Iran sent in troops and weapons to support the KPP against the PUK in Northern Iraq.

The PUK got F*K'd would be a concise way of describing what Slick Willie, Uncle Saddam and the West did to them in August of '96. The PUK represents the vast majority (70%) of the 3.2 million Kurds in Iraqi Kurdistan. They have been forced to align themselves with the Iranians who make both the U.S. and Iraq see red. This time they took it out on the yellow, the official color of the PUK party (red is the color of the KDP). Their headquarters in Sulaymaniyah was overrun in September and their followers fled towards Iran.

Kurdistan Democratic Party (KDP)

Led by Massud Barzini and backed by Iraq, because they consider him the lesser of two evils. They consider Talbani to be a pawn of the CIA (which it was until the summer of 1996) and Turkey. The KDP has stronger support amongst the rural Kurds.

Barzani controls the main border crossing at Zakhu, (see "Turkey, In a Dangerous Place") the only lifeline the north has with the Western world. They charge a tax for the *masot* or crude fuel oil that is trucked across in rusty tanks. Barzani has the support of about 30% of the Kurds inside Iraq. He was supported by the U.S. and a group of CIA people who worked out of Sulaymaniyah until the Republican Guard came to call. He know considers Saddam his ally.

Kurdish Hezbollah

A Kurdish fundamentalist group backed by Iran.

The Turkish Military and Police Forces

The presence of over 160,000 military and police has turned eastern Turkey into a war zone, and travel is strictly controlled.

The Kurds

Kurdistan became part of the Ottoman Empire about a thousand years ago. It was a feudalistic system holding together a mixture of mountain people. Today, Kurdistan is a poor region, backward, difficult to reach, and underdeveloped by Turkey for fear its neighbors, the former Soviet Union, would annex the region.

The Kurds were considered bandits (*eksiya* in Turkish). Stubborn, backward people, they refused to fit into the societies that had built countries around them. For years police and military dealt harshly with the Kurds, who not only rebelled against outside authority but continually warred amongst themselves.

Ataturk

In 1928, Mustafa Kemal, or Ataturk (Father of the Turks), began the process of unifying Turkey. As with many strong nationalistic movements his required the assimilation and subjugation of the many political and ethnic groups into one stronger group. Ataturk chose to align Turkey with the West rather than the East. The changes meant going so far as to change the written language from the Arabic form to the Latin and even banning the fez. Although the seat of the government is in Ankara and the major focus of the Turks is Istanbul, it did not address the needs of the 20 million or so Kurds who inhabit the poorer east. Kurds also are the major minority in southeastern Turkey as well as in the bordering areas of Iraq, Iran and Syria. Turkey's new love affair with the West meant that they found themselves with their Kurdish language banned and their customs under siege because of the need to Westernize all aspects of Turkish life.

The Kurdish Worker's Party (PKK)

Formed on November 27, 1978 in Siverek and led by Abdullah Ocalan who runs the operation out of a comfortable house in Damascus, Syria and the Bekaa Valley. PKK guerrillas or peshmerya (those who face death) are recruited from the villages of eastern Turkey and the refugee camps in northern Iraq. They are trained in terrorist training camps in Lebanon and Iraq. One of the main PKK bases is in Zaleh near the Iranian border with Turkey.

Politically, the Kurds found themselves a long way down in the pecking order when it came to representation, financial aid and clout, since the Turkish government has been loathe to develop the east because of the threat of invasion from the former Soviet Union, Iran and Iraq.

To fight for their rights, the Marxist Kurdish Worker's Party, or PKK, was formed to create an independent Kurdistan. Initially, the PKK pursued its demands through political actions. There were various Kurdish political parties but none that demanded absolute autonomy to the party and carried out acts of murder and intimidation like the PKK. The PKK was outlawed in 1980 for its terrorist activities against the government. Although there had been terrorist incidents since the '70s, full-scale warfare erupted in 1985, starting in Siverek (see "In a Dangerous Place: Eastern Turkey") and has continued uninterrupted now for 10 years.

In 1987 Turkey essentially declared war on the PKK and locked down the entire eastern Provinces. As of this writing, there are major military operations against the Kurds near Tuncelli and sporadic firefights and sabotage throughout southeastern Turkey.

Before and after the Gulf War, Iraq carried out a campaign of genocide to effectively push the Kurds out of Iraq and into Turkey. In 1989, Turkey accepted 150,000–300,000 Iraqi Kurds who were fleeing extermination by Saddam Hussein. It is estimated that Hussein's brutal campaign pushed 1.5 million Kurdish refugees into northern Iraq and southeastern Turkey, where many live in makeshift camps.

Iran supports the Kurds since they create conflict in one of the more Westernized and liberal Muslim nations.

The greatest damage the Kurds do to Turkey is to realign this wealthy and sophisticated country with its more backward but equally fractured Eastern neighbors. The chances of Turkey joining the EC are slim, and the increasing force that the local and national governments use against the PKK is reinforcing the brutal genocidal image the Armenians have projected.

On the other hand, the PKK has broken the cardinal rule of terrorist groups in alienating the Western press and governments. There is little sentiment for the PKK's extortion tactics against its own people. The PKK is a revolution run by an absentee landlord. They have effectively removed any constructive voice for change by being banned as a political party in Turkey. They are ineffective in providing normal fund-raising or publicity by being banned in Europe. They cannot form a workable government to take care of their own people, forcing the U.S. and U.N. to effectively run Kurdistan as an aid station in northern Iraq. This does not give them a solid footing in the international community. The atrocities committed against unarmed schoolteachers, Kurdish women, children and old men are publicized by the Turkish government and media.

The outlook for the Kurds is dim since their demands for a new homeland would not only remove a major chunk of Turkey but a major portion of Iran, Iraq and Syria as well. They also run up against Turkey's goal of uniting the various peoples within its border and the call for peaceful and political settlements to rights, but they maintain a hard line on secessionist groups. Even if Turkey was to be conciliatory, many people forget that the PKK is waging a battle on four fronts (not including its terrorist activities in Europe) and has little chance of convincing the hard-line governments of Iraq, Iran and Syria to give them concessions.

The PKK targets the local population and is on the run from the Turkish Special Ops teams. The PKK controls the countryside at night, and the government controls the major cities. There is continual warfare on a daily basis, as the Turkish government seeks to annihilate the 10,000 or so ground troops the PKK has in the country. The PKK shows no quarter to Kurds they think are sympathizers, yet are surprisingly lenient with foreigners they kidnap. Of the 20 or so foreigners they kidnap in a year, all are released without harm.

In 1993 the Kurds began a sporadic bombing campaign in Istanbul and Antalya designed to scare off Western tourists. In Europe in 1993, the Kurds created global publicity when they executed a series of terrorist activities against Turkish embassies and businesses (airline offices, banks and travel agents). Germany, with a Turkish community of over 2 million (a quarter of them, Kurds), was understandably nervous about becoming a battleground and quickly banned 36 Kurdish political organizations.

France also banned two Kurdish political groups, and Great Britain is trying to figure out how to stop the regular extortion of Turkish emigrants and/or their businesses by the Kurds.

Their efforts have been successful in creating sympathy for a people deposed. In our own humble opinion, one of the most powerful opinion shapers was Coskun's photos of the Kurdish refugees fighting for bread featured in news magazines around the world, including *Time* magazine. The problem is that there is little even a sympathetic person can do to help the Kurds.

While the U.S. turns a blind eye to the PKK atrocities in Turkey, it is actively using the Kurds to help destabilize Hussein in Iraq. "Kurdistan" was effectively created when the U.S and Turkish military (Operation Provide Comfort) created a safe zone for the 1.5 million Kurds displaced by Hussein's attempt to eliminate the Kurds. During the three-year military occupation by the Americans, they managed to form two major political parties from the diverse group of Kurds. There were actually democratic elections held among the area's 3.5 million residents in 1992. The area is essentially divided into east and west. The west is controlled by the Kurdish Democratic Party (KDP) and the east by the Patriotic Union of Kurdistan (PUK), led by Jalal Talabani, with the center being the regional capital of Arbil.

In May of 1994, fighting broke out between the two parties after a PUK leader was assassinated. The two parties then decided to settle their differences without the aid of a ballot box. Using antiaircraft guns and other heavy weaponry, they duked it out in the central mountain town of Shaqlawa.

About 200 people have been killed in a war that was conducted while the leader of the PUK was in Damascus.

In Iran the Kurds are found in the area known as Kordestan. Their language is banned and teaching of Kurdish history and culture is forbidden. After World War II, their bid for a homeland was put down and the leader was executed. After Khomeini came to power, the ayatollah bombed their villages and camps, creating a lasting insurgency that is active to this day. There are about 200,000 soldiers keeping the lid on Kordestan today, and Kurdistan Democratic party (KDPI) guerilas attack military centers on a regular basis. Iranian government agents have assassinated KDPI leaders in Austria and Germany. The leader of the KDPI is Mostafa Hejri, who is based in Iraqi Kurdistan and seems to get some support from Baghdad.

There is also a left-wing group, the Komala, which is supported by the government of Iraq.

Laos

Bombies and Zombies

From 1964 until 1973, U.S. planes averaged one sortie every eight minutes over this unfortunate slice of Spam wedged between Vietnam and Cambodia. More than 285 million bombs were dropped over Indochina during the Vietnam War, a good number of them over Laos; a good number of those remain unexploded.

Many payloads were jettisoned by B-52s, which had to get back to their bases in Thailand in a hurry; other warplanes used Laos for target practice. But mainly, Laos was pounded into oblivion to prevent Pathet Lao guerrillas from advancing from their jungle bases in the northeast toward the capital of Vientiane, as well as to wreak havoc on North Vietnamese forces shuttling up and down the Ho Chi Minh Trail, which cuts a narrow swath through the mountains of Laos.

The Laotians call the unexploded ordinance "bombies," a cute term for the cluster bombs that today take scores of Laotian lives every month. And because farmers cannot take advantage of valuable agricultural land due to the "buried treasure," thousands more Laotians face malnourishment and starvation seemingly with zombielike indifference. In heavily carpet-bombed Xieng Khouang province northeast of Vientiane, hundreds of families subsist on virtually no food at all for three to four months of every year due to the "bombies" in the fields. These "bombies" are actually small bomblets (or cluster bombs)—but very lethal—that spill from large casings as they're dropped from aircraft. The bomblets, about the size of a tennis ball, number about 650 to the case. Covered in bright yellow plastic, they make a particular curiosity to children, who comprise 44 percent of all bomb accidents in Laos. Half these accidents result in death. You don't want to see what the other half look like. Thirty-one percent of all bomb accidents occur while children are playing, giving a new meaning to Romper Room.

There aren't many soccer fields in Laos.

Macedonia

The Name Game

Imagine fighting a war over a name. Well, Greece wants some of the positive spin that comes with being the fabled land of Alexander—although things have calmed down between Greece and Macedonia. (Greece maintained that by being called Macedonia, it would claim more land.)

Meanwhile, there is a witch's brew of ethnic and religious hatred stirring. As the various ethnic factions vie for dominance in this landlocked domain that was once part of the former Yugoslavia, the United Nations is busy conducting a census of Macedonia's 2 million people to create at least a mildly accurate picture of this country's explosive ethnic composition. Sethnic Albanians and Macedonians are the major dividing lines, while Serbs, Turks, Vlachs, Greeks, Bulgarians, Gypsies and others all want to wield political power. When it's all said and done, there aren't enough flag designs left to accommodate separate countries for each of these ethnic subdivisions. And Macedonia can only exist if they are protected by big brother. It is currently the only way to get in and out of the mountainous region. The Balkans can only be crossed north to south from Belgrade to Thessalonika and from west to east from Durres to Istanbul.

An Albanian liberation group called Unikom has been set up to assist a large area of Macedonia to secede from Macedonia and unite with Albania. It is supposedly financed by Libya and Iran. On the other side is the IMRO Defense Committee, which has sworn to kill any Albanian leader to campaign for autonomous Albanian regions.

Mali

Timbuktu and Tuaregs, too

The Tuaregs, the nomadic dispossessed of the Sahel, continue to fight a mean desert war of revolution in this hot, dusty country. The light skinned Tuaregs under the leadership of Rhissa ag Sidi Mohamed ended their revolution officially in May of 1993. The black settlers from the south have a militia called Ganda Koy or "owners of the land" who are fighting or some say massacring the light skinned Tuareg nomads around Gao and Timbuktu. Smuggling is endemic so the border areas on all sides are touchy. DP visited the country and can confirm that blacks still give Tuaregs a wide berth when passing in the desert.

Morocco

Beach Blanket Bingo

The government of Morocco informs us that there are currently 30 foreign-backed Islamic fundamentalists working to advance its causes. Gee, do you think it might have something to do with the fact that it grabbed 102,675 square miles of desert without asking? Quite a windfall, when you consider all the heat Israel gets for grabbing only a cactus or two from its neighbors. Technically, the 16-year war with the Polisario Front was wrapped up in 1991, but the peace talk invitations probably didn't get delivered at every camel stop. For now, the Moroccans are doing a tidy business cultivating and exporting ganja (about US$2 billion a year), and are crossing their fingers that nobody asks them where they got all that extra beachfront property to the south. Give 'em a shout.

Sa Majeste Roi Hassan II (His Majesty King Hassan II)
Bureau de sa Majeste le Roi, Palais Royal
Rabat, Maroc (Morocco)
Telex: 0407 31744, 0407 32908,
Telegrams: sa majeste le roi, Rabat, Maroc (French or English)

Panama

Down in Noriegaville

Panama is a mean, dirty poor little place. Bombs continue to go off in public places and there's still a holdout group left that just can't get over the days when their nostrils were packed with speedballs. The M-20 Group (or 20th December National Liberation Group, named after the date the U.S. invaded Panama) is made up of Manuel Noriega's old drinking buddies. These former Panamanian Defense Force folks don't have much of an agenda or even a good press agent. Their goal is to oust the occupiers of Panama and bring the current political administration to justice as traitors.

And just think, we get to hand over the strategic Panama Canal to these folks by the end of the century.

Papua New Guinea

Treehouse Fight

PNG could stand for Pretty Nasty Guerillas who are actually called BRA or Bougainville Revolutionary Army. The rebels have been fighting for six years to secede from PNG who only got their independence in 1975. The poorly equipped but dogged rebels of the BRA control tiny pockets of Bougainville, about 5 percent in all. There is plenty of copper coming from the Panguna copper mine, about half of PNG's total income. For now, this island nation of 600 islands is busy deforesting itself to pick up the missing cash flow. DP predicts that things don't look good for these rebels wielding rusty shotguns.

South Africa

Tied Apart

A British Consumers Association survey has claimed that South Africa is one of the world's most dangerous places for tourists. It estimates that 5 percent of all tourists that visit are attacked or robbed. South Africa has the dubious distinction of having the highest crime rate of any country not at war. About 44 murders per 100,000 people.

Under apartheid in South Africa, thousands of blacks were sent to prison or exiled because of their beliefs. Millions were displaced from their homes at gunpoint. Most estimates put the number of people detained without being charged at above 50,000. Hundreds of others were tortured and even murdered while under custody. Government-sponsored death squads roamed the globe and were responsible for the assassinations in South Africa and abroad of at least 225 anti-apartheid activists.

With Mandela driving now and de Klerk in the back seat, it's time for finger pointing—and, boy, are they. While the new governments in countries such as Argentina, El Salvador, Chile and Ethiopia have established "truth commissions" to investigate crimes against humanity (i.e., war crimes) committed by previous regimes, South Africa has become embattled in whether or not to finger the culprits and, if so, what to do about them. There have been secret attempts to grant limited immunity to nearly 3480 members of the country's security forces, in addition to the police commissioner and right-wing former cabinet members. Mandela accused de Clerk of knowing about the covert immunity grants. De Clerk got pissed-off and brought the already rocky relationship to new depths. However, the new truth commission in South Africa moves unsteadily on, unsure of whom to charge and with what to charge them with.

What do politicians do when things get tough, why give themselves a raise of course. Mandela's predecessor, F.W. de Clerk, pulled down US$73,817 a year as well as US$6000 for expenses. He also received a US$77,770 car allowance every four years. And he didn't drive to the U.N. once. Mandela, on the other hand, decided he was going to make up for what he had been missing all those years in prison and he bumped his compensation to US$191,660 a year. The average annual wage in South Africa for whites is about US$4000; blacks in the townships

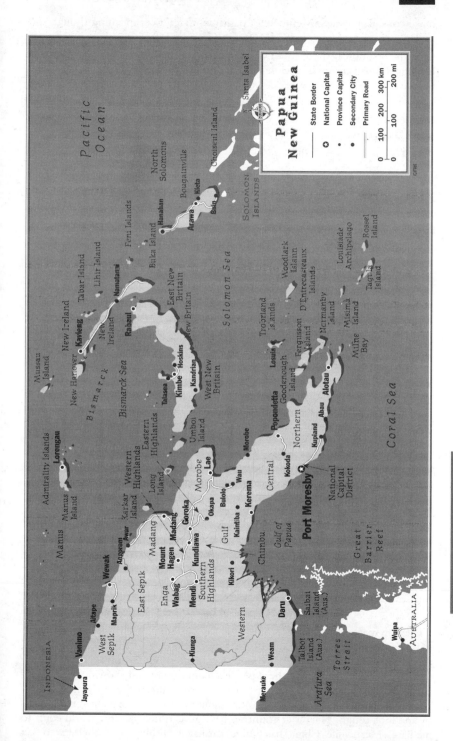

make considerably less. Members of parliament aren't complaining though they jacked their salaries from US$34,160 up to US$44,720.

On the first upscale note we can report in this book, 223 people per month are no longer killed in political violence each month in South Africa. Ninety-seven people are.

For the latest, contact Nelson Mandela. Or, for some nostalgia about the good 'ole boys in the good 'ole days, F.W. will yack your ear off.

President Nelson Mandela
☎*(012) 21-2222; FAX (012) 323-3114*

Mr. F.W. de Klerk
☎*(012) 319-1650; FAX (012) 325-4008*

Mr. A Nzo, Minister of Foreign Affairs
☎*(012) 351-0005; FAX (012) 351-0254*

South African Communication Service for updated information
☎*(031) 304-8893*

Beemmer the Redeemer

In response to the public impression in South Africa that BMWs are thieves' and carjackers' most sought-after automobiles, the German luxury car manufacturer—to protect its market share—has taken the unusual step of including antitheft and hijacking insurance in the price of a new BMW model. In 1994, vehicle thefts rose nearly 30 percent over 1993 in South Africa to 110,000. The figure in 1995 was expected to be higher. During the first 11 months of 1995, 9400 vehicles were seized by armed groups and 43 drivers murdered in Gauteng province alone (which includes Johannesburg and Pretoria).

But the biggest problem for BMW is the public misconception that BMWs are more often targeted than other marques, prompting soaring insurance premiums on BMWs that often climb as high as 25 percent of the vehicle's retail value (from a typical rate of 5-10 percent). BMW's eminence as the Holy Grail of hoodlums and hooligans is fodder for the cocktail party circuit, but indeed isn't data-based. In fact, the police and insurance companies rarely release a breakdown of statistics showing which makes of cars are favored by crooks and cods. But South Africa's National Crime Information Center did mistakenly leak numbers revealing that BMW wasn't any more prone to theft than other makes—that, in truth, the cars are stolen in numbers commensurate with or below the percentage of the automaker's market share in South Africa (6.19 percent of all vehicles stolen or hijacked; 7.59 percent market share). Toyotas are most often ripped off.

BMW is taking the fight even closer to the Bimmer-busters; the company is providing police, free of charge, with 100 of its most powerful models to chase down carnappers and other culprits.

The Spratlys

Makin' Mischief

These flyspeck islands are custom-made for a international dispute. This group of islands just north of Borneo is floating on oil close to nowhere. China, Brunei, the Philippines, Vietnam and anybody else in the neighborhood who has a half-fassed reason to lay claim to these isles is talking tough and showing off military hardware like gangs in a schoolyard. China has occupied the aptly named Mischief reef. The Philippines sent its entire fighter airforce (nine planes) to sit nearby and look tough. The other countries have gone running to the world court to mediate. Meanwhile China has built ramshackle fishing-boat shelters to get squatters rights. Looks like the court may have to separate the kids in this messy divorce.

Taiwan

The Seed of World War III

Chinese PremierLi Peng's not happy with Taiwanese President Lee Teng-hui, who's considering taking the lethal gamble of declaring Taiwan's independence from Mother China. The scarlet latter considers Taiwan a renegade province and will not tolerate such tomfoolery. China has been doing military "exercises" in the Taiwan Strait, lobbing missiles to within a few hundred meters of the Taiwanese coast, just to let the islanders considering independence know the next volley will fall on their heads. The U.S. Navy, in March 1996, sent two carrier groups close to the Strait in a show of force as the Chinese continued to splatter rockets into the waters off Taiwanese beaches. Sunbathers beware. If China decides to take the island by force, they've got a billion or so people who can help them out in the operation. Will Uncle Sam let it happen? Doubtful. Will Beijing back off at American threats. Even more doubtful. The skies again could be gillnetted by MIGs and F-16s duking it out over Formosa. This wouldn't be any Cold War, folks. The real thing. And Washington would say the hell with Bosnia, Haiti, Israel and anywhere else they've got their own guys or friendlies with M-16s and pack 'em all up on Carnival cruise ships bound for Shanghai. Look for a bunch a people to take sides, just like they did after Hitler took out Poland like a Mike Tyson fight and the Japanese sank a bunch a American steel at Pearl. Imagine Communist Vietnamese soldiers and GIs sharing C-RATs in the same trenches. Believe it.

Zimbabwe

The Justice Legal and Parliamentary Affairs Minister is looking for a hangman. He has a few applicants from locals and foreigners. Zimbabwe resumed executions in 1995 after a seven year moratorium.

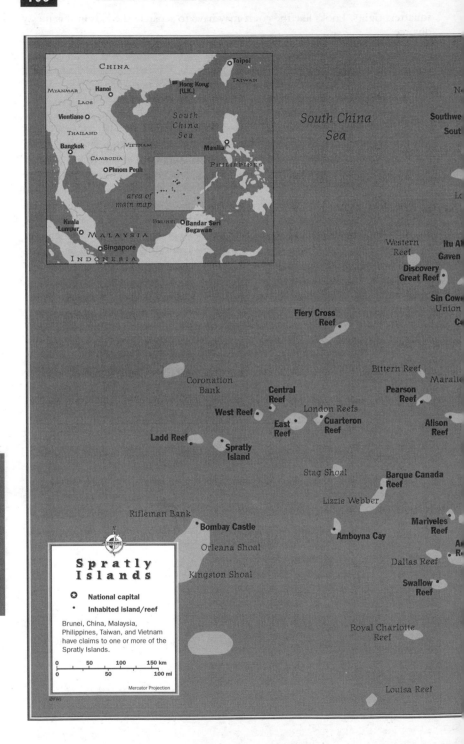

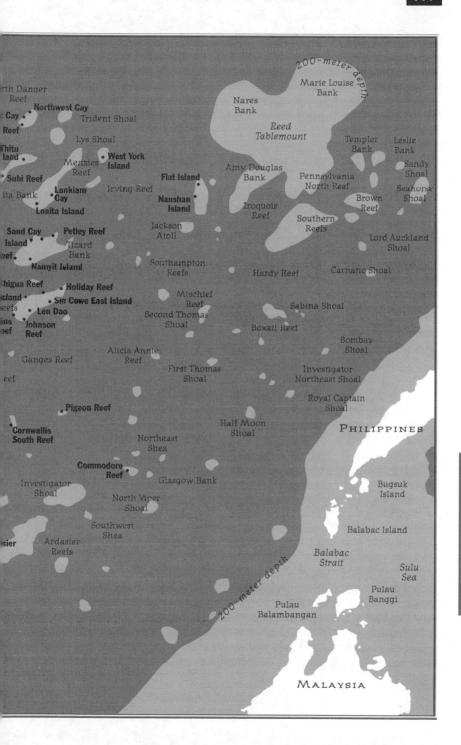

COMING ATTRACTIONS

DANGEROUS THINGS

Bribes

Crime Does Pay

Mordida, dash, spiffs, baksheesh, cadeaus, special fees, tea money, fines, gifts or whatever they are called are a regular part of travel in the Third World. In many cases, military, police and government officials will expect a gratuity to allow passage, as payment for minor infractions or to issue visas. In some cases, it may be your money or your life.

Paying Your Dues

Most travelers who are put in jail are involved in traffic- or drug-related offenses. Naturally, many countries have an unofficial method of dealing with these problems efficiently and profitably. It serves no purpose for small or poor countries to incarcerate you for lengthy periods of time. It also does not serve the purpose of policemen to spend their time filling out paperwork, when they can resolve the problem and teach you a lesson on the spot. From Minnesota to Malaysia to Mexico, I have been amazed at the solid financial education police officers have been given. (Which is better? $100 in your pocket or the policeman's pocket?) Be forewarned, there are many officers who do not accept or want bribes. The way to tell is simple. If an officer tries to resolve a problem rather than just write you up, handcuff you or arrest you, you are expected to begin the bribe process. If you feel an opening gambit has been made, then you are expected to explain to the officer your desire for a speedy amicable resolution of your problem. In most cases, the officer will shore your feelings of injustice about his having to take you all the way back to the station (always in the opposite direction you are traveling) to wait for the judge who is typically fishing or out until next week.

If he offers to take the fine back for you or to let you pay it on the spot, then bingo, the chiseling begins. Remember that bribes are a "cash-only" business and the amount you can pay will be limited to the amount of cash you have on you at that moment. Now that you have the rules of the game, please remember that offering any financial inducement to an officer, however innocently, is illegal and can put you in jail.

Delivering a Bribe

One must never discuss money or the amount or the reason for the gift. Typically, you will be presented with a "problem" that can be solved but will take time, money, or approval by a higher authority. You will naturally need to have this problem solved. You may ask if there is a fee that will expedite the solution of this problem, or if the local language fails you, you can point out your urgency and present a passport, ticket or papers with a single denomination of currency tucked inside.

DP's Guide to Bribes	
Minor traffic violation (speeding, imaginary stop signs, burned-out tail lights that magically work; usually levied on Fridays or Saturday afternoons).	$5–$10
Traffic violations (real stop signs, real speeding tickets).	$10–$50
Serious traffic violations (DUI, very serious speeding or racing).	$50–$500
Very serious traffic problem (accident with no fatalities).	$500–$1000
Accidents that involve fatalities require the application of funds to a judge, your lawyer, prosecutor and probably the police chief. Costs are usually in the $2000–$6000 range, and, yes, they will wait while your credit card clears. You will also be waiting in a jail.	$2000–$6000
If you are involved in something shady and need to correct the problem, it is wise to hire a lawyer. To make sure you get a lawyer who is sympathetic to the needs of the police, simply ask the police to recommend a good lawyer. The lawyer will negotiate fees for himself, the judge and the police.	$10,000–$45,000

The Price for Doing Bad Things

Bribes might not work if you are caught by the military, make the local papers or happen to be doing something the government is busy eradicating (usually with U.S. funds) at the time. Smuggling drugs, weapons or people requires the support of a large, covertly sanctioned organization, freelancers are usually treated roughly with little opportunity to buy their way out. Depending on how big a fish they think you are, you can expect to pay about $12,000 to get out of a South or Central American jail. It is not uncommon to have to pay $30,000–$120,000 to beat a major drug rap.

If you are kidnapped by terrorists, you might feel lucky. They will typically hit up your government of origin or your family for your ransom. Americans fetch between $100,000 to $2 million, depending on who you work for. Many times guerrillas will attach political demands or have unrealistic demands like bumping Andy Rooney on "60 Minutes" to tell their side of the story. This lowers your chances of freedom dramatically since most governments have stated policies about negotiating with terrorists, though they are fairly helpful with kidnapping cases. The catch is that your government will expect you to pay them back.

Other reasons for bribes are to bring in cars, contraband, machine parts, business samples, cash or even a wife. In many countries the police derive their sustenance from local businesses. A recent article in *Newsweek* estimated that in Hong Kong, brothels provide $120–$600 a month. In Bangkok, the city's 1000 "entertainment houses" pay $600,000 a month to the local police. Strangely, these types of businesses can provide favors to travelers if you find yourself in a squeeze or need help approaching the police on a sensitive issue.

The best way to check out bribes is to contact the local embassy, expats who live in the area, local journalists (not foreign journalists) and local lawyers. It should be stated that in many cases a demand for a bribe can be talked down if you are doing nothing wrong. Many junior customs officials will spot first-timers and shake them down for everything from their *Playboys* to their underwear. Feel free to protest, but when the man with the big hat and gold stars agrees with the peon, it's time to start rolling off the twenties.

When It Is Better to Give Than to Receive

Many people view bribery as reprehensible and evil. These are usually the ones who have to pay the bribes. Others view the practice as a normal way to supplement meager government wages (you can guess who they are). All countries including America have this affliction. Africa is the worst place for bribery, followed by South America and Central America, with northern Europe being the most incorruptible place. Nigeria has the worst reputation for *dash* but you can expect any minor official in most poor African nations to ask for a *cadeau* in exchange for providing a higher level of service. Expats detest this practice because they have to go through customs and refuse to pay it. Tourists are more easily intimidated and usually have much more to lose if they miss a flight, connection or cruise because of unnecessary delays.

Remember that small bribes are used to facilitate services that can be withheld or denied. Usually tightwads will be processed, but at the back of the line. Obnoxious tightwads who like to make loud speeches about corruption may find themselves with insurmountable visa irregularities ("The stamp in your passport must be green ink for a fifteen-day visa").

A carton of cigarettes will ensure that you are speedily processed in most African countries. A bottle of Johnny Walker will not get you far in a Muslim country but will definitely expedite your exit visa in Colombia. Border crossings into most Central American countries can be made for a one hundred dollar bill, and you can drive as fast as you want in Mexico if you have a good supply of 20 dollar bills. With such gifts, you may not need a visa entering a country and the customs official may forgo even a cursory inspection of your vehicle.

If you need to be smuggled out of a country, it is a little more complicated. First, the "coyote" will demand about twice the normal fee for your departure and there is no guarantee that he will not turn you in for a reward. Secondly, the matter of securing an exit visa without the benefit of an entry visa will cost you between $100 and $200 dollars in most Asian and Latin American countries. Eastern European and CIS countries can be crossed for as little as $5, with no guarantee that you will not be finked on 10 miles down the road.

You don't have to be a criminal to pay bribes. Criminals take great pride in their ability to extract bribes or "protection money" from honest folks. For example, in Russia, 150 criminal gangs control 40,000 businesses. Moscow has 12 major organized crime groups who've been known to extract up to 30 percent of monthly profits from businesses. So the best way to view bribes is as you would tipping. When a country lowers its wages to its police and officials below the poverty line, they look to you to make ends meet.

In summary, using bribery is like kissing in junior high school. Both parties must be willing, but you have to be given an opening before you make your move. If you are brash or unwise, you will be severely rebuked.

Dangerous Jobs

Don't have time or money for a dangerous vacation? Why not get dangerous and make money too? In fact, the odds are that you could get your kicks by being splattered on Route 66. In 1994, highway deaths accounted for 20 percent of the 6588 fatal work injuries. According to the U.S. Department of Labor, truck drivers had more fatal injuries than any other occupation, with 762 deaths that year.

Homicide was the second leading cause of job-related deaths, accounting for 16 percent of the total. Robbery was the primary motive for workplace homicide. About half of the victims worked in retail establishments, such as grocery stores, restaurants and bars, where cash is readily available. (31,000 convenience store clerks are shot every year.) Taxicab drivers, police and security guards also had high numbers of worker homicides. Four-fifths of the victims were shot; others were stabbed, beaten or strangled.

Although highway accidents were the leading manner of death for male workers, homicide was the leading cause for female workers, accounting for 35 percent of their fatal work injuries.

Falls accounted for 10 percent of fatal work injuries. The construction industry, particularly special trade contractors such as roofing, painting and structural steel erection, accounted for almost half the falls. One-fifth of the falls were from or through roofs; falls from scaffolding and from ladders each accounted for about one-eighth. Nine percent of fatally injured workers were struck by various objects, a fourth of which were falling trees, tree limbs and logs. Other objects that struck workers included machines and vehicles slipping into gear or falling onto workers, and various building materials such as pipes, beams, metal plates and lumber. Electrocutions accounted for 5 percent of the worker deaths in 1994.

Occupations with large numbers of worker fatalities included truck drivers, farm workers, sales supervisors and proprietors, and construction laborers. Industry divisions with large numbers of fatalities included agriculture, forestry, fishing, construction, transportation and public utilities, and mining. Other high-risk occupations included airplane pilots, cashiers and firefighters.

The Most Dangerous Jobs in America, or Why Don't We See More Action/Adventure Shows Starring These Folks?

1. Truck driver	8. Taxicab driver
2. Farm worker	9. Timber cutter
3. Sales supervisor/proprietor	10. Cashier
4. Construction worker	11. Fisherman
5. Police detective	12. Metal worker
6. Airplane pilot	13. Roofer
7. Security guard	14. Firefighter

Source: U.S. Labor Department

California had the highest total fatalities on the job (601) in 1994, with Texas finishing second with 497. Florida was a close third with 388. New York City led with the highest number of assaults and violent acts in the workplace (66). Apparently, something about the northeast provokes violence at work. The District of Columbia reported 76 violent acts and assaults on the job, and Rhode Island had 55. Hawaii had the highest number of work-related highway deaths with 60.

Victims of Violent Crime According to the U.S. Justice Department

Private company	61%
Government	30%
Self-employed	8%
Working without pay	1%

Source: U.S. Justice Department

Who's Out There?

The typical whacko who freaks out at work and starts banging away is typically a middle-age male over 35, withdrawn, owner of a gun, has served in the military and probably drinks or snorts too much of some substance.

The Locations Where These Crimes Took Place	
Other commercial sites	23%
On public property	22%
Office, factory or warehouse	14%
Restaurant, bar or nightclub	13%
Parking lot/garage	11%
On school property	9%
Other	8%

DANGEROUS JOBS

What's danger worth?

The U.S. Department of State thinks employees who work in dangerous places should receive an additional payment of 25 percent of their normal salary. French companies will pay up to double the standard rate to do business in remote or dangerous places. Americans are the preferred targets. Americans visiting or working in other countries are increasingly becoming targets of anti-U.S. attacks. Latin America is the most likely place for anti-American attacks, with the Middle East just behind.

Don't think that it matters to the private sector paymaster whether you are an American or a former Colombian sent to work in Colombia. You will get preferential treatment: 92 percent of U.S. companies pay the same incremental amount regardless of race or country of origin.

Dangerous Occupations

If you're seeking an adventurous career change and don't particularly like the idea of dodging bullets while you're selling Slurpies and cigarettes, here are a few other jobs you might consider:

Army Ranger

The Ranger course is 68 days and emphasizes patrolling and raiding. The course is being restricted, and very few noninfantry soldiers will be able to attend in the future. Troops from other branches can attend if they are being sent to jobs with a specific need for Ranger skills. The Ranger school is considered the toughest course in the army.

U.S. Army

2425 Wilson Boulevard
Arlington, VA 22210-3385
☎ *(703) 841-4300*

Bicycle Messenger

There are about 1500 bicycle messengers in New York City. Messengers are paid between $3 and $30 per trip. A good bike messenger should make about $125 a day. The faster you are, the more you can make, especially during rush hour. You have to supply your own bike (usually a $500 to $1200 mountain bike), safety gear and health insurance. The messenger company gives you a walkie-talkie and a big bag. Messengers work around the clock and break every rule in the book. Many practice "snatching" or grabbing onto a car or truck to speed up their trip. Contact individual messenger services in large cities for more information.

Blowout Control

If you like your work hot and dangerous, try containing oil blowouts. The most famous of these workers is, of course, Red Adair's group which inspired a movie starring John Wayne. Despite the dramatic footage of men covered in oil and being roasted, safety comes first. Red is retired, but the company lives on.

The general idea is that when oil wells catch on fire, or blow out, there is a lot of money being sprayed into the air. So these people have to work fast. Saddam Hussein overtaxed companies from eight countries when he set the Kuwaiti fields alight. There were 732 oil wells in need of capping, but not before US$60 billion worth of oil had disappeared.

Even though the companies can be paid up to a million dollars a job (mostly for equipment and expenses), a more realistic fee is between US$20,000 and US$200,000 to control a blowout. The members of the crew make about US$300 to US$1000 a day each plus room and board. The work requires a drilling background. It is tough, hard and dirty work. You also can't pick your customers, since blowouts happen anywhere, anytime.

Safety Boss	**Boots & Coots**	**Red Adair**
Red Deer,	*Houston, TX*	*Dallas, TX*
Alberta, Canada	☎ *(713) 931-8884*	☎ *(214) 462-4282*
☎ *(403) 342-1310*		

Bounty Hunter

For those of you who can't hold a day job, you might consider bounty hunting. Since the romantic notion of men being brought in dead or alive for a price on their head is almost gone, you end up working for bail bondsmen, not the most romantic of employers. They will pay you a finder's fee so that they don't have to cough up the entire amount of the court-imposed bail when their client doesn't show.

The job does not require much training or even much of anything except a pair of handcuffs and a little skip-tracing education. (Don't believe everything you see on "Renegade." It isn't necessary to have a Lorenzo Lamas physique, long hair or a Harley.) What you get for bringing in bad people is between 10 and 30 percent of the fugitives' bail from the grateful bondsmen. Their clients will not be happy to see you and, in most cases, will try to elude you, since you have neither an attractive uniform nor a big gun. If you have a permit to carry a gun, you are not always allowed to use it. You are essentially making a citizen's arrest, and if you end up with broken bones or holes in you, it's your problem. Some states don't like bounty hunters; you can't practice your business in Illinois, Kentucky or Oregon, for example.

There are about 50–100 active bounty hunters in the U.S., returning about 20,000 fugitives each year. Most of these hunters don't make much money. The lower the bail, the less serious the crime, the less money they make, the easier the errant crooks or fugitives (don't forget they are innocent until proven guilty) are to find.

There is a market for high-end bounty hunters. There are many terrorists with very big prices on their head. You will need a working command of Arabic, Persian, French and some tribal dialects. You will need to be fully conversant with Islam and the Koran and be able to pass for a Sunni or a Shiite. If you're caught, you will be lucky if you are shot. The government was recently offering US$2 million for the ring leader of the World Trade Center bombing. He was found in Pakistan and whisked back to New York.

If you want to know more about bounty hunting, contact the following:

Bob Burton

National Institute of Bail Enforcement
P.O. Box 1170
Tombstone, AZ 85638
☎ *(520) 457-9360*

Cab Driver

Taxis were introduced in 1907 in New York City. Today, it is a job usually taken by recent immigrants. In New York City, there are 11,787 Yellow Cabs, 30,000 livery cars and between 5000 and 9000 illegal gypsy cabs. Cab drivers are usually independent contractors who lease their cabs from a cab company. In New York a cabbie pays about $40 a day for the cab and maybe about $20 for gas. He gets to keep everything after that. The term for breaking even is "making the knot." There are no benefits, workers comp or holidays. The hours are flexible, and you meet a lot of interesting people, albeit briefly. The Lexan dividers in some cabs have been credited with saving lives, but driving a cab is still a dangerous business.

In 1995 in New York City, there were 40 murders of cabbies; most were drivers of livery or gypsy cabs. In a five-year period, 192 drivers were killed. There were 3700 robberies in 1994 and 3892 in 1995. The average amount of the theft was $100 in cash.

N.Y. Taxi Commission
☎ *(212) 302-8294*
FAX (212) 840-1607

CIA

The U.S. intelligence community is comprised of about 100,000 people who work for 28 different organizations. It takes eight agencies just to process and analyze the satellite images sent in by five different intelligence groups. It costs about $28 billion to find out what our friends and enemies are up to.

The job category that might attract MBAs/adventurers is what is known as *nonofficial cover.* Opportunity is knocking (or NOCing) for a few lucky business grads. Dissatisfied with the traditional foreign embassy bureaucrat or aid worker as a cover for its operatives, the CIA has decided to get creative. The CIA now recruits young executives through bogus companies usually based in northern Virginia. The ads appear in major periodicals and newspapers and seek recent business school grads who want to work overseas. The job pays well but requires training. The NOCs are not trained in Camp Peary nor do they ever appear on any CIA database to keep them safe from moles. Sounds like a great movie plot, so far.

The successful graduates are then posted with real companies overseas. Many large American corporations gladly accept these folks, since they get a real business grad who works long hours for free. Each NOC has a liaison person who must handle the intel that is provided by his charge. Many of these positions are with banks, import-export firms and other companies in such nasty places as North Korea, Iraq, Iran and Colombia. Although the CIA has to cut corners on its $28 billion dollar annual budget, NOCs cost more to train and support, but it's hoped they can provide hard information in countries where the embassy is a little light on cocktail party chatter.

If you are exposed or captured, you are officially a spy and not protected by a diplomatic passport.

CIA Employment Office
Career Trainee Division
P.O. Box A2002
Arlington, VA 22209-8727
☎ *(703) 613-8888*
FAX (703) 613-7871
To join the Clandestine service branch of the CIA you need a bachelor's degree along with strong communication and intrapersonal skills. Military experience helps. The CIA is keen on folks with backgrounds in Central Eurasian, East Asian and Middle Eastern languages (kind of tells you where the action is doesn't it?). You need to pass a medical,

psychiatric and polygraph test. You must be a U.S. citizen and can't be over 35. The starting pay is $31,459 to $48,222.

Mercenary

If someone paid you $40 million (some say $23 million), could you clean up a civil war? Well, that's what Executive Outcomes was reportedly paid to clean up things in Angola. And they did it with about 500 men. The curious thing about EO is that it is part of a larger mining group that, along with killing rebels, also looks for gold in Uganda, explores in Ethiopia, and is busy in various mining operations in Lesotho, Botswana, Sierra Leone, South Africa, and a growing number of other African nations. Although EO is a security company, it is part of a group of 32 companies. If you are wondering what the folks working for EO make, it isn't much—about $1500 a month and all the land mines you can step on. Officers are in greater demand and can negotiate monthly salaries of $4500–$6000. In-country shifts are eight weeks on and two weeks off. It helps to know a little Afrikaaner, since the officers use it as a code to confuse the bad guys. The mercs are typically black and recruited from UNITA when they fought against the well-armed and highly trained mercenaries. The kill ratio is about 50 rebels to one mercenary. Yes, they do provide insurance coverage in case you get killed or injured.

Executive Outcomes

P.O. Box 75255
Lynwood Ridge
Pretoria 0040, South Africa
☎ *[27] 12-473-789*

Minesweeper

Land mines kill or maim someone on this planet every hour. There is a big demand for former explosives and munitions experts to clean up these killers. Mine clearance personnel are paid about US$90,000 a year. There are about 20 companies that specialize in the detection and removal of land mines. Kuwait spent about US$1 billion to clean up the 7 million land mines sewn during the five-month occupation of Kuwait by Iraq; 83 mine clearance experts have been killed just in Kuwait. If you are looking for big money, be aware that local minesweepers in Angola make only US$70 a day.

Explosive Ordnance Disposal
World Services

Fort Walton Beach, FL
☎ *(904) 864-3454*

UXB

Chantilly, VA
☎ *(703) 803-8904*

Ronco

Berkeley, CA
☎ *(510) 548-3922*

Royal Ordnance

London, England
☎ *[44] (81) 012-52-37-32-32*

Navy SEAL

Specialists in Naval Special Warfare, the SEALs (SEa Air, Land) evolved from the frogman of WWII. The SEALs have been glorified in films and books. Their most recent brush with fame was their less-than-secret invasion of Kuwait City, with the world's press watching and filming with high-powered camera lights.

In 1989 the SEALs were the first into Panama, using rebreathers and midget subs. In the Gulf War they even used custom-made dune buggies to operate behind enemy lines.

The SEALs go through 25 weeks of training, either in Coronado, in San Diego or on the East Coast. The training starts with extreme physical and mental abuse. The focus is on teamwork and surviving the constant harassment. The first test is hell week, six days of misery and physical torture with little or no sleep. Then there is extensive classroom and underwater training in SCUBA (Self Contained Underwater Breathing Apparatus) diving. This phase ends with another serious physical challenge. The third and final phase is the UDT and above-water training on San Clemente Island.

SEAL teams must practice close-quarter battle drills by firing 300 or more rounds of 9-mm ammunition weekly. Each of the six-line SEAL teams is given 1.5 million rounds of ammunition annually to train its five 16-man platoons. According to the specs on their Beretta 92F pistols, this means they burn out one handgun a year. Their MP5 machine guns last a little longer.

If you just want to look like a SEAL you can shop at the same place SEALs shop. Be the first on your block to wear a shirt that says "Pain is just weakness leaving your body." **Bullshirts**, *1007 Orange Avenue, Coronado, CA 92118.*

U.S. Navy Human Resources

> *2531 Jefferson Davis Highway*
> *Arlington, VA 22242-5161*
> ☎ *(703) 607-3023*

Smoke Jumper

If the thought of being parachuted into a raging inferno and having to fight your way back until you can be airlifted out many sleepless nights later appeals to you, then you should try smoke jumping. Smoke jumpers are firefighters who must be in the air within 10 minutes and parachute into remote areas to fight fires. Dropped from small planes as low as 1500 feet in altitude, they quickly must hike to the scene of the fire, and instantly begin to chop and backburn areas to head off forest fires before they get too big. The work is all manual and requires strength, endurance and an ability to work around the clock if need be.

Most smoke jumpers are attracted by the danger and the camaraderie these jobs afford. They are known to be party animals, close friends and hard workers

Although the death of 14 firefighters in Glenwood Springs, Colorado, on July 6, 1994, reminded people that smoke jumping is dangerous, that there are only 387 smoke jumpers in the U.S. makes those deaths even more significant. The last time any smoke jumpers were killed actually fighting a fire was in 1949 during the Mann Gulch blaze in Montana. During this 45-year period of calm, one jumper pancaked into the ground due to chute failure and another hanged himself when he tried to get out of a tree where he had landed.

Like most dangerous jobs, the goal is to stay alive and healthy, and you definitely don't do it for the money. Pay for smoke jumpers starts at about $9 an hour, and there is additional pay during fires and with overtime. Most are part-time jumpers who earn the money during the hot summer fire season.

There are nine U.S. Forest Service and Bureau of Land Management regional jumper bases in the West. The supervisors react quickly to fires and send in anywhere from two or more jumpers, depending on the size of the fire. If a lightning strike starts a small blaze, fire jumpers can deal with it quickly and effectively before calling in the water bombers. Supplies can be parachuted in as soon as the jumpers are on the ground. Once done, the jumpers then get to hike out with their equipment or be picked up by helicopter.

Training requires federal certification to fell large trees and to be able to climb in and more likely, out of trees. They maintain their own chain saws and other equipment. Their protective Kevlar suits hold their equipment and protect them when landing in trees. Forest Service jumpers use round chutes and jump at 1500 feet BLM; smoke jumpers use the more modern rectangular chutes and exit at 3000 feet.

Northern California Service Center

Redding, CA
☎ *(916) 246-5467*

Redmond Air Center

Redmond, OR
☎ *(503) 548-5070*

Aerial Fire Depot

Missoula, MT
☎ *(406) 329-3402* ext. *4893*

Payette Wildlife Center

McCall, ID
☎ *(208) 634-0700*

U.N. Peacekeeper

Not many soldiers ask to be U.N. peacekeepers, and they usually find the idea of talking to a highly trained killer and making him Ghandi for a day even stranger. It's tough enough trying to figure out why someone is trying to kill his closest neighbor, or in our case, why we send pimply kids thousands of miles to whomp Third World revolutionaries. Being a U.N. peacekeeper means wearing silly blue berets and driving around in white trucks. You can be shot at, but you can't shoot back. You can be insulted, but you can't insult back. In fact, you may find yourself actually helping people kill their enemy as you protect war criminals, maintain archaic political boundaries and provide security for execution squads. You will come under shell fire, and gun fire and have to keep up with deadly bureaucratic paperwork. In Bosnia, Canadians were told to return mines they dug up to the armies that planted them. Some scratched their initials on the casings and dug up the same mines weeks later. They must use photodegradable sandbags, and the rules of engagement are so Byzantine that it requires hours to get official clearances to shoot back when they come under fire.

United Nations

Field Operations Staffing
42nd Street and First Avenue, Room 52280-D
New York, NY
☎ *(212) 963-1147*

Construction Specialists Wanted

For those who like the excitement of going into war zones with a slide rule, Brown and Root of Houston, Texas, may have a job for you. Not a military firm or even one that engages in any military activity, Brown and Root is an engineering firm owned by Halliburton. They specialize in infrastructure work, the mundane job of building sewers, pipelines and other necessary items required to restore shattered economies. The boss of this outfit is none other than Dick Cheney, former secretary of defense. Brown and Root does its work in places like Somalia, Haiti and The Balkans. For more information, call Brown and Root at ☎ (713) 676-4141.

Dangerous Diseases

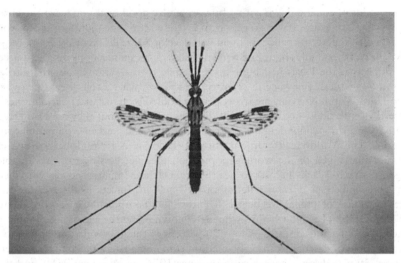

My favorite method of camping in East Africa is flat on my back under the stars. The soft wind carries past scents of the African savanna. I have spent nights listening to the lions bellow and cough their disapproval at the intruder's gall. Later, the sound of hyenas screaming and fighting raises the hair on the back of my neck even more. During the night I know the leopards will come unseen and unheard, leaving only footprints around our campsite as evidence. But the only thing I am afraid of is the sound of mosquitoes sucking my blood and possibly infecting me with deadly or disabling diseases.

Each time I stop in at my doctor's office (a tropical disease specialist with time in Vietnam), he asks me why the hell I do what I do. Yet, he takes great pains to describe the symptoms of the many and sundry tropical diseases that await me in the Third World. His lectures usually center around the lifelong pain and debilitation that can be inflicted on travelers who inadvertently ingest an amoeba, get bitten by a mosquito or become the host for a degenerative bug. I take his advice seriously, and I am as fastidious as I can be in adverse conditions. I am very careful about what I eat and how I sleep, and I follow the rules of common sense when it comes to avoiding infection. Despite this, I have spent nights shivering and delirious, lying in puddles of my own sweat on cement floors in the Sahara desert. I pay his bill gladly and trust to the cosmos and good common sense.

With this in mind, do not assume that this chapter is the be-all end-all reference source for tropical diseases. *Always confer with a specialist before taking any trip.* This way, you understand the odds and the penalties and can make an educated decision on the risks involved. Secondly, *always have full medical tests upon your return.* This means giving a little bit of yourself to the lab to run blood, stool and urine tests. Your doctor may ask you to come back again due to the long incubation time of some of these nasties. This is not hypochondria but common sense. Many people are terrified of taking an HIV test thinking that some '80s dalliance may make them a pariah. The truth is, early detection in all diseases will increase your odds of successful treatment and in the worst case allow for a better understanding of your chances.

The odds of coming down with a bug are pretty good once you leave the antiseptic Western world. If you go off on an extended trip (one month or more) you have a 60–75 percent chance that you will develop some illness or problem, most likely is diarrhea. Only about one percent will pick up an infectious disease. I used to think that the locals had built up resistance to the various bugs that strike down Westerners. But once in-country, you realize what a toll disease takes on the Third World. Not only are many people riddled with malaria, river blindness, intestinal infections, hepatitis, sexual diseases and more, but they are also faced with malnutrition, poor dental care, toxic chemicals and hard environmental conditions. The World Health Organization (WHO), in its 1995 global survey, reported that much of the world's population dies needlessly from preventable diseases due to a lack of access to health care. Of the 52 million people who died in 1995, infectious diseases killed about 17 million. Infectious diseases are the leading cause of premature death in Africa and Southeast Asia, according to WHO. Of the 11 million victims who are children under the age of five, 9 million died from infectious diseases. About 70 percent of the deaths attributed to cholera, typhoid or dysentery can be blamed on contaminated food. To make matters worse, 30 new diseases have sprung up since 1976, among them AIDS and the deadly Ebola virus. Antibiotics are becoming less and less effective in treating many of these diseases, because of resistance due to their overuse.

Malaria

Malaria is a very dangerous disease, affecting 500 million people worldwide and killing at least 2 million people every year. The mosquito-borne disease is found in 102 countries and threatens 40 percent of the world's population.

Over a million people in Africa are killed by malaria every year. Two million people died from it in 1993, according to WHO. More than 30,000 European and American travelers will come down with Malaria this year.

The female *Anopheles* mosquito is small, pervasive and hungry for your blood, and likes to bite in the cool hours before and after sunset. As they seek out blood to nurture their own procreation, they leave the Plasmodium parasites in your blood system. The symptoms can start with a flulike attack, followed by fever and chills, then lead to failure of multiple organs and then death. In many cases, the symptoms of malaria do not start until the traveler has returned home and is in a nonmalarial zone. Remember that current chemoprophylaxis does not prevent malaria. Larium, Fansidar, and chloroquinine can lower the chances of getting malaria but do not provide any guarantee of being malaria-proof. Two of my fellow travelers (one in Africa and one in Borneo) did not realize they had malaria, because they believed that Larium would protect them from the disease. Luckily, they sought treatment in time.

Malaria is a very real and common danger in most tropical countries. Most malaria in Asian and African areas is quinine-resistant and requires multiple or more creative dosages to avoid the horrors often associated with the disease. The most vicious strain of malaria (*Plasmodium falciparum*) attacks your liver and red blood cells, creating massive fevers, coma, acute kidney failure, and eventually death. There are three other types of malaria in the world: *Plasmodium malariae, Plasmodium vivax* and *Plasmodium ovale* (found only in West Africa).

The *Anopheles* mosquito is the most dangerous insect in the world, and there are few contenders for its crown. Other biting insects that can cause you grief include the *Aedes aegypti* mosquito, which carries yellow fever. His kissing cousins, the *Culex, Haemogogus, Sabethes* and *Mansonia*, can give you filariasis, viral encephalitis, dengue and other great hemorrhagic fevers. Next on the list are tsetse flies, fleas, ticks, sandflies, mites and lice. We won't even bother to discuss wasps, horseflies, African killer bees, deerflies, or other clean biters.

These insects are an everyday part of life in tropical Third World countries. They infect major percentages of the local population, and it is only a matter of time and luck before you become a victim.

Prevention is rather simple but often ineffective. Protect yourself from insects by wearing long-sleeved shirts and long pants. Use insect repellent, sleep under a mosquito net, avoid swampy areas, use mosquito coils, don't sleep directly on the ground, check yourself for tick and insect bites daily and, last but not least, understand the symptoms and treatment of these diseases so that you can seek immediate treatment, no matter what part of the world you are in.

The Gift That Keeps On Giving	
Disease	**Annual Deaths**
Infected by malaria	500 million
Infected by HIV	20 million
Infected by AIDS	4.5 million
Acute respiratory infections	4.4 million
Diarrheal Diseases	3.1 million
Tuberculosis	3 million
Malaria	2 million
AIDS	1 million

Worms

My least favorite are the helminthic infections, or diseases caused by intestinal worms. Unlike the more dramatic and deadly diseases, these parasites are easily caught through ingestion of bad water and food and cause long-term damage. Just to let you know what's out there, you can choose from angiostrongyliasis, herring worm, roundworm, schistsomiasis, capillariasis, pin worm, oriental liver fluke, fish tapeworm, guinea worm, cat liver fluke, tapeworm, trechinellosis and the ominous-sounding giant intestinal fluke (who's eating who here?). All these little buggers create havoc with your internal organs, and some will make the rest of your life miserable as well. Your digestive system will be shot and your organs under constant attack, and the treatment or removal of these buggers is downright depressing. All this can be prevented by maintaining absolutely rigid standards in what you throw or breathe into your body. Not easy since most male travelers find wearing a biohazard suit a major impediment to picking up chicks or doing the limbo.

Think of yourself as a sponge, your lungs as an air filter, and all the moist cavities of your body as ideal breeding grounds for tropical diseases. It is better to think like Howard Hughes than Pig Pen when it comes to personal hygiene.

The Fevers

The classic tropical diseases that incapacitated Stanley, Livingstone, Burton and Speke are the hemorrhagic fevers. Many of these diseases kill, but most make your life a living hell and then disappear. Some come back on a regular basis. It is surprising that most of the African explorers lived to a ripe old age. The hemorrhagic fevers are carried by mosquitoes, ticks, rats, feces or even airborne dust that gets into your bloodstream, and let you die a slow, demented death, as your blood turns so thin it trickles out your nose, gums, skin and eyes. Coma and death can occur in the second week. There are so many versions that they just name them after the places where you will stumble across them. Needless to say, these are not featured in any glossy brochures for the various regions. Assorted blood-thinning killers are called Chikungunya, Crimean, Congo, Omsk, Kyasanur Forest, Korean, Manchurian, Songo, Ebola, Argentinian, Hantaan, Lassa and yellow fever.

The recent outbreaks of the Hanta and Ebola viruses in the U.S. have proved that North America is not immune from these insect-, rodent- and airborne afflictions. So far, the Ebola Reston virus has only been found in monkeys sent by a Philippine supplier. All monkeys exposed to the virus were destroyed, and officials from the Centers for Disease Control reassured the public that Ebola Reston is a different virus from Ebola Zaire, the strain that killed 244 people in Zaire last year. Still, experts warn that the Ebola Reston strain could mutate into a strain that is fatal to humans. The outbreak of plague in India also has travelers a little edgy about the whole concept of adventurous travel. There are real dangers in every part of the world and the more knowledgeable you are about them the better your chances for surviving.

Sex

The quest for sexual adventure used to be a major part of the joy of travel. Today, the full range of sexual diseases available to the common traveler would fill an encyclopedia. Despite the continual global publicity on the dangers of AIDS, it continues to claim victims at an alarming rate. Whorehouses around the world have not gone out of business, junkies still share needles, and dentists in many Third World countries still grind and yank away with improperly sterilized instruments. Diseases like HIV, Hepatitis B and other sexually transmitted diseases that Westerners blame on the Third World, and the Third World blames on the West, are very preventable and require parking your libido. Sexually transmitted diseases are a growing health hazard. According to WHO, 236 million people have trichomoniasis and 94 million new cases occur each year. Chlamydial infections affect 162 million people, with 97 million new cases annually. And these figures don't include the increasing millions with genital warts, gonorrhea, genital herpes and syphilis. The highest rates for sexually transmitted diseases are in the 20–24 age group, followed by 15–19 and 25–29. In many countries, more than 60 percent of all new HIV infections are among the 15–24 age group.

How do you avoid sexually transmitted diseases, some people ask? Well, keeping your romantic agenda on the platonic side is a good start. The use of condoms is the next best thing. Realistically the chances of catching AIDS through unprotected sex depends on frequency and type of contact. People infected by blood transfusions, prostitutes, frequent drug users, hemophiliacs, homosexuals, and the millions of people who will get HIV this year from heterosexual sex will continue to make HIV a growing danger.

AIDS

Perhaps the most dangerous and publicized disease is AIDS. It strikes right at the heart of American phobia—pain for pleasure. AIDS is the terminal phase of HIV (Human immunodeficiency virus). HIV is usually the precursor to AIDS, and then the victim succumbs to death by cancer, pneumonia and other afflictions that attack the weakened human immune system. AIDS has roughly a nine-year incubation period.

Initially brushed aside as "the gay plague" or an "African disease," AIDS has in the last few years become the biggest killer of young American men and women. Washington, D.C., has the nation's highest AIDS rate, far higher than even New York or San Francisco, according to statistics released by the Centers for Disease Control and Prevention. The 1995 D.C. rate was 185.7 AIDS cases per 100,000 residents. Puerto Rico was second with a rate of 70.3 cases per 100,000, followed by New York, Florida and New Jersey. Nationwide, the rate of AIDS cases is 27.8 cases per 100,000. The CDC says that AIDS is spreading more among women and minorities now, while the epidemic among homosexual white men has slowed. Women accounted for 19 percent of all AIDS cases among adults and adolescents nationwide. A growing number of children are being orphaned by AIDS, which has become the leading cause of death among women of childbearing age in the United States, according to a study in the *Journal of the American Medical Association*. Experts project that about 144,000 children and young adults will have lost their mothers to AIDS by the year 2000. Blacks are six times more likely to have AIDS than whites and twice as likely to have AIDS as Hispanics.

As sobering as the U.S. statistics are, the rate of deaths caused by AIDS in other countries is alarming. The number of AIDS cases worldwide reported to the World Health Organization by governments reached 1,025,073 by January 1995. WHO said that chronic underreporting and underdiagnosis in developing countries means the actual figure is probably more than 4.5 million. More than 70 percent of the estimated cases were in Africa, 9 percent in the United States, 9 percent in the rest of the American hemisphere, 6 percent in Asia, and 4 percent in Europe. The statistics include only people with active cases of AIDS or those who have died from the disease.

An estimated one million Latin Americans could have AIDS by the turn of the century, according to the Pan American Health Organization. The group says HIV is increasing among women in the Caribbean and Central America and it is expected to increase rapidly, particularly in areas where injection drug use is prevalent. There are currently 2 million HIV-infected people in Latin America and the Caribbean. According to Italy's statistics institute, ISTAT, AIDS has become as big a killer in Italy as road accidents. An estimated 4370 Italians died from AIDS last year, compared to 6000 deaths on the roads. For young males between 18 and 29 in Italy, AIDS has overtaken drugs as the second leading cause of death. ISTAT estimates that the number of HIV-infected Italians is at least 100,000. AIDS is also on the increase in smaller countries. WHO estimates that at least 400,000 or one percent of Myanmar's citizens are infected with HIV. A high number of injection drug users, social tolerance of prostitution and large amounts of cross-border trade with nearby nations make Myanmar's populace more vulnerable. Condoms are also costly and rarely used in Myanmar, exacerbating the problem.

Ministry of Health statistics show that more than 100,000 residents of Zimbabwe have died of AIDS-related causes in the past decade. Another 100,000 or one percent of the country's population is expected to succumb to AIDS in the next year and a half. AIDS is expected to slow population growth, lower life expectancies and raise child mortality rates in many of the world's poorer countries over the next 25 years, according to a report by the U.S. Census Bureau.

By the year 2010, a Ugandan's life expectancy will decline by 45 percent to 32 years—down from 59 years projected before AIDS. A Haitian's life expectancy will fall to 44 years, also down from 59 years. Life expectancy in Thailand will drop from a projected 75 years to 45. By the year 2010, Thailand's child mortality rates are expected to increase from the current 20 deaths per 1000 children born to 110 deaths. In Uganda, the jump will be from 90 deaths to 175 deaths out of every 1000 children born. In Malawi, it will soar from 130 to 210 deaths per 1000. Overall, premature death rates in those countries will double by 2010 compared with 1985 levels.

In 16 countries—the African nations of Burkina Faso, Burundi, Central African Republic, Congo, Cote d'Ivoire, Kenya, Malawi, Rwanda, Tanzania, Uganda, Zaire, Zambia and Zimbabwe, plus Brazil, Haiti and Thailand—AIDS will slow population growth rates so dramatically that by 2010, there will be 121 million fewer people than previously forecast. Thailand's population will actually fall by nearly one percent because of AIDS deaths.

"Zoonosis"

According to journalists, AIDS first began near the Zaire-Burundi border, but did it? A 1992 Rolling Stone *article by AIDS activist Blaine Elswood places the blame on polio vaccines grown in primate kidney cells and then injected into humans in 1957 and 1958. Other researchers had injected malaria-tainted blood from chimpanzees and mangabeys into human volunteers. The first AIDS case was reportedly a British sailor (who had never been to Africa) who died in 1959. The case wasn't officially recognized by the Centers for Disease Control until 1981.*

There are two types of human AIDS virus: HIV-1, the most common type, and HIV-2, originally found only in people from Guinea-Bissau in West Africa. HIV-2 is very close to SIV (Simian immunodeficiency virus) found in sooty mangabeys. Curiously, SIV is not found in the Asian macaques normally used for research. Sooty mangabeys are commonly eaten by villagers in Africa. There is no hard proof that AIDS came from monkeys or even from Africa, but the preponderance of evidence shows that AIDS may have originated in Central Africa within the past 30 years. AIDS continues to mutate as new strains continue to appear in West Africa and Asia.

Old-Fashioned Diseases

Many travelers are quite surprised to find themselves coming down with measles or mumps while traveling. Unlike the U.S., which has eradicated much of the childhood and preventable viruses through inoculation, the rest of the world is more concerned about feeding than vaccinating their children. The recent outbreak of plague in India is a good example of what you should watch out for. Whooping cough, mumps, measles, polio and tuberculosis are common in Third World countries. (Measles claimed the lives of 1.1 million in 1995.) Although some of the symptoms are minor, complications can lead to lifelong afflictions. Make sure you are vaccinated against these easily preventable diseases.

But don't just run off to be the next bubble boy and spend the rest of your life in a hermetically sealed dome. For travelers, these diseases are relatively rare and avoidable. To put the whole thing in perspective, the most common complaint tends to be diarrhea, followed by a cold (usually the result of lowered resistance caused by fatigue, dehydration, foreign microbes and stress). The important thing is to recognize when you are sick versus very sick. Tales of turn-of-the-century explorers struck down by a tiny mosquito bite are now legend. Malaria is still a very real and common threat. Just for fun, bring back a sample of local river water from your next trip and have the medical lab analyze it. You may never drink water of any kind again.

This is not to say that as soon as you get off the plane you will automatically be struck down with Ebola River fever and have blood oozing out from your eyes. You can travel bug-free and suffer no more than a cold caused by the air conditioning in your hotel room. But it is important to at least understand the relative risks and gravity of some diseases.

The diseases listed on the following pages are important, and you should be conversant with both symptoms and cures. Please do not assume that this is medical advice. It is designed to give you an overview of the various nasties that possibly await you.

Tropical countries are the most likely to cause you bacterial grief. Keep in mind that most of these diseases are a direct result of poor hygiene, travel in infected areas and contact with infected people. In other words, stay away from people if you want to stay healthy. Secondly, follow the common sense practice of having all food cooked freshly and properly. Many books tell you to wash fruit and then forget to mention that the water is probably more filled with bugs than the fruit. Peel all fruits and vegetables, and approach anything you stick in your body with a healthy level of skepticism and distrust. If you are completely anal, you can exist on freeze-dried foods, Maggi Mee (noodles), fresh fruit (peeled, remember) and tinned food.

It is considered wise to ask local experts about dangers that await. If you do not feel right for any reason, contact a local doctor. It is not advisable to enter a medical treatment program while in a developing country. There are greater chances of you catching worse afflictions once you are in the hospital. Ask for temporary medication and then get your butt back to North America or Europe.

Remember that the symptoms of many tropical diseases may not take effect until you are home and back into your regular schedule. It is highly advisable that you contact a tropical disease specialist and have full testing done (stool, urine, blood, physical) just to be sure. Very few American doctors are conversant with the many tropical diseases by virtue of their rarity. This is not their fault, since many tourists do not even realize that they have taken trips or cruises into endemic zones. People can catch malaria on a plane between London and New York from a stowaway mosquito that just came in from Bombay. Many people come in close contact with foreigners in buses and subways and on the street from Los Angeles to New York. Don't assume you have to be up to your neck in Laotian pig wallows to be at risk.

Many labs do not do tests for some of the more exotic bugs. Symptoms can also be misleading. It is possible that you may be misdiagnosed or mistreated if you do not fully discuss the possible reasons for your medical condition. Now that we have scared the hell out of you, your first contact should be with the Centers for Disease Control in Atlanta.

African Sleeping Sickness (African Trypanosomiasis)

Found: Tropical Africa.

Cause: A tiny protozoan parasite that emits a harmful toxin.

Carrier: Tsetse fly. Tsetse flies are large biting insects about the size of a horsefly found in East and West Africa.

Symptoms: Eastern trypanosomiasis: two–31 days after the bite recurrent episodes of fever, headaches and malaise. Can lead to death in two to six weeks. Western trypanosomiasis: produces a skin ulcer within five to 10 days after being bitten. The symptoms then disappear in two to three weeks. Symptoms reappear six months to five years after the initial infection, resulting in fevers, headaches, rapid heartbeat, swelling of the lymph glands located in the back of the neck, personality changes, tremors, a lackadaisical attitude, and then stupor leading eventually to death.

Treatment: Suramin (Bayer (205), pentamidine (Lomodine), melarasoprol (Mel B)

How to avoid: Do not travel to infested areas, use insect repellent, wear light-colored clothing, and cover skin areas.

AIDS (Acquired Immune Deficiency Syndrome)

Found: Worldwide.

Cause: Advanced stage of HIV (Human Immunodeficiency Syndrome), which causes destruction of the natural resistance of humans to infection and other diseases. Death by AIDS is usually a result of unrelated diseases which rapidly attack the victim. These ranges of diseases are called ARC (AIDS-related complex).

Carrier: Sexual intercourse with infected person, transfusion of infected blood, or even from infected mother through breast milk. There is no way to determine if someone has HIV, except by blood test. Male homosexuals, drug users and prostitutes are high-risk groups in major urban centers in the West. AIDS is less selective in developing countries, with Central and Eastern Africa being the areas of highest incidence.

Symptoms: Fever, weight loss, fatigue, night sweats, lymph node problems. Infection by other opportunistic elements such as Karposi's sarcoma and pneumonia are highly probable and will lead to death.

Treatment: There is no known cure.

How to avoid: Use condoms, refrain from sexual contact, and do not receive injections or transfusions in questionable areas. Avoid live vaccines such as gamma globulin and Hepatitis B in developing countries.

Amebiasis

Found: Worldwide.

Cause: A protozoan parasite carried in human fecal matter. Usually found in areas with poor sanitation.

Carrier: *Entamoeba histolyica* is passed by poor hygiene. Ingested orally in water, air or food that has come in contact with the parasite.

Symptoms: The infection will spread from the intestines and causes abscesses in other organs such as liver, lungs and brain.

Treatment: Metronidazole, iodoquinol, diloxanide furoate, paromomycin, tetracycline plus chloroquinine base.

How to avoid: Avoid uncooked foods, boil water, drink bottled liquids, be sure that food is cooked properly and peel fruits and vegetables.

Bartonellosis (Oroya Fever, Carrion's Disease)

Found: In valleys of Peru, Ecuador and Colombia.

Cause: *Bartonella bacilliformis*, a bacterium.

Carrier: Sandflies that bite at night.

Symptoms: Pain in muscles, joints and bones along with fever occurring within three weeks of being bitten. Oroya fever causes a febrile fever leading to possible death. *Verruga peruana* creates skin eruptions.

Treatment: Antibiotics with transfusion for symptoms of anemia.

How to avoid: High boots, groundsheets, hammocks and insect repellent.

Brucellosis (Undulant Fever)

Found: Worldwide.

Cause: Ingestion of infected dairy products

Carrier: Untreated dairy products infected with the brucellosis bacteria.

Symptoms: Intermittent fever, sweating, jaundice, rash, depression, enlarged spleen and lymph nodes. The symptoms may disappear and go into permanent remission after three to six months.

Treatment: Tetracyclines, sulfonamides and streptomycin.

How to avoid: Drink pasteurized milk. Avoid infected livestock.

Chagas' Disease (American Trypanosomiasis)

Found: Central and South America.

Cause: Protozoan parasite carried in the feces of insects.

Carrier: Kissing or Assassin bugs (Triatoma insects or reduviid bugs). Commonly found in homes with thatched roofs. It can also be transmitted through blood transfusions, breast milk and in utero.

Symptoms: A papule and swelling at the location of the bite, fever, malaise, anorexia, rash, swelling of the limbs, gastrointestinal problems, heart irregularities and heart failure.

Treatment: Nifurtimox (Bayer 2502).

How to avoid: Do not stay in native villages; use bed netting and insect repellent.

Cholera

Found: Worldwide; primarily developing countries.

Cause: Intestinal infection caused by the toxin Vibrio Cholerae O group bacteria.

Carrier: Infected food and water contaminated by human and animal waste.

Symptoms: Watery diarrhea, abdominal cramps, nausea, vomiting and severe dehydration as a result of diarrhea. Can lead to death if fluids are not replaced.

Treatment: Tetracycline can hasten recovery. Replace fluids using an electrolyte solution.

How to avoid: Vaccinations before trip can diminish symptoms up to 50 percent for a period of three to six months. A threat in refugee camps or areas of poor sanitation. Use standard precautions with food and drink in developing countries.

Chikungunya Disease

Found: Sub-Saharan Africa, Southeast Asia, India, Philippines in sporadic outbreaks.

Cause: Alphavirus transmitted by mosquito bites.

Carrier: Mosquitoes who transmit the disease from the host (monkeys).

Symptoms: Joint pain with potential for hemorrhagic symptoms.

Treatment: None, but symptoms will disappear. If hemorrhagic, avoid aspirin.

How to avoid: Standard precautions to avoid mosquito bites: Use insect repellent and mosquito nets, and cover exposed skin areas.

Ciguatera Poisoning

Found: Tropical areas.

Cause: Ingestion of fish containing the toxin produced by the *dinoflagellate Gambierdiscus toxicus.*

Carrier: 425 species of tropical reef fish.

Symptoms: Up to six hours after eating, victims may experience nausea, watery diarrhea, abdominal cramps, vomiting, abnormal sensation in limbs and teeth, hot-cold flashes, joint pain, weakness, skin rashes and itching. In very severe cases victims may experience blind spells, low blood pressure and heart rate, paralysis and loss of coordination. Symptoms may appear years later.

Treatment: There is no specific medical treatment other than first aid. Induce vomiting.

How to avoid: Do not eat reef fish (including sea bass, barracuda, red snapper or grouper).

Colorado Tick Fever

Found: North America.

Cause: Arbovirus transmitted by insect or infected blood.

Carrier: The wood tick *(Dermacentor andersoni);* also through transfusion of infected blood.

Symptoms: Aching of muscles in back and legs, chills, recurring fever, headaches, eye pain, fear of brightly lit area.

Treatment: Since symptoms only last about three weeks, medication or treatment is intended to relieve symptoms.

How to avoid: Ticks are picked up when walking through woods. Wear leggings, tall boots and insect repellent.

Dengue Fever (Breakbone Fever)

Found: South America, Africa, South Pacific, Asia, Mexico, Central America, Caribbean.

Cause: An arbovirus transmitted by mosquitoes.

Carrier: Mosquitoes in tropical areas, which usually bite during the daytime.

Symptoms: Two distinct periods. First period consists of severe muscle and joint aches and headaches combined with high fever (the origin of the term "break bone fever"). The second phase is sensitivity to light, diarrhea, vomiting, nausea, mental depression and enlarged lymph nodes.

Treatment: Designed to relieve symptoms. Aspirin should be avoided due to hemorrhagic complications.

How to avoid: Typical protection against daytime mosquito bites: using insect repellent with high DEET levels, wearing light-colored long-sleeve pants and shirts.

Diarrhea

Found: Worldwide.

Cause: There are many reasons for travelers to have the symptoms of diarrhea. It is important to remember that alien bacteria in the digestive tract is the main culprit. Most travelers to Africa, Mexico, South America and the Middle East will find themselves doubled up in pain, running for the nearest stinking toilet and wondering why the hell they ever left their comfortable home.

Carrier: Bacteria from food, the air, water or other people can be the cause. Dehydration from long airplane flights, strange diets, stress and high altitude can also cause diarrhea. It is doubtful you will ever get to know your intestinal bacteria on a first name basis, but *Aeromonas hydrophila*, Campylobacter, *jejuni Pleisiomonas*, salmonellae, shigellae, shielloides, *Vibrio cholerae* (non-01), *Vibrio parahaemolyticus*, *Yersinia enterocoliticia* and *Escherichia coli* are the most likely culprits. All these bugs would love to spend a week or two in your gut.

Symptoms: Loose stools, stomach pains, bloating, fever and malaise.

Treatment: First step is to stop eating and ingest plenty of fluids and salty foods; secondly, try Kaopectate or Pepto Bismol. If diarrhea persists after three to four days, seek medical advice.

How to avoid: Keep your fluid intake high when traveling. Follow common sense procedures when eating, drinking and ingesting any food or fluids. Remember to wash your hands carefully and frequently, since you can transmit a shocking number of germs from your hands to your mouth, eyes and nose.

Diphtheria

Found: Worldwide

Cause: The bacterium *Corynebacterium diptheriae*, a producer of harmful toxins that is usually a problem in populations that have not been immunized against diphtheria.

Carrier: Infected humans can spread the germs by sneezing, or contact.

Symptoms: Swollen diphtheritic membrane which may lead to serious congestion. Other symptoms are pallor, listlessness, weakness and increased heart rate. May cause death due to weakened heart or shock.

Treatment: Immunization with the DPT vaccine at an early age (three years) is the ideal prevention; treatment with antitoxin, if not.

How to avoid: Avoid close contact with populations or areas where there is little to no vaccination program for diphtheria.

Ebola River Fever

Found: Among local populations in Zaire.

Cause: A very rare but much publicized affliction.

Carrier: Unknown, but highly contagious. In 1989 the virus was found in lab monkeys in Reston, Virginia. The monkeys were quickly destroyed. At press time, an outbreak in Zaire was rampant.

Symptoms: The virus is described as melting people down, causing blood clotting, loss of consciousness and death.

Treatment: None.

How to avoid: Unknown.

Encephalitis

Found: Southeast Asia, Korea, Taiwan, Nepal, Eastern CIS countries and Eastern Europe.

Cause: A common viral infection carried by insects.

Carrier: The disease can be carried by the tick or mosquito. The risk is high during late summer and fall. The most dangerous strain is tickborne encephalitis transmitted by ticks in the summer in the colder climates of Russia, Scandinavia, Switzerland and France.

Symptoms: Fever, headache, muscle pain, malaise, runny nose and sore throat followed by lethargy, confusion, hallucination and seizures. About one-fifth of encephalitis infections have led to death.

Treatment: A vaccine is available.

How to avoid: Avoid areas known to be endemic. Avoid tick-infested areas such as forests, rice growing areas in Asia (mosquitoes) or areas that have large number of domestic pigs (tick carriers). Use insect repellent. Do not drink unpasteurized milk.

Filariasis (Lymphatic, River Blindness)

Found: Africa, Central America, Caribbean, South America, Asia.

Cause: A group of diseases caused by long, thin roundworms carried by mosquitoes.

Carrier: Mosquitoes and biting flies in tropical areas.

Symptoms: Lymphatic filariasis, onchocerciasis (river blindness), loiasis and mansonellasis all have similar and very unpleasant symptoms. Fevers, headaches, nausea, vomiting, sensitivity to light, inflammation in the legs including the abdomen and testicles, swelling of the abdomen, joints and scrotum, enlarged lymph nodes, abscesses, eye lesions that lead to blindness, rashes, itches and arthritis.

Treatment: Diethylcarbamazine (DEC, Hetrazan, Notezine) is the usual treatment.

How to avoid: Avoid bites by insects with usual protective measures and insect repellent.

Flukes

Found: Caribbean, South America, Africa, Asia.

Cause: The liver fluke *(Clonorchis sinensis)* and the lung fluke *(Paragonimus westermani)* which lead to paragonimasis.

Carrier: Carried in fish that has not been properly cooked.

Symptoms: Obstruction of the bile system, along with fever, pain, jaundice, gallstones, inflammation of the pancreas. There is further risk of cancer of the bile tract after infection. Paragonimasis affects the lungs and causes chest pains.

Treatment: Paragonimasis is treated with Prazanquantel. Obstruction of the bile system can require surgery.

How to avoid: To avoid liver flukes do not eat uncooked or improperly cooked fish— something most sushi fans will decry. Paragonimasis is found in uncooked shellfish, like freshwater crabs, crayfish and shrimp.

Giardiasis

Found: Worldwide.

Cause: A protozoa *Giardi lamblia* that causes diarrhea.

Carrier: Ingestion of food or water that is contaminated with fecal matter.

Symptoms: Very sudden diarrhea, severe flatulence, cramps, nausea, anorexia, weight loss and fever.

Treatment: Giardiasis can disappear without treatment, but Furazolidone, metronidizole, or quinacrine HCI is the usual method of treatment.

How to avoid: Cleanliness, drinking bottled water, and strict personal hygiene in eating and personal contact.

Guinea Worm Infection (Dracontiasis, Dracunculiasis)

Found: Tropical areas like the Caribbean, the Guianas, Africa, the Middle East and Asia.

Cause: Ingestion of waterborne nematode *Dracunculus medinensis*.

Carrier: Water systems that harbor *Dracunculus medinensis*.

Symptoms: Fever, itching, swelling around the eyes, wheezing, skin blisters and arthritis.

Treatment: Doses of niridazole, metronidazole or thiabendazole are the usual method. Surgery may be required to remove worms.

How to avoid: Drink only boiled or chemically treated water.

Hemorrhagic Fevers

Some of the more well-known hemorrhagic fevers are yellow fever, dengue, lassa fever and the horror movie–caliber Ebola fever. Outbreaks tend to be localized and subject to large populations of insects, or rats. Don't let the exotic-sounding names lull you into a false sense of security; there was a major outbreak in the American Southwest caused by rodents spreading the disease.

Found: Worldwide.

Cause: Intestinal worms carried by insects and rodents.

Carrier: Depending on the disease, it can be transmitted by mosquitoes, ticks and rodents (in urine and feces).

Symptoms: Headache, backache, muscle pain and conjunctivitis. Later on, the thinning of the blood will cause low blood pressure, bleeding from the gums and nose, vomiting and coughing up blood, blood in your stool, bleeding from the skin and hemorrhaging in the internal organs. Coma and death may occur in the second week.

Treatment: Consult a doctor or medical facility familiar with the local disease.

How to avoid: Avoid mosquitoes, ticks, and areas with high concentrations of mice and rats.

Hepatitis, A, B, Non-A, Non-B

Found: Worldwide.

Cause: A virus that attacks the liver. Hepatitis A, Non-B and Non-A can be brought on by poor hygiene; Hepatitis B is transmitted sexually or through infected blood.

Carrier: Hepatitis A is transmitted by oral-fecal route, person-to-person contact, or through contaminated food or water. Hepatitis B is transmitted by sexual activity or the transfer of bodily fluids. Hepatitis Non-A and Non-B are spread by contaminated water or from other people.

Symptoms: Muscle and joint pain, nausea, fatigue, sensitivity to light, sore throat, runny nose. Look for dark urine and clay-colored stools, jaundice along with liver pain and enlargement.

Treatment: Rest and a high-calorie diet. Immune Globulin is advised as a minor protection against Hepatitis A. You can be vaccinated against Hepatitis B.

How to avoid: Non-A and Non-B require avoiding infected foods. Hepatitis B requires avoiding unprotected sexual contact, unsterile needles, dental work and infusions. Hepatitis A requires proper hygiene and avoiding infected water and foods.

Hydatid Disease (Echinococcosis)

Found: Worldwide.

Cause: A tapeworm found in areas with high populations of pigs, cattle and sheep.

Carrier: Eggs of the echinococcosis.

Symptoms: Cysts form in organs in the liver, lungs, bone or brain.

Treatment: Surgery for removal of the infected cysts. Mebendazole and albendazole are used as well.

How to avoid: Boil water, cook foods properly and avoid infected areas.

Leishmaniasis

Found: Tropical and subtropical regions.

Cause: Protozoans of the genus Leishmania.

Carrier: Phlebotomine sandflies in tropical and subtropical regions.

Symptoms: Skin lesions, cutaneous ulcers, mucocutaneous ulcers in the mouth, nose and anus, as well as intermittent fever, anemia and enlarged spleen.

Treatment: Sodium stibogluconate, rifampin, and sodium antimony gluconate. Surgery is also used to remove cutaneous and mucocutaneous ulcers.

How to avoid: Use insect repellent, a ground cover when sleeping and bed nets, and cover arms and legs.

Leprosy (Hansen's Disease)

Found: Africa, India and elsewhere

Cause: The bacterium *Mycobacterium leprae* that infects the skin, eyes, nervous system and testicles.

Carrier: It is not known how leprosy is transmitted, but direct human contact is suspected.

Symptoms: Skin lesions, and nerve damage that progresses to loss of fingers and toes, blindness, difficulty breathing and nerve damage.

Treatment: Dapsone, rifampin and clofazimine.

How to avoid: Leprosy is a tropical disease, with over half the cases worldwide occurring in India and Africa. There is no known preventive method.

Loaisis

Found: West and Central Africa.

Cause: The loa loa parasite.

Carrier: Chrysops deer flies or tabanid flies in West and Central Africa.

Symptoms: Subcutaneous swellings that come and go, brain and heart inflammation.

Treatment: Diethylcarbamazine.

How to avoid: Deerflies are large, and their bites can be avoided by wearing full-sleeved shirts and thick pants. Hats and bandannas can protect head and neck areas.

Lyme Diseases

Found: Worldwide

Cause: A spirochete carried by ticks.

Carrier: The Ixodes tick, found worldwide and in great numbers during the summer. Ticks are found in rural areas and burrow into skin to suck blood.

Symptoms: A pronounced bite mark, flulike symptoms, severe headache, stiff neck, fever, chills, joint pain, malaise and fatigue.

Treatment: Tetracyclines, phenoxymethylpenicillin or erythromycin if caught early. Advanced cases may require intravenous penicillin.

How to avoid: Do not walk through wooded areas in the summer. Check for ticks frequently. Use leggings with insect repellent.

Malaria

Malaria is by far the most dangerous disease and the one most likely for travelers to pick up in Third World countries. Protection against this disease should be your first priority. As a rule, be leery of all riverine, swampy or tropical places. Areas such as logging camps, shantytowns, oases, campsites near slow moving water, and resorts near mangrove swamps are all very likely to be major areas of malarial infection. Consult with a local doctor to understand the various resistances and the prescribed treatment. Many foreign doctors are more knowledgeable about the cure and treatment of malaria than domestic doctors.

Found: Africa, Asia, Caribbean, Southeast Asia, the Middle East.

Cause: The Plasmodium parasite is injected into the victim while the mosquito draws blood.

Carrier: The female Anopheles mosquito.

Symptoms: Fever, chills, enlarged spleen in low-level versions; plasmodium falciparum, or cerebral malaria, can also cause convulsions, kidney failure and hypoglycemia.

Treatment: Chloroquinine, quinine, pyrimethamine, sulfadoxine and mefloquine. Note: Some people may have adverse reactions to all and any of these drugs.

How to avoid: Begin taking a malarial prophylaxis before your trip, as well as during and after (consult your doctor for a prescription). Avoid infected areas and protect yourself from mosquito bites (netting, insect repellent, mosquito coils, long-sleeve shirts and pants) especially during dusk and evening times.

Measles (Rubeola)

Found: Worldwide.

Cause: A common virus in unvaccinated areas.

Carrier: Sneezing, saliva and close contact with infected or unvaccinated humans.

Symptoms: Malaise, irritability, fever, conjunctivitis, swollen eyelids and hacking cough appear nine to 11 days after exposure. Fourteen days after exposure, the typical facial rash and spots appear.

Treatment: Measles will disappear, but complications can occur.

How to avoid: Vaccination or gamma globulin shots within five days of exposure.

Meliodosis

Found: Worldwide.

Cause: An animal disease (the bacillus *Pseudomonas pseudomallei*) that can be transferred to humans.

Carrier: Found in infected soil and water, and transmitted through skin wounds.

Symptoms: Various types, including fever, malaise, pneumonia, shortness of breath, headache, diarrhea, skin lesions, muscle pain and abscesses in organs.

Treatment: Antibiotics such as tetracyclines and sulfur drugs.

How to avoid: Clean and cover all wounds carefully.

Meningitis

Found: Africa, Saudi Arabia.

Cause: Bacteria: *Neisseria meningitis, Streptococcus pneumoniae* and *Haemophilus influenzae*. Children are at most risk. There are frequent outbreaks in Africa and Nepal.

Carrier: Inhaling infected droplets of nasal and throat secretions.

Symptoms: Fever, vomiting, headaches, confusion, lethargy and rash.

Treatment: Penicillin G.

How to avoid: Meningococcus polysaccharide vaccine. Do not travel to areas where outbreaks occur (the Sahel from Mali to Ethiopia) in the dry season.

Mumps

Found: Worldwide.

Cause: A virus found worldwide. Common in early spring and late winter and in unvaccinated areas.

Carrier: Infected saliva and urine.

Symptoms: Headache, anorexia, malaise, and pain when chewing or swallowing.

Treatment: Mumps is a self-innoculating disease. There can be complications which can lead to more serious lifetime afflictions.

How to avoid: Vaccination (MMR).

Plague

Found: India, Vietnam, Africa, South America, the Middle East, Russia.

Cause: A bacteria *(Yersinia pestis)* that infects rodents and the fleas they carry.

Carrier: Flea bites that transmit the bacteria to humans. Ticks, lice, corpses and human contact can also spread the disease.

Symptoms: Swollen lymph nodes, fever, abdominal pain, loss of appetite, nausea, vomiting diarrhea, and gangrene of the extremities.

Treatment: Antibiotics like streptomycin, tetracyclines and chloramphenicol can reduce the mortality rate.

How to avoid: Stay out of infected areas, and avoid contact.

Poliomyelitis (Polio)

Found: Worldwide.

Cause: A virus that destroys the central nervous system.

Carrier: Occurs through direct contact.

Symptoms: A mild febrile illness that may lead to paralysis. Polio can cause death in 5 to 10 percent of cases in children and 15 to 30 percent in adult cases.

Treatment: There is no treatment.

How to avoid: Vaccination during childhood with a booster before travel is recommended.

Rabies

Found: Worldwide.

Cause: A virus that affects the central nervous system.

Carrier: Rabies is transmitted through the saliva of an infected animal. Found in wild animals, although usually animals found in urban areas are most suspect: dogs, raccoons, cats, skunks, and bats. Although most people will automatically assume they are at risk for rabies, there are only about 16,000 cases reported worldwide. The risk is the deadly seriousness of rabies and the short time in which death occurs.

Symptoms: Abnormal sensations or muscle movement near the bite, followed by fever, headaches, malaise, muscle aches, tiredness, loss of appetite, nausea, vomiting, sore throat and cough. The advanced stages include excessive excitation, seizures and mental disturbances leading to profound nervous system dysfunction and paralysis. Death occurs in most cases four to 20 days after being bitten.

Treatment: Clean wound vigorously, injections of antirabies antiserum and antirabies vaccine. People who intend to come into regular contact with animals in high-risk areas can receive HDCV (human diploid cell rabies vaccine) shots.

How to avoid: Avoid confrontations with animals.

Relapsing Fever

Found: The louseborne version is found in poor rural areas where infestation by lice is common.

Cause: *Borrelia spirochetes.*

Carrier: Lice and ticks. Ticks are found in wooded areas and bite mainly at night.

Symptoms: The fever gets its name from the six days on and six days off of high fever. Other symptoms include headaches, muscle pains, weakness and loss of appetite.

Treatment: Antibiotics.

How to avoid: Avoid infected areas, and check for ticks.

Rift Valley Fever

Found: Egypt and East Africa.

Cause: A virus that affects humans and livestock.

Carrier: Mosquitoes, inhaling infected dust, contact with broken skin and ingesting infected animal blood or fluids.

Symptoms: Sudden one-time fever, severe headaches, muscle pain, weakness, sensitivity to light, eye pain, nausea, vomiting, diarrhea, eye redness and facial flushing. Blindness, meningitis, meningoencephalitis and retinitis may also occur.

Treatment: Seek medical treatment for supportive care.

How to avoid: Avoid contact with livestock in infected areas; protect yourself against mosquito bites.

River Blindness (Onchocerciais)

Found: Equatorial Africa, Yemen, the Sahara and parts of Central and South America.

Cause: The roundworm *Onchocerca volvulus.*

Carrier: Transmitted by blackflies found along rapidly flowing rivers.

Symptoms: Itching, skin atrophy, mottling, nodules, enlargement of the lymph nodes, particularily in the groin, and blindness.

Treatment: Invermectin or Diethylcarbamazine(DEC), followed by suramin, followed by DEC again.

How to avoid: Insect repellant, long-sleeve shirts and long pants. Avoid blackfly bites.

Rocky Mountain Spotted Fever

Found: Found only in the Western Hemisphere.

Cause: A bacterial disease transmitted by tick bites.

Carrier: Rickettsial bacteria are found in rodents and dogs. The ticks pass the bacteria by then biting humans.

Symptoms: Fever, headaches, chills, and rash (after fourth day) on the arms and legs. Final symptoms may include delirum, shock and kidney failure.

Treatment: Tetracyclines or chloramphenicol.

How to avoid: Ticks are found in wooded areas. Inspect your body after walks. Use insect repellent. Wear leggings or long socks or long pants.

Salmonellosis

Found: Worldwide.

Cause: A common bacterial infection; *Salmonella gastroenteritis* is commonly described as food poisoning.

Carrier: Found in fecally contaminated food, unpasteurized milk, raw foods and water.

Symptoms: Abdominal pain, diarrhea, vomiting, chills and fever usually within eight to 48 hours of ingesting infected food. *Salmonella* only kills about one percent of its victims, usually small children or the aged.

Treatment: Purge infected food, replace fluids. Complete recovery is within two to five days.

How to avoid: Consume only properly prepared foods.

Sandfly Fever (Three-day Fever)

Found: Africa, Mediterranean.

Cause: Phleboviruses injected by sandfly bites.

Carrier: Transmitted by sandflies, usually during the dry season.

Symptoms: Fever, headache, eye pain, chest muscle pains, vomiting, sensitivity to light, stiff neck, taste abnormality, rash and joint pain.

Treatment: There is no specific treatment. The symptoms can reoccur in about 15 percent of cases, but typically disappear.

How to avoid: Do not sleep directly on the ground. Sandflies usually bite at night.

Schistosomiasis (Bilharzia)

Bilharzia is one of the meanest bugs to pick up in your foreign travels. The idea of nasty little creatures actually burrowing through your skin and lodging themselves in your gut is menacing. If not treated, it can make your life a living hell with afternoon sweats, painful urination, weakness and other good stuff. There is little you can do to prevent infection, since the Schistosoma larva and flukes are found where people have fouled freshwater rivers and lakes. Get treatment immediately, since the affliction worsens as the eggs multiply and continue to infect more tissues. About 250 million people around the world are believed to be infected.

Found: Worldwide.

Cause: A group of parasitic Schistosoma flatworms (*Schistosoma mansoni, Schistosoma-japonicum* and *Schistosoma haematobium*) found in slow moving, tropical freshwater.

Carrier: The larvae of Schistosoma are found in slow moving waterways in tropical areas around the world. They actually enter the body through the skin and then enter the lymph vessels and then migrate to the liver.

Symptoms: Look for a rash and itching at the entry site, followed by weakness, loss of appetite, night sweats, hivelike rashes, and afternoon fevers in about four to six weeks. Bloody, painful and frequent urination, diarrhea. Later victims become weaker and may be susceptible to further infections and diseases.

Treatment: Elimination of *S. mansoni* requires oxamniquine and praziquantel. *S. japonicum* responds to praziquantel alone, and *Schistosoma haematobium is treated with* praziquantel and metrifonate.

How to avoid: Stay out of slow moving freshwater in all tropical and semitropical areas. This also means wading or standing in water.

Syphilis

Found: Worldwide.

Cause: A spirochete *(Treponema pallidum)* causes this chronic venereal disease, which if left untreated progresses into three clinical stages.

Carrier: Syphilis is spread through sexual contact and can be passed on to infants congenitally.

Symptoms: After an incubation period of two to six weeks, a sore usually appears near the genitals, although some men and women may not experience any symptoms. Some men also experience a scanty discharge. A skin rash appears in the second stage, often on the soles of the feet and palms of the hands. It may be accompanied by a mild fever, sore throat and patchy hair loss. This rash generally appears about six weeks after the initial sore. The third phase of the disease may develop over several years if the disease is left untreated and may damage the brain and the heart or even cause death.

Treatment: Antibiotics are used to treat syphilis, and infected people should abstain from sex until treatment ends. Blood tests should be performed again in three months after the round of treatment. Sexual partners need to be tested and treated. Victims of syphilis should also be tested for other sexually transmitted diseases.

How to avoid: Abstain from sexual activities or use a latex condom.

Tainiasis (Tapeworms)

Found: Worldwide.

Cause: A tapeworm is usually discovered after being passed by the victim.

Carrier: Ingestion of poorly cooked meat infected with tapeworms.

Symptoms: In advanced cases, there will be diarrhea and stomach cramps. Sections of tapeworms can be seen in stools.

Treatment: Mebendazole, niclocsamide, paromomysi and praziqunatel are effective in killing the parasite.

How to avoid: Tapeworms come from eating meats infected with tapeworm or coming into contact with infected fecal matter.

Tetanus (Lockjaw)

Found: Worldwide.

Cause: A bacteria caused by the bacteria *Clostridiium tetani*.

Carrier: Found in soil and enters body through cuts or punctures.

Symptoms: Restlessness, irritability, headaches, jaw pain, back pain and stiffness, and difficulty in swallowing. Then within two to 56 days, stiffness increases with lockjaw and spasms. Death occurs in about half the cases, usually affecting children.

Treatment: If infected, human tetanus immune globulin is administered with nerve blockers for muscle relaxation.

How to avoid: Immunization is the best prevention, with a booster recommended before travel.

Trachoma

Found: Common in Africa, the Middle East and Asia.

Cause: A chlamydial infection of the eye, which is responsible for about 200 million cases of blindness.

Carrier: Flies, contact, wiping face or eye area with infected towels.

Symptoms: Constant inflammation under the eyelid that causes scarring of the eyelid, turned-in eyelashes and eventual scarring of the cornea and then blindness.

Treatment: Tetracyclines, erythromycin, sulfonamide, surgery to correct turned-in lashes.

How to avoid: It is spread primarily by flies. Proper hygiene and avoidance of fly-infested areas are recommended.

Trichinosis

Found: Worldwide.

Cause: Infection of the *Trichinella spiralis* worm.

Carrier: Pig meat (also bear and walrus) that contain cysts. The worm then infects the new hosts' tissues and intestines.

Symptoms: Diarrhea, abdominal pain, nausea, prostration and fever. As the worm infects tissues, fever, swelling around the eyes, conjunctivitis, eye hemorrhages, muscle pain, weakness, rash and splinter hemorrhages under the nails occur. Less than 10 percent of the cases result in death.

Treatment: Thiabendazole is effective in killing the parasite.

How to avoid: Proper preparation, storage and cooking of meat.

Tuberculosis

Found: Worldwide.

Cause: A disease of the lungs caused by the *Mycobacterium tuberculosis* bacteria or *Mycobacterium bovis*.

Carrier: By close contact with infected persons (sneezing, coughing) or, in the case of *Mycobacterium bovis*, contaminated or unpasteurized milk.

Symptoms: Weight loss, night sweats and a chronic cough usually with traces of blood. If left untreated, death results in about 60 percent of the cases after a period of two and a half years.

Treatment: Isoniazide and rifampin can control the disease.

How to avoid: Vaccination and isoniazid prophylaxis.

Tularaemia (Rabbit Fever)

Found: Worldwide.

Cause: A fairly rare disease (about 300 cases per year) caused by the bacteria *Francisella tularnesis* passed from animals to humans via insects.

Carrier: The bite of deerflies, ticks, mosquitoes and even cats can infect humans.

Symptoms: Fever, chills, headaches, muscle pain, malaise, enlarged liver and spleen, rash, skin ulcers and enlargement of the lymph nodes.

Treatment: Vaccination is used. Streptomycin primarily. Tetracycline and chloramphenicol are also effective.

How to avoid: Care when handling animal carcasses, removal of ticks and avoidance of insect bites.

Typhoid Fever

Found: Africa, Asia, Central America.

Cause: The bacterium *Salmonella typhi*.

Carrier: Transmitted by contaminated food and water in areas of poor hygiene.

Symptoms: Fever, headaches, abdominal tenderness, malaise, rash, enlarged spleen. Later symptoms include delirium, intestinal hemorrhage and perforation of the intestine.

Treatment: Chloramphenicol.

How to avoid: Vaccination is the primary protection, although the effectiveness is not high.

Typhus Fever

Found: Africa, South America, Southeast Asia, India.

Cause: Rickettsia.

Carrier: Transmitted by fleas, lice, mites and ticks found in mountainous areas around the world.

Symptoms: Fever, headache, rash and muscle pain. If untreated, death may occur in the second week due to kidney failure, coma and blockage of the arteries.

Treatment: Tetracyclines or chloramphenicol.

How to avoid: Check for ticks, avoid insect bites, attend to hygiene to prevent lice and avoid mountainous regions.

Yellow Fever

Found: Africa, South America.

Cause: A virus transmitted by mosquito bites.

Carrier: The tiny banded-legged *aedes aegpyti* is the source for urban yellow fever, and the haemogogus and sabethes mosquito carries the jungle version.

Symptoms: In the beginning, fever, headaches, backaches, muscle pain, nausea, conjunctivitis, albumin in the urine and slow heart rate. Followed by black vomit, no urination and delirium. Death affects only 5 to 10 percent of cases and occurs in the fourth to sixth day.

Treatment: Replace fluids and electrolytes.

How to avoid: Vaccination is mandatory when entering or leaving infected areas.

DANGEROUS DISEASES

Drugs

War's Bastard Son

No list of dangerous things would be complete without mentioning drugs. Not the danger of drugs, but the drugs that cause danger, and the lands that are dangerous because of them.

Heroin

The *Papaver somniferum*, or Eurasian poppy, was introduced to Asia by Arab traders in the 12th century and was cultivated for its medicinal properties. This innocent little flower originally came from the Mediterranean area. It's now grown up and discovered it's the half-brother of war. Lebanon, Turkey, India, Myanmar, China, Pakistan, Laos, Thailand, Mexico, Uzbekistan and Afghanistan are the troubled homes of this gentle, unassuming weed that blows in the wind. Wars have been fought over opium since the 1839–1842 Opium War between Britain and China. Today, the battles are taking place on the streets of St. Louis, Miami, L.A. and small-town America. Crime experts say that as turf battles among drug lords decline in the cities, America's small towns are becoming the growth markets. A recent survey found that 47 percent of small town police chiefs consider drugs a serious problem and two-thirds say drug problems in their area have increased over the last five years. Millions of people are currently enslaved by the by-products of the opium poppy. And heroin's slaves today aren't just junkies in backalleys. The media recently has had a field day exposing heroin addict movie stars and fashion models. Since the drug can now be snorted like cocaine or smoked rather than injected into veins, it has begun increasing in popularity with the terminally hip seeking the ultimate high.

Seventy percent of all illicit drugs in the U.S. are derived from heroin, originating in the land of desperadoes—the Golden Triangle of Southeast Asia. The current purity of heroin found on the street in the United States has jumped from an average 7 percent in 1984 to 36 percent today, a testament not only to its grip on a nation, but to the seemingly ceaseless world supply of the narcotic. Heroin shipped into the U.S. comes from at least 11 different countries. The DEA estimates it stops only 30 to 40 percent of drugs illegally entering the country.

Poppies can be grown in the cool plateaus above 1500 meters. The plants grow rapidly and propagate easily. Planted at the end of the wet season (in Asia in September and October), the poppy heads are later scraped after the petals fall off. The scraping creates an oozing sap that is removed from the plant and packed tightly into banana leaves. The crude opium is then packed out of the hills via pony or armed human convoys to the middlemen. For those who grow opium, few are spared. Hilltribe growers swiftly become addicts themselves. Up to 30 percent of Southeast Asia's Hmong tribe is addicted to opium. Most of the income into northern Laos is dope money. In fact, small nickel bags, or *parakeets* as they are called locally, can be used as a form of currency.

The poppy is usually cultivated in Third World countries with little or no political, military or police interference. Mexico, Lebanon and Turkey have faded from the scene and been replaced by Afghanistan, Pakistan, Laos and Myanmar. The DEA says that 60–70 percent of the heroin coming into America is brought in by four groups: the United Wa State Army and Shan in Southeast Asia, and the Quetta Alliance and the Haji Baig Organization in Pakistan.

Opium

Opium has been used to kill pain, cure diarrhea and even as a social drug since 300 BC. Today, the legal use of opium is mainly to create morphine and codeine for medicinal purposes. Worldwide, there were an estimated 4000 metric tons of the stuff in 1995, double the amount produced in 1986.

If You Want Something Done Right

A curious sidebar to the opium business is that the U.S. government almost put notorious Khun Sa out of business in the mid and late 60's when it assisted Laotian hill tribes in transporting their opium without the usual middleman's taxes and archaic transportation. In some cases the government-owned cargo planes of Air America replaced the tired mules of the hill tribes. When the CIA left Laos, Khun Sa was back in business.

Heroin

Heroin (from the Greek root, meaning "Hero") is the most refined by-product of the opium poppy and causes a sense of power, creates a feeling of euphoria, relieves pain and induces sleep. Heroin has only been around since 1874 and was originally used for medicinal purposes without knowledge of its addictive properties. Today, 60 percent of the world's heroin supply comes from Myanmar and Laos, not northern Thailand as assumed by most tourists. The U.S. government has vacillated between encouraging the production of heroin (as it did in its support of Laotian rebels during the Vietnam War) and condemning it (through its covert military ops in Thailand aimed at stemming the heroin tide washing up on the shores of New York City).

Even in its heavily cut street form (nickel bags diluted with sugar, starch, powdered milk or quinine to less than 10 percent purity), it is highly addictive, and its victims require larger and larger doses and more direct methods of ingestion to deliver a high. In New York City, the street price for a gram of 90 percent pure heroin is about $100, and a nickel bag goes for about $10; its dearth of purity means junkies can snort it instead of having to inject it. Some estimates tag the heroin trade as a US$4 to 10 billion a year business. There are about 600,000 users; half of them are concentrated in New York City. Heroin is becoming more popular; there was a 50 percent increase in heroin-induced overdoses as tracked by ER rooms in the first half of 1995 in the U.S.

Morphine

Morphine is bitter to the taste, darkens with age and is derived from opium (at a strength of between 4 and 21 percent). Most of its addicts are former soldiers who were treated with morphine as a pain killer after being wounded in combat.

Codeine

Codeine (0.7 to 2.5 percent concentration of opium) is an alkaloid by-product of the poppy and is found in a variety of patent medicines around the world. In the U.S., codeine is only available in prescribed medications. However, these same medicines (i.e., Tylenol with Codeine) can be had over the counter in many countries, particularly in Central and South America and Southeast Asia.

Just Say No in Mexico

Mexico rigorously prosecutes drug cases. Under Mexican law, possession of and trafficking in illegal drugs are federal offenses. For drug trafficking, bail does not exist. Mexican law does not differentiate between types of narcotics: Heroin, marijuana and amphetamines are treated the same. Offenders found guilty of possessing more than a token amount of any narcotic substance are subject to a minimum sentence of seven years. It is not uncommon for people charged with drug offenses to be detained for up to one year before a verdict is reached. Remember if narcotics are found in your vehicle, you are subject to arrest and your vehicle can be confiscated.

Major Drug Producers

Afghanistan

A common harvest of lawlessness is drugs. When the Soviets pulled out of Afghanistan, they left little government and less of an economy. So the gaps were filled in by industrious Afghans who raised poppies and sold them to the equally industrious Pakistanis. The Pakistanis jumped in when Iran's fundamentalist government got tough on drugs and Afghan routes to the west were interrupted by war. Today, Pakistan exports between 65 and 80 tons of heroin every year. Not much when you compare it to the 2630 tonnes from the Golden Triangle, but enough to generate US$1.5 billion in revenue.

The major drug producing regions in Afghanistan are Helmand, Kandahor, Uruzgan and Nangarhar provinces. Less productive regions for poppies are the provinces of Badakhstan, Kunar, Farah and Nimroz. In 1995 Afghanistan produced 2400 tonnes of dry opium gum, down from 1994 by 32% according to the U.N. Things don't look good for drug producers in the *taliban* held provinces. The *taliban* have told *DP* that will cut the throats of drug dealers and are sending 150 men to patrol the Afghan/Iranian borders. Iran will also send in troops to patrol their side. Afghanistan is the world's leading producer of opium.

The Haji Baig Organization

This is a Lahore, Pakistan-based group loosely modeled after the 1980s American S&L structure; in other words, most of the key players are currently in jail while making millions of dollars. This organization lacks the political halo and the tens of thousands of armed men the Myanmar groups possess, and they are paying the price. Haji Mirza Iqbal Baig, 66, Anwar Khan Khattak, 44, and Tariq Waheed Butt, 44, are all killing time in Pakistan on drug charges awaiting extradition to the States. Meanwhile, their organization relies on Haji Ayub Afridi to carry on business as usual. Afridi lives a half-hour outside Peshawar in a compound protected by antiaircraft guns and armed tribesmen. His responsibility is to keep the flow of heroin and hashish moving to local distribution and sales groups in New York, Newark, NJ, L.A. and San Francisco.

The Quetta Alliance

The DEA-named Quetta Alliance is a coalition of Afghan tribes (the Issa, Notezai and the Rigi) based along the Pakistan-Afghani border. The tribes control the output and shipment of processed opium (mostly morphine) to Turkey for further processing into heroin. The PKK and other terrorist groups in Turkey and Iran take care of security, and the final product is trucked from Istanbul to Europe for the last leg of the journey into America. The leader of the Notezai, Sakhi Dost Jan Notezai, is serving his third term in the provincial assembly, while concurrently serving time in prison on drug charges.

Drugs are also sent from Quetta to the Makran coast, where they are shipped via freighter to Marseilles and New York.

Crack

Crack has replaced heroin as the new "jones" that is dragging down the inner city. Not as addictive as heroin, it has an intense high that is psychologically addictive. In some American cities, three out of 100 first-graders are addicted to crack, thanks to their mothers. In 1995, 18 per 1000 live births were crack babies. Crack pushes users to violent criminal acts, sexual trading and other desperate measures to feed their habit. According to the Bureau of Justice Statistics, the typical crack user is low-income, white (49.9 percent) and desperate; 35.9 percent are black and 14.2 percent Latino.

The PKK

Although they are known as a Kurdish liberation group, these folks have enough dough to run a TV station in London, 30 radio stations and a host of newspapers and rent time on two satellites (for a reputed 2 billion English pounds). You don't get this kind of money selling Free the Kurds T-shirts. Dope is protected through east Turkey and into Cypress and then shipped to sales networks in Europe and the U.S. These guys should sell stock!

The Balkans

The well-maintained roads and compliant customs officials of the former Yugoslavia were the home leg of the long road from the poppy fields of Asia. The war messed up this convenient leg and now most heroin is smuggled through Albania, Macedonia and Bulgaria. About 70 percent of the heroin is smuggled under the direction of the Albanian Mafia to customers in Germany and Switzerland. They are bosom buddies with the Italian Mafia. The Albanian Mafia is comprised primarily of the Kosovar clan. Heroin is also processed in Albania by the Mafia to increase profits.

Colombia

In the early '70s Colombia started out primarily as a grower of pot, with cocaine being a small part of the then $500 million a year export. Pot was mostly cultivated along the Atlantic coast. Today, it is estimated that Colombia's drug industry pockets about 3 billion a year in profits from the drug trade. They have a lock on 75 percent of the world's cocaine, and about 80 percent of the toot goes to Uncle Sam. To get an idea of what a narco government is, you have to understand that the entire gross domestic product of Colombia is only $5 billion.

Most coca is grown on 8–20 acre farms. The Colombian farmers get in 3–4 harvests a year. Some farmers are taking the next step and creating coca paste which sells for about $1100 per kilo. Most of the 135,000 acres of coca farms in Colombia are in the far south. It is estimated that there are 35,000 farmers in the business of growing coca and poppies. Only about 7000 families have switched to legal crops in the last two years.

Egypt

There are large opium and marijuana plantations in the remote valleys of the Sinai Peninsula. The government launched a military offensive to eliminate them in March of 1996. The flow of cash from the drug trade is supposed to have made the drug cartels' assets an estimated $15 to $60 billion. Bill Gates looks like a pauper next to these people.

The Golden Triangle

Just under 70 percent of the world's heroin seized by U.S. law enforcement in 1995 came from the Golden Triangle. The Golden Triangle is not really a geographic triangle but a loosely defined area that covers eastern Myanmar, northern Laos and scattered parts of northern Thailand. The common elements are remoteness and inaccessibility, lack of law enforcement and the right altitude and climate to permit the cultivation of poppies.

Visitors to this area will find the locals decidedly reserved and openly belligerent if pressed for details on their trade.The U.S. State Department estimates that Myanmar exports about 2300 tonnes of raw opium a year, primarily from the Kachin and north Shan states. Laos moves about 300 tonnes and Thailand about 30 tonnes.

The Hill Tribes

The real dirty work is taken care of by the region's poor but industrious hill tribes. Poppies in the Golden Triangle are grown and harvested by the Lahu, Lisu, Nfien and Hmong tribes, and cultivated among less odious but less profitable crops like maize. Since smart farmers maximize the use of their land and labor, it's not surprising that the annual opium production has tripled in Myanmar in the last 10 years. Depending on which drug lord's auspices the farmer falls under, the raw product is sent to processing labs either along the Chinese border (Wa) or along the Thai border (Shan).

The Mong Tai Army

As broken as the surrounding topography, the Mong Tai Army, led by the notorious and elusive Khun Sa, disintegrated into factions in mid-1995 as the drug warlord cut a deal with Myanmar's ruling SLORC. Khun Sa, 62, lives in the village of Ho Mong in temporary exile and protected by Myanmar army troops, nine miles from the Thai border. Ho Mong is a wealthy, well-administered town paid for with drug money and has little use for outside visitors or missionaries. Khun Sa had his own army based here, the Mong Tai Army, a group of 19,000 men who, in addition being an industrial security force, also carried a big political club when the outside world threatened to crack down. Now tattered and split into factions (those that remain), the Shan guerrillas continue to do battle with SLORC, both for protecting the lucrative drug trade and to continue the fight for Shan independence, which they believe Khun Sa abandoned out of greed for dope bucks. Depending which PR spin you like, he was either an oppressed freedom fighter forced to tax drug growers to support his peoples' fight for freedom, or a greedy drug king who enslaved an ethnic minority to do his dirty work. Nonetheless, Khun Sa had a knack for business. He's rich, and Robin Leach may be paying a visit to Ho Mong in the near future. The U.S. government still has a US$2 million bounty on his head.

The United Wa Army

Khun Sa's biggest competitor was the United Wa State Army, still quite operational. Back in 1989, the Wa decided to dump Khun Sa as an ally and get into bed with the generals who run Myanmar. The Wa is run by two men, Chao Nyi-Lai and Wei Hsueh-Kang, who operate out of the town of Pan Hsang in the easternmost corner of Myanmar. They control an army of between 15,000 to 35,000 men and once provided raw opium to Khun Sa. The two leaders have political ambitions and claim that they want to shift the Wa people into legitimate crops once they have representation within the country of Myanmar, whose leaders are allegedly benefiting from everything from timber smuggling to drug trafficking.

A third group led by Ai Hsiao-shih and Wei Hseuh-kang specializes in the transportation of raw and processed heroin into China and Thailand.

The Wa and the Shan—or more accurately the former Khun-Sa factions and Nyi-Lai/Hsueh-kang—account for 75 percent of the opium leaving the Golden Triangle. Most of Myanmar's opium is transported in pony caravans along simple trails into China's Yunnan province and eventually to the drug syndicates in Hong Kong, or it moves south through Chiang Mai in northern Thailand down to Bangkok. Once the pony caravans reach minor towns, the heroin is then trucked to major cities, from where it is shipped or flown to the United States or Mexico.

A third route is from Moulmein in southern Burma into Bangkok and, surprisingly, into Malaysia and Singapore. Malaysia and Singapore widely publicize their imposition of a mandatory death penalty for drug smuggling, while also serving as major centers for the export of drugs.

Mexico

As a supplier of a third of the cocaine that reaches the United States, Juan Garcia Abrego, "The Doll," was the first international drug trafficker to get his name pasted to post office walls as an elite member of the FBI's Ten Most Wanted list. He joked to his captors after he was busted by the FBI in January 1996, saying, "I never thought you'd get me." He probably had good reason to think they wouldn't, considering that he was cozy with former Mexican president Carlos Salinas de Gortari's brother, Raul. In fact, Raul used to party regularly with the boys of the Gulf cartel, one of Mexico's big four, and stashed some US$84 million into frozen Swiss bank accounts. The stinger was Raul Salinas de Gortari's alleged trip to Colombia to pick up US$10 million from the Cali drug cartel, which he then tried to use to fund Luis Donaldo Colosio's bid for the presidency. When Colosio turned down the contribution, he was wasted by the Gulf cartel in March 1994. Raul is now in prison for plotting the September 1994 murder of one of Mexico's top politicians. When Carlos Salinas de Gortari was in office, the Gulf cartel rose to the top among Mexico's drug syndicates. Now this conglomerate of traffickers is on the downslide. Seventy of its members have been convicted in three U.S. states.

Juarez Cartel

With the capture of Abrego and other gold-chained fat dudes of the Gulf cartel, the Juarez cartel has emerged as Mexico's strongest dope alliance. Cartel kingpin Amado Carillo Fuentes, under indictment in Dallas and Miami, is chummy with the Cali cartel and is accused of facilitating huge jetloads of dope into Mexico from Colombia. From Ciudad Juarez, the coke moves to American cities like Los Angeles, Dallas, Houston and New York.

Sonora Cartel

Miguel Caro Quintero's northwest Sonora cartel mostly runs ganja into Nogales, Arizona and the western United States but also dabbles in the white stuff. Quintero, 32, assumed the helm of the cartel after his brother Rafael was busted for the murder of DEA agent, Enrique "Kiki" Camarena. The softspoken Quintero is under indictment in Denver and Tucson.

Tijuana Cartel

Ruthless and territorial, Benjamin Arellano Felix is supposedly running the most violent dope syndicate in Mexico. His brother is wasting away in a Mexican jail cell. The Tijuana cartel is behind the massive quantities of methamphetamine that have been flooding into San Diego, Los Angeles and points east. Arellano Felix's enforcers are thought to have been the trigger men in the 1993 assassination in Guadalajara of Catholic Cardinal Juan Jesus Posadas-Ocampo.

Panama

The Darien region of Panama is a hot spot for coca cultivation for the Colombian drug czars. Local Indians are goaded into cultivating crops under the watchful protection of Colombian guerillas. In 1995, officials destroyed more than five tons of cocaine, broke up six coca paste labs and burned down 200 acres of a coca plantation. Still, Panama retains its reputation as an ideal shipment point for drugs and is a major center for laundering drug money.

Peru

Coca is Peru's second largest crop (after maize) with 930 square miles under cultivation. The major areas are the Huallaya Valley and the Apurimac-Enc Valley east of Lima. Coca leaf is worth 40–50¢ a kilo (down from $3 in 1994). The drugs are grown by peasants who sell to shippers and processors under the control of the Shining Path and oddly enough the Peruvian military.

Russia

Russia's geographical position makes it a major drug producing and shipping point. Its neighbors make good use of the corrupt and inefficient police and border guards. Drugs from the Golden Crescent (Pakistan, Afghanistan and Iran) are transported to major centers like Tashkent in Uzbekistan, or through the states of Chechnya, Tajikistan, Georgia and Azerbaijan. There are also major growing areas in southern Russia and the western Ukraine, as well as the states of Uzbekistan, Kazakhstan and Krygyzstan. The presence of foreign troops during the Balkan War has disrupted the once traditional smuggling routes into Europe, which are being replaced by Afghanistan to Tajikistan to St. Petersburg to Cyprus and then out through ports on the Baltic Sea and Mediterranean.

Russian officials estimate there are about 5.7 million drug users in Russia, with hashish being the drug of choice. A U.N. report says there may be 100,000 opium poppy fields and more than 2.5 million acres of marijuana under cultivation within the country. Drug-related crime is up 15 percent and 23 tons of drugs were seized in raids last year. About 80 percent of drug dealers arrested in Moscow are Aberbaijanis; the rest are Chechens. The total drug business adds up to an unimpressive US$25 million (compared to our US$500 billion narcotics industry Stateside). A kilo of hash in Russia goes for as little as US$15, compared to US$200 in Europe. Russian gangs are also expanding into Europe and the United States.

The Drugstore

Cocaine

Cocaine is a bitter crystalline alkaloid obtained from coca leaves. It creates a euphoric effect in users as well as a compulsive psychological need. It has limited medical applications as a local anesthetic agent. It is readily absorbed by the mucous membranes lining the nose and throat. Crack is a derivative of cocaine.

Marijuana

Mary Jane, grass, weed, or pot is a drug derived from *cannabis sativa*, a tall, leafy plant that is easily cultivated. The chemical that causes the high in pot is THC, or delta 9-tetrahydrocannabinol. More than 400 other chemicals are found in the cannabis plant. Marijuana is usually smoked in loosely rolled cigarettes and is considered a social drug consumed at parties or at home. There are many varieties, with the effects dependent on the amount of THC in the plant. Due to better strains of the plant being cultivated, the marijuana sold today is estimated to be 10 times stronger than the weed sold in the 1970s.

The effect of marijuana varies with the user, but typically results in a faster heart rate, bloodshot eyes and dry throat and mouth. Marijuana can cause acute panic, memory loss and a lack of motivation. Proponents of its use praise its medicinal effects, enhancement of mental powers and increased sensitivity, especially during sex. Others experience drowsiness, giddiness and stupor.

Hashish

Hash is derived from the resin of hemp plants. It is stronger than marijuana and can contain up to 50 percent pure THC. It is usually smoked in a pipe or smoked inserted into regular cigarettes. THC is a chemical that many times contains PCP.

PCP

PCP, phencyclidine, also called angel dust, was originally developed as an anesthetic in the 1950s. Today, it is illegal but it is easily manufactured. PCP acts as a stimulant and can stretch time, numb pain centers, and slow body movements. Some users have a sense of power and strength. Overdoses can create violent behavior, which may lead to rash acts when the victim feels invincible (jumping from high places, drownings, car accidents). Heavy users can develop symptoms of paranoia, fearfulness and anxiety.

LSD

LSD is manufactured from lysergic acid, which is a common fungus typically in grains or bread. LSD was discovered in 1938 and is odorless, tasteless and colorless. It is often in liquid or tab form. Hallucinogenics create a rush of unusual emotions, visions, experiences and sensations. They also increase heart rate, dilate pupils, and increase body temperature and blood pressure. Use of hallucinogens may unmask or exacerbate emotional problems. In some cases, LSD is cut with other drugs to change the high.

Mescaline

Mescaline comes from the peyote cactus, and its effects are similar to those of LSD, though less extreme. It is usually smoked or swallowed in pill form.

Psilocybin/Mushrooms

Psilocybin is a hallucinogen found in mushrooms. It is taken in its raw form (mushrooms) or in a powdered tablet.

"Khat's Fancy"

Although most countries outlaw the chewing of khat, a mildly stimulating drug, it is still legal in hot, dusty Yemen. It is estimated that half of Yemen's population is moderately drugged for at least part of the day. Khat, or gat, costs about US$3 for a day's hit and is chewed mostly by men. It is issued to soldiers to reduce tension and anxiety. It can also diminish sexual potency, as well as create loss of appetite or gastritis, inflammation of the gums, and quirky side effects. One of the side effects is the perception that the user can regale people with long speeches and stories. They seem inspirational and fascinating to the user, but sound ridiculous to the listener. Khat is a social drug, usually chewed in the afternoon or evening. It is not known to be addictive, but it may prevent users from falling asleep. The leaves of the plant are bitter and are left in the mouth like chewing tobacco and formed into a plug or ball.

DRUGS

Getting Arrested

Oh Won't You Stay...Just a Little Bit Longer

You're catching some rays on the beach in Manzanillo. The low tangerine shafts of sunlight trickle across the purple Pacific as you wipe the piña colada foam from your lips. It's your last day. Monday, it's back behind the desk at Shrapnel-Wesson Bros., the brokerage people, in beautiful downtown Gary, Indiana. You lament the week ahead, as you notice the young Mexican kid approach your towel. Another souvenir or massage parlor tout. Jeez, they get these kids young, you think. Instead of balsawood dolphins, hammocks or whorehouse flyers, the kid pulls from his pocket a bag of weed. You do a double take. *Sensimilla*, the kid says. Twenty bucks. What the hell, you say. It's your last day. You're grabbed from behind. Someone's got your hair. Your face gets stuffed into the sand. Then a boot in the left ear. Christ, that hurt! Thirty minutes later, you're pissing against a stained cement wall. Your left eye has swollen over. You've signed a confession.

What the hell. It's your last day.

Approximately 3000 Americans are arrested abroad every year, about one percent of all U.S. international travelers. At the end of 1995, there were 2434

Americans in foreign jails, according to the U.S. State Department. The majority (about 70 percent) of the cases are drug-related. Mexico and Jamaica are responsible for the bulk of the drug-related incarcerations, filing 72 percent of all drug charges against Americans traveling abroad.

The top five destinations for Americans seeking free room and board are Mexico, Germany, Canada, Jamaica and Great Britain. At the end of 1995, Mexico had 525 gringos on ice and had arrested 768 that year. Fifty-five of those weren't happy campers and filed complaints of mistreatment. The Mexican judicial system is based on Roman and Napoleonic law and presumes a person accused of a crime is guilty until proven innocent. There is no trial by jury. Trial under the Mexican system is a prolonged process based largely on documents examined on a fixed date in court by prosecution and defense counsel. Sentencing usually takes six to 10 months. Bail can be granted after sentencing if the sentence is less than five years. Pretrial bail exists but is never granted when the possible sentence is greater than five years.

Even those folks have it good. In places like Malaysia and Singapore, move dope and die. Zero tolerance. Deal dope and you'll get the rope. Getting beaten up in a Mexican jail may be inconvenient, but at least the *federales* are trying to teach you a lesson, one you might learn from in later life. In Southeast Asia, there is no later life.

Here are a few survival tips (at the risk of sounding like your mother) for those who don't want to die as a skinny, frazzled, psychotic wimp in a Pakistani jail:

Have nothing to do with drugs or the drug culture.

Those pleasant men in pressed uniforms are employed for a single purpose, to find your drugs. Once they've found them, make no mistake, you will be busted. Once you're tried (if you ever are), you will be going away for a long time. And then it will take a lot of money to get you out. A lot of it. And you'll look different, too. Not good.

Do not take anything illegal through customs, or anything that doesn't belong to you.

Do not be an unwitting mule and carry a package for a friend. Do not think you can sneak a few joints through. Customs officers live by two words: How much? How much is it going to cost you to get out of this mess? How much time are you going to do? How much will it cost to repatriate your remains?

Be careful with unmarked drugs.

Combining drugs or putting prescription drugs into reminder boxes may create questions of legality. Your personal appearance, the quantity of the drugs and the general demeanor of your inquisitor will determine if you are let off.

Avoid driving.

Car accidents are a great way to go to jail. In many countries, the Napoleonic code of justice is utilized. In other words, by law, you are guilty until proven innocent. For instance, if someone smacks into your car in Mexico, you'll go to jail. No witnesses and it may be a long time. Hire a driver and you're off the hook.

Be judicious in your enthusiasm to photograph military or government facilities.

Soldiers in Africa love camera equipment. If you want it back, you'll have to pay a fine. In most of the former Soviet republics, you will be arrested for taking pictures of army bases or airports. We have spent plenty of time fast-talking our way out of jail simply for carrying cameras in countries that demand you have national and regional permits to carry them.

Get the right kind of help.

The U.S. embassy will not lift a finger to get you out of jail. They may assist you, but if you have broken the law in that country, you are expected to do the time. Many countries will assume you are guilty and hold you until trial. It may take an extraordinary amount of time for your case to go to trial, and you may even be required to pay your room and board while in jail. Hire a local lawyer and explore all options for your release, including bribes and being smuggled out. Communicate your case to friends, and tell them to contact journalists in the local and national media. If you really did something stupid and you don't have any money, be prepared for the worst.

Country	Currently in Custody	Country	Currently in Custody
Antigua & Barbuda	15	Italy	21
Australia	59	Jamaica	107
Austria	8	Japan	72
Bahamas	31	Korea	13
Barbados	8	Mexico	525
Belize	29	Netherlands	26
Bermuda	19	Netherlands Antilles	21
Bolivia	13	Nigeria	1
Brazil	25	Panama	42
Canada	102	Peru	20
Colombia	40	Philippines	23
Costa Rica	22	Russia	2
Cuba	11	Saudi Arabia	3
Denmark	6	South Africa	3
Dominican Republic	51	Spain	33
Ecuador	58	Sweden	6
France	50	Switzerland	13
Germany (Fed Rep)	114	Taiwan	2
Greece	20	Thailand	67
Guatemala	10	Trinidad & Tobago	16
Honduras	14	United Arab Emirates	17
Hong Kong	5	United Kingdom	94
India	7	Venezuela	41
Ireland	1	Yemen Arab Republic	1
Israel	24		

Source: U.S. State Department Consular Affairs Office

Guns

Boys and Their Toys

If you travel to dangerous places you will meet a lot of people with guns. You should know what guns can and cannot do. But you should never carry or use one in a war zone. Television is not a good role model for those who want to learn about guns. On TV, puny handguns fire off hundreds of rounds without re-loading, and bullets seem lethally attracted to bad guys. In reality guns are rather simple and deadly. Imagine throwing a pea-size pebble at someone. Now imagine using a slingshot, projecting that pea-size objective at 1200 feet per second. Ouch. Bullets are just heavy projectiles that puncture flesh, bounce off and shatter bone and turn people into trauma cases more efficiently than a club.

There are more than 200 million guns in the United States. It is estimated that firearm injuries in the States cost about $20 billion in medical costs and lost wages. Firearms send almost 40,000 Americans to their graves each year (19,000 Americans use guns to commit suicide each year, another 18,500 are murdered with a gun, and at least 1500 more are accidentally shot to death). Gun-related homicides rose 18 percent in the last decade—30 percent among people ages 15 to 24.

The most dangerous handheld weapons are rifles. Handguns require short ranges and careful aim to be lethal. Handguns tend to be the weapons of choice for domestic violence and robberies. Most handguns lose any effectiveness after 25 yards. In fact, the Western movies where men bang away from across the street without hitting anyone are not too far from reality.

On the other hand, if someone is shooting a rifle at you, you will probably end up dead.

Gun Statistics

- There are 216 million firearms in America; 72 million of them are handguns, and 3 million of those are 9-mm semiautomatics. Seventy-five percent of all gunshot victims are under the age of 30. The top guns found at crime scenes are 9-mm.

- By 2003, it is estimated that gunshots will surpass car accidents as the leading cause of injury and death in the United States.

- It is believed that young shooters aim for the neck to cause lifelong spinal injury but not kill their victim. Just the first-year costs are estimated to be around $400,000, with $74,000 each year thereafter (not accounting for inflation).

- Eighty percent of gunshot victims do not have private health insurance, according to *U.S. News and World Report,* July 1, 1996.

- For every patient who dies from a gunshot wound, there are three who are hospitalized. One of those will spend his life with a disabling injury.

- Gunshot victims cost $20 billion a year—20 percent of that in medical expenses, about $200 for every household. In some cities, 70% of gunshot victims are criminal offenders. The average gunshot wound costs $14,541 to treat, compared to $6446 for a stab wound, (1992 figures).

- There were 39,720 deaths by gunshot in 1994/1995.

In the 1850s, rifles were called muskets. They were smooth bore, and long barreled (about 4–5 feet in length) and could kill a man at 100 meters. Loading slowed down the killing process to about eight shots a minute.

In 1855, the Crimean War introduced the rifled bullet, a major advance that pushed the killing range out to 600 yards. The French invention meant that armies could now battle without the standard volley, advance and hand-to-hand combat. Armies were slow to adapt the deadly new Minié ball, and the Civil War still saw armies facing each other 50 to 100 yards apart, firing at point-blank range and then charging.

The next big advances were in the late 1800s, when breech-loading weapons like the Mauser rifle and metal-cased bullets were introduced. The next step was the 1903 Springfield rifle and the later 1917 Enfield. These rifles were deadly out to 1200 yards and could be loaded and fired quickly.

WWI trenches were typically spaced 300 to 1200 feet apart and dictated rifle design. The ideal weapon was one that fired accurately, from rest with a minimum of maintenance and training. The focus was on careful killing of fleeting targets. When fighting got close, bayonets and pistols were the choice. Machine guns were heavy and water-cooled and used for withering fire during assaults or attacks. In 1917 came the introduction of the first semiautomatic weapon that could fire 20 rounds as fast as the trigger could be pulled. The simple Pedersendevice modification to the 1903 Springfield rifle was ordered too late to make a difference in the Great War but changed the use of rifles in warfare.

WWII introduced the idea of rapid-fire, portable weapons that could intimidate rather than kill. The M1 Garand (designed by John C. Garand) was a semiautomatic, gas-operated rifle that could fire 30•06 cartridges in eight-round clips. Later, it would be found that the number of rounds fired for every person actually killed was 15,000 rounds, even though the range of engagement closed to half WWI distances. Heavy bolt action rifles were still the infantry weapon of choice, but the Germans and Russians used machine guns and infantry attacks to good effect. The Germans were the first to create the Sturmgewehr (assault rifle), but the first successful version was the post- war Russian AK47.

Assault weapons provide killing power out to about 600 meters, although battlefield results showed that 350 meters was the maximum practical range in combat. Most firefights occurred with opponents 200 to 300 yards apart.

Vietnam and a host of other dirty bush wars introduced the ambush concept of very high rates of fire, light ammunition and firepower. Ammunition had to be light, weapons cheap and easy to fix, and general tactics dictated spraying thousands of rounds during short firefights. The number of rounds per kill tripled from WWII levels to a staggering 50,000 rounds for each kill. In Vietnam, the light and deadly M-16 became the overwhelming choice of ground troops.

The future of rifle design is anyone's guess. Everything from all-plastic bullets to nonlethal ammunition is being developed. In the meantime, it seems to take a major war to change the face of battle and eventually the use of weapons.

Here's a quick primer on things that go bang:

Handguns

Small weapons with 2"-8" barrels designed for personal protection and intimidating people at close range. Typically, the number of bullets is five–20. Average is about eight–13. Lethal range is from up close to about 50 meters when fired at rest. In combat or tense, moving situations, they are deadly out to about 25 meters. Most people miss when they use handguns as a defensive weapon and hit people when they use them as offensive weapons. Consistent training, long barrel length and small caliber play a big part in attaining accuracy.

What to Wear If You're Not Superman

The 9mm cartridge was designed in 1902 to kill soldiers who were not wearing body armor. Current bulletproof vests constructed with 24 layers of Kevlar can easily stop a 9mm bullet at one meter.

Rifles/Submachine Guns

Modern military rifles are usually fully automatic. They can be fired in single shots or on full automatic. Full automatic is the least accurate but most intimidating. If a soldier is careful when squeezing off single shots, he is probably trying to kill you. If soldiers are using full automatic (common at night and in attacks), it means you have scared the shit out of them. Sniper rifles are the world's most dangerous weapons, simply because they are only used to kill. Rifles are issued to most troops, however bullets are sometimes not issued to some African troops (or Iraqis). Submachine guns like the MAC-10 and Uzi were designed for spraying fast bursts of pistol-sized (9mm and smaller) bullets in close quarters. Assault rifles like the AK-47 and AK-

74 have high burst rates but longer barrels and better accuracy. Most terrorist or liberation movements carry AK-47 assault rifles because they are cheap, easy to fix and accurate.

Most Asian and African soldiers tend to fire fast and aim high under stress. Middle Eastern and Central Asian countries like Afghanistan and Pakistan breed deadly shots, since they grow up using guns for hunting and engage in warfare at long distances. Jungle fighters like to spray bullets.

Machine guns hold about 20–70 bullets and go through them pretty quickly at full auto. An Uzi kicks out 600 rounds per minute but has a maximum clip of 40 rounds. About 10 bullets a second gives you exactly four seconds of looking good until you have to reload. Killing range can extend to 1400 meters (over a mile with tripod-mounted sniper rifles with scopes) and are effective between 400 and 600 meters. Assault rifles (the ones with large clips and short barrels) are designed to kill between 20 and 200 meters.

AK-47 (Avtomat Kalishnikova Obrazets 1947g)

If there is one visual symbol or prop that symbolizes the Soviet/revolutionary influence, it is the unmistakable profile of the AK-47. Once it was the hammer and sickle; now it is the banana-shaped clip and pointed barrel of the world's most dangerous rifle.

These weapons are cheap (between $50 and $350), available around the world, rock-hard reliable, and in use from Afghanistan to Zaire. It is estimated that there are about 30 to 50 million copies of the rugged rifle in existence. They can pour out 600 rounds a minute and are designed to be manufactured and repaired in primitive conditions.

In 1941, the 23-year-old tank commander Mikhail T. Kalishnikov was wounded in the battle of Bryansk by the German invaders. While recuperating, he listened to the complaints of Russian soldiers about their archaic bolt-action rifles. Kalishnikov made use of his downtime to copy the current German machine pistol. His pistol never made it into the arsenal of the Russian army, but in 1943 it got him an entry to compete with other Russian gun designers to create the first Soviet assault rifle. An assault rifle is designed to be light, possess high rates of fire, and do double-duty as an accurate defensive rifle.

His design was chosen based on its durability and simplicity. The AK-47 and variants thereof have been manufactured in 12 countries from Bulgaria to Yugoslavia. The AK-47 and the AKM (a simpler-to-make variant) are sighted in to about 1000 meters, field-strip down to six parts, fire 30 rounds of the 7.62 X 39 mm cartridge and will deliver three-inch patterns at 25 meters. The rifle is accurate to about 200 meters when fired from the shoulder at rest, and accurate to about 50 yards fired from the hip. The newest version of the classic assault rifle is the AK-74 (adopted in 1974 by the Soviets), which uses a lighter but more accurate 5.45 X 39mm cartridge.

Kalishnikov was born in the Siberian town of Izhevsk, west of the Ural mountains. Today, Izhevsk is home to Izhmash, a former major arms manufacturing company that exports hunting rifles under the name, The Kalishnikov Joint Stock Co.

Kalishnikov still designs hunting rifles and has never received a royalty for his innovative design, though he has received many medals for it.

M-16

The M-16, or the civilian version called the AR-15, was introduced in 1965. By this time, the light and powerful AK47 was the best weapon available. In Vietnam, the light and deadly M-16 suffered initially because of ammunition that caused fouling. And the lighter bullet was deflected by brush. After the problem was sorted out, it became the standard issue for all ground troops (replacing the M-14). The M-16 used a lighter (5.56) bullet compared to the Viet Cong 7.62 used in the AK-47. The M-16 round had just as much impact at 200 yards as the AK47 round.

The M-16 lays down 700 rounds per minute with a muzzle velocity of 3250 feet per second. It comes with 20 or 30 round clips. With a weight of 6.6 pounds, it has been adopted by Asian armies as the weapon of choice.

The G3

Heckler & Koch are known for high-precision German weapons. A relative newcomer to the arms trade, they were formed in 1949 by three partners; Seidel is the modest one. Originally, the postwar German army used old M1 Garands and the FAL rifle. The G3 was adopted in 1959 and was the first entirely German designed and made rifle (based on the Spanish CETME). The G3 used the standard 7.62 X51 NATO cartridge, and its accuracy and durability led it to being adopted by more than 50 other countries. The basic rifle design was made in everything from sniper to.22 calibre versions.

The ultimate H&K version is the PSG1, a $5000 sniper version for military and police use.

The UZI

The UZI is the brainchild of Israeli designer Major Uziel Gal, borrowing heavily from Czech models 23 and 25. The Uzi is designed to spray a room with bullets or be used as an infantry weapon. The 9mm version has a rate of fire of 10 bullets per second. The magazine inserts through the pistol grip, and the UZI comes in 16"-long barrel or ultra-compact machine pistol size. The UZI is also a favorite of the U.S. Secret Service because of its small size and high rate of fire. Originally designed for 9mm NATO standard ammunition, the UZI was manufactured in a more powerful.45-calibre format for the U.S. market. Magazines come in 20-, 25- and 32-round capacity (the.45-calibre version comes in a meager 16-round capacity).

Medium-Range Weapons

When bullets just won't communicate how much you hate people, the military can whip out some other gizmos. Mortars look like tubes with legs on three plates. They are designed to throw shells short distances in a high trajectory. The soldier drops the hand-sized missile down the tube and it fires. When it lands, it spreads shrapnel in a 20- to 60-yard perimeter, depending on the shell. The only good thing about mortars is that you can tell where they come from and they tend to target specific areas.

Artillery is another matter. Artillery sends medium to large shells screaming in waves. The shells are used either to demoralize troops or create havoc before an attack. Artillery kills more people than bullets. If you come under artillery attack, it is not a good sign. You should try to change your travel plans in a direction other than towards the guns.

Rockets (RPG)

Those funny-looking green things on the end of long sticks are RPG, or Rocket Propelled Grenades. They are very much in vogue in Afghanistan and West Africa. Rocket RPGs are used to attack small to medium-sized groups of men, trucks and sometimes tanks. They usually signal the start of an attack and kill with concussion and shrapnel.

Machine Guns

Machine guns were put to good use in the trenches of World War I, where a team of two men with a Maxim could mow down hundreds of attacking troops. The only limitation was how much ammunition they had and if the gun would jam due to the barrel overheating. Travelers will only see the big machine guns at checkpoints and on top of tanks and bunkers. They are used to pin down or decimate large groups of attacking soldiers. They are also mounted on the back of trucks in places like Somalia. Machine guns fire belt-fed ammunition (great for wearing in bandoliers and posing for bad guy pictures) and require a tripod (unless you are Arnold Schwarzenegger) for accuracy. They are loud and require someone to make sure the bullets are feeding properly. They are deadly out to 2500 meters and can also fire armor-piercing bullets. If you are in an area that has a preponderance of these weapons, you can safely assume you are in an active war zone.

Long-Range Weapons

Those of you who were lucky enough to see our $5 million cruise missiles go streaking overhead understand why war sucks. Today, there are so many exotic weapons delivery systems that they fill their own Jane's book. Travelers won't come across too many of these weapons, unless they are on the wrong side of Uncle Sam. Some groups like to use Stinger surface to air missiles like the Chechens, the Afghans and the Hutus, but they are lethal and unexpected and there is no advice one can give on avoidance except take the train.

Dirty Harry School

Citizens and law enforcement personnel can hone their shooting skills at the Smith and Lesson Academy in Springfield, Massachusetts. Among the tips the professionals impart are the following:

• Keep your finger off the trigger, with your trigger finger extended alongside the pistol frame.

• Shoot for the center of the target, and practice with static, moving and interactive targets (targets that shoot back).

• Size doesn't matter. The gun that works best for you is the one you should carry. For more information, contact **Smith and Wesson Academy**, *2100 Roosevelt Avenue, Springfield, Massachusetts 01102 or call* ☎ *(800) 331-0852 ext. 255 or (413) 781-8300. Check with your local law enforcement agencies and gun shops for weapons instruction courses and target ranges in your area.*

Kidnapping

"I'll see your envoy and raise you two hostages."

You're in Good Hands

Kidnappings by such groups as the PKK in Turkey, Al-Faran in Kashmir, Abu Sayeff in the Philippines, the Khmer Rouge in Cambodia, the Chechens in Europe and Hezbollah in Lebanon have made travelers realize that they can be targets just by being Westerners. Kidnapping is an ancient sport designed to generate cash, embarrass your enemies and, in some countries, find wives. Today, it is a big business. Consider yourself a blue chip, a pork belly, a regular over-the-counter commodity in many countries. A mid-level American executive can fetch US$500,000–800,000 for the kidnappers; ransoms of US$2 million for corporate brass aren't unusual. In areas such as Colombia, Venezuela and Russia—where kidnappers have perfected kidnapping to a fine art—people don't hesitate to meet the kidnappers' demands to get their boys home safe. In countries like Pakistan, the U.S. and the Philippines, negotiators can usually work out a discount—if you don't get killed in an aborted rescue attempt.

Hijacking is a more lucrative and dangerous version of kidnapping. Chechens have found that they can squeeze bonzo rubles out of cash-poor Moscow by commandeering buses, airplanes or even ferryboats.

The trick is not to get greedy. Once kidnappers become too outrageous in their demands, it is much easier to send in groups of specially-trained (or in the case of the Russians, specially untrained) commandos to rescue the hostages. This usually results in success, but there have been bloodbaths.

Latin America is the most dangerous place in the world for kidnapping. More than 6000 people were kidnapped in Latin America in 1995. Colombia accounted for 4000 of those. Half of the kidnappings were carried out by FARC and ELN. It is estimated that ransoms, extortions and thefts paid out totaled about $800 million in Colombia between 1990 and 1994. A typical ransom demand is $2–6 million for foreign workers. That's between 50,000 and 150,000 barrels of oil you better pump to justify your job if you work in this oil patch.

Brazil accounts for 800 kidnappings a year with 104 in Rio alone. In Mexico, there are as many as 1400 kidnappings a year. In 1994, a Mexican banker had to scratch together $30 million for his freedom. That same year a supermarket magnate was snatched and released after his family paid an estimated $50 million in ransom. About 100 people are grabbed in Guatemala, mostly children of wealthy families and foreign workers. Ecuador and Venezuela each report around 200 kidnappings a year, and Peru estimates 100 hostages are taken annually.

Most victims are ranchers and small businessmen. Foreign executives who work in the oil and energy industries are tops on most kidnappers' wish lists but aren't numerically high because of the security provided. Kidnapping and ransom insurance covers the cost of the ransom, the fee for a hostage negotiation team and any wages lost during captivity.

Before you head out on your next business trip or accept a long-term post in another country, take this brief test. You may want to apply for the ambassadorship to Disneyland instead.

The DP "Should I Really Go?" Test

- Are you traveling to a country that is hostile to American political policy?
- Are you traveling to a country that has regular kidnappings?
- Do you work for an American company? Is it a Fortune 500 company?
- Is your business in oil, mining or food?
- Are you a non-Muslim?
- Do you have substantial personal assets?

You've got the point. But there is hope.It's called abduction insurance or KR&E (Kidnapping, Rescue and Extortion insurance). It makes it easier for the bad guys, and it makes it easier for the good guys.

These days, Chubb, Fireman's Fund, Kroll & Associates, AIG and Lloyds of London will insure you if you get abducted. The premiums run from US$1000 to $100,000 a year, depending on where you plan to go and how long you plan to stay. Lloyds of London has experienced a 50 percent jump in policies written over the last five years, and more insurance companies are looking into offering the coverage.

What do you get for your money? Actually quite a bit. Insurers will pay the ransom payment, medical treatment, interpreters and even your salary, while you are gagged and bound. If you hire a freelance Rambo or security company to help spring you, it's included in the coverage.

Chubb has the best deal in town; annual payments total about US$1000 for every $10 million of ransom payments released. If you are deemed to be "high profile" or the target of previous kidnapping attempts, the premium skyrockets to US$25,000 a year. Kidnapping and ransom insurance for dangerous countries like Colombia costs around $20,000 a year for a million dollar policy. Coverage is about half that for Brazil.

Who is high profile? Senior American executives who work for high-profile companies overseas. Most victims are ranchers and small businessmen. Foreign executives who work in the oil and energy businesses are tops on most kidnappers' wish lists, but aren't numerically high because of the security they are provided. Where are you most likely to get snatched?

The World's Most Dangerous Places for White-Collar Expats	
Brazil	Italy
India	Mexico
Pakistan	Peru
Philippines	Spain
Colombia	Venezuela

These 12 countries are the sites for 90 percent of all kidnappings. The hot spots are South and Central America and Mexico. Lawlessness in Russia and Eastern Europe will soon put these areas toward the top of the list. The number of kidnappings worldwide grew from 369 in 1984 to 862 in 1995. It is important to remember that a large number of kidnappings are never reported for fear of attracting further attempts. In America, 95 percent of kidnappers are brought to justice; the record for the rest of the world is not as impressive.

What is the real danger of being held hostage? The primary motivation of most kidnappers is to generate cash—lots of it. So being worth more alive than dead is comforting. According to Control Risks Group out of London, about 40 percent of all hostages are released safely after the ransom is paid. Having an insurance policy will make your chances of generating the necessary number of bucks a lot easier. But you won't have a choice should someone try to storm the joint in a rescue effort. About 34 percent of hostages are rescued from their captives before the ransom is paid. This is perhaps a hostage's greatest threat.

Approximately 79 percent of all hostages are killed during rescue attempts, according to Kroll Associates. Nearly 11 percent of kidnapping victims are released without payment, either through negotiation or the abductors' realization that no one really gives a damn you took their sorry-ass employee, who was about to get fired anyway.

How to Survive a Kidnapping

- **Don't freak out; there is little you can do.**

- **Do whatever your captors tell you to do without argument.**

- **Communicate with your captors to make them understand that you want to stay alive.**

- **Take control of your mental and physical state. Develop a routine that will include mental and physical exercise.**

- **If you think you can escape, do so, but stop if you are under threat of death or being shot.**

- **If you are being rescued by armed troops or police, stay on the ground. Make it difficult for your captors to drag you away, but do not resist. The greatest risk of death is during a rescue attempt.**

Want to know how to avoid being kidnapped? First make sure you answered "no" to each of the questions in our rigged quiz. Secondly, follow these slightly paranoid tips:

How to Avoid a Kidnapping

- **Try to de-Westernize your mode of dress. Do not wear jewelry or American flag accessories.**

- **Do not follow a regular routine.**

- **Do not enter taxis, buildings, cars or areas where you feel you have been seen often. Avoid public transport, expensive cars or limousines.**

- **Do not book hotels or restaurants in a corporate name or even your name.**

- **Keep family, colleagues and other trusted people informed of your whereabouts. Do not use a cellular phone to do this.**

- **Remember that most victims are snatched as they are traveling between places in relatively close proximity to each other.**

Hijacking/Hostage Situations

The most dangerous phases of a hijacking or hostage situation are the beginning and, if there is a rescue attempt, the end. At the outset, the terrorists typically are tense and high-strung and may behave irrationally. It is extremely important that you remain calm and alert and manage your own behavior.

- Avoid resistance and sudden or threatening movements. Do not struggle or try to escape, unless you are certain of being successful.

- Make a concerted effort to relax. Breathe deeply and prepare yourself mentally, physically and emotionally for the possibility of a long ordeal.

- Try to remain inconspicuous; avoid direct eye contact and the appearance of observing your captors' actions.

- Avoid alcoholic beverages. Consume little food and drink.

- Consciously put yourself in a mode of passive cooperation. Talk normally. Do not complain, avoid belligerency, and comply with all orders and instructions.

- If questioned, keep your answers short. Don't volunteer information or make unnecessary overtures.

- Don't try to be a hero, endangering yourself and others.

- Maintain your sense of personal dignity, and gradually increase your requests for personal comforts. Make these requests in a reasonable low-key manner.

- If you are involved in a lengthier, drawn-out situation, try to establish a rapport with your captors, avoiding political discussions or other confrontational subjects.

- Establish a daily program of mental and physical activity. Don't be afraid to ask for anything you need or want, such as medicines, books, pencils and papers.

- Eat what they give you, even if it does not look or taste appetizing. A loss of appetite and weight is normal.

- Think positively; avoid a sense of despair. Rely on your inner resources. Remember that you are a valuable commodity to your captors. It is important to them to keep you alive and well.

Security Firms, Hostage Negotiation and Rescue Firms

Pinkerton Risk Assessment Services

1600 Wilson Boulevard, Suite 901
Arlington, VA 22209
☎ *(703) 525-6111*
FAX (703) 525-2454

Once on the trail of bank robbers in the Wild West, Pinkerton has gone global and high-tech. Today, you can get risk assessments of over 200 countries on-line or in person. Pinkerton offers access to a database of more than 55,000 terrorist actions and daily updated reports on security threats. For the nonactive, you can order printed publications that range from daily risk assessment briefings to a monthly newsletter. Their services are not cheap, but how much is your life worth? Annual subscriptions to the on-line service start at about US$7000, and you can order various risk and advisory reports that run from US$200–700 each. Pinkerton gets down and dirty with its counterterrorism programs, hostage negotiators, crisis management and travel security seminars.

The service is designed for companies who send their employees overseas or need to know what is going on in the terrorist world. Some reports are mildly macabre, with their annual businesslike graphs charting maimings, killings, assaults and assassinations. Others are truly enlightening. In any case, Pinkerton does an excellent job of bringing together the world's most unpleasant information and providing it to you in concise, intelligent packages.

Unlimited on-line access to their database on 230 countries will run you US$6000 a year. You will find the information spotty, with a preponderance of information on South and Central America. Many of the write-ups on everything from Kurds to the Islamic Jihad are written by young college students with little in-country experience. On the other hand, there are many holes that are filled by CIA country profiles (available at any library for free).

If you want to save a few bucks, for US$4000 a year (US$5000 overseas), you can get a full subscription of daily, weekly, quarterly and annual risk assessments, as well as analysts' commentaries, a world status map and a fax service that keeps you abreast of fast breaking events.

Cheapskates can opt for the US$2250 standard package, which eliminates the daily reports sent via fax, but provides you most of the other elements. If you want to order à la carte, expect services that range from a US$30 personalized trip package, to US$250 printouts of existing risk and travel advisories, to accessing the company's Country Data bank for US$1000 per country.

Ackerman Group

166 Kennedy Causeway
Suite 700
Miami Beach, Florida 33141
☎ *(305) 865-0072*

Control Risks Group

8200 Greensboro Drive, Suite 1010
McLean, Virginia 22102
☎ *(703) 893-0083*
FAX (703) 893-8611

Control Risks Group, London

83 Victoria Street
London, England SW1H-OHW
☎ *[44] (171) 222-1552*

This international management consulting company specializes in political, business and security risk analysis and assessments, due diligence and fraud investigations, preventative security and asset protection, crisis management planning and training, crisis response and unique problem solving. With extensive experience in kidnapping, extortion and illegal detention resolution, they have handled more than 700 cases in 79 countries. Control Risks has 14 offices around the world including Washington, D.C., London, New York, Bogota, Mexico City, Bonn, Amsterdam, Manila, Melbourne, Moscow, Paris, Singapore, Sydney and Tokyo. Their international, political and security risk analysis research department is the largest of its kind in the private sector and has provided hundreds of companies with customized analyses of the political and security risks they may face doing business around the globe. An on-line Travel Security Guide addresses security issues in more than 100 countries.

Employment Conditions Abroad

Anchor House, 15 Britten Street
London, England SW3 3TY
☎ *(071) 351-7151*
FAX (071) 351-9396

This company provides assessments of employment opportunities, and rates business and living conditions abroad. They offer several profiles on more than 100 countries.

The American Society for Industrial Security (ASIS)

FAX (703) 243-4954

Holds three-day meetings where topics ranging from terrorism, espionage and neo-Naziism are discussed.

Kroll Associates

900 Third Avenue, 7th Floor,
New York, New York 10022
☎ *(212) 593-1000*

Land Mines

If there was ever a reason to pay attention in history class, land mines would be one. Why? Because travelers to dangerous places need to know more than the current situation; they must also know why and where wars were fought in the past. There may be peace in Mozambique, Eritrea, China, Jordan and the Ukraine, but there are plenty of souvenirs from past wars hiding in the ground. Someone is killed or injured by a land mine every 15 to 20 minutes.

The world has between 105 and 110 million land mines buried in 64 countries, according to the United Nations. Nobody actually knows exactly how many there are since the people who placed them never bothered to remember exactly where they buried them. The people who find them remember for the rest of their lives—if they survive the blast.

What, Me Worry?

Even though land mines maim and kill between 20,000 and 24,000 men, women and children every year, many governments claim they are not a threat to travelers. Even when the temples of Angkor Wat were mined and booby-trapped, the government was careful to put up little red signs. Greenpeace says the death toll is more like 9600. Mine clearance groups estimate that the number is 15,000, with about 80 percent being civilians and a third of those being young children. (Some anti-mine groups estimate 37, 000.) The truth is there are few little red signs in the boonies. No one knows exactly how many Iraqis were killed during the Gulf War, let alone how many shepherds stepped on land mines. In the remote parts of Afghanistan, there are no medical or government groups to keep track of the numerous maimings and murders, let alone mine victims.

Death by land mine is nasty and lonely. Most victims bleed to death in remote places or are maimed for life. Being injured by a land mine is one of the most traumatic experiences, both mentally and physically, a human can live through.

Eighty-five percent of current mine-related casualties are in Afghanistan, Angola and Cambodia—all sites of past and present dirty little wars where land mines are the perfect weapon.

With so many mines, it only takes one false step to be killed or maimed for life. When *DP* was in Cambodia, we came across a young child dying from a land mine blast. He was walking behind a cow who stepped on the mine, but the shrapnel degutted the child like a fish. The cow's death at least had a benefit. When it comes to mines, all you get is angry, maimed or dead.

More Than You Ever Want to Know About Mines

The next time someone tells you that it is those crazy Russians and liberation groups that sprinkle the world's mines, you might want to check the receipts of the countries that are buying the land mines. According to Janes Intelligence Review, Iran, Israel, Cambodia, Thailand, Chile, El Salvador, Malaysia and Saudi Arabia top the list. Tsk, tsk, you say. Well, those folks have good reasons to buy those land mines. Iran has a nasty border with Iraq, Israel gets grief from Southern Lebanon, Cambodia has the Khmer Rouge to contend with, Thailand has drug runners, Chile has Paraguay, El Salvador has jungle insurgents, and Malaysia still has vivid memories of a nasty war with Indonesia back in the early '60s. Saudi Arabia figures land mines are cheaper than picket fences to mark its southern boundaries. We are sure there must have been good reasons for placing 400 million land mines after World War II. The scary problem is there are still between 65 and 110 million of those mines sitting under the ground. The real bad guys may be the people who cash in from making the grizzly leg poppers.

Who Makes 'em	
Country of Origin	**Places Used**
Belgium	*Angola, Iraq (Kurdistan), Kuwait, Mozambique, Namibia, Somalia*
Brazil	*Nicaragua*
Bulgaria	*Cambodia*
Canada	*Iraq*
Chile	*Iraq (Kurdistan)*
China	*Afghanistan, Angola, Cambodia, Mozambique, Namibia, Somalia*

Who Makes 'em	
Country of Origin	**Places Used**
Czech (ex)	*Afghanistan, Angola, Cambodia, Mozambique, Namibia, Nicaragua, Somalia*
Egypt	*Afghanistan, Nicaragua, Iraq*
France	*Iraq (Kurdistan), Iraq (Kuwait), Mozambique, Somalia*
Germany (former East)	*Angola, Cambodia, Mozambique Namibia, Somalia*
Hungary	*Cambodia*
Italy	*Angola, Iraq (Kurdistan), Iraq(Kuwait)*
Pakistan	*Somalia*
Romania	*Iraq (Kurdistan)*
Russia	*Afghanistan, Angola, Cambodia, Iraq (Kurdistan), Iraq (Kuwait), Mozambique, Namibia, Nicaragua, Somalia, Vietnam*
Singapore	*Iraq (Kuwait)*
South Africa	*Angola, Mozambique, Somalia*
Spain	*Iraq (Kuwait)*
United Kingdom	*Afghanistan, Mozambique, Somalia*
United States	*Angola, Cambodia, Iraq (Kurdistan), Mozambique, Nicaragua, Somalia*
Vietnam	*Cambodia*
Yugoslavia (ex)	*Afghanistan, Cambodia, Mozambique, Namibia, Zimbabwe*

Source: Janes Intelligence Review

Land mines are cheap and can be laid in relative safety, cripple economies, stall advances and create fear. The most industrious and creative producers of land mines are not the Cold War vassal states but the high-tech Western countries who make such a big stink about all those little kids who get blown to bits. There are 100 different companies in 55 countries that make land mines. Of the 55 countries who design and manufacture antipersonnel mines (about 75 percent of all land mines), 36 of the countries allow them to be exported. Keep in mind that many mines are bought through shell companies who import them into "nice" countries and then export them to "nasty" countries. Even Switzerland makes and sells five models, while Iran, Cuba and Myanmar only can figure out how to make one model of land mine.

The U.S. has taken steps to remove mines from its base in Guantanamo Bay in Cuba but will leave them in the ground in Korea. They will destroy about $10 million worth of $2 antipersonnel mines and will use instead smart mines that destroy themselves or become inert when their batteries die. Here's a list of where you can shop for the 362 different models of land mines:

Stumps 'R Us: Who designs 'em	
Country	# of Models Sold
United States	37
Italy	36
Russia	31
Sweden	21
China	21
Germany	18
Vietnam	18
France	14
Bosnia Herzegovinia	16
Austria	16

Source: Janes Intelligence Review

How Are They Used?

Land mines are supposed to be laid according to preagreed patterns. The area should be marked and maps kept to facilitate cleanup. Land mines are laid about six feet apart. One such NATO pattern is an A pattern with one antitank mine surrounded by three antipersonnel mines: one above and one on each side like a triangle with the antitank in the middle.

During hostilities, these mine fields are carefully marked with skull and cross-bones "Beware of mine" signs, backed up with accurate maps showing placement and layout. Once hostilities cease, the winning side then quickly and efficiently removes every single land mine, allowing people to live their lives free from fear. In your dreams!

That is wishful thinking, since the most effective way to sow land mines is to drop millions of small plastic mines by shell or from aircraft. Small bomblets, 247 to a pod, are dropped as part of cluster bombs. Most rebel groups will put mines in potholes, in detours, along walking paths and in fields; they'll even booby-trap intriguing items that villagers, soldiers or children will pick up. Guerillas don't follow patterns. Nobody knows how many mortar rounds, artillery shells and discarded ordnance will be discovered by curious children or diligent farmers. No one bothers to keep notes of where mines are planted as booby traps or nightly security perimeters.

The problem of land mines has become the largest single threat to the health of rural populations in countries that once suffered warfare. Mines can be part of a major defensive region, as in some parts of China, the Middle East and Europe. Mines are also used in combat operations to provide security and early warning or create surprises. Bosnia, Iraq and Kuwait are examples of countries that were heavily mined but stand a chance of being cleaned up. Other countries have actually become dumping grounds for millions of cheap mines laid down to terrorize the population. Most of the African countries, Afghanistan and Cambodia are full of land mine junkyards.

How Do They Work?

Most people picture the movie cliché of a careless GI hearing a soft click and then sweating buckets, while his buddy slides his knife under his boot to keep the detonator depressed. Not quite. Yes, mines are essentially dumb explosive devices that are detonated by pressure, but weapon specialists have learned a few tricks since those WWII movies.

First of all, a mine contains extremely explosive material that creates a wall of air and debris that expands outward at almost 7000 meters per second. Some mines add metal projectiles like ball bearings, sharp flechettes or even nails that puncture soft flesh and shred bone into a fine spray. The shock waves are so strong that many victims find their feet still in their boots and their bones turned into projectiles that kill other people.

If you don't die of blood loss, shock or as a result of being turned into Swiss cheese, infection is your worst enemy. The explosion will imbed bits of clothing, grass, mud, dirt and your trusty guide into the shredded mass of meat that used to be your legs. You will need to apply a tourniquet and get to a hospital (yeah, sure) ASAP. Once you're under medical care, the mashed bits will be quickly amputated, you'll be punched with an IV and given enough morphine to kill a junkie.

Liquid Lunch in a Crunch

Many times victims of gunshot wounds, mine blasts and injuries caused by blood loss don't have to die. In order to provide an IV solution to provide minimum nutrition and increase blood pressure, it is important to know how to administer an IV injection. If you do not have a sterile IV solution, one can be made by taking one liter of sterile freshwater (filtered, then boiled for five minutes and cooled while covered). Add 25 grams of glucose and 4.5 grams of table salt. In emergency cases, the juice from a green coconut can be used with just the salt added.

Other mines have cute names like Bouncing Betty, because they spring up and explode at eye level, releasing a lethal explosion of ball bearings, killing everything within 25 meters and wounding everyone else within 200 meters. Road mines are so large and powerful that there is a crater and little else left over. Enough scary stuff, let's get specific. Here are the basic types of land mines used today:

Scatter Mines

The Soviet-made PFM-1 butterfly-type mine delivers specialized deadly services. These small mines are sprinkled all over Afghanistan by Russians to injure, but not kill *mujahedin*. The idea is that a wounded person slows down two healthy people. That the Ruskies don't have the balls to go up into the mountains to plant them is another major attraction. These mines are dropped from helicopters and burrow into the ground using tiny wings. They explode when twisted or pressed firmly. The mines were a last-ditch effort by the Russians in Afghanistan, but now they mainly injure children since adults know not to pick them up. These mines have not found wide usage but are a disturbing use of lethal force. They do not always explode when first handled and can actually be kicked, dropped and twisted before they explode, leading some people to believe that the Russians designed them to kill curious children. There also are "smart" scatter mines that can arm themselves, detonate without direct pressure and self-detonate after a specified period. These smart mines are delivered by cannon, airplane or rocket.

DP's visit to Afghanistan proved that small scatter mines are still doing their deadly work, having seen many maimed children and young men missing their feet.

Antipersonnel, Small

Foot soldiers can't carry big heavy mines, so they make a lot of little plastic blast mines that can be sprinkled in villages, latrines and rice paddies. These mines are about the size of an oversized hockey puck and have a pressure-sensitive plate that the victim steps on. These mines are usually not buried but placed under brush, streams, wet potholes, rice paddies and mud. The mine takes very little pressure to set it off, and the victim will usually lose a foot and/or a leg up to the knee. These mines are not designed to kill but to create serious, incapacitating injury which effects the morale of the other side. No one feels gung ho when they see the results of a mine. Top sellers in this category are the Chinese Type 72, Italian TS-50 and US M14. These mines are very difficult to find, since many of them use plastic casings and cannot be readily picked up by normal metal detectors.

Antipersonel, Large

These killer-blast mines usually pack about 200 grams of explosive (compared to 40 grams in the small category). The best-selling Soviet PMN likes to deliver leg-shattering wounds caused by small mines with higher explosive content. They are used to maim groups of soldiers, with severe wounds to groin and buttocks and loss of both legs common. These and their smaller cousins are the most popular mines in existence. They cost about US$3 each and can be found killing people in most Third World war zones. There are also large versions of these pressure mines that can kill entire platoons. These mines are typically buried just under the surface and can be easily found if they have metal parts.

Fragmentation Mines

Fragmentation mines like the Russian POMZ-2 or US M18A1 "Claymore" are designed to spray large areas with big pieces of metal fragments. These mines are set up as booby traps (usually with trip wires) and are used to protect camp perimeters or ambush columns. There is a detonator pin that is attached to a wire. The mines are placed above ground, on trees, across narrow paths, inside buildings, along roads, or anywhere a group of soldiers would collect. One soldier trips over the wire, and instantly he and his buddies are killed. If the mines are never tripped, they sit waiting for the next victim.

There is also the Bouncing Betty type of fragmentation mines called "bounding" mines. They are designed to be buried in the ground in open areas, and when one of the whiskerlike sensors is triggered, the mine will project upwards and explode ball bearings or shrapnel in a lethal 360-degree radius. The Italian-made Valmara-69 is the most famous example of this mine. The explosion occurs at a three- to five-foot height maximizing the "kill ratio" (a popular term in all military sales films). Some mines have over 1000 individual pieces of shrapnel, so the chances of surviving by ducking or turning sideways are slim to none.

These mines are designed to be lethal and are left behind to slow down advancing armies, decimate charges and create maximum casualties.

Road Mines

The mines that do the most damage to wartime soldiers and peacetime mine clearance workers are the big plate-sized and plank-size tank killers. These are mines laid down in active war zones to kill and disable vehicles, kill the occupants and destroy the road. The British L9 and the Italian VS-22 are popular mines used in the Gulf War and in other combat zones. Road mines are also used in Somalia, Southern Lebanon and other active zones. Since these mines are easy to detect and placed around major transportation corridors, they are usually the first ones to be cleared up (or to be run over). Mines are almost always laid at night and rarely under paved roads. They are laid on dirt roads and along the side of the road.

Other Mines and Hidden Dangers

If you really are kinky about mines, you can pick up a Jane's directory or send for brochures. There are many booby traps that are not technically mines. There are also extraordinary amounts of unexploded ordnance in the ground that may not jump up and bite you, but can be found displayed in villager's homes and souvenir shops.

What are your chances of finding one of these millions of mines? It simply depends on how far off the beaten path you travel and the military history of your country of choice. Off-roading in Angola would not be a good idea. Playing hide and seek around Cambodia is also not a good idea.

Where Are the Mines?

Eighteen African countries have between 18 and 30 million mines each; Angola has the most, between 9 and 20 million uncleared mines, and even the "lightly mined" countryside of Mozambique (with about 2 million) has turned many small roads into death traps and caused large game to vanish. Somalia has 1 million mines; Sudan has between 1 and 2 million (and growing); Zimbabwe and Ethiopia have major uncleared minefields (about half a million each). Bosnia Herzegovina, Cambodia and Croatia are the most mined countries in the world, with an average of between 92 and 142 land mines per square mile. This can be misleading, since the mines in Egypt are sitting in the remote northern deserts and the mines in Angola are in small towns and fields. All of East Asia has 15 to 23 million land mines. The Middle East has 17 to 24 million land mines, mainly in Iraq, Iran, Kuwait and the Israeli border. Saddam Hussein went a little overboard during his brief occupation of Kuwait and turned the entire country into a minefield, most of which has been cleaned up at great expense. Europe is home to 7 million mines, mostly along the former Soviet border. During World War I, seven countries fired nearly 1.5 billion shells. Ninety-five percent of them were conventional explosives; the rest were chemical shells. It is estimated that 30 percent of the chemical shells landed without ever exploding and have been sitting around since 1918. Most of the shells were used in Belgium. The Ukraine is home to over a million mines. Russia has both new minefields and WWII fields that were never cleared. Bosnia-Herzegovina has many uncleared fields, and new mines were being laid at a rate of 60,000 a week. At last count, there were 152 mines per square mile in this torn-up land.

The Land Mine Top 20			
Rank	Country	# of mines	Avg per sq mile	Area found
1.	Egypt	23,000,000	59	*North toward border with Israel*
2.	Iran	16,000,000	25	*Along border with Iraq*
3.	Angola	15,000,000	31	*Rural areas*
4.	Afghanistan	10,000,000	40	*Scattered by air, also around Kabul*
5.	Cambodia	10,000,000	142	*Rural areas*
6.	China	10,000,000	3	*Along border with Russia*
7.	Iraq	10,000,000	60	*Along border with Iran*
8.	Bosnia-Herzegovina	3,000,000	152	*Throughout country*

The Land Mine Top 20				
Rank	Country	# of mines	Avg per sq mile	Area found
9.	Croatia	2,000,000	92	Throughout country
10.	Mozambique	2,000,000	7	Rural areas
11.	Eritrea	1,000,000	28	Along border with Ethiopia, rural
12.	Somalia	1,000,000	4	Along border with Ethiopia
13.	Sudan	1,000,000	4	Southern areas
14.	Ukraine	1,000,000	4	Old battle fields
15.	Ethiopia	500,000	1	Along border with Eritrea, Somalia
16.	Yugoslavia	500,000	13	Throughout country
17.	Jordan	207,000	5	Along border with Israel
18.	Chad	100,000+	6	Along northern border with Libya
19.	Rwanda	100,000+	5	Primarily in north
20.	Vietnam	100,000+	8	Southern areas, DMZ

Source: U.S. Department of Humanitarian Affairs

Up to a million uncleared mines are left in South America. There are mines in Colombia, Chile and most areas of Nicaragua, Guatemala and even Cuba. Some areas of the Falklands are permanently off-limits because the British could not spare the men to clear the minefields. There is a lot of splattered mutton every week in the Falklands.

Most countries in Southern Africa have large mined areas, as do the entire Horn of Africa, all areas of Middle East conflict and most border areas from the Cold War. Although there are no mines in North America, we did send a few overseas. If you thought the U.S. doesn't do those types of things, think again. Remember that Uncle Sam used to clean out our bomb loads over Laos, leaving millions of cluster bombs for little Laotians to discover. More than 300,000 tons of bombs were dropped on northern Laos during the Vietnam War. No one has any idea how much unexploded ordnance still lies in the jungles of Northern Vietnam. The overly cautious should understand that, along with cigarette butts, ammo containers and mixed-race children, land mines are just the litter of war.

A Thousand and One...a Thousand and Two...BOOM! Places Where They Haven't Counted All the Land Mines	
North, Central and South America	
Mexico	Reports of land mine injuries, number unknown
Guatemala	Under 100,000
Cuba	Reports of land mine injuries, number unknown
Honduras	Under 100,000, along border with Nicaragua
El Salvador	Under 100,000, throughout country
Costa Rica	Under 100,000
Colombia	In remote areas, under 100,000
Ecuador	Along border with Peru
Peru	Along border with Ecuador

A Thousand and One...a Thousand and Two...BOOM!
Places Where They Haven't Counted All the Land Mines

Falkland Islands	*Throughout region*
Africa	
Libya	*Less than 100,000*
Uganda	*Along border areas, less than 100,000*
Burundi	*Newly laid mines, less than 100,000*
Zimbabwe	*Throughout country, more than 100,000*
Zaire	*Less than 100,000*
Namibia	*Less than 100,000*
Western Sahara	*Less than 100,000*
Mauritania	*Less than 100,000*
Senegal	*Less than 100,000*
Guinea Bissau	*Less than 100,000*
Liberia	*Throughout country*
Sierra Leone	*Throughout country*
Tunisia	*Less than 100,000*
Middle East	
Oman	*Throughout country, along borders*
Turkey	*Eastern areas, along eastern borders*
Lebanon	*Southern Lebanon, mined daily*
Syria	*Along border areas*
Cyprus	*Along Turkish/Greek division*
Yemen	*Along border areas*
Europe	
Germany	*In former Eastern Germany, along border areas*
Slovenia	*More than 100,000*
Greece	*Less than 100,000*
Czech Republic	*Less than 100,000*
Denmark	*Less than 100,000*
Latvia	*Less than 100,000*
Asia	
Belarus	*Throughout country*
Armenia	*Areas of conflict*
Azerbaijan	*Throughout country*
Tajikistan	*Border areas*
Burma	*Throughout country*
Mongolia	*Border areas, less than 100,000*
Laos	*Throughout country, unexploded ordnance*

LAND MINES

How Do You Get Rid of Land Mines?

There are movements by both military and civilian groups (about 300 in total) to ban the manufacture and use of land mines. The chances are good of convincing First World countries of a ban, but the facts are that the most heavily mined countries are a result of dirty wars, not major conflicts. The United Nations called for a worldwide ban on land mines, but nobody seems to care. In conflicts between major powers, land mines are usually cleaned up. The majority of land mines have been planted in the last 20 years with 2 million planted in 1994 alone. Currently, 36 nations build land mines and most countries use them. These countries produce about 10 to 20 million units a year.

The U.S. asked the countries that manufacture land mines to voluntarily suspend exports for three years, yet the U.S. budgeted $89 million for land mine warfare in 1996.

Land mines are cleared in a variety of ways. In large open areas, tracked vehicles with flailing chains can clear most mines. In less accessible or poorer areas, the old-fashioned metal detector is used. Some new Scheibel-type models can detect many plastic versions. Some countries use the old-fashioned method of probing at a shallow angle with knives. Sniffing dogs can be used, along with a raft of new high-tech methods employing radar, sonar, thermal neutron, microwave, and even satellites. For now, most mines are detected and dug up the old-fashioned way, by hand.

Wildly speculative estimates on the costs to remove the world's land mines come in at about $33 billion.

In Cambodia, a burgeoning adventure travel destination, estimates are it will cost US$12 million annually for 10 years to remove the 10 million land mines left from the war. There are a few groups like HALO working in Cambodia, but they still have to put up with being kidnapped and harassed. There are 60,000 victims of land mines in Cambodia today. Every 237th Cambodian is an amputee. The reality is that unlike handicap-friendly America, losing a limb in the Third World is a fast ticket to poverty and begging.

Land mines can be found in Angola, Afghanistan, Bosnia-Herzegovina, Cambodia, Ethiopia, Eritrea, the Falklands, Iraq, Iran, Laos, Mozambique, Somalia, Thailand, Kuwait and Vietnam. In addition to carefully planted land mines, there is a significant amount of unexploded ordnance in Europe, Southeast Asia and the South Pacific.

One Small Step...

If you can't dig them up and you can't stop them from planting them, what can you do to help? First, write your local and federal politicians to make them aware that the U.S. and its allies manufacture these insidious killers. If you have experience in explosives or mine clearance, read the "Dangerous Jobs" section to contact a number of mine clearance companies. If you would like to donate money or time to help the innocent victims of mines, contact EMERGENCY, via Bagutta 12, 20121 Milan Italy (☎ 39-2-7600-1104, or FAX 39-2-7600-3719),

There were 7 million land mines laid in Iraq and Kuwait before and during the Gulf War. Kuwait spent $800 million clearing out land mines after the Gulf War.

It costs between $500 and $2000 per mine to remove them. In 1993, 80,000 - 100,000 mines were removed around the world at a cost of $100 million. To remove all the mines in the world would cost $58 billion. Unfortunately, 2 to 5 million mines are put in the ground every year.

A *DP* reader who spends much of his time in mined areas while working for the U.N. Rapid Response Unit has sent in these tips:

Wheel of Misfortune:
How to Avoid Land Mines

1. Never take a trip on a mined road before 9 or 10 a.m. Most mines are laid at night to surprise regular convoys or patrols. Try to follow heavy trucks. Keep at least 200 yards behind but do not lot lose sight of the truck.

2. Never take point. (Let others start walking or driving before you.) Keep a distance of at least 60-100 feet to avoid shrapnel. If someone is wounded by a mine, apply a tourniquet immediately to the damaged limbs to prevent death by blood loss.

3. When possible, follow local vehicles or stay on fresh tracks. If a mine goes off, DO NOT RUN. Stay where you are, and walk backwards in your own tracks.

4. Always stay on the pavement. In heavily mined areas, NEVER leave the pavement (even to take a leak). If you must turn around, do so on the pavement.

5. If you have a flak jacket or bullet-proof vest, sit on it when driving.

6. Know the mining strategy of the combatants. Do they place mines in potholes (as in northeastern Somalia) or on the off-road tracks made by vehicles avoiding potholes (as in Rwanda, Burundi and Zaire)?

7. If you think you may have strayed into a mined area, go back on your tracks. Mines are usually planted at a shallow depth with their detonators requiring downward pressure. As a last resort, mines can be probed with a long knife or rod at a very shallow angle and a very gentle touch. Do not attempt to remove the mine, but mark it for later removal or detonation.

8. Never touch unusual or suspicious objects. They may be booby-trapped.

9. Travel with all windows open. Preferably with doors off or in the back of pickup trucks. This will release some of the blast if you hit a land mine.

10. If you have reason to believe that there has been mine activity (new digging, unusual tire tracks and footprints), mark the area with a skull and crossbones and the local or English word "MINES." Notify local and/or foreign authorities.

A ROGUE'S GALLERY OF LAND MINES
PMN—Antipersonnel mine

The plastic, four-inch mine contains enough explosive to remove a leg at the hip.

Made by: Chinese, common in former Soviet states.

Cost: US$3.00

Found in: Zones throughout Africa, Middle East and Southeast Asia.

Est. in-ground: 20 million.

TYPE 72-A—Antipersonnel mine

Tiny, cheap and difficult to detect because of its plastic case. The perfect recipe for a best selling land mine.

Made by: China North Industries (Beijing).

Cost: US$3.00

Found in: Afghanistan, Angola, Cambodia, Iraq, Mozambique, Somalia, Thailand, Vietnam, Kuwait.

Est. in-ground: 20 million.

A ROGUE'S GALLERY OF LAND MINES

POM-Z-2—Antipersonnel Fragmentation Mine

Small and crude, the POM is mounted on a stick and has the same force as a hand grenade.

Made by: Chinese and common in former Soviet state arsenals.

Cost: US$3.30.

Found in: Zones worldwide.

Est. in-ground: 16 million.

PRB 409—Antipersonnel Mine

Three inches wide, mildly powerful, popular with rebel groups.

Made by: Paoudres Reunie de Belgue, a subsidiary of Giat Industries (Versailles, France).

Cost: US$4.00

Found in: Afghanistan, Iraq, Iran, Mozambique, Somalia, Lebanon.

Est. in-ground: 11 million.

PT-MI-BA III—Antitank Mine

Made of plastic, the 13-inch mine contains 16 pounds of explosive, enough to disable heavily armored vehicles.

Made by: Czechoslovakian state factories.

Cost: US$38.00

Found in: Iran, Iraq, Kuwait, Mozambique, Somalia.

Est. in-ground: 11 million.

VS 2.2—Antitank Mine

Plastic, nine-inch diameter mine containing 2.2 kilograms (4.8 pounds) of explosive.

Made by: Valsella Mecannotecnica S.P.A., a subsidiary of Fiat Motors (Brescia, Italy).

Cost: US$26.00

Found in: Afghanistan, Iraq, Iran, Kuwait.

Est. in-ground: 10 million.

L-9—Antitank Mine

The "bar" mine is pressure sensitive along its entire 47-inch length. Buried under roads it is designed to destroy small personnel carriers and disable tanks by blowing off their tracks.

Made by: Royal Ordnance, a division of British Aerospace (London).

Cost: US$38.00

Found in: Iraq, Kuwait.

Est. in-ground: Six million.

M18A1 'Claymore'—Antipersonnel Mine

A rectangular mine usually mounted as part of defensive construction or used for ambushes. The Claymore has a killing zone 50 yards wide and comes with helpful notice telling you which side to face towards the enemy.

Made by: Thiokol Corporation (Shreveport, LA.); widely imitated.

Cost: US$27.47

Found in: Angola, Mozambique, Central America, Southeast Asia.

Est. in-ground: Six million.

Military and Paramilitary Organizations

How to Travel Free, Meet Interesting People and Then Kill Them

There is a small group of people who think that planting seedlings and buying running shoes made out of recycled garbage bags is not doing enough. Young men with a hunger for action should be lining up to be cabbies or donning the polyester warrior garb of the late-night convenience store clerk. Instead, our young are force-fed a diet of well-armed soldiers barfing out endless rounds of 9mms and steroid-pumped knuckleheads causing serious dental bills—at least on TV. In the inner city there is less plot but a lot more action. With all this violence becoming the Muzak of the'90s, it is no surprise that the more ambitious think the best way to make the world a better place is to start by eliminating some of the bad guys. Jimmy Carter doesn't have a show called "Have Mouth Will Travel" and it is unlikely that Stallone will star as a softspoken peace broker anytime soon. For now, we just shoot first and negotiate later.

But adventure stirs deep in the loins of youth. What can they do to make this world a better place and tell stories to their grandkids? In the old days you could ride off to the Crusades, discover the New World or just raise hell in some wealthy potentate's army. Since then, there have been enough great wars to occupy the heroic and romantic. Between our great and not-so-great wars (when Uncle Sam made you volunteer), poets, thugs and the bloodthirsty have volunteered for a variety of noble causes, from the Russian Revolution to the Spanish Civil War. Today, those who seek to make a difference by direct action can choose to join an army or group that is actively fighting for independence, freedom or any other cause. Keep in mind that you can lose your American citizenship if you do, and your chances of being summarily executed by the side of the road if captured are high. The shadowy nature and basic illegality of the mercenary business means we can't provide you with neat little addresses and phone numbers of all the people who recruit or hire mercenaries, but we can give a general overview of what is out there and a few interesting highlights of this ancient and much maligned profession.

Happiness Is a Warm Gun: The Army

Today's armed forces look pretty good to the hordes of young men and women who can't find jobs. Despite the dire warnings and foreign rumblings, there is little chance for good versus evil action in today's globocop environment. The world's businesses are just too tightly interwoven to allow another Axis versus Allied confrontation. The U.S military has officially seen action in Korea, Vietnam, Lebanon, Iraq, Grenada, Panama, Libya, Somalia and Haiti. Strangely, none of these have been official wars but rather police actions or showing up international brigades fighting to support victimized countries. There have been few guts-and-glory movies about our covert action in Angola, Cuba, Cambodia, Nicaragua, El Salvador and numerous other covert operations. Most of our military expenditures and efforts have been concentrated on a Cold War with the Soviet Union and China. With today's lack of clear objectives, simple villains or even positive role models, it is no surprise that the U.S. military is having trouble attracting the caliber of soldier it had with the draft. Scores are down, as are average IQ levels, while the equipment and technology get more complicated. Although political science and sociology are not required of grunts, it is very difficult for modern-day veterans of Somalia, Haiti and Beirut to understand why they risked their lives.

It would be hard to get excited about fighting for America's freedom while sitting in a peacekeeping checkpoint in Beirut or baby-sitting missiles pointed at Moscow. What can you expect if you sign up in today's army? The Army's nine-week basic training program at Fort Jackson, South Carolina, transforms civilians to soldiers 60 raw recruits at a time. At bases like Fort Jackson, 70,000 military personnel are trained annually, 3 million since the base's opening in 1917.

Upon arrival, you can expect to fill out horrendous amounts of paperwork. You spend the first six days at the Reception Battalion, where you pick up your uniforms, get a shaved head and shots and are given 16-hour doses of KP, or kitchen patrol. The second week is filled with 12-hour days (with reveille at 4 a.m. and ending at 8 p.m.), drill and ceremony movements, classroom work, land and navigation courses, bayonet assault training and an obstacle course centered around the Victory Tower.

The second month begins with basic rifle marksmanship. You will learn to understand and care for your M-16 like no other physical object you will own. You will learn to fire at targets as far as 300 meters away. Based on your performance, you will be called a marksman, sharpshooter or expert. Toward the end of the second month, the weaponry gets serious, with the M-60 machine gun, AT4 anti-tank weapon and hand grenades. Instead of firing your weapon, you get a taste of what it will be like on the receiving end, as you learn how to move around under fire complete with barbwired obstacles, dynamite going off and M-60 rounds being fired over your head as you crawl 300 meters on your belly.

The last week of training intensifies with PT testing and working with explosives. The climax is a three-day field exercise, where trainees get to play war by digging foxholes and taking eight-mile hikes with full packs. The last few days are spent cleaning barracks in preparation for the next cadets. How tough is it? New recruits will say very; the old salts will say not as tough as it used to be. Corporal punishment was banned in the mid-1970s, and sexual harassment has been added to the list of subjects taught. Minor punishment is confined to "smoke sessions," for the less than motivated. These semipunitive periods of intense physical training are designed to remind the errant soldier who is in charge. Soldiers are chewed out using the entire spectrum of profanity.

The front-leaning rest position (a push-up that is never completed) is also used as punishment. There is no form of entertainment, since there technically is no rest time. Television, newspapers and radios are taboo. Mail and occasional phone calls are allowed. Three washing machines and five showerheads are considered enough to keep 60 active men clean.

Once out of basic training, you can expect to be posted to an area in line with your specialty. The military is still using technology about 10–20 years behind what you find on the outside. The main focus in the military is changing from '40s style ground wars to '70s style rapid-deployment tactics. The Army provides lousy pay, good benefits and a chance to pack in two careers in a lifetime. As for furthering a cause or making the world a better place, one only has to look at Lebanon, Kuwait, Somalia and Vietnam to see the results of gunboat diplomacy.

Since McDonald's is not hiring any Green Berets or Navy SEALS to take down Burger Kings, just who is hiring military experts? Well technically, nobody. Although many countries like Brunei (which uses Ghurkas), the Vatican (which has about 100 Swiss guards), the Spanish Foreign Legion (the poor man's legion) and Oman have armies staffed by paid foreigners (about 360 British officers were "seconded" to the Sultan to fight rebels), you will have to be hired out of an existing army (typically the British Army) to be considered. Many foreign armies are happy to enlist your services and the Canadian, British or Australian armed forces will even give you citizenship when you are finished. Times are tough, so there are plenty of people who like the idea of paid housing and training. You can expect stringent entry requirements and a thorough check of your police record and passport. These groups have had a dismal record of mismanagement and failed causes from Beirut to Mogadishu. The recent action in Haiti looked more like a replay of the L.A. riots, except that Haiti had a happy ending. If you endorse the retro concept of keeping the natives from getting restless, or just want to hang out with men who have bad tattoos, you might want to consider enlisting in the Foreign Legion. For those who want to get dangerous we have some other options:

Beau Geste: The French Foreign Legion

The more romantic and politically insensitive might want to consider joining the Legion. The Legion does France's colonial housekeeping work, oppressing minorities, liberating missionaries and generally keeping the natives from getting too restless. The Legion knows it does France's dirty work and recruits accordingly. They will take all comers, preferably foreigners and men who will not draw too big a funeral procession. The Legion is tough and disposable.

The best example of the Legion's mindset is the single most revered object in their possession—the wooden hand of Captain Jean Danjou on display in the museum in Aubagne. Danjou lost his hand when his musket misfired and blew up. He then died with the 59 worn-out survivors defending a hacienda on April 30,

1864, in a small hamlet called Camerone in Mexico. His men, exhausted after a long forced march to evade the 2000-strong Mexican army, decided to die rather than surrender. His wooden hand was found by the tardy relief column and enshrined to commemorate his courage. Over 10,000 legionnaires died at Dien Bien Phu in 1954 in a similar debacle. One unit suffered 90 percent losses at Cao Bang, only to have 576 out of 700 killed four years later at Dien Bien Phu.

A normal army would tut tut the lack of reinforcement, bad strategies and resulting waste of manpower. The Legion (like all of French Military history) myopically elevates folly into legend and attracts thousands of eager recruits every year. The basic lesson is that with only 75 percent of the Legion being French, they are considered disposable.

Despite its notoriety, the Legion is still the army of choice when young men dream of adventure. The Legion is the tough guy's army, tailor-made for Hollywood film scripts, home for intellectuals, criminals and outcasts. It's a close-knit band of hardy, brutal men who are either escaping misguided pasts or seeking adventure in exotic places and doing heroic deeds. The lure of the Legion is communicated to us via simplistic movies like *Beau Geste,* or simplistic books that romanticize its violence and bloodshed. What they don't tell you is that the Legion has always been brutal, ill-equipped and, worst of all, disposable. But you get to learn to be a professional killer and chances are high that you will get to use those skills on other people.

The Legion was created in 1831 by King Louis Phillipe to assist in the conquest of Algeria. The king correctly assumed that paid mercenaries would not complain about the conditions or political correctness in carrying out his orders. Since then, the Legion has been used to fight France's dirty little wars in Algeria, Indochina, Africa and the Middle East. Although there have been many heroic battles fought in some of the world's most remote and hostile regions, you are better served by reading the multitudes of books about the Legion. The reality today is that the Legion has been downsized and specialized.

The Legion is one of the few action outfits (like the former Selous Scouts of Rhodesia or Oman's mostly British army) which offers the professional adventurer a steady diet of hardship broken up by short bursts of excitement and danger. This format has attracted many of the world's best-trained soldiers, like the SS after WWII or Special Forces vets from Vietnam. The world of adventure is shrinking, however. Today the French Foreign Legion is made up of 8500 officers and men from more than 100 countries. They no longer have any ongoing wars that require constant replacements. They now focus on picking and choosing from amongst the world's tough guys to enable them to field soldiers who are fluent in many languages and specialities without many of the religious, political or ethnic barriers that hamper other peacekeeping or expedition forces.

How to Get in

There are 16 Legion recruiting centers in France, the most popular being Fort de Nogent in Paris. Just ask at the police station for the *Legion Etrangere*. The more focused head straight for Aubagne, just outside of the dirty Mediterranean port of Marseille. You will be competing with over 8000 other eager Legionnaire wannabe's for the 1500 slots available. East Europeans make up about 50 percent of the eager candidates these days. Candidates are tested for their intelligence and physical fitness, and special skills are a definite plus. If you just murdered your wife's boyfriend the week before, be forewarned that all candidates are run through Interpol's data banks and the Legion cooperates with them to weed out murderers. If you just want to escape the IRS or alimony payments, the Legion could care less. After all, what better inducement is there to staying after your third year in Djibouti than the thought of spending that same time in jail Stateside.

You don't have to bring any ID or proof of anything; when you sign up, you will be assigned a *nom de guerre* and a nationality. Being Canadian is popular, and calling yourself Rambo is definitely an old joke.

You must pass the same general standards as the French Army, but then the Legion takes over. You will learn to march like a mule in hell—long forced marches with heavy packs; jungle, mountain and desert training. You can bail during the first four months of training, but from then on you will speak the thick, crude French of the Legionnaire and learn to be completely self-sufficient in the world's worst regions.

There is basic training in Castelnaudary (between Carcassone and Toulouse, just off the A61), commando training in St. Louis near Andorra, and mountain training in Corsica. Four weeks into your training, you will be given the *Kepi blanc,* the white pillbox hat of the Legionnaire. Unlike the Navy SEALS or Western elite forces, the accommodations are simple and the discipline is swift, and other than special prostitutes who service the legion, there is little to look forward to in the mandatory five years of service. Legionnaires can get married after 10 years of service.

Once you pass basic training, you will be trained in a specialty: mountain warfare, explosives or any number of trades that make you virtually unemployable upon discharge (except in another mercenary army). French citizens cannot serve, except as officers. Those French officers who do sign on do so for a taste of adventure. In troubled times, the Legionnaires are always the first to be deployed to protect French citizens in uprisings or civil wars.

With this international makeup, it is not surprising that Legionnaires today find themselves as peacekeepers, stationed in the tattered shreds of the French empire or with the U.N. You may be assigned to protect the European space program in Kourou, in the steamy jungles of French Guiana, or to patrol the desert from Quartier Gaboce, in the hot baked salt pan of Djibouti.When it hits the fan as in Kolwezi or Chad, you can expect some excitement, a quick briefing, an air drop into a confused and bloody scene, followed by years of tedium, training and patrol.

Since the Legion attracts loners and misfits and since many of them spend their time in godforsaken outposts, it is not hard to understand that the Legion becomes more than a job. In fact, the motto of the Legion is *"Legio Patria Nostra,"* or "The Legion Is Our Homeland," which describes the mindset and purpose. Many men serve out their full 20 years, since they are unable to find equally stimulating work on the outside.

When you get out, you don't get much other than a small pension, and the opportunity to become a Frenchman (Legionnaires are automatically granted French citizenship after five years). After a lifetime of adventure, and divorced from their homeland, the men of the Legion can look forward to retirement at Domaine Danjou, a château near Puyloubier (12 miles west of St. Maxim, north of the A7) in southern France, where close to 200 Legionnaires spend their last years. This is where the Legion looks after its own, its elderly, wounded and infirm. Here, the men have small jobs, ranging from bookbinding to working in the vineyards. Later, they will join their comrades in the stony ground of the country that never claimed them but for which they gave their lives. Remember, the Legion has always been disposable.

Happiness Is a Dead Infidel: The *Mujahedin*

If the Legion seems a little too Euro or confining, you can try the next level down. If you are Muslim, don't mind being completely disposable and hate infidels more than the IRS, maybe you should become an Afghan. The most volunteering folks on this planet are the Afghans, or veterans of the war in Afghanistan against Russia. You should want a front row seat in the Superbowl of religious wars: Jihad. There is always Jihad, or the Holy War, being exported by Iran against Russia, the Great Satan (us) and all its allies. Think of it as the Crusades of the 21st century.

Jihad started in 1979, when the Soviets decided to install a puppet ruler and then back him up with the Soviet Army. As with all foreign countries who decided to roll armies into Afghanistan, they forgot that the tribes of Afghanistan love a good fight. In fact, when there is no occupying power, they love to fight amongst themselves.

The Afghans are the direct effect of too much money, training and weapons being funneled into one of the world's poorest regions—Pakistan and Afghanistan. The U.S. decided this would be a great time to give the Russians a bloody nose and sent in massive amounts of money to support every tiny tribal religious or political group that hated the Russians. All the Afghan groups had to do was provide a head count, a list of weapons, an area of operations, and they were in business. Naturally, the real *mujahedin* looked upon the money from the infidels warily and the most wacky kept coming back for more.

The result is that the States and the Gulf States (through the CIA, through Pakistan) created an entire 7-11 chain of warrior clans armed to the teeth with the common goal of causing the Russians grief. Simple gun-happy tribesmen were trained in everything from how to make explosives out of fertilizer to how to use Stinger missiles. The CIA not only provided more than enough money; they created an unholy network where these factions could swap war stories and business cards.

Over 10,000 volunteers traveled to Afghanistan to fight the Russians lured by money, principal and a chance to poke the bear in the nose. Many more people, after hearing of the plight of the Afghan people, sent funds and were predisposed to the total annihilation of the Russian soldiers in Afghanistan. Recruits and funding were actively sought in 28 states in America, but the number of U.S. volunteers was minuscule.

The war in Afghanistan was the largest covert operation of the Reagan era. Over the course of the war, Western countries pumped in $25 million to several billion dollars a year. The CIA, Saudi government and Gulf States signed most of the checks, with 70 percent of the U.S. aid going to training and arming the Islamic radicals. Pakistan was hired to provide training to the volunteers, and nobody ever thought about what these people were going to do after the war. The Russian people simply went bankrupt and flushed the Communist Party down the drain; the Russian army went into business for itself, renting and selling weapons to any social or political group that wanted them, and the well-trained and ideologically infused Afghans became terrorists for hire. Keep in mind that the term "Afghan" refers to fighters who traveled or were trained in Pakistan to fight Russians. They are typically young Muslim men (now in their thirties) turned on by clerical haranguing and with little financial incentive to remain in their home country. Their home countries are usually Muslim, have high birth rates, high unemployment and strong representation by Iranian-backed political and religious groups (usually from Egypt, Sudan, Algeria, Libya or Pakistan).

It is no coincidence that all the men arrested in the World Trade Center bombing were trained or involved in the war in Afghanistan.

Ahmad Ajaj, 28, learned how to make bombs in Afghanistan; Mahmud Abouhalima, 34, a New York taxi driver, fought in Afghanistan; Clement Hampton-El, 55, born in America, but a veteran of Afghanistan, provided materials to the bombers, Ramzi Yousef, 26, was captured in Islamabad, and their reputed ring leader, Sheik Omar Abdel-Rahman, 55, has direct connections with the Afghan resistance movement and even sent two sons to fight the Russians in the Afghan war.

It is no coincidence that all these men have links to Afghan Prime Minister Gulbuddin Hekmatyar, who was the most entrepreneurial and most dedicated anti-Soviet. He spent over $1 billion of U.S. aid during the war against the Soviets. That Hekmatyar hated the West didn't seem to bother Ronald Reagan. In the mid-'80s Hekmatyar set up an Afghan refugee center to coordinate and support the works of fundamentalist activities in America. The *taliban* recently told *DP* that when they took control of Hekmatyar's stockpile of arms, they acquired enough weapons and ammunition to fight a war for 10 years.

Most of the Afghan volunteers whom Hekmatyar recruited and trained did not come from America but ended up in America as refugees from Afghanistan. The CIA facilitated the handing out of visas and green cards, and many of these recent transplants can be found driving taxis in New York City. Using the funds supplied by the CIA, Hekmatyar set up a center in Brooklyn to raise funds to supply arms to the *mujahedin* in Afghanistan and to send volunteers to fight in Afghanistan. The center also organized paramilitary training in the United States for Muslims. One of the refugee center graduates was El Saaid Nosair, charged and then acquitted of killing Rabbi Mayer Kahane in a Manhattan hotel. Police have also implicated Mahmud Abouhalima, who was alleged to be Nosair's getaway driver. When police investigated Nosair's apartment, they found a variety of training materials and information in Arabic that were the beginnings of the WTC bombing. We still hadn't figured out what was going on.

How to Get in

If you are a traditional Westerner, forget it. You are the enemy. If you are from Sudan, Pakistan, India, Egypt, Turkey, Syria, the Middle East or a Shiite, you stand a good chance. If you fought in the war against Russia and have contacts, you are in like Flynn. The problem is now finding an employer or a cause. Peshawar is still the major clearinghouse for Afghans. Peshawar was also the headquarters of Gulbuddin Hekmatyar's party, which trained four of the New York bombing suspects.

Other Volunteer Activities

Harkat-ul Jehad Al Islami, or Holy War for Islam, plans to send at least 3000 activists as *mujahedin*, or holy warriors, to Kashmir and is recruiting Bangladeshi volunteers to join Muslim militants fighting Indian troops for the independence of Kashmir, according to Dhaka's privately run PROBE news agency.

Their founder, Abdur Rahman Faruqi, was among 25 Bangladeshi *mujahedin* killed in Afghanistan in action against the Soviets in 1989. They provided Bangladeshi volunteers during the Soviet occupation of Afghanistan. The current head of the group, Chief Mufti Shiftier Rahman, is currently recruiting volunteers but denies that they are being mobilized. The volunteers are being recruited from the Madrashas, or Islamic schools, in southern districts of Cox's Bazaar and the northeastern district of Sylhet.

Harkatul Jihad al Islami has an organization in Pakistan and provides training in Bangladesh and Pakistan. Bangladesh is a predominately Muslim nation. The young men are being convinced in handouts written by clerics that it is their Islamic duty to fight against Hindu India. There are between 20 and 24 Islamic fundamentalist groups in Bangladesh; some are currently recruiting volunteers to join the Muslim separatist war. It is estimated that there are 3000 new volunteers who are waiting to join the 200 Bangladeshi Moslems currently fighting in the secessionist war that has killed at least 9150 people in Kashmir since 1990. The group insists that any volunteers who end up in Kashmir do so at their own effort and Harkatul Jihad al Islami does not send them.

Happiness Is a Hired Gun: Mercenaries

Er, excuse us, we meant to say "volunteers"—a curious career choice for folks who have gone to Military U and can't seem to find a direct application or reward for their skills in the outside world.

The Hague 1907 Convention banned operation on the territory of neutral states of offices for recruitment of soldiers (volunteers or mercenaries) to fight in a country at war. In 1977 part of a supplementary protocol to the 1949 Geneva Convention on the Protection of Civilian Population in Time of War made freelancers liable to court trial as criminals if they are taken POW. If found guilty, they can be simply shot on the spot as bandits.

The U.N. General Assembly reached a consensus in 1989 on recruiting, training, use and financing of mercenaries. If you are interested in volunteering, make sure you understand the laws and penalties that will suddenly apply to you. If you think fighting for money will make you popular and chicks will dig you, think again. On the other hand, if Uncle Sam has spent five years and about half a million dollars turning you into all that you can be, there are employment choices other than flipping burgers or working at Jiffy Lube.

Americans have not always been the ideal volunteers. In fact, the last two great wars showed that the majority of Americans held back until they were pushed into it, But once they were in it they finished the job.

For now, many foreign armies don't want American volunteers. They want too much money, they complain too much, and they create too many political overtones when captured or killed. American mercenaries have fought in Angola, Rhodesia, Guatemala, El Salvador, Nicaragua, Lebanon, Bosnia and Russia.

Many are motivated by religion (black Muslims in the Middle East), background (Croats in Yugoslavia), money (Central America) or a misguided sense of adventure (Angola). The U.S. is not adverse to hiring or supplying mercenaries, starting back when Benjamin Franklin hired the Prussian officer Friedrich von Steuben to instill discipline into the Continental Army, or when Claire Chennault was hired to give China grief with his Flying Tigers. In modern times U.S.-hired mercenaries have been as diverse as the Ray-Banned pilots that flew for Air America, the Nung or Montagnard tribes in Vietnam or the doomed Contras in Nicaragua. Mercenaries continue to do *our* dirty, or covert, work, but our government does not like the idea of *you* running off to fight in other people's wars.

Today, those who wish to be wild geese or soldiers of fortune will find few clear career paths. You will need the minimum service and training provided by a Western military power. Special forces members, explosives experts, pilots, and officers with training experience and other specialized skills are in demand.

Although the need for foreign volunteers cannot be predicted, there are certain hot spots that are excellent starting points. The main centers for recruitment of mercenaries (almost always ex-soldiers) are Pretoria, Johannesburg, Istanbul, Bangkok, London, Belgium, Marseille and Beirut. Remember, if you find a recruiter who is looking for a few good men, they are usually filling grunt and junior-officer levels only. The players have already cut their deal up at the top. For example, Executive Outcomes got $20 million for supplying 2000 soldiers and another $20 million for arms and supplies. Not bad, considering they paid their mercs (mostly ex-SWAPO vets) about $2000 a month for risking their lives.

There are also horror stories about hucksters preying on the gullible, as in Angola in the '70s. Even if you do find someone who has a gig for you, remember that they get paid by the head count, and once in that country you can be turned down, arrested or sent into action on your first day without training, weapons, gear or ammo. The reality is that most experienced mercenaries simply fly to the capital city of an emerging war zone and offer their services directly to the military advisors for whichever side they feel is the most desperate. Their services usually include rounding up cannon fodder like you. Other mercenary groups are organized and funded by local militia funded and directed by CIA operatives. Some like the Falangists and Chamounists in Beirut in the '80s brought in eager French Falangist Party students and trained them, but most look for trained, hardened professionals with special skills. Things like first-aid kits and even blankets aren't luxuries they are nonexistent. Your paycheck is an occasional bad meal and a place in heaven for fighting the good fight. Isn't war fun?

Because of the old-boy network and need for inside contacts, many soldiers of fortune do not make their money fighting on the ground in wars, but make themselves available for transportation contracts using leased aircraft, organizing jail breaks, and negotiating hostage releases. "Employment with a difference" was how the classified ad placed by Mike Hoare read when he set out to recruit mercenaries to fight in the Belgian Congo. Having neither the budget nor the time to train men, he put together what he called his "Wild Geese," the name of an Irish band of soldiers for hire.

Today's mercenary is not a cigar-chomping, muscle-bound adventurer with a bandolier of 50mm bullets and grenades hung like Christmas ornaments. He is more likely to be an unemployed soldier 30–35 who can't find work with his specialized skills. The pay is lousy (mercenaries make between $1200 and $3500 a month, depending on your skills or rank), the benefits slim to none, and the chances of getting killed pretty low depending on which side you pick. Americans will lose their passport or citizenship if they fight in the service of a foreign army. Others will most definitely be jailed and tried for war crimes.

Are there any loopholes? If you are hired to invade another country, destroy property, kill or hurt people, or even to destabilize a democratic or undemocratic government, you are breaking the law. If you do not live in the attacked country, have a foreign citizenship, have come in to rescue someone, or you're just hanging around a war zone, you can be shot as a spy or foreign agent. If you are in a country that has declared a state of war, remember it is much easier and cheaper to shoot questionable characters than to fill out the paperwork.

If you want to truly be a volunteer like Steiner (the Sudan) or Che Guevara (Bolivia), remember that Steiner was tried, imprisoned and tortured, and Guevera was ventilated by CIA operatives.

There are some grey areas that afford some (but little) protection. Make sure you enlist in a recognized foreign army. Join a foreign legion like the Spanish or French Foreign Legion; have a civilian work contract for a recognized government. You could fight with a recognized army in a foreign territory (like our army in the Gulf or Vietnam) that is not technically at war but helping someone else win a war.

The skinniest loophole is offering your services for a higher pay rate in a foreign army where you are seconded to another army. Technically, you can join as a regular service member if there are no local troops with comparable experience. Will that stop the opposing side from parading you around like a zoo animal, then doing a flamenco dance on your testicles? No.

Be warned that there are plenty of cheap movies and bad books attempting to add the luster of righteousness and adventure to the mercenary life. These books tend to be short on facts and long on gun talk. They provide hard-to-find tips like "never handle explosives carelessly" (from the *Mercenary's Tactical Handbook* by Sid Campbell) to "take no unnecessary risks" (from the *African Merc Combat Manual* from Paladin Press).

There are some good books on this nasty business, most long out of print and yellowed: *The Brother's War* by John St. Jorre, *Legionnaire* by Simon Murray, *Mercenary* by Mike Hoare, *The Last Adventurer* by Rolf Steiner, *Mercenary Commander* by Jerry Puren, and probably the most accurate, well-written and depressing of the bunch, the *Whores of War, Mercenaries Today* by Wilfred Burchett and Derek Roebuck. *Whores*, published in 1977, chronicles the misfortunes of 13 American and British mercs in Angola who were captured, tried and executed or imprisoned. Sobering stuff for wannabe's.

Movies like the *Dogs of War* and *The Wild Geese* had some credible origins in real events, and real mercenaries were used to advise the writers and filmmakers. But once the scriptwriters, directors and editors get going, it turns into pure gun love and cigar chomping.

Who reads *Soldier of Fortune*? (By their ads ye shall know them.) Here, the terminally tough can order "Combat Babe" posters for $10, buy military medals they never won, learn how to be a private eye and even correspond with "gorgeous" and obviously lonely Russian, Asian and Latin ladies. For those who can read without the need for large pictures, there are articles on "Screw the Bitch, Divorce Tactics," secrets on how to hit a man 11 times in one second or less, or help on where to buy steroids and how to convert your SKS to full auto. For those who want to leave the mercenary life behind, the reader can choose from classes on **Bounty Hunting** ☎ *(602) 457-9360,* **Locksmithing, Private Eye,** ☎ *(213) 879-1165,* **Bodyguarding** and even the vaguely defined **Outdoor Careers!** ☎ *(800) 223-4542.* Most, of course, require a hefty payment for an inversely thin brochure. My favorites are "How to Make a Potato Cannon" and "Worse than Tailhook" actual videos of off-base (in more ways than one) military parties in the Philippines.

The bottom line is the merc business is about 99 percent bullshit and one percent reality, and the reality part sucks. Despite having to buy your own beret, cigars and big knife, you will end up spending time in the most godawful parts of the world and if a land mine doesn't get you, then the bugs will. If the bugs don't get you, the long arm of the law will.

Any time you leave the apron strings of Uncle Sam's army, you are on your own, and even if you are not in violation of any laws, you will be accused of being a criminal (actually, a criminal has rights—you won't) without any rights and dealt with accordingly.

The true movers and shakers in the mercenary world are the classic megalomaniacs, self-promoters and verbose ex-soldiers who see their role beyond that of a short-term gun toter—as a potential ruler of faraway kingdoms. So our advice, if you are going to get into this nasty business (the retirement program sucks), is to think big, don't take any checks and make sure you remember your hat size when you order your crown.

The late '60s and early '70s were the glory years for mercenaries like "Mad" Mike Hoare, "Black" Jacques Schramme, and Bob Denard. Tin pot rulers unable to field trained armies turned to freelancers so that they could continue to rifle treasuries and shop in London and Paris without being overthrown while on vacation. Stories of evil mercs laying waste to natives in the Congo, Angola, Biafra, Uganda, Gabon, Benin, Rhodesia and Mozambique became part of literature and Hollywood screenplays. In some cases, the scene became truly Chaplinesque and Kiplingesque.

WARNING

Joining any military or paramilitary organization and/or fighting with a foreign army may subject you to prosecution, imprisonment or execution by other countries. If you are a U.S. citizen, you can lose your citizenship and be liable for international crimes. Association or contact with mercenary recruiters and groups can make you subject to investigation by U.S. and international law enforcement agencies.

The Men Who Would Be King

The late '60s and early '70s were the glory years for mercenaries like "Mad" Mike Hoare, "Black" Jacques Schramme, and Bob Denard. Tin pot rulers unable to field trained armies turned to free-lancers so they could continue to rifle treasuries and shop in London and Paris without being overthrown while on vacation. Stories of evil mercs laying waste to natives in the Congo, Angola, Biafra, Uganda, Gabon, Benin, Rhodesia and Mozambique became part of literature and Hollywood screenplays. In some cases the scene became truly Chaplinesque and Kiplingesque.

The Man Who Would Be King: Part I

A more successful attempt was made by Frenchman Bob Denard who actually managed to run the Comoros Islands between 1978 and 1989. The Comoros are an Indian Ocean island group just northwest of Madagascar. The major export of the long forgotten islands is *ylang-ylang*, a rare flower used in the production of aromatic oils. On May 12, 1978 Denard landed with 46 men in a converted trawler named the *Massiwa*. He had sailed from Europe with his black uniformed crew to claim ownership of this tiny but idyllic group of islands.

Denard had been here before to train the soldiers of Marxist ruler Ali Soilih. Soilih was busy kicking out Ahmed Abdallah. Abdallah fled to Paris and later, short on funds but high on ambition, offered to cut Denard in on the deal if he would return him to power. Denard enjoyed his new role as "man who would be king." Abdallah took all the political heat as his puppet. Denard, a former vacuum cleaner salesman and policeman, had seen what a handful of trained soldiers could do in his various adventures as a mercenary in Katanga, Yemen and Benin. This time he was in charge. He took a Comoran wife, bought a villa, converted to Islam and became Said Mustapha Madjoub.

His presence angered the other African states to such a degree that the French arranged for Denard's ouster in 1989. Denard, disappointed and back in South Africa, spent his evenings planning his return to paradise. Sounds like a great premise for a sequel (See "The Man Who Would Be King Part V.")

The Man Who Would Be King: Part II

The Dogs of War, by Frederick Forsyth, was published in 1974. In the book and in the film, a group of white mercenaries are hired to take over a West African country on behalf of an industrialist who finds it cheaper to take over the country rather than pay for its mineral resources. The movie ends with the mercenaries suddenly having a change of heart and installing an idealistic and honest leader. Naturally, the book and the film are fiction. Well, not completely, said an investigative report by London's *Sunday Times*. They claimed that *The Dogs of War* was based on a real incident instigated by the author. The *Times* claimed that in 1972 Forsyth allegedly put up just under a quarter of a million dollars ($240,000) to overthrow President Francisco Macias Nguema of Equatorial Guinea. Forsyth was no stranger to the murky world of mercenaries, since he had spent considerable time in Nigeria covering the Biafran civil war. While he was there, he met a Scottish mercenary named Alexander Ramsay Gay. Gay was only too happy to train and equip a small group of men who would set up a homeland for the defeated Biafrans. It is reputed that Gay was able to purchase automatic weapons, bazookas and mortars from a Hamburg arms dealer, then hire 13 other mercenaries along with 50 black soldiers from Biafra. They then purchased a ship called the *Albatross* out of the Spanish port of Fuengirola. The plot was blown when one of the British mercs shot himself after a gunfight with London police. The mercenaries were denied an export permit for their weapons and ammunition, and the ship and crew were arrested in the Canary Islands en route to their target.

Forsyth denies the story or any participation in the plot and admits to nothing more than writing a solidly researched book.

The Man Who Would Be King: Part III

Dublin-born "Mad" Mike Hoare was hired by persons unknown to take over the Seychelles, a nation of 92 islands 1000 miles off East Africa. Hoare served in the Royal Armored Corps in World War II and left with the rank of Major. He emigrated to South Africa after the war and made ends meet by being a safari guide, car dealer and accountant, until he was hired by Moise Tshombe in 1964 to help him defeat rebels. Hoare put together about 200 male white mercenaries and led probably the last efficient use of a mercenary army in Africa—to save lives and put down a revolt in the Belgian Congo.

Hoare's last big gig (Major Hoare does not work too often due to his high price tag) was a Keystone cops affair that would seem to be the result of a bad script-writer rather than real political intrigue. They were supposed to overthrow the socialist government of President Albert Rene of the Seychelles and to take control of the idyllic Indian Ocean archipelago. In December of 1981 their plan of flying in as a visiting rugby team quickly unraveled when customs inspectors found heavy weapons in the bottom of their gym bags. A brief shoot-out between the 52 raiders and police ensued on the tarmac with the mercenaries' transportation being quickly hijacked and flown back to safety in South Africa. It was not known for whom or why this was done, but suspicion falls on the South African government. Some analysts believe that Hoare backers were South African businessmen looking for a tax haven. A Durban newspaper charged that several of the mercenaries were South African policemen.

The leniency with which the mercenaries were treated back in South Africa adds to that suspicion. The 44 mercenaries who made it back were put on trial (wearing beach shirts and khakis) not for hijacking the Air India aircraft, which would have meant a mandatory five to 30 years in jail; they were charged with kidnapping which requires no mandatory penalty.

The South African Cabinet also approved the freeing on bail of 39 of the 44 mercenaries on the condition they keep a low profile and not discuss the coup attempt. Five mercenaries were arrested in the Seychelles and it is assumed that three others are dead or hiding in the hills.

Others blame ousted Seychelles President James Mancham, who was exiled after Rene's successful 1977 coup. Although Mancham denied the accusation, one of the captured mercenaries had a tape recording of Mancham's victory speech intended for broadcast after the coup. The soldiers for hire were paid $1000 each and were promised a $10,000 if the coup was successful.

The Man Who Would Be King: Part IV

Rolf Steiner was a member of Hitler's Youth, or Werewolves, He joined the French Foreign Legion at the age of 17 in 1950. He fought at Dien Bien Phu and in Algeria and made the mistake of joining the anti–De Gaulle OAS—finding himself a drummed out corporal chef and a civilian.

In the fall of 1967, Biafra was busy spending oil money and French secret service funds on hiring mercenaries from Swedish pilot Count von Rosen (pilots were paid between $8000 and $10,000 per month in cash to fly in supplies) and paying Swiss public relations firms to publicize their plight. Money flowed freely; grisly battle-scarred veterans like Roger Faulques were paid 100,000 British pounds to hire 100 men for six months but only delivered 49. He was asked to leave, but Steiner, one of the mercenaries he had hired, chose to stay.

In July of 1968 Steiner asked for and was given a group of commando-style soldiers and had great successes against the Russian-backed Nigerians. He was later given the rank of colonel and given command of thousands of soldiers. This created an instant Napoleonic complex and Steiner experienced a series of military defeats and routs. He was reigned in by removal of his Steiner Commando Division and after an angry confrontation with the Biafran leader, Sandhurst-educated General Emeka Ojukwa, he was shipped out of the country in handcuffs.

Steiner then showed up in the Southern Sudan among the Anya Na fighting the Islamic North. He taught agriculture, defense, education and other essential civic skills to the animist tribes. For a brief shining moment, he was their de facto leader, until he was captured by the Ugandans and put on trial in Sudan in the mid-'70s. He was released after spending three years in a Sudanese prison where he was tortured and beaten. Some say he was a crazed megalomanic; other say he tried to apply his skills to aid a tiny struggling nation. He died in South Africa of a kidney ailment.

The Man Who Would Be King: Part V

They say sequels are never as interesting as the originals, and, in this case, they're right. Remember Bob Denard (see "The Man Who Would be King: Part I"). It seems that staring out the window got to be too much for him, so at the crusty old age of 66, Denard decided to give it one more go. On October 4, 1995, Denard and a group of 33 mercenaries (mostly French) rented a creaking fishing trawler and sailed back to the Comoros to recapture his little Garden of Eden where he had been King (actually, head of the Presidential Guard, watching over a puppet ruler) from 1978–1989.

They landed at night and quickly sprung their old buddies out of the islands' main jail; then they captured the two airports, the radio station and the barracks. After that, they rousted the doddering, 80-something Said Mohamed Djohar out of bed. By morning, Denard was on top and Djohar was a criminal charged with misrule and stealing government funds.

Two days later, the French government landed 600 troops and after a brief but halfhearted fight, the mercenaries were rounded up and Denard was shipped to France for trial

It's Not a Job, It's an Adventure

For now, the job opportunities for mercenaries are limited. South Africa and Great Britain are really the only places where ex- (and current) soldiers are actively recruited for "security" work overseas. Other groups, such as the Ghurkas, the Swiss Guards, and the Spanish and French Foreign Legions, are not your classic "Dogs of War" type of mercenaries. Right now, stinking rich flyspeck states are eager employers but usually by contract with another country. Oman, Brunei and the Holy See all need outside help to keep things quiet. Other countries like Myanmar, Angola, Croatia, Namibia, Guatemala, El Salvador, Afghanistan and other war-torn regions use foreign advisors to keep their army trained and dominant.

But in the days of rapid-reaction forces, the U.N., and political correctness, the days of the Wild Geese, Colonel Bob (Robert Denard) and Steiner are long gone

But for old diehards, *DP* snooped around and came up with a few open offers. (For the record, the authors of *DP* do not kill people, carry weapons or even side with any faction. Anyway, the health benefits suck.) Sierra Leone is paying $15,000–$22,500 a month for British SAS vets on three-month contracts. Most of them bailed after Bob Mackenzie was killed in action, even thought they had been paid in advance, and the Bosnian Croats pay a measly $600–$1200. Colonel Bob was paying $4000–$6000 a month, but with a houseboy, car and villa thrown in for free. Lots of people have picked up freelance work, and there has been no shortage of unpaid volunteer work in Bosnia, Afghanistan, the southern Philippines and Central America.

South Africa is the major supplier of mercenaries for work around Africa. Enterprising firms have no problem finding well-trained, bush-savvy soldiers to prop up dictators. By the year 2000, it is estimated that the South African government will lay off 60,000 soldiers.

The only two legit organizations that were hiring mercenaries (they call them security advisors) are Executive Outcomes in Pretoria and GSG on the isle of Jersey.

Executive Outcomes

Eeben Barlow is managing director of Executive Outcomes, based in Pretoria, South Africa. Executive Outcomes was founded in 1989 by the 17-year veteran and former long-range reconsoldier from South Africa's 32nd battalion.

EO has obtained between 2000 to 5000 troops and about 30 pilots for Angola. The firm trains and supplies pilots and security personnel for corporations in Africa. They recruit primarily from the South African military, typically hiring men who have combat experience. A $140,000 contract in September of 1993 was to protect a diamond mine in Canfunfo in Lunda Norte, Angola. EO has supplied around 1000 soldiers to fight UNITA. They consider themselves security guards that stabilize mining operations. (An important job when a country gets all of its allowance from diamonds that require no processing and can be used instead of hard currency.) For example, Angola's diamond fields generate $350–$450 million dollars a *month*. Estimates put EO's Angola contract at $40 million (about half for soldiers and half for equipment and supplies). Soldiers of UNITA (National Union for the Total Independence of Angola) finally overran the mine, leaving 36 people dead, most of them from the security firm. The men were provided as military trainers and allowed to carry out preemptive strikes against UNITA if they felt they or the mine were threatened. Since things have quieted down in Angola, they are training MPLA soldiers to handle the upcoming peace.

After their success in Angola, Barlow made a sales call with his unusual wares in March of 1995 to the beleaguered Valentine Strasser and got busy shortly thereafter. The deal is supposedly worth between $500,000 and $1.5 million a month. It could be the latter figure, since the payment was based on EO securing the diamond fields from the rebels and part of the payment was made by giving Branch Energy the concession to the Koidu diamond field (the Sierra Leone government still holds a 60 percent ownership). Branch Energy is owned by Strategic Resources Group, a British company based in the Bahamas, that in turn owns Executive Outcomes. Naturally, EO captured the Kono diamond district from the rebels in two days, instead of the nine they estimated. Other reports say that Bahamas-based but British-owned Heritage Oil and Gas (part of the same group that owns EO) financed the EO intervention in exchange for diamond concessions and that the fee was 1.5 million *pounds* per month. Branch Energy is reputed to be the largest shareholder in Heritage (which also owns Branch Mining) to develop the diamond fields (worth an estimated 180 million pounds).

It gets even more confusing when the alleged links of the Heritage Board of Directors are explored, revealing vague but interesting connections to British liberal newspapers and a former Liberal leader. There are also direct connections between South African military intelligence officers and officers of Heritage Oil and Gas. Far too shady for *DP*, but a good story for "60 Minutes."

Troops were in-country by April, and they quickly managed to push back the rebels from 36km to 126km from the capital in just nine days. They then pushed the rebels out of the Kono diamonds fields (about 216 km east of Freetown) in just two days using helicopter gunships.

It seems the folks in Freetown need a little security. Their spokesperson, Colonel Andy Brown in Sierra Leone, says they have been asked to provide 150–200 soldiers. Currently, they are supplying men and expertise to seven countries in Africa, among them Kenya, Angola and Uganda. They are discussing deals with customers in Malawi, Mozambique, Sudan, and even a client in Southeast Asia.

It seems that Executive Outcomes is not a drinking club or hairy-chested group of killers but just one of 80 companies. For example, the company that owns EO is **Strategic Resources**, based in Pretoria. ☎ *[27] 123-481-352*. That company owns a percentage of Branch Mining, which has been given mining concessions as partial payment for EO providing security in Sierra Leone. Now this is either a great yarn, a fantastic movie plot or an indication of how wars may be fought in the future. You decide.

Gurkha Security Guards (GSG)

Reputedly a front for the British Government set up to facilitate sending Ghurkas to Sierra Leone to defend the diamond mines. Nick Bell, a former officer in the Gurkha regiment of the British army managed to provide a few good men. The salary is as high as $8000 a month. Not bad for the wages of war.

GSG Brits who have had service with Her Majesty's Forces or other security work. Obviously, they leans toward hiring men from Nick's old outfit. His last client was the government of Sierra Leone, which was fighting an all-out war against RUF, a rebel faction. Nick does his recruiting out of hotel rooms in places like Banbury, Oxfordshire, according to the *New African.*

Job security is a little dicey since the leader of the GSG contingent in Sierra Leone, American Bob MacKenzie, was killed in the Malal Hills in February of 1995. He was also reportedly eaten by the rebels. After MacKenzie was killed, the Ghurkas returned to Nepal.

Other groups like Pretoria, South Africa–based Mecham supply soldiers, but primarily for removal of land mines and unexploded ordnance. There were also rumors of an SAS group that was to be paid up front $22,500 per person per month for a three-month contract.

Coup School

The School of the Americas (SOA) in Fort Benning, Georgia, has turned out 56,000 "elite military personnel" since its founding in Panama in 1946. Nicknamed "Escuela de Golpes" (School of Coups), it has been at Fort Benning since 1984, after intense political pressure in Panama forced its relocation. In order to avoid the school being shut down due to base closures, other sites such as Fort Bragg, North Carolina, headquarters of the Green Berets Special Forces and locations in Bolivia are being considered as potential sites.

The SOA operates on a $5.8 million annual budget and has an interesting list of graduates: the ex-dictator of Panama, Manuel Noriega; Bolivia's Hugo Banzer Suarez; Guatemalan intelligence chief in the 1970s and 1980s, General Manuel Antonio Callejas y Callejas; Honduran Chief of Staff Humberto Regalado, and Salvadoran death squad leader Roberto D'Aubuisson.

The school has been under a cloud ever since it was revealed that 19 out of the 27 Salvadoran officers implicated in the San Salvador massacre of six Jesuit priests and their housekeeper in 1989 were SOA graduates. The 1993 United Nations Truth Commission Report on El Salvador cited 60 Salvadoran officers for ordering, carrying out and concealing major atrocities during 10 years of civil war; 48 of the officers were SOA graduates.

Military Professional Resources

Now there is an option for those with a little silver around the temples and a tire around the middle. Billed as the "greatest corporate assemblage or Military Expertise in the World," Military Professional Resources, Inc. (MPRI) is a group of former military professionals who train armies and do what retired generals do. They are based in Alexandria, Virginia, and claim to pull in about $12 million a year in assignments. Not bad for an eight-year-old company with 160 employees and about 2000 top kicks on call. Although their brochure copy would not get them much ink in *Soldier of Fortune*, their terminology sounds ominously like the doublespeak of Executive Outcomes. What does MPRI offer their well-heeled but disorganized customers? Their brochure offers Doctrine Development, Military Training, War Game Support, and even Democracy Transition. *DP* could not find Advanced Medal Polishing, Golf 101 or Cocktail Party Banter in the list, so we are somewhat suspect of their credentials. However, they are credited with training the Croat army who smacked the bejeezuz out of the Serbs in Krajina province back in August of '95. If you are tired of wearing your medals at home, give MPRI a call at ☎ *(703) 916-1780.*

Military/Adventure Resources

Books International

69B Lynchford Road
Farnborough
Hampshire, England GU14 6EJ
☎ *01252-376564*
FAX 01252-370181

Books International specializes in military reference books for the modeler, collector, researcher or curious. You won't find too many cerebral products here but plenty of hard-to-find illustrated books on past wars, equipment, history and military reference works. Where else would you find an illustrated reference guide to Polish military helicopters or a real life photo book of the Navy SEALS?

Brassey's Inc.

8000 Westpark Drive
First Floor
McLean, Virginia 22102
☎ *(703) 442-4535*
FAX (703) 790-9063

Brassey's is the publisher of choice when British military men want to fill their mahogany bookcases. They are known for their annual *Defence* yearbook that keeps the Brits up to date on the rest of the world. Each issue has essays and intros on the leading political and military topics. If you want to be the model of a modern major general, you should look into their books on biological, nuclear, naval, historical and military warfare. Their annual update of *The World in Conflict* is a must-read for professional adventurers. There are drier books on ammunition, land force logistics and radar and other technical reference manuals. It is no surprise that their U.S. rep is based in McLean, Virginia.

Covert Action

1500 Massachusetts Ave., N.W., #732
Washington, D.C. 20005
☎ *(202) 331-9763*
FAX (202) 331-9751

A magazine written by some ex-company folks who have no qualms about telling it like it is. Plenty of facts, numbers, dates, photos and other material to back their statements up.

For Your Eyes Only

Tiger Publications
Post Office Box 8759
Amarillo, Texas 79114
☎ *(805) 655-2009*

Billed as an open intelligence summary of current military affairs. Editor Stephan Cole puts together the biweekly eight-page newsletter to provide an excellent update on military, political and diplomatic events around the world. Somewhat right-wing and hardware-oriented, it still provides a balanced global view of breaking events. An annual subscription costs $65 (26 issues). Sample copies are $3 each. Back issues are available for $1.25–$2, depending on how many you order. FYEO is also available on NewsNet, ☎ *(800) 952-0122* or *(215) 527-8030*.

Jane's Information Group

1340 Braddock
Suite 300
Alexandra Virginia 22314
☎ *(703) 683-3700*
FAX (703) 836-1593

Jane's is the undisputed leader in military intelligence for the world's armies. About a quarter of a million people subscribe to their annual guide on aircraft, but only about 11,000 need to know what's new in nuclear, biological and chemical protection clothing. Just as teenagers await the new car catalogs in the fall, the world's generals eagerly await the new Jane's reports on weapon systems, aircraft, ships, avionics, strategic weapons and other hardware. Esoteric fans thumb through their yearbooks on "Electro-optics, Image Intensifier Systems" (not to be confused with their guide to thermal imaging systems) or Air Launched Weapons. Arms dealers never travel without their *World Markets for Armoured and Military Logistics Vehicles*. Prices for the books or CD-ROMS run between $400 and $9000. If you are buying an update of an existing book or CD-ROM, the price drops about 25 percent. For your money, you get one annual guide, 11 monthly updates and a summary report. Jane's also publishes a monthly intelligence review, *Jane's Intelligence Review,* that provides background on global conflicts, terrorist groups and arsenals.

Jane's Security and Counterintelligence Equipment Yearbook

A new service is *Jane's Sentinel*, a series of regional security assessments with monthly updates and a broadcast fax service. *Sentinel* breaks down the world into six regions and provides reports on physical features, infrastructure, defense and security, as well as general information like maps and graphs.

In case the world is smitten with a bad case of peacefulness, Jane's also dabbles in the mundane. They have guides to airports, the container business and railways.

If you have ever have been torn between buying a Vigiland Surveillance Robot or a Magnavox Thermal Sniper Scope, Jane's makes it as easy as shopping at Victoria's Secret. The book contains an overview and listing of all major equipment used by security, antiterrorist and civil defence organizations.

The New Press

450 West 41st Street
New York, New York 10036
☎ *(212) 629-8802*
FAX (212) 268-6349
This publisher of "serious books" can be counted on for interesting new books. Their titles include *Civil Wars: From L.A. to Bosnia* by Hans Magnus Enzensberger, a book that helps readers understand the new forces that shape conflicts, and two books by Gabriel Kolko—*Century of War*, a new view of wars since 1914 with some excellent insights to war after WWII, and *Anatomy of a War*, the story of the Vietnam conflict from the Vietnamese, U.S. and Communist Party viewpoints.

Paladin Books

Post Office Box 1307
Boulder, Colorado 80306
Your best source for militaria, gung-ho adventure books and such classics as *Advanced Weapons Tactics for Hostage Rescue Teams*. Send for a listing or catalog. Much of the material is flatulent diction, tough guy fantasies from military manuals or bizarre "get even" tomes. But there are some gems among the stones.

Soldier of Fortune

5735 Arapahoe Avenue
Boulder, Colorado 80303
☎ *(800) 877-5207 (subscriptions)*
☎ *(303) 449-3750 (editorial)*
The political left imagines the SOF reader as a gun-polishing, beer-drinking closet Rambo who actually cleaned latrines in Nam. Well, they are probably half right. It's the other half of the readership and content that is impressive. For every three articles on self-defense, gun control or new fighting knives, there is a good firsthand description of one of the world's dirty little wars. SOF does provide some very interesting on-the-ground reporting from countries undergoing Third World turmoil. Their editorial position is somewhat to the right of Ronald Reagan and Wyatt Earp, but the magazine is still an important source for information on weapons and little-known conflicts. Subscriptions are $28 a year with newsstand issues going for $4.75

Soldier of Fortune Expo

P.O. Box 693
Boulder, Colorado 80306
☎ *(303) 449-3750*
☎ *(800) 800-7630*
Alone in your room, dreaming of foreign adventure and glory? Why not get those army surplus fatigues cleaned and pressed, get a suitable buzz cut, suck in your gut, and hang out with thousands of other "military/survivalist" enthusiasts? Every September this Expo is more than just row after row of guns and survival equipment; it's also a chance to see real men fire off real machine guns. You get to see things blow up and watch real men

fight with pugil sticks; worship real mercenaries, tough guys and heroes up close, as you strut around the convention center terrified that people might think you are actually a wimp; hear speakers tell you why our government can't be trusted and learn what you can do to maintain your God-given right to own metal tubes that propel projectiles.

The Stockholm International Peace Research Institute

FAX (46) 8 655 97 33
This group publishes an 870-page annual on the world's military expenditures, arms production and trade.

Play That Funky Music White Mercenary Boy

In an effort to give the men of Executive Outcomes a kinder, more gentle image, they put together a country music video called "And They Call Us the Dogs of War." The video shows EO staff distributing Bibles and working on do-gooder projects like building water purification plants in Angola. It has not hit MTV yet. EO's headquarters is at Cabo Leda about 60 miles south of Luanda, if you want to stop by their camp for a beer and a sing-a-long under the cow skull that decorates the bar.

Terrorism

I Hear You Knocking, But You Can't Come In

Terrorism can be easily defined as "premeditated, politically motivated violence perpetrated against noncombatant targets by subnational groups or clandestine agents usually intended to influence an audience" as it is by United States Code Section 2656(d). This definition is obviously the work of leaders of established and recognized countries, most with democratic political processes. It should be remembered that the United States of America, Russia, China, France and Israel, along with numerous other now respectable countries, began their road to independence using terrorist methods and actions against their past leaders.

Today, few can argue that terrorism is a legitimate and sadly productive method to gain international attention, demand concessions and eventually establish legitimate states and political parties. Despite what the world governments espouse, there are few minority groups that can use the existing political process to gain their independence or freedom without resorting to outrageous tactics.

The less potent the group is as a political force and the thinner the support base, the more likely the group will resort to more dramatic methods to secure world attention. The leaders of these groups tend to be from the upper classes, well educated, creative, egotistical and flamboyant almost to the point of ridiculousness. Che Guevara, Yasir Arafat, Carlos the Jackal and Rafael Sebastin Guillen Vicente, a.k.a. Subcommandante Marcos, the pipe-smoking, wisecracking son of a furniture salesman...coming soon to a movie theater near you (courtesy of Oliver Stone).

According to the U.S. State Department's report, "Patterns On Global Terrorism," in 1995 there were 440 international terrorist incidents. This is up from 322 in 1994. The fatality total from terrorism was 165, down from 314. Unfortunately, while the international fatality total decreased, the number of wounded increased from 663 in 1994 to 6291 in 1995 (5500 were injured in the gas attack on the Tokyo subway system.

As if to prove the State Department as liars, nineteen Americans were killed and more than 230 seriously injured on June 25, 1996 when a truck bomb was planted by terrorists outside the U.S. Air Force Housing Complex in Dhahran, Saudi Arabia. The F.B.I. and Saudi officials believe the incident may have been in retaliation for the terrorists who were caught and beheaded for committing the November 1995 bombing of the Riyadh headquarters of the Office of the Program Manager/Saudi Arabian National Guard. That bombing killed seven people, including five U.S. citizens, and seriously injured 42 others. Not much later a TWA 747 taking off from New York exploded killing all aboard. Are the '80s back?

There are various proven methods of gaining the world's attention. The first is to execute or kidnap Americans while they are abroad. This will guarantee at least two to five minutes on CNN, with 30-minute repeats every half-hour until the situation is resolved.

The next is usually hijacking; the third and most frequent is bombing, the last and possibly least effective are attacks on military or police forces. Sending a well-written political proposal with workable, fair solutions to the ruling party won't even get you a return phone call. You gotta have a gimmick, and fear among the populace will definitely get you attention.

There is another level of terrorism activity that doesn't make the headlines but is necessary for the ongoing support of organizations and activities. If terrorist groups are not funded by a government (such as Iran, Iraq, Libya or private sources), they must resort to extortion (demanding money in exchange for lack of violent attacks), robbery (theft of money or possessions by force or threat of force), kidnapping (abducting people who then are released in exchange for negotiated amounts of money) or drug or weapons smuggling (payment for safe transport of illegal goods). Other groups are for hire and will conduct assassinations, kidnappings, warfare, bombings or other criminal attacks for a fee. Many times these acts are carried out under the name of a terrorist group but are simply criminal acts. There are various freelance terrorists like Abu Nidal and the now forcibly retired Carlos. They would provide spectacular sound bites and video clips for a fee and/or a piece of the action. All that was missing was a director and a producer.

It is important to note that terrorists would like to attack at the heart of the intended enemies' strongholds but are neither strong, wily or powerful enough. Worse yet, there are few terrorist groups who can handle the ideologically numbing bureaucracy it would take to pick up the trash and clean out parking meters.

TERRORISM

Just look at the poor Palestinians who are now faced with beating their own people to quell rioting and protect Israelis. So most groups content themselves with chipping away at the public confidence, gaining a hollow importance but taking no real steps toward bettering the plight of the people they represent. Some groups like Hezbollah and Hamas are strong political entities with equally strong military arms. Other groups like the Kurdish independence groups are caught in a Catch-22, with their political structures banned forcing them to continue as terrorist organizations.

Terrorists Attacks on Americans

Americans don't like the idea of terrorism. When *Condé Nast Traveler* did a misguided and somewhat '70s view of the terrorist threat in their July '96 issue, they focused on the threat of airport security and Middle Eastern terrorists. They claimed quite rightly that out of the 60 million Americans who traveled abroad last year, only 12 were killed as a result of a terrorist attack. Five were killed in a blast at a military installation in Riyadh, two died in Karachi when their shuttle bus was attacked, two were missionaries kidnapped and killed in Colombia, one was a tourist who took a ride about 40 km north of the Angkor Wat temples in Cambodia and never came back, one was killed in a suicide attack on an Israeli bus in Gaza, and another was killed in a similar attack in Jerusalem. That article was published prior to the TWA jet explosion that killed 230 people, an incident that sent chills down the spine of every American. They also forgot about Project Bojinka, the World Trade Center and other unknown attempts that if successful would have killed hundreds of Americans.

The problem is that for every tourist who was actually killed, many were a whisker away from being kidnapped, robbed, blown up or shot. Many travelers spend their time worrying about hijacking, bombs, random shootings and kidnapping—all the more understandable considering the 5000-pound bomb that was recently driven in front of an apartment complex housing U.S. Air Force personnel in Dhahran, sending 19 Americans home in aluminum cases. So much for being smug about terrorism. Saudi Arabia has one of the lowest crime rates, the military has the highest security precautions (in this case, a safe zone created by cement barriers and chain-link fences), and once again the culprits are badly shaven men who are fighting for something Americans have yet to figure out.

The reality is that terrorism is successful by its ability to create terror. The fact that every major and minor airport in the world has metal detectors, security guards and X-ray machines is testament to the terrorists' effectiveness—as is the fact that Americans can rattle off two or three well-known terrorist groups but couldn't possibly tell you the legal political parties in Israel, Cambodia or Colombia.

Follow the Leader

The writing may be on the wall for the old terrorist groups of the past 20 years. The demise of Marxist-style terrorism may crumble under the weight of paperwork and the fundamental inability of these groups to grasp success. The IRA ran out of patience to outtalk the verbose Brits, the PLO still can't manage its own people, and Fidel has started to wear natty Western business suits while stumping for investors. Terrorism requires polite attacks to avoid alienating future investors.

While the PLO is figuring how to write parking tickets and the IRA is busy beating drug dealers to death with hammers, other groups ponder the benefit of actually getting what they want. They know that sooner or later their actions will force compromise and integration. Freedom fighters, from the Kurds to the Afghans to the Sudanese, are dividing into smaller warring factions. If the truth be known, these folks are happiest channeling eons of subjugation and oppression into some pretty spectacular and brutal events but have little stomach for politicking.

Some of the most dramatic terrorist acts have been the bombing of the Marine Barracks in Beirut, the bombing of the World Trade Center in New York, the downing of Pan Am 107 over Lockerbie, Scotland, the total destruction of the William P. Murrah building in Oklahoma City, and the world's first large-scale chemical gas attack on five Tokyo subway trains. It is important to note that in each one of these cases the perpetrators were either apprehended, identified or are killed in the act. Crime does not pay and wages of fear suck.

Terrorism: No Longer a Growth Industry

Terrorism is running out of money, and, with the rash of suicide bombings in Sri Lanka and Israel, terrorist groups may be running out of recruits. The former and current supporters of terrorism against the West find themselves banished from the world marketplace and proudly trying to pretend they never needed all that Western money anyway. Libya, Iraq and Iran all make hollow speeches, while privately their emissaries desperately try to get invited back into the real world's economic cocktail party. When you make it big in the terrorism network, you are guaranteed to have a short career. When Carlos was an embarrassment to the terror network, he was shuffled between Libya, Iraq, Jordan, Syria and Yemen and finally ended up in the Sudan before he was then served up to the French to entice the U.S. to lift sanctions.

The thought that should give Westerners pause is that these folks are emulating the early actions that led to the nations of China, France, Israel and the U.S.

Terror Mutates

The pure ideology of '70s terrorism is slowly evolving into a cash-based, self centered ideology better suited for the '80s (we never said terrorists are up on trends—after all, they do spend a lot time in hiding). Despite the lack of big-time sponsors, terrorism will continue to be a threat to all Western travelers. Westerners are high-profile pawns in the publicity game. The savvy traveler needs to understand the difference between the Algerian terrorist (who will cut your throat without even rifling through your pockets), a Mexican terrorist (who has no reason to harm an American tourist), a Filipino terrorist (who will trade you like a used car salesman), a Kurdish terrorist (who will use you as a political pawn and usually release you unharmed and well fed), a Khmer Rouge (who wants his $10,000 or you get whacked) or a plain ol' thug who may have been fighting for some funky acronymic rabble, but just likes the Rolex you have and can't be bothered asking you politely for it. Terrorism may also be faceless in the case of bombings in Paris, Tel Aviv, Karachi and other urban centers. So keep in mind that carrying around a copy of Mao's little red book or Gadhafi's green book or even Carlos' black book won't get you as far as carrying a Gold card. Money is the primary goal of most terrorism groups in the Third World, publicity is second, and achievement of political objectives is a distant third. From Colombia to Kashmir, bad guys are taking the money and running.

For those who want to understand more about the aims of various political, terrorist or freedom groups, they can be contacted at the address below. Keep in mind that any contact with this group may put you under the direct scrutiny of U.S., European and Israeli intelligence agencies and lead to criminal charges being filed if any collusion or support is proven.

Hezbollah

Mekteb-1 Hezbollah
South Suburb
Bir-al Abed
Beirut, Lebanon

PKK

Mekte-Bi Amele-1 Kurdistan
Barelias-Chotura
West Bekaa, Lebanon

Along the Afghan Trail

There are 14,000 foreign veterans of the Russian/Afghan war. This network of experienced veterans are members of hard-line Islamic groups in Algeria, Egypt, Jorgan, Palestine, Pakistan, China and even The Philippines. (Nearly 3000 Algerians, 2000 Egyptians and 10,000 Arabs fought in Afghanistan.) Most of the members of the GIA are former Afghans.

Only 100 full time U.S. spooks and diplomats actually controlled Operation Cyclone from Pakistan and Washington from 1986 to 1989. Massive amounts of weapons and supplies were shipped in to the resistance fighters. The U.S. spent half a billion dollars a year while the Saudis kicked in $240 million a year. The operation not only dumped containers and storage yards worth of weapons in Afghanistan but also created a generation of out of work fighters, many of whom continue to train or actually fight in Algeria, Chechnya, Tajikistan, Egypt, Sudan, The Philippines, Afghanistan, Morocco, Kashmir and other Muslim conflicts.

Although the press is quick to blame Afghans for recent terrorism attacks, the rash of bombings, killings and events have been sponsored by Iran, Libya and Syria.

Ramzi Ahmed Yousef was known as "The Chemist." He is credited with the World Trade Center bombing, Project Bojinka, being a collaborator with the Iraqis in Kuwait, planning an attempt on the Pope's life, and training Abu Sayyef terrorists in the Philippines. The World Trade Center was blown up because of the U.S. support of Israel.

The major training center for *mujahedin* used to be Peshawar, Pakistan on the border with Afghanistan. Now terrorists can find sanctuary in Iran, Sudan, Libya, Pakistan, Afghanistan, Cuba, Iraq, Lebanon and North Korea. In many cases, the leaders of those countries utilize the services of terrorist groups.

The U.S. State Department puts out rewards of up to 4 million dollars to find over 30 leading terrorists and international criminals. Drug dealers like Khun Sa, terrorists like Dursun Karatas, the leader of Dev Sol, or even the two Libyan intelligence agents, Lamen Khalifa Fhimah and Abdel Basset Ali Megrahi, the two men accused of masterminding the destruction of Pan Am Flight 103 over Lockerbie, are all worth serious cash to Uncle Sam.

The Merchant of Menace

Ok, you have about $300 million burning a hole in your pocket, and you're young good-looking and single. Well, 38-year-old Osama bin Laden is a member of one of Saudi Arabia's richest construction families, and he has an interesting hobby. He likes to play sugar daddy to terrorists. He is allegedly behind a number of specific terrorist incidents, including:

* *the Algerian bombing by the GIA in France,*

* *the assassination attempt on Egypt's President Hosni Mubarek, and*

* *the hotel bombings in Aden that killed two Austrian tourists.*

Laden actually fought against the Russians in Afghanistan. He bummed some bulldozers from his dad and shipped them to Pakistan. There, he helped build defense works to protect fighters from the Russian helicopters. He later took up soldiering in places like Shaban and Jaji where he gathered a reputation as a fierce fighter and devout mujahedin.

Currently targeted by the U.S. as a major instigator and supporter of terrorist activities, Laden feels he is just helping out. He is forbidden from entering Britain and has not been charged with any crime.

He then recruited other Arabs to fight in Afghanistan and even set up the largest training camp for mujahedin.

Not only is he supposed to be behind the current turmoil in his homeland, but he can be counted on to pitch in when something nasty needs to be done. He currently provides and helps to raise money from other Muslim businessmen to fund Islamic extremists around the world. Besides his day job in Sudan of running a construction company, and exporting goat hides and sunflower seeds, he keeps three training camps in the Sudan, where Algerians, Tunisians and Egyptians train, and the major training camp in Afghanistan (Kunar) that trains the Egyptian terrorist groups, Islamic Jihad and the Islamic groups.

No one really knows if he is the man behind all these activities or if he is just a rich kid who likes slumming in Sudan. But wait–it gets better. Osama's son-in-law is Mohammed Jamal Khalifia, who is being held for deportation in California. According to a highly classified Philippine intelligence report leaked by Japan's Kyodo news service, Khalifia is the glue that binds. U.S. authorities to believe that Khalifia is a key figure in the World Trade Center bombing, a plot to blow up an airliner from L.A. to Hong Kong, and the Abu Sayyef group in the southern Philippines. A Jordanian court has convicted Khalifia in absentia of plotting terrorism and sentenced him to life in prison.

Khalifia is also suspected of being the central support behind terrorist cells in Iraq, Jordan, Turkey, Russia, Malaysia, the United Arab Emirates, Romania, Lebanon, the Netherlands, Morocco, Albania, Syria and Pakistan. That's a lot of frequent flyer miles.

Terrorism in Europe

There are about 5 million non-European immigrants living in Germany, of which about 45,000 are known to be members of extremist groups. About half of this latter group are considered to be prepared for violence.

The total numbers are not impressive, but the support they provide to terrorism groups is. Europe provides a much more lucrative and unsuspecting field of battle for groups from the PKK of Turkey to the GIA of Algeria. A rough estimate of expats from countries with potential sympathies to terrorist groups include 70,000 Tamils and Sikhs, 30,000 Afghans, 300,000 Kurds (3500 are known members of PKK), 650,000 Yugoslavs, 70,000 Palestinians and 85,000 Iranians. The disenchantment of these recent immigrants and the intolerance shown by their host countries (some with insurmountable citizenship laws) have created fertile ground for groups like Hezbollah and the PKK.

The PKK has a network that covers 26 cities in Western Europe. The PFLP is estimated to have 50–60 terrorists in Europe; al-Fatah has 1700 supporters in West Germany; the PFLP GC has 30 expert terrorists in West Germany. A sleeper network of Abu Nidal was exposed in Portugal, and the ranks are growing, not shrinking, despite a get-tough attitude by Germany, Spain and France.

Qaddafi was an ardent supporter of the IRA, training Irish Republican soldiers and providing explosives and arms. Libya also supports the Basque ETA, Charles Taylor in Liberia and the RUF in Sierra Leone. These groups are now being supplied by Iran and Syria. The new austerity of the '90s was evidenced by the dropping of the expensive SEMTEX as an explosive device and shifting to more available and cheaper fertilizer chemicals for explosives.

The Terrorism Club

Terrorists is what they call freedom fighters before they come into power, right? Well, you decide. Here is the latest list of folks who'd like to bring a little fear and loathing into your day:

Iran

The land the Ayatollah built remains the most dangerous sponsor of sanctioned terrorism and the greatest source of concern. Iran's surrogate political and military arm, Hezbollah, was responsible for the bombing of the Israeli Embassy in Buenos Aires in early 1992 and remains the leading suspect in the July 1994 bombing of the Argentine-Israel Mutual Association in Buenos Aires that killed 96 people. Iran opposes the Middle East peace process and arms and funds rejectionist groups who espouse violence.

Libya

The colonel's ties with terrorists and insurgents are ongoing, despite the continual pleading by Gadhafi to be allowed back into the political and financial playpen of the world market. He continues to harbor those responsible for placing the bomb on Pan Am flight 103 in 1988, and the French want to chat with him regarding the bombing of UTA flight 772. United Nations Security Council Resolution 883 froze selected Libyan assets and banned the sale of many categories of oil-industry equipment. Gadhafi has made a series of silly demands in exchange for the suspected terrorists but has yet to show any good faith. He also backs homemake insurgents in West and Central Africa.

Gadhafi has been busy building a subterranean factory to manufacture chemical weapons. Seems he knows how to get in on the ground floor on what may be a big business.

Syria

Hassad continues to support groups that carry out terrorist attacks against its two neighbors, Israel and Turkey. Syria harbors the leader of the PKK and provides a safe headquarters for other terrorist groups. They also control Lebanon, which is home to the Lebanese Hezbollah. Hassad is mad at Turkey for stealing his water and Israel for stealing his land.

Sudan

This tortured country has provided safe haven to a number of international terrorist groups, not least the Abu Nidal organization. Sudan-based fundamentalist organizations have carried out acts of terrorism in Egypt, Tunisia and Algeria. They also were caught red handed in the attempted assassination of Hosni Mubarek. A Sudanese national, who pleaded guilty in February 1995 to various charges of complicity in the New York City bomb plots foiled by the F.B.I., alleged that a member of the Sudanese U.N. Mission had offered to facilitate access to the U.N. building in pursuance to the bombing plot. The Sudanese official reportedly had full knowledge of other bombing targets. Sudan's support of terrorist groups includes paramilitary training, indoctrination, money, travel documentation, safe passage and refuge in Sudan. Several Iranian-backed terrorist groups use Sudan as a transit point and meeting place.

Cuba and North Korea

These two anachronisms have not been tied directly to acts of international terrorism for some years now. Both of these countries are having a hard time feeding their people, let alone making payroll for their armies. The idea of bankrolling outside terrorist groups seems to be more a Cold War perception carried over from the '70s. However, Havana still provides safe haven to several terrorists who sought sanctuary several years ago. A number of Basque Fatherland and Liberty (ETA) terrorists live on the island, along with some Latin American terrorists and a few U.S. fugitives.

Algeria

This hard place poses the most dangerous threat to Western visitors and expats, though not through government-sanctioned terrorism but rather Islamic fundamentalists opposed to the Western-backed military government of President Liamine Zeroual. The Salvation Islamic Front, which is seeking to transform Algeria into a fundamentalist Islamic state, is using terrorism to frighten Western nations supporting Zeroual's authoritarian government, particularly in the wake of canceled elections in 1991 and 1992. Since the canceled 1992 Algerian elections, radical fundamentalists have assassinated more than 11,000 people, including 70 journalists. In addition to journalists, among the victims have been playwrights, politicians and even schoolgirls who refuse to don the *hejab* Muslim head scarf.

Terrorists tend to strike countries where there is the potential for the greatest amount of economic damage. Tourists and tourism facilities are prime targets, because crippled tourism cuts off vital foreign hard currency. Following the 1985 hijacking of TWA flight 847 enroute to Athens, the Greek government estimated that the subsequent tourism damage topped out at more than US$100 million.

Does terrorism work? In Egypt, Islamic fundamentalists have been waging a bloody terrorist campaign against foreign tourists. Cruise ships, tour buses and public gathering areas have especially been targeted. It's estimated that earnings from Egypt's tourism industry may be down by as much as 50 percent since the start of that campaign. The president of Egypt got tough and was nearly assassinated for his trouble. Slowly, the tourists came back. Then in April of '96, nineteen Greek tourists were gunned down in Cairo, killing with them the positive tourism spin the government had been sending out over the previous year. Yes, terrorism works.

ADVENTURE GUIDE

Adventure Calls

Think adventure is a calling for nut cases? Now you can blame your thirst for adventure on your parents. A study published in *Nature Genetics* reported that people who are prone to be exploratory and excitable have a longer version of a gene called D4DR found on chromosome 11. The gene helps regulate dopamine which controls pleasure and emotion in the brain. Although the research is not conclusive, the researchers believe that finding this gene may help identify thrill-seekers.

If you have that extra gene, you will find that there is no one perfect source for information on travel or adventuring to far-flung places. This is only a sampler of what is out there. We encourage readers to send in any sources they have come across to expand our list and to report on the experience.

A few things to keep in mind when dealing with these folks: Tell them why you are calling. Ask them for more information. Ask them to describe the typical member, client etc., and then ask for references. Do not take brochure or PR material at face value.

There is no one way to join or organize an expedition. By definition, all you have to do is walk out your door. Most expeditions have goals, structure, deadlines, budgets, and so forth, and require more planning than execution. Most are scientific in nature. Many are adventurous or exploratory, with little of the painstaking information recording required of expeditions in the old days.

Expeditions

Expeditions are simply formalized trips. Like any great endeavor, they should have an objective, a unique sense of purpose and maybe a dash of insanity. A lot of people dream about doing great things and being lauded for their superhuman status.

An expedition is a way to say "Here is what we said we would do, and here is what we did." There is little to no reward for climbing Mt. Everest blindfolded or swimming the Atlantic while towing a barge. There is far more reward in being an actor portraying the adventurer. Sigourney Weaver (as Dian Fossey) and Patrick Bergen (as Sir Richard Burton) put more in the bank than their characters ever made in a lifetime—a sobering thought. Fame does await the bold. And after that fame comes an endless procession of rubber chicken dinners and outdoor store openings. The more literate will write a book that will grace remainder lists for years to come. So consider an expedition as a good use of your skills and talents, with the only reward being the satisfaction of fellowship, a job well done and a better understanding of our world. Along the way, you will enter an elite club of men and women who have tested themselves and found themselves to be comfortably mortal.

Now a warning to the adventurous who view expeditions as an interesting way to see the world. All expeditions have some hardship involved. In fact, more and more of them seem to feature physical discomfort. Rannulph Fiennes' jaunt to the pole on skis is an example of this craziness. He could have flown, but he wanted to do something that had never been done before. Other expeditions like the recent attempt to climb Mt. Kinabalu in Borneo the hard way turned into a fiasco because a group of men decided to do whatever they felt like and got lost. They were found later, close to starvation on a mountain that is routinely climbed by schoolchildren. Expeditions are usually led by tough, experienced men who think there is nothing unusual about forcing physical and mental discomfort on others. So it is not surprising than many expeditions tend to be run either by emotionless, sadomasochistic, raving egomaniacs, men who were dressed as girls when they were young or questionable characters with overstated credentials who are forced by their lack of job skills to make their living in godforsaken places.

If you can combine all these characteristics into one person, then you stand the chance of mounting a successful expedition. Why would someone want to walk to the North Pole, bake in the Sahara or pick ticks out of their private parts, you may well ask? The answer is always unsatisfactory. Most expedition junkies are always testing themselves, proving other people wrong and seeking to top themselves in their next harebrained adventure.

Why do I sound so cynical here? Maybe because I have watched various expedition leaders lose it and seen many of my well-trained friends throw their hands up in disgust. The biggest single enemy of the expedition is bad chemistry, usually caused by the fearless leader's inability to lead men by example rather than brute force.

My more pleasurable expeditions have always seemed leaderless, where the group reacted in unison allowing creative interpretation of directions, deadlines and goals. Also, you must truly know your fellow expedition members. Men and women react very strangely under stress. Some revert to childish whining, others become combative, and still others simply lose it both mentally and physically.

The best way to see if you have picked the right partners in an expedition is to have a dry run that includes at least 48 hours without sleep, in adverse conditions. Sleep deprivation, combined with some mental and physical abuse at the 36-hour stage, will show a person's real mettle. Strangely enough, in my experience, white-collar workers, physical fitness nuts, city dwellers, businessmen, triathletes and sportsmen do very poorly in the ill-defined noncompetitive expedition environment. People with military experience, medical personnel, aboriginals, photographers, blue-collar laborers, and folks with rural backgrounds do very well.

The attributes to look for are experience in hard conditions, physical fitness, a sense of humor, a levelheaded approach to stress, pain and discomfort, and a genuine desire for knowledge and fellowship.

Expedition members should be chosen for specific knowledge, such as medical, language or bushlore; always get references. Members should never be chosen for prestige, ability to provide funding, or university credentials, and absolutely stay away from taking on journalists, relatives of backers and good-looking members of the opposite sex.

How to Launch an Expedition

1. **Pick a region or topic that is newsworthy or beneficial to sponsors.**

2. **Select a specific task that you will accomplish and one that will make the world a better place or create publicity.**

3. **State specifically how you will generate publicity (book, speeches, press releases, photographs, magazine articles).**

4. **Write a one-page query letter that states your purpose, method of execution and perceived result. Ask for a written show of support (do not ask for money) and other people who should be made aware of your expedition.**

5. **Gather letters of support from high-profile politicians, community members and scientists, and include them in your proposal.**

6. **Write an expedition plan (much like a business plan), and explain the benefits to the backers and sponsors.**

7. **Create a sponsorship program. Tell and show the primary sponsor what they will get, secondary sponsor and so on. As a rule of thumb, ask for twice as much money as you predict you will need, and come up with something to present to a recognized nonprofit charity at the end of your expedition.**

8. **Once you have your expedition goal figured out and raison d'etre, send a one-page press release and your outline to all news organizations, telling them that you are going to do this and you need sponsors. It is important to set a date to let sponsors know that you are going with or without their funds.**

9. **Gather lists of potential sponsors, and then phone to get the owner, president or founder's name. Send in your pitch, along with any early PR you generated. If the president or owner likes it, they will delegate it downward. If you send it in blind, most companies will put you in the talk-to-our-PR-company-who-then-promise-to-talk-to-the-client loop.**

10. **Follow up with a request for a meeting (money is never pledged over the phone), and thrill them with your enthusiasm and vision.**

11. Send a thank-you letter with a specific follow-up and/or commitment date. Promise to follow up with a phone call on a certain date and time.

Do this thousands of times, and you will have enough money to do any harebrained thing you want.

Just as Columbus had to sweet-talk Isabella after the banks turned him down, you have to be creative and ever hopeful. Everyone wishes they could go with you and their investment is just a way of saying I am part of this adventure.

The best sources for tough expeditions are the Royal Geographical Society in London and the National Geographic Society in Washington. Local newspapers will carry features on "brave young men and women" who are setting out to do whatever has not been done. In most cases, they will be looking for money (always an automatic entree into an expedition) or someone with multiple skills (doctor, cook, masseuse) to fill out the team. Be careful, since it all comes down to personality fit. Many people have never spent more than a weekend in close proximity to their spouse, let alone a total stranger; shakedown cruises are well advised, and go with your first impression. Things usually only get worse.

The up side is that you can be the first person on your block to pogo-stick to the North Pole, balloon across the Sahara or kayak Lake Baikal. Fame and fortune may await. You will need lots of money, time and the enthusiasm of a Baptist preacher. Remember that 99 percent of your time will be spent raising funds and planning. The best single source in the world is the Expedition Advisory Centre of the Royal Geographical Society in London.

Expeditions are usually funded by universities or governments, and there are no real grapevines other than reading scientific journals, staying in touch with universities or talking to expeditioners and outfitters. Most participants will be scientists and will often bring interns (for a fee) to help defray costs. The best way to find out what is happening is to contact a university directly to see if any expeditions are being mounted.

Expedition Planning

The National Geographic Society

The august and venerable National Geographic Society has become the best and most popular means for the world to understand itself. Back in 1888, it was simply a group of philanthropists who wanted to increase and diffuse geographical knowledge. Since then, they have funded almost 5000 expeditions and educated and entertained hundreds of millions, and today are the largest geographic group of any kind on this planet. They manage to maintain a rough edge and an accessible front. Unlike the tiny, musty adventurer's clubs, the National Geographic Society has gone global. You can sit in your own musty den and travel to more countries, experience more expeditions and learn more about our world, thanks to their efforts.

Many adventurers were weaned on their yellow tomes. A generation further back was titillated by sights of unclothed natives and exotic locales. If any magazine could be called adventurous, it would be good old *National Geo*.

National Geographic Society has 9.7 million members in almost 200 countries. Over 44 million people read each issue of the magazine, 40 million watch their documentaries on PBS and 15 million watch "On Assignment" each month. Though not exactly an elite group, being featured in or by a National Geographic publication thrusts you into the mainstream of adventure/entertainment. If you are written up or have an article in the *National Geographic Magazine*, you can work the rubber chicken circuit for the next decade. If you are featured on any of their television specials, like Jacques-Yves Cousteau ("The Voyages of the Calypso") or Bob Ballard ("The Search for the Titanic"), you can contemplate licensing and even your own TV series.

Despite being Valhalla for adventurers, the National Geographic does its bit to generate content. In 1992 the Society awarded 240 grants for field research and exploration. The Nat Geo is also on a mission to create higher awareness of geography among students, because they would have little product to sell if people didn't know the difference between Bahrain and the Bahamas. If you are young and a whiz at geography, you can try to join the 6 million people who take part in the National Geographic Bee.

The National Geographic is probably the biggest and best source for just about any information about the world and adventure. They offer a staggering range of books on everything from the Amazon to Zaire. They now offer *World*, a kids magazine with three million readers a month, *Traveler Magazine* with another three million and "National Geographic Explorer" (8 million viewers a month), a radio station (a million listeners a day) and home videos with 5.4 million viewers a year. You wouldn't think there was enough adventure, geography and science info out there, but Nat Geo just keeps on churning it out with CD-ROMs, Geoguides, popup action books, news features, on-line services, globes, atlases, a museum and more. How do they do it? For starters, they pull in about half a billion dollars in tax-free income. Just call ☎ *(800) 638-4077* for a catalog of what interests you and join today.

National Geographic Research & Exploration Quarterly

1145 17th Street North West
Washington, D.C. 20036
☎ *(800) 638-4077*
A quarterly journal with a definitely scientific bent. Better laid out and illustrated than other dry journals.

National Geographic Magazine

1145 17th Street North West
Washington, D.C. 20036
☎ *(800) 638-4077*
The old standard (requires membership) at $21 a year is still a great bargain. Editorial stance is getting tougher. More articles on pollution, politics and natural threats, in addition to the standard "purdy" pictures. The magazine has launched a small but well-traveled group of photographers who capture the world for a handsome fee.

The Royal Geographical Society

1 Kensington Gore
London, England SW7 2AR
☎ *[44] (71) 589 5466*
The fabled exploration society that still requires nomination by an existing member to join. When in London, nonmembers can visit the Map Room in their creaky Victorian headquarters on Hyde Park near Albert Hall. They also have an impressive photo archives and reference book selection.

The Royal Geographical Society Magazine

Stephenson House, 1st Floor
Bletchley, Milton Keynes
MK2 2EW
☎ *(0908) 371981*
A monthly magazine that is a lot drier and a lot less pretty than a *Nat Geo* publication but much tougher and smarter in its editorial focus. Covers expeditions, environment, travel, adventure—all with a scientific bent.

RGS Expedition Advisory Centre

1 Kensington Gore
London, England SW7 2AR
☎ *[44] (71) 5812057*
Contact the Expedition Advisory Centre. Don't be shy about calling or ordering any one of their excellent (but very British) books on expedition planning. They have an incredible selection of how-to books, and you can also get listings of past expeditions, contact other people interested in expeditions and get in touch with experts who have been to your area of interest.They do not sponsor expeditions but have a handbook on how to raise money.

All Inclusive Expeditions

The line between soft and hard adventure is the word "expedition." Experienced rafters, climbers, canoeists, hikers and divers usually seek out the small category of hard-core trips that may or may not provide any touristic benefit but push them to the limit. The common goal is to do something first, more intensely or just better than anyone has done before.

Mountain Travel/Sobek Inc.

6420 Fairmont Avenue
El Cerrito, California 94530
☎ *(800) 227-2384*
MTS is always trying to open up new areas or try new rivers. Usually trips are offered as part of their catalog, or if you call them directly they might have the same idea you have and help you put together a run (at a cost, of course). MTS does the old-fashioned type of expediting and running expeditions.

The Sports Advisory Bureau

Sports Council
16 Upper Woburn Place
London, England WC1H 0PQ
☎ *[44] (71) 388 1277*
They can put you in touch with the major specialist sport and adventure groups in the UK. From there, you can ask around as to who's climbing what mountain or running what river.

Expedition Organizers

If you would like to do more than wander around a country, try joining an expedition. Americans haven't quite caught on to this method of travel, but Europeans and the Japanese are crazy about it. Accordingly, they offer a lot more variety than some of their Stateside counterparts.

Brathay Exploration Group

Brathay Hall
Ambleside
Cumbria, England LA22 0HP
☎ *[44] (53) 9433942*
The Brathay Group has launched more than 550 expeditions since 1947. Every year about 125 young people (15–25 years old) in groups of about 20 set off on a variety of scientific trips. There are sponsorships for the financially disadvantaged and most members contribute toward the cost of each expedition.

Trekforce Expeditions

134 Buckingham Palace Road
London, England SW1W 9SA
☎ *[44] (71) 824 8890, FAX [44] (71) 824 8892*
Trekforce has six-week expeditions to Indonesia between June and November. Trips include four days of jungle training and require the ability to work side by side with scientists at a variety of scientific sites. Some of the projects have included Sumatran Rhino surveys, trips to the Baliem valley in Irian Jaya, grasshopper studies and even restoring a

British fort in Sumatra. You must be over 18 years old and are expected to raise the $4000 or however much it takes for airfare and your expenses.

Environmental Careers Organization

68 Harrison Avenue
Boston Massachusetts 02111
(617) 426-4783
Helps find paid, short-term positions for college students and graduates.

Earthwork

The Student Conservation Association
Post Office Box 550
Charlestown, New Hampshire 03603
(603) 543-1700
Provides lists of internships for students in the natural resources area.

Green Corps

Field School for Environmental Organizing
3507 Lancaster Avenue
Philadelphia, Pennsylvania 19104
☎ *(215) 879-1760*
Selected applicants can join annual training programs in environmental studies and campaign organizing.

University Research Expeditions Program

University of California
Berkeley, California 94720
☎ *(510) 642-6586*
Local and worldwide field research programs are available throughout the California State University Network.

Oceanic Society Expeditions

Fort Mason Center
Building "E", Suite 230
San Francisco, California 94123-1394
☎ *(415) 441-1106*
OSE manages research projects around the world and promotes the collection and analysis of scientific evidence that can be used in the protection of marine and terrestrial natural habitats. Natural history and volunteer-assisted research expeditions are guided by OSE naturalists and use local guides when possible. Encounter the legendary pink dolphins of the Amazon River, help a research team document bottleneck dolphins in Belize, get up close to Costa Rican humpback whales, or study sea turtles in Suriname. More than 30 unique expeditions are offered each year.

Wexas International

45 Brompton Road
London, England SW3 1DE
☎ *[44] (71) 589 3315, FAX [44] (71) 589 8418*
A British travel club with members in 130 countries. Its *Traveller* magazine is a good source for finding expedition members, discounts or travel partners. You can also find deals on airfares, insurance, car rental and hotels.

World Challenge Expeditions

Soane House
305-315 Latimer Road
London, England W10 6RA
☎ *[44] (81) 964 1331, FAX [44] (81) 964 5298*
World Challenge Expeditions puts together young people in groups of 12–16 members, and sends them off to foreign lands to conduct an environmental field project. These are not real scientific projects but tasks designed to build leadership skills and self reliance. Each member of the team has a chance to lead at least once during the month-long expedition.

Applicants must be between 16 and 20 years old, and the cost runs about $3000. Applications should be in before February.

Running with the Bulls

Have you ever dreamed of being one of the corredores in the annual encierro of Pamplona? Probably not, but many of us have dreamed of running with the bulls ever since we read Hemingway's account of it in the Sun Also Rises. Little did he know that he would elevate the running of the bulls in the medieval city of Pamplona to the level of the Holy Grail for adventurers. Twelve people have been killed in the run. No one bothers to keep track of the trampled, tripped and torn. The consumption of alcohol is considered to be mandatory, and the cost and scarcity of hotel rooms means that sleeping is completely on a "when available/as needed basis."

The running of the bulls is part of the Festival of San Fermin, July 6-14, every year in the Spanish province of Navarre. As if it matters anymore, Saint Fermin was martyred in the third century.

The bulls are let loose from a corral about 800 meters away from the bull ring, and they run through the barricaded streets on their way to it.

A rocket is fired off to start the run on Calle Santo Domingo at 7 a.m. on the seventh day of the seventh month. Don't eat breakfast first, since it is customary to celebrate afterwards with hot chocolate and deep-fried churros, essentially a long Spanish donut. Get there early. The students from the local university tend to be the most enthusiastic members of the crowd. Foreigners are usually too damn serious. The course is a lot shorter and tighter than most people expect it to be. Novices (or Los Valientes, the Brave Ones) get about a five-minute head start on the bulls but are quickly overtaken. The most dangerous part of the course is the tight turn onto Estafeta Street. Here, bulls and corredores discover that two objects can't occupy the same place at the same time. The lack of space is aggravated by lines of policemen who prevent the more timid from bolting over the barricades. The bulls are prodded on by the less valiant (those running behind or spectating) who smack them with rolled-up newspapers. Once bulls and runners stream into the bull ring, free-form amateur bullfighting breaks out. Once you get bored, head into the old quarter for breakfast or to the cafes to continue your celebrating. If you end up feeling like a Union 76 ball on a car antenna, the Red Cross is nearby to attend to any minor injuries.

If for some strange reason you do not spend the evening drinking and carousing, the best accommodations are to be found in the nearby town of Olite, about 40 kilometers away.

In July of 1995 an American from Chicago was gored in the chest and thrown 23 feet in the air, becoming the first fatality in over 20 years.

Sounds like a great concept for a Reebok commercial.

Volunteer Vacations

For those of you who flunked science but still want to do something meaningful with your time, consider volunteering in a foreign region. You can do anything from writing pamphlets to cleaning toilets. In most cases, there will be a "goal" and you will help in "achieving that goal." You, of course, will pay for all the expenses involved and will have to make a donation as well. Once on site, you will be working with motivated people who are trying to change whatever it is that causes problems in the local region. It can be lonely, frustrating and ultimately depressing. On the other hand, there is no better way to understand the world's problems. There are thousands upon thousands of opportunities for people who want to give of their time and skills. There are even more opportunities for people who don't mind paying to volunteer. In some cases, state agencies have replaced paid workers with paying volunteers for maintenance of trails, parks, and so forth. Archaeological digs are popular, as are works projects in Third World countries. The list and choice of volunteer vacations is so extensive that there are over 40 books and directories currently in print on the subject. There are enough of these opportunities to ensure that you will end up in the dangerous place of your choice, whether it's digging ditches in Sierra Leone, working on a Kibbutz in areas occupied by Israel or counting trout in the good old U.S.A. You can choose from mild to wild.

An excellent resource is *Volunteer Vacations*, by Bill McMillon, and published by the Chicago Review Press, or call any one of the clearing houses for volunteer opportunities listed below.

Archaeological Institute of America

675 Commonwealth Avenue
Boston Massachusetts 02215
☎ *(800) 338-5578, (617) 353-9361, FAX (617) 353-6560*
Call to order their annual listings of digs around the world that are looking for volunteers.

Council on International Educational Exchange

205 East 42nd Street
New York, New York 10017
☎ *(212) 661-1414*
Field programs and summer academic programs in Latin and South America.

Earthwatch

680 Mt. Auburn Street
Box 403N,
Watertown, Massachusetts 02272
☎ *(800) 776-0188, (617) 926-8200, FAX (617) 926-8532*
Offers working vacations on 155 field research expeditions around the world. Document the decay in the coral reef off Maui, excavate Mayan sites in Guatemala, or help scientists in Siberia study active volcanoes.

GAP Activity Projects Limited

44 Queen's Road
Reading
Berkshire, England RG1 4BB
☎ *[44] (734) 594914, FAX [44] (734) 576634*
The "gap" is a British term to describe the year between grade school and college. The GAP places young people in a variety of work situations in Russia, Hungary, Japan, China and Poland. Positions include business, medical, adventure training, conservation and teaching.

ADVENTURE CALLS

Institute for International Cooperation and Development

Post Office Box 103-F
Williamstown, Massachusetts 01267
☎ *(413) 458-9828*
Semester-long programs worldwide that combine cultural and educational experiences.

Raleigh International

Raleigh House
27 Parsons Green Lane
London, SW6 4HZ England
☎ *[44] (71) 371 8585, FAX [44] (71) 371 5116*
Can you swim 500 meters? Can you speak English? Good, you're on. Raleigh International sends eager young (17–25 years old) volunteers to the far corners of the world. The goal is to work on community, research and conservation projects while having a bit of adventure. The charity likes to challenge young people and develop their leadership skills and self-confidence.

UNIPAL (Universities' Education Fund for Palestinian Refugees)

33A Islington Park Street
London, N1 1QB, England
☎ *[44] (71) 2267997, FAX [44] (71) 2260880*
UNIPAL provides teaching and social services to the Palestinians in Israel and Jordan.

Volunteers for Israel

330 West 42nd Street
Suite 1318
New York, New York
☎ *(212) 643-4848*
Those who want to work on kibbutzim, Israel Defense Fund bases or in hospitals can expect to pay between $500 and $1000 for the privilege. Age is no object, other than you must be more than 18; over 15,000 people have signed up with this 13-year-old agency.

Volunteers for Peace

43 Tiffany Road
Belmont, Vermont 05730
☎ *(802) 259-2759*
A work camp–type environment with placement worldwide.

Volunteers in Technical Assistance

1815 North Lynn Street
Suite 200
Arlington, Virginia 22209
☎ *(703) 276-1800*
If you have a specific technical skill that you would like to share or apply with others, contact this group. They prefer to communicate by mail and will ask you some specific questions before referring you to one of the many volunteer groups in their listings.

Volunteer, The National Center

1111 North 19th Street
Suite 500
Arlington, Virginia 22209
☎ *(703) 276-0542*
If you want to narrow down your choices, make this group your first stop. They will simply refer you to a group of organizations they think will match your interests.

Working Overseas

Working overseas is a lot more romantic than it is financially rewarding. My stepfather pulled down a mediocre wage looking for oil in Canada but managed to get a six-figure tax-free salary with a simple idea. He figured he would find the thing of most value to the wealthiest people in the world. What's that, you ask. Water and the Saudis, of course. Most jobs overseas require training and lengthy job searches. There are some shortcuts: The military, the diplomatic corp, multi-national corporations, airline stewards, aircraft ferry pilots, even foreign correspondents all will guarantee you air time and broken marriages. On the other hand, the world will be your playground and you will develop an understanding and enjoyment of the world few people will ever appreciate.

Vacation Work Publications

9 Park End Street
Oxford, England OX1 1HJ
☎ *[44] (865) 241978*
FAX [44] (865) 790885

A British source for publications on summer jobs, volunteer positions and other new ways of travel. If you cover the postage, they will send you their latest catalog about books and specific publications on subjects that cover teaching or living and working in various countries around the world. A small sampling of publications can show you how to teach English in Japan, work on a kibbutz in Israel, choose an adventure holiday, get au pair and nanny jobs, find summer employment in France and much more.

EcoNet and PeaceNet

18 De Boom Street
San Francisco, California 94107
☎ *(415) 442-0220*

An on-line group that can link you up with like-minded conservationists and possibly a job.

Foundation for Field Research Programs

Post Office Box 2010
Alpine, California 91903
☎ *(619) 445-9264*

A comprehensive directory of Field Research Programs around the world.

Archaeology Abroad

31-34 Gordon Square
London, WC1H 0PY England

AA puts out three bulletins a year advertising overseas excavations that need volunteers and staff. They are primarily looking for people with excavation experience (grave digging and gardening don't necessarily qualify you).

The Astrid Trust

Training Ship Astrid
9 Trinity Street
Weymont, DT4 8TW England
☎ *[44] (305) 761916*

Every year the square rigger *Astrid* offers two 3-month, transatlantic voyages for 26 young people. The seven-week trip heads to the Caribbean from Weymouth in September and from St. Lucia to Weymouth in mid-May. There are also short summer cruises while in England, where the crew can learn to sail and scuba dive and take part in expeditions onshore.

Transitions Abroad

Box 3000

Denville, NJ 07834
☎ *(413) 256-3414, FAX (413) 256-0373*
This bimonthly magazine is targeted for people who want to live and work in a foreign country. It includes a directory of international volunteer positions and lists job opportunities including teaching and technical positions. $38 for 12 issues.

Rules of Politically Correct Travel

• *Try to learn and use the local language.*

• *Dress conservatively.*

• *Try to use nonpolluting conveyances (bike, hike, canoe).*

• *Use public transport (bus, train, plane) to save fuel.*

• *Stay to marked paths; do not litter.*

• *Respect local cultures.*

• *Try to choose locally run establishments (restaurants, hotels, tour guides) rather than chains.*

• *Hire a local guide to add to your knowledge and exchanges with locals.*

Destination: Adventure

For the less organized and mildly impetuous, we offer straight shots into the unknown. We all yearn to stuff a few things into a faded knapsack and hit the road. For those who look a little farther down the road, it means a dirt-cheap ticket from a bucket shop and a bunch of needles and expensive pills. Where do you want to go? We have put together a smattering of rough-and-tumble places that will get you started. For those who like a baby-sitter to keep them out of trouble, I have included the addresses of tour packagers and outfitters.

Say "Cheese!"

A plane ride is a plane ride, but when they crack open those aluminum doors and the heat and smell clobber you like a hammer, you know you have arrived. Outside, the heat rises in waves and the reddish-brown earth tells you that you have come a long way. On one such trip, I had to take a picture of the UTA DC-10 on the broken and potholed tarmac. I had to capture the silver bird crowned by a single monstrous cumulus cloud incongruously surrounded by soldiers with faded green uniforms. No sooner had I raised my camera to my eye than I was arrested by two scowling soldiers. Stupid, I should have known better than to take a picture in a West African airport. Thinking quickly as they grabbed for my Leica, I waved toward the cockpit. The soldiers balked, trying to figure out who I was waving to. Why, of course, I was taking a picture of the pilot. I explained quickly to the French ground crews to tell the pilot that I had taken a picture of him, not the airplane. The guards frog-marched me up the ladder, and, to my relief, the pilots played along. The soldiers let me go and explained how lucky I was that I wasn't taking pictures of the airport. There was no law as far as they knew against taking pictures of the pilots.

—Coskun Aral

Arctic/Antarctic

We used to say the Arctic was a great place to live if you were a Fudgsicle. Having been born in Edmonton, Alberta, and having participated in snowshoe marathons in my youth, all I can say is the frozen food section in the grocery store is about as close as I want to get to the colder climes these days. But don't let me stop you if your idea of fun is trying to unstick your private parts from your zipper after relieving yourself in a blizzard.

For cold-weather travelers, the most popular place is Antarctica, where legions of red survival–suited tourists create more photos of penguins and icebergs than ever could be viewed by their warmer relatives; second is Alaska and then the Northwest Territories. Siberia and Kamchatka are a distant fourth, but ripe for development. People who venture to the poles have to be a little crazy, since there is essentially nothing to see. The folks who pay a minimum of 10 grand to get to the North Pole are really sitting over a mass of water. Weather permitting, you get a few hours before you are bundled back on the plane for the long return flight. April is really the only hospitable month that the Pole can be visited with some certainty. There is some awe-inspiring and desolate scenery along the way, and you will be sick of flying as you must first get to Yellowknife, then Resolute, then a weather station on the edge of Ellesmere Island. From there, you wait until the weather clears and off you go. Make sure you know there is a geographic North Pole and a magnetic North Pole. The Magnetic North Pole wanders around like a bedouin looking for an oasis. A visit to the geographic North Pole may be all in good fun, but a visit to the South Pole is a different story. As bad as the weather is up north, it is much worse in the south. The vibes are very different as well. Scientists want nothing to do with the variety of adventurers, tourists and nuts who want to do everything from ski to motorcycle to the South Pole. Most of these people require very expensive and difficult extraction once they come face to face with the harsh realities of Antarctica. Cruise ships are considered a major evil, with their disturbance of animal populations, litter and general disruption of this pristine area.

Is it dangerous in the colder climes? Well, what to you think? You can start with the cold. Hypothermia, exposure, frostbite and plain old freezing to death are the constants. Falling through thin ice, predatory polar bears, crevasses, fires caused by unattended heaters and the list goes on. Being an old hand in the north, I won't bore you with long descriptions of 100-mph winds, helicopter crashes, drilling through blood blisters with pocket knives to relieve the pain, how flesh sticks to metal, why engines have to be run 24 hours a day and what frostbite can do to your toes. If you want all the gory details, contact the following:

Adventure Canada

1159 West Broadway
Vancouver, British Columbia, Canada V6H 1G1
☎ *(604) 736-7447*
OK, you've been there, done that, visited all 235-some-odd countries. What is left to impress your friends? How about a round of golf on the North Pole? You can also claim to visit Greenland, Russia, Canada and the U.S.A. as you whack your ball around the four international zones that meet at the North Pole. The trip costs $10,200 and golf clubs are provided.

Adventure Network International

200-1676 Dranleau Street
Vancouver, British Columbia, Canada V6H 3S5
☎ *(604) 683-8033, FAX (604) 689-7646*
Nothing to do in late November or early December? Then the Antarctic is the place to be. Pat Morrow and those crazy adventurers at ANI (founded in 1985 by a group of expedition guides) have put together a two-week ski and snowmobile trip, where an intrepid few can stay at Patriot Hills base camp (the only private base camp in the Antarctic) and then visit the surrounding area on skis or via snowmobile. Flights are available to overfly Mt. Vinson and the Ellsworth mountains. Campers can participate in the two-week ski trip that includes outside camping. If that sounds too tame, how about flying down to the South Pole and driving some *Ski-Doos* back to the base camp? All you need is $50,000 (that's not a typo) for the three-week stint. If this seems cheap, then get in line for a month-long trip that crosses the Ross Ice Shelf to Cape Evans, where you will be met by an expedition ship. The ticket is $100,000 per person. That's a lifetime of Club Meds for most folks.

Arctic Experience

29 Nork Way
Banstead SM7 1PB, England
☎ *[44] (737) 362321*
A small outfit specializing in putting together European-based Arctic expeditions for small groups.

Borton Overseas

5516 Lyndale Avenue South
Minneapolis, Minnesota 55419
☎ *(800) 843-0602, FAX (612) 827-1544*
Every spring Borton runs eight-day tours of Greenland that include two days of dog sledding. Participants can visit a remote Inuit village as well as tour Ammasalik and Sarfagajik Fjord.

Ecosummer Expeditions

1516 Duranleau Street
Vancouver, British Columbia, Canada V6H 3S4
☎ *(604) 669-7741*
A neighbor of ANI on picturesque Granville Island, this group is the best kayak outfitter in North America. They will send you to both warm and cold climates to get eye level

with the world. Their trips to Ellesmere Island are not strenuous and cover only about five to 20 miles a day, leaving plenty of time to get to see the wide variety of wildlife that becomes visible in the summer.

Special Odysseys

3430 Evergreen Point Road
Post Office Box 37A
Medina, Washington 98039
☎ *(206) 455-1960*
If you really want to get to the North Pole, it will cost you about eight days and 10 grand just to land, walk around and then get back in the plane the same day. The trip leaves every April, and I am sure can provide you with some type of sporting event other than golf.

Arctic Adventure Aps

Aaboulevarden 37, DK-1960
Frederiksberg
Copenhagen, Denmark
☎ *[45] (1) 37 12 33*
The experts on the massive island of Greenland. They can get you there just about any time you want to go.

Quark Expeditions

980 Post Road
Darien, Connecticut 06820
☎ *(800) 356-5699 or (203) 656-0499*
Eighteen grand will put you in a nuclear-powered Russian icebreaker with a bunch of pre-fab living quarters bolted on. The 500' Sovetskiy Soyuz puts its 75,000 horses into crushing through up to 16 feet of ice. Quark puts an ecospin on this trip, so expect to be educated by scientists and come back knowing more about the Arctic than you ever wanted to know. The Soyuz will cut a hole right on up to the geographic North Pole (the magnetic Pole is too flaky).

Adventure Trips

For those who have no particular method of transportation in mind, you might want to contact these groups:

Above The Clouds Trekking

P.O. Box 398E
Worchester, MA 01602
☎ *(800) 233-4499*
If you're seeking in-depth exploration of remote lands and exotic cultures, this travel outfit provides expert guides and average group size of eight. Destinations include Bhutan, Pakistan, Tibet, Madagascar, Nepal, Norway, France, UK, Costa Rica and Hawaii. Call for a free brochure.

Adventure Center

1311 EP 63rd Street
Emeryville, California 94608
☎ *(510) 654-1879*
☎ *(800) 227-8747*
Since 1976, Adventure Center has offered more than 160 affordable adventure programs worldwide. Programs include hiking, trekking, wildlife, natural history, sea treks, river journeys and cultural adventures. Discover ancient Mayan sites, sail Turkey's Aegean coast, experience the rain forests of Costa Rica.

MIR Corporation

85 S. Washington Street, Suite 210
Seattle, Washington 98104
☎ *(800) 424-7289*

Discover off-the-beaten-path Russia, Czech Republic, Uzbekistan, Mongolia, Hungary, Ukraine, Poland and China, including Trans-Siberia rail journeys and Central Asian explorations.

Turtle Tours

5924 East Gunsight Road
Cave Creek, Arizona 85331
☎ *(602) 488-3688*
FAX (602) 488-3406
Post Office Box 1147
Carefree, Arizona 85377

For 11 years Irma Turtle has specialized in introducing small groups of travelers to the world's dwindling nomadic and tribal peoples. Starting with trips to the Sahara to visit the Turegs, she has expanded her offerings to cover South America, the Middle East and Asia. If you want to experience the Wodaabe gerewol festival in Niger, the Pushkar camel fair in Rajashtan in India or the Asmats of Irian Jaya, she can provide an existing itinerary or put together a custom trip. Turtle offers a good selection of destinations for groups as small as two. Choose from Trans Sahara, The Empty Quarter, Northern Kenya, Namibia, Ethiopia—all designed to add an element of contact with culture, and peoples that other operators don't offer. Ground costs, per person for group tours run about $3500 for 14 to 18 day trips.

Discovery Expeditions

Expedition Base
Motcombe, near Shaftesbury
Dorset, England SP7 9PB
☎ *[4] (747) 54456*

Colonel John Blashford-Snell runs a variety of very adventurous and rewarding trips for "active mature adults." There are no age limits or special requirements, but they do ask that prospective team members get together at a briefing weekend (in England) to determine their compatibility and for a briefing on the realities that await them. Blashford-Snell's reputation as a "famous explorer" truly has the credentials to make any expedition interesting and worthwhile.

Other adventure-minded agencies include the following:

Backroads

1516 5th Street
Berkeley, California 94710
☎ *(800) GO ACTIVE, FAX 510-527-1444*

Twickers World

20/22 Church Street
Twickenham, England TW1 3NW
☎ *[44] (81) 892 7851, FAX (081) 892 8061*

Explore Worldwide

Aldershot, England GU11 1LQ
☎ *[44] (252) 344161 (24 hr)*

Karakoram Experience

32 Lake Road
Keswick, Cumbria C12 5DQ
☎ *(07687) 73966, FAX (07687) 74693*

Foundation for Field Research

P.O. Box 2010
Alpine California
☎ *(619) 445-9264*

Brathay Exploration Group

Brathay Hall
Ambleside, Cumbria LA22 OHP
☎ *(05394) 33942*

InnerAsia

☎ *(800) 777-8183*

Butterfield and Robinson

☎ *(800) 678-1147*

Bolder Adventures

P.O. Box 1279
Boulder, Colorado 80306
☎ *(800) 642-ASIA*

Adventure Center

1311-E 63rd Street
Everyville, California 94608
☎ *(800) 227-8747*

Ecotour Expeditions

Post Office Box 1066
Cambridge, Massachusetts 02238
☎ *(800) 688-1822, (617) 876-5817*

Natural Habitat Wildlife Adventures

1 Sussex Station
Sussex, New Jersey 07461
☎ *(800) 543-8917, (201) 702-1525*

The Nature Conservancy

International Trips Program
1815 North Lynn Street
Arlington, Virginia 22209
☎ *(703) 841-4880*

Tread Lightly

1 Titus Road
Washington Depot, Connecticut 06794
☎ *(203) 868-1710*

Wilderness Southeast

711-J Sandtown Road
Savannah, Georgia 31410
☎ *(912) 897-5108*

Overseas Adventure Travel

349 Broadway
Cambridge, Massachusetts 02139
☎ *(800) 221-0814*

International Expeditions

1 Environs Park
Helena, Alabama 35080
☎ *(800) 633-4734*

National Audubon Society

700 Broadway
New York, New York 10003
☎ *(212) 979-3066*

Sierra Club Outings

730 Polk Street
San Francisco, California 94109
☎ *(415) 923-5630*

University Research Expeditions

University of California
Berkeley, California 94720
☎ *(510) 642-6586*

World Wildlife Fund Travel Program

1250 24th Street, N.W.
Washington D.C. 20037
☎ *(202) 293-4800*

Ballooning, Hang Gliding and Flying

Balloons are not really a method of travel, unless you are Richard Branson. Balloons are expensive, vicarious, and sometimes deadly as a method of long-distance travel. As a vehicle for short, breathtaking ascents, they are a blast. Zeppelins have fallen out of favor (and out of the sky), so for now any desire to float through the sky is limited to balloon tour operations, hang gliding and soaring (glider flight). The newest adventure twist is bungy jumping from balloons.

Balloons travel with the prevailing wind, so you can't really determine your path. A variety of balloon safaris are available in Africa. For example, a balloon ride with champagne breakfast in the Masai Mara in Kenya will set you back about $250 per person for the four-hour event. If you are really nutso about starting every day with a balloon ride, then give one of these folks a call. If you are more interested in emulating Tom Cruise in *Top Gun*, you can sign up to a fly a fighter plane at the International Fighter Pilots Academy.

Adventure Balloons

3 Queens Terrace
Hanwell
London, England W7 3TS
☎ *[44] (81) 840-0108*
A specialist in balloon holidays in Great Britain, France and Ireland.

Air Escargot

Remigny, France 71150
☎ *[33] (85) 87 1230*
Balloon trips in the Burgundy area with evenings at fine restaurants. Expect to pay about $300 a day per person and stay in luxury accommodations complete with daily balloon rides.

Bombard Balloon Adventures

6727 Curran Street
McLean, Virginia 22101
☎ *(800) 862-8537, (703) 883-0985*

Where would you like to go? Bombard is the world's largest balloon tour operator and can take you just about anywhere you want to go. They claim to have sent more than 14,000 people on trips over the last 18 years.

Air Combat USA

230 Dale Place
Fullerton, CA 92833
☎ *(800) 522-7590 or 714-522-7592*
If you're dying to use a nickname like "Iceman" or "Maverick" and have always salivated over fighter planes, this is the place for you...if you have the guts and enough big bucks. For $695, you can man the controls of a tactical fighter trainer and engage in simulated aerial dogfighting with other *Top Gun* wannabes. For your money, you get a one-hour ground course, one-hour of flight time, a videotape of your experience and a one-hour debriefing afterwards. No flying experience is required. An instructor sits next to you the entire time, but even novices get to take the controls. Flights are conducted daily and reservations are needed.

Fly a MIG

Incredible Adventures
6604 Midnight Pass Road
Sarasota, Florida 34242
☎ *(800) 644-7382*
Just think the Russians spent all this money so that well-heeled dentists and plastic surgeons can fly a real MIG. The rather steep fee includes flying to Russia, lots of training and warning and your choice of a MIG-21, 25 or 29. For a few extra bucks ask them if you can drop bombs on Chechen or Tajik rebels (just kidding).

Vanuatu Land Diving

Vanuatu National Tourism Office
☎ *(408) 685-8901*
Kiwis claim bungy jumping started in New Zealand, but natives of Vanuatu say they started it all. On southern Pentecost Island, you can take a leap with jungle vines wrapped around your ankles. Vine lengths are custom-cut to fit each diver, and your hair will just barely brush the grass before you are hurtled back into the air. Unfortunately, one unlucky vine clinger bit the dust while land diving for the Queen.

Four-Wheel Drive

Adventure Racing

Racing originated with the marathon, based on the distance a messenger ran from the battlefields of Marathon to Athens. (He died of course). Th concept of pushing oneself past the limits has evolved from polite joggers to Triathlons and Iron man competitions where swimming and biking is integrated so that the competitors could tan and have an excuse to buy a $2000 bike to ride through the park on weekends. It seems that when TV and sponsors become involved these simple tests of personal best became more akin to the events held at the coliseum of ancient Rome. Now people who desperately fear aging or being a wimp can travel to exotic lands and do silly things for the benefit of cameras and sponsors. The Camel Trophy (which sells off road vehicles, clothing and subliminally cigarettes), The Raid Gauloise (which sells those nasty Francophone cancer sticks) and the Eco Challenge (which sells anything you want to wear logos for) are the new breed of adventure racing. Of course there is also the Olympics with mountain biking, pentathlon and other rugged sports. The only major difference is that you have to beat out 1. 6 million people to be part of the Camel Trophy and the rest require a checkbook and a disclaimer.

The World's Toughest Cigarette Commercial

The Camel Trophy is the major marketing effort of Land Rover and World Brands, Inc. (WBI), a fully owned subsidiary of RJR Nabisco, the makers of Camel cigarettes and Oreo cookies. No longer directly flogging Camel cigarettes, The Camel Trophy is an event designed to create the imagery that sells about $400 million a year in licensed watches and about 80 different styles of boots–the logo stays the same as the cigarettes though. Pretty sneaky. This is an ideal way to push imagery (sans cigarette) in countries that don't allow overt cigarette advertising. WBI does not release budgets for The Camel Trophy, but DP estimates the total marketing cost worldwide at between $20 and 30 million, with each division kicking in funds from their advertising budgets. They fly in 120 journalists from around the world to cover not only the main event but also the qualifications trials usually held in a European location. Simple math would tell even the most gullible that licensing revenue (typically 5–15 percent of the gross) from $400 million sales would barely cover the event cost, let alone the corporate and advertising campaign. There is also a "coincidental fascination" with countries that are open to this macho brand image. You don't see a lot of Camel Trophies in North America or Europe. In fact, there have been none. Asia, South America and Africa are the venues of choice. There is also a growing disaffection by journalists who find the increased emphasis on yuppie sports, macho posturing, unabashed posing for the PR cameras and RJR's denial of tobacco hype to be a little too much.

Many yearn for the bad old days when it was a group of young men trying to get from Point A to Point B in their Land Rovers. The fact that a cigarette company paid the tab to sell more smokes in Europe and the Third World was fine since it was no secret. Now team members come from countries where the people smoke a lot of cigarettes but don't buy a lot of adventure wear. For example, why do the Canary Islands (I never knew RJR could confer sovereignty on areas), Russia and Poland compete when Canada and Mexico do not? It obviously has to do with the presence of RJR cigarette entities not potential clothing purchasers. Now things are a little too posey and murky, and the journos I talk to don't like it. U.S. journalists who want to participate should contact Glenn Campbell, public relations representative for Land Rover North America, (818) 799-0877 FAX (818) 799-0878, or Bill Baker at Land Rover North America, (301) 731-9041.

The actual event can range from comical to magical to pathetic, as the organizers try to create as much havoc and "toughness" as possible. I enjoy the camaraderie and exotic locations of the event, but the overall mindset of the organizers should be questioned once in a while. My claim to fame in Africa was having a knife pulled on me by event leader Ian Chapman, who was terrified that I would throw him in the swimming pool with his pretty little kilt on.

The Camel Trophy does afford the regular Joe an opportunity to compete for and get a spot in a world-class competition that pits him against the best that other countries have to offer. Rather than compete, the participants are united by adversity, and winning the team spirit award can provide a lot more weight than the actual trophy. The team spirit award is voted on by the competitors, while the overall trophy is decided by some voodoo method only the organizers understand.

What kind of people make the cut? Triathletes, joggers, weight lifters and racers shouldn't even waste the postage. The key is teamwork, a sense of humor and the stamina to go through a lot of crap and keep smiling. Hard-core athletes rarely have the team spirit or stamina required for a two-week event. Musclemen and racers couldn't handle the bad days, when two to three miles seem like a long way. Finally, who makes it? Stable, good-humored people, who can endure being squeezed in a vehicle with three other people for two weeks. Professional racers are disqualified automatically, and females are welcome.

The World's Toughest Cigarette Commercial

The initial cut is based on experience–can you drive off-road, pitch a tent, read a map or change a tire? Once accepted, you will spend a miserable frozen weekend in Grand Junction, Colorado, with team organizer Tom Collins. You will be run through the standard officer candidate tests, silly things like sliding people through rope webs, balancing on a log, even winching vehicles places they should never fit into. Forty-eight hours later, sleepless, bagged and tired, you will find out if you made the first cut. If you make it, you get to go to the finals, usually held in Europe. Here, they mess with your mind and run you through junior commando school, fun things like dragging a Land Rover half a mile with its wheels locked the wrong way (it can be done), building bridges, getting dumped in freezing cold water and playing the Flying Wallendas while crossing high wires–all posed for the cameras and designed to generate a sinking feeling of self-doubt for the real event.

The real event is quite different. A convoy of yellow vehicles will snake its way across some fetid hell-hole. There are few roads and fewer reasons why trucks should pass here.The event is usually run in the wet season so that there are plenty of opportunities to use your winch or slide down hills. The competitions are great fun and deadly serious. High-speed driving is not a factor in any of this. Rally driving is being phased out in favor of more ecosensitive events like building research facilities. You are graded on how well you perform in these tasks as well as how you perform as an overall team member.

Few people can claim the honor of having been on the Trophy, and most people would never want to. But, hey, that's adventure.

The Camel Trophy

Tom Collins
U.S. Camel Trophy Team Coordinator
Snowmass, Colorado
FAX (303) 927-9308

Eco Challenge

9899 Santa Monica Boulevard
Los Angeles, CA 90212
☎ (310) 553-8855, FAX (310) 553-7497
The Eco-Challenge is sort of a Raid Gauloise-Lite. Designed to appeal to American Yuppies who buy a lot of brightly colored gear and created by Mark Burnett, the event is a direct, unashamed attempt to sell sponsorship and provide a TV show load of pathos and agony by people who actually pay for the experience. Burnett got the idea after he took part in three Raid Gauloises and despite some rather disastrous setbacks he decided that Americans would pay to be lost in the woods and grimace a lot. Like any new venture the Eco Challenge had its financial setbacks, screw ups, outraged environmentalists and tenuous existence. But now the Eco Challenge has graduated from MTV and has a multimillion dollar deal with Discovery Channel so it should hit the big time soon. You know things are getting a little too Yuppified when you have team names like Team Land Rover, Team Rolex, Team Nike and Team Reebok.

Here's the scoop. You must go from point A to B, a distance of around 350 miles. You must enter as a team of five people with at least one person being certifiably female, (women buy yuppie gear too you know). It costs about $15,000 - $40,000 to compete, $10 grand for the entry fee and the rest for travel, gear and training outings. Between points A and B contestants must utlilize a virtual sporting goods store of conveyances: canoes, horses, rafts, mountain bikes, canoes and climbing gear. It is expected that about half of the logo-festooned teams will drop out. (If one of your team flakes, you're out) and the race is usually won by Europeans who have been doing these things for years.

In Utah it took the winning team 7 days, 16 hours and 12 minutes to win. Not bad considering they had a 35 mile horseback ride and run, 25 mile hike/swim through a canyon, a 60 mile desert hike, 30 mile mountain bike ride and a 75 mile raft trip (23 miles of it whitewater), a 24 mile hike through the mountains, a 1200 foot vertical ascent, a 14 mile hike through a canyon, and a final 52 mile canoe trip.

Burnett figures it costs $2.5 million to stage the event and with about 75 teams competing it should be around for a while.

Marlboro Adventure Team

A newcomer and somewhat panty-waisted event asks that team members have expertise in four wheeling, dirtbiking, whitewater rafting and horseback riding. An 11-day adventure that covers 600 miles in the American Southwest, the Adventure team event is beautifully photographed be Pete Turner and amply promoted complete with Adventure Gear and plenty of print advertising. This event is open to anyone who can fill out a form and pass the initial knowledge tests.

Applications can be had by calling ☎ *(800) MARLBORO.* (Closing date is around April 22 each year.)

Raid Gauloise

470 Waverly Drive
Beverly Hills, California, 90211
☎ *(310) 271-8335*
Created in 1988 by a French journalist who felt that the Camel Trophy was too easy. Gerard Fusil put together a 300 mile, 10 day torture test that attracts masochists from around the world. Unlike the Camel Trophy which is free, participants in the Raid Gauloise must pay their own way plus the $13,000 entry fee for the privilege of walking, climbing, riding, rafting, parachuting and canoeing themselves to exhaustion. There is no cash prize, little fame and a lot of camaraderie. The event takes place in a different exotic location each year.

Alies Kar, The Adventure Company, Inc.

8855 Appian Way
Los Angeles, California 90046
☎ *(213) 848-8685*
Everything's clear to this outfitter that can take you on four-wheel-drive tours around Southern California and Baja.

Borneo Safari

P.O. Box 171 888 68
Kota Kinabalu, Sabah, Malaysia
FAX 088-426-180
An event that's been around for 6 years winds and grinds through Northern Borneo (Sabah). DP always has a blast but if you don't like mud, very large insects, not sleeping and noodles, forget it. Open to competitors, participants and journalists.

Bush Trek 4WD Services

44 Tulloch Avenue
Maryland, New South Wales 2287
☎ *(049) 515815*
Garry Walthers will yank you out of a tight spot, train you not to get into a tight spot or set up four-wheel-drive tours.

Four-Wheel Drive

Cape York Guides
Post Office Box 908
Atherton, Queensland 4883
☎ *(070) 911978*
FAX (070)912545
Four-wheel drive trips through the top end of Australia. You can bring your own or rent one of theirs. Travelers can rely on good cooking and expert guidance.

Land Rover Adventure Outfitters

McVeigh Associates, 7 12th Street

Garden City, New York 11530
☎ *(800) 726-5655*
FAX (516) 742-9103
Land Rover organizes off-road expeditions worldwide with itineraries including a seven-day safari in North Africa, eight days in Colorado's Rocky Mountains, five days on the pioneer trail in the Red Rock canyons of Moab, Utah, a 10 day safari through the dunes and wadis of Oman, nine days in Australia's Outback, and more. Accommodations are ultradeluxe, and the tab isn't cheap, but what price can you put on unforgettable experiences?

The Lost Patrol

Suite 172
11919 North Jantzen Avenue
Portland, Oregon 97217
☎ *(503) 731-3030*
Billed as the longest, coldest, toughest winter rally in the world, The Lost Patrol is a quick run up the Alcan highway in the dead of winter. Using standard TSD rally methods, the idea is to have the most accurate and consistent times. Sometimes this means driving as fast as the law of gravity and friction will allow and sometimes crawling to make up time. The Rally leaves Seattle at the beginning of February with about 30 entries and ends up in the Arctic about a week later.

The winner might pick up about a grand (depending on who donates the purse) and side bets are encouraged. Economically, the entry fee of $2500 doesn't make this a paying proposition, but what better things could you be doing in the dead of winter?

Richard Petty Driving Experience

6022 Victory Lane
Harrisburg, North Carolina, 28075
☎ *(800) BE PETTY*
Talk slow, spit far and drive fast in a real Winston Cup stock car. There are five courses to choose from and three locations (Las Vegas, Atlanta and Charlotte). Does not include oversized hat or sunglasses.

Southern Traverse

☎ *[011] (64) 3442-3660*
The grand daddy of them all, The New Zealand race was the forerunner in covering long distances in short periods and then tossing in mountains, roaring rivers and no sleep to make it interesting.

Warn Adventure

G.P.S Expeditions
Antonia Lopez, 115
28026 Madrid, Spain
☎ */FAX: 34-1475-6841*
If you have a hankering to explore the uncharted terrain of the North African desert, try this event sponsored by Warn Winches (who sponsored a muddy and cold trip to Transylvania a while back). The event is called Adventure Morocco and is looking for 20 teams comprised of three trucks and six participants. You need to be 17 or over and healthy and have insurance and a properly outfitted vehicle. The event is a competition that stresses teamwork. There are a series of tasks that must be performed to gain points. Although, like most adventure concepts, this one stresses that every challenge can be met by protecting the environment through "ecological sensitivity," there is no supervision of the tasks. All team members simply show a Polaroid of the checkpoint. The entry fee for each vehicle is a paltry $450, with the ferry from Spain to Morocco about $250 per car. Contestants must supply all food, lodging etc. If you win, you will receive an unspecified prize.This year the five-day event kicks off in the spring and will wind through the Atlas

mountains, through forests, across riverbeds and finally into the great sand dunes of the Sahara.

Jungle Trekking

Many people would never think of going to a tropical jungle with a tour operator while others wouldn't think of going without one. Keep in mind that most of these folks will hook you up with local ground operators, so expect to find the same trips offered by many agencies. Top jungle destinations are Irian Jaya, Papua New Guinea, Borneo, Sumatra, Vietnam and the Amazon; the most popular are Costa Rica and Belize.

Adventure Center

1311 63rd Street
Suite 200
Emeryville, California 95608
☎ *(800) 227-8747,* ☎ *(510) 654-1879*
A lower-cost alternative.

Ecosummer Expeditions

1516 Duranleau Street
Vancouver, British Columbia, Canada V6H 3S4
☎ *(604) 669-7741*
I know you are getting sick of "sea"ing this company in here, but it just so happens that they are one of the best packagers to Papua, New Guinea.

Journeys/Wildland Adventures

4011 Jackson Road
Ann Arbor, Michigan 48103
☎ *(800) 255-8735*
An excellent choice for trips to Madagascar, Brazil and Venezuela.

Mountain Travel/Sobek Inc.

6420 Fairmont Avenue
El Cerrito, California 94530
☎ *(800) 227-2384*
Although they are primarily a rafting company, they have developed good contacts and a good nose for exotic tours.

SafariCenter

3201 North Sepulveda Boulevard
Manhattan Beach, California 90266
☎ *(800) 223-6046, in California (800) 624-5342*
An excellent selection of adventure and jungle tours.

Kayaks

The Shotover in New Zealand, the Sun Khosi in Nepal, the Rogue River in Oregon and the Cheat, the Upper Yough, the Gauley and the Tygart in the Allegheny mountains in West Virginia are some of the top spots. West Virginia probably offers the widest selection of Class IV to V runs on the continent. Rafters can conquer these rivers with impunity, but kayakers need a healthy dose of Class IV skills before venturing out. Kayakers need look no further than Ecosummers located in Vancouver for the widest selection of kayak trips.

Ecosummer Expeditions

1516 Duranleau Street
Vancouver, British Columbia, Canada V6H 3S4
☎ *(604) 669-7741*
Ask for their annual catalog of trips along the West Coast of North America as well as some intriguing Arctic and foreign destinations.

Motorcycle

Motorcycle touring comes in four flavors: the classic Harley/Gold Wing big-butt road riders; the leather-clad, bug-splattered BMW crowd; the brightly colored and over-revved sport

Tourers, and the sunburnt, trans-Sahara off-road crowd. All can be considered adventurous and dangerous, but the choice is ultimately yours. There is a law of diminishing returns if you are crossing Mali dehydrated, stricken with dysentery and nursing a broken ankle. You will probably dream of cruising the Grand Tetons adjusting the air suspension and the radio on your Gold Wing. There are happy mediums. Usually BMWs are found in scenic places like New Zealand, California and the Alps. If you want to ship your own bike, expect to pay between $1500 and $3000 for the roundtrip. You might want to look into BMWs European delivery plan, where you will pay about what the discounted price is in the States. You then pick up your bike in Munich, drive all over Europe and bring it back to Munich where they will pay for the crating, shipping and taxes. You can also look into buy-back deals, where you sell the bike back at the end of the trip. Stateside, you can arrange rentals through Von Thielman or Western States Motorcycle Tours. Bikes rent for about $500–$800 per week, with insurance extra. If you are interested in touring Vietnam, I should plug Wink Dulles' book *Vietnam on 2 Wheels*, the best (and only) guide to motorcycling through South Vietnam. Call ☎ *(800) FW-2-GUIDE* to order your copy.

The first step is to contact the companies that strike your fancy and then start packing your leathers:

Alaska Motorcycle Tours

Post Office Box 622
Bothell, Washington 98041
☎ *(800) 642-6877, (206) 487-3219*
Timothy McDonnel runs shiny new Honda Gold Wings through the summer wilds of Alaska. The tour covers about 1600 miles over seven days. Figure on about $250 a day; that includes your gas, high-end hotels and the bike rental. You pay for your own food.

Adventure Center

1311 63rd Street
Suite 200
Emeryville, California 95608
☎ *(800) 227-8747, (510) 654-1879*
The Center reps the Australian Motorcycle Touring ☎ *(011 61) 3 233-8891*, where owner Geoff Coat runs eight- and 10-day trips beginning in Melbourne. You can expect a well-serviced BMW R80 and twin share accommodations. Tours run about $120 a day, and watch out for those kangaroos.

Baja Off Road Tours

25108 Marguerite Parkway
Suite B-126
Mission Viejo, California
☎ *(714) 830-6569*
A former Team-Honda dirt-bike racer will put you on a Honda 250 or 600cc dirt bike and send you off to La Paz (seven days) or San Felipe (four days). You will experience one of the primo desert riding and scenic runs in Mexico. The all-inclusive trips will cost you about $300–$400 a day. You pay the airfare to Southern California.

Beach's Motorcycle Tours

2763 West River Parkway
Grand Island, New York 14072
☎ *(716) 773-4960, FAX (716) 773-5227*
Why not buy your bike overseas? Beach's will set you up on a rental or your very own BMW as you tour the Alps. They have trips to New Zealand, Great Britain and Australia as well. You can also ship your own bike for the ride. Beach's will handle the crating, shipping and customs involved. Expect to pay about $800–$1800 each way to Europe; New Zealand is about 30 percent more. Tours are longer than most (16–22 days) but are great deals and highly recommended. Costs are about $200 a day, plus about $50 a day for the rental of the bike.

Desmond Adventures

1280 South Williams Street
Denver, Colorado 80210
☎ *(303) 733-9248, FAX (303) 733-9601*
One of the best ways to see the Alps is on a 16-day Alpentour devised by the Desmonds. You can choose from East or West. Expect to pay about $4000 per rider and about $500 less for the passenger. It includes roundtrip airfare from New York, meals, bike rental and insurance. The trip is van-supported, so bring lots of camera gear and luggage. You can also choose your weapon, from mighty CBR 1100cc sport bikes to nimble Honda Trans Alps (Beemers, Trans Alps, CBR's Katanas sport bikes or Kawasaki Concours).

Edelweiss Bike Travel

Armonk Travel
146 Bedford Road
Armonk, New York 10504
☎ *(800)255-7451, (914) 273-8880*
The U.S. agents for Edelweiss Bike Travel (*Steinreichweg 1, A6414 Meiming, Austria*) can send you just about anywhere, including the CIS. Its homegrown 12-day Alpine ride is one of the most popular (and the best deal) for mountain rippers. They like to stick you on BMW 750s, the ridcable but standard for many bike rentals, but larger bikes are available for 10–20 percent more. Edelweiss provides support vans.

Explo-Tours

Arnulfstasse 134
8000 Munich 19, Germany
☎ *(49) 89 160 789, FAX (49) 89 161 716*
Africa nuts who like chipped teeth and sandblasted eyeballs will love the offerings of Explo-Tours. They arrange tours across the Sahara, through Central Africa and into South Africa on spartan but reliable Yamaha XT350s. Naturally, only Germans are crazy enough to keep this company in business, but most Germans speak English. This is some serious riding, so participants must be physically fit and ready to ride thousands of miles in sweltering heat. The trips are great bargains at about $150 a day, including bike rental. There is a support van if you or your bike conk out, and when you return, you'll know more than a plasterer about mud and sand.

Great Motorcycle Adventures

8241 Heartfield Lane
Beaumont, Texas 77706
☎ *(800) 642-3933, (409) 866-7891*
If you are looking for a little danger, how about a mix of Mexican roads and fast bikes? Well, OK, how about offroading on slow bikes? GMA organizes off-road trips to Copper Canyon, the Yucatan and the Sierra Madre mountains on dual-purpose bikes. Tour costs include food, lodging, tours, gas and insurance. Trips are about $160 a day, not including bike rental (dual-purpose bikes are only $500 a week). If you really want to do it on a fast road-bike, then expect to pay another $600 a week.

MHS Motorradtouren GmbH.

Donnersbergerstrasse 32
D-8000, Munich, Germany
☎ *[49] (89) 168 4888*
FAX [49] (89) 1665 549
MHS offers a wide array of bike tours (including Southern California). You can choose from their popular week in southern Italy tour or any one of the other tours, including northern Italy, Kenya, Sicily, Tunisia, Hungary, the U.S.A. and South Africa. European tours run about $150 a day, with bike rentals (BMWs or Suzukis) costing about $900 a week. A cool idea for *Easy Rider*-wannabes is the one-way Drive U.S.A. program, where riders can pick up a bike at either coast and drop it off on the other.

Motorrad-Reisen

Jean Fish
Post Office Box 591
Oconomowoc, Wisconsin 53066
☎ *(414) 567-7548*
The U.S agent for Motorrad-Reisen, *Postfach 44 01 48, D-8000, Munich 44, Germany,*
☎ *(011 49) 89 34 48 32,* can send you on a motorcycle adventure (we don't use the word "holiday") to Kenya, southern France, the Alps, Italy or Russia. As with most German companies, it offers less expensive tours with less frills. You can also purchase a new BMW, ride it on your trip and ship it back home.

Villa Moto-Tours

9437 E.B. Taulbee
El Paso, Texas
☎ *(800) 233-0564*
☎ *(915)757-3032*
One of the few companies that can stick you on a Harley. As you guessed from the name, Pancho Villa specializes in tours through Mexico down to the Yucatan Peninsula. They also can take you through Costa Rica, Baja, the Sierra Madre central coast and the Southwest U.S. Harleys and the Southwest—what a combo. The prices are fair, about $110 a day, with bike rental running about $50–100 a day extra.

Rocky Mountain Moto Tours Ltd.

Post Office Box 7152
Station E
Calgary, Alberta T3C 3M1
☎ *(403) 244-6939*
FAX (403) 229-2788
Touring the dramatic countryside of Alberta and British Columbia may be a good second choice to the Alps. Using Honda 600cc dual-purpose machines, RMMT takes you on the remote backcountry routes. Their rates of about $120 a day, including bike rental, are downright cheap. Choose from seven-day tours of the Bugaboos and 10-day trips through Big Sky country.

Western States Motorcycle Tours

1823 East Seldon Lane
Phoenix, Arizona 85021
☎ *(602) 943-9030*
Western states will put a fire-breathing Harley between your legs and point you in the right direction. You can arrange a buy-back deal if you plan on being gone a long time, or you can rent everything from a Gold Wing to a Harley for about $100 a day.

Von Thielman Tours

Post Office Box 87764
San Diego, California 92138
☎ *(619) 463-7788*
FAX (619) 234-1558
If you are a jaded biker and view the Alps and New Zealand as commonplace, then Von Thielman has the antidote. This company has been around long enough to put together tours that bring the jaded back. How about Southern California, Thailand, China, Argentina or even Jamaica? The company has really got its act together. They can send you out alone, help you buy a new bike, ship yours or give you a wide selection of dual-purpose and touring bikes.

Mountaineering

There is little argument that the Hindu Kush in Nepal is the *ne plus ultra* of peaks and trekking. Only about 40 years ago, the ascent of a major peak would put you on the rubber chicken circuit until you grew old. Now, even Mount Vinson in the Antarctica has had 130 successful summit trips. Up and coming places include the peaks of Alaska, Argentina and Pakistan, with the Alps looking like a drive-through window at McDonald's. The Holy Grail is to conquer the seven summits or climb the highest mountain on each continent. Many guides will require that you have proof of your skills before taking you along.

The international UIAGM or the local AMGA provides certification and standards for guides. See the listings under schools in the "Save Yourself" chapter, or to find out more about schools, guides and programs, contact the following:

American Mountain Guides Association

Post Office Box 2129
Estes Park, Colorado 80517
☎ *(303) 586-0571*

Canadian Mountain Guide Association

Post Office Box 1537
Banff, Alberta, T0L 0C0, Canada
(403) 678-4662

Himalayan Kingdoms

20 The Mall
Clifton
Bristol, BS8 4DR, England
☎ *[44] (272) 237163, FAX [44] (272) 744993*
One of the leaders in expedition and advanced quality climbs.

Summits

Post Office Box 214
Mount Rainier, Washington 98304
☎ *(206) 569-2992, FAX (206) 569-2993*

The World's Most Dangerous Mountain

K2 is called the killer mountain, simply because on average it kills every second person who tries to conquer the summit. The 50 percent fatality rate makes Everest's 25–30 percent fatality rate seem almost safe.

Mount Everest has been climbed more than 650 times, and to date about 100 people have died in the attempt. The 45˚ slopes are fairly easy to negotiate, so Everest's notoriety as the world's highest mountain continues to attract thrillseekers and climbers. Tens of thousands have made the trek to the 17,500-foot-elevation base camp. A permit costs $10,000. K2 is 236 meters lower, but it is considered the world's most dangerous mountain to climb. Only 100 people have reached the 8611-meter summit of K2, and more than 45 people have died trying. The slopes of K2 average about 60˚ and the storms are so violent that no one managed to conquer the mountain between 1986 and 1991. Avalanches are frequent, and the most dangerous segment involves passing through a bottleneck area prone to avalanches.

In 1993, 40 people reached the summit of Everest the same day, and in May of 1996, eight out of 30 climbers died on Everest when a storm hit. There were 11 different groups trying to make it to the top at the same time. Over a million people followed the disaster online.

The odds are one in three climbers will die attempting to reach Mt. Everest's summit. The total cost to risk your life on Everest or K2 is between $30,000 and $100,000, depending on what your guide thinks his life is worth.

Overlanding

Although not technically four-wheel driving, you will be sitting in a four- or six-wheel-drive Bedford as you bump and lurch across Africa. Any old African hand knows that you use a Bedford to pull out a Land Rover and you will need a tank to pull out a Bedford.

Overlanding became all the rage in the early seventies when companies could take you all the way from London to South Africa for only $1200 bucks. Today, prices are up around $5000, and the conditions and roads have since worsened. Most overlanding is done on a communal basis. Cooking and other camp chores are usually shared. Most only invite young people along. You can imagine the social dynamics of young people usually on their first or second major trip away from home. Cliques emerge, rebellions soon form, people leave and seats, toilet paper and girlfriends are fought over. In the end, everyone departs firm friends.

Himalayan Travel, Inc.

Post Office Box 481
Greenwich, Connecticut 06836
☎ *(800) 225-2380, (203) 622-6777*
The agent or Tracks Africa can send you on a 15-week overland trip from Fez in Morocco to Dar es Salaam in Tanzania. The route changes or the trip is cancelled, depending on who's killing whom along the way. If things are relatively quiet, expect to pay about $4000 per person.

Dragoman c/o Adventure Center

1311 63rd Street
Suite 200
Emeryville, California 95608
☎ *(800) 227-8747, (510) 654-1879*
Contact the Adventure Center if you want more punishment than Tracks Africa delivers. If you want to do 19 weeks, Trans-Africa will weave you through West Africa as well as hit most countries in Central and East Africa. Dragoman is a British company that uses Mercedes trucks. The 20-year-old company can also take you on a seven-week tour down the spine of South America.

Forum Travel International

91 Gregory Lane
Suite 21
Pleasant Hill, California 94523
☎ *(510) 671-2900, FAX (510) 946-1500*
If you want to travel 5000 miles from the headlands of the Amazon to the tip of Patagonia, then mark five months off your calendar and call Forum Travel. Probably a little too much of South America for anyone, so you can bail on any one of the 11 sections, each lasting about 12 days. The cost is $1800 per stage, but do you really want to spend $20,000 bouncing around in a modified Mercedes troop truck?

Trans Continental Safaris

James Road
Clare, South Australia 5453
☎ *(61) 88 423 469, FAX (61) 88 422 586*
The continent of Australia may look small, but it is very big from the windshield of a Toyota Land Cruiser about to run out of gas. Although there are many operators who will run you around in a four-wheel-drive truck for the day, it is best to stick with a pro who puts together long-distance safaris. TCS will provide one- to 37-day tours of Australia's outback, complete with driver/cooks/guides who know how to fix the air conditioning and also tell you enough dirty jokes to make the long distances bearable. They supply all the camping equipment you will need; all *you* need is the stamina.

World Expeditions

Suite 747
920 Yonge Street

Toronto, Ontario Canada M4W 3C7
☎ *(800) 387-1483*
World Expeditions will show you the most remote sections of the Australian outback on a 15-day trip from Marlin Coast to Cape York. Starting and returning in Cairns, they will introduce you to the aborigines, the Australian rain forest and the rugged scenery of northern Australia.

Diving

Scuba (Self Contained Underwater Breathing Apparatus) was invented by Jacque-Yves Cousteau and a partner back in the 1940s. Since then, SCUBA tourism has taken Americans to some of the most beautiful places on the planet.

The highest percentage of underwater species is found around the island of Borneo, decreasing as you get farther away. The U.S. has only about 250 species, Hawaii about 450, Indonesia about 2500. There is much talk about where the best dive sites are. There is always a hard-core crowd that will invariably travel to the next best place. I was on Sipadan in Sabah, Malaysia, during the early years, and it was spectacular. At that time, they were busy creating a new dive site in Indonesian Borneo—Kalimantan. Now that Sipadan is known worldwide, there are many more dive sites waiting to be discovered in Indonesia. The best dive sites in the world for pure color and variety are in Indonesia, followed by Thailand, Malaysia and then the South Pacific and the Red Sea. The adventurous will choose the Sea of Cortez for its amazing proliferation of large fish; others prefer wreck diving in Truk or even the frigid waters of the Inside Passage in British Columbia. Having dived from the Seychelles to Hawaii, my personal preferences are the island of Sipadan and live-aboards in the remote Nusa Tenggara islands of Indonesia. The more adventurous claim that Papua New Guinea has much to be explored and that the Galapagos is the next big place. The top dive sites are Indonesia, Micronesia, Truk, Bajal, Australia, Hawaii and Papua New Guinea.

As you probably already know, you need to be certified to dive (although I was on a dive trip where Mexican dive masters certified the rookies with about 90 seconds of boat-side instruction). Most dive tour companies will link you up with the dive site of your choice. Don't hold high hopes for luxury or gourmet food.

Many people can't decide whether to bring all their shiny new gear or to rent. If you just spent $3000 on all the gear, then you are more than likely going for one reason, so bring the whole kit. Many airlines offer extended luggage or weight allowances if one of your bags is dive gear. If you are going to bring your gear, take a small tool kit, including spare O-rings, straps and batteries.

My experience is that, at a minimum, it is best to bring your mask along with octopus, regulator and gauges. The next level would be booties and BC. Pack your dive knife, tanks, flippers and wet suit for warm water dives. Photographers will want to bring their certification card, logbook, camera, film, flash, batteries and maintenance pack.

There is a caveat. I ran out of air at 90 feet below in the clear waters of the Cayman Islands. The reason? The vibration from the plane flight had loosened my regulator, and, I went through 3000 psi of air in about eight minutes. Speaking of close calls, there is also divers insurance that will make sure you get repatriated or flown to the nearest decompression center. Contact **Divers Alert Network**, ☎ *(800) 446-2671*, or **Divers Security Insurance**, ☎ *(800) 288-4810*. Remember to wait that extra day to fly home after diving. To start planning your next great dive trip, contact the following:

Avalon Aquatics
   615 Crescent Ave.
   Avalon, California 90704
   ☎ *(800)MR-SHARK*
   ☎ *(310) 510-1225*

All types of diving adventures are offered here, from introductory to instructor level. An all-day shark diving adventure costs $250 per person, which includes transportation, tanks and food.

HydroSphere

860 de Lima Paz, Suite D3
Pacific Palisades, CA 90272
☎ *(310) 230-3334*

This company offers intense shark diving experiences in the world's largest cage, plus the opportunity to assist university researchers with a shark tagging program. Day and night shark tagging and research expeditions are offered, with student prices from $79, adults $99 and special rates for groups. The expeditions to see kelp forests, sea lions and sharks are led by former Cousteau Society team member and documentary film producer, Yehuda Goldman. Programs are also offered for children, snorkelers, nondivers and even nonswimmers.

Innerspace Adventures

13393 Sorrento Drive
Key Largo, Florida 34644
☎ *(800) 833-SEAS, FAX (813) 596-3891*

A 20-plus year old dive travel agency that can get you deals as well as great dive sites. Micronesia is a specialty.

Island Dreams Travel

7887 Katy Freeway
Suite 105
Houston, Texas 77024
☎ *(800) 346-6116*

Specialists in the Western Caribbean.

San Diego Shark Diving

P.O. Box 881037
San Diego, CA 92168-1037
☎ *(800) 888-SD-SHARK*
☎ *(619) 299-8560*

If you've seen *Blue Water, White Death* or *Jaws*, it might interest you to know that you can dive with live sharks and experience the same feeling as a worm on the end of a hook. The place is called Sharksville, and it's about 20 miles off the coast of San Diego, California. After a rolling, choppy boat ride, you get to sit in a 16' x 8' shark cage about 10 feet below the surface while they throw chum in to attract sharks. The chances are good you will see blue sharks ranging in size from five to eight feet. You may also see mako sharks and albacore tuna. The water is cold, so bring a wet suit. Tough guys get to go outside the cage for more adventurous escorted shark dives. Those with a more scientific bent can take part in a blue shark tagging program. The San Diego dive master also has a chain mail arm that he lets the sharks chew on while you get some great photos.

Sea Safaris Travel, Inc.

3770 Highland Avenue
Suite 102
Manhattan Beach, California 90266
☎ *(800) 821-6670, in California (800) 262-6670*

An agency staffed by divers that can set you up in Asia, the Caribbean, the South Pacific and the Middle East.

See & Sea Travel Service, Inc.

50 Francisco Street
Suite 205
San Francisco, California 94133
☎ *(800) 348-9778, (415) 434-3400*

A good choice for more exotic and far-flung dive trips. See & Sea has an excellent selection of live-aboards.

Safaris

Arguably, safaris were the first adventure or ecotour. Back then, you would save wildlife by collecting samples for museums by shooting and mounting them. Now, all you hear is the clicking of cameras and whirring of videotapes. Most safaris in Africa today are nothing more than small tours conducted via zebra-striped buses carrying tourists in floppy bush hats brandishing new auto-everything cameras.

Masai Mara and Krueger Parks are glorified zoos without bars. The sight is still spectacular, and the photographs make everyone feel like they were the first one to set eyes on a lion kill or multihued African sunset. Despite the rampant commercialism, there is still a primitive joy in drinking a bloody Mary while watching the sun go down in Africa. I also enjoy the raw fear of camping without a tent in hunting areas of Tanzania and listening to the lions coughing and roaring at the intruders.

It is quite easy to fly directly to Nairobi or Dar es Salaam and book your own safari. You can also rent your own four-wheel-drive vehicle and stay at the various game parks or campsites. In fact, *Fielding's Guide to Kenya*, the most complete guide to homestays, game lodges and campsites, will show you how easy it is.

The best safaris in the world are private tented safaris to the lesser-visited areas of Africa's parks. In terms of wildlife, South Africa has an overabundance of it, along with clean, efficient facilities. Kenya has the creaky colonial ambience many people expect, and Tanzania is the stronger and more realistic of the two. My personal favorite is the rugged and remote Ruaha in Tanzania.

If you want to get your money's worth, the best way to get around is by air. That way, you can hit as many regions as you want and get a good grounding in geography as you bump and shudder through the hot African sky. Masai Mara has the most wildlife per square foot but has an equal number of tourists. Northern Kenya is plagued with bandits but has more dramatic scenery. Tanzania can be tedious (Selous) or dramatic (Ngorongoro Crater) but is what most people expect Kenya to look like. The Okavongo Delta and Namibia are becoming ideal second safari areas, and regions in Uganda, once the most beautiful country in Africa, are supposed to be coming back slowly. If you want to set up a safari in Africa, we recommend these groups:

Abercrombie & Kent

1520 Kensington Road,
Oak Brook, Illinois 60521
☎ *(800) 323-7308, (708) 954-2944*
The most famous African Safari and adventure tour operator does tours on the "cushy side" but the Kents run a first-class show. They also can put together custom expeditions, since they know most of the major ground operators on every continent.

American Museum of Natural History Discovery Tours

Central Park West at 79th Street
New York, New York 10024
☎ *(800) 462-8687, (212) 769-5700*
One of the best sources for high-end natural history tours. Although the tours are set up using a variety of ground operators, the museum provides stimulating guides and guest lecturers.

Borton Overseas

5516 Lyndale Avenue South
Minneapolis, Minnesota 55419
☎ *(800) 843-0602, (612) 824-4415*
A ground operator who specializes in Tanzania.

Ker, Downey, Selby

Box 41822
Nairobi, Kenya

☎ *(254) 2 556466*
The classic tented safari is the specialty of this group of independent outfitters and former big-game hunters.

Tamu Safaris

Post Office Box 247
West Chesterfield
N.H. 03466
☎ *(800) 766-9199)*

Wildland Adventures

3516 Northeast 155th
Seattle, Washington, 98155
☎ *(800) 345-4453*

Walking/Trekking

This is the most laid-back method of travel. You will meet people, get healthy and presumably do most of your travel in the world's most beautiful places. There is some danger of kidnapping and robbery as well as the usual penalties caused by tripping, falling and general wear and tear. Most trekkers hire porters and spend the evenings in small huts or villages. Trekking does not have to be set up from home, since most countries that are known for trekking supply the manpower for tour packagers overseas. Make sure, however, that you bring all the camping do-dads and clothing you will need.

The most popular trekking sites are Annapurna in Nepal, Zanskar in Ladakh, Bernese Oberland in the Alps, the Milford Track in New Zealand and Chiang Mai in Northern Thailand.

L.L. Bean Outdoor Discovery Schools

☎ *(800) 341-4341 x 6666*
Hands-on instruction and wilderness trips for beginners and experienced outdoor enthusiasts. Good preparation before you tackle more adventurous treks outside the United States.

The Ramblers Association

1 -5 Wandsworth Road
London, SW8 2XX, England
A group that can advise you on where to hike in Britain and set you up with the resources you might need for a European walking holiday. As you may have guessed from the name of this group, their members are not triathletes or mountain climbers. For actual tours, contact Rambler's Holidays below.

Mountain Travel-Sobek

6420 Fairmount Avenue
El Cerrito, California 94530
☎ *(800) 227-2384*
The IBM and GM of adventure tours can send you anywhere that's worth trekking to. Although their expertise is really rafting and climbing, their trekking expeditions make use of many of the same contacts and guides.

Rambler's Holidays

P.O. Box 43
Welwyn Garden City AL8 6PQ, England
☎ *[44] (707) 331133*
A British group that can set up walking tours in Europe and Britain.

The Sierra Club

730 Polk Street
San Francisco, California 94109
☎ *(415) 776-2211*
One of the better sources for trekking, hiking or climbing trips around the United States and the world.

White-Water Rafting

Rafting has captured the imagination of Americans. In fact, when you ask most people what adventure is, they will reply, "a rafting trip on the Colorado." The truth is that rafting is among the safer aquatic sports. Bobbing like a cork on thundering white water, large flexible rafts carry thousands of people a year down the nation's major rafting rivers. As a method of travel, rafts, canoes and kayaks are a pain. They must be trucked in to the river and trucked out, and you are always wet and soggy and cold. But rafts and canoes provide the best way to see a lot of the primitive world. I have traveled by canoe in Africa, North America and Asia and found that the purity and simplicity cannot be beaten for communing with nature. I also have despised the primitive method of transportation after carrying a water-logged six-man canoe across the nine-mile Grand Portage.

The top domestic rivers for white-water rafting are the Tatshenshini in Alaska, the Colorado in Arizona, the Chiclo/Chicoltin in British Columbia, Canada, and the Upper Youghiogheny in West Virginia. Internationally, there are many rivers yet to be run, among them the upper reaches of the Mahakam in Borneo, the Bio Bio in Chile, the Obihingoú in the CIS and the Zambesi in Zimbabwe.

To find out where you can eat H_2O, contact U.S.A. Whitewater at ☎ *(800) USA-RAFT* for a selection of outfitters in the U.S.

In this country, these two international outfitters stand head and shoulders above the rest:

Mountain Travel/Sobek Inc.

6420 Fairmont Avenue
El Cerrito, California 94530
☎ *(800) 227-2384*
The granddaddy of adventure tour companies, Sobek joined Mountain Travel to create the Thomas Cooks of ecotourism. I once stayed with a remote tribe in Borneo who used the word "sobek" to ask for money. They explained that an American rafting expedition had been through and when the natives said the word "sobek," the rafters gave them money. Such is ecotourism. MTS has specialized in Asia and Africa and are really the only sources for reliable rafting trips in Papua New Guinea, Ethiopia and Borneo.

Steve Curry Expeditions Inc.

Post Office Box 1574
Provo, Utah 84603
☎ *(801) 224-6797*
The master of the Yangtze in China, Curry also provides expertise in Latin America and the Soviet Union.

Adventure Travel Publications

Business Traveler International

51 East 42nd Street
New York, New York 10017
☎ *(212) 697-1700*
FAX (212) 697-1005
Geoffrey H. Perry has about 40,000 avid readers who need to know facts, not gushy descriptions of the world's regions. The magazine can be counted on to provide on-the-ground information, comparative charts and travel tips that are always useful. A year's subscription is $29.97. Single copies are $3.

EcoTraveler

9560 S.W. Nimbus Avenue
Beaverton, Oregon 97008
☎ *(800) 285-5951*
Definitely on the fluffy side, an adventure magazine in the genre of: "Oh Muffy, won't we look so butch in hiking boots!" This is the latest in the wave of new ecozines that

channels college guilt into politically correct travel experiences. This bimonthly lacks the veracity of *Escape* but does cover faraway regions. I can't help feeling like I'm being scolded as I am being lectured on proper etiquette for scuba divers ("Get involved in local environmental issues"). There are lots of "I was there and this is what I did" articles for the politically correct and ecologically aware. On the positive side, there are lots of local getaways, plenty of pictures and, of course, lots of ads. A subscription to *EcoTraveler* costs $11.97 for a year (six issues), or you can buy it off the rack for $3.95

The Educated Traveler

P.O. Box 220822
Chantilly Virginia 22022
☎ *(800) 648-5168*
A newsletter that covers museum-sponsored tours, learning vacations, cultural tourism and more for $65 a year. A little stuffy but a good source for unusual travel opportunities.

Escape Magazine

3205 Ocean Park
Santa Monica, California 90405
☎ *(800) 738-5571*
An outdoor /adventure/world music pub that features a good mix of Third World adventure stories with practical info. The editor/founder, Joe Robinson, has a good eye and ear for real adventure and you never know what will crop up in this quarterly magazine. *Escape* also covers world music and sociopolitical issues in between stories about blisters and leeches. Good stuff and available at major bookstores or by subscription.

Great Expeditions

5915 West Boulevard
Vancouver, British Columbia
☎ *(604) 257-2040*
A magazine that gets down and dirty with firsthand information on trips by its readers to exotic places. The magazine is tough to find but worth it for the up-close info it provides.

Maplink

25 E. Mason
Santa Barbara, California 93101
☎ *(805) 965-4402*
One of the best sources for maps from around the world. Call for a free catalog.

Outside Magazine

400 Market Street
Santa Fe, New Mexico 87501
☎ *(505) 989-7100, (800) 678-1131*
Created by Jann Wenner who founded *Rolling Stone*, *Outside* is now published in New Mexico by Mariah Media, Inc. The monthly magazine includes colorful features on destinations and activities for outdoor-loving travelers. Off-the-beaten-path places are spotlighted, along with profiles of adventurers. Departments include travel tips, environmental news, sports reports, and consumer reviews of travel gear, including apparel, camping gear, mountain bikes, etc. A yearly subscription is $14.97.

South American Explorers Club

Lima Clubhouse
Avenida Portugal 146
Brena District
Lima Peru
Mailing address:
Casilla 3714
Lima 100, Peru
U.S. Associate address:
126 Indian Creek Road
Ithaca, New York 14650
☎ *(607) 277-0488*

Books, maps, trip reports, rain-forest advice. The main clubhouse in Peru has an excellent library of maps and other helpful publications. Membership is open to all and includes their magazine: *The South American Explorer*.

Travel Guides

Travel guides are an odd source of travel information, more for what they don't tell you than what you can find inside. Most travel writers write champagne tour guides on beer budgets. Budget guides tend to stick to inner cities, known hiking trails or tourist ruts (even though they profess not to), simply because they avail themselves of the local tourism industry to get around. The other problem is that the data can be horribly outdated or wrong. Check the copyright in the front of the book, get to know the writer, and get at least a couple of opinions before you go.

Fielding Worldwide, Inc.

308 South Catalina Avenue
Redondo Beach, California 90277
☎ *(800) FW-2 GUIDE*
FAX (310) 376-8064
Internet: http://www.fieldingtravel.com

Hey, it's my company, so I get to plug it shamelessly. Fielding was started by New England blue blood Temple Fielding who got his start writing disinformation pamphlets for Tito while in the employ of the OSS in World War II. After that auspicious start, he also wrote one of the wittiest, right-on travel guides to Europe back in 1947. Carrying on that tradition, Fielding guides continue to focus on the unusual, the unknown and the unique.

FWI does its best to gather firsthand information from people on the ground. Our authors range from college professors who read Mayan hieroglyphics, to war correspondents, to Americans living in Vietnam—not just folks with a notebook and a penchant for freebies. We look beyond the standard tourism ruts to deliver fresh information. Of course, when we cover areas like the Caribbean, Hawaii and Europe, we also focus our laser-sharp eye on the standards and experience that the tourism industry provides. Our books are controversial, a little wacky (you bought this book, didn't you?) and never boring.

The Government Printing Office

Superintendent of Documents
U.S. Government Printing Office,
Washington, D.C. 20402
☎ *(202) 783-3238*

If you trust and believe our government, then you might want to try their version of travel guides. The information is surprisingly helpful. The following publication is available for $1.25:

Your Trip Abroad—offers tips on obtaining a passport, considerations in preparing for your trip and traveling, and other sources of information.

The following two publications are available for $1 each from the U.S. Government Printing Office:

Safe Trip Abroad—contains helpful precautions one can take to minimize the chance of becoming a victim of terrorism or crime, and other safety tips.

Tips for Americans Residing Abroad—offers information for U.S. citizens living abroad on dual citizenship, tax regulations, voting, and other overseas consular services.

Passports—Applying for Them the Easy Way gives detailed information on how and where to apply for your U.S. passport. It is available for 50 cents from the Consumer Information Center, *Pueblo, Colorado 81009*.

Background Notes are brief, factual pamphlets describing the countries of the world. They contain the most current information on each country's people, culture, geography, history, government, economy and political conditions. Single copies are available from the U.S. Government Printing Office for about $1 each. Yearly subscription for updated copies is available. Confirm price by calling ☎ *(202) 783-3238.*

Health Information for International Travel contains detailed information on international health requirements and is available from the U.S. Government Printing Office for $6.50.

Lonely Planet Publications

Embarcadero West,
112 Linden St.,
Oakland, California 94607
☎ *(415) 893-8555*
Web site: http://www.fieldingtravel.com
The '70s and '80s bible of adventure travelers and expats. Plenty of good practical info served up with a sense of juvenile naiveté. The books are worth it for the maps alone. Most of the 190-plus books are updated on a two- or three-year cycle, so check the copyright date.Tony and Maureen Wheeler built Lonely Planet from the kitchen table to a $12 million publishing business. Their recent shot at guides to civilized countries falls well short of the standard they set for Third World countries. Their books on Asia are excellent.

Moon Publications

722 Wall Street
Chico California 95938
☎ *(800) 345-5473, (916) 345-5473*
Web site: http://www.fieldingtravel.com
A company launched by their flagship book on Indonesia by founder Bill Dalton. Moon is quietly building a following and slowly building a library of good, comprehensive, intelligent books on the world. Well researched, well written and very practical. They cover domestic locations very well and are updated when needed.

Rough Guides

1 Mercer Street
London WC3H 9QJ
☎ *[44] (71) 379-3329*
Web site: http://www.fieldingtravel.com
A new entry over here but over in Europe, Rough Guides have out–lonely planeted Lonely Planet by emphasizing detail, attitude and opinions as well as facts. They tend to dwell on places you have no intention of going to, and their information is lacking on anything above backpacker budgets. Better written than most books.

Trade & Travel Publications

6 Riverside Court
Riverside Road
Lower Bristol Road
Bath BA2 3DZ
☎ *[44] (225) 469141, FAX [44] (225) 469461*
Among the most compact and well-researched travel guides to the world's remote regions. These tiny, expensive travel bibles contain phone numbers, maps, sidebars, intros and just about everything needed for reference. They are thin on accommodation reviews. They began at the turn of the century with their South America guide and have expanded into Asia, the Caribbean and Africa.

Other Publications

New Internationalist/Third World Guide
Post Office Box 1143

Lewiston, New York 14092
☎ *(905) 946-0407*
FAX (905) 946-0410

Founded in 1970, the *New Internationalist* "exists to report on the issues of world poverty and inequality: to focus attention on the unjust relationship between the powerful and powerless in both rich and poor nations...." Well, you get the point. This rather biased magazine does provide a good second look at the world's people and has some interesting things to add to any cocktail political discussion. A good source for folks looking for information to make their case against the world's military/industrial complex. Subscriptions are $35.98 per year, with corporations being dunned $60 (as you would expect from these folks).

Third World Guide

New Internationalist
55 Rectory Road
Oxford OX4 IBW
☎ *(0865) 728 181*
FAX (0865) 793 152

If the *New Internationalist* magazine is a little too strident in its bashing of the U.N., big business and First World countries, at least you should own its most illuminating product, a fascinating annual called *Third World Guide*. This unusual guide covers 173 countries, is put together by researchers, journalists and academics in Third World countries and provides information on arms, housing, aid, refugees, food and country profiles on newly formed nations. The 630-page '93/'94 issue covers 30 emerging nations and has 55 maps, 780 diagrams and 6800 references. The full-sized book will set you back a hefty $38.95, plus $3.95 shipping and handling. Now in its ninth edition. Stick this hefty guide next to your CIA handbooks and you have a fairly balanced portrait of the world.

World Press Review

200 Madison Avenue
New York, New York 10016
☎ *(212) 889-5155*

The *World Press Review* consists of material excerpted from the press outside the United States. *WPR* is a nonprofit organization/educational service and seeks to foster the international exchange of information. The magazine does a good job of providing updates on news from various countries but, more importantly, showing the variety of responses on global affairs, whether it is the U.S. invasion of Haiti or what the rest of the world thinks of Saddam Hussein. Their choice of news sources is quite good and varied. The leaning of the publication is noted before the clip (pro-government, centrist, liberal, conservative business, etc.). The *Review* also makes good use of political cartoons from around the world. Subscriptions are $24.97 for 12 issues.

The Economist

111 West 57th Street
New York, New York 10019
(212) 541-5730,
☎ *(800) 456-6086*
FAX (212) 541-9378

The granddaddy of world mags is devoid of the cheesy stereo ads of the *New York Times* or the "grow new hair" ads found in *Time* and *Newsweek*. Their readers just don't have time to read the ads. In fact, the *Economist* probably has the most time-starved readership of all the news magazines—a blue-chip collection of world leaders, policy makers, big business, etc. If they get something wrong, chances are the person that they are writing about will contact them to correct it. Their lofty and somewhat ludicrous goal is to "take part in a severe contest between intelligence which presses forward, and an unworthy, timid ignorance obstructing our progress." I suppose they mean that their subscription drives are hampered by stupid people who don't see the value of paying $125 a year (for

51 issues) to bone up on global and financial news. The magazine's easy-to-use format and impressive attention to facts before opinions make this a must-have for globally aware readers. Their special sections are packed full of first generation information, and they even throw in charts, graphs and other helpful graphics. If you can't get enough, the *Economist* also puts out quarterly indexes and some very impressive year-end wrap-ups in book form.

Geographical

Post Office Box 425
Woking GU21 1GP
☎ *0483 724122*
FAX 0483 776573
A surprisingly intelligent magazine that explores adventure, science, politics and geography. A monthly published for the Royal Geographic Society. Very little posturing, long on facts, with maps and research; the magazine provides coverage other magazines can't deliver. Definitely a recommended publication for adventurers. $57 for an annual subscription or $5.50 on the newsstands.

United Nations Publications

Sales Sections
2 United Nations Plaza
Room DC2-853, Department 403
New York, New York 10017
FAX (212) 963-3489
The United Nations provides an enormous amount of important information on the world and its people. The first step is to send away for their catalog of publications. Their rather dry but informative publications cover narcotics, disasters, agriculture, economics, hunger, poverty, war and just about anything else of interest. They range from thrilling books like *ESCAP Atlas of Stratigraphy IX: Triassic Biostratigraphy* and *Paleography of Asia—Mineral Resources Development Series and Stratigraphic Correlation Between Sedimentary Basins of the ESCAP Region* to *Urban Crime Global Trends and Policies.*

Travel Book Stores

Adventurous Traveler Bookstore

P.O. Box 577
Hinesburg, Vermont 05461
☎ *(800) 282-3963*
http://www.gorp.com/atbook.htm
More than 3000 books and maps for hiking, biking, kayaking, snorkeling, fly-fishing, trekking and general travel worldwide. Call for a free catalog or find it on the World Wide Web.

Stanfords

12 -14 Long Acre
London England WC2E 9LP
☎ *[44] (71) 836 1321*
FAX [44] (71) 836 0189

Also at

156 Regent Street
London, England W1R 5TA
Billed as the world's largest map and travel book shop, this is a great source for hard-to-find maps and books.

AAA

600 S.W. Market Street
Portland, OR 97201
☎ *(503) 222-6720*

Adventure 16 (chain)

4620 Alvarado Canyon Road
San Diego, CA 92120
☎ *(619) 283-2374*

California Map Center

 3211 Pico Boulevard
 Santa Monica, CA 90405
 ☎ *(310) 829-6277*

Rand McNally (chain)

 8255 Central Park Avenue
 Skokie, IL 60076
 ☎ *(708) 329-8100*

Travel Emporium

 20010 Ventura Boulevard
 Woodland Hills, CA 91364
 ☎ *(818) 313-9452*

Traveler's Choice Bookstore Inc.

 111 Green Street
 New York, NY 10012
 ☎ *(212) 941-1535*

Complete Traveller

 199 Madison Avenue
 New York, NY 10016
 ☎ *(212) 685-9007*

Travel Books & Language Center

 4931 Cordell Avenue
 Bethesda, MD 20814
 ☎ *(301) 951-8533*

Travelfest Superstores

 1214 W. 6th Street
 Austin, TX 78703
 ☎ *(512) 479-6131*

Voyager's Travel Store

 19009 Preston Road #300
 Dallas, TX 75252
 ☎ *(972) 732-9373*

Internet Travel Sites

If you spend much time with your computer on the Information Superhighway, otherwise known as Cyberspace, you may want to check out some of the travel information sources listed here. As the World Wide Web grows, more and more companies are creating their own Web Pages. You can access information ranging from State Department Consular Information Sheets and Travel Warnings to foreign exchange rates and which immunizations you need for traveling to New Guinea or any other destination in the world. To access these sources, you'll need a computer, modem and communications software and membership with an on-line service such as **America Online**, ☎ *(800) 827-6364*, **CompuServe**, ☎ *(800)848-8199*, or **Prodigy**, ☎ *(800)-PRODIGY*. Monthly fees are generally $9.95 per month, with five hours of access time; additional charges of $2.95 per hour thereafter. Various other value plans are available for heavy on-line users. It would take too many pages to list every travel address on the Internet, but you should find the following sources helpful.

Adventurous Traveler Bookstore

Internet: http://www.discribe.ca/other/bluep.htm
This on-line warehouse of adventure titles will have you considering travel to countries you never knew existed. The catalog of 2200 titles can be accessed through keywords and handy indexes. You can order choices, access phone numbers or download an order form on-line. A hot list includes new titles and additions added weekly.

Centers For Disease Control

Internet: http://www.cdc/gov/travel/html
Here, you'll find warnings for disease outbreaks, immunization requirements for countries around the world, cruise ship inspection ratings and the latest information on malaria pills. General travel hints for dealing with traveler's diarrhea, insect bites and other maladies likely to haunt travelers.

City.Net

Internet http://www.city.net
Tourism and cultural information on cities worldwide.

Fielding Worldwide

Internet: http://www.fieldingtravel.com
If you're enjoying this book, you'll want to check out Fielding's catalog of other travel guides. The Fielding Web Site includes excerpts from bestselling travel guides, such as *Fielding's Guide To Worldwide Cruises*, sample maps, photos and charts, plus news on upcoming travel guides and itineraries for adventure-oriented travelers.

Foreign Exchange Rates

Internet: http://www.dna.lth.se/cgi-bin/kurt/rates/
This site lists current exchange rates and helps you do the math to find out how much your dollar will buy in countries around the world.

Foreign Languages for Travelers

Internet: http://insti.physics.sunysb.edu/mmartin/languages.html
How do you say "Where is the bathroom?" in St. Petersburg? This site helps travelers learn rudimentary phrases in French, Italian, German, Spanish, Russian, Portuguese, Dutch and Polish. The site includes basic phrases and links to dictionaries and sound.

GNN Travel Center

Internet: http://nearnet.gnn.com/gnn/meta/travel/res/countries.html
Region, country, city and state guides with a wealth of information on places ranging from Tucson, Arizona, to Kuwait.

International Travel and Health

Internet: http://www.who.ch/Travelandhealth/home.html
The World Health Organizations's Web site issues bulletins on malaria, vaccination requirements and other health topics grouped by region.

Internet World Travel Review

Internet: http://www.stempler.com/punchin/internet.html
Summaries on many locations worldwide including insider tips on attractions and hotels, plus links to Convention and Visitor Bureau resources.

Magellan Basic Maps

CompuServe: gomagellan
This collection of on-line maps shows 500 regions. You must read the licensing agreement before accessing the maps, but if you accept the agreement, you can download the world.

National Geographic Traveler

America Online: keyword national geographic
The world-famous magazine and documentary folks now help transport on-line users to remote and exotic destinations. The text of *National Geographic* is combined with travel information, and the photos that have made the publication famous are featured here, too.

Perry-Castaneda Library Map Collection

Internet:http://www.lib.utexas.edu/Libs/PCL/Map-Collection/
This huge map collection includes satellite maps of the planet, islands, oceans, countries, national parks and a variety of other topics.

Round The World Travel Guide

Internet:http://www.digimark.net/rec-travel/rtw/html/faq.html
Along with general information on a plethora of places, this guide offers information on offbeat travel options, such as freighters that book passengers. Topics such as Transportation, People, Money Matters, Communications and Major Decisions help on-line travelers plan the perfect trip.

21st Century Adventures

Internet: http://www.10edesign.com/centadv/
Aimed at adventure travelers, this Web Site offers articles on white-water rafting and exploring Borneo and a wealth of advice from travel professionals. A forum answers on-line questions, such as when to go, what to pack, etc.

Time Zone Converter

Internet:http://hibp.ecse.rpi.edu/cgi-bin/tzconvert
Type in a date, time and two cities, and get back the time for each. This site can be very helpful for planning trips, booking flights and scheduling long-distance phone calls.

Traveler's Corner and Traveler's Edge

America Online: keyword travel, traveler's corner
Weissman Travel Reports hosts forums and provides short summaries of national and international destinations. Helpful information includes safety tips, restaurants, hotels and costs.

Travel Industry Magazine

Internet:http://www.newspage.com /NEWSPAGE/cgi-bin/
Aimed at travel agents and others in the travel industry, this site offers a wealth of tips for consumers as well. The site includes travel articles gathered from UPI, AP and Reuters news wires.

Travel Safety

Internet: http://www.solutions.net/rec-travel/general/safety/txt
This Web site offers tips on avoiding travel scams, how to recognize and avoid suspicious characters when you are traveling, specific dangers in certain regions, plus a variety of safety tips, from how to carry your backpack, to steps for avoiding stolen baggage, to dangerous drinks and much more.

U.S. State Department Travel Warnings and Information Sheets

Internet:http://www.stolaf edu/network/travel-advisories.html/
Anyone planning a trip outside the country should check out this site for the latest warnings and visa/customs regulations for each country in the world. Digesting the red tape in advance of your trip may save you some hassles and embarrassment later, or even save your life.

Ulysses

Internet:http://www.demon.co.uk/ulyssesbooks/travel.html
Hard-to-find and out-of-print travel and adventure books can be located here. The books are organized by geographic area, with brief summaries and the cost of each book.

Virtual Tourist

Internet: http://wings p.buffalo.edu/world/
This site connects to several national and international travel guides, including cultural information, weather, maps and cost estimates.

World Factbook

Internet: http://www.odci.gov/96fact/fb96toc/fb96toc/html
The CIA's country profiles for every nation in the world include geographic, political and social information, along with an abundance of statistics. Maps are provided with each profile.

World Sex Guide

Internet: http://www.paranoia.com/faq/prostitution/
A comprehensive guide to finding adult activities in major cities around the world.

Yahoo Travel Links

Internet: http://www.yahoo.com/Recreation/Travel/
You can book a plane or train ticket, check rental car rates or find a bed-and-breakfast in England at this site. If travel information exists, you're likely to find it here.

A word of caution: Unless a web site is developed by a known provider of content, be somewhat skeptical of the veracity or purpose of the content. Also, there is more change than Las Vegas odds in the web business, so don't be surprised if some of these folks vaporize.

Adventure Clubs

Okay, you feel a little strange at cocktail parties. Your friends jabber on about mutual funds, car leases and football games. You, on the other hand, want to discuss the pros and cons of female circumcision, the relative merits of Chinese vs. Bulgarian–made AK-47s, the quality of polo played at Chitral vs. Gilgit, or even the archaeological merits of Nemrut Dagi. Your friends think you are talking about a new rock group and then slowly fade to the opposite corner. Seems like you need to find the right social circle. Well, take heart. There are actually clubs for adventurers. Obviously, these groups have their share of toupee-wearing, bring-'em-back-alive bullshitters, but you can probably find someone who can engage you in a spirited discussion about which side of the rift valley their ancestors came from in Swahili.

Adventurers are lone wolves, social misfits or even outcasts. Misunderstood by their friends and inept in their mundane existence, they tend to travel alone, romanticize the esoteric and only later realize that they are trendsetters. Occasionally, by choice or by circumstance, we find ourselves in the company of other adventurers, huddled in bomb shelters, squeezed into native huts or killing time in Central American jails. For a brief shining moment, we have found an equal, only to be dumped back into the real world, where most people think we're crazy.

The reality is that danger creates a special fellowship. You'll find instant camaraderie whether you are sitting around a small fire drinking bad cognac and discussing politics as the sun rises in an Asian jungle, or shivering in a mountain hut in Pakistan while arguing about the firing rates of automatic weapons. These serendipitous friendships under adversity create bonds and memories. It is not surprising that these adventurers would seek to re-create the boisterous warm feelings that many of them had around foreign campfires. Back in the real world, we do long for those clear, crisp moments when minds met and the world made sense.

Keep in mind that I believe in the words of Marx (Groucho, that is): "I would never join a club that would have me as member." But if you like wildlife and animals of the social kind, you may want to check out an adventure club in your neighborhood. There tends to be a liberal sprinkling of windy Baron Munchausen's complete with pencil mustaches and Faustian guts, as well as honest-to-goodness adventurers. In any case, the clubs can be an excellent way to learn about the world of adventure and the quixotic people that make it tick.

Be forewarned that each club has a unique personality. Many of the clubs demand that you earn your spurs before joining, some have a prepubescent abhorrence of females, and others are more businesslike and adopt the patina of adventure only as a decorating trend. Obviously, geographic proximity will dictate your choice, so it is up to you to inspect and decide. My personal favorites? I prefer the less arthritic and gravitate toward the scientific. The Royal Geographical Society is probably the best blend of historical and dynamic. There is a constant list of presentations and events that lean toward the scientific. If you prefer hanging out with aging astronauts or port-soaked big-game hunters, the American clubs may appeal to you. If you would like to cultivate a wider social circle, the foreign clubs may be ideal. If you would like to trade witticisms à la Oscar Wilde, then maybe the Savage Club is for you. In any case, here are descriptions of clubs designed for fellowship among the adventurous.

The Adventurer's Clubs

These are clubs where kindred souls can gather to swap tall tales and compare adventures. The Adventurer's Club originated in New York in 1912 and was the brainchild of a group of 34 men, among whom were soldiers, sailors, hunters, trappers, explorers, travelers, journalists, authors and scientists. Their goal was to promote the exchange and dissemination of knowledge in the areas of exploration, geography and natural history, as well as provide a social center for adventurous types. Today, these antique clubs have a hard time attracting the new breed of ecosensitive, bungy-jumping rock and rollers. The average age is 50 plus, but some young people are still attracted by the club's aura of history and tradition.

The concept of manly men surrounded by dusty trophies in creaky surroundings has kept these clubs alive and active. Within their confines, you can make such butch toasts as "To every lost trail, lost cause and lost comrade" or "To Adventure, the shadow of every red-blooded man" without fear of ridicule. The original New York club spawned similar clubs in Chicago (1913), Los Angeles (1921), Copenhagen (1937) and Honolulu (1955). Although the Chicago club will boast they predate the New York club, they are essentially cut from the same cloth—superannuated boys clubs where members can proudly display their trophies and tell tales of adventures past.

Here, members can attend or give weekly presentations of their most recent exploits. Presentations cannot cover subjects that are controversial, religious or political in nature. (That puts DP fans out of the running.) If you have just come out of the jungle and are looking for a little female companionship, this is definitely the wrong place. The club is very politically incorrect in its very male membership but does hold Ladies Nights "occasionally."

To be eligible for active membership, you must prove you are a real adventurer, not just someone with tattoos and a devil-may-care smirk. You must show "competent proof" of having:

- had outstanding adventure in travels off the beaten trail, hunting, mountaineering, aviation, sailing, diving, sports or similar activities;
- held responsible positions in official expeditions and explorations, the results of which have been published;

- taken calculated risks above and beyond the call of duty in military or public service;
- achieved distinguished and outstanding success and recognition for your research and explorations in the fields of geography, geology, archaeology, anthropology, natural history and kindred arts and sciences.

The clubs generally offer active memberships, associate memberships and consular memberships, with fees based on how much money you are willing to contribute.

Membership to any level provides for visiting membership in the other Adventurer Clubs as well as the Savage Club in London and the Explorers Club of New York.

The Adventurer's Club of Chicago

300 West Grand Avenue, Suite 270
Chicago, Illinois 60610
☎ *(312) 822-0991*

The Chicago club was started by journalist (Major) W. Robert Foran. He and a group of adventurers, big-game hunters and military men used to meet informally until 1911, when during a boozy meeting they decided to form a club and even came up with the motto "a hearth and home for those who have left the beaten path and made for adventure" at the same meeting. It might have something to do with Foran having just returned from one of Teddy Roosevelt's big-game expeditions in Africa and feeling like he needed a permanent watering hole. In any case, the strangely nomadic club has occupied eight locations in its 83-year history. A real bitch, considering what a pain it is to move those shrunken heads, mounted trophies, stuffed bears, weapons, photos and other bric-a-brac that adorn the club.

Only 200 adventurous posteriors can be warmed by the clubhouse's fire at any one time. Both men and women (since 1989) are invited to an "exploratory visit." Membership is open to men and women. You simply write a letter to the president or drop off your application at the club.

The Chicago club prides itself on not having relaxed its membership standards and provides a rough but incomplete list of what they consider adventurous activities.

The list of adventurous pursuits that would qualify one for membership starts with "travel to remote areas not readily accessible by tour guides" and continues with hunting, fishing, photography (in remote areas) white-water rafting, ballooning, underwater activities, extended stays in remote areas and environmental testing, and winds up with archaeologists, treasure hunters and astronauts.

The board of directors will look for the element of risk to life and limb and prefers that your adventure be far from home and off the beaten path. They are open to new interpretations of adventure, so those four days you spent blindfolded, drunk, condomless and in heat in a Thai whorehouse may possibly qualify you for membership.

Once you have been initiated, you get to do silly, adventurous, manly things like "worship Wahoo," the household god, by donating to the baksheesh bowl (a charitable fund used for members in need), carry club flags to far-off places and then bring them back, and enjoy the hospitality of the Long Table, the lubricated fellowship at the "sign of the whale bar," and the general adventurous ambience of swapping yarns amongst the formaldehyde, rust and dust of an adventurer's club.

The Adventurer's Club of Los Angeles

2433 North Broadway
Los Angeles, CA 90086-2541

☎ *(213) 223-3948*

The Adventurer's Club of Los Angeles meets in downtown L.A. every Thursday evening. The spacious club boasts trophies that would dignify many museums. Members and guests gather at 6 p.m. in the club's dining room and engage in sprightly conversations over dinner. At 8 p.m. they convene in the central meeting hall where a featured speaker recalls his exploits in adventure, exploration, arts and science. Most of the presentations contain "off-the-record" and "behind-the-scenes" stories not covered in commercial presentations. Controversial and religious subjects are not presented in the weekly assemblies, and the "manly men" deign to hold Ladies Nights about six times a year. The hand of good fellowship is extended to visiting members of the Savage Club of London, the Explorer's Club of New York, the Adventurer's Club of Chicago, the Adventurer's Club of Copenhagen, the Adventurer's Club of Moscow and the Adventurer's Club of Honolulu.

Los Angeles Explorers Club

706 West Pico Boulevard
Los Angeles, California 90015

A somewhat aging male-only and nomadic club of 200 male members, who recently voted down accepting women members 95 to 5. Unlike the grand New York Adventurer's Club, the L.A. club has kept its trophies and bric-a-brac in storage for years. The membership is diverse, and the meetings have included entertaining presentations by interesting people, such as Will Rogers, who spoke on the eve of his departure on his round-the-world journey. He died two weeks later, when the plane he was riding in, piloted by Wiley Post, crashed in Alaska. Dues are $150 per year; members pay for their meals.

The Explorer's Club of New York

46 East 70th Street
New York, NY 10021
☎ *(212) 628-8383*

This club is 90 years old and a popular hangout for media types. The Explorer's Club was formed in 1904 by Henry Collins Walsh, when he invited a group of buds to create a club "to encourage explorers in their work by evincing interest and sympathy and especially by bringing them in the bonds of good fellowship."

The nonprofit club began in 1905, and the founding members consisted of an Indian fighter, museum curator, Arctic explorer, mountaineer, archaeologist, war correspondent and hunter.

What makes the Explorer's club a must is the fascinating decor created by 90 years of collecting trophies and junk from around the world. The six-story 1910 town house with its magnificent library is an "in"site for parties in New York.

For those who do not live in New York, there are 27 regional chapters, seven of them in other countries (Australia, Britain, India, Norway, Poland and Western Europe).

The club likes to lend out numbered flags, so that you can take them to some godforsaken place on some harebrained quest, and then throw a party when you return the dilapidated piece of cloth.

They sponsor some expeditions, award medals (the Explorer's Medal) and provide local support to scientific and educational programs, all based on merit. The club publishes a quarterly journal and a newsletter and offers a 25,000-item library, a 500-item map room and historical archives.

Membership includes 3000 men and women, with 500 of them outside the New York area.

As with most of these clubs, to join the Explorers Club or New York you have to have some type of experience in being "adventurous." Driving a cab in Harlem probably won't impress them, nor will big-game hunting trips, extensive travel without a scientific purpose or photography in remote parts of the world. But if you provide sponsoring letters, fill out the application form and fork over the hefty membership fee, your chances are good.

You can be a "fellow" if your exploits are published, or try for regular membership if you are modest about your exploits. In any case, it will depend on what the membership committee and the Board of Directors say.

Also available are student memberships (16–24 years of age, over 24 if you are pursuing a graduate degree), and corporate memberships.

Savage Club

> 1 Whitehall Place
> London, England SW1A 2HD
> ☎ (071) 930 8118

The Savage Club is one of the more unusual clubs for adventurers. It was founded in 1857 by a group of "merry fellows" at the Crown Tavern. Their quaint logo features a Plains Indian, but the club members do not know how the club and the members became known as "Savages." Some say it was a dead poet or a poverty-stricken journalist; others say it was a sick joke since the club consists mostly of men of the arts. The Savages are writers, doctors, lawyers, actors, musicians and artists. They welcome "solitary men or irrelevant characters, kind or quirky ones" and those who have "packed their accolades (but not their psyches) in their knapsacks and pursued in common cause the Savage fellowship."

The club has rules which must be obeyed. No guests may buy drinks, no one may enter the bar with an overcoat (the penalty is a round for all present), tipping is forbidden, and any member is encouraged to expostulate at the drop of a hat. The accent here is on being somewhat eccentric and entertaining.

The posh Savage Club is famous for holding on to two cases of bourbon requested by writer Samuel Clemens (Mark Twain). When asked if he wanted to take the liquor with him, Clemens requested that the club hold on to it until his return. When a prewar visitor informed them that Clemens had been dead for quite some time, they said they were bound by duty to honor his wishes and to hold on to it until his return. The clubhouse and Clemen's liquor were destroyed during a WWII air raid, ending what could have been a long running joke. Why is the Savage Club a great adventurer's club? Well, there is a bald-pated dullness when surrounded by people of the same persuasion. How many big-game-hunting stories or eating-grubs-with-the-pygmy stories can you endure? The mix of intellectuals at the Savage Club encourages lively discourse and a chance to find an appreciative audience.

Joining is not as difficult as it may seem. The club welcomes applications from "gentlemen over 18 connected professionally with literature, art, music, drama, science or law in their creative and interpretive aspects, and to such other gentlemen as are deemed to have contributed to one or more of these disciplines." Attainment in hobbies, pursuits and other interests go a long way to impress the qualifications subcommittee. Two sponsors (both must be "Savages") are required to nominate a candidate. They must write a lengthy letter explaining why the candidate will make a great Savage. A resume, or curriculum vitae, along with a month-long probationary period are required.

The Royal Geographical Society

> 1 Kensington Gore
> London SW7 2AR

☎ *(011 71) 581 2057*
FAX (011 71) 584-4447

Not technically a "club" but a vital social and scientific institution. The RGS was founded in 1830, with the goal of advancing geographical science and the "improvement and diffusion of geographical knowledge." The London-based society takes its mandate seriously, and although most Americans will remember the great expeditions of Sir Richard Burton and John Hanning Speke to discover the source of the Nile, few may know that they continue to send adventurous men to the far corners of the world.

Their focus today is a little more politically correct, centering on a range of environmental issues. The RGS welcomes any member regardless of nationality, etc. The only trick is you have to be nominated by other members and seconded by another if you wish to be a Fellow. The 12,000 or so members typically have academic qualifications or expedition experience or are widely traveled. It is somewhat difficult to be nominated as a Fellow (30 pounds per year—most are graduates and work in geographical professions) but there are also Associate Members (24 pounds), Educational Corporate Members (60 pounds) and Corporate Members (200 pounds).

Once you are a member, you can subscribe to the 164-year-old *Geographical Journal*, the largest circulation of any British academic journal. The rather staid and colorless journal is published three times a year and contains original research papers and important articles on geography. The monthly *Geographical Magazine* is more colorful and deals with more contemporary issues. There is also a newsletter that keeps members aware of upcoming events and activities in the RGS.

The RGS is headquartered in Lowther Lodge, a Victorian-era brick building across the street from Hyde Park and close to major museums. From the outside, statues of Shackleton and Livingstone peer around the corner from their niches in the walls. Inside, you find the exact kind of casual bric-a-brac you would expect to find in a house that has been storing other people's stuff for more than 150 years. Stuffed penguins are crammed in stairwells, portraits of the great explorers glare down on you, and there are more maps and books than you could possibly read in a lifetime. The library holds more than 150,000 books, periodicals and reference materials; the Map Room is stacked floor to ceiling with over 850,000 maps, globes and atlases. The Picture library has an excellent but somewhat confused selection of period photographs. The Archives holds the crown jewels of the RGS, the personal papers, diaries and observations of the world's great explorers. The RGS continues to sponsor expeditions and organize major field research programs.

There is also an excellent Expedition Advisory Center that is invaluable for anyone considering traveling the hard way or desiring to meet up with other like-minded people. The 15-year-old EAC is open to all and has assisted more than 500 expeditionary teams in providing training and advice to primarily university-level groups. Their impressive publications assist adventurers with tips on everything from the fund raising phase to gaining a publication contract for expeditions.

On the social side, activities surround the ongoing lecture program. RGS holds regular lectures on subjects as diverse as screening adventure films to nuts-and-bolts presentations on geomorphology. There is daily lunch, cocktails are served before and after lectures, and events can be held at the Society's headquarters.

The Expedition Advisory Centre

Royal Geographical Society
1 Kensington Gore
London SW7 2AR
☎ *(011 71) 581 2057*
FAX (011 71) 584-4447

Not a club or even a place where more than five people can sit down at one time. The EAC's home is in a crowded set of offices about the Royal Geographic Society's headquarters in London. They do a yeoman's job of singlehandedly running the only support group for expedition planning.

The Centre provides information, training and, most importantly encouragement for anyone planning an expedition overseas. Their cumulative knowledge and vast contacts can help you decide what type of flashlight works best underwater, the best place to buy snake venom antidote, or even if there are other equally eager folks who want to join on. Nobody at the center writes checks for great ideas or does any work for you, but they can point you in the right direction and show you how and why expeditions are funded.

There is an annual program of meetings that brings seasoned pros together with fresh-faced explorers. In November there is an expedition planning seminar that generates enough enthusiasm to send anyone to the North Pole. For Americans the major source of help is the list of publications that pack years of solid experience into a bookshelf of manuals.

The Centre keeps a list of people who are interested in joining expeditions (people with medical and multidisciplinary scientific skills are most in demand; photographers and folks who just are looking for something to keep them busy are the least in demand).

If you would like to get the latest prices and listings, just send a fax to the address above and request a list of publications (you can use your credit card and there is a discount of 10 percent if you order more than 3 to 9 copies of the same publication, 25 percent if you order more than 10 of the same one).

There are books on fund-raising for expeditions, joining an expedition, writing expedition reports, reference sources, expedition field techniques on collecting and studying everything from meteors to reptiles to people and handbooks on expeditions to polar, tropical, desert, underwater, underground and rain forest sites, and their expedition yearbooks detail the various expeditions the EAC has assisted or kept track of.

ADVENTURE CLUBS

Fielding's
The
World's
Most Dangerous
Places

What to Pack

Travel light, wash often, dress casually and buy what you need when you get there. I have traveled with nothing (after all my luggage was stolen) and lots (on assignment, complete with tripod, tape recorders, video cameras and camera), and nothing is the way to go. Most travelers travel with less and less as they gain experience. The only exception would be specialized expeditions, where you are expected to come back with footage or samples of your discoveries. Even if you consider porters for your gear, maintain your credo of traveling light.

Luggage

I prefer a frameless backpack and a fanny pack. Avoid outside pockets, or fill them with your dirty laundry. Locks and twist ties from garbage bags are good to slow down thieves.Put everything inside large heavy-duty Ziploc freezer bags, and then put those inside large garbage bags. Bring some spares of both types of bags. Some people like to use thick rubber "rafting" sacks, but in my experience they are useless, being neither waterproof nor durable. Inside my pack, I like to put a small Pelican case with the delicates and expensives. I also carry a second fanny pack for toiletries and personal stuff. I use clear Tupperware containers to store first aid, medicines, and other assorted small objects. Don't scrimp on your pack but remember it will come back foul smelling, ripped and covered in dirt.

Tent

North Face's Bullfrog is about as good and as light as it gets. Not cheap, but I have yet to find anything close in space and weight. Two people won't fit. You can substitute a groundsheet with rope for warmer climes or a jungle hammock if you are going to be in the swamps. After your first night on the ground in the jungle, you will realize why the apes sleep in the trees. It is wet, very wet down on the ground. L.L. Bean, *Freeport, ME 04033,* ☎ *(800) 221-4221,* makes a great jungle hammock (make sure that where you are going there are at least two Land Rovers from which to hang).

Sleeping Bag

Get a light cotton-lined sleeping bag that has anything but down stuffing. Down does not insulate in the wet. Get a sleeping bag, small enough so that it can be washed (it will get funky!).

Toiletry Kit

Combination comb/brush, toothbrush, toothpaste, floss, deodorant, toilet paper, tampons, condoms, small Swiss Army knife with scissors and nail file, shaver, shampoo, liquid soap.

Compass

Even if you don't know how to use a compass, you should have one. If you take along the manual you learn how to use compasses to tell time, measure maps, navigate by the stars, signal airplanes, shave with and, God forbid, even plot your course if you get lost. The best compasses are made by Silva, *P.O. Box 966, Binghampton, NY 13902,* ☎ *(607) 779-2200*, and are available at just about any sporting goods store.

Flashlight

There are only two kinds you should consider buying—a small Tekna waterproof flashlight (get a yellow one so that you can find it when you drop it); better yet, get two or three because they make great gifts for your guide. The other kind is a Petzl or REI waterproof head-mounted flashlight. You will use both. Try putting up a tent with a handheld flashlight. Maglites are great but are a bitch to hold on to in the mud. Get lots of AA Duracell batteries.

Mosquito Netting

REI sells a nifty mosquito tent. Mosquitoes like to start feeding as soon as you drift off to sleep, so this light tentlike mesh will keep your head and arms safe. It can also be used to catch fish, strain chunks out of water and strain gasoline. Bring bug repellent with the highest DEET content. Wash it though, because it may cause some nasty rashes if not washed off. In hotel rooms, mosquito coils can make life bearable. They do not scare off large rats.

Clothing

Cotton is about the only fabric worth wearing, and don't get carried away with too many changes. After one week, everything you own will be stinky, damp and wrinkled, so it's best to rotate three shirts, three T-shirts, two pants, one shorts, three socks, three underwear, a hat, poncho, one pair of sneakers, hiking boots and flip-flops. And that's it.

Pants: The plain khaki army fatigues made in Korea are your best bet. You will find them in any surplus or Army Navy store. Cabellas is also an excellent source. Banana Republic used to be the place for adventurers, but the only thing they make that is worthwhile now is their correspondent's vest, which has to be special-ordered.

Light cotton T-shirts: Preferably with the name of where you are from or a *DP* shirt (use as gifts later).

Wool socks: Take three pairs—one to wear, one to wash and another to wear because you forgot to wash the first pair. Do not get the high-tech synthetic socks, just the funky rag type.

Underwear: Loose cotton boxers; get groovy-looking ones so that they can double as swim trunks.

Shirt: long-sleeved cotton, not too butch so you can wear it to dinner.

Poncho: cheap plastic to protect pack and camera gear and to sleep on.

Hat: wide-brimmed canvas hat. Tilleys are the best, but who wants to look like a geriatric on safari? Another choice is to pick up a cheap straw hat when you get there. Natty and disposable.

Hiking boots: Lightweight mesh and canvas or leather, no foam padding if possible.

Sneakers: I use Chuck Taylor's Converse in beige. Get 'em one size larger 'cause your feet will swell up. The world's greatest (and cheapest) jungle boots.

Cooking

I bring a standard stainless-steel cooking set that doubles as an eating set: a knife, fork and spoon with a hole in the handle so that they can be carried on a belt ring. (That way, I am always ready to eat.) Other people just bring the old military mess tin and one spoon. I notice that the more I travel and the friendlier I get, the less I use my own mess kit and end up eating at other people's homes.

If you are on an expedition, you need a cooking stove that burns not just stove fuel but diesel and every grade of automotive gasoline. (You haven't lived until you have tasted a dinner cooked over diesel fuel.) Bring a multifuel stove and a small fuel bottle. They work best with white gas, since car fuels clog up the stove and require frequent cleaning (so bring the kit and a spare O-ring). When it comes to freeze-dried food, don't be swayed by those high-end organic meals. You won't hear many complaints when you serve up those cheese-and-potato meals they sell at regular supermarkets (at about a tenth of the price). Remember to bring fruits and treats. I can live off peanut butter, beef jerky and warm beer, but I can't stand some of the healthy meals. (By the way, some African termites and caterpillars have between 600 to 700 calories per 100 grams. Insect fatty acids are low in cholesterol. The food value of ants, grubs and caterpillars is about the same as liver or sausage.) Power Bars can be a life saver but taste like hell.

First Aid Kit

A prescription from your doctor or a letter describing the drugs you are carrying can help. Pack wads of antidiarrheals, electrolyte powder, antibiotics, insect-sting kit, antacids, antihistamines (for itching and colds), antibiotic ointment, iodine, water purifier, foot powder, antifungal ointment and a syringe or two.

Camera

If you are a total idiot, bring an auto-everything camera and find out when you return how it turns on and what batteries you should have packed. If you are an idiot-in-training, bring a brand-new outfit with too many lenses and never use it. Pros bring two or more bodies, a 300mm 2.8, a zoom to cover the middle and then a 20mm. The new autofocus lenses suck in moisture and dust. Try to stick to the old manual metal mount lenses. I shoot with a Leica range finder and R system. Nikon, Canon and Zeiss systems are just as good.

Video

I love the now discontinued Sony TR-200, Hi-8 system and consider it a must-have on any trip. It's light, tiny (even with all the accessories) and easy to shoot. Anyone will do.

Binoculars

Don't bring binoculars. You can always bum somebody else's, unless you are going to Africa or want to avoid gunships—then they are a must. Leica and Zeiss roof prisms are the only ones to consider.

Survival Kit

Down in the bottom of your pack is the best spot for your survival kit. It's like an African fetish, and we hope that just having these items around means we will never have to use them. Bring a first-aid kit, two space blankets, Bic lighters, Swiss Army knife (get the one with the saw), a whistle, Power Bars (get one of each flavor), plenty of rope, fishing line with hooks (not too helpful in the desert), candle butts, Stop Trot or any other electrolyte replacement product and headache pills. Also bring a sewing kit, and buy a surgical needle shaped like a fishhook. You will need this to sew up your skin if you suffer a severe gash. I recommend a tiny first-aid manual to refer to if things go wrong. Baby wipes are handy for many uses. Hydrogen Peroxide is a nasty but useful disinfectant.

Water Bottle

Bring a metal water bottle that can double as a spare fuel bottle (use a large silver one for your water and a small red one for fuel). Condoms can hold water in a pinch.

Essentials

Your passport, airline tickets, money, credit cards, traveler's checks, drivers license, malaria pills, sunscreen, lip salve, spare contacts, glasses, sunglasses.

Letters of Recommendation

If you get in a jam or need special dispensations, it doesn't hurt to have plenty of glowing letters about you on fancy stationery. Lots of official stamps help too. Money is better.

Gifts

Most of the Third World views you as a rich capitalist pig. Because you think you are a *poor* capitalist pig doesn't let you off the hook when it comes to giving gifts. Keep it simple and memorable and have plenty to go around. Mirrors, beads and shiny paper were big in Columbus' time, but you are expected to do better than that today. Here are a few suggestions to make you the hit of the village:

Pens

Call an advertising specialty company to get cheap pens printed with your name and message on them. They will still be as cheap as drugstore Bics and a lot cooler as gifts.

Stickers

Buy a bag of them from party stores; if you can't resist a little self-promotion, have your own stickers printed up on foil and give 'em out to the eager hordes.

Cigarettes

I know it is not cool to smoke, but male bonding through passing around the smokes is still very big in the rest of the world. In the Muslim world where men don't drink, they smoke enough to make up for it. Even if you don't smoke, carry a couple of packs of cigarettes as gifts and icebreakers. I know for a fact that peoples' intentions to shoot me have been altered by the speed with which I have offered up the smokes.

Balloons

Kids love the farting sound they make, and they will play with the balloons until they mysteriously pop—at which point, they will head straight back to you asking you to repair it. So carry lots.

Holograms

I carry stacks of cheap hologram stickers. They will amaze, confuse and delight your hosts.

Weird Stuff No Adventurer Should Be Without

Everyone tells you to pack light (including me), so here are all the little items that can make your day or night in the bush:

Travel Clock Calculator

I can never find the kind I like, so I buy them in the duty-free shops. The Sharp EL-470 acts as an international timepiece, alarm clock, calculator, currency converter and business card holder. Some of the new personal assistants put this tiny thing to shame, but think about packing one along.

Adventurer Watch

A number of companies make waterproof watches with all sorts of gee whiz features including alarms, compasses and dual dials for different time zones. Divers will want a watch made for specific underwater depths.

Utility Vest

Not the kind that holds grenades or ammunition clips, but the fishing, cruising or photo vests they sell in various adventure stores. They make great organizers hung over the back of your seat or hanging in the tent. Don't wear the damn thing; you might be mistaken for a tourist.

Books

Buy them by thickness. My faves are *Information Please Almanac*, the *Book of Lists*, Penguin compendiums of classic stories and fat chunky adventure novels like *Three Musketeers* or *Les Miserables*. The Bible or the Koran will do in a pinch, and I have been known to write a book out of boredom. Trade 'em or give them away as gifts along the way. We hope the first thing you pack is a Fielding guidebook. Also think about phrase books, survival manuals, and even poetry if you know all is lost. Address books are useful too.

Maps

Good maps are very difficult to get in Third World countries. Especially in war zones. Spraying them with a spray fixative available at any art store will help to waterproof them.

Business or Calling Cards

If you are the sociable type, have a bunch of cheap cards with plasticized ink made up (be sure moisture doesn't make the ink run). Look in the phone book for a translator if you would like them in two languages. Leave enough room for your new friends to write their name and address on them. Make sure you also bring plenty of extra passport photos.

Shortwave Radio

Now that Sony makes those teensy-weensy shortwave receivers, you need never spend a 10-hour bus ride without entertainment.

A Notebook and Pens

For the nontechnical, a notebook is an indispensable part of the travel experience. You will have plenty of time to wax poetic and capture your thoughts.

Caribiners

Use them to snap your pack to a bus rail or bike frame, hold items on your belt, hang things from trees, rescue people and use as a belt when you lose weight.

Yellow and Black Danger Zone Tape

I use the heavy striped tape to mark my luggage, tape rips, pack boxes and even fix my runners.

Syringes

Just visit a Third World hospital.

Razor Blades

Boils, slivers, infected cuts—all may require a little field surgery.

Hydrogen Peroxide

Cleans out cuts, hurts like hell, stops major infections.

Ziploc Freezer Bags

Organizes, holds anything, waterproofs everything from passports to cameras. Use it for everything but food. The plastic transmits an icky plastic taste to food when kept in hot climates.

Trash Bags

Heavy-duty garbage bags make great waterproofers. They also double as ponchos, groundcovers, umbrellas, water catchers, spare windows, sails and even garbage bags.

Tupperware

It organizes and waterproofs, and you can eat out of it and give it away as gifts. Get the clear stuff and size it to the pockets or corners in your luggage.

Bubblegum

Get the kind that Amerol makes in the tape form. It's sold in a plastic snuff tin. Get the dayglo pink stuff; it drives the natives crazy to watch you blow those bubbles.

Empty Film Cannisters

The clear kind that Fuji film comes in. Take the top off, squeeze them and they act like suction cups. Squeeze them with the tops and they are like tiny popguns. You can amuse the little ones for hours.

Polaroid Camera

I could create peace in the world and brotherly love if I just had enough Polaroid film to take pictures of every headhunter, mercenary, tribal warrior, soldier and politician. They love it, and smiles break out all around. Think about it: How many times does somebody take your picture where you work and actually give you a copy?

If any of our rabid readers have more gizmos or tips send them in or fax them (310) 376-8064 or email fielding@fieldingtravel.com.

Save Humanity

I always get a little nervous when I see the amount of money and time that goes into animal, ecological, art and entertainment special-interest groups. The images of small children dying of starvation and disease seem to have less impact than the image of a baby seal having its brains bashed in. We eat animals and we wear their skins on a daily basis, but if you shot a calf on TV and ate it I am sure it would spawn hundreds of letters about cruelty, etc. There is a hidden Darwinian ethos among many Westerners who assume that AIDS in San Francisco, starvation in Africa, the plague in India and earthquakes in Indonesia are just God's way of cleaning up the mess. There are others who realize more correctly that civilization is a machine that does not offer an instruction manual. Humans are constantly learning cause and effect the hard way. Cut down trees to grow crops, and the dirt washes away. Start a war over oil, and an entire nation is plunged into the Middle Ages. Pocket aid money to buy seed from Western governments and use it to go shopping in Paris, and entire populations starve. We don't see the cause a lot of times, but we do see the effect.

Americans are getting thicker hides than the endangered rhino. Reality shows spawn like flies from maggots, and people watch the pain and suffering of total strangers interrupted every eight minutes by commercials that sell toothpaste and new cars. The 4 o'clock, 6 o'clock, 7 o'clock, 8 o'clock, 9 o'clock and 10 o'clock news cut together the world's woes and wars into 15 minutes, complete with snazzy graphics, logos and maps. Designed to stop channel surfers and fire freaks, television zooms in with nice clean images of blood, explosions, screaming and "you are there" action. The trouble is, you aren't there, and even if you are, television makes it seem more distant, less painful and, with the flick of a remote control, less fixed.

People helping people can make a difference. It might be teaching kids a song or working for 10 years for their indigenous rights. Every time you do something for someone instead of just watching, a life is changed. Dangerous places need people who can help push back the danger. You don't need to be a bomb disposal expert or a facial reconstuction expert to make a difference; you can also pick up a shovel or mend a net.

Those seeking a productive outlet for their urges to make the world a better place should look into the variety of groups that strive for global peace. Many of the groups are bad hangovers from the Cold War era. Some engage in endless discussion to provide solutions, while other groups get their hands dirty and clean up the mess. We would advise you to investigate the results of a group's efforts rather than its intentions. Don't waste your time polluting the world with more hot air.

The more people who look for solutions and actively carry out the remedies, the better off the world will be. There are groups that can provide an outlet for your need to make the world a better place. Some require major commitments of time; others can take your money and put it toward projects that do good. There is no way we could list every charitable organization that seeks to elevate the position of people in the world, but here is a start:

Life Enhancers

American Field Service Intercultural Programs

220 East 42nd Street, Third Floor
New York, New York 10017
☎ *(212) 949-4242*
☎ *(800) 876-2377*
FAX (212) 949-9379

Since 1947 AFS has been a global leader in promoting intercultural understanding through high school student exchanges. AFS offers U.S. students more than 100 programs in 46 countries around the world. Students live and study abroad for a year or a semester of high school. Or they can take time out between high school and college to do valuable community service work in another country. AFS also offers opportunities for families and high schools in the United States to host selected students from 50 countries who come to live and study in America for a semester or a year.

The Carter Center

One Copenhill
Atlanta, Georgia 30307
☎ *(404) 331-3900*
FAX (404) 331-0283

Jimmy Carter has been busy since he left office. His peace negotiations in North Korea, Haiti and Bosnia have been effective in achieving short-term results as well as angering many hard-liners by his friendly approach to our enemies. Carter shows that a mild-mannered, ever smiling good ol' boy from the South can play the perfect good cop to the

U.S. military's bad cop. Jimmy Carter seems to be working overtime for the Nobel peace prize. Not because he needs more stuff to hang on his wall, but because he really believes that all people have good in them and he has a responsibility to make the world a better place.

Jimmy and Rosalynn's "keep busy and do good" organization is the Carter Center. Eternally miffed by Reagan's skunk job on the Iran hostages, Jimmy is in the good guy business in a big way. He works out of a 100,000-square-foot complex, complete with chapel, library, conference facilities and museum. Seeded by $28 million in donations, the center works to fight disease, hunger, poverty, conflict and oppression in 30 countries. The center is linked to Emory University and operated by the Federal government. Jimmy Carter has been busy acting as a force for good and justice everywhere, from doing Bill's dirty work in Haiti and North Korea to monitoring elections in Africa. It could be argued that Carter has done better out of office than in. Some programs could be considered downright useless (preparing for democratic elections in Liberia and teaching CIS TV journalists how to cover elections), to down-home practical (like eradicating the Guinea worm and immunizing kids). The center is always happy to receive donations and resumes of motivated individuals who want to volunteer their time. With Jimmy's upstaging of fellow Southerner Clinton, you might just be making it to the Soviet Union, northern Ireland and elsewhere.

Connect US-USSR

☎ (612) 333-1962

A nonprofit Minneapolis organization that arranges sister-city projects between the Twin Cities and Novosibirsk, a Soviet city of 1.5 million people. They also develop projects for other Americans and Soviets seeking exchanges and relationships.

Cultural Survival Inc.

215 First Street
Cambridge, Massachusetts 02142
☎ *(617) 495-2562*
FAX (617) 621-3814

There is much talk that there is more work being done to save the rain forest than the people who live in it. Nomadic forest dwellers have no money, own no land and in many cases do not integrate into societies who are pushing them out of their homeland. Having seen the havoc wreaked on our own native Indians and Inuit, it is difficult to come up with viable alternatives to their eventual extinction.

This is an organization of anthropologists and researchers whose goal is to help indigenous peoples (like tropical forest dwellers) develop at their own pace and with their own cultures intact. Cultural Survival's weapon is the almighty dollar, and they put it in the hands of the groups they help. Working with indigenous peoples and ethnic minorities, they import sustainably harvested, nontimber forest products. What are those, you ask? Well, handicrafts, cashew and Brazil nuts, babassu oil, rubber, bananas, even beeswax. The end result is that indigenous peoples gain lands, develop cash crops and don't have to live in shantytowns or timber camps to support themselves.

Founded in 1972, the group has a variety of methods of achieving its goals: education programs, importing and selling products, providing expertise to larger aid groups and providing technical assistance to local groups seeking economic viability.

The organization has projects in Brazil, Guinea-Bissau, Guatemala, Ecuador, the Philippines and Zambia. Membership ($45) gets you a subscription to the *CSE Matters* and the quarterly journal *Cultural Survival Manual*. Ask for a free catalog of products. By purchasing the products for sale, you directly support the peoples who gather and manufacture them, something very rare in this world of markups and middlemen.

If you would like to work as an intern, they are looking for people to help crank out the newsletter, raise funds, handle the office work and expand the network of indigenous groups and supporters. To receive an application, contact Pia Maybury-Lewis, Director of Interns, Cultural Survival, *46 Brattle Street, Cambridge, Massachusetts 02138,* ☎ *(617) 441-5400,* or fax your resume and a letter that explains your personal interests to *(617) 441-5417.*

The Eisenhower Exchange Fellowships Inc.

256 South 16th Street
Philadelphia, Pennsylvania 19102
☎ *(215) 546-1738*
FAX (215) 546-4567

You don't have to be a pimply-faced student to do good in the world. Captains of industry, artists, farmers and educators can do their bit too. Based on the premise that the best leadership is by example, the Eisenhower Exchange Fellowship (EEF) is looking for prime examples of successful people from education, business and government. The organization allows you to submit your own ideas on what needs to be done and how you intend to do it. In other cases host countries ask for specific expertise and they try to fill the need. Either way, you will find the opportunity offered by the EEF rewarding and stimulating. You can reach out and touch someone, and EEF will pick up the bill.

If you have a few years, a little knowledge and a yen for travel, but don't have too much money, you might want to apply for an Eisenhower Exchange Fellowship. They offer two shades of the same color, the USA-EEF program and the USA Emerging Democracies Program. The former is a one-month gig in October that will take you and your spouse to a selected foreign country (this year's choices are Argentina, Taiwan and Turkey), where you'll speak on topics like journalism, international relations and human rights. The EEF will take care of all the arrangements (and the basic bills) on this short but intense trip.

The Emerging Democracies will require three months of your life and will usually plunk winning candidates in places like the Czech Republic or Romania, talking on topics like information technology, arts management and helping extend the growing season in Romania. Candidates should be "mid-career professionals who have demonstrated outstanding achievements in their professions." You will compete with other overachievers, but once selected, expect the foundation to pick up airfare, domestic travel, housing and meals for you and a spouse (yours, of course). Leave the kids at home. You will conduct workshops, attend numerous meetings, get one on one and, it is hoped, inspire and enlighten your hosts. You must be an American citizen and have some experience in leadership and participation in organizations outside of your regular place of work. The bowling league won't cut it.

The Eisenhower Exchange Fellowship was founded in 1953 to honor and emulate then President Eisenhower. Their goal is to promote the exchange of ideas, information and perspectives throughout the world.

National Charities Information Bureau (NCIB)

☎ *(212) 929-6300*

NCIB regularly publishes listings and reports on charities, monitoring which groups meet their standards. Ask for a copy of their *Wise Giving Guide.* Individual contributions of $25 or more and corporations and foundations contributing $100 or more will be sent the *Wise Giving Guide* for one year. NCIB also publishes detailed evaluations about organizations. As many as three reports at a time are available without charge.

Overseas Development Network

333 Valencia Street, Suite 330
San Francisco, California 94103
☎ *(415) 431-4204*

FAX (415) 431-5953

The ODN is primarily for students who want to work overseas in an intern (read no pay) position.This is also called "alternative tourism" in the San Francisco area. The benefit is that you get to get in there and do something about hunger, poverty and social injustice. The 12-year-old organization has placed over 200 interns overseas and in the Appalachian area of the States (yes, Third World standards do still exist in America). If you want to do your good deeds even closer to home, ODN membership($15 Student, $25 for a regular member) will introduce you to other like-minded students. There are also positions with ODN requiring about 12–20 hours a week. You can gain experience organizing, promoting, writing and marketing and get a good "foot in the door" position if you want to get serious in global affairs. All positions are unpaid and require a minimum commitment of three months and eight hours a week. You can take part in a local ODN chapter, work to build sustainable locally initiated development programs within your local community or just contribute to the ODN's ongoing programs.

The most tangible fund-raising program is the annual Bike-Aid program. The "spin" has been toward AIDS awareness over the last two years. The cross-country event is in its eighth year and has raised over $1 million for international grassroots development programs. The idea is for small (25–30) groups of cyclists to cover any one of five routes (Seattle, Portland, San Francisco, Montreal and Austin), converging on Washington, D.C., in late August. There is even an all-women route that starts in Portland. You find people to sponsor you at about a buck a mile. Along the way, participants meet local leaders and help in community projects about once a week. All ages are welcome. If you are not a bike rider, you can help out by hosting riders in your home, sponsoring riders, even acting as a local publicist.

An information packet on the Bike-Aid program will cost you five bucks. They also offer publications that provide insight into opportunities for alternative travel:

Pros and Cons of the Peace Corps ($7)

A compilation of articles written by former Peace Corps members. It also includes a list of publications that can lead you to employment and intern positions around the world.

The Peace Corps and More ($10, students $7)

120 Ways to Work, Study and Travel in the Third World

Last updated in 1993, this book will give you the names, addresses and requirements of over 100 organizations that can get you overseas and working

A Handbook for Creating your Own Internship in International Development ($7.95)

This is a how-to book on financing your internship and finding placement with an international development firm, written by interns who have been there and done that.

Peace Corps

1990 Street, N.W.
Room 9320
Washington, D.C. 20526
☎ *(800) 424-8580*

When most people in the '60s and '70s thought about how they could change the world, the Peace Corps came to mind. It may surprise you to know that the Vietnam-era hearts and minds division of the U.S. Government is still hard at work making the world a better place without killing or maiming.

The Peace Corps is pure American do-goodism from its Woodstock-style logo (the Peace Corps was formed in 1961) to its Puritan slogan "The Toughest Job You'll Ever Love" and goes straight to the soul of every Midwestern farm boy. The Corps appeals to the American love of doing good things in bad places. In the 30 years of the Peace Corps' existence, 140,000 Americans have heeded the call and the world has truly benefited by an outpouring of American know-how. Last year there were about 6500 volunteers spread out over 90 countries. What do you get? Well, the answer is better stated as what do you give. Successful applicants go through two to three months of language, technical and cultural training for each "tour." You will get a small allowance for housing, food and clothing, airfare to and from your posting and 24 days of vacation a year.

While in-country, you will work with a local counterpart and may be completely on your own in a small rural village or major city. The payoff is that you can actually make things happen, understand a different culture and say that you did something about the world. Does the reality meet the fantasy? Apparently it does. The average length of time spent in the Peace Corps is six years with nine months of training. That works out to three two-year tours with the minimum training. All ex-Peace Corps volunteers we talked to said it was among the most rewarding years of their lives.

Getting in is not that easy, but once in, you join a club that can benefit you greatly in your career. Being an ex-Peace Corps member says that you are about giving and hard work and a little more worldly than most.

You must be a U.S. citizen and at least 18 years old and healthy. Most successful applicants have a bachelor's degree. You must also have a minimum 2.5 grade point average for educational assignments or experience in the field you want to enter. Although there is no limit on age, the Peace Corps is typically a young person's game and considered to be an excellent way to get a leg up in government and private sector employment. The government will give you $5400 when you get out, find you a job in the government on a noncompetitive basis and even help you apply for the over 50 special scholarships available for ex-Peace Corps members.

The emphasis is on training and education in the agricultural, construction and educational areas. There are not too many fine arts requirements, although they do have a category for art teacher. Couples with dependents are a no no, and couples are strongly discouraged. It helps if you know a foreign language, have overseas experience and have a teaching/tutoring background.

The Peace Corps does not mess around in countries that are overtly hostile or dangerous to Americans, like Peru, Colombia, Angola, Algeria and Iran. Also, you will not be posted to Monaco or Paris. You can be posted to Fiji, Thailand, Central Africa or most countries in the CIS. If you are curious, the Peace Corps recruiters hold two-hour evening seminars at their regional offices. Don't be put off by the slightly '80s banner of "Globalize Your Resume." You can meet with returning volunteers and ask all the questions you want.

Philanthropic Advisory Service (PAS)
of the Council of Better Business Bureau (CBBB)

☎ *(703) 276-0100*

The Council and its Philanthropic Advisory Service (PAS) promote ethical standards of business practices and protect consumers through voluntary self-regulation and monitoring activities. They publish a bimonthly list of philanthropic organizations that meet the Council of Better Business Bureau's (CBBB) Standards for Charitable Solicitations. The standards include Public Accountability, Use of Funds, Solicitations and Informational Materials, Fund-Raising Practices and Governance. Ask for a copy of *Give But Give Wisely* ($1.00). Many of the groups have e-mail addresses, databases and on-line services.

Save the Children

50 Wilton Road
Westport, Connecticut 06880
☎ *(203) 221-4245*
☎ *(800) 243-5075*
FAX (203) 222-9176

SCF is a nonprofit, nonsectarian organization, founded in 1932, to make positive and lasting differences in the lives of disadvantaged children both in the United States and abroad. SCF has more than 60 years of experience in 59 countries and throughout the United States providing emergency relief and community development assistance. The group targets four key sectors: (1) health/population/nutrition, (2) education, (3) economic opportunities and (4) commodity-assisted development/emergency response.

UNICEF

338 East 38th Street
New York, New York 10016
☎ *(212) 686-5522*
(800) FOR-KIDS
UNICEF is the leading advocate for children throughout the world, providing vaccines, clean water, medicine, nutrition, emergency relief and basic education for children in more than 140 nations. Children in Rwanda and the former Yugoslavia have been recent recipients of emergency relief. UNICEF is an integral but semiautonomous agency of the United Nations with its own executive board. Financial support for its work comes entirely from voluntary contributions. UNICEF's budget is not part of the dues paid by the member governments of the United Nations. An extensive network of volunteers work for UNICEF throughout the world, and local volunteers are always needed.

UNHCR

P.O. Box 2500
1211 Geneva 2, Depot, Switzerland
☎ *41-22-739-8502*
The United Nations High Commission for Refugees works to prevent refugees from being forcibly returned to countries where they could face death or imprisonment. It also assists with food, shelter and medical care. *Refugees Magazine* focuses on a different refugee movement each month. The U.N. defines a refugee as anyone who flees his home country in fear of loss of life or liberty.

U.S. Committee For Refugees

1717 Massachusetts Avenue, N.W., Suite 701
Washington, D.C. 20036
USCR In Review compiles statistics and reports from more than 100 field workers. The U.S. Committee documents and defends the rights of refugees worldwide, regardless of their nationality, race or religion.

World Learning Inc.

Kipling Road, P.O. Box 676
Brattleboro, Vermont 05302-0676
☎ *(802) 257-7751*
☎ *(802) 258-3248*
This organization offers a school for international training in teaching languages, intercultural management and world issues as well as college semester abroad programs in 30 countries. Citizen exchange and language programs include summer abroad programs for students and seniors, corporate language projects and youth adventure camps. Au pair arrangements and exchange programs are also offered. Projects in international development and training strive to improve economic and social conditions around the world through development management, human resource development and development training.

Youth Exchange Service (YES)

4675 MacArthur Court
Suite 830
Newport Beach, California 92660
☎ *(800) 848-2121*
☎ *(714) 955-2030*

An international teenage exchange-student program dedicated to world peace. If you are interested in hosting an international teenage "ambassador," contact this group.

Medical Aid Groups

There are angels in Rwanda, Somalia, Angola, Afghanistan and Iraq. They are not there to convert souls or play harps. They are not soldiers or politicians but white-coated volunteers who sew back limbs, pull out shrapnel from babies' heads and minister to the sick and dying. They are the men and women who try to ease the suffering caused by violent actions. Natural disasters also tax the resources and stamina of aid workers to the limit. If you don't mind stacking bodies like firewood or can live with the ever-present stench of too many sick people in one place, you will do just fine.

The world needs people who clean up the mess caused by governments. If there is a disaster, chances are you will see these folks in there long before the journalists and the politicians try to grab air time. These are nondenominational groups that are found in the world's most dangerous places. If you have medical skills and want to save more lives in a day than a tentful of TV evangelists in a lifetime, this is the place to be. Conditions are beyond primitive, usually makeshift refugee camps on the edges of emerging conflicts. Many groups will walk or helicopter in to war-torn regions to assist in treating victims. Many aid workers have been targeted for death because of their policy of helping both sides. There is constant danger from rocket attacks, land mines, communicable diseases and riots. These people are not ashamed to stagger out of a tent after being up 48 hours straight, have a good cry and then get back to work saving more lives. It hurts but it feels good. Contact the following organizations for more information:

American Red Cross

National Headquarters
17th and D Street, N.W.
Washington, D.C. 20006
☎ *(202) 737-8300*
For 115 years, whenever there has been a disaster or war, these folks have been on the scene knee-deep in bandages, blood and cots, helping the injured and consoling those who have just lost everything. They always have a need for volunteers, particularly people with medical and technical skills. If you can't volunteer your time or skills, blood donors are desperately needed.

AmeriCares

161 Cherry Street
New Canaan, Connecticut 06840
☎ *(203) 966-5195*
☎ *(800) 486-4357*
AmeriCares is a private, nonprofit disaster relief and humanitarian aid organization that provides immediate response to emergency medical needs and supports long-term health care programs for people around the world, irrespective of race, color, creed or political persuasion. Since 1982 AmeriCare has delivered more than $1.4 billion worth of medical and disaster aid around the world. AmeriCare works with corporate America to secure large donations of supplies and materials. Cash contributions are used primarily for logistical costs. For every $1 donated, AmeriCare is able to deliver $22 worth of relief supplies.

Amnesty International USA

322 Eighth Avenue
New York, New York 10001
☎ *(212) 807-8400*
Amnesty International likes to shine light in dark places. When the London-based organization organizes the dissemination of thousands of letters, they tend to send jailors and governments scattering like cockroaches scurrying for cover. By showing these governments that they are aware, they hope to embarrass or pressure governments into better

treatment of political prisoners. Their method is simple and easy to effect. They coordinate the writing and mailing of letters to the captors of prisoners of conscience. Their methods have been proven successful and the international group was awarded the Nobel peace prize in 1977 for their efforts to promote observance of the U.N. Universal Declaration of Human Rights.

The membership is over 500,000 people in over 150 countries. Together, they can create an avalanche of mail and global protest over the mistreatment of prisoners. Amnesty International has groups that focus on health needs, legal support, human rights awareness and education and even a writers group that writes three prisoner appeals each month to government authorities. There is an Urgent Action network which will step up the pressure to aid prisoners who are in immediate danger of execution or torture.

Amnesty International began in London in 1961 and so far claims they have come to the rescue of 43,000 prisoners. Today, the staff of 200 monitors news and information and communications from around the world to seek out cases of mistreatment. Their goal is to pressure governments to end torture, executions, political killings and disappearances, to ensure speedy trials for all political prisoners and to effect the release of prisoners of conscience provided they have neither used nor advocated violence. Many countries with political prisoners (don't be so smug, the U.S. is on their list) insist that they are just meddlers. They are the only global organization that can really apply enough pressure to save the health and life of many political prisoners.

As a member, you can provide letter writing assistance, organizing skills or financial support. Memberships run $25 a year ($15 for students), and you are urged to participate in as many programs and networks as you would like. Freedom writers are sent sample letters which are then written and mailed by the member. Lawyers can contribute research and defense skills. Doctors can work to dissuade medical practitioners from participating in torture and executions. Students can join a 2000-school-wide student network that works in groups of five to 100 people to write letters, educate peers and gather signatures for petitions. Regular Joes can get writer's cramp sending letters to prisoners identified in the *Amnesty Action* newsletter. Amnesty International has local chapters in 47 states as well as four regional offices and their national office in Washington, ☎ *(202) 544-0200.* If you want to attend the monthly orientation session held in New York leave a message on Randy Paul's machine, ☎ *(212) 873-1073.*

A Few Tips on Writing Letters to Governments

AI encourages members to write letters, but telegrams are more effective in gaining the attention of the reader. State the purpose of your letter in the first sentence and make sure you end it with your request. If you are writing about a specific person, clearly state his name. The letters should be short. Be polite and state your concern as simply and honestly as possible. Always assume that the person you are writing to is a reasonable person. Tell the reader what you do for a living and what country you are from. Do not bring up politics, religion or opinions. Use the proper title of the addressee, write in English, write it by hand and sign the letter "Yours respectfully."

CARE

Worldwide Headquarters
151 Ellis Street
Atlanta, Georgia 30303
☎ *(404) 681-2552*
FAX (404) 577-4515

CARE was founded when 22 American organizations joined to help European survivors of World War II. It is the world's largest private, nonprofit, nonsectarian relief and development organization. In 1994, CARE provided $367 million in goods and services to more than 30 million people in developing countries. There are programs for disaster relief, food distribution, primary health care, agriculture and natural resource management, population, girls' education, family planning and small-business support. Ongoing self-help projects are in place in 61 of the least developed countries of Africa, Asia and Latin America, and programs are in progress for the emerging economies of Eastern Europe and the former Soviet Union. CARE responds to disasters overseas and has sent emergency aid to victims of famine and war in Rwanda, Haiti and the former Yugoslavia.

CARE Austria

11 Invalidenstrasse
Vienna, Austria 1030
☎ *[43] 171-50-715*
CARE Austria provides mobile gynecological and women's clinics in Bosnia and Croatia. They also offer care to ex-Yugoslavia's refugees. To help out, contact them at the number above or in Croatia at *Poljickih Knezova 15, Stroxanac, 58312 Podstrana, Croatia*.

Doctors Without Borders (Medecins Sans Frontieres

11 East 26 Street, Suite 1904l
New York, New York 10010
☎ *(212) 679-6800*
France: ☎ *[72] 73-04-14*
Doctors Without Borders, founded 25 years ago, is the largest international emergency medical organization in the world. Every year around 3000 volunteers leave for three to six months of service in more than 70 countries around the world. Many of the countries are in a state of war. Sixty percent of the volunteers are medically trained and come from 45 countries around the world. Most are 25–35 years old. The organization assists victims of natural disasters and health crises like Ebola, and ministers to refugees and war victims. To deploy people as quickly as possible (within 24 hours when possible), special emergency kits were created with strict operational and medical procedures. Today, these kits and manuals are used by other international organizations around the world.

Human Rights Watch

1522 K Street, N.W.
Suite 910
Washington, D.C. 20005
☎ *(202) 371-6592*
This organization promotes and monitors human rights worldwide. Human Rights Watch serves as an umbrella organization to Africa Watch, Asia Watch, Americas Watch, Middle East Watch, Helsinki Watch and the Fund for Free Expression.

International League for Human Rights

432 Park Avenue South
New York, New York 10016
☎ *(212) 684-1221*
ILHR is a nongovernmental organization with a history of human rights advocacy since 1942. Originally a voice for those fleeing Nazi-occupied Europe, the League became a force for the promotion and protection of human rights throughout the world. With the Universal Declaration of Human Rights as its platform, the League addresses a full range of international human rights issues and holds consultative status with the United Nations, UNESCO, the ILO and the Council of Europe. The Children of War project aims to improve state protection of human rights for children. The Religious Freedom project attempts to improve the protection of persecuted religious groups. The Eastern European Gender Discrimination project strives to achieve more equal treatment of women in Eastern European countries. The Human Rights and Business project works

with transnational business for the promotion and protection of human rights around the world. ILHR conducts briefing sessions with U.N. delegates regarding human rights issues and offers a number of publications, including *Mission Reports*, *Critiques*, and the ILHR *Human Rights Bulletin*.

Anti-Defamation League (ADL)

833 United Nations Plaza
New York, New York 10017
☎ *(212) 490-2525*
Skinhead International: A Worldwide Survey of Neo-Nazi Skinheads is published by ADL. It details skinhead activities in 33 countries. According to ADL, the Neo-Nazi skinhead movement has 70,000 members. Send US$10.50 to the address above for a copy of the directory and a list of ways you can help ADL combat the skinheads.

Reporters Sans Frontieres

International Secretariat
5, rue Geoffroy-Marie
Paris, France
☎ *33-144-838-484*
RSF was founded in 1985 and has offices in Belgium, Canada, France, Germany, Italy, Spain and Switzerland with members in 71 countries. Their job is to defend imprisoned journalists and press around the world. Their annual report offers tips for journalists on 152 countries, including the ones where journalists have been harassed, threatened and murdered. The annual report is available for US$20.

They will send protest letters and provide lawyers (if possible) and other forms of assistance to reporters in jail. If you want to convert to journalism after you are jailed, these folks can't help you.

Political Action Groups

Peace Links

729 8th Street S.E.
Suite 300
Washington, D.C. 20003
☎ *(202) 544-0805*
FAX (202) 544-0809
Founded in 1982 at a kitchen table by Betty Bumpers and a group of friends, Peace Links is a group of about 30,000 citizens (mostly female) who work to eradicate conflict and the threat of nuclear war. Although Peace Links is a relic of the Cold War, they feel that the threat of nuclear war is not past and they have shifted their focus to eliminate armed violence, warfare, conflict and other violent ways of settling differences. Peace Links creates local citizen groups to pressure politicians; they provide educational programs to schools on how to resolve conflicts without violence, and they have an unusual Pen Pals for Peace program that sends and receives letters stressing goodwill and peace.

They are developing exchange programs between the CIS, China and the U.S. and are looking for donations to continue their work. You can also buy a Peace Pal Bunny (a 7.5"-high stuffed rabbit with the world in her paws) for $10 or a video of a Peace Links' trip to the former Soviet Union.

Contact them about the U.S./C.I.S. Letter Links, which organizes people from those countries to write and receive letters.

Other Political Action Groups

Center on Budget and Policy Priorities

236 Massachusetts Avenue, N.E.
Washington, D.C. 20002
☎ *(202) 546-9737*

Citizen Exchange Council

12 West 31st Street
New York, New York 10001-4415
☎ *(212) 643-1985*

Foreign Policy Association

729 Seventh Avenue
New York, New York 10019
☎ *(212) 764-4050*

Institute for Policy Studies

1601 Connecticut Avenue, N.W.
Washington, D.C. 20009
☎ *(202) 234-9382*

World Policy Institute

777 U.N. Plaza, 5th floor
New York, New York 10017
☎ *(212) 490-0010*

Educational Organizations

Foundation for Global Community (Formerly Beyond War)

222 High Street
Palo Alto, California 94301
☎ *(415) 328-7756*
FAX (415) 3328-7785

Before the red AIDS ribbon was the hip lapel pin, there was the ubiquitous earth pin, the San Francisco version of the Midwesterner's Rotarian pin. The group originally wanted to show the Soviet Union that it could be good-vibed out of existence (maybe it worked) and had to refocus their efforts once the Evil Empire went bankrupt. Since 1991 they have been working on building a global community.

They are a New Age group whose goals are mired in PC-speak. Their mission statement, "Discover, live and communicate what is needed to build a world that functions for the benefit of all life," has a Berkleyish happy-face ring to it. Their list of current projects includes the Heroic Choice (learning how to move beyond self-interest to a larger purpose) educational process, a Fifth Discipline Team (how to integrate the process of systems thinking) and The Enneagram learning process (understanding the nine personality types to instill a deeper appreciation of people) are probably too obtuse for New Yorkers or Midwesterners. In plainspeak, they hope to offer nonviolent alternatives to resolving conflict. They also offer educational programs that teach that all life is one interconnected whole.

For example, they have brought together Armenians and Azeris at the Sequoia Seminar retreat in Ben Lomond, California, to discuss how to end the war in Nagorno-Karabakh. They then sent four participants to Azerbaijan to work toward the peace process. It will be interesting to see if the northern California free thinkers can roll back five centuries of ethnic hate or the Armenian tanks. Some may find the mental gymnastics and endless intellectual stroking a little like showing drive-in intermission films in Somalia. Positive, entertaining but ultimately ineffective.

The important thing is that they search for answers and they try to effect change in people's thinking. It's up to you what you do with all that positive energy and clear thinking. For now, they have members in 32 states and offer a variety of materials (audio- and videotapes, posters, stickers, cards, pins and books that offer imagery and information that reinforce the idea of a global community). If you are committed to embracing incongruent lifestyles and engaging others while learning and want to show that all of life is one interconnected whole, then donate over $25 or order their catalog of materials. The 5000-plus members receive their bimonthly copy of *Timeline*, a 24-page newsletter.

Global Education Associates

475 Riverside Drive
Suite 456
New York, New York 10115
☎ *(212) 870-3290*

Institute for Peace and Justice

4144 Lindell, #122
St. Louis, Missouri 63108
☎ *(314) 533-4445*
Sültzburgstrasse 140
D-5000 Köln Germany
☎ *(0) 221 14 76 05*

Save the Planet

Save the Rain Forest

The statistics fly around on deforestation like curses at a barroom brawl. Typically, like the curses, the numbers are half-right, half-wrong, but rooted in truth. Rain forests comprise only 2 percent of the planet's surface, yet they contain half the world's species. Half of the world's rain forests have disappeared since World War II, which is understandable when you consider the value of the timber and the need for emerging countries to develop their wilderness into towns, factories and grazing land.

Many conservation groups paint a Disneyesque picture of sunny glades populated with singing birds, bright flowers, romping animals and happy native peoples. The reality is much darker. Triple-canopy tropical forests have one of the lowest biomasses of mammals and birds. They are typically dark, dank, still and oppressively hot—ideal incubators for plant life. The native people live in isolation, sometimes culling each other in violent tribal conflicts, a natural thinning process that is also accelerated by disease and early death. When cleared, the land is barren and provides at most two years of scanty crops. Forest dwellers are forced to use swidden, or slash-and-burn cultivation, a method whereby trees are cleared, the ground burned, crops are planted for one or two years, and then the area is left to regenerate for up to 10 years before any nutrients are put back in the soil.

The term "rain forest" pertains to a variety of environments. There is no single way to saving the montane moss forests and the mangrove swamps, since they are in jeopardy from a variety of sources. The major enemies of the Asian forests are logging companies that pull out first-generation hardwood using crude and inefficient methods. Because of the low cost of this wood, tropical hardwoods are turned into everything from concrete construction forms to coffee table veneers. Decline is also accelerated by repopulation programs that clear large areas for cultivation and grazing. The country itself has the most to lose, but there are few options. Many countries, like Malaysia, point to our denuded forests and first World prosperity, then ask us why we think we have the right to tell them not to develop the same resources to achieve the same success.

The West's view of the rain forests seems to be as a potential location for tourism (if they ever get there) and as the lungs of the world. The East's view of the rain forests are that they provide short-term jobs and income. They still view the forests as the wilderness and as a symbol that they are not fully developed like the West. Both sides seem to agree that the rain forests are a resource, but the two hemispheres don't see eye to eye on how they should be used. We say to cut at sustainable yields, and they say they need the money now. The hitch is that the valuable timber in those triple-canopy forests is well over a hundred years old; unlike our fast-growing softwoods, they will not be back in our lifetime. There are answers and there are groups that are coming up with solutions and programs. The major thrust seems to be toward finding higher returns on the same resources. For example, over 70 percent of plant species that may help in the fight against cancer come from the rain forest, yet only one percent of the species has been tested for this property. Many foods, such as rice, potatoes, chocolate, tomatoes, oranges and cinnamon, have come from the tropical forests.

Although experts on both sides duke it out over how much rain forest is lost every minute, there is no denying that a lot more forest is being cut down than is being planted. Does it matter? Of course. Can you stop it? Of course not. Can you slow it down? Absolutely.

If you want to save the rain forest, or any forest for that matter, there are groups that make a difference. Joining any one of the following groups supports their activities as well as introduces you to other like-minded people. The variety of programs is bewildering, but then the answers required for solid preservation and management are even more complex.

Start by asking for information and attending some meetings. You can communicate with many of these people via computer. Many groups have needs for active volunteers as well as members. If you are looking for more active pursuits, as was the case of Bruno Manser, a Swiss national who helped the Punan organize against the timber companies in Sarawak, they can introduce you to sponsors, legal funds, mentors, and so forth.

You may just be happy to receive the ever-present newsletter and know that your money is supporting a good cause.

American Forests
Post Office Box 2000

Washington, D.C. 20013
☎ *(800) 873-5323*

OK, so everyone wants to save the rain forests, but when was the last time you visited Washington, Alaska or Hawaii? It seems we like to cut our rain forests as fast as our Third World cousins do. The American Forestry Association is about cutting down trees and about growing trees, but mostly about the need to grow trees. I worked on both sides of the fence, both for the Forest Service (basically counting trees) and as a logger (cutting them down). I, like most people, prefer walking through virgin forests to cutting them down. I just don't know whose forests we are going to cut down if we don't rebuild and manage ours.

Both sides of the fray (loggers and environmentalists) agree that we need to preserve trees. They just don't agree about how. Loggers say grow 'em as fast as you cut 'em down, and conservationists say don't cut 'em. Loggers like to ask who is going to supply the timber to build the house you return to after your hike in the woods. The fact is we still consume them a lot faster that we replace them. Joining American Forests puts your money toward replanting trees. Whether you shell out $30 to plant 10 trees or $1000 to plant an entire acre of trees (500), your money gets right to the heart of the matter. The 120-year-old organization is the creator of the Global ReLeaf program and works to make the country and the city a more livable place by planting more trees. It should be known that this group views trees as a renewable resource and not as sacred plants, so the more strident preservationists may want to spend their money with the Sierra Club or other "preservation-only" groups. For now, as long as we continue to use wood as a resource, management is the first step to better logging practices. The group also offers trips to forested places like New Zealand and even has a magazine on urban forests.

American Forestry Association (AFA)

☎ *(202) 667-3300*
To donate $5.00 for Global ReLeaf, ☎ *(900) 420-4545*
To plant trees, contact their Global ReLeaf Campaign.

Better World Society

☎ *(202) 331-3770*
Become a BWS video advocate and obtain *Profits from Poison*, a documentary about the dangerous misuse of pesticides in developing countries.

Conservation International

1015 18th Street, N.W.
Suite 1000
Washington, D.C. 20036
☎ *(202) 429-5660*
FAX (202) 887-5188
CI tries to integrate people into its conservation efforts. Their major focus is the rain forest in 24 countries in Latin America, Africa and Asia. They strive to integrate economics, community development and scientific solutions. Being down to earth, they tell you exactly what your donation can provide. Whether it is a $100 donation that buys a grinding wheel for making handicrafts from sustainable rain forest products in Ecuador, or $1000 that provides one thousand tree seedlings and planting equipment in Costa Rica, they do a good job of putting your money to work. Their idea of being able to create economic benefit seems a refreshing alternative to the eco-Nazis who demand natural preservation at the cost of local development.

Earth Island Institute

300 Broadway, Suite 28
San Francisco, California 94133
☎ *(415) 788 3666*
FAX (415) 788- 7324

EII is somewhat of an incubator for conservation, preservation and restoration projects. In 1982 David Brower, the founder of Friends of the Earth and first executive director of the Sierra Club, set up an institute to support creative solutions to the world's problems. Projects that have sprung from the institute include films, conferences and a variety of organizations. The Rain Forest Action Network, International Rivers Network and the International Marine Mammal Project all went on to become self-sustaining separate organizations. Earth Island Institute supports numerous projects around the world, from protecting mangrove forests to educating Australian aborigines about uranium waste disposal. Annual membership is $25 and gets you a subscription to the quarterly *Earth Island Journal*.

Greenpeace

1436 U. Street, N.W.
Washington, D.C. 20009
☎ *(202) 462-1177*
Their Toxics Campaign seeks to solve the toxic pollution problem through waste prevention. Greenpeace takes direct action against the polluters, fighting to cut off toxic substances at their source. Ask for a copy of *Toxics: Stepping Lightly on the Earth, Everyone's Guide to Toxics in the Home* (free).

National Audubon Society

700 Broadway
New York, New York 1003-9501
☎ *(212) 979-3000*
Ask for a copy of "The Audubon Activist Carbon Dioxide Diet," a worksheet that explains how to reduce your household's production of carbon dioxide, CFCs and trash ($2.00).

Rainforest Action Network (RAN)

450 Sansome Street
Suite 700
San Francisco, California 94111
☎ *(415)398-4404*
FAX (415) 398-2732
RAN is a feisty little group (13 full-time employees) formed in 1985 that yaps around the heels of big business. Their Darth Vader of the rain forest is Mitsubishi, "the worst corporate destroyer of rain forests in the world." They have also targeted oil companies like Texaco and Unocal and anybody who destroys rain forests or endangers indigenous peoples. They use public pressure, direct action and the coordinated actions of hundreds of like-minded groups around the world to force change and conservation.

They claim to have forced Burger King to stop importing beef from Central America— beef raised on land formerly occupied by rain forests. Their boycott caused a 12 percent drop in income and BK now no longer makes Whoppers out of Third World cows.

Their biggest weapon is a group of 150 independent Rain Forest Action Groups (RAG), which raise funds, educate their community and conduct campaigns to save the rain forest. RAN is proud of the fact that at least 82 percent of donations go directly toward rainforest preservation. Their most effective program is the Protect-an-Acre program. RAN uses funds to help forest peoples secure communal land titles and helps them develop livelihoods and long-term protection programs. To date, they have secured more than 2.5 million acres of land title.

They offer a variety of publications including the monthly *Action Alert* and the quarterly *World Rainforest Report*, and produce numerous fact sheets and brochures targeting specific rain-forest issues. There are directories of over 250 groups that are working to save the rain forest in the Amazon and 250 groups in Southeast Asia.

If you would like to get involved, you can start your own RAG, join one, support the group with funds or work as an unpaid intern in their San Francisco headquarters. You must put in 12 hours a week for three months.

Sierra Club

739 Polk Street
San Francisco, California 94109
☎ *(415) 776-2211*
☎ *(202) 547-1141 (D.C.)*
The granddaddy of ecoclubs, with 102 years under its belt and 600,000 members. The Sierra Club was founded in 1892 by John Muir with the idea that the natural areas of America needed to be saved from the industrialists who were ravaging the West.

Backed up by a staff of 350 paid volunteers, 20 regional field offices, 32 chapter offices and a rapidly growing membership roster, the Sierra Club is by far the most effective voice for conservation in America. They track the environmental profiles and voting history on environmental issues of members of the U.S. Senate and House of Representatives. They support their activities by publishing an impressive array of books, calendars, licensed products and *Sierra* magazine. They also lead about 300 trips every year and fight a number of legal battles from their six Legal Defense Fund Offices in San Francisco, Denver, Juneau, Honolulu and Washington, D.C.

You don't have to be a reformed lumberjack to help out. You can join as a member, or you can apply for a paid (or unpaid) job in their head office in San Francisco or in one of the regional offices. The Sierra Club is looking for low-paid, hardworking staff to work on books and their magazine. They need human resources, financial, data-entry, management, public affairs, travel, conservation and campaign workers. Their Washington office needs lobbyists, support people, media reps and issues specialists. If you are hoping to be paid to hike around the parks and take those amazing photographs in *Sierra* magazine or their books, sorry, its all on spec or freelance. They welcome submissions though, so keep trying if you get turned down the first time. The Sierra Club can give you a reduced fee on one of their outings in exchange for some trail clearing and maintenance work. Twenty lucky interns can work for nothing throughout the organization with the hopes of getting a full-time job later. If you do get a job, expect full dental, medical and life insurance programs, a pension plan and generous vacation accrual (that means you will work plenty of OT) and discounts on calendars, outings, etc. If you are interested, contact the Human Resources Department at ☎ *(415) 923-5581.*

Worldwatch Institute

1776 Massachusetts Avenue NW
Washington, D.C. 20036
☎ *202-452-1999*
A global environmental research organization. Ask for publications such as *Clearing the Air: A Global Agenda, Air Pollution, Acid Rain, and The Future of Forests,* and *The Bicycle: Vehicle for a Small Planet.*

Save the Animals

Animal rights activists are not always bulimic models and washed-up celebrities. There are plenty of square-jawed park rangers who hunt down and kill poachers on a nightly basis. I spent three days badgering the Tanzanian game wardens in Selous park to take us man hunting with them at night. I found out why they didn't want me along; it seems they left their remote little hut, drove about half a mile away and slept. Oh, well. In any case, you can make a difference, whether you are on the ground or in your living room. Your meager contribution is a spit in the ocean and is guaranteed not to save an animal species from extinction, but a lot of people chipping in a few bucks and a few hours will go a long way to doing something concrete.

If you just can't stand by and watch another elephant get chain-sawed for his tusks, then there are active outlets for you. One of the best ways to visit dangerous places is to do good. The image of the great white hunter as adventurer has been replaced by the great white conservationist as adventurer. If you have dreams of getting sunburnt, dusty and wrinkled while bouncing around Africa in an old Land Rover 88, your best bet is to look into the many conservation groups that need volunteers and support. Those who preferred *Indiana Jones* to *Born Free* can also check into the many archaeological digs that need helping hands. If you just want to read about and keep one more white rhino on the planet, then by all means tuck in your love gift and get warm fuzzies (and usually a colorful newsletter).

African Elephant Conservation Coordinating Group

c/o Dr. David Weston
Wildlife Conservation Intl.
P.O. Box 62844
Nairobi, Kenya
☎ *[254] 2245-6922-1699*
FAX [254] 2159-6922-1699
This group works with other wildlife protection groups to help protect elephants and ensure that they do not fall victim to poachers.

African Wildlife Foundation

1717 Massachusetts Avenue, N.W.
Washington, D.C. 20036
☎ *(202) 265-8393*
Founded in 1961 with the belief that only Africans can save African wildlife, the AWF operates two colleges of wildlife management. Their colleges have trained hundreds of game wardens and rangers for parks all over Africa. AWF is unique in that it works with Africans within Africa to manage African wildlife. They also educate children on conservation, help local communities benefit from wildlife preservation and show them ways to make more efficient use of land.

The AWF developed programs and trained staff in Rwanda's Parc des Volcans to protect the remaining 650 mountain gorillas. They have continued their support of the rangers throughout the recent bloodshed and report that no gorillas were harmed. They also run the longest continuous study of elephants in Africa in Kenya. They have been tracking the 790 elephants in Amboseli National Park to understand elephant behavior and social patterns. There are a field office in Nairobi and a fund-raising center in Washington. Supporters receive a thrice yearly newsletter *Wildlife News,* and contributions are tax-deductible.

Convention on International Trade in Endangered Species (CITES)

c/o UNEP
DC2-0803 United Nations
New York, NY 10017
☎ *(212) 963-8093*
The United Nations Environment Program (UNEP) was created in 1972 as a result of the Stockholm Conference on the Human Environment. Its original purpose was to raise environmental awareness and promote action at all levels of society worldwide. UNEP monitors and assesses the state of the world environment, develops policies, and provides a forum for global environmental concerns. UNEP is the guardian of international environmental law. At the 1992 U.N. Earth Summit in Brazil, UNEP's role was reconfirmed and strengthened by its ambitious Agenda 21 plan. Endorsed by world leaders, this doc-

ument provides a plan of action for dealing with ongoing problems including the deple-
tion of the ozone layer, biological diversity, hazardous wastes and droughts.

The Cousteau Society

Membership Center
870 Greenbriar Circle
Suite 402
Chesapeake, Virginia
☎ *(800) 441-4395, or (804) 523-9335*

This worldwide organization, started in 1973, serves to protect the oceans, marine animals and ultimately humans from pollution and abuse. Their noble but somewhat ambitious goal is to "provide a centralized facility for continuing studies of man and his
world." They also strive to "protect and improve the quality of life for present and future
generations," another goal that I am sure would be difficult to oppose. They freely admit
that their job is to "bridge the gap between specialists and the public," meaning doing
cool things with a scientist as baby-sitter. Their methodology might be overly dramatic
and Inspector Clouseau/Captain Cousteau's voiceover horribly mangled and poetic, but
many of my generation can't imagine going diving without saying at least once: "Luuk at
zee leetle feeshes adrrrift in zeee vaaast ocheoon."

Well anyway, join the club and let me know. In the meantime, if you like diving as I do
you have to give Jacques-Yves his due for being the coinventor of the aqualung and making diving such a popular sport.

If you join up, you'll get a free bimonthly mag called *The Calypso Log* and the *Dolphin
Log* for kids. The money goes toward supporting the activities of the Cousteau Society
and publicizing their ongoing activities, which consist primarily of creating films on various regions of the world and acting as PR agents for whales and other wet things. Cousteau is currently on his rediscovery of the world, which means they have pretty much
blown through it once before. His shows are bankrolled by Ted Turner and continue to
be the best aquatic filmmaking out there. On the downside, Cousteau seems to keep discovering places that people have lived in for thousands of years. Simplification and a
somewhat lopsided view of the world (ocean) make for great entertainment but sometimes provide only sketchy scientific content. Oh hell! I admit I love bumper stickers that
say things like "Nuke the gay whales for Jesus" and I do eat fish. Can you actually do anything or come along for the ride? No. But you can watch their television specials, buy the
books and join the society. Membership is $20 for an individual and $28 for families.

National Wildlife Federation

1400 16th Street, N.W.
Washington, D.C. 20036
☎ *(202) 797-6800*
FAX (703) 790-4040

The National Wildlife Federation was founded in 1936 as a nationwide network of grassroots conservationists. Its mission is to educate, inspire and assist individuals and organizations of diverse cultures to conserve wildlife and other natural resources and to protect
the Earth's environment in order to achieve a peaceful, equitable and sustainable future.
Representatives of 45 state and territorial affiliates meet annually to establish NWF's conservation policy. The National Conservation Office based in Washington, D.C., campaigns in Congress, federal agencies and the courts for these priority issues: endangered
species, clean water, wetlands, farm policy, public lands reform, environmental justice and
environmental quality. The International Affairs Department works to assure environmental considerations are incorporated into U.S. trade agreements, to assure citizen
access to environmental decision-making, and to encourage economic, cultural, human
welfare and population initiatives.

The Nature Conservancy

1815 North Lynn Street
Arlington, Virginia 22209
☎ *(800) 628-6860, (703) 841-5300*
FAX (703) 841-4880
The Nature Conservancy seeks out, develops and works to create conservation areas around the world. Its goals are to assist in the development of local conservation institutions, provide on-the-ground protection assistance, create sustainable conservation financing and generate improved conservation information. The group sets up Conservation Data Centers for developers trying to avoid vulnerable species and for conservationists designing preserves. It is active in the Caribbean and Latin America with programs in Mexico, Panama, Costa Rica, Ecuador and Brazil. It also is working to build and protect parks in the South Pacific.

The Student Conservation Association, Inc.

Post Office Box 550
Charlestown, New Hampshire 03603
☎ *(603) 826-4301*
FAX (603) 826-7755
The SCA offers 12-week positions assisting in the management and protection of U.S. national Parks, forests and other conservation areas. You might be maintaining trails, educating visitors, helping archaeology surveys and telling people to turn their ghetto blasters down in campsites. You will get to work in the great outdoors, have food and housing supplied, as well as have your travel expenses covered in the U.S.

The year-round program is open to those over 18, and it helps if you have academic qualifications. The list of positions available is published every July and December and is available by contacting the recruitment director.

Wilderness Conservancy

1224 Roberto Lane
Los Angeles, CA 90077
☎ *(310) 472-2593*
FAX (310) 476-7527
This nonprofit conservation organization, headed by Dr. Robert Cleaves, provided four anti-poaching aircraft for governments in Zimbabwe and Kwazulu, supplies for game scouts in Zambia and funds for a preschool in Zimbabwe. They are now raising funds for four more aircraft for Southern Africa. If you are interested in getting involved in the real world of conservation and the effort to prevent the extinction of black rhinos, elephants, cheetahs and other species, give them a call.

Wildlife Conservation International

☎ *(212) 220-5155*
Their Tropical Forest Campaign supports field researchers and conservation action plans at work in 37 tropical forests around the globe.

World Wildlife Fund

1250 24th Street, N.W.
Washington, D.C. 20037
☎ *(202) 293-4800*
For more than 30 years, World Wildlife Fund (WWF) has worked to save endangered wildlife. Their activities include halting global trade in endangered animals and plants, training and equipping anti-poaching teams, undertaking research on wildlife behavior and habitat needs, and mounting international campaigns to save flagship species like tigers, rhinos and giant pandas. WWF has helped to create and preserve hundreds of parks and other protected areas around the world. WWF also works with local leaders, grassroots groups, governments, and international funding institutions to improve living standards and to integrate conservation into public and private-sector development programs.

SAVE THE PLANET

Save Yourself

How to Stay Alive and Well (for At Least Four Weeks)

I guess just about any type of school can be called a survival school (translating Homeric poems from the original Greek could help you survive British boys school reunions). Knowledge is power and power creates self-confidence. America offers little in the normal school curriculum that would help us survive in either urban or rural environments. In fact, most high school kids don't even know how to open a bank account, let alone trap, skin and cook a rabbit.

There are three types of survival schools. The first is sport- or location-specific (mountain, diving, jungle, jumping); the next deals with bush lore, and the last type is the southern "be a mercenary" school that does little but promote the sales of black T-shirts with skulls, and cheap beer. Having never received any formal military training, I learned my survival skills from a variety of eclectic sources: guides, boatmen, headhunters, Indians, trappers, botanists and others.

The first tool for survival is knowledge, the second is self-confidence, and the third is ingenuity. I would like to say that luck is by far the most important element of survival, but let's put that aside for now.

Armies have long known that training can replace thinking in men. If someone is exposed to rote learning, common experience and instinctive reaction, they will often do the unthinkable. In the trenches of WWI, thousands of men crawled out of relative safety to follow their dead comrades into withering machine-gun fire. Intensive training can suppress our natural instinct to run away, cower in fear or scream at the top of our lungs.

What does that have to do with survival training? First of all, most people have never been in a life-threatening situation. Or more correctly, most people don't know how to deal with life-threatening situations. Second, most urban people left in remote places don't have the foggiest idea about how to build a fire, construct shelter and find food.

Most adventurers eagerly look forward to the serendipity of being thrust into unforeseen or harsh circumstances. Many of them have a smattering of training and good sense, but few are honest-to-god bushmen, so if you want the odds stacked in your favor, try spending some time at one of the training spots listed in this section.

The best sources for survival training are the special forces or commando sections of the British, American, Australian and French military. Most require a minimum of four to five years and will consume the flower of your youth. You may find yourself with skills that lead you to a life of hard-core adventure, since the first place security and mercenary recruiters go is to the bars that the SAS and French Foreign Legion frequent. If you wish to sidestep the endless years of boredom spent on military bases and go straight for the good stuff, you can look into these schools, many taught by the cream of the SAS or American special forces vets. Don't be shy about setting up a one-on-one itinerary if you have special educational needs.

If you gravitate toward the more earthbound, then be prepared to learn survival the politically correct way: no killing, no field stripping of weapons and a definite slant toward New Age thinking. Will these skills save your life when you have to E&E Khmer Rouge terrorists? Maybe. Will they make you more comfortable and secure in the wild? Yes.

Adventure/Recreation Schools

OK we should say schools for dangerous people, or schools that will make your adventures less dangerous; Oh hell, it sounds better our way. Herein you can find a list of institutions, events and resources that will help the curious and adventurous add to their survival skills.

Bremex

Expedition Leadership Training Scheme
London Information Center
18 Westbourne Park Villas
London, England W2 5EA
☎ *[44] (71) 229-9251*
Bremex operates a school in expedition planning, leadership and survival skills. The briefings and lectures are on Tuesday evenings, with weekend training wilderness expeditions in the winter. All courses are London-based and vary from "Weekend Taster" courses to nine-month qualifying courses for expedition leaders. Training includes first aid, survival skills, mountain rescue, leadership studies, canoeing, snow and ice climbing, navigation and orienteering.

Fees are about $50 a month, with transportation provided to weekend moor and mountain locations.

National Outdoor Leadership School

Post Office Box AA
Lander, Wyoming 82520
☎ *(307) 332-6973*
FAX (307) 332-3031

This school gets past the superficial imagery of some survival schools and right down to business. People who want to make money in the outdoor adventure business come here to learn not only survival aspects, but the nuts and bolts of adventure travel outfitting. You can also take the 34-day, $2100 NOLS instructor's class once you have passed a basic wilderness class. The emphasis here is on safety, since your future charges will be less than amused if they end up living off the land because you forgot to pack their favorite pudding. Choose from, sea kayaking, winter camping, telemark skiing, backpacking or mountaineering. Some courses qualify for college credit.

Entry-level classes are in reality great adventure vacations depending on your area of interest. Mountaineering classes are taught in Alaska, British Columbia and even Kenya. Expect to spend two weeks to three months on location learning the specialized skills you will need to lead other groups. If you want to cram in a class on your vacation, then opt for their selection of two-week courses on horsepacking, winter skiing, rock climbing or canoeing. If you flunk, well you had a good time on a well-organized adventure tour.

School for Field Studies

16 Broadway
Beverly, Massachusetts 01915
☎ *(508) 927-5127*

A nonprofit group that runs 40 month-long and semester-length programs that allow students to gain field research experience. Targeted to high school and college students, the college credit courses are run all around the world. There is a wide choice of topics, from coral reef studies (the Caribbean), marine mammals (Baja, Mexico), tropical rain forests (Australia) and wildlife management (Kenya). Scholarships and interest-free loans are available.

SOLO (Stonehearth Open Learning Opportunity)

Rural Federal District 1
Box 163
Conway, New Hampshire 03818
☎ *(603) 447-6711*
FAX (603) 447-2310

A school for professionals, SOLO is designed to teach wilderness guides what to do in an emergency. They offer a four-week, $1200 Emergency Wilderness Training Certification course that will get you on the preferred list of just about any expedition. Shorter two-day seminars are taught around the country for $100. The areas of specialization are wilderness emergencies (such as frostbite, hypothermia, bites and altitude sickness), climbing rescue, and emergency medicine (wounds, broken limbs, shock and allergy). Participants are expected to have a basic grounding in climbing and outdoor skills.

Adventure Experience Organizations

British Schools Exploring Society

Royal Geographical Society
1 Kensington Gore
London, England SW7 2AR
☎ *[44] (71) 584-0710*
FAX ([44] (71) 581-7995

BSES sets up an expedition for young people (16-1/2 to 20 years old) every year. The six-week expeditions are usually to the arctic regions of Europe (Canada to Russia) and are during the summer holidays. They have been sneaking in expeditions to tropical climes and offer four- to six-month expeditions to Botswanna, Greenland, Alaska and Svalbard.

Over 3000 people have taken part since 1932, and interviews take place in London in November. Participants pay a fee to cover costs; membership to BSES is by election after the successful completion of a BSES expedition.

Castle Rock Center for Environmental Adventures

412 County Road 6NS
Cody, Wyoming 82414
☎ *(800) 533-3066, (307) 527-6650*
FAX (307) 527-7196

Here's a place that is about halfway between the Boy Scouts and Outward Bound, targeted directly to bored teens. Called "Man and His Land Expeditions," they allow you to choose from fishing, ice climbing, white-water rafting, horse packing, mountain biking and llama trekking, or you can do all of them. The eight-week Full West program will pack more rootin' tootin' Western adventure than a year of *National Geographic* TV specials. How about a seven-day backpack trip in the Rockies; then you're off to the Grand Canyon; then you zip over to the Green River for a little white-water rafting, and zoom, you blast up to Mount Rainier for mountain climbing and rescue training. Still not totally bagged? More thrills and spills await, as you tour the rain forests of the Olympic Peninsula and then more river running, then in one last eco-adventure blast in the Absaroka Range in Wyoming, you spend the next week mountain biking, llama trekking, horse packing and camping. If there are any survivors, the final week is spent climbing mountains in the Tetons as part of the Exum school of Mountaineering. And all you thought there was for teenagers to do in the summer was play video games and listen to heavy metal.

Earth Skills

570 Shepard Street
San Pedro, CA 90731
☎ *(310) 833-4249*

There is a school where you can learn tracking, survival, plant uses and general bush lore. The Earth Skills school was founded in 1987 by Jim Lowery to introduce people to the great outdoors in a very practical way. Most of the classes are over a three-day weekend and run between $50 to $160. The wilderness skill course is a three-day class that will teach you how to trap, identify edible plants, weave baskets, build shelters, start a fire with an Indian bow, make primitive weapons, purify water and generally learn how to survive more than 50 miles from a Seven-11.

The one-day classes, usually held on a weekend, teach tracking skills or plant uses. Once you have graduated from tracking or wilderness, you can move up to the advanced levels where you can learn Earth Philosophy. Using the methodology and philosophy of aboriginal peoples, Lowery will show you how to apply your inner vision to communicate with the animals. If this is a little too California for some folks, you can skip Earth Philosophy and go into Advanced Tracking and Awareness. This class is taught in the Los Padres mountains at an elevation of 8000 feet in the summer or in Joshua Tree in the winter. Both are spectacular sites.

Ready for graduate work? Once you have completed the above, you are ready for the Track-Reading workshop, a one-day class that teaches you foot movement and biomechanics so that you will essentially be reading the animals' mind and actions as you follow the tracks of wild animals. If that is not enough, there is a whole weekend of tracking in Nipomo dunes near Pismo Beach. Here, you will track coyote, bobcat, raccoons, opossums and other small animals.

The school has had about 3000 graduates who have spent serious "dirt time" with Jim. He recommends his class for nature center leaders, biologists, Scout leaders and anyone who wants to understand our world a little better. He offers a quarterly newsletter called *Dirt Times* for $10 a year.

Four Corners School of Outdoor Education

East Route
Monticello, Utah 845535
☎ *(800) 525-4456*
Four Corners provides outdoor skills, natural sciences and land stewardship in the Colorado Plateau. The activities include rafting, jeeping, hiking and backpacking. Costs are between $375 to $2495, with courses given between February and November.

The Hardt School of Wilderness Living and Survival

Post Office Box 231-A
Salisbury Vermont 05769
Ron Hardt and those rugged Vermonters must specialize in the lighter side of survival. Here you can spend six days doing all the things the Indians did without being banished to the wilderness to prove your self-sufficiency. Better yet, you can look forward to a cozy cabin and three robust meals a day, while you learn how to skin rabbits and make tepees. The summertime classes cost $525, with a weekend program for about $200.

International Journeys Inc.

☎ *(800) 622-6525*
Travel up the Amazon on a research vessel ($1695 from Miami); extensions to Macchu Pichu and Cuzco are available.

Outward Bound

384 Field Point Road
Greenwich, Connecticut 06830
☎ *(800) 243-8520, (203) 661-0797*
Colorado School: ☎ *(800) 477-2627*
Pacific Crest School: ☎ *(800) 547-3312*
Do you want to develop that calm, steely-eyed approach, that strong warmth that exudes from those '40s male movie stars with an unshakable faith in your abilities and courage? All right, how about just being able to sleep without your Mickey Mouse nightlight on? Outward Bound starts with the mind, and the body follows. The program has been used with the handicapped, the criminal and the infirm, and it creates magical transformations in all. What is the secret? Well, like the tiny train that said, "I think I can, I think I can," OB teaches you to motivate yourself, trust your companions and step past your self-imposed limits. What emerges is self-confidence and a greater understanding of your fellow man.

The idea for the school was developed in 1941. Today, there are 31 Outward Bound schools around the world, with seven in North America: Colorado, Maine, New York, North Carolina, Oregon, Minnesota and Toronto. The instructors are not strutting, barking ex-marines but warm, caring individuals who hold safety and understanding above pushing limits. So now that you're sold, what actually happens to effect this magical change in people? Well, first you must put aside about two grand for the two-day-long programs; shorter programs cost about half that.

You can choose from hiking, rafting, winter camping, climbing, trekking, canoeing and ski mountaineering. Each program is broken into four phases (I sense a heroic structure through these schools.) First, students are instructed in the sport-specific skills they need. Phase two is the journey. Small groups of eight to 12 people tackle a specific journey via their chosen mode of travel. Phase three is the Challenge, where students now must go into the wilderness (their instructors check in on them daily) and be self-sufficient, meditate and reflect on their general state of affairs (40 days and 40 nights is probably too extreme, so the usual length of time is one to three days). Phase four lets the students break into smaller groups without the benefit of instructors and complete their own mini-expedition. At the end of the course, the students are reunited and they participate in one last activity. Whew! After all that, most students rave about the change in their self-confidence, their lust for life and their re-centering (a California word that means they are on the right track).

If you find this process stimulating and rewarding, Outward Bound has leadership courses to prepare you for positions as a guide or just to help you teach other people to expand their self-confidence and awareness.

Outward Bound has expanded to include executive training courses, but the results are not as glorious as anticipated. In one recent session, instructors in England divided executives into two groups and told them to rescue two injured people on the side of a mountain. One group then proceeded to steal the other's stretcher, brought their "victim" to safety, then stood and cheered while the other victim lay stranded on the mountain. Oh, well. Maybe learning to survive the urban jungle makes men tougher than we thought.

John Ridgeway Adventure School

Ardmore, Rhiconich
By Lairg, Sutherland, Scotland IV27 4RB
☎ *[44] (97) 182-229*
The Ridgeway School is an established (since 1969) place for young people to learn outdoor skills. For those young people jaded by the choices offered by the Wild West, John Ridgeway can put them on a 57-foot sailing ketch, teach them how to sail a dinghy and provide a different angle on survival training, backpacking, canoeing, rock-climbing and interpersonal skills. Open to 12- to 15-year olds and 15- to 18-year olds, these two-week summer courses run about $800. An interesting alternative if you are spending the summer in Europe and are looking for something to occupy the teens.

U.S. Space Camp

Huntsville, Alabama
☎ *(800) 63-SPACE*
All right, this one is not quite a life-and-death experience, but for the young it is a great way to understand why astronauts need the right stuff. It might be the beginning of a life of adventure for the next generation.

This commercial enterprise (no pun intended) strives to deliver a youthful replica of the space program and will really turn on science geeks and flight nuts. During the weeklong experience students will perform water survival training, and eventually earn Space Academy wings.

If you can cough up an additional $75 or $225, trainees can either fly as an observer, or get behind the controls of a *Tampico Club* training aircraft when instructors from the University of North Dakota's aerospace department fly Space Academy and Aviation Challenge trainees in single-engine planes.

More than 183,000 trainees have graduated from U.S. Space Camp programs in Alabama and Florida in the past 12 years, more than enough to supply the next few generation of astronauts. Campuses also are located in Japan and Belgium, with Space Camp Canada scheduled to open soon.

Survival Training

Boulder Outdoor Survival School

Post Office Box 3226
Flagstaff, Arizona 86003
Summer: ☎ *(801) 335-7404*
Winter: ☎ *(208) 356-7446*
If you want to live like a native (no, they do not offer casino management courses), check out the BOSS progam. The big one is the 27-day course in Utah, where you will go

through four phases. For openers, you will spend five days traveling without food or water. The second phase is 12 days, with the group learning and practicing your survival skills.The third phase has you spending three to four days on a solo survival quest with minimal tools (no credit cards or Walkmans), living off the land until you finally make the grade by spending five days in the wild traveling a substantial distance. Graduation ceremonies are somewhat informal and muddy. For this, you pay about $1300. Naturally, food, accommodations and transportation are not included. One added benefit is that most participants lose about 5 to 8 percent of their body weight after taking the month long course.

For those who don't have a month to spend on a forced weight-loss system, or can't miss reruns of "McGyver," there are one- to three-week courses that range from basic earth skills and aboriginal knowledge for $550, to winter survival courses that include making snowshoes, mushing dog sleds and cold weather first aid for $565. The one that appeals to me is the seven-day desert and marine (as in water) survival course held in the Kino bay area of Sonora, Mexico. This course teaches you how to find your food underwater and on land, finding water, what there is to eat in arid lands and general desert survival knowledge. BOSS is consistently held above the others as the toughest and most rewarding survival school.

A Great Place to Visit... If You're a Fudgsicle

A sparse naval-science outpost at the base of a towering iceberg at the mouth of Independence Fjord—this is "Cool School," Arctic survival training for the 109th Air National Guard unit from Scotia, N.Y. It's not just a job; it's an ordeal. For 50 hours, the students endure continuous exposure to minus 35°F off the coast of northeastern Greenland, learning how to use the resources from their aircraft and the environment to sustain themselves in an emergency.

Taught by four active-duty airmen from Eielson Air Force Base in Alaska, Cool School is an adaptation of the Arctic survival training course they teach 20 weeks each year in the woods outside Fairbanks, Alaska. The course includes a full day of classroom briefings on the environment, clothing, shelter, signaling and cold injuries, followed by a minimum of two days in survival conditions.

The 109th airlift group flies missions for the armed forces and National Science Foundation to both the North and South Poles and is one of only two United States military units capable of landing cargo aircraft on skis. All flight crew members are required to complete the training at some point in their guard service; 23 braved the cold at this year's session.

Green Mountain Wilderness Survival School

Post Office Box 125
Waitsfield, Vermont 05673
☎ (802) 496-5300

Green Mountain offers a softer and lower-cost approach than BOSS to survival training, and, in the process, the owner, Mike Casper, has more takers. He runs 10-day courses in the summer in Vermont State Parks and wilderness areas. Students will learn how to gather food via tracking, trapping, hunting or fishing. Edible plant identification, cooking without the aid of pots or pans and finding and purifying water round out the culinary aspect of this $950 course. You don't need to be Hawkeye to join, and you might actually have some fun.

Executive Outcomes Ltd.

P.O. Box 75255
Lynwood Ridge
Pretoria 0040 South Africa
☎ *[27] 12 473-789*
This group can teach you all about war. They conduct clandestine warfare and special forces training and offer sniper courses. Five African governments have reportedly used their services.

International Adventure

7 Melbourne Street
Royston, Hertfordshire, England SG8 7BP
☎ *[44] (763) 242-867*
This British school will send you off to train under Preben Mortensen, a survival instructor who also provides military survival training to the armed forces. The course is held in the Varmland area of Southern Sweden during the winter and the summer. There is little Indian lore or men barking at the moon—just how to stay alive in wilderness conditions. Expect to pay about a grand for 10 days.

Survival School for Reporters

Most reporters brag about trial by fire or the red badge of courage. The reality is that very, very few war correspondents have any military or survival training. Much like the effect of those Drivers Ed. movies in high school, hours of watching mangled bodies and gimpy people might make them think twice about journalistic heroics.

It is safe to say that the 125 journalists who were killed in 1994 and 1995 didn't deliberately get up in the morning and decide to lay down their lives in hopes of gaining eternal fame. They just screwed up. The wrong place at the wrong time, an overenthusiastic sniper, a leftover land mine, ricochets, booby traps—you name it.

There is an interesting course designed to at least lower the odds of violent death for journalists. The four-day Battlefield First Aid Training Course run by the British Army has certified more than 500 journalists since 1992. Journalists are taught how to stay alive: avoiding snipers, identifying and understanding mines and booby-traps, and the effects and damage of weapons of various calibers, as well as first aid and basic training rules. Some tips gleaned from the course:

• Learn to estimate the source and direction of shooting.

• Understand the various calibers and weapons used.

• Seek cover and stay low (most people shoot high).

• Stay off rooftops.

• Wear dark colors but do not wear green.

• Do not carry military equipment, including military food rations.

• Stay alert.

• Watch all openings for snipers or combatants.

• When entering buildings, push windows or doors slowly in case of booby traps.

A watered-down version of hand-to-hand combat is taught along with first-aid techniques. The first-aid classes teach more than just how to administer for shock and bleeding as a result of gunshot wounds. The students are shown and then asked to use hypodermic needles on themselves in case they need to inject morphine. To minimize the need for first aid, attendees are educated on the amazing variety and types of land mines and booby traps.

For information on course dates and fees, contact the following:

British Army Medical Services Training Center
☎ *[44] 125-234-0237*

Security/Health

Who do you turn to when things get nasty? Chances are you are not going to get shot, kidnapped, beaten up, robbed, infected, conned, knifed, raped, scammed or just sick, but as they say, waste matter happens. The first stop for most folks is the embassy. When they find out just how little the embassy can do for them, they usually are referred to other sources.

Emergency/Rescue

If you become seriously ill or injured abroad, a U. S. consular officer can provide assistance in finding medical services and informing your the next-of-kin, family or friends. A consular officer can also assist in the transfer of funds from the United States, but payment of hospital and other expenses is your responsibility.

It is wise to learn what medical services your health insurance will cover overseas before you leave on your trip. If you do have applicable insurance, don't forget to carry both your insurance policy identity card as proof of such insurance, and a claim form. Many health insurance companies will pay customary and reasonable hospital costs abroad, but most require a rider for a Medivac flight back to the States. This is usually done via private plane or by removing airline seats. You will be accompanied by a nurse or medical assistant who will also fly back to the country of origin. Medivacs can burn money as fast the *Lear Jet* you charter, so plan on spending a minimum of five grand up to $30,000. If you are really banged up, you may need more medical technicians, special equipment and a higher level of care during your flight. The Social Security Medicare program does not provide for payment of hospital or medical services outside the U.S.A.

If you're getting toward the back end of your adventuring career, the American Association of Retired Persons (AARP) offers foreign medical care coverage at no extra charge with its Medicare supplement plans. This coverage is restricted to treatments considered eligible under Medicare. In general, it covers 80 percent of the customary and reasonable charges, subject to a $50 deductible for the covered care during the first 60 days. There is a ceiling of $25,000 per trip. This is a reimbursement plan so you must pay the bills first and obtain receipts for submission to the plan. Keep in mind that many insurance policies may not cover you if you were injured in a war zone.

To facilitate identification in case of an accident, complete the information page on the inside of your passport, providing the name, address and telephone number of someone to be contacted in an emergency. The name given should not be the same as your traveling companions, in case the entire party is involved in the same accident. Travelers going abroad with any preexisting medical problems should carry a letter from their attending physician. The letter should describe their condition and cover information on any prescription medications, including the generic name of any prescribed drugs that they need to take.

Any medications being carried overseas should be left in their original containers and be clearly labeled. Travelers should check with the foreign embassy of the country they are visiting to make sure any required medications are not considered to be illegal narcotics.

Access America, Inc.
Post Office Box 90310
Richmond, Virginia 23230
☎ *(800) 284-8300*

Air Ambulance Services:

Air Ambulance Inc.
Hayward, California, ☎ *(800) 982-5806, (510) 786-1592*

Aero Ambulance International
Ft. Lauderdale, Florida, ☎ *(800) 443-8042, (305) 776-6800*

Air Ambulance Network
Miami, Florida, ☎ *(300) 327-1966, (305) 387-1708*

Air-Evac International
8665 Gibbs Drive
Suite 202
San Diego, California 92123
☎ *(800) 854-2569*

Air Medic - Air Ambulance of America
Washington, Pennsylvania, ☎ *(800) 321-4444, (412) 228-8000*

Care Flight - Air Critical Care Intl.
Clearwater, Florida, ☎ *(800) 282-6878, (813) 530-7972*

National Air Ambulance
Ft. Lauderdale, Florida, ☎ *(800) 327-3710, (305) 525-5538*

International Medivac Transport
Phoenix, Arizona, ☎ *(800) 468-1911, (602) 678-4444*

International SOS Assistance
Philadelphia, Pennsylvania, ☎ *(800) 523-8930, (215) 244-1500*

Mercy Medical Airlift
Manassas, Virginia, ☎ *(800) 296-1217, (703) 361-1191*
(Service area: Caribbean and Canada only. If necessary, will meet commercial incoming patients at JFK, Miami and other airports.)

AIRescue
7435 Valjean Avenue
Van Nuys, CA 91406
☎ *(800) 922-4911, (818) 994-0911*
FAX (818) 994-0180
(This number can be called collect by patients and customers from anywhere in the world.)
AIRescue is a company whose services you hope you never need. AIRescue was started in 1991by former UCLA MEDSTAR physician Francine Vogler, with the primary goal of providing emergency aeromedically trained physician/nurse teams along with chartered aircraft to get your butt back in the U.S.A. Naturally, they assume you're sick and that your insurance company won't faint when they see the bill. The cost for getting you home can run up to $100,000. In some cases, a small commercial jet can be chartered or normal airliners can be used. In the case of using regularly scheduled airlines, you will be dinned for four to 12 seats to accommodate the stretcher, equipment and staff required. The majority of emergency flights are national, but they can come and get you just about anywhere you can call them.

Keep in mind that many insurance policies do not cover repatriation costs, yet the extra coverage is minimal. (Don't tell them you're off to liberate Angola under "Reason for travel.") You can and should buy this coverage if you know you are heading out of town. The older you get and the farther you travel should make the coverage that much more compelling. Don't think the coverage is only for the wild and dangerous. It shouldn't take a car accident in Senegal; it could be a rancid taco in Mexico or a burst appendix in Aruba to make you call in a dust-off.

American Red Cross
National Headquarters
17th and D Street, N.W.
Washington, D.C. 20006
☎ *(202) 737-8300*
For 115 years, whenever there has been a disaster or war, these folks have been on the scene knee-deep in bandages, blood and cots, helping the injured and consoling those who have just lost everything in a disaster. They always have a need for volunteers, partic-

ularly people with medical and technical skills. If you can't volunteer your time or skills, blood donors are always needed.

Anca De Jica

Worldwide Operations Manager
International SOS Assistance
15 Rue Lombard,
1205 Geneva, Switzerland
☎ *22-347-6161*
FAX 22-347-6172

Médecin Sans Frontière

Amsterdam
FAX 20-205 170
Equilibre Association L01 1901
France
☎ *[72] (73) 04-14*

This medical-aid assistance organization goes into countries where no one else will dare. They provide essential medical services to war victims and countries in transition for whom medical care would be nonexistent without their services. Emergency kits are provided in large part through donations from large corporations. Doctors and medical technicians are recruited from all over the world.

Medico International

Frankfurt, Germany
☎ *[49] (69) 94-43-80*

Healthcare Abroad

243 Church Street, N.W.
Suite 100-D
Vienna, Virginia 22180
☎ *(800) 237-6615, (703) 281-9500*

Political and World Affairs

CIA World Factbook

An accurate if frumpy look at 250-odd countries of the world. Covers government statistics and economics. Order from U.S. Government Information Office.

Superintendent of Documents

P.O. Box 371954
Pittsburgh, Pennsylvania 15250-7954
☎ *(202) 512-1800*
FAX (202) 512-2250

État des Drogues, Drogue des États

Hachette ISBN 2 01 278701 0
A 322-page, annually updated guide to the world of illegal drugs from the Geopolitical Observatory of Drugs in Paris.

This unique guide breaks down the world of illicit drugs into three levels of intensity. It provides a country-by-country analysis of the global drug trade. With 63 sections on individual countries. Identifies "narco states" such as Myanmar, states under the influence like Colombia, and "fragile states" like Italy where corruption as a result of drug trafficking is a problem.

National Institute of Standards and Technology (NIST)

$32, on disc $140
The CIA/KGB fact book is also available on CD-ROM from Compton New Media for $40.

Pinkerton Risk Assessment Services

200 N. Glebe Road
Suite 1011
Arlington, Virginia 22203-3728

☎ *(703) 525-6111*
FAX (703) 525-2454
Pinkerton provides risk assessments of over 200 countries on-line or in person. Some are in-depth, and some are simply rehashes of outdated State Department info. They offer access to a database of over 55,000 terrorists' actions and daily updated reports on security threats. The nontechie can order printed publications that range from daily risk-assessment briefings to a monthly newsletter. Their services are not cheap, but then again, how much is your life worth? Annual subscription to the on-line service starts at about $7000, and you can order various risk and advisory reports that run from $200–$700 each. Pinkerton's can still get down and dirty with counterterrorism programs, hostage negotiators, crisis management and Travel Security seminars.

The service is designed for companies who send their employees overseas or need to know what is going on. Some reports are mildly macabre, with their annual report–like graphs of maimings, killings, assaults and assassinations. Others are downright enlightening. In any case, Pinkerton does an excellent job of bringing together the world's most unpleasant information and providing it to you in concise, intelligent packages.

Reporters Sans Frontières Annual Report

John Libbey & Co. Ltd.
13 Smiths Yard
Summerley Street
London SW18 4HR
☎ *[44] (181) 947 2777, FAX [44] (181) 947 2664*
This fact-filled book covers the state of freedom of the press in every country in the world and tells you the scoop on what to expect in the way of murders and disappearances, arrest, imprisonment and torture, threats and harassment, administrative, legal or economic pressure and obstacles to the international free flow of information. It is an exhaustive, informative and obviously self-serving reference book that should be required reading for every traveling journalist.

I.B. Tauris

c/o St. Martins Press
257 Park Avenue South
18th Floor
New York, New York 10010
☎ *(212) 982-3900*
FAX (212) 777-6359
I.B. Tauris is an English publisher who specializes in political and nontraditional books on world affairs. Their coverage of the Middle East, Balkan region and the religion of Islam is excellent. Titles like *A Modern History of the Kurds*, *The Making of the Arab-Israeli Conflict* and *Violence and Diplomacy in Lebanon* are useful reference guides. They also publish books on Yemen, Turkey, Jordan, Algeria, Pakistan, Iran, Syria and Albania. Books on assassins, gypsies, mythology, politics, war and Africa are a great addition to the politically astute reader's library.

Understanding Global Issues

FREEPOST GL496
The Runnings
Cheltenham, England GL51 9BR
☎ *[44] (242) 245252*
FAX [44] (242) 224137
UGI publishes 10 minibriefings (18–22 pages) that range from *The Kurds, Caught Between Two Nations* to *The Rubbish Mountain, Tackling Europe's Waste*. The almost monthly mailings are well illustrated, somewhat simplistic (which, in this case, is good), politically unaligned and an ideal overview of the world's global issues. Although it is published by a German schoolbook company, the teenage-level presentation, complete with charts, graphs, maps and photos, does provide an easy entry point into complex social issues.

An annual subscription (10 issues) is £22.50; back issues are £2.50. You can order your binder for £4.95.

The World Bank

1818 H Street, N.W.
Washington, D.C. 20433
☎ *(202) 473-2941*
The World Bank can provide you with some interesting information on world population projections, saving the rain forest, health care, literacy and general information on global financial topics. Although this agency has been blamed for many of the world's woes by financing large mining, development and dam projects, it would be best to understand why they are so busy developing the world while some ecologists are busy trying to undevelop it.

The World's Statistics on CD-ROM

DSI Data Service & Information
CD-ROM Department
Post Office Box 1127
D-47476 Rheinberg, Germany
☎ *[49] (28) 43 3220*
FAX [49] (28) 43 3230
or
American Overseas Book Company
550 Walnut Street
Norwood, New Jersey 07648
☎ *(201) 767-7600*
Number crunchers can pig out with statistics from the United Nations and Europe, even census information from a variety of countries. The information is very expensive but worth it for those who make their living by knowing the right numbers. Relevant titles would be *International Statistical Yearbook* (DM 5000), *World Climate Disc* (DM 2300), *United Nations* (on CD-ROM contains over one million entries for all countries and regions of the world) and the CD *Atlas of France* (DM 2600).

Organizations

The American Society for Industrial Security (ASIS)

FAX (703)-243-4954
They hold three-day meetings where topics ranging from terrorism, espionage and neo-Nazism are discussed.

Committee To Protect Journalists (CPJ)

333 Seventh Avenue, 12th Floor
New York, New York 10001
☎ *(212) 465-1004*
This group defends the rights of journalists worldwide. Their mission is to promote freedom of the press throughout the world by defending the right of journalists to report the news without fear of reprisal. CPJ's professional staff based in New York City includes an area specialist for each region of the world. These specialists track press conditions through independent research, reports from the field and fact-finding missions. The Committee's activities are directed by a board of prominent U.S. journalists. The committee's activities are funded entirely by donations from journalists, news organizations and foundations. CPJ also publishes a database of local journalist contacts around the world as well as practical safety guides offering advice to journalists on dangerous assignments. Membership is $35 per year.

Control Risks Group

8200 Greensboro Drive
Suite 1010
McLean, Virginia 22102
☎ *(703) 893-0083*

FAX (703) 893-8611

Employment Conditions Abroad

Anchor House, 15 Britten Street
London SW3 3TY
☎ *[44] (71) 351-7151*
FAX [44] (71) 351-9396

Organization Resources Counselors

Rockefeller Center
1211 Avenue of the Americas
New York, New York 10036
☎ *(212) 719-3400*
FAX (212) 398-1358

Reporters Sans Frontieres

5 rue Geoffroy-Marie
Paris, France
☎ *[33] 144-838-484*
RSF was founded in 1985 and has offices in Belgium, Canada, France, Germany, Italy, Spain and Switzerland with members in 71 countries. Their job is to defend imprisoned journalists and press around the world. Their annual report, available for $US20, covers 152 countries and offers tips for journalists working in dangerous countries.They will send protest letters and provide lawyers (if possible) and other forms of assistance to reporters in jail.

Travel Assistance International

1133 15th Street, N.W.
Suite 400
Washington, DC 20005
☎ *(800) 821-2828, (202) 331-1609*

Travmed

Post Office Box 10623
Baltimore, Maryland 21285
☎ *(800) 732-5309*

World Care Travel Assistance

1150 South Olive Street, Suite T-2233
Los Angeles, California 90015
☎ *(800) 253-1877*

Security/Hostage Negotiations

Pinkerton Risk Assessment Services

1600 Wilson Boulevard
Suite 901
Arlington, Virginia 22209
☎ *(703) 525-6111*
FAX (703) 525-2454
Once on the trail of bank robbers in the Wild West, Pinkerton has gone global and high-tech. Today, you can get risk assessments of over 200 countries on-line or in person. They offer access to a database of over 55,000 terrorists' actions and daily updated reports on security threats. The non-techie can order printed publications that range from daily risk-assessment briefings to a monthly newsletter. Their services are not cheap, but then again, how much is your life worth? Annual subscription to the on-line service starts at about $7000, and you can order various risk and advisory reports that run from $200–$700 each. Pinkerton's can still get down and dirty with counterterrorism programs, hostage negotiators, crisis management and travel security seminars.

The service is designed for companies that send their employees overseas or need to know what is going on. Some reports are mildly macabre, with their annual report–like graphs of maimings, killings assaults and assassinations. Others are downright enlightening. In any case, Pinkerton does an excellent job of bringing together the world's most unpleasant information and providing it to you in concise, intelligent packages.

Political Risk Services

6320 Fly Road
P.O. Box 248
East Syracuse, New York 13057
☎ *(315)431-0511*
FAX (315) 431-0200

Providing international, political, economic and business risk assessments, this company offers forecasts for 148 countries. They claim to be politically and economically non-plussed and employ a network of 250 experts on various countries who provide input for the reports. The series of reports are designed to provide many levels of information, including political stability, investment and trade restrictions, AND economic forecasts, and are also available on CD-ROM. A 50-page printed report on one country costs US$325. Two or more reports are $250 each. CD-ROM are available by region for $2000, or you may purchase a CD with condensed reports on hundreds of countries. A monthly 14-page newsletter summary of the latest forecasts is available for $435 per year. A 450-page bound volume, published twice each year, summarizes the current forecasts for 100 countries from all country reports and executive reports. Extensive tables compare and analyze global and regional rankings. Rates are $350 for one volume or $545 for a one-year, two-issue subscription.

Seitlin & Company Insurance

2001 N.W. 107th Avenue
Suite 200 Miami Florida 33172
☎ *(305) 591-0090*
FAX (305) 593-6993

Providers of insurance for Kidnaping, Recovery and Prevention

The Travel Watch

A new, free travel service is available to warn about crime, medical concerns and even such hazards as missing manhole covers (stolen by the thousands in Beijing to be sold as scrap metal). The reports are compiled from about 270 cities in 89 countries (including the United States). The Travel Watch is produced and distributed by Kroll Associates, a firm offering security and "risk-assessment" to corporate clients. The reports fill one 8-by-11-inch page and are delivered to the computers of about 29,000 travel-agency clients of SABRE, one of the industry's principal electronic reservation systems. Within the first two weeks of offering the reports in June, Kroll Travel Watch reported about 10,000 requests. The reports are free through travel agency requests. For more information or a Travel Watch for your destination, contact your travel agent.

Security Paraphernalia

Counter Spy Shop of Mayfair London

360 Madison Avenue
6th Floor
New York, New York 10022
☎ *(212) 557-3040*
FAX (212) 983-1278

The ideal upscale store for the paranoid. Counter Spy sells a variety of gizmos that will put you back in control of your life. Start by securing your phone lines from tapping, bullet proofing your car and body from terrorist attacks, and even use a voice stress analyzer to see if your spouse is really working late.

For those who never imagined how easy it is for other people to eavesdrop, attack, bug, tail, photograph, track and rob, they offer two videos. The videos are catalogs that provide background and information on intercepting faxes, sniffing out bombs, booby trapping your valuables, and even scrambling your phone messages.

The videos also give a little insight on how you can be tracking, bugging, snooping and checking up on all those people you know are out to get you before they get you. Counter Spy has retail outlets in London, Mexico City, New York, Beverly Hills, Miami and Washington as well.

Tape One (cellular and fax intercept, night vision systems, video and audio surveillance, bulletproof vests, tracking systems and miniature transmitters) is $89.00, and tape two (telephone stress analyzers, hidden recorders, data encryption, audio recorders, bulletproof cars, lie detection and digital tracking systems) is $79.00, and both are available in English, Spanish, Russian, French and Arabic. You can deduct the cost of the tape from your first purchase.

You can also order brochures and information by calling the following other companies:

Executive Protection Products Inc.

1325 Imola Avenue West
#504S
Napa, California 94559
☎ *(707) 253-7142*
FAX (707) 253-7149
Need another source for spy and surveillance gizmos at discount prices? How about a pinhole video camera system for only $2500?

Fuji Safety

P.O. Box 190430
San Francisco, California 94119
☎ *(415) 677-5140*
The place to go for a Fuji escape mask guaranteed to provide helpful protection from smoke and harmful fumes.

International Medcom

7497 Kennedy Road
Sebastopol, California 95472
☎ *(707)823-0336*
The Radalert Nuclear Reaction Monitor contains a beeper that sounds when radiation reaches "alert" level ($290).

Magellan Systems

960 Overland Court
San Dimas, California 91773
☎ *(909) 394-5000*
The Trailblazer Satellite Navigator ($400) picks up signals from 21 satellites. The global positioning system can pinpoint your location anywhere in the world. A mere $8000 will get you a communications system the size of a portable computer that will enable you to send faxes, e-mail or voice messages via Inmarsat-M satellites.

Quark Research Group

537 Third Avenue
New York, New York 10016
(212)889-1809
Budding spies and undercover types will find bulletproof umbrellas ($2500), Kiss of Death lipsticks ($39 and a blade pops up instead of lip color) and other James Bond–inspired paraphernalia here.

Romero Close, CAFOD

Stockwell Road
London, SW9 9TY
☎ *[44] 171-733-900*
Run For Your Life is a board game for those who want to experience the life of a refugee. The object of the game is to get from your village to the refugee camp while dodging

obstacles along the way, such as land mines and artillery attacks. Send US$12.50 to the address above or call for more information.

Spy Supply, Inc.

1212 Boylston Street
#120 Chestnut Hill, Massachusetts 02167
☎ *(305) 340-0579, (617) 327-7272*
Specialists in phone systems. They can program two phones to one number.

Tele-Adapt

☎ *(408) 370-5105*
FAX (408) 370-5110
UK +44 (0) 81-421-4444
Adaptors for U.S. phone plugs to foreign plugs.

Health and Safety

Adventure Link, Inc.

Post Office Box 510434
Melbourne Beach, Florida 32951
☎ *(407) 724-5368*
Oceanese waterproof reference cards provide medical information on how to treat injuries from marine animals. They also have illustrations of animals for easy identification and avoidance. The information is sparse but could save your life. There is one card for the Atlantic and another for the Pacific; they run $4.95 each.

American Society of Tropical Medicine and Hygiene

6436 31st St. N.W.
Washington, D.C. 20015-2342
☎ *(301) 496-6721*
Ask for *Health Hints for the Tropics.*

Centers for Disease Control and Prevention

1600 Clifton Road, N.E.
Atlanta, Georgia 30333
☎ *(404) 639-3311*
The Centers for Disease Control in Atlanta maintains the international travelers hot line at ☎ *404-332-4559.*

Citizens Emergency Center

☎ *202-647-5225*
U.S. State Department Consular Information Sheets and Travel Warnings may be heard anytime by dialing the Citizens Emergency Center using a touch tone phone, or by contacting any of the 13 regional passport agencies, field offices of the U.S. Department of Commerce and U.S. embassies and consulates abroad, or by writing and sending a self-addressed, stamped envelope to the Bureau of Consular Affairs.

The Citizens Emergency Center maintains a travel notice on HIV/AIDS entry requirements. Call to obtain these requirements. A number of countries require foreign visitors to be tested for the AIDS virus as a requirement for entry. This applies mostly to those planning to reside overseas. Before traveling, check the latest entry requirements with the foreign embassy of the country to be visited.

Foreign Entry Requirements

A listing of foreign entry requirements is available for 50 cents from the Consumer Information Center, *Pueblo, Colorado 81009.*

Directory of Medical Specialists

The authoritative reference is published for the American Board of Medical Specialists and its 22 certifying member boards; it contains detailed information on physicians abroad. This publication should be available in your local library. If abroad, a list of hospitals and physicians can be obtained from the nearest American embassy or consulate.

Emergency Medical Payment/Information Services

Available to American Express:

1) A directory of *U.S. Certified Doctors Abroad* (price: $3.00).

2) A health insurance plan is available through the Firemens Fund Life Insurance Company, *1600 Los Gamos Road, San Raphael, California 94911.* Attention: American Express Card Service.

Health Information for International Travelers

By the Centers for Disease Control; ☎ *(404) 639-3311.*
Publication No. HHS-CDC 90-8280 ($6.00 each) is an annual global rundown of disease and immunization advice and other health guidance, including risks in particular countries; may also be obtained from the Government Printing Office.

IAMAT International Association for Medical Assistance to Travelers

736 Center Street
Lewiston, New York 14092
☎ *716-754-4883*
A medical directory, clinical record and a malaria-risk chart are sent without charge; however, a contribution is requested for World Climate Charts.

Immunization Alert

P.O. Box 406
Storrs, Connecticut 06268
☎ *203-487-0611*
For $25, a traveler is provided with an up-to-date, detailed and personalized health report on up to six countries to be visited. It will tell you what diseases are prevalent and what precautions are recommended or advisable.

The following are vendors that can supply non-FDA-approved drugs. Remember, it is best to use Federal Express to ship drugs.

Medical Sea Pak Company

1880 Ridge Road East
Suite 4
Rochester, New York 14622
☎ *(800) 832-6054*
Most first-aid kits are great for homes and construction sites, but what about for divers? How about Sea Paks, a selection of four different kits for divers? The largest is the $900, 30-pound Trans Ocean Pak and the smallest is the Day Pak, a seven-pound, 15"x 6"x 3"day pack with instruction booklet.

U.S. Assist

Two Democracy Center
Suite 800
6903 Rockledge Drive
Bethesda, Maryland 20817
☎ *(301) 214-8200*
FAX (301) 214-8205
Since 1988, U.S. Assist has been the American headquarters of the SFA Group, a world leader in assistance services based in Paris, France. A network of 14 operating centers includes Washington, D.C., Paris, Hong Kong, Mexico City, Buenos Aires, Sao Paulo, Milan, Barcelona, Lisbon, Munich, Cardiff, Brussels, Stockholm and Taipei. The company assists travelers with a variety of medical, financial and legal services. It offers 24-hour service every day of the year and is accessible worldwide. A network of 54,000 agents and correspondents cover more than 210 countries. The multilingual staff speak 40 languages. The company's newest product for travelers is a MedData card, a wallet-sized card with a microfiche of an individual's medical history. It can easily be read with a magnifying glass. Other products available include medical kits, vaccination recommendations, site surveys, predeparture packages and city profiles.

International Travel Health Guides

Travel Medicine

351 Pleasant Street
Suite 312
North Hampton, MA 01060
☎ *(800) 872-8633, (413) 584-0381*
An annualy updated guide that is much more comprehensive and far more useful than the government info. It is 456 pages, updated annually and costs $25.95. *DP's* favorite pick for health advice.

Health and Safety Information

National Safety Council

Accident Facts
Customer Service
1121 Spring Lake Drive
Itasca, Illinois 60143
☎ *(708) 285-1121*
Every year the National Safety Council adds up all the dead bodies, severed limbs, infections, etc., and puts together a 115-page guide to what's dangerous in America. It is good reading for people who worry about bacon causing cancer or just how dangerous flying is.

Security Intelligence Report

More than 25 specialists on terrorism come together to create a reference book on misery. SRI is a biweekly newsletter concentrating on terrorism and security issues and provides coverage of terrorism, bombs, crisis management, forensics, civil disorder and other fields The book is divided into six sections. It provides an overview of terrorism, Middle East assassinations, terrorism financing, and aviation security. The book also addresses trends and has in-depth coverage of security issues affecting the U.S. There is a section on executive protection, disguised weapons, assassination devices, information protection and forensics.The expanded information on explosive devices, bombing incidents and tactics, vehicle and mail bombs and other topics alone makes the publication worth the price. The back end provides data on 1600 incidents that occurred around the world and a listing of dates significant to terrorist groups—such as dates of attacks and independence anniversaries.

Insurance

The following companies provide international travel insurance to travelers who live in the U.S. (Because of varying insurance regulations, Canadian policies differ.)

Access America Intl
☎ *(800) 284-8300*

American Express
☎ *(800) 756-2639*

Berkeley Carefree
☎ *(800) 323-3149*

CSA
☎ *(800) 348-9505*

Global Emergency Medical Services
☎ *(800) 249-2533*

Health Care Abroad
☎ *(800) 237-6615, (540) 687-3166*

International SOS Assistance
☎ *(800) 523-8930*

Travel Guard
☎ *(800) 826-1300*

Travel Insurance Service
☎ *(800) 937-1387*

The Travelers
☎ *(800) 243-3174*

Worldwide Assistance
☎ *(800) 821-2828*

The Web

If you have been incarcerated or shipwrecked for the last few years you might be the only person who doesn't know that the Web is the hottest thing out there for those with a fast (28,800) modem and a computer. Cruising the Web is like browsing through the world's largest magazine newstand except you don't have to pay for most of the info out there. Keep in mind that this is the golden age of the Web because many info-rich corporations are experimenting with putting their "content" on line. For now there is a wealth of information available to anyone who can stand the phone bill and has the patience to watch funky little graphics download. Any estimate of how many web sites there are is outdated—right now there are over 55,158,536 million web sites from tiny geek pages to massive online ventures from Microsoft.

A few tips from DP on using the Web for info.

•**Start with a major web searcher that searches content. We always start with excite (http://www.excite.com) or Lycos (http://six.srv.lycos.com/lycs-inc./index.html) to search for keywords. We usually get about 10 - 3000 choices. You can find non web sources by using Nlightn (http://www.nlightn.com) An excellent search tool for books and other sources.**

• **Use your bookmark function to build a library of other indexers and esoteric sites.**

• **Don't be surprised if you get dumped back in the same old web sites. For example just about every web site likes to puff up their site by linking you back to the CIA World Factbook.**

• **Send e-mail and ask. I am surprised how many responses you can get if you ask a succinct answerable question such as "Do you have a list of web sites for Afghanistan?" as opposed to "what is your opinion on the recent tri-party political structure in Kabul?"**

• **Send good links to your favorite links. This way everyone benefits.**

• **Turn graphic downloading off. We have yet to see any graphics that have enhanced our information. Eye candy is great for movie intros and newscasts but sitting for 2 minutes while a background page or a sponsor loads art is a waste of time.**

Dangerous Web Sites

http://www.nsi.org

An excellent starting point for intelligence and security informaton from everyone from the Mossad to the Canadian Security Intelligence Service.

The Security Resource Net is devoted exclusively to the needs of individuals with an interest in security—featuring a daily news service, computer alerts, travel advisories, personal security tips, a directory of products and services, and access to an extensive virtual security library.

National Security Institute
57 East Main Street, Suite 217
Westborough, MA 01581
☎ *508-366-5800*
FAX: 508-898-0132
infoctr✩nsi.org

http://www.capital.net.com

Another gathering point for resources on spying, intelligence and terrorism info. They even have a classified section for those looking for a job in intel-land.The IWR Intelligence Employment Service helps companies looking for individuals with security experience. Companies can list openings for $75 per position for two months and individuals can post resume information for $25 for two months.

http://www.awpi.com

The Intelligence Watch Reports site has a handy country by country index that also includes the latest CIA factbook updates as well as cross indexed information on security updates.

http://www.imex.com

International Export Import Business Exchange has some practical info for business travel and web links.

http://www.accessasia

A gathering of web sites on Asia. It takes a little searching to find the good ones but it is worth the trouble.

http://www.cdc.com

The Center for Disease Control in Atlanta has the information you normally get in their printed or fax info.

http://www.icrc.org/

The International Committeee of the Red Cross provides background on their organization in French and English as well as a search engine.

http://www.economist.com

The magazine of the same name and a chance to have information sent to you by subscription.

http://www.fbi.gov

The G-Men dish out the same old tired and officious info on crime and terrorism.

http://www.sofmag.com

Soldier of Fortune Magazine online.

http://www.suul.st.no/~cyrinus/ltte/vol101.html

The Tamil Tigers home page out of London. Mostly one sided press releases.

http://www.actlab.utexas.edu/~zapatistas/index.html

This is what happens when trendy students meet trendy revolutionary movements. Tons of graphics complete with revolutionary icons and slow to load graphics. As they say: "The Revolution Will Be Digitized!"

http://www.vtek.chalmers.se:80/~v93saeid/kurdistan.html

A link site for information on Kurdistan and the Kurds.

http://www.xs4all.nl/~covert/index/html

Pretty chunky information on the PKK, Kurdistan and the Kurdish Information Network.

http://www.ib.be/med

Web site for the Kurdish Television Station in London

http://wmbr.mit.edu/stations/list.html

An indexed list of Radio stations that broadcast on the Internet

http://frankenstein/worldweb.net/afghan/Taliban

One of the most comprehensive sites we have cruised. In depth usable information that gets as useless as a five day weather report for Kabul (early morning low clouds with slight chance of rockets in the afternoon), addresses for the Taliban, music clips and very useful links.

http://www.mynet/~msanews/Launchpad/hamas.html

A resourse page on Hamas from the Islamic News center with articles and background information on Hamas.

http://medic.dickenson.edu/russian/chechen.html

Good background on the Chechen peoples and their side of the Chechen conflict.

http://sun.aacc.cc.md.us/~haq/chech/mujahid.html

A sort of "Chechen Lite" site. You won't find anything meaty here. Just the flag, music clips, pictures of Raduyev (before his plastic surgery), field commanders and that's about it for now.

http://www.imran.com/newspapers/Kashmir_News.html

Daily updated newspapers from Pakistan with a special section on Kashmir.

http://www.sile.gmu.edu./~cdibona/index.html

Terrorist Profiles (usually from the outdated State Department files)

http://link.lanic.utexas.edu/menic/oil/game/simulation/profiles/1996/0031.html

A bizarre way to get some of the most complete information DP has seen on terrorist and political groups. As far as we can tell these are profiles to help in war and political simua-lation games. The information the GIA and HAMAS shows that somebody has been doing their homework at the U of T.

Presented without comment or endorsement but our readers waste plenty of time on sites like these:

http://www.mediafilter.org/MFF/USDCO.idx

http://www.paranoia.com

http://www.sysnews.com/personal/octopus.html

http://www.efn.orgl~marc/hotlist/covert.html

Visas and Entry Requirements

VISAS AND ENTRY REQUIREMENTS

IMPORTANT: THIS LISTING IS PREPARED FROM INFORMATION OBTAINED FROM THE STATE DEPARTMENT AND FOREIGN EMBASSIES PRIOR TO PUBLICATION. THIS INFORMATION IS SUBJECT TO CHANGE. CHECK ENTRY REQUIREMENTS WITH THE CONSULAR OFFICIALS OF THE COUNTRIES TO BE VISITED WELL IN ADVANCE.

Passports

U.S. citizens who travel to a country where a valid passport is not required will need documentary evidence of their U.S. citizenship and identity. Proof of U.S. citizenship includes an expired passport, a certified (original) birth certificate, Certificate of Naturalization, Certificate of Citizenship, or Report of Birth Abroad of a Citizen of the United States. To prove identity, a valid driver's license or government identification card are acceptable, provided they identify you by physical description or photograph. However, for travel overseas and to facilitate reentry into the U.S., a valid U.S. passport is the best documentation available and it unquestionably proves your U.S. citizenship.

Some countries require that your passport be valid at least six months beyond the date of your trip. If your passport expires before the required validity, you will have to apply for a new one. Please check with the embassy or nearest consulate of the country you plan to visit for their requirements.

Some Arab or African countries will not issue visas or allow entry if your passport indicates travel to Israel or South Africa. Consult the nearest U.S. passport agency for guidance if this applies to you.

A visa is an endorsement or stamp placed by officials of a foreign country on a U.S. passport that allows the bearer to visit that foreign country. VISAS SHOULD BE OBTAINED BEFORE PROCEEDING ABROAD. Allow sufficient time for processing your visa application, especially if you are applying by mail. Most foreign consular representatives are located in principal cities, and, in many instances, a traveler may be required to obtain visas from the consular office in the area of his/her residence. The addresses of foreign consular offices in the United States may be obtained by consulting the Congressional Directory in the library. IT IS THE RESPONSIBILITY OF THE TRAVELER TO OBTAIN VI-

SAS, WHERE REQUIRED, FROM THE APPROPRIATE EMBASSY OR NEAREST CONSULATE OF THE COUNTRY YOU ARE PLANNING TO VISIT.

Immunizations

Under the International Health Regulations adopted by the World Health Organization, a country may require International Certificates of Vaccination against yellow fever. A cholera immunization may be required if you are traveling from an infected area. Check with health care providers or your records to ensure other immunizations (e.g., tetanus and polio) are up to date. Prophylactic medication for malaria and certain other preventive measures are advisable for travel to some countries. No immunizations are required to return to the United States. Detailed health information is included in *Health Information for International Travel*, available from the U.S. Government Printing Office for $6.50 or obtained from your local health department or physician or by calling the Centers for Disease Control at ☎ *(404) 332-4559.*

An increasing number of countries have established regulations regarding AIDS testing, particularly for long-term visitors. Although many are listed in the chart that follows, check with the embassy or consulate of the country you plan to visit to verify if this is a requirement for entry.

All international flights are subject to U.S. Immigration and U.S. Customs fees paid in advance as part of your ticket. In addition, many countries have departure fees that are sometimes collected at the time of ticket purchase.

Entry Information for Foreign Countries

COUNTRY	ENTRY
AFGHANISTAN	Passport and visa required. No tourist or business visas are being issued at this time. For further information, contact the Embassy of the Republic of Afghanistan, *2341 Wyoming Avenue, N.W., Washington, D.C. 20008,* ☎ *(202) 234-3770/1.*
ALBANIA	Passport required. a Visa is not necessary for a stay up to 30 days. For further information, contact the Embassy of the Republic of Albania at *1150 18th Street N.W., Washington, D.C. 20036,* ☎ *(202) 223-4942.*
ALGERIA	Passport and visa required. Obtain visa before arrival. Visa valid up to 90 days, requires two application forms, two photos, proof of onward/return transportation, sufficient funds and $22 fee (money order or certified check). Company letter (plus one copy) required for business visa. Visa not granted to passports showing Israeli visas. Enclose prepaid self-addressed envelope for return of passport by registered, certified or express mail. For currency regulations and other information, contact the Consular Section of the Embassy of the Democratic and Popular Republic of Algeria, *2137 Wyoming Avenue, N.W., Washington, D.C. 20008,* ☎ *(202) 265-2800.*
ANDORRA	(See France.)
ANGOLA	Passport and visa required. Tourist/business visas require an application form, letter stating purpose of travel, and two color photos. Applications by mail require prepaid return envelope. Yellow fever and cholera immunizations required. For additional information, contact the Embassy of Angola, *1899 L Street, N.W., 6th Floor, Washington, D.C. 20036,* ☎ *(202) 785-1156),* or the Permanent Mission of the Republic of Angola to the U.N., *125 East 73rd Street, New York, NY 10021,* ☎ *(212) 861-5656.*
ANTIGUA AND BARBUDA	Proof of U.S. citizenship required, return/onward ticket and/or proof of funds needed for tourist stay up to six months. AIDS test required for immigrant, student and work visas. U.S. test accepted. Check with the Embassy of Antigua and Barbuda, *Suite 4M, 3400 International Drive, N.W., Washington, D.C. 20008,* ☎ *(202) 362-5122/ 5166/5211,* for further information.
ARGENTINA	Passport required. Visa not required for tourist stay up to three months. Business visa requires company letter detailing purpose of trip and length of stay. For more information, contact the Argentine Embassy, *1600 New Hampshire Avenue, N.W., Washington, D.C. 20009,* ☎ *(202) 939-6400* or the nearest consulate: CA ☎ *(213) 739-5959* and ☎ *(415) 982-3050,* FL ☎ *(305) 373-1889,* IL ☎ *(312) 263-7435,* LA ☎ *(504) 523-2823,* NY ☎ *(212) 603-0415,* PR ☎ *(809) 754-6500* or TX ☎ *(713) 871-8935.*
ARMENIA	Passport and visa required. For additional information, contact the Consular Section of the Embassy of Armenia, *122 C Street, N.W., Suite 360, Washington, D.C. 20001,* ☎ *(202) 393-5983.*
ARUBA	Passport or proof of U.S. citizenship required. Visa not required for stay up to 14 days, extendable to 90 days after arrival. Proof of onward/return ticket or sufficient funds for stay may be required. Departure tax $9.50. For further information, consult the Embassy of the Netherlands ☎ *(202) 244-5300,* or nearest Consulate General: CA ☎ *(212) 380-3440,* IL ☎ *(314) 856-1429,* NY ☎ *(212) 246-1429* or TX ☎ *(713) 622-8000.*

VISAS AND ENTRY REQUIREMENTS

COUNTRY	ENTRY

VISAS AND ENTRY REQUIREMENTS

AUSTRALIA

Passport, visa and onward/return transportation required. Transit visa not necessary for up to eight-hour stay at airport. Visitor visa valid one year for multiple entries up to three months, no charge, requires one application and one photo. Applications for a stay of longer than three months or with a validity longer than one year, require fee of $25 (U.S.). Need company letter for business visa. Departure tax, $20 (Australian), paid at airport. Minors not accompanied by parent require notarized copy of the child's birth certificate and notarized written parental consent from both parents. AIDS test required for permanent resident visa applicants age 15 and over; U.S. test accepted. Send prepaid envelope for return of passport by mail. Allow three weeks for processing. For further information, contact the Embassy of Australia, *1601 Massachusetts Avenue, N.W., Washington, D.C. 20036,* ☎ *(800) 242-2878 or (202) 797-3145* or the nearest Consulate General: CA ☎ *(213) 469-4300* or *(415) 362-6160*, HI ☎ *(808) 524-5050*, NY ☎ *(212) 245-4000* or TX ☎ *(713) 629-9131.*

AUSTRIA

Passport required. Visa not required for stay up to three months. For longer stays, check with the Embassy of Austria, *3524 International Court, N.W., Washington, D.C. 20008,* ☎ *(202) 895-6767,* or nearest Consulate General: Los Angeles ☎ *(310) 444-9310*, Chicago ☎ *(312) 222-1515* or New York ☎ *(212) 737-6400.*

AZERBAIJAN

Passport and visa required. Visa (no charge) requires one application form, one photo and a letter of invitation. For additional information, contact the Embassy of the Federal Republic of Azerbaijan, *927 15th Street, N.W., Suite 700, Washington, D.C. 20005,* ☎ *(202) 842-0001.*

AZORES

(See Portugal.)

BAHAMAS

Proof of U.S. citizenship, photo ID and onward/return ticket required for stay up to eight months. Passport and residence/work permit needed for residence and business. Permit required for firearms and to import pets. Departure tax of $15 must be paid at airport. For further information, call the Embassy of the Commonwealth of the Bahamas, *2220 Massachusetts Avenue, N.W., Washington, D.C. 20008,* ☎ *(202) 319-2660* or nearest Consulate: Miami ☎ *(305) 373-6295* or New York ☎ *(212) 421-6420.*

BAHRAIN

Passport and visa required. No tourist visas issued at this time. Transit visa available upon arrival for stay up to 72 hours; must have return/onward ticket. Business, work, or resident visas valid for three months, single-entry, require one application form, one photo, letter from company or No Objection Certificate (NOC) from Immigration Department in Bahrain and $30 fee ($20 for bearer of NOC). Yellow fever vaccination needed if arriving from infected area. Send SASE for return of passport by mail. For departure tax and other information, contact the Embassy of the State of Bahrain, *3502 International Drive, N.W., Washington, D.C. 20008,* ☎ *(202) 342-0741,* or the Permanent Mission to the U.N., *2 United Nations Plaza, East 44th Street, New York, NY 10017* ☎ *(212) 223-6200.*

BANGLADESH

Passport, visa and onward/return ticket required. Tourist/business visa requires two application forms, two photos. Business visa also requires company letter. For longer stays and more information, consult the Embassy of the People's Republic of Bangladesh, *2201 Wisconsin Avenue, N.W., Washington, D.C. 20007,* ☎ *(202) 342-8373.*

BARBADOS

U.S. tourists traveling directly from the U.S. to Barbados may enter for up to three months stay with proof of U.S. citizenship (original or certified copy of birth certificate), photo ID and onward/return ticket. Passport required for longer visits and other types of travel. Business visas $25, single-entry and $30 multiple-entry (may require work permit). Departure tax of $25 is paid at airport. Check information with the Embassy of Barbados, *2144 Wyoming Avenue, N.W., Washington, D.C. 20008,* ☎ *(202) 939-9200,* or Consulate General in New York ☎ *(212) 867-8435.*

BELARUS

Passport and visa required. Visa requires one application form and one photo. The visa processing fee is $30 for seven working days, $60 for next day, and $100 for same day processing. (No charge for official travelers.) Transit visa is required when travelling through Belarus ($20). For additional information, contact the Embassy of Belarus, *1619 New Hampshire Avenue, N.W., Washington, D.C. 20009,* ☎ *(202) 986-1604.*

COUNTRY	ENTRY

BELGIUM
Passport required. Visa not required for business/tourist stay up to 90 days. Temporary residence permit required for longer stays. For residence authorization, consult the Embassy of Belgium, *3330 Garfield Street, N.W., Washington, D.C. 20008*, ☎ *(202) 333-6900*, or nearest Consulate General: Los Angeles ☎ *(213) 857-1244*, Atlanta ☎ *(404) 659-2150*, Chicago ☎ *(312) 263-6624* or New York ☎ *(212) 586-5110*.

BELIZE
Passport, return/onward ticket and sufficient funds required. Visa not required for stay up to 30 days. If visit exceeds one month, a stay permit must be obtained from the Immigration Authorities in Belize. AIDS test required for those staying more than three months; U.S. test accepted if within three months of visit. For longer stays and other information, contact the Embassy of Belize, *2535 Massachusetts Avenue, N.W., Washington, D.C. 20008*, ☎ *(202) 332-9636*, or the Belize Mission in New York at ☎ *(212) 599-0233*.

BENIN
Passport and visa required. Entry/transit visa for stay up to 90 days, requires $20 fee (no personal checks), two application forms, two photos, vaccination certificates for yellow fever and cholera, proof of return/onward transportation (guarantee from travel agency or photocopy of round-trip ticket) and letter of guarantee from employer. Send prepaid envelope for return of passport by certified or express mail. Apply at the Embassy of the Republic of Benin, *2737 Cathedral Avenue, N.W., Washington, D.C. 20008*, ☎ *(202) 232-6656*.

BERMUDA
Proof of U.S. citizenship, photo ID and onward/return ticket required for tourist stay up to 21 days. Departure tax of $10 is paid at airport. For further information, consult the British Embassy ☎ *(202) 986-0205*.

BHUTAN
Passport and visa required. Visa requires $20 fee, one application and two photos. Tourist visas arranged by Tourism Department and issued at entry checkpoints in Bhutan. Apply two months in advance. Yellow fever vaccination required if traveling from an infected area. For further information, call the Consulate of the Kingdom of Bhutan in New York ☎ *(212) 826-1919*.

BOLIVIA
Passport required. Visa not required for tourist stay up to 30 days. Business visa requires $50 fee and company letter explaining purpose of trip. Send SASE for return of passport by mail. AIDS test required for resident visa. U.S. test sometimes accepted. For more information, contact the Embassy of Bolivia (Consular Section), *3014 Massachusetts Avenue, N.W., Washington, D.C. 20008*, ☎ *(202) 232-4828* or *483-4410* or nearest Consulate General: San Francisco ☎ *(415) 495-5173*, Miami ☎ *(305) 358-3450*, New York ☎ *(212) 687-0530* or Houston ☎ *(713) 780-8001*. (Check special requirements for pets.)

BOSNIA AND HERZEGOVINA
Passport required. At the time of publication, Bosnia-Herzegovina entry permission is being granted at the border on a case by-case basis.

BOTSWANA
Passport required. Visa not required for stay up to 90 days. For further information, contact the Embassy of the Republic of Botswana, *Suite 7M, 3400 International Drive, N.W., Washington, D.C. 20008*, ☎ *(202) 244-4990/1*, or nearest Honorary Consulate: Los Angeles ☎ *(213) 626-8484*, San Francisco ☎ *(415) 346-4435* or Houston ☎ *(713) 622-1900*.

BRAZIL
Passport and visa required. Visa must be obtained in advance. Multiple-entry visa valid up to 90 days (extendable); requires one application form, one photo, proof of onward/return transportation, and yellow fever vaccination if arriving from infected area. No charge if you apply in person; $10 service fee if you apply by mail. Provide SASE for return of passport by mail. For travel with children or business visa, contact the Brazilian Embassy (Consular Section), *3009 Whitehaven Street, N.W., Washington, D.C. 20008*, ☎ *(202) 745-2828*, or nearest Consulate: CA ☎ *(213) 651-2664*, FL ☎ *(305) 285-6200*, IL ☎ *(312) 464-0244*, LA ☎ *(504) 588-9187* or NY ☎ *(212) 757-3080*.

BRUNEI
Passport required. Visa not required for tourist/business stay up to 90 days. Yellow fever vaccination needed if arriving from infected area. For more information, contact the Embassy of the State of Brunei Darussalam, *Suite 300, 2600 Virginia Avenue, N.W., Washington, D.C. 20037* ☎ *(202) 342-0159* or Brunei Permanent Mission to the U.N., *866 United Nations Plaza, Room 248, New York, NY 10017* ☎ *(212) 838-1600*.

COUNTRY	ENTRY
BULGARIA	Passport required. Tourist visa not required for stay up to 30 days. AIDS test may be required for those staying more than one month; U.S. test not accepted. For business visas and other information, contact the Embassy of the Republic of Bulgaria, *1621 22nd Street, N.W., Washington, D.C. 20008,* ☎ *(202) 387-7969.*
BURKINA FASO	Passport and visa required. Single-entry visa valid three months for visit up to one month, extendable; requires $20 fee, two application forms, two photos and yellow fever vaccination (cholera immunization recommended). Send passport by registered mail, and include postage or prepaid envelope for return by mail. Payment accepted in cash or money order only. For further information, call the Embassy of Burkina Faso, *2340 Massachusetts Avenue, N.W., Washington, D.C. 20008* ☎ *(202) 332-5577,* or Honorary Consulate in Decatur, GA ☎ *(404) 378-7278,* Los Angeles, CA ☎ *(213) 824-5100* or New Orleans, LA ☎ *(504) 945-3152.*
BURMA	(See Myanmar.)
BURUNDI	Passport and visa required. Obtain visa before arrival to avoid long airport delay. Multientry visa valid for two months (must be used within two months of date of issue); requires $11 fee, three application forms, three photos, yellow fever and cholera immunizations and return/onward ticket (meningitis immunization recommended). Company letter needed for business travel. Send U.S. postal money order only and SASE for return of passport by mail. For further information, consult the Embassy of the Republic of Burundi, *Suite 212, 2233 Wisconsin Avenue, N.W., Washington, D.C. 20007,* ☎ *(202) 342-2574,* or Permanent Mission of Burundi to the U.N., ☎ *(212) 687-1180.*
CAMBODIA	Passport and visa required. Airport visa valid for a 30-day stay is available upon arrival in Cambodia from the Ministry of National Security; requires $20 fee. Visas can also be obtained from a Cambodian embassy or consulate in a country which maintains diplomatic relations with Cambodia. There is no Cambodian embassy in the U.S. at this time.
CAMEROON	Passport and visa required. Obtain visa before arrival to avoid difficulty at airport. Multiple-entry tourist visa for stay up to 90 days; requires $65.22 fee, two application forms, two photos, yellow fever and cholera immunizations, proof of onward/return transportation and bank statement. If invited by family or friends, visa available for up to three months, may be extended one month. Invitation must be signed by authorities in Cameroon. Multiple-entry business visa, valid 12 months, requires company letter to guarantee financial and legal responsibility; include exact dates of travel. Enclose prepaid envelope for return of passport by registered, certified or express mail. For additional information, contact the Embassy of the Republic of Cameroon, *2349 Massachusetts Avenue, N.W., Washington, D.C. 20008,* ☎ *(202) 265-8790 to 8794.*
CANADA	Proof of U.S. citizenship and photo ID required. Visa not required for U.S. tourists entering from the U.S. for a stay up to 180 days. However, anyone with a criminal record (including a DWI charge) should contact the Canadian embassy or nearest consulate before travel. U.S. citizens entering Canada from a third country must have a valid passport. For student or business travel, check with the Canadian Embassy, *501 Pennsylvania Avenue, N.W., Washington, D.C. 20001,* ☎ *(202) 682-1740,* or nearest Consulate General: CA ☎ *(213) 687-7432* and *(415) 495-6021,* GA ☎ *(404) 577-6810,* IL ☎ *(312) 427-1031,* MA ☎ *(617) 262-3760,* MI ☎ *(313) 567-2340,* MN ☎ *(612) 333-4641,* NY ☎ *(212) 768-2400 or (716) 852-1247,* OH ☎ *(216) 771-0150,* TX ☎ *(214) 922-9806* or WA ☎ *(206) 443-1777.*
CAPE VERDE	Passport and visa required. Single-entry tourist visa (must be used within 120 days of issue); requires $11.31 fee, one application form, one photo and yellow fever immunization if arriving from infected area. Include SASE for return of passport by mail. For further information, contact the Embassy of the Republic of Cape Verde, *3415 Massachusetts Avenue, N.W., Washington, D.C. 20007,* ☎ *(202) 965-6820,* or Consulate General, *535 Boylston Street, Boston, MA 02116,* ☎ *(617) 353-0014.*
CAYMAN ISLANDS	(See West Indies, British.)
CENTRAL AFRICAN REPUBLIC	Passport and visa required. Visa must be obtained before arrival. To obtain a visa, you need two application forms, two recent photos, yellow fever immunization, onward/return ticket, SASE for return of passport by mail, and $30 fee. Company letter needed for business visa. For further information, contact the Embassy of Central African Republic, *1618 22nd Street, N.W., Washington, D.C. 20008,* ☎ *(202) 483-7800 or 7801.*

COUNTRY	ENTRY
CHAD	Passport and visa required. Transit visa valid for up to one week; requires onward ticket. Single-entry visa valid two months for tourist/business stay up to 30 days (extendable); requires $25 fee (no personal checks), yellow fever and cholera vaccinations, three application forms and three photos. For business visa, need company letter stating purpose of trip. Send prepaid envelope for registered/certified return of passport. Apply Embassy of the Republic of Chad, *2002 R Street, N.W., Washington, D.C. 20009,* ☎ *(202) 462-4009*, and check specific requirements.
CHILE	Passport required. Visa not required for stay up to three months, may be extended. For official/diplomatic travel and other information, consult the Embassy of Chile, *1732 Massachusetts Avenue, N.W., Washington, D.C. 20036,* ☎ *(202) 785-3159*, or nearest Consulate General: CA ☎ *(310) 785-0113* or *(415) 982-7662*, FL ☎ *(305) 373-8623*, PA ☎ *(215) 829-9520*, NY ☎ *(212) 980-3366*, TX ☎ *(713) 621-5853* or PR ☎ *(809) 725-6365*.
CHINA, PEOPLE'S REPUBLIC OF	Passport and visa required. Transit visa required for any stop (even if you do not exit the plane or train) in China. Visitors must show hotel reservation and letter of confirmation from the China International Travel Service (CITS) or an invitation from an individual or institution in China. CITS tours may be booked through several travel agencies and airlines in the United States and abroad and are often advertised in newspapers and magazines. Visas for tour group members are usually obtained by the travel agent as part of the tour package. Visa requires $10 fee (no personal checks), two application forms and two photos. Allow at least 10 days processing time. Medical examination required for those staying one year or longer. AIDS test required for those staying more than six months. For further information, contact the Chinese Embassy, *2300 Connecticut Avenue, N.W., Washington, D.C. 20008,* ☎ *(202) 328-2517*, or nearest Consulate General: Chicago ☎ *(312) 346-0287*, Houston ☎ *(713) 524-4311*, Los Angeles ☎ *(213) 380-2506*, New York ☎ *(212) 330-7409* or San Francisco ☎ *(415) 563-4857*.
COLOMBIA	Passport, proof of onward/return ticket, and entry permit required for tourist/business stay of up to six months. Entry permits are granted by the immigration authorities at the port of entry. Minors (under 18) traveling alone, with one parent or in someone else's custody, must present written authorization signed before a notary and authenticated by the Colombian embassy or consulate from the absent parent(s) or guardian. Persons suspected of being HIV-positive may be denied entry. For information about longer stays and business and official travel, contact the Embassy of Colombia (Consulate), *1825 Connecticut Avenue, N.W., Washington, D.C. 20009,* ☎ *(202) 332-7476*, or nearest Consulate General: CA ☎ *(213) 362-1137* or *(415) 362-0080*, FL ☎ *(305) 448-5558*, GA ☎ *(404) 237-1045*, IL ☎ *(312) 341-0658/9*, LA ☎ *(504) 525-5580*, MA ☎ *(617) 536-6222*, MI ☎ *(313) 352-4970*, MN ☎ *(612) 933-2408*, MO ☎ *(314) 991-3636*, OH ☎ *(216) 943-1200*, NY ☎ *(212) 949-9898*, PR ☎ *(809) 754-6885* or TX ☎ *(713) 527-8919*.
COMOROS ISLANDS	Passport and onward/return ticket required. Visa for up to three weeks (extendable) issued at airport upon arrival. For information, consult the Embassy of the Federal and Islamic Republic of Comoros, *336 East 45th Street, 2nd Floor, New York, NY 10017,* ☎ *(212) 972-8010*.
CONGO	Passport and visa required. Single-entry $30 or multiple-entry $50, for tourist/business stay up to three months, requires yellow fever and cholera immunizations and onward/return ticket. First-time applicants need three application forms and three photos, returning visitors need only two. For business visa must have company letter stating reason for trip. Include SASE for return of passport by mail. Letter of introduction stating reason for trip, three applications and three photos required. Apply to the Embassy of the People's Republic of the Congo, *4891 Colorado Avenue, N.W., Washington, D.C. 20011,* ☎ *(202) 726-5500*, or the Permanent Mission of the Congo to the U.N., *14 East 65th Street, New York, NY 10021* ☎ *(212) 744-7840*.
COOK ISLANDS	Passport and onward/return ticket required. Visa not needed for visit up to 31 days. For longer stays and further information, contact the Consulate for the Cook Islands, *Kamehameha Schools, #16, Kapalama Heights, Honolulu, HI 96817,* ☎ *(808) 847-6377*.

COUNTRY	ENTRY

COSTA RICA

Passport required. Travelers are sometimes admitted with (original) certified U.S. birth certificate and photo ID for tourist stay up to 90 days. Tourist card issued upon arrival at airport. U.S. citizens must have onward/return ticket. For stays over 90 days, you must apply for an extension (within the first week of visit) with Costa Rican Immigration and, after 90 days, obtain exit visa and possess a valid U.S. passport. Visitors staying over 90 days must have an AIDS test performed in Costa Rica. For travel with pets and other information, contact the Consular Section of the Embassy of Costa Rica, *1825 Connecticut Avenue, N.W., Suite 211, Washington, D.C. 20009,* ☎ *(202) 328-6628,* or nearest Consulate General: CA ☎ *(415) 392-8488,* GA ☎ *(404) 370-0555,* FL ☎ *(305) 377-4242,* IL ☎ *(312) 263-2772,* LA ☎ *(504) 467-1462,* NY ☎ *(212) 425-2620* or TX ☎ *(713) 266-0485.*

COTE D' IVOIRE

Passport required. Visa not required for stay up to 90 days. Visa $33, requires four application forms, four photos, yellow fever vaccination, onward/return ticket and financial guarantee. Include postage for return of passport by registered mail. For further information, contact the Embassy of the Republic of Cote D' Ivoire, *2424 Massachusettes Avenue, N.W., Washington, D.C. 20008,* ☎ *(202) 797-0300,* or Honorary Consulate: CA ☎ *(415) 391-0176.*

CROATIA

Passport and visa required. Visa can be obtained at port of entry. There is no charge for business or tourist visa. Check requirements with the Embassy of Croatia, *236 Massachusetts Avenue, N.E., Washington, D.C. 20002,* ☎ *(202) 543-5580 or 5586.*

CUBA

Passport and visa required. Tourist visa $26, business visa $36, valid up to six months; requires one application and photo. Send money order only and SASE for return of passport. Apply to the Cuban Interests Section, *2639 16th Street, N.W., Washington, D.C. 20009,* ☎ *(202) 797-8609 or 8518.* AIDS test required for those staying longer than 90 days. Note: U.S. citizens need a Treasury Department license in order to engage in any transactions related to travel to and within Cuba. Before planning any travel to Cuba, U.S. citizens should contact the Licensing Division, Office of Foreign Assets Control, Department of the Treasury, *1331 G Street, N.W., Washington, D.C. 20220,* ☎ *(202) 622-2480.*

CURACAO

(See Netherlands Antilles.)

CYPRUS

Passport required. Tourist/business visa issued on arrival for stay up to three months. Departure tax of $8 paid at airport. AIDS test required for certain entertainers; U.S. test accepted. For other information, consult the Embassy of the Republic of Cyprus, *2211 R Street, N.W., Washington, D.C. 20008,* ☎ *(202) 462-5772* or nearest Consulate: CA ☎ *(213) 397-0771,* LA ☎ *(504) 388-8701* or New York ☎ *(212) 686-6016.*

CZECH REPUBLIC

Passport required. Visa not required for stay up to 30 days. All foreigners must register with the proper authorities within 48 hours of arrival. For more information, contact the Embassy of the Czech Republic, *3900 Spring of Freedom Street., N.W., Washington, D.C. 20008,* ☎ *(202) 363-6315.*

DENMARK (Including GREENLAND)

Passport required. Tourist/business visa not required for stay of up to three months. (Period begins when entering Scandinavian area: Finland, Iceland, Norway, Sweden.) Special rules apply for entry into the U.S.-operated defense area in Greenland. For further information, contact the Royal Danish Embassy, *3200 Whitehaven Street, N.W., Washington, D.C. 20008,* ☎ *(202) 234-4300,* or nearest Consulate General: CA ☎ *(213) 387-4277,* Chicago ☎ *(312) 329-9644* or New York ☎ *(212) 223-4545.*

DJIBOUTI

Passport and visa required. Visas must be obtained before arrival. Single-entry visa valid for 30 days, extendable; requires $15 fee, two applications, two photos, yellow fever immunization, onward/return ticket and sufficient funds. Company letter needed for business visa. Send prepaid envelope for return of passport by registered, certified or express mail. Apply to the Embassy of the Republic of Djibouti, *1156 15th Street, N.W., Suite 515, Washington, D.C. 20005,* ☎ *(202) 331-0270,* or the Djibouti Mission to the U.N., *866 United Nations Plaza, Suite 4011, New York, NY 10017,* ☎ *(212) 753-3163.*

DOMINICA

Proof of U.S. citizenship, photo ID and return/onward ticket required for tourist stay up to six months. For longer stays and other information, consult the Consulate of the Commonwealth of Dominica, *820 2nd Avenue, Suite 900, New York, NY 10017,* ☎ *(212) 599-8478.*

COUNTRY	ENTRY
DOMINICAN REPUBLIC	Passport or proof of U.S. citizenship and tourist card or visa required. Tourist card for stay up to two months, available from consulate or from airline serving the Dominican Republic, $10 fee. Visa issued by consulate, valid up to five years, no charge. All persons must pay $10 airport departure fee. AIDS test required for residence permit. U.S. test not accepted. For business travel and other information, call the Embassy of the Dominican Republic, *1715 22nd Street, N.W., Washington, D.C. 20008,* ☎ *(202) 332-6280,* or nearest Consulate General: CA ☎ *(415) 982-5144,* FL ☎ *(305) 358-3221,* IL ☎ *(312) 772-6363,* LA ☎ *(504) 522-1007,* MA ☎ *(617) 482-8121,* NY ☎ *(212) 768-2480,* PA ☎ *(215) 923-3006* or PR ☎ *(809) 725-9550.*
ECUADOR	Passport and return/onward ticket required for stay up to three months. For additional information, contact the Embassy of Ecuador, *2535 15th Street, N.W., Washington, D.C. 20009,* ☎ *(202) 234-7166* or nearest Consulate General: CA ☎ *(213) 628-3014* or *(510) 223-2162,* FL ☎ *(305) 539-8214,* IL ☎ *(312) 329-0266,* LA ☎ *(504) 523-3229,* MA ☎ *(617) 523-2700,* MD ☎ *(301) 889-4435,* MI ☎ *(313) 332-7356,* NV ☎ *(702) 735-8193,* NY ☎ *(212) 683-0170/71,* PR ☎ *(809) 781-4408* or TX ☎ *(214) 747-6329.*
EGYPT	Passport and visa required. Transit visa for stay up to 48 hours available. Tourist visa, valid three months; requires $15 fee (cash or money order), one application form and one photo. Visa may be issued at airport upon arrival for fee of $20. For business travel, need company letter stating purpose of trip. Enclose prepaid envelope for return of passport by certified mail. Proof of yellow fever immunization required if arriving from infected area. AIDS test required for workers and students staying over 30 days. Register with local authorities or at hotel within seven days of arrival. Travelers must declare foreign currency on Form "D" on arrival and show Form "D" and bank receipts upon departure. Maximum Egyptian currency allowed into and out of Egypt is LE20. For additional information, consult the Embassy of the Arab Republic of Egypt, *2310 Decatur Place, N.W., Washington, D.C. 20008,* ☎ *(202) 234-3903,* or nearest Consulate General: CA ☎ *(415) 346-9700,* IL ☎ *(312) 443-1190,* NY ☎ *(212) 759-7120* or Houston ☎ *(713) 961-4915.*
EL SALVADOR	Passport and visa required. (Length of validity of visa will be determined by immigration authorities upon arrival.) Requires one application form and two photos. Allow three working days for processing. Send SASE for return of passport by mail. AIDS test required for permanent residence permit. U.S. test not accepted. Apply to the Consulate General of El Salvador, *1010 16th Street, N.W., 3rd Floor, Washington, D.C. 20036,* ☎ *(202) 331-4032,* or nearest Consulate: CA ☎ *(213) 383-5776 or (415) 781-7924,* FL ☎ *(305) 371-8850,* LA ☎ *(504) 522-4266,* NY ☎ *(212) 889-3608* or TX ☎ *(713) 270-6239.*
ENGLAND	(See United Kingdom.)
EQUATORIAL GUINEA	Passport and visa required. Obtain visa in advance. For further information, contact the residence of the Ambassador of Equatorial Guinea at *57 Magnolia Avenue, Mount Vernon, NY,* ☎ *(914) 667-9664.*
ERITREA	Passport and visa required. Tourist/business visa valid for a stay of up to six months; requires one application, two photos, $25 fee (no personal checks). Business visa can be extended up to one year, requires company letter stating purpose of travel. Include SASE for return of passport by mail. Allow three working days for processing. For more information, contact the Embassy of Eritrea, *910 17th Street, N.W., Suite 400, Washington, D.C. 20006,* ☎ *(202) 429-1991.*
ESTONIA	Passport required. Visas not required for stay of up to 90 days. AIDS test required for residency and work permits. U.S. test sometimes accepted. For further information, check the Embassy of the Republic of Estonia, *9 Rockefeller Plaza, Suite J-1421, New York, NY 10020,* ☎ *(212) 247-1450.*
ETHIOPIA	Passport and visa required. Tourist/business visa valid for stay up to two years, fee $50 or transit visa for 48 hours, $20; requires one application, one photo and yellow fever immunization. Business visa requires company letter. Send $2 postage for return of passport or $15.30 for Federal Express and $9.95 for Express Mail service. (Money orders only.) Allow two weeks for processing. Exit visas are required of all visitors remaining in Ethiopia for more than 30 days. For longer stays and other information, contact the Embassy of Ethiopia, *2134 Kalorama Road, N.W., Washington, D.C. 20008,* ☎ *(202) 234-2281/2.*

VISAS AND ENTRY REQUIREMENTS

FIJI	Passport, proof of sufficient funds and onward/return ticket required. Visa issued on arrival for stay up to 30 days and may be extended up to six months. For further information, contact the Embassy of Fuji, *2233 Wisconsin Avenue, N.W., #240, Washington, D.C. 20007,* ☎ *(202) 337-8320,* or Mission to the U.N., *One United Nations Plaza, 26th Floor, New York, NY 10017,* ☎ *(212) 355-7316.*
FINLAND	Passport required. Tourist/business visa not required for stay up to 90 days (90-day period begins when entering Scandinavian area: Sweden, Norway, Denmark, Iceland). Check Embassy of Finland, *3216 New Mexico Avenue, N.W., Washington, D.C. 20016,* ☎ *(202) 363-2430* or nearest Consulate General: Los Angeles ☎ *(310) 203-9903* or New York ☎ *(212) 573-6007.*
FRANCE	Passport required to visit France, Andorra, Monaco, Corsica and French Polynesia. Visa not required for tourist/business stay up to three months in France, Andorra, Monaco and Corsica, and one month in French Polynesia (officials/diplomats, journalists on assignment, ship or plane crew members, and students are required to obtain a visa in advance). For further information, consult the Embassy of France, *4101 Reservoir Road, N.W., Washington, D.C. 20007,* ☎ *(202) 944-6200/6215,* or nearest Consulate: CA ☎ *(310) 479-4426* or *(415) 397-4330,* FL ☎ *(305) 372-9798,* GA ☎ *(404) 522-4226,* HI ☎ *(808) 599-4458,* IL ☎ *(312) 787-5359,* LA ☎ *(504) 523-5774,* ME ☎ *(617) 482-3650,* MI ☎ *(313) 568-0990,* NY ☎ *(212) 606-3600,* PR ☎ *(809) 753-1700* or TX ☎ *(713) 528-2181.*
FRENCH GUIANA	Proof of U.S. citizenship and photo ID required for visit up to three weeks. (For stays longer than three weeks, a passport is required.) No visa required for stay up to three months. For further information, consult the Embassy of France, *4101 Reservoir Road, N.W., Washington, D.C. 20007,* ☎ *(202) 944-6200/6215.*
FRENCH POLYNESIA	Includes Society Islands, French Southern and Antarctic Lands, Tuamotu, Gambier, French Austral, Marquesas, Kerguelen, Crozet, New Caledonia, Tahiti, Wallis and Furtuna Islands. Passport required. Visa not required for visit up to one month. For longer stays and further information, consult the Embassy of France at ☎ *(202) 944-6200/6215.*
GABON	Passport and visa required. Visas must be obtained before arrival. Single-entry visa valid up to one month, multiple-entry visa valid for two–four months. Both visas require two application forms, two photos, small pox and yellow fever vaccinations, and $50 fee (no personal checks accepted). Also need detailed travel arrangements, including flight numbers, arrival and departure dates, accommodations and next destination. Business visa requires company letter stating purpose of trip and contacts in Gabon. Accompanying family must be included in letter. For longer stays and other information, call the Embassy of the Gabonese Republic, *2034 20th Street, N.W., Washington, D.C. 20009,* ☎ *(202) 797-1000,* or the Permanent Mission of the Gabonese Republic to the U.N., *18 East 41st Street, 6th Floor, New York, NY 10017,* ☎ *(212) 686-9720.*
GALAPAGOS ISLANDS	Passport and onward/return ticket required for visits up to three months. For further information, consult the Embassy of Ecuador at ☎ *(202) 234-7166.*
GAMBIA	Passport and visa required. Tourist/business visa for a stay of up to three months; requires one application, one photo, and yellow fever immunization certificate (no fee. For business visa, you also need company letter stating purpose of visit and itinerary. Allow at least two working days for processing. Include prepaid envelope for return of passport by mail. Apply to the Embassy of the Gambia, *Suite 720, 1030 15th Street, N.W., Washington, D.C. 20005,* ☎ *(202) 785-1399,* or Permanent Mission of The Gambia to the U.N., *820 2nd Avenue, 9th floor, New York, NY 10017,* ☎ *(212) 949-6640.*
GEORGIA	Passport, visa and letter of invitation (issued upon arrival) required. For additional information, contact the Embassy of the Republic of Georgia, *Suite 424, 1511 K Street, N.W., Washington, D.C. 20005,* ☎ *(202) 393-6060.*

COUNTRY	ENTRY
GERMANY	Passport required. Tourist/business visa not required for stay up to three months. For longer stays, obtain temporary residence permit upon arrival. AIDS test required of applicants for Bavaria residence permits staying over 180 days; U.S. test not accepted. Every foreigner entering Germany is required to provide proof of sufficient health insurance. For further information, contact the Embassy of the Federal Republic of Germany, *4645 Reservoir Road, N.W., Washington, D.C. 20007*, ☎ *(202) 298-4000*, or nearest Consulate General: CA ☎ *(415) 775-1061*, FL ☎ *(305) 358-0290*, GA ☎ *(404) 659-4760*, IL ☎ *(312) 263-0850*, MA ☎ *(617) 536-4414*, MI ☎ *(313) 962-6526*, NY ☎ *(212) 308-8700* or TX ☎ *(713) 627-7770*.
GHANA	Passport and visa required. Tourist visa required for stay up to 30 days (extendable). Requires one application form, four photos, copy of onward/return ticket, bank statement or pay stub and yellow fever immunization. Single-entry visa requires $20 fee, multiple-entry $50. Allow three working days for processing. Include prepaid envelope for return of passport by certified mail. For additional information, contact the Embassy of Ghana, *3512 International Drive, N.W., Washington, D.C. 20008*, ☎ *(202) 686-4520*, or Consulate General, *19 East 47th Street, New York, NY 10017*, ☎ *(212) 832-1300*.
GIBRALTAR	Passport required. Visa not required for tourist stay up to three months. For further information, consult the British Embassy at ☎ *(202) 986-0205*.
GILBERT ISLANDS	(See Kiribati.)
GREAT BRITAIN AND NORTHERN IRELAND	(See United Kingdom.)
GREECE	Passport required. Visa not required for tourist/business stay up to three months. If traveling on diplomatic/official passport, visa required and must be obtained in advance. AIDS test required for performing artists and students on Greek scholarships; U.S. test not accepted. For additional information, consult the Consular Section of the Embassy of Greece, *2221 Massachusetts Avenue, N.W., Washington, D.C. 20008*, ☎ *(202) 232-8222*, or nearest Consulate: CA ☎ *(213) 385-1447 or (415) 775-2102*, GA ☎ *(404) 261-3313*, IL ☎ *(312) 372-5356*, LA ☎ *(504) 523-1167*, MA ☎ *(617) 542-3240*, NY ☎ *(212) 988-5500* or TX ☎ *(713) 840-7522*.
GREENLAND	(See Denmark.)
GRENADA	Passport is recommended, but tourists may enter with birth certificate and photo ID. Visa not required for tourist stay up to three months, may be extended to maximum of six months. For additional information, consult the Embassy of Grenada, *1701 New Hampshire Avenue, N.W., Washington, D.C. 20009*, ☎ *(202) 265-2561*, or Permanent Mission of Grenada to the U.N., ☎ *(212) 599-0301*.
GUADELOUPE	(See West Indies, French.)
GUATEMALA	Passport and visa or tourist card required. Visas no charge, valid one year, multiple entries of 30 days each; requires passport, one application form, one photo and $5 fee. Provide SASE for return of passport by mail. For travel by minors and information, about tourist cards, contact the Embassy of Guatemala, *2220 R Street, N.W., Washington, D.C. 20008*, ☎ *(202) 745-4952*, or nearest Consulate: CA ☎ *(213) 365-9251/2 or (415) 788-5651*, FL ☎ *(305) 443-4828/29*, IL ☎ *(312) 332-1587*, NY ☎ *(212) 686-3837* or TX ☎ *(713) 953-9531*.
GUIANA, FRENCH	(See French Guiana.)
GUINEA	Passport and visa required. Tourist/business visa for stay up to three months; requires three application forms, three photos, yellow fever immunization and $25 fee (cash or money order only). Malaria suppressants are highly recommended. For business visa, need company letter stating purpose of trip and letter of invitation from company in Guinea. Provide SASE for return of passport by mail. For more information, contact the Embassy of the Republic of Guinea, *2112 Leroy Place, N.W., Washington, D.C. 20008*, ☎ *(202) 483-9420*.

VISAS AND ENTRY REQUIREMENTS

COUNTRY	ENTRY
GUINEA-BISSAU	Passport and visa required. Visa must be obtained in advance. Visa valid up to 90 days; requires two application forms, two photos, health certificate, financial guarantee to cover stay, letter staying purpose of travel and $12 fee (payment by money order only). Include prepaid envelope for return of passport by express mail. Apply to the Embassy of Guinea-Bissau, *918 16th Street, N.W., Mezzanine Suite, Washington, D.C. 20006,* ☎ *(202) 872-4222.*
GUYANA	Passport required. For more information, consult the Embassy of Guyana, *2490 Tracy Place, N.W., Washington, D.C. 20008,* ☎ *(202) 265-6900/03,* or Consulate General, *866 U.N. Plaza, 3rd Floor, New York, NY 10017,* ☎ *(212) 527-3215.*
HAITI	Passport required. For further information, consult the Embassy of Haiti, *2311 Massachusettes Avenue, N.W., Washington, D.C. 20008,* ☎ *(202) 332-4090,* or nearest Consulate: FL ☎ *(305) 859-2003,* MA ☎ *(617) 723-5211,* NY ☎ *(212) 697-9767* or PR ☎ *(809) 766-0758.*
HOLY SEE, APOSTOLIC NUNCI-ATURE OF THE	Passport required (for entry into Italy). For further information, consult the Apostolic Nunciature of the Holy See, *3339 Massachusettes Avenue, N.W., Washington, D.C. 20008,* ☎ *(202) 333-7121,* or call the Embassy of Italy, ☎ *(202) 328-5500.*
HONDURAS	Passport and onward/return ticket required. For additional information, contact the Embassy of Honduras (Consular Section), *Suite 319, 1612 K Street., N.W., Washington, D.C. 20006,* ☎ *(202) 223-0185,* or nearest Consulate: CA ☎ *(213) 383-9244* and *(415) 392-0076,* FL ☎ *(305) 447-8927,* IL ☎ *(312) 772-7090,* LA ☎ *(504) 522-3118,* NY ☎ *(212) 269-3611* or TX ☎ *(713) 622-4572.*
HONG KONG	Passport and onward/return transportation by sea/air required. Visa not required for tourist stay up to 30 days, may be extended to three months. Confirmed hotel and flight reservations recommended during peak travel months. Departure tax 150 Hong Kong dollars (approx. $20 U.S.) paid at airport. Visa required for work or study. For other types of travel, consult the British Embassy at ☎ *(202) 986-0205.*
HUNGARY	Passport required. Visa not required for stay up to 90 days. For business travel and other information, check the Embassy of the Republic of Hungary, *3910 Shoemaker Street, N.W., Washington, D.C. 20008,* ☎ *(202) 362-6730,* or Consulate General, *8 East 75th Street, New York, NY 10021,* ☎ *(212) 879-4127.*
ICELAND	Passport required. Visa not required for stay up to three months. (Period begins when entering Scandinavian area: Denmark, Finland, Norway, Sweden.) For additional information, call the Embassy of Iceland, *2022 Connecticut Avenue, N.W., Washington, D.C. 20008,* ☎ *(202) 265-6653-5,* or Consulate General in New York, ☎ *(212) 686-4100.*
INDIA	Passport and visa required. Obtain visa in advance. Tourist visa valid for stay up to one month, requires $5 fee, up to six months $25 fee and up to 12 months $50 fee, one application form, two photos, onward/return ticket and proof of sufficient funds. Visa must be obtained before arrival. Business visa requires $50 fee, two application forms, two photos and company letter stating purpose of trip and itinerary. Include prepaid envelope for return of passport by certified mail. Allow two weeks for processing. Yellow fever immunization needed if arriving from infected area. AIDS test required for all students and anyone over 18 staying more than one year; U.S. test sometimes accepted. Check requirements with the Embassy of India, *2536 Massachusettes Avenue, N.W., Washington, D.C. 20008,* ☎ *(202) 939-9839/9850,* or nearest Consulate General: Chicago ☎ *(312) 781-6280,* New York ☎ *(212) 879-7800* or San Francisco ☎ *(415) 668-0683.*
INDONESIA	Valid passport and onward/return ticket required. Visa not required for tourist stay up to two months (non-extendable). For longer stays and additional information, consult the Embassy of the Republic of Indonesia, *2020 Massachusettes Avenue, N.W., Washington, D.C. 20036,* ☎ *(202) 775-5200,* or nearest Consulate: CA ☎ *(213) 383-5126* or *(415) 474-9571,* IL ☎ *(312) 938-0101,* NY ☎ *(212) 879-0600* or TX ☎ *(713) 626-3291.*
IRAN	Passport and visa required. The United States does not maintain diplomatic or consular relations with Iran. Travel by U.S. citizens is not recommended. For visa information, contact the Embassy of Pakistan, Iranian Interests Section, *2209 Wisconsin Avenue, N.W., Washington, D.C. 20007,* ☎ *(202) 965-4990.*

COUNTRY	ENTRY

IRAQ

Passport and visa required. AIDS test required for stay over 5 days. The United States suspended diplomatic and consular operations in Iraq in 1990. Since February 1991, U.S. passports are not valid for travel in, to, or through Iraq without authorization from the Department of State. Application for exemptions to this restriction should be submitted in writing to Passport Services, U.S. Department of State, *1425 K Street, N.W., Washington, D.C. 20524, Attn: CA/PPT/C, Room 300*. Note: U.S. citizens need a Treasury Department license in order to engage in any transactions related to travel to and within Iraq. Before planning any travel to Iraq, U.S. citizens should contact the Licensing Division, Office of Foreign Assets Control, Department of the Treasury, *1331 G Street, N.W., Washington, D.C. 20220*, ☎ *(202) 622-2480*. For visa information, contact a country that maintains diplomatic relations with Iraq.

IRELAND

Passport required. Tourists are not required to obtain visas for stays under 90 days, but may be asked to show onward/return ticket. For further information, consult the Embassy of Ireland, *2234 Massachusettes Avenue, N.W., Washington, D.C. 20008*, ☎ *(202) 462-3939*, or nearest Consulate General: CA ☎ *(415) 392-4214*, IL ☎ *(312) 337-1868*, MA ☎ *(617) 267-9330* or NY ☎ *(212) 319-2555*.

ISRAEL

Passport, onward/return ticket and proof of sufficient funds required. Tourist visa issued upon arrival valid for three months, but can be renewed. Departure tax of $15 payable at airport. Tourists should not travel by bus and should avoid crowded areas and bus stops. Due to threat of terrorist activities, tourists are advised to exercise extreme caution and be aware of their surroundings at all times. Consult the Embassy of Israel, *3514 International Drive, N.W., Washington, D.C. 20008*, ☎ *(202) 364-5500*, or nearest Consulate General: CA ☎ *(213) 651-5700* or *(415) 398-8885*, FL ☎ *(305) 358-8111*, GA ☎ *(404) 875-7851*, IL ☎ *(312) 565-3300*, MA ☎ *(617) 542-0041*, NY ☎ *(212) 351-5200*, PA ☎ *(215) 546-5556* or TX ☎ *(713) 627-3780*.

ITALY

Passport required. Visa not required for tourist stay up to three months. For longer stays, employment or study, obtain visa in advance. For additional information, consult the Embassy of Italy, *1601 Fuller Street, N.W., Washington, D.C. 20009*, ☎ *(202) 328-5500*, or nearest Consulate General: CA ☎ *(310) 820-0622* or *(415) 931-4924*, FL ☎ *(305) 374-6322*, IL ☎ *(312) 467-1550*, LA ☎ *(504) 524-2272*, MA ☎ *(617) 542-0483/4*, MI ☎ *(313) 963-8560*, NJ ☎ *(201) 643-1448*, NY ☎ *(212) 737-9100*, PA ☎ *(215) 592-7329* or TX ☎ *(713) 850-7520*.

IVORY COAST

(See Cote d' Ivoire.)

JAMAICA

Passport (or original birth certificate and photo ID), onward/return ticket and proof of sufficient funds required. (Photo ID is not required for U.S. citizens under 16 using birth certificate.) Tourist card issued on arrival for stay up to six months; must be returned to immigration authorities on departure. For business or study, visa must be obtained in advance, no charge. Departure tax of $15 paid at airport. Check information with the Embassy of Jamaica, *Suite 355, 1850 K Street, N.W., Washington, D.C. 20006*, ☎ *(202) 452-0660*, or nearest Consulate: CA ☎ *(213) 380-9471* or *(415) 886-6061*, FL ☎ *(305) 374-8431*, GA ☎ *(404) 593-1500*, IL ☎ *(312) 663-0023* or NY ☎ *(212) 935-9000*.

JAPAN

Passport and onward/return ticket required. Visa not required for tourist/business stay up to 90 days. Departure tax of $15.50 paid at airport. For specific information, consult the Embassy of Japan, *2520 Massachusettes Avenue, N.W., Washington, D.C. 20008*, ☎ *(202) 939-6800*, or nearest Consulate: AK ☎ *(907) 279-8428*, CA ☎ *(213) 624-8305* or *(415) 777-3533*, FL ☎ *(305) 530-9090*, GA ☎ *(404) 892-2700*, Guam ☎ *(671) 646-1290*, HI ☎ *(808) 536-2226*, IL ☎ *(312) 280-0400*, LA ☎ *(504) 529-2101*, MA ☎ *(617) 973-9772*, MI ☎ *(313) 567-0120*, MO ☎ *(816) 471-0111*, NY ☎ *(212) 371-8222*, OR ☎ *(503) 221-1811*, TX ☎ *(713) 652-2977* or WA ☎ *(206) 682-9107*.

JORDAN

Passport and visa required. Visa requires one application form, one photo, letter stating purpose of visit and itinerary. Entry into Jordan is sometimes denied to persons holding passports with Israeli visas stamps. (This is especially true when the holders are U.S./Jordanian dual nationals.) Send SASE for return of passport by mail. For details, check the Embassy of the Hashemite Kingdom of Jordan, *3504 International Drive, N.W., Washington, D.C. 20008*, ☎ *(202) 966-2664*.

KAZAKHSTAN

Passport and visa required. For additional information, contact the Embassy of Kazakhstan, *3421 Massachusettes Avenue, N.W., Washington, D.C. 20007*, ☎ *(202) 333-4504 or 07*.

COUNTRY	ENTRY

KENYA

Passport and visa required. Visa must be obtained in advance. Single-entry visa for tourist/business stay up to six months, $10 (money order only); requires one application form, two photos and onward/return ticket. Yellow fever immunization is recommend. Anti-malaria pills are recommended for those travelling to the western or coastal regions. Multiple-entry business visa valid for up to one year, $50. Payment by cashiers check or money order only. Airport departure tax is $20. Consult the Embassy of Kenya, *2249 R Street, N.W., Washington, D.C. 20008,* ☎ *(202) 387-6101,* or Consulate General: Los Angeles ☎ *(310) 274-6635* or New York ☎ *(212) 486-1300.*

KIRIBATI (Formerly Gilbert Islands)

Passport and visa required. For additional information, consult the British Embassy at ☎ *(202) 462-1340.*

KOREA, DEMOCRATIC PEOPLE'S REPUBLIC OF (North Korea)

U.S. passports are valid for travel to North Korea. The United States does not maintain diplomatic or consular relations with North Korea. U.S. government interests are represented on an interim basis by Sweden, which is able to provide limited emergency services to U.S. citizens. U.S. travel service providers are authorized to organize group travel to North Korea, including transactions with North Korean carriers. However, U.S. citizens may spend money in North Korea only to purchase items ordinarily used in travel such as hotel accommodations, meals and goods for personal consumption during travel. Purchases of goods and services unrelated to travel are prohibited. Before planning any business transactions with North Korea, U.S. citizens should contact the Licensing Division, Office of Foreign Assets Control, Department of the Treasury, *1331 G Street, N.W., Washington, D.C. 20220* ☎ *(202) 622-2480.* Visa information may be obtained from a consulate in a country that maintains diplomatic relations with North Korea or from the North Korean Mission to the United Nations in New York. ☎ *(212) 772-0712.*

KOREA, REPUBLIC OF (South Korea)

Passport required. Visa not required for a tourist stay up to 15 days. For longer stays and other types of travel, visa must be obtained in advance. Tourist visa for longer stay requires one application form and one photo. Business visa requires one application form, one photo and company letter. Fine imposed for overstaying visa and for long-term visa holders not registered within 60 days after entry. AIDS test required for anyone staying over 90 days; U.S. test accepted. For further information, check the Embassy of the Republic of Korea, (Consular Division), *2600 Virginia Avenue, N.W., Suite 208, Washington, D.C. 20037,* ☎ *(202) 939-5660/63,* or nearest Consulate General: AK ☎ *(907) 561-5488,* CA ☎ *(213) 385-9300* and *(415) 921-2251,* FL ☎ *(305) 372-1555,* GA ☎ *(404) 522-1611,* Guam ☎ *(671) 472-6109,* HI ☎ *(808) 595-6109,* IL ☎ *(312) 822-9485,* MA ☎ *(617) 348-3660,* NY ☎ *(212) 752-1700,* TX ☎ *(713) 961-0186* or WA ☎ *(206) 441-1011.*

KUWAIT

Passport and visa required. AIDS test required for work visa; U.S. test accepted. For further information, contact the Embassy of the State of Kuwait, *2940 Tilden Street, N.W., Washington, D.C. 20008,* ☎ *(202) 966-0702,* or Consulate, *321 East 44th Street, New York, NY 10017,* ☎ *(212) 973-4318.*

KYRGYZ REPUBLIC (Kyrgyzstan)

Passport and visa required. Visa requires one application form, and two photos, (plus a letter of invitation from a Kyrgyz citizen or organization if staying more then 21 days). Multi-entry visa $100 (no personal checks). Include SASE for return of passport by mail (or proper fee for express mail service). For additional information, contact the Embassy of the Kyrgyz Republic, *1511 K Street, N.W., Suite 707, Washington, D.C. 20005,* ☎ *(202) 628-0433.*

LAOS

Passport and visa required. Visa requires $35 fee, three application forms, three photos, onward/return transportation, sufficient funds, cholera immunization and SASE for return of passport by mail. Transit visas for stay up to five days requires onward/return ticket and visa for next destination. Visitor visas are issued for one entry and must be used within three months of issue date. Period of stay: one month can be extended for another 30 days (visitor visa application must be accompanied by letter from relative or friends in Laos). Tourist visas are issued only to those who apply through a tourist agency. Business visa requires letter from counterpart in Laos, is valid for one entry and must be used within three months of issue date. For more information, check with the Embassy of the Lao People's Democratic Republic, *2222 S Street, N.W., Washington, D.C. 20008,* ☎ *(202) 332-6416/7.*

COUNTRY	ENTRY
LATVIA	Passport and visa required. Tourist/business visa issued at embassy or point of entry. One application form, one photo and $5 fee are required. For further information, contact the Embassy of Latvia, *4325 17th Street, N.W., Washington, D.C. 20011,* ☎ *(202) 726-8213.*
LEBANON	Passport and visa required. AIDS test required for those seeking residence permits; U.S. test accepted. Since January 1987, U.S. passports are not valid for travel in, to or through Lebanon without authorization from the Department of State. Application for exemptions to this restriction should be submitted in writing to Passport Services, U.S. Department of State, *1425 K Street, N.W., Washington, D.C. 20524, Attn: CA/PPT/C, Room 300.* For further visa information, contact the Embassy of Lebanon, *2560 28th Street, N.W., Washington, D.C. 20008,* ☎ *(202) 939-6300,* or nearest Consulate General: Los Angeles ☎ *(213) 467-1253,* Detroit ☎ *(313) 567-0233* or New York ☎ *(212) 744-7905.*
LEEWARD ISLANDS	(See Virgin Islands, British.)
LESOTHO	Passport and visa required. Visa requires one form. Single-entry visa requires $5 fee and multiple-entry $10. For more information, check with the Embassy of the Kingdom of Lesotho, *2511 Massachusettes Avenue, N.W., Washington, D.C. 20008,* ☎ *(202) 797-5533.*
LIBERIA	The U.S. Department of State warns U.S. citizens against travel to Liberia. Although the U.S. embassy remains open, it is closed for visa services and is providing only emergency services for U.S. citizens. Travelers who plan a trip to Liberia, despite the warning, are required to have a passport and visa prior to arrival along with evidence of yellow fever vaccinations. An exit permit must be obtained from Liberian immigration authorities before departure. For more information on entry requirements, direct inquiries to the Embassy of the Republic of Liberia, *5201 16th Street, N.W., Washington, D.C. 20011,* ☎ *(202) 723-0437* or ☎ *(202) 723-0440.*
LIBYA	Passport and visa required. AIDS test required for those seeking residence permits; U.S. test accepted. Since December 1981, U.S. passports are not valid for travel in, to or through Libya without authorization from the Department of State. Application for exemptions to this restriction should be submitted in writing to Passport Services, U.S. Department of State, *1425 K Street, N.W., Washington, D.C. 20524, Attn: CA/PPT/C, Room 300.* Note: U.S. citizens need a Treasury Department license in order to engage in any transactions related to travel to and within Libya. Before planning any travel to Libya, U.S. citizens should contact the Licensing Division, Office of Foreign Assets Control, Department of the Treasury, *1331 G Street, N.W., Washington, D.C. 20220,* ☎ *(202) 622-2480.* Application and inquiries for visas must be made through a country that maintains diplomatic relations with Libya.
LIECHTENSTEIN	Passport required. Visa not required for tourist/business stay up to three months. For further information, consult the Swiss Embassy at ☎ *(202) 745-7900.*
LITHUANIA	Passport and visa required. Visa requires one application form and $25 fee. AIDS test required for permanent residence permits. U.S. test sometimes accepted. For further information, contact the Embassy of Lithuania, *2622 16th Street, N.W., Washington, D.C. 20009,* ☎ *(202) 234-5860.*
LUXEMBOURG	Passport required. Visa not required for tourist/business stay up to three months. For additional information, contact the Embassy of Luxembourg, *2200 Massachusettes Avenue, N.W., Washington, D.C. 20008,* ☎ *(202) 265-4171,* or the nearest Consulate: CA ☎ *(415) 788-0816,* FL ☎ *(305) 373-1300,* GA ☎ *(404) 668-9811,* IL ☎ *(312) 726-0355,* MO ☎ *(816) 474-4761,* NY ☎ *(212) 888-6664* or OH ☎ *(312) 726-0355.*
MACAU	Passport required. Visa not required for visits up to 60 days. For further information, consult the nearest Portuguese Consulate: Washington, D.C., ☎ *(202) 332-3007,* San Francisco ☎ *(415) 346-3400,* New Bedford ☎ *(508) 997-6151,* Newark ☎ *(201) 622-7300,* NY ☎ *(212) 246-4580,* Providence ☎ *(401) 272-2003,* or Portuguese Consulate in Hong Kong ☎ *(231-338.*
MACEDONIA, (FORMER YUGOSLAV REPUBLIC OF)	Entry permission can be obtained at border points. Macedonia does not currently maintain an embassy in the U.S. For more information, check with the Former Yugoslav Republic of Macedonia's Office, *1015 15th Street, N.W., Suite 402, Washington, D.C. 20005,* ☎ *(202) 682-0519.*

COUNTRY	ENTRY

MADAGASCAR

Passport and visa required. Visa valid six months for single-entry up to 90 days, $22.50, or multiple-entries, $44.15 (no personal checks). Requires four application forms, four photos, yellow fever and cholera immunizations, proof of onward/return transportation and sufficient funds for stay. Include a prepaid envelope for return of passport by registered mail. Allow four months to process visa for longer stay. For additional information, contact the Embassy of the Democratic Republic of Madagascar, *2374 Massachusettes Avenue, N.W., Washington, D.C. 20008,* ☎ *(202) 265-5525/6,* or nearest Consulate: NY ☎ *(212) 986-9491,* PA ☎ *(215) 893-3067* or CA ☎ *(800) 856-2721.*

MALAWI

Passport required. Visa not required for stay up to one year. Strict dress codes apply for anyone visiting Malawi. Women must wear dresses that cover their shoulders, arms and knees and may not wear slacks except in specifically designated areas. Men with long hair cannot enter the country. For further information about this and other requirements, contact the Embassy of Malawi, *2408 Massachusettes Avenue, N.W., Washington, D.C. 20008,* ☎ *(202) 797-1007,* or Malawi Mission to the U.N., *600 3rd Avenue, New York, NY 10016,* ☎ *(212) 949-0180.*

MALAYSIA (and the Borneo States, Sarawak and Sabah)

Passport required. Visa not required for stay up to three months. Yellow fever and cholera immunizations necessary if arriving from infected areas. AIDS test required for work permits; U.S. test sometimes accepted. For entry of pets or other types of visits, consult the Embassy of Malaysia, *2401 Massachusettes Avenue, N.W., Washington, D.C. 20008,* ☎ *(202) 328-2700,* or nearest Consulate: Los Angeles ☎ *(213) 621-2991* or New York ☎ *(212) 490-2722.*

MALDIVES

Passport required. Tourist visa issued upon arrival, no charge. Visitors must have proof of onward/return transportation and sufficient funds (minimum of $10 per person per day). Check with the Embassy of Maldives in Sri Lanka, *25 Melbourne Avenue, Colombo 4, Sri Lanka,* or the Maldives Mission to the U.N. in New York, ☎ *(212) 599-6195,* for further information.

MALI

Passport and visa required. Visa must be obtained in advance. Tourist/business visa for stay up to four weeks; may be extended after arrival; requires $17 fee (cash or money order), two application forms, two photos, proof of onward/return transportation and yellow fever vaccination (cholera immunization is recommended). For business travel, must have company letter stating purpose of trip. Send SASE for return of passport if applying by mail. Apply to the Embassy of the Republic of Mali, *2130 R Street, N.W., Washington, D.C. 20008,* ☎ *(202) 332-2249.*

MALTA

Passport required. Visa not required for stay up to three months (extendable); extension must be applied for prior to end of 3-month period or expiration of original visa. Visa requires three application forms, two photos, proof of onward/return transportation and $46 fee (check or money order). Transit visa available for $31. For additional information, consult the Embassy of Malta, *2017 Connecticut Avenue, N.W., Washington, D.C. 20008,* ☎ *(202) 462-3611/2,* or nearest Consulate: CA ☎ *(213) 939-5011* or *(415) 468-4321,* MA ☎ *(617) 259-1391,* MI ☎ *(313) 525-9777,* MO ☎ *(816) 833-0033,* MN ☎ *(612) 228-0935,* NY ☎ *(212) 725-2345,* PA ☎ *(412) 262-8460* or TX ☎ *(713) 497-2100* or *(713) 999-1812.*

MARSHALL ISLANDS, REPUBLIC OF THE

Proof of U.S. citizenship, sufficient funds for stay and onward/return ticket required for stay up to 30 days (extendable up to 90 days from date of entry). Entry permit not needed to bring in seagoing vessel. Obtain necessary forms from airline or shipping agent serving Marshall Islands. Departure fee $10 (those over age 60 exempt). Health certificate required if arriving from infected areas. AIDS test may be required for visits over 30 days; U.S. test accepted. Check information with Representative Office, *Suite 1004, 1901 Pennsylvania Avenue, N.W., Washington, D.C. 20006,* ☎ *(202) 234-5414,* or the nearest Consulate General: CA ☎ *(714) 474-0331* or HI ☎ *(808) 942-4422.*

MARTINIQUE

(See West Indies, French.)

MAURITANIA

Passport and visa required. Obtain visa before arrival. Visa valid three months, requires $10 fee (money order only), two application forms, four photos, yellow fever and cholera immunizations and proof of onward/return transportation. Business travelers must have proof of sufficient funds (bank statement) or letter from sponsoring company. For further information, contact the Embassy of the Republic of Mauritania, *2129 Leroy Place, N.W., Washington, D.C. 20008,* ☎ *(202) 232-5700/01,* or Permanent Mission to the U.N., *211 East 43rd Street, Suite 2000, New York, NY 10017,* ☎ *(212) 986-7963.*

COUNTRY	ENTRY

MAURITIUS Passport, sufficient funds for stay and onward/return ticket required. Visa not required for tourist/business stay up to three months. AIDS test required for permanent residence and work permits; U.S. test sometimes accepted. For further information, consult the Embassy of Mauritius, *Suite 441, 4301 Connecticut Avenue, N.W., Washington, D.C. 20008,* ☎ *(202) 244-1491/2,* or Honorary Consulate in Los Angeles, ☎ *(818) 788-3720.*

MAYOTTE ISLAND (See France.)

MEXICO Passport and visa not required of U.S. citizens for tourist/transit stay up to 90 days. Tourist card is required. Tourist card valid three months for single entry up to 180 days; no charge; requires proof of U.S. citizenship, photo ID and proof of sufficient funds. Tourist cards may be obtained in advance from Consulate, Tourism Office, and most airlines serving Mexico upon arrival. Departure tax of $10 is paid at airport. Notarized consent from parent(s) required for children travelling alone, with one parent or in someone else's custody. (This permit is not necessary when a minor is in possession of a valid passport.) For other types of travel and details, check with the Embassy of Mexico Consular Section, *2827 16th Street, N.W., Washington, D.C. 20009-4260,* ☎ *(202) 736-1000,* or nearest Consulate General: CA ☎ *(213) 351-6800, (415) 392-5554* or *(619) 231-8414,* CO ☎ *(303) 830-6702,* FL ☎ *(305) 441-8780,* IL ☎ *(312) 855-1380,* LA ☎ *(504) 522-3596,* NY ☎ *(212) 689-0456,* PR ☎ *(809) 764-0258* or TX ☎ *(214) 522-9741, (713) 463-9426, (512) 227-9145* or *(915) 533-3644.*

MICRONESIA, FEDERATED STATES OF (Kosrae, Yap, Ponape and Truk) Proof of citizenship, proof of sufficient funds, and onward/return ticket required for tourist visit up to six months, extendable (up to 12 months from date of entry) after arrival in Micronesia. Entry permit may be needed for other types of travel; obtain forms from airline. Departure fee $5 (U.S.). Health certificate may be required if traveling from infected area. Typhoid and tetanus immunizations are recommended. AIDS test required if staying over one year; U.S. test is accepted. For further information, contact the Embassy of the Federated States of Micronesia, *1725 N Street, N.W., Washington, D.C. 20036,* ☎ *(202) 223-4383,* or nearest Consulate: HI ☎ *(808) 836-4775* or Guam ☎ *(671) 646-9154.*

MOLDOVA Passport and visa required. Visas issued at authorized entry points at the airport or along the Romanian border. Moldova does not currently maintain an embassy in the United States.

MIQUELON ISLAND Proof of U.S. citizenship and photo ID required for visit up to three months. For further information, consult the Embassy of France at ☎ *(202) 944-6000.*

MONACO Passport required. Visa not required for visit up to three months. For further information, consult the French Embassy, ☎ *(202) 944-6000* or nearest Honorary Consulate of the Principality of Monaco: CA ☎ *(213) 655-8970 or (415) 362-5050,* IL ☎ *(312) 642-1242,* LA ☎ *(504) 522-5700,* NY ☎ *(212) 759-5227* or PR ☎ *(809) 721-4215.*

MONGOLIA Passport and visa required. Transit visa for stay up to 48 hours requires onward ticket, visa for next destination and $15 fee ($30 for double transit). Tourist visa for up to 90 days requires confirmation from Mongolian Travel Agency (Zhuulchin) and $25 fee. Business visa requires letter from company stating purpose of trip and invitation from Mongolian organization and $25 fee (multiple-entry $50). Submit one application form, two photos, itinerary and prepaid envelope for return of passport by certified or special delivery mail. AIDS test required for students and anyone staying longer than three months; U.S. test accepted. For additional information, contact the Embassy of Mongolia, *2833 M Street, N.W., Washington, D.C. 20007,* ☎ *(202) 333-7117,* or the U.N. Mission of Mongolia, *6 East 77th Street, New York, NY 10021,* ☎ *(212) 861-9460.*

MOROCCO Passport required. Visa not required for stay up to three months, extendable. For additional information, consult the Embassy of Morocco, *1601 21st Street, N.W., Washington, D.C. 20009,* ☎ *(202) 462-7979 to 7982,* or Consulate General in New York, ☎ *(212) 213-9644.*

COUNTRY	ENTRY
MOZAMBIQUE	Passport and visa required. Visa must be obtained in advance. Entry visa valid 30 days from date of issuance; requires two application forms, two photos, immunization for yellow fever and cholera, $20 fee and letter (from company or individual) giving detailed itinerary. Visitors may have to exchange $25 at point of entry and declare all foreign currency. Apply to the Embassy of the People's Republic of Mozambique, *Suite 570, 1990 M Street, N.W., Washington, D.C. 20036,* ☎ *(202) 293-7146.*
MYANMAR (Formerly Burma)	Passport and visa required. Single-entry visas for stays up to four weeks require $16 fee for tourist visa and $30 fee for business visa, two application forms, three photos and itinerary. Tourists visas are issued for package or group tours as well as Foreign Independent Travelers (FITs). FITs holding tourist visas must change a minimum of $300 (U.S.) upon arrival. Business visa requires company letter and invitation from a Myanmar company; extendable after arrival. Overland travel into and out of Myanmar is only permitted at certain points (check with the Embassy). Enclose prepaid envelope for return of passport by registered/certified mail. Allow two–three weeks for processing. Minimum of $100 must be changed for local currency on arrival. For further information, contact the Embassy of the Union of Myanmar, *2300 S Street, N.W., Washington, D.C. 20008,* ☎ *(202) 332-9044-5,* or the Permanent Mission of Myanmar to the U.N., *10 East 77th Street, New York, NY 10021,* ☎ *(212) 535-1311.*
NAMIBIA	Passport, onward/return ticket and proof of sufficient funds required. Visa not required for tourist or business stay up to 90 days. Consult the Embassy of Namibia, *1605 New Hampshire Avenue, N.W., Washington, D.C. 20009,* ☎ *(202) 986-0540,* for further information on entry requirements.
NAURU	Passport, visa, onward/return ticket and sponsorship from a resident in Nauru required. For more information, contact the Consulate of the Republic of Nauru in Guam, *P.O. Box Am, Agana, Guam 96910,* ☎ *(671) 649-8300.*
NEPAL	Passport and visa required. Tourist visa for stay up to 30 days extendable to three months. Single-entry visa $40, double $70 and multiple $100 (postal money order); requires one application form and one photo. For other types of travel, obtain visa in advance. For additional information, contact the Royal Nepalese Embassy, *2131 Leroy Place, N.W., Washington, D.C. 20008,* ☎ *(202) 667-4550,* or Consulate General in New York, ☎ *(212) 370-4188.*
NETHERLANDS	Passport required. Visa not required for tourist/business visit up to 90 days. Tourists may be asked to show onward/return ticket or proof of sufficient funds for stay. For further information, contact the Embassy of the Netherlands, *4200 Linnean Avenue, N.W., Washington, D.C. 20008,* ☎ *(202) 244-5300,* or nearest Consulate General: CA ☎ *(213) 380-3440,* IL ☎ *(312) 856-0110,* NY ☎ *(212) 246-1429* or TX ☎ *(713) 622-8000.*
NETHERLANDS ANTILLES	Islands include Bonaire, Curaçao, Saba, Statia and St. Maarten. Passport or proof of U.S. citizenship required. Visa not required for stay up to 14 days, extendable to 90 days after arrival. Tourists may be asked to show onward/return ticket or proof of sufficient funds for stay. Departure tax of $10 when leaving Bonaire and Curaçao, $4 in Statia, $10 in St. Maarten. For further information, consult the Embassy of the Netherlands, ☎ *(202) 244-5300,* or nearest Consulate General: CA ☎ *(213) 380-3440,* IL ☎ *(312) 856-0110,* NY ☎ *(212) 246-1429* or TX ☎ *(713) 622-8000.*
NEW CALEDONIA	(See French Polynesia.)
NEW ZEALAND	Passport required. Visa not required for tourist/business stay up to three months, must have onward/return ticket, visa for next destination and proof of sufficient funds. For additional information, contact the Embassy of New Zealand, *37 Observatory Circle, N.W., Washington, D.C. 20008,* ☎ *(202) 328-4800,* or the Consulate General, Los Angeles, ☎ *(213) 477-8241.*
NICARAGUA	Passport and onward/return ticket required. Check further information with the Embassy of Nicaragua, *1627 New Hampshire Avenue, N.W., Washington, D.C. 20009,* ☎ *(202) 939-6531 to 34.*

COUNTRY	ENTRY
NIGER	Passport and visa required. Visa valid between seven and 12 months (from date of issuance), depending on type/category of travelers. Requires three application forms, three photos, yellow fever vaccination (cholera vaccination is recommended, but not required), proof of onward/return transportation, letter of invitation and $56.07 fee. For further information and fees, contact the Embassy of the Republic of Niger, *2204 R Street, N.W., Washington, D.C. 20008,* ☎ *(202) 483-4224.*
NIGERIA	The U.S. State Department warns that travel to Nigeria is extremely dangerous. Violent crime is acute, and business scams targeting foreigners are a pervasive problem. Persons contemplating business deals are urged to check with the U.S. Department of State or U.S. Department of Commerce before providing any information, making any financial commitments or traveling to Nigeria. Under no circumstances should American citizens travel to Nigeria without a valid visa. Invitations to enter Nigeria without a visa are normally indicative of illegal activity. U.S. citizens cannot legally depart Nigeria unless they can prove by entry visa that they entered legally. Consular services for all of Nigeria are available only at the U.S. Embassy in Lagos. Passport and visa required of U.S. citizens and all other foreigners. Evidence of yellow fever and cholera vaccinations also required. For further information, contact the Embassy of the Republic of Nigeria, *2201 M Street, N.W., Washington, D.C. 20037,* ☎ *(202) 822-1500 or 1522,* or the Consulate General in New York, ☎ *(212) 715-7200.*
NIUE	Passport, onward/return ticket and confirmed hotel accommodations required. Visa not required for stay up to 30 days. For additional information, consult the Embassy of New Zealand, ☎ *(202) 328-4800.*
NORFOLK ISLAND	Passport and visa required. Visa issued upon arrival for visit up to 30 days; extendable; requires confirmed accommodations and onward/return ticket. Australian transit visa must also be obtained in advance for travel to Norfolk Island. For both visas, consult the Australian Embassy, ☎ *(202) 797-3000.*
NORWAY	Passport required. Visa not required for stay up to three months. (Period begins when entering Scandinavian area: Finland, Sweden, Denmark, Iceland.) For further information, contact the Royal Norwegian Embassy, *2720 34th Street, N.W., Washington, D.C. 20008,* ☎ *(202) 333-6000,* or nearest Consulate General: CA ☎ *(415) 986-0766 to 7168* or *(213) 933-7717,* MN ☎ *(612) 332-3338,* NY ☎ *(212) 421-7333* or TX ☎ *(713) 521-2900.*
OMAN	Passport and visa required. Tourist/business visas for single-entry issued for stay up to three weeks. Requires $21 fee, one application form, one photo and cholera immunization if arriving from infected area. AIDS test required for work permits; U.S test not accepted. Allow one week to 10 days for processing. For transit and road travel, check with the Embassy of the Sultanate of Oman, *2535 Belmont Road, N.W., Washington, D.C. 20008,* ☎ *(202) 387-1980-2.*
PAKISTAN	Passport required. No visa required for stays up to 60 days. For longer stays, visa must be obtained before arrival. Tourist visa requires one application form, one photo and proof of onward/return transportation. Validity depends on length of visit (minimum three months), multiple entries, no charge. Need letter from company for business visa. Include prepaid envelope for return of passport by registered mail. AIDS test required for stays over one year. For applications and inquiries in Washington area, contact the Consular Section of the Embassy of Pakistan, *2315 Massachusettes Avenue, N.W., Washington, D.C. 20008,* ☎ *(202) 939-6295.* All other areas apply to Consulate General, *12 East 65th Street, New York, NY 10021,* ☎ *(212) 879-5800.*
PALAU, THE REPUBLIC OF	Proof of U.S. citizenship and onward/return ticket required for stay up to 30 days (extendable); $50 fee for extension (must apply for extension in Palau). Obtain forms for entry permit from airline or shipping agent serving Palau. For further information, consult with Representative Office, *444 N. Capitol Street, Suite 619, Washington, D.C. 20001,* ☎ *(202) 624-7793.*
PANAMA	Passport, tourist card or visa and onward/return ticket required. Tourist card valid 30 days, available from airline serving Panama for $5 fee. For longer stays and additional information, contact the Embassy of Panama, *2862 McGill Terrace, N.W., Washington, D.C. 20008,* ☎ *(202) 483-1407.*

COUNTRY	ENTRY
PAPUA NEW GUINEA	Passport, onward/return ticket and proof of sufficient funds required. Tourist visa not required for a stay of up to 30 days. Business visa requires two application forms, two photos, company letter, bio-data and $10.25 fee (single entry) or $154.00 (multiple entry). AIDS test required for work and residency permits; U.S. test accepted. For longer stays and further information, contact the Embassy of Papua New Guinea, *Suite 300, 1615 New Hampshire Avenue, N.W., Washington, D.C. 20009,* ☎ *(202) 745-3680.*
PARAGUAY	Passport required. Visa not required for tourist/business stay up to 90 days (extendable). AIDS test required for resident visas; U.S. test sometimes accepted. For additional information, consult the Embassy of Paraguay, *2400 Massachusettes Avenue, N.W., Washington, D.C. 20008,* ☎ *(202) 483-6960.*
PERU	Passport required. Visa not required for tourist stay up to 90 days, extendable after arrival. Tourists may need onward/return ticket. For official/diplomatic passport and other travel, visa required and must be obtained in advance. Business visa requires company letter stating purpose of trip and $27 fee. For further information, contact the Embassy of Peru, *1700 Massachusettes Avenue, N.W., Washington, D.C. 20036,* ☎ *(202) 833-9860-9,* or nearest Consulate: CA ☎ *(213) 383-9896* or *(415) 362-5185,* FL ☎ *(305) 374-1407,* IL ☎ *(312) 853-6173,* NY ☎ *(212) 644-2850,* PR ☎ *(809) 763-0679* or TX ☎ *(713) 781-5000.*
PHILIPPINES	Passport and onward/return ticket required. For entry by Manila International Airport, visa not required for transit/tourist stay up to 21 days. Visa required for longer stay, maximum of 59 days, one application form, one photo, no charge. Company letter needed for business visa. AIDS test required for permanent residency; U.S. test accepted. For more information, contact the Embassy of the Philippines, *1600 Massachusettes Avenue, N.W., Washington, D.C. 20036,* ☎ *(202) 467-9300,* or nearest Consulate General: CA ☎ *(213) 387-5321* or *(415) 433-6666,* HI ☎ *(808) 595-6316,* IL ☎ *(312) 332-6458,* NY ☎ *(212) 764-1330,* TX ☎ *(713) 621-8609* or WA ☎ *(206) 441-1640.*
POLAND	Passport (must be valid at least 12 months past date of entry) required. Visa not required for stay up to 90 days. Visitors must register at hotel or with local authorities within 48 hours after arrival. Check with the Embassy of the Republic of Poland (Consular Division), *2224 Wyoming Avenue, N.W., Washington, D.C. 20008,* ☎ *(202) 232-4517,* or nearest Consulate General: Chicago, IL, *1530 Lakeshore Dr., 60610,* ☎ *(312) 337-8816,* Los Angeles, CA, *3460 Wilshire Blvd., Suite 1200, 90010,* ☎ *(213) 365-7900,* or New York, NY, *233 Madison Avenue, 10016,* ☎ *(212) 889-8360.*
PORTUGAL	(Includes travel to the Azores and Madeira islands.) Passport required. Visa not required for visit up to 60 days (extendable). For travel with pets and other information, consult the nearest Consulate: Washington., D.C. ☎ *(202) 332-3007,* CA ☎ *(415) 346-3400,* MA ☎ *(617) 536-8740* or *(508) 997-6151,* NJ ☎ *(201) 622-7300,* NY ☎ *(212) 246-4580* or RI ☎ *(401) 272-2003.*
QATAR	Passport and visa required. Single-entry visa $33; multiple-entry visa, valid three–six months for $60 or 12 months for $115 fee; transit visa $6. Visas require No Objection Certificate from Qatar Ministry of Interior, two application forms, two photos and SASE for return of passport by mail. Business visa must be obtained through sponsor in Qatar. AIDS test required for work and student visas; U.S. test accepted if within three months of visit. For specific information, contact the Embassy of the State of Qatar, *Suite 1180, 600 New Hampshire Avenue, N.W., Washington, D.C. 20037,* ☎ *(202) 338-0111.*
REUNION	(See France.)
ROMANIA	Passport and visa required. Transit and tourist visa may be obtained at border in Romania or from the Romanian embassy or Consulate before departure. Transit visa for stay up to four days, single-entry $21 or double-entry $31. Tourist/business visa, single-entry, valid six months for stay up to 60 days, $31 (multiple-entry, $68). No application or photos needed. Provide SASE for return of passport by mail. Allow one to three days for processing. For additional information, consult the Embassy of Romania, *1607 23rd Street, N.W., Washington, D.C. 20008,* ☎ *(202) 232-4747-9,* or the Consulate General, New York, ☎ *(212) 682-9120, 9121, 9122.*

COUNTRY	ENTRY

RUSSIA

Passport and visa required. Tourist visa, no charge, requires one application form, three photos, confirmation from tourist agency in the Commonwealth of Independent States (CIS) and processing fee (visa processing fee is $20 for two weeks, $30 for one week, and $60 for three days processing time). Business visa requires one application, three photos, and letter of invitation from a CIS company. Multiple-entry business visa $120 plus processing fee. Fee paid by money order or company check only. AIDS test required for anyone staying over three months; U.S. test accepted. For additional information, contact the Consular Section of the Embassy of Russia, *1825 Phelps Place, N.W., Washington, D.C. 20008,* ☎ *(202) 939-8907, 8911 or 8913,* or the nearest Consulate General: San Francisco ☎ *(415) 202-9800* or Seattle ☎ *(206) 728-1910.*

RWANDA

The State Department warns U.S. citizens to defer travel to Rwanda. Sporadic fighting, poor communication, transportation and health services continue to make travel in Rwanda extremely difficult and dangerous. The U.S. embassy in Kigali can provide emergency services to U.S. citizens. Passport and visa required, plus evidence of yellow fever immunization. Airport visas are not available. There is also a departure tax. For more entry information, contact the Embassy of the Republic of Rwanda, *1714 New Hampshire Avenue, N.W., Washington, D.C. 20009,* ☎ *(202) 232-2882.* U.S. citizens who plan to enter Rwanda are urged to register at the U.S. Embassy in Kigali, *Boulevard de la Revolution,* ☎ *(250) 75601.*

SAINT KITTS AND NEVIS

Proof of U.S. citizenship, photo ID and onward/return ticket required for stay up to six months. AIDS test required for work permit, residency or student visas; U.S. test is accepted. For further information, consult the Embassy of St. Kitts and Nevis, *2501 M Street, N.W., Washington, D.C. 20037,* ☎ *(202) 833-3550,* or Permanent Mission to the U.N., *414 East 75th Street, Fifth Floor, New York, NY 10021,* ☎ *(212) 535-1234.*

SAINT LUCIA

Passport (or proof of U.S. citizenship and photo ID) and return/onward ticket required for stay up to six months. For additional information, contact the Embassy of Saint Lucia, *2100 M Street, N.W., Suite 309, Washington, D.C. 20037,* ☎ *(202) 463-7378/9,* or Permanent Mission to the U.N., *820 Second Street, 9th Floor, New York, NY 10017,* ☎ *(212) 697-9360.*

ST. MARTIN (Sint Maarten)

(See West Indies, French, or Netherlands Antilles.)

ST. PIERRE

Proof of U.S. citizenship and photo ID required for visit up to three months. For specific information, consult the Embassy of France at ☎ *(202) 944-6000.*

SAINT VINCENT AND THE GRENADINES

Proof of U.S. citizenship, photo ID, onward/return ticket and/or proof of sufficient funds required for tourist stay up to six months. For more information, consult the Embassy of Saint Vincent and the Grenadines, *1717 Massachusettes Avenue, N.W., Suite 102, Washington, D.C. 20036,* ☎ *(202) 462-7806 or 7846,* or Consulate, *801 Second Avenue, 21st Floor, New York, NY 10017,* ☎ *(212) 687-4490.*

SAN MARINO

Passport required. Visa not required for tourist stay up to three months. For additional information, contact the nearest Honorary Consulate of the Republic of San Marino: Washington *1899 L Street, N.W., Suite 500, Washington, D.C. 20036,* ☎ *(202) 223-3517,* Detroit ☎ *(313) 528-1190* or New York ☎ *(516) 242-2212.*

SÃO TOME AND PRINCIPE

Passport and visa required. Tourist/business visa for visit up to two weeks, requires two application forms, two photos, yellow fever immunization card, letter stating purpose of travel and $15 fee (money orders only). Company letter is required for a business visa. Enclose prepaid envelope or postage for return of passport by certified or special delivery mail. Apply to the Permanent Mission of São Tome and Principe to the U.N., *122 East 42nd Street, Suite 1604, New York, NY 10168,* ☎ *(212) 697-4211.*

COUNTRY	ENTRY
SAUDI ARABIA	Passport and visa required. All Americans should exercise caution and be extremely vigilant at all times of their personal security and surroundings. Tourist visas are not available for travel to Saudi Arabia. Transit visa valid 24 hours for stay in airport, need onward/return ticket. Business visa requires $15 fee (money order only), one application form, one photo, company letter stating purpose of visit, invitation from Foreign Ministry in Saudi Arabia and SASE for return of passport by mail. Meningitis and cholera vaccinations are highly recommended. Medical report, including AIDS test, required for work permits; U.S. test accepted. For details and requirements for family visits, contact the Royal Embassy of Saudi Arabia, *601 New Hampshire Avenue, N.W., Washington, D.C. 20037,* ☎ *(202) 342-3800,* or nearest Consulate General: Los Angeles ☎ *(213) 208-6566,* New York ☎ *(212) 752-2740* or Houston ☎ *(713) 785-5577.*
SCOTLAND	(See United Kingdom.)
SENEGAL	Passport required. Visa not needed for stay up to 90 days. U.S. citizens need onward/return ticket and yellow fever vaccination. For further information, contact the Embassy of the Republic of Senegal, *2112 Wyoming Avenue, N.W., Washington, D.C. 20008,* ☎ *(202) 234-0540.*
SERBIA AND MONTENEGRO	Passport required. For further information, check with the Embassy of the Former Federal Republic of Yugoslavia (Serbia and Montenegro), *2410 California Street, N.W., Washington, D.C. 20008,* ☎ *(202) 462-6566.* Note: U.S. citizens need a Treasury Department license in order to engage in any commercial transactions within Serbia and Montenegro. Before planning any travel to Serbia and Montenegro, U.S. citizens should contact the Licensing Division, Office of Foreign Assets Control, Department of the Treasury, *1331 G Street, N.W., Washington, D.C. 20220,* ☎ *(202) 622-2480.*
SEYCHELLES	Passport, onward/return ticket and proof of sufficient funds required. Visa issued upon arrival for stay up to one month, no charge, extendable up to one year. Consult Permanent Mission of Seychelles to the U.N., *820 Second Avenue, Suite 203, New York, NY 10017,* ☎ *(212) 687-9766* for further information.
SIERRA LEONE	The State Department warns U.S. citizens to defer travel to Sierra Leone. Travel within the country is considered extremely hazardous. Passport and visa required. Cholera and yellow fever immunizations required and malarial suppressants recommended. Adult travelers (over age 16) must exchange $100 minimum upon arrival and declare other foreign currency on an exchange control form (M), certified and stamped at the port of entry. For further information, consult the Embassy of Sierra Leone, *1701 19th Street, N.W., Washington, D.C. 20009,* ☎ *(202) 939-9261.*
SINGAPORE	Passport and onward/return ticket required. Visa not required for tourist/business stay up to two weeks, extendable to three months maximum. AIDS test required for some work visas; U.S. test is not accepted. For additional information, contact the Embassy of Singapore, *3501 International Place, N.W., Washington, D.C. 20008,* ☎ *(202) 537-3100.*
SLOVAK REPUBLIC	Passport required. Visa not required for stay up to 30 days. For longer stays and other types of travel, contact the Embassy of the Slovak Republic, *2201 Wisconsin Avenue, N.W., Suite 380, Washington, D.C. 20007,* ☎ *(202) 965-5164.*
SLOVENIA	Passport required. Visa not required for stay of up to 90 days. Additional information can be obtained from the Embassy of Slovenia, *1300 19th Street, N.W., Washington, D.C. 20036,* ☎ *(202) 828-1650.*
SOLOMON ISLANDS	Passport, onward/return ticket and proof of sufficient funds required. Visitors permit issued on arrival for stay up to two months in one-year period. For further information, consult the British Embassy at ☎ *(202) 986-0205.*
SOMALIA	Passport required. For further information, contact the Consulate of the Somali Democratic Republic in New York, ☎ *(212) 688-9410.*
SOUTH AFRICA	Passport required. Visa not required for tourist stay up to 90 days. Malarial suppressants are recommended. For business travel, a visa and company letter are required. For more information, contact the Embassy of South Africa, Attn: Consular Office, *3201 New Mexico Avenue, N.W., Washington, D.C. 20016,* ☎ *(202) 966-1650,* or nearest Consulate: CA ☎ *(310) 657-9200,* IL ☎ *(312) 939-7929* or NY ☎ *(212) 213-4880.*

COUNTRY	ENTRY

SPAIN

Passport required. Visa not required for tourist stay up to six months. For additional information, check with the Embassy of Spain, *2700 15th Street, N.W., Washington, D.C. 20009*, ☎ *(202) 265-0190/1*, or nearest Consulate General: CA ☎ *(415) 922-2995* or *(213) 658-6050*, FL ☎ *(305) 446-5511*, IL ☎ *(312) 782-4588*, LA ☎ *(504) 525-4951*, MA ☎ *(617) 536-2506*, NY ☎ *(212) 355-4080*, PR ☎ *(809) 758-6090* or TX ☎ *(713) 783-6200*.

SRI LANKA

Passport, onward/return ticket and proof of sufficient funds ($15 per day) required. Tourist visa not required for stay up to 90 days. For business or travel on official/diplomatic passport, visa required and must be obtained in advance. Business visa valid one month; requires one application form, two photos, a company letter, a letter from sponsoring agency in Sri Lanka, a copy of an onward/return ticket and $5 fee. Include $6 postage for return of passport by registered mail. Yellow fever and cholera immunizations needed if arriving from infected area. For further information, contact the Embassy of the Democratic Socialist Republic of Sri Lanka, *2148 Wyoming Avenue, N.W., Washington, D.C. 20008*, ☎ *(202) 483-4025*, or nearest Consulate: CA ☎ *(805) 323-8975* or *(504) 362-3232*, HI ☎ *(808) 373-2040*, NJ ☎ *(201) 627-7855* or NY ☎ *(212) 986-7040*.

SUDAN

U.S. citizens are warned against all travel to Sudan because of violence within the country. The U.S. has suspended its diplomatic presence in Sudan. Emergency consular services are severely limited. Passport and visa required. Visa must be obtained in advance. Transit visa valid up to seven days; requires $50 fee (cash or money order), onward/return ticket and visa for next destination, if appropriate. Tourist/business visa for single entry up to three months (extendable), requires $50 fee, one application form, one photo, proof of sufficient funds for stay and SASE for return passport. Business visa requires company letter stating purpose of visit and invitation from Sudanese officials. Malarial suppressants and vaccinations for yellow fever, cholera, and meningitis recommended. Visas not granted to passports showing Israeli visas. Allow four weeks for processing. Travelers must declare currency upon arrival and departure. Check additional currency regulations for stays longer than two months. Travelers must register with police headquarters within three days of arrival and must reregister if they change their location. Curfews are strictly enforced and violators of curfews are arrested. Contact the Embassy of the Republic of the Sudan, *2210 Massachusetts Avenue, N.W., Washington, D.C. 20008*, ☎ *(202) 338-8565 to 8570*, or Consulate General, *210 East 49th Street, New York, NY 10017*, ☎ *(212) 421-2680*.

SURINAME

Passport and visa required. Multiple-entry visa requires two application forms and two photos. Business visa requires letter from sponsoring company. For return of passport by mail, send $5 for registered mail or $9.95 for Express Mail. For additional requirements, contact the Embassy of the Republic of Suriname, *Suite 108, 4301 Connecticut Avenue, N.W., Washington, D.C. 20008*, ☎ *(202) 244-7488 or 7490*, or the Consulate: Miami ☎ *(305) 593-2163*.

SWAZILAND

Passport required. Visa not required for stay up to 60 days. Temporary residence permit available in Mbabane for longer stay. Visitors must report to immigration authorities or police station within 48 hours unless lodging in a hotel. Yellow fever and cholera immunizations required if arriving from infected area, and anti-malarial treatment recommended. For further information, consult the Embassy of the Kingdom of Swaziland, *3400 International Drive, N.W., Suite 3M, Washington, D.C.*, ☎ *(202) 362-6683*.

SWEDEN

Valid passport required. Visa not required for stay up to three months. (Period begins when entering Scandinavian area: Finland, Norway, Denmark, Iceland.) For further information, check the Embassy of Sweden, *Suite 1200, 600 New Hampshire Avenue, N.W., Washington, D.C. 20037*, ☎ *(202) 944-5600*, or nearest Consulate General: Los Angeles ☎ *(310) 575-3383* or New York ☎ *(212) 751-5900*.

SWITZERLAND

Passport required. Visa not required for tourist/business stay up to three months. For further information, contact the Embassy of Switzerland, *2900 Cathedral Avenue, N.W., Washington, D.C. 20008*, ☎ *(202) 745-7900*, or nearest Consulate General: CA ☎ *(310) 575-1145* or *(415) 788-2272*, GA ☎ *(404) 870-2000*, IL ☎ *(312) 915-0061*, NY ☎ *(212) 758-2560* or TX ☎ *(713) 650-0000*.

COUNTRY	ENTRY
SYRIA	Passport and visa required. Obtain visa in advance. Single-entry visa valid six months, or double-entry for three months, $15; multiple-entry visa valid six months, $30. Submit two application forms, two photos (signed) and fee (payment must be money order only). Enclose prepaid envelope (with correct postage) for return of passport by mail. AIDS test required for students and others staying over one year; U.S. test sometimes accepted. For group visas and other information, contact the Embassy of the Syrian Arab Republic, *2215 Wyoming Avenue, N.W., Washington, D.C. 20008,* ☎ *(202) 232-6313.*
TAHITI	(See French Polynesia.)
TAIWAN	Passport required. Visa not required for stay up to five days. AIDS test mandatory for anyone staying over three months; U.S. test sometimes accepted. For business travel, longer stays or other information, contact the Coordination Council for North American Affairs (CCNAA), *4201 Wisconsin Avenue, N.W., Washington, D.C. 20016-2137,* ☎ *(202) 895-1800.* Additional offices are in Atlanta, Boston, Chicago, Guam, Honolulu, Houston, Kansas City, Los Angeles, Miami, New York, San Francisco, and Seattle.
TAJIKISTAN	Passport and visa required. In the U.S., visas for Tajikistan are issued by the Russian Embassy, Consular Division, *1825 Phelps Place N.W., Washington, D.C. 20008,* ☎ *(202) 939-8907,* or the Russian Consulates in New York, San Francisco or Seattle. Tajik visas granted by these offices are valid for a stay of five days in Tajikistan. These visas are also valid in other Commonwealth of Independent States for five days, except in Uzbekistan, where they are valid for three days only for transiting to another country. If travelers plan a longer stay, they may apply at the Ministry of Foreign Affairs for a longer visa. The U.S. embassy provides a full range of consular services to Americans but is very limited in services it can provide outside Dushanbe. Tourist facilities within the country are limited, and many goods and services are unavailable. Tajikistan is a cash-only economy, and international banking services are not available. Credit cards and traveler's checks are not accepted, and travel with large amounts of cash is dangerous.
TANZANIA	Passport and visa required. Obtain visa before departure. Visas for mainland Tanzania are valid for Zanzibar. Tourist visa (valid six months from date of issuance) for one entry up to 30 days may be extended after arrival. Requires one application, one form and $10.50 fee (no personal checks). Enclose prepaid envelope for return of passport by certified or registered mail. Yellow fever and cholera immunizations recommended (required if arriving from infected area), and malarial suppressants advised. Allow one month for processing. For business visa and other information, consult the Embassy of the United Republic of Tanzania, *2139 R Street, N.W., Washington, D.C. 20008,* ☎ *(202) 939-6125,* or Tanzanian Permanent Mission to the U.N., *205 East 42nd Street, 13th Floor, New York, NY 10017,* ☎ *(212) 972-9160.*
THAILAND	Passport and onward/return ticket required. Visa not needed for stay up to 15 days if arrive and depart from Don Muang Airport in Bangkok. For longer stays, obtain visa in advance. Transit visa for stay up to 30 days, $10 fee; tourist visa for stay up to 60 days, $15 fee. For business visa valid up to 90 days, need $20 fee and company letter stating purpose of visit. Submit one application form, two photos and postage for return of passport by mail. Apply to the Embassy of Thailand, *2300 Kalorama Road, N.W., Washington, D.C. 20008,* ☎ *(202) 234-5052,* or nearest Consulate General: CA ☎ *(213) 937-1894,* IL ☎ *(312) 236-2447* or NY ☎ *(212) 754-1770.*
TOGO	Passport required. Visa not required for stay up to three months. Americans travelling in remote areas in Togo occasionally require visas. Yellow fever and cholera vaccinations are required. Check further information with the Embassy of the Republic of Togo, *2208 Massachusettes Avenue, N.W., Washington, D.C. 20008,* ☎ *(202) 234-4212/3.*
TONGA	Passport and onward/return ticket required. Visa not required for stay up to 30 days. For additional information, consult the Consulate General of Tonga, *360 Post Street, Suite 604, San Francisco, CA 94108,* ☎ *(415) 781-0365.*
TRINIDAD AND TOBAGO	Passport required. Visa not required for tourist/business stay up to three months. Business visa requires passport and company letter. For further information, consult the Embassy of Trinidad and Tobago, *1708 Massachusettes Avenue, N.W., Washington, D.C. 20036,* ☎ *(202) 467-6490,* or nearest Consulate in New York, ☎ *(212) 682-7272.*

COUNTRY	ENTRY
TUNISIA	Passport and onward/return ticket required. Visas not required for tourist/business stay up to four months. For further information, consult the Embassy of Tunisia, *1515 Massachusettes Avenue, N.W., Washington, D.C. 20005*, ☎ *(202) 862-1850*, or nearest Consulate: San Francisco ☎ *(415) 922-9222* or New York ☎ *(212) 272-6962*.
TURKEY	Passport required. Visa not required for tourist/business stay up to three months. For other travel, visa required and must be obtained in advance. For further information, contact the Embassy of the Republic of Turkey, *1714 Massachusettes Avenue, N.W., Washington, D.C. 20036*, ☎ *(202) 659-0742*, or nearest Consulate: CA ☎ *(213) 937-0118*, IL ☎ *(312) 263-0644*, NY ☎ *(212) 949-0160* or TX ☎ *(713) 622-5849*.
TURKMENISTAN	Passport and visa required. At the time of publication, visa issuances are being handled by the Russian Consulate. The visa process must be initiated in Turkmenistan by the sponsoring agency or by the travel agent involved; no visa request is initiated at the Russian Consulate. Visas are not issued until an approval cable arrives from the Ministry of Foreign Affairs in Turkmenistan to the Russian Consulate.
TURKS AND CAICOS	(See West Indies, British.)
TUVALU	Passport and onward/return ticket and proof of sufficient funds required. Visitors permit issued on arrival. For further information, consult the British Embassy, ☎ *(202) 986-0205*.
UGANDA	U.S. citizens should avoid travel to northern Uganda as it is extremely dangerous. Travel to Murchison Falls National Park north of the Victoria Nile is not recommended. Passport required. Immunization certificates for yellow fever and cholera are required (typhoid and malaria suppressants recommended). For business visa and other information, contact the Embassy of the Republic of Uganda, *5909 16th Street, N.W., Washington, D.C. 20011*, ☎ *(202) 726-7100-02*, or Permanent Mission to the U.N., ☎ *(212) 949-0110*.
UKRAINE	Passport and visa required. Visas may be obtained at the Ukraine Embassy in the U.S. (visas limited to three days may be obtained at airports in Ukraine, or at any border crossing point). Visa requires one form, one photo and $30-100 fee, depending upon processing time (company check or money order only). AIDS test may be required for anyone staying over three months. U.S. test is sometimes accepted. For additional information, contact the Embassy of Ukraine, *3350 M Street, N.W., Washington, D.C. 20007*, ☎ *(202) 333-7507*, or the nearest Consulate: IL ☎ *(312) 384-6632* or NY ☎ *(212) 505-1409*.
UNITED ARAB EMIRATES	Passport and visa required. Tourist visa must be obtained by relative/sponsor in UAE, and sponsor must meet visitor at airport. Business visas issued only by embassy, and require company letter and sponsor in UAE to send a fax or telex to embassy confirming trip. Single-entry visa valid two months for stay up to 30 days, $18 fee. Multiple-entry visa (for business only), valid six months from date of issue for maximum stay of 30 days per entry, $225 fee, paid by cash, money order or certified check. Submit two application forms, two photo and prepaid envelope for return of passport by certified/registered mail. AIDS test required for work or residence permits; testing must be performed upon arrival; U.S. test not accepted. For further information, contact the Embassy of the United Arab Emirates, *Suite 740, 600 New Hampshire Avenue, N.W., Washington, D.C. 20037*, ☎ *(202) 338-6500*.
UNITED KINGDOM (England, Northern Ireland, Scotland, and Wales)	Passport required. Visa not required for stay up to six months. AIDS test required for anyone staying over six months and for resident and work visas; U.S. test usually accepted. For additional information, consult the Consular Section of the British Embassy, *19 Observatory Circle, N.W., Washington, D.C. 20008*, ☎ *(202) 986-0205*, or nearest Consulate General: CA ☎ *(310) 477-3322*, GA ☎ *(404) 524-5856*, IL ☎ *(312) 346-1810*, MA ☎ *(617) 437-7160*, NY ☎ *(212) 752-8400*, OH ☎ *(216) 621-7674* or TX ☎ *(713) 659-6210*.
URUGUAY	Passport required. Visa not required for stay up to three months. For additional information, consult the Embassy of Uruguay, *1918 F Street, N.W., Washington, D.C. 20008*, ☎ *(202) 331-1313-6*, or nearest Consulate: CA ☎ *(213) 394-5777*, FL ☎ *(305) 358-9350*, IL ☎ *(312) 236-3366*, LA ☎ *(504) 525-8354* or NY ☎ *(212) 753-8191/2*.

COUNTRY	ENTRY
UZBEKISTAN	Passport and visa required. Apply to the Uzbekistan Consulate, *866 United Nations Plaza, Suite 326, New York, NY 10017,* ☎ *(212) 486-7570.*
VANUATU	Passport and onward/return ticket required. Visa not required for stay up to 30 days. For further information, consult the British Embassy at ☎ *(202) 986-0205.*
VATICAN	(See Holy See.)
VENEZUELA	Passport and tourist card required. Tourist card can be obtained from airlines serving Venezuela, no charge, valid 60 days, cannot be extended. Multiple-entry visa valid up to one year; extendable; available from any Venezuelan consulate; requires $30 fee (money order or company check), one application form, one photo, onward/return ticket, proof of sufficient funds and certification of employment. For business visa, need letter from company stating purpose of trip, responsibility for traveler, name and address of companies to be visited in Venezuela and $60 fee. All travelers must pay departure tax ($12) at airport. Business travelers must present a Declaration of Income Tax in the Ministerio de Hacienda (Treasury Department). For additional information, contact the Consular Section of the Embassy of Venezuela, *1099 30th Street, N.W., Washington, DC 20007,* ☎ *(202) 342-2214,* or the nearest Consulate: CA ☎ *(415) 512-8340,* FL ☎ *(305) 577-3834,* IL ☎ *(312) 236-9655,* LA ☎ *(504) 522-3284,* MA ☎ *(617) 266-9355,* NY ☎ *(212) 826-1660,* PR ☎ *(809) 766-4250* or TX ☎ *(713) 961-5141.*
VIETNAM	Passport and visa required. Tourist visa, valid 30 days, requires application form(s), two photos and $90 fee. Allow at least three weeks for processing. (Visas are not being issued in the U.S. at this time. You must apply in a country that maintains diplomatic relations with Vietnam.) For other types of travel and more information, contact the Vietnamese Permanent Mission to the U.N., *20 Waterside Plaza, New York, NY 10010,* ☎ *(212) 679-3779.*
VIRGIN ISLANDS, (British)	Islands include Anegarda, Jost van Dyke, Tortola and Virgin Gorda. Proof of U.S. citizenship, photo ID, onward/return ticket and sufficient funds required for tourist stay up to three months. AIDS test required for residency or work; U.S. test accepted. Consult the British Embassy for further information at ☎ *(202) 986-0205.*
WALES	(See United Kingdom.)
WEST INDIES, (British)	Islands include Anguilla, Montserrat, Cayman Islands, Turks and Caicos. Proof of U.S. citizenship, photo ID, onward/return ticket and sufficient funds required for tourist stay up to three months. AIDS test required for residency or work; U.S. test accepted. Consult the British Embassy for further information at ☎ *(202) 986-0205.*
WEST INDIES, (French)	Islands include Guadeloupe, Isles des Saintes, La Desirade, Marie Galante, Saint Barthélémy, St. Martin and Martinique. Proof of U.S. citizenship and photo ID required for visit up to three weeks. (For stays longer than three weeks, a passport is required.) No visa required for stay up to three months. For further information, consult the Embassy of France at ☎ *(202) 944-6200/6215.*
WESTERN SAMOA	Passport and onward/return ticket required. Visa not required for stay up to 30 days. For longer stays, contact the Western Samoa Mission to the U.N., *820 2nd Avenue, Suite 800, New York, NY,* ☎ *(212) 599-6196.*
YEMEN, REPUBLIC OF	Passport and visa required. Visa valid 30 days from date of issuance for single entry; requires one application form and two photos. For tourist visa, need proof of onward/return transportation and employment and $20 fee. Visitors visa requires letter of invitation and $20 fee. Business visa requires $20 and company letter stating purpose of trip. Payment by money order only, and include postage for return of passport by registered mail. Entry not granted to passports showing Israeli or South African visas. Yellow fever and cholera vaccinations and malaria suppressants recommended. Check information with the Embassy of the Republic Yemen, *Suite 705, 2600 Virginia Avenue, N.W., Washington, D.C. 20037,* ☎ *(202) 965-4760,* or Yemen Mission to the U.N., *866 United Nations Plaza, Room 435, New York, NY 10017,* ☎ *(212) 355-1730.*

VISAS AND ENTRY REQUIREMENTS

COUNTRY	ENTRY
ZAIRE	Passport and visa required. Visa must be obtained before arrival. Transit visa for stay up to eight days, single-entry $45, double-entry $70. Tourist/business visa, valid one month $75–120, two months $140–180, three months $190–220 and six months $264–360; requires three photos, three applications, yellow fever immunization and onward/return ticket. Business visa also requires company letter accepting financial responsibility for traveler. No personal checks; send money order and enclose SASE for return of passport by mail. Apply ato the Embassy of the Republic of Zaire, *1800 New Hampshire Avenue, N.W., Washington, D.C. 20009,* ☎ *(202) 234-7690/1,* or Permanent Mission to the U.N., *747 Third Avenue, New York, NY 10017,* ☎ *(212) 754-1966.*
ZAMBIA	Passport and visa required. Obtain visa in advance. Visa valid up to six months; requires $10 fee (no personal checks), two application forms and two photos. Business visa also requires company letter. Yellow fever and cholera immunizations recommended. Apply to the Embassy of the Republic of Zambia, *2419 Massachusettes Avenue, N.W., Washington, D.C. 20008,* ☎ *(202) 265-9717-21.*
ZANZIBAR	(See Tanzania.)
ZIMBABWE	Passport, onward/return ticket and proof of sufficient funds required. Visitors must declare currency upon arrival. For regulations, check with the Embassy of Zimbabwe, *1608 New Hampshire Avenue, N.W., Washington, D.C. 20009,* ☎ *(202) 332-7100.*

NOTES:
SASE is self-addressed, stamped envelope. If applying in person, remember to call about office hours. Many consulates are only open in the morning.

VISAS AND ENTRY REQUIREMENTS

Tourist Offices

If you need information about a country not listed here, call the United Nations at ☎ *(212) 963-1234,* wait through the recorded message for an operator, and ask for the number of the country's U.N. delegation. If it is not a member of the U.N., call the Ministry of Tourism or government office in that country directly, using the area code of the capital city.

Antigua and Barbuda
> *Antigua and Barbuda Department of Tourism*
> *610 Fifth Avenue, Suite 311*
> *New York, New York 10020*
> ☎ *(212) 541-4117*

Argentina
> *Argentine Government Tourist Office*
> *3550 Wilshire Boulevard, Suite 1450*
> *Los Angeles, California 90010*
> ☎ *(213) 930-0681*

Armenia
> *Embassy of Armenia*
> *122 C Street, N.W., Suite 360*
> *Washington D.C. 20001*
> ☎ *(202) 393-5983*

Aruba
> *Aruba Tourism Authority*
> *1000 Harbor Boulevard*
> *Weehawken, New Jersey 07087*
> ☎ *(800) 862-7822 or (201) 330-0800.*

Australia
> *Australian Tourist Commission,*
> *2121 Avenue of the Stars, Suite 1200*
> *Los Angeles, California 90067*
> ☎ *(310) 552-1988*

Austria
> *Austrian National Tourist Office*
> *11601 Wilshire Boulevard, Suite 2480*
> *Los Angeles, California 90025*
> ☎ *(310) 477-3332*

Bahamas
> *Bahamas Tourist Office*
> *3450 Wilshire Boulevard, Suite 208*
> *Los Angeles, California 90010*
> ☎ *(213) 385-0033.*

Barbados
> *Barbados Tourism Authority*
> *3440 Wilshire Boulevard, Suite 1215*
> *Los Angeles, California 90010*
> ☎ *(213) 380-2198*

Belgium
> *Belgian Tourist Office*
> *780 Third Avenue, Suite 1501*
> *New York, New York 10017*
> ☎ *(212) 758-8130*

Belize
> *Consulate General of Belize*
> *5825 Sunset Boulevard, Suite 203*
> *Hollywood, California 90028*
> ☎ *(213) 469-7343*

Bermuda
> *Bermuda Department of Tourism*
> *310 Madison Avenue, Suite 201*
> *New York, New York 10017*
> ☎ *(212) 818-9800*

Bhutan
> *Bhutan Travel Service*
> *120 East 56th Street, Suite 1130*
> *New York, New York 10022*
> ☎ *(212) 838-6382*

Bolivia
> *Embassy of Bolivia*
> *Tourist Information*
> *3014 Massachusetts Avenue, N.W.*
> *Washington D.C. 20008*
> ☎ *(202) 483-4410*

Bonaire
> *Tourism Corporation Bonaire*
> *444 Madison Avenue, Suite 2403*
> *New York, New York 10022*
> ☎ *(800) 826-6247 or (212) 832-0779*

Brazil

Consulate General of Brazil
Brazilian Trade Center
Tourist Information
8484 Wilshire Boulevard
7th Floor
Beverly Hills, California 90211
☎ (213) 651-2664, ext. 200

British Virgin Islands

British Virgin Islands Tourist Board
1686 Union Street, Suite 305
San Francisco, California 94123
☎ (800) 835-8530

Bolivia

97-45 Queens Park, Suite 600
Rego Park
New York, New York 11374
☎ (800) BOLIVIA or (718) 897-7956
FAX (718) 275-3943

Bulgaria

Balkan Holidays
Tourist Information
41 East 42nd Street, Suite 508
New York, New York 10017
☎ (212) 573-5530

Canada

Canadian Consulate General
Tourist Information
300 S. Grand Avenue
10th Floor
Los Angeles, California 90071
☎ (213) 346-2700

Caribbean

Caribbean Tourism Organization
20 East 46th Street, 4th Floor
New York, New York 10017
☎ (212) 682-0435

Cayman Islands

Cayman Islands Department of Tourism
3440 Wilshire Boulevard, Suite 1202
Los Angeles, California 90010
☎ (213) 738-1968

Chile

Chilean Consulate General
Tourist Information
1110 Brickell Avenue, Suite 616
Miami, Florida 33131
☎ (305) 373-8623

China, People's Republic of

China National Tourist Office
333 W. Broadway, Suite 201
Glendale, California 91204
☎ (818) 545-7505

Russia/CIS

(and most former Soviet republics)
Intourist U.S.A. Inc.
610 Fifth Avenue, Suite 603
New York, New York 10020
☎ (212) 757-3884

Cook Islands

Cook Islands Tourist Authority
6033 W. Century Boulevard, Suite 690
Los Angeles, California 90045
☎ (800) 624-6250 or (310) 216-2872

Costa Rica

Consulate General of Costa Rica
3540 Wilshire Boulevard, Suite 404
Los Angeles, California 90010
☎ (213) 380-7915

Curaçao

Curaçao Tourist Board
400 Madison Avenue, Suite 311
New York, New York 10017,
☎ (800) 270-3350

Cyprus

Cyprus Tourism Organization
13 East 40th Street, 1st Floor
New York, New York 10016
☎ (212) 683-5280

Czech Republic (and Slovakia)

Cedok Central European Tours & Travel
10 East 40th Street, Suite 3604
New York, New York 10016
☎ (212) 689-9720

Denmark

Danish Tourist Board
655 Third Avenue, 18th Floor
New York, New York 10017
☎ (212) 949-2333
For information on Greenland contact:
Atuakkiorfik
Post Office Box 840 DK-3900
Nuuk Greenland
☎ (299) 22 122
FAX (299) 22 5 00

Dominican Republic

Consulate General of the Dominican
Republic Tourism Department
1 Times Square, 11th Floor
New York, New York 10036
☎ (212) 768-2481

Ecuador

Ecuadorian Consulate
Tourist Information
548 S. Spring Street, Suite 602
Los Angeles, California 90013
☎ (213) 628-3014

Egypt

Egyptian Tourist Authority
8383 Wilshire Boulevard, Suite 215
Beverly Hills, California 90211
☎ (213) 653-8815

Estonia

Consulate General of Estonia
Tourist Information
630 Fifth Avenue, Suite 2415
New York, New York 10111
☎ (212) 247-7634

Fiji

Fiji Visitors Bureau
5777 W. Century Boulevard, Suite 220
Los Angeles, California 90045
☎ (310) 568-1616

Finland

Finnish Tourist Board
655 Third Avenue, 18th Floor
New York, New York 10017
☎ (212) 949-2333

France

French Government Tourist Office
9454 Wilshire Boulevard, Suite 715
Beverly Hills, California 90212
☎ (310) 479-4426
☎ (900) 990-0040
(calls cost 50 cents a minute)

French Guiana

French Government Tourist Office
9454 Wilshire Boulevard, Suite 715,
Beverly Hills, California 90212
☎ (310) 479-4426
☎ (900) 990-0040
(calls cost 50 cents a minute)

Germany

German National Tourist Office
11766 Wilshire Boulevard, Suite 750
Los Angeles, California 90025
☎ (310) 575-9799

Ghana

Embassy of Ghana
Tourist Information
3512 International Drive, N.W.
Washington D.C. 20008
☎ (202) 686-4520

Great Britain

British Tourist Authority
551 Fifth Avenue, Suite 701
New York, New York 10176
☎ (800) GO2 BRITAIN
Free fax-on-demand service (213) 628-
1216; you must call from a fax machine

Greece

Greek National Tourist Organization
611 W. 6th Street, Suite 2198
Los Angeles, California 90017
☎ (213) 626-6696

Grenada

Grenada Tourist Office
820 Second Avenue, Suite 900-D
New York, New York 10017
(800) 927-9554

Greenland

See Denmark

Guadeloupe

See French Government Tourist Office

Guam

Guam Visitors Bureau
1150 Marina Village Parkway, Suite 104
Alameda, California 94501
☎ (800) US3-GUAM

Guatemala

Guatemala Consulate General
2500 Wilshire Boulevard, Suite 820
Los Angeles, California 90057
☎ (213) 365-9251

Haiti

Haitian Consulate
271 Madison Avenue, 17th Floor
New York, New York 10016
☎ (212) 697-9767

Honduras

Honduras Consulate
3450 Wilshire Boulevard, Suite 230
Los Angeles, California 90010
☎ (213) 383-9244

Hong Kong

Hong Kong Tourist Association
10940 Wilshire Boulevard, Suite 1220
Los Angeles, California 90024
☎ (310) 208-4582.

Hungary

Ibusz Travel
1 Parker Plaza, 4th Floor
Ft. Lee, New Jersey 07024
☎ (201) 592-8585

Iceland

Icelandic Tourist Board
655 Third Avenue, 18th Floor
New York, New York 10017
☎ (212) 949-2333

India

Government of India Tourist Office
3550 Wilshire Boulevard, Suite 204
Los Angeles, California 90010
☎ (213) 380-8855

Indonesia

Indonesia Tourist Promotion Office
3457 Wilshire Boulevard, Suite 104
Los Angeles, California 90010
☎ (213) 387-2078

Ireland

Irish Tourist Board
345 Park Avenue
New York, New York 10154
☎ (800) 223-6470 or (212) 418-0800

Israel

Israel Government Tourist Office
6380 Wilshire Boulevard, Suite 1700
Los Angeles, California 90048
☎ (213) 658-7462

Italy

Italian Government Tourist Board
12400 Wilshire Boulevard, Suite 550
Los Angeles, California 90025
☎ (310) 820-0098

Ivory Coast

Tourism Cote d'Ivorie North America
2424 Massachusetts Avenue, N.W.
Washington D.C. 20008
☎ (202) 797-0344

Jamaica

Jamaica Tourist Board
3440 Wilshire Boulevard, Suite 1207
Los Angeles, California 90010
☎ (213) 384-1123

Japan

Japan National Tourist Organization
624 S. Grand Avenue, Suite 1611
Los Angeles, California 90017
☎ (213) 623-1952

Jordan

Jordan Information Bureau
2319 Wyoming Avenue N.W.
Washington D.C. 20008
☎ (202) 265-1606

Kenya

Kenya Consulate
Tourist Office
9150 Wilshire Boulevard, Suite 160
Beverly Hills, California 90212
☎ (310) 274-6635

Korea (South)

Korea National Tourism Corp.
3435 Wilshire Boulevard, Suite 350
Los Angeles, California 90010
☎ (213) 382-3435

Latvia

Latvian Embassy
4325 17th Street, N.W.
Washington D.C. 20011
☎ (202) 726-8213

Liechtenstein

See Swiss National Tourist Office

Lithuania

Embassy of Lithuania
Tourist Information
2622 16th Street, N.W.
Washington D.C. 20009
☎ (202) 234-5860

Luxembourg

Luxembourg Tourist Office
17 Beekman Place
N.Y. 10022
☎ (212) 935-8888

Macau

Macau Tourist Information Bureau
3133 Lake Hollywood Drive
Los Angeles, California 90068
☎ (213) 851-3402

Madagascar

Embassy of Madagascar
Tourist Information
2374 Massachusetts Avenue, N.W.
Washington D.C. 20008
☎ (202) 265-5525

Malaysia

Malaysia Tourism Promotion Board
818 West 7th Street
Los Angeles, California 90017
☎ (213) 689-9702.

Malta

Malta National Tourist Office
249 East 35th Street
New York, New York 10016
☎ (212) 213-6686

Martinique

See French Government Tourist Office

Mauritius

Mauritius Tourist Information Service
8 Haven Avenue
Port Washington New York 11050
☎ (516) 944-3763

Mexico

Mexican Government Tourism Office
10100 Santa Monica Boulevard, Suite 224
Los Angeles, California 90067
☎ (310) 203-8191

Monaco

Monaco Government Tourist & Convention Bureau
845 Third Avenue, 19th Floor
New York, New York 10022
☎ (800) 753-9696 or (212) 759-5227

Morocco

Moroccan National Tourist Office
20 East 46th Street
New York, New York 10017
☎ (212) 557-2520

Myanmar (Burma)

Embassy of Myanmar
2300 S Street, N.W.
Washington D.C. 20008,
☎ (202) 332-9044

Nepal

Royal Nepalese Consulate
Tourist Information
820 Second Avenue, Suite 202
New York, New York 10017
☎ (212) 370-4188

Netherlands

Netherlands Board of Tourism
225 N. Michigan Avenue, Suite 326
Chicago, Illinois 60601
☎ (312) 819-0300.

New Zealand

New Zealand Tourism Board,
501 Santa Monica Boulevard, Suite 300
Santa Monica, California 90401
☎ (800) 388-5494 or (310) 395-7480

Nigeria

Embassy of Nigeria, Tourist Information
2201 M Street, N.W.
Washington D.C. 20037
☎ (202) 822-1500

Norway

Norwegian Tourist Board
655 Third Avenue, 18th Floor
New York, New York 10017,
☎ (212) 949-2333

Papua New Guinea

Air Niugini
5000 Birch Street, Suite 3000
Newport Beach, California 92660
☎ *(714) 752-5440*

Paraguay

Paraguay Embassy
Tourist Information
2400 Massachusetts Avenue, N.W.
Washington D.C. 20008
☎ *(202) 483-6962*

Peru

Peruvian Consulate
Tourist Information
3460 Wilshire Boulevard, Suite 1005
Los Angeles, California 90010
☎ *(213) 383-9895*

Philippines

Philippine Department of Tourism
3660 Wilshire Boulevard, Suite 216
Los Angeles, California 90010
☎ *(213) 487-4525*

Poland

Orbis Polish Travel Bureau
342 Madison Avenue, Suite 1512
New York, New York 10173
☎ *(212) 867-5011*

Portugal

Portuguese National Tourist Office
590 Fifth Avenue, 4th Floor
New York, New York 10036
☎ *(212) 354-4403*

Puerto Rico

Government of Puerto Rico Tourism Co.
3575 W. Cahuenga Boulevard, Suite 560
Los Angeles, California 90068
☎ *(213) 874-5991*

Romania

Romanian National Tourist Office
342 Madison Avenue, Suite 210
New York, New York 10173
☎ *(212) 697-6971*

Russia/CIS

(and most former Soviet republics)
Intourist U.S.A. Inc.
610 Fifth Avenue, Suite 603
New York, New York 10020
☎ *(212) 757-3884*

St. Barthélemy

See French Government Tourist Office

St. Kitts and Nevis

St. Kitts and Nevis Tourist Office
414 East 75th Street, 5th Floor
New York, New York 10021
☎ *(212) 535-1234*

St. Lucia

St. Lucia Tourist Board
820 Second Avenue, 9th Floor, Suite
900E
New York, New York 10017
☎ *(800) 456-3984 or (212) 867-2950*

Sint Maarten

Sint Maarten Tourist Office
275 Seventh Avenue, 19th Floor
New York, New York 10001-6788
☎ *(212) 989-0000*

St. Martin

See French Government Tourist Office

St. Vincent

St. Vincent & the Grenadines Tourist
Office
801 Second Avenue, 21st Floor
New York, New York 10017
☎ *(212) 687-4981*

Samoa

American Samoa Government Office
Tourism Information
401 Waiakamilo Road, Suite 201
Honolulu, Hawaii 96817
☎ *(808) 847-1998*

Senegal

Senegal Tourist Office
888 Seventh Avenue, 27th Floor
New York, New York 10106
☎ *(202) 234-0540*

Seychelles

Seychelles Tourist Office
820 Second Avenue, Suite 900-F
New York, New York 10017
☎ *(212) 687-9766*

Singapore

Singapore Tourist Promotion Board
8484 Wilshire Boulevard, Suite 510
Beverly Hills California 90211
☎ *(213) 852-1901*

Slovakia

Cedok Central European Tours & Travel
10 East 40th Street, Suite 3604
New York, New York 10016
☎ *(212) 689-9720*

Slovenia

Slovenian Tourist Office
122 East 42nd Street, Suite 3006
New York, New York 10168-0072
☎ *(212) 682-5896*

Solomon Islands

Solomon Islands Tourist Authority
P.O. Box 321
Honiara, Solomon Islands
☎ *(011) 677-22-442*

South Africa

South African Tourist Board
9841 Airport Boulevard, Suite 1524
Los Angeles, California 90045
☎ *(800) 782-9772 or (310) 641-8444*

Spain

National Tourist Office of Spain
8383 Wilshire Boulevard, Suite 960
Beverly Hills, California 90211
☎ *(213) 658-7188*

TOURIST OFFICES

Sri Lanka

Embassy of Sri Lanka
Tourist Information
2148 Wyoming Avenue, N.W.
Washington D.C. 20008
☎ (202) 483-4025

Sweden

Swedish Travel & Tourism Council
655 Third Avenue, 18th Floor
New York, New York 10017
☎ (212) 949-2333

Switzerland

Swiss National Tourist Office
222 N. Sepulveda Boulevard, Suite 1570
El Segundo, California 90245
☎ (310) 335-5980

Tahiti (French Polynesia)

Tahiti Tourism Board
300 N. Continental Boulevard, Suite 180
El Segundo, California 90245
☎ (310) 414-8484

Taiwan (Republic of China)

Taiwan Visitors Assn.
166 Geary Street, Suite 1605
San Francisco, California 94108
☎ (415) 989-8677

Tanzania

Tanzania Mission to the U.N.
205 East 42nd Street, Suite 1300
New York, New York 10017
☎ (212) 972-9160

Thailand

Tourism Authority of Thailand
3440 Wilshire Boulevard, Suite 1100
Los Angeles, California 90010
☎ (213) 382-2353

Tonga

Tonga Consulate General
Tourist Information
360 Post Street, Suite 604,
San Francisco, California 94108
☎ (415) 781-0365.

Trinidad & Tobago

Trinidad & Tobago Tourism
Development Authority
25 West 43rd Street, Suite 1508
New York, New York 10036
☎ (800) 232-0082

Tunisia

Embassy of Tunisia
Tourist Information
1515 Massachusetts Avenue
N.W. Washington D.C. 20005
☎ (202) 862-1850

Turkey

Office of Tourism Information Attache
821 United Nations Plaza
New York, New York 10017
☎ (212) 687-2194

Ukraine

Kobasniuk Travel
157 Second Avenue
New York, New York 10003
☎ (212) 254-8779

Uruguay

Consulate of Uruguay
Tourist Information
747 3rd Avenue, 21st Floor
New York, New York 10017
☎ (212) 753-8191

Vanuatu

National Tourism Office of Vanuatu
520 Monterey Drive
Rio del Mar, California 95003
☎ (408) 685-8901

U.S. Virgin Islands

U.S. Virgin Islands Division of Tourism
3460 Wilshire Boulevard, Suite 412
Los Angeles, California 90010
☎ (213) 739-0138

Venezuela

Embassy of Venezuela
Tourist Information
1099 30th Street N.W.,
Washington D.C. 20007
☎ (202) 342-6850

Zambia

Zambia National Tourist Board
237 East 52nd Street
New York, New York 10022,
☎ (212) 308-2155.

International Long-Distance Access Codes

Dial these numbers from within the countries to reach your preferred carrier.

COUNTRY	AT&T	MCI	SPRINT
Albania	00-800-0010	No MCI Access	No Sprint Access
American Samoa	6332-USA	633-2MCI	633-1000
Angola	199	No MCI Access	No Sprint Access
Anguilla	1-800-872-2881	No MCI Access	1-800-877-8000
Antigua	1-800-872-2881	#2	1-800-366-4663
Argentina	001-800-200-1111	001-800-333-1111	001-800-777-1111
Armenia	8*14111	No MCI Access	8-10-155
Aruba	NO AT&T ACCESS	800-8888	800-8870
Australia	1800-881-001	1800-551-111	1-800-5511-10
Austria	022-903-011	022-903-012	022-903-014
Bahamas	1-800-872-0881	1-800-888-8000	1-800-389-2111
Bahrain	800-001	800-002	800-777
Barbados	1-800-872-2881	1-800-888-8000	1-800-534-0042
Belarus	8*800101	No MCI Access	No Sprint Access
Belgium	0-800-100-10	0800-10012	0800-10014
Belize	555	815	812
Benin	102	No MCI Access	No Sprint Access
Bermuda	1-800-872-0881	1-800-888-8000	1-800-623-0877
Bolivia	0-800-1112	0-800-2222	0800-3333
Bosnia	00-800-0010	No MCI Access	No Sprint Access
Brazil	000-8010	000-8012	000-8016
Brunei	800-1111	No MCI Access	No Sprint Access

COUNTRY	AT&T	MCI	SPRINT
Bulgaria	00-1800-0100	00-800-0001	00-800-1010
Cambodia	1-800-881-001	No MCI Access	No Sprint Access
Canada	1-800-225-5288	1-800-888-8000	1-800-877-8000
Cape Verde	112	No MCI Access	No Sprint Access
Cayman Islands	1-800-872-2881	1-800-888-8000	1-800-366-4663
Chile	800-800-0311	800-207-300	00*0317
China	10811	108-12	108-13
Columbia	980-11-0010	980-16-0001	980-13-0010
Cook Islands	09-111	No MCI Access	No Sprint Access
Costa Rica	0-800-0-114-114	0800-012-2222	0800-0013-0123
Croatia	99-385-0111	99-385-0112	99-385-0113
Cyprus	080-90010	080-90000	080-900-01
Czech Republic	00-42-000-101	00-42-000112	0042-087-187
Denmark	8001-0010	8001-0022	800-1-0877
Dominican Republic	1-800-872-2881	1-800-888-8000	1-800-751-7877
Ecuador	999-119	999-170	999-171
Egypt (Cairo)	510-0200	355-5770	356-4777
Egypt (All Others)	02-510-0200	02-355-5770	02-356-4777
El Salvador	800-1785	800-1767	800-1776
Estonia	8-00-8001001	No MCI Access	No Sprint Access
Fiji	004-890-1001	004-890-1002	004-890-100-3
Finland	9800-100-10	9800-102-80	9800-1-0284
France	19-0011	19*00-19	19*0087
French Antilles	19-00-11	No MCI Access	No Sprint Access
French Guiana	19-00-11	No MCI Access	No Sprint Access
Gabon	00*001	No MCI Access	No Sprint Access
Gambia	00111	00-1-99	00-155
Germany	0130-0100	0130-0012	0130-0013
Ghana	0191	No MCI Access	01-99-00
Gibralter	8800	No MCI Access	No Sprint Access
Greece	00-800-1311	00-800-1211	008-001-411
Grenada	1-800-872-2881	1-800-888-8000	1-800-877-8787
Guam	018-872	950-1022	950-1366
Guatemala	190	189	195
Guyana	165	No MCI Access	No Sprint Access
Haiti	183	001-800-444-1234	170-171
Honduras	123	122	121

COUNTRY	AT&T	MCI	SPRINT
Hong Kong	800-1111	800-1121	800-1877
Hungary	00*800-01111	00*800-01411	00*800-01-877
Iceland	800-9001	800-9002	800-9003
India	000-117	000-127	000-137
Indonesia	001-801-10	001-801-11	001-801-15
Ireland	1-800-550-000	1-800-55-1001	1-800-55-2001
Israel	177-100-2727	177-150-2727	177-102-2727
Italy	172-1011	172-1022	172-1877
Ivory Coast	00-111-11	No MCI Access	No Sprint Access
Jamaica	0-800-8722881	1-800-888-8000	0-800-877-8000
Japan (KDD)	0039-111	0039-121	0039-131
Japan (IDC)	0066-55-111	0066-55-121	0066-55-877
Jordan	18-800-000	18-800-001	18-800-777
Kazakhstan	8*800-121-4321	No MCI Access	No Sprint Access
Kenya	0800-10	080011	0800-12
Korea (DACOM)	009-11	0039-12	0039-13
Korea (KT)	550-HOME	009-14	009-16
Kuwait	800-288	800-MCI	800-777
Latvia (Riga)	7007007	No MCI Access	No Sprint Access
Latvia (Others)	8*27007007		
Lebanon (Beirut)	426-801	600-MCI	No Sprint Access
Lebanon (Others)	01-426-801	01-600-MCI	No Sprint Access
Liberia	797-797	No MCI Access	No Sprint Access
Liechtenstein	155-00-11	155-0222	155-9777
Lithuania	8*196	No MCI Access	8*197
Luxembourg	0-800-0111	0800-0112	0800-0115
Macao	0800-111	0800-131	0800-121
Macedonia	99-800-4288	No MCI Access	No Sprint Access
Malaysia	800-0011	800-0012	800-0016
Malta	0800-890-110	0800-89-0120	No Sprint Access
Mexico	95-800-462-4240	95-800-674-7000	95-800-877-8000
Micronesia	288	No MCI Access	555
Monaco	19-0011	19*00-19	19*0087
Montserrat	1-800-872-2881	No MCI Access	No Sprint Access
Morocco	002-11-0011	00-211-0012	No Sprint Access
Netherlands	06-022-9111	06-022-91-22	06-022-9119
Netherlands Antilles	001-800-872-2881	001-800-950-1022	001-800-745-1111

COUNTRY	AT&T	MCI	SPRINT
New Zealand	000-911	000-912	0-800-760-877
Nicaragua	174	166 (Managua)	171
*Nicaragua		02-166 (Others)	
Norway	800-190-11	800-19912	800-19877
Palau	02288	No MCI Access	02-222
Panama	109	108	115
Paraguay	0081-800	008-11-800	008-12-800
Peru	171	170	176
Philippines	105-11	105-14	105-16 (PLDT)
Philippines			105-01 (ETPI)
Poland	0*0-800-111-1111	00-800-111-21-22	00-800-111-3115
Portugal	05017-1-288	05-017-1234	05017-1-877
Puerto Rico	1-800-225-5288	1-800-888-8000	1-800-877-8000
Qatar	0800-011-77	0800-012-77	0-800-01-777
Romania	01-800-4288	01-800-1800	01-800-0877
Russia (Moscow)	755-5042	8*10-800-497-7222	155-6133
Russia (Others)	8-095-755-5042	8*10-800-497-7222	8095-155-6133
St. Kitts/Nevis	1-800-872-2881	No MCI Access	No Sprint Access
St. Vincent	1-800-872-2881	No MCI Access	No Sprint Access
Saint Lucia	1-800-872-2881	1-800-888-8000	1-800-277-7468
Saipan	235-2872	950-1022	235-0333
San Marino	172-1011	172-1022	172-1877
Saudi Arabia	1-800-10	1-800-11	1800-15
Sierra Leone	1100	No MCI Access	No Sprint Access
Singapore	800-0111-111	8000-112-112	8000-177-177
Slovak Republic	00-420-00101	00-42-000112	00-42-087-187
South Africa	0-800-99-0123	0800-99-0011	0-800-99-0001
Spain	900-99-00-11	900-99-0014	900-99-0013
Sri Lanka	430-430	440100	No Sprint Access
Suriname	156	No MCI Access	No Sprint Access
Sweden	020-795-611	020-795-922	020-799-011
Switzerland	0-800-550011	155-0222	15-9777
Syria	0-801	0800	0888
Taiwan	0800-10288-0	0080-13-4567	0080-14-0877
Thailand	0019-991-1111	001-999-1-2001	001-999-13-877
Trinidad & Tobago	NO AT&T ACCESS	1-800-888-8000	23
Turkey	00-800-12277	00-8001-1177	00-800-1-4477

COUNTRY	AT&T	MCI	SPRINT
Turks and Caicos	1-800-872-2881	No MCI Access	No Sprint Access
Ukraine	8*100-11	8*10-013	8-100-15
United Arab Emirates	800-121	800-111	800-131
United Kingdom	0800-890011	0800-89-0222	0800-89-0877
United States	1-800-225-5288	1-800-888-8000	1-800-877-8000
Uruguay	00-0410	000-412	000417
Uzbekistan	8*661-7440010	No MCI Access	No Sprint Access
Venezuela	1-201-0288	800-1114-0	800-1111-0
Vietnam	1-201-0288	1201-9999	1201-1111
Virgin Islands (U.S.)	1-800-225-5288	1-800-888-8000	1-800-877-8000
Virgin Islands (U.K.)	1-800-872-2881	1-800-888-8000	1-800-877-8000
Zambia	00-899	No MCI Access	No Sprint Access
Zimbabwe	1-201-0288	No MCI Access	No Sprint Access

INDEX

Order Your Guide to Travel and Adventure

Title	Price	Title	Price
Fielding's Alaska Cruises and the Inside Passage	$18.95	Fielding's London Agenda	$14.95
Fielding's The Amazon	$16.95	Fielding's Los Angeles	$16.95
Fielding's Asia's Top Dive Sites	$19.95	Fielding's Malaysia & Singapore	$16.95
Fielding's Australia	$16.95	Fielding's Mexico	$18.95
Fielding's Bahamas	$16.95	Fielding's New Orleans Agenda	$16.95
Fielding's Baja	$18.95	Fielding's New York Agenda	$16.95
Fielding's Bermuda	$16.95	Fielding's New Zealand	$16.95
Fielding's Borneo	$18.95	Fielding's Paris Agenda	$14.95
Fielding's Budget Europe	$17.95	Fielding's Portugal	$16.95
Fielding's Caribbean	$18.95	Fielding's Paradors, Pousadas and Charming Villages	$18.95
Fielding's Caribbean Cruises	$18.95	Fielding's Rome Agenda	$14.95
Fielding's Disney World and Orlando	$18.95	Fielding's San Diego Agenda	$14.95
Fielding's Diving Indonesia	$19.95	Fielding's Southeast Asia	$18.95
Fielding's Eastern Caribbean	$17.95	Fielding's Southern Vietnam on 2 Wheels	$15.95
Fielding's England	$17.95	Fielding's Spain	$18.95
Fielding's Europe	$18.95	Fielding's Surfing Indonesia	$19.95
Fielding's European Cruises	$18.95	Fielding's Sydney Agenda	$16.95
Fielding's Far East	$18.95	Fielding's Thailand, Cambodia, Laos and Myanmar	$18.95
Fielding's France	$18.95	Fielding's Vacation Places Rated	$19.95
Fielding's Freewheelin' USA	$18.95	Fielding's Vietnam	$17.95
Fielding's Hawaii	$18.95	Fielding's Western Caribbean	$18.95
Fielding's Italy	$18.95	Fielding's The World's Most Dangerous Places	$19.95
Fielding's Kenya	$16.95	Fielding's Worldwide Cruises '97	$19.95
Fielding's Las Vegas Agenda	$14.95		

To place an order: call toll-free 1-800-FW-2-GUIDE
(VISA, MasterCard and American Express accepted)
or send your check or money order to:
Fielding Worldwide, Inc., 308 S. Catalina Avenue, Redondo Beach, CA 90277
add $2.00 per book for shipping & handling (sorry, no COD's), allow 2–6 weeks for delivery

International Conversions

TEMPERATURE

To convert °F to °C, subtract 32 and divide by 1.8.

To convert °C to °F, multiply by 1.8 and add 32.

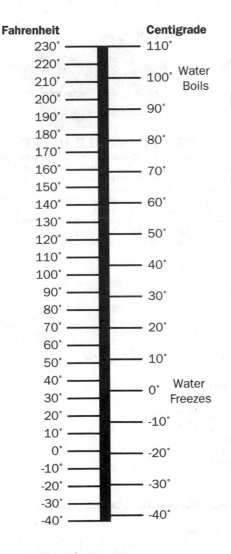

Fahrenheit	Centigrade	
230°	110°	
220°		
210°	100°	Water Boils
200°	90°	
190°		
180°	80°	
170°		
160°	70°	
150°		
140°	60°	
130°		
120°	50°	
110°		
100°	40°	
90°	30°	
80°		
70°	20°	
60°		
50°	10°	
40°	0°	Water Freezes
30°		
20°	-10°	
10°		
0°	-20°	
-10°		
-20°	-30°	
-30°		
-40°	-40°	

WEIGHTS & MEASURES

LENGTH

1 km	=	0.62 miles
1 mile	=	1.609 km
1 meter	=	1.2936 yards
1 meter	=	3.28 feet
1 yard	=	0.9144 meters
1 yard	=	3 feet
1 foot	=	30.48 centimeters
1 centimeter	=	0.39 inch
1 inch	=	2.54 centimeters

AREA

1 square km	=	0.3861 square miles
1 square mile	=	2.590 square km
1 hectare	=	2.47 acres
1 acre	=	0.405 hectare

VOLUME

1 cubic meter	=	1.307 cubic yards
1 cubic yard	=	0.765 cubic meter
1 cubic yard	=	27 cubic feet
1 cubic foot	=	0.028 cubic meter
1 cubic centimeter	=	0.061 cubic inch
1 cubic inch	=	16.387 cubic centimeters

CAPACITY

1 gallon	=	3.785 liters
1 quart	=	0.94635 liters
1 liter	=	1.057 quarts
1 pint	=	473 milliliters
1 fluid ounce	=	29.573 milliliters

MASS and WEIGHT

1 metric ton	=	1.102 short tons
1 metric ton	=	1000 kilograms
1 short ton	=	.90718 metric ton
1 long ton	=	1.016 metric tons
1 long ton	=	2240 pounds
1 pound	=	0.4536 kilograms
1 kilogram	=	2.2046 pounds
1 ounce	=	28.35 grams
1 gram	=	0.035 ounce
1 milligram	=	0.015 grain